Dumont d'Urville

Jules-Sébastien-César Dumont d'Urville, oil on canvas, 1845, by Jérome Cartellier (1813–1892).
Château de Versailles

Dumont d'Urville

EXPLORER & POLYMATH

Edward Duyker

OTAGO

For Ivan Barko,
in friendship and gratitude

Publisher: Rachel Scott
Editor: Jane Connor
Design/layout: Jane Connor
Index: Diane Lowther

Printed in China through Asia Pacific Offset

Australian Government

Contents

List of illustrations

List of maps

Introduction

But you shall shine more bright in these contents
Than unswept stone besmear'd with sluttish time.
When wasteful war shall statues overturn
William Shakespeare*

On Thursday, 23 April 1942, in the Saint-Sauveur quarter of Condé-sur-Noireau (in the *département* of Calvados), Normandy, local residents were surprised to see a truck arrive with a team of workers equipped with ladders, long pieces of wood, ropes and chains. Acting under the instructions of the occupying Germans, their object was the one-tonne bronze statue by Dominique Molknecht of the town's great son, Jules-Sébastien-César Dumont d'Urville, one of the most famous explorers of the age of sail and sometimes called 'France's Captain Cook'. With the aid of a tripod scaffold, the men soon hoisted the statue from its pedestal and slid it into their waiting truck.[1] Many French towns had been similarly despoiled of their bronze monuments by the German war machine, but the loss to Condé-sur-Noireau, on that spring day in 1942, was made all the harder to bear because the residents were to commemorate the centenary of the explorer's death in a fortnight. Worse was to come.

In the three months after the D-Day landings of June 1944, the town was bombed 26 times by the Allies. There were 235 civilian deaths and 94 percent of its buildings were destroyed. One shocked worker arriving from Marseille wrote to his wife: 'Here, you stand on a brick and you see the whole town.'[2] A substantial part of the house in which d'Urville was born survived the bombing largely intact[3] but bereft of one wing, its attic gutted, standing alone and perhaps unsafe amid the devastation. The architects of the new Condé-sur-Noireau preferred a clean slate to one marred with the scattered and cracked remnants of the town's pre-war past, so what was left of the house was soon demolished. Now, only a bronze plaque marks the explorer's birthplace, and at the end of rue Dumont d'Urville, in front of the rebuilt church of Saint-Sauveur, where the explorer was baptised on 23 May 1790, another statue stands. This stone copy of the stolen bronze, sculpted by Robert Delandre, was paid for by local subscription and bears the original bronze bas-relief panels of important episodes in d'Urville's life –

---

*Sonnets (1609), no. 55, lines 2–4

Postcard, ca.1930s (photograph by Pierre Levasseur) of the
original statue (1846) of Dumont d'Urville, by Dominique
Molknecht, at Condé-sur-Noireau. It was seized by the
occupying Germans in 1942 and melted down for its bronze.
Author's collection

saved by courageous residents[4] who removed and hid them in the middle of the night
before the Germans could take them for smelting.

Given the devastation Condé-sur-Noireau suffered, it is not surprising that recent
biographers have assumed that there were few original documentary sources to be
found in the explorer's home town. Reading the post-war biographies of d'Urville by
Jacques Guillon (1986), Yves Jacob (1995) and John Dunmore (2007), one is struck by
the extent to which they repeated what their predecessor, the novelist, historian and
classical scholar Louis-Auguste-Camille Vergniol,[5] published (sometimes in error) in

his biography in 1931. Admiral Jacques Guillon even declared: 'For all that concerns the childhood and youth of Dumont d'Urville, one is referred in great part to the book of M. Camille Vergniol. This author had had, in effect, the possibility of accessing archives today disappeared or dispersed as a result of the destruction of the war of 1939–1945.'[6] Guillon went on to discuss the lacunae in d'Urville's personal journals. Yet a number of the gaps he identified are covered by original journals bequeathed to the municipality of Condé-sur-Noireau after the death of the explorer's unmarried great-nephew Louis-Charles-Henry Dumont de la Londe.[7] They remain there to this day, long overlooked by previous scholars.[8]

There are also rich sources in Paris. Letters in d'Urville's Paris apartment at the time of his death are now preserved in the Archives nationales.[9] They were apparently seized on the orders of the navy minister, Admiral Victor-Guy Duperré. Another precious collection of documents, donated in January 1884 by Luc-Frédéric-Antoine Malcor,[10] is preserved in the Service historique de la défense, Château de Vincennes. Malcor had acquired these documents from a nephew[11] of Captain Louis-Clement Salvy. At the time, Malcor described the elder Salvy as the 'proper nephew of Mme Dumont d'Urville'.[12] In fact, Salvy was the explorer's stepfather-in-law, the man his wife's divorced mother, Josephine-Hélène Las de Guérin, married in Toulon on 24 November 1817.[13] Madame Salvy inherited part of d'Urville's papers on her daughter's death in 1842, and her second husband inherited them from her when she died in 1861.[14] His beneficiary would keep them for another two decades before entrusting them to Malcor for donation. The balance of the papers from the Salvy estate (including d'Urville's private journals from 1830 to 1837) that did not go to the Château de Vincennes were acquired by the Bibliothèque municipale de Toulon.[15] Malcor also gave transcriptions of a number of shorter documents (together with some personal observations on d'Urville, his family and his writings) to the naval archives in Vincennes. This was fortuitous because some of the originals in Toulon disappeared during World War II.

Back in 1931, Vergniol cited the 'Archives Colein-Dubusq' as one of his principal sources for 'almost all that concerns the relations between d'Urville, his mother, his uncle, his sisters, nephews and nieces'.[16] Yet it would seem that Vergniol never actually sighted these documents. In his foreword, he alluded to his correspondence with a Monsieur P. Colein-Dubusq[17] of Condé-sur-Noireau and thanked him for providing 'all the information on the Dumont d'Urvilles, with the memories and traditions of the whole family' and deemed him his 'true collaborator'.[18] However, Colein-Dubusq's kinship with the explorer's family was *par alliance* (by marriage);[19] he asserted in a letter to Vergniol that d'Urville's great-niece was his 'cousin'.[20] Although he evidently had access to some personal letters, much of what he passed on to Vergniol seems to have been a filtered précis of published sources (some erroneous) from the mid-to late nineteenth century. I also suspect that Colein-Dubusq deliberately avoided communicating one unsavoury detail in the process: the fact that one of his eponymous forebears had signed a warrant for d'Urville's mother's arrest during the Reign of Terror!

D'Urville fascinated me long before I read Vergniol's influential biography. For more than half my life, I have been in possession of a 1:100 scale model of the *Coquille*, the vessel in which he first circled the globe; d'Urville would command her again, renamed the *Astrolabe*, on two more great voyages. My model[21] was made in the house my great-great-grandfather built and in which my mother grew up on Mauritius – an island d'Urville visited twice. It is hardly surprising that I pondered life aboard her crowded decks and sought out accounts of her visits, not only to Mauritius in 1824 and 1828 but to Australia and New Zealand between 1824 and 1840, and to the coast of Antarctica in 1838 and 1840.

Although francophone readers have long had access to d'Urville's original accounts, he has only gradually become accessible to the English-speaking public. Between 1907 and 1909, the surveyor and ethnographer Stephenson Percy Smith[22] introduced many New Zealand readers to him[23] with annotated English translations of his accounts of exploration of Tasman Bay, Tolaga Bay, Whangarei, Waitemata and the Thames in 1827.[24] Olive Wright,[25] seemingly unaware of Smith's pioneering work, covered much of this same ground again in a translation published in 1950 but with a substantial biographical introduction and appendices. She followed up five years later with a fine translation of d'Urville's 1840 New Zealand journals.[26] D'Urville has an anonymous entry in the *Australian Encyclopaedia* (1958) but is absent from *An Encyclopaedia of New Zealand* (1966), the *Dictionary of New Zealand Biography* (1991–) and the *Australian Dictionary of Biography* (1966–). The Australian scholar Helen Rosenman[27] introduced him to a broader English readership with her impressive two-volume abridged translation *Two Voyages to the South Seas* (1987). In 1992, Carol Legge produced a skilful translation of d'Urville's manuscript *Les Zélandais ou histoire australienne*, the first New Zealand novel – albeit unpublished for 167 years. It was a product of d'Urville's first visit to the Bay of Islands in 1824 and bore his detailed ethnographic notes.

Other biographical and scholarly studies helped shed further light on the events recounted in the primary texts. In 1988, Isabel Ollivier[28] published an illuminating article on the life of Pierre-Adolphe Lesson, surgeon-naturalist on d'Urville's first *Astrolabe* expedition.[29] Roger Collins advanced the study of d'Urville's artists with *New Zealand Seen by the French (1769–1846)*, the catalogue for an exhibition held at the National Library of New Zealand in 1991, and later with individual monographs on Louis-Auguste de Sainson (1997) and Louis Le Breton (2012). Similarly, Susan

Hunt, Martin Terry and Nicholas Hunt produced an informative catalogue, *Lure of the Southern Seas: The Voyages of Dumont d'Urville 1826–1840*, for an exhibition on d'Urville's voyages at the Museum of Sydney (2002–03). In 2007, New Zealand scholar John Dunmore[30] gave us the first book-length biographical study of d'Urville in English: *From Venus to Antarctica: The life of Dumont d'Urville*. He had previously surveyed d'Urville's voyages in his *French Explorers in the Pacific* (1965–69).

Despite the breadth of this scholarship, there are important sources that have been overlooked, and there is a great deal more that can be set down, and set straight, regarding d'Urville's parents and his family's experiences during the Revolution; his studies and early naval career (including the discovery and acquisition of the Vénus de Milo); his passionate but emotionally fraught marriage; his scientific legacy in the Pacific, Australia, New Zealand and Antarctica; his confirmation of the fate of Jean-François de Galaup, comte de Lapérouse; his secret orders to search for the site for a French penal colony in the Antipodes; his role in precipitating pre-emptive British colonisation in several parts of Australia; his radical political views and participation in the Revolution of 1830; and his linguistic ideas and conceptualisation of the Pacific and its people, including his coining of the terms Melanesia and Micronesia.

Although France failed to colonise Australia or New Zealand, d'Urville's voyages and writings ultimately strengthened a French colonial impulse in other parts of the Pacific. Within two years of d'Urville's death, his secretary, César Desgraz, and his hydrographer, Clément-Adrien Vincendon-Dumoulin, had co-authored books that summarised considerations for colonial enterprise in Tahiti and the Marquesas.[31] A decade later, another two of his officers, Joseph-Fidèle-Eugène Dubouzet and Louis-François-Marie Tardy de Montravel, played their part as early French colonial administrators.

Regardless of his empathy and understanding of others, d'Urville's writings on race give particular pause and provoke critical judgement. One can't simply resort to apologia and assert that he was 'a product of his times'. Firstly, unlike his racist polygenist colleagues Jean-Baptiste Bory de Saint-Vincent,[32] Prosper Garnot[33] and Jacques-Bernard Hombron,[34] d'Urville believed in the fundamental unity of the human species and he never had any abhorrence of miscegenation, calling such attitudes 'stupid prejudice'.[35] It is not surprising, therefore, that he had sympathy and respect for those of mixed race living on the fringes of their parent communities. Numerous examples are recorded in his journals: the savant Jean-Baptiste Lislet Geoffroy, whom he visited on a number of occasions in Mauritius; the 'coloured' Canadian Richard Symons, whom he invited to join the crew of the *Astrolabe* at King George Sound; the Hispano-Chamorran Luis de Torres, whom he visited in Guam; the soldiers and mistresses of the Spanish, whom he met in Zamboanga; Madame Tissot and her daughters, with whom he socialised in Semarang, Java; and Madame Tielman, whom he met in Timor. Secondly, for all his writings on the different peoples of the globe – and at times his attitude to Australian Aborigines and Melanesians was harsh, sweeping and peppered with stridently racist judgments of intellectual inferiority and intractability – d'Urville was capable of more favourable opinions to the contrary, particularly when he gained vocabularies and linguistic tools for communication. For example, at Jervis Bay in New South Wales, where his expedition recorded 158 Wandandian words,[36] he judged the local Aborigines to have 'a degree of intelligence superior to any he knew'.[37]

Although he sometimes described faces (and skull shape) as betraying impoverished intellect, generally he did not hold entrenched views regarding intelligence being immutably constrained by race, class or gender. He clearly had ethnocentric aesthetic prejudices – and was quick to use the words 'hideous' or 'ugly' to describe the physical appearance of some of the peoples he encountered during his voyages – but once again, his views must be qualified. Apparently echoing the notions of Georges-Louis Leclerc, comte de Buffon, and Johann Friedrich Blumenbach on the influence of climate, environment and nutrition on humanity, he asserted that abundant food probably accounted for the Aborigines of Jervis Bay being 'less ugly, more vigorous, and above all better proportioned' than others on the continent.[38] Similarly, skin colour was not a measure of intrinsic inferiority for him.[39]

What interested him most when he assessed those that he met was intellectual cultivation, personal merit, compassion and honesty. Once again, d'Urville's friendship and profound admiration for Jean-Baptiste Lislet Geoffroy is relevant to this discussion; he was not only a brilliant, highly respected thinker of mixed race but the emancipated son of an African slave. When d'Urville encountered slavery, he intervened whenever he felt able, for example when he enabled two Bandanese men – Nohor and Gueberar –enslaved by Palauans, to escape aboard the *Astrolabe*. Similarly, he approved of the Boutonese slave Kakou gaining freedom from Jolo pirates with passage aboard the *Zélée*. Earlier still, in March 1827, he allowed the former Māori slave Kokako to join the *Astrolabe*'s crew. He saw men and women[40] as full of promise and capable of redemption, and for this reason he had great admiration for Governor Lachlan Macquarie's efforts to uplift those stigmatised by penal servitude in Australia. His compassion and clemency towards the deserter Charles Simonet reveal that his humane principles were not simply abstract notions but personally applied. Finally, his extensive reading (see Appendix) and his life-long interest in the languages, literature, philosophies and religions of other peoples of the world are evidence of an open and expansive intellect – something not normally associated with intemperate and immutable prejudice. D'Urville's passion for Hebrew (and what would appear to be a complete lack of anti-Jewish comments in his writings) would suggest that he was not fired from the same clay as those who later poisoned French political life with anti-Semitism.

Aside from being 'one of France's foremost authorities on geographical discovery',[41] d'Urville was also one of the major travel writers of the nineteenth century. In his autobiography, the great Russian composer Nikolai Rimsky-Korsakov alluded to the explorer firing his youthful imagination for the navy when he wrote: 'I fell in love with the sea, conceived a passion for it without ever having seen it, read Dumont d'Urville's voyage around the world, rigged up a brig, played sea voyager.'[42] D'Urville and his voyages seeped into popular culture, fiction, and broader scholarly and scientific discourse, and he was referred to or cited in many hundreds of reference works, books and articles after his death. Jules Verne, who must have read d'Urville extensively, mentions him in at least nine of his novels and one of his historical compilations.[43] There are passing references to d'Urville in Victor Hugo's *Les travailleurs de la mer* (1866) and *L'homme qui rit* (1869); Alexandre Dumas' *Les drames de la mer* (1853) and *Mémoires* (1863); Émile Zola's *L'amour sous les toits* (1865); Pierre Loti's *Le mariage de Loti* (1880); and even Marcel Proust's *À la recherche de temps perdu* (1913). Eric Hunter Christie, in *The Antarctic Problem* (1951), observed: 'Whether writing of the form of a marble statue, the colours hidden in the depths of an iceberg or the physical attributes of the Patagonian women of Tierra del Fuego, d'Urville's descriptive passages contain a Gallic flash and fire which the less inspired Anglo-Saxon can rarely emulate.'[44] Christie was guilty of an injustice to his fellow Anglo-Saxon authors, but there is indeed a 'flash and fire' in d'Urville's writing. His historical accounts are born of deep sensitivity and broad polymathic humanism. In 1951, the botanical historian Auguste Chevalier compared d'Urville's botanical work to that of Alexander von Humboldt, Aimé Bonpland, Johann Reinhold Forster and Robert Brown, and celebrated his major contribution to biogeography. Despite the lack of a detailed inventory, Chevalier estimated the number of species d'Urville collected, or enabled to be collected, at between 5000 and 6000, including those gathered during the expeditions of the *Chevrette* and the *Coquille*.[45] He could have added that the extraordinary breadth of this collecting and the ecological and biogeographic detail that suffused d'Urville's historical accounts also had significance for later evolutionary biology.

The first voyage of the *Astrolabe* is referred to a number of times in Charles Darwin's account of the voyage of the *Beagle* (1839).[46] Although Darwin does not mention the explorer in *On the Origin of Species by Means of Natural Selection* (1859) or *The Descent of Man* (1871),[47] d'Urville's article on the distribution of ferns ('De la distribution des fougères sur la surface du globe terrestre') and his work on the plants of the Falklands ('Flore des Malouines') are both mentioned in Darwin's notebooks on the transmutation of species.[48] There are also numerous references to d'Urville's works in Darwin's 'books to be read' and 'books read' notebooks,[49] and he is repeatedly referenced in *The Structure and Distribution of Coral Reefs* (1842).

One sees sparks of astute scientific understanding early in d'Urville's career. His article of 1822, on the islands within Thera's crater rim in the Aegean, revealed an impressive ecological understanding of species succession on virgin volcanic substrata.[50] Similarly, in 'Flore des Malouines', he not only published descriptions of 44 new plant species but offered several highly prescient ecological, geomorphological and palaeobotanical observations. 'De la distribution des fougères sur la surface du globe terrestre' also offered eco-mathematical observations on the percentage of local flora composed of pteridophytes and occupying similar habitat niches. The distractions and responsibilities of leading his own expeditions would later limit such individual scientific forays, but during the first *Astrolabe* voyage, d'Urville combined his interest in botany and entomology to make habitat notes on the associations between particular plants and insects. During the second *Astrolabe* voyage, he noted the transformative role of fire in anthropogenic ecological change in Tierra del Fuego and also recognised the association between glaciers and icebergs. The detailed meteorological and ocean-temperature observations undertaken during his voyages also have continued relevance to climatologists and those seeking to understand the nature and pace of global warming.[51]

D'Urville has something to offer all who encounter him, but before we re-explore the explorer, a few textual explanations are necessary (with further assistance available in the glossary at the end of the book).

RANKS, TITLES & NAUTICAL TERMS[52]

During the *ancien régime*, the usual way in which young nobles joined the French naval officer corps was through one of the three companies of *gardes de la marine* located in the ports of Brest, Rochefort and Toulon. In the immediate wake of the Revolution, young nobles entering the navy in this manner became known as *élèves de la marine*. Non-nobles, other than *volontaires*, entered as *aspirants*. However, by the time d'Urville joined the navy, this was a term that covered all prospective naval officers. During the Restoration, the term *élèves de la marine* was resurrected. Although I have used these original titles, I have also used the English translation 'midshipman'; this is despite the fact that it can be argued that an *élève de la marine* and an *aspirant* approximated a combination of naval cadet and midshipman in the British Royal Navy. Where the rank of ensign appears in the text, it is a translation of *enseigne de vaisseau*, and where I have referred to someone as a lieutenant, this is an abbreviation of *lieutenant de vaisseau* (which was roughly equivalent to a British lieutenant-commander). I have avoided translating many other institutional names and military and administrative terms, particularly those without an exact English equivalent.

When citing the names of French institutions (such as museums, archives and academies), I have generally followed French grammatical rules and capitalisation styles; likewise, titles of nobility (such as marquis, comte and duc) are lower case. I have also avoided the acute accent in Napoleon. Except when referencing correspondence and other documents, throughout my narrative I have chosen to refer to d'Urville's wife as 'Adélie', using his affectionate diminutive. Although she was christened 'Adèle', and d'Urville also wrote lovingly of his 'good Adèle' and his 'gentle Adèle', it was his 'Adélie' he chose to immortalise on the coast of Antarctica. She, in turn, usually referred to her husband as 'd'Urville', and I have done so too. My final authority in the translation of French nautical terms has been the classic *Dictionnaire de la marine à voile* by Pierre-Marie-Joseph de Bonnefoux, first published in 1848 and revised in 1856 by his son-in-law Édouard Pâris, himself a veteran of d'Urville's first *Astrolabe* voyage.

MEASUREMENTS

For old French measurements, such as, *milles, brasses, pieds, pouces* and *livres* – which appeared in everyday writing and conversation long after the metric reforms of the Revolution – I have freely translated miles, fathoms, feet, inches and pounds in quotations. Elsewhere I have used metric equivalents, including for nautical miles and the weight of British and American ships. However, *livre* still appears in the text when I am referring to the common monetary unit of France prior to the introduction of the *franc* on 7 December 1793.

DATES

Although a revolutionary calendar was enforced in France between 1793 and 1805, I have generally converted such dates to the familiar Gregorian equivalent or given the two dates together.

PLACE NAMES

I have tried to orient my readers with reference to the old provinces of France (such as Normandy, Brittany and Dauphiné), but when referring to small towns and hamlets, I have generally given the name of the surrounding present-day *département* in brackets alongside. While I have abandoned some archaic Anglicisms – using Livorno and Genova (instead of Leghorn and Genoa), and Marseille and Lyon (instead of Marseilles and Lyons) – other than exact citations in my bibliography, I have not forsaken familiar English equivalents such as Rome, Geneva and Athens (instead of Roma, Genève and Athína).

My references to cartographic discoveries are generally references to first published use rather than simply a European world view. I am mindful of my friend John Mulvaney's remark in 1969 that, 'Europocentric historians of explorations have been inclined to assume that those lands unknown to Europeans existed in some limbo of uncharted and static seas, awaiting redemption by some imaginative navigator.'[53] Although d'Urville's most important discoveries were of uninhabited lands, he was not indifferent to the discoveries of Polynesians and other navigators in the Pacific and, as we shall see, frequently went to great lengths to record and reinstate indigenous names on his charts.

Aside from some former colonial or European explorers' place names (which have generally been followed by present-day equivalents in parentheses), two archaic Australian toponyms are used in the text: New Holland and Van Diemen's Land. Like the name New Zealand, they date from Abel Tasman's voyage of 1642. After the Dutch explorer effectively circumnavigated Australia and established that it was an island continent, the 'South Land' was given the name Nova Hollandia (Latin for New Holland) on the Eugene Map (*ca.* 1644),[54] which consolidated Tasman's discoveries with those of earlier Dutch navigators. Tasman also named one of his southern landfalls of 1642 'Anthonie van Diemensland', in honour of the then governor of the Netherlands East Indies.[55] Unlike his subsequent landfall New Zealand, Tasman was unaware that Van Diemen's Land was separate from New Holland. The name 'Tasmanie' occasionally occurs in d'Urville's journal, but Tasmania did not become the official name for the island until 1854. Similarly, d'Urville occasionally used the name 'Australie' when referring to New Holland; however, Australia did not become the official name for the continent until federation of its British colonies in 1901.

PLANT AND ANIMAL NAMES

Modern scientists name and revise the names of plants and animals on the basis of their knowledge of a species and its relationship to other species. In the past, botanists studying plants in different parts of the world sometimes gave different names to the same species. Under the International Code of Botanical Nomenclature, a species can have only one name. Beginning with those published in Carl Linnaeus's *Species Plantarum* (1753), the oldest name has priority. Similarly, under the International Code of Zoological Nomenclature, the starting date for animals is the tenth edition of Linnaeus's *Systema naturae* (1758). Taxonomic revision can take place not simply as a result of discovering an older name; it can take place as a result of a better understanding of the differences or similarities in a taxon.[56] Thus a given species can be moved from one genus to another; although its generic name can change, its specific epithet usually does not. Decisions are made by the International Commission on Zoological Nomenclature, which was founded in 1895. Although one of the particular emphases of this present biography is d'Urville's contribution to modern science, I have not felt it necessary to cite the name of every botanical or zoological author after every species mentioned in the narrative. In referring to species collected during d'Urville's voyages, I have often inserted the generally accepted modern scientific name in parentheses. When d'Urville or one of his naturalists collected a species that had already been described and revised, I have not gone to the extent of citing the author of the original name.

D'URVILLE'S MISSING MEMOIRS

Where I refer to d'Urville's now-missing manuscript memoirs, I am alluding to a document, formerly in the possession of the Bibliothèque municipale de Toulon, that disappeared during World War II. It should not be confused with the spurious memoir, dated 1 September 1838, that was perpetrated by Aloysia Soudry du Kerven in her strange romanticised work *Dumont d'Urville pages intimes*.[57] Although Isidore Le Brun and Sabin Berthelot offered a number of brief extracts from d'Urville's genuine *mémoire autobiographique* in their respective elegies, I have cross-referenced and quoted from two more-substantial, though incomplete, transcriptions. The first, dated 31 May 1884, was undertaken by Malcor and is held at the Château de Vincennes.[58] The second, by the archivist and historian Pierre Margry, forms part of a manuscript collection on the 'Mers Australes' acquired by the Bibliothèque nationale de France on 1 February 1896.[59] When I refer to d'Urville's 'Ms journal de la *Coquille*', I am alluding to a manuscript held by the mairie de Condé-sur-Noireau (Ms 11), which to my knowledge has not been used by any other scholar. It is a very personal and highly significant account but incomplete[60] and should not be confused with d'Urville's sparse summary (Ms 1602) preserved in the Bibliothèque centrale du Muséum national d'histoire naturelle, Paris.

All of d'Urville's surviving original manuscripts present great challenges because of their exceedingly difficult legibility. In 1931, Vergniol described d'Urville's handwriting as 'galloping … atomic and especially fragmentary, because the words and letters are composed of juxtaposed "fly prints".' He added, 'D'Urville does not shorten the words, but he subtilises them. Some parts of sentences, lines, resist the most powerful magnifying glasses and the best founded interpretations, even by those who know the general sense and guess the particular meaning.'[61] Eight decades later, I faced the same challenge, in some fields harvesting a mere fraction of what d'Urville had sown; yet I hope few will go hungry from the grist I have ground.

Edward Duyker
Australian Catholic University/University of Sydney
March 2014

PART I

'… a sort of reputation'

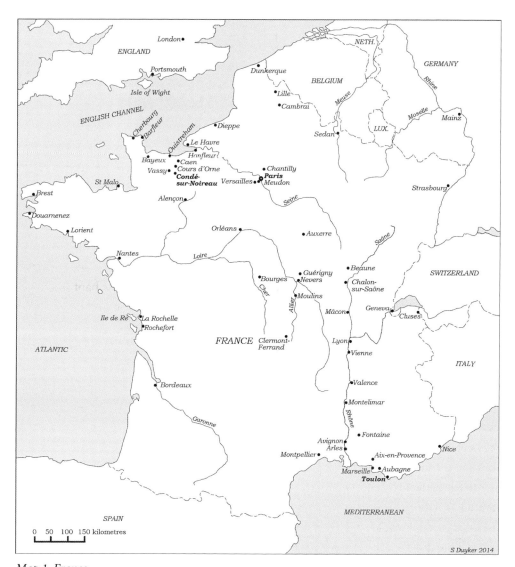

Map 1. France

1

Childhood

*That is the way of youth and life in general: that we do not understand the
strategy until after the campaign is over.*
Johann Wolfgang von Goethe*

Jules-Sébastien-César Dumont d'Urville was born in Condé-sur-Noireau (in the
department of Calvados) on 23 May 1790.[1] His father, Gabriel-Charles-François
Dumont d'Urville, was then in his early sixties and some 26 years older than his mother,
born Jeanne de Croisilles. The future explorer's parents had married in August 1774.[2]
Despite their significant age difference, their marriage lasted more than two decades
and produced at least nine children, only four of whom appear to have survived early
infancy: Jules, his two older sisters and a younger brother.[3] Jules was baptised in the
church of Saint-Sauveur the day after he was born. His father, the hereditary bailiff
of Condé-sur-Noireau, was not present. According to a travel document drafted four
years later, Gabriel stood 153 centimetres tall, had greying brown hair, grey-blue eyes,
a large round face with a dimpled chin and a large mouth.[4] Another more romantic
description (with no definite provenance) presents him as having 'a noble and gentle
physiognomy' and being 'very well built although somewhat boxlike, with an arm
which had been injured in his youth'.[5] This reference to an injured arm suggests a
possible confusion with Jules himself, for he is known to have fallen onto a glowing
brazier at the age of two and to have borne scars on his arm for the rest of his life.[6]

In the sixteenth century, the Dumont family resided in the village of Poulhaye near
Frênes (Orne) in Lower Normandy. It was Jules' great-grandfather, Gilles Dumont,
who acquired the fiefdom of Urville, near Condé-sur-Noireau, through his marriage to
Jacqueline de Prépetit in 1672. She in turn had inherited the fiefdom from her father,
whose maternal ancestors had apparently possessed it since the thirteenth century.
While Gilles Dumont belonged to the *noblesse de robe* as a result of his position in
the rural magistracy, his wife had deeper roots in the local rural nobility, and his son,
the explorer's grandfather, also named Gilles, consolidated the family position by

Dichtung und Wahrheit (1833), part iv, book 20

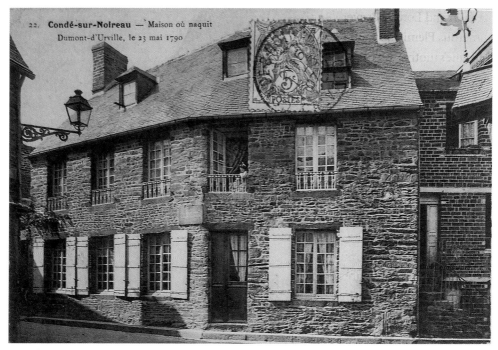

'Condé-sur-Noireau, maison où naquit Dumont-d'Urville, le 23 mai 1790', postcard, ca.1907, of the house in which Dumont d'Urville was born. It was badly damaged by Allied bombing in 1944 and subsequently demolished. Courtesy Jean-Jacques Thomas, Condé-sur-Noireau

purchasing the hereditary Bailly of Condé.[7] Gabriel would inherit this title of bailiff when his older brother Louis died shortly before the Revolution.[8] Condé-sur-Noireau became home to the family, and Jules was born in a corner townhouse with two storeys and an attic on rue Entre-les-Murs (now renamed rue Dumont d'Urville in his honour). Built of stone, it had a slate roof, two chimneys and shuttered ground-floor windows.[9] By this time, the d'Urville feudal manor house, 'Le Fouques', on an elevated escarpment above the river Tortillon near Saint-Germain-du-Crioult (between Vassy and Condé-sur-Noireau), was in ruins. Its reconstruction, by Jules' nephew Stanislas Dumont de la Londe,[10] would not begin until the Bourbon Restoration.

Jules' mother, Jeanne, was reputedly a very beautiful woman – 'tall, noble and relaxed in bearing', with a fine figure and 'the most lively blue eyes'.[11] It is a description that bespeaks her Viking Norman heritage and the blonde hair and blue eyes her son Jules inherited. She was born in the village of Saint-Rémy near Thury-Harcourt (Calvados), where her father, Jacques-François de Croisilles, was an advocate. The Croisilles were also from the nobility but not simply by virtue of office; they boasted a distinguished Norman lineage that included one of the chevaliers who accompanied Robert Curthose to Jerusalem during the First Crusade (1096–99).[12] Jeanne was also a descendant of Charlemagne and several Western Frankish kings, including Charles the Bald and Louis II; several Anglo-Saxon monarchs, including Alfred the Great; and numerous Flemish, Lombard, Burgundian and Germanic royal lines.[13] As we shall see, d'Urville's mother was a woman of formidable character, vivacity, conservative religious piety and confidence born of the assumptions of noble station and the established certainties of the *ancien régime* – certainties that were about to unravel.

At the time of the Revolution, which began less than a year before Jules was born, Condé-sur-Noireau was a town of perhaps 3500 individuals,[14] whose principal industries were linen- and hemp-spinning, weaving, tanning, hat-making and horse-trading. Located on a basin of schist on the strategic confluence of the Noireau and the Druance rivers, Condé was regularly subject to flooding. For much of the year, water stagnated in the main thoroughfare and 'it was not rare to see all communication between the north and the south of the town interrupted'.[15] When news of the storming of the Bastille reached muddy, sunken Condé-sur-Noireau, an excited mob burned local tax records. In neighbouring Caen, a mob stormed the citadel and killed a young dragoon officer. Fearing similar disturbances, the mayor of Condé-sur-Noireau banned the use of masks during the forthcoming summer carnival. Order was re-established by a town militia, whose flag was blessed by the vicar of Saint-Sauveur on 3 September and whose ranks were later formalised as a part of the National Guard.[16]

Among the very early revolutionary reforms enacted by France's new National Assembly, on the night of 4 August 1789, was the abolition of the feudal rights and fiscal privileges of the nobility, clergy, towns and provinces.[17] Exclusive military ranks and hereditary offices for the nobility were prohibited; seigneurial fiefs such as Urville were dissolved, and positions such as hereditary bailiff, held by Jules' father in Condé-sur-Noireau, were abolished. Gabriel is said to have fulfilled this 'honorable place' in the magistracy with 'much intelligence and integrity'.[18] It does appear that he undertook his duties fairly; how else can one explain the apparent respect in which he was held by the local revolutionary administration, even after he lost his hereditary post? Such a past, however, was no apparent barrier to advancement under the new order. One of the first revolutionary mayors of Condé-sur-Noireau, Michel Aubin, was himself a colleague and fellow hereditary bailiff of the town.[19] Under the *ancien régime*, Condé-sur-Noireau had been the chief seat of justice for 35 parishes, but when the National Assembly abolished the ancient provinces of France in favour of 83 new administrative departments, the number of new tribunals was strictly limited. Condé-sur-Noireau lost its judicial significance and became part of the new district of Vire, which in turn became part of the department of Calvados, with Caen as its capital.[20] Even if Jules' father had wanted to pursue a legal career in the wake of these administrative and legal changes, Condé-sur-Noireau would probably have offered limited opportunities. A year or two after Jules was born, with his principal reason for living in Condé-sur-

Noireau ended, his health failing and (as we shall see) his wife at risk of revolutionary vengeance, Gabriel moved his family to what appears to have been a residual portion of the fiefdom of Urville, 12 kilometres away in Vassy. Little did he know that it would soon become a focus of counter-revolutionary insurgency.

At the time, the vast majority of French citizens thought of reform in terms of constitutional monarchy. Even if they resented the loss of their privileges, it seems likely that the d'Urville family hoped for a secure monarchy and an end to France's fiscal crisis. Even Jules' uncle, abbé Jean-Jacques-François de Croisilles, is said to have been a supporter of the 'new ideas' while Canon of Cambrai in the early days of the Revolution.[21] It should not be forgotten that it was defections by enlightened noble and clerical members of the Estates-General that emboldened the non-noble Third Estate to declare the formation of a National Assembly and catalyse the Revolution. This support for reform by some members of the clergy and nobility was limited; it waned with the abolition of privileges, dismantling of ancient institutions and confiscation of properties, and as heartfelt religious beliefs were offended, and economic insecurity, war and violence left no level of French society untouched.

Aside from the personal loss of privilege that had been enjoyed by the nobility, there were a number of key events in this process of alienation for conservative Catholics such as Jules' mother. On Sunday, 30 January 1791, in Condé-sur-Noireau's church of Saint-Sauveur, as in churches throughout France, members of the local clergy were obliged to swear allegiance to a new civil constitution and effectively become government employees.[22] Jeanne appears not to have attended the ceremony, despite the fact that it was dignified with a solemn *Te Deum*. Her lack of attendance at this and other revolutionary festivals was noticed. Some priests refused to submit to the authority of the state and became known as refractories; Jules' mother was soon identified with them. The church was not only divested of its power and authority but also its property, and clerical properties throughout France were sold. In Condé-sur-Noireau, this sale took place at the end of April 1791 and raised a total of 18,873 francs.[23] Six weeks later, on 13 June 1791, Jules' mother was arrested for having spitefully thrown, or caused to be thrown (it was 1.00 am and the culprit could not actually be seen), the contents of a chamber pot full of filth onto the clothes of passing 'patriots'. After being denounced at the municipality, she was imprisoned for eight days.[24] On 21 June 1791, the day she was presumably released from prison, Louis XVI and the royal family were arrested at Varennes while attempting to flee the country to join émigrés menacing the fledgling French democracy. Another of Jules' maternal uncles, Jacques-François de Croisilles, a former member of the king's body guard, was one of the officers in the regiments of these émigré princes.[25] Austria and Prussia, united in their fear of the missionary zeal of the French Revolution, issued a joint declaration in August 1791 that threatened force if the French royal family was not released. For many in the National Assembly, particularly the deputies from the Gironde, this foreign menace was sufficient reason for war. Both France and her foreign enemies had miscalculated. The Austrians and Prussians thought France was on the verge of financial and administrative chaos and incapable of resisting a military assault, let alone mounting an effective attack. In contrast, the government in Paris mistakenly believed that Austria and Prussia were on the verge of a revolution and that French troops would be welcomed by downtrodden populations devoid of nationalist sentiments. With opportunistic enthusiasm for territorial conquest on both sides and few diplomatic initiatives to avert hostilities, armed conflict became inevitable. France declared war on Austria on 20 April 1792 and promptly invaded the Habsburg-ruled Southern Netherlands. Although the Austrians counter-attacked and were soon joined by the Prussians, on 20 September, the French thwarted their invasion at Valmy and set the scene for protracted war.

Initially, the volunteers who stepped forward to meet this foreign challenge to the Revolution were ardent and enthusiastic recruits, but in the wake of growing casualties, revolutionary excesses and the economic strain caused by the absence of able-bodied men sent to the front, the new 'volunteers' for military service were reluctant individuals bought, substituted or coerced by local councils to fill quotas for new battalions. Money was also needed by regional authorities to pay, feed and arm these men. The National Guard in Condé-sur-Noireau was armed only with locally made wooden pikes. The 'donations' to meet these provisioning costs, like the 'voluntarism' of many of the recruits, were in many respects a resigned response to a forced requisition or levy. In Condé-sur-Noireau, Jules' parents were obliged to pay 25 livres. In the nearby parishes where they also owned property, they gave even larger sums: 50 livres in Vassy, 60 livres in Saint-Pierre d'Entremont and 50 livres in Saint-Germain; this was in addition to 18 livres in 'donations' made to revolutionary authorities in Vassy and Condé-sur-Noireau in September 1791.[26]

In late 1792, to expunge any hint of Bourbon associations,[27] the name Condé-sur-Noireau was changed to Noireau ('black water'). Much dark water would indeed pass under the bridge before peace would return to this part of Normandy. On 21 January 1793, Louis XVI was executed. His death further fuelled the royalist insurgencies in Normandy and in the neighbouring Vendée and Brittany. By now, the French army was very much over-extended. The threat posed by foreign enemies and insurgents inevitably had internal political repercussions: the relatively moderate Girondin deputies in the National Convention (which replaced the National Assembly when France became a republic on 21 September 1792) were overthrown in early June 1793 and executed. Draconian powers were granted to a 12-member executive known as the Committee for Public Safety. Dominated by Maximilien Robespierre and the 'mountain' faction[28] of the Jacobin leadership, the committee met the counter-revolutionary crisis with utter ruthlessness. In August 1793, it ordered universal conscription, which ultimately created the largest army Europe had ever seen,[29] and on 5 September 1793, the 'Reign of Terror' (the Terror) was unleashed to crush all domestic opposition. By the end of July 1794, some 16,594 people had been guillotined. Many thousands more died in prison or as a result of summary mass executions during counter-insurgency operations in the cities and provinces.[30] Some idea of the cold-blooded amorality of the times can be gained from General François Westermann's report to the convention on the crushing of the Vendée insurgency in December 1793: 'There is no more Vendée. I have buried it in the marshes of Savenay. I have crushed the children under the hooves of the horses and massacred the women. I don't have a prisoner to reproach me. I have exterminated them all.'[31]

Earlier biographers have confused the fate of individual members of d'Urville's family during these tragic events. According to Aimable Matterer, one of the explorer's closest friends and one of his obituarists, Jules' father was taken before the 'frightful revolutionary tribunal of Caen' but freed thanks to the 'most persuasive eloquence' of his remarkable wife, who succeeded in extracting him from the 'bloody hands of these murderers'.[32] What Matterer wrote of this supposed episode, more than 50 years after the events, was very likely based on his faded memory of conversations aboard the survey vessel *Chevrette* in the Mediterranean and the Black Sea in 1819–20. This testimony apparently inspired Just-Jean-Étienne Roy, who, under the pseudonym Fr[ançois]. Joubert, published a highly unreliable biography of the explorer in 1871.[33] In it, he fictionalised the elder d'Urville's arrest and trial to such an extent that it took up almost a quarter of his book! The 1889 edition even contained an engraving by Aristide Pannetier representing the purported arrest, with Jules' father leaning on a faithful servant in front of a château far grander than any home he actually lived in.[34]

There is no surviving or verifiable primary documentary evidence to suggest Jules' father was ever the personal victim of the Terror. Vergniol asserted that he was tried before the Revolutionary Tribunal in Caen in February 1794 for 'conspiracy with foreigners and plotting against the safety of the fatherland', and that Madame Dumont d'Urville went to plead his case and convinced the judges that 'this demi-paralytic, capable of pronouncing a few words and a few lines with difficulty, was even less able to conspire for the ruin of the Republic'.[35] Vergniol gives no source for his assertions. There is no doubt that Jules' father was old and possibly even infirm by February 1794. According to Matterer, he was unable to go to his son's rescue when he fell on the glowing brazier around 1792. Nevertheless, he retained his mental faculties and on 8 July 1794, prior to travelling to Maltot near Caen, signed his name, albeit with an unsteady hand.[36]

'L'arrestation du père de Dumont d'Urville', engraving by
Aristide Pannetier, from Fr. Joubert [Just-Jean-Étienne
Roy], Dumont d'Urville, A. Mame et Fils, Tours, 1889.
In fact, it was d'Urville's mother, not his father, who was
arrested during the Terror. Mitchell Library, State Library of
New South Wales

Like a great deal of oral history, there is a kernel of truth in the story, even if
the events and the principal actors are confused or transposed. There is ample
documentary evidence that it was Jules' mother, rather than his father, who was
arrested by a detachment of the National Guard acting under the orders of the local
Jacobin Committee of Surveillance on 14 October 1793. This was for having a brother
who was a member of the 'bodyguard of the tyrant Capet [Louis XVI]', for 'never
having given any proof of her attachment to the Revolution' and for having 'insulted
the patriotism of the good citizens on days of civic celebration'.[37] Other documents,
co-signed by Colein-Dubusq, provide more specific details. Her accusers declared that

she had never attended any festivals or parades and raked up the earlier incident in
which the stinking chamber pot had been emptied onto passing patriots. Jeanne was
again arrested while still breastfeeding her youngest child.[38] It was perhaps then that
the family was obliged to engage a wet nurse named Nicole, who was herself arrested
some months later for her loyalty and dedication to the d'Urvilles.

Jules' father, abundantly aware of the mortal threat to his wife, went to her defence
and wrote several appeals for her to be released on bail or kept under house arrest. On
9 February 1794, he wrote to the local revolutionary authorities and acknowledged
that his brother-in-law was indeed an émigré; that his wife might outwardly appear
unattached to the Revolution but that for a very long time she had had no contact with
her brother; that she was a good Republican; that she had 'devoted her time to the
education of her daughters … in the principles of equality'; that she had abandoned
her vain noble titles; and that she did not participate in civic or public festivals because
of his infirmities and because by nature she was 'strongly misanthropic'. Even before
the Revolution, she had not attended festivals because she was exclusively devoted to
the care of her children. Furthermore, he insisted, she had not insulted local patriots;
rather it was 'a clumsy servant', distracted by one of his little children, who emptied a
'potty which unfortunately splashed some of the passers-by'.[39]

To this litany of excuses, the anxious old man catalogued his and his wife's payments
to local 'volunteers' and was at pains to point out that he had only a house and a
small garden in Condé-sur-Noireau, where he no longer lived, but that his wife had
nevertheless still given 25 livres there. Indeed, all their properties earned less than
1000 livres in rent. Despite his able advocacy, the members of the local Committee of
Surveillance reaffirmed their belief in Jeanne's guilt and now made additional mention
of a bundle of her letters, 'without reference to the Revolution, but very injurious to the
commune of Noireau'.[40] Unsure what to do (or perhaps reluctant to show leniency or
compassion at a local level), the revolutionaries in Condé-sur-Noireau decided to refer
her case to a higher, more-dangerous authority: the Committee of General Security or
a representative of the people. Despite the initial reforms to the judicial system, France
had once again been reduced to summary legal process.

Jeanne appeared before a representative of the people, Henri-Gaspard-Charles
Bouret, on 5 April 1794. This was the day the former leading revolutionary Georges
Danton was condemned to death and executed – a reminder of the perilous, ruthless
times. Bouret was originally a notary and former mayor of Riez in the provençal
Basses-Alpes. Although a committed republican and deputy to the convention who
had worked ferociously against clerical influence in Cherbourg (in order to prevent
a naval mutiny and support for an expected British-assisted émigré landing), he was
also against the excesses of the Terror and later took a leading role in dismantling

it, calling its perpetrators 'cannibals'.[41] Bouret's treatment of Jeanne suggests he was indeed a man of some humanity. By now, she had fallen ill in the cold, crowded prison. A report by the medical officers (later called into question) attests that she was prostrate, her pulse was feeble and that she was suffering from dysentery. In another report, they expressed their concern at the presence of this contagious disease in the centre of Condé-sur-Noireau. An earlier letter from her husband, dated 1 brumaire in the new revolutionary calendar (23 October 1793), also reported that she was spitting blood as a result of a chest condition, but this was not confirmed by the medical officers. It would seem that she also had an anal fistula, perhaps as a result of a difficult childbirth. The medical reports convinced Bouret to give her verbal permission to return home, which she did three days later. Jeanne's apparent freedom to return must have angered the Condé Jacobins because she was taken from her bed the next day by four local guardsmen. Now confident of fairer treatment in Caen, she boldly asked to be returned there rather than incarcerated once again in the small local prison in Condé-sur-Noireau. Two days later, she did in fact present herself to Robert Benard, commissioner of police in Caen. However, he was not prepared to lock her up without a formal order of arrest and, on 24 germinal an II (13 April 1794), wrote a perplexed letter advising the gendarmerie in Condé what had happened.[42] In the meantime, Jeanne, accompanied by her married eldest daughter, Adélaïde-Jeanne-Victoire, herself the mother of an infant child, returned home yet again. The gendarmerie in Condé-sur-Noireau provided the required summary of her case and also questioned whether she was as ill as she maintained (presumably on account of her numerous journeys between Condé and Caen). On 27 germinal (16 April), the authorities in Caen ordered that she be locked up in the city's ancient former Benedictine abbey.[43]

By now, Jeanne had made several petitions for release, including being released under guard. In these petitions, she frequently mentioned her young children, who must have been deeply traumatised by these events. She was eventually granted bail in early fructidor (the third week of August 1794) but with the condition that she pay for a guard on her home. Nevertheless, her enemies made further accusations against her on 10 fructidor an II (27 August 1794), co-signed once again by Citizen Colein-Dubusq; 'suspect persons, even refractory priests' were believed to frequent her home.[44] (In that month, priests who had refused to swear allegiance to the civil constitution were ordered to be arrested; the church of Saint-Sauveur had already been ordered closed on 27 April.) The 'patriots of the commune' entered and searched her house in Vassy and found made-up beds with still-warm sheets! Jeanne had had enough of these violations of her home and, in breach of her bail conditions, she apparently fled to Caen. Her embarrassed guard, who can't have been too good at his job, grumbled about not being paid! Indeed, the accusers of 'La Durville' complained that she had exposed not only the guard but her husband, the officer sent to arrest her and the committee to the strongest reproaches. Furthermore, her evasion had occasioned a costly search.

While there were calls for a wider net of culpability – one tortuous recapitulation even cast aspersions on one of the medical officers, the two guards, Jules' sisters and the faithful family servant Nicole – no one sought to implicate Jules' father. Nicole was the only additional arrest, and a certain sympathy was extended to Citizen Dumont d'Urville and those who had guaranteed his stubborn wife's bail. Her flight had exposed them all to financial liability.

How long Jeanne's ordeal lasted and whether she was granted her liberty or simply came out of hiding post-thermidor is unclear. The fall of the Jacobin 'mountain' faction did not bring immediate peace to the area around Condé-sur-Noireau. Royalist Chouan attacks, led by Louis de Frotté, became bolder and more frequent. Vassy was attacked on 23 September 1794, and its republican garrison retreated to Saint-Germain. An inn-keeper was killed, and several houses were pillaged by the royalist forces. A degree of calm returned during the winter, but Vassy, Saint-Germain and other neighbouring villages where the d'Urville family owned property once again came under insurgent control in March 1795. Local food prices increased tenfold: by December 1795, a one-pound loaf of bread cost 30–35 francs.[45] By this time, Jules' family had fled this scene of bitter irregular civil war that would rage until 1800. According to his life-long friend, the writer Isidore Le Brun,[46] they took refuge in the Collège du bois in Caen. Founded in 1441, it belonged to the university until the Revolution.[47] Today, the remains of its impressive gothic vaulting can still be seen in Caen.[48] Although Le Brun (who was himself born in Caen) states that they remained in the college for two years and that they left for the manor house of Cours d'Orne in 1795, it seems likely that they resided in Caen only for perhaps the last trimester of 1794 and part of 1795.

Cours d'Orne, near Feuguerolles-sur-Orne (Calvados), is an open rectangular ensemble of stone buildings set on a gentle slope down to the tree-lined banks of the river Orne. Although it appears in local records as early as the thirteenth century, and its southeastern corner is probably its most ancient, Cours d'Orne has evolved over many centuries. Its two circular dovecotes date from the fifteenth century, the first storey of the northern façade from the sixteenth century, the southern façade from the seventeenth century and the northern end of the eastern façade from the last quarter of the eighteenth century.[49]

The move to Cours d'Orne was not by chance; the manor was an ancestral property on Jules' mother's side. Jules' maternal grandmother was the daughter of Jean-Jacques Fortin, the seigneur of Maltot and Feuguerolles, to which Cours d'Orne belonged. It was to Maltot, very close to Feuguerolles-sur-Orne, that Jules' father obtained a

The southern façade and dovecote of Cours d'Orne, where d'Urville's family took refuge in the years 1795–99, and where his father died in October 1796; illustration from Commandant H. Navel's Monographie de Feuguerolles-sur-Orne (Calvados) des origines à la Révolution, Caen, Jouan et Bigot, 1931. Bibliothèque de Caen, FN B 130

document (signed by nearly a dozen Condé revolutionaries) to travel in July 1794.[50] This would suggest a measure of careful planning, with him perhaps moving there before the rest of the family but as tenant rather than owner. According to several accounts, they were not alone; a number of refractory priests appear to have joined them in their refuge. Despite secularisation and concomitant attempts to establish a competing 'Religion of the Supreme Being', by 1795 there was a degree of liberalisation and toleration as the Catholic clergy began to reassert itself in the homes of the devout. In Normandy, where the republic remained suspicious of clerical involvement in the royalist insurgency, these tentative steps were more cautious. The archives of the Bishopric of Bayeux reveal that between 9 February 1796 and 6 September 1798, abbé Antoine-Thomas Delafontaine celebrated three marriages and five baptisms in the chapel of a private house in the parish of Feuguerolles. The fact that Jules' mother, his eldest sister Adélaïde and, on 13 February 1796, a Charles Dumont (most probably Adélaïde's husband) were formal witnesses to these sacraments would suggest that the chapel in question was at Cours d'Orne, and that abbé Delafontaine resided with the d'Urville family over several months of the summer of 1796.[51] Whether it was a private world of silk chasubles and gold chalices or the simple peasant homespun and pewter *calix stanneus* of a persecuted church we do not know. Nor do we know if abbé Delafontaine was present, on 12 October 1796, when Jules' father died at Cours d'Orne at the age of 68. Doubtless, the family prepared his body for burial and observed an office for the dead with or without a priest. Gabriel Dumont d'Urville was not laid to rest beside Feuguerolles' beautiful romanesque church but was buried in the commune of Fresne (Orne), close to the hamlet of Poulhaye, where he was born.[52]

Jules' infancy had already been marked by his family's loss of power, status and wealth in the wake of revolutionary reforms. While he must have spent long periods with his father (especially during his mother's imprisonment and flight), he could not have received normal paternal mentoring. Jules' father must often have seemed more like a feeble grandfather, but a man who cannot play rough and tumble with his son can still find ways to offer solace, tell a story, or teach a child to read – even from an invalid bed. There is no surviving image of Jules as a child, but the bleak word portrait we have of him during this harsh and painful period is evocative of both physical and emotional deprivation: a 'weak and sickly child, short of stature … straight hair, the legs thin, big belly, big head and a morose air which almost never left him'. [53]

In his family's rural isolation, Jules' early education was haphazard. According to Le Brun, there were few books available to him at Cours d'Orne, but at the age of seven he began to read (and re-read) Isaac-Joseph Berruyer's *Histoire du peuple de Dieu*.[54] In this three-part, multi-volume work, published between 1728 and 1757, the Jesuit author Berruyer offered an engaging, lively, even romantic account of the history of the Jews, Jesus and the early Christians. His popular religious history was translated into German, Italian, Spanish and Polish but soon aroused controversy and accusations of heresy. Since each section was quickly placed on the papal index of prohibited books – it was not until 1828 that an edited version managed to pass the Vatican censor – young Jules was fortunate to have access to the original.[55] The presence of Berruyer's book also suggests that Jules' family, or perhaps the refractory priests who took refuge with them, were not as dogmatic or conservative in their beliefs as one might have thought. How much a seven-year-old child, even a precocious and highly intelligent one, can read and understand is another matter, but the second part of Berruyer's work also contained maps and other appendices to engage a young mind. It is tempting to speculate that at an early age it stimulated his interest in Hebrew, a language he would later devote himself to with great seriousness and even engage rabbinical assistance to study.[56]

Cours d'Orne is surrounded by lush green fields punctuated with buttercups and other wildflowers. Isolated and bounded by the river Orne, it was probably in the surrounding fields that Jules first began to study plants. Nature had other lessons to offer too, for the river was rich in aquatic life, which in turn attracted numerous birds. Jules' family had a strong respect for nature, and more than 50 years before, in January 1740, one of his hot-tempered maternal great-uncles had stabbed and wounded a gardener at Cours d'Orne after he found him shooting waterbirds in large number on the otherwise tranquil river! The maternal side of his family would certainly leave an indelible mark on the boy, for in 1798, Jules' forceful mother was joined by her erudite brother, abbé Jean-Jacques-François de Croisilles. A decade earlier, he had been vicar-general in Cambrai (Nord) and would probably have succeeded the bishop had the Revolution not thrown the French church into turmoil. Now he gained refuge and purpose at Cours d'Orne as his nephew's exclusive tutor. Jules later wrote: 'The little that I am, I owe to my good uncle, whose learning was as obliging as it was varied. After two years, I could readily translate Quintus Curtius and Virgil [and] I had learned arithmetic and geography.'[57]

Jules' childhood was unquestionably austere. Matterer wrote that he rose early and that his mother accustomed him to long and tiring journeys through the countryside, 'barefoot and without a hat'. It was character-building and he acknowledged this maternal discipline positively: 'I owe the force of my temperament to my respectable mother.'[58] According to Lesson, Jules' mother was also emotionally austere, and he asserted that she disdained 'gentle affection and the ordinary tenderness of a mother for her son'. Her plan of education was to give her child 'a proud and manly character, free of the usual affectations of community life'. According to Lesson, she employed the formal word *vous* rather than *tu* with her son so as to exclude familiarity and maintain a certain 'ceremonial habit' in the family. This was in contrast to the warm and informal relationship Jules enjoyed with his uncle. Although Lesson acknowledged, with surprise, Jules' affection for his domineering mother, he also felt that she had given him a manner 'dry in the expression of his emotions, [and] rugged in form, which the naval profession maintained in no small measure'. At the same time, Jules developed habits that were always 'calm, serious and solitary',[59] and he later acknowledged that his habit of 'plunging into reflection' had given him 'a cold and serious air, unusual for my age'.[60]

Despite the austerity perceived by others, Jules looked back on his childhood and the Norman countryside with joy: 'The marshes, the rain and the bad roads, nothing stopped me,' he wrote. 'With what pleasure I frolicked barefoot in the woods and clambered up mountains! ... A wood, meadows, a stream, birdsong, were enough to give me the truest joy compared to all the finest works of art.'[61] He enjoyed early-morning swims, became a good horseman and swordsman, but had little interest in music or dance (the latter he considered ridiculous exercise) and paid little attention to his physical appearance. Although shy and lacking in social graces, he was also ambitious. One day, on a visit to a fair at Condé-sur-Noireau, he reflected on the fact that his birthplace had produced no great name in the affairs of men, so he promised himself that he would 'redouble his efforts' and would one day bestow his name among the ranks of the famous. Later in life, he acknowledged, self-deprecatingly, that he had had 'so much arrogance ... in the soul of a brat!'[62]

2

The lycée & the sea

… profane men living in ships like the holy men gathered together in
monasteries develop traits of profound resemblance … for simplicity
is a good counsellor and isolation not a bad educator.

Joseph Conrad*

All the published biographies of d'Urville state that he commenced his naval career in 1807; however, a document in his personal dossier at the Château de Vincennes, dated 23 July 1808, states that he had 24 months' service beginning on 1 vendémiaire an VIII (23 September 1799), the equivalent of New Year's Day, which roughly coincided with the end of the two years' tutelage he received from his uncle. He joined the 16-gun cutter *Sandwich* at only nine and a half years of age, as a novice sailor with a meagre salary of 12 francs per month. Although such youthful entry to the navy was not unheard of,[1] it was often a brief interlude under the care of a trusted relative or family patron with the aim of later seniority and promotion. The *Sandwich*, as her name suggests, was originally a British vessel – under lease to the Royal Navy when captured by the 16-gun French lugger *Affronteur* in June 1799.[2] Her new French commander, Jean-Marie Le Bastard de Kerguiffinec, had joined the navy just before the Revolution and gained rapid promotion with the emigration of many other noble officers. He had commanded the corvette *Biche* during the expedition to Ireland in 1798 and then the *Lazare Hoche* in the Mediterranean. Le Bastard de Kerguiffinec was given command of the *Sandwich* in August 1799. She appears to have been based, or rather was blockaded by, Admiral William Cornwallis's Channel Fleet, in Douarnenez (Finistère) on the Pouldavid estuary in Brittany. D'Urville's service aboard was attested by naval authorities in Brest,[3] so we can assume that he took part in a battle between the *Sandwich* and the 12-gun British cutter *Nile*, drawn into Douarnenez Bay on 9 May 1801. During the engagement, Le Bastard de Kerguiffinec attempted to disable the *Nile* and capture her, but the British cutter, with a crew of 45 men under the command of

* *Chance* (1913), part i, chapter i

Lieutenant Newton, put up stiff resistance. The *Sandwich*, damaged and leaking, was forced to withdraw and seek protection underneath the guns of a shore battery.

In the meantime, d'Urville's family had left Cours d'Orne and moved back to Vassy. This was in the year following Bonaparte's coup d'état of 18 brumaire (9 November 1799), when the young dictator sought to crush the royalist Chouan insurgency in Normandy once and for all with an injection of 60,000 troops. The marquis de Frotté, who had returned secretly to Normandy from England on the day d'Urville entered the naval registers, was tricked into negotiations with promises of safe conduct only to be arrested and summarily executed.[4] Late in the same year, secret overtures to the papacy commenced the process that led to the signing of the concordat with Rome, including the rescission of anti-clerical legislation, the recognition of Catholicism as the religion of the majority of French citizens, and the return of places of worship not already alienated or sold. Among the pope's concessions in the agreement (signed in September 1801 and promulgated in France in April 1802), was the rationalisation of the number of dioceses in France from 136 to 60.[5] Such a reduction greatly impeded abbé de Croisilles' prospects of promotion ahead of those forced to relinquish 76 now-redundant sees; nevertheless, when the French church reconstituted itself from the shadows, he became vicar-general and secretary-general to Charles Brault, bishop of Bayeux. It was a return, for he had received his tonsure, taken his minor vows and served as deacon of the cathedral in Bayeux more than 30 years before.[6]

Bonaparte's overtures to the church and ultimate reconciliation with Rome removed clerical agitation and the religious outrage that drove ordinary peasants and their former noble seigneurs to risk their lives as royalist guerrillas. The Treaty of Lunéville (February 1801) and the Treaty of Amiens (March 1802) also starved the insurgency of foreign support by temporarily ending hostilities between France and her British and European enemies. Furthermore, resolute military action and the destruction of the Chouan leadership made the price of rebellion more and more costly for a population that essentially craved peace, order and stability, and had already regained the right to worship in its own churches. Consolidating his dictatorship, Bonaparte gave France order and an ersatz monarchy by crowning himself emperor, with the pope's blessing, in December 1804.

D'Urville's perhaps partly nominal 24 months' service on the *Sandwich* ended in the month Bonaparte signed his concordat with Rome. Soon after, he rejoined his uncle, living in a narrow street near the bishop's residence in Bayeux. D'Urville seems to have made a positive impression on the influential Bishop Brault,[7] judging by the latter's supportive testimonials to the navy minister a decade later. He continued to devour books: Plutarch's *Parallel Lives*, the plays of Racine, the history of the discovery of America and, especially, Homer, all works he treasured until the end of his life. His memory was prodigious, and Le Brun later recorded that he could recite an entire canto of Virgil's *Aeneid* without fault.[8] Lesson wrote similarly of his capacity to recite from Homer's *Odyssey*. According to Le Brun, at the very early age of 12, d'Urville completed his *rhétorique* – then the final year of college before Bonaparte's educational reforms. He also studied mathematics and Greek at the Collège de Bayeux, under the direction of a certain abbé Le Comte, in the rue Saint-Patrice. Le Brun tells us that he was soon translating the witty satirical works of Lucian of Samosata – presumably including the fantastic travel tale *The True History*, which contains an account of a voyage to the moon with the aid of a waterspout in the Atlantic. During this period, he remained pious and fervent in his religious devotions. Despite d'Urville's early engagement with the navy, his mother is said to have harboured ambitions that he should follow his uncle into the priesthood, but Bayeux, close to the windswept English Channel, seems only to have reaffirmed his desire for a naval career, and it was to his uncle he turned for support in resisting his mother's plans.[9]

Yet another document in d'Urville's service dossier, dated 3 November 1808, indicates that from 4 prairial an X (24 May 1802) until 21 messidor an XIII (10 July 1804), he served aboard a Cherbourg-based naval schooner *Les Deux Amis* as a novice sailor under the command of Captain François-Claude Le Tellier.[10] There is some uncertainty regarding this vessel; the name belonged to more than one naval vessel and to a number of privateers within a short period of time. D'Urville must have joined *Les Deux Amis* during the Peace of Amiens and presumably remained with her for nearly 14 months after hostilities resumed on 17 May 1803. He nevertheless maintained his precocious scholarly interests; in February 1803, not yet 13 years of age, he delivered a Latin philosophical *prolegomena* (introductory essay) to a mainly ecclesiastical audience in Bayeux.[11] According to Le Brun, his essay was printed but no copies appear to have survived. Extracts from a letter he wrote to his uncle around this time offer some insights into his philosophical musings, linguistic researches and remarkable youthful intellect:

> There is room to believe that one day, disabused of the value of this state of things to fill the emptiness of my heart, I will be freed of these researches into several branches of literature. [With] strong erudition, endowed not of genius but of a sufficiently proper judgement, I would have become an able commentator, a judicious critic or a savant glossarist. It was written in the book of destiny that I will have none of this … Like you, I believe that with the light of firm and strict reason, with the sole aid of philosophy, man can fulfil with dignity the duties imposed on him on this earth. Perhaps the sage is more admirable than the real devotee. Philosophy is the throne of wisdom; religion is nothing but the support; but how few mortals are capable of being true philosophers![12]

In the meantime, Antoine-François de Fourcroy, director-general of public instruction, had begun to reorganise France's education system, which had been much altered by the Revolution and particularly as a result of the ejection of religious teaching orders from schools and colleges. Fourcroy's aim, under Bonaparte's orders, was to ensure a broad secular curriculum (of languages, literature, science and mathematics), under strong central control, to train the nation's civil and military leaders. At the outset, 30 new colleges, known as *lycées*,[13] were established throughout France, with a defined program of six years' study. To gain a civil service position, enter a university, tertiary college or the officer corps of the army or navy, a *baccalauréat* from a lycée became an essential prerequisite – and still is.

In July 1804, d'Urville became a student of the new Lycée impérial de Caen (now the Lycée Malherbe), with a scholarship from Bayeux.[14] This was the month that his service record indicates that he left *Les Deux Amis*. Although his mother heeded clerical opposition to the secular lycées and their seemingly godless dormitories, she was pragmatic enough to accept that they held the key to her son's future and is said to have compromised by allowing him to attend as a day student.[15] Surviving documents for this period are very fragmentary, but d'Urville started a notebook for his physics lessons at the lycée on 22 pluviôse an XIII (11 February 1805).[16] His name also appears among the list of bursary holders in July 1806.[17] In that same year, there were 176 boarders.[18] Although not all the lycée's students were destined for a military career, they were divided into companies of 25, subject to military discipline under the command of a sergeant and four corporals; a sergeant-major liaised with the instructing officer. A navy-blue military tunic with high collar and brass-buttoned doublet in celestial blue[19] was worn by boarders and was forbidden to day students; in 1808, the uniform became compulsory for all those enrolled.[20] D'Urville, who remained a day student until his matriculation in 1807, thereby avoided this additional regimentation. As we shall see, for most of his life he tended to avoid wearing a uniform whenever he could.

Although the *proviseur* (headmaster), Louis Vastel, was a jurist, the *censeur* (assistant-headmaster), Charles-Alexandre de Mouy, was the former canon of Nancy in Lorraine. Indeed, despite Madame Dumont d'Urville's religious anxieties about the lycée, it had a chaplain, and many, if not most, of the school's administrative and teaching staff were former clergymen. The eight teachers (three for Latin, four for mathematics and one for French and Latin literature) were largely drawn from the former colleges of Caen and Alençon. One of the Latin masters, Monsieur Ribard, was a former Benedictine monk who had been driven out of the abbey of Saint-Étienne in 1790, only to return as a teacher when its buildings were handed over to the lycée.[21] This was the same former Benedictine abbey where d'Urville's mother was briefly imprisoned during the Terror – which might also explain some of her negative sentiments towards the new institution.

Occupied by the lycée between 1804 and 1959 (and now the Hôtel de Ville), the abbey is a magnificent collection of historic limestone buildings. The original abbey and abbey church were built by William the Conqueror in the eleventh century, and his grave can still be seen in the chancel. A gothic choir was constructed in the thirteenth century, and major reconstruction and additions to the southern side of the abbey took place in the sixteenth, seventeenth and eighteenth centuries, giving this wing of the former abbey a neo-classical façade. The four storeys were linked by sweeping cantilevered limestone staircases, held together, in precise compression, without mortar and seemingly suspended in mid-air. The chapter room, refectory and sacristy were endowed with richly carved oak panelling and grand oil paintings of religious and secular scenes. In short, it was an extraordinary architectural edifice for a new school.

The lycée also had a modest library of 1500 volumes from which all students could borrow.[22] D'Urville continued to devour books, including accounts of the voyages of George Anson, Louis-Antoine de Bougainville and James Cook (which further fired his romance with the sea), and every work of drama he could lay his hands on. The fact that he also gained a grounding in English at this time suggests that some of the accounts of exploration that he read were in their original language. Even after officially abandoning literature in favour of mathematics and science to better his prospects of admission to the elite École polytechnique, d'Urville could not resist reading his way through more than 100 novels.[23]

At some stage, probably when he was a student at the lycée, d'Urville began a lifelong friendship with Pierre-Aimé Lair, director of the Jardin des plantes in Caen and for 40 years councillor of the prefecture. The Norman botanical historian Auguste Chevalier also suggested that during this period, d'Urville got to know the entomologist Jean-Baptiste Boisduval, the marine biologist Jean-Vincent-Félix Lamouroux and the botanist (and later photographer) Louis-Alphonse de Brébisson,[24] but this is doubtful. Although they certainly did become friends and colleagues in the following decades, Boisduval and Brébisson were respectively nine and eight years d'Urville's junior, and Lamouroux did not become a teacher at the Académie de Caen until 1808, the year after d'Urville departed. Nevertheless, d'Urville sent Lamouroux natural history specimens from the Mediterranean (they shared a keen interest in marine algae) in 1819[25] and sought his professional assistance in 1822. After Lamouroux's death, d'Urville's mother went to live with his widow in Caen, which suggests earlier family associations. Similarly, Boisduval's friendship went beyond entomological collaboration; he also became d'Urville's family doctor in Paris.

Because the Lycée de Caen opened its doors after d'Urville had already completed his *rhétorique*, he did not begin his studies there at entry level, deliberately choosing a lower class than was first proposed, to be better assured of winning prizes and perhaps to be with students his own age. Despite his obvious intelligence, ability and familiarity with parts of the curriculum, he was not as gifted (or perhaps disciplined) in mathematics and the sciences as he was in languages. Unlike his close friend Louis-Charles Lefébure de Cerisy,[26] he was not accepted by the École polytechnique after sitting the selective examination in September 1807. (His teachers were apparently surprised, but Le Brun speculated that, had d'Urville spent his final year at the lycée as a boarder, presumably with a tutor and free of other distractions, the result might have been otherwise.) D'Urville was offered a respectable place at the École militaire in Fontainebleau but declined. Instead, in November 1807, the thin, awkward 17 year old set off for Brest to rejoin the navy.[27]

D'Urville left Caen in the gathering winter of late 1807 with a letter of introduction from the prefect of Calvados, Charles-Ambroise de Caffarelli du Falga. Before the Revolution, Caffarelli had been a priest and canon of the ancient diocese of Toul in Lorraine. He was also a classical Greek scholar, and it seems that the precocious talents of the young student from the lycée had drawn his attention during an official inspection; it also seems likely that abbé de Croisilles made representations on behalf of his talented nephew. Caffarelli came from a distinguished family of erudite soldiers and clergymen from Languedoc. Two of his brothers were generals (one of whom died during Bonaparte's Egyptian campaign);[28] another, a former refractory canon of Montpellier, became bishop of Saint-Brieuc in the wake of the concordat. Yet another brother, Louis-Marie-Joseph Caffarelli, was the maritime prefect of Brest,[29] and it was to him that d'Urville had a personal letter of introduction.[30]

Brest is still home to France's largest and most important naval base. Like Caen and Condé-sur-Noireau, it was badly bombed in 1944, and the rebuilt town and port are very different from what d'Urville would have known in 1807. On the extremity of the Finistère Peninsula, which juts into the Atlantic, it was strategically located on the American, African and Asian trade routes, and was windward of British naval dockyards. Within the protective embrace of the Plateau du Léon and the Crozon Peninsula, the harbour was also readily defended. Nevertheless, the chronically under-funded French navy, which less than two years earlier had been routed off Cape Trafalgar in Spain, was powerless to deal with the continuous British naval blockade. On the western tip of Brittany, it was also far from the estuaries of the Seine and Loire, and had poor road access and no canals. The large number of naval personnel in the complex of docks, warehouses, barracks, shipyards, Vauban-designed fortifications, forges and armouries lived in relative isolation from the rest of France.

D'Urville was warmly received in Brest by the intelligent and conscientious Intendant Caffarelli. Granted the rank of *aspirant provisoire*, he joined the 74-gun

Aquilon (ex-*Nestor*), under the able and well-respected mariner Captain Jacques Rémy Maingon, who had been in command since December 1805.[31] An experienced teacher of hydrography and mathematics, and the author of several scientific monographs, Maingon was a captain who had risen from the lower deck and was an ideal instructor for a bright young recruit destined for the officer corps.[32]

Despite the state of war that raged in Europe, the French navy could mount little more than occasional coastal sorties when the winds and fogs rendered the British blind. When not studying for his admission examination for officer training, d'Urville occupied himself studying Hebrew, Greek and Latin in the naval library.[33] Brest also had impressive botanical gardens, established in 1694 to grow medicinal herbs for the adjoining naval hospital and enriched by species brought back from all over the world by French naval officers. Furthermore, two senior naval medical officers had founded an associated 'natural history cabinet', which in the nineteenth century grew into a formal museum.[34] Given d'Urville's interest in botany, it is hard to believe he was not drawn to this splendid oasis (tragically destroyed during the siege of Brest in 1944).

When d'Urville passed his examination for officer training and formally became an élève de la marine (midshipman), his annual salary jumped nearly three-fold to 600 francs. He served on the *Aquilon* until 23 July 1808 and was therefore spared the disaster that befell her nine months later. Joining Admiral Zacharie Allemand's squadron, Maingon sailed her to Rochefort in March 1809. There, off the Île d'Aix on 13 April 1809, she and three other French vessels were attacked by fireships deployed by Lord Thomas Cochrane's Royal Navy squadron. Maingon, who had so much to offer as a teacher and hydrographer, was killed in the course of the attack – one of so many gifted men whose lives were squandered in the conflict.

Because d'Urville's next vessel was not yet completed, he was given more than six months' leave, punctuated by three days aboard the *Requin* (a small naval ferry commanded by a helmsman) before being posted to Le Havre in Normandy. He used this as an opportunity to cross Brittany, largely on foot, and to visit his family in Bayeux. At this time, he also began to read the works of Arthur Young, the enlightened English social and political observer and agricultural writer, who had travelled widely in France during the Revolution. Although Young's works had been translated into French, d'Urville chose to read them in the original English. Similarly, with his growing passion for natural history, he began to read classic works of German botany and zoology. His object appears to have been as much absorbing the contents of these books as the language they were written in. Of the process, he himself later wrote: 'I read … the whole of a grammar with the greatest attention; then I got myself a dictionary and a work in the language which occupied me, I boldly began to translate, often at the risk of spending many hours to discover the meaning of a sentence; after two months, the dictionary served me little.'[35] We do not know how well he spoke the languages he learned, and there is some evidence that his English was heavily accented. [36]

D'Urville finally joined the *Amazone* in February 1809.[37] She was a 1100-tonne, 40-gun frigate, launched in Le Havre in May 1807. Fitted out in Cherbourg and commissioned in January 1809,[38] she was under the command of Captain Bernard-Louis Rousseau, who had 34 years' experience in the navy and merchant marine. D'Urville served aboard her as an *aspirant* second class, on what Matterer called a 'very arduous cruise'[39] in the English Channel and the Atlantic until May 1810, but which Rousseau's service dossier suggests was largely confined to Le Havre and the estuary of the Seine.[40] D'Urville joined the *Amazone* convinced that she was destined for the Indies and that he would escape 'insignificant service in ports and harbours' and 'visit distant countries'.[41] He would have to wait longer for such opportunities. Before she was assigned elsewhere in the spring of 1810, the *Amazone* was inspected by the Emperor Napoleon and his new wife, Princess Marie-Louise of Austria. According to Le Brun, d'Urville saw only 'the conqueror in the emperor, and that was nothing to admire'.[42] He was not interested in battlefield glory and spurned the blood-drenched martial culture of the Empire, declaring:

> I found that nothing was more noble and worthy of a generous spirit than to devote one's life to the progress of the sciences. Because of this my interests were pushing me towards the navy of discovery rather than the purely military navy. Without dread of the chances of battle, my naturally republican spirit could not conceive of any real glory attached to the act of risking one's life and killing one's fellow men for differences of opinions over things and words.[43]

His declaration of a 'naturally republican spirit' affirmed a democratic detachment not only from the imperial megalomania of Napoleon but also from the monarchical values of the *ancien régime*. For all Napoleon's efforts to embolden d'Urville and his comrades aboard the *Amazone*, the emperor neither understood what his navy required nor comprehended what it was capable of in the face of the ruthless discipline, efficiency and resources of the British navy. After taking a company of 51 gunners to Antwerp, the *Amazone* was attacked by a British division near Barfleur on 23 March 1811. Fleeing her attackers, she accidentally grounded on rocks and was ignominiously burned the next day lest she fall into enemy hands. After just over two years' service, all that was left of the *Amazone* was a charred carcass picked clean of copper and other metal by naval salvors.[44]

D'Urville was not aboard the *Amazone* when she was burned. Orders from his superiors that placed him elsewhere seem to have been a direct result of letters to the navy minister from abbé de Croisilles (with significant personal annotations by the bishop of Bayeux), who urged his advancement and promotion to the rank of *enseigne de vaisseau*.[45] He was ordered to join the 80-gun *Suffren* in Toulon. Given the blockading British, there was no question of getting there by joining the Mediterranean fleet on a transport sailing through the Strait of Gibraltar. Instead, he traversed the length (and much of the breadth) of France via Bourges and Clermont-Ferrand by coach.

Toulon, then a town of some 33,000 people,[46] made a great impression on d'Urville. He would later write that it was 'built in a half-circle in front of one of the most beautiful ports of the Mediterranean' and that the town was 'the advanced sentinel of France'.[47] He reflected on how the Toulonnais had twice repelled the Saracens, and how the British occupation in support of the royalists during the Revolution had given the young artillery officer Bonaparte the opportunity to demonstrate his brilliance in recapturing the town. He thought, too, of the abandoned royalists and the victims of the Terror who had suffered in the Champs-de-Mars when it was converted into a 'theatre of bloody reprisals'[48] by the republic. He encountered pitiful gangs of convict labourers engaged in backbreaking work in the shipyards and arsenal, and daily clearing filth from the streets. Their plight moved him to reflect on the criticisms of the French penal system by Saint Vincent de Paul. This was typical of d'Urville: in the cascade of his emotions there was a constant collision of beauty and ugliness. Nevertheless, he fell in love with Toulon. Of this 'maritime citadel', he would later write:

> One's view is lost in the multitude of vessels, frigates, corvettes, schooners, flutes, transports, message-boats etc., anchored in the harbour and basins with picturesque symmetry. This forest of masts and rigging partly obscures the coast. A mountain dominates the town and protects it from the north winds. A variety of crops traverse the flanks of this mountain; between groups of olive trees, orange groves, trees from Africa and Italy, as far as the eye can see one perceives burgeoning dovecotes, villas, white-washed cottages, where the Toulonnais go in little caravans for festivals and light rustic meals … The first view of Toulon is confused. The roads are narrow, the places irregular, but decorated with fountains which combat the heat of summer. The profusion of hydraulic works is one of the riches of the town. These basins of stone, covered with moss and vegetation, are natural embellishments which the good taste of the people respect as utter poetry, issuing salutary freshness day and night.[49]

Walking through the town, he found the houses generally elegant. He was impressed by the monumental caryatids of the Hôtel de Ville[50] but felt that the cathedral 'merited little to speak of'.[51] The arsenal reminded him of naval establishments that he had already come to know in Rochefort, Brest and Cherbourg: 'pyramids of grenades, bar-shot, bombs forming many rows which separated heavy mortars of cast iron, canons and carronades'. In the magazine, many thousands of muskets lined the walls; pikes, halberds and pistols were 'arranged symmetrically in parallel lines'; sabres were arranged on the ceiling with points touching, with blades diverging and forming 'suns and roses on the ceiling'. But reflecting on the history of all this weaponry, his fundamental disgust for war welled up and moved him to express his astonishment 'that there were still men remaining on the earth'.[52]

The arsenal where his friend Cerisy now worked in naval-ship construction (until his transfer to Civitavecchia in Italy in 1812)[53] was a hive of remarkable human activity and technical achievement. D'Urville surveyed the 700-foot-long *corderie*, where six enormous cables could be wound simultaneously, and the 300-foot-long dry dock, built by Antoine Groignard nearly three decades before. There were also foundries, mechanised forges, carpentry workshops, a cooperage, a bakery and a room full of models where one could study a great range of ship designs. As he would later write, it was 'a nursery of the brave … for perilous expeditions which would one day carry the commerce of France to unknown peoples, under the protection of our flag'.[54]

D'Urville joined the *Suffren* in mid-October 1810; a month later, he was promoted to *aspirant* first class. He spent more than a year aboard the *Suffren*, with a great deal of time at sea, and occupied himself studying mathematics, physics and chemistry, and became increasingly interested in astronomy. He also began translating the works of the Roman historian Tacitus and studied Italian and Spanish. Nevertheless, it was a shipboard life amid 'general scattered ignorance' until a recently promoted ensign, named Louis-Isidore Duperrey, joined the *Suffren* in late September 1811. One day, he and d'Urville would circle the globe together. With Duperrey's 'imagination, his knowledge of mathematics and love of study', he was soon drawn to d'Urville. For his part, d'Urville admitted that he was prone to be 'mistrustful and suspicious' and often promised himself 'not to search for friends' but to content himself 'to have comrades'. Duperrey succeeded in drawing him out of his reserve and they began to exchange ideas and opinions and to confide in each other. Within a month or two, they were almost always dining together and making plans for the future. 'Our intimacy', wrote d'Urville, 'several times astonished those who surrounded us', although, according to d'Urville, Duperrey became more and more opinionated and even more presumptuous. D'Urville felt that his role was now to approve all that Duperrey would say, 'good or bad, true or false'. Matters came to a head when they disagreed on the operation of a particular piece of equipment – whether to double or quadruple the force applied. Their lieutenant was asked to arbitrate, and when d'Urville was deemed correct, Duperrey went pale with rage and 'poured out his bile against the judgement'. According to d'Urville, Duperrey then made him understand that the difference in their ranks no longer permitted familiarity between them. As a result, d'Urville would not address a single word to Duperrey for another six months.[55]

In the meantime, d'Urville's uncle made renewed representations seeking his promotion (once again including a testimonial from the bishop of Bayeux), and in August 1811, the navy minister received a letter on his behalf from the influential senator for Nîmes, Louis-Thibault Dubois-Dubais, who asserted that his wife was related to d'Urville.[56] Dubois-Dubais was also born in Calvados, but there was another important connection: the senator and d'Urville's maternal uncle, Jacques-François de Croisilles, had both been members of Louis XVI's personal guard.[57] Five days after his twenty-second birthday, d'Urville was promoted to *enseigne de vaisseau* and in early July went to sea aboard the *Borée*. Although he had already enjoyed seven months' leave after quitting the *Suffren*, on 9 August 1812, his mother wrote to the navy minister asking that her son again be accorded leave 'to come for some days to his family' so that she could divide property among her children according to the law.[58] (It is possible that this related to property left by d'Urville's younger brother, who apparently died while living in the rue du Battoir, Paris, in January 1812.[59])

Given his extended absences and the overwhelming nature of British naval power, which kept the French navy largely port-bound, d'Urville did not participate in any battles during this period. However, he served with a number of seasoned veterans, including (for six weeks in late 1812) Louis-Antoine-Cyprien Infernet, famous for his resolute command of the *Intrépide* during the Battle of Trafalgar, and (for much of the next two years) Captain Louis-André Senez, who had commanded the *Vénus* during the ill-fated French attempt to support Wolfe Tone's rising in Ireland in 1798.[60] In his poem 'Au peuple anglais', d'Urville made reference to being seated in a shed in the arsenal and hearing Julien-Marie Cosmao-Kerjulien give a personal account of Trafalgar. He also gave his own vivid account of seeing the 74-gun *Romulus*, belonging to Cosmao's squadron, return to Toulon in February 1814, 'shaven like a tomb', her deck holed, her capstan full of shrapnel, her masts floating in the water and all her midshipmen 'cut to pieces' after close combat with three British navy vessels.[61] Despite the cries for revenge in every part of the port, more than two decades of war were nearly at an end.

Napoleon, with the impaired judgement of megalomania and the advice (when he heeded it) of sycophants, continued to drain France and her vassal states of yet another generation of young men. He now fought enemies who had learned to deal with his massed artillery and his tactics of shock and speed with flexible tactics and carefully planned defences of their own. Thousands of his men were tied down in the ports of his empire, enforcing his continental blockade of British trade. His divisions were withering under protracted guerrilla attacks and in the face of Wellington's resolute advances on the Iberian Peninsula, and thousands more were starving and freezing to death in the retreat from Moscow. Napoleon's defeats now began to outweigh his past glories and, powerless to prevent the allies entering Paris, he was forced to abdicate at Fontainebleau on 31 March 1814.

By then, d'Urville had followed Captain Senez from the *Borée* to another vessel, the *Ville de Marseille*. Unfortunately, his time aboard was marred by long-standing personal disagreements with an unnamed officer or officers, which induced his uncle to request his transfer to another vessel of the squadron;[62] the request was denied. In April 1814, with the Bourbons restored and Napoleon exiled to Elba, Senez was charged with conducting Louis-Philippe, duc d'Orléans, head of the cadet branch of the Bourbon family, to Palermo so that he could return to France with his family. The duke was accompanied to Sicily by his aides-de-camp, comte Camille de Sainte-Aldegonde and baron Louis Athalin.[63] However, during this same period many other Frenchmen, out of favour with the new Bourbon administration, went into exile.

D'Urville's visit to Sicily during the First Bourbon Restoration was his first voyage to another country. We have none of his letters or journals for this period, but with his classical training, Palermo's Phoenician, Greek, Roman and Arab roots very likely engaged his historical sensibilities, and the city's rich Norman heritage (1074–1194) must also have had a personal resonance, given his own origins and maternal crusader forebears. Among d'Urville's books auctioned after his death was a four-volume history of the Arabs in Sicily, published in German.[64] This was almost certainly Philipp Wilhelm Gottlieb Hausleutner's translation of Giuseppe Vella's fraudulent *Codice diplomatico di Sicilia sotto il governo degli Arabi* (1788).[65] We have no way of knowing whether d'Urville knew that the Maltese cleric Vella had been tried for his monumental historical forgery in 1795 and died after nine years' house arrest in Palermo in the year d'Urville visited Sicily.

The *Ville de Marseille* returned to France with the liberal duc d'Orléans, his pregnant wife Maria-Amalia, daughter of King Ferdinando I of the Two Sicilies, and their three young children. In the fading summer of 1814, d'Urville could neither have guessed that he would one day play a part in the rise of this colourful duke as 'king of the French' nor that he would later survey uncharted corners of the globe in his name.

3

Adélie

Woman and the sea revealed themselves to me together, as it were: two mistresses of life's values. The illimitable greatness of the one, the unfathomable seduction of the other working their immemorial spells from generation to generation fell upon my heart at last.

Joseph Conrad*

Ensign Dumont d'Urville's posting on the *Ville de Marseille* ended on 18 September 1814. Having returned to France from Palermo, he found himself without appointment and on half-pay; the new Bourbon administration focused on demobilising a great part of the armed forces and redirecting the nation's resources to peaceful ends. At the time, he resided in one of the brightly rendered stone tenement buildings on the narrow rue Riaux, close to Toulon harbour. He had also fallen in love with a pretty brown-haired Toulonnaise. D'Urville would later write of paying a 'tribute' to the '*coquetterie*' of the women of Toulon. He liked their sensuous dresses, which he declared never 'descended to the ankle leaving the best view of the leg and the foot', and he wrote affectionately of their broad-brimmed hats of straw or beaver fur that 'preserved their complexion from the reach of the sun'.[1] Perhaps it was beneath just such an ample brim that he first saw Mademoiselle Adèle-Dorothée Pépin rather than under the formal ribboned bonnet she wears in the imaginary portrait by Michèle Garreau on a 1981 French postage stamp.

Adélie, as d'Urville affectionately called her, was the 16-year-old daughter[2] of Joseph-Marie Pépin, a successful watchmaker and optician. He was originally from Cluses (Haute-Savoie)[3] and had close relatives in Switzerland.[4] Accurate chronometers were already well established as essential aids to navigation and the determination of longitude. D'Urville had a strong professional interest in timepieces,[5] and it is very possible that he met Adélie as a customer of the Horlogerie Pépin in Toulon. We know nothing of the smiles and laughter they exchanged, the books they discussed or the walks they took, but their romance clearly blossomed, and d'Urville soon asked for

* The Arrow of Gold (1919), part i, chapter iv

Terres Australes et Antarctiques Françaises stamp (1981) honouring d'Urville's wife, Adèle Dumont d'Urville. Alas, the portrait by Michèle Garreau, engraved by Pierre Bequet, is imaginary. Author's Collection

Adélie's hand in marriage. Twice divorced,[6] Monsieur Pépin might have had grounds to caution his daughter against such a youthful betrothal, but he and Adélie's mother, Josephine-Hélène Las de Guérin, who was herself to remarry in November 1817, both gave their consent to the union. Despite the fact that he had reached his majority, as a naval officer, d'Urville required the permission of his superiors to marry, and they required his mother's approval, which was potentially problematic. Would his devout Catholic mother recoil from a bride whose family was tainted by divorce and civil marriage? If she made enquiries, she might also learn that Adélie was born less than five months after her parents were wed! Moreover, his mother probably placed a high value on ancient seigneurial bloodlines and powerful family alliances. One way to avoid marrying 'beneath' yourself was to marry your kin; d'Urville's eldest sister had married her first cousin. Whatever her preferences for her son, Madame Dumont d'Urville knew that he was far from his family milieu in Normandy, and that ultimately he could still marry the woman he loved if he left the navy. She clearly did not want to place obstacles in the way of his happiness, and she forwarded her notarised consent from

Vassy on 26 January 1815.[7] Past biographers have stated that, regardless of this formal consent, she steadfastly refused to accept her daughter-in-law, which is untrue. As we shall see, Adélie was accepted by her mother-in-law and by her husband's conservative family in Normandy, although the relationship was not without difficulties.

Whether d'Urville anticipated more resistance from his mother is uncertain, but on 18 January 1815 – just over a week before she finally gave her consent – he requested three months' leave to attend to family matters. His leave was approved in early February, but he may not have travelled to Normandy. Soon after, with his mother's permission appended, the maritime prefect of Toulon solicited the minister's approval for d'Urville to marry. In his letter, the prefect stated that Mademoiselle Pépin belonged to a family 'respected in the area' and that she was an 'only daughter'.[8] In the formal marriage contract that d'Urville and his bride drew up on the afternoon of 28 April 1815, a dowry of 8500 francs was declared. Adélie's father contributed 3500 francs towards this as the agreed value of his daughter's wearing apparel, trousseau, rings, jewellery and linen. Her mother contributed the remaining 5000 francs. D'Urville acknowledged both sums, which he and his bride then gave as reciprocal gifts to each other 'in consideration of their marriage and to give proof of their love'. However, should they have no living children, these reciprocal gifts were to become 'null and void', and should their marriage be dissolved, Adélie's possessions and money would all be restored to her.[9] It was both a generous and a cautious arrangement facilitated by the loving parents of the bride, who had themselves experienced the misfortune of marital breakdown but who apparently maintained cordial relations despite living separate lives. (Little did they know that, at the behest of the clergy, the Bourbons would soon abolish divorce in France.)

On the evening of 1 May 1815, d'Urville and Adélie married in Toulon in the presence of the bride's parents, a judge of the Civil Tribunal and several of the groom's fellow naval officers.[10] Theirs was a true love match. In Adélie, d'Urville gained a life partner and soul-mate. Adélie's love for her children was intense and matched only by the depth of her despair and grief when she lost them to illness. Her letters are those of an intelligent and articulate women who loved, longed and ached for her frequently absent husband. Vergniol correctly asserted that she had 'an education, rare at that time among the young girls of the best families of Toulon'.[11] Although she might not have had her husband's degree of learning, she sought to share his joy in languages and no doubt surprised him (as she surprised this biographer) with a stream of letters written in near-perfect English. With some justification, Luc-Frédéric Malcor, a fellow Toulonais who was 15 years old when Adélie died (and knew her stepfather's family and probably Adélie personally), described her as 'not lacking a certain eccentricity which, like her real beauty, captivated the mind and heart of the young officer'.[12] While Adélie was considered beautiful, d'Urville might not have been considered handsome. Several artists portrayed him as a pleasant-featured man, but in one profile sketch preserved in Toulon, his chin protruded prominently. Le Brun tell us that d'Urville stood '1 metre 84 centimetres', which was very tall for a nineteenth-century Frenchman. He also asserted that his features were 'very regular' and that he had a 'piercing gaze'.[13] Pierre-Adolphe Lesson (who sailed with d'Urville on the first *Astrolabe* voyage) agreed that he was 'tall' but added that he was 'tart, misshapen, badly attired' and had 'bones a little big, hair curling naturally, high, large and bare forehead, blue eyes, small nose, thin tight lips, prominent heavy chin, rather strong teeth without space in between … pale chestnut hair, rather thick, fair complexion'.[14] But, as we shall see, the younger Lesson had strong personal animosity towards his commander that might have coloured his description of d'Urville as 'tart' and 'misshapen'.

When d'Urville married Adélie in early May 1815, France was in the midst of great uncertainty. Napoleon, having escaped from his exile on Elba, had landed at Cannes on 1 March. (D'Urville would refer to it as 'Bonaparte's invasion'.[15]) Three weeks later, he had reclaimed 'his' throne, and the Bourbons had once more been put to flight. For much of the 'Hundred Days', before the Battle of Waterloo finally put paid to Napoleon's vanity and imperial ambitions, d'Urville remained on leave. In the wake of these tumultuous events, abbé de Croisilles asserted that 'during the interregnum', his nephew's 'conduct was pure and irreproachable' and that he was 'constantly loyal to the cause of the king'. He added that d'Urville had 'inscribed his formal refusal to accept the *actes additionnels* (Napoleon's new constitution)'.[16] Although d'Urville's personal loyalty to the Bourbons is highly questionable, it seems likely that he was indeed part of the abstention *en masse* from the plebiscite aimed at gaining approval for a renewed imperial government (albeit with liberal concessions that echoed the recent Bourbon constitution). There is no evidence that d'Urville identified with Napoleon – unlike his eldest sister, Adélaïde, and her husband, Louis-François-Charles Dumont de la Londe (d'Urville's first cousin),[17] who had apparently named their youngest son Louis-Napoléon in the emperor's honour some four years before.[18] Perhaps the best clues to d'Urville's own confused emotions, divided loyalties and sense of national humiliation at the time come from the first stanza of his unpublished poem 'Au peuple anglais', written more than 15 years later:

> Et moi, longtemps aussi, vieux français d'un autre âge,
> Au seul nom des anglais je sentis un outrage,
> D'enfantins préjugés l'œil encore obscurai,
> En pleurant, Waterloo, je songeais à Crécy:
> Chaque page où l'histoire exaltait l'angleterre
> Aiguisait mon venin de haine hériditaire.

[And I, so long a Frenchman of a bygone age,
Only with the English I felt an outrage,
Childish prejudices still obscured the view,
I thought of Crécy, while crying Waterloo:
Each page which lauded England's history,
Sharpened my venom of hereditary antipathy.][19]

As we shall see, these were indeed 'childish prejudices' and a 'hereditary antipathy' that he would outgrow. Although d'Urville was without a naval posting during the Hundred Days and for much of the year following the Second Bourbon Restoration, Vergniol's assertion that he resigned his commission as an ensign in order to join the army with the brevet of a captain of the infantry is without any documentary reference. Vergniol conveniently added that Waterloo left 'resignation and request unresolved'.[20] No letter of resignation has survived in d'Urville's service dossier; he remained in the navy but declared: 'Tired of the kind of shipboard service I had done, I promised myself to stay ashore the more that I could cultivate science and letters in peace.'[21] Among the visitors to d'Urville's home on 'numerous occasions' during this period was Duperrey. In the previous two years, he and d'Urville had not seen much of each other but they had been reconciled. D'Urville wrote that 'he seemed to me to have changed for the better', and he expressed his desire to retain Duperrey's 'candid reflection'.[22]

Within three months of marriage, Adélie was pregnant, and at 9.00 am on 29 April 1816, she gave birth to their first child: Jules-Eugène-Gustave.[23] D'Urville was able to sign the registration of birth in Toulon, but on the same day, in what would be the first of many difficult separations from his family, he was ordered to join the three-deck *Royal Louis*, flagship of Admiral Edouard-Thomas de Burgues, comte de Missiessy. A veteran commander with 60 years' service in the navy, Missiessy was ordered to bring the bride of Charles-Ferdinand d'Artois, duc de Berry, to France from Naples. After negotiations conducted by the French ambassador to the Two Sicilies, Carolina, the 18-year-old daughter of King Francesco I, had agreed to marry her Bourbon cousin Charles-Ferdinand (nephew of the childless Louis XVIII), in the hope of producing an heir to the throne. Bans were published in the church of Saint-Germain l'Auxerrois – the duke's marriage to an English woman, Amy Brown Freeman, by whom he had two daughters, had conveniently been annulled in 1814 – and the couple were married by procuration on 25 April 1816. When the *Royal Louis* returned to France with the new duchesse de Berry and her Sicilian bodyguard, they were taken ashore in a gilded longboat manned by 44 rowers clad in white satin uniforms and blue and gold scarves. Marseille was festooned with flags and flowers, and the duchess was met by an assembly of dignitaries and a detachment of the Royal Guard.[24] D'Urville later remarked wryly: 'I smiled to myself, I, whose already pronounced ideas were entirely republican, was confused with the troops of the paladin generals of the [Bourbon] Legitimacy.'[25]

A large measure of compromise was inherent in the new Bourbon regime, despite the braying ultras (including the duc de Berry) who demanded a return to the status quo prior to the storming of the Bastille. Although Louis XVIII retained executive power, with ministers personally responsible to him, many of the progressive gains of the Revolution (with regard to taxation and equality before the law) were confirmed. Louis XVIII retained the Napoleonic Civil Code. The king nominated judges, but they were independent and could not be dismissed. The officer corps did not, once again, become the exclusive preserve of the nobility. Louis also found it very convenient to retain the highly centralised state apparatus that had evolved in the wake of the Revolution and was consolidated during the Consulate and Empire. He did not devolve power to the old provinces, instead retaining the revolutionary departments, and the administrative titles and even the decorations (including the *Légion d'honneur*) of the Empire, but not the tricolour flag. Nationalised properties, which had already been sold, were not resumed. The concordat remained in place, although some episcopal sees were re-established and Catholicism became, once more, the state religion (not just the religion of the majority). Despite a measure of personal liberty, the press remained censored. National representation took the form of a Chamber of Peers and a Chamber of Deputies, but with the franchise and electoral eligibility very much restricted by age and income. D'Urville, for example, had no vote because he was under 30 years of age and would also have had to pay 300 francs per year in direct tax. He could not have stood as a deputy because he was under the age of 40 and paid less than 1000 francs per year in tax.[26]

On 5 July 1816, a month after leaving the *Royal Louis*, d'Urville joined the *Alouette* under the command of Claude-Caprais Rigodit, who had distinguished himself as an ensign aboard the *Duguay-Trouin* at Trafalgar. The *Alouette* was a 380-tonne *gabare écurie*, essentially a floating stable, purpose-built four years earlier at La Seyne-sur-Mer, near Toulon, for the navy to transport livestock, in particular military horses.[27] D'Urville sailed with her to Elba and then Civitavecchia, the port of the Papal States on the western coast of the Italian Peninsula. The hot Mediterranean summer months and perhaps the stench of a hold full of animals, not to mention his thwarted ambitions, might explain his recorded antipathy to the navy during this period.[28] Nevertheless, the voyage gave him the opportunity to visit his friend and former classmate Cerisy (employed as an engineer in the naval arsenal in Civitavecchia until the following year),[29] and to visit Rome for the first time.[30] D'Urville left the *Alouette* on 18 October 1816, after she had sailed out of the Mediterranean and north to Lorient in Brittany.[31] He rejoiced at leaving the 'bad precedents' of his career in Lorient,[32] but he was more fortunate than he knew. In June the following year, with Rigodit still in command, the *Alouette* was lost near Simon's Bay on the Cape of Good Hope.[33]

D'Urville remained in France with his heart set upon joining Louis-Claude de Saulces de Freycinet's planned circumnavigation aboard the *Uranie*, which was fitted out before his eyes and left Toulon in September 1817. His approaches to Freycinet were 'without success', and he was bitterly disappointed when he was not selected to participate. The fact that Duperrey was selected once again strained their friendship, with d'Urville admitting he was envious and detected a 'hint of haughtiness' in Duperrey's attitude. Nevertheless, he 'embraced him on his departure' and with all his heart wished Duperrey 'a fortunate voyage and much success'.[34] Like the *Alouette*, the *Uranie* would also founder, but in the even more-distant southern latitudes of the Falkland Islands in February 1820,[35] and d'Urville would later visit her wreck site.

Having failed to gain a place on Freycinet's expedition, botany became d'Urville's 'refuge'. More than a decade later, he reminisced:

> In the company of several friends, I spent all of the summer of 1817 scouring the environs of Toulon to study the flora and I soon formed a considerable herbarium; it was a fortunate time for me. Having become a stranger to all other pastimes, I dreamt of nothing but recording all the plants which carpeted the Mediterranean peaks and valleys.[36]

His stalwart mentor and life-long friend was Gaspard Robert, director of the navy's botanical garden in Toulon. According to Lesson, who was then Robert's counterpart in Rochefort, d'Urville soon made the transition from 'student' to 'master', and, with a kind of 'feverish ardour', his botanical perseverance was such that he neither stopped for 'hunger, thirst nor the sun'.[37] He gathered 1200 local plants, which he identified, described and provided habitat statements for in a manuscript *Flore Toulonnaise*, which was never published. Although the 'troop of botanophiles' was eventually reduced to two and then one (as its naval members were posted elsewhere), in the spring of 1818 he was joined, on a number of his excursions, by a fellow Norman, Rear Admiral Jacques-Félix-Emmanuel Hamelin, a passionate botanist and also a veteran explorer who had commanded the *Naturaliste* during Nicolas Baudin's expedition to Australian waters (1800–03). Baudin had the misfortune to die in Mauritius, in September 1803, before being able to return to France and publish the results of the expedition. This was done instead by François Péron and Freycinet, both of whom loathed Baudin and blackened his posthumous reputation in their *Voyage de découvertes aux Terres australes*.[38] Significantly, d'Urville would be the first to publish a portrait of Nicolas Baudin – honouring him with Bougainville, Cook and Lapérouse – as part of the frontispiece of the first and second volumes of his *Voyage pittoresque autour du monde*. It is tempting to speculate that this rehabilitation of Baudin began with conversations between d'Urville and Hamelin during botanical excursions in the hills surrounding

Toulon in 1818, and very likely Hamelin's reminiscences made d'Urville even more determined to be part of a major voyage of exploration.

In early 1819 it would appear that, thanks to Hamelin, d'Urville finally received an opportunity to participate in a significant scientific mission. On 23 March, he joined the *Chevrette*, bound for hydrographic work in the Greek Islands. Apparently built to an identical plan to the *Alouette* and launched in Toulon in 1811, the *Chevrette* was also originally a military livestock transport.[39] She had already completed three survey missions under her seasoned commander, Captain Pierre-Henri Gauttier-Duparc. Born in Saint-Malo, Gauttier-Duparc had begun his career in the merchant marine at the age of 16 (sailing to Africa, America and northern waters) and then distinguished himself in the fighting navy during the Revolution. His talents as a marine surveyor were first recognised in the Antilles and then on the French coast during the Empire. Among his fellow officers, he was known as *Gauttier-horloge* (Gauttier the clock) because of his 'scrupulous exactitude'.[40] D'Urville probably already knew Gauttier-Duparc, who had surveyed the port of Toulon and parts of the coast of Provence before taking command of the *Chevrette*,[41] but it was with her second-in-command, Matterer, yet another Trafalgar veteran, that d'Urville formed a lifelong friendship. Although he would be intimately involved in the *Chevrette*'s hydrographic and ancillary astronomical operations (for double-checking longitude determined with marine chronometers), d'Urville embraced the secondary role of expedition naturalist and antiquary with passion.

4

Aphrodite & the isles

... all the wonder of the Venuses
revered and rendered by the chisel of the Greeks.
Honoré de Balzac*

The *Chevrette* left Toulon on 3 April 1819 and sailed first to Milos, in the western Cyclades, anchoring within the deep, well-protected bay that offers sanctuary from the northerly winds. Gauttier-Duparc would use the island's longitude as a reference point for his hydrographic work in the region, returning a number of times to rate and re-rate his chronometers. Milos was formed by volcanic eruptions that began about 3.5 million years ago and ended some 90,000 years ago.[1] Lack of surface water has limited agriculture on the island to vines and olives, but Melian obsidian (volcanic glass) was prized for bladed tools and weapons, and was widely traded, perhaps as early as 10,000 BC. Even in the iron age, it continued to be mined for ornaments, mosaics and mirrors.[2] In antiquity, there were also silver mines on the island.[3] Despite the cessation of volcanic activity on Milos, magma is relatively close to the surface and there are numerous thermal springs, which d'Urville visited – as many before him had done since ancient times.[4] He wrote:

> On the island of Milos everything suggests the existence of underground fires; in many places one finds hot springs where the temperatures reach up to 98 degrees of the centigrade thermometer; sulphur crystals [and] feather alum carpet the inner lining of some grottos, and at certain times sulphurous vapours, often even in flame, escape over the rocks which border the southern coast.[5]

The *Chevrette* sailed from Milos on 5 May 1819, but d'Urville would make two more visits to the island. The next day, the expedition reached Thera (d'Urville uses the old Venetian name Santorin in his account), an island where the heritage of volcanic activity was far more visible and recent than on Milos. The Minoan eruption, in the middle of the second millennium BC, blew the heart out of the island and created a 10-kilometre-diameter (multiple) caldera, which was also flooded by the sea.[6] The

* *Sarrasine* (1830), ch. ii

destruction of the Bronze Age settlements on the island has some eerie parallels with Plato's story of Atlantis.[7] D'Urville was aware that eruptions in more recent times had created the islands of Kameni and Nea Kameni within the 300-metre cliffs of the crater rim, and gases still bubbled from the sea floor, forming a sulphuric acid solution that attacked the *Chevrette's* copper-sheathed hull. He was unable to visit Nea Kameni but collected 45 plants and two insect species that had colonised the recent lava of Kameni. In his article on the island group, he speculated on how this was achieved from Thera by the wind, birds and the sea – offering a brief but interesting testament to his ecological understanding and prefiguring later empirical studies of the establishment of living organisms and ecosystems, and species succession on similar pioneer substrata on islands such as at Krakatoa (post-1883) in the Indonesian Archipelago and Surtsey (post-1963) off Iceland.

The expedition then carried out survey work on Cos, Samos, Lesbos and Tenedos (Bozcaada), situated close to the entrance to the Dardanelles. Unfortunately, as the *Chevrette* sailed west along the Thracian coast via the island of Thasos, d'Urville came down with a persistent fever that left him weak and wracked with violent headaches for the next six weeks. Despite his febrile state, his mind remained full of classical references, and he even speculated on the location of the channel constructed by Xerxes for his fleet across the sandy isthmus of Athos in 483 BC.[8]

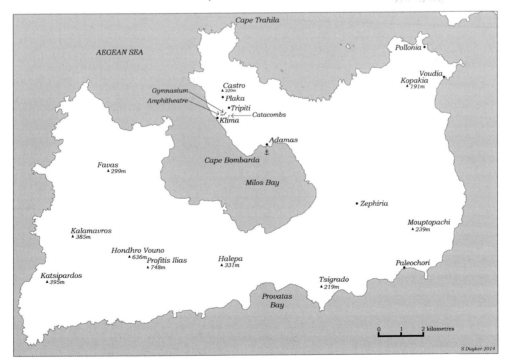

Map 2. *The Greek island of Milos.*

After skirting the coast of Thessaly and the islands of Euboea and Tinos, the *Chevrette* anchored in Piraeus harbour, a short distance from Athens. There d'Urville saw the Parthenon and met the artist, cast-maker, collector and French vice-consul Louis-François-Sébastien Fauvel, who received him with politeness, friendship and 'particular goodwill'.[9] Remembered as the 'Nestor of antiquities' and as one of Lord Elgin's rivals in the quest for the Parthenon marbles, Fauvel lived in a house located on the old Athenian agora with a splendid view of the Acropolis.[10] He was long associated with the comte de Choiseul-Gouffier, Louis XVI's last ambassador in Constantinople, who acquired the two sections of the Parthenon frieze bequeathed to the Louvre; in the year the Revolution began, it was Fauvel who found Choiseul-Gouffier's famous bust of Marcus Aurelius (purchased by the Louvre after the former ambassador's death).[11] Both Fauvel and Choiseul-Gouffier offered examples of the fame and kudos that could be gained by someone instrumental in embellishing French collections. Was it perhaps a lesson for d'Urville, who had read the first part of Choiseul-Gouffier's *Voyage pittoresque de la Grèce* and who would boldly make his own recommendations to the French ambassador in Constantinople the following year? On a more modest level, we know from his private correspondence that d'Urville undertook to search for medallions and coins on behalf of Théodose-Cyriaque Prost, postal director at Mende in the upper valley of the Lot. Unfortunately for Prost, d'Urville was not prepared to dabble in a market where competition from wealthy English and Russian collectors had driven prices to 'exorbitant' levels.[12]

The *Chevrette* returned to Toulon on 15 November 1819, but d'Urville's reunion with his family would be further delayed, as one of the sailors aboard the survey vessel had died during their return voyage and the entire crew was confined to the port's lazaret for *quarante jours* (hence our word 'quarantine'). D'Urville nevertheless used the time to put his herbarium in order and to prepare duplicate plant and insect specimens to be dispatched to the distinguished Swiss botanist Augustin-Pyramus de Candolle and his friends Jean-Vincent-Félix Lamouroux[13] and Théodose-Cyriaque Prost. Three weeks after his release from quarantine, he wrote to Prost of his satisfaction with the voyage:

> My campaign has been very fortunate and very agreeable: all the countries that I visited are very capable of exciting the interest of the voyager: natural history, antiquities, grand memories, even the spectacle of the degraded Greek, vile slave of the ignorant and stupid Turk. Although overburdened with calculations and astronomical observations, which formed the purpose of our voyage, I often escaped to scour the diverse islands of Greece and I have collected all that appeared to me new or, at least, rare in France.[14]

*The Vénus de Milo (upper detail) in the Musée du Louvre,
Paris.* Author's collection

There was also sad news on his return, for he must soon have been informed that
his beloved uncle and teacher had died of a stroke in Bayeux in May 1819.[15]

After wintering in France, the *Chevrette* left Toulon once again on 3 April 1820. A
fortnight later, she was back in Milos, once more to enable Gauttier-Duparc to rate his
chronometers.[16] D'Urville was drawn to the remains of what was once the ancient city
of Klima. A marble amphitheatre (from the Roman period) had been uncovered below
the village of Trypiti in 1814[17] and three years later was purchased by Crown Prince
Ludwig of Bavaria, a passionate philhellene and collector of antiquities. D'Urville
noted that the French vice-consul on the island, Louis Brest[18] – who at the time lived
on the towering weathered lava dome of Kastro, overlooking the white-washed village
of Plaka[19] – had been involved in excavations 'beneath the ancient ramparts' and had
found a number of 'very rare fragments'.[20] On arrival, it is clear that he learned of one

particularly exciting find and, according to Matterer, asked Brest to take him to it.[21] In his own account, d'Urville gives little detail of who else knew of this discovery or the train of events that led to it.

From other sources, we know that on 8 April 1820,[22] nine days before d'Urville arrived in Milos, a local farmer named Theodoros Kendrotas[23] was working in the field he owned about 150 metres from the amphitheatre beneath Trypiti. He appears to have been aided by at least two of his three sons, Antonis and Giorgios[24] – the latter referred to phonetically as 'Yorgos' in a number of accounts because at one stage he claimed credit for the discovery and was confused with his father.[25] Ostensibly in the process of taking stone from a ruined chapel on the boundary of his property, Kendrotas discovered an oblong underground cavity 1.2 to 1.5 metres deep with three wings, presumably like many such cavities and catacombs in the surrounding volcanic tuff. Lying on the ground in the cavity was a vague mass partly buried in soil. Kendrotas began to uncover what proved to be the upper part of a Parian[26] marble statue of a beautiful young woman carved in the classical Hellenistic style (but probably during the Roman period of the first or second century BC). Kendrotas's terraced land is believed to have been located on what was once a Roman gymnasium decorated with statuary.

Coincidentally, just 20 paces away, others were at work in search of archaeological finds at the foot of the Kastro escarpment. They were Olivier Voutier, a young ensign from the visiting nine-gun French naval schooner *Estafette*, and two of her sailors. According to Voutier's testimony, written 54 years later,[27] he soon realised that Kendrotas had found something. As he approached, the farmer appeared to be covering up his discovery. Voutier later suggested that he did so because he could see no use for the statue as building stone, but this implies that its beauty left Kendrotas unmoved and that he thought the statue worthless, despite a rash of excavations in the area for ancient artifacts, which found an immediate and direct market among visiting foreigners, even Bavarian royalty.[28] Other art historians have adopted the unsupported assertions of Salomon Reinach, in the *Gazette des Beaux-Arts* of May 1890,[29] that the statue was destined for a lime kiln![30] Such claims, like arguments employed to condone Lord Elgin's activities, conveniently absolve those who later dispossessed Greece of her treasures. It seems much more likely that Kendrotas was trying to keep his find secret until he could assess it and decide what to do without onlookers. If so, he failed. Simple peasant farmers like Kendrotas lived with the certainty of hard work, heavy taxation, the potential conscription of every fifth son as a janissary, and the caprice of local rulers (including Christian vassals) who represented the sultan on the island. Kendrotas also knew that a foreigner, whose nation enjoyed special relations with the Sublime Porte[31] in Constantinople and whose consular agent lived nearby, had to be treated with deference and respect. He was, therefore, as likely to rebuff the inquisitive uniformed Voutier as an Orthodox priest or a visiting Turkish pasha. In return for a 'few piastres', Kendrotas agreed (or perhaps resigned himself) to uncovering the statue. The head and naked torso were revealed in one part, but the arms were broken off and the lower half was clearly separate. Apparently after further urging, the farmer located the clothed lower portion. The absence of a smaller middle section (on the statue's left hip) still prevented vertical reassembly. With 'much patience and new encouragements', Kendrotas was induced to keep digging on his land until he exposed the missing marble wedge that kept the top half of the statue in stable compression. Aided by the two sailors, the heavy pieces were lifted into place. With 'stupefaction',[32] Voutier gazed upon a sensuous statue of Aphrodite, standing for perhaps the first time in 2000 years (although without her arms), with a naked torso and a gown that barely clung to her hips and buttocks. Destined to achieve iconic status as one of the greatest works of western art, she is now known as the Vénus de Milo and is arguably the most famous statue in the world.[33] Yet according to Ensign Voutier, he could not convince Brest to purchase this treasure for 400 piastres (roughly equivalent to what a humble artisan might earn in a year or, for perverse balance, what Van Gogh earned from a lifetime of painting). In a letter he wrote 40 years later, Voutier derisively recorded Brest's response: 'Are you really sure it is worth that much?'[34] Brest, who was already very involved in the antiquities trade, would endow the island with two Catholic churches and owned substantial property, was probably not so naïve. Very likely he had his own agenda, which did not include the involvement of a young ensign seven years his junior. In his letter, Voutier also claimed that he convinced Captain Robert, commander of the *Estafette*, to return immediately to Constantinople to plead for the acquisition of the statue.[35] This also seems unlikely, since Robert apparently had orders to proceed to Smyrna before returning to Constantinople.[36] Three days after Kendrotas's discovery, another French naval vessel, the flute *Bonite*, arrived at Milos. Her commander, Captain Alexandre Dauriac, was taken to see the statue. He then wrote to Pierre David, consul in Smyrna, and informed him that Brest was seeking to buy it for the Musée royal for 1000 piastres but that he did not have the means and wanted to be assured of reimbursement.[37] The apparently increased price was not explained but seems to confirm that Brest knew the statue was worth more than 400 piastres. Less than a week later, the *Chevrette* arrived in Milos.

By the time d'Urville saw the statue of Aphrodite, in the company of Brest and Matterer, the upper part had been moved by Kendrotas to his stable for safe-keeping. The farmer had also found two statues of the god Hermes and marble pieces of an upper left arm, a left hand clasping an apple, a right hand holding a belt or harness and an inscribed pedestal. Matterer thought the statue very beautiful but did not trust his

Pierre-Henri Gauttier-Duparc, commander of the Chevrette, *portrait by Jacques-François Peynaud. Among his fellow officers, he was known as 'Gauttier-horloge' ('Gauttier the clock') because of his 'scrupulous exactitude'.* Musée Trochu, Belle-Ile

own judgment in such matters; he even recounted that he had forgotten it by the time they left the island.[38] D'Urville, however, like Voutier before him, knew he was in the presence of a masterpiece; but unlike Voutier, he had the good fortune to be bound for Constantinople – Gauttier-Duparc had precise orders to determine the exact longitude of the Ottoman capital – where the French ambassador resided and where he would ultimately make a personal case for the statue's acquisition.

On the morning of 25 April, the *Chevrette* reached the entry to the Dardanelles and was confronted by the extraordinary sight of more than 60 vessels that had been unable to enter the channel because of contrary winds. As she sailed past the high cliffs of Gallipoli (which d'Urville mentions by name), the number of vessels increased to at least 150, 'of diverse nations, of all kinds, of all sizes, moving with speed and all sails unfurled',[39] along the length of the European and Asian coasts of the channel. Because the Ottomans forbade military vessels in their waters, Gauttier-Duparc stowed his guns in the hold and gave the *Chevrette* the appearance of a commercial vessel. On 28 April, amid this extraordinary mêlée of vessels in the Sea of Marmara – some bound for the Golden Horn, others bound for the Bosphorus and the Black Sea ports – the crew of the *Chevrette* discerned the southern limits of the fifth-century walls of Byzantium, the domes and thrusting minarets of Sancta Sophia, the Blue Mosque and the Süleymaniye Mosque. (They did not impress d'Urville: he would write of the 'poverty and bad taste of the Turkish edifices'![40]) The *Chevrette* then dropped anchor in the port of Constantinople.

According to Matterer, even before their arrival, d'Urville had drafted a 'scholarly historical notice' on the statue they had seen on Milos and which he now dubbed the 'Venus Victrix' – alluding to a Roman appropriation of Aphrodite as 'Venus Victorious', a goddess of war rather than love. Be that as it may, on disembarking in Constantinople, he did not go directly to the French ambassador, Charles-François de Riffardeau, marquis (later duc) de Rivière,[41] although he may have dispatched a

Bronze bas relief panel (1846), by Dominique Molknecht, portraying Dumont d'Urville and the discovery of the Vénus de Milo; it decorates the pedestal that supports the explorer's statue in Condé-sur-Noireau. In fact, by the time d'Urville saw the statue, its upper half had been moved to a stable for safe-keeping. Author's collection

letter to him. In fact, d'Urville did not disembark until 6.00 am on 30 April and not on the European shore. Instead, he botanised in Üsküdar on the Asian shore for eight or 10 hours, finding seven or eight plant species new to him, before dining on the summit of Bulgurlu. The weather was beautiful and he gained a magnificent view of the Bosphorus, the adjoining countryside and the teeming city of Constantinople.[42] He did not record his movements in the next two days, but if he was free of duties, he very likely explored the city's monuments and colourful bazaars, perhaps in search of a gift for his son, who had turned four the day after he arrived in Constantinople, and his beloved Adélie, who was to celebrate her 22nd birthday in Toulon in a little over a week. It is also possible that he visited local bookshops and purchased the Turkish grammar we know he later had in his library in Toulon. Similarly, he owned a copy of James Dallaway's *Constantinople Ancient and Modern: With excursions to the shores and islands of the archipelago*, which may also have been purchased at the same time.[43]

On 2 May, d'Urville ventured north of the Ottoman capital on the European shore to Büyükdere, where a river of the same name flows into the Bosphorus at its widest point. There he joined Gauttier-Duparc for dinner with the Russian ambassador, the famous gourmet Baron Grigori Alexandrovich Stroganoff. If he had not already met the French ambassador's secretary, Marie-Louis-Jean-André-Charles Demartin du Tyrac, comte de Marcellus, by this time, he certainly met him at Büyükdere, because he tells us that Marcellus guided him on the route to Therapia in order to botanise.[44] A handsome elegant young man with a romantic air (judging from his portrait by Ingres),[45] Marcellus came from a family that had suffered greatly during the Revolution – his maternal and paternal grandparents had been guillotined during the Terror – and he had rallied to the royalist cause after Napoleon's first abdication and joined the diplomatic service after the Hundred Days. Marcellus had been in Constantinople since mid-1816 and had pursued a number of scholarly interests there, including the collection of folksongs.[46] In his memoir of his time in the Levant, *Souvenirs de l'Orient* (1839), Marcellus mentions his meeting with d'Urville and how they had talked of the statue of 'Venus' while they walked 'in the woods and fields of the Bosphorous' and botanised in the 'mountains of Thrace', how he 'multiplied his questions on the excavations in Milos and their results', and how d'Urville's very casual answers increased his curiosity. According to Marcellus, he then submitted this information to the ambassador and requested permission to go to Milos.[47] However, d'Urville, only months after the events, recorded that it was the ambassador who had 'questioned' him on the statue and that he had told the diplomat what he thought before he gave 'M. de Marcellus, secretary of the embassy, the copy of the notice'.[48] This is also asserted by René de Chazet, Rivière's biographer.[49] The two accounts are not necessarily contradictory; Marcellus's initial report to the ambassador might very well have led to d'Urville's visit to the embassy and his provision of a copy of his historical notice to Marcellus.

The day after d'Urville and the *Chevrette* left Constantinople, Voutier arrived from Smyrna on the *Estafette*, the vessel Marcellus already expected would take him on his planned inspection of Christian sites in the eastern Mediterranean and to Milos. Marcellus does not mention Voutier in the planning of the embassy response, probably because the decision had already been made, and the newly arrived young ensign played no part in making it. Nevertheless, it is doubtful whether Voutier, a staunch Bonapartist, would have received a warm reception from the haughty marquis de Rivière. The ambassador was a royalist ultra with bitter memories and prejudices to match. During the Revolution, he had emigrated with the comte d'Artois (the future Charles X) and served as his emissary among the royalist Vendée insurgents. Arrested in Nantes in 1795, Rivière managed to escape and evade recapture. However, in 1804 he was once again arrested and condemned to death for his part in Georges Cadoudal's conspiracy to assassinate Bonaparte. Although his sentence was commuted after the personal intervention of Madame Bonaparte (soon to become the Empress Joséphine), Rivière spent the next four years imprisoned in Fort de Joux before being deported. After the Restoration, he was made a peer of France. In the wake of the Battle of Waterloo, he was sent to Toulon (when d'Urville was also there) to take control of the garrison from the unfortunate marshall Guillaume Brune, who was murdered shortly after by a royalist band in Avignon.[50] In 1816, Rivière was appointed ambassador to Constantinople, ironically another post held previously by Brune with distinction. Rivière, however, failed spectacularly in this post, signing a treaty with the Ottomans in 1819 that imposed on Marseille trade a tariff two and a half times higher than that imposed on other nations! Denounced in the Chamber of Peers, his recall, in the year d'Urville arrived in Constantinople, was inevitable.[51] It seems likely that he believed that the statue of Aphrodite, if he could acquire it, might provide him with an incomparable gift with which to salvage his reputation and standing with the king.

On 15 May, the comte de Marcellus left Constantinople for Milos aboard the *Estafette*, with orders to purchase the statue,[52] but the acquisition did not proceed smoothly. After the departure of the *Chevrette*, Kentrotas had come under pressure from the local orthodox clergy following representations made by a priest named Vergis Milioti,[53] acting on behalf of Nicolaki Mourouzi, the recently appointed grand dragoman (translator) of the Ottoman admiralty. Mourouzi was not a Turk; he was a Greek nobleman,[54] a passionate scholar and private collector,[55] an advocate of Hellenic culture and a patriot, and he would become a martyr in the Greek Revolution the following year.[56] By the time Marcellus reached Milos on 23 May, the statue had already been dragged aboard a brig from Galaxidi[57] about to sail for Constantinople.

Marcellus's initial attempts to cajole the local clergy into confirming the sale of the statue to France (to whose consular agent it was first offered) instead of the dragoman proved fruitless. According to Marcellus, contrary winds kept the brig from Galaxidi in Milos harbour. More likely, it was the menacing presence of the *Estafette*. Whatever, it was long enough for Marcellus to succeed in his negotiations – held in the consular agent's home overlooking Plaka – and settle on a price of 8000 francs. To allay the possibility of any additional claims, he paid Kentrotas his asking price directly and, with diplomatic flourish, provided the primates with an explanatory letter to the dragoman, whom he knew personally in Constantinople.[58] Finally, he wrote to the ambassador seeking protection for the clergymen. (These gestures apparently proved useless: Brest, Marcellus and Rivière all asserted that Mourouzi ordered the Orthodox primates – Petros Tatarakis, Archimandrite Mikelis and Œconomos Armenis – to come to him on the neighbouring island of Siphanto, where he personally flogged them on their knees and fined them 7000 piastres.[59]) On 25 May, the statue was transferred from the Galaxidi brig to the *Estafette*. French sources would have us believe that this was done without coercion, resistance or acrimony.[60] Greek sources, however, indicate that Brest was armed with a sword and a stick, and 20 armed French soldiers were deployed by Captain Robert to seize the statue. Brest even slapped one of the priests, and the ear of one islander was slashed. It is uncertain whether the pieces of the arms of the statue were lost in a struggle during the transfer or whether they were already overlooked by those who took the statue aboard the *Estafette*.[61] It has even been suggested that Kendrotas might have withheld them as an act of retribution.[62] If they were sent to Mourouzi as proof of Melian resistance to the French, they presumably disappeared after his execution the following year.[63]

Aphrodite would remain aboard the naval schooner for much of the remainder of 1820 while Marcellus completed his diplomatic rounds in the Mediterranean – sailing to Thera, Rhodes, Cyprus, Lebanon, Palestine, Egypt, back to Rhodes, Crete, Paros, Smyrna, Piraeus (where the statue was viewed by Vice-Consul Fauvel) and then back to Smyrna.[64] Finally, on the Anatolian coast, she was put aboard another French vessel, the *Lionne*, and dispatched to the marquis de Rivière. She did not reach him in Constantinople until 24 October. Five days later, the ambassador finally quit the diplomatic post that he had long detested and sailed for France with the 'Venus'. Alas, Aphrodite, for all her beauty and mystique, would not enhance the marquis' career: dismissed from the diplomatic service for his neglect of French commercial interests in the Levant, his next posting was as a captain in the king's bodyguard. In the last two years of his life, however, Rivière was governor to Henri, duc de Bordeaux, the posthumous son of the assassinated duc de Berry – born in the Louvre, on 29 September 1820, the very palace that became home to the Vénus de Milo.[65]

5

The Bosphorus & beyond

… to the Pontic Sea,
Whose icy current and compulsive course
Nev'r keeps retiring ebb, but keeps due on
To the Propontic and the Hellespont.

William Shakespeare*

During the complicated events surrounding the acquisition and delivery of the Vénus de Milo to France, the *Chevrette* continued her survey mission. After determining the longitude of Constantinople and the entry to the Bosphorus, Captain Gauttier-Duparc weighed anchor on 5 May 1820.[1] Sailing east through the Bosphorus, d'Urville could not help but think of the dangers that had threatened his mythological precursors Jason and the Argonauts. His Homeric heroes had supposedly entered the Black Sea amid the clashing of the floating Symplegades: 'two rocky and very arid islands', d'Urville wrote, 'now well-attached to their bases'![2] Other classical references came to mind as the *Chevrette* continued her survey of the northern Anatolian coast and sailed past Eregli (ancient Heraclea, where Hercules is said to have killed Cerberus) and the former Paphlagonian towns of Amastris, Sesamus, Cytorus and Cromna – allied to Troy and mentioned in Homer's *Iliad*. After reaching Cape Kerempe, Gauttier-Duparc sailed north across the Black Sea until he reached Feodosiya, on the south of the Crimean Peninsula. Formerly the Ottoman trading port of Kaffa, it had been captured along with the entire peninsula by the Russians in 1783. When ruled by the Genoese and besieged by the Mongols in 1347, refugees from the town are believed to have been the first carriers of the Black Death into Europe.

Some historical lessons are well learned: the plague still raged in the Ottoman Empire, so when the *Chevrette* arrived on the evening of the 13 May 1820, the Russians isolated her in the port's lazaret. Ironically, its walls may have offered welcome protection for Gauttier-Duparc, who had his own 'extreme fear of the plague'[3] and no desire to expose his crew to the risk of contracting the disease, let alone passing

* *Othello* (ca.1603), act iii, scene iii, lines 450–53

it on; quarantine works both ways. Nevertheless, he was still able to fulfil his orders and determine Feodosiya's exact longitude from within the lazaret. While d'Urville was frustrated by the time-consuming demands of astronomical observation,[4] he still managed to comb the sides of the lazaret for plant specimens – exacting a 'considerable tribute' of some 15 species, including the Syrian bean caper *Zygophylum fabago*, which he found 'very common on the seaside'.[5]

Leaving Feodosiya on 19 May, the *Chevrette* resumed the survey of the Crimean coast to Kerch and the eponymous strait that provides access to the Sea of Azov.[6] When his duties permitted, d'Urville collected more than 20 plant species in the thick waist-high steppes and gathered a great number of insects, which swarmed in clouds wherever he walked.[7] Eventually, the Crimean steppes would provide him with 'more than 300 beautiful plants'.[8]

Gauttier-Duparc then charted points on the northern and eastern arc of the Black Sea from Anapa (ancient Gorgippia) to the coast of Georgia. Along the way, d'Urville sought to recognise the ancient coastal settlements mentioned by the Greek geographer Strabo. Many had disappeared, like the tribes that he named, but the same proud spirit of independence that characterised those who once resisted the might of Rome could now be seen in those, like the Abkhaz, who resisted the might of Russia. On the morning of 1 June, off Pitsunda on the coast of Abkhazia, two large boats, each carrying between 60 and 80 armed men, attempted to attack the *Chevrette*. Did they think that she was Russian or would they have attacked a vessel of any nation? There was little wind, and the raiders apparently thought they could take the *Chevrette* by surprise from the poop. Fortunately, the alarm was sounded by a young midshipman named Delaroque, and Gauttier-Duparc ordered warning shots. When these seemed only to hasten the advance of the boats, he ordered several volleys from all his guns, and although these shots still fell short of the boats, the rowers finally lost their nerve and broke off their attack.[9] The following day, the *Chevrette* received a warmer reception when she reached the port of Sukhum, on the coast of Abkhazia, amid a large flock of pelicans. This was disputed territory, captured by the Russians from the Ottomans in July 1810 and stipulated for return under the Treaty of Bucharest in 1812, but still held tenuously by a Russian garrison commanded by Major Petr Vasilievitch Mogilyansky.[10] Gauttier-Duparc deftly managed to maintain good relations with Mogilyansky, holed up in his fortress a few kilometres away, and with the young local Abkhaz chieftain, whom d'Urville names as Hassan Bey.[11] The latter was received aboard the *Chevrette* with full military honours and given a Jecker telescope and double-barrel shotgun. A small, dignified man with a lively face, he made a strong impression on d'Urville.

While Gauttier-Duparc rated his chronometers and determined the port's position (he found Sukhum to be some 55 kilometres further east than his Russian chart suggested), d'Urville botanised on the 'flanks of the Caucasus'.[12] The Russians urged caution: they frequently lost men kidnapped from the very walls of their fortress, the last only two months before. D'Urville himself noted that the Roman general Pompey had lost three entire cohorts trying to cross these same mountains. Mogilyansky, and later Hassan Bey, recommended an armed escort, so D'Urville resigned himself to botanising in the hinterland in the company of a dozen Russian soldiers. The sullen Abkhaz, who were better armed than they were clothed, kept their distance. D'Urville returned to his ship with an interesting botanical bounty, including *Galega officinalis* (goat's rue) and *Periploca graeca* (silk vine).

From Sukhum, the *Chevrette* sailed diagonally across the Black Sea to the then largely Pontic Greek and Armenian coastal port of Trebizond (now the Turkish port of Trabzon). During their brief visit, d'Urville hoped to gather *Rhododendron ponticum* on the same hill where the French botanist Joseph Pitton de Tournefort had collected this now-popular garden plant more than a century before. With the aid of the long-serving French consul Pierre Dupré (who died less than three months after d'Urville's visit),[13] he found rhododendrons still growing there but no longer in flower. He added some 20 other species to his herbarium before Gauttier-Duparc called his men aboard to resume charting the northern Anatolian coast as far as Sinop. The *Chevrette* then cut across the Black Sea to commence mapping the western coast of the Crimea. She reached Sevastapol on the morning of 4 July,[14] and once again d'Urville was forced to botanise within the confines of a port lazaret. Despite this, he managed to add specimens of *Dianthus*, *Gallium*, *Salvia* and *Sideritis* to his burgeoning collection. It was now mid-summer, and he took advantage of good weather to press and dry many duplicate specimens for other French botanists. However, the weather began to deteriorate soon after the *Chevrette* left Sevastapol on 8 July, the cloudy skies and indefinite horizon no doubt complicating the astronomical observations Gauttier-Duparc used to double-check his longitudinal positions. After surveying the coast to the mouth of the Dnieper, the *Chevrette* reached the Ukrainian port of Odessa on 16 July. The city impressed d'Urville, and he was reminded that the duc de Richelieu – then serving for the second time as France's prime minister – had spent much of his exile during the Revolution in Russian service as governor of Odessa (and the neighbouring Crimea), bringing great prosperity to the region.[15]

After fulfilling his orders on the Romanian and Bulgarian coasts of the Black Sea (including the determination of the position of a channel in the Danube delta), Gauttier-Duparc sailed back to Constantinople, anchoring at Therapia, close to the

Following pages: 'Carte réduite de la Mer Méditerranée et de la Mer Noire, première feuille (left)' and 'deuxième feuille (right)' (1821), and showing the fruits of the Chevrette's surveys. Médiathèque Intercommunale André Labarrère, Pau, Service Patrimoine, cote 220039

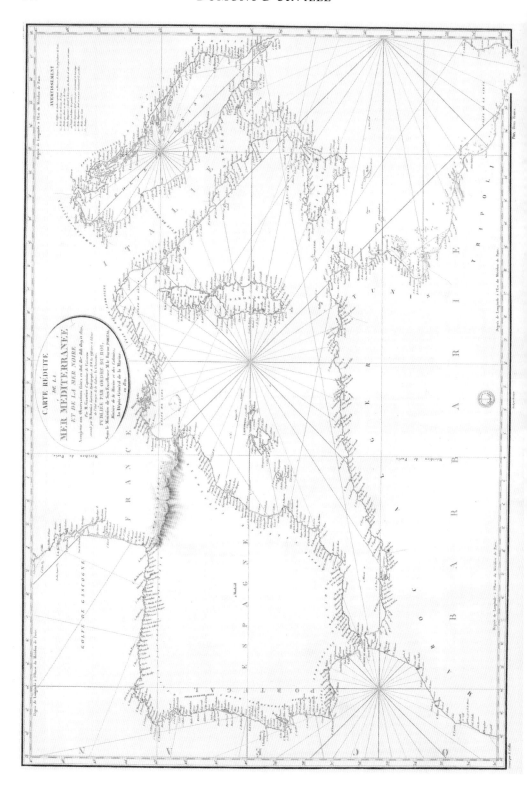

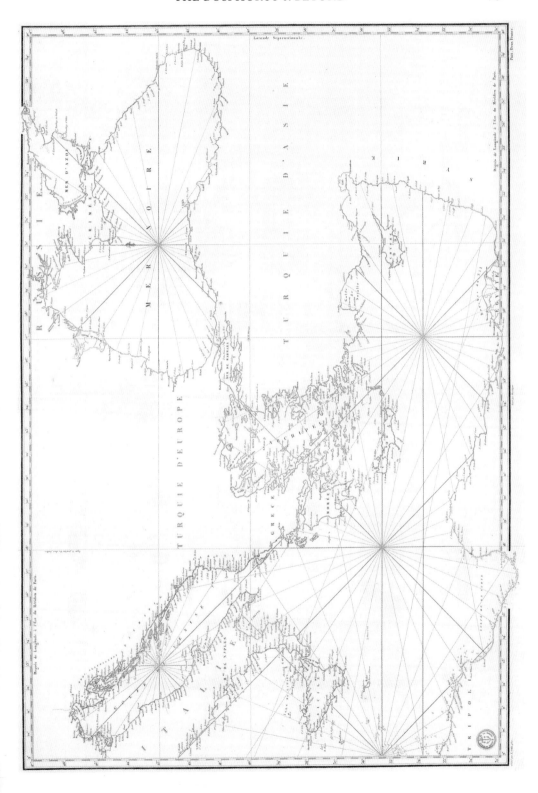

home of the French ambassador, on 3 August 1820.[16] The marquis de Rivière was still in residence (he had not yet taken delivery of the Vénus de Milo), and d'Urville appears to have been genuinely touched by the friendship and hospitality extended by the ambassador and his wife and their personal interest in his work. He would even acknowledge their engaging seven-year-old son as the source of several insect specimens he brought back to France.[17]

On 9 August, the *Chevrette* briefly relocated to an anchorage at Tophane, not far from Constantinople's famous Galata tower. With his firman (permit) to pass through the Dardanelles in hand, Gauttier-Duparc left the Ottoman capital the next day. The *Chevrette* would make a deliberately slow farewell, taking 12 days to sail through the Sea of Marmara, crossing it width-ways five times and anchoring seven times at different points, apparently for purely hydrographic reasons.[18]

Surprisingly, after leaving the Hellespont, the *Chevrette* sailed directly to Spetses in the Saronic Islands. D'Urville went ashore with Gauttier-Duparc and climbed the island's highest point to conduct astronomical observations. Spetses is a rocky island with little arable soil, and d'Urville noted a sparse flora of stunted pine, Phoenician juniper, wild thyme and sage. Most of the inhabitants were engaged in commerce and navigation rather than farming, and he remarked that their houses were 'clean and well built'.[19]

Although d'Urville does not mention it, Spetses was home to Laskarina Bouboulina, member of the secret nationalist organisation Philikí Etaireía (founded in Odessa) and soon to become a legendary heroine of the Greek War of Independence.[20] At this very time, she was storing arms, food and ammunition for the uprising against the Turks that would begin seven months later.[21] At her own expense, Bouboulina was also completing construction of the *Agamemnon*, which must have been visible to d'Urville but without him realising that he was looking at the largest warship in the nascent rebel navy. Bouboulina had already built three other vessels, which were successfully used the following year to blockade nearby Nafplion in the Peloponnese.

It is another striking coincidence that the *Chevrette*'s next port of call was Nafplion – beneath the very fortress of Palamede, which was successfully besieged by the rebels.[22] Although it is tempting to speculate that Gauttier-Duparc had secret orders regarding Spetses, we have no proof of this. We may have to content ourselves with d'Urville's guarded philhellenic declaration that Spetses 'gives a faint idea of what the Greeks can become again, if one day they succeed in throwing off the yoke of the Turks'.[23] While the charting of the Aegean, the Dardanelles, the Sea of Marmara, the Bosphorus, the Black Sea and the Crimea was outwardly a scientific hydrographic exercise, there can be no doubt that the voyage of the *Chevrette* was also a military intelligence mission. The maps Gauttier-Duparc drafted, with precise longitudinal placement of key points in the region, undoubtedly laid the foundations for a whole new generation of naval charts that were employed during the Anglo-French interventions on the side of the Greek rebels in 1827–28, during the Crimean War of 1854–56 and even during the allied landings in the Dardanelles in 1915.

While d'Urville would live to see the first of these naval actions and the founding of modern independent Greece, for the moment her ancient past absorbed his attentions. The expedition's sojourn in Nafplion provided him with a precious opportunity to visit nearby Argos and the remains of the citadel of Mycenae – capital city of Homer's King Agamemnon – extraordinary monuments of Greek civilisation dating back more than 3500 years and famously excavated by Heinrich Schliemann more than 50 years later. Judging by the names he employs, d'Urville, like Schliemann, appears to have been armed not only with a copy of the *Iliad* but with Pausanias's second-century AD *Description of Greece*. He visited the so-called Treasury of Atreus (actually a *tholos* or beehive tomb that predates the period of the Trojan Wars by some 400 years) and gazed upon the massive Cyclopean block walls of the citadel. Despite the profound mythological and historic resonance of these stones, they seem to have left him unmoved. It will surprise anyone who has walked through and been thrilled by the ancient grandeur of the lion gate – with its carved rampant sentinels above the enormous stone lintel – to learn that d'Urville considered the imposing ensemble to be in 'very bad taste'![24]

Before returning to Toulon, Gauttier-Duparc wanted to take advantage of an eclipse of the sun to double-check his longitudinal calculations at Milos. The *Chevrette* left Nafplion on 31 August and made such a good passage that she reached Milos on 1 September, with a week to spare before the celestial event. During this week, one of the *Chevrette*'s officers chanced upon the island's catacombs outside the ramparts of the ancient city of Klima and west of the present village of Trypiti. With plenty of time on his hands, d'Urville explored these underground tunnels, thinking himself a pioneer archaeologist of the site. (Although he does not mention it in his account, he also carved his name on one of the walls.[25]) It was only after he returned to Paris that he learned that Guillaume-Antoine Olivier had visited the same underground galleries three decades before. D'Urville published a detailed description with plans and sections in the *Nouvelles annales des voyages*, together with copious quotations from the first volume of Olivier's *Voyage dans l'empire Othoman, l'Égypte et la Perse*. He also speculated on possible pagan ceremonial origins, suggesting they were smaller versions of the 'labyrinths of Crete, Egypt and Lemnos', and that with the coming of Christianity, they may have become 'prisons to lock up malefactors' or a 'place of refuge, to withdraw women, children and the most precious property of the islanders from the rapacity of the pirates who often infested their locality'.[26] Despite his own family experience of persecution and clandestine worship, d'Urville appears not to have suspected that these underground passages were among the earliest Christian places of burial and religious observance in Europe, dating from the Roman persecutions of the second to the fourth centuries AD and to a considerable degree analogous to the Christian catacombs outside Rome. They are certainly the largest Christian catacombs in Greece. D'Urville's detailed drawings and description in his pioneering article on these underground monuments appears to have been largely forgotten in the subsequent archaeological literature.[27]

Well-versed in classical references to volcanic catastrophe and having already witnessed the handiwork of the elemental forces of nature in the archipelago, the officers of the *Chevrette* were apparently anxious about the geological stability of the region and highly susceptible to the power of suggestion. As the solar eclipse was about to take place at Milos on the afternoon of 7 September 1820, all eyes and instruments were directed to the sky. Suddenly detonations were heard, and smoke was seen rising from a mountain. Thinking it was the beginning of a volcanic eruption, people panicked, and the order was given to return immediately to the ship. In reality, the detonations were canon shots from a vessel signaling for a pilot, and the smoke on the mountain flank was simply a fire lit by shepherds. When the confusion subsided, the officers of the *Chevrette* successfully observed the eclipse.[28]

The *Chevrette* returned to Toulon on 7 October 1820, via Malta and the Sardinian coast.[29] Yet again, d'Urville's reunion with his family was delayed by more than a month in quarantine, but he was able to send letters and he eagerly began reporting his adventures.[30] On 24 November 1820, within a week of being released from quarantine, he presented an account of his travels to the Académie du Var, which had recently elected him a member.[31] It would be the first of many such honours.

6

Paris & plans

*For my part, my natural history work, my memoir and
my statue give me a sort of reputation.*

Dumont d'Urville*

Within a month of leaving quarantine in Toulon, d'Urville was ordered to the navy's hydrographic office, the Dépôt des cartes et plans, in Paris to assist in the editing of the results of the *Chevrette* expedition. Travelling from Toulon to Paris in December 1820 was no casual undertaking, as the roads and bridges of Restoration France were in serious disrepair after three decades of neglect and war.[1] Travellers from Paris to Provence could at least avail themselves of barges down the swiftly flowing Rhône from Lyon to the Mediterranean, but for the voyage upstream, large teams of horses took weeks (40 days from Arles to Lyon) to drag these same barges back. It seems likely that d'Urville and his family travelled by mail or stage coach from Toulon to Paris – a journey of about a week or more, depending on the number of breaks. According to Adélie, in a letter to Louis-Charles Lefébure de Cerisy, they travelled via Lyon (which they 'had time to visit'), Mâcon and Chalon-sur-Saône. Because of the transport costs, d'Urville left his books and general herbarium in Toulon,[2] but he still took his enormous collection of plants and insects from the Aegean and the Black Sea.

Despite traversing almost the length of France, d'Urville and his family arrived in the capital on 15 December 1820, as Adélie put it: 'without accident and without experiencing any fatigue'.[3] From their correspondence, we know that they resided in the Hôtel de Valois, 38, rue Saint-André-des-Arts; it is difficult to identify this building now. Although one of the oldest streets in Paris, the rue Saint-André-des-Arts was shortened with the creation of the place Saint-Michel and later the boulevard Saint-Michel. The church of Saint-André-des-Arts, where Voltaire was baptised and which once stood at one end of the street, has also disappeared. At the other end was the port de Buci – the notorious gate that a traitor allowed the Burgundians to pour through in 1481 and begin a massacre unrivalled until Saint Bartholomew's Day 1572.[4] Despite

*Dumont d'Urville to Louis-Charles Lefébure de Cerisy, 25 August 1821

all that has been written by d'Urville's previous biographers about his mother's never receiving or accepting Adélie, she had travelled from Normandy to see her son, and to meet her daughter-in-law and her young grandson for the first time. In early January 1821, Adélie informed Cerisy:

> My mother-in-law has been with us since our arrival; you know from d'Urville's conversations that I thought her hard and severe, but I was agreeably disabused; she appears, on the contrary, to have much affection for me; she is kind, gay [and] very amiable for her age.[5]

It is not known when d'Urville's mother returned to Normandy, but it is clear that she was with her son's family for a number of weeks at the very least. D'Urville presumably had some free time before he began work at the Dépôt des cartes et plans. Adélie informed Cerisy that they had visited the Tuileries and the Palais royal; perhaps d'Urville's mother accompanied them. Later Adélie would tell Cerisy that Sundays were their only family days because of d'Urville's work obligations. With or without him, she began to explore Paris. At the Louvre, she was impressed by the works of Raphael, Rubens, Poussin, Albanis and 'the Dominican' – presumably Fra Angelico's 'Coronation of the Virgin', which had entered the collection in 1812. She also enjoyed the Jardin des plantes but not as much as the botanical gardens in Toulon, where she felt far more at ease.[6]

From Adélie's correspondence, we know that one of the couple's first friends in the city was Achille Richard, who taught at the École de médecine and with whom d'Urville would later collaborate on the botany of the voyage of the *Astrolabe*. The son of the botanist and famous plant collector Louis-Claude Richard, who also taught in the medical school until his death in June that year, Achille was married to the daughter of yet another renowned professor of medicine, Antoine Dubois. At that time, Dubois was Louis XVIII's surgeon; the year before, he had attempted to save the life of the mortally wounded duc de Berry; and in 1811, he had famously delivered Napoleon's son, the 'king of Rome', and revived him with mouth-to-mouth resuscitation.[7] During his sojourn in Paris, d'Urville frequently botanised 'on foot, box on his back and filament in hand … in the woods surrounding the capital as far as Fontainebleau'.[8] It seems likely that this was in the company of Richard and his students.

Despite his famous friends, with his modest ensign's salary of 2000 francs per annum, d'Urville was forced to live and entertain frugally in what remains France's most expensive city. Aside from his demanding work at the Dépôt des cartes et plans, which occupied all his time 'from 10.00 to 4.00' on the short winter days,[9] he continued putting his natural history collections into order with the aid of fellow naturalists. It is clear from his correspondence that he used gifts of duplicate plant specimens as a means of securing taxonomic determinations for species that he did not recognise. According to Le Brun, he gave away 8000 plant specimens to other naturalists in Paris and kept an almost equal number.[10] In 1822, he would publish his 'Enumeratio plantarum quas in insulis archipelagi aut littoribus Ponti-Euxini annis 1819 et 1820' in the *Mémoires de la Société Linnéenne de Paris*. It was essentially a list of 219 plants species collected during his two voyages on the *Chevrette*, with corresponding references to descriptions by previous botanists, including Linnaeus, Sibthorp, de Candolle, Pitton de Tournefort, Lamarck, Loiseleur-Deslongchamps and Desfontaines.

Regardless of all his efforts, his article included descriptions of no new species. The Société Linnéenne de Paris (Linnéan Society of Paris), which published it entirely in Latin, had been 're-established' in May 1820,[11] and d'Urville was a corresponding member for the department of Var. The sexual system of plant classification established by the Swede Carl Linnaeus never held sway in France as it did in England,[12] and now it was decidedly in decline among the minority of French botanists who had favoured it.[13] While the amateur d'Urville organised his work on effectively obsolete Linnaean lines, the leaders in the discipline had acknowledged the advances being made in plant physiology and morphology, and the need for a systematic approach to classification that went beyond the mere examination of the sexual parts of the flower.

Despite being a novice smitten by the simplicity of the superseded Linnaean system, d'Urville did draw favourable attention. In Paris, on Tuesday 29 January 1821, he delivered an account of the voyage of the *Chevrette* to a meeting of the Académie des sciences. The minutes of the meeting indicate that 60 of the greatest scientists of the age were among the audience, including Richard.[14] His subsequent correspondence and his journal reveal that d'Urville befriended several others present, including the distinguished Breton botanist René-Louïche Desfontaines and the gentle unassuming entomologist Pierre-André Latreille, who became a regular visitor to d'Urville's lodgings and began to help him with the organisation of his insect specimens.[15] A former priest, Latreille famously survived the Terror after discovering a previously unknown species of beetle in his prison cell, which generated sufficient public attention for him to be released![16] D'Urville also got to know the great Jean-Baptiste-Pierre-Antoine de Monet, chevalier de Lamarck, through the academy but principally because of his friendship with Latreille.[17] One of the founders of evolutionary biology, Lamarck was by then completely blind, impoverished and thrice widowed, but he was still a man of engaging intellect who continued to work with the aid of one of his daughters. As referees for d'Urville's paper, the academy appointed the botanist Labillardière and the hydrographer Élisabeth-Paul-Edouard de Rossel – ironically once bitter enemies after d'Entrecasteaux's expedition fragmented on royalist and republican lines in the Netherlands East Indies in 1793.[18] The original manuscript has survived in Toulon but it was also published in the *Annales maritimes et coloniales*.[19] It was essentially the same paper d'Urville gave in Toulon, in November 1820, to the Académie du Var.[20] One foreign member of the academy, who did not hear his paper but whom he met in March 1821, was the celebrated traveller and scientist Alexander von Humboldt. Their meeting was perhaps inevitable: Humboldt frequented the famous Café Procope around the corner from d'Urville's lodgings.[21]

In his paper, d'Urville mentioned many geographical, botanical and historical details, as well as the statue he had seen on Milos and reported on in Constantinople. Three weeks later, the marquis de Rivière himself arrived in Paris with the statue, and on 1 March the former ambassador offered it to Louis XVIII for the Louvre. The offer was accepted. There is no doubt that d'Urville's presence in Paris at the time of the arrival of the statue would have important repercussions for his career – particularly as word spread of how wonderful it was. Even though the principal focus of d'Urville's writings remained botanic and hydrographic, the American historian Gregory Curtis has asserted that:

> [He] began to create the legend that would first make him famous. From that moment everything he did or wrote was a mixture of truth, errors, and lies of omission designed to make d'Urville himself, and only him, the discoverer of the Venus de Milo. He tried and almost succeeded in sweeping everyone else, including the faithful Matterer, off the stage and out of history.[22]

When one compares d'Urville's printed text with the manuscript of what he read before members of the Académie des sciences, brief omissions become apparent.[23] Originally, d'Urville included an additional note of thanks to Gauttier-Duparc, who permitted him to land at all their ports of call, and to Matterer, whom he described as an 'officer of great merit' and one of his 'good friends'. This was dated 6 November 1820, when he was still in quarantine in Toulon. It did not appear in the article when it was published in the *Annales maritimes et coloniales*, but presumably it was read to the academy in January 1821.[24] Similarly, although d'Urville mentioned Marcellus's purchase of the statue, his more detailed original paragraph on the negotiations and payments (and the reprisals against the primates of Milos by the dragoman Mourouzi), which presumably was also read, was deleted in the published article – hardly proof of dishonourable behaviour. Editors frequently insist on space-saving cuts and the deletion of details they consider superfluous or unwarranted; the *Annales maritimes* was a densely set journal with little blank space. The end of d'Urville's article is immediately followed by a letter to the editor, so it would hardly be surprising if it was edited. While d'Urville might have deliberately omitted what he knew (second-hand) of Olivier Voutier's role in Kendrotas's discovery and failed to mention that Matterer and Louis Brest were in his company when he first saw the statue, Gregory Curtis's additional assertion that his 'self-promotion'[25] forced the hand of the director of the Louvre to display the Vénus de Milo sooner rather than later would appear to be an exaggeration. Aside from the marquis de Rivière, who had his own agenda, few could compete with the statue's own powers of self-promotion!

D'Urville's surviving correspondence for the period contains a number of brief references to the statue. To Cerisy, he wrote in early March: 'The famous Vénus de Milo is in Paris; M. de Rivière has asserted publicly that it was in great part due to my notice and M. Marcellus has confirmed that he purchased it without seeing it, trusting what was said. I was very fortunate in my judgment, M. Fauvel has ranked it between the Venus of the Capitol and that of Arles and valued it at 100,000 francs.'[26] D'Urville also wrote to his friend Théodose-Cyriaque Prost, on 8 April 1821: 'The statue of which I speak at the beginning of my memoir and of which I had the good fortune to give the first news to our ambassador, is actually here, where it is admired by artists and connoisseurs. It has been classed among the ranks of the best pieces known from antiquity.'[27]

As the statue's fame grew, there can be little doubt that d'Urville sought to be identified with it. For example, on 25 August 1821, he wrote to Cerisy in Toulon: 'My Vénus de Milo continues to be classed in the first order.'[28] And a week later, in a letter in which he sought membership of the Académie de Caen, he wrote: 'Thanks to a fortunate chance occasion, I was the first to visit, to describe and to make known the celebrated Venus victrix of Milos.'[29]

Throughout this period, however, D'Urville's principal object remained promotion in the navy. Four days after presenting his paper before the Académie des sciences, he complained to Cerisy: 'in this immense town one must take infinite trouble and … often one doesn't get anywhere.'[30] On 17 April, he wrote to the marquis de Rivière seeking promotion to *lieutenant de vaisseau*. It might have provoked the attention of the king because in May he received prior notice that he was to be decorated. Le Brun also tells us that Louis XVIII promised him a copy of the *Description de l'Égypte* (1809), the great work produced under Napoleon's orders.[31] Although d'Urville would come to own two copies of Vivant Denon's *Voyage dans la basse et la haute Égypte* and did get to know a number of members of the Commission of Egypt while in Paris in 1821, Le Brun appears to have been in error about the king's gift. D'Urville himself informed Cerisy that for his 'work relating to the beautiful antiquity [the Vénus de Milo]', the king had 'accorded' him 'Visconti's *Iconographie grecque*'.[32] Since we know that Ennio Quirino Visconti's *Iconographie ancienne* was indeed part of his personal library,[33] we can assume that he was given the first three volumes relating to famous Greeks. (The remaining four of the total seven volumes provide illustrations of illustrious Romans and were published later.[34])

'Dumont d'Urville', lithograph by [Antoine?] Maurin from a portrait by Émile Lassalle, presumably based on the work of an earlier artist, from Victor Frond's Histoire de la marine française au XIXe siècle, *Abel Pilon, Lemercier, Paris, 1868, vol. 2. It portrays d'Urville in his early thirties, wearing the medal of a chevalier de la Légion d'honneur. The same lithograph was also used in Frond's* Panthéon des Illustrations Françaises au XIXème siècle. Author's collection

Louis Isidore Duperrey

Né en 1780.

'*Louis Isidore Duperrey (1786–1865)*', *etching by A. Lefevre, from the frontispiece of Dumont d'Urville's* Voyage pittoresque autour du monde, *L. Tenré, Paris, vol. ii, 1835. D'Urville first met Duperrey in September 1811 aboard the* Suffren. *He later circled the globe with Duperrey as his second-in-command on the* Coquille. Author's collection

Still impatient and frustrated by his lack of advancement – and financially stressed by the needs of his young family – d'Urville remarked ungraciously to his friend Prost that 'a ribbon' had been his 'entire recompense'[35] and used almost identical words to Cerisy in Toulon.[36] The official letter advising him that the king had named him a *chevalier de la Légion d'honneur* at just 31 years of age was dated 8 June 1821.[37] One should not underestimate the honour, especially in peacetime; his distinguished friend Latreille received the same decoration in the same year, but he was nearly 30 years d'Urville's senior and one of the founders of modern entomology.

D'Urville was not a happy man when he arrived in Paris, and he was determined to leave under different circumstances. In a frank autobiographical statement he wrote:

> Disgusted by thirteen years of poverty, humiliation and fruitless efforts, my ardour was extinguished and the illusions of my youth had dissipated, my ambition was destroyed; I have dragged my sad harness for the sole reason that my means do not permit me to quit. Well, I will not leave the capital, after a sojourn of sixteen months, without my name having become known and to execute a project worthy of a mariner who has long had an established reputation. Thanks to the plants and insects I collected in the Levant to distract myself and this Venus which has arrived in Paris causing general satisfaction among peers and deputies, even the generals, colossi of the navy; here is the obscure ensign, aged thirty-one and a half, with more than seven years in the rank, here, sought out by artists, appreciated by scientists, received by eminent persons.[38]

In early July, d'Urville planned to leave for Normandy with his family, originally intending a sojourn of six weeks. It is possible that they travelled down the Seine from Paris – via Rouen and Honfleur, so that Adélie could see some of the jewels of Norman architecture – and by coastal vessel to Ouistreham on the Orne estuary. According to Le Brun, d'Urville botanised at Ouistreham, the closest port to Caen. Another possibility is that they travelled to Caen (where he spent much of his time) via the port of Abbeville, the hometown of Prosper-Abbeville Tillette de Clermont-Tonnerre, a decorated former army officer and an amateur botanist, whom d'Urville specifically mentions befriending during his sojourn in Normandy.[39] D'Urville also travelled to Bayeux to visit the tomb of his beloved uncle abbé de Croisilles. Le Brun, however, states that d'Urville cut short his visit to family in Vire as a result of an unravelled attempt to revive contact with relatives.[40] Le Brun did not name d'Urville's mother, but it would seem that Vergniol had no doubts: 'He avoided,' he wrote, 'seeing any of his relatives, even his mother.'[41] This is plainly incorrect, unless we are to believe that d'Urville, alone, was estranged from his family, rather than his wife, the alleged cause of the estrangement! In a letter to Cerisy, Adélie wrote: 'I was expected with impatience by my mother-in-law, of whom I have already spoken and who received me with the greatest joy.'[42] After leaving Caen, she went to the countryside to attend the wedding of d'Urville's nephew (to the daughter of a wealthy landholder) and to visit the youngest of d'Urville's sisters – a beautiful, intelligent woman in her late thirties who looked 10 years younger than her age and who had adopted simple country ways, despite her formal upbringing. In contrast, she found d'Urville's formidable eldest sister, Adelaïde (who had shared much of d'Urville's mother's ordeal during the Terror), very different. 'She has conserved the customs and the usages of high society', wrote Adélie, 'I did not find her to my taste and I did not bond with her.'[43] Yet Adélie would write more warmly of d'Urville's maternal cousins, also raised in the manners of 'high society.' She was 'well received' by Louise de Croisilles; she 'frequently saw' the beautiful Stéphanie de Croisilles, who resided in Caen; and she gained 'much affection' from Stéphanie's younger sister Laure.[44] Adélie, direct and irrepressible, appears to have relished the Norman countryside of d'Urville's youth. She might have raised eyebrows with her provençal ways, but one can almost hear her laughing as she gleefully told Cerisy of following d'Urville home from church on horseback and getting caught in pouring summer rain, with her crêpe-garnished straw hat sodden, sagging and covering her eyes, and her previously pristine white collar covered in mud, just like the back of her dress.[45] We know from their private papers that d'Urville was back in Paris by late August, but that Adélie remained in Normandy until he returned to collect her a month later.

On 22 August 1821, two and a half months after being decorated with the *Légion d'honneur*, d'Urville was finally promoted to *lieutenant de vaisseau*, with an increase in his annual salary of 665 francs. He would later reflect on his circumstances at the time and the enormous personal significance of the promotion:

> Recently arrived in the capital with my wife and my child, I proposed to reside long enough to be able to profit from the luminaries and the encounters in this immense depot of knowledge. Unfortunately, I was not long in realising that our expenses there surpassed my means and [as a] result the 3–4000 francs that I wanted to sacrifice each year, saw me submit myself to a thousand privations which were so much more cruel because they fell in large part on my kind and virtuous companion. I therefore saw the necessity of renouncing, for the moment, my designs on Paris, even if it cost me infinitely to return to Toulon to resume ordinary port service or to embark under the orders of some chiefs without merit and to have supported these caprices without [any] other compensation than voyages without glory and positions without point … I drifted in this painful certitude until 25 August 1821 raised me to the rank of *Lieutenant de vaisseau*, terminated my doubts and made me take a decisive part. I felt that I could not reappear … in the navy other than for a brilliant mission which even forced the envious to silence.[46]

In the same month that he was promoted, he was joined at the Dépôt des cartes et plans by Duperrey, who had been ordered to Paris[47] to edit the geographical findings of Freycinet's *Uranie* expedition. According to d'Urville, they had both arrived in the capital around the same time and had renewed contact in March. D'Urville wrote in his journal that Duperrey spoke to him of 'diverse parts of the globe still unexplored, notably the Carolines and New Guinea'.[48] Both young men were ambitious and began to discuss collaboration. 'Well!', d'Urville informed Cerisy, 'we have formed a plan to go and explore the islands of the Pacific Ocean which are still entirely unknown. Duperrey will assume responsibility for all the nautical and hydrographic work. I will take the descriptive part and the diverse branches of natural history. With our zeal … we will obtain important results.' D'Urville added that the project would be presented 'incessantly' to the minister and that he would lobby those friends he had made among the members of the Institut royal de France. Although he had not ruled out the construction of a purpose-built vessel, mindful of the costs of such an expedition, he asked Cerisy in Toulon to scout for available écuries-gabares, similar to the *Chevrette*, which were fit for 'two or three years of sea keeping'. He was enjoined to respond as quickly as possible but also to observe strict secrecy: 'you know', he wrote, 'that such projects should not be spread about, above all in the ports'.[49] D'Urville, by his own admission, left the proposed route of the expedition 'entirely' to Duperrey's 'disposition'.[50]

Although d'Urville found interest and approbation among numerous members of the Académie des sciences, this did not translate into action at the navy ministry. He was disappointed after returning from Normandy with Adélie, in September 1821, to discover that Duperrey's pompous assertion of representations to the ministry were apparently a charade. Knowing that he would not be able to remain indefinitely in Paris and that their plans would falter as soon as he left, d'Urville took it upon himself to see Rear Admiral François d'Augier, director of naval personnel. The admiral listened politely and attentively as d'Urville outlined their ideas and how they intended to employ the most stringent economies to minimise the cost of the expedition. According to d'Urville, d'Augier responded: 'My friend, your enthusiasm pleases me; I like to see young people animated with desire to work ardently for glory. After tomorrow I will have private audience with the Minister and I will put your project before him and I promise to support it with all my means; count on my word.'[51] If we are to believe d'Urville, two days later Duperrey was summoned to the ministry, and the day after that they were both warmly received by the minister, baron Portal d'Albarèdes, at a soirée.

According to Duperrey, their predecessors in the age of exploration had left only 'fragments of archipelagos to explore, or polar ice to pass beyond', but their discoveries had 'expanded the theatre of our meditations'. He added, 'nature has not divulged all of her mysteries; she is very fertile and her phenomena are very complex ... savants will always obtain new observations and precious discoveries'. Duperrey's proposal, made conjointly with d'Urville, was for a voyage of circumnavigation that would involve hydrography (particularly confirming and rectifying the position of a great number of points on the globe, including islands, banks and reefs, and tracing new routes through dangerous archipelagos) but also geophysical observations (including magnetism, the shape of the globe and meteorology), natural history and the 'language, character, manners and physiognomy of the islanders'.[52] The principal focus of these efforts would be the Pacific. They proposed to cross the Atlantic and to enter the Pacific via the South Shetland Islands, sail to the Society Islands via Easter Island and refine cartographic knowledge of the islands west of Tahiti and as far north as the Marianas, using European colonies on the periphery of the region to re-provision. Ultimately, the South Shetlands and Easter Island were removed from the proposed route. Baron Portal responded favourably in November 1822, but he would not remain minister for much longer.

This was a period of instability in French politics. In the wake of the duc de Berry's assassination, the persistent attacks of both the ultra royalists and the liberals eventually made the position of the prime minister, the duc de Richelieu, untenable. He resigned on 12 December 1821 and was succeeded by the leader of the reactionary ultra royalists, Finance Minister Joseph de Villèle.[53] Fortunately for Duperrey and d'Urville, the new prime minister was sympathetic to naval issues. As a young man, he had served in the navy in the Caribbean and the Indian Ocean. Villèle had also spent much of the Revolution on the island of Bourbon (now La Réunion), where he married the daughter of a wealthy colonist. He had seen the sister island of Mauritius – French for the better part of century and with a significant French population – captured by Britain in 1810 and never returned. It is possible he saw further French exploration as a means to new territorial acquisitions, however modest: on 9 May 1822, *Le moniteur universel* reported the government's wish to have 'in the islands of Polynesia and Australasia a few places where French ships could transplant civilisation and its benefits' and then went on to extol the work of naturalists as 'missionaries of science gathering on all the points of the globe the brilliant products of the three kingdoms [of nature]'.[54] Aimé-Marie-Gaspard, marquis de Clermont-Tonnerre, had also been appointed navy minister on 14 December 1821.[55] A student of the École polytechnique before he joined the army, Clermont-Tonnerre was a man sympathetic to the sciences[56] and, a few days after his appointment, called Duperrey to his office. Duperrey's and d'Urville's plan was discussed and 'adopted with enthusiasm and without modification'.[57] The proposed circumnavigation was then taken to Louis XVIII for royal assent. Duperrey was appointed commander of the expedition and d'Urville second-in-command.

As was the case with most previous French voyages, the Académie des sciences prepared detailed instructions for those who would assume responsibility for the various branches of science during the expedition. Duperrey's formal instructions from the minister reaffirmed that a principal focus of the voyage would be geographical and that he was expected to conduct 'all kinds of astronomical observations' to obtain latitude and longitude, and rate his marine chronometers. 'The position of the town of Sydney' was considered particularly important, because it could 'serve with success to either rectify or verify a great number of others'.[58] Aside from the determination of the latitude and longitude of numerous points in the Pacific, special focus for exploration would be the Caroline and the Gilbert islands. The expedition also had important political instructions with regard to French colonial ambitions in Australia:

> For several years, researchers have gone to the most distant countries … to find land preceded by a harbour or a port, which by its fertility and the gentleness of its climate, could receive an establishment formed uniquely for Europeans. The place where attention has turned is situated on the western coast of New Holland along the shores of the Swan River. The latitude of 32° 4½′ south of the equator located outside the torrid zone and in a temperate climate would [allow?] Europeans to cultivate the earth and [aid?] their subsistence with the aid of a foreign population … the river was visited during the expedition to the southern lands commanded by Captain Baudin. Its shores present all the advantages proper to give the hope that an establishment will prosper there and will become, in a short time, very flourishing. It is this place, M. Duperrey must visit … He must examine scrupulously and in the most minute detail, all the local circumstances which could favour the endeavours of an initial settlement.[59]

As d'Urville desired, a stout écurie-gabare, the *Coquille* (seashell), was made available for the voyage, although she required four months' repairs high and dry in the stocks of the naval arsenal. It was time well spent; this sturdy little vessel would circle the globe twice and serve the French navy for nearly 40 years in both war and peace. Weighing 380 tonnes, with three masts and armed with 12 carronades, her 30-metre-long keel had been laid down at nearby La Seyne-sur-Mer in 1811. Her generic hull, originally designed by the naval engineer François-Timothée-Benjamin Pestel to transport 46 horses, was well suited to the task of storing the provisions for a voyage of circumnavigation,[60] and her 3-metre draught would save her on numerous occasions in shallow waters.[61]

A talented group of young officers and scientists was also assembled for the expedition, many of whom d'Urville already knew. Twenty-six-year-old ensign

Charles-Hector Jacquinot was from Nevers in Burgundy, the son of a banker. Tall, well built and auburn haired, he had served in the Mediterranean on the *Chevrette* and *Lionne* (when the latter had transported the Vénus de Milo from Smyrna to Constantinople). A fastidious, non-smoking bachelor, Jacquinot was also an amiable ladies' man, a raconteur and a teller of bawdy provençal jokes who was considered excellent company. D'Urville was keen to sail with him again. He would prove to be d'Urville's stalwart companion on all his remaining voyages.[62] Another veteran of the *Chevrette*, and thus of Gauttier-Duparc's rigorous training in hydrography, was Victor-Charles Lottin. Even earlier, Lottin had served with d'Urville aboard the *Ville de Marseille* on the expedition that took the duc d'Orléans to Sicily. He was originally from Paris and was about to turn 27.[63] Ensign Auguste Bérard, 26 years old, was from Montpellier. He too had served on the *Chevrette* between 1815 and 1816 and then with Duperrey under Louis Freycinet aboard the *Uranie*; he would eventually reach the rank of rear admiral[64] and was the brother of Jacques-Étienne Bérard, who pioneered the study of the chemical processes involved in fruit maturation. Ensign Théodore-Julien Deblois de la Calande was a 23-year-old Breton from Morlaix. The son of a naval officer, he had joined the service through the elite École spéciale de la marine in Brest and had served mainly in Atlantic waters. According to d'Urville, he was 'proposed' by Admiral Rossel, which made his inclusion among the staff officers difficult to reject. A capable hydrographer, he reached the rank of lieutenant but squandered the advantages of birth, education and noble patronage with an impulsive resignation after the July Revolution of 1830.[65]

The minister himself proposed two members of the expedition. One was Paris-born Jules-Alphonse Poret de Blosseville, who would serve as a midshipman and was promoted to ensign by the end of the voyage. He would embrace hydrography and geophysical observations with a passion and rise rapidly in the navy, only to disappear in Greenland waters while in command of the *Lilloise* in 1833, at just 31 years of age.[66] The minister's other candidate was the 18-year-old artist François-Louis (aka Jules or Jules-Louis) Lejeune, who would make an important visual record of the expedition. Although described as the 'nephew' of General Louis-François Lejeune, he appears to have been the general's natural son. His service record states that he was the son of General Louis-Alexandre Berthier's aide-de-camp, but this was his 'uncle's' position at the time.[67] The genetic connection is all the more credible because General Lejeune had himself turned to painting – with considerable success as the visual chronicler of Napoleon's military exploits – while recovering miraculously from a Spanish guerrilla attack, in 1811, that wiped out his detachment of dragoons, killed his horse with a hail of 30 gunshots and left him with 10 musket balls in the chest.[68]

Not all the appointments were to d'Urville's liking. He found himself in conflict with two of the towering figures of the biological sciences in France: Étienne Geoffroy Saint-Hilaire and Georges Cuvier, who favoured the nomination of an unnamed employee of the laboratory of the Muséum national d'histoire naturelle as a professional 'naturalist' to the expedition.[69] D'Urville saw this as a direct challenge to the primary role he envisaged for himself during the voyage and dismissed the candidate contemptuously as a 'valet', apparently rallying the support of the equally influential botanist René Desfontaines and André Thouin, head of the Jardin des plantes.[70] Regardless of Cuvier's 'irritation', the navy was probably reluctant to approve the appointment of a civilian. During the earlier French voyages of d'Entrecasteaux[71] and Baudin, the medically trained civilian naturalists Labillardière, Riche and Péron had done profoundly important scientific work, but they had also seriously undermined the authority of their expedition commanders because they were not subject to naval discipline. D'Urville was, therefore, very pleased when the chief physician of the navy, Pierre-François Keraudren, proposed the naval pharmacist René-Primevère Lesson for the expedition. Twenty-eight years old and born in Rochefort on the Atlantic coast, he was a graduate of his hometown's famous naval medical college and had served as an assistant surgeon then gardener–botanist in the navy's botanical gardens before training in pharmacy and becoming conservator of the navy's natural history cabinet (museum) in Rochefort.[72] He would write an important two-volume account of the voyage and contribute significantly to its results in the natural sciences. D'Urville was also pleased when Keraudren proposed 28-year-old Prosper Garnot to be surgeon to the expedition, because he, too, seemed well qualified to assume additional responsibilities in zoology. Garnot, after whom the plant genus *Garnotia* would later be named by Adolphe-Théodore Brongniart, was born in Brest; he had served for many years in the naval hospital of his home port but had also made a number of voyages to the Antilles.[73]

In marked contrast, d'Urville was angered when, without consultation, Duperrey nominated his friend Charles-Félix-Victor Lesage to join the staff of the expedition. They were both Parisians (from the same parish of Saint-Germain) and, as young midshipmen, Lesage and Duperrey had served together on the *Républicain*. Lesage had been an ensign for almost a decade. D'Urville, who had been promoted over Lesage, detested him for his egotism and his exaggerated claims. Possibly d'Urville also saw him as a rival to his authority as second-in-command, because Lesage was two years his senior and had long experience in the fighting navy. Ultimately Lesage, like Prosper Garnot, would not complete the circumnavigation aboard the *Coquille* and would return home separately from Port Jackson.[74]

It was perhaps inevitable that someone with d'Urville's ambition and force of character would find it difficult to play second fiddle to Duperrey. However unusual it was for two officers to jointly formulate an expedition, there could only ever be one captain. When their official orders were received on 13 April 1822, Duperrey began to assert his authority in a manner that d'Urville found offensive. 'So', he wrote, 'Duperrey, having nothing more to desire, began to neglect me and to speak to me with that haughtiness so common to officers ridiculed in the navy. It was obvious to me that I had served none other than an ingrate, but that the folly was committed and I would either have to drink from the chalice or renounce the navy.'[75] Adélie, aware of her husband's unhappiness and no doubt recognising an opportunity to keep him in France, pressed him 'several times to abandon' the expedition.[76] D'Urville knew that if he was to achieve anything in the navy, he could not squander the opportunity to participate in the voyage of the *Coquille*, so he submitted to Duperrey's authority.

7

La Coquille

The anchor heaves, the ship swings free,
The sails swell full. To sea, to sea!
Thomas Lovell Beddoes*

D'Urville returned to Toulon from Paris on 10 May 1822 and promptly surveyed the refitting and repairs to the *Coquille* being undertaken in the naval dockyard by Cerisy.[1] This work included strengthening the hull with a 200 millimetre-thick false keel, renewing all its copper sheathing and replacing iron with copper in the area of the quarterdeck to prevent interference during future magnetic observations.[2] The *Coquille* was also fitted with a 30-litre alembic for distilling fresh water in case of emergency and an oven large enough to bake bread daily for the entire crew of 60 men and 12 officers. After the repairs were finished, she was loaded with provisions sufficient, depending on the kind and quantity, for 15–24 months of voyaging, including many tablets of dried soup and 2-kilogram tins of beef and vegetables prepared using Nicolas Appert's method of sterilisation and preservation developed for the Napoleonic military.[3] The *Coquille* was also supplied with exchange goods to barter for fresh supplies in the Pacific. Her crew members were issued with greatcoats, oilskins, flannel trousers and vests, and were paid six months' wages in advance to ensure the security of their families during their absences.[4] Finally, her officers were supplied with an up-to-date selection of navigational and scientific instruments.[5]

D'Urville was greeted warmly by Duperrey when he arrived in Toulon, but he soon received reports of unflattering comments made behind his back by his commander. 'All the jealousy returned,' d'Urville wrote, and Duperrey 'once again became cold, whimsical and several times dishonest.' He chose to show no indignation, hoping his 'passive obedience' would banish Duperrey's suspicions and lead to a resumption of 'more reasonable sentiments'.[6] In this state of false harmony, the two senior officers of the expedition completed their final preparations.

The *Coquille* set sail from Toulon on the morning of 11 August 1822. One of her

*'Song from the Ship', lines 15–16

master gunners, Thomas-Pierre Rolland, noted in his journal that 'the preparations for casting off were carried out in the blink of an eye'.[7] Although the crew was confident of a successful voyage, there was silence aboard as she cleared the harbour and the coast of Provence. D'Urville had made his farewells to his family the night before, knowing it would be years before he would return; this same knowledge had underscored the departure of every other man aboard. At first, even the sea remained silent for lack of agitation but, when finally stirred, condemned the novices to seasickness. Some days later, the *Coquille* sailed past the Balearic Islands. The sight of the tiny island of Cabrera, where 12,000 French troops were left to starve between 1809 and 1814, brought back painful memories for Duperrey, who had served as second-in-command of the *Rose* – the first vessel sent to their aid after the Restoration. After rounding the Iberian Peninsula and passing through the Strait of Gibraltar, the *Coquille* entered the Atlantic and made for the Canary Islands. The towering Mount Teide on Tenerife was sighted at dawn on 28 August. Although the *Coquille* dropped anchor in Santa Cruz harbour that same day, the Spanish authorities determined that the presence of yellow fever on the Mediterranean coast required her to spend two weeks in quarantine. The real reason, not mentioned by Duperrey in his published account, was probably retaliation for French troops massing on the Spanish border and threatening intervention against the new liberal constitutional government that had made a captive of Fernando VII – yet another Bourbon cousin of Louis XVIII.[8] Under the circumstances, Duperrey decided not to stay and weighed anchor within three days. Before doing so, he took on a quantity of the famous local Malmsey wine and other supplies with the aid of the French vice-consul. He also performed geophysical and astronomical observations, including the calculation of 86 lunar distances to verify the longitude of the pier of Santa Cruz – the very pier, d'Urville later noted, where Horatio Nelson had lost his arm and 500 men in 1797.[9] Unfortunately, the prospect of enforced quarantine deprived d'Urville and his colleagues of the opportunity to visit the island, climb its volcanic peak and collect natural history specimens. While Lesson regretted the lost scientific opportunity, as a medical officer, he believed it a blessing that the crew had been denied contact with the local women, who were notorious for their high rates of venereal disease.[10]

The *Coquille* set sail for the Cape Verde Islands in calm seas on the evening of 1 September. Four days later, the Tropic of Cancer was crossed and, on 8 September, the lookouts sighted Santo Antonio, the most westerly of the Cape Verde Islands and, as d'Urville later put it, 'the most populated of the archipelago and dominated by a very elevated peak'.[11] In the midst of the Northern Equatorial Current, the sea was covered with seaweed, and d'Urville collected specimens of the well-known *Sargassum natans*.[12] In the course of the voyage, he would make a major contribution to the collection of many new species of marine flora, which would be described by Jean-

Baptiste Bory de Saint-Vincent, who had been one of the original botanists of Nicolas
Baudin's expedition to Australian waters.

On the evening of 10 September, the crew beheld yet another spectacle on the
surface of the sea: a display of phosphorescence, which d'Urville described graphically
in his journal:

> It is above all noticeable in the waves broken by the vessel: large sheets of fluid, very
> much like … some of the most brilliant portions of the Milky Way, sliced at each
> instant on the sombre hue of the sea. The rays of light very much like exploding Ro-
> man candles in fireworks displays, gushing in every sense on the surface of the sea,
> drawn out along the side of the ship in the form of flaming globules … [13]

With his classical learning, d'Urville was no doubt aware that phosphorescence
at sea had been discussed by both Aristotle and Pliny the Elder. His travels in the
Mediterranean might already have led him to observe luminescent zooplankton
known as *Noctiluca*, first identified in the Adriatic in the eighteenth century. While
Benjamin Franklin had erroneously speculated that such phosphorescence was the
result of electrolytic discharges in sea water, and François Péron, naturalist of Baudin's
expedition, had correctly suggested that it was a phenomenon 'peculiar to marine
animals',[14] d'Urville began his own investigation:

> These globules above all drew my attention, and I was persuaded that they were
> emitted by some animal. Armed with a fine net, I endeavoured to seize some of
> them; but as soon as the net left the water the luminous globe was reduced to a point
> and soon disappeared without it being possible to determine what produced it. Ul-
> timately, after long research, I discovered that the luminous point came from an
> animated atom like a speck of dust, and, with the aid of a strong lens, I recognised
> that this animalcule was an infinitely small and almost diaphanous crustacean.[15]

Even today, bioluminescence is imperfectly understood. D'Urville could only have
guessed at chemical reactions in marine creatures, let alone light-emitting bacteria or
photophores. He came to the conclusion that it was to 'the strongly refractive property
of the droplets of water which surround them that one can attribute without doubt the
lively light that these animated atoms are capable of emitting'.[16] To be fair, d'Urville's
'droplets of water' might have contained still-smaller luminescent life forms, but
his speculations, although linked to microscopic marine fauna, were suggestive of a
belief in a coincidental optical effect rather than a purely biological phenomenon for
the purposes of sexual attraction, luring food, warning predators of stinging cells or
providing camouflage against background surface light – to name just a few possible
explanations for marine bioluminescence.

The following night, the officers and crew of the *Coquille* observed yet another striking phenomenon: a 'globe of fire' suddenly appeared in the west-northwest and traced an arc across the sky before plunging into the sea to the south with a sound like distant thunder. Duperrey remarked that the falling meteorite was a portent to 'strike superstitious men with terror'.[17] Ironically, there were indeed ominous events in distant France: Louis XVIII lay on his deathbed with gangrene spreading through his legs. Within the week, he would be the last French king to die while occupying his throne.[18] He was succeeded by his reactionary brother, Charles X, who was so averse to compromise and constitutional restraint that he declared: 'I would rather saw wood than be an English-style king.'[19]

With the benefit of favourable but gentle winds, the *Coquille* made a slow but serene passage across the waist of the Atlantic towards Brazil. On 24 September, she crossed the equator. The crew engaged in the traditional initiation ceremonies – cathartic release, tinged with sanctioned opportunistic sadism, in a normally strict disciplinary environment. D'Urville and the other officers who had not crossed the line before were spared Neptune's customary demands, apparently after augmenting the rations for the festivities. Ensign Auguste Bérard also composed a witty song for the occasion.[20] Of the commissioned and scientific staff, only the young artist Lejeune was the physical butt of the sailors' fun. He was dunked in sea water and then pursued with the firehose as far as his cabin. The next day, military discipline returned as if there had never been any kind of lapse.[21]

On 6 October, they sighted the islands of Martin Vaz and Trindad – the latter surrounded by numerous whales – and three days later, they crossed the Tropic of Capricorn. Soon after, sea birds heralding land began to escort the *Coquille* and, on 16 October, she entered the bay of Santa Catarina Island off the verdant southern Brazilian coast. At first the crew could not understand the cool reception from the local garrison, but when d'Urville, bearing a letter from the king of Portugal, was dispatched to announce their arrival to the governor, he was informed that Brazil had declared independence on 7 September. Dom Pedro, prince of the royal house of Braganza and Bourbon, had been proclaimed Emperor Pedro I of the Empire of Brazil, an empire that would survive in name until 1889. Despite initial Brazilian suspicions, the French were permitted to cut firewood and conduct scientific work. D'Urville was drawn to the island's interior. 'For the botanist', he wrote, it was characterised by 'immense forests … innumerable shrubs … impenetrable thickets, which each moment arrest his view and his path.'[22] It was here that he apparently collected the type specimen of the epiphytic bromeliad *Tillandsia geminiflora*. In 1768, it had been collected at Rio de Janeiro by Joseph Banks and Daniel Solander[23] and illustrated in a watercolour by Sydney Parkinson during the voyage of the *Endeavour* but never published. (That honour would go to Adolphe-Théodore Brongniart, who would co-edit the botanical

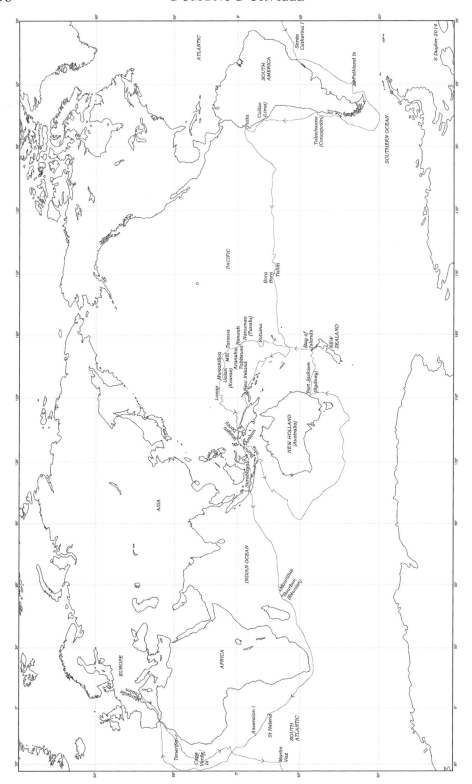

results of the *Coquille* voyage along with d'Urville and Bory de Saint-Vincent, and publish a separate volume on phanerogams (plants that bear flowers and true seeds).[24]) Santa Catarina was also the source of the type specimen of the exquisite *Epidendrum fulgens*,[25] belonging to the same genus as the popular crucifix orchid. Here too, d'Urville collected the type specimens of a number of Brazilian grass species, including *Ichnanthus fastigiatus* and *Deyeuxia splendens*, later described by Brongniart.[26] Under fallen leaves, he also collected the type specimen of a previously unknown species of segestrid spider, *Segestria ruficeps*, belonging to a genus named by Latreille in 1804; it has a largely dark-brown body and is characterised by brilliant green mandibles.[27]

The *Coquille* left Santa Catarina Island on 30 October – not having been able to purchase much in the way of fresh victuals – and headed south for the Falkland Islands (known in French as the Malouines and to the Spanish as the Malvinas). She reached the eastern island in the group on 18 November, and Duperrey sailed her into what is now Berkeley Sound. It took three cautious days, in contrary winds, to anchor in French Bay, safely short of where the *Uranie* had foundered in early 1820. This had been the site of the French settlement of Port Saint-Louis – founded by Louis-Antoine de Bougainville in 1764 but handed over to Spain at the insistence of France's Spanish allies in 1767. By the time the *Coquille* arrived, the Spanish settlement had been abandoned for more than a decade. Although an American privateer, in the employ of an Irish merchant in Buenos Aires, had raised the flag of the United Provinces of the Río de la Plata (soon to be renamed Argentina) in November 1820, there were no inhabitants. The men of the *Coquille* had the island to themselves, with the exception of the native fauna and the feral descendants of the once-domestic animals of the early colonists, including rabbits, oxen, wild horses and pigs. For his part, d'Urville thought that if other South American states, such as Peru and Chile, finally achieved independence from Spain, the Falklands would become a very important port of call as they sought to develop commercial relations with Europe.[28]

It was then late spring in the southern hemisphere, but the mountains remained snow-covered and the weather was bitterly cold and wet. The bleakness of the climate heightened empathy for those who had been marooned for four months when the *Uranie* foundered. She was still visible: according to d'Urville, 'the officers found the hull of the *Uranie* on the beach, half-buried in the sand, [along with] the caronades, iron chests and debris of all kinds'.[29] Her veterans, like Master Gunner Rolland, had returned to the island with valuable knowledge of its rich hunting grounds. In his journal, Rolland remarked: 'It is nigh impossible to convey to the reader how easy hunting is on these islands.'[30] D'Urville recorded that during their sojourn, they 'killed

Opposite: *Map 3. The circumnavigation of the* Coquille, *August 1822 to 25 March 1825.*

an enormous quantity of birds and rabbits, in addition to several wild pigs and two bullocks'.[31]

The *Coquille* remained in the Falklands for a month, during which an observatory was established ashore. In the early stages of the expedition, to give a clear impression of submission to Duperrey's authority, d'Urville had made astronomical observations twice a day like the other officers. However, some two months into the voyage, Duperrey, in a 'black mood', rebuked him and declared that such work was not his responsibility. It might have been just the pretext d'Urville was looking for. From that moment onwards, he did neither astronomical nor geographical work and withdrew almost exclusively into natural history. On several occasions, Duperrey sought to engage him in celestial observations, but d'Urville rebuffed him with what appears to have been sullen firmness.[32] After d'Urville's death, Lesson would write of the manner in which his relationship with Duperrey changed:

> The mutual understanding that had existed between the two chiefs of the expedition unceasingly faded after the first months of the campaign, to be replaced by senti-ments contrary to those which had initially united them towards a common pur-pose. Changeable and impressionable, the head of the expedition was continually annoyed by the cold, tenacious, trenchant character of the second-in-command; the result was clashes, discord, which added their vexations to those which natu-rally tested officers full of force and ambition, enclosed in narrow cabins and always face to face. Then the antipathy of the heads soon engendered misunderstandings between the subordinates who took the side of one or the other. M. d'Urville always lived in feigned peace with his superior in the military hierarchy, because both were of the same grade. He confined himself entirely to the completion of his duties as an officer, utilising all the landings for exhaustive explorations and for the conservation of his collections. As first officer, he had facilities to lodge the products of his col-lecting … His cabin was perfectly fitted out by M. de Cerisy, and M. d'Urville closed himself up to write minutely, day by day, the journal of his observations. He soon stopped occupying himself, like the other officers, with astronomical observations, and he concentrated entirely on his natural history work.[33]

In the Falklands, d'Urville would make an intensive study of the local flora. For him, the contrast with the lush vegetation of Brazil was striking:

> [There were] plains without boundaries and bare coasts. Not a tree, not a veritable shrub breaks the uniformity of this vast solitude. The traveller, assailed by the wind, the rain and the hail, can cover several miles without encountering the least shelter; for the earth itself, as uniform as its vegetation, does not offer any of its rocks in the midst of vales, no hollows so frequently encountered in uncultivated countries. Yet, despite this extraordinary nudity, perhaps the surface of no land was covered with

a carpet so compact, despite the lack of height. Most of the plants and the ground cover are provided with rampant roots and running shoots which strongly attach themselves to the soil and interlace tightly in every sense: a useful precaution employed no doubt by nature to counter the destructive action of the violent winds which frequently reign in these parts.[34]

During 12 botanical excursions conducted over 26 days, d'Urville collected 217 species, including 108 distinct species of phanerogams in 80 genera, 11 species of moss, six ferns, 55 lichens, two lycopods and numerous introduced weeds, all of which he published under the title 'Flore des Malouines' in the *Mémoires de la Société Linnéenne* in 1826. He also studied the islands' coastal marine flora, including *Durvillea*, a genus of bull kelp that Bory de Saint-Vincent would name in his honour. D'Urville's flora of the Falklands was not the first. That honour belongs to Charles Gaudichaud-Beaupré, Freycinet's botanist, who published his 'Rapport sur la flore des îles Malouines' in the *Annales des sciences naturelles* in 1825; d'Urville would make frequent references to Gaudichaud's work in the course of preparing his own publication. His own flora was a major study because it contained original descriptions of 44 new species,[35] which were also included in the published expedition volumes on flowering plants and cryptogams, written respectively by Brongniart and Bory de Saint-Vincent.

On 30 November 1822, d'Urville accompanied Lesson to the mountains south of their anchorage.[36] According to d'Urville, they traversed a plain covered in heath and reached mountains that were completely bare, except for occasional 'green scarfs' of moss. The weathered stone had a monumental quality, and in the clearly exposed strata there was evidence of faulting or, as d'Urville verbosely put it, 'powerful causes of the destruction of their parallelism in certain places'.[37] His description of *éboulemens de blocs* indicates that he saw the island's famous 'stone runs', or 'streams of stones' as Charles Darwin called them.[38] Here, and also during a later two-day excursion with Bérard to the 585-metre summit of Mont Châtellux (now Mount Simon), d'Urville was the first to collect *Nassauvia serpens* (snakeplant), which rears like a serpent from the cascade of stones; unique to the Falklands, this striking plant is now a threatened species. To cover the 27 kilometres to the mountain and then return, d'Urville and Bérard pushed themselves to walk 15 hours each day in the wet, wind-chilled sub-Antarctic wilderness.[39] Of the view from the mountain, d'Urville would later write:

> The island is dominated in the centre by Mount Chastellux, the culminating point, from which a multitude of small chains radiate, between which streams snake, or bays, lakes and ponds lie. Meadows with their reddish tint, a sky very often dull and uncoloured, in the distance whales in the sea and much closer, on land, troops of horses galloping freely – such is the general aspect of this land.[40]

In ecological terms, d'Urville's study displays great appreciation of the highly adapted Falklands' flora; he saw 'nature, that mother so wise, so prudential, for all the living things that she has created' providing 'guarantees against the efforts of the tempests'.[41] There is canny perceptiveness, in a geomorphological and palaeo-botanical sense at least, in his writing on these islands. From his knowledge of the botanical collections of Philibert Commerson (described posthumously by Lamarck and others) and Johann Georg Adam Forster,[42] he correctly recognised that the flora of the Falklands was related to the flora of Tierra del Fuego and the Strait of Magellan. This led him to ask if the Falkland Islands were 'none other than a detached fragment of this extreme point of South America'.[43] Of course, his perspicacity did not extend to tectonic-plate movements, the breakup of a supercontinent (Gondwana) or the enlargement of crust fragments with basalt intrusions. The flora itself, the respective positions of the land masses, the matching latitudes, and the relative shallowness of the sea between the Falklands and the tip of South America provided sufficient justification for his hypothesis.[44]

The expedition was ready to leave the Falklands on 16 December 1822, but contrary winds delayed its departure for another two days. On the evening of 28 December, the lookouts sighted Staten Land – the island south of Tierra del Fuego discovered by Willem Schouten and Jacob Le Maire in 1616[45] – and rounded Cape Horn by passing through the Strait of Le Maire. D'Urville described the strait as a 'dangerous passage for vessels', and added that it was bounded by mountains 'varying from between six to two hundred feet in height' and that several of these summits presented 'a grandiose and imposing aspect' with 'a scarlet lichen, which carpets their precipitous sides' and 'slices the dark green of less abrupt slopes'.[46] Several times, snow and hail covered the deck of the *Coquille*, and 'a thick fog did not cease to veil the sky', but the winds remained moderate and belied the cape's fearsome reputation as the ship left the Atlantic behind her.[47]

Prior to their departure, Duperrey had decided that d'Urville would dine with him aboard the *Coquille*. D'Urville had agreed, but their meals together had become tense affairs and required a disciplined façade.

> During more than six months, neither observation, nor reproach left my mouth in public and yet my fierce colleague unceasingly drenched me with disgust and disagreement; each day he made me listen to indecent tirades against natural history and those occupied with it, unjust reproaches on ship-handling, offensive allusions and perpetual complaints about the staff-officers and the crew. I bore all in silence or I contented myself in consigning some of these grievances to paper.[48]

D'Urville had no illusions: 'the friend doesn't like me at all and my presence aboard offends'.[49] The silence and resignation on d'Urville's part – observed, recorded and perhaps not fully understood by Lesson, who did not sail on his later voyages – would form the basis for posthumous character assessments of a cold and taciturn man. To be fair, d'Urville's defensive behaviour probably exacerbated the insular traits of a man who had sought solace in books and the natural world from an early age, but Duperrey also withdrew from his second-in-command. As d'Urville put it: 'his reports to the Minister, his operations and his projects are absolutely foreign to me and I am nothing in the publication of the voyage'.[50]

8

The Pacific

*The winds and waves are always on the
side of the ablest navigators.*
Edward Gibbon*

After entering the Pacific, the *Coquille* sailed north and, on 20 January 1823, reached Talcahuano, the port of Concepción on the Chilean coast. Once again, d'Urville found himself in the midst of tumultuous events. In the wake of the Chilean War of Independence, General Bernardo O'Higgins Riquelme, illegitimate son of the Irish-born Spanish viceroy of Peru, had become 'supreme director' of the Chilean Republic. Despite significant nation-building achievements, the liberal reforms of his benign dictatorship alienated the local clergy and Chile's large landowners. In mid-December 1822, his erstwhile ally General Ramón Freire Serrano had attacked him in the local press, and on 26 January 1823, the 42-gun corvette *Independencia*, loyal to Freire's conservative faction, had entered Talcahuano harbour from Valdivia with a regiment of 300 uniformed men under the command of Colonel Georges Beauchef, a Grande Armée veteran of Austerlitz, Jena, Marengo, Friedland and the war in Spain. Beauchef had other refugee French Bonapartists as officers under his command. In the wake of the Napoleonic Wars, there were many such men who continued to live by their swords rather than beat them into ploughshares, and they would not be the last the *Coquille* would encounter in her circumnavigation. According to Lesson, among the soldiers of fortune who arrived at Talcahuano was a grandson of Jean-Baptiste Drouet, the postmaster who recognised Louis XVI at Varennes during his attempt to flee France in 1791.

On 2 February, news reached Concepción that O'Higgins had been taken prisoner by an artillery battalion of his own troops in Santiago. The following day, d'Urville, Lesson and Lottin set off on the road from Talcahuano to Concepción. The edge of the road was broidered with wildflowers and shaded in places by overhanging myrtles, heavy with scented blossoms, and Lesson wrote of their fifteen-kilometre walk: 'A

Decline and Fall of the Roman Empire (1781), vol. ii, chapt. lxviii

botanist naturally finds the most vivid contentment in such a short journey.'[1] They soon reached Concepción, then a town of 10,000 inhabitants, which 'seemed to have been taken by assault and pillaged'.[2] Here the three French officers attended a revue of Freire's troops, Lesson recording: 'The drum rolls, the cavalry fanfares, the officers in ponchos, the Araucans armed with long javelins, formed a mélange difficult to describe. I thought myself transported among hordes of Tartars or into a Cossack camp.'[3] At 2.00 pm, these same soldiers set off for Talcahuano in order to board the *Independencia* bound for Santiago, where their general intended to consolidate his hold on power.

Calm finally descended on Concepción, and d'Urville and his colleagues resumed their botanising to the amusement of the locals, who could see no value in the species they collected. Returning to Talcahuano, the officers of the *Coquille* were obliged to attend yet another parade of Freire's troops. Freire also dined aboard the *Coquille* and provided passports for the expedition after singing the praises of the French. However, before he departed, there was still one final act in his revolutionary operetta. This involved two Englishmen, both vying for his favour: the commander of the *Independencia* and the port captain at Talcahuano; the latter expected the incumbent's dismissal for loyalty to O'Higgins and believed he was promised command of the *Independencia*. When Freire retained his existing commander, the port captain struck his rival's head with the blade of his sabre and left him covered in blood. To the consternation of the French, despite this subaltern's brutality and indiscipline, he managed to walk freely in Talcahuano and, according to Lesson, was soon after made Freire's aide-de-camp![4]

With the departure of Freire's troops, Duperrey accelerated the revictualling of the *Coquille*. 'The greater part of the households of Talcahuano,' he wrote, 'took part in the preparation of the biscuits we had need of.'[5] As fuel for their shipboard bread oven and galley stove, they availed themselves of a local deposit of lignite (brown coal), which simply required them to open a six- or seven-foot-deep pit themselves and pay only for mules to transport the coal to their vessel. The local people proved to be warm and hospitable, and the staff officers were invited to two lively balls. Garnot and Lesson tended the local sick and received much gratitude in a town that had only one doctor and where dysentery, enteritis and syphilis were rife.[6] While Jacquinot established the expedition's astronomical observatory at Fort Galvez, 800 metres north of the centre of Talcahuano, and determined the latitudinal and longitudinal co-ordinates with precision, d'Urville and the other naturalists occupied themselves collecting.[7] Aside from the type specimen of *Spartina densiflora* (southern cordgrass), found in the salt marshes,[8] d'Urville collected the fern *Lomaria blechnoides* (*Blechnum blechnoides*)[9] and, on the coast, at least seven previously undescribed seaweeds, including two species of marine algae later named in his honour by Bory de Saint-Vincent: *Polyides durvillei*

(*Ahnfeltiopsis durvillei*) and *Dawsonia durvillaei* (*Hymenena durvillaei*).[10] From under a rock, while exploring the mountains in the area of Penco (also served by the harbour of Talcahuano), he collected the type specimen of a new species of scorpion, *Buthus vittatus*, later described by Félix-Édouard Guérin-Méneville.[11]

Duperrey and his men entrusted their letters home and official reports to Captain James Choyce of the visiting English whaler the *Sarah-Anne*.[12] Almost certainly d'Urville dispatched letters to Adélie and his son, but he also sent some 50 packets of seeds he had collected in South America to André Thouin, director of the Jardin des plantes in Paris.[13] On 13 February 1823, the *Coquille* weighed anchor and set sail for Peru, reaching the busy port of Callao on the evening of 26 February. Peru was yet another newly independent republic after three centuries of Spanish rule. Unfortunately, the visiting French expedition generated suspicion and mistrust. While d'Urville botanised and Auguste Bérard collected bird specimens on the rocky flanks of Mount San Cristobal, overlooking the capital Lima, they were reported to the National Guard as Spanish spies. A picket of mounted peasants, under the command of a lieutenant, was dispatched to arrest them. But for the intervention of the officer, who wanted his trophies alive, the guardsmen would have shot them on sight. Offering no resistance, d'Urville and Bérard failed to convince their proud captors of their bona fides, and their safe-conduct passes, recently issued at Fort Callao, were rejected. Tethered behind one of the nags of the mounted guardsmen, the two French officers were taken into Lima in the fierce midday sun and thrown into prison, their money and watches stolen, as was the double-barrelled shotgun Bérard used to shoot his bird specimens. Some hours later, after the intervention of the commanding general – perhaps the very general who had signed their safe-conduct passes – they were released. They recovered their possessions with difficulty, but the lieutenant who had bound and humiliated them (and who had already sought a promotion for his zeal and 'successful' counter-espionage!) still refused to believe that they were French.[14] D'Urville was able to laugh about this misadventure later, but the number of botanical specimens he collected appears to have been comparatively small. They included half a dozen species of coastal grasses (*Sporobolus, Polypogon, Leptochloa, Chloris* and *Paspalum*),[15] all of which had previously been described.

The *Coquille* left Callao on 4 March and sailed north for more than 1000 kilometres, reaching the small northern Peruvian port of Paita on 10 March. This was to enable the expedition to conduct geophysical observations at the magnetic equator, which would be crossed six times during the course of the entire expedition.[16] Duperrey was able to purchase several hundred kilograms of dried peas and beans, and a quantity of fresh mutton, several chickens, and even citrus and coconuts from trading barques that entered the port.[17] Meanwhile, d'Urville and the *Coquille*'s Toulon-born steward

André-Paul Gabert, another veteran of Freycinet's circumnavigation,[18] and an erudite and capable linguist with a 'good heart',[19] took the opportunity to accompany the port captain, Manuel Gonzáles y Otoya, to visit Rinconada, an estate on the Chira River. It was an arduous journey, across the desert northwest of Paita – often in loose sand, which swallowed the horses' hooves and blew up unpleasantly in the wind. Otoya, in a large straw hat and with a cigar perpetually between his lips, proved to be an unreliable guide; he several times took the wrong route, obliging them to climb the slopes of the Western Cordillera to scout the correct way ahead. For d'Urville, there were always compensations: as they approached the fertile Chira River valley, they encountered *Prosopis juliflora* var. *horrida* (algarrobo) and *Colicodendrum scabridum* (zapote del perro). The ground was also strewn with Oligocene[20] marine fossils.

The centre of Rinconada, amply irrigated by the fresh water of the river some 19 kilometres inland from the sea, was a large single-storey house of lime-rendered brick surrounded by a garden of tropical fruit trees, citrus and watermelon, and fields of cotton, rice, maize, sugar cane and tobacco. D'Urville, Gabert and Otoya were well received by the owner of the estate, Don Joaquín Helguero y Gorgoña, who fed them a splendid meal of many and diverse courses. Ruling Rinconada with feudal authority, Helguero even counted his workers like 'sheep', according to Gabert, at the ringing of the chapel bell to ensure their attendance at evening prayers. Surprisingly, for the *Coquille*'s staunchly anti-clerical republican steward, the pious fervour of the members of the congregation – their Latin prayers, litany and hymns amid the lush moonlit surroundings – made a deep impression and plunged him into reveries.[21] D'Urville's emotions at this point are unknown, except that some months later, when he wrote about the opinionated Gabert's atheism, implacable hatred of priests and Christianity, he declared, 'Certainly, I far from merit the title of devout, but I will honour all my life the religion in which I was born and which I solemnly profess and I will respect all religions in which the maxims are not obviously opposed to the laws of society, persuaded that they tend rather to confirm and corroborate them.'[22]

It appears that at one stage d'Urville's and Gabert's tranquillity in Rinconada's garden of Eden was disturbed by a 'serpent' or, more precisely, the movements of a nearby alligator.[23] After a visit to the hamlet of Amotape, four and a half kilometres to the northwest, they left the Chira River valley for Paita and returned to the *Coquille* on 19 March.[24] Three days later, the expedition began its traverse of the Pacific, setting sail in a south-southwest direction with the benefit of the South Equatorial Current.

Easter 1823 was celebrated with the opening of a number of tins of Nicolas Appert's preserved food. As befitted a scientific expedition, there was an empirical purpose to the meal, and the officers made a detailed statement of the condition of the contents more than seven months after their departure from Europe. The beef was found to have an 'agreeable coloured appearance', with a taste and aroma usual for meals 'prepared with fresh meat [and] vegetables'.[25]

After another month at sea without human contact other than a chance meeting with a Nantucket whaler, the *Charles*, d'Urville thought he heard breaking waves early on the morning of 22 April. Sunrise revealed a narrow low-lying atoll, less than 25 kilometres long, previously unknown to Europeans. As the *Coquille* approached the island, rising smoke indicated it was inhabited. On the eastern limits of the widely dispersed Tuamotu Archipelago, it would prove to be the expedition's first geographical discovery. Duperrey named it Clermont-Tonnerre in honour of the navy minister, but its inhabitants, who still number only a few hundred, know it as Reao. The *Coquille* hove to as a canoe approached, but the islanders aboard remained wary and kept their distance. After waiting 30 minutes and attempting verbal communication without any further approach from the locals, Duperrey decided to sail on.[26] Those aboard the canoe would be the first Polynesians d'Urville ever saw, but the beginnings of his cultural and linguistic exploration of Polynesian society, which would occupy a great deal of his life, would have to wait. Soon, other islands were sighted, but all had already been charted by earlier European explorers.

On 3 May, five weeks after leaving the Peruvian coast, the *Coquille* arrived at Matavai Bay in Tahiti, but she was not greeted by a throng of outriggers; much had changed since the visits of Samuel Wallis, Bougainville and Cook. As d'Urville put it, 'What one does not find is the women, so gracious and so vaunted by these navigators.'[27] The island had been transformed by the fire and brimstone of English missionaries, and the sailors soon discovered that the local girls, who once traded their sexual favours for iron nails or trinkets, appeared resolutely unmoved by all their gifts. But in time, according to Lesson, clandestine romantic trysts, behind hibiscus thickets and beyond the puritanical scrutiny of the missionaries and their local invigilators, did eventually take place.[28]

There were other European vessels at Tahiti at the time. One was the schooner *Endeavour*, under the command of Captain John Dibbs, which regularly brought supplies from New South Wales; the other was the pearling brig *Active*, under the command of Captain Richard Charlton.[29] It was the Cornishman Charlton who introduced Duperrey and his officers to a number of the local English missionaries, including Henry Nott, originally a bricklayer, who arrived aboard the *Duff* with the first London Missionary Society (LMS) contingent in 1797. (In his personal library, d'Urville had William Wilson's account of this voyage,[30] although we do not know exactly when he acquired it.) D'Urville described Nott as the 'doyen of the missionaries of Tahiti, and recently governor of the young [King] Pomaré'.[31] According to Lesson, it was Nott who 'presented' Duperrey and other officers to Pomare Nehoraii, the morbidly

René-Primevère Lesson, engraving, frontispiece from his Voyage autour du monde entrepris par ordre du gouvernement sur la corvette la *Coquille, P. Pourrat frères, Paris, 1838, 2 vols.* Alexander Turnbull Library, Wellington

obese 16-year-old brother-in-law of the infant King Pomare III and the consort of the future Queen Aimata Pomare IV.[32] Nott drafted the Pomare Law Code of 1819, shortly after the previous Tahitian monarch, Pomare II, was converted to Christianity. This code prohibited murder, infanticide, theft, bigamy, adultery, false witness, divorce and not keeping the Sabbath holy.[33] The punishment for the latter 'crime' in this new theocracy was labour for the king, specifically construction of just over a hundred metres of roadway, a penalty that later provoked François-René de Chateaubriand's wry comment that if 'such equal laws existed in France, we would have the most beautiful roads in Europe'.[34] The *Coquille* had dropped anchor on a Saturday, and it was hardly surprising that when d'Urville landed the next morning, he found the churches full of worshippers and those reluctant to become road-workers. Nott, whose simple grave can still be seen near those of Tahiti's Pomare dynasty, would later publish the first Tahitian translation of the Bible (1836). D'Urville, who had himself studied the Bible in the original Hebrew and who would make a comparative study of Tahitian and other Polynesian languages, would no doubt have found much in common with Nott.

On 6 May, Duperrey requested the use of a hut from Nott to store trade goods to be exchanged for fresh provisions. The hut was carried to the foreshore by a group of 20 islanders the following day; within it, Rolland and Gabert supervised the exchange of pins, fish-hooks, files, saws and printed calico for local fruit, pigs, chickens and goats.[35] On 10 May, to continue his astronomical and geomagnetic research, Duperrey put up a tent as an observatory at Point Venus, where Cook had observed the Transit of Venus in 1769. Nearby fluttered the new flag of independent Tahiti (a white star on a red field), designed with the aid of the missionaries in yet another gesture of compliance to European mores. Meanwhile, d'Urville continued his natural history work.

Early in his sojourn in Tahiti, he met and befriended a young Tahitian named Otouri, with whom he exchanged names according to the local custom of becoming bond-friends (*tau'a hoa*).[36] It seems likely that he was introduced to d'Urville by the missionaries, who were well aware of Otouri's local botanical knowledge, and he acted as d'Urville's guide and scientific protégé. One could also add 'host' because d'Urville was apparently a frequent dinner guest at the home of Otouri and his wife. Towards the end of the first volume of his *Voyage pittoresque autour du monde*, d'Urville mentions Otouri and his personal assistance during the visit of the *Coquille* and then describes his assistance to a fictional European visitor seven or eight years later. The account appears strongly autobiographical and was probably based on a now-missing part of d'Urville's journal of 1823. This is further reinforced by Lesson's glowing acknowledgement of Otouri's aid to d'Urville. According to Lesson, Otouri (whose portrait appears in both Duperrey's *Atlas* and d'Urville's *Voyage pittoresque*) acted as a skilled plant collector, providing d'Urville with specimens from distant corners of the island and with personally written ethnobotanical notes detailing local names and uses. Although fearful of the remonstrations of the missionaries, with whom he was closely associated, Otouri also performed a Tahitian war dance on the deck of the *Coquille* at the behest of her officers.[37]

In his account of the voyage, Lesson tells us that the officers of the *Coquille* wore tough Breton cloth fatigues when engaged in hunting or work details. This, combined with their familiarity with the lower ranks, caused confusion among the missionaries, who normally distinguished British naval officers by their rigorous dress code. Lesson added that d'Urville was 'more than once' mistaken for an 'assistant cook', although the zoologist thought that he looked more like a 'market gardener'. With seeming delight, he could not resist recording the 'simplicity' of d'Urville's 'scientific undress' for posterity. In Chile, d'Urville had purchased a straw hat for a few cents, and Lesson noted it was now battered and perforated. His duck drill jacket had 'forgotten when it was new', and his trousers, of a canvas-like cloth, were threadbare and unravelling. Furthermore, he wore neither cravat nor stockings and was shod in hobnailed shoes.[38]

Ironically, d'Urville, oblivious to his own image, would write that he struggled not to laugh at the Tahitians, who, when they attended church on a Sunday, dressed as if for a 'masquerade' or with 'frippery'.[39]

Among d'Urville's first excursions was a visit to the Vaitepiha Valley, on the Taiarapu Peninsula. Five kilometres from the sea, beyond the coconut, mango and breadfruit groves, he and Otouri soon reached the steep flanks of the mountains, carpeted with ferns and studded with luxuriant trees. White-tailed tropicbirds, fruit doves and green parrots swooped overhead as the canopy of the rainforest gradually closed above the serpentine watercourse in the narrowing valley. Collecting plants and other natural history specimens along the way, they reached an area of columnar basalt similar to that of Ireland's Giant's Causeway and Scotland's Isle of Staffa, and the beautiful waterfall of Piha, where the wind over the cascade still fills the air with a fine mist. (The same waterfall was also visited by the *Coquille's* artist Lejeune, who sketched it in the company of Lesson.[40]) By now, evening was approaching in the dense forest, which was illuminated by the overhead sun for only a few hours each day. Tired and faced with scaling a peak without any defined track, d'Urville finally agreed to return to Matavai Bay but via Otouri's home for a welcome dinner of roast goat and fish.[41]

The *Coquille* would remain in Tahiti for almost three weeks. During his earlier landfalls, d'Urville set himself numerous demanding exertions, and Tahiti appears to have been no different. For him, the time ashore was precious; in the first volume of his *Voyage pittoresque autour du monde*, he wrote: 'A tireless and ardent walker, I did not take more than four hours' rest during our sojourn at Matavaï. I saw all that one could see; I seized on all the sites mentioned by the [earlier] voyagers; I even created itineraries for the geologist and the naturalist.'[42] During other probes of the island's mountainous interior and visits to pre-Christian religious sites, such as the marae in Papara, d'Urville continued his natural history work. Even on the coast, there were important discoveries to be made. One of the significant zoological finds was a species of *Ocypode* (ghost) crab, which inhabits the intertidal and littoral fringe of the island. Since the species was named *O. urvillei* in his honour by Guérin-Méneville,[43] we can assume that d'Urville collected the type specimen. We cannot be as certain of the type specimen of *Garnotia stricta*, belonging to a hitherto unknown grass genus. Brongniart would coin the generic name in honour of the surgeon of the *Coquille*, but there is no indication that Garnot, rather than d'Urville, was the first to collect it in Tahiti.[44] D'Urville gathered many other plant specimens (including seaweed) while at the island, but most were not new to science. Unfortunately, he also lost much of his herbarium because of the prevailing atmospheric conditions. It rained incessantly for the last few days of the *Coquille's* sojourn in Tahiti, and the humidity and heat engendered mould and decay – despite his diligence in changing the paper between his pressed plants. Lesson's herbarium was affected even worse, because he had far less space at his disposal to dry his specimens.[45]

Ten days after his arrival in Tahiti, d'Urville (under orders to wear full naval uniform) joined Duperrey, Jacquinot, Bérard, Blosseville and Lesson at the annual gathering of all the missionaries in the archipelago. Those who attended included the LMS inspectors Daniel Tyerman and George Bennett, who had already made a formal visit to the *Coquille*, and Charles Wilson, whom both d'Urville and Lesson mention in their respective accounts of Tahiti.[46] Duperrey, who would attend many other missionary gatherings during his stay,[47] was keen to make a good impression. One reason was that another of the missionaries, the fiery evangelist John Muggridge Orsmond, had informed the Tahitians in a sermon that the French were a 'poor people, without manufacturing industry, inhabiting a meagre territory, inferior in power to the English their conquerors'![48] Captains Charlton and Dibbs were also in attendance, and after the missionary meeting, d'Urville offered them passage by boat back to their ships in Matavai Bay. He very likely thought this a necessary courtesy to be extended to two captains from another country but, according to Lesson, it infuriated the young midshipman Blosseville, whom d'Urville bluntly ordered to walk back in the heavy rain to make room for them. D'Urville, who was used to long walks in all weather, probably thought such exertions a trifling matter for a young man of Blosseville's age. However, Lesson, who was also obliged to make the same muddy return journey of one and a half hours on foot, declared that Blosseville's unceasing dislike for d'Urville began from this moment.[49] It should be noted that when Lesson published these comments, he knew he could not be contradicted by Blosseville, who had been missing and presumed dead for some five years. Lesson's account should also be questioned because we know that d'Urville had an extremely high opinion of Blosseville, despite the fact that he was the expedition's most junior officer. Animosities tend not to flourish in an atmosphere of admiration and respect. After 16 months in Blosseville's company, d'Urville wrote glowingly in his private journal:

> He had surpassed, without doubt, all his colleagues in instruction, in judgement, in means and in experience. Alone of them all, having done very good studies in his youth, he has continued, after his entry into the navy, to acquire new knowledge and he is still today the most studious of the *Coquille*'s officers. Born with the best disposition, endowed with a good temperament, the regularity of his conduct and his distance from pleasures and dissipation … add to his love for work. Since he embarked on the *Coquille*, this amiable timidity, this great modesty and this extreme politeness which are so good in a young man of twenty at the beginning of his career, are noticeable in all his conversations and in all his actions and add a new lustre to his merit. I avow that he seems to me to be the most distinguished aspirant I have ever known and he could offer an example to all who pursue the same career.[50]

Blosseville was also Duperrey's favourite among the junior officers and, according to d'Urville, became his close companion and 'almost his aide-de-camp'. Indeed, Duperrey also relied heavily on Blosseville's facility with English during his many conversations with the missionaries. Although d'Urville thought Duperrey's trust in Blosseville well placed and was pleased to see this gentle reserved young man grow in confidence and independence, he appears to have been a little disappointed, or perhaps annoyed, by Blosseville's tendency to treat him (d'Urville) 'as a colleague rather than as a superior'.[51]

The *Coquille* sailed from Tahiti on 22 May, after two days awaiting a favourable wind. On board were a number of passengers whom Duperrey had agreed to transport to Bora Bora. They included Orsmond, a master carpenter by trade, who the year before had constructed the first Christian church on the island.[52] Bora Bora has a rugged mountainous axis that is, in fact, the weathered coral-fringed rim of a flooded crater, part of the same chain of extinct seven-million-year-old volcanoes that formed Tahiti. When the officers of the *Coquille* went ashore on 26 May, they were surprised to land on a 140-metre jetty that Orsmond and his congregation had built on coral-block foundations. It gave access to an avenue leading directly to the church, which, as in Tahiti, had become the central focus of the islanders' lives, thanks to what Lesson called the 'sombre and incessant fanaticism of missionaries who governed these islands by religious despotism', in his opinion 'the most intolerable of dominations'.[53]

During their stay of more than six weeks at Bora Bora, Duperrey undertook magnetic observations at Point Paoua, on the western side of the village of Beula, and Jacquinot and Lottin conducted astronomical observations to determine the latitude and longitude of this same village, the mission church, the summit of Mount Pahia, and the southern and northern extremities of the reef surrounding the island.[54] Meanwhile, Blosseville was seconded to the *Endeavour* to do survey work at the islands of Maupiti and Motu-iti.[55] Bérard and Lottin circumnavigated and charted Bora Bora, and the *Coquille*'s naturalists surveyed the island's flora and fauna. Among the species d'Urville collected were a number of grasses, the epiphytic orchid *Oberonia equitans* and a sedge known locally as *mo'u upo'o taratara*; back in France, the latter was thought by Brongniart to be a new species, but it was in fact *Cyperus cyperoides*, belonging to the same genus as the papyrus of Egypt first described by Linnaeus.[56] The most unexpected acquisition for d'Urville, however, was a George III medal struck in 1772 for Cook's second voyage. It must have been presented to one of the islanders during Cook's visit to Bora Bora in December 1777. D'Urville obtained it from a man named Temena in exchange for two shirts and some printed cloth.[57]

The *Coquille* left Bora Bora on 9 June and was escorted as far as the reef by a large number of islanders disappointed to see the expedition depart. Duperrey was originally intent on sailing directly to Port Jackson to re-victual, but contrary winds made him

decide on Tongatapu instead. A number of islands in the Tongan Archipelago were
sighted, but unfortunately, the winds once again frustrated plans to land. Instead,
Duperrey sailed on to New Ireland, en route sighting Santa Cruz on 2 August, and
Bougainville and Bouka islands on 9 August.

On the evening of 12 August 1823 – a year and a day after their departure from
France – the *Coquille* anchored in a bay northwest of Cape Saint George. This was the
bay Philip Carteret had called Gower's Harbour in August 1767[58] and Bougainville
called Port Praslin when he anchored there in July 1768.[59] The next morning, three
canoes approached the ship bearing dark men with ochred hair and pierced noses.
For d'Urville, it was his first encounter with 'Melanesians', an ethnographic term he
would later coin. Friendly relations were soon established, and they began trading
with each other. Nevertheless, because of the fierce reputation of the New Irelanders,
Duperrey initially forbade his men from going ashore. Not to be thwarted in his quest
for botanical specimens, d'Urville proposed to Rolland, Blosseville and Lejeune that
they explore ashore secretly. This they did, according to Rolland's journal, but how
d'Urville reconciled their insubordination and the specimens he gathered is unclear.[60]
D'Urville largely botanised alone, while the rest of the landing party went in search of
the nearby village of Likiliki. Again, friendly relations were established with the local
men, although they kept their women hidden from the French. On 15 August 1823,
presumably this time with the commander's approval, d'Urville, accompanied by Lottin,
Blosseville and Lesson, used the whaleboat to visit the offshore island of Lambon.[61]
It appears their visit was inspired by Bougainville's description of its conchological
treasures; more than 50 years before, he called the island 'Île aux Marteaux' in honour
of the hammer-shells his expedition found there.

D'Urville would also gather a number of important marine specimens during his
visit to New Ireland. These included a syntype for *Sargassum pacificum* (which he had
previously collected on the Chilean coast) and the type specimen for the red seaweed
Halymenia durvillaei, described and also named in his honour by Bory de Saint-
Vincent.[62] While Jacquinot conducted astronomical observations – to compare their
calculated latitude and longitude with Bougainville's determinations – Bérard, Lottin
and Deblois surveyed the peninsula to Lamassa Bay. Then, having filled their water
casks and replenished their firewood, Duperrey and his men set sail on the morning of
21 August.[63]

After traversing the Bismarck Sea and the length of the northern coast of New
Guinea, late on the afternoon of 6 September the *Coquille* dropped anchor in Offak
Bay on the island of Waigeo – separated from the Doberai (Vogelkop) Peninsula of
West Papua by the Dampier Strait. Early on the morning of 8 September, d'Urville
took a boat to visit Port Fofaag (now Teluk Fofag), the western arm of the bay, in the

company of Lesson, Rolland and a party of sailors, including an American, William Taylor,[64] who had joined them in Bora Bora seeking passage to Port Jackson. The coast was flanked by heavily wooded mountains shrouding deep dark valleys, thick with ferns and palms, and cleaved by innumerable cascades and streams all making their way to the sea. As the moisture-laden wind changed, so too did the weather in the bay, which alternated between thick mist and torrential rain, according to d'Urville, and soaked them to the bone in a few minutes. It was still raining when they reached what would be christened 'Lottin Cove' at 7.30 am, so they decided to have breakfast in the boat, hoping the weather would improve by the time they had finished. They were to be disappointed.

Undaunted by the rain and the dense *Brugiera* mangrove swamp that covered the shore, at 8 am, d'Urville, Rolland and Taylor began to cross the steep neck of land that separates Offak Bay from what would be christened Chabrol Bay to the southwest.[65] The presence of two pirogues on the shore promised contact with the indigenous inhabitants. Lesson, however, who had received a painful wound in his hand from the spine of a 'pimelode' (possibly a goatfish or member of the Mullidae), decided not to accompany them.[66] After following a stream inland, d'Urville and his party reached a path (the 'chemin d'Offak' on the chart Blosseville later drafted) used by the locals to communicate between the two bays. However, even when they reached the highest point on the isthmus, the forest remained so dense that they could not see the bay they had come from. The rain also remained so heavy that pressing plant specimens became very difficult – all the more frustrating because of the diversity of remarkable species. Here, for example, d'Urville encountered *Nepenthes mirabilis* (swamp pitcher-plant), with its 'goblets always full of water'.[67] This remarkable carnivorous species had first been described by the Portuguese Jesuit physician and botanist João de Loureiro under the name *Phyllamphora mirabilis*,[68] but d'Urville astutely considered it to be part of the widespread Linnaean genus *Nepenthes*, even though its formal transfer to this genus did not take place until 1916.[69]

Fortunately, the party's safe descent on the slippery, rain-drenched slope was aided by large branches that had been deliberately positioned along the way by the locals. Shells from countless meals were also in evidence along the track, but nowhere did they encounter the indigenous inhabitants. Back at sea level, their progress yet again became painfully slow through the mud and buttressed roots of the mangroves. Taylor, whose long residence in Tahiti had made him used to walking in such difficult conditions, pushed ahead about 800 metres to reconnoitre a small marshy cove containing two small islands. Waiting for the American to return, d'Urville collected a number of new plant species and several richly coloured butterflies. Rolland's journal indicates that they became lost at this stage.[70] On returning to the highest point on the isthmus, d'Urville managed to climb a tree to get his bearings, his own account indicating that he was also able to view the cove Taylor had found to the west – confirming that it was part of the larger Chabrol Bay. (Regardless of its indigenous toponym, it would be named Port Blosseville in honour of the young officer who surveyed it in the subsequent days.) D'Urville, Rolland and Taylor were reunited with Lesson at 12.30 pm. On their way back to the *Coquille*, they visited a cove with a grove of coconut trees and a house elevated on stilts above the tidal flats. Earlier, Bérard had visited this same island and left a number of knives in exchange for taking a quantity of coconuts without the consent of the owners. On d'Urville's arrival, he found the same knives beside more coconuts and felt at ease drinking from them in the tropical heat. Soon after, the young Papuan who had harvested them appeared. D'Urville, keen to reaffirm friendly intentions, recorded that he bestowed gifts of ear pendants and a necklace on the Papuan. He then spent 'one or two hours in the forest' making a 'good collection of beautiful lepidoptera'. These included what he called 'the superb butterfly *Urania orontes*', vaulting in 'leaps and bounds' on the mangrove leaves and abundant in the marshes.[71] D'Urville was not to know that phylogenetically the Uraniidae are moths, not butterflies – despite their wing shape, coloration and diurnal habits – and that just the year before, the great German entomologist Jacob Hübner had established the new genus *Alcides*, which now includes the species d'Urville collected at Offak Bay. When d'Urville and Rolland returned to the boat, they found 'ten or twelve Papuans playing and eating with the boat crew as if they were old acquaintances'.[72] This friendly contact provided the basis for some limited trading in fresh supplies for the expedition.

D'Urville continued his botanical work in the days that followed. It is possible that he trekked north of the *Coquille*'s anchorage, since a cove on the ocean shore of the eastern peninsula was named 'Anse Adèle' on Blosseville's chart, presumably in honour of d'Urville's wife. Among the important type specimens he collected at Offak Bay were that of the delicate yellow orchid *Thelasis micrantha*[73] and the fern *Pleocnemia brongniartii*.[74] Duperrey established an observatory facing the *Coquille*'s anchorage, and after further survey work, mainly undertaken by Blosseville, the expedition set sail from Waigeo on 16 September.

Duperrey initially set a course for the island of Ceram, but unfavourable winds made him head instead for Buru further to the west. The *Coquille* reached the isolated Dutch outpost of Cajeli (now Kajeli) on the northeastern side of the island on 23 September. Such a visit would usually have been problematic for a French vessel, as the Dutch jealously guarded their spice-producing monopoly and normally forbad foreign vessels from calling. Duperrey, however, had letters patent, signed by the king of the Netherlands, requesting that he be accorded assistance in all Dutch possessions.

Some fresh supplies were acquired but 'not without difficulty'.[75] During his week on Buru, d'Urville enriched his entomological collection, particularly with beetles,[76] and collected many plants. Given Dutch sensitivities, it is not clear exactly how far afield he was permitted to wander on the island, but he would later recall that the highlands were 'almost always enveloped in thick mist'.[77] Although most of the plants he gathered were not new to science, there were some exceptions, including the type specimens of at least three grasses later published by Brongniart.[78] Duperrey also took advantage of their visit to compare his calculations of the latitude and longitude for Cajeli with those calculated during the visit of d'Entrecasteaux's expedition in August 1793.[79]

The *Coquille*'s next port of call was the Moluccan island of Ambon, where she dropped anchor in the harbour beneath Fort Victoria on 4 October. At first, Duperrey was informed that this was forbidden, but he received a warmer reception after the *Coquille*'s papers were examined. Nevertheless, the Dutch provincial governor, Pieter Merkus, fearing that the French might make clandestine purchases of cloves and nutmegs, demanded that her crew be confined aboard. Duperrey managed to allay his concerns to some degree and secured permission for the officers and petty officers to go ashore as they wished but for the sailors to have much more restricted opportunities.[80]

To the surprise of the officers and crew of the *Coquille*, the day after their arrival, they were visited by several Frenchmen in Dutch service. According to Rolland, they were 'renegades', which suggests that they were perhaps refugee Bonapartists or Republicans like those they had met previously in Chilean service. Whatever their past allegiances, the men of the *Coquille* welcomed their compatriots aboard and hoped that they might be a source of news from home. Alas, their most recent reports of France predated the *Coquille*'s departure from Toulon by a month![81]

Merkus was new to his job, having been appointed only the previous year, but he was apparently a man of ability, educated in law at Leiden, who eventually rose to become governor-general of the Netherlands East Indies. Erudite visitors such as the officers and savants of the *Coquille* were a rare occurrence in Ambon, and Merkus invited the staff officers to dine with him almost daily.[82] At one such gathering, according to d'Urville, there were 26 for a meal that was 'gay and excellent'.[83] D'Urville was astonished to discover how well paid the Dutch officers in Ambon were. Even a humble clerk of the Dutch East India Company earned the equivalent of 900 francs per month – almost half his recent annual salary as an ensign. The governor's salary was the equivalent of a staggering 30,000 francs per month, necessary, judged d'Urville, for the Dutch to retain their 'very precious advantages and their dependencies in these feverish climates'.[84] Unfortunately, despite the apparent personal wealth of the Dutch officers, they had virtually no substantive supplies to offer the *Coquille* for the next stage of her voyage.

From a botanical perspective, the *Coquille*'s visit to Ambon was significant for the collection of a specimen that enabled Brongniart to establish not just a new species but an entirely new genus: *Lophatherum*. The grass in question, *L. gracile*,[85] was new to western science but has a long-established use in Chinese medicine as *dan zhu ye* (淡竹叶),[86] as has the kindred species *L. elatum*.[87] With its verifiable antipyretic and diuretic properties, it is still used by Chinese herbalists to treat fevers and anxiety, and to ease urination. Whether it was found growing wild in Ambon or whether d'Urville acquired it from local Chinese is uncertain. We know that he visited the Chinese quarter of Ambon on 25 October, but in his journal, he recorded only the purchase of two pieces of timber (to make a table for his home) and an unsuccessful attempt to purchase Japanese cloth for a pair of trousers.[88]

   D'Urville was certainly not oblivious to his botanical precursors on Ambon. For example, one of the 'new' orchids he collected, *Habenaria rumphii*,[89] although unpublished according to modern binomial conventions, had been described as *Orchis ambonica minor* by the remarkable seventeenth-century naturalist Georg Eberhard Rumphius[90] in the sixth volume of his posthumously published *Herbarium amboinense*).[91] Rumphius spent most of his life on Ambon and died there. D'Urville and Lesson made a pilgrimage to his tomb, but unfortunately, the grave, which stood on private land, had been plundered for its fine-grained European sandstone by the landowner some 20 years earlier. Lesson spoke to Governor Merkus about this vandalism and he promised to restore the violated grave at the expense of the state. Four years later, when d'Urville next visited the island, he would find 'this promise accomplished with dignity'.[92]

   The *Coquille* did not leave Ambon without burying some of her own on the island. Two of the English sailors who had signed on for the passage from the Society Islands to Port Jackson died ashore – of cholera, according to Blosseville.[93] Taylor, who had been d'Urville's indefatigable companion on Waigeo, was not one of them.[94] Four others of the original crew – Charles Mercier, Julien Jaffray, Joseph Le Gallic and another sailor named Métour – attempted to desert.[95] They were all young men in their early to mid-twenties, and at least three (and possibly all) had previously served together on the 74-gun *Annibal* (formerly HMS *Annibal*, captured by the French in 1801).[96] All had had limited time ashore because of Governor Merkus' restrictions. Mercier, the oldest, worked as a medical orderly aboard the *Coquille*. Could his anxieties about the epidemic of dysentery (or even cholera) on board have precipitated the flight of all four? The deteriorating state of the provisions aboard and the obvious lack of fresh supplies acquired in Ambon may also have provoked the desertions. All four were apprehended by the Dutch authorities and returned to the *Coquille* just before her departure on 28 October. They received punishment of 20 lashes each and were fined. D'Urville increasingly found such punishment distasteful but, as he put it, 'the unacceptable had become indispensable'.[97] Some months later, reflecting on his normal gentleness with the men but still troubled by the floggings, he wrote, 'I believe I have kept the esteem of those I have been obliged to punish despite myself … my conscience is clear'.[98] For all his criticisms of Duperrey, d'Urville also conceded that the expedition's commander 'rarely tormented the sailors' and was 'very much disposed to accord all the leniency that circumstances permitted'.[99]

The *Coquille* cleared Ambon with two Dutch vessels, the *Comete* and the *Anna-Pawlona*, but soon parted company with them, sailing southwest across the Banda Sea to the Ombai Strait (between Timor and the Alor Archipelago), then entered the Savu Sea, en route determining geographical positions for the islands of Wetar, Babi, Cambi, Alor and Pantar. In these tropical waters, conditions became oppressive aboard the corvette. Cockroaches, which had come aboard in Ambon, began to multiply in plague proportions, infesting the cabins, fouling food, eating furniture and even drinking the inkwells dry. According to Lesson, he and d'Urville quit their cabins and, for what would amount to 'more than ten months', slept on native mats on the deck regardless even of the rain.[100] On 16 November, while still in the Savu Sea and close to the island of Sumba, Duperrey made it clear to his officers that they would not be visiting the Western Australian coast. D'Urville wrote in his private journal:

It appears that Duperrey had decidedly renounced any kind of landing up until Port Jackson. Blaming in part what he had promised the staff officers who would find themselves without provisions during this long and disagreeable passage. I left entirely happy. Now I am impatient to stand into more southerly and more temperate regions, and I very much want to see Port Jackson …[101]

Duperrey had clear instructions to investigate the Swan River estuary as a possible location for a French settlement in Western Australia and to conduct detailed surveys of the river, and scout for locations for crops and the first residences and warehouses;[102] rather than fulfil his orders, he allowed the winds to take him in a sweeping arc around the continent. He would later use these winds as his principal excuse for not complying with his orders when he wrote to the minister from Port Jackson.[103] Leslie Marchant, in reviewing Duperrey's decision, has criticised him for his dangerously depleted provisions on leaving Ambon and for not replenishing his stores elsewhere in the East Indies,[104] but he ignores the fact that the *Coquille* had already called at the island of Buru with similar lack of success. Marchant also argues that Duperrey could have called at King George Sound to take on fresh water and abundant fish and wild game.[105] Be that as it may, Duperrey must have known that survey work on the Swan River or a visit to King George Sound would have been time-consuming and would still have put considerable stress on what was left of his dried and salted provisions, even if they were partly augmented by fishing and hunting. Moreover, his official instructions obliged him to be in Port Jackson by mid-January 1824 to fulfil other important orders. It is perhaps not surprising that he changed his plans.

Despite the detailed and emphatic instructions Duperrey received, it is hard to know how quickly the French government could and would have acted on any survey he had completed. Ultimately, his failure to comply with his instructions provided d'Urville with an important reason to propose an expedition of his own. However, given the pre-emptive element in Britain's own settlement established in 1829, Duperrey's failure arguably cost France the possibility of a foothold on the western coast of New Holland.

On 1 December, after entering the Indian Ocean, the *Coquille* encountered a 304-tonne whaler, the *Melantho*, bound for Japanese waters. She had left London on 17 July 1823 and it was from her skipper, Captain Noah Pease Folger, that Duperrey and his men gained European news, including details of France's relations with Spain.[106] What had been threats of military action at the time of their visit to the Canary Islands had now become actual French intervention in support of the Spanish Bourbons. It was known that Britain did not approve of this action. Given Duperrey's need for fresh provisions and shore leave for his men, it was only natural that he should worry about possible repercussions when he arrived at Port Jackson.

From the Indian Ocean, the *Coquille* entered the Southern Ocean and traversed the length of the Great Australian Bight before approaching Van Diemen's Land (now Tasmania) in the closing days of 1823 – all without landfall. Given the serious tensions that existed within the expedition, it is surprising that when a rupture occurred between Duperrey and one of his staff officers, it did not directly involve d'Urville but Ensign Charles Lesage, who had been Duperrey's personal choice for the expedition; the two had known each other for almost two decades. 'Normally', wrote d'Urville, the eldest of the ensigns would 'inspire the most confidence and possess the most knowledge'. However, in Lesage's case, the reverse was true. D'Urville added that 'he had neither instruction, judgment, dignity nor natural ability'. Despite a passion for astronomy, despite devoting more time to calculations and observations than all the other officers, and despite a mountain of 'scrap paper covered in figures', it became evident, by the time the *Coquille* reached the Falklands, that his results were 'unworthy of any confidence'.[107] In ship-handling he offered no more guarantees, and his heedlessness, grimaces and frequent capriciousness enraged the sailors. Throughout the voyage and presumably because of his incompetence, he had submitted to the 'most humiliating reproaches' from Duperrey.[108] However, on the evening of 30 December, Lesage snapped.[109] According to d'Urville, Duperrey addressed him with his 'usual insulting and coarse remarks', but this time Lesage 'responded with vigour'.[110] For his insubordination,

Duperrey had him thrown into the brig and threatened to keep him there for the rest of the voyage. Not only did d'Urville consider this an abuse of power, but he felt that Duperrey had lost his dignity and the respect of his crew in the process.[111]

When d'Urville asked his fellow officers to accompany him in a New Year's Day courtesy call on their captain, several formally refused. For all Lesage's faults, d'Urville had no doubt of his sincere commitment to the expedition, and for once he had shown some 'character'.[112] Duperrey, however, had painted himself into a corner with his heavy-handed response and remained completely silent about Lesage and his punishment. The following day, without consulting d'Urville, he informed Lesage in writing that he did not require his services any longer and insisted that he disembark when they arrived at Port Jackson. This was conveniently achieved with a medical certificate signed by Garnot, who would himself quit the *Coquille* in New South Wales. Lesage would return to France via Mauritius and Bourbon. Although promoted in 1823 and decorated with the Order of Saint-Louis in 1827, he never rose beyond the rank of *lieutenant de vaisseau* and retired in 1831.[113] He died in the naval hospital in Rochefort in June 1834, a month after his forty-sixth birthday.[114] While d'Urville thought Lesage's expulsion from the expedition dishonourable and disagreeable, he also thought it 'unimportant to the success of the campaign', and he admitted that he was delighted to have Jacquinot take Lesage's place as his immediate subordinate because he was someone on whom he could 'count'.[115] The two had become firm friends and would become professional partners in two successive voyages.

In the days that followed, the *Coquille* rounded Van Diemen's Land and, on 10 January 1824, entered the Tasman Sea. After sailing north and then west, she approached the coast of New South Wales, and on the night of 16 January, the Macquarie Lighthouse was sighted on the south head of Port Jackson.

9

New South Wales

… one walks continually on the ridge of high mountains which are covered with timber and are completely uncultivated and uninhabited. Sometimes their sheer hewn flanks, forming gigantic walls 80 to 100 fathoms in height, dominate frightening precipices.

Dumont d'Urville [on the Blue Mountains]*

It was a cloudy morning with a few drops of light rain when the pilot boarded the *Coquille* to take her into Port Jackson on 17 January 1824. As she entered, d'Urville was 'astonished' by his first sight of the expansive harbour, 'with its numerous beaches and its wild shores covered in *Eucalyptus* and *Casuarina*'. At 10.00 am, the port officer, Captain John Piper, came aboard. He did not stay long, presumably having been shown the expedition's passports, which would have precluded the collection of normal harbour dues. Piper had first arrived in the colony as an ensign in the New South Wales Corps in February 1792 and, despite a chequered career, had prospered. As port officer, he was entitled to keep a percentage of the customs and other duties he collected.[1] D'Urville's eyes were soon drawn to evidence of Piper's success and prosperity in his office: the 'sumptuous habitations' of Henrietta Villa, which he thought could 'pass for a beautiful château'. The young colony was thriving, with a population of around 35,000, mainly in Sydney. Indeed, the town, then just 36 years old, seemed to d'Urville to 'resemble the most beautiful towns of Europe'.[2] Master-gunner Rolland, who, like Duperrey and Bérard, had visited Port Jackson aboard the *Uranie*, was surprised at the number of new churches and houses constructed over the previous four years.[3] D'Urville noted the impressive beginnings of Sydney's first Catholic church[4] and felt certain that the city and its people had a great destiny.[5]

Two days after their arrival, Duperrey, d'Urville, Gabert and Blosseville travelled to Parramatta,[6] nestled on the banks of the river of the same name, 23 kilometres from Sydney. As they approached, d'Urville's attention was quickly drawn to the spires of St John's Church, which had been constructed during Governor Lachlan Macquarie's

* *Les Zélandais ou histoire australienne* (1825), canto ii

'Vue de Sydney' engraving by Jean-Denis Nargeot from a sketch by Louis-Auguste de Sainson, for Dumont d'Urville's Voyage pittoresque autour du monde, L. Tenré, Paris, vol. ii, 1835, plate xxxvii. Author's collection

administration. In his journal, he mentions the church's first rector, the Reverend Samuel Marsden, but it is unclear whether d'Urville was aware then of Marsden's controversial reputation as a harsh magistrate, as an individual intolerant and unaccepting of emancipated convicts, and as a minister equally concerned with personal profit and the propagation of Christian principles[7]. What particularly impressed him was that Marsden had visited New Zealand,[8] and d'Urville would later make many references to his writings on New Zealand gleaned from the *Missionary Register*.[9] However, it was not Marsden whom they had come to see in Parramatta; it was Sir Thomas Brisbane, who had arrived as governor of New South Wales in November 1821.

Brisbane was a Scot and a soldier with a distinguished military career, having commanded a brigade in the Peninsular War. He was familiar with France, having taken part in Wellington's capture of Tarbes and Toulouse in 1814, and having commanded a division of the allied occupation force from 1815 to 1818,[10] but he was also a man of science. His passion for astronomy had been engendered by his experience of a near shipwreck in 1795 and an appreciation of the navigational applications of celestial observation. He had built an observatory at his home near Largs in Ayrshire, Scotland, in 1808 and had been elected a Fellow of the Royal Society in 1810. Soon after his arrival in New South Wales, he had set to work building a private observatory behind Government House in Parramatta. It was completed in May 1822, and here he recorded 7385 stars of the southern hemisphere.[11] D'Urville noted that Brisbane was assisted in this task and even in the publication of an almanac in Sydney by the German-born astronomer Karl Rümker, whom the governor had brought out at his own expense.[12] Given Brisbane's extraordinary commitment to astronomy, it is not surprising that he warmly welcomed an expedition that had nautical astronomy as one of its primary objectives. For his part, Duperrey was well aware of the identity of the new governor (his arrival in Sydney had been reported in *Le moniteur universel* in Paris on 3 June 1822).[13] Even before leaving France, he had been advised that Brisbane was a man who cultivated the sciences in the colony 'with much zeal' and that he had 'very amicable communications with the Bureau des longitudes and the Académie des sciences' in Paris.[14] Although Brisbane made his own observatory available at Parramatta and it was used by Blosseville, Duperrey's principal observations were conducted at Fort Macquarie at Bennelong Point.[15]

When Duperrey received his instructions prior to commencing his voyage, he was also advised that 'the English colony would offer the resources of all kinds to repair the vessel and to procure refreshment of victuals for the crew'.[16] Thanks to the willing and generous co-operation of Brisbane, this proved to be the case. Duperrey wrote: '… all that we needed was delivered by the government stores'.[17] D'Urville confirmed that 'one finds in Sydney all the resources of European ports', but noted that it was all 'very much more expensive'.[18] During his visit to Parramatta, d'Urville took the opportunity to inform Brisbane of his desire to see more of New South Wales, in particular to cross the Blue Mountains and visit Bathurst. This too was approved by the governor, who provided letters of introduction[19] and arranged for a four-wheeled cart, two horses and a guide. Despite his kind assistance, d'Urville had mixed feelings about Brisbane and would later write that he was 'an affable, gentle, sober man, esteemed by savants for his astronomical knowledge, but cold, timid and unsuited to high office'.[20] From his reading, and from his conversations with all walks of life in the colony and with veterans of the Freycinet expedition, d'Urville had become a firm admirer of the legacy of the humane and visionary builder Governor Macquarie. His opinion of Brisbane appears to have been greatly influenced by his perception that Macquarie's successor had done little to heal divisions between the free immigrants and the emancipated convicts. As d'Urville put it: 'Surrendering always to the influence of the free immigrants, he accorded no public favour to the emancipated and none among them appeared at his table.'[21] D'Urville was also aware that Brisbane did not have the kind of budgetary support in New South Wales that had enabled Macquarie to construct 'just about all the beautiful monuments and noble institutions which nowadays make it so interesting'. It was not surprising, therefore, that under Brisbane, the colony had 'fallen into a very evident state of languor'.[22]

Before departing for Bathurst, d'Urville, accompanied by Lesson, Bérard, Lottin and Blosseville, visited the southern shore of Botany Bay – where Cook had landed in April 1770 and where Banks and Solander had made botanical discoveries that had occasioned the very naming of the bay[23] – and the northern shore, where Lapérouse had last been seen alive by Europeans in March 1788. On the latter shore, they found and re-marked the tomb of Lapérouse's naturalist, the Franciscan friar Claude-François-Joseph Receveur, who was buried there on 17 February 1788.[24] En route, they were amused to pass through a locality named Waterloo in honour of Napoleon's defeat in 1815.[25] D'Urville's journal contains numerous references to familiar Australian plant genera that he encountered.[26] He also hastily wrote letters destined for France, which appear to have been entrusted to Garnot in case the latter, who was leaving the expedition because of chronic dysentery contracted in Peru, set sail for Europe while d'Urville was in the Blue Mountains.[27] In fact, Garnot (and Lesage) did not sail on the *Castle Forbes* for another month. On 29 January, d'Urville, accompanied by Lesson, a sailor from the *Coquille* and a young convict driver and guide named Ashley, set off to cross the Blue Mountains, first traversed by Europeans only a decade before. Although they planned to obtain other fresh provisions along the way, aside from their bags, they loaded their cart with 23 kilograms of biscuits, 30 bottles of wine and three bottles of brandy.[28]

Taking the excellent convict-maintained road to Parramatta once more, d'Urville was not bored. He later wrote:

> I have made the trip from Sydney to Parramatta several times and I can testify that nothing is as interesting, nothing is as capable of provoking profound reflection in the observer's mind, as the sight offered by this beautiful region which was only recently snatched from the hands of unspoiled nature and was already covered with pleasant estates and numerous residences, thanks to the ingenuity of an active people and the good offices of a generous and enlightened government.[29]

Of Parramatta itself, d'Urville wrote that it 'occupies a considerable surface area; but the majority of the houses are separate and have a single storey, often with a simple ground floor, surrounded by courtyards and gardens. The streets are wide, following a straight line although still uninhabited in great part'.[30] The travellers stayed at the Woolpack Hotel, then owned by the emancipated convict Andrew Nash, whom d'Urville specifically mentions in his journal.[31] This was the same hotel where Péron lodged two decades earlier; it was then owned by 'James' Larra, a Sephardic Jew from Bayonne, and known as the Freemason's Arms.[32] It is perhaps because of Larra's previous ownership – he sold the hotel in 1821 – that Lesson mistakenly identified the then proprietor as 'a Jew or an Arab at least'.[33]

While in Parramatta, d'Urville and Lesson sought out Allan Cunningham, one of the great figures of early Australian botany. Cunningham had begun his career assisting William Aiton, director of the Royal Botanic Gardens at Kew, a fact that particularly impressed d'Urville.[34] It was at Kew that he had met Banks, who recommended Cunningham's appointment as a plant collector aboard HMS *Duncan*, bound for Rio de Janeiro in 1814. After 18 months in Brazil, he was requested to proceed to New South Wales via the Cape of Good Hope aboard the convict transport *Surry*. Cunningham arrived in Sydney in December 1816, and soon after, at the suggestion of Macquarie, he began collecting plants as a member of the expeditions of John Oxley and then Phillip Parker King.[35] In December 1820, Cunningham began exploring and botanising between Bathurst and the Cudgegong River, and then between Bathurst and the Hunter River and the Liverpool Plains.[36] His participation in all these expeditions was particularly noted by d'Urville in his journal.[37] D'Urville could not have asked advice and guidance from a better authority regarding their route to Bathurst; Cunningham gave d'Urville a 'very detailed note of the stages … in the mountains and of the rare and interesting plants most particularly to be found there'.[38] Cunningham also showed the two French naturalists his collection of insects and molluscs from 'the northern coasts of New Holland'.[39] In 1925, it was asserted by Ida Lee that Cunningham accompanied d'Urville and Lesson to Bathurst.[40] This assertion was repeated by Tom Perry in the *Australian Dictionary of Biography*,[41] but d'Urville's and Lesson's journals do not support this. Furthermore, Cunningham's biographer, Greg McMinn, pointed out that the botanist was 'prevented from accompanying them on excursions by the work of preparing for another long journey, the southern limits of contemporary knowledge of New South Wales'.[42] McMinn also wrote that when drought prevented d'Urville from making 'large botanical collections', Cunningham 'gave him many of his own duplicate specimens'.[43]

In d'Urville's journal, there are indications that he received assistance from Cunningham in reviewing his plant collection, and on his return from Bathurst, he did indeed receive additional specimens from him,[44] but the number is unclear. One belonging to the Xanthorrhoeaceae was later published by Brongniart with Cunningham's manuscript name *Xerotes filamentosa*.[45] Although Brongniart thought the specimen was distinct from Robert Brown's *Xerotes leucocephala* (*Lomandra leucocephala*), his name is now regarded as a mere synonym for this species. Cunningham also appears to have given him at least three beetle specimens, which were included among the 219 insect species d'Urville gathered in New South Wales.[46] Jean-Baptiste Dechauffour de Boisduval named Cunningham as the source of the following species: *Panagaeus australis* (*Craspedophorus australis*)[47] and *Rembus goryi* (*Dicrochile goryi*) from northern Australia, and the carabid beetle *Catadromus lacordairei*, published among those collected during d'Urville's subsequent *Astrolabe* voyage.[48]

According to Lesson, on the evening of 29 January, he and d'Urville dined with Brisbane at Government House, Parramatta, in the company of a number of officers. D'Urville, however, recorded that they ate with Cunningham then returned to their hotel to change before joining him again for tea (rather than dinner) with the governor, Lady Brisbane and a Major McDougall and his sister.[49] The later part of the evening probably assumed more significance for Lesson, who, unlike d'Urville, appears to have been making his first call on Brisbane. Lesson was unimpressed with the governor's residence and the gardens in Parramatta, but he did admire Brisbane's astronomical observatory and instruments. He also found Brisbane personally gracious and keen to remind his guests that he was a corresponding member of the Institut de France.[50]

Early on the morning of 30 January, after making their farewells to Cunningham, d'Urville and Lesson left Parramatta and headed west. At Prospect Hill, they took in the view and for the first time saw the 'thick haze of a very bluish tint', the ozone that gives the Blue Mountains their name. Further on, at the toll-bar at Eastern Creek, they called at the Corporation Inn, kept by William 'Lumpy' Dean, another emancipated former convict.[51] Although d'Urville did not mention Dean (only that they bought a bottle of beer at the inn), he would make a profound impression on Lesson, who wrote: 'I have never been able to recover from my astonishment at the immense corpulence of the proprietor.'[52] On reaching the tranquil Nepean River, d'Urville thought it comparable – presumably in width and flow – to the 'Seine at Paris or the Rhône at Lyon.'[53] According to Lesson, they hoped to catch sight of platypuses – those strange creatures with mammalian fur, anomalous duck-like beaks and egg-laying reproductive systems that had perplexed the scientific community since the arrival of the first specimens in Britain in 1799 – but their search was in vain. However, before crossing the river by ferry, they did observe sulphur-crested cockatoos screeching in the nearby trees.[54] This was at Penrith, then a mere cluster of houses.

At Emu Plains, they called on Lieutenant Peter Murdoch, superintendent of the 200 convicts working on the government farm that grew wheat, fruit and vegetables, reared cattle, horses, sheep and pigs, and produced profitable salted meat for nautical provisions. The government farm also had vineyards, and d'Urville appears to have had a much more positive impression of the manner in which they were tended by the 'careful and intelligent gardener'[55] than Lesson, who thought that they lacked proper pruning. Thanks to a letter of introduction from Brisbane, they were warmly received by Murdoch, a Scottish Waterloo veteran who had fulfilled occupation duties in Paris and had accompanied Brisbane to New South Wales in 1821.[56] Murdoch gave them a 'good dinner with tea' and invited them to spend the night at his residence on an eminence overlooking the Nepean. Aided by only two free overseers and a number of trusted convicts rewarded for their good behaviour and honesty,[57] the government farm run by Murdoch impressed the two Frenchmen for its productivity, but d'Urville was very uneasy about the penal system:

> I was standing at my window at 5 am, looking at the countryside and following the progress of the emerging day; a thick mist delineated the course of the Nepean, and as usual the disk of the sun, firm and red as blood, rose slowly above this veil; suddenly the sound of a bell was heard and the prisoners were leaving their barracks to start their work in the fields. An interesting spectacle, but much more revolting for the philosopher to witness these condemned men, weighted with iron, leaving early in the morning to continue their work in the arsenal. Having completed their time, and back into society, these men no longer criminals are often more troubled than during the time of their condemnation. [58]

While d'Urville believed that 'their most harsh treatment' and their work in the fields had undoubtedly advanced the country, he felt that no visitor to New South Wales could fail to notice the reach of the disciplinary system. 'I do not hesitate to believe', he added, 'that progress would be no less fulfilled if the convicts of a free society could receive just rewards from the government, especially if it erased the shame attached to them, and which accompanies them even to their posterity – a shame that was unfortunately confirmed by Commissioner Bigges' report.'[59]

D'Urville would later write and publish more of his thoughts on the plight of those who had served their sentences:

> The emancipists are those who came to the colony under the weight of condemnation; there they recovered liberty, either by the expiration, or the partial or entire remission of the sentence. This class is quite numerous and many of the emancipists have already acquired important properties. If the collective conception of Australian colonisation is comprised of all who are today members, these men returning to the bosom of society, washed of their guilt by time and penalty, must be regarded as the equal of others, and seen to be received, as if the past did not exist, by the members who never had a bone to pick with the law … In Sydney, the individuals of free origin already constitute an insulting aristocracy for the emancipists. These poor penitents are not admitted in any patrician society; they are effectively excluded from all the posts of minor distinction and their attempts to re-establish an equality which is within their rights often result in the most scandalous scenes. This

reprobation does not stop with the person who incurred it, it passes from one generation to the other; the mark on the forehead goes from father to son ... it becomes hereditary.[60]

Given his sympathy for the process of emancipation, it is not surprising that d'Urville considered Commissioner John Thomas Bigge's savage report on Macquarie's administration unfortunate.[61] He would later be openly scathing of Bigge in his 'Histoire de la colonie de la Nouvelle-Galles du Sud', published as chapter ix of the first historical volume of his *Voyage de la corvette l'*Astrolabe. Five years later, in the second volume of his *Voyage pittoresque autour du monde*, he wrote: 'The report of the Briggs [sic] Commission of Enquiry, an extremely ill-advised work, opened old wounds and old hatreds; it furnished the patricians with a complete justification for their disdain for the concerns of the emancipists; it became for the colony a new, interminable, rumbling source of dissension.'[62]

D'Urville was not the only member of the *Coquille* expedition to write on the British convict system in Australia. Lesson wrote at length on the subject in his book and suggested that the treatment of the emancipists and their children would ultimately lead to the colony's declaring its independence from Britain.[63] Blosseville's observations, most notably, would later have important historiographic significance. Impressed by New South Wales and its economic success, on his return to France he wrote a report on the prospects for similar proposed French penal colonies in Western Australia and New Zealand.[64] Blosseville also intended to write an article on the British colonies in Australia but was distracted by his naval duties. Instead, his notes and journals were used by his brother Bénigne-Ernest Poret de Blosseville – who also comprehensively surveyed all the published literature on Australia – to write his *Histoire de la colonisation pénale et des établissements de l'Angleterre en Australie*, which Colin Forster argued was the 'first history of the European settlement in Australia'.[65] (In this historiographical context, d'Urville's chapter 'Histoire de la colonie de la Nouvelle-Galles du Sud' also deserves recognition, although it was not a book in its own right.[66]) As we shall see, the reports from the expedition also further stimulated ambitions to establish French penal colonies.

The rugged Blue Mountains, which had thwarted numerous crossings in the initial quarter-century of the British colony's existence, were first traversed by Gregory Blaxland, William Charles Wentworth and William Lawson in May 1813. The first primitive road was completed by William Cox in February 1815, after just seven months' construction.[67] Yet despite more than a decade of improvement, widening and realignment, in January 1824, the route to Bathurst was still 'excessively rough',[68] and d'Urville's and Lesson's young convict guide, Ashley, was now unwilling to drive the cart alone. (The horses frequently slipped as they dragged the cart along the steep serpentine road following the summits and crests of the ridges, bounded by the sheer sandstone cliffs that had thwarted earlier explorers.) Murdoch must have considered the convict's anxieties warranted because he provided the visiting Frenchmen with an additional driver. He also augmented their twelve days' supplies with fruit, vegetables and other provisions, including fodder for their horses. Within 20 minutes of setting out from Emu Plains on the morning of 31 January, they began their ascent of the mountain range. Amid the dominant eucalypts and *Allocasuarina*, their attention was drawn to *Acacia taxifolia* and *Lambertia speciosa*. Because it was summer, there were few plants in flower other than grasses, and water was also scarce in the dry sclerophyll forest. Like two other wagon parties on the road at the same time, they stopped at Springwood, then a small military post occupied by six soldiers and a corporal. Despite its name, drinking water had to be 'drawn from a distant ravine'.[69] Here they had breakfast, according to d'Urville dining on two chickens, watermelon and tea. Their only disappointment was not sighting any lyrebirds.[70] These beautiful birds of the forest floor, famous for the lyre-like tail of the male during display, are no less reclusive today. It is possible that the Frenchmen unwittingly heard them, for they are the most extraordinary mimics of the avian world; be it the call of other birds, the buzzing of a chainsaw or the bark of a dog, they can master almost any sound and confuse and astound the visitor to their domain.

Despite taking plentiful provisions and equipment to preserve their natural history specimens, d'Urville and Lesson had not had sufficient foresight to carry any significant cooking utensils – an omission that 'occasioned some privations' during their 12 nights in the open. They appear also to have been surprised by the cold nights while camped in the mountains. The party reached Kings Tableland (930 metres) on 1 February. Lesson noted 'scattered pieces of spectacular iron ore'[71] and one can still see bands of ironstone and limonite in the Aboriginal rock shelter on Kings Tableland, the oldest known site of human habitation (22,000 years ago) in the Blue Mountains. The plateau south of Wentworth Falls, which d'Urville referred to as 'Campbell's Cataract' (the name bestowed by Macquarie in honour of his secretary),[72] afforded sweeping views of the Jamison and Kedumba valleys, and the vast complex of sandstone ridges and mountains stretching on to the western horizon. Smoke from forest fires was also evident in the distance. Lesson described them as a result of the 'carelessness of the savages',[73] but we now know that these fires were the product of a far more complex symbiosis with the land and its flora. In the vicinity of Kings Tableland, presumably in a wet soakage area[74] given its particular habitat, d'Urville found *Grevillea acanthifolia*.[75] He was nevertheless disappointed that other species were 'no longer in flower'.[76]

Near present-day Katoomba, d'Urville and Lesson visited Pitts Amphitheatre and enjoyed 'the view of enormous precipices, deep chasms, in short the ruins of nature'.[77]

D'Urville wrote that they could 'distinguish several considerable peaks', and that one or two were reminiscent of the 'Peak of Tenerife' (Mount Teide).[78] Later, from Pulpit Hill, he described the view as that of an 'immense diorama'. It has long been suspected that this same Pulpit Hill was a convict burial place.[79] Lesson wrote cryptically of what for him was 'Mount Sepulchre' because of the 'still fresh grave' of a young man who died there in 1822, but he added no other detail. D'Urville, however, recorded in English what was written on the tomb, and his journal now provides us with an opportunity to reinstate the inscription for posterity: 'Sacred to the Memory of Edgard [sic] Church who has departed this life, the 20 Juny [sic] 1822, aged 27 years.'[80] He also guessed, correctly, that this young man was 'an unfortunate convict'[81] who had died during road construction.[82] That same day, after breakfasting in the Jamison Valley, they encountered several bullock drays driven by convicts and laden with wool from government-owned farms to the west. Several herds of cattle also passed them and then 'two young Australians well mounted and followed by a pack of hounds'.[83] The two men were the Macarthur brothers returning from their vast holdings on the Bathurst plains. At the time, d'Urville and Lesson were on foot collecting insects. Although d'Urville did not mention the encounter in his journal,[84] Lesson recounted that 'with that mechanical instinct that accompanies the courteous man, I greeted them politely, but these two noble gentlemen, taking us for convicts at least, cast us a deep glance of scorn which I here return publicly to those two ill-bred Australians'.[85] As we have already seen, in Tahiti, Lesson recorded something of d'Urville's idiosyncratic habits in dress. In 1844, he published yet another revealing portrait of his companion. While it might not excuse the snobbish haughtiness of the Macarthurs on the road to Bathurst, it might at least explain why they mistook d'Urville for a convict:

> Everything, in his physique as in his habits and dress, recalled in d'Urville a man of primitive times: he combined the excessive sobriety of a Spaniard with the disdain of a [Neapolitan] Lazzarone for his appearance. I joked with him, when he was alive, about his usual shipboard attire. In fact d'Urville wore his uniform on very rare occasions and only when constrained by service obligations that he could not avoid; but his customary clothing was shabbier than that of the sailors, which was very untidy in those days. So this coarse exterior would give rise to some amusing incidents when English officers would come aboard to greet the commander of the French ship. One knows the care and rigour British officers have for their uniform, yet they were greeted on deck and on equal terms by a big untidy man, without stockings or tie, wearing torn canvas trousers, and unbuttoned twill jacket, and crowned with a battered straw hat full of holes. I was always amazed at the effect of the word 'lieutenant' in the ear of the visitor and the surprise that resulted.[86]

On the evening of 1 February, d'Urville and his party set up their tent at Blackheath and slept soundly in their blankets. Waking to a heavy dew the next morning, they proceeded to the top of Mount York (1061 metres). Here, their cart, already the worse for wear, was repaired with the assistance of the local convict overseer. While they waited, they looked for echidnas but were disappointed. D'Urville's and Lesson's journals indicate that they believed Mount York, or more precisely the steep descent of Cox's Pass, to be the place where another visiting naturalist, the Bohemian Franz Wilhelm Sieber,[87] had acquired two echidnas for three dollars each,[88] one of which he gave to their colleague Garnot to take back to France.[89] (Alas, although Garnot recorded important observations of its habits in his cabin, the echidna only survived as far as Mauritius.[90]) Rejoining Cox's Road, the travellers cleared the mountains and entered the southern Vale of Clywdd, carpeted with meadows that d'Urville found reminiscent of Europe, yet also incongruously dressed 'in *Banksia, Grevillea, Pultenaea, Acacia* etc'.[91] They then headed south to Cox's River, presumably to the military post at Glenroy, where they collected rock specimens and lunched with an obliging corporal who tended a beautiful garden and had to be pressed to accept a payment of two shillings for their meal. D'Urville's journal suggests that the corporal had earlier been involved in anti-bushranging operations in the Wellington Valley. Lesson recorded that he purchased the skin of a flying possum (possibly a sugar glider) shot by the corporal in the same distant valley. After a two-hour break, no doubt partly spent searching for platypuses and other fauna, they crossed the granite-boulder-strewn Cox's River[92] and proceeded beyond Mount Blaxland to what appears to have been Jock's Creek. Along the way, they encountered a wretched group of three escaped convicts turned bushrangers (bandits), who had been apprehended by carriers and were being taken back to Parramatta to face justice. With darkness approaching, they camped at what d'Urville and Lesson both referred to as 'Yorck's Bridge' (possibly a misapprehension of Jock's bridge). There they dined on the flesh of the bird specimens they had collected during the day and retired to their tents with their guns loaded – evidently fearful of fugitive convicts.

The next morning, 3 February, d'Urville's party headed for Fish River, where they once again had great hopes of observing platypuses. Unfortunately, despite three hours of motionless silence, they failed to see their quarry – just as they had failed to see them on Nepean and Cox's rivers, and just as they had failed to see any of their egg-laying kin, the echidnas, on Mount York. (As most Australians know, platypuses are rarely seen, mainly because they are largely nocturnal or crepuscular. It was at dusk, 12 years later, that Charles Darwin, following an almost identical route to Bathurst, had more success observing 'several of the famous *Ornithorhynchus paradoxus* … diving and playing about the surface of the water'.[93]) The desire for platypus specimens, which were extremely rare in Europe, must also be seen in the context of the classificatory and physiological debate that raged over these puzzling animals. Many of the leading individuals in the debate were also personally familiar to d'Urville. In 1803, Geoffroy Saint-Hilaire, on the basis of Sir Everard Home's dissections, had placed the platypus and the echidna in a separate order, Monotremata (meaning 'one hole', an allusion to the single cloaca they have in common with birds and reptiles). He believed them egg-producing mammals but without mammae. In 1809, in his *Philosophie zoologique*, Lamarck had seen them as 'animals intermediary between birds and mammals'.[94] Then, in 1817, in the first volume of his *Le règne animal*, Cuvier classified them (with the echidna) among the Edentata –the toothless anteaters and sloths, which are placental mammals – despite evidence that they produce eggs.[95] Crucially, shortly before the *Coquille*'s return to Europe, the German anatomist Johann Friedrich Meckel published a paper in Leipzig announcing that the platypus had primitive mammary glands that opened directly onto the skin without nipples. Although Geoffroy Saint-Hilaire remained recalcitrant about the nature of these glands and what they secreted, other anatomists, such as Richard Owen and Henri de Blainville, would eventually reaffirm evidence that the platypus suckled their young with milk from mammary glands yet produced eggs. Ultimately, none of this was possible without additional specimens for dissection, like the two Lesson would eventually bring to France. In Britain, Richard Owen clung tenaciously to his belief that platypus was ovoviparous (producing eggs that hatched within the body of the mother). It was not until 1884 that the Scottish zoologist William Hall Caldwell obtained irrefutable evidence that the platypus was oviparous (laying eggs that hatch outside the mother's body).[96]

Leaving the mountainous confines of the Sidmouth Valley, d'Urville and Lesson entered the plains and called on William Webb Shannon, superintendent of the farm at Raineville. Established just six months earlier by Captain Thomas Raine – who had skippered the convict transport *Surry*, on which the botanist Cunningham arrived in 1816 and on which Macquarie returned to Britain in 1822 – the farm cultivated wheat and raised sheep, cattle and horses. Shannon, a former soldier who had faced the French in battle and had a high opinion of their valour,[97] had no idea who his modestly dressed visitors were but nevertheless received them courteously in his simple hut and gave them a welcome meal of 'tea, milk and potatoes'. They then spent 'an excellent night' as Shannon's guests, waking next day to the sound of myriad lorikeets before breakfasting from a menu much the same as their previous night's dinner.[98]

That day, 4 February, d'Urville and Lesson crossed O'Connell Plains, lunched on the Fish River (above its confluence with the Macquarie River), then entered the Bathurst plain before reaching their destination at 4.00 pm. Bathurst was then a village of about a dozen houses, including the convicts' quarters and a government barn that had lost its roof during a severe gale a few days earlier. The commanding officer, Major James Morisset, had replaced William Lawson the previous November. Like their previous host, Shannon, Morisset had fought the French during the Peninsular War and had been wounded at the Battle of Albuera in 1811. Indeed, d'Urville specifically noted in his journal that he was a 'big man' whose 'face had evidently been disfigured by a [musket] ball in … Portugal'.[99]

Morisset warmed more to his former French foes after reading their letters of introduction; nevertheless, he excused himself from accommodating them on the grounds that his official residence remained unfinished. In his journal, d'Urville made a point of comparing this with the warmth of Shannon's reception. He and Lesson were obliged to pitch their tent at the foot of Morisset's flagstaff on the banks of the Macquarie River. Lesson nevertheless wrote appreciatively that Morisset had received them with 'urbanity' and facilitated their research 'with all his means'.[100] D'Urville's journal indicates that his colleague obtained two platypus specimens, apparently thanks to Morisset,[101] but strangely, Lesson does not mention this.

Morisset was a strict disciplinarian. Later that year, as the indigenous Wiradjuri continued to resist the unrelenting British expropriation of their tribal lands and the defilement of their sacred places, he enforced Brisbane's order of martial law with ruthless determination. D'Urville and Lesson, however, had little apparent contact with the indigenous inhabitants during their journey, only seeing their fires in the distance or their bark shelters and camping places along their route. It is not clear whether they even saw any of the 60 Aborigines whom they were told lived near the settlement, but the two Frenchmen remained for only two full days in Bathurst. D'Urville and Lesson collected flora and fauna from the Macquarie River and its banks, where the Wiradjuri commonly fished, and each day they too ate fish from the river. Indeed, their fishing at Bathurst yielded the type specimen of a genus of Australian fresh-water fish entirely new to science, the Macquarie perch, which Georges Cuvier and Achille Valenciennes later named *Macquaria australasica*.[102]

On his second night in Bathurst, d'Urville developed severe colic and nausea, suggestive of gastroenteritis, and he seems to have been able to consume nothing more than tea for lunch and broth in the evening, his 'sole treatment'. He was so unwell that he had to lie down all the next day (6 February); ironically, it was Morisset who ministered to him by giving him the use of an 'excellent bed'.[103] Lesson recorded that d'Urville was ill for two days, which might have included the first day of their return journey. The party left Bathurst on 7 February, with provisions of English tinned meat (which they would later find as good as Appert's canned meat aboard the *Coquille*) and bread supplied by Morisset. The weather had suddenly turned cold. Retracing their footsteps, they were once again generously received by those who had accommodated them en route from Sydney, and they also revisited Cunningham and Brisbane in Parramatta. Early on the evening of 12 February, after 'fifteen days of continuous walking and fatigue', d'Urville and Lesson returned to Sydney. Lesson's natural history bounty included 'fifteen birds, two *Ornithorhynchuses*, several quadrupeds, two fluvial fish, reptiles, freshwater eels and a series of rocks from the Blue Mountains'. Although d'Urville returned with 'three boxes full of insects and several packets of dried plants', he was dissatisfied. He confided in his journal that, if he had been able to begin his excursion two months earlier (presumably when there were many more plants in flower), it would have been 'infinitely more agreeable and, above all, fruitful'.[104] Ironically, on his return to Sydney, d'Urville purchased several bouquets of artificial flowers, presumably for the women of his family!

Despite some dissatisfaction in New South Wales, d'Urville recorded that he 'was able to gather there in the space of two months 330 kinds of plants in flower'.[105] They included a number of important specimens with enduring botanical significance. Three were new species belonging to the Euphorbiaceae. One, *Monotaxis linifolia*, was not just the type for a new species; it formed the basis for an entirely new genus established by Brongniart,[106] of which there are now 10 Australian species. The other specimens were two species of *Poranthera* (one collected by d'Urville and the other by Lesson), respectively *P. corymbosa* and *P. microphylla*. They have syntype status, because when Brongniart published his descriptions of them,[107] he also consulted specimens gathered by Gaudichaud during the Freycinet expedition's visit to Port Jackson and, in the case of *P. microphylla*, a specimen gathered during the Baudin expedition's visit to the D'Entrecasteaux Channel in Van Diemen's Land.[108]

On his return to the *Coquille*, d'Urville rearranged the watch schedule and duties for the officers and men in the wake of the departures from the expedition and supervised repairs to the vessel.[109] He also arranged and dried his new specimens, visited the botanical gardens in Sydney and strengthened his friendship with Cunningham on a number of visits.[110] He entrusted more seeds to Garnot to give to André Thouin at the Jardin des plantes in Paris,[111] as well as additional letters for his mother, his wife and several members of the Académie des sciences, including his friends Latreille, Richard and Desfontaines.[112] Garnot also took three cases of the expedition's natural history collections, including 365 bird specimens and his live echidna, and sailed from Port Jackson on the *Castle Forbes* (447 tonnes, Captain John Windsor Ord) on 1 March 1824, bound for Mauritius. Unfortunately, nothing entrusted to Garnot would arrive; he was shipwrecked at Saint Sebastian Bay, on the eastern coast of the Cape of Good Hope, on the second leg of his voyage aboard the *King George IV* (Captain John Prissick), losing all his collections. Garnot survived the disaster and, after three months at the Cape of Good Hope, boarded another vessel for France and reached Paris on 14 March 1825.[113]

Two days before Garnot's departure from Sydney, d'Urville went with the Irishman John Fitzgerald Uniacke, superintendent of distilleries in New South Wales,[114] to meet Bungaree, the first indigenous Australian to circumnavigate the continent, with Matthew Flinders, and also, like Cunningham, a veteran of Phillip Parker King's *Mermaid* expedition of 1817.[115] Originally from Broken Bay and invariably portrayed by colonial artists wearing an officer's uniform coat and cocked hat, Bungaree was a colourful character then living at Georges Head (Mosman) on the north shore of Sydney Harbour. He informed d'Urville that a 'great assembly' would take place with several other tribes to punish several individuals 'accused of various crimes'.[116] D'Urville was keen to attend and promised Bungaree brandy if he would inform him further of the gathering when passing by the *Coquille* the next morning. Sure enough, Bungaree arrived at 6.00 am with a group of companions in two boats to keep the bargain. By this time, Duperrey, Lottin and Blosseville were also keen to attend, but when d'Urville was informed that the gathering would not take place before 10.00 am, they all went to breakfast with Uniacke. It was at Uniacke's home that Bungaree, accompanied by his wife and his friends, called once again and bade the Frenchmen to hurry.

The excited group proceeded some three kilometres inland, with Bungaree and his companions leaping and prancing through the scrub, until they reached a large flat area with expansive views of both Port Jackson and Botany Bay. (Lesson stated that the location was 'between the route to Botany Bay and Brich-Field' [*sic*], presumably the present-day suburb of Surry Hills.[117]) Members of other tribes were already present. Bungaree then began a martial dance, and others did the same on their arrival. There were five to six groups[118] of 15–20 armed men from 'Parramatta, Kissing Point, Sydney, Liverpool, Windsor, Emu [Plains], Broken Bay, Five Islands and even Hunter River',[119] essentially a gathering of the Dharawal, Dharug, Gandangara and presumably Darginung language groups of the region. The men from Cowpastures impressed d'Urville the most: they were short but 'vigorous and perfectly formed'.[120] He referred to them as the 'Mericon', which would appear to be a corruption of Muringong,[121] the indigenous name for Cowpastures. Later he sought out and interviewed their formidable leader, whose name he recorded as 'Douel', presumably Duall, who had served as Hamilton Hume's guide on his expedition to Berrima in 1814, only to be declared a 'hostile native' by Macquarie in 1816 and exiled to Port Dalrymple (Van Diemen's Land) until Charles Throsby secured his release to serve as a guide on his expedition to the Illawarra in 1819.[122] Kristyn Harman considered him a member of the Dharawal language group, but the Muringong have been described as a band of the Dharug.[123]

The proceedings, essentially aimed at the dissolution of feuds, commenced with six women placed in a semi-circle and two men nearby. All were implicated in the killing of a man from the 'Windsor tribe' (presumably the Buruberongal band of the Dharug language group), whom d'Urville tells us were allied to a tribe (presumably the Gandangara) led by Cogai. Each of the women singled out for punishment had a long stick to support themselves and to deflect blows. Five received only perfunctory blows across the staves they held, but one, considered more culpable (a 'witch', according to Lesson), was singled out for fierce blows to her throat, head and chest. The two men, carrying long wooden shields, which d'Urville calls 'helomans', had to endure some 60 spears thrown in turn by 15 aggrieved men from less than 10 metres away. Boomerangs (d'Urville calls them 'womerangs') were also thrown from a distance of 12–15 metres; all the missiles were either successfully deflected or missed. Within half an hour, all those subject to punishment were released. They were unharmed, except for the one unfortunate woman who had been mercilessly clubbed. She could hardly stand and was dragged away by the other women.

Then a general combat began between two groups of about 20 men in the form of a 'regulated tournament' with much 'sang-froid'.[124] One young man appears to have been singled out for a concentrated rain of spears from Bidgee Bidgee and his (presumably Wallumedegal, Dharug) clansmen from Kissing Point. He retaliated only two or three times, which led d'Urville to believe that he was ritually constrained. D'Urville later added that this young (Dharawal) man from Five Islands on the Shoalhaven River had been implicated, in a dream, in the strangling of Bidgee Bidgee's nephew at the school in Parramatta. The fighting lasted a matter of minutes and appears to have ended when the young suspect from Five Islands was deeply wounded in the lumbar region as he turned in an unsuccessful attempt to avoid a spear. As d'Urville put it:

> Probably it sufficed for the offended tribe to have spilt the blood of the guilty one, and their allies were not at all anxious to push the affair any further. Some of the natives spoke again, women moaned and some new warriors issued threats with spear and womerang; but all that promptly abated; at 11.45 everyone retreated to their side through the bush.[125]

There was still more drama in the ebb and flow of retribution on this field of ritual combat. Suddenly two men from Cowpastures seized a young woman and dragged her away. Although Uniacke assured him that this was simply the prelude to a marriage, d'Urville determined from others present that this abduction was payback for the kidnapping of two young girls by men (possibly Wallumedegal) from the northern shore of Port Jackson. The young woman, however, was briefly and willingly rescued by a brave Englishman, who then found himself surrounded and forced by superior numbers to yield her again to her abductors. There was more brief combat between two men from the opposing tribes but without injury. The unfortunate woman, 'covered with blood and dust', was then dragged to a tree 'against which she remained glued, without strength or movement'. Duall then 'challenged to combat anyone who was disposed to claim her',[126] but no one came forward to fight such a formidable warrior. Despite this highly charged situation, d'Urville tried to speak with Duall, to whom he had spoken earlier. Probably because his prestige was at stake and because he was uncertain how to deal with this strange Frenchman under these circumstances, Duall simply did 'not deign to pay the least attention' to him.[127] The incident and the previous combat, with spears and shields, must have reminded d'Urville of both the *Iliad* and the Age of Chivalry, for he saw a 'valiant Paris' and 'knight' in the Englishman – actually a Sydney boot-maker – who had apparently already rescued another of the kidnapped women. D'Urville was sensitive enough to realise that 'all was going according to established practice and custom, [and] since no one came forward to claim the beautiful distressed [maiden], all returned to order and quiet, and several tribes soon made their preparations for departure'.[128]

D'Urville's attention then turned to the amazing aerodynamics and performance of the boomerang, which was entirely new to him and which he described in detail in his journal.[129] He later recorded that Bungaree promised him one but failed to deliver it on the expedition's last day in the colony.[130] It seems clear that, despite his own ethnographic observations and questioning of indigenous men such as Duall, Cogai and Bungaree, d'Urville relied heavily on the explanations of the Cambridge-educated Uniacke, son of the member for Younghall in the Irish House of Commons and nephew of the Marquis of Waterford. Three months later, Uniacke was appointed sherriff and provost master for the colony of New South Wales. The *Coquille* set sail from Port Jackson on 20 March 1824. Like the boomerang, d'Urville was destined to return; sadly, he would not be able to renew his friendship with Uniacke, for the latter died of fever the following January, not yet 27 years of age.[131]

10

New Zealand

*These singular people exaggerate all their sentiments and carry everything
to excess: their love and devotion as well as their hatred and vengeance.*

Dumont d'Urville [on the Māori]*

Shortly before the *Coquille* left Sydney on 20 March 1824, she was visited by the
Reverend Samuel Marsden, seeking passage to New Zealand for the missionary
George Clarke, his wife Martha, their Australian-born infant son George,[1] and two
young Māori men, Rawiri (later David) Taiwhanga and his servant Hapai. With
Duperrey's consent, all five embarked.[2] During the crossing of the Tasman Sea,
d'Urville got to know Taiwhanga, who was the great-nephew of the formidable Ngā
Puhi chief Hongi Hika, who had already used European firearms to dominate much of
northern New Zealand.[3] Taiwhanga had been in Sydney for 18 months and, according
to d'Urville, 'boasted of having arranged for a great supply of weapons and munitions
to be sent to his uncle'. He added that he was 'a big lad, robust, jovial and very good
looking but he appeared to have been endowed with very limited [intellectual?] means
and after this very long period away [in Sydney], he had hardly retained more than
a few words of English'.[4] It appears he also became a figure of fun for the crew of the
Coquille, one of whom maliciously sprinkled flour on a prized old coat he was taking
back to New Zealand. As a rangatira or Māori leader, Taiwhanga clearly saw this as an
act of whakamā or social shaming. In a rage at his affronted dignity, he 'tugged at his
hair, stamped his feet, cried like a child and ended up throwing his coat into the sea'.
All d'Urville could do to console him, aside from forbidding the crew to molest him,
was to give him a 'good grey overcoat, which he immediately put on'.[5]

Taiwhanga was not the only passenger seeking respect for his status. George Clarke
was originally a gunsmith, and it was on this basis that he had been recommended by
Marsden to Hongi Hika, who wanted someone 'in his service to repair his muskets
and keep them in good working order'. D'Urville, however, wrote that Clarke, 'in his
new position as a missionary', had 'assumed manners and pretensions far above those

---

* *Les Zélandais ou histoire australienne* (1825), canto i, note 46

of a simple worker' and doubted that he would ever 'lower himself to practice his first trade'.[6] This proved to be the case but, to be fair to Clarke, there were sound moral reasons not to aid and abet Hongi Hika and the Ngā Puhi in repairing weapons that could be put to further ruthless purpose. D'Urville was no less aware that 'the only reason Chongui [Hongi Hika] was so highly regarded was because he alone in [New] Zealand was in a position to assemble a thousand warriors armed with guns'.[7]

After crossing the Tasman Sea, the northern coastal tip of the North Island of New Zealand was sighted on 31 March 1824. The expedition then determined the position of North Cape, Knuckle Point and the entrance to Doubtless Bay before surveying the entrance to Whangaroa Harbour (where the crew of the *Boyd* was massacred in 1809) and the Cavalli Islands, and then entering the vast expanse of the Bay of Islands on 3 April. Here the *Coquille* anchored south of the island of Motukaori, off the northwestern tip of the Orokawa Peninsula, and less than three kilometres from Te Hue Cove, where the French explorer Marc-Joseph Marion Dufresne and 24 of his men were massacred by local Māori in June 1772.[8] Duperrey and d'Urville were both well aware of this tragic history and of the savage French reprisals, and they must have had some degree of disquiet when more than 400 Māori swarmed all over the deck of the *Coquille* in an 'extraordinary tumult'.[9] Eventually, most left, but a chief named Tuhi,[10] who had visited England in 1818 and who wore European clothing, remained with his brother and a large number of women.[11] According to d'Urville, the women were 30–40 slaves who performed lascivious dances and songs 'in the hope of obtaining a few trinkets in return for their disgusting favours'.[12]

Much of the excitement of the *Coquille*'s arrival was directed at Taiwhanga, who had a very emotional and tearful reunion with his relatives, so much so that d'Urville observed: 'These singular people exaggerate all their sentiments and carry everything to excess: their love and devotion as well as their hatred and vengeance'.[13] Despite his joy at returning home, Taiwhanga even came back on board 'two or three times' to offer his services to d'Urville as a guide on an inland botanical excursion. D'Urville, however, was pessimistic about the prospects for a productive journey and declined, mainly because of bad weather and the 'advanced season'.[14] He would later complain that he collected only 12–15 plants in flower while in New Zealand.[15] He was drawn to the nearby kauri forests, where Marion Dufresne had attempted to secure timber to re-mast the *Marquis de Castries*, unwittingly violating the sacred prohibitions of tapu with tragic consequences.

The day after the *Coquille* arrived in the Bay of Islands, she was again visited by Tuhi and then by Hongi Hika, both of whom were greeted with a five-gun salute.[16] Hongi Hika was accompanied by a number of his principal warriors, and they entertained the officers and crew of the *Coquille* the whole evening with dances and songs.[17] D'Urville

'Touaï [Tuhi]', engraving (detail) from a sketch by Louis-Auguste de Sainson, for Dumont d'Urville's Voyage pittoresque autour du monde, *L. Tenré, Paris, vol. ii, 1835, plate xlvii. The Māori Tuhi was an important source of cultural and linguistic information for d'Urville during his first visit to New Zealand.* Author's collection

was impressed by the 'precision, suppleness and energy'[18] of these dances and by the spiritual and emotional response of Māori such as Tuhi.[19] Although d'Urville did not have the opportunity to see the chiefs in their finest cloaks (having noted that for a long time they had been exchanging them with Europeans for weapons and powder!), he wrote: 'I can testify that their garments, far from producing a disagreeable effect, suited them very well and gave them a certain air of dignity and gravity which matched their naturally serious character, their generally imposing height and their truly martial bearing.'[20]

While Jacquinot and Lottin established an observatory in Te Angamate Bay below Tangitu pā on the Orokawa Peninsula, Bérard, Deblois and Blosseville began their survey of Manawaora Bay (radiating lines of soundings from the anchorage and between the headlands),[21] and Gabert purchased fresh fish, a few pigs and vegetables for the crew.[22] D'Urville dined aboard the *Coquille* with the lapsed Church Missionary Society (CMS)[23] missionary Thomas Kendall on 5 April, the day Clarke's possessions were taken by canoe to his new home.[24] D'Urville also visited Kendall at his home on Matauwhi Bay, south of Kororareka (now Russell) and part of the inner harbour of the Bay of Islands. Here Kendall lived in trusting harmony with the Māori without walls or palisades around his home, in marked contrast to his former CMS colleagues.[25] He had resided in New Zealand for most of the previous decade (except for his visit to England, accompanied by Hongi Hika, in 1820–21), and his ethnographic and linguistic knowledge was of enormous interest to d'Urville, who wrote: 'He alone, among all the missionaries who live in these wild regions, appeared to me to be able to furnish science with useful data for the study of mankind. The others simply have no idea of the interest such research can have in the eyes of educated people.'[26]

Kendall was the author of a Māori–English primer, *A Korao no New Zealand*, and, with the Cambridge Orientalist Samuel Lee, had published *A Grammar and Vocabulary of the Language of New Zealand* (1820). D'Urville either already knew about the latter book or would soon become familiar with it in New Zealand.[27] By the time d'Urville arrived at the Bay of Islands, Kendall was a fallen angel who had been dismissed by the

'*Village de Korora-Reka*', *engraving by Jean-Denis Nargeot for Dumont d'Urville's* Voyage pittoresque autour du monde, *L. Tenré, Paris, vol. ii, 1835, plate xlv.* Author's collection

'*The Rev Thomas Kendall and the Maori chiefs Hongi and Waikato*', *oil on canvas, 1820, by James Barry. The disgraced English missionary Thomas Kendall was a highly sensitive scholar of Māori language and culture. D'Urville was quickly drawn to him during his first visit to New Zealand in 1824. Four years before, Kendall had visited London with the formidable Ngā Puhi chief Hongi Hika – who would use European firearms to dominate much of northern New Zealand – and the younger Ngā Puhi leader Hohaia Parata Waikato.* Alexander Turnbull Library, Wellington, G-618

CMS. Although married with five children, he had fallen in love with one of his Māori students, Tungaroa, and lived with her for the better part of a year at Matauwhi Bay. He was also prone to heavy drinking with visiting mariners and had been repeatedly involved in the musket trade.[28]

D'Urville discussed Māori religion with Kendall. While d'Urville seemed prepared to accept that Māori had 'a God who was superior to all the others, unique and truly spiritual' and that their other divinities were like 'good and bad Angels, [or] what were for the Ancients good and bad genies', he found Kendall's tendency to rationalise Māori spirituality with aspects of the Old Testament 'ingenious' but more often 'far from … satisfactory'.[29] Kendall also explained the great importance attached to the manner in which Māori greet each other by pressing their noses together (hongi). At first d'Urville thought it was just 'simple contact' but was deeply impressed by what Kendall told him of the notion of the intermingling of breath, carrying with it the special attributes of the spirit.[30] D'Urville quizzed Kendall on tapu; the pronunciation of Māori words, building on his knowledge of Polynesian languages gained in Tahiti and Bora Bora; and also on local natural history. Some confusion resulted when d'Urville asked him if there were emus in New Zealand. Kendall affirmed that there were but that they were called kiwis! It was left to Tuhi to set the record straight.[31]

Kendall revisited the *Coquille* after d'Urville's first attempt to have Tuhi assist him in the correction and translation of Kendall's published transcription of a traditional Māori *pihe* (a dirge-like ode). (Tuhi had been Kendall's first instructor in Māori language when they met in Parramatta in early 1814.[32]) Although d'Urville had quizzed Tuhi in his cabin for three hours, the results were far from satisfactory. D'Urville later wrote: '... a few isolated passages did indeed appear to make some sense but taken overall it was disjointed, incoherent and perfectly unintelligible'. Even with Kendall's renewed help as an interlocutor, there was little additional progress, to the point that d'Urville concluded that Tuhi seemed 'incapable of giving the real meaning of all the passages of the *Pihe*', possibly because 'the allusions of which it is composed are already too ancient and their meanings escape the modern islanders'. He likened it to a Hindu questioning Christians about the meaning of the 'several parables of the Gospels'.[33] D'Urville had little doubt about the emotional power of the pihe: 'When several hundred warriors intone this solemn and sacred hymn, the resulting effect must be something funereal, impressive and terrifying'.[34] Despite d'Urville's failure at translation, his efforts had ethnomusicological significance: Mervyn McLean, in his book *Maori Music*, commented that d'Urville confirmed the pihe as 'a funeral song ... related to the war dance'.[35]

There was certainly more war, dance and death to come, with Hongi Hika's attack on the Ngāti Whatua at Hokianga on the west coast of the North Island in 1825. Moreover, his ally, Tuhi, chief of Kahuwera, would be dead six months to the day after the *Coquille*'s departure. According to the *Missionary Register*, 'one slave was sacrificed by his tribe in an attempt to avert his death; and four more were sacrificed to appease his manes [soul]'.[36]

Before his departure from the Bay of Islands, d'Urville also met the missionary Henry Williams, a former Royal Navy officer who had seen action against the Danes, Americans and French, and had been wounded during the Battle of Tamatave (Madagascar, 1811).[37] Although d'Urville considered Williams a 'trustworthy' ethnographic observer and got to know him better during subsequent visits to New Zealand, he clearly did not warm to him in the manner in which he warmed to Kendall, whose days in the Bay of Islands were numbered. Unable to gain the forgiveness and acceptance of his fellow Christians and heavily burdened with guilt, Kendall left for

South America the following year. For a brief time, he regained respectability as a chaplain and schoolmaster to the British Consul and the small English Protestant community in Valparaiso, but in 1827, the community reconsidered its subscription for a minister and paid him £100 to return to New South Wales from Chile. Based in Ulladulla, he became involved in the coastal cedar trade. An anguished alcoholic, Kendall drowned in August 1832 when his cutter *Brisbane* (manned by Aborigines, Māori and convicts) was wrecked near the entrance to Jervis Bay during a storm.[38]

The *Coquille* sailed from New Zealand on 17 April 1824 after a stay of two weeks in the Bay of Islands. During the 11 months of the *Coquille's* return voyage to France, d'Urville would begin writing a novel set in New Zealand, with some events set in New South Wales. Entitled *Les Zélandais ou histoire australienne*, it was divided into six cantos and was completed by the time he returned to France in March 1825. It is reputed to be the first New Zealand novel, although it remained unpublished until 1992, when an English translation was published as *The New Zealanders: A story of Austral lands*. Soon after the *Coquille* left the Bay of Islands, a stowaway was found and was allowed to join the crew. D'Urville wrote that he was an Englishman named Burns, but other sources describe him as an Irishman named O'Brien. Whatever his real name, he inspired the character of the fictional narrator of d'Urville's novel. According to d'Urville's notes, he was a former convict who had served a seven-year term in New South Wales before shipping out of Sydney on the American schooner *Cossack* in March 1823, only to be shipwrecked on the bar of Hokianga Harbour in the following month.[39]

Les Zélandais is written in the contrived style of a Greek epic, with numerous Greek allusions but with strongly didactic and melodramatic elements, and multitudinous additional notes completed in August 1825. The principal characters are the sage-like Moudi-Pangui, chief of the peaceful Tiami tribe of the west coast, his wife Momona, their intelligent and noble son Tawiro, and their radiant and virtuous daughter Marama. The villain of the story is the ruthless and barbarous Chongui, whose son has been rebuffed in his quest for Marama's hand in marriage and who has designs on the lands of the Tiami. Although Chongui attacks the Tiami with European firearms, Moudi-Pangui initially manages to outwit him tactically. During the peace that follows, a young man who gives his name as Koroké is captured by Moudi-Pangui's warriors in the wake of a shipwreck. His real name is Taniwa and he is another of Chongui's sons but by a woman who is the daughter of a French survivor of a massacred boat crew from Marion Dufresne's expedition. Like Ferdinand in Shakespeare's *The Tempest*, the son of one of Prospero's old adversaries, Koroké falls in love with the Miranda-like Marama. Koroké, however, has come under the influence of Christian missionaries, including Keni (Kendall), who accompanied his father to England and has even been educated near Sydney by another missionary named Madden (clearly inspired by Marsden).

Like a true Christian, Koroké abjures violence. After another battle, the hero and heroine are captured by Chongui and are saved from execution at the last moment when Koroké reveals to Chongui that he is his son Taniwa. The novel ends with operatic melodrama as Madden arrives with the Christian message to change the hearts of the warring Māori. Although d'Urville claims in his preface only to have translated the novel, it is clearly his work. At one point in the second canto, he even has Koroké recount passing three men on the road to Bathurst in the Blue Mountains and cheekily declares that 'their faces carried the mark of gentleness, intelligence and goodness'. Koroké is then told that they are French, which causes him great excitement since he realises that they are compatriots of his maternal grandfather. Koroké is also told that they are accompanied by an officer to 'ensure that wherever they go, they are treated with the respect they deserve. Their reason for crossing these mountains is to discover things which have been overlooked in the research work of other mortals and to investigate nature in all its detail.' Their vessel, flying the white Bourbon flag, is in Sydney and 'it has to make a complete tour of this globe that we inhabit and, wherever it calls, carry out operations of the greatest importance and belonging to the most elevated sphere of human knowledge'. Koroké concludes favourably that the Frenchmen are exceptional 'men who are prepared to leave their homelands, face all sorts of perils and endure all forms of privations, solely in the interests of science'. Later, d'Urville has Koroké visit their ship in Port Jackson and he cannot resist having him declare that 'the English, who in my presence had often displayed a feeling of hatred towards them and a partiality which revolted me, showed that they really did appreciate their merit.'[40]

D'Urville's New Zealand novel was never published in its original French, possibly because its author recognised his literary shortcomings. Lesson, who saw the novel as deeply steeped in the *Iliad* and grounded in d'Urville's perceptions of Homeric parallels in Māori New Zealand, was convinced that it was indeed intended for publication, but that as its author's fame as an explorer grew, 'he feared, with good reason, that the public might confuse the accounts of his voyages with the fiction of poetic prose narrative'.[41] However, d'Urville did insert many of the notes into the account of his second voyage. This was only the beginning of his romance with Polynesia.

11

Completing the circle

And every one who heard of my return came and questioned
me of my adventures and of foreign countries, and
I related to them all that had befallen me ... Anon.*

On 1 May 1824, having sailed in a northerly direction from New Zealand for a fortnight, the expedition reached the volcanic island of Rotuma, located 12 degrees south of the equator. It was first sighted by Europeans in 1791, during the voyage of HMS *Pandora* in search of the *Bounty* mutineers. Although the *Duff*, dispatched by the London Missionary Society, had called there in 1797, the island had not yet attracted the serious attention of Christian missionaries.[1] There had been brief visits by other vessels, including the English whaler *Rochester* (Captain Benjamin Hodde) in 1823. Part of the rebellious crew of the *Rochester*, which included the captain's brother-in-law, the assistant carpenter and four other sailors, had deserted there.[2]

When the *Coquille* arrived, one of these deserters, a man named William John (originally a cooper from Northumberland)[3], pleaded with Duperrey to be allowed to return to Europe. This displeased the local chief, who did not wish to lose a man who had become an accepted member of the local Polynesian population of some 8000 and had even taken a local wife. According to d'Urville, the chief was eventually placated with an 'exchange' in the form of two English sailors, who had joined the crew of the *Coquille* in Port Jackson and were happy to make a new life on Rotuma. John would become the expedition's principal source of ethnographic information about the island.[4] During the *Coquille*'s day-long visit, the location of the island was fixed for comparison with that calculated by earlier navigators, and a chart was also drafted by Bérard.[5] Throughout the day, more than 100 islanders came aboard the *Coquille*. They were delighted to welcome the French but were unrelenting in their theft of items from the ship, particularly objects made of iron and copper. The sailors attempted to stop them with whips made of cord, but this appears to have engendered only laughter rather than an end to the pillaging.[6]

'The Second Voyage of Sinbad Hight the Seaman' (*ca.* IXth century), Burton trans., vol. vi

Eight days later, continuing to sail in a northerly direction, the expedition sighted the island of Nanumanga in the Tuvalu group, which they recognised as 'Gran Cocal', discovered by Francisco Antonio Mourelle de La Rúa in early 1781. The next day, 10 May, they sighted neighbouring Nanumea, which Mourelle had named 'San Agustin' and which was charted by Lottin.[7] Five days later, the *Coquille* reached 'Drummond Island' (Tabiteuea) in the Gilbert Islands (now Kiribati).[8] D'Urville recorded the following description:

> We could easily distinguish several natives with their women, their children and their dogs, occupying the beach and watching us attentively. During this time, some 15 pirogues, each containing three to nine men, made every effort to reach us, aided at times by their sails and their paddles; they also waved their mats from far away to signal to us to wait for them. Two or three among them, approached to within a half-cable of the rear of the vessel, having taken a long time to catch up with us, although we were doing only three miles an hour … At last we heaved to and one of them, carrying three men, drew alongside after a moment of hesitation. These men, of medium height, had very dark complexions, and skin covered in leprous lesions. Their only clothing was reduced to small pieces of coarsely woven fabric wound around the neck and bonnets of the same stuff. Their features were not very agreeable; their limbs were very thin, and their language completely different from the idioms of the Polynesians. Their pirogues were of a very coarse construction, as were their sails. None of them was tattooed, and, as their only provisions, they carried giant clams (*Tridacna*) which they exchanged for knives and fishhooks. These islanders demonstrated very little intelligence and all our efforts to obtain the names of their islands were useless. Within a half-hour, they left us and returned to their island.[9]

On 16 May, the *Coquille* reached Nonouti.[10] D'Urville believed the inhabitants 'resembled perfectly those of Drummond'. The first Europeans to sight both these islands, in 1799, were Charles Bishop and the crew of the *Nautilus*, which included George Bass, the discoverer of Bass Strait.[11] For d'Urville, the realisation that the language of the people of the Gilbert Islands was 'completely different from the idioms of the Polynesians' was profoundly significant because it led him to separate Polynesia from what, in 1831, he would call 'Micronesia'. In 1835, after discussing Rotuma and the islands discovered by Mourelle, d'Urville declared how important it was 'to obtain positive observations on the language and the manners of the natives who occupy the islands … Only then will the definitive line of demarcation which separates Polynesia from Micronesia be traced.'[12]

On 17 May, after crossing the equator, the expedition sighted another island in the Gilbert Chain, 'Henderville' (Aranuka Atoll). It had been sighted by Thomas

Gilbert, captain of the 'First Fleet' transport *Charlotte*, after whom the Gilbert Islands are named, and John Marshall, captain of the *Scarborough*, after whom the Marshall Islands are named. They sailed from New South Wales to China in 1788 and made numerous discoveries en route.[13] On 'Henderville', a large number of naked islanders assembled on the beach, and several pirogues unsuccessfully attempted to reach the *Coquille* as she passed by.[14] Soon after, to the northwest, they sighted 'Woodle' (Kuria) Island, comprised of two small, low-lying, wooded atolls, which had also been charted by Gilbert and Marshall in 1788. D'Urville's particular attention was drawn to the shore, where he saw:

> … a house of at least twenty-four feet in length and covered with an immense roof. Here and there enclosures surrounded by palisades were visible. Close to two hundred natives were spread over the beach. Some came beside the *Coquille*, all were naked, hairless and lightly tattooed on the back and the chest. They brought no kind of provisions and were content to exchange several shell and scale necklaces for knives, fishhooks and nails. The latter article is what they prized most.[15]

According to Duperrey, the weather, which had become very stormy, did not permit them to locate 'Hopper Island' (Abemama) to the east.[16] 'Hall Island' (Maiana) was sighted on 18 May, and the locations of its southern, eastern and northern points were determined. Over the next two days, 'Knox Island' (Tarawa), 'Charlotte Island' (Abaiang) and then, 'from afar',[17] what they thought was 'Mathews Island' were sighted.[18] It has been suggested by Andrew Sharp that this latter, distant sighting was in fact the first European discovery of Marakei Atoll.[19]

On 26 May, the *Coquille* encountered the Mulgrave Islands, including Mili Atoll, in the Ratak (or Sunrise) Chain of the Marshall Islands. Although the latitude and longitude of the southern and northwestern part of the chain were determined, and some people were seen, no communication was established with the inhabitants. The Bonham Islands were sighted on 28 May. Ninety-one of these tiny islands make up Jaluit Atoll, which has a total land mass of just 11 square kilometres yet embraces an enormous lagoon of 690 square kilometres; the first European sighting of these islands was by the brig *Elizabeth* (Captain Patterson) in 1809.[20] After confirming their position, Duperrey decided to divide the islands into two and name the southern part 'Elizabeth', in honour of the original vessel of discovery, and the northern part 'Îles de la Coquille', in honour of his own ship.[21] These names, however, have not survived; quite appropriately, indigenous names have been re-asserted, many of which were made famous in the annals of World War II.

Although Duperrey largely confirmed the discoveries of earlier navigators and established more-precise locations, there were new discoveries to be made in these waters. On 30 May, the *Coquille* encountered the Nantucket whaler *Boston*, which had also been in the Bay of Islands. Her captain, George Joy, informed Duperrey that, less than a week before, he had discovered a small island group that he had called the 'Nantucket Islands' (Ebon Atoll) at the southern extremity of the Ralik Chain. A week later, the *Coquille* would reach another island 'discovered' by another American navigator, Captain Crozer, of the Boston whaler *Nancy*, on 20 December 1804. Although Duperrey's expedition would call the island 'Oualan' or 'Ualan' (Ualang) in acknowledgement of its indigenous name, Crozer had named it 'Strong Island' in honour of Caleb Strong, governor of Massachusetts.[22] Today, Ualang and the adjoining islet of Lelu are known collectively as Kosrae (previously rendered as 'Kusaie'), one of the four Federated States of Micronesia. From a distance, Ualang, with its two principal peaks, resembles a woman reclining on her back. Despite this alluring feminine form, Crozer did not land on the island. It appears that the men of Duperrey's expedition were the first Europeans to do so, after the *Coquille* dropped anchor in present-day Okat Harbour – which Duperrey named 'Coquille Harbour' – on the island's northwestern coast.

Although Lesson and Blosseville went ashore on 6 June, d'Urville remained aboard the *Coquille*, 'detained,' he wrote, 'because of the duties of my rank'. He indicated that Lesson was no longer his travelling companion of choice: 'But I knew also, from more than one experience, that our colleague Lesson was a very sad walker; fatigue had, without doubt, tripled the distances for him.'[23] Lesson would take this comment very personally. In his own book, published three years after d'Urville's *Voyage pittoresque autour du monde*, he bristled with resentment and wrote that the cold water of the shaded riverbed that he followed inland had occasioned a 'fibrous rheumatism', which had made it 'almost impossible' for him to return aboard. In a footnote on the same page, he asserted that this rheumatism, which had persisted for 10 years, had continued to menace his days and was 'the cause of d'Urville's banter'. Lesson added: 'If I had the character of M. d'Urville, I would take cruel revenge, but I disdain such means and I would leave to Mr d'Urville the use of all that his irony has of cold cruelty, against a gravely ill companion.'[24] As we have already seen, Lesson's resentment would persist after d'Urville's death and tinge his writings on his fellow explorer.

After nearly two months at sea, at 6.00 am on 7 June 1824, d'Urville headed off in the ship's boat with Jacquinot, Bérard, Lottin, Gabert and two other young crew members to carry provisions and a 'beautiful and well-sharpened axe' as a gift for the as yet unknown paramount chief or ruler of the island. Because of the shallowness of the surrounding waters, they were forced to disembark some distance from dry land and 'throw everything into the sea and send the boat back'.[25] Under the circumstances, they also stripped off their wet clothes and dressed like the locals. According to d'Urville, they were received at 'Lual' in a large communal house, which also served as a workshop for two or three workers hollowing out a large pirogue with adzes fashioned from sharpened clam shells. There they asked for a guide to take them across the island to 'Leilei' (Lelu). After some initial anxiety on the part of the locals, they were guided along a narrow pathway that traversed carefully tended plantations of taro, bananas and sugar cane, then passed a palisaded cemetery and crossed over several slow-running streams beneath an almost continuous natural vault of trees. After walking three-quarters of an hour, they reached a village inhabited by about 40 people.

Their arrival caused great excitement, and a number of the men and women approached to touch and marvel at their pale skin. D'Urville and his party responded with gifts of glass-beaded jewellery, nails and knives. After a half-hour stop, they took leave of their delighted hosts and continued on the path into the island's mountainous interior. The dense tropical vegetation reminded d'Urville of his earlier visit to

'*Course dans l'intérieur des bois à Ualan*', *engraving by Boilly presumably from a sketch by Lejeune, for Dumont d'Urville's* Voyage pittoresque autour du monde, *L. Tenré, Paris, vol. ii, 1835, plate lviii. The crew of the* Coquille *were the first Europeans to land on the island of Ualang. When d'Urville visited the adjoining islet of Lelu, he was astonished to find a settlement of hundreds of people with paved streets and a substantial exterior stone wall. Today, Ualang and Lelu are known collectively as Kosrae, one of the four Federated States of Micronesia.*
Author's collection

Waigeo.[26] One of the ferns he collected, belonging to the genus *Scolopendrium*, proved to be new to science and was named *S. durvillaei* in his honour by Bory de Saint-Vincent.[27] He was disappointed by the lack of insect diversity on the island, except for a few butterflies. Similarly, he could see only five or six bird species. In the valley between the island's two principal peaks, mounts Finkol and Mutunte, d'Urville and his companions encountered a plain covered in sugar cane, watered by numerous streams. Here they found yet another large communal house and some 60 locals, who welcomed them warmly. The road from this village, possibly Tofol (now the capital of the island), was more substantial; by 9.30 am, they reached a major stream bounded on both banks by 'two very well-made dry stone walls'.[28] This obliged them to proceed with difficulty along the stream bed, with water up to their waists. After 100 paces, however, they were relieved to meet two large pirogues, which had been dispatched to take them to Lelu, built on the eponymous islet within the embrace of Lelu Harbour,[29] on Ualang's eastern coast.

When they arrived, they were amazed to find a veritable town inhabited by at least 800 people.[30] D'Urville was deeply impressed by its 'beautiful houses surrounded by high walls [and] well-paved streets'.[31] By now, d'Urville and his party assumed that the uros or paramount chief of the ruling Ton clan, which controlled this substantial domain, was worthy of royal appellation. D'Urville was warmly received by the thin elderly 'king' and his consort. The French officers presented gifts of glass beads, mirrors, knives, nails, handkerchiefs and presumably the splendid axe they had brought with them. However, when the uros of the Ton demanded d'Urville's botanical specimen case, plant knife and other possessions, he responded that he too was a ruler and that he would decide what gifts he would bestow. It is not exactly clear how this was communicated, but with a gallant flourish, d'Urville then presented the 'queen' with a brilliant necklace of cut and faceted glass.[32]

Here, in the midst of the seemingly endless Pacific, the men of the *Coquille* had found a new world in microcosm that no other Europeans had seen before. D'Urville's admiration of Lelu's architecture was further excited when he surveyed the royal precinct, a vast enclosure with walls 'no less than twenty feet in height and ten to twelve in thickness'.[33] He found it hard to understand how the builders of such enormous walls had transported and lifted the heavy basalt blocks without the aid of machines. Although much of this impressive neolithic heritage has been swallowed up by modern Lelu, significant vestiges remain, and archaeological research since World War II has revealed that the town was built over a period of 600 years – from about the middle of the thirteenth century onwards, with the largest walls constructed between 1400 and 1600.[34] D'Urville correctly guessed that some of the structures had a public ceremonial function, and his account of Lelu is an important first-contact document.

Despite his sensitivity and understanding, it is clear that d'Urville committed a number of breaches of local etiquette, particularly with regard to deference to the island's ruler. For example, he and his fellow officers failed to prostrate themselves before the uros, and they ate in his presence. Nevertheless, d'Urville extricated his men with linguistic skill, good humour and charm. By 5.30 pm, they were back aboard the *Coquille* after what d'Urville considered an 'agreeable promenade'.[35]

Duperrey would make his own excursion into the interior of the island on 8 June. He was accompanied by the artist Lejeune, who made numerous sketches of the islanders, some of which later formed the basis for engravings published in d'Urville's *Voyage pittoresque autour du monde*. While astronomical observations and a survey of the island were completed by Bérard and Lottin, the *Coquille* took on fresh water and firewood, and a quantity of breadfruit and bananas. Few fish were to be had, but one of the naturalists collected the type specimen of a new species of shrimp, *Hippolyte leachii*.[36] Today, it is preserved in the Academy of Natural Sciences in Philadelphia.[37]

On 15 June, the expedition set sail once again.[38] Two days later, a group of low-lying islands was sighted and recognised as the 'McAskill Islands', sighted by Allan McAskill, master of the *Lady Barlow*, en route from Sydney to Canton in October 1809. Comprising three islands, the atoll is known as Pingelap to its inhabitants. On the morning of 18 June, another three small islands were sighted, but they were previously unknown on any chart. According to Duperrey, his officers wished to name the islands after him, so he accepted; however, the locals, who came in their boats to trade coconuts, breadfruit and taro for nails, axes and other iron implements,[39] were asked the names of their individual islands, and French renderings of these names were recorded on the expedition's charts. The 'Duperrey Islands' were, in fact, all part of Mwoakilloa (also known as Mokil Atoll), which, like Pingelap, is now part of the State of Pohnpei and thus the Federated States of Micronesia. On 23 June, yet another island, seemingly unknown to Europeans,[40] was sighted at 6° 53' 44" N, 152° 44' 1" E. It was tiny, 'no more than a mile east to west', and named 'Île d'Urville'; today, however, it is known by its indigenous name, Losap. In the days that followed, the *Coquille* encountered many more small islands belonging to what Duperrey refers to as the 'Îles Hogoleu', now known as the Chuuk (formerly Truk) Island group, where one of the major naval battles of World War II took place.

Duperrey had previously visited the Tamatam Islands (now Poluwat Atoll), in the western Caroline Islands, with Freycinet's expedition, and he saw an opportunity to recalculate its longitude and compare it with the earlier determination, so on 30 June, 1850 metres south of the atoll, he made reference to his chronometers and the position of the sun. The difference in his and Freycinet's calculated positions proved to be only 1' 27". Although no one from the expedition went ashore, the *Coquille* was soon greeted by 27 canoes full of islanders.[41] Despite the brevity of the encounter, d'Urville later wrote that the inhabitants, like those of Ualong, had 'gentle and gracious' features and 'decent and reserved' manners.[42]

At the beginning of July, Duperrey set a southwesterly course for New Guinea. The expedition would do no more northerly exploration of the Carolines, and from this point, the *Coquille* began her return voyage. After sailing close to the Schouten Islands, the expedition reached the well-enclosed harbour of Dorey (now Manokwari) on the Doberai Peninsula of West Papua on 26 July. The local Melanesian population received them warmly and began trading bows, arrows, mats, birds of paradise, taro, bananas, fish and shells. Here, as at earlier landfalls, Duperrey established an observatory ashore in order to map the harbour, fix the positions of its principal points and rate his chronometers. In his *Voyage pittoresque autour du monde*, d'Urville included an account of a visit to Dorey and of an excursion inland to hunt for birds of paradise. He described the inland vegetation as:

> … composed of immense plants, which often form two stages of verdure; that is to say, on the first level, the *Pterocarpus*, figs, *Inocarpus*, a kind of *Acacia* or *Mimosa*, and other species that I could not recognise at all, raising their bare stems to a height of a hundred feet and blooming then in high tops which enlarge again in equal proportion; at the second level, the less tall trees, like the *Tectona*, *Hibiscus*, *Hernandia* or the palms of the genera *Areca*, *Corypha*, *Sagus*, *Cycas*, sometimes as high as eighty feet and which meanwhile compose the secondary forest. Beneath this double vault, the ground, which receives no ray of sun, only offers rare and meagre shrubs, and almost no herbaceous plants, if they are not orchids, reeds, legumes, ferns or lycopodes common to the equator.[43]

D'Urville also made notes on the customs, material culture and religious beliefs of the locals. After a two-week sojourn, the *Coquille* weighed anchor and set sail on the morning of 9 August.

After rounding Kaap de Goede Hoop (now Tanjung Yamursba) and the small island of Rawak off Waigeo, the expedition sighted Gebe, sailed across the Halmahera Sea and then the Sea of Ceram, before passing through the straits separating Buton and Wangiwangi islands in the southeastern Celebes (Sulawesi). The *Coquille* then passed through the Selayar Strait and arrived at Surabaya in west Java on 29 August. Here, Duperrey conducted astronomical observations to facilitate a comparison with the latitude and longitude fixed in 1794 by d'Entrecasteaux's expedition.[44] D'Urville's attention was inevitably drawn to the white-walled Dutch colonial houses of the port, which he would later describe as having 'beautiful covered galleries with exterior colonnades'.[45] On the shore opposite the customs house was a battery that commanded the river. Duperrey and his officers were warmly received by the senior officers of the

Dutch garrison and naval station.[46] As in Ambon, however, d'Urville appears to have been drawn to the Chinese quarter: 'clean, noisy, animated, like all the towns where these nomads have planted their merchant tents'.[47] He would retain a passion for Chinese language and culture for the rest of his life.

On 17 September 1824, six days after leaving Surabaya and sailing the length of the northern coast of Java, the *Coquille* left the Sunda Strait and entered the Indian Ocean. On 3 October, she reached Port Louis in Mauritius (the former Île-de-France), part of the Mascareigne group. D'Urville's attention was inevitably drawn to the 812-metre peak of Le Pouce, which framed the port, along with 'other chains of rock seeded with forest'.[48] The island had been under British rule for 14 years, but most of the colonists had been born French subjects – whether free or slave – and were the product of nearly a century of French colonial enterprise on an island that had no indigenous inhabitants. Thus the men of the *Coquille* found themselves in a French-speaking community for the first time since leaving Toulon. As d'Urville put it, 'I was among compatriots; although the English had de-baptised this land, they had not de-nationalised it. Mauritius is still French, although conquered since 1810.'[49] The Mauritian planters, merchants and former privateers chafed under foreign rule and their limited democratic institutions, but like the Québécois, who had become reluctant British subjects more than 50 years earlier in North America, they too had no alternative but to accept the rule of their former foes and prosper. The British also had to resign themselves to stubborn cultural realities. When Charles Darwin visited Mauritius in April 1836, he remarked: 'Although the island has been so many years under the English government, the general character of the place is quite French: Englishmen speak to their servants in French, and the shops are all French; indeed, I should think that Calais and Boulogne [were] much more Anglified.'[50] D'Urville himself found Port Louis a 'little Paris', full of French products with nothing from London or Liverpool.[51]

The governor of Mauritius at the time of d'Urville's first visit to the island was Dublin-born Sir Galbraith Lowry Cole, second son of the Earl of Enniskillen. (Duperrey recorded and published his name as 'Lauricol'.[52]) A distinguished veteran of the Peninsular War, he had missed the Battle of Waterloo because of his marriage, two days before, to the daughter of the Earl of Malmsbury. Sir Galbraith and Lady Frances Cole had arrived in Mauritius in June 1823 and were generally popular with the conservative local sugar planters.[53] They received the officers of the *Coquille* warmly, and Governor Cole allowed Duperrey to conduct observations near the hospital in Port Louis and at Trou Fanfaron. This enabled comparisons with the longitudinal determinations of the distinguished eighteenth-century hydrographer Jean-Baptiste d'Après de Mannevillette, the astronomer abbé Nicolas de La Caille and others.[54]

During his visit to Mauritius, d'Urville called on the Belfast-born doctor and naturalist Charles Telfair at his 'Bel Ombre' estate, probably with a letter of introduction from Cunningham.[55] D'Urville and Telfair were both *chevaliers* of the *Légion d'honneur*; Telfair had received his decoration for services to French scientists during a visit to Paris the year before d'Urville was honoured. Their meeting would engender an enduring friendship. Given his passion for botany (we know he collected 270 plants in Mauritius),[56] it also seems likely that d'Urville visited the island's world-famous botanical garden at Pamplemousses. Soon after, Telfair would become its superintendent.[57]

Another impressive friend d'Urville made in Mauritius was Jean-Baptiste Lislet Geoffroy,[58] a man who had risen from slavery to be inscribed on the list of correspondents of the Académie des sciences (section géographie et navigation) in 1821. Born on the neighbouring island of Bourbon (La Réunion), the son of a slave-woman from Guinea and a Compagnie des Indes engineer, Lislet Geoffroy was taught mathematics and drawing by his father and studied physics and astronomy with the aid of books lent to him by the chevalier de Tromelin. He rose to prominence as an able hydrographer after drafting charts in Madagascar, the Seychelles, the Île de France and Réunion. Lislet Geoffroy's interests, however, extended to geology, geography, climatology, meteorology, botany, zoology, astronomy and physics.[59] It is hardly surprising that a man such as d'Urville should have been drawn to him.

The *Coquille* left Mauritius on 16 November and reached the sister island of Bourbon the following day. For d'Urville, the harbour of Saint-Denis seemed as if it was set within 'an amphitheatre of rock', with high basalt walls 'bathed in the sea'.[60] Because Bourbon lacked a true harbour (like Port Louis in Mauritius) and was unlikely to become another nest of corsairs in any future conflict, the island was returned to France after the Treaty of Paris (1814). The French governor was Henry Saulces de Freycinet, a veteran, like his brother Louis, of the Baudin expedition to Australian waters. He had followed the voyage of the *Coquille* from Duperrey's dispatches to the minister; now Duperrey would carry his dispatches back to France.

The expedition sailed from Bourbon on 28 November. A total solar eclipse took place on 20 December, the day after the Cape of Good Hope was sighted. Having already replenished her stores and water, *Coquille* did not call at the former Dutch colony, now in British hands, but proceeded directly to the island of Saint Helena. D'Urville would later write that the island, which became visible on 2 January 1825, seemed like 'a dark and sombre château, rising from the water'. Thousands of birds wheeled about the rugged cliffs of volcanic rock, plunging furiously into the waves after fish. For d'Urville, 'the elements' appeared 'still in conflict', and the sea about the island 'seemed to batter it as if it wanted to uproot it one day'. Saint Helena was 'a land distant from all continents, solitary on this expanse of water, dismal, wild, without greenery'.[61]

On closer inspection, the natural order seemed reversed: the summits, continually bathed in condensing clouds, bore trees, but the valleys were 'arid and naked'. The *Coquille* reached Jamestown on the morning of 3 January 1825.[62] A little more than three and a half years before, the island's most famous resident, the exiled Napoleon Bonaparte, had died. It was, in d'Urville's words, an 'island of grand memories'.[63] Until Napoleon's death, the island had been tightly garrisoned under the command of Governor Sir Hudson Lowe and its famous resident held largely incommunicado. The visit of a French naval vessel would have been problematic, given fears that the former emperor might have tried to escape, as he had from Elba. Now, the island's new governor, Brigadier-General Alexander Walker, could afford to be more welcoming to French visitors, and his kindness was suitably acknowledged by Duperrey.[64] Four years later, when d'Urville returned to Saint Helena, he was disappointed not to meet the governor again and described him as the 'honest M. Walker, from whom I received much kindness'.[65] He was clearly a scholar after his own heart. As a young man, the Scottish-born Walker had participated in James Strange's expedition along the northwestern coast of America and had become very interested in ethnography and the language of the Nootka Indians. During his later service in India, he had also acquired a valuable collection of Arabic, Persian and Sanskrit manuscripts, which were later donated to the Bodleian Library.[66]

When d'Urville went ashore, he passed the East India Company warehouse before entering an arched gateway. On the left he found Government House; on the right he observed a modest church. Jamestown was enclosed within a narrow ravine and flanked by protective batteries. Overlooking the town was 'The Briars', the bungalow belonging to the merchant William Balcombe, where Napoleon was housed for the first three months of his exile and where he first met and befriended Balcombe's young daughter Betsy.[67] D'Urville followed the main road, lined with painted or varnished wooden houses belonging to local merchants. The road then divided: in one direction lay the barracks and hospital; in the other, to the east, lay the interior of the island and the serpentine route to 'Longwood'. The latter was the cold, mist-enveloped, wind-blown 'Thébaïde', as d'Urville put it,[68] where Napoleon had finally been lodged – at the suggestion of the Duke of Wellington, who had visited the island in 1805 – and where he had pitted his wits against the petty tyrannies of the much-maligned Lowe – emancipator of the island's slaves. Here, too, he nurtured the cult of his martyrdom and dictated his memoirs like the Christ of his own gospel. All the while, his small but portly body was absorbing arsenic, detectable to this day in locks of his hair souvenired after his death. Some have suggested that this was a result of a deliberate poisoning orchestrated by Lowe;[69] others have pointed the finger at Charles-Tristan de Montholon, head of Napoleon's household at 'Longwood' and cuckolded husband of his mistress Albine de Vassal.[70] More recently, and perhaps more convincingly, it has been argued that Napoleon was unintentionally poisoned by arsenic dispersed from his fashionable green wallpaper (by the damp mouldy atmospheric conditions prevailing at 'Longwood'), and that this toxic burden then fatally exacerbated his already ulcerated stomach.[71] Perhaps Napoleon also had a genetic predisposition to stomach cancer, the disease his father died from. For his part, d'Urville thought Napoleon had died of a liver disease.[72]

Despite the fact that only a few years before, 'Longwood' had been the focus of so much British military scrutiny, and Napoleon had lived there with a measure of austere elegance – surrounded by a select group of sycophants, servants, medical staff and eventually clergy – it was now largely derelict. Although d'Urville provided a semi-fictional context in his *Voyage pittoresque autour du monde*, there seems little doubt that he was speaking from his personal experience when he wrote:

At the time I visited 'Longwood', the home of Napoleon was in a ramshackle state impossible to describe. The drawing rooms had become a sifting room for grain; the Emperor's room was a stable; a manger occupied the corner where his bed had been, the corner where he died. It would have been better to burn this debris of little value, than to profane it with this usage.[73]

D'Urville also visited Napoleon's grave, as did Lesson and other members of the expedition.[74] (This was 15 years before Napoleon's remains were returned, with British permission, to France.[75]) In the nearby Sane Valley, d'Urville found the tomb set in a small lawn by a stream and beneath several weeping willows. Its flat stones, surrounded by a metal balustrade, bore 'no name, no coat of arms, no emblem'.[76] It is hard to imagine that d'Urville was not reminded of his time aboard the *Amazone*, as a young aspirant in 1810, when she was inspected by the emperor whose grave now lay before him. Although he was not a Bonapartist, he was not indifferent to Napoleon's achievements – calling him 'the Prometheus of glory'[77] – or his plight. With his emotions provoked, he wrote: 'In front of the tomb of so vast a genius, it is impossible for the perceptions of a traveller, sad and religious, not to be heightened.'[78]

After further positional determinations, the *Coquille* departed from Saint Helena on 11 January. Sailing directly to Ascension Island, she anchored in Sandy Bay a week later. The British garrison was commanded by Irish-born Lieutenant-Colonel (later General Sir) Edward Nicolls of the Royal Marines, who had distinguished himself in North America during the War of 1812.[79] D'Urville noted that the island had had no British garrison until 1815, and that one had only been established out of fear that Ascension might become the base for an attempted rescue of Napoleon from Saint Helena. With the former emperor's death, this was no longer a strategic consideration, but d'Urville observed that the naval station had grown from 25 men in 1815 to 225 under Nicolls,[80] and with the demands of empire, it would continue to grow.

Ascension Island is essentially a barren volcanic peak thrusting out of the South Atlantic. As d'Urville put it, 'as far as one can see, one discovers only a red volcanic soil, without any kind of vegetation. Everywhere one walks on piles of scoria.'[81] Although there were numerous insects, the island did not offer much promise for a botanist, but in some humid locations and on Green Mountain (859 metres), d'Urville did find some vegetation, mainly ferns. The island does have 27 species of flowering plants and ferns, of which seven are endemic, including two that are probably extinct.[82] It was on the southeastern side of Green Mountain that the explorer and buccaneer William Dampier found fresh water after his decrepit ship, *Roebuck*, foundered on the island in February 1701. This remained a vital source for the British garrison; according to d'Urville, each of the Royal Marines was restricted to a gallon and a half ration of water per day, per man, all year round.[83]

After further navigational astronomy, the *Coquille* left Ascension Island on 28 January and headed for Europe. Nearly six weeks later, on 9 March, she once again passed through the Strait of Gibraltar and entered the Mediterranean. On 24 March 1825, faced with strong easterly winds, Duprerrey decided to enter the port of Marseille rather than wait indefinitely for favourable winds to sail directly to Toulon.[84] After an absence of more than two and a half years, d'Urville's first circumnavigation – to which his biographer Vergniol devoted just a single page! – was over. He was safely back in France but not yet in Adélie's arms.

PART II

'… the progress of geography'

'Jules Sébastien César Dumont d'Urville', etching by A. Lefevre, from the frontispiece of Dumont d'Urville's Voyage pittoresque autour du monde, L. Tenré, Paris, vol. ii, 1835. Author's collection

12

Command

One inch of delay more is a South Sea of discovery.
William Shakespeare, [Rosalind]*

D uring his long absence, d'Urville had received no news whatsoever from his family, and they had not received any of his letters.[1] On the very day the *Coquille* arrived in Marseille, he set off for Toulon full of anticipation. Nothing could have prepared him for what he faced on arrival.

> What sad news awaited me! During my voyage I had had a cruel loss; my son Jules having already reached the end of his seventh year and having given at an early age the highest hopes of the double qualities of the heart and the mind, had been dead for almost two years; his unfortunate mother inconsolable at this loss and moreover tormented by the anxieties of the dangers that I had to face, had for almost fifteen months been in a state of little less than despair and at the moment of my return was still in precarious and debilitated health.[2]

Regardless of any soothing reassurances to Adélie, d'Urville was not about to curtail his ambitions. He promptly wrote to Emmanuel Halgan, the navy's new director of personnel, requesting that he be ordered immediately to Paris. He received no reply. He had more luck when he wrote to the maritime prefect of Toulon, François Daugier, who responded with a very warm letter. A few days later, the *Coquille* arrived in Toulon, and d'Urville and Lesson received orders by the aerial *télégraphe* – a cumbersome semaphore communications system of raised and lowered arms atop steeples and towers[3] – to proceed to Paris. D'Urville disembarked his collections from the *Coquille* and loaded a hired wagon to take him (and presumably Lesson and his zoological collections) to the capital, a journey they completed in 18 days.[4]

Despite a warm reception from his superiors in Paris, d'Urville was disappointed not to receive an immediate promotion.[5] Apparently, on Duperrey's promotion to *capitaine de frégate* in May 1825, he wrote to the new navy minister, comte Christophe

* *As You Like It* (*ca.*1599), act iii, scene ii, lines 192–93

Chabrol de Crouzol, pleading his own case;[6] this was from his new lodgings at 18, rue des Petits Augustins, now the rue Bonaparte. (Four years before, Victor Hugo had resided with his mother and brother in the same building.[7])

Although d'Urville did not receive his promotion to *capitaine de frégate* until 3 November 1825 – Duperrey's seniority was probably the main reason he had to wait – he was made a *chevalier de Saint-Louis* on 12 July.[8] Established by Louis XIV in 1693, this order of chivalry rewarded outstanding military service and held forth the prospect of a pension. Non-nobles were eligible to receive the decoration, but recipients had to be Catholic – the order was closed to all other religious denominations – and they had to reaffirm their faith. This was one reason the order was abolished during the Revolution. Louis XVIII, however, reinstituted it soon after the Bourbon Restoration. How readily d'Urville pledged to live and die a Catholic is uncertain; in the years that followed, his faith was further eroded by still more family tragedies.

Throughout his stay in Paris, d'Urville had to care for his wife, broken in spirit by the loss of their son. This is not to suggest that his grief was any less than Adélie's, but he was keenly aware that his absence and the non-arrival of his letters had exacerbated her suffering and further weakened her mental health. His return must have been healing, so too, perhaps, the work he gave her as his amanuensis; we know she rendered his New Zealand novel in a clearer hand. Carol Legge pointed out that many of the errors are French homonyms, suggesting that d'Urville dictated the novel rather than force her to deal with his forbidding handwriting.[9] It was a time-consuming task that kept them close together and absorbed in a project he had contrived. D'Urville also completed the explanatory notes for the novel in August 1825. By this time, Adélie was several weeks' pregnant with a son who would also be named Jules, no doubt a welcome prospect of a new family life and a renewed focus for her shattered maternal love. Nevertheless, d'Urville's ambition, fierce desire to command an expedition of his own and inevitable future absence must have haunted her.

The principal reason for d'Urville's presence in Paris was to communicate the results of the voyage of the *Coquille* and to work on forthcoming publications from the expedition. This work would progress over the next five years, with the appearance of the initial botanical, zoological[10] and hydrographic volumes and atlases. D'Urville had hoped to write the historical account of the voyage, but long before the expedition had ended, Duperrey had insisted on undertaking this task. According to d'Urville, 'the example of [François] Péron', who destroyed the posthumous reputation of Nicolas Baudin when he gained editorial control of the official account of Baudin's voyage, made Duperrey 'tremble'; ironically, it was the prospect of René Lesson's account rather than that of d'Urville that made him most fearful.[11] Ultimately, only 202 pages of Duperrey's historical account (up to the expedition's visit to Concepción in Chile) would appear before the Revolution of 1830 brought its publication to a grinding, mid-paragraph, mid-sentence, mid-word halt. This was all the more surprising because d'Urville noted that Duperrey had 'taken care to repeat very frequently' that his journal was 'completely ready to be delivered to the printer on his arrival in France'.[12] The official account of the *Coquille* voyage begun by Duperrey was never resurrected. In the more liberal political climate after the fall of Charles X, however, d'Urville was able to include substantial parts of his journal in his *Voyage pittoresque autour du monde* in 1834–35, and Lesson was able to publish his two-volume historical account in 1838–39. The incomplete printed record appears to be one reason Duperrey's voyage has been studied less thoroughly than other major voyages of exploration.

Aside from assisting Brongniart and Bory de Saint-Vincent with the botanical volumes, d'Urville published (in 1825) a 20-page note on the collections he had gathered during the expedition, another article on the worldwide distribution of ferns in the *Annales des sciences naturelles*,[13] and, in 1826, 'Flore des Malouines' in the *Mémoires de la Société Linnéenne de Paris*. Undoubtedly, d'Urville's scientific efforts were appreciated. On 18 July 1825, Cuvier (assisted by d'Urville's friend Latreille) reported on the zoological results of the *Coquille* expedition to the Académie des sciences, including glowing praise for d'Urville's entomological efforts:

> … it is principally thanks to M. Durville that we have the rich collection of insects among the results of this expedition. This able mariner was charged with this work, in some respects, by supererogation, and could not carry it out other than in moments of spare time after his principal duties. In addition, the gift that he has made of these insects to the Muséum can be regarded as an act of pure generosity. He has already ministered to the interests of the Muséum from his survey of the Black Sea with Captain Gauttier; but in this voyage, he can be seen again to have proved his zeal and his unselfishness. The insects he has deposited number close to twelve hundred, comprising around eleven hundred species, namely: three hundred and sixty-one coleoptera, four hundred and twenty-eight lepidoptera, and the rest in other orders.[14]

Surprisingly, it was François Arago, better known as an astronomer (and later as a bitter critic of d'Urville), who summarised the botanical results of the expedition in the penultimate part of the commission of report to the Académie des sciences, dated 22 August 1825. Like Cuvier, he acknowledged that d'Urville, as second-in-command of the *Coquille*, had numerous responsibilities while in port – particularly reprovisioning and supervising the crew – but that he had nevertheless achieved significant scientific results. The plant collections he gathered during his landfalls, wrote Arago, 'comprised almost three thousand species; of this number, it is estimated that there are four hundred new. Several others, including those already known, are rare and are not found in the collections of the Muséum d'histoire naturelle.'[15]

Duperrey, who disparaged the natural sciences,[16] would very likely have agreed with the sentiments of Ernest Rutherford, who once declared: 'All science is either physics or stamp collecting.'[17] Yet the physical scientist Arago acknowledged that, as a botanist, d'Urville was 'not content to gather the plants offered to view; he has analysed and described them with care'.[18] Understanding why species are different from each other is what would eventually elevate the natural sciences beyond mere cataloguing and taxonomy (the 'stamp collecting' Rutherford alluded to).

Soon after his arrival in the capital, d'Urville set about making a case for a new expedition under his own command. Inevitably, his proposal focused on the unfinished work of the *Coquille* expedition. On 23 May 1825, he completed a plan for a voyage of exploration on the coasts of New Guinea, New Britain and the Louisiade Archipelago.[19] He would later write:

> The campaign of the *Coquille*, that I had jointly conceived and presented the plan of with M. Duperrey, my colleague, had ended. Its navigation was almost always out of sight of the coasts, offering little danger … The natural sciences and physics had obtained interesting results from it. Geography had also had some discoveries and, above all, rectification of badly determined points; but there had been no reconnaissance following the coasts, no complete exploration of the archipelago with the exception of the Gilbert and Mulgrave Islands; geography, therefore, claimed the new attention of the navigator in these seas.[20]

Despite his particular attention to botany and entomology during the voyage of the *Coquille*, d'Urville asserted that he had assiduously studied 'the direction of the winds and the currents, the march and influence of the seasons' and the exact 'progress of geography made in the diverse archipelagos of the South Sea', thereby conceiving the 'plan of a campaign to render the greatest service to this science'.[21]

He gained a sympathetic hearing from the navy minister, who had previously been minister of the interior.[22] The comte de Chabrol considered d'Urville one of the most erudite officers in the navy,[23] and he was very favourably disposed to investigating the site for an overseas French penal colony. Discussion on such a colony in New Zealand had been precipitated by the visit to Paris of baron Charles-Philippe-Hippolyte de Thierry. Raised in England, the son of an émigré nobleman and a godson of Charles X, Thierry had been studying law in 1820 when the missionary Thomas Kendall visited Cambridge with the Ngā Puhi chiefs Hongi Hika and Waikato. He claimed to have struck a deal with Kendall to purchase land for him in New Zealand with £800 worth of goods. In August 1822, however, Kendall apparently purchased a 40,000-acre parcel of land from the Ngā Puhi chiefs Patuone and Nene, and the Popoto chief, Muriwai, for a mere 36 axes. Thierry later accused Kendall of misappropriation, but his own history of extravagant claims and dubious financial dealings casts doubt on this. Thierry's attempts to gain British support for his colony made no progress, so he then approached the Dutch ambassador, seeking to become 'Viceroy of New Zealand' and making fantastic projections of revenue for the Dutch Crown. Once again, he got nowhere.[24]

In late April 1825, a month before d'Urville submitted his outline, Thierry was in Paris hovering around the fringes of the court and making still more grandiose proposals. He would cede his 'territory' in New Zealand to the French government on condition of being nominated 'Governor'. Although he requested no salary, he wanted to be given Stewart Island as his fiefdom, 10 per cent of government revenue from the colony and an unspecified sum of money from the public purse to enable him 'to bring that which will be necessary'. Oh, and France would also have to supply two frigates, six transport vessels (with provisions for a year) and a military force of 500 men, artillery and munitions for the 'protection of the new colony'! He then went on to list the land grants he would make for nominated values of capital goods brought by settlers to the colony or for years of indentured labour.[25] Thierry was specifically mentioned by the comte de Chabrol in his secret instructions to d'Urville, but it is clear that the minister did not accept his claims of land ownership in New Zealand. While it is hardly surprising that his pompous expensive demands were rejected by the frugal French court, the very mention of his name in d'Urville's orders suggests that he did contribute to serious discussion on the subject of a French colony. Ironically, after bankruptcy, further wanderings and more fantastic schemes – Ruth Ross wrote pointedly of his 'Ruritanian absurdities' – Thierry did eventually settle in New Zealand and died there in 1864.[26] He was not the sole advocate of colonial schemes around this time: in 1826, Chabrol would be addressed personally by a pamphleteer, Jean-François Ginouvier, who urged the establishment of a French Botany Bay.[27]

Although formal royal assent was not requested for d'Urville's expedition until 4 December 1825,[28] by mid-September, d'Urville had received in-principle approval for his proposal. On 12 September, the director of naval movements wrote to the minister seeking approval to rename the *Coquille* – *La Découverte*, *La Recherche* or l'*Astrolabe* – to differentiate d'Urville's forthcoming voyage from Duperrey's.[29] The latter name was that of one of Lapérouse's ships, and it would be chosen in the wake of renewed discussion on the fate of the missing French explorer, thanks to yet another visitor to the capital. On 8 September 1825, *Le moniteur universel* reported that Rear Admiral Thomas Manby RN, recently arrived in Paris, had brought new evidence of the location where Lapérouse had perished in the Pacific. According to Manby, a whaling vessel had visited an island between New Caledonia and New Guinea where a chief had come on board wearing a cross of the order of Saint Louis 'as an ornament' in one ear.

Other islanders had swords made in Paris and carried 'medals of Louis XVI'. When interviewed, the middle-aged chief said that when he was young, 'a large ship was wrecked in a violent storm on a coral reef and all who were aboard perished'.[30] The comte de Chabrol would later make specific reference to Manby's assertions in the context of d'Urville's proposed voyage in a letter to Vice-Admiral de Rosily, director-general of the Dépôt des cartes et plans de la marine.[31] Manby, who as a young man had sailed with George Vancouver's expedition, had rented a house in Chantilly (Oise) for the winter. D'Urville wrote to him there on 9 December but did not receive a reply until after Christmas. Although d'Urville sought to question Manby in person, the Englishman politely stated that he had 'nothing more to add, [than] what the public journals have stated'.[32] D'Urville's instructions would contain explicit orders to try to 'discover the traces of La Pérouse and his unfortunate companions' and not to 'neglect anything that could render [the search] fruitful'.[33]

On 15 December 1825, the comte de Chabrol wrote five letters to set d'Urville's expedition in motion. One was written to the naval intendant in Toulon, telling him that the *Coquille* would be renamed *Astrolabe* and ordering that the vessel be scrupulously repaired with particular attention to the integrity of her hull. She was also to be fitted out in a manner 'absolutely the same as that for the last campaign', with the sole exception of a few 'light modifications' specified by d'Urville.[34] Another letter was to Rosily, advising him of the proposed expedition and its general route and asking him to draft 'nautical instructions' for the 'observations' d'Urville was 'to make during the course of his navigation'.[35] Another letter was addressed to baron Maxence de Damas, the minister of foreign affairs, asking him to obtain passports for the expedition from London, Madrid, Lisbon and The Hague.[36] Yet another letter was to baron Aimé de Puymaurin, director of the Paris Mint, asking him to have 50 silver and 150 bronze medallions – similar to those for the *Coquille* expedition – struck for presentation purposes during the proposed voyage.[37] (The number of bronze medallions was later increased to 450.)

In the coming months, still more letters left the minister's office. One was written to baron Armand-Louis-Maurice Séguier, the French consul-general in London, requesting the purchase of James Horsburgh's *Directions for Sailing to and from the East Indies, China, New Holland, Cape of Good Hope and the Interjacent Ports* (1809– 11), James Horsfield's *Zoological Researches in Java and the Neighbouring Islands* (1824), John Latham's anachronistic *Index Ornithologicus* (1790), and charts and atlases from the expeditions of Adam Johann von Krusenstern, Matthew Flinders and Phillip Parker King.[38] Two new iron chains were also ordered for the expedition from the royal foundry at Guérigny (Nièvre).[39] (The 90-metre chains proved to be too heavy for the *Astrolabe*, so d'Urville took only one after obtaining permission to purchase another during the voyage.[40]) On 26 December, the comte de Chabrol wrote to the perpetual secretaries of the Académie des sciences requesting scientific instructions for d'Urville's expedition.[41] More than two months later, he still had no reply from either Cuvier or Joseph Fourier (the first proponent of the 'greenhouse effect'). However, one member of the academy did write promptly on learning of d'Urville's proposed expedition. This was Jean-Pierre-Joseph d'Arcet, who offered to 'cooperate in the preparation … of gelatine … to serve as food for the crew of the vessel'.[42] D'Arcet had pioneered a new process of gelatine production from animal bones in 1817. At the time, there were exaggerated claims about the nutritional value of this food product. It was believed, for example, that '60 grams of this gelatine were regarded as equivalent to 1,500 grams of meat'.[43] Not surprisingly, there was disquiet when, for economic reasons, alms-houses and hospitals began to serve bouillon made from gelatine instead of real meat, and patients suffered dramatic weight loss. The Académie des sciences appointed the notorious vivisector François Magendie, whom we will meet again in the final chapter of d'Urville's life, to chair a commission of investigation. Its findings were very unfavourable to gelatine; indeed, Magendie reported experiments that showed that animals preferred to starve to death rather than eat it![44] We now know that gelatine lacks several vital amino acids, but d'Arcet clearly wanted to add d'Urville and his sailors to his list of guinea pigs.

Although the minister thanked d'Arcet for his offer, it is uncertain how much gelatine, if any, was actually taken on the expedition. Indeed, the supplies given to d'Urville were ordered to be 'of the same nature as had been provided to M. Duperrey'.[45] Similarly, when the minister replied to a letter from d'Urville, dated 16 December, regarding the supply of trade goods (to be used in exchange for fresh provisions, firewood, water and even natural history specimens), he gave approval on condition that they too were 'the same as those that had been employed during the expedition of M. Duperrey'.[46] The stage was set for d'Urville to show what he could do with almost identical resources as had been allocated to his rival three years before. Over the coming months, the passports from foreign governments arrived, firstly from Britain, then Portugal and the Netherlands, and finally from Spain. Similarly, the specialised cartographic and zoological publications from Britain were gradually acquired by the French consul-general in London and forwarded to Paris. D'Urville left Paris, apparently with Adélie, in the New Year of 1826 and arrived in Toulon on 28 January. There he received the instructions from the Académie des sciences and finalised the muster roll for his crew.

13

Astrolabe

T' explore the world, and search the ways of life,
Man's evil and his virtue. Forth I sail'd
Into the deep illimitable main,
With but one bark, and the small faithful band
That yet cleav'd to me.

Dante Alighieri*

As his second-in-command, d'Urville chose Charles-Hector Jacquinot, veteran of the *Coquille* expedition, now promoted to *lieutenant de vaisseau*. Another *Coquille* veteran who also agreed to sail again was the tall, thin, chestnut-haired Ensign Victor-Charles Lottin, whom d'Urville considered 'cultivated' and 'naturally quiet and retiring'.[1] With the exception of the master carpenter Alexandre Béringuier,[2] the rest of the crew was entirely new. (The purser Joseph Imbert was not the same man as the sailor on the *Coquille* expedition.) Some, however, were relatives of the previous crew, including surgeon Pierre-Adolphe Lesson, the blue-eyed brother of René Lesson and an equally bitter critic of d'Urville,[3] who had begun his working life as an apprentice carpenter before studying medicine in Rochefort.[4]

One of the two new ensigns was Victor-Amédée Gressien, who had previously served with d'Urville on the *Chevrette*. Very hairy, with a receding forehead and swarthy complexion,[5] Gressien was impecunious, rash and prone to depression. He would eventually marry an Algiers hotel-keeper of questionable character without the approval of his naval superiors, and their son would later be murdered. Although Gressien's tarnished family associations affected his naval career, and he later attempted suicide, d'Urville had a high opinion of him, as did the other officers. Thrice decorated, Gressien reached the rank of *capitaine de vaisseau* after the Revolution of 1848.[6]

The other ensign was Pierre-Edouard Guilbert, a pale, blonde-haired Breton, with a small nose and large eyes. The son and brother of respected naval medical officers, he had joined the navy as a cabin boy at the age of 11 and had experienced active service

---

* *Divina Commedia*, 'Inferno' (*ca.* 1300), canto xxvi, lines 97–101, Carey trans.

Terres Australes et Antarctiques Françaises
stamp honouring Jean René Quoy (1990),
engraved by Pierre Bequet. Author's collection

in the convoy-escort *Aigle*, even before reaching his teens. Charming, intelligent, congenial and zealous, Guilbert was esteemed by his fellow officers and the crew alike. He would later serve in the Algerian and Crimean wars, and retire as a *capitaine de vaisseau* and *commandeur de la Légion d'honneur*.[7]

D'Urville was fortunate in the choice of the expedition's two naturalists. Jean-René-Constant Quoy was a surgeon and anatomist, pale, dark-haired, of medium height, with a largish mouth and a delicate constitution. He was so thin that he still wore his original midshipman's coat from his entry into the navy, minus its original embroidery. Like Bérenguier, a veteran of Freycinet's circumnavigation, Quoy (pronounced *kwa*) was not only a methodical zoologist, he was also an accomplished draughtsman who would execute 6500 drawings during the expedition. Although a native of Maillé, in the staunchly royalist and Catholic Vendée, Quoy was a philosophical sceptic, and his political sympathies were decidedly republican.[8] Very well read and with a prodigious memory – he could recite much of Rabelais by heart[9] – Quoy would share his scientific work with Joseph-Paul Gaimard. Born in Saint-Zacharie (Var) to a family of crystal-cutters, Gaimard had been Quoy's zoological collaborator on Freycinet's expedition. A short, stocky, womanising *bon vivant* with black curly hair, dark brow and expressive eyes, Gaimard was as outgoing and extroverted as Quoy was austere and taciturn.

Joseph-Paul Gaimard, surgeon-naturalist on d'Urville's first Astrolabe *voyage, lithograph by [Alfred-Léon?] Lemercier, from a painting by François-Gabriel-Guillaume Lépaulle.* The Royal Library, Copenhagen, Collection of Prints and Photographs

Together, however, they formed a potent scientific partnership, immortalised by their many jointly published descriptions. Both men were veterans of the Napoleonic navy, and Gaimard – an ardent Bonapartist who regulated his life with anniversaries of the Empire and its victories[10] – had recently returned from a study tour of natural history collections in England, Holland and Belgium. He later studied the epidemiology of cholera in Russia, Prussia and Austria, and participated in four expeditions to search for traces of d'Urville's former *Coquille* colleague Jules-Alphonse Poret de Blosseville in Iceland and Greenland.[11]

The official artist of the expedition was Louis-Auguste de Sainson, a short, plump, jovial, round-faced man with a thin moustache and dark complexion who was liked by all aboard the *Astrolabe*. As the son of an army engineering officer who had served

Louis-Auguste de Sainson, artist of d'Urville's first Astrolabe
*expedition, detail from 'Toumboua-Nakoro conversant à
bord', unknown engraver, from Dumont d'Urville's* Voyage
pittoresque autour du monde, *L. Tenré, Paris, vol. ii, 1835,
plate xi.* Author's collection

in the West Indies, Hanover, Russia and on fortifications throughout France, Sainson
was already much travelled. He had also been the private secretary of the liberal duc
de la Rochefoucauld-Liancourt before joining the navy in Rochefort in 1825. Later he
would become the secretary of the wealthy Russian Count Anatole Demidoff.[12]

There were also three midshipmen who joined d'Urville's staff officers aboard the
Astrolabe. The eldest was Henry-Antoine Faraguet, 160 centimetres tall, with chestnut
hair, grey eyes, fair complexion, oval face, large mouth and a long pointy nose.[13] He was
the son of a battle-hardened officer of the Grande Armée, who had fought at Austerlitz
and in Spain and Russia (where he was wounded and taken prisoner). A graduate of the
elite École polytechnique, Faraguet had entered the navy the previous November. His
roots, however, were far from the sea: born in the frontier town of Sedan (Ardennes),
his father's family came from Auxonne in Burgundy.[14] More than two years his junior
was Midshipman François-Edmond Pâris, who would later command some of the first
steam vessels in the French navy and retire a highly decorated vice-admiral.[15]

The youngest of the midshipmen was Ésprit-Justin-Gustave Girard Dudemaine, from
Marseille. Although his dossier has disappeared from the naval archives at Vincennes,
we know that he entered the Collège royal de la marine in Angoulême as an *élève* in
April 1823,[16] later married a baroness, and that his father, Jean-Louis-Vincent Girard
Dudemaine, was a decorated army officer, who had served in the king's bodyguard and
was well regarded as a poet and member of the Académie de Marseille.[17]

D'Urville's secretary, Barthélémy Lauvergne, was from Toulon, the son of a cutler. He had studied mathematics, rhetoric and drawing at the Collège communal de Toulon between 1816 and 1821, and had a clear neat hand. His brother taught *materia medica* in Toulon and was probably already known to d'Urville. Well respected as an artist and draughtsman, Lauvergne would later participate in the *Favorite* expedition of Cyrille Laplace, the *Bonite* expedition of Auguste Vaillant and then an expedition to Lapland, Finland and Russia (1839–41).[18]

The vast majority of the sailors selected for the *Astrolabe* were men from Toulon and other parts of Var, but there were also a few men from Brittany, Normandy, Corsica and other littoral regions. Perhaps mindful of James Cook's experience, d'Urville also embarked a corporal and five marine fusiliers (2e régiment d'infanterie de marine) to provide additional protection for the expedition. They were mostly men from eastern and south-central France, born far from the coast and in many cases familiar with rugged mountain terrain.[19]

D'Urville's final instructions from the minister were dated 8 April 1826 and reached him five days later. Although these orders were published at the beginning of the first volume of d'Urville's historical account, several pages of secret instructions that appear in the original manuscript were omitted. A reference to 'special instructions' was cut from the end of the eighth paragraph and, after the twenty-second paragraph, the equivalent of four hand-written pages were excised from the printed text. There can be little doubt that the French government did not want the British to know what d'Urville was requested to do. Among these sensitive orders, he was particularly asked to

> … search for anchorages in which the king's ships could find resources in time of war if they have to make a long sojourn in the Great Ocean, either following combined operations that they have to conduct, or as a result of general events which bring them there … France possesses no colony where large ships-of-war can be secure and where it could be possible to supply them, other than by military occupation of several distant points where Europeans do not yet occupy fixed establishments.[20]

With regard to such locations, in addition to 'hydrographic work', d'Urville was expected (as Duperrey had been earlier) to provide detailed reports on the number and character of local inhabitants and to undertake detailed surveys of water and other resources that would best suit 'the first French' settlers. In addition to these military and maritime reports, the comte de Chabrol informed him that he was expected to search for

> … a place conducive to the establishment of a colony where we would deport criminals we now condemn to irons. For a very long time we have wanted to imitate what the English have done in this respect on the east coast of New Holland; but we have always been frustrated by the difficulty of finding a location which was appropriate

for such an establishment. It is necessary that its latitude be where Europeans can work without succumbing to the excesses of fatigue and the epidemics and will not develop contagious diseases that are the scourge of a great part of America.[21]

On 28 March 1826, the *Astrolabe* left the naval dockyard and entered the main harbour of Toulon. The next day, d'Urville became a father again, when Adélie gave birth to their son, Jules-Eugène-Hector. By 17 April, all of d'Urville's officers and men were aboard the *Astrolabe*. Yet again, his departure from Adélie and their new-born son must have been heart-wrenching. He knew he would be absent for at least three years.

Although the *Astrolabe* weighed anchor on the morning of 22 April 1826, violent winds suddenly threatened her near the only reefs in the harbour, and she was forced to anchor for another 30 hours to avoid going aground. The delay enabled d'Urville to take delivery of four Bunten 'thermometrographs' that had been dispatched from Paris to replace five that had arrived broken in the care of Lottin and could not be repaired. They were to be used to record sea temperatures at depth during the voyage. (François Arago of the Académie des sciences had specifically criticised the voyage of the *Coquille* for failing to conduct just such experiments.[22]) On 25 April, the *Astrolabe* entered the Mediterranean. Although the weather remained unpredictably violent and challenged the crew, d'Urville was heartened by their apparent synergy. They acted like men who had already served six months at sea together. For his part, d'Urville resumed his old habits. Lesson described him in terms very similar to his brother:

> Stiffly dressed; wearing the round hat even when in uniform (it is true that it was the fashion at the time for sailors on board), without deportment, untidy most of the time, rarely wearing a tie, his stockingless feet bare in shoes shaped like slippers and wearing one of the [cotton] cloth trousers which had seen better times during the *Coquille* campaign, one of which was composed of seven pieces, the other of eleven! In good weather his headdress consisted of an old straw hat, and in doubtful weather an otter-skin cap worn in the previous campaign, which he often wore, reserving the hat for the trips ashore. In good weather he wore a drill vest, but more often a very old threadbare uniform frock-coat, and he constantly kept his field-glasses. It is not necessary to add that he was careless to his person.[23]

With the first calm weather, d'Urville began his initial observations with one of the thermometrographs,[24] sending it down 300 fathoms (548.6 metres) in a copper cylinder. This was not a new field of research. Numerous experiments had been conducted in the eighteenth century, both at the surface and at depth. Benjamin Franklin, for example, was the first to identify the Gulf Stream during one such series of experiments. D'Urville recorded 13.8°C at 300 fathoms, which was little different from the relatively constant temperatures recorded by Luigi Marsigli, Horace-Bénédicte de Saussure, and later

François Péron and Charles-Alexandre Lesueur in the Mediterranean.[25] In the much deeper Atlantic, however, temperature changes were far more dramatic. In most cases, these earlier experiments were conducted with water brought on deck from deep below, but d'Urville considered this method very inaccurate and, like Péron, he sent down a mercury thermometer capable of recording minimum and maximum readings.[26]

The *Astrolabe* initially made rapid progress across the western Mediterranean. Minorca was sighted far to the west-northwest on 27 April, Cartagena at dawn on 1 May and Gibraltar on 3 May. Unfortunately, as she approached the strait, contrary winds, strong currents and fog suddenly thwarted her entry to the Atlantic for over a month. The long and frustrating delay provided an opportunity for d'Urville to go ashore with most of his officers, botanise and visit the impregnable British fortifications on Gibraltar, honeycombed with tunnels and bristling with 600 heavy guns. D'Urville believed that this very freedom to visit the rock was the means by which Britain 'paraded all her power' and sought to impress upon the nations of Europe that she would never be expelled from such a strategic redoubt. However, he also believed that famine, betrayal or diplomatic necessity might yet return Gibraltar to 'the hands of its legitimate and natural masters'.[27] Helen Rosenman, in summarising d'Urville's Gibraltar visit, declared that he 'indulged his latent dislike of the British when describing the fortifications',[28] but this ignores his objectivity as an observer, his many British friendships and the many other examples of his Anglophilia. D'Urville also visited the Spanish towns of San Roque and Algesiras, together with the sparsely vegetated neighbouring countryside, and was entertained by the local governor on the occasion of the king of Spain's birthday.

Early on the morning of 7 June, conditions finally became favourable for the *Astrolabe* to leave the Mediterranean and pass through the Strait of Gibraltar. A week later, she reached Tenerife in the Canary Islands and dropped anchor in the port of Santa Cruz. There she was met by the French consul, Alexandre Brétillard. D'Urville was disappointed to learn from the consul that Captain Phillip Parker King, whose Australian survey work, books and charts he greatly admired,[29] had departed only two days before in the sloop HMS *Adventure*, bound for the coast of South America to undertake hydrographic work in company with HMS *Beagle*. All the more disappointing was that King had apparently delayed his departure for five days in the hope of meeting d'Urville. Nevertheless, the two would eventually correspond.[30] During his previous visit to the island, d'Urville, like the rest of the crew of the *Coquille*, had not been permitted to go ashore because of a quarantine order imposed by wary Spanish authorities loyal to the then-liberal government in Madrid. In the wake of the successful French intervention in the Spanish Civil War of 1820–23 and the victory of the reactionary Bourbons, the *Astrolabe* now received a friendlier reception.

Leaving Jacquinot in charge of reprovisioning, astronomical observations and other duties, d'Urville was able to visit the Jardín de Aclimatación founded by Alonso Nava y Grimón, marquis de Villanoeva del Prado, outside the charming highland town of La Orotava.[31] This beautiful botanic garden contains striking examples of endemic Canary Islands flora, such as the monocotyledenous dragon tree *Dracaena draco*, which deeply impressed d'Urville, as it had Humboldt before him.[32] At the time of his visit, the garden was under the direction of Sabin Berthelot (1794–1880), a former midshipman in the Napoleonic navy, who would later co-author the monumental nine-volume *Histoire naturelle des Îles Canaries* (1836–50) with the English botanist Phillip Barker Webb and become the French consul on the island. D'Urville struck up a warm friendship with Berthelot, who would later write his obituary for the *Bulletin de la Société de géographie*. He even stayed at Berthelot's home in La Orotava and was given numerous botanical specimens by him.[33] Coincidentally, d'Urville would later reside in the same street in Paris as Phillip Barker Webb and they too would became good friends.

While in the Canary Islands, d'Urville climbed Mount Teide (the 'Peak of Tenerife'), rising 3718 metres above sea level. In company with the naturalists Quoy and Gaimard, he camped on the volcanic mountain in bitterly cold conditions and collected a number of plant specimens, including the yellow-flowered *Hypericum canariense*, the delicate *Viola cheiranthifolia*,[34] and, on the exposed, pumice-strewn flanks of the caldera, the remarkably resilient broom *Spartocytisus supranubius*.[35]

Like Péron a quarter of a century before, d'Urville read the work of the naturalist and historian José de Viera y Clavijo while in Tenerife.[36] In doing so, he gained some idea of the stubborn valour of the indigenous Guanche during the Spanish conquest of the island. With characteristic historical sensitivity, he realised that his botanical and entomological excursions between San Cristóbal de La Laguna and Santa Cruz took place in what had once been a grimly contested landscape. When shown a Guanche mummy in the collection of the commanding officer in Santa Cruz, Lieutenant-Colonel Juan de Megliorini y Spínola, he was moved to reflect on the 'unique vestiges of a gentle, peaceful and dignified race of humans … exterminated to the last'.[37]

After a sojourn of a week, completing astronomical observations, replenishing the *Astrolabe*'s much-diminished water supplies, purchasing 900 litres of local wine, and dispatching reports, letters and natural history specimens back to France via the French consul, d'Urville gave the order to set sail on 21 June. As the *Astrolabe* drew away from Tenerife, Mount Teide was shrouded in the clouds, with the exception of the summit, which remained visible far out to sea, like an island in the sky.

D'Urville then made directly for Praia in the Cape Verde Islands in the hope of catching Phillip Parker King and gaining advice for the *Astrolabe*'s planned survey work in New Guinea waters. The *Astrolabe* arrived on 29 June, but unfortunately King had departed 36 hours before. Instead, d'Urville encountered HMS *Leven* (which he mistakenly recorded as *Level*) and HMS *Barracouta*, under the command of William Fitzwilliam Owen, who had undertaken impressive survey work on the coasts of east Africa and Madagascar during the previous four years.[38] While d'Urville considered Owen's masterly efforts worthy of comparison with those of Flinders and King, they were clearly of little relevance to his own orders. The heat, parched aridity and decrepit state of Praia disgusted d'Urville, and with King departed, he saw no reason to stay any longer and promptly set sail the next morning.

Frequently becalmed by light winds, the *Astrolabe* sailed slowly down the west African coast. Seeking some profit from the inertia, the naturalists collected numerous floating pelagic marine creatures, particularly members of the Porpitidae and Physaliidae. It rained on 4 July, and the sailors were able to wash their clothes. Two days later, d'Urville continued his sea-water temperature observations, plunging his instrument 400 fathoms (731.5 metres) in a copper cylinder weighted with 30 kilograms of lead. He noted a drop in temperature of 21°C from the surface. Once again, this was consistent with earlier observations by Henry Ellis, William Wales, Charles Irving and François Péron. On 10 July, d'Urville attempted to measure the temperature at more than 800 fathoms (1463 metres). After two hours, the instrument was hauled to the surface and found to have been shattered by the immense pressure of 156 atmospheres: the copper cylinder was 'completely flattened', and the glass thermometer was 'broken in a thousand pieces'.[39]

Under the Bourbons, the anniversary of the fall of the Bastille was no longer the French national day, and there were no shipboard festivities on 14 July. The only remarkable event of the day was a meeting with a Russian vessel, the *Ercole*, which they had previously encountered off Gibraltar. Her captain sought their assistance determining his longitude. While the reversal of monarchical authority in 1789 was not celebrated, King Neptune briefly usurped traditional naval authority aboard the *Astrolabe* on 20 July. On that day, the expedition crossed the equator, and there was much drinking and festivity as the uninitiated were ritually dunked by those who had previously endured the same ritual humiliations of the male seafaring fraternity.

For a man (albeit a naval officer) entranced by the plant kingdom, the sea was frequently a tedious, even incongruous place; and for a man who had left a beautiful wife and infant child for a monastic world of men, occasional bouts of melancholy were hardly surprising. Aboard the *Astrolabe* were two cases of olive seedlings that d'Urville had agreed to transport to New South Wales for the Macarthur family (some of whose members he had encountered on the road to Bathurst in 1824). This was at the behest of his friend Gaspard Robert, director of the navy's botanical garden in Toulon. In the warm sultry weather the olive seedlings had thrived, despite the otherwise rough seaboard conditions. D'Urville looked lovingly upon their green leaves: 'In the middle of the wearisome monotony of the ocean,' he wrote, 'this vegetation delights the eye, diverts the dejected imagination, and returns one to thoughts less sad.' He added, 'I would like to decorate my cabin with several cases of flowers, without regard to their cost, only with regard to their verdure.'[40]

Like Duperrey in 1822, d'Urville took advantage of the equatorial current and the northeasterly trade winds to sail the *Astrolabe* towards Brazil and the islands of Martin Vaz and Trindad, which were reached on the morning of 31 July. However, instead of heading for the Falklands and Cape Horn, as Duperrey had been ordered to do, d'Urville picked up the westerlies and swung back across the South Atlantic to then traverse the Cape of Good Hope and cross the Southern Indian Ocean. He did not sail below 38° 42′ S on this leg of the voyage,[41] so the *Astrolabe* did not exploit the true 'Roaring Forties', later used so effectively by the clippers. The passage across two of the globe's major oceans was rough, stormy and without landfall. The *Astrolabe* did pass close to the islands of Amsterdam and St Paul, but they were not sighted.

Although d'Urville's crew remained free of disease, sailing in southern waters – with powerful winds and waves un-blunted by any significant landmass – was inherently dangerous. On the morning of 12 September, a young sailor named Benoît-Antoine Binot was attempting to remove a bucket caught in the main chainwale when a large wave washed him overboard. D'Urville was fast asleep at the time, but the duty officer, Gressien, threw two chicken coops into the water to give Binot something to cling to. Unfortunately, he could not swim. Although his red shirt kept him visible and the air in his clothes kept him afloat for some minutes, by the time the *Astrolable* was brought about and the yawl was bravely launched in the dangerous seas by Charles Simonet and several other sailors, Binot had disappeared beneath a large wave and was never seen again.

There were other casualties. The quarter-master, Michel Vignale, a Toulonnais like Binot, received a head injury when he fell on deck as the *Astrolabe* pitched in the heavy seas. The injury was not fatal, but two years later, Vignale would succumb to dysentery and never see Toulon again. Despite the capriciousness of the sea, d'Urville could see beauty in its moods. On 19 September, he wrote:

> … as if tired of its efforts, the wind had suspended its violence and allowed a brief respite to the billows. At that moment, the waves, less irregular, seemed like so many chains of moving hills, cut by so many valleys and on the backs of which our corvette glided peacefully. A truly majestic spectacle, admirable, and one that the most able pen could only give a feeble impression of![42]

But it was only a matter of days before d'Urville wrote again of a 'monstrous sea', waves that had become 'veritable mountains', and all his books, charts and linen being soaked in his cabin as his 'poor vessel' took in 'seven inches of water in six hours'.[43]

14

New Holland

On the arrival of the French discovery ship Astrolabe, *it was reported
pretty currently that she had not only visited several ports and harbours
on the coast of New Holland, but had actually hoisted the drapeau blanc
at King Georges Sound, Western Port and Jervis' Bay, and taken possession
of these places ... all on board seeing what they could and acquiring as
much knowledge of the coast as they were enabled.*

The Australian*

On 12 September 1826, the day young Benoît Binot drowned, d'Urville made the decision to head for the Western Australian coast and put into King George Sound. 'This place,' he wrote, 'promises me a rich mine to exploit in all fields.'[1] It would be as much a mistake to believe that this was a purely personal decision as it would be to accept the assessment of historian Leslie Marchant that the documents associated with d'Urville's landing point to an accidental and unplanned event.[2] It should be remembered that the comte de Chabrol secretly ordered d'Urville to 'search for anchorages in which the King's ships could find resources in time of war' and for 'a place conducive to the establishment of a colony [to which to] ... deport criminals.'[3] Duperrey had received similar instructions to investigate the Swan River estuary further to the north[4] but had not fulfilled his orders. Even before the *Astrolabe*'s return to France, d'Urville's former subordinate on the *Coquille*, Jules-Alphonse Poret de Blosseville, would single out King George Sound in his report to the minister on a favourable location for a French penal settlement.[5]

Early in the afternoon of 5 October 1826, 19-year-old Jean-Victor Cannac, at work above one of the *Astrolabe*'s topgallants, sighted the Western Australian coast to the northeast. That evening, d'Urville identified Point D'Entrecasteaux and set an easterly course along the coast. Forty-eight hours later, the *Astrolabe* sailed into King George Sound, making land after 108 consecutive days at sea – a sea 'almost always in fury.'[6]

First charted by George Vancouver in September 1791, King George Sound covers over 100 square kilometres, including two inner basins. Although d'Urville particularly wished to enter the western basin – Princess Royal Harbour, where the port of Albany now stands – the winds were unfavourable, so on the morning of 8 October, accompanied by Lottin in the *Astrolabe*'s whaleboat, he entered Oyster Harbour to the north. As they approached Green Island ('Ile du Jardin' on Lottin's chart), 30–40 pelicans took off, leaving their nests unprotected, so d'Urville and his party took about a dozen hapless pelican chicks for their breakfast and for the *Astrolabe*'s larder. D'Urville then made for the shore of Oyster Harbour, where his sailors had reported the smoke of a fire, almost certainly Aboriginal. Here they encountered a man of about 40 years of age, with a long beard, straight black hair, pierced membrane between his nostrils and wearing an animal-skin cloak.[7] D'Urville thought his manner, skin colour and thin limbs very similar to those of the indigenous inhabitants of New South Wales. The man approached the French visitors with a 'quite resolute air', but when d'Urville offered him a piece of bread, he began 'to laugh, dance, sing and call his friends'. He also climbed into the whaleboat without fear and happily went aboard the *Astrolabe*. According to d'Urville, this man 'did not lose, for an instant, his gaiety and his confidence'.[8] Everyone aboard made friends with him, and he was delighted to receive so many presents that he could not hold them all. He also spent the night on board in a bed improvised from sails and tarpaulins. On the shore opposite the *Astrolabe*, a significant number of his kinsman – almost certainly members of the Minang clan of the Nyungar language group – began to congregate. They and others in the bay were also very friendly in their dealings with the French. One, Mokaré,[9] whose portrait was sketched by Sainson,[10] would later play a vital part in fostering peaceful European–Aboriginal relations in the region.[11]

D'Urville appears to have had mixed feelings about Oyster Harbour: 'I assured myself that in case of necessity a ship could anchor in four or five fathoms of water near the Oyster Harbour Channel and would find wood and water close by. But there would be no hunting at all and the north-west winds would be felt with the greatest violence'.[12] More encouraging were Jacquinot's and Lottin's reports of a 'very fine watering place' on the northern bank of the Princess Royal Harbour channel and, nearby, 'a very commodious esplanade' to establish their observatory. D'Urville satisfied himself that 'water and wood were easily available' and concluded that if a vessel was anchored in the channel itself, 'there would only be a cable's length to the watering place'.[13] Indeed, he considered it preferable to Flinders' anchorage near Seal Island. D'Urville saw other possibilities, which leave little doubt that he appraised King George Sound according to his secret orders: 'I have no hesitation but to think that if one wanted to establish a colony here, one would not find a more suitable site than where we have placed our observatory'.[14]

Although d'Urville avoided making other explicit references to a possible French

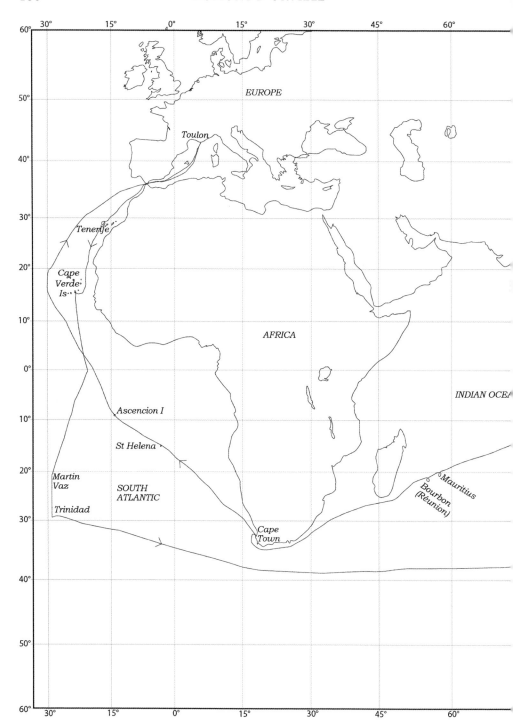

Map 4. The route of the Astrolabe, *25 April 1826 to 26 March 1829*

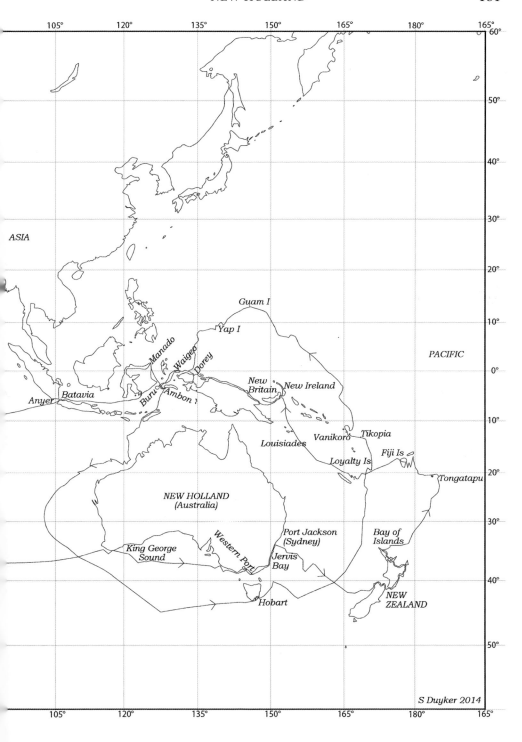

ASIA

Guam I

Yap I

Manado

Waigeo

Dorey

New
Britain

New Ireland

PACIFIC

Buru

Ambon

Batavia

Anyer

Vanikoro

Tikopia

Louisiades

Loyalty Is

Fiji Is

Tongatapu

NEW HOLLAND
(Australia)

Port Jackson
(Sydney)

Bay of
Islands

King George
Sound

Western Port

Jervis
Bay

NEW
ZEALAND

Hobart

S Duyker 2014

settlement in his published account of his sojourn, he did state that 'the soil, despite being sandy, seemed to me susceptible to fertility, if it were carefully cultivated'.[15] With regard to potential irrigation, d'Urville added: '... there are marshy areas concealing springs, the waters of which would be easy to bring together in a canal'.[16] This was not the comment of a captain simply concerned with replenishing his vessel's water supply. As would be expected in an assessment of a potential site for a colony, a survey was undertaken. The concerted and premeditated approach to the task was described by Guilbert in his personal journal: 'Immediately we arrived at the anchorage, the commander designated our geographical work. M. Lottin found himself charged with the large bay. M. Gressien was to draft the plan of Princess Royal Harbour and I, that of Oyster Bay[;] we will then bring together our particular work to form the general plan of the port.'[17] Once again, it is hard to reconcile these deliberate methodical actions with dismissive assertions that d'Urville's visit was accidental or even incidental.

D'Urville was well aware that after Vancouver's discovery of King George Sound in 1791, it had been visited by Matthew Flinders, Nicolas Baudin and twice by Phillip Parker King. There were unmistakable signs of European timber cutting, but d'Urville could not be certain of more recent visitors until 12 October. Late on that evening, the *Astrolabe* received a surprise visit from a boat manned by a party of sealers. They had been left by the schooner *Governor Brisbane* eight months earlier when their captain, Samuel Nolbrow, had apparently sailed for the Netherlands East Indies and not returned. Numbering eight men, they were mainly English, but one was a Māori from Kerikeri in the Bay of Islands. Although they spoke of peaceful relations with the local Aboriginal community, d'Urville did not know whether the two Aboriginal women who had joined them on Breaksea Island had done so freely. D'Urville was particularly interested in the question of relations with the indigenous inhabitants, almost certainly because of their likely attitude to any future French colonists. This was another issue the comte de Chabrol expected him to address. His own expedition's experience had certainly been positive and friendly. Although the sealers from the *Governor Brisbane* had managed to survive by fishing and seemed eager to escape their privations by joining the *Astrolabe*, their reticence in accepting d'Urville's offer of passage to Port Jackson led him to suspect that some were escaped convicts. Only three of the sealers took up the offer: one to work his passage and the other two to go as passengers to New South Wales; the rest chose to remain at King George Sound.[18]

On 17 October, another two whaleboats were sighted near Observatory Island; they were from the schooner *Hunter*. Once again, d'Urville faced the entreaties of men who wished to join the *Astrolabe*. Anxious about his diminishing stores as well as what a dozen 'audacious and determined' men might do at night, he accepted half the sailors from one boat and only one from the other, a 'coloured' Canadian

'Vue du Port du Roi Georges, Nouvelle-Hollande', lithograph by Victor-Jean Adam and Louis-Julien Jacottet, from a sketch by Louis-Auguste de Sainson, Voyage de la corvette l'Astrolabe, Atlas historique, *Paris, 1833, plate 16. D'Urville visited King George Sound, Western Australia, in October 1826, armed with secret orders to search for the location for a potential French penal colony.* National Library of Australia PIC U1725 NK3340

named Richard Symons, who impressed d'Urville with his ability to speak French.[19] Two days later, the same whaleboats returned bearing 'fish, petrels, oysters, a female seal, a small possum and several blue penguins',[20] all of which were exchanged for a small quantity of gunpowder and rope yarn. These animals were acquired for both victualling and natural history purposes. The trading session even had ethnographic significance, because this time the party comprised two young Tasmanian Aboriginal women (from near Port Dalrymple), a young man and a young woman from the South Australian coast near Kangaroo Island, and an eight-year-old girl from King George Sound. All were interviewed by Gaimard to record as many words of their respective languages as possible.[21] D'Urville and Faraguet would also record Aboriginal words at King George Sound. All these vocabularies were later published in the second volume of the expedition's philological account compiled by Dumont d'Urville.[22] In the case of King George Sound, d'Urville would augment the expedition's consolidated list with words collected in 1826–31 by Isaac Scott Nind, surgeon with the 39th Dorsetshire Regiment, and published in the *Journal of the Royal Geographical Society of London* in 1831.

The Tasmanian women kept their heads close-shaven, so d'Urville could not discern what kind of hair they had. It seems likely that he had read Bory de Saint-Vincent's entry on 'Man' in the eighth volume of the *Dictionnaire classique d'histoire naturelle.*

(D'Urville was mentioned several times in this dictionary entry, so curiosity, genuine scientific interest and perhaps even vanity are likely to have drawn him to its pages.) Bory de Saint-Vincent, who it will be remembered had named the genus *Durvillea* in d'Urville's honour, was a polygenist who considered the Tasmanians 'frizzy [haired] *Mélanien[s]*'[23] and members of a separate human species, '*Homo Melaninus*'![24] The residents of the Australian mainland belonged, in his judgement, to yet another species, '*Homo Australasicus*', who had 'hair neither frizzy nor woolly'.[25] Although d'Urville would coin the geographical term 'Mélanesie' from Bory de Saint-Vincent's term 'Mélanien', he did not accept his polygenist ideas that divided humanity into separate species.[26] However, d'Urville believed that the Australian mainland was inhabited by more than one race and he appears to have based this on his own aesthetic prejudices and comparative observations. This is evident in his description of the young South Australian couple he met at King George Sound: 'These two, fairly well proportioned, have a much darker hue, regular features, rather beautiful eyes and very smooth black hair; they are far from being repulsive like most of the natives of Australia and seem to belong to a less degraded race [*une race moins dégradée*].'[27] What did d'Urville mean by 'degraded race'? It is possible that he implied the 'degeneration' and racial differences envisaged by Georges-Louis Buffon[28] and Johann Friedrich Blumenbach[29] as a result of climate, environment and nutrition. Clearly, d'Urville did not link darkness of skin colour to any intrinsic *dégradation* – the word in French also has a specific meaning with regard to the graduation or scaling of colour from dark to light in painting – because the South Australian Aborigines encountered by the expedition had 'a much darker hue' yet were supposedly 'less degraded'.

In his official instructions, reference was made to d'Urville's knowledge of the 'great progress of the inhabitants of the Society Islands in civilisation, in morality and in industry' and alluded to the value of such 'points of comparison', not only for the public in general but 'for those who specifically study the path that savage people follow leaving their primitive condition, to reach the perfect state of civilisation'.[30] D'Urville did make comparisons between the indigenous people of King George Sound and those he had seen in New South Wales – the only other 'Australians' (his preferred term) that he had met. Although one should be cautious attributing the sentiments of a fictional character to an author himself, in d'Urville's unpublished novel, *Les Zélandais ou histoire australienne*, the Māori Koroké acknowledges the admirable qualities of the Aborigines near Sydney. They are not cannibals and do not make human sacrifices; 'they are gentle, tranquil and humane'. Yet he considers them ugly inferior beings: 'their features are hideous, their limbs deformed and, on reaching a certain age, some of them seem to tend more towards brute than man'. Worse, Koroké presents them living harsh, intellectually intractable lives and incapable of social advancement:

In spite of the example of Europeans and the advantages that civilisation offers them, in spite of the efforts of the English to lead them to more gentle and sociable ways, they have persisted in their wandering and precarious lives and none of them appears to have been tempted to renounce it. Only those who live near the towns have covered their loins with rags and they roam the streets of Sydney and Parramatta, begging bread and especially a kind of strong liquor from white people, which they crave although it … robs them entirely of the little reason that nature has given them.[31]

The *Astrolabe*'s visit to King George Sound would not yield any significant new contributions to d'Urville's other great passion: botany. Indeed, there would be no account of Western Australian flora in the botanical volume of the expedition published by Pierre-Adolphe Lesson and Achille Richard in 1832. This was mainly because King George Sound had already been well explored by the Scottish botanist Robert Brown during his visit with Matthew Flinders in December 1801.[32] D'Urville, in his own account, mentions only a few genera already familiar to him from his visit to New South Wales, including *Eucalyptus*, *Banksia*[33] and *Xanthorrhoea*.[34] However, Lesson did collect the previously unknown 'downy' *Stackhousia pubescens* at King George Sound, and its description was published in the expedition's botanical volume.[35] From a zoological perspective, the sojourn was more significant. Aside from numerous mollusca, Quoy and Gaimard collected the type specimens of several birds found at King George Sound, whose descriptions they published in 1830. These included the white-breasted robin (*Eopsaltira georgiana*), the splendid fairy wren (*Malurus splendens*) and the Australian ringneck parrot (*Barnardius zonarius semitorquatus*).[36]

With repairs to the *Astrolabe* finished, fresh water replenished and Jacquinot's astronomical and magnetic declination observations completed ashore,[37] on 25 October the expedition departed from King George Sound, making final soundings between the mainland and Breaksea and Michaelmas islands before entering the Southern Ocean. Originally, d'Urville had been instructed to visit Port Dalrymple in Van Diemen's Land. He had been expected to arrive there around 25 August so was already two months behind schedule. His provisions were greatly diminished – on 1 November he found that more than half of his nearly 300 remaining tins of Appert preserved meat were putrefied and had to be thrown overboard – and he feared further delay entering the difficult channel from Bass Strait to reach the British settlement of Port Dalrymple. He was also concerned about being distracted entertaining resident colonists, so instead he decided to sail to Western Port Bay on the southeastern Australian mainland. This was still within the bounds of his flexible secret orders – just as King George Sound had been – to search for potential strategic anchorages and the site for a penal colony. He considered Western Port still 'very incompletely

known',[38] despite George Bass's pioneering survey in the whaleboat *Tom Thumb* in
1798, James Grant's and John Murray's respective surveys aboard the *Lady Nelson* in
1801, and Hamelin's visit in April 1802 (after the *Naturaliste*'s separation from Baudin's
Géographe).[39] Perhaps more attractive was the knowledge that Western Port Bay had
no formal European settlers, save perhaps occasional sealers.

On 4 November, as the *Astrolabe* completed her traverse of the Great Australian
Bight, her crew celebrated the feast of Saint Charles Borromeo, patron saint of King
Charles X, with coffee at breakfast, double rations of wine at dinner and punch after
supper. D'Urville noted, with apparent amusement, that two of his new recruits, the
Canadian Richard Symons and another man from the *Hunter* named Cloney, took
a very active part in the festivities. On 7 November, the southern Australian coast
near Mount Gambier was sighted. Cape Otway was sighted four days later, and on
12 November, after a night battling the westerly current off Cape Schanck, d'Urville
entered Western Port Bay and anchored off the north coast of Phillip Island. D'Urville
believed he had been guided to Flinders' anchorage by another of his new British
recruits, a man identified as 'Hambilton', but Flinders never entered Western Port (he
only skirted the bay's eastern and western entrances aboard the *Investigator* in May
1802), and the anchorage on his chart was that of Bass or Grant.

No sooner had the *Astrolabe* anchored than she was visited by a group of sealers.
Their leader presented his papers to d'Urville for inspection, but the latter returned
them without looking at them, remarking that they were not within his jurisdiction
and that, like his own expedition, they could consider themselves 'perfectly free on this
deserted soil, until now unoccupied'.[40] This was in fact a pointed political statement.
D'Urville was as much rejecting any purported British permission for the sealers to
pursue their labours in Western Port as he was reaffirming the French government's
view (of a nation in search of a site for a colony of its own) that the bay was officially un-
colonised and under no European authority. In referring to '*sol désert*', d'Urville also
conveniently ignored the sealers' huts and gardens and effectively affirmed a doctrine
of *terra nullius*, negating the rights of the indigenous people of the area. The local
Boonwurrung people were not encountered during the *Astrolabe*'s visit – d'Urville
suspected that the presence of the sealers had something to do with this – but their
numerous bark shelters were observed, and some skulls and other human remains
were collected for Quoy. The fact that, on one occasion, the sealers assumed that the
French had been attacked by the Aborigines and that it was necessary to go to the
aid of the visitors when there was no such attack – indeed no encounter of any kind –
suggests heightened suspicion and strained ongoing relations with the Boonwurrung.
D'Urville later learned of violence between the two groups and the death of one of
the sealers, who had five Tasmanian Aboriginal women with them. Whether these

'Habitation de pêcheurs de phoques au Port Western (Nouvelle-Hollande)', lithograph by Langlumé, figures by Victor-Jean Adam, from a sketch by Louis-Auguste de Sainson, Voyage de la corvette l'Astrolabe, Atlas historique, Paris, 1833, plate 21. The Astrolabe's visit to Western Port heightened British anxieties about French colonial intentions in southern Australia. This lithograph, published two years before the founding of Melbourne, is (with plate 20 of the Atlas historique) one of the two earliest printed images of any part of Victoria. State Library of Victoria

women had been abducted is unclear, but their very presence at Western Port (like King George Sound) raises questions about the manner in which sealers related to the indigenous people along Bass Strait.

D'Urville's first landfall was near Mangrove Creek, on the eastern shore of Western Port. There are large tidal mudflats in this area, and d'Urville also noticed volcanic rocks on the shore: the Oligocene basaltic lava flows in the vicinity of Western Port are in places more than 600 metres thick. Beyond the mangroves, d'Urville entered the thick coastal scrub comprising *Banksia*, *Eucalyptus*, *Casuarina*, *Podocarpus*, *Leptospermum* and *Dampieria*. During the *Astrolabe*'s week-long sojourn at Western Port, Jacquinot and Lottin conducted astronomical observations to determine the coordinates of the bay. Meanwhile, Quoy and Gaimard gathered numerous natural history specimens. Although several birds were collected, most were already familiar to science. One, however, proved to be the type specimen of a subspecies of the silvereye (*Zosterops lateralis westernensis*), a tiny passerine familiar to most Australians and

New Zealanders.[41] Six new species of beetle[42] and a member of the order Hemiptera, *Lygaeus pacificus* (*Spilostethus pacificus*), were also discovered at Western Port, very possibly as a result of d'Urville's personal collecting efforts. In the bay itself, Quoy and Gaimard collected numerous mollusca and the type specimens of a sea-squirt, *Clavelina cylindrica*,[43] a species now the subject of interest for the unusual alkaloids it produces; the southern calamari (*Sepioteuthis australis*); the krake or webfoot octopus (*Octopus membranaceus*); and the air-breathing sea snail or false limpet, *Siphonaria denticulata* – all of which they later described and published.[44] However, the discovery that excited them the most was a live specimen of the bivalve *Trigonia pectinata* (*Neotrigonia pectinata*). A shell from this genus, first collected by Péron in Van Diemen's Land during the Baudin expedition and later described by Lamarck,[45] had caused great excitement because it had hitherto been thought to exist only as a fossil. Quoy and Gaimard prized their living fossil so much that when the *Astrolabe* was later threatened by the reefs of Tongatapu, it was the only specimen they took when it appeared that they might have to abandon the ship.[46]

Early on the morning of 19 November, the *Astrolabe* set sail and tacked between Phillip Island and the rocks off the mainland before being drawn out of Western Port by the ebbing tide. Wilsons Promontory was sighted at first light the following day. Aware of anomalies between the charts of Flinders and Freycinet with regard to the location of Rodondo Island and the Crocodile Reef in Bass Strait, d'Urville charged Gressien with making a determination; Flinders was upheld over Freycinet. After entering the Tasman Sea, the *Astrolabe* made for Cape Howe and then surveyed the coast between Twofold Bay and Cape Dromedary from a distance of five and a half kilometres. The landscape below Mount Dromedary revived frustrations for the botanist in d'Urville, but there was no time to explore its 'delicious glades'.[47] It was only when contrary winds frustrated the expedition's northward progress between Cape St George and Point Perpendicular that d'Urville decided that a visit to Jervis Bay would be more productive than time at sea.

At 2.30 pm on 26 November, the *Astrolabe* rounded rugged Bowen Island and a half-hour later dropped anchor in the southern part of the bay. Jacquinot and Lottin set up an observatory on what is now Hole-in-the-Wall Beach and also established friendly relations with the indigenous people. During their visit, Gaimard would record a vocabulary of 158 Wandandian Aboriginal words at Jervis Bay.[48] Meanwhile, d'Urville commenced a preliminary examination of the local flora and fauna. The following day, he charged all his ensigns with the task of surveying Jervis Bay. On 28 November, gale-force winds from the north continued to thwart their departure for Port Jackson, so d'Urville allowed all his officers to go ashore on condition that they did not venture far and were prepared to return at the first signal from the *Astrolabe*.

During their stay, members of the crew cast nets and caught many fish, sharing part of their catch (actually less-desirable species such as shark and trigger fish) with the local Wandandian people. Two crew members also went line fishing off Bowen Island and caught about 100 kilograms of fish per day. Furthermore, the rocks yielded oysters and other delectable shellfish. According to d'Urville, this abundant food probably accounted for the local Aborigines being 'less ugly, more vigorous, and above all better proportioned' than those of Port Jackson. He considered them to have 'a degree of intelligence superior to any he knew',[49] and he was also impressed by their oblong, beehive-shaped bark huts covered in seagrass, which were clean and spacious enough to accommodate a family of eight to ten. He admired the drawings of 'cutters and longboats' on the sandstone, considering them 'quite well sketched'. In his opinion, these were people who displayed 'a probity, a gentleness and even a circumspection very remarkable for this class of men'.[50] Despite the latent racism still evident in his comments, it would seem that the more Aboriginal people he met (especially those who lived traditional lives), the more he esteemed them.

'*Baie Jervis, Nouvelle Hollande, les marins de l'*Astrolabe *partagent leur pêche avec les naturels'*, *lithograph by Victor-Jean Adam, from a sketch by Louis-Auguste de Sainson,* Voyage de la corvette l'Astrolabe, Atlas historique, *plate 34. The* Astrolabe *visited Jervis Bay, New South Wales, in November 1826. During the visit, members of the crew caught a large number of fish, sharing part of their catch with the local Wandandian people. Surgeon Gaimard also recorded a vocabulary of 158 Wandandian words.* National Library of Australia, PIC U1743 NK3340

The *Astrolabe* resumed her voyage on the morning of 29 November, but continued contrary (at times even gale-force) winds made for a slow passage to Port Jackson, which she entered on the morning of 2 December. D'Urville received a very warm reception from Captain Piper, who invited him to dinner that evening, along with Jacquinot and Lottin. Like Duperrey, d'Urville anchored in front of Fort Macquarie, where the Sydney Opera House now stands. Three British warships were also at anchor nearby: HMS *Warspite*, HMS *Volage* and HMS *Success*. *Warspite*'s commander, Commodore James Brisbane, a cousin of former Governor Thomas Brisbane, was too ill to call on d'Urville (he died 17 days later of dysentery), but Captain Richard Dundas of the *Volage* and James Sterling of the *Success* promptly offered their services. Sterling would later play a major part in the colonisation of the Swan River in 1828 and became a future governor of Western Australia – events, as we shall see, directly related to British perceptions of French intentions in the area.

Early on the afternoon of his arrival, d'Urville made his own courtesy call on Governor Ralph Darling, Thomas Brisbane's successor in New South Wales, whom he described as 'an elderly man of quite cold politeness'.[51] Darling had earlier been military commander and acting governor of Mauritius, and had been very unpopular for allowing a British frigate (HMS *Topaze*) to breach quarantine and start an epidemic of cholera. He then suspended Port Louis' newly established municipal council when it protested his actions.[52] In New South Wales, despite initiating numerous important administrative reforms, he also gained a reputation for severity and contempt for civil liberties and democratic institutions. Ten days before d'Urville's arrival, Darling had drummed out of the 57th Regiment two soldiers – privates Joseph Sudds and Patrick Thompson – who had deliberately committed theft (a transportable offence) in order to leave the army and settle in Australia. He also illegally increased their sentences to seven years' hard labour and had them both put in leg irons and collars. Unfortunately for Darling, five days later (just before d'Urville left Jervis Bay), Sudds died in custody and there was uproar in New South Wales and eventually in Britain.[53] Among the governor's fiercest opponents were the barrister-journalists William Charles Wentworth and Robert Wardell, who together owned the newspaper *The Australian*. Significantly, on Wednesday 6 December 1826, after reporting the *Astrolabe*'s landfalls in King George Sound, Western Port and Jervis Bay, and mischievously asserting that France had taken possession of them 'with a view to forming settlements', *The Australian* then linked French interest in the region to the struggle for civil liberties in New South Wales, declaring:

> It might render England fearful of quarrelling with us, [and] incline her, in conse-
> quence, to treat us not only with common fairness but with magnanimity. It would

induce her to give us government to our liking and a Constitution that we could revere and teach others to revere. She would be afraid to quarrel with us if we had the scion of a foreign power near us.[54]

The British, however, did not need two braying democrats in Sydney to underline strategic imperatives in the region. The government was already well aware of plans for d'Urville's expedition long before its departure. Not only had d'Urville written to Vice-Admiral Thomas Manby (on 9 December 1825), alerting him to his impending voyage, he also wrote to Phillip Parker King seeking advice.[55] In mid-December, the comte de Chabrol had asked baron Maxence de Damas, the minister for foreign affairs, to obtain a passport for the expedition from London; it was received in Paris on 31 January 1826.[56] In London, the French consul's quest for charts and atlases from the expeditions of Flinders and King would also have been strongly suggestive of French interest in New Holland, and finally, the British ambassador in Paris, Lord Granville Leveson-Gower, very likely had his own informants at the French court.

It would seem that news of the *Astrolabe*'s imminent departure from Toulon and perhaps knowledge of d'Urville's general orders (in the wake of the French navy's other recent expeditions) precipitated a British response aimed at preventing France from gaining a toehold on the Australian continent. On 1 March 1826, the secretary of state for war and the colonies, Lord Bathurst, wrote twice to Governor Darling. In his first letter, he instructed Darling to prepare for the establishment of a settlement at Western Port.[57] In a second letter (marked 'private'), Bathurst wrote:

The sailing of Two French Ships on a Voyage of Discovery ... led to the considera-tion how far our distant possessions in the Australian Seas may be prejudiced by any designs which the French may entertain of establishing themselves in that quarter, and more especially on that part of the coast of New South Wales, which has not as yet received any colonists from this country. I allude to that line of Coast, which extends to the Westward from the Western point of Bathurst Island in 129° East Longitude, where the North West boundary of the New South Wales Government has been lately fixed ... As this tract of shore is understood to be for the most part barren and devoid of all circumstances, which could invite a settlement, it is proba-ble, if the French Government should entertain any serious intention of forming an Establishment on that side of the Continent of New Holland, that so advantageous a port as Western Port would not be neglected by them; and it is therefore with a view of avoiding any pretensions, to which the touching at that Port of either of the Discovery Ships in question, might give rise for the formation of a Settlement there, that your attention has been so earnestly directed to the formation of a Colony at that place in the manner and for the objects pointed out in my Instructions. In giving that Instruction, you will observe that I have carefully avoided any expression which might be construed (in the event of the Instructions being hereafter referred to) as an admission of there not having been a preoccupancy by us before the French may have admitted to establish themselves there; and you will regulate your language accordingly. The Establishment to be formed at Shark Bay, is, as you are aware, partly for a different object, but it is equally necessary that our projects in that quarter should not be anticipated.[58]

D'Urville sailed with only one vessel, so Bathurst's reference to 'Two French Ships on a Voyage of Discovery' may have been a collective reference to the expeditions of the *Coquille* and the *Astrolabe*, or to the *Thétis* and the *Espérance*, under the command of Hyacinthe de Bougainville. Although the latter two vessels spent almost three months at Port Jackson in 1825, they were well on their way home by the time Lord Bathurst wrote to Governor Darling.[59]

On 11 March 1826, Lord Bathurst wrote an additional letter to Darling asking him to survey for a settlement at King George Sound rather than Shark Bay.[60] Darling obeyed his orders, and on 9 November, HMS *Fly* sailed from Sydney under the command of Captain Wetherall, in company with the brigs *Dragon* and *Amity*, to establish settlements at Western Port and King George Sound.[61] Aboard the *Dragon* was Captain Samuel Wright of the 'Buffs' – yet another veteran of the bloody Battle of Albuera and presumably an officer unlikely to be sentimental in his dealings with the French[62] – in charge of a party of 20 soldiers and 20 convicts. They reached Western Port on 24 November, very likely passing the *Astrolabe* on the way.[63] Had they found the French at Western Port, Wright was ordered by Darling to 'signify that their Continuance, with any view of Establishing themselves or Colonisation, would be considered an unjustifiable intrusion on His Britannic Majesty's Possessions'. He was also ordered to 'warn them immediately to desist from any such attempt [at colonisation], as their perseverance must be attended with unpleasant consequences, and might interrupt that harmony, which it is so desirable should be preserved inviolate between the two Countries'.[64] Aboard the *Amity* was Major Edmund Lockyer, bearing similar orders and in charge of a detachment of soldiers and a party of 24 convicts. They arrived at King George Sound on Christmas Day 1826 and landed the next day to establish a settlement.[65] Although Leslie Marchant, in *France Australe*, appears to have considered Lord Bathurst's orders to establish settlements to have been coincidental, the very nature of those orders suggests that the British had accurate intelligence (or at the very least had made a shrewd guess) on where d'Urville was likely to call and for what reason. If so, it is hard to escape the conclusion that the *Astrolabe* expedition played a very real part in precipitating pre-emptive British colonisation of Western Australia and Victoria.

Two days after d'Urville's arrival in New South Wales, Governor Darling informed him of HMS *Fly*'s mission. On 4 December 1826, in a letter to Robert William Hay, under-secretary for the colonies in London, Darling reported on what he had gleaned of the voyage of the *Astrolabe* and of d'Urville's declared intentions (which he appears not to have accepted):

> I find that she touched on her way out, both at King George's Sound and Western
> Port, having remained six days at the latter; but Captain D'Urville would lead me to
> believe that the object of his Expedition is solely for the purposes of general science.
> He has applied for Stores, which will be supplied, and for assistance in refitting his
> Ship. He has intimated his intention, as soon as this is accomplished, of proceeding
> to New Zealand; and I should not be surprized to find that the French have some
> intention of establishing themselves there, from the wish he affected to express, that
> we had, or surprize, that we had not, made a Settlement at those Islands. It is per-
> haps a fortunate event that he has found His Majesty's Ships *Warspite*, *Success* and
> *Volage* lying here, knowing at the same time that the *Fly* has sailed with the Expedi-
> tion Southward, as he may in Consequence be more circumspect in his proceedings
> than he otherwise would have been.[66]

Although Darling informed d'Urville that he had taken steps to establish colonies at both King George Sound and Western Port, the governor appeared to exhibit 'considerable anxiety'[67] when d'Urville informed him that he had no knowledge of this and had not encountered the settlement parties en route. Clearly, Lord Bathurst's political message would have been more potent if d'Urville had actually *seen* a British settlement in either, or both, ports. Any apparent anxiety or disappointment Darling had regarding this question was very likely tempered by the fact that he knew that his government was in earnest.

The departure of three vessels to establish settlements at King George Sound and Western Port not only negated the value of d'Urville's survey work on the Western Australian and Victorian coasts, it also put pressure on available resources at Port Jackson. The competing demands of three other British men-of-war in the harbour made refitting and re-supplying the *Astrolabe* more difficult, and in addition, d'Urville had great difficulty finding skilled shipwrights and sufficient caulking. Somehow he was able to scrounge what he needed to replace a rotting plank that had allowed water to leak into the hull on the *Astrolabe*'s starboard side. Similarly, two urgently needed cables were supplied from the government store, despite Governor Darling's equivocation that necessitated sourcing additional back-ups privately. D'Urville also purchased 6000 kilograms of English biscuits from the colonial administration. They had travelled all the way from Europe and were already infested with weevils, but d'Urville thought them better quality than those produced by Sydney bakers. With patience and persuasion, he also obtained vegetables, tobacco, salt, rum, salted meat, coffee, sugar, coal (for his cooking stoves and ovens) and fresh water. D'Urville declared that the *Astrolabe* left New South Wales as well provisioned as when she had sailed from France.

D'Urville found Sydney had grown visibly since his visit just three years before, but to his surprise, there was still little progress in the construction of the Catholic church, which he had noted soon after his arrival aboard the *Coquille*.[68] Sainson would sketch a number of Sydney scenes, including Government House and a view of George Street from what is now Grosvenor Street, with d'Urville's Aboriginal acquaintance Bungaree in the foreground.[69] Despite the colony's evident growth, drought had afflicted the countryside, and bushfires burned in numerous areas: *plus ça change*! D'Urville was also disappointed to learn that his friend the botanist Allan Cunningham was away visiting New Zealand. However, he did make new friends, such as the French-speaking, Corsican-born police chief, Francis Nicolas Rossi, whose previous posting had been in Mauritius. He was also able to renew his friendship with the Reverend Samuel Marsden in Parramatta. At dinner at the home of the new colonial secretary and fellow entomologist, Alexander McLeay, d'Urville used the evening as an opportunity to gather further intelligence on New Zealand from Marsden. In his published account, d'Urville boasted of 'imperceptibly' returning Marsden's dinner conversation to the subject of New Zealand and confirming what he had already read in the missionary's published accounts. However, judging from Darling's comments to Under-Secretary Hay in his letter of 4 December, d'Urville was not as 'imperceptible' or subtle as he thought he was. The following day, Marsden lunched with d'Urville aboard the *Astrolabe*, bringing with him a pale-eyed man with a rounded nose and large mouth: the Reverend Frederick Wilkinson, the new Anglican assistant chaplain. Wilkinson gave d'Urville letters for missionaries in Tonga and, surprisingly, the skulls and bones of an Aboriginal adult and child, presumably for Quoy's anthropological collection. The return of such bones, taken with dubious authority by men such as Wilkinson, d'Urville and Quoy, remains a vexed issue for indigenous communities and museums around the world.

Given the brevity of the *Astrolabe*'s visit to Port Jackson and the limited opportunities for significant excursions beyond the town, it is not surprising that there were few significant entomological[70] and botanical results – it was very late in the season to collect flowering plants. Nevertheless, it is apparent that d'Urville now had a broader ecological vision, since he supplied insect specimens to Jean-Baptiste de Boisduval with important habitat notes on particular insect-plant associations.[71] In the animal kingdom, a specimen from the Cucumariidae (sea cucumber family) that Quoy and Gaimard collected in Port Jackson and named *Holothuria spinosa*[72] is worthy of comment. In 1946, the French zoologist Gustave Cherbonnier used it as the type specimen for an entirely new genus, *Plesiocolochirus*.[73]

Just before leaving Port Jackson, d'Urville entrusted Alexander McLeay with his report to the minister of the navy and colonies, under cover of a letter to the French ambassador in London. It is not present in French archives and its fate is unknown. However, we know it contained a request for promotions for several of his officers (and the expectation of a reply in Ambon, which was not fulfilled).[74] We can assume it also contained an account of the expedition's Australian survey work and perhaps even a disheartening statement of Darling's actions to establish British colonies where France might soon have done.

D'Urville had dined with Darling on 13 December and returned again on 16 December to make his farewells. Leaving aside subliminal anger at being thwarted by Darling, it is abundantly clear that d'Urville did not warm to the governor as a man and that he could not help but contrast him with his predecessors Brisbane and Macquarie. Opening his chapter on the present state of the colony of New South Wales, d'Urville wrote that Darling

> … enjoyed the reputation of a just, but very severe man; and I readily saw that he was little-liked. In fact, in the few meetings I had with him, he appeared to me to have a dryness of character, a stiffness of manner and a form of austerity which must have been all the more unsuitable in his position, given that these kinds of negative qualities are rarely encountered in the English of a certain rank, without being mitigated by gracious etiquette. Without doubt, I did not receive anything but politeness on the part of the new governor, but I did not encounter in him the distinguished manners and the courtesy of M. Brisbane, even less the obliging good will and careful consideration that M. Macquarie lavished on the officers of the *Uranie*.[75]

After recapturing two deserters, d'Urville set sail for New Zealand on 17 December. Aboard the *Astrolabe*, he now had an Australian crew member: a cockatoo purchased in Port Jackson, which he described as 'malicious'.[76] During his visit to New Ireland, it would break the *Astrolabe*'s precious marine barometer, and Lesson would later write sarcastically that 'it was the same friendly bird' that made d'Urville laugh uproariously when it grabbed with its beak 'a toe or the heel of a member of the crew'.[77] Singularly devoted to d'Urville, it died at sea a year later.

15

Return to New Zealand

Each to his business, tending ropes and gear,
navigating or cooking, keeping log,
fulfilling in each act our sacrament
and simple story … A.R.D. Fairburn *

D'Urville was full of anticipation and excitement as the *Astrolabe* began her traverse of the Tasman Sea. The Dutch explorer Abel Tasman had charted much of the west coast of New Zealand in 1642 – not realising that he had coasted two islands separated by a strait.[1] James Cook, during six months of running survey that began in late October 1769, circumnavigated the North and South islands and discovered the strait now named in his honour. Many parts of his survey, however, required more detail. There had also been brief visits by the French expeditions of Jean-François-Marie de Surville, Marion Dufresne and d'Entrecasteaux, but they made only localised coastal contributions to the cartography of New Zealand. D'Urville saw an opportunity to contribute precise surveys of major sections of the coast. 'An immense prospect,' he wrote, 'unfolded before us, offering us the least known places and the most vaguely traced coasts in all the Pacific Ocean as an objective.'[2] The past bloody history of contact with New Zealand Māori also bore warnings. D'Urville began to drill his men in gunnery and the use of small arms, lest they fall victim to a surprise Māori attack, as did Marion Dufresne's expedition in 1772,[3] and the passengers and crew of the *Boyd* in 1809.[4]

On Christmas Day 1826, despite its being mid-summer in the southern hemisphere, the weather became cold and wet, and deteriorated into one of the violent storms for which the Tasman Sea is so notorious. D'Urville thought it comparable to the worst of winter weather in France. As a result of the unfavourable winds, the *Astrolabe* made little significant progress. For a time, as d'Urville contemplated human feebleness in the face of such potent natural forces, his buoyant optimism deteriorated into melancholy depression.

---

* 'The Voyage' (1952), verse xi

The New Year of 1827 brought calm weather, and d'Urville returned to measuring sea-water temperatures at depth. Originally he had ambitions to sail to Chalky Inlet, a fiord on the southwestern tip of the South Island, and then to survey the entire west coast of the island before fulfilling his orders in Cook Strait and on the coast of the North Island. However, after more than a fortnight of uselessly battling the elements in the Tasman, d'Urville decided to proceed directly to Cook Strait to begin his survey from Cape Farewell. Ironically, on 14 January 1827, he realised that the *Astrolabe* had already been drawn directly towards the cape. As the coast became visible, he recognised significant differences with Cook's charts:

> Advancing towards the south, we saw that the vast bay between Cape Farewell on one side and that of Cape Stephens on the other, and which Cook named Blind Bay on his first voyage, is divided into two very distinct basins by a remarkable point that I have named *Pointe de Séparation* [Separation Point]. The basin to the west [Golden Bay], that Cook named Massacre Bay,[5] is only vaguely traced on our map, because at the distance we passed, we could only grasp a general view. On the contrary, the southern basin, for which I have retained the name Tasman Bay according to Cook's second voyage, became the object of our particular attention …[6]

At 4.00 pm on 14 January, the *Astrolabe* dropped anchor off Separation Point. The next day, the position of the newly discovered promontory was fixed by Ensign Guilbert, who went ashore with the whaleboat, accompanied by the naturalists Quoy and Gaimard and Midshipman Dudemaine. On their return, d'Urville was furious to learn that members of Guilbert's boat crew had found a number of empty Māori huts and had taken items from them. He was convinced that similar actions had provoked Māori violence in the past. Although he decided that it was impractical to return the stolen artefacts, he threatened severe punishment for any repeat offence and confiscated all the objects for the royal collection.[7]

The *Astrolabe* continued her pioneering survey of the coast of Tasman Bay. On the afternoon of 15 January, Dudemaine appears to have sighted the valley of the Motueka River from the crosstrees. That evening, the *Astrolabe* anchored northeast of Moutere Bluff. Close to the southern limit of Tasman Bay, the next day she approached its eastern coast and anchored off Wakapuaka (just north of present-day Nelson).[8] Here she was approached by two canoes bearing a mixture of high-ranking and other Māori (presumably Ngāti Tumatakokiri). D'Urville called out to them in Māori: 'Come on board ship; we are friends.' After some initial hesitation, they did come aboard and were warmly welcomed. D'Urville soon found that he could communicate using the vocabulary compiled by missionaries such as Thomas Kendall. The only difference was pronunciation of some words rather than their meaning.

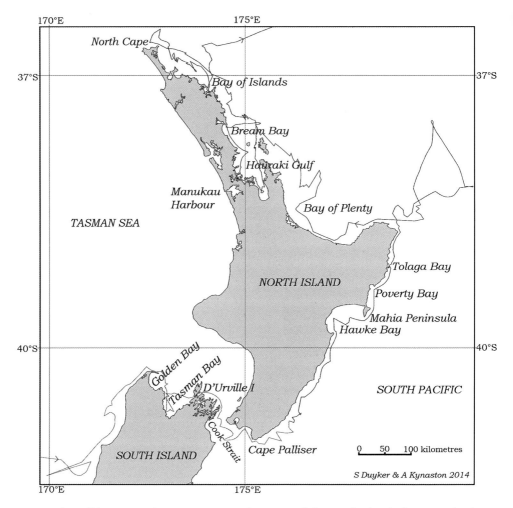

Map 5. D'Urville's surveys of Tasman Bay, Cook Strait and the North Island of New Zealand, January–March 1827, during the first Astrolabe *voyage.*

Although the local Māori appeared to have some comprehension of the power of firearms – in the hands of raiding rival iwi (tribes) from the northwest, whom they hoped the French would 'kill and eat'![9] – they had little knowledge of Europeans or of metal. One Māori traded a fine flax cloak for an old blue shirt, having first refused to exchange it for 'beautiful axes and even a sword'.[10] D'Urville was impressed by their bearing, honesty and trust. Despite considering these Māori 'incontestably very inferior both in industry and culture to those of the North Island, of which they are probably mere colonies',[11] his explanatory reasons are noteworthy, since they confirm once again that he did not see intellectual and cultural development constrained by racial characteristics: 'A less productive soil, a more rigorous climate, and much greater privations have prevented the human race from reaching the same development and forming such powerful tribes here as has been done on Ika-Na-Mawi [North Island].'[12] Four Māori remained aboard overnight, and their kin returned in three canoes the following day to trade once again.

Further to the north, still on the eastern side of Tasman Bay, d'Urville located other possible anchorages off Pepin Island (named in honour of his wife's family) and in Croisilles Harbour (after his mother's family) but decided to return to the western side of the bay to what appeared to be a safe anchorage between the coast and two small offshore islands sighted on 15 January. The larger of these islands ('Motuarero-nui') was named Adele Island in honour of his wife. With Lottin sounding the way ahead, the *Astrolabe* entered the channel and, just after 6.00 pm on 16 January, dropped anchor between Adele Island and the coast. The channel is still called Astrolabe Roadstead in honour of d'Urville's anchorage.

On 17 January d'Urville set his men to work ashore. Jacquinot and Lottin established an observatory on present-day Observatory Beach,[13] while Guilbert and Dudemaine commenced further surveys of Tasman Bay. Meanwhile, d'Urville, accompanied by Lesson and the sailor Charles Simonet, went ashore at the expedition's 'aiguade' (present-day Watering Cove)[14] to pursue natural history specimens. He recorded that he was able to collect at least seven birds, and it would appear that two of these (published by Quoy and Gaimard) would prove to be new species: the grey gerygone (*Curruca igata*),[15] belonging to the Acanthizidae or thornbill family, and the New Zealand fernbird (*Bowdleria punctata*), belonging to the Sylviidae or old-world warbler family.[16] Although few plants were in flower, in the days that followed, d'Urville gathered three entirely new species in Tasman Bay; these would be named in his honour by botanist Achille Richard: *Pimelea urvilleana*, *Dracophyllum urvillianum* and *Peperomia urvilleana*.[17] A number of new species of lichen (including *Sticta latifrons* and *Nephroma australe*)[18] and two new species of *Senecio* (*S. neglectus* and *S. argutus*) would also be collected.[19] Two new species of terrestrial gastropod (*Arthracophorus bitentaculatus* and *Onchidium nigricans* [*Onchidella nigricans*]) and two new marine gastropods (*Trochus tiaratus* [*Coelotrochus tiaratus*] and *Diloma zelandica*) were also collected in Tasman Bay and later described by Quoy and Gaimard.[20] For his part, Pierre-Adolphe Lesson, like his brother René, would come to detest his excursions ashore with d'Urville:

> Ambitious for fame and glory, he wanted to shine at all cost, and since he was as proud as he was vain, he believed himself much superior to the other men of his corps … He would even claim that he was the navy's top walker, even the Globe's. In fact he was not hindered by fat and possessed such an advantageous stature that his steps were worth two of those of his companions. In three years I have never seen

him miss the opportunity of glorifying himself of such a faculty, which is of course a rare occurrence with navy officers. Before me, my brother had noticed the same thing during the campaign of the *Coquille*; he had even allowed himself to observe how comfortable it was to follow him![21]

On 18 January, d'Urville landed on Observatory Beach with Charles Simonet and proceeded inland, following a stream before climbing a number of bluffs dominating the coast. After traversing difficult terrain, he succeeded in 'reaching the top of a high hill'[22] to the S.W. of the anchorage'. D'Urville then described discovering 'a second basin' beneath his feet 'no less safe than Astrolabe Cove from which it is separated by an isthmus of only five or six hundred toises in width'.[23] This was his 'Anse des Torrens' (modern Torrent Bay), immediately to the north.

On 23 January, the *Astrolabe* made for a channel that had been noticed from a distance and appeared to offer a connection between Tasman Bay and what Cook had named Admiralty Bay. It required the *Astrolabe* to make her way tentatively up the channel, relying on her cables and anchors – snapping one of each in the process! – to secure her gains and even to kedge forward against the difficult tidal current, before trimming her sails and passing through with the receding high tide. Now known as French Pass, this narrow rock-strewn stretch of water also divides D'Urville Island from the mainland of the South Island. On 25 January, d'Urville tested the narrow pass in a ship's boat, as Lottin and Gressien had done two days before in two other boats, and on the 28th, he succeeded in sailing, or rather scraping, the *Astrolabe* through. He recorded the chilling moments his vessel struck twice in the passage:

> … the first shock was light, but on the second occasion an ominous and general cracking accompanied a prolonged jolt, a noticeable pause in the progress of the corvette and a heavy list to portside, making us feel certain that she would remain on the rocks and break up. The crew, at this moment, gave an involuntary cry of terror. *'It's nothing, we've cleared it'*, I cried out in a loud voice to reassure them. In fact, the current continuing to carry the vessel, prevented her from remaining on the fatal rock; furthermore, the wind rose; we were able to steer and very soon, free of all fear, we entered the calm waters of Admiralty Bay under full sail. We only lost some fragments of the false keel which the shock detached and which floated in the wake of the ship.[24]

This bold yet carefully calculated manoeuvre was immortalised by Sainson, who depicted the *Astrolabe* leaning heavily to port and just clearing the exposed rocks.[25] Like the naturalists, he had been sent ashore by d'Urville to be gainfully employed but 'above all to dull the sailors to the approaching dangers' by showing them 'that work was persisting just as it did under the happiest circumstances'.[26] Significantly, this scientific

'L'Astrolabe *dans la Passe des Français, Nouvelle Zélande', lithograph by Achille Saint-Aulaire, from a sketch by Louis-Auguste de Sainson,* Voyage de la corvette l'Astrolabe, Atlas historique, *Paris, 1833, plate 40. The* Astrolabe *boldly sailed through French Pass – a narrow, rock-strewn stretch of water that divides D'Urville Island from the mainland of New Zealand's South Island – on 28 January 1827.* National Library of Australia PIC U1749 NK3340

excursion occasioned the discovery of a branched perennial herb with white daisy-like flowers, which would prove to be not only a new species, *Vittadinia australis*,[27] but the founding member of an entirely new genus that now includes Australian, New Caledonian, Hawaiian and South American species. D'Urville accepted the request of his officers to name D'Urville Island in his honour, but surprisingly, he made it a temporary acceptance until the indigenous name became known; that name, Rangitoto ki te Tonga, has now been restored as a dual name along with the French toponym bestowed in 1827. While d'Urville's modesty may have been sincere, and he certainly did his best to use Māori toponyms, he made no such undertaking to rescind the naming of Adele and Pepin islands or Croisilles Harbour if the existing indigenous names were determined.

After leaving Admiralty Bay and rounding Cape Jackson, the *Astrolabe* traversed the mouth of Queen Charlotte Sound and entered the narrowest part of Cook Strait. Had the wind been more favourable, d'Urville would have explored Te Whanganui-a-Tara (Wellington Harbour). Instead, he sailed towards Turakirae Head, the southern terminus of the Rimutaka Range. Shortly after midday on 29 January, the *Astrolabe* was approached by a canoe. Among those on board was Tehi Noui, a Māori chief in his early thirties who, with his companion Koki Hore, was determined to join the expedition.[28] D'Urville, having decided that they could be useful interpreters and capable of providing him with details of local place names, agreed to their request but repeatedly warned them that they might never be able to return home.

Soon after, the *Astrolabe* anchored in Palliser Bay (between Turakirae Head and Cape Palliser, the southernmost tip of the North Island), where the landscape reminded d'Urville of volcanic islands such as Milos, Lemnos and Santorini in the Aegean. His attempts to land in the whaleboat were foiled by the rough surf, and he decided to weigh anchor, lest the *Astrolabe* be surprised by a southerly squall. On 30 January, the expedition left Cook Strait, having made its first significant contributions to New Zealand hydrography. With the help of his new Māori expedition members, d'Urville also commenced a toponymic revision. 'Instead of Tera-Witi [Cape Terawhiti] and Palliser given by Cook', d'Urville wrote, 'they gave me those of Poli-Wero and Kawa Kawa which I restored on our map to the capes which should bear them, convinced that it would be ridiculous not to adopt designations applied to points, for centuries perhaps, by tribes as numerous and as intelligent as those of New Zealand.'[29]

In the rough waters beyond Cook Strait, seasickness added to the depression and discontent of the *Astrolabe*'s new Māori recruits, who now regretted their departure from home. Tehi Noui, in particular, had left three wives and four children behind. When his pleas and supplications failed to make the *Astrolabe* turn about, he began to use threats, abuse and insults, and then to wail like a child. Despite earlier emphatic cautions to Tehi Noui regarding the finality of his decision to join the expedition, d'Urville resolved to put him and his companion ashore at the earliest opportunity. On 3 February, when another Māori canoe approached the *Astrolabe*, d'Urville thought he had found a convenient means. However, he mistook the excitement of his guests – in fact, eager for the *Astrolabe* to exterminate their enemies in the canoe – for enthusiasm for an imminent landing. Horrified at the prospect of being handed over to their foes, who might make slaves of them or kill and eat them, Tehi Noui and Koki Hore begged for more honorable deaths at the hands of the French! D'Urville had no choice but to crowd sail and avoid an encounter with the approaching canoe.

The next day, his capricious Māori travellers – having surmounted their seasickness and now thankful for not being handed over to their enemies – put their petulance and wavering behind them and once more affirmed their desire to sail to Europe with the *Astrolabe*. That day, 4 February, the expedition made remarkable progress up the east coast of the North Island: traversing Hawkes Bay, then rounding Portland Island (off the southern tip of Mahia Peninsula), passing the white cliffs of Young Nicks Head[30] at the southern approaches to Poverty Bay, then Whangara and Pourewa islands, before reaching the southern approaches of Tolaga Bay. Initially, d'Urville had no intention of landing. However, when a Māori canoe approached bearing news that there were pigs and potatoes aplenty to trade, and when the hitherto favourable winds dropped, he changed his mind. On 5 February, the *Astrolabe* anchored where Cook had anchored the *Endeavour* in October 1769. To the local Māori, the bay was known as Uawa (d'Urville would render it Houa-Houa); none recognised the name Tolaga. It is possible that the men of the *Endeavour* mistakenly recorded the Māori word *tauranga*, meaning anchorage.

Because of the shallowness of Tolaga Bay, which later necessitated one of the longest wharves in the world, d'Urville chose a small cove, named Oputama (now Cooks Cove), within the southern arm of the bay to take on fresh water and make astronomical observations as Cook had done before him. The Māori who traded with the *Astrolabe* in February 1827 were intent on acquiring iron axes to replace stone implements like those that can still be seen protruding, along with broken shells and charcoal, from eroded middens in the cove. It soon became clear to d'Urville that the *Astrolabe* had attracted rival iwi, some of whom employed various ruses (either urging the French to fire on their competitors or spreading fear of French violence) in attempts to exclude other eager contenders for trade goods. D'Urville would do his best to allay such fears in his increasingly fluent Māori, but ever watchful for misunderstandings and the possibility of violence, he did not leave his ship the whole time she was anchored in the bay. Although deprived of opportunities for botany and entomology ashore, d'Urville nevertheless gained further information on Māori toponyms from the many visitors who came aboard.

At Tolaga Bay, d'Urville was also able to free himself of Tehi Noui and Koki Hore, who finally went ashore under the protection of a local chief, who promised them a canoe to return home. They were even given a quantity of gunpowder to gratify this chief for his trouble. By now, the 'shouting and chatter'[31] of the Māori traders on deck had begun to annoy d'Urville, and he was glad to put to sea again on 6 February. However, contrary winds prevented the *Astrolabe* from making significant progress, and yet another canoe (thought to have come from Anaura Bay) was able to paddle out bearing yet another chief, named Oroua. He and his companions had some 20 hogs aboard and wanted the expedition to make land and trade. With the *Astrolabe* already brimming with hogs, d'Urville declined. Nevertheless, he permitted the exchange of the hogs aboard the canoe for knives and invited Oroua to dine with him. D'Urville was particularly pleased to learn that Oroua was familiar with the pihe, the dirge-like ode he had first encountered in the Bay of Islands in April 1824. He had quizzed all the Māori he had met since returning to New Zealand, and until now none had any knowledge of this haunting archaic Māori song that had captivated him.

The *Astrolabe* sailed north then rounded East Cape and Cape Runaway before following the concave arc of the Bay of Plenty. On 15 February, near Plate Island (Motunau, northeast of Maketu), she was struck by a storm of 'extraordinary violence'[32] that, the following day, came very close to overwhelming her in dangerous reef-strewn waters.[33] Ship-handling became almost impossible as the vessel pitched deeply in the waves, pulley-blocks gave way and ropes were torn from the hands of the men. The *Astrolabe*'s new jib was also ripped by the wind, and the vibrating foremast appeared to be in danger of coming down. D'Urville hesitated to send men up on the yards in such perilous conditions; nevertheless, the jib was replaced, and the main foresail was reefed. For four hours, the *Astrolabe* battled the elements. In his official account, d'Urville admitted that he had considered driving his vessel aground on the eastern Bay of Plenty in the hope that at least some survivors from the wreck 'could render testimony to what we had done until that moment and a few friends of science would perhaps applaud our efforts and pity our fate'.[34] It has been suggested that stress, exhaustion and pain may have affected d'Urville's ability to give effective commands and that he faced a technical mutiny on the part of his first officer, Jacquinot, who took decisive action to crowd sail and pull away.[35] Lesson's journal supports the contention that it was Jacquinot who took the decisive action not to allow the ship to be run aground, despite d'Urville's initial fatalistic decision.[36] Guilbert's journal, however, indicates that, despite the 'imminent danger' that menaced the crew, 'each conserved the utmost coolness' and all was done 'with order and without confusion and the command[er] gave his orders with the calm that we have always seen in the most critical circumstances'.[37] Ultimately, it appears to have been a combination of d'Urville's ability to heed Jacquinot's resolve, the resilience of the corvette and the fortuitous clearing of the weather that saved the expedition.[38] Pierre-Adolphe Lesson, however, handed down a harsher judgement:

> I have said that I did not believe that Monsieur d'Urville was a great mariner, but what was most obvious to us was the facility with which he sank into discouragement. It is also true that he often forgot the reason for his discouragements and that with the same coolness, he would start his clumsiness all over again.[39]

Although Lesson added that d'Urville 'lost his head during great danger', he contradicted himself two sentences later by stating: '… one was convinced that he was incapable of appreciation of real dangers'.[40] Shortly before sailing into this tempest, d'Urville had reflected on the 'easy' expeditions of Freycinet and Duperrey in comparison with the dangerous survey work of his own. In the wake of the tempest, he compared his grumbling, storm-weathered sailors with those of Bougainville, Lapérouse and d'Entrecasteaux, and found them wanting. For his officers, he had kinder words, but we do not know what criticisms he had in his heart for himself.

The *Astrolabe* then sailed north along the Coromandel Peninsula, rounded Cape Colville and traversed the mouth of the Hauraki Gulf.[41] Off Cape Rodney, bad weather made d'Urville decide to seek shelter in Whangarei Harbour, but a sand bank and unfavourable winds off Bream Head forced him to anchor at the mouth of the harbour on 21 February. Here the expedition undertook further surveys, and d'Urville met a Māori chief, whom he refers to as 'Rangui', who had resided for a time at Port Jackson and wore European clothes. This was Rangituke, a high-born Ngā Puhi, whom d'Urville rightly suspected, and confirmed, was involved in a military expedition. According to the historian S. Percy Smith, he commanded 'the advance guard of a fleet on its way to make war on the Ngāti-Paoa of Tamaki'.[42] The attack proved a disaster, with fatal consequences for Rangituke, but his meeting with d'Urville 'served to fix the exact date of an important event in the history of the Auckland isthmus'.[43]

From Rangituke, d'Urville would collect still more Māori place names, which he once again substituted for Cook's on his chart. He would continue this process of toponymic revision when, following up on Cook's less-detailed surveys, the *Astrolabe* headed southeast, again passed Cape Rodney, rounded Tokatu Point and sailed into the Hauraki Gulf. After passing the island of Tiritiri Matangi, the corvette sailed southwest and anchored off the coast of Rangitoto Island at 7.00 pm on 24 February.[44] The next day, she faced contrary winds as she began to navigate the Rangitoto Channel, so d'Urville decided to go on ahead in the whaleboat, accompanied by Lottin, Gaimard and Lesson. They disembarked on the shore of Devonport (probably present-day Torpedo Bay) so that Lottin could conduct observations from the top of Takarunga (Mount Victoria, 87 metres).

Just after midday on the same day (25 February), d'Urville crossed to the southern shore of the entry to Waitemata Harbour, this time accompanied by Lottin, Gaimard and Simonet. Only Simonet was armed, but no Māori were seen; most of the inhabitants had fled, the whole region having only recently been conquered by Hongi Hika and 4000 musket-bearing Ngā Puhi warriors from the Ngāti Whātua and Ngāti Paoa. Since d'Urville's objective was to cross the Auckland Isthmus, or at least reach the summit of the central volcanic cone of Maungawhau (Mount Eden, 196 metres), he and his men probably landed in the vicinity of either Judges Bay or Hobson Bay and walked up Parnell ridge. The track they followed passed through scrub, then disappeared in denser woodland intersected by gullies, streams and, finally, impassable swamp. When Gaimard was injured in a fall, d'Urville, himself exhausted, decided to abandon the excursion and return to the whaleboat. In the meantime, Jacquinot, with the help of a favourable tide, had brought the *Astrolabe* into the Rangitoto Channel, and d'Urville was back on board by 4.00 pm. With the further assistance of a southwesterly breeze, the expedition rounded the southern coast of Rangitoto and anchored for the night off Browns Island (Motukorea) at the mouth of the Tamaki River.[45]

The next day, d'Urville made the acquaintance of Rangi-hue, a well-built Ngāti Paoa[46] chief, whom he refers to as 'Te Rangui'. He would be another important source of local toponyms and other information for d'Urville during protracted conversations aboard the corvette. Here, too, given the menace of the Ngā Puhi to the north, there was a desperate desire for European weapons and ammunition. Lottin gained the services of a Māori pilot, Makara, in return for gunpowder, a large axe and other trinkets.[47] Gaimard was surprised that one of Rangi-hue's fellow chiefs, Tawiti, was prepared even to breach tapu and prostitute his wife to satisfy his desire for a repeating firearm,[48] and Rangi-hue got his slave to steal the Astrolabe's sounding lead for musket balls.[49]

Between 25 and 27 February, the Astrolabe would make a significant contribution to the hydrography of the western side of the Hauraki Gulf, including Waitemata Harbour and the Rangitoto and Motukorea channels, which connect to the gulf. Lottin, with Guilbert, Gaimard, Faraguet and their guide Makara, proceeded up the Tamaki River in a whaleboat, crossed the Auckland Isthmus (at its strategic narrowest point)[50] and also visited Manukau Harbour[51] – traversed seven years earlier by Samuel Marsden.[52] While d'Urville believed that these surveys were as significant as d'Entrecasteaux's discoveries in Van Diemen's Land in 1792–93,[53] the name 'Astrolabe Channel' has not survived to honour the expedition's running survey of much of the littoral boundary of the present-day city of Auckland.[54]

From Hauraki Gulf, the Astrolabe proceeded to North Cape. D'Urville saw it as a natural terminus for his expedition's New Zealand surveys as well as another opportunity to link their labours to that of d'Entrecasteaux, who had plotted the location of North Cape in March 1793. From North Cape, the Astrolabe sailed south to the Bay of Islands, where she arrived on 12 March. Despite d'Urville having had a chart drafted three years earlier on the Coquille, his corvette went aground on a sand bank,[55] and the crew had to run out a kedge anchor in the longboat to haul her free. An hour later, she was safely moored in Te Rawhiti Inlet off Paeroa (on Moturua Island), where the pā (fortified place) had been destroyed by the French in 1772 in reprisal for the deaths of Marion Dufresne and two of his boat crews. Although rebuilt, its residents had more recently been dispersed by the Ngā Puhi in the wake of Tuhi's death in 1824.

D'Urville did not learn of Tuhi's death until he went ashore and met with the missionary Henry Williams at Paihia on 13 March. He also learned that his friend, the botanist Allan Cunningham, had returned to New South Wales two months earlier and that Hongi Hika (who he had earlier been told had been killed in battle) was still alive, although he had sustained a musket ball through the chest while attacking the Ngāti Uru and the Ngāti Pou at Whangaroa in January. Despite his wound emitting 'a mournful whistle at every breath', Hongi would linger for another 14 months before succumbing to infection.[56] In the meantime, the missionaries,

who had enjoyed his protection, dreaded the uncertainties that his imminent death
might bring.

When d'Urville visited the Paihia mission settlement in the western Bay of Islands
on 13 March, it was not only to renew his friendship with Henry Williams but to
question him on various aspects of Māori ethnography, particularly since his earlier
trusted informant, Thomas Kendall, was no longer resident.[57] He would also question
Williams on the veracity of baron de Thierry's grandiose territorial claims. D'Urville
would conclude that Thierry's pretensions were 'absurd' and that at best the 'self-styled
sovereign of our Antipodes'[58] might have had a claim on 14,000 acres, but that this
was tenuous given his lack of continuous occupancy and the ever-present threat of
conquest by invaders. Williams and his missionary colleague Richard Davis, a former
farmer who had arrived from New South Wales in 1824, visited the *Astrolabe* the
following day. On 15 March, d'Urville returned the courtesy but also landed at Paihia
to see more of the forested interior. He was accompanied on this excursion by his
secretary Barthélemy Lauvergne, together with Lottin, Gaimard and William Williams,
who had been asked by his elder brother Henry to act as their guide. D'Urville thought
William Williams inexperienced and lacking in knowledge of Māori language and
culture. He also distrusted him because of his lack of frankness. While in the company
of the younger Williams, d'Urville became convinced that they had stumbled on a
location where a human sacrifice had recently taken place, and that both the local
Māori and the missionaries were anxious to keep the French from seeing the evidence –
the former to avoid the reproaches of Europeans, and the latter to avoid giving proof of
the 'little progress they had made up to now on the minds of these barbarous people'.[59]
D'Urville's discussion of tapu and Māori religion – dismissed as inconsequential by
earlier explorers and even by European residents such as William Williams[60] – reveals
his sensitivity and understanding of how visitors to Polynesia, such as Cook and Marion
Dufresne, may have breached local prohibitions with tragic consequences. The next day,
16 March, d'Urville sent Midshipman Pâris to Paihia with his letters and reports home,
entrusting them to the missionaries for dispatch via a London-bound whaler expected
within two months. He was accompanied by Sainson, who was sent to sketch a view
of 'their little establishment'.[61] His work that day was later lithographed by Jacques
Arago for the expedition's 'Atlas historique' (plate 56). It included the extensive timber
palisades around the settlement and even a field gun on the foreshore,[62] testament to
the deep-seated fears of the missionaries living on a bay that had become a funnel for
European weapons enveloping the lands to the south in war.

During the *Astrolabe*'s brief sojourn in the Bay of Islands, around a dozen Māori
slave women plied a lively trade for their sexual favours among the crew. Despite his
annoyance and disgust at the exploitation of these women and, almost certainly, his

health concerns (three of the crew would contract venereal diseases during their visit), d'Urville was reluctant to prohibit the prostitutes. He believed they helped his sailors 'forget their past troubles and their long privations', and that they acted as guarantors against any Māori plots.[63] D'Urville engaged in a body trade of his own: giving a coloured dress to the Ngā Puhi chief Wetoi, nephew of Pomare I, in exchange for the preserved head (known as a toi moko) of a heavily tattooed rangatira (chief) named 'Hou'. This man had been killed very recently at Waitemata (possibly at the Battle of Te ika a Ranganui) and was presumably a Ngāti Whātua. D'Urville would also investigate the manner in which such heads were preserved, essentially through desiccation after the removal of the brains, followed by the insertion of wax in the eye-sockets. Later he presented the head he had acquired to the Musée de Caen in his native Normandy, but its location, if it survived the bombing of 1944, is now unknown. To be fair, d'Urville was not without moral qualms in this matter; he appears not to have enquired about such heads – waiting instead for one to be offered to him – lest it lead directly to the decapitation of an unfortunate victim simply to gratify his request.[64]

Before leaving the Bay of Islands, d'Urville also re-visited Paeroa pā, on Moturua, and was very surprised at the enormous changes since his visit during the *Coquille*'s sojourn. Although the deep ditches and some of the palisades were still visible, grass pushed through the walls of the ruined houses, and he was convinced that in two or three years, travellers would 'have difficulty determining whether this hill was [ever] inhabited'.[65] Today, two large ditches can be detected across what was once the narrow land access to the pā, and scattered midden debris continues to signal past human habitation. (This pā was excavated by a team of University of Otago archaeologists in 1965.[66])

Aside from a subspecies of the glabrous willowherb *Epilobium billardierianum*,[67] the Bay of Islands would not yield any new botanical discoveries for the expedition. Achille Richard believed that d'Urville had personally collected a new species of kauri there, but he was mistaken.[68] He was similarly mistaken with regard to what he thought was a new species of *Metrosideros*.[69] None of the dozen New Zealand beetles described by Boisduval came with precise habitat locations, and in any case, none were new. However, Quoy and Gaimard collected two new species of marine gastropod, *Vermetus zelandicus* (*Serpulorbis zelandicus*) and *Ascidia coerulea* (*Asterocarpa coerulea*),[70] and a new species of white ribbon worm *Borlasia novae-zelandiae* (*Amphiporus novae-zelandiae*)[71] in the inter-tidal zones of the bay.

With her water, firewood and provisions replenished and her navigational observations completed, the *Astrolabe* set sail from New Zealand on 18 March 1827. On board was a new Māori member of the crew, a former slave named Kokako, who had already served on two whaling vessels and who would prove to be a diligent and cheerful seaman. D'Urville would further distil his knowledge of the Māori and their country in an impressive scholarly essay of 321 pages, taking up more than half of the second volume of his historical account of the voyage of the *Astrolabe*.[72] It was followed by a further volume of nearly 800 pages of supporting documents, extracts and notes – all testament to his remarkable erudition and meticulous personal observations. This biographer, however, is still drawn more naturally to d'Urville's historical narrative. On several occasions during his visit to New Zealand, the fortified Māori pā on the coast and the gathering of sea-going war canoes about to leave on raids had reminded d'Urville of the *Iliad*, the Greek Archipelago and also the humble origins of some of the world's great nation states. His historical musings and prophetic observations about the shared destinies of Australia and New Zealand deserve to be quoted at length:

> I was reminded of the Gauls, brigands, so frowned upon by the refined Greeks; of the Britons, savages whom Rome disdained to conquer in the most brilliant periods of her empire: twenty centuries have sufficed to raise them to the first rank of the nations. One of these has just made Europe tremble at the sound of its arms, and today the other dominates the whole world by the influence of its wealth and the overwhelming power of its ships … If, as everything leads one to think, Australia is destined to become the seat of a great empire, it is impossible for New Zealand not to follow her impulse, and her children, civilised and mixed with the posterity of England, will themselves become a powerful and formidable people. Everything seems to presage, particularly, a high destiny on the sea. Like Great Britain, New Zealand, surrounded on every side by ocean waters, and provided with excellent ports, also possesses forests capable of producing the finest timber for masts and construction, a plant yielding fibre suitable for making the best cordage, and a soil capable of lending itself to the cultivation of all the crops of temperate climates. It is without doubt, therefore, that the inhabitants will make very rapid progress towards civilisation, when Europeans or Australians are willing to assume responsibility for the task, or when from among themselves there emerges a genius of extraordinary powers, capable of becoming the legislator of his fellow citizens and uniting them in one national body. Then these coasts, at present deserted or populated by a few isolated *pas*, will present flourishing cities; these silent bays traversed from time to time by frail canoes, will be highways for ships of every kind. And in a few centuries hence, if the press is not there to record by its indestructible means the deeds and discoveries of modern times, future members of the Academy of New Zealand will undoubtedly question or at least argue laboriously about the narratives of the earliest navigators, when they found them speaking of the wilderness and savages of their country …[73]

16

Ill winds in Tonga

The winds … are heard wheresoever they go, but they give ear to none. Their acts resemble crimes. None know on whom they cast their hoary surf; with what ferocity they hover over shipwrecks, looking at times as if they flung their impious foam-flakes in the face of heaven. They are the tyrants of unknown regions.

Victor Hugo*

The *Astrolabe* sailed north after leaving the Bay of Islands on 18 March 1827. Feeble winds meant she covered little more than 165 kilometres in the following week. In addition to the cases of venereal disease reported aboard, three members of the crew (including Ensign Lottin) soon showed symptoms of colic and tenesmus. Whether this led d'Urville to check the quality of some of his provisions is unclear. Perhaps as a consequence, on 27 March, 56 of the remaining 68 tins of Appert's braised chicken were thrown overboard because they were found to have putrefied.

D'Urville's initial objective was the Tongan Archipelago, so that he could compare longitudinal observations with those of d'Entrecasteaux. Other comparisons became possible, on 2 April, when the expedition sighted Curtis and Macaulay islands,[1] grouped together as part of the Kermadec Islands by d'Entrecasteaux's hydrographer, Beautemps-Beaupré. Soon after, the weather deteriorated into torrential rain and fierce winds, which did not ease until very early on 11 April. That morning, d'Urville was surprised to find the sea covered in *'chrysippe'* (*Cethosia chrysippe*?) butterflies, which he believed had been blown all the way from Tonga by the storm. Nine days later, on 20 April, the *Astrolabe* passed the Tongan islands of 'Eua (Tasman's 'Middleburg Island') and Euaiki. That same day, d'Urville hoped to negotiate a narrow break in the reef off Pangaimotu, an offshore islet east of Nuku'alofa on the main island of Tongatapu (literally 'sacred Tonga').

At first all went well, but when the wind dropped, the *Astrolabe*, which had advanced about eight kilometres into the channel, was suddenly without motive power and at the mercy of the current. The situation was worsened by the fact that the waters had

---

* *Les Travailleurs de la mer* (1866), part ii, book iii, chapter ii

'La corvette l'Astrolabe *en perdition sur des récifs, Tonga-Tabou*', *lithograph by Achille Saint-Aulaire and Victor-Jean Adam, from a sketch by Louis-Auguste de Sainson,* Voyage de la corvette l'Astrolabe, Atlas historique, *Paris, 1833, plate 67.* National Library of Australia, PIC S2319 LOC 6042

been made murky by the recent storm and the reef was not visible. Despite the crew's best efforts, the *Astrolabe* was sucked sideways onto the coral. No serious damage was done, but it took more than four hours to free her by dropping a kedge anchor with one of the boats and hauling her off the reef with the cable and capstan. Nevertheless, the corvette remained in a highly vulnerable position because, once again, the wind shifted and she failed to reach her intended anchorage, and she was also unable to withdraw from the channel as the tide ebbed. Although aligned with the reef and secured with two hawsers, the failure of one, combined with a strong wind, could easily have thrown the *Astrolabe* back onto the reef with even more violence.

Despite her vulnerable position, the *Astrolabe* was soon surrounded by canoes full of Tongans. In an effort to prevent a mass boarding, d'Urville restricted access to chiefs alone.[2] Around 3.00 pm, a young Englishman named James Read boarded the *Astrolabe*. He had lived in the Friendly Islands (Cook's name for the Tongan Archipelago) since being shipwrecked, as a cabin-boy aboard the *Ceres*, on the reef at Lifuka in 1821 and surviving the massacre of much of the crew.[3] D'Urville received him warmly, promptly recognising him as 'a useful interpreter with the natives'.[4] Read bore a letter of introduction from the Reverend John Thomas, a Wesleyan missionary, who was established at Hihifo in northwestern Tongatapu.

At 4.00 pm, another canoe arrived bearing a polite and gentle Englishman[5] named

William Singleton. He was a survivor of the Tongan attack on yet another British vessel, the privateer *Port-au-Prince*, at Lifuka in December 1806[6] and had then settled on Tongatapu, where he now had a Tongan wife. D'Urville took an instant liking to Singleton and discerned yet another valuable interlocutor with a deep knowledge of the Tongans. The cavalcade became more operatic with the arrival of a mysterious Englishman named 'Ritchett'. With a shrill pretentious voice and wearing a dirty grey frock coat riddled with holes, his bizarre appearance and eccentric manners soon led the crew to nickname him the 'school master'.[7] D'Urville quickly realised that Rickett had far less facility in the local language than the other Englishmen on the island and that he would be of limited assistance to the expedition. Nevertheless, he received him courteously and would later acknowledge his services as a guide.

All three visitors delighted in European food and, especially, wine for the first time in many years. During Singleton's visit, d'Urville sought his counsel on the *Astrolabe*'s predicament and what would happen should she be wrecked on the reef. Singleton assured him that the Tongans would spare the lives of the crew but would pillage everything except the men's immediate personal effects. D'Urville was advised to

'Maison des missionnaires à Hifo', *engraving probably by Charles (Carl Traugott) Beyer, from a sketch by Louis-Auguste de Sainson, for Dumont d'Urville's* Voyage pittoresque autour du monde, *L. Tenré, Paris, vol. ii, 1835, plate viii. With the* Astrolabe *in danger of breaking up on the reefs of Tongatapu, d'Urville briefly entrusted his expedition's papers to Reverend John Thomas, a Wesleyan missionary who was established at Hihifo in the western part of the island.* Author's collection

D'Urville (seated second from left) and his officers, presumably with their English interlocutor William Singleton (seated centre, barefoot), Tongatapu, detail from 'Visite des Officiers de l'Astrolabe à la Tamaha', engraving by Boilly from a sketch by Louis-Auguste de Sainson, for Dumont d'Urville's Voyage pittoresque autour du monde, *L. Tenré, Paris, vol. ii, 1835, plate lx.*
Author's collection

seek the protection of Tongatapu's most powerful chiefs. One, Palu (chief of Mu'a on the eastern side of the island), called on the *Astrolabe* about an hour after the last of the Englishmen had come aboard. D'Urville noted the pronounced deference of the English to the tall, fat chieftain with closely shaven hair and gave Palu the use of his day cabin on the poop deck for the duration of his visit. D'Urville was particularly interested to learn that he had childhood memories of d'Entrecasteaux's visit to Tonga in 1793.

Despite the *Astrolabe*'s critical predicament, d'Urville allowed all but a handful of the sailors to retire at 7.00 pm. His optimism was ill-placed. Two hours later, one of the hawsers snapped, and the corvette swung round and strained on her solitary tether no more than 'eight or ten feet from the reef'.[8] The crew was roused, and the long boat was lowered once again to do battle with the violent swell and drop yet another anchor a safer distance from the coral.

The next morning, more Tongans came to trade plentiful supplies of pigs, chickens, coconuts, yams, bananas and other fruit. D'Urville was surprised by the keen appetites of the sailors and their apparent disregard for the expedition's peril, but he seems to have been happy for them to eat and distract themselves. That morning, yet another missive arrived from the Reverend Thomas, seeking answers to numerous questions about the expedition and also requesting soap and candles. D'Urville, however, had more important things on his mind and put off replying to the missionary.

Not for the first time in his life, d'Urville had landed in a country where traditional authority had recently been overthrown. In the year before the *Astrolabe* arrived, Fatafehi Laufilitonga, of the once-great Tu'i Tonga dynasty of Tongan kings, had been defeated in the Battle of Velata by the Tupou chieftain Tufa'hau, who would later proclaim himself King George Tupou I when baptised a Christian in 1831. (The current Tongan royal family are his descendants.) Tahofa, the nephew of Pulaho Taufu'i'aevalu, one of Tufa'hau's most important allies in the Battle of Velata, was the next visitor to the corvette. D'Urville gave Tahofa and Palu a military firearm and a length of printed Indian cloth each, requesting their protection in the event that the *Astrolabe* was wrecked on the reef.

In the wake of these assurances, and given the likely loss of life should the *Astrolabe* founder, d'Urville decided to send half the crew to the safety of the offshore islet of Pangaimotu. He hoped that they would be able to return aboard as soon as the danger passed. Although the sailors were ordered to take only a packet of essential supplies and two or three shirts, most ignored their orders and tried to take bundles weighing 'forty to fifty pounds'.[9] The loading of the longboat and the yawl was suspended until all the bags were emptied in front of Lieutenant Jacquinot and only the most necessary items selected to accompany each man. As the swell worsened, and the prospects for the *Astrolabe* looked more grim, the boats made ready to go ashore, with 35 sailors under the command of Lottin and accompanied by Guilbert, Quoy, Bertrand, Lesson and Sainson. It was planned that Dudemaine would then return to the *Astrolabe* with the longboat. However, just before they got underway, a canoe arrived bearing two unnamed English missionaries, one of whom may have been John Hutchinson. Learning of d'Urville's plan, they were aghast and pleaded with him not to send the men ashore, for they were convinced that the promises of Tahofa and Palu would be inadequate to protect the crew from Tongan avarice and from a massacre for their possessions.

Unable to ignore such a stern warning, d'Urville halted the partial evacuation of his vessel and ordered all the men, and their bags, back on board. He placed all the expedition's official journals in a metal chest and asked the missionaries to take them back to Hihifo under the guard of a sailor named Louis-Alexandre Martineng. In addition, for safe-keeping by the missionaries, d'Urville decided to send Lottin ashore in the yawl with James Read, bearing the charts the expedition had drafted, along with atlases, navigational instruments, the commander's personal journals, scientific notes and uniform, Sainson's sketchbook and the vessel's foreign passports. As Lottin pulled away from the *Astrolabe* – pitching helplessly in the narrow, reef-constrained channel – he was convinced that he would never see her in one piece again.

Despite the anxieties of the French, the chiefs Palu and Tahofa remained aboard the *Astrolabe* and slept peacefully. Unbeknown to them, d'Urville ordered all the rifles, pistols and hunting weapons to be stowed in the magazine beneath his cabin and the hatch nailed down. Explaining his orders, he wrote: 'I was not at all pleased by the idea of seeing the French become the musketeers of the chiefs of Tonga-Tabou, which would undoubtedly have happened, as soon as the vessel was lost, without the precaution which I took.'[10]

The following day, another Tongan chief, Lavaka, boarded the *Astrolabe*, and around midday, he was followed by the Reverend John Thomas. Formerly a village blacksmith in Hagley, Worcestershire, Thomas had arrived in Tonga only the previous year, and we know now that he was considering abandoning his mission for lack of support from Britain.[11] An impatient and stressed d'Urville soon saw that, although Thomas was respected by the Tongans, he had no local influence or authority, his judgement was flawed, and effectively he was of no use to the *Astrolabe* other than as a safe-keeper of specific items. D'Urville was also annoyed by his lukewarm enthusiasm for sheltering the French at the mission. Although Thomas repeatedly enjoined d'Urville to stay with his ship, he himself was clearly anxious about remaining aboard the corvette any longer than was necessary. D'Urville made 'no effort to keep him,'[12] and Thomas departed at 3.00 pm.

An hour later, the wind shifted to the east, and d'Urville thought he had an opportunity to extricate the *Astrolabe*. He even sought the aid of the Tongans to help tow her out of danger. Of the chiefs, only Palu seemed sincere in his efforts to assist them; the others seemed deliberately half-hearted. D'Urville was forced to rely on his own boats and ordered all the *Astrolabe*'s sails unfurled. For about eight or ten minutes, it seemed that the wind would deliver the corvette from the menace of the coral, but then the water suddenly shallowed to a little over a metre, and the *Astrolabe* settled once again on the reef.

The Tongan canoes now appeared 'like a cloud of vultures who awaited a favourable moment to pounce on their prey'. D'Urville was convinced that all was lost. He bade Singleton and the Tongan chiefs follow him to his cabin. Pointing to the portrait of Charles X, he informed the Tongans that the king was the supreme chief of the French and capable of 'graciously rewarding their generosity' or 'taking conspicuous vengeance'. With Singleton's assistance as translator, he mournfully acknowledged the *Astrolabe*'s 'most critical position'. His crew, he told the chiefs, could 'without doubt land on their island, arms in hand, brave all their forces and vanquish them', but, he told them, he would rather 'rely on their loyalty' and place himself and his companions 'under their protection'. In return, aside from a 'small number' of necessary objects, d'Urville promised that he would 'leave to them, without restriction, the possession of the arms and the numerous riches, such as iron utensils, glassware, cloth and mirrors' on board the vessel.[13] To d'Urville's relief, the chiefs listened attentively and solemnly promised to become allies of the French and even give their lives to protect them. Throughout these sombre discussions, d'Urville expected to hear the hull jarring on the coral, but he heard nothing. To his surprise, when he went back on deck, he found the *Astrolabe* afloat; nevertheless, within 20 minutes, the current had effectively reversed this change in fortune. Gressien had then located their anchor buoy, and Jacquinot had lost no time in re-securing the corvette. D'Urville would write that it became 'a kind of presentiment guaranteeing me that we were not destined to leave the *Astrolabe* on the reefs of Tonga', adding, 'this supernatural confidence in our destiny did not leave me during the rest of the campaign'.[14]

Despite their prize slipping from their grasp, the Tongan chiefs continued to profess their friendship. Palu, in particular, asserted that he and his countrymen were not now disposed 'to pillage and despoil foreigners who fell into their hands'.[15] The numerous fires which burned along the shore, he explained, were lit on his orders in celebration of the good fortune of the French in regaining their anchorage. D'Urville had little choice but to play along with this charade.

On 23 April, Lottin returned safely from Hihifo, guided by James Read. With the sea a little more tranquil, d'Urville attempted to recover his anchors in the passage. Although he succeeded in salvaging only one in addition to a chain, the *Astrolabe*'s most favourable circumstances in three days occasioned a meal with the officers, joined by the Reverend Thomas, that verged on the jubilant. That night, d'Urville gained two hours of peaceful sleep.

The next day, with the sails strategically set to take advantage of the slight east-northeasterly wind, the longboat and the whaleboat once again began to tow the *Astrolabe* out of the channel. With the assistance of Singleton as their pilot, all went well until the current suddenly became violently turbulent near Monuafe Reef. The towlines snapped, and the corvette was once more dragged onto the coral. Fortunately, she floated again at high tide on 25 April – the first anniversary of their departure from France – and calm waters kept her from further danger. That day, on behalf of the 'great chief of the French', d'Urville distributed gifts to the three Tongan chiefs he sought to propitiate. Each received 'a musket, two pounds of gunpowder, three ells of scarlet cloth and two large cutlasses' in addition to a number of other gifts. The fact that each sought to hide their bounty from the chiefs ashore convinced d'Urville that their power was obtained by 'usurpation, rather than birth or legitimate rights'.[16] Finally, on 26 April, the *Astrolabe* made her way to anchor safely off the southern point of Pangaimotu, just as d'Entrecasteaux had done in March 1793.

Shortly after anchoring, d'Urville received a branch of green kava (*Piper methysticum*) from ashore. William Singleton explained that this sacred branch had been sent by the dowager Tu'i Tonga *fefine* (great-aunt of the now powerless Tu'i Tonga monarch Fatafehi Laufilitonga) as a sign of her spiritual protection.

D'Urville's first priority was clear: he immediately dispatched Gressien to recover the expedition's papers, instruments and other precious items from the missionaries. One consequence of this safe-keeping exercise was that the expedition's chronometers had not been wound and had stopped keeping the time of the (Paris) reference meridian. This thwarted the very purpose of the *Astrolabe*'s visit to Tonga: re-calculating the longitude of Pangaimotu for comparison with d'Entrecasteaux's determination of 1793. Now they had no choice but to use this explorer's longitude as their reference meridian, thereby embedding any error in his calculation into their own.

Four men (quarter-master and carpenter François-Bernard Chieusse and the sailors Joseph-Antoine Audibert, Jean-Joseph Bérenguier, and Jean-Pierre-Melchior Bertrand) began diving under the *Astrolabe*'s hull to search for any harmful consequences from the groundings on the reef. Fortunately, they found only minor additional damage to the false keel and only a few leaves of copper missing from the sheaving on the port side. D'Urville also sent Lottin and Pâris, and then Gressien and Faraguet, in two boats to drag for the *Astrolabe*'s lost anchors and cables in the channel. To his great regret, they failed in their salvage mission and had to abandon their efforts when the weather deteriorated.

Soon after anchoring, d'Urville went ashore and called on the missionaries at Hihifo, meeting the Reverend Thomas's wife, Sarah, for the first time. He also took on fresh supplies of food and water, the latter of poor quality, which would prove to be a problem. Because the Tongan Islands are coral formations, there are no surface streams (despite rainfall of 1500–1800 mm per year), and the islanders are dependent on wells. One such water source was located in the centre of Pangaimotu, and d'Urville resented demands for payment from the chief who controlled it. Although d'Urville asserted that water was a universal human right, he knew that it was of the utmost importance for the *Astrolabe* to depart with her water supplies fully replenished, and he appears to have resolved the situation by declaring his preparedness to pay an enhanced price for food.

During the expedition's stay, the naturalists were accompanied by Singleton in their search for specimens. Ethnographic items were also acquired for the royal museum;

d'Urville made copious ethnographic notes, and Sainson completed numerous sketches. Gaimard, Sainson, Pâris and Lauvergne also attended a kava ceremony at Palu's village of Mu'a. When d'Urville made his own visit to the same village for an expected feast, in company with Jacquinot, Lottin, Gressien, Quoy and Faraguet, he was surprised not to be met by anyone of distinction and to find Palu far from his usual cordial and happy self. A kava ceremony was performed, but d'Urville soon learned, from Singleton, that Palu had recently lost a son and that yet another was now very seriously ill. Not surprisingly, he found the chief's depressed spirits 'very natural'. Given the sad and unexpected circumstances, it was little wonder that, instead of the promised 'copious meal', d'Urville received a mere two bananas and a coconut.[17]

D'Urville also met the 'tamaha'[18] Amelia Fakahiku'o'uiha (belonging to the family of the late Tu'i Tonga monarch Fuanunu'iava and the deposed Fatafehi Laufilitonga). Because she had personal memories of the visits of both Cook and d'Entrecasteaux, d'Urville thought it opportune to ask whether another expedition (that of Lapérouse) had also visited in between. According to the tamaha, two European vessels, flying white flags, had indeed anchored off Nomuka (in the Ha'apai group) for 10 days, a few years prior to the arrival of d'Entrecasteaux. Singleton added weight to the expedition's being French by recounting that he had seen two pewter plates bearing French names that were said to have come from these vessels. They were subsequently buried with the chief who owned them when he died. The Englishman Ritchett also advised d'Urville of the presence of a European anchor on the island of Lakemba in Fiji's southern Lau Archipelago. As we shall see, this proved to be from an American vessel.

As the expedition's departure grew nearer, d'Urville entrusted a packet of letters, including his report to the minister, to the Reverend Thomas for dispatch via the first vessel bound for Europe to call at Tonga. He also decided to visit Nuku'alofa and, further to the east (facing Pangaimotu), the sacred religious site of Ma'ufanga, burial place of numerous Tongan chiefs, and then Mu'a to bid farewell to Palu. However, this hitherto friendly chief was still too distracted by his critically ill son's condition to entertain visitors.

On his return to the *Astrolabe*, d'Urville received a letter from the Reverend Thomas warning him that several of his sailors intended to desert and remain in the archipelago. D'Urville took the warning very seriously. He knew that among his men were several undesirables who had convictions for theft or for previous desertions. He also knew that in South America, the *Uranie* had lost nearly a quarter of her crew to desertions, and that the *Coquille* had lost 14 men. Furthermore, he knew that while the unforgiving Australian wilderness, the harsh regime of the penal colony of New South Wales and the fierce Māori in New Zealand had acted as deterrents against desertions, Tonga offered a warm seductive contrast, with several English castaways providing examples of the comfortable life that could be had there. To forestall the deserters' plot, d'Urville decided to set sail the next morning. Jacquinot urged secrecy, and the officers were ordered to maintain close surveillance during the night. The only officer who was not yet aboard was Dudemaine, who, enjoying local hospitality, was unaware of his commander's plan. But for other unfolding events, he was very nearly left behind.

On the morning of 13 May, the *Astrolabe* was surrounded by a larger than usual number of canoes. When the chief Tahofa attempted to sell several more pigs, d'Urville made it clear that he had no need of additional provisions because he was leaving. Tahofa and all the canoes then disappeared on what appears, in retrospect, to have been a prearranged signal; even young James Read vanished.

In the meantime, d'Urville had sent his longboat to raise the *Astrolabe*'s northern anchor. He had also sent the yawl to collect the bosun, Jacques-Philippe Jacon, who had been dispatched ashore at dawn to observe the tide and, at Jacquinot's request, to load a small quantity of sand for cleaning the decks during the next leg of the voyage. D'Urville also planned to use the yawl to guide the *Astrolabe* through the channel. Under the command of Midshipman Faraguet, it reached the shore a few minutes ahead of the Tongan canoes. So confident was d'Urville that all was going according to plan that he decided to have a quick breakfast in his cabin, but this ended abruptly when he received a frantic report that the yawl and its crew were under attack from a large number of Tongans. With his telescope, he soon saw that the Tongan numbers had swelled to some 500. In retrospect, we know that Tahofa's objective was to kidnap, rather than to assault (or massacre) and rob, a number of the French, apparently in the hope of keeping some of the French among his entourage for their technical and military skills. He was clearly encouraged in this plan by knowledge that some of the French did indeed wish to stay but had been thwarted by d'Urville's plan to sail early.

D'Urville's first inclination was to fire a couple of cannon shots over the heads of the Tongans, but he changed his mind because of the risk of killing some of his own men in the process. It took another 20 minutes to arm and embark 23 men in the longboat, under the command of Gressien, in order to give chase. Although they failed to overtake the Tongan assailants, who had dispersed into the forest, they did recapture the yawl. D'Urville then sent the whaleboat under the command of Guilbert – with Sainson, Bertrand and Imbert as reinforcements – with orders for Gressien to set fire to all the houses he could find as an initial punitive action.

To d'Urville's satisfaction, Guilbert and the whaleboat returned to the *Astrolabe* having rescued Dudemaine, the bosun Jacon and Jacques-Philippe-Ésprit Cannac. He would also bring news that Faraguet and the yawl crew (Antoine Bellanger, Joseph Gras, Étienne Bouroul, Barthélemy Reboul, Lambert Fabry, Louis Martineng and Joseph de La Maria) had all been abducted by the Tongans. When the longboat returned three

'*Combat des Marins de* l'Astrolabe', *engraving probably by Charles (Carl Traugott) Beyer from a sketch by Louis-Auguste de Sainson, for Dumont d'Urville's* Voyage pittoresque autour du monde, *L. Tenré, Paris, vol. ii, 1835, plate ix. In 1827, when a number of his men were taken hostage on Tongatapu, d'Urville ordered an attack on the sacred religious site of Ma'ufanga, in an attempt to secure their release.* Author's collection

hours later, having set fire to the houses on Pangaimotu and Manima islands, d'Urville also learned that one of the crew, Simonet, had used the opportunity to desert. He had earlier been seen speaking to Tahofa, and his bag was later found cached and ready for his departure, but he had been forced to amend his plan because of the new circumstances. Simonet's collusion with Tahofa appears to have been confirmed by the fact that he had been seen among the Tongans still carrying his firearm, while his captured comrades had all been stripped of their weapons and possessions.

D'Urville was determined to maintain pressure on Tahofa as long as his men remained prisoners ashore. There was no lack of volunteers for another landing, but Gressien's report of the indiscipline and disorder of the sailors in the longboat crew convinced d'Urville to use officers who could be relied upon to obey orders and maintain a coherent formation ashore. Command of the landing party was once again given to Gressien. As the party was about to leave, Corporal François Richard came forward and pleaded with d'Urville to be allowed to go too, claiming his exclusion dishonoured him as commander of the expedition's marine detachment; with evident reservations, d'Urville gave in to his request.

Having reduced the habitations of Pangaimotu to ashes, Gressien's party now landed on Tongatapu and began setting fire to villages and canoes along the coast before heading for the religious site of Ma'ufanga. He had orders to fire only at those who displayed hostility, and he was told to respect women, children and those who did not resist. Meanwhile, Pâris followed the party along the reef with the longboat, thereby ensuring a rapid and favourable means of retreat in case of imminent encirclement. As Gressien's column approached Ma'ufanga, Tongan numbers began to swell, and it became clear that they intended to defend the religious site. Although the French started to come under sniper fire, Gressien and his men continued to advance and reply with musket fire of their own, but it was obvious that they were outnumbered and too exposed.

Just before Gressien ordered a retreat, the eager volunteer Corporal Richard had felled a Tongan some distance to the rear of the column and, with an apparent appetite for more blood, he imprudently broke formation to pursue another Tongan in the surrounding thicket. He was surprised and set upon by eight or ten men, who clubbed him unconscious and bayoneted him with his own weapon. Although his comrades responded to his cries, and Joseph-Victor Castel, the *Astrolabe*'s cook, apparently killed one of his assailants, Richard was carried back to the longboat with terrible wounds. The accuracy and rapidity of the fire directed at Gressien's retreating party – one rifle ball grazing Dudemaine's elbow – gave rise to suspicions that the deserter Simonet was responsible.

The longboat returned to the *Astrolabe* at 5.30 pm. Richard was unconscious when he was brought aboard, died of his wounds two and a half hours later and was buried on Pangaimotu the next day. A shocked d'Urville strongly supported Gressien's decision to retreat. Had his party, made up of so many of the expedition's best men, been surrounded and overwhelmed, it would have represented 'an irreparable loss for the *Astrolabe*'.[19] The obvious risk of further casualties fighting a numerous yet elusive enemy on home ground made d'Urville decide on another strategy: he would sail the *Astrolabe* directly in front of Ma'ufanga and menace the religious site with destruction from his heavy guns. His hope was that such a threat would force the other chiefs to take action against Tahofa and make him return his French prisoners. D'Urville's plan was underpinned by profound psychological reasoning. Having visited Ma'ufanga only a few days before, and having read William Mariner's account of Tongan religion and customs, he knew that it was where some of Tonga's greatest chiefs were buried, that it was considered a sacrilege to do battle or resist landings there, and that enemies had to be treated as friends within its less than a kilometre square confines – all on pain of divine displeasure and untimely death.[20] Weapons were made ready. A number of small field guns were installed in the corvette's forecastle, and a platform was constructed on the bow of the longboat in case it was necessary to mount such a field piece for a landing. Sentries were put on a state of alert in case an attempt was made to rush the corvette during the night. Meanwhile, the Tongans, aware of the French threat, worked feverishly through the night to construct defences of their own in front of their sacred site.

The next morning, a canoe was seen approaching. It contained Faraguet and yet another European castaway, a Swede named Thom. Faraguet asserted that, after the kidnapping, he had fallen into the hands of one of Palu's sisters, and that Singleton had then taken him to the chief. According to Faraguet, Palu had treated him well and had tried to get him to remain in his service, claiming that Tahofa had captured the *Astrolabe*. Faraguet had then been taken to Ma'ufanga, where he saw the sailors Fabry and Gras, and where he attended a kava ceremony with Palu, Tahofa and their warriors. He once again refused to remain in Tonga and was eventually released by his captors. (D'Urville was surprised to learn that Palu had parted with Faraguet by requesting a necklace of blue beads from his captain!) Singleton, who had also returned to the *Astrolabe*, advised d'Urville that the seizure of the yawl and the abduction of the sailors had been entirely the work of Tahofa, and that the other chiefs were unhappy with his actions but that they considered him too powerful to challenge. D'Urville responded by stating his preparedness to make common cause with the other chiefs against Tahofa.

By now, however, d'Urville did not entirely trust Singleton and decided to use him as a means of impressing upon the Tongans that if his men were not returned, he would begin destruction of Ma'ufanga the next day. If his 2700 kilograms of gunpowder and 15,000 bullets were not enough, he blustered, he would seek the aid of two French frigates stationed in Peru to exterminate the entire population of Tonga. A message was also received from Reverend Thomas, who stated that the Tongans had asked for his intercession, regretted their actions and feared Ma'ufanga would be destroyed. D'Urville replied that he would depart immediately, without firing a shot, if his men were returned.

With no Tongan reply and his men still in captivity, d'Urville took the *Astrolabe* along the reef to Ma'ufanga, guided by Lottin in one of the boats. He then anchored four hundred metres in front of the sacred burial site and saw several white flags flying on the shore. Guilbert, armed with a blunderbuss, was sent by boat to investigate whether they were flags of surrender. When he approached, he was surprised to see that the Tongans had constructed impressive sand ramparts, behind which hundreds of warriors sheltered in a trench up to one and a half metres deep. Then Martineng was released onto the beach and began to walk into the water calling out to Guilbert that the Tongans were prepared to release their French prisoners if an officer would come forward, unarmed and accompanied by one or two men, to 'conclude this affair with the chiefs'.[21] Guilbert was just about to comply when a gun shot rang out and a ball penetrated both sides of his boat, passing between the arms of the oarsmen, so he began to withdraw on d'Urville's orders. Martineng then took off his clothes and attempted to swim to the boat. When he too was shot at, he turned back, but not before pleading with Guilbert to return to the *Astrolabe* and not to fire back, lest he be killed by the Tongans.

D'Urville now took the *Astrolabe* even closer to the shore and anchored with Ma'ufanga within range of his guns. Martineng reappeared on the beach, and d'Urville sent an officer ashore to reiterate that there was no need for an unarmed French officer to meet with the chiefs; the prisoners could simply be returned by canoe, and peace would be concluded. He also passed on d'Urville's request to speak with Singleton, but Martineng replied that he too was detained by the Tongans and could not appear. D'Urville was now convinced that the call for an officer and men, without arms, was simply a deadly ruse. The rifles, bayonets and lances along the Tongan defences showed clearly what was intended. He then called all his officers to his cabin and asked for their opinions, beginning with the youngest, Pâris. All favoured opening fire, and some expressed surprise that d'Urville had taken so long to do so. For his part, d'Urville made it clear that he thought it better 'to sin by a little slowness, than to incur the reproach of speed, which in the eyes of some people would be charged with unjust severity'.[22]

At 10.30 am on 16 May, the *Astrolabe* opened fire. The first cannonball hit the branch of a large fig tree and brought it down on the Tongans below, who ran away screaming. Other balls caused some commotion when they hit the trunks of coconut palms or huts overlooking Ma'ufanga, but the vast majority thudded uselessly into the sand ramparts. One wonders whether these highly effective defences were conceived by the Tongans as a result of their own military experience facing Europeans, or whether they were thrown up at the suggestion of the castaways or deserters now in Tahofa's service. Undoubtedly, men such as Simonet would have had knowledge of the kind of improvised fortifications that would best offer protection under such circumstances. Given the removal of the French prisoners from harm's way (they might otherwise have been used as human shields), d'Urville began to suspect that many were would-be deserters.

Over the next hour, the veteran master gunner François Raynaud, one of the oldest men aboard the corvette, fired 30 cannonballs ashore. The Tongans (and presumably their European allies) returned fire with muskets aimed at men on the decks and rigging of the *Astrolabe* and at Guilbert, who had been ordered to move one of the anchors with the longboat. When the breech lashings on almost all the *Astrolabe*'s guns failed, probably because of prolonged exposure to moisture, the firing had to stop for repairs to be made. The Tongans used the respite to fortify their ramparts. When Raynaud recommenced fire, he did so with grapeshot directed to fall behind the Tongan sand barriers. The ensuing screams suggest that these shots told, but what seemed like a call for a truce (in the form of the Tongans waving a piece of cloth) came to nothing. A dozen of the next 24 shots were also charged with grapeshot, and yet again, screams punctuated the deep silence ashore, but there was still no sign of any Tongan willingness to negotiate. Quite to the contrary, at sunset, a volley of a dozen Tongan musket shots raked the *Astrolabe*, and the French responded by once more directing grapeshot at the village. Throughout the night, the felling of still more trees could be heard, and it was obvious that the Tongans were building additional defences. The following day, the *Astrolabe* fired only 17 shots, of which six were grapeshot, but they were regularly spaced. For much of the day, there was also torrential rain, and d'Urville, despite his growing respect for the Tongan warriors, hoped that the wet weather would diminish their morale in the exposed trenches.

With his telescope, d'Urville could see that his imprisoned men were still closely guarded, although two sailors, Fabry and Bellanger, whom he respected, were seen alone on the beach. Fabry was evidently wounded in the right leg and walked with difficulty. D'Urville thought he and Bellanger were placed on the beach as bait, but he refused to be drawn ashore with a rescue boat; with his telescope, he could see that they too were being carefully watched by men hidden in the woods. For the moment, d'Urville confined his response to occasional musket fire, but at sunset, the *Astrolabe* once more poured grapeshot on Ma'ufanga. Although Lottin communicated the desire of several aboard to participate in another armed landing, d'Urville dismissed the idea. The Tongan defences clearly provided considerable protection to Ma'ufanga, and the proximity to the reef posed a much greater risk to the *Astrolabe*. D'Urville had decided to remain only one more day and then cut his losses and leave with the first favourable winds. However, should disaster befall the *Astrolabe*, Dudemaine was given precise orders to blow her up 'to give a stern lesson to the perfidious islanders of Tonga-Tabou and to remove in an instant to the regret and to the consideration of future explorers, the sad debris of our brilliant expedition'.[23] Fortunately, it did not come to this.

The firing recommenced the next day, 19 May, but at 3.30 pm, Tahofa sent Martineng back to the *Astrolabe* by canoe. He brought news that there were 3000 well-armed Tongan warriors dug in at Ma'ufanga and that the *Astrolabe*'s protracted cannonade had produced only one fatality – with grapeshot the previous evening. (Apparently, this fatality was a chief who was hit by a piece of shot that ricocheted from an ironwood tree.[24]) That night, the chiefs held a long conference and successively called

'Tonga-Tabou, Vadodai vient demander la fin des hostilités', lithograph by Victor-Jean Adam, from a sketch by Louis-Auguste de Sainson, Voyage de la corvette l'Astrolabe, Atlas historique, Paris, 1833, plate 88. The Tongan Wai-Totai – who had befriended Ensign Victor-Amédée Gressien – boarded the Astrolabe bearing a pig, yams and several hands of bananas from the chief Tahofa, in the hope of ending hostilities with the French. Sainson captured the moment a trembling Wai-Totai prostrated himself on the deck. National Library of Australia PIC U1797 NK3340

and interrogated each of the French sailors (presumably with regard to their personal desire to stay or leave), then Tahofa agreed to release them. D'Urville no longer trusted Martineng and kept him away from the rest of the crew. He gave him time to drink some wine and smoke some tobacco, then sent him straight back in the longboat to reiterate to Tahofa that, as soon as the prisoners were released, hostilities would end and he would quit Tonga. By 4.30 pm, Martineng had conveyed this message to Tahofa and had reappeared on the beach to inform the officer in the waiting longboat that Simonet and Reboul were no longer present at Ma'ufanga, but that all the sailors would be returned together the following morning.

As the weather worsened again, once more threatening grim consequences for the *Astrolabe*, d'Urville received disturbing news from the second mate, Pierre Collinet, that only five or six sailors in the entire crew could be relied on; the rest were prepared to desert to the Tongan side! Although a violent wind blew the entire night, the following morning it dropped, the sky cleared and the rain stopped. Ashore, the Tongans began to demolish their fortifications and made a breach in the ramparts to launch a canoe carrying Wai-Totai, who had formed a particular friendship with Gressien during their sojourn, and a pig, yams and several hands of bananas as a peace offering. A trembling Wai-Totai prostrated himself on the deck of the *Astrolabe* (a moment captured by Sainson in a sketch later published as a lithograph in the 'Atlas historique' of the expedition)[25] and explained that he had been charged by Tahofa to report that Simonet and Reboul had fled to the interior and could not be returned immediately with the other French captives ashore. D'Urville knew well that Simonet, in particular, would be reluctant to return because his desertion and subsequent actions made him liable to face capital punishment. Since Simonet had previously been convicted of theft and had been suspected of other crimes, d'Urville considered him no great loss. He had a kinder opinion of Reboul, whom he considered a passable sailor but a tranquil imbecile, easily corrupted. He decided to cut his losses, not simply with regard to the deserters – Tahofa was welcome to them – but also the muskets taken from Dudemaine and the unfortunate Richard, and even the items stolen from the yawl. A quarter of an hour after this message of quittance was conveyed ashore by Wai-Totai, Guilbert was able to embark Martineng, de La Maria, Bellanger, Bouroul, Fabry and Gras, all clad in local tapa, having been stripped of all their own clothes when they were captured. Of all of them, only Martineng appears to have equivocated, apparently contemplating desertion until the very last minute. The former prisoners returned with testimony that Tahofa had indeed harboured plans to capture the *Astrolabe* and had been intent on luring the longboat ashore in the hope of dealing a fatal blow to her officers. His ruses had failed and, despite Tongan numbers and ample weaponry, three days of bombardment and torrential rain had weakened Tahofa's hold over the other chiefs. Although he had gained kudos through his spirited defence of Ma'ufanga, the one death from grapeshot – although insignificant in terms of the total number of 3000 warriors – had nevertheless engendered fear and weakened the resolve of Tahofa's army. So too, d'Urville believed, had his other emphatic threats conveyed through Singleton, but there is no proof of this.

On 21 May, with Lottin leading the way in the yawl and Guilbert serving as a lookout from the fore-topgallant crosstree, the *Astrolabe* carefully made her way through the reef without incident and once more entered the vast expanse of the Pacific. The closing paragraphs of d'Urville's account of his visit to Tonga contain a summary of Simonet's perfidious behaviour based on the testimony of other members of the crew. As we shall see, his path was destined to cross d'Urville's again.

17

Any other captain would probably have hesitated

To hear him, none other than himself would ever have attempted the exploration of the Fijis when deprived of anchors and cables, such as was the case with the Astrolabe; *in fact any other captain would probably have hesitated.*

Pierre-Adolphe Lesson*

After leaving Tongatapu, the *Astrolabe* sailed north-northwest towards the Fiji Islands. On 24 May 1827, shortly after sighting the small island of Ongea Levu in the southeast of the archipelago, she was approached by two canoes. Five of the occupants immediately came on board. One, a man named Mediola, was a Chamorro from Guam who had taken refuge on the island of Lakemba after being shipwrecked near Viti Levu on a Spanish sandalwood vessel, the *Concepción*. All the others, including a chief named Mouki, were Tongans. They asked to remain aboard the *Astrolabe* and, recognising that they were potentially useful as interpreters in Fijian waters, d'Urville agreed. They also provided information about an anchor, apparently abandoned on Lakemba by an American whaler (possibly the *Argo*, which ran aground there in 1800). Lakemba was reached two days later. There, d'Urville encountered a sailor named Guittierez and two other Spaniards from Manila, who were also survivors of the *Concepción*. All three asked permission to join the crew of the *Astrolabe* and were gladly accepted as replacements for the men lost in Tonga. Although the presence of the American anchor was confirmed, the aggressive posturing of the inhabitants of the village who controlled it and the need to renegotiate the reef to land there led d'Urville to abandon any further attempt to acquire it as a replacement for one of the several he had lost.

The *Astrolabe* then sailed on to Vatu Vara, Taveuni and neighbouring Nggamea. Unfortunately, deteriorating weather made survey work difficult, so d'Urville altered course and headed south. On 2 June, after depositing his now gift-laden but anxious

* 'Portrait de l'état-major de l'Astrolabe', 1828

Tongan passengers on the island of Moala (which was also located with accuracy for the first time), d'Urville sailed south-southeast and made, in Andrew Sharp's words, the 'first firm record' of the islands of Totoya and Matuku.[1] He then set a reverse north-northeasterly course, catching sight of the island of Ngau and then the main Fijian island of Viti Levu, but a dangerous reef far offshore reminded him of the fate of the brig *Eliza* – wrecked off Nairai in 1808 on what he thought was a continuation of the same reef – so he turned south yet again.

Soon after, the *Astrolabe* was hit by a fierce electrical storm. As howling winds and torrential rain enveloped the corvette, visibility was reduced to less than 100 metres, but luckily she was in open waters. The storm persisted until the following morning, but when it was over, the *Astrolabe* had been blown even further to the southwest. Finding himself within 90 kilometres of Kandavu, discovered by William Bligh in 1792, d'Urville decided to confirm the island's position on the (1810) chart of the Russian explorer and circumnavigator Adam von Krusenstern. In doing so, the expedition once again came close to disaster. On the night of 5 June, d'Urville was wakened by the cry of a terrified crewman, who had noticed breakers just over half a kilometre to leeward and fortuitously illuminated by the clearing moon. The previously unknown reef, which was only narrowly avoided, now bears the *Astrolabe*'s name. After locating Kandavu, still more coral shoals frustrated the expedition's renewed attempt to approach Viti Levu. Several canoes were encountered off the island's west coast and south of Malolo, and they provided an opportunity to exchange gunpowder, axes and scissors for pigs, chickens, yams, coconuts and traditional Fijian weapons – and to make brief ethnographic observations.[2]

After 18 days zigzagging in the Fijian Archipelago – hampered by storms, heavy seas, dangerous reefs and overcast skies that prevented navigational astronomy – d'Urville set sail for the Loyalty Islands off the east coast of New Caledonia. No new discoveries were made in this chain, other than a previously unknown reef, to the northwest of Beaupré Island, that was yet again named after the *Astrolabe*. According to his instructions, d'Urville sailed on to the Louisiades and New Ireland. Still hungry for further discoveries, he did not slavishly follow d'Entrecasteaux's route, but he did make follow-up comparisons with several positions d'Entrecasteaux fixed, such as Rossel Island (Yela), and also those of other navigators, such as Louis-Charles-Ruault Coutance, whose Mauritian commercial expedition discovered an islet nearby in 1803.[3] The islet, little more than an exposed rock, had remained unnamed on Krusternstern's chart, so d'Urville christened it 'Île Adèle'. He was at pains to tell his readers that this was in honour of Coutance's vessel the *Adèle*[4] – making no reference to his beloved wife, though he must have had her in mind.

D'Urville also remained mindful of d'Entrecasteaux's primary mission, which

'Aiguade de l'Astrolabe au Havre Carteret, N[ouv]elle Irelande', lithograph by Achille Saint-Aulaire, from a sketch by Louis-Auguste de Sainson, Voyage de la corvette l'Astrolabe, Atlas historique, Paris, 1833, plate 110. In July 1827, the Astrolabe took shelter in Carteret Habour (now Lamassa Bay) on the coast of New Ireland and replenished the expedition's water supplies. National Library of Australia, PIC U1819 NK3340

meshed with his own subsidiary instructions: determination of the fate of Lapérouse. D'Entrecasteaux died during his search for his missing compatriot and was eventually succeeded as commander of the expedition by Elisabeth-Paul-Edouard de Rossel, whom d'Urville knew well as the director-general of the navy's hydrographic office in Paris. Rossel would die shortly after the Astrolabe returned to France but not before reviewing d'Urville's charts and rekindling disturbing personal memories of the dangers he had faced in these same waters.[5]

After finding nothing to support the rumours, sourced to Admiral Thomas Manby RN, regarding an unnamed American whaler coming across traces of Lapérouse's expedition (on what was thought to be an island in the Louisiades), d'Urville sailed on to New Ireland. He was still unaware that Lapérouse had met his fate about 1800 kilometres to the southeast. Although d'Urville intended to put into English Cove, named by Philip Carteret in late July 1767,[6] but did not wish to revisit Port Praslin, which he had visited with Duperrey in August 1823, the deteriorating weather made this difficult. English Cove is at the head of Breton Harbour, and the entry is north of Lambon Island (Carteret's 'Wallis's Island') in Saint George's Channel. Instead of passing through the eastern channel, between Lambon and the mainland of New

Ireland, d'Urville decided to round the island from the west on the afternoon of 5 July. However, off the western point of Lambon, torrential rain reduced visibility almost to nil, and d'Urville felt he had no choice but to seek shelter further to the north in Carteret Harbour, now Lamassa Bay. Lottin sounded the way ahead in the yawl. Unfortunately, in the continuing deluge, he and his crew of eight men became separated from the *Astrolabe* on entering the harbour. Given the winds and the strong southerly current, d'Urville believed that the *Astrolabe* might never be reunited with the yawl if she re-entered Saint George's Channel, and on such an apparently inhospitable coast, he became deeply anxious over the fate of the men in the yawl. For their part, Lottin and his crew were also on the verge of despair, but in taking refuge in the southeast of the harbour, they soon saw the *Astrolabe* dragged north by the current towards Carteret's 'Coconut Island', now Lamassa Island. The yawl was therefore able to rejoin the mother ship at her night's anchorage, safe from the nearby shoals but with d'Urville's men furling her sails in the pouring rain until late at night. Regrettably, it was a mooring that would cost the expedition yet another precious anchor (albeit one with only one fluke), when the cable and buoy rope snapped on being hauled in by the capstan.

Firing several cannons, d'Urville announced the *Astrolabe*'s arrival at Lamassa Bay. The following morning, a swollen, rain-fed stream was located in a nearby cove, and a longboat crew was put to work replenishing the expedition's water barrels. Sainson sketched the water being funnelled into the longboat via a hose strung along a causeway of barrels. The watering party also met a group of local inhabitants fishing nearby and recognised them as the same race as those encountered by the *Coquille* at Port Praslin in 1823. From them, the officers traded a fish and a possum. Meanwhile, d'Urville, in need of exercise and suffering from a 'dullness of mind and a general indisposition',[7] landed on Lamassa Island. One wonders whether he also wanted to expose himself to danger as an antidote to his depressive state. The day before, Guilbert had encountered a large crocodile on the same island, and d'Urville recorded that this dangerous animal had put everyone on guard but had also engendered a desire to acquire 'the skeleton or the skin' to augment their natural history collections.[8] There were further sightings of crocodiles on the coast, and one was finally shot on 15 July. However, by the time its body (over 3.7 metres long) was found by Dudemaine two days later, it had putrefied so much that it could only be sketched by Sainson before its severed head was preserved in alcohol. There were other prizes for the naturalists, and Quoy and Gaimard would eventually publish the first scientific description of the Bismarck hawk-owl, *Noctua variegata* (*Ninox variegata*) from a specimen collected at Lamassa Bay.[9]

The geology of this part of New Ireland essentially consists of 'Punam' limestone laid down in the Pliocene,[10] and d'Urville noted compacted madrepores (coral) as he climbed to the highest point of Lamassa Island. Although 44 plant species were listed as collected at 'Havre Carteret', only one among them was new to science: a beautiful epiphytic orchid that Achille Richard named *Oberonia gladiata*, later included in the genus *Phreatia* by the German botanist Friedrich Kraenzlin. Richard specifically mentions that this species was collected on 'Île aux Cocos' (Lamassa Island), growing on the bark of trees,[11] so it is entirely possible that d'Urville was its collector on the morning of 7 July 1827. Ironically, despite the name Carteret gave the island, d'Urville did not find a single coconut tree among its lush vegetation.

On going ashore, d'Urville had given orders to Béringuier and Chieusse to cut cabbage palms (*Livistona australis*) to be distributed as vegetables among the crew. According to d'Urville's official account, they mistakenly returned with toxic cycads, which they then began to eat with disastrous consequences. Pierre-Adolphe Lesson, however, was adamant that his commander's account of these events was untruthful:

> On that day, I had landed with the commandant and the two carpenters. On arriving on the spot in the interior of the island, and finding no palm-trees but a lot of cycads, Monsieur d'Urville said to Master Béringuier that since palm-trees were so scarce, they could knock down the cycads which would provide the equivalent cabbage. This was done by the carpenters who brought them on board and ate them that same evening and suffered colic and vomiting, which finished up with one being cured, and the other [Béringuier] dying three months after. Thankfully … the officers [and], the sailors abstained from eating them, being suspicious of their bitterness. Only the commandant wanted to do the like of the carpenters and ate some of it, being taken likewise by colic and after-pains which lasted eight days. He had been wrong to declare to the carpenters that the cabbage of the cycads could replace those of the palm-trees, and without this invitation, Béringuier and Chieusse would have abstained from felling the cycads. I have mentioned on several occasions that Monsieur d'Urville did not like to own up to his mistakes. I have been witness to this, as I heard his words.[12]

Cycads contain the glycoside toxins cycasin and neocycasin. D'Urville surely knew that several members of d'Entrecasteaux's expedition suffered severe gastrointestinal effects from eating cycad nuts. He might have been aware that members of Cook's *Endeavour* expedition had suffered similarly in northern Queensland.[13] From reading Labillardière's *Relation*, d'Urville would also have known that the indigenous inhabitants of New Ireland carefully prepare cycad nuts before they eat them. Although Labillardière noted that the nuts were roasted in New Ireland, it was not until he reached the Moluccas that he realised the need to macerate them in order to remove their 'hurtful qualities'.[14] Freycinet also recorded processes of cycad detoxification during his visit to Guam.[15] While d'Urville blamed Béringuier's and Chieusse's 'imprudence' in eating the cycad-palm heart, he admitted that he had tried the same heart, boiled, in the hope that 'cooking would remove its harmful qualities',[16] perhaps thinking the 'heart' of new leaves less of a risk than the nuts. It was an experiment that failed: d'Urville spat out the bitter cooked morsel and quickly ordered the remaining palms thrown overboard. Even if Lesson offers us the more accurate record of events, his accusation regarding Béringuier's death three months later is questionable. A study of cycad toxicity, published in 2004, suggests that severe vomiting is the only significant symptom: out of 21 cases of poisoning, there were no recorded fatalities, and all patients recovered fully within 24 hours.[17] However, the ingestion of incompletely de-toxified cycads in the Mariana Islands and the Kii Peninsula in Japan has been suggested (but not proved) as a cause of neurodegenerative disorders such as amyotrophic lateral sclerosis (ALS) and the related Parkinsonian dementia complex (PDC).[18] The medicinal use of cycads has also been linked to neurodegenerative disorders in Irian Jaya. Furthermore, cycads are known to cause hind-quarter paralysis in cattle, and gastro-intestinal and liver damage in sheep and pigs: 2200 sheep in a flock of 6000 merinos died over a three-week period after one *Macrozamia* grazing incident in the Piliga Scrub, near Coonabarabran, New South Wales, in 1929.[19]

There can be little doubt that the 22-year-old Pierre-Adolphe Lesson disliked d'Urville even more than his older brother René did. 'He always displayed offhandedness, whether ashore or on board,' wrote Lesson, 'always aiming straight to his target, disdaining social conventions by design, as much as by personality.'[20] Although Lesson recognised that d'Urville was 'a studious man, erudite and possessing a solid knowledge of botany', he, very surprisingly, believed that his expedition leader was 'not very knowledgeable in matters of the sea'. Yet he himself had only served aboard one other vessel: the storeship *Durance*. In Lesson's opinion, the *Astrolabe*'s survival was due to the fact that she 'had good officers', whose 'glorious labour' d'Urville acknowledged in his 'good moments'. There was obviously a personality clash between the resentful young surgeon and his commander. Lesson's personal journal contains unrelentingly negative comments about d'Urville, and he could see little to admire in his commander. His speech was 'short, harsh' and his tone 'sharp, scornful, always unpleasant'; his character was 'cold, tenacious, obstinate'; his language contained 'a malicious causticity'; he was 'personal and selfish … vindictive'; he was 'not very sincere'; he 'had the highest opinion of himself'; he 'liked to say that he was the most independent man in the world'; he was 'convinced of the superiority of his mind'; and so on.[21]

There can be little doubt of d'Urville's eccentricities, bluntness, intellectual aloofness, ambition, vanity and hunger for glory. For all his initiative and tenacity, his self-confidence appears to have been frequently impaired by depressive mood swings.[22] Indeed, d'Urville, who frequently preferred solitude to the company of his men, was unlike any of the charismatic heroes extolled by two of his favourite authors: Plutarch and Homer.

Despite his personal idiosyncrasies and failings, d'Urville's two principal officers, Jacquinot and Lottin, had both circumnavigated the globe with him before and freely chose to sail with him again – in Jacquinot's case, on d'Urville's final expedition as well. The master carpenter Alexandre Béringuier was also a fellow veteran of the *Coquille* expedition. For d'Urville, personal command was clearly very important; he burned with envy and frustration under Duperrey's authority aboard the *Coquille*. Significantly, despite his belief that officers should maintain distance from their subordinates, and (at that time but not later in his life) that corporal punishment was necessary to counter indiscipline and insubordination, his own command style was not inflexibly authoritarian. Although he reserved the right to make final decisions, he regularly sought the opinions and counsel of his subordinate officers, and at several critical junctures – such as during the storm in the Bay of Plenty in New Zealand – effectively surrendered power when he was too exhausted or incapable of offering leadership. He also regularly delegated authority to those in command of landing or surveying parties (or in charge of the *Astrolabe* when he went botanising) and did not always strictly dictate steps to be taken in his absence. Through all of this, and despite his obvious failings, his potent intellect maintained a clear strategic overview of the historical, political and scientific context of his mission and how the resources at his disposal might best be utilised to bring his orders to fruition.

After gathering firewood and water, completing repairs (including scrubbing the hull with sand), surveying the harbour and conducting limited trade with the indigenous inhabitants – whom d'Urville described in very unflattering terms of stupidity, indolence, apathy,[23] hideousness and dirtiness[24] – the *Astrolabe* was ready to depart from Lamassa Bay on 10 July. However, ill with a severe case of enteritis, d'Urville decided not to set sail. Lesson would blame his captain's intestinal sensitivity on eating 'heavy things, cheap, badly prepared, to which he naturally adds spices, or following this bad habit he prefers smoked or salted meats'.[25] Yet d'Urville would complain about his 'sad ration of beans and salt pork' aboard ship, for which he had 'little liking'.[26] Given his concomitant fever, his enteric condition appears to have been caused by a bacterial or protozoal infection rather than from any preference for dried or salted naval rations over fresh food.

During his illness, d'Urville took nothing but 'light broth', and Gaimard treated him with leeches, enemas and hot baths. It is hardly surprising that he felt worse after such ministering. Fearing that he might die, he drafted a 'kind of memoir to guide M. Jacquinot for the rest of the campaign'.[27] Although still very weak, d'Urville left his sick bed on 18 July, and that night, the longboat was embarked for departure. The following morning, d'Urville rose at 4.30. All around him, men – some almost naked – were fast asleep on the deck in the tropical heat. They were soon roused from their torpor and begrudgingly set to work hoisting the anchors. No sooner was the *Astrolabe* underway than the capricious wind drove her towards the coral, and it was necessary to drop anchor once again. Fortunately, the delay was brief, and the current soon took the corvette out of Saint George's Channel. D'Urville's relief was tempered by exhaustion and lingering fever. The strong current in this part of the Bismarck Archipelago also dragged the *Astrolabe* to the southwest and away from his next objective, the southern coast of New Britain. Gale-force winds and torrential rain made navigational astronomy only occasionally possible and further sapped the psychological reserves of the captain and his crew, but after sailing north, the expedition sighted mist-shrouded Cape Orford early on the evening of 23 July. The next day, the position of this cape was fixed, and the *Astrolabe* continued sailing southwest along the coast. A large peak in the distance (presumably Mount Yeno) and a cape east of Waterfall Bay were named in honour of Quoy, but only the cape, albeit in a phonetically mutated pidgin form as Cape Kwoi, has survived. Jacquinot was also honoured, and to this day Cape Jacquinot and Jacquinot Bay further to the west bear his name.

The occasional glimpses of the coast of New Britain, largely shrouded by the constant bad weather, were the 'torment of Tantalus' for d'Urville.[28] Such poor visibility made inshore surveying dangerous and obliged the *Astrolabe* to withdraw a safe distance out to sea. Although Dampier had written that 'no Meadow in England appears more green in Spring, than these'[29] and had named the island 'Nova-Britannia' because it reminded him of his homeland, a dispirited d'Urville challenged such idyllic accounts – including those of his compatriot of Charles 'Président' de Brosses.[30] Indeed, the torrential rain soon began to remind d'Urville of Genesis and the Noachic flood.

At the beginning of August, the *Astrolabe* passed through Dampier Strait – briefly striking reefs twice in the process but without any significant damage – and entered the Bismarck Sea. In sailing along the northern coast of New Guinea, d'Urville would christen Astrolabe Bay, Cape Croisilles, Humboldt Bay and Cape d'Urville. These toponyms have endured to this day, unlike those he gave to three small islands close to Aitape on the West Sepik coast after Faraguet (Seleo), Sainson (Ali) and Dudemaine (Tumelo). Finally, the imposing Gauttier Mountains (west of the Foja Range) and Matterer Bay were named in honour of his former superiors aboard the *Chevrette*. After traversing Geelvink Bay on 25 August 1827, the *Astrolabe* slowly made her way into the harbour of Dorey (Manokwari) on the Doberai Peninsula of West Papua. Three years earlier, d'Urville had visited this same harbour with Duperrey, and he felt confident of acquiring water, firewood and fresh provisions for his expedition. His expectations were only partly met.

Only limited provisions were traded by the local coastal Papuans. Firewood and water were obtained, but the still-constant rain also made inland travel unpleasant, swelled local watercourses and apparently flushed most of the fish from the bay. Much more successful was the trade in zoological specimens, and the *Astrolabe* left Dorey with a rich trove of previously unknown birds, including the little shrike-thrush *Muscicapa megarhyncha* (*Colluricincla megarhyncha*);[31] two species of Papuan frogmouth, *Podargus ocellatus*[32] and *P. papuensis*[33] (the latter also found in northern Queensland); the emperor fairy-wren, *Todus cyanocephalus* (*Malurus cyanocephalus*);[34] and the purple-tailed imperial pigeon, *Columba rufigaster* (*Ducula rufigaster*).[35] The local Papuans also traded a large number of insects, many of which were published in the expedition's entomological volumes. This was along with those collected by d'Urville during the visit of the *Coquille*, so it is difficult to separate the collection dates.

As was his habit, d'Urville undertook a number of exploratory excursions during his sojourn in Dorey. Unfortunately, his imagined physical reserves did not match the demands of the topography or the arduous wet conditions. From a botanical perspective he was also disappointed. The vast majority of plants collected at Dorey were already known to science, but they did include one previously undescribed species: the spleenwort *Asplenium cyatheaefolium*.[36] D'Urville returned 'bored and tired' from an excursion on 26 August,[37] but it was not just steaming, soaking, slippery Dorey that seemed different. The commander of the expedition recognised a change in himself: 'My altered temperament could no longer take these long excursions which were nothing but a frolic for me during my campaigns in the Levant, and which I repeated without difficulty during the voyage of the *Coquille*.'[38] Nevertheless, D'Urville made several other day-long excursions, accompanied by his secretary Lauvergne and another sailor. He hoped that these forays would prove beneficial to his health, but returning to the *Astrolabe* on 31 August, he was forced to admit defeat: 'A kind of general langour, a weakness in all the parts of the body made me lose the taste for long excursions.'[39] Though only 37 years of age, he was no longer the physically powerful man whose steps, Pierre-Adolphe Lesson asserted, 'were worth almost two of those of his companions.'[40]

During the final part of his sojourn at Dorey, aside from preparing his vessel for departure, d'Urville appears to have occupied himself drafting ethnographic notes on the coastal Papuans and their feared head-hunting highland neighbours, the 'Arfaki' (*Arfak* is a term covering a number of tribes in the neighouring mountains).[41] The day before the *Astrolabe* set sail for the Moluccas, a watering party comprising Guillaume Quemener, André Vignau and Antoine Bellanger was attacked by these very same Arfak highlanders intent on taking their bucket. In the surprise assault, Bellanger was seriously wounded by an arrow in his back. Fortunately, his lung was not punctured and he survived, but d'Urville did not rest easy until all his shore parties had returned safely. At 5.30 am on 6 September 1827, the *Astrolabe* weighed anchor and began to slip out of Dorey, followed by numerous canoes bearing Papuans still keen to engage in one last trading session. By 8.00 am, however, even they had withdrawn, and the departing corvette was once again separated from the rest of humanity.

The *Astrolabe* rounded Cape Goede Hoop (Tanjung Yamursba) on 10 September and the same day approached Waigeo. D'Urville's original intention was to pass between Waigeo and Batanta as William Dampier had done. Instead, the winds forced him to round Waigeo from the north as Duperrey had done four years earlier. His desire to differentiate his route from Duperrey's by sailing between the islands of Gag and Waigeo was also thwarted by unfavourable winds. The *Astrolabe* therefore sailed through the southern Halmahera Sea between Gebe and Gag. Near the island of Boo, a *kora kora* (planked Moluccan double-outrigger canoe) flying a Dutch flag was sighted. D'Urville altered course, west-northwest, to communicate with her, but she appears to have deliberately avoided a meeting. After crossing the Sea of Ceram, on 20 September the *Astrolabe* entered the Banda Sea by passing through the strait separating the islands of Buru and Manipa. On 24 September, she reached Ambon and was greeted by the port captain, Andries Adolph Ellinghuijsen, whom d'Urville tells us he had met previously in Surabaya in 1824.[42]

The *Astrolabe* anchored temporarily next to an English whaler (probably the *Castor*) before anchoring beneath Fort Victoria the following day. Ensign Lottin went ashore to present the expedition's papers – including a letter of recommendation from Willem I, the first king of the previously republican Netherlands – to the Dutch colonial authorities. Pieter Merkus, who was provincial governor when the *Coquille* visited Ambon in 1823, was absent on an inspection tour, so d'Urville made an official call on Presiding Judge Johan Moorrees, who was acting governor. He recorded that he was amiably and cordially received by Moorrees, in the company of Colonel Stijman (the military commander at Fort Victoria), Captain Lang (in charge of the battery), the port captain Ellinghuijsen and two other officers, Paoli and Roos. D'Urville added that he was promised that all his requests 'would be accorded immediately' and that he received 'offers of the most obliging service'.[43] These do not appear to have been idle promises. D'Urville wrote in glowing terms that he received everything he needed from the Dutch magazines, including 'anchors and hawsers', and that he purchased 4000 kilograms of 'good quality' biscuits and 1500 kilograms of 'very ordinary' rice. Acting Governor Moorrees also permitted the French to establish an observatory in the port captain's garden.[44] Furthermore, two of the expedition's sick cases, Bérenguier and Aubry, were admitted to the Dutch colony's hospital.

D'Urville was not the kind of person to conceal irritation or bitterness, but in Ambon,

'Un Marché au Campong Chinois', engraving by Boilly from a sketch by Louis-Auguste de
Sainson, for Dumont d'Urville's Voyage pittoresque autour du monde, *L. Tenré, Paris, vol. ii,
1835, plate xxiv. D'Urville visited the island of Ambon in the Netherlands East Indies several
times and was drawn to its Chinese quarter. It is possible that he purchased his first Chinese
books at this market place. By the time of his death he owned over 60 books in Chinese. His study
of Chinese language became more serious after the Revolution of 1830. His young son Jules also
began to translate Chinese texts under his father's tutelage.* Author's collection

he complained only of the smell of the tobacco smoke, which hung heavy in the air
during dinners and musical recitals. Yet Pierre-Adolphe Lesson would have us believe
that 'in the presence of Dutchmen', d'Urville's behaviour appeared 'unseemly and
unpleasant'.[45] Even if one discounts Lesson's chronic antipathy towards his commander,
one way that d'Urville might have offended the Dutch is by an undiplomatic expression
of admiration and sympathy for Diponegoro, Prince of Yogyakarta, leader of the
Javanese insurgency, whom he believed he had seen as a prisoner during his previous
visit to the Netherlands East Indies. We know that d'Urville considered him 'a man of
energetic character … [whose] heart was embittered by the bad treatment he received
from the Dutch'.[46] Indeed, he had already acknowledged that the 'consequences of
this war caused a marked disquiet among most of the colonial functionaries'.[47] But if
d'Urville did give offence, it cannot have been lasting, for he was repeatedly invited to
dinner and other social gatherings by Dutch officials.

As he had during the *Coquille* expedition, d'Urville visited Ambon's Chinese quarter. There can be little doubt of his admiration and respect for the Chinese and for his interest in their language. He wrote: 'I have admired the propriety, the tranquillity and the honesty of these small merchants, in all respects very superior to Europeans, so proud of their civilisation.'[48] D'Urville compared these Chinese traders to the Jews of Europe, without anti-Semitic connotations. He also attended a Chinese wedding in Ambon with J.R. Paape, the acting governor's secretary.[49]

At Ambon, Guittierez and the two other Spanish survivors of the wreck of the *Concepción* left the expedition. So too did the Māori Kokako, who had joined the expedition at the Bay of Islands; he would apparently join four other Māori aboard the English whaler *Castor*.[50] Of the crewmen recruited in the Pacific, only the Chamorro Mediola remained aboard the *Astrolabe*, and d'Urville was happy to pay this 'brave boy' sailors' wages of 28 francs per month.[51] Despite Pierre-Adolphe Lesson's accusations about d'Urville's attitude to his men, at Ambon he unilaterally raised all their wages and wrote to the minister seeking his confirmation.

D'Urville, however, failed to receive any mail from France in Ambon, including a reply from the navy minister regarding a request for the promotion of several of his staff officers. After entrusting still more correspondence to the port captain in a tin box sealed with solder, wrapped in tar-cloth and addressed to the French ambassador in The Hague, d'Urville set sail from the Dutch colony on 10 October 1827. He recorded his destination as 'la Tasmanie' – an early French use of the modern toponym for an island that was still officially called 'Van Diemen's Land' by the British. His intention, he wrote, was 'to visit Hobart-Town, capital of this interesting establishment; a place which no French vessel had seen since d'Entrecasteaux made his discovery'.[52] D'Urville then planned to return to the west coast of New Zealand before heading west and passing through Torres Strait on his way back to France. Events in Hobart would soon dramatically alter these plans.

18

Van Diemen's Land

... O! I have suffer'd
With those that I saw suffer: a brave vessel,
Who had, no doubt, some noble creatures in her
Dash'd all to pieces. O! the cry did knock
Against my heart.

William Shakespeare [Miranda]*

After leaving Ambon, d'Urville toyed with the possibility of 'dropping anchor for a day or two' at Kupang, in Timor, but the winds were unfavourable.[1] Sailing beyond the islands of the Indonesian Archipelago, he saw no need for his officers to pursue significant geographic and hydrographic work, given the prior efforts of d'Entrecasteaux, Freycinet and Duperrey.[2] With a number of sick cases – he had left Ambon with François-Pierre-Michel Aubry, Béringuier, Collinet, Fabry and Faraguet afflicted with fever – d'Urville declared his intention to visit Exmouth Gulf on the Western Australian coast in the hope that they might benefit from a sojourn ashore – or so he asserted in his official account. His principal intention might, in fact, have been to investigate yet another site for a possible French penal colony and perhaps also to fix the position of North West Cape, which had not been visited by d'Entrecasteaux, Baudin or Freycinet. Once again, these ambitions were frustrated by contrary winds. On 18 November 1827, d'Urville profited from a complete calm in Australian waters to resume his sea-water temperature studies: plunging his thermométrographe 820 fathoms (1499.6 metres), he recorded a temperature of only 4.5°C, compared to 23° at the surface and 21.8° for the air at sea level. He also searched unsuccessfully for the Tryal Rocks, where the English East India Company vessel the *Tryal* was wrecked in 1622;[3] because he could not find these rocks, he incorrectly came to the conclusion that they did not exist.

At 2.20 pm on 29 November, the *Astrolabe*'s hardworking master carpenter Alexandre Bérenguier died of a painful gastrointestinal condition and recurrent fever.

---

* *The Tempest* (1611), act i, scene ii, lines 4–7

He was 47 years old and was buried at sea with full naval honours. D'Urville was deeply saddened by his death and clearly held him in very high regard, even recording in a footnote that he had unsuccessfully sought a decoration for him.[4] The son of a baker from Six-Fours, near Toulon, Béringuier had joined the navy in 1797 and had been taken prisoner by the British on the *Généreux* in February 1800. After his release during the Peace of Amiens, he served on a dozen other French naval vessels, circled the globe twice and was shipwrecked in the Falklands with Freycinet. His wife, Anne-Marie Pelliccia, 13 years his junior, was a native of La Spezia, and Béringuier had two children by her in Italy before they were married. There can be little doubt that d'Urville made a determined effort to secure a pension for Béringuier's Italian widow, writing to the minister on 9 April 1829 that her late husband was 'a model of zeal, and of devotion and continual application to work'.[5] Although Béringuier probably died from a combination of dysentery and malaria rather than the direct effects of cycad poisoning (as Lesson asserted), it is possible that d'Urville considered himself partially to blame for his demise.

By the beginning of December, the *Astrolabe* rounded Cape Leeuwin and entered the Southern Ocean far from the Australian coast. On 10 December, she reached the same latitude as the southern tip of Tasmania, but her crew did not sight the island until six days after. On 16 December, after more than two months at sea, the *Astrolabe* entered the southern D'Entrecasteaux Channel, rounded Partridge Island, where she anchored briefly, and then proceeded to anchor 1800 metres from Satellite Island at 8.00 pm. D'Urville was at pains to remind his readers that this channel was discovered by the French and noted, with subtle political import (given his secret orders), that it bore no sign of any settlement. Nevertheless, a signal mast was soon spotted at 'Pointe Riche' (now Simpsons Point), on the northern tip of South Bruny Island, and d'Urville was convinced that their arrival had already been reported to the British authorities in Hobart. Along the coast and particularly on Bruny Island, the dry bushland was aflame. Since there was no sign of indigenous inhabitants, d'Urville believed that these fires had been lit by colonists clearing the land.

The following morning, the *Astrolabe* weighed anchor and continued sailing up the D'Entrecasteaux Channel. Meanwhile the naturalists made an excursion ashore, with the intention of catching up with the main expedition later. At 3.45 pm, the corvette reached the mouth of the Derwent River. Shortly after 6.00 pm, harbour master James Kelly and pilot Michael Mansfield came aboard and greeted the expedition. Kelly, born in Parramatta, the son of a cook and a convict woman, dismissed Mansfield (who, nevertheless, remained on board) and took personal charge of conducting the first French warship ever to visit Hobart to her anchorage. Unfortunately, he gained little glory for himself. By 11.00 pm, the *Astrolabe*, with apparently most of her sails unfurled, had hardly progressed two kilometres up the Derwent and was forced to anchor five kilometres from the town on the western bank. In conversation with Mansfield during this protracted passage up-river, d'Urville received the startling news that debris from Lapérouse's expedition had been reported on an island in the Pacific, and the governor of Bengal had dispatched a merchant vessel to investigate. This vessel had sailed via Hobart six months before the *Astrolabe* arrived, and one of her crew members, a Prussian, was apparently still in Hobart. These salient facts were confirmed and clarified by James Kelly, who further informed d'Urville that the island where the debris was found was Vanikoro, and that the captain who had reported the debris to the government of Bengal was a Mr Dillon, whom he knew personally. Although Kelly had a high regard for Dillon, d'Urville soon realised that this intriguing captain – who supposedly held the key to a mystery that had gripped French public imagination for 40 years – was a controversial figure with a very mixed reputation in Hobart. When George Frankland, the colony's assistant surveyor (d'Urville refers to him as the governor's aide-de-camp), called on the *Astrolabe* on 19 December, d'Urville was surprised to hear Dillon described as a 'fool, an adventurer and that his pretended discovery was nothing but a fable'.[6]

Peter Dillon, born in Martinique of Irish parents and educated in Ireland before commencing an adventurous life in merchant shipping between Calcutta, Sydney and the Pacific, was no fool. In 1814, as master of the *Active*, he was engaged by Samuel Marsden to take d'Urville's friend Thomas Kendall to New Zealand on his pathfinding missionary expedition. Hongi Hika and another of d'Urville's friends, Tuhi, were among the Māori passengers Dillon and Kendall brought back to Sydney. The same year, Dillon married the daughter of Sydney merchant (and emancipated convict) Patrick Moore, and in 1816, he made Calcutta his trading base. Nearly a decade later, in October 1825, Dillon had set sail from Chile bound for India, via Tahiti and New Zealand, in command of his own vessel, the *St Patrick*. Two days out of the Bay of Islands, the aged *St Patrick* was struck by a gale and sprang a leak. Dillon thought first of heading for refuge in Sydney, but the winds did not favour such a course, so he headed for the island of Tikopia, in the Santa Cruz group of the Solomon Islands. It was not a casual choice; he knew this island. Twelve years earlier, while in command of the 35-tonne cutter *Elizabeth*, he had taken a Stettin-born Prussian sandalwood cutter named Martin Burchardt, the Prussian's Fijian wife and a Bengali named Achowlia (also known as 'Joe') to Tikopia. This was after a spirited defence and narrow escape from a Fijian attack on the island of Vanua Levu, which had first brought Captain Dillon to public attention.[7] Dillon returned to Tikopia on 13 May 1826 (when the *Astrolabe* was still struggling to leave the Mediterranean). His three acquaintances were still alive: the Indian Achowlia was the first to come aboard the *St Patrick* and he was followed by Burchardt. Soon after, Dillon was surprised to discover that his armourer had acquired the silver guard of a sword-hilt from Achowlia. When he questioned the Prussian about this, Dillon learned that on arriving at the island in 1813, Burchardt had seen 'the sword-guard, several chain-plates belonging to a ship, also a number of iron bolts, five axes, the handle of a silver fork, a few knives, tea-cups, glass beads and bottles, one silver spoon with a crest and cipher, and a sword, all of French manufacture'[8] in the possession of the Tikopians. He learned, further, that these objects had come from 'Manicolo' (Vanikoro), also in the Santa Cruz group. Believing that the sword-guard bore Lapérouse's initials, Dillon questioned some of the Tikopians with the assistance of Burchardt and Achowlia. From them he learned that, many years before, two large ships had been wrecked off Vanikoro, that the survivors from the vessel wrecked on one part of the island (Whanoo or Wannow) had all been killed, but that those from the other vessel, who came ashore at 'Paiou' (Paiu),[9] built another boat from the wreckage and sailed away. Although they left some of their compatriots and promised to return with help, they were never seen again. Those left behind remained with various chiefs, apparently until their deaths, but uncertainty over this lingered.

Dillon was determined to visit Vanikoro and investigate further, but the winds were unfavourable, his vessel was still leaking, he had very limited provisions and he was travelling with a disgruntled supercargo anxious to reach his destination. He therefore resumed his original course and arrived in Bengal on 30 August 1826 with Burchardt. Why Dillon waited three weeks to write to the chief secretary of the government of Bengal is unclear. The state of his vessel was probably his principal consideration, but it is possible that he first wanted to do research on Lapérouse's expedition. His lengthy letter, when he finally did write it, bore the mark of some reading on the subject. It is also possible that he wanted to investigate a whaling vessel that Burchardt told him had visited Tikopia a year to 18 months before the *St Patrick*. This vessel might very possibly have been the source of the report, disseminated by Admiral Manby, that d'Urville investigated in Paris shortly before his departure. When Dillon did write to the chief secretary of the government of Bengal on 19 September 1826, he gave a lengthy account of what he had discovered at Tikopia and offered his services to 'revisit the islands, and bring off the Europeans if alive, and ascertain more accurate details relative to the wrecked vessels'.[10] In further correspondence, he asked the government to repair the *St Patrick* for the voyage, but the East India Company baulked at the expense and eventually provided a vessel of its own, the 257-tonne *Research*, with strict conditions.

Dillon set sail on 23 January 1827, and his first port of call was Hobart, which he reached on 5 April. Even before the *Research* left India, Dillon had found himself in simmering conflict with the East India Company surgeon Robert Tytler,[11] whom he had met at the Asiatic Society of Bengal and had foolishly accepted as a member of his expedition. In seeking to reassert his authority at sea, he had confined Tytler to his cabin (although he did allow him to take exercise on deck). In Hobart, Tytler alleged he had been assaulted by Dillon (when the captain had put his hand on his shoulder to arrest him!) and had abused his authority in confining him. Tytler even asserted that the expedition was his idea and that it was he, not Dillon, who had revealed the cipher on the French sword-guard. In the court case that followed, the jury of six military officers upheld Tytler's charge. The severity of the fine of £50 and two months in prison surprised many in Hobart; four of the six jurors even signed a petition seeking Dillon's release. Many locals thought Dillon had been convicted for affronting Tytler's supposedly superior social status as an East India Company surgeon and officer rather than for any actual violence. Given the voices raised in his support and concern for the future of his politically sensitive expedition, Governor George Arthur and his executive council decided to remit Dillon's sentence on 9 May. Nevertheless, with his fine and his legal expenses, Dillon was out of pocket £521. Tytler left the *Research*, and Dillon sailed to Port Jackson, where the local press reported sympathetically on his misfortunes in Hobart.

Wasting as little time as possible, Dillon sailed to the Bay of Islands, Tongatapu, Rotuma, Tikopia and finally Vanikoro on 7 September. Although he would learn of d'Urville's movements at the Bay of Islands and Tongatapu (where he met the Reverend John Thomas and other Europeans residents but refused to meet deserters from the *Astrolabe*), he appears to have seen the *Astrolabe* expedition as a potential rival for the glory of confirming the fate of Lapérouse, even before leaving Calcutta. Dillon wrote that he had instructions from the Bengal government to 'meet with, if possible, and communicate to him [d'Urville] all the intelligence … respecting the expedition and the fate of the Count de la Pérouse',[12] and he left explanatory messages for d'Urville at Rotuma and Tikopia. Ironically, on his return to Port Jackson on 29 December 1827 – with artefacts that left no doubt that Lapérouse had indeed been wrecked at Vanikoro – Dillon learned from one of the Sydney pilots that d'Urville had recently anchored in the Derwent.[13] He would wait in Sydney until 1 February in the vain hope of meeting d'Urville,[14] but the *Astrolabe* would set a different course.

In Tasmania, the *Astrolabe* moved to a new anchorage in Sullivans Cove on 20 December. That day, d'Urville, Gaimard, Sainson, Faraguet, Gressien and Bertrand attended an outdoor reception at Government House. Although Governor Arthur received them with great politeness and undertook to provide the *Astrolabe* with all that she needed from the government storehouses, the French and the other invited guests were soon decidedly uncomfortable as the afternoon temperature plunged to

10 degrees. The indoor soirée that followed was warmer and convivial, but d'Urville soon had his own taste of the partisan conservative opinion that denigrated Captain Dillon and his quest as 'tales forged … with the aim of extorting money from the [East India] company'.[15] Whatever Dillon's lack of social polish, for d'Urville, 'it was not a reason for his veracity to be doubted'.[16] It would seem that there were some in Hobart who would stop at nothing, even forgery, to prevent d'Urville's following up on Dillon's claims. When he met with James Ross, editor of the *Hobart Town Gazette*, he was told that Dillon's former advocate Joseph Gellibrand had received a letter from Dillon purportedly sent from the Bay of Islands. When d'Urville went to see Gellibrand, the advocate read the letter out loud. In it, Dillon supposedly asserted that he had abandoned his mission because of lack of water and a contrary monsoon, which prevented his sailing to Tikopia. D'Urville was soon suspicious and wrote that 'this latter assertion on his part, seemed to me so absurd, that I developed doubts on the origin of the letter. In effect, anyone who has sailed this part of the Pacific knows that there is no monsoon that can prevent a ship from getting to Tikopia from New Zealand.'[17] When d'Urville asked if the letter was in Dillon's hand, he was told that most of it was not because the captain was barely literate!

D'Urville was now in a difficult, potentially embarrassing position. Would he indeed confirm the fate of his unfortunate compatriot Lapérouse, or would he be abandoning his 'glorious work' on the basis of mere nonsense 'to undertake a search as fruitless as it was dangerous'? According to d'Urville, all his companions thought the idea of breaking off their mission to visit Vanikoro was a 'joke'.[18] When he dined with Chief Justice John Pedder and confided his intention to sail to the Solomons to investigate, he was told that Dillon's account was nothing but a 'tissue of lies'.[19] D'Urville might finally have abandoned any further investigation had he not, on New Year's Day 1828, received a copy of the *Sydney Gazette and New South Wales Advertiser*, dated 5 December 1827, from the captain of a vessel recently arrived in the harbour. In the newspaper, d'Urville found the text of a letter, sent to Sydney by the now apparently literate Captain Dillon from New Zealand, via the schooner *Herald*; in the letter, Dillon announced his return from the Solomon Islands and reported diverse objects from the wreckage of Lapérouse's expedition, including 'the altar and mess plate … ship's bells, a brass mortar, five brass guns, several copper kitchen utensils, the greater part of which are marked with the arms of France: namely, three *fleur-de-lis* … the rudder irons, the brass shieves [*sic*] of the frigate's topmast, and many other things too tedious to mention'.[20]

On 28 December, d'Urville had already entrusted to Captain Plunkett of the *Persian* (bound for London) all his letters, dispatches, tracings of eight new charts and other scientific reports and documents in a sealed tin box weighing about 14 kilograms.

'*Hobart-Town, vue prise d'un ravin au nord, Van Diemen*', *lithograph by Edouard-Jean-Marie Hostein, from a sketch by Louis-Auguste de Sainson,* Voyage de la corvette l'Astrolabe, Atlas historique, *Paris, 1833, plate 157. D'Urville first visited Hobart in 1827 and, using Van Diemen's Land as a base for his second Antarctic descent, returned again in 1839 and 1840.* National Library of Australia, PIC U1866 NK3340

However, in the wake of the publication of Dillon's letter in the Sydney press, he felt obliged to inform the minister of the navy of the new development. Fortunately, Plunkett had not yet sailed for Europe, so d'Urville was able to send a supplementary report. As an additional precaution, he sent a duplicate report to the minister via another vessel, the *Harvey*, on 4 January. Half a world away, in Caen, d'Urville's anxious mother, now living with the widow of his botanist friend Lamouroux, had just a few days before written to the same minister pleading for news of her son.[21]

D'Urville still had one more burning desire to fulfil before leaving Hobart. This was to climb the brooding peak of Mount Wellington, then still generally known by the name Flinders had given it: Table Mountain. Provided with good horses courtesy of surveyor George Frankland, and accompanied by Dudemaine, Lesson and two young sailors,[22] he set off on the morning of 2 January. Lesson insisted on walking, presumably to better spot botanical specimens. As anyone who has ascended Mount Wellington knows, the climb is steep and arduous, and the summit is exposed to fierce winds and is frequently covered in snow, even in summer. It is perhaps no surprise that Lesson was soon exhausted, feeling poorly and unable to reach the top. Even d'Urville, mounted on a good horse but recently ill himself, felt almost defeated by the sun and the stiff ascent. Although it was eventually necessary for everyone to dismount, d'Urville rallied and made it to the summit. He soon recognised the affinities of the Tasmanian flora with that of Port Jackson and the Blue Mountains in New South Wales and Western Port in what is now Victoria. On reaching the plateau of the summit and seeing the carpet of clumped and stunted windblown vegetation, he was immediately reminded of the summit of 'Mount Chastellux' (now Mount Simon), which he had climbed in the Falklands in December 1822. D'Urville was also impressed by the magnificent panorama of the Derwent River, the D'Entrecasteaux Channel, Storm Bay and the Tasmanian interior.

D'Urville tells us that on Mount Wellington, he collected several plant species that he thought 'still unknown'.[23] It is uncertain what they were. Four new species of *Senecio* were collected by the expedition in Tasmania: *S. hispidulus*, *S. rupicola*, *S. pinnatifolius* and *S. spathulatus*.[24] The last two type specimens were known to have been gathered along the D'Entrecasteaux Channel, and the others are unlikely to have been collected on Mount Wellington.

Although D'Urville made a pointed remark about a noticeable lack of birds compared to his visit to Western Port,[25] the expedition's time in Tasmania yielded the first scientific description of the flame robin – familiar to most Australians for the male's brilliant orange breast and the attractive trill of its high-pitched call. This was published by Quoy and Gaimard in 1830 under the name *Muscicapa chrysoptera*[26] and appears to have been based on a specimen of an immature male they collected near Hobart. Ironically, seven years later, John Gould published his description of the same bird under the name *Petroica phoenicea*, and this was universally adopted and ultimately protected. Thus, despite Quoy's and Gaimard's precedence, their name is now treated as a *nomen oblitum*.[27] Although d'Urville also noted a lack of insects in the area, nine Tasmanian beetles were described by Boisduval in the second part of the expedition's entomological volume, including *Cryptocephalus consors* (*Aporocera consors*), personally collected by d'Urville in the environs of Hobart.[28]

There were other significant zoological discoveries in Tasmanian waters. At low tide in Hobart harbour, Quoy and Gaimard collected the type specimen of the sea anemone *Actinia punctulata* (*Spyractis punctulata*).[29] Yet another sea anemone, *Actinia clavus* (*Anemonactis clavus*),[30] was discovered in Bass Strait, in addition to a new species of siphonophore, *Diphes bassensis* (*Bassia bassensis*).[31] In the D'Entrecasteaux Channel, the expedition collected another creature new to science: the intertidal pulmonate *Siphonaria diemensis*[32] (closely related to *S. denticulata*, collected at Western Port).

D'Urville would draft a detailed account of Van Diemen's Land, based on his own observations and, it would appear, the accounts of others, such as the recently deceased Lieutenant Charles Jefferys, author of *Geographical and Descriptive Delineations of the*

Island of Van Diemen's Land (1820). He also surveyed the principal timbers of the island, writing with particular admiration of the Huon pine, and described Tasmania's significant fauna, including the now extinct carnivorous thylacine, which 'always fled at the approach of man'.[33] D'Urville was impressed by the standard of life and industry in Hobart, which he compared favourably to that of many major French towns, and he was surprised by Hobart's active commerce and regular maritime links with London and thus the rest of the world. Of the island's indigenous human inhabitants, he had a pessimistic, racist assessment: they were 'incapable of ever being civilised'. He believed that in 40 or 50 years, they would completely disappear, like the Guanches, Caribs and Mohawks. Moreover, he thought that this would also be the fate of the mainland Australian Aborigines.[34]

A man of liberal political persuasion, it is hardly surprising that d'Urville was uneasy about the administration of Governor Arthur. Where d'Urville's hero Lachlan Macquarie saw the potential good in the hearts of the convicts in his charge, Arthur only saw innate wickedness and enthusiastically embraced the stern disciplinary régime advocated by Commissioner Thomas Bigge: transportation was once more to become 'an object of real terror' in the hearts of felons.[35] D'Urville had also seen something of the arbitrary nature of the rule of the governor and his council and the manner in which Peter Dillon had been treated. Of George Arthur, he wrote: 'The severity of his character and his military haughtiness often inspired acts of despotism which aroused angry complaints and bitter recriminations.'[36]

After a sojourn of 15 days, the *Astrolabe* weighed anchor and set sail from Hobart on the morning of 5 January. On the expedition's final night in Tasmania, d'Urville had maintained close surveillance of three of his sailors, whom he believed were preparing to desert: Frédéric Bernard, Joseph de La Maria and Louis Martineng; they were thwarted in their plans, if indeed they had them. One member of the expedition was left behind deliberately because of a deteriorating mental illness: Honoré-François Coulomb, a Toulonnais who fulfilled domestic duties for the officers. His place was filled by a young English recruit named 'Jack'. Almost left behind was Joseph-Paul Gaimard, who had fallen ill. However, he rejoined the corvette at the very last minute – with the pilot who guided the *Astrolabe* from the harbour. By 11.00 am, the corvette had reached Storm Bay, and the pilot bade her farewell.

19

Vanikoro

*Rather perplexed, Dumont d'Urville didn't know if he should give credence
to these reports … nevertheless, he decided to start on Dillon's trail.*

Jules Verne*

After a stormy traverse of the Tasman Sea, the *Astrolabe* headed for the northern tip of New Zealand and then sailed close enough to Norfolk Island for d'Urville to see the distinctive green fringe of Norfolk Island pines (*Araucaria heterophylla*) on the coast. Soon after crossing the Tropic of Capricorn, he took the opportunity to find and fix the position of volcanically active Matthew Island – first recorded in 1788 by Captain Thomas Gilbert of the 'First Fleet' convict transport *Charlotte*.[1] D'Urville appears to have had some satisfaction in informing his readers that Duperrey had orders to locate this same island during his expedition but failed to do so. He himself was unable to find neighbouring Hunter Island (70 kilometres to the east) and incorrectly suggested that it might be one and the same as Matthew Island.

On 8 February 1828 – coincidentally the birthday of Jules Verne, who would later include these events in *Vingt mille lieues sous les mers* (1870) – the expedition sighted Mitre Island and, two days later, Tikopia. D'Urville was determined to visit the latter, in order to verify Peter Dillon's story, before sailing on to Vanikoro, 200 kilometres to the west-northwest. Tikopia is small – a mere five square kilometres in surface area – and essentially an extinct volcano, the weathered rim of which rises from the sea to a peak of 380 metres: Mount Reani. The rim also embraces an 80-metre-deep brackish crater lake, Te Roto. When the *Astrolabe* visited Tikopia, it was inhabited by perhaps 1000 Polynesians.[2] D'Urville was pleased that one of the first people to come aboard was the Prussian Martin Burchardt, wearing a red shirt, white trousers and a woollen cap. After participating in Dillon's expedition, he had returned to his idyllic home from the Bay of Islands as a passenger on the *Governor Macquarie*. D'Urville questioned him at length about Vanikoro and thought that he had gained his agreement to act as a guide there (even reluctantly agreeing to take Burchardt's

* *Vingt mille lieues sous les mers* [*20,000 Leagues Under the Sea*] (1870), ch. xix

'*Tikopia*', *engraving from a sketch by Louis-Auguste de Sainson, for Dumont d'Urville's* Voyage pittoresque autour du monde, *L. Tenré, Paris, vol. ii, 1835, plate xv. Metal artefacts brought from the island of Vanikoro to Tikopia, sometime after 1788, provided vital clues to the fate of the missing French expedition of Lapérouse in the Solomon Islands.* Author's collection

attractive young Māori wife as a passenger on the *Astrolabe*); however, the Prussian failed to join the expedition. There were other Europeans at Tikopia – a number of sailors who claimed to have been deserters from a whaler, the *Harriet*, nine months earlier. They told d'Urville that Burchardt had changed his mind because of pressure from one of the island's *ariki* (chiefs), who was unhappy at the prospect of his leaving with his weapons and goods. Although d'Urville exerted counter-pressure of his own – keeping some 30 Tikopians, including chiefs, aboard the *Astrolabe* – and forced Burchardt's reappearance, the Prussian asserted that he had changed his mind freely. D'Urville also questioned Burchardt's nervous Indian companion, Achowlia, well aware that it was he who possessed the French sword-hilt from Vanikoro that first attracted Peter Dillon's attention. Unfortunately, as with Burchardt, d'Urville failed to recruit Achowlia's services, declaring that the Indian 'employed all of his eloquence to dissuade me from going to Vanikoro, assuring me that we would all die if we landed'.[3] It would seem that the main reason Achowlia was reluctant to leave Tikopia, which had been his home since 1813, was the uncertainty of returning.[4] Apparently a native of

Calcutta, he had adopted Polynesian dress and tattoos and was barely distinguishable from the local people. D'Urville was fascinated by his Pacific travels and lamented his lack of literacy. He observed that, despite having melted into the population, Achowlia's face was 'different … more oval and less rounded'. Was there perhaps a phrenological subtext to this casual comment? There can be no doubt of racist preconceptions, for he added that the Indian's 'traits also announced a more intelligent race'.[5]

After being assured of the friendliness of the islanders, who were already trading coconuts and fish with the expedition, d'Urville ordered Guilbert to take Gaimard and Lesson ashore to gather natural history specimens and Sainson to make a pictorial record, while he himself remained aboard with his guests. Aside from gathering information about Vanikoro and the vestiges of the Lapérouse expedition, d'Urville sought ethnographic information about the Tikopians and the inhabitants of the neighbouring islands, aware that he was probably on the extremities of Polynesian settlement in the Pacific.

Although rebuffed by both Burchardt and Achowlia, d'Urville took on board two of the mysterious English castaways, the self-declared deserters from the whaler *Harriet*, who had gained some useful knowledge of local customs and language during their nine-month stay. He referred to them as English and recorded their names as 'Hambilton' and 'Williams', but one wonders whether these were now his *omni-nomen* for English-speaking recruits, especially those with dubious pasts.[6] Peter Dillon was told by Achowlia that no vessel named *Harriet* had ever visited Tikopia and that these men, whom he also met, were part of a group of five Englishmen who arrived together by longboat. Some of the castaways told Dillon that they had been wrecked east of Tikopia on a whaler named *Mary*, but he did not believe them. He was convinced that they were convicts on the run: 'There can be no doubt', he wrote, 'but that these men had escaped from New South Wales within the last year.'[7]

D'Urville also found himself with a number of unwilling Tikopian passengers. Most of the higher-ranking islanders he had detained aboard the *Astrolabe* (while trying to determine whether or not Burchardt was acting of his own volition) had been able to leave the vessel on canoes summoned from the shore. However, four Tikopians of lower rank, together with a castaway named Brini-Warrou from Ouvéa in the Loyalty Islands, found themselves without transport as the expedition weighed anchor, but d'Urville was reluctant to defy the tide and turn back at their behest. Despite the fact that the current had already taken the *Astrolabe* thirteen kilometres leeward of the island, the remaining Tikopians pleaded for pieces of wood before preparing to jump overboard. D'Urville, horrified by what seemed like suicidal behaviour, was relieved when the Englishman 'Hambilton' allayed their anxieties by assuring them that they would be free to leave at Vanikoro.

That same day, the expedition reached a point where the volcanic peaks of both Tikopia and Vanikoro were visible from the *Astrolabe*. D'Urville recorded the rising emotions aboard the corvette, which suggests that their doubts had been dispelled in Tikopia. The very proximity of Vanikoro seemed to add weight to what had already been established about the fate of Lapérouse's ships.

> … our hearts were agitated by an indefinable impulse of hope and regret, of pain and satisfaction. At last, before our eyes, we had the mysterious place which had hidden so long from France, from the whole of Europe, the debris of a noble and generous entreprise; we were going to tread this fatal soil, investigate its shores and question its inhabitants. But what was to be the result of our efforts? Would it only be possible to pay our tearful tribute to the memory of our unfortunate compatriots? Such were the sad reflections which left us deep in mournful reveries …[8]

On 14 February, d'Urville cautiously approached the reef surrounding Vanikoro and kept the *Astrolabe* windward of the breakers on the island's eastern coast, while Guilbert and Lottin, in separate boats, went ahead to reconnoitre. The following day, Lottin was given command of an armed party comprising Gaimard, Pâris, the Englishman Hambilton and the Ouvéan Brini-Warou. They were ordered to resume sounding a passage to a safe anchorage and, if possible, to establish where Dillon had anchored and where Lapérouse had been shipwrecked. Furthermore, in an attempt to gain the co-operation of the locals, Hambilton was ordered to take a gift to a chief named Nelo, whom Burchardt had advised was a man of great local influence. Although Dillon's anchorage was found, and Nelo came out in his canoe to meet the French, it was soon discovered by Gaimard that Lapérouse's vessels had foundered on the opposite side of the rugged forested island – which at its highest point rises to 923 metres – and that violence had ensued between the survivors and the people of a village named 'Vanou' (Fono). For the moment, the wind did not favour entering Dillon's anchorage in front of 'Ocili' (Usili), so d'Urville decided to search the west coast of Vanikoro for an island named Taumako, where some of the locals asserted that Lapérouse had foundered. He spent two days doing so, without success, only to focus again on Paiu and 'Wannow' (Fono), as reported by Dillon.

From the accounts that he had obtained in Hobart, d'Urville suspected that Vanikoro might be a collection of islands. He was not able to confirm this in Tikopia, but on arrival, his assumption proved correct. On 20 February, Lottin sounded a channel ('Birch's Passage' on Dillon's chart) between Banie and 'Tevai' (Teanu),[9] the two largest and the only inhabited islands of the five that make up Vanikoro – all of which are surrounded by a single coral reef; the three other small islands are Manieve, Nomianu and Nanuga. D'Urville, however, would refer to the largest island, Banie

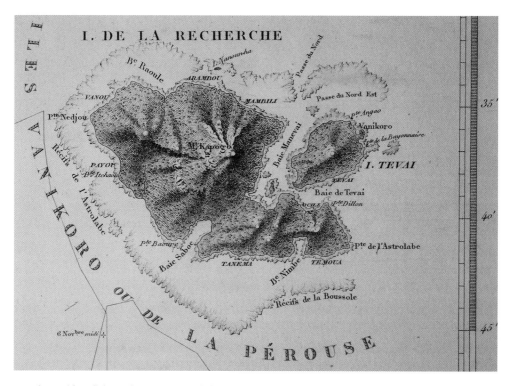

Vanikoro, (detail) 'Des Iles Santa Cruz', from Dumont d'Urville's Voyage au pôle sud et dans l'Océanie, Atlas hydrographie, *Paris, 1847, plate 18. At Vanikoro in the Solomons, d'Urville confirmed Peter Dillon's reports of the fate of Lapérouse.* Mitchell Library, State Library of New South Wales

(190 square kilometres), as Vanikoro and the larger reef-bound complex by the name d'Entrecasteaux gave it in 1793: 'Recherche Island'.

While the *Astrolabe* stood off the reef, she was visited by a large outrigger canoe with a triangular sail, bearing three men of striking appearance, one of whom proved to be the son of Chief Nelo. Their small, dark, well-proportioned bodies were copiously oiled; they had pieces of bamboo through their nasal membranes; and they wore numerous sea-shell and tortoise-shell ornaments on their ears and limbs. D'Urville received them warmly, gave them gifts (including floral printed cloth) and sought to assure them of his good intentions. Before they departed, he learned from them that fresh water and pigs could be had ashore. The following day, 21 February, with the yawl and a boat as pathfinders, and Guilbert cautiously surveying the way ahead from atop a mast, d'Urville took the *Astrolabe* through the passage. Although she dropped anchor at 3.30 pm, d'Urville became fearful that she might ultimately have difficulties departing, so he chose to look for a more sheltered anchorage to the south of Teanu Bay. When he also found fresh water close to the shore, his mind was made up: at 8.00 pm, the *Astrolabe* was secured with a kedge anchor and three hawsers at a new mooring opposite Usili on the Banie Island side of the bay. Ironically, Peter Dillon rightly considered this anchorage dangerous and named it 'Treacherous or Tytler's Bay' on his chart, an obvious act of vengeance towards his nemesis surgeon Robert Tytler. D'Urville would himself discover the dangers of this mooring when he tried to leave.

Usili was uninhabited, apparently in the wake of internecine fighting with the people of nearby Teanu. The *Astrolabe* was soon welcomed by Chief Nelo and a clutch of canoes from Teanu. Because the chief was a man of at least 55 years of age, d'Urville hoped that he might have personal memories of Lapérouse's ships, but he proved to be a disappointing source of information. Four days later, d'Urville was told by Nelo that Lapérouse's men had fired on and killed some 20 islanders at 'Vanou' (Fono) and had then departed. Nelo was adamant that none of the French had remained on Vanikoro or the neighbouring islands, but nevertheless he promised to make someone available to guide the *Astrolabe*'s boat to Paiu and Fono, assuring d'Urville that Dillon had done this easily as a return day-trip on several occasions.

Peter Dillon had brought a bountiful supply of trade goods from India and had distributed these very generously among the islanders, and d'Urville found that the *Astrolabe*'s meagre trinkets excited little interest at Vanikoro. Although their iron axes were more coveted, promised exchanges could not be relied upon to take place. D'Urville felt that he was lucky to extract himself without serious injury or death from Nelo's village after the chief reneged on a bargain struck over a pig. Unable to purchase fresh fruit, vegetables or meat other than at highly inflated prices, the French had to resort to their all-too-familiar dried and salted shipboard rations. The only exceptions were wild pigeons and water hens, which they were able to hunt ashore, and fish, which were plentiful in the local waters. The debased currency in trade goods also undermined the interest of local women – whom d'Urville described uncharitably as 'very hideous'[10] – in prostituting themselves; so the commander of the expedition took some consolation at the unlikely prospect of sailors deserting on the island. The next day d'Urville would write, with unequivocal racism, of 'a kind of natural antipathy of the black races towards the white, an antipathy which many voyagers have proved the fatal consequences of'.[11]

D'Urville was determined that all his officers should progressively visit the site of Lapérouse's wreck so that each could bear witness on his return to France. The first boat, under the command of the taciturn Gressien, departed very early on the morning of 23 February with Quoy, Gaimard, Faraguet, Bertrand and Hambilton, accompanied by two local guides from Teanu, whom Hambilton had brought back from Nelo's village. Meanwhile, Jacquinot and Lottin commenced astronomical observations to fix the location of the *Astrolabe*'s anchorage with precision.

Gressien and his boat party returned around midday on 24 February, having circumnavigated the island within the inner reef. Although Hambilton went ashore at Paiu, all but two very elderly residents fled at his approach, and they were not forthcoming with any information. At Ngama, the boat party purchased several pieces of iron and copper that had come from the wreck sites, and an old man was able to tell them that at least two Frenchmen, who had floated ashore on pieces of wood, had settled in Paiu but had long since died. Although the other villagers professed no knowledge of Lapérouse's expedition, Gressien believed that their stubborn silence was engendered by fear of French vengeance rather than ignorance of the events of 1788. This opinion, however, was possibly influenced by what Gaimard had learned, on 15 February, of violence between Lapérouse's surviving crewmen and the locals. That same day, while hunting ashore, Guilbert met two islanders, Tangaloa and Barbaka, who produced a certificate attesting their assistance to Dillon in October 1827. They told Guilbert of five bronze cannons, a copper mortar and dishes that had been found on Vanikoro, and from them he traded a piece of pierced copper, which appeared to have come from a yardarm. When d'Urville followed up on this meeting, he remarked that Tangaloa had a 'perfect understanding of the language of Tikopia',[12] which would suggest that he was perhaps Polynesian. Most of the population of Vanikoro are Melanesian, but Banie has a small Polynesian minority of Tikopian descent in the south. It was these Polynesians who were almost certainly responsible for the transfer of artefacts from Lapérouse's expedition to Tikopia, where they were then seen by Peter Dillon; and it was these people who welcomed d'Urville's Tikopian passengers and whose chief, Moembe, provided them with a canoe to return to Tikopia.

On 26 February, while Gressien continued his survey of 'Manevai' (Manieve) Bay and Pâris surveyed Teanu Bay, d'Urville dispatched Jacquinot to Paiu, in command of a boat carrying Lottin, Sainson, Dudemaine, Lesson, Gaimard and Hambilton. Gaimard was a late inclusion in the party. D'Urville's original plan was to leave Hambilton at Paiu for several days to gather information and gain the confidence of the locals, but Gaimard had pleaded to be allowed to join him – despite the fact that he spoke no English and Hambilton spoke no French. Since Quoy would remain with the *Astrolabe* and there would be at least one medical officer left if Gaimard was lost to the expedition, d'Urville reluctantly gave his consent. One wonders whether Gaimard's libido and his ethnological interests (perhaps better described as a fetish) coalesced in this regard. Of this study of female body hair, Pierre-Adolphe Lesson wrote:

> … just as some savants had established the distinction between different human races in the form of their hair, Monsieur Gaymard likewise seemed to establish this distinction in the hair of different parts of the body. It seems … by the selection of his subjects, that he wanted to collect that of women … restricting his research to them, wrapping them carefully, labeling them with precise indications of the

*The missing explorer Jean-François de Galaup de Lapérouse, last
seen by Europeans in March 1788, etching by A. Lefevre, from the
frontispiece of Dumont d'Urville's* Voyage pittoresque autour du
monde, *L. Tenré, Paris, vol. ii, 1835.* Author's collection

places, the times and circumstances. One was led to believe that in acting thus,
Monsieur Gaymard had an ulterior motive. But one must agree that the idea was
original. It would be curious to know if that collection will one day be deposited in
the Museum.[13]

Jacquinot's party sailed firstly to Fono. There the women fled into the forest, and
the men remained anxious, fearful and tight-lipped in their responses to questions
about Lapérouse's ships and men. One subordinate chief, a man named Valié, was
on the verge of confiding to the French but was silenced by his angry kinsmen. At
'Nama' (Ngama), Jacquinot dramatically overcame the silence of one of the residents by
spreading a length of red cloth. So anxious was he to acquire the coloured cloth that he

*'Chaloupe de l'*Astrolabe *sur le lieu du Naufrage', engraving by Boilly from a sketch by Louis-Auguste de Sainson, for Dumont d'Urville's* Voyage pittoresque autour du monde, *L. Tenré, Paris, vol. ii, 1835, plate xvii. The engraving shows the salvaging of an anchor from the Lapérouse expedition off Vanikoro.* Author's collection

promptly jumped into the boat and took Jacquinot's party to a small opening in the reef four or five kilometres from the shore, opposite Ambi. When they looked at the seabed a few metres beneath them, they soon discerned four anchors, a number of cannons, cannon balls, sheets of lead and other objects all encrusted with coral. The position of the four anchors suggested that they had gone down with the ship – which we now know was the *Astrolabe*, namesake of d'Urville's vessel – which had been trapped in the narrow, gorge-like opening in the reef. Another two anchors appeared to have been cast earlier in an attempt to secure the vessel. It would seem that the survivors, who came ashore at Paiu and who, according to the expedition's informants, later built a small boat to leave the island, came from this wrecked vessel. They assumed that the other vessel had foundered and sunk on the outer reef.

Although Jacquinot dived on one of the anchors and attempted to raise it with a block and tackle, it was so heavily embedded in the coral that the stress of hauling on the salvage rope almost caused the stern of the boat to cede to the water, so the attempt had to be abandoned. Given that it was now 4.00 pm, Jacquinot decided to drop Gaimard and Hambilton ashore at Ngama and return to the *Astrolabe*, but he did not go back empty-handed. He and Lottin were able to acquire from the locals 'a cat hook, the end of a lightning conductor chain, a copper powder measure, an instrument

pedestal or a heavy copper stanchion … a cubic copper vase with heavy lead lining …
[and] finally an iron kentledge weighing a hundred pounds.[14]

D'Urville now had no doubt that he had confirmed the fate of Lapérouse's ships.
On the afternoon of 28 February, as he bathed ashore in the shade of *Barringtonia*
and *Calophylum* trees, he reflected on his mission and felt satisfaction on completing
subsidiary orders that his superiors could only have had a vague hope that he would
fulfil. Nevertheless, his personal resentment towards the people of Vanikoro, and what
he saw as their greed, dishonesty and violent menace, welled up in racist anger. That
day, he wrote in his journal:

> As a whole, like all those of the black race of Oceania, these people are disgusting,
> lazy, stupid, savage, avaricious and with neither qualities nor virtues that I know of.
> Only our strength makes an impression on them, and I believe that our lives would
> be compromised, if we were, or they thought us weaker.[15]

Imagining the fate of the survivors of the Lapérouse expedition ashore, he added:

> It was without doubt cruel for our illustrious Lapérouse to succumb in a manner so
> unfortunate at the end of his brilliant expedition; but if he had had the time to get
> to know the hideous beings into whose hands his misfortune had thrown him, be-
> fore perishing, his shipwreck would have seemed ten times more deplorable again.
> Everywhere else, among the peoples of the Polynesian race, such as in Tahiti, Tonga,
> Rotouma, Tikopia, etc., [once] the first moment of anxiety and fear at the savages
> passed, he would have been able to treat with them and gain respect and even help
> and victuals. The cannibals of New Zealand have sometimes shown themselves hos-
> pitable to Europeans wrecked on their shores. But at Vanikoro, Lapérouse's com-
> panions must not have found anything but cupidity, barbarism and perfidy.[16]

Perhaps, had he known more of the languages of the Melanesian Vanikorans, as he
did of the languages of the Polynesians, he might have been better able to apply the
cultural sensitivity and intellectual curiosity that usually characterised his temperament.

D'Urville now determined to move to a more secure anchorage, all the better if it
was marginally closer to the wreck site. He was also determined to salvage an anchor
and a cannon as further evidence of Lapérouse's fate. By this time, Pâris had finished his
survey of Teanu's coast, and the expedition's supplies of water and firewood had been
replenished. Ironically, as if the inhabitants of Teanu had got wind of the expedition's
impending relocation (and thus the disappearance of a potentially lucrative market),
a large trading party arrived with two pigs and a substantial quantity of bananas and
coconuts. According to d'Urville, their prices remained 'outrageous' and thus they
made no sales to the expedition. Nor did they bring Nelo's payment for his iron axes –
which only confirmed d'Urville's low opinion of the chief.

The *Astrolabe* left her anchorage in front of Usili on the morning of 29 February. Initially, all went well, but then there was a change of wind from the north, which left no option but to kedge forward. By the end of the day, the crew had 15 times taken anchors secured with Ambon cables ahead in the longboat, dropped them and then used them to pull the corvette towards the eastern channel. By evening, the men were exhausted. The following day, the process was repeated 22 gruelling times before the vessel was secured for the night. On several occasions, the *Astrolabe* came perilously close to the reef in the heavy swell. With large waves breaking close by, d'Urville was inevitably reminded of his experience in Tongatapu.

On the morning of 2 March, d'Urville took advantage of a calm to find a safe anchorage near Manieve Island in the yawl. When he returned with the corvette, 15–20 of the local people, including their elderly chief Moembe, came aboard. D'Urville gained a good opinion of these people and soon came to call Moembe his friend. When he discovered that one of the local men, a sagacious individual named Kavaliki, was the brother of Tangaloa (the proficient Tikopian speaker he had met some days before), he wondered whether he was the son of a Tikopian father and a Vanikoran mother. It would appear that these people did have a (perhaps mixed) Polynesian heritage and that some knowledge of their language was the key to understanding and friendship. The next day, d'Urville, in the company of his secretary, Barthélemy Lauvergne, visited the fruit and vegetable gardens of Moembe's village with its amiable chief. Significantly, he also brought the Englishman Williams, who had a knowledge of the language of Tikopia. In conversation with the chief, he gained information about their local customs, gods and religious beliefs. Moembe also told him that he was a very young child when Lapérouse was shipwrecked on Vanikoro. According to the accounts he had heard, 'the inhabitants of Vanou [Fono] went to the wrecked vessel to pillage it, but they were repulsed by the whites who fired on them and killed twenty of them and three chiefs'. In turn, the islanders killed, with arrows, all the whites 'who wanted to land on their territory'. He added that 'only two men landed at Païou [Paiu] and did not live there more than three moons'.[17] This account had more detail than Gaimard had gathered on 15 February but mirrored many of its essential points.

The following day, d'Urville dispatched Guilbert, Pâris and Sainson in the longboat with 14 armed men to drag the wreck site and to endeavour to raise an anchor and a cannon, and also to collect Gaimard and Hambilton. Meanwhile, Gressien was ordered to continue the survey of the coast in the whaleboat. Both boats were given supplies for two days and returned early on the morning of 5 March. Despite the difficult currents and cracking the stern of the longboat during these salvage operations, Guilbert's party succeeded in raising a very corroded and coral-encrusted anchor weighing 800 kilograms, together with a bronze swivel gun,[18] a copper blunderbuss, a lead ingot, a large sheet of lead and fragments of porcelain. Significantly, both the salvaged weapons carried ordnance numbers on their trunnions. Ashore at Ngama, Guilbert purchased the remains of a kettle. For his part, Gaimard returned disappointed from the west coast. Pierre-Adolphe Lesson described him as usually 'welcomed everywhere on account of his amiable qualities … attracting a good opinion even from savages, above all through his largesse, since one of his qualities was generosity', but Vanikoro was the exception: 'the reception was not very good and even became perilous at one stage. And the illness he contracted ashore even put his life in danger for a time.'[19] D'Urville would describe this illness as a 'very violent fever'[20] and make comparisons with the lingering fever that had afflicted him personally in the northern Aegean nine years before.[21] It seems likely that Gaimard contracted malaria, which remains endemic in the Solomon Islands to this day. It is not known whether the intrepid surgeon returned with any new additions to his collection of female pubic hair, although he did learn the local words for it (along with 'virile erect member' and 'vulva') among the 230 local terms he collected![22]

Vanikoro would also yield a significant scientific booty. The naturalists collected a number of new species, which included the lichens *Parmelia latiloba* and *Opegrapha unicolor* and the orchids *Dendrobium calcaratum*, *D. macranthum* and *Macrolepis longiscapa* (*Bulbophyllum longiscapum*).[23] Meanwhile, Quoy and Gaimard discovered a subspecies of the widely distributed island thrush (*Turdus poliocephalus*), *T. p. vanikorensis*.[24] They also collected and described the uniform swiftlet, *Hirundo vanikorensis*[25] (*Aerodramus vanikorensis*), and the Vanikoro flycatcher, *Platyrhynchos vanikorensis*[26] (*Myiagra vanikorensis*), both of which have habitats beyond the Solomon Islands. Although they collected a fruit bat they thought was a new species and named *Pteropus vanikorensis*,[27] there is still debate on its taxonomic status[28] and whether it might, in fact, be a subspecies of *Pteropus mariannus*, collected on Guam and first described in 1822.[29] The intertidal zone of the island yielded the first specimens of the pulmonate gastropod *Auricula lutea* (*Melampus luteus*)[30] and yet another pulmonate, *Siphonaria atra*,[31] closely related to two species already collected in Australian coastal waters. It was among the mangroves that they made the first collection of the now widely traded *Nerita communis*,[32] sometimes called the 'zigzag nerita' because of its distinctive striped shell. The coastal waters yielded still more new gastropods[33] and other marine species new to science, such as the sea cucumber *Holothuria miliaris* (*Actinopyga miliaris*); the sea anemones *Actinia aurora* (*Heteractis aurora*) and *A. vas*; the stony coral, *Fungia crassitentaculata*; and two species of soft coral, *Clavularia viridis and C. violacea*[34] (both of which have since been found to contain a number of exciting new anti-inflammatory steroids and cytoxins with cancer-fighting potential).[35] These species (excluding the soft corals) are also found in Australian waters. Significant entomology was also undertaken on Vanikoro, and d'Urville himself appears to have taken an active part when his duties permitted. Descriptions of 34 beetles collected on the island, many of which were completely new to science, were published in 1835 by Jean-Baptiste Boisduval. They included a black snout-beetle, *Elytrurus lapeyrousei*,[36] endemic to the island (not collected again until 2005).[37] Another notable find was a jewel beetle that Boisduval first published under the name *Buprestis xanthocera* but which was later designated the type specimen for an entirely new genus, *Paracupta*, established by Henri Deyrolle in 1864.[38] *Buprestis helopioides*[39] (*Paracupta helopioides*), also collected by the expedition, has undergone similar taxonomic revision. The type specimen for the palmfly *Dyctis agondas*[40] (*Elymnias agondas*), a brown and yellow nymphalid butterfly, also found in Australia's wet tropics, was collected by the expedition in Vanikoro.

D'Urville was determined to construct a memorial to Lapérouse before he left Vanikoro and received the enthusiastic support of his men. It would not be the first such monument. In Mauritius, in 1805, Matthew Flinders, on parole as a prisoner-of-war, had been the principal instigator of a monument to Lapérouse at Mesnil, where the explorer had owned land and lived. Hyacinthe de Bougainville had also paid for another monument to Lapérouse on the shores of Botany Bay, in New South Wales, in 1825.[41] It was decided to build a cenotaph at Paiu, where the French had taken refuge and where they had built the boat in which they left the island. The design d'Urville settled on was a quadrangular prism framed in local timber: 1.8 metres high with four foundation blocks of coral and in-filled with courses of smaller coral blocks. It would be set among the mangroves in an intertidal area at the end of the reef. For the pyramidical capital of the monument, an additional 1.8 metres in height, d'Urville decided on New Zealand 'koudi' (kauri) that he had purchased the year before at the Bay of the Islands, possibly for his own use. Lottin was charged with supervising the construction and was ordered not to use any nails or ironwork that might tempt the islanders to destroy the monument.

That same day, 5 March, d'Urville received a visit from a chief named Valiko, from the village of Vanikoro on the northeastern tip of Teanu. Once again, he had to reassess his prejudices. Valiko was a grizzled man of 50–55 years of age but, according to d'Urville, 'lively, active and seemingly more intelligent than all of the natives of the black race that I had so far seen'.[42] He too recounted oral history of the wreckage of Lapérouse's ships and the fate of the 'maras' who came ashore. D'Urville thought this word might have been 'a corruption of the word *mer* [sea]',[43] which Lapérouse's men might have used to explain where they had come from. Valiko was adamant that one of the vessels sank off Paiu and that some 30 men came ashore to build a small vessel; the other ship sank off Tanema but beyond the reef. He too reiterated that there was violence between the 'maras' and the people of Vana but put the casualties at five rather than 20, including three *ariki* (chiefs). According to Valiko, two 'maras' were killed at Paiu, and at the beginning of five moons, the rest sailed away. Hambilton would find yet another elderly witness at Manieve who asserted that the ships were wrecked during strong winds, and that some 30 survivors got ashore from the vessel, which sank off Tanema, and they were united with survivors who landed at Paiu. Although he saw only the vessel that foundered off Tanema, his account of the casualties at Paiu and among the people of Vanou essentially tallied with Valiko's account. It is significant to note that in the first quarter of the twentieth century, a number of amateur excavations took place at Paiu; objects with an apparently eighteenth-century French provenance were recovered but were poorly documented.[44] While these suggested that there were indeed survivors at Paiu, it was not until 1999 that their campsite was discovered by French archaeologists, who conducted further systematic excavations in 2000 and 2003.[45] The wreck on the reef off Tanema was discovered by the New Zealander Reece Discombe in 1964. Although it was then thought to be Lapérouse's flag-ship *Boussole*, it was not until 2005 that this was confirmed by marine archaeology, which revealed the remains of scientific instruments known, from archival sources, to have been aboard this vessel.[46]

These friendly new contacts with the Vanikorans heralded improved trade in fresh produce, but unfortunately, illness had already begun to appear among the previously healthy crew. On 8 March, aside from Gaimard, at least two other crew members and d'Urville himself were afflicted with fever. By 10 March, there were eight fever cases aboard the *Astrolabe* and another five two days later. One of the Tikopian passengers (who each night still slept aboard the corvette for fear of fever) also contracted the illness, and this precipitated his departure with his compatriots. The Tikopians made their farewells on 9 March, appearing untroubled by the fragility of their borrowed outrigger and their lean provisions of dried coconut and taro. The crew of the *Astrolabe* gave them many presents, including biscuits. Vanikoro receives an average 5000 mm of precipitation per year, so it is hardly surprising that during the *Astrolabe*'s visit, there was some heavy rain. On the day that the Tikopians departed, it was of such 'inconceivable force' that Lottin found it impossible to work on the monument to Lapérouse, and d'Urville began to fear the worst for the islanders attempting to return to their native island in their small open craft, which must surely have been inundated.

On the morning of 11 March, d'Urville dispatched the methodically efficient Gressien to reconnoitre the northern coast of the island with a view to finding a favourable exit for the *Astrolabe*. D'Urville, who had still not visited the west coast of the island, was determined not to leave until the monument was completed. Despite heavy rain and strong winds, Lottin continued to work with his carpenters. Early on

14 March, he placed the kauri capital on the cenotaph and crowned it with a facetted wooden finial. He then added a small lead plaque bearing the engraved words:

A LA MÉMOIRE
DE LAPÉROUSE
ET DE SES COMPAGNONS,
L'ASTROLABE.
14 MARS 1828

Still wracked with fever aboard the *Astrolabe*, d'Urville reluctantly deferred to Jacquinot to inaugurate the monument. At 10.30 am, the expedition's second-in-command went ashore at Paiu with a detachment of 10 men, who solemnly paraded thrice in front of the monument and discharged three volleys of rifle fire. A lithograph by Hippolyte Vanderburch after Sainson's drawing of the inauguration was published in the expedition's 'Atlas historique'.[47] The National Library of Australia, in Canberra, also has a version in oil on canvas, which Roger Collins has attributed to Louis-Philippe Crépin. In the foreground, the artist depicted 12 officers, even though we know that d'Urville was not the only officer who was ill with fever at the time. In the middle ground, behind the monument, Sainson showed a detachment of at least two dozen men with muskets, when we know that there were only 10 dispatched. Finally, in the background, he painted the *Astrolabe* firing her guns in salute when, in fact, she was anchored near Manieve Island and would have found it very difficult, if not impossible, to sail so close to Paiu, given her size and draught. For all Sainson's romantic confection, his sketch does give us a sense of the simple dignity of the monument and the solemnity of the day.

Despite his absence, d'Urville did fire a salute from the *Astrolabe*'s guns on that day but on the other side of the island. To maximise the psychological impact on the locals, he gave them no warning. An uncertain Moembe and another chief, Kalaï, soon came aboard. With Hambilton's aid, d'Urville sought to reassure them but then drove home his intended condescending message:

> … the shots that they had heard were only fired in honour of the *Atoua Papalangui*, the god of the Europeans, which we had placed on the reef. I requested them to engage their compatriots to respect the house of our God, and not to seek to destroy it. If the ship which came after us, to their island, saw this house intact, this would be for them a pledge of our friendship with the inhabitants of Manevai [Manieve], and the latter would only be better treated by their visitors. If the monument was overturned, the whites would be angered and if they were of our nation, they would severely avenge this outrage. To banish all anxiety on their part, I made them un-

*'Inauguration du monument élevé par l'*Astrolabe *a La Pérouse à Vanikoro, 14 March, 1828', oil on canvas, ca. 1831, attributed to Louis-Philippe Crépin, after Louis-Auguste de Sainson. This painting is a confection. Twelve officers are depicted, even though d'Urville's staff was ravaged by malaria at the time. Similarly, at least two dozen men with muskets are portrayed, when we know that there were only 10 dispatched. Finally, the* Astrolabe *is seen firing her guns in salute in the background when, in fact, she was anchored near Manieve Island and would have found it very difficult, if not impossible, to sail so close to Paiu given her size, draught and debilitated crew.* National Library of Australia, NK11641

derstand that this would be the only vengeance that we would take for the deaths of the *Maras* killed long before, to understand that the God that we had placed on the shoal would from now on protect the spirits of the *Maras*; that this ceremony satisfied us, and that now there remained not the least reason for war against the people of Vanikoro. I pointed out to them that, so as not to provoke the anger of the *Atouas* of Vanikoro, ours had been placed on the reef, in the middle of the water, whereas the *Atouas* of the country, Banie and Loubou, were established on land; a precaution which would avoid all collision of powers between these diverse gods.[48]

Although d'Urville believed that Moembe and Kalaï were sincere, he knew that they could not give undertakings on behalf of the whole of Vanikoro. Indeed, he declared that he would count little on the word of people who were 'coarse and stupid', if his men hadn't used building materials unlikely 'to tempt their cupidity'. He also thought that the effort required to destroy the monument would yield only pointless fatigue, unlikely to appeal to people whom he uncharitably characterised as marked by laziness and 'natural indolence'.[49] Ironically, it would appear to have been the same periodic cyclonic forces that wrecked Lapérouse's expedition, rather than the iron-hungry Vanikorans, that would in time destroy the monument, leaving only its coral foundations.

By 17 March, there were 40 crew members affected by fever. Ailing himself and with more crewmen being infected by the day, d'Urville felt he had to leave as soon as possible. Despite the fact that so many men were weakened by fever and would be unable to cope with protracted kedging or other heavy tasks should the *Astrolabe* ground on the reef, d'Urville decided to set sail. Another factor was his strong suspicion that the islanders sensed the number of sick cases aboard the corvette was so large that they now had an opportunity to capture the vessel. He even suspected that the people of Manieve and Teanu might have put their past differences aside in a sinister pact to this end. When the people of Manieve declared that they had now made peace with the people of Teanu, and he saw Teanu canoes full of men armed with bows and arrows, bearing no provisions for trade and making for the *Astrolabe*, he ordered all his Manieve visitors to leave. When they refused, he promptly had the armoury opened and pointed to 20 gleaming muskets. The gravity of d'Urville's implied threat produced the desired result: the decks were cleared.

D'Urville had now burned his bridges and felt that he had no choice but to weigh anchor. He was confident of the excellence of Gressien's work charting the north coast of the island and its reef. This was also a significant moment in the history of the expedition: the *Astrolabe* would now begin her return voyage to France. What d'Urville had found on Vanikoro had to be reported to his superiors as soon as possible. He knew that Peter Dillon would likely achieve a measure of fame as a result of his prior efforts, but he had no way of knowing whether Dillon would actually seek his rewards in person at the court of Charles X. D'Urville was determined to claim his share of the glory in unravelling the mystery of Lapérouse. Being second at Vanikoro might not necessarily mean being second in Paris, as his part in the acquisition of the 'Vénus de Milo' had demonstrated. Peter Dillon might yet prove another Olivier Voutier.

The knowledge that the *Astrolabe* was now finally homeward bound had enormous psychological importance. The combined efforts of the crew were henceforth vested in collective return rather than abstract scientific and political ends that they did not fully understand. The men rallied. As d'Urville put it, 'I exhorted … the crew to redouble their courageous efforts, and I hastened the moment of setting sail as much as my feeble means permitted. The sick themselves put their debilitated hands to the task … on 17 March 1828, at 11.15 in the morning, *Astrolabe* unfurled her sails and finally winged her way out of Vanikoro.'[50] Little did they know that it would be yet another year before they saw Toulon again.

20

The voyage home

… La Pérouse, whose remains Dumont d'Urville brought back …
Marcel Proust*

D'Urville initially hoped to chart more of the Santa Cruz group en route to Torres Strait, but he reconsidered, given the growing number of fever cases among his crew and his own feeble state. By 26 March 1828, only Gressien and Guilbert remained fit among all of his officers, but two days later, Gressien also fell ill. Although a still-weak Lottin took his place, d'Urville had no choice but to put one watch under the command of the second mate, Pierre Collinet. He had known Collinet since they had sailed together on the *Chevrette* and held him in high regard. Although Collinet had joined the navy in 1804 and was a veteran of Trafalgar, he had spent almost nine years as a prisoner of war before returning to France in July 1814.[1]

So large was the number of sick cases that d'Urville considered returning to New South Wales to seek medical assistance in Sydney. However, the torrential rain and recurrent gales already battering the *Astrolabe* convinced him that the crew would be utterly incapable of sailing south, and he feared that in doing so, the winds might drag the *Astrolabe* through the potentially dangerous waters of the New Hebrides. Instead, he resolved to sail to Guam in the Marianas, which proved to be a slow passage because the *Astrolabe* could not carry many sails for lack of fit men to handle them. Those who were able were no doubt worked to the limits of endurance, including the cheerful medical orderly Jean-François-Guillaume Berre, who tended the sick. Sensibly, the fever cases were treated with quinine, but while suffering was further eased with laudanum, it was also needlessly exacerbated with leeches and blistering vessicatories.[2]

Despite her skeleton working crew, the *Astrolabe* avoided mishap and reached Guam on 2 May 1828. She anchored in palm-fringed, mountain-framed Umatac Bay, where Magellan had landed three centuries before. D'Urville was promptly greeted by José Flores, the *alcalde* or district magistrate,[3] and was pleased to learn from him that the Spanish governor of the Mariana Islands was Lieutenant-Colonel José de Medinilla

* *À la recherche de temps perdu*, vol. i (1913)

y Pineda, a Seville-born nobleman who was governor when Freycinet visited Guam in 1819. D'Urville knew that Freycinet had been well received during his three-month sojourn,[4] and he drafted a letter to the governor asking to be allowed to disembark his sick cases and to purchase supplies from the locals. Medinilla promptly arrived in person, offered the use of an old convent to house the sick, extended an invitation to d'Urville to stay in his pompously named 'palace' on the northern shore of Umatac harbour (rather than in the capital Agaña, 32 kilometres to the north) and ordered Flores to supply all the expedition's needs – albeit after warning d'Urville that local resources were almost exhausted by four months of drought and by his predecessor's allowing 'illicit' trade with English whalers. This so-called 'illicit' trade was emblematic of the restrictive nature of Spanish colonial rule. D'Urville became aware that the locals (who numbered a mere 4000 inhabitants) had warmly welcomed the previous liberal administration of José Ganga Herrero, for he had allowed them to prosper by trading freely with foreign vessels. In the neighbouring harbour of Apra (now the site of a major US naval base), d'Urville became aware of the presence of two vessels captured from South American separatist traders who also chafed under the monopolistic yoke of the Spanish crown. Despite his own liberal sympathies, d'Urville remained very grateful to the generous but conservative Governor Medinilla, who dispatched his aide-de-camp, Captain Manuel Tiburcio Garrido, with a gift of 10 pigs, 62 chickens, more than five dozen eggs, two baskets of potatoes, a case of tea, a 22-kilogram case of sugar, 17 bottles of beer and two flagons of aniseed cordial for the French.[5]

There were still more than 40 sick cases with varying degrees of fever on the *Astrolabe*. Quoy, Lottin and Dudemaine chose to remain aboard, along with five other ailing sailors, rather than move to the convent hospital ashore. On the morning of 4 May, d'Urville inspected this convent with Jacquinot and Flores and found it clean, spacious and airy. Sainson's sketch of the building, published as a lithograph in the expedition's 'Atlas historique', shows a two-storey building with rendered stone walls, thatched roof, slated windows and a stone stairway to the entrance.[6] In contrast, the governor's residence in Umatac, although very agreeably located, appeared to have been 'abandoned for a very long time' and retained 'only the feeble vestiges of its ancient splendour'.[7] Flores also took them to visit Fort San Ángel – little more than an isolated rock with a platform for two bronze cannons protecting part of the town and harbour – with a view to establishing the expedition's temporary observatory there. D'Urville was informed that the Italian-born Spanish explorer Alessandro Malaspina had used this very same fort (and the battery near the church) to conduct his observations in navigational astronomy when he visited in 1792. However, Jacquinot thought that San Ángel was far too vulnerable to high winds that might affect his instruments and opted instead for the governor's residence at Umatac.

After an absence of just three hours ashore, d'Urville returned to the *Astrolabe* so exhausted that he decided not to move from the corvette, regardless of the attractions on land. This would have implications for the expedition's botanical work on Guam, since Lesson was also kept busy assisting in the treatment of the sick cases and had little time for natural history. A list of 94 species collected on the island by the *Astrolabe* expedition was ultimately published, but none were identified as new.[8] Charles Gaudichaud-Beaupré, the botanist on Freycinet's expedition, had done three months of thorough collecting during his earlier visit. No new birds, fish or insects were collected by Quoy and Gaimard either, but they too had done their own thorough collecting in Guam with Freycinet in 1818. Similarly, Gaimard's Chamorro vocabulary, published in the second of the *Astrolabe*'s philological volumes, was largely gathered among the people of Guam during his earlier visit.[9] Like Lesson, they had their own onerous medical obligations among the crew.[10] Despite this, they did manage to gather the type specimen for a previously unknown gastropod: *Nerita guamensis*, endemic to Guam and the Southern Marianas.[11]

Guillaume Quemener, a Breton from Lorient, would be the first of the sick cases to return to the *Astrolabe* on 10 May. Regrettably, several of the others, already seriously weakened by fever, would fall victim to other tropical ailments such as dysentery in the weeks and months that followed. D'Urville was particularly saddened by the death of Hambilton on the night of 19 May. Despite his clouded past, his intelligence and knowledge of local languages had been of enormous assistance to the expedition in Vanikoro. His death appears not to have been solely the result of malaria. He is known to have imbibed a large quantity of coconut arrack shortly before his demise; alcoholic poisoning very possibly exacerbated the effects of malaria, which include enlargement and inflammation of the liver and other organs. D'Urville dispatched Dudemaine and a detachment of sailors to assist the magistrate Flores in burying Hambilton the following afternoon.

There were a number of other departures from the expedition but fortunately not because of death. The Chamorro sailor Mediola (originally shipwrecked on Lakemba), who joined the *Astrolabe* off Ongea Levu in Fijian waters, recovered from fever and was happily reunited with his relatives. An English sailor named 'Jack', who had joined the expedition in Hobart, also departed with d'Urville's blessing. Less happy was the temporary parting of another foreigner: John Maclean. It is not certain whether he joined the *Astrolabe* in Tasmania or King George Sound. He was brought back to the corvette by the magistrate Flores after absconding to Agaña from the hospital and then unsuccessfully attempting to join the crew of an English whaler. D'Urville had no intention of keeping any foreigner in the expedition against his will, but he resented the panic and prejudice he believed Maclean had spread regarding the fever aboard the *Astrolabe*. The whaler had sailed from Guam convinced of an impending epidemic. Not surprisingly, Governor Medinilla became anxious too and threw a sanitary cordon around the hospital. Aside from this quarantine measure, he ordered the port captain (his formal title was 'Port Adjutant') to investigate conditions aboard the *Astrolabe*. Commissioned only the previous December, he was a Scot named John Anderson. Known as 'Don Juan', he had come to Guam in 1818 aboard the *Uranie*, having served briefly as Freycinet's chief helmsman.[12] He was thus already well acquainted with Lottin, Quoy and Gaimard, spoke very good French and was particularly receptive to the reassurances of the expedition's medical officers. He ended up spending 'a good part of the evening on board',[13] engaged in conversation on a number of subjects relating to the Marianas, which d'Urville thought interesting enough to summarise on nearly three printed pages. When Anderson departed, d'Urville entrusted him with a letter and a fine percussion firearm of French manufacture (together with 5000 fulminate firing caps) for the governor. D'Urville knew full well that such a gun was an extremely valuable, state-of-the-art weapon, destined to render the flintlock musket obsolete and completely unknown in Guam. It was an act of generosity calculated to make an impression on Medinilla.

By this time, there were only four or five complete cures among all the *Astrolabe*'s sick cases. Of the officers, Gaimard, Bertrand, Lesson, Faraguet, Pâris and Dudemaine had still not completely shaken off the fever, and Quoy also had occasional relapses. Nevertheless, d'Urville was determined to set sail by the end of the month. To assist him, Governor Medinilla even provided additional men to help the *Astrolabe*'s withered crew raise her anchors. Yet again, the governor dispatched his faithful aid Captain Garrido with another splendid selection of provisions, including 'nine handsome pigs … eighty pounds of sugar, a case of sago biscuits, six bags of fresh rice, a bag of sago flour, twenty bottles of Madeira, six dozen eggs and a quantity of marrows, water-melons, bananas, pineapples, tomatoes [and] purslaine'.[14] As a final token of thanks to Medinilla for this generosity, d'Urville entrusted Garrido with silver and bronze *Astrolabe* commemorative expedition medals and a portrait of Alexander von Humboldt – whom he knew the governor had met in South America and admired.

The *Astrolabe* left Guam on 30 May, bound for Ambon. D'Urville wanted to explore the Western Caroline Islands en route, particularly those islands imperfectly charted by Freycinet a decade earlier. This was also a follow-up on Duperrey's exploration of part of the widely dispersed Carolines, named in honour of Carlos II (Carolus II in Latin) of Spain. Unfortunately, d'Urville's ambitions did not match the physical reserves of his men. On 2 June, although they skirted the reef that surrounds the Egoi group, they did not land, but Guilbert, charged with the survey work, was able to discern 13 islands from the topmast. While there was some satisfaction in meeting some of the friendly inhabitants who came aboard, communication was difficult, and d'Urville was surprised that the name Egoi meant nothing to them. Similarly, hoving-to on the west of the island of Yap, on 4 June, he was greeted yet again by friendly locals but was forced to accept that his men were still too sick to explore the island. D'Urville soon had a closer approximation of how the islanders pronounced the name of their island, recording the name 'Gouap'.[15] He would no doubt have found the island fascinating, particularly its stone-money culture. In his account, he wrote dejectedly: 'How agreeable it would have been to anchor at Gouap and, over several days, to study the manners of the inhabitants there and the products of the soil! But the *Astrolabe* was nothing but a floating hospital. A general demoralisation reigned aboard.'[16]

On the following day, the small, low-lying Ngulu Islands (the most westerly in the Carolines) were sighted. D'Urville found them imprecisely located on Arrowsmith's map and sailed closer to investigate. These atolls were little more than 'two small plateaux of sand and coral, covered with trees, and each being around a half-mile in circumference', with 'no trace of population'.[17] Having fixed their position but faced with tempestuous weather and the very worrying proximity of surrounding reefs, d'Urville broke off his investigation and headed southwest for the Palau Islands. On 7 June, the *Astrolabe* passed close by Babelthuap, Koror, Beliliou and Angaur, which enabled Guilbert to draft an incomplete chart that added to knowledge of these little-known islands.[18]

Heading in a generally southwesterly direction, on 17 June, for the second time in the course of the expedition, the *Astrolabe* came within sight of the mountains of New Guinea between Dorey and Cape Goede Hoop. Once again, d'Urville hoped to pass between Waigeo and Batanta as William Dampier had done, but unfortunately, as in September 1827, the winds once more forced the *Astrolabe* to round Waigeo from the north, just as they had the *Coquille*. Nevertheless, he was able to differentiate his route from Duperrey's by sailing close to the little-known Ayu Islands north of Waigeo, before rounding Sayang Island and entering the Halmahera Sea on 23 June. The next day, the *Astrolabe* sailed between Gebe and Giolo (Halmahera). Although initially there appeared to be an improvement in the health of the crew, by the third week of June, there was another malignant complication, presumably as a result of contaminated water aboard the corvette: dysentery began to infect the crew. The first fatality was Michel Sper, a servant to the officers, who died on 24 June. Five days later, another sailor of the same age, Marius Maille, died. By this time, most of the officers were suffering from yet another recurrence of malaria.

Faced with deteriorating weather conditions, critically shorthanded and with men dying, d'Urville decided to seek refuge at the small Dutch outpost of Cajeli on the island of Buru.[19] The *Astrolabe* arrived there on 30 June. Initially, the French had a cool reception from the resident Dutch East India Company officer, a man named Janszen, but he became decidedly friendly after reading the expedition's Dutch passports. Although he spoke only Dutch, he entertained the officers with the aid of his half-Indonesian daughter and did his best to assist the expedition with some fresh food until the weather conditions improved. While the sick languished in the tropical heat, Sainson completed a number of portraits and views of the island, and d'Urville found the energy to make a collection of local insects.[20]

On 6 July, the *Astrolabe* sailed out of Cajeil harbour and, two days later, reached Ambon. Port Captain Andries Ellinghuijsen, whom d'Urville had met in 1824 and 1827, once again guided her to anchorage. Soon after, d'Urville renewed his friendship with other Dutch colonial officials, including the provincial governor, Pieter Merkus, whom he had first met in 1823; the presiding judge, Johan Moorrees, who had been acting governor during the *Astrolabe*'s previous visit; the military commander Colonel Stijman; and Captain Lang, in charge of the battery at Fort Victoria. D'Urville received no mail in Ambon, not even official correspondence from the minister. Of the whole crew, only Lesson found a letter waiting for him from his brother René, who undoubtedly knew well the emotional privations of voyaging without family news. Lesson was among the crew members admitted to the local hospital. He proved a difficult patient, and his papers indicate that he favoured leeches over the ipecac prescribed (with some justification)[21] by the local Dutch medical officer 'Langaker' (Lange?).[22] Although still weak and despite contracting a cold in Ambon, d'Urville avoided hospital and recovered enough to revisit the Chinese quarter, to walk to the outskirts of the Dutch settlement and to collect over a dozen beetles.[23] Here the tropical fruit and the 'delicious freshness' of the 'rich and brilliant vegetation' made his spirits soar and reminded him of the seemingly fantastic descriptions in the *One Thousand and One Nights*.[24] Others aboard the *Astrolabe* also returned to familiar pursuits. Quoy's attention was drawn to a dead dugong in the harbour. This herbivorous marine mammal had arrived on the colonial brig *Siva* as a specimen for the Dutch medical officer, but unpreserved and weighing hundreds of kilograms (both Dampier and Baudin had mistaken dead dugongs for hippopotami!), it soon putrefied in the tropical heat and was so offensive that there seemed no alternative to throwing it overboard. Quoy seized the opportunity to make a careful study of its discarded body and had Sainson sketch it before appropriating its skull.[25]

Despite the continuing serious ill-health of so many crew members, the lure of still more natural history specimens induced d'Urville, incredibly, to break off his return voyage and accept Governor Merkus's invitation to accompany him on an official visit to Manado on the northern tip of Sulawesi. This meant backtracking some 400 kilometres north, and the *Astrolabe* and her weary crew left Ambon in the wake of the governor's vessel, the *Bantjar*, on 18 July. It took nine long days to reach Manado, and they were piloted into the harbour by an émigré Frenchman named Barbier, who commanded a little schooner, the *Lucifer*, engaged in the Moluccan trade.[26] The visit was an extravagant diversion, although some significant natural history specimens were acquired, including a dwarf buffalo or anoa (*Bubalus depressicornis*)[27] and a breeding pair of babyrousas (*Babyrousa celebensis*).[28] The latter, belonging to the pig family and native to Sulawesi, were unrepresented in live zoological collections in Paris. Cages were built for them on the *Astrolabe*, and they were consigned to the special care of the medical orderly Berre. While d'Urville, Sainson, Gaimard and Guilbert made an excursion to undertake fresh-water temperature studies at Lake Tondano (a crater lake 30 kilometres away in the Lambean Mountains),[29] Pâris surveyed the bay. Gaimard also compiled a vocabulary of some 86 local words.[30] Unfortunately, during their 'very agreeable' stay, two more crew members died of dysentery: Lambert Fabry, from Marseille, and Michel Vignale, a second mate from Toulon.

The *Astrolabe* set sail on 3 August, and Sainson commemorated the visit to Manado with a colourful sketch of Governor Merkus farewelling the French in front of Fort Amsterdam (built in 1658). In it, a fully uniformed d'Urville and his officers are portrayed shaded by a servant bearing a parasol; the babyrousas – tethered limb, snout and tusk on the beach – await embarkation; Quoy handles a live python like an accomplished circus performer; a uniformed Manadonese soldier bears a parrot bound for France; turbaned labourers shoulder the anoa suspended by its legs on a portage pole; and, in the foreground, a Celebes crested macaque (*Macaca nigra*) – probably the one given to the expedition by Captain Lang at Ambon – freely observes the proceedings![31] Sadly, the macaque would die at sea on 13 August, the same day as the assistant caulker Jean-Baptiste-Mathieu Richaud.

The *Astrolabe* reached Batavia, the Dutch colonial capital, on 29 August, bearing still more dysentery cases, including d'Urville himself. Once again, the French were warmly received, not simply because of their official passports but because of generous letters of introduction furnished by Pieter Merkus. In the large colonial metropolis, d'Urville was able to catch up with the European newspapers. Given his liberal political sympathies, he recorded his pleasure at learning of the fall of the ultra-royalist cabinet of Joseph de Villèle and the rise of the less-conservative administration of vicomte de Martignac, which would seek to restore freedom of the press in France. As the 'natural enemy of Turkish barbarism and the sincere partisan of the liberation of the Greeks',[32] he was pleased to learn of the defeat of the Turkish-Egyptian fleet at the Battle of Navarino 10 months earlier, although he believed that the three most powerful naval powers in the world – Britain, France and Russia – had little to boast of in defeating a 'half savage nation'.[33] Very likely, d'Urville's unflattering comments about the allied

'Mr Merkus, Gouverneur des Moluques, offrant des babi-rousses a l'expédition de l'Astrolabe, Célèbes', lithograph by Victor-Jean Adam, from a sketch by Louis-Auguste de Sainson, Voyage de la corvette l'Astrolabe, Atlas historique, Paris, 1833, plate 216. The Astrolabe set sail from Manado, in Sulawesi, on 3 August 1828. Governor Pieter Merkus gave the expedition two babyrousas (belonging to the pig family) on its departure. They are shown tethered limb, snout and tusk in front of Fort Amsterdam (built in 1658). Surgeon Quoy handles a live python like an accomplished circus performer; a uniformed Manadonese soldier bears a parrot bound for France; turbaned labourers shoulder the anoa suspended by its legs on a portage pole; and, in the foreground, a Celebes crested macaque (Macaca nigra) freely observes the proceedings. National Library of Australia, PIC U1925 NK3340

intervention on the side of the Greeks stemmed partly from his annoyance at the complete lack of reportage on the Astrolabe voyage in the French press and the absence of any correspondence from the navy minister when he arrived in Batavia. Not only was his vanity wounded at seemingly being forgotten, in a letter received by Lottin from Jules-Alphonse Poret de Blosseville (his former shipmate on the Coquille, who just two months earlier had visited Batavia aboard the Chevrette), d'Urville learned that he risked his thunder being stolen by Louis Le Goarant de Tromelin, commander of the Bayonnaise, who had been ordered to investigate Peter Dillon's claims regarding the fate of Lapérouse on Vanikoro. In response, d'Urville drafted a detailed report to the minister on the expedition's activities from Hobart through to Batavia. He also asked for promotions and decorations for members of his staff and sent Sainson's tableau 'representing the ceremony of the inauguration of the monument erected to the memory of La Pérouse on the shores of Vanikoro'. [34]

Although d'Urville wanted to explore Batavia and its southern hinterland – in particular the famous Buitenzorg Botanic Gardens at Bogor – the region's unsanitary reputation and its potential to further devastate his crew weighed heavily on his mind and he decided to stay aboard the *Astrolabe*. D'Urville's decision was also influenced by the fact that the Dutch would not supply him with horses without charge, and local prices were inflated thanks to generous Dutch colonial salaries. Perhaps more fundamentally, his determination to secure his share of glory in Paris also influenced his decision to leave Java as soon as he had replenished his supplies; he would not re-victual in Batavia, which he left on 1 September. Rather, he reprovisioned the *Astrolabe* at the western Javanese port of Anyer[35] on the Sunda Strait – taking on four small buffaloes, firewood, 8000 litres of water, brooms and fresh vegetables before setting sail for Mauritius on 7 September.

A fortnight into the voyage across the Indian Ocean, there were still almost a dozen sick cases aboard the *Astrolabe*. The corvette's veteran master gunner, François Raynaud, was almost completely paralysed from his illness. He would survive although he would not return to France with the *Astrolabe*. Jean-Julien Gemeir, a sailor from Brittany, was not so lucky; ravaged by dysentery, he succumbed just after midnight on 19 September. In the tropical heat, his body was soon committed to the deep; and deep it was, for soon after, d'Urville sounded 1160 fathoms (2121.4 metres) during his sea-water temperature studies.

The *Astrolabe* reached the beautiful island of Mauritius, Gaimard's 'colony of predeliction',[36] on 29 September 1828. After a medical inspection, the corvette was allowed to anchor at Trou-Fanfaron, the inner harbour of Port Louis. On 1 October, seven dysentery cases, one fever case and the paralysed Raynaud were then moved to the hospital at Grande-Rivière. One of the dysentery cases, Jean-Pierre-Melchior Bertrand, a sailor from Toulon, would not survive. Another fever case and two other dysentery cases were sent to the hospital the following day, and still more would require hospitalisation in the days that followed. The *Astrolabe* also needed ministering to; the caulkers found that her protective timber wale was completely rotten and had to be replaced.

D'Urville was politely received by the new governor of just three months, Lieutenant-General Sir Charles Colville, a veteran of campaigns against the French in the West Indies, Egypt, the Peninsula (where he was shot through the left thigh and lost a finger) and Waterloo. Colville was now in charge of an island of stubborn, French-speaking British subjects whose past spectacular success as privateers in support of the French navy, preying on British Indian shipping, sealed their fate under the terms of the Treaty of Paris (1814).

One of those who had begun his career in privateering (as an assistant pilot) was

Jean-Baptiste Lislet Geoffroy, who, it will be remembered from d'Urville's earlier visit, was the son of a slave woman. A man of extraordinary erudition and learning despite never having visited Europe, Geoffroy challenged all the preconceptions and prejudices of those who believed that the mind was constrained by race. Freed with his mother on the day he was baptised and taught by his enlightened father, Geoffroy was living testament to the potency of emancipation and education. He rose to become the island's most senior engineering officer, handing over its fortifications when the French capitulated in 1810, only to be quickly re-employed by the British. He was also the first 'mulatto' to be accorded academic honours in Europe, and he was one of the first people d'Urville sought out on his return to Mauritius. Although Geoffroy would live another eight years, continuing to research and write in his house in the rue d'Artois on an extraordinary range of subjects (mainly in the physical sciences), he trod a difficult and lonely path astride the worlds of black and white in a society in which slavery was still to run its malignant course. Though his skin was not white, his once-black hair now was. D'Urville found the aging savant residing in the 'Malabar' (Indian) quarter and thought him 'very crestfallen and very broken' since his earlier visit.[37]

Another friendship d'Urville renewed was with the Irishman Charles Telfair, intimately associated with the first days of British administration in Mauritius under Governor Robert Townsend Farquhar but also with British science and agricultural enterprise on the island. He was then at the apogee of his financial success, with a town house in Port Louis and ownership of the still-famous estates of Bel Ombre, Beau Manguier, Bois Chéri and Bon Espoir.[38] D'Urville would visit the latter of these estates and commented that his slaves were treated with 'gentleness and humanity'.[39] A trained doctor, who made a point of providing clean quarters, nourishing food, recreation, less-strenuous work for elderly slaves and education for his young slaves, Telfair was undoubtedly enlightened and humane by the standards of the time, but he was soon to be named and shamed as a slave-owner in Zachary Macaulay's *Anti-Slavery Monthly Reporter*.[40] Although Telfair sought to challenge the most serious accusations against him in a 250-page polemic published in 1830[41] (and enlisted numerous testimonials from his friends, which might explain d'Urville's comments), he could not expunge the fact that he owned and used African slave labour on his estates. Ultimately, even the fruits of this enslaved labour could neither sufficiently underwrite his scientific pursuits, generous hospitality to visiting savants, and dispatch of plant and animal specimens to scientists around the world, nor save his grand horticultural schemes. When he died, five years after d'Urville's visit, he was financially ruined and bereft of his beloved wife, the talented botanical artist Annabella Telfair, who predeceased him by a year. It was no doubt Telfair the naturalist (founder of the Royal Society of Arts and Sciences of Mauritius) rather than Telfair the slaveholder who attracted d'Urville. He is remembered to this day with the *Telfairia*, a genus of pumpkin named in his honour by William Jackson Hooker, and Telfair's skink (*Leiolopisma telfairii*), endemic to Round Island off Mauritius.

Yet another of the wealthy planters d'Urville met in Mauritius was Adrien d'Epinay. He was already famous as a barrister and advocate for freedom of the press and, like Telfair, he would rail against the abolitionists and champion the cause of his fellow slave-owners who sought compensation from the British when their 'property' was emancipated.[42] His statue in Port Louis' Jardin de la Compagnie (cast by his son, the celebrated sculptor Prosper d'Epinay, in 1866) is regularly besmirched with the grafitto '*esclavagiste*' (slave owner).[43] On 11 October, d'Epinay and his brothers sent their carriage to collect d'Urville from the *Astrolabe* and took him northeast to visit the gardens at Pamplemousses, then superintended on an honorary basis by Telfair. D'Urville spent that night at d'Epinay's brother-in-law's estate, Beau Séjour, overlooking the reef where the *Saint-Géran* was wrecked in 1744. This was a disaster that later provided inspiration for Bernardin de Saint-Pierre's famous novel *Paul et Virginie* (1787), and d'Urville was amused to learn from d'Epinay that it was a male passenger who drowned after refusing to undress to save himself rather than the modest putative heroine Virginie. 'Much less romantic!', remarked d'Urville.[44] He was also surprised to learn that Lapérouse, the object of so much of his attention on Vanikoro, had married in Mauritius in 1784[45], and that his sister-in-law still resided on the island. Curiously, he does not mention seeking her out, but he does note spending the night at the home of the widow of a surgeon from Bougainville's expedition.

Initially, d'Urville was disappointed that the only mail that awaited his expedition in Mauritius largely comprised very old family letters. His rivalry with Duperrey surfaced when he was reminded that the captain of the *Coquille* had at least received an official letter of congratulations on his arrival in Mauritius. Similarly, there was no joy in the newspapers, only outrage at the local re-publication of what he considered the 'most false and most calumnious' report in the *Sydney Gazette*, sourced to the missionaries John Thomas and John Hutchinson, regarding the *Astrolabe*'s misadventures in Tonga.[46] Surprisingly, through Telfair, d'Urville had the day before encountered yet another of his Pacific acquaintances: the London Missionary Society inspector George Bennett, whom he had first met in Tahiti in 1823. Bennett gave him a Tahitian grammar and an Indian copper figurine.[47]

D'Urville's linguistic studies (with a particular reference to Polynesia) would take another significant turn on Mauritius. On 7 November, at the home of Emmanuel Victor Singery, a Paris-born teacher who had lived on the island for some 14 years, he tells us he spoke of his desire to obtain a complete Malagasy vocabulary 'to compare its roots with those of the Malays and the idioms of Polynesians'. He then tells us that he learned of a local person who had long been engaged in 'this kind of work' and that the man in question 'very politely' received him and put at his disposal 'his immense materials'.[48] Curiously, d'Urville does not name him, in either his historical account, or in the introduction to his philological volumes. We know now that he was the planter Barthélemy Huet de Froberville, author of *Sidaner*, the first novel published in the southern hemisphere, and that he sought anonymity because in 1815 he had signed a contract to sell a half-right in his lexical work to Governor Farquhar – seeking to increase British influence in Madagascar and to encourage Protestant missionary activity there.[49]

D'Urville tells us that he transcribed extracts over several days aboard the *Astrolabe*. His initial impression was a lack of affinity between Malay and Malagasy, but he later concluded that 'Malagasy much resembles Polynesian'.[50] In the first of his philological volumes, d'Urville not only included anonymous extracts from Froberville's manuscript 'Grand dictionnaire de Madagascar' (with some changed orthography) but republished an 'Éssai de Grammaire Madekass', which René Lesson had published in 1827 and wrongly attributed to Louis-Armand Chapelier.[51] It was actually the work of a Lazarist priest in Mauritius, Antoine Flageollot, edited by Froberville.[52] Knowledge of Polynesian and Malay affinities with Malagasy was not new; they had first been recognised more than a century before by the Dutch scholar Adriaan van Reeland.[53] It remains to be said that there is also genetic[54] and archaeological evidence that voyagers from Southeast Asia (in particular Kalimantan and Sulawesi) arrived in Madagascar in the middle of the first millennium AD, and linguistic evidence of affinities between Malagasy and the languages of Polynesia (which also have Southeast Asian origins).[55]

The naturalists Quoy and Gaimard collected a number of new marine species on Mauritius, including the type specimen of a large sea slug, *Aplysia cirrhifera*,[56] on the Îles aux Cerfs; two new corralines, *Actinia gracilis* and *A. strigata*[57] in Port Louis; and *Chiton mauritianus*[58] on an un-named part of the coast. They also received specimens from their friend Julien Desjardins, including the type specimen of the knife razorfish, found at Flacq, which they named *Julis praetextata* (*Cymolutes praetextatus*).[59]

On 17 October, some mail finally reached the expedition via the neighbouring French island of Bourbon. One letter received by Dudemaine confirmed that d'Urville's official reports on the Bay of Islands and Tonga had been received in France. Two of the *Astrolabe*'s midshipmen, Pâris and Faraguet, both received confirmation that they had been promoted to *enseigne de vaisseau* by virtue of seniority and were promptly seen wearing their new insignia in town. D'Urville was particularly pleased for Pâris, whom he thought possessed 'all the qualities conducive to becoming a good officer'.[60] He made no comment in favour of Faraguet and did not mention him among the names of the officers working on the expedition's hydrographic results in a room he rented in Port Louis on 4 October. As we shall see, Faraguet's life was about to take a surprising turn.

On 18 October, another letter arrived for d'Urville from Bourbon, this time from Louis Le Goarant de Tromelin, commander of the corvette *Bayonnaise*, announcing his imminent arrival in Mauritius. The two commanders met a few days later in Port Louis. D'Urville was surprised to see how generously equipped the *Bayonnaise* was compared to the *Astrolabe*. In particular, he envied her capstan, the likes of which would have spared his crew much labour. D'Urville learned from Le Goarant that the *Bayonnaise* had received a hostile reception in Tikopia and that his men had not been permitted to land because of an epidemic that had killed 115 islanders in the wake of the *Astrolabe*'s visit. Nevertheless, the Lascar Achowlia had joined his expedition and had decided to journey to France with Le Goarant, thinking he would be honoured by the king of France. (D'Urville dissuaded him and he chose instead to return to Bengal.) D'Urville was also very surprised that Le Goarant had not explored his anchorage in Vanikoro and had been 'content to send his boats in reconnaissance'.[61] Furthermore, he learned that the *Astrolabe*'s cenotaph at Paiu had been respected by the Vanikorans and that the sailors of the *Bayonnaise* had done little more than nail a copper medal to the monument once they had discovered its existence. D'Urville must have been put at ease by this report, and it seems that he waited to receive it before sending his own duplicate reports to the minister, sealed in a tin box, the following day.

The *Astrolabe* remained in Mauritius for some seven weeks. Although a much sought-after dinner guest, d'Urville was forced to decline invitations because of his recurrent dysentery. By mid-November, he knew that his remaining sick cases would probably have to be taken to Bourbon and left in the care of the French naval hospital there. The *Astrolabe* set sail on 18 November 1828 and arrived there the following day. For d'Urville, the contrast between the sister islands was striking. Mauritius had been characterised by 'the order, maintenance, vigilance and wealth of the administration'. However, at Bourbon, under the French, 'everything suggested the negligence, indifference and poverty of the administration'.[62] Indeed, if he hadn't seen the French flag flying, d'Urville thought he could have imagined himself back at one of the islands of Polynesia.

Because of his difficulty communicating with Achille de Cheffontaines, the French governor of Bourbon, and the time required to bake a sufficient number of sea-biscuits for their voyage home, d'Urville had ordered his purser François-Esprit Bertrand to purchase supplies in Mauritius; Cheffontaines gave retrospective approval for these measures. Consequently, d'Urville needed to spend very little time in Bourbon. His priority was to send his sick cases to hospital and to find replacement men. His ailing sailors were joined by Gaimard, who suffered a recurrence of fever, Lesson (although d'Urville does not mention him) and then by Faraguet, who requested hospitalisation. The severity of the latter's illness was questionable. He remained in the hospital in Saint-Denis at least until the *Astrolabe* departed on 24 November 1828 but then sought permission to 'go to Mauritius for some days to await an opportunity to return to France'. However, from Mauritius, on 3 March 1829, he sent his resignation to the governor of Bourbon, stating that the slow recovery of his health and the continued weakening of his eyesight would never permit him to 'command or navigate in division'.[63] In Port Louis, on 29 July 1829, Faraguet married a Mademoiselle Marie-Joseph-Henriette Durand, the daughter of a former notary. It is not certain whether he had met Henriette during the visit of the *Astrolabe* and whether his illness in Bourbon and return to Mauritius prior to his resignation from the navy were part of a preconceived plan, but the circumstantial evidence is suggestive of romantic intent. Faraguet became a teacher of chemistry and physics at the Royal College in Mauritius. He also retained an interest in natural history and particularly astronomy, sighting the 'Great Comet' from Mauritius on 16 March 1830 and calculating its orbit.[64] He remained prominent in local educational and scientific circles for the better part of two decades before returning to France.[65]

Aside from taking on fresh provisions and water, the *Astrolabe* would make a number of subsequent stops on her return voyage to facilitate longitudinal observations. With the exception of the Cape of Good Hope, these observations would be compared with those made during the *Coquille* expedition. The *Astrolabe* reached the Cape on 23 December 1828, aided by 10 or more replacement sailors transferred from the *Colibri* and other vessels stationed at Bourbon. At the Cape, d'Urville was pleased to meet the naturalist Victor Jacquemont, who had arrived two days before him and whom he had first met in Paris and had exchanged plants with. He was on his way to India, where he would achieve fame for his travels in Rajasthan, Punjab, Ladakh and Bengal, chronicled in his posthumous letters (he died in Bombay aged just 32), including those from the Cape, which he entrusted to d'Urville to take back to France. In one of these letters, dated 28 December 1828, Jacquemont wrote:

> M. d'Urville … has just cast anchor at the Cape. We are constantly together. I have just spent the whole day on board the *Astrolabe*, which he commands. He is a capable man, very capable, and I like him very much. I here saw one of the sacred anchors and cannons of La Pérouse, which he raised from the bottom of the sea, on the reefs of Vanikoro, with immense trouble and danger. His vessel is dreadfully shattered; and many of his men have been killed or have died. But, on these hard conditions, he has succeeded beyond all sea voyagers. He sails in two days, as we do, but for Toulon.[66]

Jacquemont and d'Urville climbed Table Mountain together with Quoy, Lottin and Lesson. The view proved 'most beautiful', but the summit disappointed d'Urville from an ornithological and entomological perspective, and even with regard to 'species of plants very particular to this station'.[67] Quoy, however, had more success scouring the waters of Cape Town harbour, where he found the type specimen of a previously unknown sea cucumber *Holothuria aurea* (*Thyone aurea*).[68]

D'Urville also renewed his acquaintance with Sir Galbraith Lowry Cole, now the British governor of the Cape, whom he had previously met when Cole was governor of Mauritius in 1824. He savoured the famous wines of Johannes Colijn at Klein Constantia (now Hoop-op-Constantia) and found them very much to his liking. Colijn also presented a young 'Boschisman' woman in her early to mid-teens to him. His reference to her not being 'deformed' but of 'the type of this race disgraced by nature'[69] is troubling. It could have been a quirky, off-hand, racist or subjective, ethnocentric aesthetic comment, but given the recurrent fascination of European explorers with the genitalia of Bushmen (San) women and, in particular, their large and elongated *labia minora*, this comment might have contained gynaecological allusions.[70] To be fair to d'Urville, his principal interest in the girl appears to have been linguistic, given that he devoted a whole paragraph to the click-consonant Khoisan language he heard her speak.

D'Urville mentions being entertained and dining with several other prominent Dutch colonists. He also dined aboard another visiting French corvette, the *Zélée*, destined to play an important part in his final expedition more than a decade later but then bound for Pondicherry in India with his friend Jacquemont. As with the *Bayonnaise* at Mauritius, the generous manner in which the *Zélée* was fitted out engendered bitterness when he compared her with the humble *Astrolabe*, which he believed did no justice to the honour of France:

> One can economise on vessels destined to carry consular mail, horses, forage, or even to explore Corsica or a neighbouring coast; but when one must show the flag at the extremities of the globe, to people who often have never seen it; when a vessel is preceded by a sentiment of interest and curiosity which is involuntarily attached to missions of discovery, it is not acceptable to remain beneath English whalers which travel the same regions.[71]

The *Astrolabe* left the Cape of Good Hope on 2 January 1829. As she set sail, d'Urville had the misfortune to have a sailor accidentally drop a capstan bar on his foot. As a result, he found it difficult to walk and perhaps for this reason chose to review his insect collections; unfortunately, he found many had been destroyed by humidity. His living specimens, the babyrousas, were still in good health, but on the morning of 14 January, they managed to escape into the hold for a time. There was some anxiety at what they might do during their liberty, but they eventually returned to their cages of their own accord. The next morning, Saint Helena was sighted, and the *Astrolabe* was able to anchor in front of Jamestown in the mid-afternoon. Gressien was dispatched to call on Governor Charles Dallas and to present the expedition's British safe-conducts. He was very politely received, and the governor would send the commander of the *Astrolabe* 'diverse refreshments' and several invitations to join him. That evening, however, d'Urville and his officers were entertained by a local merchant named Saul Solomon, who had grown wealthy on the back of the exiled Napoleon – firstly because of the large military establishment that was deployed to guard the fallen eagle, but also through the hefty charges for the delicacies and luxury goods ordered by his household. Solomon doubled as an undertaker and buried Napoleon's valet Cipriani for the tidy sum of 1400 gold francs; in 1840, he would accompany Napoleon's remains back to France on the *Belle Poule* (in yet another capacity as honorary consul for France).[72]

D'Urville did not revisit Napoleon's former habitation at Longwood (which by this time had become a silk factory) or his willow-fringed grave. However, Quoy, Gressien, Guilbert, Pâris, Dudemaine and Sainson made the excursion. The latter would complete a number of sketches, which still feature among the familiar images of Napoleonic hagiography. Alas, poor Gaimard, left behind in the Mascareignes, was not to visit the tomb of his Corsican Messiah. D'Urville excused himself from accompanying his officers because of his injured foot and an east-southeasterly wind, which required his vigilance aboard the *Astrolabe*. Such a 'pilgrimage' (the word d'Urville himself uses to describe his officer's excursion) by the commander of a French naval vessel might have been viewed with political suspicion by his then-Bourbon masters, but in his historical account, published after the fall of Charles X, d'Urville referred sympathetically to Napoleon's exile as the 'long agony of the most extraordinary man of modern times'.[73] Since d'Urville's previous visit, the island had gained a new prison, constructed in 1827; its ultramarine façade is still the first thing visitors see on entering Jamestown's main gate. Close by was a new staircase of 699 steps cut into the basalt flank of the town in 1828 and rising 270 metres to the citadel above.[74] Neither appears to have made an impression on d'Urville, who stated that Jamestown 'had not changed appearance in four years', but he was struck by the fact that the town was virtually deserted because almost all the inhabitants were attending the horse races.[75]

After a stay of just two days, the *Astrolabe* left Saint Helena at 2.30 am on 17 January, reaching Ascension Island and anchoring in Sandy Bay less than a week later. Lieutenant-Colonel Edward Nicolls, who commanded the British garrison during d'Urville's previous visit, had departed just two months before. It would appear that mentioning his name engendered no affection: Nicolls had been recalled because of his imperious, arbitrary, 'even tyrannical' administration of the island. Captain William Bates, now in command, received d'Urville and his officers warmly, albeit with little more than rum and biscuits on the first occasion. He sent a sea turtle each day for the expedition's consumption (and another 11 on their departure), which was very much appreciated. D'Urville also put the *Astrolabe's* crew to good use each day catching an 'incredible number of fish' at their anchorage. One of the species caught during their visit proved to be the type specimen of a previously unknown wrasse, the greenfish, which Quoy and Gaimard named *Julis ascensionis* (*Thalassoma ascensionis*).[76]

Probably because of his injured foot, d'Urville initially decided against revisiting Green Mountain, where Dampier had sourced his fresh water in 1701 and where Bates's garrison still filled its water barrels. The following year, Bates would begin work on an effective scheme of pipes and tunnels to bring the water directly to Georgetown. On the morning of 26 January, however, he accepted Bates's offer of horses and set off with Quoy, Jacquinot, Lottin and Pâris. During his previous visit, he had been drawn to the island's mosses, lichens and pteridophytes.[77] During this visit, a seemingly new liverwort, staghorn club moss and *Cyperus* sedge were collected – very likely in the moist vicinity of Green Mountain, since the rest of the island is largely barren. Unfortunately, these 'discoveries' later proved to be already-known species.

On 27 January, d'Urville invited eight members of the British garrison to dine aboard the *Astrolabe* as a gesture of thanks for their generosity and kindness. It proved a very joyous affair, with numerous toasts and then affectionate farewells. The lonely British, stranded on their isolated volcanic rock in the midst of the Atlantic (Bates would die there),[78] were determined to extend their adieux by hosting yet another meal the following afternoon. After this, at 5.00 pm on 28 January, the *Astrolabe* set sail for France – four years to the day after the *Coquille* had made her departure.

The final leg of the expedition's return voyage to France was relatively uneventful. D'Urville recorded sea-water temperatures at depth and conducted regular firearms and cannon drills, the latter in case the corvette was attacked by Barbary pirates flushed into the Atlantic as a result of the French blockade of Algiers, which he had no doubt recently read about in the European papers or been warned of at Ascension Island.[79] The *Astrolabe* passed rapidly through the Strait of Gibraltar on 16 March, in marked contrast to her tortuous exit from the Mediterranean in mid-1826! Like Duperrey, d'Urville thought it better to sail to Marseille rather than waste time battling the northeasterly winds and currents to reach Toulon. He also thought Marseille offered a more direct route to Paris for the many natural history specimens aboard. Despite the reservations of the local quarantine officers – given the history of fever aboard the *Astrolabe* – she was allowed to anchor in the port of Marseille at midday on 25

March. There, d'Urville was delighted to be reunited with Gaimard, who had arrived back in France aboard the *Bayonnaise* two days before the *Astrolabe*. (Lesson was with Gaimard, but d'Urville makes no mention of his arrival.) In his published account, d'Urville tells his readers that the *Astrolabe* remained in Marseille only for the time that was absolutely necessary to disembark and pack the numerous cases destined for the museum in the capital. Since he wrote to the minister from Toulon on 26 March 1829,[80] he must have arrived in his home port within a day. With so many Toulonnais among his crew, d'Urville was undoubtedly not the only one anxious to weigh anchor and return to Toulon and the embrace of his family.

21

France & revolution

Not all the water in the rough rude sea
Can wash the balm from an anointed King.
William Shakespeare*

The joy of d'Urville's previous homecoming from the *Coquille* expedition had been utterly subverted by news of his first son's death and Adélie's psychological breakdown. His return in the spring of 1829 was an immeasurably happier event, though Adélie must have found his face aged by three more years at sea, his body thin and gaunt after repeated attacks of malaria and dysentery, and his uniform loose on his towering frame. Three days after arriving in Toulon, d'Urville's second son, Jules-Eugène-Hector, turned three. The child was the anchor of Adélie's sanity during d'Urville's absence. We do not know how the family celebrated that day; there is a lacuna in d'Urville's surviving journals between late March 1829 and the end of June 1830. D'Urville had last held his son in his arms when he was barely three weeks old. Now he was old enough to walk and talk with the father he did not know. It was not an uncommon experience for sailors, like anguished separation from a loving wife. One wonders whether d'Urville's repeated resentment of Freycinet in his journals[1] sprang in part from the jealous knowledge that Freycinet's beautiful young wife, Rose, had been secreted aboard the *Uranie* from the very beginning of his circumnavigation.[2]

Although Adélie was soon pregnant again, d'Urville found it hard to disengage from the *Astrolabe* and his expedition. With his characteristic bluntness, he challenged his superiors regarding the unanswered requests he had made for the promotion of his men and the bestowal of decorations. The day after his arrival in France, d'Urville wrote to the new navy minister, Jean-Guillaume Hyde de Neuville, descendant of an émigré English Jacobite family:

> [The *Astrolabe*'s] long and painful campaign is at last ended with success, and the immense materials that we have collected with so much suffering and danger are

* *Richard II (ca.1595)*, act iii, scene ii, lines 54–55

now safe from all events. We are convinced of having fulfilled with honour the mandate that was imposed on us, and, in this regard, our conscience is clear. It is up to Your Excellency, now, to prove to scientific Europe what value he places on such endeavours. For my part, I will not repeat the requests that I have already made in favour of my companions, too convinced that such attempts will be useless if the first were without success, and above all if an account of our long ordeals has not been sufficient to fix the opinion of the public and the Minister towards us.[3]

He then reiterated that he had given a general promotion to his crew in Ambon, and that in Hobart he had promised a further promotion once the evidence of Lapérouse's shipwreck had been established. 'Have my promises to my crew been illusory?' he asked, adding: 'Your Excellency will be kind enough to end my uncertainty in this regard.'[4] Hyde de Neuville was a little surprised by such boldness. In the margin of d'Urville's letter, he pencilled a note for baron Jean Tupinier, director of port movements: 'Reply to M. d'Urville that the King knows how to appreciate and recompense, and that justified reclamations are never without success before the ministers of His Majesty.' He added wryly: 'M. d'Urville announces that the *Astrolabe* anchored yesterday, at Marseille, and already he is unhappy. That was quick!'[5] Ironically, two days before d'Urville reached Marseille, baron Tupinier *had* drafted an official letter acknowledging receipt of his reports. It was sent to Toulon to await d'Urville's arrival.[6] Given the timing and the references to the 'Île de France' (Mauritius), it would appear that Tupinier's letter was initiated by the arrival of d'Urville's duplicate dispatches aboard the *Bayonnaise*.

D'Urville's bitterness over what he considered the meagre rewards received by his men would be sustained. More than four and a half years later, at the end of his official account of the *Astrolabe* voyage, he noted that he still hoped his steadfast second-in-command, Charles-Hector Jacquinot, would be promoted. In fact, Jacquinot would have to wait until 1836, although he was decorated *chevalier de la Légion d'honneur* in October 1829.[7] While Victor-Charles Lottin was made a *chevalier de Saint-Louis* on 6 November 1829, his promotion to *lieutenant de vaisseau* was effective only from 27 July 1827,[8] which d'Urville took to mean it was in consideration of the *Coquille* rather than the *Astrolabe* voyage. Similarly, Jean-René-Constant Quoy was made a *chevalier de la Légion d'honneur* five years after the *Uranie* expedition and before his voyage with d'Urville; furthermore, his promotion to second chief medical officer was dated almost a year before the *Astrolabe* returned to France; he would not be promoted again for seven years. Victor-Amédée Gressien was made a *chevalier de Saint-Louis* on 6 December 1829, but his promotion to *lieutenant de vaisseau* was effective from 30 December 1828[9] and was thus seen by d'Urville to be based merely on seniority. It is further evidence of d'Urville's sincere democratic values that for years he continued to press for decorations for Pierre Collinet and Joseph-Marie Nivière, both non-commissioned sailors who had assumed important leadership roles when the crew was ravaged by disease. Similarly, he repeatedly sought a decoration for Victor-Marie-Denis de La Noy, who, although only a corporal for two months, assumed command of the detachment of marines after François Richard was killed in Tonga. While d'Urville approved of the promotions of the artist Louis-Auguste de Sainson[10] and the purser François-Ésprit Bertrand (who was still suffering from malaria contracted in Vanikoro),[11] he did not approve of the promotion of Pierre-Adolphe Lesson, whom he considered 'estimable' but not having 'rendered to the mission the most important services'.[12] Indeed, Lesson had not yet turned 25 when he returned to France on the *Bayonnaise* but was promoted to surgeon second class effective from 7 July 1827.[13] From the beginning of the voyage, Lesson had been classed with the midshipmen in rank and had to compete with d'Urville for botanical kudos. At the end of the voyage, he was given a humble bronze commemorative expedition medal rather than the silver medal given to the other officers. Yet despite the faint praise given to Lesson, d'Urville ultimately requested his secondment to Paris to work on the botanical results of the voyage with Achille Richard.[14]

D'Urville's own order to report to Paris was sent on 28 March 1829 by aerial telegraph;[15] it reached Toulon on 30 March. He did not set off immediately but had a fortnight of rest with his family and arrived in the capital at the beginning of May 1829 to begin 'editing of the materials collected in the course of the campaign'.[16] It is not clear whether Adélie and young Jules accompanied him or whether they joined him later, perhaps by 9 May, when Adélie celebrated her twenty-ninth birthday. The d'Urvilles also employed a maid-servant named Toinette, who might also have been from Toulon. What is clear from their private papers is that the d'Urville family found lodgings in what appears to have been an apartment (with its own kitchen) in the ancient rue du Battoir-Saint-André. Close to the Sorbonne and the Paris medical school, this street had once been the home of the court physician Jean-Adrien Helvetius, who pioneered the use of ipecac, the same drug that very probably saved d'Urville from the fatal consequences of dysentery. In 1829, it ran between rue Hautefeuille and rue de l'Ésperon. However, in 1851, the prefect of the Seine, baron Georges Haussmann, fused it into the present rue Serpente, close to what became the junction of the boulevard Saint-Michel and the boulevard Saint-Germain.[17]

Perhaps inevitably in the wake of the family reunion came a number of 'conjugal tribulations', as d'Urville described them: petty differences during excursions with their young son, disagreements over domestic economies, trivial quirks and foibles – all chronicled in his surviving personal journals.[18] Those who command ships are used to giving orders and having them obeyed. Adélie, however, had been accountable to herself while her husband was absent (although she also received 3000 francs from her father not long after the *Astrolabe* set sail).[19]

One of the first things d'Urville did in Paris was to attend a meeting of the Académie des sciences on 12 May 1829, where he read a long summary of all the scientific work conducted during the *Astrolabe* voyage.[20] Six months later, his friend and patron Rear Admiral de Rossel, director-general of the navy's Dépôt des cartes et plans, died. One of Rossel's final official acts had been to read to the academy his own very favourable report on the hydrography of the *Astrolabe* voyage.[21] This was just over a week after d'Urville was promoted to *capitaine de vaisseau* on 8 August 1829.[22] Rossel had been a member of the Académie des sciences since 1811, and on his death, d'Urville was induced to accept nomination for election to his vacant place in the geography and navigation section. The result was a humiliation for d'Urville, who was fourth on the list of seven candidates, which included his rival Duperrey.[23] The winner, elected on 25 January 1830, was Admiral Albin-Reine Roussin, a member of the Bureau des longitudes, who had undertaken significant cartographic work in Brazil and on the coast of Africa.[24] Roussin received 49 votes, while d'Urville received a mere five votes. Although d'Urville did have a number of firm supporters in the academy, the astronomer François Arago would later rake up this contest and mock him by suggesting that three of the five votes he received were, in fact, mere sympathy votes by those who already knew that Roussin's election was a forgone conclusion.[25] The early months of 1830 were indeed a winter of discontent for d'Urville. Not only was he seemingly spurned by the scientific community, but during many bitterly cold weeks, he walked to work beside the Seine frozen in the very heart of Paris.

While d'Urville had the consolation of being promoted to *capitaine de vaisseau* on the recommendation of navy minister Hyde de Neuville and with the approval of Charles X, he resented the fact that he was not officially presented to the king on his return to France after his 'incomparable' expedition.[26] Ironically, within a year, he would have a protracted audience of an entirely unexpected kind, but for the moment the king had other things on his mind. The blockade of Algiers was still in force, and there was no sign that the Dey would agree to the reparations demanded by France for having thrice struck the French consul Pierre Deval during a dispute over a debt dating back to the Revolution. Less than a week before d'Urville received his promotion, the French parley vessel, *Provence*, was fired upon 80 times as she left the port of Algiers. News of this further affront reached Paris just as Charles X and his ultra-royalist supporters succeeded in engineering the fall of the liberal–monarchist Martignac Government (having thwarted its program of moderate administrative reform at every turn) and replacing it with the reactionary Polignac Ministry. Initially, Polignac conspired with Mohammed Ali Pasha of Egypt to use Egyptian troops to attack Algeria, but Mohammed Ali demanded four French warships and 20 million francs to conclude the bargain. Hyde de Neuville's replacement as navy minister, baron d'Haussez, refused to countenance such a transfer of vessels, and the minister of war, Ghaisnes de Bourmont, finally convinced Polignac of the unlikely prospect of the Egyptians' being able to deploy 40,000 troops across 3000 kilometres of desert. By the end of January 1830, the Polignac Ministry decided on a full-scale French invasion using 103 naval vessels, 350 transports (including the *Astrolabe* put to use as a cattle carrier),[27] 27,000 sailors (including many of d'Urville's fellow officers), 37,000 troops, 83 siege guns and commensurate supplies and equipment. Despite delays and stern British protests and threats, the landing in North Africa began in mid-June, and Algiers was conquered by early July 1830.[28]

If Charles X and his new prime minister thought that the French public would be distracted by this rapid military victory and that their government could pursue its reactionary domestic agenda without resistance, they were wrong. Similarly, any thought that stiffer military resolve, as demonstrated in North Africa, was a solution to liberal political resistance at home would also prove wrong. In the naïve belief that there would be no disturbances and that they could turn back the liberal tide, on 25 July the king signed four ordinances that reinstated censorship of the press, dissolved the newly elected chamber of deputies, drastically reduced the number of future deputies, dramatically restricted the franchise of the urban bourgeosie in favour of the landed rural nobility, and called for the electoral colleges to meet in the first half of September.[29] In order to ensure surprise, there was no reinforcement of the Paris garrison prior to the promulgation of the July ordinances, and the king went hunting at Rambouillet, 32 kilometres from Versailles. The strategy would prove a major blunder.

On the morning of Monday 26 July, d'Urville was visited by Lottin, who appears to have told him of the dissolution of the chamber of deputies and the suppression of freedom of the press. He confirmed this by obtaining a copy of *Le moniteur universel* and in his journal recorded his disgust that the constitutional charter of 1814 had been 'trampled under foot' and that the electoral law had been changed by a 'simple caprice'. He had no doubt that rebellion was likely. 'The masses aroused,' he wrote, 'who will stop them?' Walking in the Luxembourg Gardens, he sensed the uneasy mood of the populace and noticed that 'every face' was 'sad'.[30] That same day, the editors of the major opposition newspapers – including the new opposition daily *Le National*, funded by the liberal banker Jacques Lafitte and edited by Adolphe Thiers – met, deemed the ordinances illegal and refused to submit. With the support of their journalists, they determined to print their papers the next day and called for the illegally dissolved chamber of deputies to resist the violation of the laws. Although warrants were issued for the arrest of journalists whose protests appeared in these papers, they were not acted upon, but the police commissioner did seize the presses of the newspaper *Temps*. On 26 July, industrialists and merchants also voted to close their workplaces and thus fuel agitation, with their employees on the streets along with the already elevated numbers of unemployed – disgruntled by three years of economic recession and soaring bread prices.[31] Students and printing workers began to assemble around the Bourse and the Palais-Royal.

On 27 July, 30 of the deputies met to protest the ordinances but stopped short of calling for insurrection. D'Urville had no doubt that Paris was 'in combustion'.[32] That same day, Marshal Auguste Viesse de Marmont reluctantly accepted command of the Paris garrison and began to deploy his troops. 'What a choice!', d'Urville wrote disparagingly when he learned of the appointment.[33] D'Urville had no doubt that the troops were there to 'repress the people'. He noticed that the Tuileries were now closed, cannons were aligned along the length of the gardens and the cour du Carrousel was occupied by detachments of cuirassiers, lancers and royal guards. Yet he was pleased to see that the soldiers and non-commissioned officers were 'sad and disheartened'. Might they still side with the people? Despite his sympathies for the democratic cause, his reaction to the growing agitation in the streets was to return home and 'barricade' himself.[34] That afternoon, the first of the street demonstrators was killed by the gendarmerie. Despite the declaration of a state of siege, the troops were returned to their barracks as the disturbances appeared to die down. In fact, in a dozen Paris arrondissements, armed rebellion was now being organised.

The next day, Wednesday 28 July, d'Urville heard the first cries of 'Down with the King!' and 'Long live the Republic!' At 8.00 am, he left his home and noticed groups of workers in the streets. He also saw the *fleur-de-lis* and other monarchical symbols being torn down. After lunch, he went out again and saw that the same streets were full of armed civilians and members of the National Guard. 'All the gun-shops have been pillaged,' d'Urville recorded in his journal. Crossing the city, he noticed the revolutionary tricolour flag flying from the towers of Notre Dame Cathedral.[35] The momentum of the rebellion began to build as military depots and magazines were captured, and the insurgents began to isolate vast sections of the city with thousands of barricades (which d'Urville referred to as 'palisades'). Recognising the danger, that morning Marmont sent his famous note to Charles X at Saint-Cloud: 'This is no longer a riot, it is a revolution. It is urgent for Your Majesty to resort to some means of pacification. The honour of the crown can still be saved. Tomorrow perhaps it will be too late.'[36]

In the absence of royal instructions or any hint of a political settlement, Marmont and his troops attempted to clear major roads and occupy strategic points, but new barricades sprang up behind them, and gunfire and stones (ripped up from the streets) rained down on them from the rooftops. According to d'Urville, between 4.00 pm and 6.00 pm there was a 'continual fusillade' and royalist troops had the 'turpitude to fire grapeshot'.[37] D'Urville was not able to get to sleep until almost midnight, when the sound of gunfire ceased. That day, a delegation from the elected deputies had been sent to Marmont in an attempt to end the bloodshed through a political solution involving a withdrawal of the ordinances and the appointment of a new ministry. Marmont, however, did not feel empowered to negotiate, and Polignac, who was apparently in the next room, was not prepared to make any concessions.[38] By this time, the resolve of the outnumbered royalist troops had begun to waver as they were cut off by barricades and their ammunition ran out in the face of withering insurgent fire. There was a steady stream of individual desertions, then two whole regiments defending the place Vendôme defected on Thursday 29 July. Ironically, the colonne de Vendôme was the only place d'Urville saw the Bourbon ensign still flying that day. Marshal Marmont had already sought to reinforce his troops with royal guards from Beauvais, Orléans, Rouen and Caen, but now he was obliged to deploy the Swiss guards defending the royal palaces in Paris.

When d'Urville left his home at 7.30 on the morning of 29 July, he found all the bridges free and soon realised that the royal troops had retreated to the Louvre and the Tuileries, and were firing from the windows. Rumours were rife. A student told d'Urville that 4000 'men of the people' had been killed, and that 'Raguse' (an allusion to Marshal Marmont's Napoleonic title of duc de Raguse)[39] had perished the previous night with 1500 of his men. This was untrue. Crossing the Pont Neuf, d'Urville realised that a bold insurgent assault on the Louvre was in progress. He probably did not know it at the time, but the attack was led by veteran officers of the Empire and students from the École polytechnique. D'Urville was thankful that the attack succeeded with 'no deaths, no excesses of any sort'.[40] Nor were there bloody reprisals as occurred in the wake of the fall of the Bastille in 1789 or the fall of the Tuileries in 1792. He saw 20 captured Swiss guards under the protection of armed bourgeois volunteers in the passage Dauphine. The Swiss had fled rather than fire on the people, no doubt mindful of their compatriots massacred by a vengeful populace in 1792.

Two years after the events, Louis Rozet, son-in-law of the botanist Antoine de Jussieu, wrote definitively that d'Urville 'took part' in the Revolution,[41] and in his biographical notice on d'Urville (1846), Clement-Adrien Vincendon-Dumoulin told his readers that d'Urville's involvement in the events of the Revolution of July 1830 was not 'indecisive' and that 'he took part personally in the glorious days'.[42] A century after the events, in two articles published in La Revue de France, Camille Vergniol was the first to make direct reference to d'Urville's own journal in order to argue that he was more a witness than a participant.[43] Yet he was not an entirely passive witness. In his journal, aside from expressing contempt for the Bourbons, d'Urville recorded distributing 'money and counsel' to the insurgents.[44] He was also part of the physical presence of the population in the streets of the capital. Every riot or demonstration is characterised by varying levels of vociferousness and action – be it violent or non-violent – the passive sympathisers, fellow-travellers and the purely curious all adding to the momentum and spontaneity of events, along with the premeditated actions of committed militants. As a serving naval officer, how much was d'Urville prepared to record in his journal? He was certainly concerned for the bigger picture and a return to stability and order.

By 3.00 pm on 29 July, d'Urville's quarter of the city (the parish of Saint-Sulpice) was calm: 'No more gunshots,' he wrote, 'not the sound of a carriage'. He left his home once again after dinner and noticed that 'even women' were returning to the streets. The remaining royal troops had completely evacuated the city and, according to d'Urville, 'the people reigned sovereign there'. It was the absence of the mayor and the deputy-mayor, 'legally and honestly constituted' in the 11th arrondissement, that finally disposed d'Urville to pay 40 francs to join the National Guard that evening.[45] Soon after, he would proudly declare that he was 'one of the first (and perhaps the very first) naval officers' to offer his services.[46] His colleague Vincendon-Dumoulin saw his membership of the National Guard as 'bringing his tribute to the national cause and enlisting in the commune to pay in person, as a simple citizen, in case it became necessary'. In assessing his political beliefs, Vincendon-Dumoulin added: 'except for some aristocratic prejudices, the last memories of maternal education, d'Urville was profoundly liberal'.[47] In his now-missing manuscript memoir, d'Urville admitted that at the beginning of the Revolution of 1830, his 'possibly immoderate ardour inspired him with very advanced opinions'.[48]

Whether d'Urville joined the National Guard out of conservative fear of disorder or to consolidate a liberal political victory, his actions were not passive. Others were certainly fearful that the political vacuum and revolutionary mood might have dangerous, unpredictable consequences. D'Urville was aware that some deputies favoured Charles X's abdicating in favour of his grandson, the young Henri duc de Bordeaux, with the liberal duc d'Orléans of the cadet branch of the Bourbon family acting as regent. For their part, the republicans offered the marquis de La Fayette the presidency. However, at 6.00 am on Saturday 31 July, La Fayette refused the republican offer and threw his support behind those who advocated an Orléanist solution. Two hours later, a deputation from the chamber of peers and the chamber of deputies offered the duc d'Orléans the 'lieutenant-generalship of the realm'. He accepted. The stage was set for what La Fayette called 'a popular throne, surrounded by republican institutions'.[49]

The day before, d'Urville had decided to report to the navy ministry, entering via the rue Royale. He was told by the doorman that neither the minister, the chief-of-staff nor the director of ports was present. Climbing the stairs, he encountered Vice-Admiral Jean-Baptiste-Philibert Willaumez, veteran of d'Entrecasteaux's expedition, who lashed out at 'those who had deserted their post'. D'Urville tells us that he vainly tried to convince Willaumez of the need to form a provisional naval council 'for the conservation of the registers'. The admiral, according to d'Urville, responded with 'absurd obstinacy that he must receive his orders from the king alone'. Only recently promoted *capitaine de vaisseau*, d'Urville lacked the seniority and evidently the confidence to press the matter personally with the provisional government. Had he been a 'rear admiral', he recorded in his journal, he would have been 'sure to take certain useful measures for the conservation of our navy'. Instead, he decided to keep his own counsel and left the building, stating that he would be at home if he was needed. And home he went, for he found it difficult to proceed any further with 'quays de-paved and palisades everywhere'. He added, 'I found groups of workers, with the tricolour flag; orators on trestles who speak of liberty and even the Republic.'[50]

When d'Urville learned of the formation of a provisional government, he once more headed for the navy ministry. On the way he met a Monsieur Bailly (possibly the mineralogist and hydrographer Charles-Joseph Bailly, veteran of the Baudin expedition)[51] and, it would seem, Admiral Ange de Mackau, the director of naval personnel but recently elected a deputy for Morbihan in Brittany.[52] He shared with them his delight regarding the events of the previous few days. Further on, he found the Archevêché (archbishop's palace) 'entirely sacked', which evoked no outrage in the once-devout Catholic d'Urville – quite the opposite. After crossing the Petit Pont, he made his way to the place de Grève (the present place de l'Hôtel de Ville), crowded with people of the 'lowest orders'. There he met a Monsieur 'Renaudier' – possibly the future foreign minister Anatole Brénier de Renaudière – who, d'Urville wrote, 'shared with me the joy of seeing the hopes of the Jesuits destroyed'.[53]

From a 'good source', he learned that the king had left Saint-Cloud with a mere 2000 men. For d'Urville, this epitomised the fate of a sovereign 'who wished to rule illegally'. In fact, Charles X withdrew from Saint-Cloud to the Château de Rambouillet only on 1 August. Back in Paris, as the crowd waited at the place de Grève, d'Urville noted the cries of 'Liberty' and 'Down with the Bourbons!' He recorded that the rue du Palais-Royal was crowded with people – all 'well dressed' and with the national colours (the tricolour had been prohibited for 15 years) adorning their hats. D'Urville wrote that the duc d'Orléans was 'received with a unanimous explosion of applause' and that this left him 'satisfied and full of hope for the future'.[54] Here d'Urville's testimony and participatory affirmation fold into each other.

At Rambouillet, Charles attempted to maintain a semblance of monarchical control by appointing the duc d'Orléans lieutenant-general of the realm, but the duke promptly rebuffed him with a reply that stated that he already held his power from the representatives of the people. That same day, d'Urville decided on a walk in the Tuileries with his wife and son. He noted that 'all was tranquil' and that the streets were once again 'becoming practicable for carriages'.[55] D'Urville was still to play a part in the last dramatic chapter of the Revolution of 1830.

At noon on 2 August, Charles assembled his family and abdicated in favour of his grandson. Yet he still resisted attempts to get him to leave Rambouillet with a safe conduct. It was only the impending arrival of a ramshackle body of members of the National Guard, dispatched from Paris to menace him, that made him decide to move to Maintenon (Eure et Loire). This decision was also influenced by a deliberately exaggerated report by Marshal Nicolas-Joseph Maison on the number of approaching guardsmen. Maison told Charles that 60–80,000 men were on their way, when there was only a ragtag band of 15–20,000 men, described by one observer as a 'rout in reverse'.[56] While the remnant royal artillery might have been able to scatter the hastily assembled militia, they could not have influenced the broader contest. Charles knew that the tide of events had turned irrevocably against him. But how was he to extricate himself?

Some three hours before the abdication, d'Urville once more left his lodgings for the navy ministry. There he learned that baron Tupinier, director of ports, had been summoned by Orléans. In fact, Tupinier, who lived virtually opposite the ministry, had been confronted on his doorstep by a student of the École polytechnique, who had been ordered to find him and request his presence at the Palais-Royal. Determined not to be excluded, d'Urville decided to make his own attempt to see the duke but was stopped by a 'kind of aide-de-camp'. He once more offered his services before returning home, 'little satisfied at not having been honourably received'. D'Urville then attempted to see Joseph Tastu, the publisher of the official account of the *Astrolabe* voyage, but waited fruitlessly for an hour for him to arrive before returning home yet again. This time there was a message from Tupinier requesting his presence. Now a 'provisional commissaire' of the new administration, Tupinier informed d'Urville of a special mission he wanted him to undertake and informed him that 'Charles X and [the duc] d'Angoulême had requested safe conduct to leave France'.[57] D'Urville listened and agreed to take them into exile after assuring himself of constitutional formalities. In Tupinier's draft instructions to d'Urville, dated the same day, he was ordered to 'go to Le Havre without the least delay'. There he was to deliver an accompanying letter of instruction to Commissaire-Général Denois. Together they were to 'lease the two best American packet boats to be found in the port' but with the condition that they 'add to the American crew, a French crew of equal number'. They were then to sail to Cherbourg (Manche), where they would receive 'new instructions'.[58] After leaving Tupinier, d'Urville organised a carriage to collect him early the next morning and then went home to pack; he did not finish his preparations for departure until after midnight.[59] Although he had barely three and a half hours sleep, he was underway at 6.00 am.

After leaving the dirt and clutter of Paris and entering the tranquillity of the countryside, he reflected on nature 'so calm and insensitive, in the midst of the flux and reflux of human passions'. He travelled alone, paying the driver of the carriage 250 francs for the privilege. D'Urville's route took him via Magny-en-Vexin. There he saw small feeble detachments of national guards from Rouen marching on Paris. 'The 30,000 national guards announced,' he wrote, 'were reduced to 300 poor devils, badly equipped.' In referring to them and recognising their importance, d'Urville revealed his hatred of political extremes: 'It is necessary,' he added, 'to defy insurrections as much as Jesuit ministers.' After dining in Rouen, he travelled on the road that touched the northern bank of the Seine in various places, including Caudebec, which he appears to have reached around sunset. The rest of his traverse of his native Normandy was in the dark. It was unexpectedly cold for August, and he slept as best he could wrapped in his coat in his carriage.[60] D'Urville reached Harfleur[61] at dawn and soon after was in Le Havre. After taking a room at the Hôtel de la Paix, he changed and at 6.30 am, went to the home of Etienne-François Denois[62] – just as the naval *commissaire-général* was rising.

With Denois' assistance, d'Urville learned that the two American packet boats in the harbour were the *Great Britain* (737 tonnes, Captain Francis French)[63] and the *Charles Carroll* (417 tonnes, Captain James Clark).[64] When he visited the two ships, he wrote that they 'far surpassed the opinion I had formed'. Describing them as 'superb vessels', d'Urville added, 'how fortunate I would have been if the *Astrolabe* had approached them!'[65] The nationality of the vessels was clearly chosen intentionally to avoid the possibility of Charles X's entering a foreign port under the Bourbon ensign. According to the acting navy minister, Admiral de Rigny, 'the flag of the United States' would 'fulfil perfectly … the goal'.[66] Denois and d'Urville had to negotiate with the two American captains without revealing the purpose of the lease or the ultimate destination of the vessels after they left Cherbourg. In fact, they themselves did not know Charles X's final destination. They had to make contingencies in case he chose Naples[67] – which would have required rounding the Iberian Peninsula, entering the Strait of Gibraltar and crossing half the Mediterranean. Not surprisingly, the Americans quickly sensed a significant profit to be had. The agreed price for each vessel, reported to the minister on 6 August, was 30,000 francs per month if the voyage lasted more than two months, 50,000 francs 'for the whole voyage' if it lasted 'less than two months' and 10,000 francs for each additional fortnight after two months, with 30,000 francs payable within 10 days of the signing of the contract. If the passengers were to be disembarked other than in a Channel port or in the United States, 10,000 francs was to be paid to each captain 'in addition to the stipulated cost'. In each port after leaving Le Havre, the needs of the vessel and the crew would be met by the government.[68] The cost of victualling the passengers would also be at the expense of the French government. The following day, the new administration, eager to have Charles X leave France, allocated 200,000 francs to cover the possible cost of the expedition.[69] At 8.00 am on 7 August, the *Charles Carroll* arrived in Cherbourg harbour with d'Urville aboard.[70] He found the *Great Britain* at anchor the following morning. Reporting his safe arrival in Cherbourg, d'Urville took the opportunity to request that Lottin, then in Paris, serve again as his first officer.[71] Tupinier promptly granted this request.[72]

On the day d'Urville reached Cherbourg, Charles X and his entourage had only reached Le Merlerault (Orne). The deposed king maintained a deliberately slow pace, ostensibly to spare his horses and to arrive with his entourage in one body but in reality because the British ambassador, Lord Charles Stuart de Rothesay, had sent his attaché, Colonel John Hobart Cradock, to slow him down in the hope of gaining time to install the young duc de Bordeaux on the throne. Despite a sojourn in Argentan (Orne), these delays came to nought: on 9 August, the duc d'Orleans accepted the crown offered to him by the chamber of deputies and thereby ended the regency.

Charles, nevertheless, continued his stubborn stately progress. He did not arrive in Cherbourg until 16 August, having travelled through d'Urville's birthplace, Condé-sur-Noireau, then Vire (Calvados), Saint-Lô and Valognes (Manche). It took him a fortnight to cover much the same distance d'Urville had covered in a day and a night. Asked by the local authorities to enter Cherbourg with a simple escort rather than with his 600 guardsmen, Charles agreed – despite the anxieties of some of his retinue. His boarding of the *Great Britain* – calculated to coincide with the tide – was tranquil, except for a trumpet fanfare, the emotional farewells of those of his party who were to remain in France, and the jeers and taunts of the gloating labourers in the naval arsenal.[73] Among the 80 or so individuals[74] who embarked with the crestfallen 73-year-old Charles X were the young duc de Bordeaux (the would-be Henry V) and his Neapolitan mother, the duchesse de Berry, who, two years later, would fail in an attempt to once more raise the Vendée in royalist counter-revolution; the inflexible former prime minister Polignac, whose fanatical reactionary policies had directly precipitated the disaster; and the hapless Marshal Marmont, who had wielded the blunted sword of the Bourbons against his own people and against his own better judgement.[75] In his journal, d'Urville noted that Marmont, duc de Raguse, 'had aged twenty years in twenty days'.[76] Had they met before, or had d'Urville simply seen him in the streets at the beginning of the Revolution? Whatever, during the coming voyage, the two would talk frankly for hours about the events that had recently unfolded.

Still unable to determine where Charles X would seek refuge, the new navy minister, General Horace Sébastiani de La Porta, had written to the maritime prefect in Cherbourg with supplementary orders for d'Urville. Under no circumstances would the government accept the Low Countries, another French port or the Channel Islands as a destination. Charles had to propose a specific port before the American vessels set sail, and he could not change his mind once they were under way. If he would not nominate a destination, he was to be taken directly to Portsmouth.[77] The new administration was determined to treat Charles X very differently from the manner in which Louis XVI had been treated when he was deposed. D'Urville hardly needed to be told that he was expected to give Charles X and his family all the respect that their former positions entitled them to and to assure them of their liberty.[78] However, it was a qualified liberty. Almost certainly under official instructions, d'Urville armed the *Charles Carroll* with two four-pounder guns and four swivel guns, and the *Great Britain* with four six-pounder guns and four swivel guns.[79] As an added precaution, the two American vessels were to be shadowed by two French naval vessels, the flute *Seine* (800 tonnes, 24 guns, Captain Thibaut) and the small fisheries patrol cutter Rôdeur (six guns, Captain Quesnel),[80] presumably in case Bourbon partisans (or even the passengers themselves) attempted to seize control. According to Louis Rozet, 50 French naval personnel were also meant to travel on board the American ships to give d'Urville 'a strong hand if needed',[81] but Charles absolutely refused to embark if they remained. D'Urville complied with his wishes, little worried because he knew (and Charles did not) that reinforcements remained close at hand aboard the *Seine* and the *Rôdeur*. For good measure, he removed his own uniform – in any case habitual behaviour on his part as we have seen! – and Lottin apparently did the same. The former king and his son had also shed their uniforms and insignias of rank before entering Cherbourg. There was one other potential complication: Charles had made it known that he would not set foot on the vessel if he saw a single tricolour cockade. Since the whole of Cherbourg was bedecked in the tricolour, and some of the crew of the *Great Britain* were French citizens displaying their enthusiasm for the Revolution, d'Urville deftly overcame the problem by dismissing the cockades as the American red, white and blue.

At the last minute, it was discovered that there was no bread aboard the *Great Britain*, and their departure from Cherbourg was delayed for almost two hours while sufficient loaves were located ashore. Meanwhile, the principal members of the deposed regime, anxious to set sail, conversed with an attentive d'Urville. In his personal journal, d'Urville recorded that his passengers behaved in a very amiable manner towards him and Lottin: '… all spoke with me at length and with goodwill'. And he added, 'the most witty is the King'.[82] D'Urville gave an account of these conversations to the *Revue des deux mondes*[83] and to Louis Rozet, who incorporated them into his book on the July Revolution, *Chronique de juillet 1830*. According to Rozet, Charles X asked d'Urville if he was '*the* Captain d'Urville'. When d'Urville answered 'Yes, Sire', Charles replied, 'I am fortunate to be conducted by so distinguished an officer: I know you already, and I count on you.' D'Urville responded graciously: 'Sire, your desires are my orders so long as they are not opposed to my instructions; and I am forced to prevent them.' Finally, Charles answered the question foremost in d'Urville's mind. He told him that he wished to sail firstly to Spithead and anchor in 'front of Cowes' because he did not know 'at all the harbour of Portsmouth'.[84] This would have been very pleasing news for d'Urville, because Cowes is almost due north of Cherbourg and only required him to sail across the Channel to the Isle of Wight and into the Solent. The flotilla under d'Urville's command got underway. Only after they set sail did Charles realise that they were being shadowed by two warships flying the tricolour. D'Urville fended off accusations of breached undertakings by stating that the escort was 'by virtue of new orders received from Paris'.[85] Although displeased, Charles was powerless to do anything.

The voyage across the Channel took 24 hours because of unfavourable winds – long enough for seasickness to affect many of the passengers. The duchesse de Berry bravely tried to maintain her dignity, both vomiting and smiling as she promenaded on deck. The stores of sumptuous delicacies and wines stowed for a possible two-month voyage were barely touched. D'Urville dined with the American captain and never shared a table with his distinguished guests. When the *Great Britain* finally anchored off Spithead, and boats bearing English produce came alongside in the hope of sales, the duchesse de Berry, rather than avail herself of the fine French cheeses that were no doubt available on board, settled on a large morsel of what d'Urville and the former king considered foul-smelling Chester. In his private journal, d'Urville described the duchesse de Berry as 'the best soul in the world, the most simple and the most playful; but she is empty-headed, and one could not follow a word of her conversation'.[86]

There were still more conversations with the fallen monarch as the duc de Luxembourg and the duc de Choiseul were dispatched by Charles X to London from Spithead to negotiate their refuge in Britain with the prime minister, the Duke of Wellington. According to Rozet, Charles asked how d'Urville had come to command this special mission. He replied that it was simply because there had not been 'another naval officer who had offered his services to the *lieutenant-général*'.[87] D'Urville's personal account of his conversations with the royal party reveals that they did not comprehend the reasons for the fall of the Bourbon dynasty. They sought explanations in conspiracies rather than their own flawed autocratic policies.[88] For his part, d'Urville, alluding to the role of foreign troops in restoring the Bourbons in

1814 and 1815, told Charles X that while 'anarchy could one day return the enemies to France, and, as a result, the duc de Bordeaux', he 'by no means wished it'. Surprisingly, if we are to accept d'Urville's private journal, the former sovereign 'appeared happy' with such frank 'sincerity' and several times took d'Urville's hand and thanked him for his 'behaviour towards his family'.[89] By this time, Charles X already knew that there would be no foreign troops to restore the Bourbons. On 19 August, d'Urville had written in his journal that 'it appears that the English people are exasperated by the aristocracy and the king of England dares not receive Charles X in his kingdom'.[90] However, the next day, 20 August, Admiral Sir Thomas Foley, commander-in-chief, Portsmouth, and hero of the 'Battle of the Nile', came aboard the *Great Britain* and informed d'Urville that Charles X was authorised to land in England, but as a 'simple individual'.[91] Implicitly, there would be no government in exile and no honours of state.

It soon became clear that the pragmatic British government was reconciled to the process of democratic change in France. On 21 August, Charles X informed d'Urville that he would establish himself at Lullworth Castle, near Weymouth in Dorset,[92] but it was not until 8.00 am on 23 August that he boarded the steamboat that took him ashore. Before leaving, he thanked d'Urville and offered him his best wishes; he also gave 500 francs to the French sailors aboard the *Great Britain* and 160 francs to those aboard the *Charles Carroll*.

Curiously, after d'Urville's death, he was accused by the duc de Bordeaux of having had 'shortcomings' in his treatment of the king and his family.[93] The duke, though, was not yet 10 years old at the time of the actual events. D'Urville was also accused of having said that 'if he [Charles X] wants to return to France, I will sink him'.[94] However, d'Urville was on the same vessel as the king and this blustering threat is strikingly similar to the one attributed to Captain Thibaut of the *Seine* by Louis Rozet in 1832. It was uttered in the context of a coded emergency signal agreed upon in advance by d'Urville and the commanders of the two French naval vessels that shadowed the *Great Britain* and the *Charles Carroll*. If a red flag was flown from the *Great Britain*, this meant that d'Urville had been the subject of violence, and the vessel was being forced to sail to a prohibited destination. In such a case, Thibaut was to fire warning shots in the air and then into the *Great Britain*'s topsails until she 'resumed the fixed route'. According to Rozet, Thibaut swore that this was 'not a pleasantry' and that he would send her 'to the bottom!'[95]

There were other unflattering reports of d'Urville's conduct during the voyage published in the memoirs of various members of the royal entourage. For example, the duchesse de Gontaut – soon to be dismissed by Charles X because her views were considered too liberal! – resented d'Urville's command of the vessel, his suggestion that her berth face that of the 'governor' and his 'walking constantly on deck, near His

Majesty!'[96] Guillaume-Isidore de Montbel, who had served successively as Polignac's minister for ecclesiastical affairs and public instruction, the interior and finance, asserted that 'during the crossing Dumont d'Urville exhibited an arrogant harshness towards the royal family';[97] while baron d'Haussez, the former navy minister, asserted that d'Urville eavesdropped on conversations, affirmed his liberal beliefs, disavowed his noble origins and, when criticised for not taking his cap off in the presence of the king, retorted: 'What do you want, I don't have the habits of the court.'[98] None of these criticisms were based on the personal complaints of Charles X. What they have in common is a belief that d'Urville should have behaved in a more obsequious and formal manner, yet what we know of d'Urville's abrupt manners and relaxed dress code would suggest that he probably behaved according to his usual habits. Ultimately, his eccentricities and political frankness were ammunition for those who wanted to find insults where likely there were none. In 1871, the Bourbon legitimist historian Alexandre de Saint-Albin even declared that, 'during the entire crossing, Captain Dumont d'Urville, sought by his attitude and his gestures to insult malevolently, speaking to the king as he would not have spoken to another elderly person: brusquely, with cap on his head and pipe in his mouth'.[99]

In 1833, perhaps already subject to, or expecting, legitimist criticism, d'Urville wrote, in the concluding remarks of the fifth and final historical volume of the *Astrolabe* expedition, that Charles X was the victim of 'perfidious counsel', and that he accorded him and all those consigned to his care 'all the respect ... all the kind attentions due to a great unfortunate'. He added: 'It seemed to me that nothing was left to be desired in this respect: at the time of leaving me, Charles X himself and the various members of his family and his retinue renewed their thanks in the most affectionate way'.[100] Be that as it may, d'Urville must have breathed a sigh of relief when his passengers disembarked.

22

Paris & the pen

He who cannot limit himself has ever been able to write.
Nicolas Boileau-Despréaux*

As soon as Charles X had left the *Great Britain*, d'Urville drafted a report for the minister, which he gave to Captain Michel Quesnel to take immediately to Le Havre aboard the *Rôdeur*. Ironically, having just taken one fallen monarch out of France, he suddenly sought to return another, for he added a postscript stating that he had read 'in several newspapers … that the king of France would request the return of the remains of Napoleon Bonaparte to Paris', that if this came to be, and if the minister was satisfied with the mission he had just accomplished, he hoped that eyes would again fall on him.[1] Not known for any past Bonapartist sympathies but having visited the island of Saint Helena twice, this might have been a deliberate sycophantic ploy on d'Urville's part to draw the further attention of a new minister who was both Corsican and known for his military career under the former emperor. Ultimately, Louis-Philippe would not order the repatriation of Napoleon's remains for another decade, and when he did, it was his third son, François d'Orléans, prince de Joinville, who commanded the mission.[2]

Because of contrary winds, d'Urville was not able to leave the Solent until 26 August 1830 and did not return to Cherbourg until 27 August. From there, he reported to General Sébastiani that he would leave for Caen on the evening of Monday 30 August, and that he would only 'remain long enough to find a place [in a coach] for the capital' before returning immediately for further orders.[3] Conveniently, this gave d'Urville the opportunity to see his elderly mother and some of his friends. En route, he passed through Bayeux, redolent with childhood memories, but he wrote unequivocally in his journal: 'I prefer Provence.' He arrived in Caen, at the Hôtel de la Place, on Tuesday 31 August and found his mother waiting for him along with his friends Pierre-Aimé Lair (director of Caen's botanical gardens) and, it would seem, Jean-Augustin Marescot.[4] D'Urville wrote that he embraced them 'with joy' before leaving his baggage in the

* *L'Art poétique* (1674)

doorway of the hotel in readiness for his imminent departure and dining with 'gaiety' at his mother's home.[5] There is no indication of any maternal censure for d'Urville's part in the fall of the Bourbons. A proud conservative noble, a devout Catholic and a stubborn royalist she might have been, but perhaps she was not quite the inflexible 'ultra' that some of d'Urville's biographers have painted her as being, and perhaps she had already come to terms with the new Orléanist régime.

After his brief interlude in Caen, no doubt recounting his recent adventures and exchanging news of family and friends, d'Urville was once again on the road to Paris. He had been away from home a month, and he recorded in his journal that the following morning he hoped to 'surprise' his 'gentle and charming Adèle in bed'.[6] The coach reached its Paris terminus at 4.30 am on 2 September. Grabbing his bag, he took a cab to the rue Battoir Saint-André, and in a few extra minutes, he was home. D'Urville wrote: 'My gentle friend, excited herself by a supernatural presentiment, rose and waited. I flew into her arms and love enabled me to forget the anguish of the wait.'[7]

Four and a half hours after d'Urville returned home from Cherbourg, his reunion was interrupted by a visit from Paul Gaimard, hastening him to report to the navy minister. Less than an hour later, he was warmly received by General Sébastiani and complimented on the success of his special mission. D'Urville then decided to seek an audience with the new monarch, Louis-Philippe. Was this an investment in his future naval career or did he simply want to be noticed? It was 10.00 am, and he waited for the king to finish his breakfast. After an hour, the king's aide-de-camp, the comte de Rumigny, took d'Urville's card and assured him that he would not have to wait much longer. However, Louis-Philippe remained occupied, and d'Urville gave up and went home. There, at 3.00 pm, he received a message from Rumigny telling him that the king would see him at 10.00 the following morning. He returned to the Palais-Royal the next day, only to watch 10 or 12 deputations receive audiences with the king while he waited … and waited. Five hours after the appointed time, d'Urville finally gained admission.

Seventeen years d'Urville's senior, Louis-Philippe was the most worldly and widely travelled monarch to sit on the French throne. Initially a supporter of the Revolution of 1789, he had served with some distinction in the French army and reached the rank of lieutenant-general. His father, the duc de Chartres, who changed his name to 'Philippe Égalité', even voted for the execution of Louis XVI but himself fell victim to the Terror and was guillotined. Louis-Philippe spent years as an impoverished exile in Switzerland, Scandinavia, the United States, Cuba, Britain and Italy (where he married), before returning to France from Palermo after Napoleon's first abdication.[8] D'Urville was clearly pleased that Louis-Philippe remembered that they had voyaged together from Palermo in 1814. According to d'Urville, the king asked him about his 'last campaign' –

King Louis-Philippe, by an unknown engraver, frontispiece from George Newenham Wright's Life and Times of Louis Philippe, King of the French, *Fisher, Son & Co., London, [1842?], vol 1.* Author's collection

the voyage to England – and listened 'with much interest' as he recounted the details.[9] Aside from d'Urville's private journal, we have a detailed account of the conversation in the second volume of Alexandre-Ernest Billault de Gérainville's *Histoire de Louis-Philippe*. Not surprisingly, Louis-Philippe was most anxious to know what had been said in various conversations during the voyage, particularly about himself. He was disappointed to learn that Charles X and his party believed him to be the head of a conspiracy that had toppled the Bourbon monarchy.[10] As d'Urville was descending the stairs to leave the palace, he was stopped by one of the king's aides, who informed him that he was invited to dinner on Sunday evening.[11]

When d'Urville and Adélie arrived at 6.00 pm two days later, 'close to a hundred people were there already'. They sat at the same table as Louis-Philippe's teenage son, the duc de Nemours, and d'Urville was engaged in animated conversation with Frédéric-Christophe

(Detail) 'Carte pour l'intelligence du mémoire de M. le capitaine d'Urville sur les Îles du Grand Océan', from Dumont d'Urville's Voyage de la corvette l'Astrolabe, Atlas hydrographie, Paris, 1833. This map shows d'Urville's division of the Pacific using the ethno-geographical terms 'Micronésie' and 'Melanésie', which he coined. Dixson Library, State Library of New South Wales

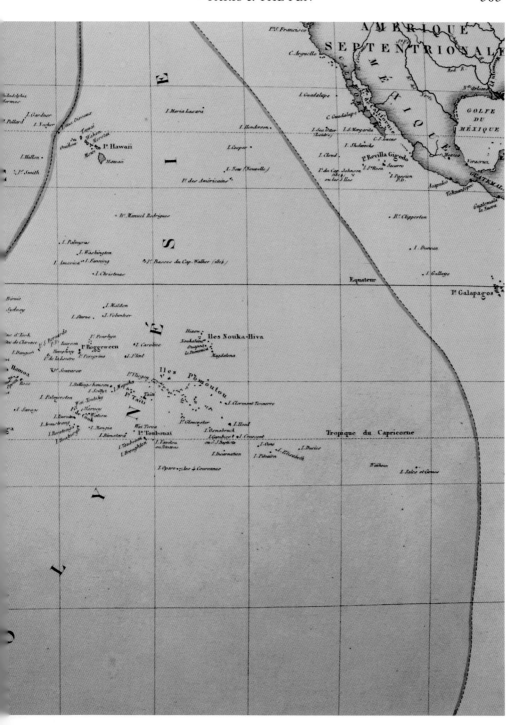

de Houdetot, member of the Chamber of Peers, and Frédéric Gaëtan, marquis de La Rochefoucauld-Liancourt, member of the chamber of deputies. He also spoke to Marshal Maison for quarter of an hour. The guests appear to have been much more interested in his voyage to England with Charles X than his contribution to global exploration and the sciences. It was clearly a time of political opportunity for the ambitious, but despite the fact that d'Urville was present as much for his ambition as his liberal idealism, he was quick to view the evening in negative terms. In his journal, he remarked that 'the atmosphere of these salons of baseness and of intrigue made me feel ill'.[12] D'Urville and Adélie left at 10.00 pm, travelling home on the Saint-Sulpice omnibus,[13] incongruously dressed in their finery but feeling egalitarian kinship with their fellow passengers. Of these humble folk, d'Urville remarked in his journal: 'kings are not richer'.[14]

There can be no doubt that d'Urville was soon disillusioned with the July Monarchy. This appears partly to have stemmed from his lack of promotion under the new régime. He believed that his 'perhaps immoderate ardour' inspired by his 'very advanced opinions' and his reluctance to 'dissimulate' were viewed negatively in the navy, a service that required 'passive and almost blind obedience'. D'Urville also wrote that the new navy minister, Marie-Henri-Daniel Gauthier, comte de Rigny, had 'given irrefutable proof of his ill-disposition' towards him,[15] but there appears also to have been a strong idealism underpinning his criticisms. In 1834, he stated publicly:

> On my return to France, the new king made me the most flattering declarations and the most brilliant promises. But the direction that the government took soon showed me that I would be just as much out of place among them as I had been among their predecessors. Wrongly or rightly, I was one of those who had regarded the July Revolution as something more than a simple event, who had looked upon it as the dawn of a noble, generous, equitable administration and founded, above all, on the most liberal and selfless ideals. The eagerness with which they devoted themselves to consecrating the errors of the Restoration and the Empire soon proved to me that these hopes were nothing but illusions; once again I had to resign myself to necessity.[16]

According to Isidore Le Brun, d'Urville's name appeared on the list of supporters of a particular party – presumably republican. Despite attending 'some meetings, he soon resolved to get rid of demagogue visitors, to refuse their printed papers and seldom read, without choice, some newspapers'. Yet, according to Le Brun, still suspected by the police of being a factious 'malcontent', he retired from the political arena to study 'the Chinese language and the hieroglyphs'.[17] While his journal indicates that he did indeed embrace the study of Chinese and Ancient Egyptian, he wrote of this period that he devoted his 'entire time' to the education of his only son and 'to the study of the ethnography and philology of the peoples of Oceania'.[18]

On 27 December 1831, d'Urville delivered, to the members of the Société de géographie (of which he had been elected secretary the previous April),[19] a paper that would have a seminal influence.[20] The paper, which was published in January 1832, addressed a longstanding debate by geographers on the division of the islands of the Pacific and the racial taxonomy of its people. Effectively, d'Urville began with the demarcations of the Danish geographer Conrad Malte-Brun, who had categorised the peoples of what he called '*Océanique*'[21] – rendered '*Océanie*' by the French cartographer Adrien-Hubert Brué in 1822[22] – as belonging to two races, Oceanic Negroes and '*Polynésiens*', the latter word adapted from the term '*Polynésie*' (Greek *polýs* = many + *nēsos* = island), first proposed by Charles de Brosses in 1756 for 'all that is contained in the vast Pacific Ocean'.[23] On the basis of his own travels and ethnographic and linguistic studies, d'Urville further divided '*Océanie*'. He retained the name '*Polynésie*' but restricted it to Easter Island, Tahiti, Hawaii, Tonga, New Zealand and the islands in between – inhabited by 'copper-coloured' people who spoke essentially the same language and were united by common religious practices such as *tapu* (ritual prohibition or sacred restriction). The Malay-Indonesian Archipelago he labelled '*Malaisie*', a term he appropriated, with acknowledgement, from René Lesson. Northern Oceania, or the small dispersed islands north of the equator, including the Gilbert, Marshall, Caroline, Mariana and Pelew islands, he named '*Micronésie*' (from Greek *mikros* = *small* + *nēsos* = island). The residual part of Oceania, between the limits of *Polynésie* and *Micronésie*, essentially the continent of Australia and its adjacent islands – Tasmania, New Guinea, New Britain, New Ireland, the Louisiades, New Hebrides (Vanuatu), New Caledonia, the Loyalty Islands, Fiji and the Solomons – he named '*Mélanésie*', a term coined from the Greek (*melas* = black + *nēsos* = island) but more directly adapted from the ethnographic designation '*Mélaniens*' of Bory de Saint-Vincent.

The ethnocentric prejudices that sometimes characterised his journal descriptions during his landfalls in the southwestern Pacific now condensed unequivocally on the page within his stridently racialised conception of '*Mélanésie*': 'All the nations which live in this great division of Oceania are men of a more or less dark colour, with curly or frizzy hair, or sometimes almost woolly, with a flat nose, a large mouth, unpleasant features and limbs often very thin and seldom well-formed. The women are even more hideous than the men.' In a sweeping, poorly informed generalisation, he wrote: 'Much closer to a state of barbarity than the Polynesians and Micronesians, one finds among them neither a form of government, nor laws, nor regularly established religious ceremonies. All their institutions appear still to be in infancy; their disposition and their intelligence are also generally much inferior to those of the copper race.' Although he acknowledged that many of these people were still 'very imperfectly known', he arrogantly added that they were 'natural enemies of whites' and they had

'always displayed a defiant opinion and a pronounced antipathy towards Europeans'.[24]
His most unkind judgement, however, was reserved for the indigenous Australians:
'The islanders of Australia and of Tasmania have been described in a rather exact
manner, and according to these descriptions these men are probably the most limited
beings, the most stupid and essentially the closest to brutes without reason'.[25] Within
the context of his hierarchical conception of Melanesians he wrote:

> Finally, those which occupy the lowest degree of this race are obviously the inhabit-
> ants of Australia and of Tasmania. Weak and miserable beings, joined together in
> feeble tribes, curiously disgraced by nature, and reduced by the poverty of their soil
> as by their indolence and their stupidity, to a very precarious existence, they speak
> extremely limited languages which vary almost from tribe to tribe, and offer no
> analogy with any of those whose rules are better established. All their industries are
> reduced to the manufacture of nets, spears, wretched bark canoes, and coats of pos-
> sum or kangaroo skin. Some can build huts of tree bark rather well enclosed, others
> simple shelters with branches covered by brush; but they are always wandering and
> living in the open air, content during their sleep, to cover their shoulders with a
> piece of bark torn off a nearby tree. These men have no trace of religious ideas other
> than vague notions concerning the existence of malignant spirits always disposed
> to torment them, and the confused sense of a new life which awaits them after their
> death.[26]

In his article, d'Urville suggested that the Melanesians were the original
inhabitants of Oceania. Like Johann Reinhold Forster, naturalist on Cook's second
voyage, he also asserted that the Polynesians had migrated into the Pacific 'from the
west and even Asia'.[27] While he saw evidence of the 'fusion of the two races'[28] in New
Zealand, Micronesia and even Tahiti, d'Urville believed that in Ualan (Kosrae in the
Carolines) and Tahiti, the lower 'castes' had a Melanesian appearance. D'Urville also
asserted that the Melanesians were a branch of 'the black race of Africa' and that the
Polynesians were a branch of the 'yellow race originally of Asia'.[29] Although others
had already drawn attention to Malay-Polynesian linguistic affinities, d'Urville noted
that he had 'discovered around sixty words which are evidently common between
the two languages and that these are enough to attest to ancient communications'.[30]
Furthermore, d'Urville's identification of the 'white' race with Caucasians[31] would also
suggest that he was influenced by the racial classifications proposed by Johan Friedrich
Blumenbach in the third edition of his *De generis humani varietate nativa* (1795),
although he did not have this work in his library at the time of his death.

While the English-speaking world has never fully embraced the term Oceania and
has suffered its organisational use by the United Nations and a number of sporting
organisations, such as the International Olympic Committee and FIFA,[32] d'Urville's

ethno-geographical divisions of Micronesia and Melanesia have gained much wider international acceptance and, ironically, formal adoption by the inhabitants of the region itself. Examples of this can be seen in the national name the Federated States of Micronesia, the Pan-Melanesian Economic Union proposed by the Solomon Islands, Melanesian Socialism advocated by Father Walter Lini of Vanuatu, and the nationalist political party Union progressiste mélanésienne, formed in New Caledonia. However, Australians – inhabiting a vast continent with separate cultural traditions stretching back 50,000 years – have no natural affinity with the term Oceania and have long recognised the sharp cultural differences between indigenous Australians and the peoples of Papua New Guinea (formerly administered by Australia under a League of Nations mandate) and other islands to the northeast. Consequently, with the exception of the Torres Strait islanders, they have long excluded Australia from the original boundaries d'Urville proposed for Melanesia.

On 6 April 1832, d'Urville was elected vice-president of the Société de géographie,[33] no doubt a consolation after the snub he received from the Académie des sciences. Less than a month later, on Thursday 4 May 1832, his mother died in Caen. D'Urville did not receive word from his nephew abbé Louis-François-Paul Dumont de la Londe[34] until Sunday 6 May. His visit to Caen in late August 1830 was apparently the last time he saw his mother alive. In his journal, d'Urville wrote that despite her 'conduct towards me, this news affected me deeply'.[35] Mercifully for d'Urville, his last visit to his mother had been a joyful one, but there seems little doubt that the relationship was difficult and perhaps even marked by a period of estrangement. While the often-repeated claims that d'Urville's mother never accepted his wife have been proven false by Adélie's own letters, cruel barbs might nevertheless have been flung at least once. As her children died, Adélie never forgot what she called the 'cruel prophecy' of her mother-in-law: '… in your last days you will have no more children'.[36] We do not have the context of these words, dragged up by Adélie more than six years after d'Urville's mother's death. They might simply have been a tactless reprimand, or caution with regard to the raising of the children (she herself lost five of her nine children). D'Urville entrusted his nephew with dealing with his share of his mother's estate, and they remained in contact by mail. For much of the third quarter of 1832, cholera raged in Caen, and this would have discouraged travel.[37] (The epidemic had been present in Paris as early as 26 March,[38] claiming the life of, among others, the great biologist Georges Cuvier on 13 May.) According to Le Brun, d'Urville made a brief visit, incognito, to Caen in 1833 in the wake of his mother's death, and this was the last time he visited his native Normandy. D'Urville's journal, however, does not substantiate any such visit.

In sharp contrast to the emotional austerity of his relationship with his mother, d'Urville delighted in the 'charms' of his family life. He lavished attention on his children and made his son Jules' education his principal objective outside his naval and scholarly obligations in Paris.[39] They both shared a gift for languages, and the child had a precocious intelligence. When Jules was seven years of age, d'Urville wrote proudly to Le Brun to inform him that his son was translating the fables of Aesop.[40] Not yet eight, he was studying Arabic, frequently translating Chinese texts and reading Chateaubriand. Within a year, d'Urville's journals (and Le Brun's testimony)[41] indicate that the boy was translating Lucian, Homer, Virgil and Tacitus, and in March 1834, Jules began studying English.[42]

Fourteen months after his mother died, d'Urville became a father again with the birth of a daughter. While others might have named their first daughter in honour of a recently deceased grandmother, Sophie was given her mother's name Adèle and Julie (the feminine version of her father's name) as her second and third names respectively. Lottin, who was a frequent morning visitor to the family (often bearing charts, drafts and proofs of the *Astrolabe* volumes), accompanied d'Urville to Saint-Sulpice to register the birth of the child on 6 July 1833.[43]

D'Urville also pressed on with the massive task of publishing the results of the *Astrolabe* voyage. Much of 1833 was taken up with vocabularies for his philological volumes. He still found time to publish a number of other scholarly articles during his Paris sojourn, including ethnographic, oceanographic and hydrographic studies, and book reviews for the *Bulletin de la Société de géographie*, the *Revue des deux mondes* and *La France littéraire*. He also published a substantial biographical article on James Cook, whom he described as 'figuring eternally at the head of the navigators of all the centuries and of all the nations', for the sixth volume of the *Encyclopédie des gens du monde*. Furthermore, in April 1834, d'Urville wrote an article entitled 'Australie', which dealt, in part, with convict transportation, but it is not known whether it was ever separately published.

D'Urville's articles were sometimes a means of airing his criticisms of the government. For example, when he reviewed Frederick Beechey's *Narrative of a Voyage to the Pacific and Beering's Strait* (1831) in the *Bulletin de la Société de géographie*, he noted that Beechey's work was published less than three years after the British explorer's return home, unlike most French accounts of exploration. He went on to lament: 'Sums allocated for the publication of the combined voyages of the *Uranie*, the *Coquille* and the *Astrolabe*, will always be much less than the nearly one million [francs] lavished on so many ridiculous ceremonies, and expended to feed a crowd of sinecures useless to the state.'[44] His complaints did not end there. Once again, in 1834, after detailing the meagre sums allocated to commission and provision the *Astrolabe*, he commented that the published results of such voyages were 'glorious monuments' and, by way of contrast, drew attention to the incalculable sums expended to bring the Obelisk of Luxor from the upper Nile to Paris.

Relocating the enormous carved red-granite obelisk of Ramses II, which had been given to King Louis-Philippe by the Khedive of Egypt, Mehmet Ali, had required the construction of a purpose-built transport vessel, the *Luxor*.[45] This had had to cross the Mediterranean before being towed up the Nile, deliberately sunk on a bed of sand and de-masted prior to embarkation of the 23-metre, 250-tonne obelisk. Aside from the engineering works associated with removal of the obelisk and its transportation to the Nile (including the demolition of 30 houses), the *Luxor* then had to be refloated and re-masted before commencing a voyage to the Atlantic and then up the Seine to the French capital,[46] all of which took longer than d'Urville's first *Astrolabe* voyage! On one level, d'Urville's criticisms appear remarkably sensitive and advanced for his time (although he did not apply the same logic to the acquisition and relocation of the Vénus de Milo):

> ... and when it is finally planted with great expense on one of our places, what will we have other than a block of ancient and undoubtedly very worthy granite, but which will offer nothing more to the meditations of the archaeologist, who would have made an accurate sketch and traced on large scale, its form, its dimensions and its covering hieroglyphs? I find, for my part, that these ancient and gigantic witnesses of past centuries lose much of their value when they are no longer on the spot where they were [originally] erected.[47]

Despite his undoubted personal interest and respect for the patrimony of ancient Egypt – as evidenced by the books in his library, including several by Jean-François Champollion, the decipherer of the hieroglyphs (see Appendix) – is it possible that d'Urville's criticisms were also sour grapes? It should be noted that the captain of the *Luxor*, Raymond-Jean-Baptiste de Verninac Saint-Maur, whose name can still be seen on the pedestal of the obelisk in the place de la Concorde and who published a popular account of the voyage, had succeeded d'Urville as captain of the *Astrolabe* and had brought the philologist Champollion back to France from Egypt in December 1829 aboard the same corvette.[48] It is not known whether d'Urville sought the *Luxor* mission, but given his strong interest in Egypt's monuments, ancient language and the work of Champollion, and his astounding offer to command an expedition to transport Napoleon's remains from their original resting place on the island of Saint Helena, it is possible.

With the final publication of the *Astrolabe* voyage, d'Urville embarked on a private literary venture, his *Voyage pittoresque autour du monde*, which was based on the journals and published accounts of the great Spanish, Dutch, British, French and Russian maritime explorers from the sixteenth century onwards. Much of the editorial work, particularly in the first volume, was done by the left-wing journalist and political economist Louis Reybaud,[49] but as we have seen, it also contained numerous extracts from d'Urville's unpublished journal during his voyage aboard the *Coquille*. Furthermore, it seems likely that his article on Australia formed the basis of chapters XXXII–XXXIX of the second volume. D'Urville's journal indicates that he worked assiduously on this project, often writing 10 pages a day but still finding time to work on his Chinese translations – beginning with texts from the Confucian canon by Kŏng fū zǐ, Mèng Zǐ and Zǐsī– and to take his daily promenade in the Jardin du Luxembourg (or occasionally the Tuileries), sometimes with members of his family, and often to sit and read liberal newspapers such as *Le Courrier, Le Journal des Débats* and *Le National*, which had played such an important role in the Revolution of 1830. The first edition of the *Voyage pittoresque autour du monde*, published in Paris by Louis Tenré, was issued in parts beginning in 1833, with volume i completed in 1834 and volume ii in 1835. The whole work was very liberally illustrated by Sainson and others and was an impressive popular success, with the rapid sale of more than 20,000 copies.[50] Prior to his final voyage, d'Urville would sell his share of the rights to the engraver Ambroise Tardieu;[51] thereafter, an abridged version was produced under the title *Voyage autour du monde*, in numerous editions over the next 30 years.

Aside from his navy colleagues Lottin and Gaimard, the writer Le Brun, the botanist Achille Richard, and the doctor and entomologist Jean-Baptiste Boisduval, the most frequent visitor to the d'Urvilles' home was Madame Antoinette Dombrowski, widow of a Polish émigré.[52] Madame Dombrowski was Adélie's closest friend in Paris, but the whole family, including d'Urville, also returned her frequent visits. D'Urville made a number of firm new friends of his own in Paris, including the zoologist and anatomist Henri de Blainville, the sinologist Aignan-Stanislas Julien, the ethnographer Grégoire-Louis Domeny de Rienzi, and the librarian and archaeologist Jacques-Joseph Champollion-Figeac, older brother of the Egyptologist Jean-François Champollion and editor of his posthumous works.[53] Furthermore, on 2 July 1833, d'Urville was visited by Sabin Berthelot, the dark-haired, dark-eyed naturalist and traveller whom he knew from both the Canary Islands and the Société de géographie. He was in the company of the English botanist Phillip Barker Webb, with whom he would co-author the monumental nine-volume *L'Histoire naturelle des Îles Canaries*. Educated at Harrow and Oxford, Webb was trained as a lawyer but on his father's death came into possession of a significant fortune and was able to indulge his passion for botany, geology, languages and travel. Prior to meeting d'Urville, aside from the Canary Islands, he had visited Sweden, Spain, Portugal, North Africa, Madeira, Brazil, the Mediterranean, the Aegean and Turkey. Like d'Urville, he was steeped in Homer and Strabo. In Paris, Webb soon established himself in the rue Madame and set about building a magnificent private library and one of the finest private herbaria in France, including specimens from d'Urville's own travels.[54] He and d'Urville, both blond-haired and with so much else in common, would become enduring friends.[55]

Although a passionate bibliophile in his own right (and in possession of a significant private herbarium), d'Urville still required access to the Bibliothèque royale and specialised texts in order to research his various publications.[56] According to Le Brun, this was the principal reason he prolonged his stay in Paris once he had completed his work on the *Astrolabe* voyage in May 1835, but as a serving naval officer, d'Urville would not have had such discretionary freedom. He tells us that, once the publication of the *Voyage et découvertes de l'Astrolabe* was completed, he requested permission to return to Provence. 'The order pure and simple to return to my port, Toulon, was addressed to me and I returned.'[57]

PART III

' … towards the polar ice'

23

La Juliade

When men come to like a sea-life, they are not fit to live on land … it is then too late to choose another profession; as indeed is generally the case with men, when they have once engaged in any particular way of life.

Samuel Johnson[*]

D'Urville and his family left Paris on 2 July 1835.[1] It took 15 days, travelling via Sens, Joigny, Arnay, Chalons, Mâcon, Saint-Vallier, Montélimar, Saint-Cannat and Marseille, to reach Aubagne in the Huveaune Valley. Here, a day's travel from Toulon, they halted. During their journey, d'Urville had anxiously noted reports of cholera, and we know that an epidemic had raged in Marseille until the end of March. A new epidemic began in Provence in June 1835 and reached its height in the fourth week of July, with 1500 deaths.[2] Because of reports of the epidemic raging in Toulon, the family decided, for the moment, to remain in Aubagne. D'Urville went on ahead to inform Adélie's father, and it appears he returned with him. On 23 July, however, d'Urville learned that cholera had reached Aubagne. There must have seemed little point in remaining; they could just as easily sit out the epidemic at home. But which home?

D'Urville and Adélie co-owned a building of several storeys on a corner of Toulon's place de l'Intendance, facing the city gate of the same name. They had acquired it while they were still in Paris, from Adélie's father,[3] possibly with the aid of money d'Urville had inherited from his mother. It was very likely a building that Monsieur Pépin had allowed them to live in after their marriage. As early as 1827 (when the cadastral plan for the semi-rural western outskirts of Toulon was drawn up and her name appeared on it),[4] Adélie is known to have been in possession of a property, roughly a third of a hectare in size, in the parish of Saint-Roch. According to René Lesson, she purchased it for 20,000 francs and named it after her son,[5] but the name 'La Juliade' could just as easily have been coined from the first three letters of the first names of her husband and herself.[6] It would now become the d'Urville family home in Provence.

[*] Quoted by Boswell, *Life of Samuel Johnson*, 12 March 1776

The surrounding parish took its name from a Franciscan chapel dedicated to the fourteenth-century French mendicant Saint Roch. The chapel, on the outskirts of Toulon's Vauban-designed fortifications, was destroyed by the Austrians during the siege of 1707 but rebuilt seven years later next to a bridge over the Béal,[7] a canal constructed by the Romans in the second or third century A.D. , used in the Middle Ages for irrigation and as a sewer, and harnessed, from the late sixteenth century, to supply water to the fountains of Toulon. 'La Juliade' stood on a road that followed this same canal. Along its route, the Béal also powered many water mills and supplied numerous *lavoirs* (laundries) servicing Toulon.[8] Ensuring the potable quality of the water of the Béal had long been a concern of the municipality of Toulon. Whether the d'Urvilles drew their drinking water directly from the canal (they did pay the municipality 2.50 francs per annum for water rights)[9] or from a well in their garden is not clear. Whatever the state of the Béal, wells were also vulnerable to ground-water contamination, and the local laundries could have spread the cholera epidemic through the discharge of waste water after washing soiled and infected clothing. In d'Urville's time, however, this was not suspected; many believed that a malevolent miasma was to blame. Unfortunately, it was not until the pioneering epidemiological work of the London physician John Snow, who plotted cholera cases around the Broad Street pump in Soho in 1854, that it was realised that sewage-contaminated drinking water was the principal vector for the disease.[10] In the same year (and thus three decades before Robert Koch, who has generally been credited with the discovery), the Italian anatomist Filippo Pacini isolated the bacterium *Vibrio cholerae* as the specific cause.[11]

Day after day, d'Urville noted the number of new local cholera cases and the number of deaths in his journal. His daughter Sophie, who had only just celebrated her second birthday during the family's journey from Paris, was acutely vulnerable to infection from contaminated water and to the severe dehydration and electrolytic imbalance caused by cholera's vomiting and diarrhoea. In the last week of July, she fell ill with the disease. Despite rallying on 30 July, Sophie died at 11 am on Friday 31 July. Three hours later, a traumatised d'Urville and his father-in-law undertook the sad task of registering the child's death before the mayor of Toulon.[12] There were 13 others before them that day and another nine to follow, and this did not include the cholera deaths in the adjoining parishes.[13] Almost certainly, it is tears that blotched d'Urville's long, grief-stricken and barely legible journal entry for that Friday in the summer of 1835; their traces are visible on the page to this day. The epidemic did not end until late October. Among the casualties, less than a week after Sophie died, was François-Esprit Bertrand, the highly regarded purser of the *Astrolabe*, who was 37 years old.[14] Officially, 4600 individuals contracted the disease in Toulon; of them, 1757 died – a mortality rate of 38 per cent. According to one account, 'life seemed to stand still; Toulon resembled

View of the northwestern outskirts of a scale model of Toulon, completed in 1800, with arrow showing the location of d'Urville's home 'La Juliade' in the parish of Saint-Roch. The Béal canal flowed on the northern boundary of the property. Although the house is not represented on the vacant block (it might have post-dated the model), one can assume it was built in the same vernacular style as those nearby. Musée des Plans-Reliefs, Paris

a deserted town … grass grew between the cobblestones of the streets; a lugubrious silence weighed on this ravaged city'.[15] One can only begin to imagine the fear, dread and sorrow that must have pervaded the d'Urville family during this period.

Despite the children she lost there (and who were interred in the garden), Adélie would write that 'La Juliade … is an Eden for me when I am here with my husband and my son.'[16] Toulon's population has grown tenfold since the d'Urvilles resided in the parish of Saint-Roch. Their home no longer stands; in 1868, it was taken over and demolished for a road-widening project, which created the present rue Henri Vienne. A decade earlier, the southern end of its garden had been requisitioned for the creation of the avenue de l'Amiral Collet. Indeed, that avenue's junction with the avenue de Saint-Roch effectively marks the former property's southern limits. By 1904, in the wake of railway construction and further redevelopment, the historic Béal was vaulted over and rendered little more than a stormwater drain.[17]

Surviving cadastral plans indicate that the d'Urville residence ran east–west across the width of the northern limits of the block, fronting the road and the Béal. The neighbouring houses were also similarly aligned along the canal. There was a path on the eastern side of the house that gave access to the garden and a narrow outbuilding running north–south on the western boundary of the property. This small *dépendance* was a cottage with a kitchen and salon on the ground floor and an upstairs bedroom. (In 1842, it was furnished and rented to a Mademoiselle Victoire Faberd for 500 francs per annum, plus a share of the vegetables grown in the garden.[18]) 'La Juliade', like all the neighbouring properties, was enclosed by stone walls, and its garden was further subdivided by an east–west wall at its waist. It was almost certainly built in the same vernacular style, with pink or yellow stucco and a terracotta roof, that characterised neighbouring houses.[19] A number of trees offered a shaded canopy and seasonal fruit. Isidore Le Brun described it as a *bastide*,[20] the provençal word for a villa. In the Middle Ages, this same word had defensive military connotations for a blockhouse. Certainly the walls of the house and its perimeter, and the orientation of most of the windows onto the interior grounds, are suggestive of a defensive embrace, but 'La Juliade' was also well appointed for sunlight and cooling sea breezes. Le Brun (who perhaps never visited it) went on to describe it as 'one of the most isolated and least obvious' of residences,[21] but in fact it was one of numerous houses lining the road to Toulon with deep gardens to the rear. The d'Urvilles' immediate neighbour to the east was the erudite and cultured pharmacist André Honnoraty who, like d'Urville, was a member of the Académie du Var. Later, he would purchase 'La Juliade' from Adélie's heirs.

The house itself was of two storeys. From the inventory drafted by the notary Maître Elzéar Vallavielle in 1842, we know that on the ground floor was a kitchen with a walnut bench, a lockable two-drawer buffet and a number of presses and cupboards of grey-painted poplar. The kitchen had a window and internal and external doors, the latter accessible under a wooden trellis, probably covered in grapevines, which appears to have fringed the whole southern side of the house. A vestibule off the kitchen led to an antechamber, furnished, perhaps as a guest room or maid's quarters, with a small bed, a commode, two paintings and a clock. The vestibule also provided access to a salon illuminated by two windows facing the enclosed grounds and screened with white calico hung from curtain rods with gilded ends. This salon was furnished with a mahogany desk known as a *bonheur du jour* (usually used by the lady of the house), an oval poplar dining table and four matching chairs, antique armchairs upholstered in white calico and a velour-covered sofa of cherry wood. The walls were decorated with antique mirrors and four framed lithographs of Louis-Auguste de Sainson's scenes from the voyage of the *Astrolabe*. There was also a scullery on the ground floor for utensils, table glasses and hardware, and a wine cellar with a dirt floor. We know about the cellar because two and a half years before his death, in a codicil to his last will and testament, d'Urville declared that he had left 18,000 francs in gold and silver either in the sand of the cellar or in two possible locations in his library![22] Did he or his heirs recover the hoard (it is not mentioned in the inventory of his estate), or does it now lie buried under the present rue Henri Vienne?

Upstairs, there were a number of bedrooms with south-facing windows, all curtained with white calico and furnished as one would expect with beds, wardrobes, dressers, mirrors and commodes. In one room hung d'Urville's portrait. In another, with two south-facing windows, there were 14 framed pictures of mainly maritime subjects and landscapes. Its sofa bed and armchairs were upholstered in yellow and red. It also contained d'Urville's herbarium (comprising his plant specimens from around the world, pressed on grey paper and eventually arranged in 102 volumes) and his *coquillier* – a wooden cabinet painted white with 30 copper-handled drawers, containing an impressive collection of 'shells of diverse genera and diverse species'.[23] In 1839, they were catalogued by d'Urville's son Jules according to Lamarck's classifications.[24] Another upstairs room, with only one south-facing window, appears to have been d'Urville's study and library. It contained numerous natural history objects, curiosities and bookcases; and it was decorated with an ensemble of 16 landscapes, works of botanical art and other subjects. The 'objects of curiosity' appear to have been ethnographic objects, for they were separately described as fishing instruments, cooking utensils, items of wood, bone and cord from the 'diverse countries that … Dumont d'Urville … visited during his diverse voyages around the world'. There were other such items in the house, including numerous 'carpets of tree bark' (almost certainly tapa from Polynesia), and 'lances, bows, arrows and other objects of curiosity from the islands of Oceania'. There were also commemorative medallions struck for d'Urville's voyages.[25]

The d'Urville library contained many of the classics of French history and literature; ancient history and classical studies; dictionaries and grammars of some 30 languages; many books in European and Asian languages (including, by the time of his death, 65 books in Chinese); and books on Egyptian, Persian, Chinese, Indian and Arab history and literature; many scientific works (with a particular emphasis on botany and the natural sciences); numerous encyclopaedias and biographical reference works; many works of ethnography; and very many accounts of travel and maritime exploration (see Appendix).[26] Here, d'Urville withdrew to pursue his scholarly endeavours. Yet despite the solace of his family, his life was not entirely tranquil.

D'Urville was now in his mid-forties, and his health had already been undermined by the privations and serious illnesses of his last voyage. The painful attacks of gout that began a few years before appear to have worsened during this period. This acute inflammatory arthritic condition is caused by the under-excretion of uric acid by the kidneys and its appearance in the joints. Genetics, lifestyle and diet are known to influence the incidence of gout. In d'Urville's case, it is possible that his condition was symptomatic of long-term kidney damage. A possible cause of this damage was lead in the solder used to seal tins of preserved food taken on his voyages[27] and also the leaded glass used to store and decant wine and spirits at the time. However, what is more likely is that long periods of water rationing at sea and highly salted provisions combined to affect the state of his kidneys. This was almost certainly a factor in the early death from nephritis of another explorer, Matthew Flinders. How d'Urville initially treated his gout is uncertain. According to René Lesson, he had a 'blind confidence' in the supposed panacea of Leroy's purgative[28] – a concoction of scammony (*Convolvulus scammonia*), turpeth root (*Operculina turpethum*), jalap (*Ipomoea purga*) and *Senna alexandrina*, which became fashionable in Paris in the early 1820s. Lesson, however, believed that this very purgative had 'compromised' d'Urville's health and that of other naval officers too,[29] but whether Leroy's purgative actually damaged his kidneys is another matter. While he might very well have taken this purgative during the *Coquille* voyage, d'Urville's gout had not then manifested itself. With his profound botanical knowledge and wide reading, it is not surprising that d'Urville would later repeatedly take a preparation of *Colchicum autumnale*,[30] which has been known for its anti-gout properties since the days of Pedanius Dioscorides and is still used to treat the condition. It contains an alkaloid, colchicine (first isolated in France in 1820 and further refined in 1833). Unfortunately, it is also quite toxic and can cause nausea and severe intestinal pain.[31]

By late October 1835, Adélie was pregnant again and gave birth to another son, Émile-Jules-Léon, early on the evening of 30 July 1836,[32] a year and a day after their beloved daughter Sophie's death. In the months that followed, however, it would become clear that Adélie's familial joy was threatened by d'Urville's dream of yet another voyage of exploration. Curiously, he rationalised this desire for another expedition as 'several sacrifices on my part to assure one day the fate of my children in a more honourable manner'.[33] It was an argument calculated to gain Adélie's agreement.

When d'Urville returned to Toulon, the navy minister was Victor-Guy Duperré, hero of the Battle of Grand-Port (1810)[34] and, more recently, commander of the naval flotilla during the French invasion of Algiers. He was the fourth to hold the office after the comte de Rigny's resignation in April 1834. D'Urville's first 18 months back in Toulon largely coincided with Duperré's ministry. In his own words, it was a period in which he had little choice but 'to fulfil the obscure functions to which are assigned a *captaine de vaisseau* in the port'.[35] D'Urville, nevertheless, was grateful to Duperré for accepting his recommendations for the decoration of his junior officers who had distinguished themselves during the *Astrolabe* voyage.[36] When Duperré was forced to resign, after his patron Adolphe Thiers left office as president of the Council of Ministers (an alternative designation for prime minister) on 6 September 1836, d'Urville's prospects would brighten further. Under the new government of Mathieu Molé, Vice-Admiral Claude du Campe de Rosamel was appointed navy minister. Originally from Frenq in the Pas-de-Calais, Rosamel had served in the navy with distinction during the Revolution, the Empire and the Restoration. In the wake of the July Revolution, he had been appointed maritime prefect for Toulon, and in June 1834, he was elected to the Chamber of Deputies as a representative for the Var.[37] Although more politically conservative than d'Urville, the two had made Toulon their home and enjoyed cordial relations. D'Urville wrote to Rosamel with a proposal for a new voyage of exploration on 2 February 1837. He also recorded the concomitant emotional tensions in his family at the time:

> … many considerations kept me ashore; the happy and tranquil existence that I had in my cottage, the company of a cherished partner who had suffered such a long time from my absences, the pleasure that I had to see the rapidly developing faculties of my son, all acted forcibly against my new plans. Finally my wanderlust won once again and I only had to obtain the approval of my wife. One can easily imagine the sorrow with which she received my initial overtures; however, after having thoroughly weighed-up my reasons, especially with regard to the wellbeing of her children, she consented to this long and painful separation, she even occupied herself with the preparations for my departure with a courage, a zeal and a devotion for which I will be grateful all my life.[38]

What d'Urville does not mention is that on 15 January 1837, Adélie's kind and generous father, Joseph-Marie Pépin, died.[39] He had been close at hand during all of d'Urville's absences; now Adélie would not be able to call on him if she needed help during another of her husband's expeditions. It was d'Urville who made yet another sad journey to the office of the mayor of Toulon to register Pépin's death. It seems likely that he was drafting his proposal to the minister at the time. When he finally sent it, it was accompanied by detailed notes.[40] In this separate document, d'Urville proposed departing from France on 1 September 1837, traversing the Atlantic via La Praya in the Cape Verde Islands and passing through the Strait of Magellan to reach the Pacific. D'Urville told the minister, 'no French vessel, that I know of, has revisited this strait since [Louis Antoine de] Bougainville'. D'Urville alluded to the five years of complex hydrographic work done by Phillip Parker King on the coast of Tierra del Fuego and in the Strait of Magellan in HMS *Adventure* but asserted that 'there was still more [work] to do of all kinds'. His proposed expedition would then visit Chile, cross the Pacific to survey Vava'u, Vanikoro and Santa Cruz in the Solomon Islands, replenish in Ambon, and visit New Zealand and Mindanao in the Philippines before returning to France in April 1840. Despite his complaints about the Spartan commissioning of his previous expeditions, he dared not make extravagant demands, so once again, he requested a vessel like the *Astrolabe*, or the *Astrolabe* conveniently repaired.

To his surprise, d'Urville received a prompt and favourable response from the minister but one qualified by likely delay occasioned by the heavy financial demands of fitting out the respective expeditions of Abel-Aubert Dupetit-Thouars in the *Venus* and Cyrille Laplace in the *Artémise*. Initially, d'Urville thought that he had been politely fobbed off, but when he wrote asking for a frank assessment from the minister's private secretary, his friend Lieutenant François-Charles Chaucheprat, he was informed that the cost was the only reason for delay and that baron Jean Tupinier, still director of port movements, had been asked to report on the proposed voyage. Then, towards the end of February 1837, d'Urville was surprised to receive a letter informing him that King Louis-Philippe had now taken a personal interest in the planning of his expedition and had expressed a desire for him to include an approach towards the South Pole. Consequently, he would be offered command of not one but two vessels.

D'Urville tells us that his first reading of this unexpected plan left him 'stunned and undecided' and that a 'thousand thoughts' passed through his mind. The suggestion was for exploration in waters that had no connection to his 'tastes' and 'studies', presumably meaning that the frozen south offered few opportunities for botany and entomology, let alone ethnographic and linguistic research. Earlier, he had also recorded having dreams 'almost every night' that he was following the example of Cook's third voyage towards the pole and that these dreams usually finished with his steering the *Astrolabe* 'in narrow channels, shallows or even proceeding on firm ground'. Although he did not describe these recurrent dreams as nightmares, he confessed that, despite his admiration for the 'courageous efforts of Cook, Ross and Parry, across the ice', he 'never wanted to follow in their wake'.[41] Like King Louis-Philippe, he had also read the published accounts of the British sealer James Weddell and the American whaler Benjamin Morrell, both of whom had sailed into Antarctic waters. D'Urville owned a copy of Benjamin Morrell's *A Narrative of Four Voyages to the South Sea* (1832) in his library but described him as 'already known as a fabricator of tales'. Although he also believed Weddell's claims required verification, he was clearly tantalised by the possibility that the Weddell Sea might offer access all the way to the South Pole. Just 17 years before, no person had laid eyes on the Antarctic continent, only the icy seas that surrounded it. Ever hungry for glory, d'Urville wrote that he recognised that 'an attempt to reach the South Pole would, in the eyes of the public, have a character of novelty, grandeur and even wonder, which could not fail to draw their attention'.[42]

D'Urville accepted the amended mission and, on 25 February, he responded with observations occasioned by the changed objectives. Aside from the usual passports and safe conducts, 'conserved' food, he thought – given the obvious lack of revictualling points in Antarctic waters – would be 'indispensable'.[43] By the beginning of March, d'Urville had once again been given command of the *Astrolabe* as well as an identical escort, the corvette *Zélée*, which had also begun service as a military horse/cattle transport in 1812. During the Restoration, the *Zélée* had been deployed in the intervention in Spain and had sailed to the island of Bourbon. In 1831, she had made a voyage to the Antilles and had then helped re-supply French troops in Algeria. Between 1833 and 1837, she had undergone a complete refit. Indeed, both the *Astrolabe* and the *Zélée* would be heavily reinforced prior to their voyage into southern waters: their prows were strengthened with timber and bronze to resist the impact of collision with ice; their hulls were double-sheathed in copper and they were fitted with two false keels.[44]

While his faithful friend Charles-Hector Jacquinot – who had married in 1832 and was now the father of a three-year-old daughter – agreed to command the *Zélée*, d'Urville could not convince the thin and pensive Victor-Charles Lottin, who had married in 1830,[45] or the blond and bright-eyed Pierre-Édouard Guilbert, who had taken part in the invasion of Algeria and who had married in 1834,[46] or the balding, bear-like Victor-Amédée Gressien, who had already made a series of poor choices in life,[47] to join him as his executive officer. Although all three had now been decorated with the red ribbon and white star of the *Légion d'honneur*, thanks to his recommendations, a disappointed d'Urville declared: 'I could not blame them: they had grown old in the harness, their attitudes had changed with age, above all they had been so coldly received at the end of the first voyage, that they were little desirous of exposing themselves to even more painful tests.'[48] Others, like Pierre Collinet, the son of a humble day labourer and the only one of the *Astrolabe*'s non-commissioned officers to be decorated at d'Urville's repeated request, had already retired from the navy.[49]

Ironically, Lottin was also destined for frozen latitudes. Between 1838 and 1839 he would be a member of the 'Commission scientifique du Nord', which visited Lapland. He returned to Paris via Stockholm and, in July 1839, was presented to King Karl XIV Johan of Sweden, formerly Napoleon's Marshal Jean Bernadotte, and decorated with the *Svärdsorden* (Order of the Sword).[50]

On 28 March 1837, the minister sent an aerial telegraphic dispatch to the naval prefect in Toulon, summoning d'Urville to Paris and ordering Jacquinot to assume command of the preparations aboard the *Astrolabe* and *Zélée* while d'Urville was absent.[51] Travelling without his family and via Lyon and Auxerre, d'Urville arrived in the capital on the morning of 10 April. He soon met with Chaucheprat and then the minister (who promoted him to *capitaine de vaisseau, 1ère classe*, effective 10 April),[52] but also old friends such as Madame Dombrowski. Aside from official consultations, he was in Paris to do research and purchase instruments for his expedition.[53] However, it quickly became clear to d'Urville that he needed to visit London in order to obtain additional reference works and charts, and 'to procure the most positive and most authentic information concerning recent discoveries in the Antarctic regions'.[54] He was promptly given leave and funding to travel to England.[55]

Amid the ebb and flow of Englishmen beginning or ending their 'grand tours' of the continent, d'Urville reached London on 26 April 1837. This was less than two months before Queen Victoria's accession to the throne and the birth of the Victorian Age. D'Urville would remain in the British capital for 10 days, buying books and maps but also seeking out British mariners familiar with Antarctic waters. One fruitful meeting took place on the evening of 1 May, when he dined with the Raleigh Club, probably at the Thatched House Restaurant, in St James Street. This club, founded in 1826 by the traveller to Lapland Sir Arthur de Capell Brooke, was the parent organisation of the Geographical Society of London (later the Royal Geographical Society), established in 1830. It provided a convivial social circle for distinguished explorers and travellers. One of those present at the Raleigh Club dinner and mentioned by d'Urville was Commander John Washington, who was also the secretary of the Geographical Society. Another of d'Urville's hosts was the Irish hydrographer (of French Huguenot descent) Captain Francis Beaufort RN, remembered to this day for the invention of the Beaufort Scale of wind force.[56] Yet another of those present was Charles Enderby, whose family owned a fleet of whaling and sealing vessels that had already made numerous discoveries in Antarctic waters.[57] D'Urville does not mention Enderby, but he does mention the voyage of his employee, John Biscoe, who, in April 1832, completed the third circumnavigation of Antarctica after that of James Cook and Fabian von Bellingshausen.[58] The voyage of James Weddell and the veracity of his claim (to have proceeded three degrees further south than Cook) was also a topic of dinner conversation.[59]

We also know that in London, on 4 May, d'Urville met James Deville, a phrenologist and sculptor of Swiss descent. In 1823, Deville was one of the founders of the London Phrenological Society, located in the Strand. Historian David de Giustino has described him as a 'crude figure who spoke rough language and knew nothing of contemporary philosophy'. Although he was 'haughty and impossibly arrogant', as 'one of phrenology's first popular lecturers, he soon accumulated a fortune while his colleagues still had nothing'.[60] Phrenology was not an uncommon interest at the time, and Deville is known to have made cranial examinations and casts of the heads of William Blake, William Makepeace Thackeray, Ann Radcliffe, the Duke of Wellington, George Elliot (Mary Ann Evans) and later Albert the Prince Consort. D'Urville also consented to a cranial examination. It seems he was introduced to Deville by the naturalist John Edward Gray, one of the founders of the Entomological Society of London (later the Royal Entomological Society). It was Gray who recorded Deville's dictated phrenological report on d'Urville. His original repetitive report has disappeared, but a translation by Jean-Baptiste Berrier-Fontaine of Toulon survives among d'Urville's papers at the Château de Vincennes. Like a practised soothsayer who keenly observes his subject, who has perhaps already been apprised of other private and public information, who offers generalisations and who knows how to deliver what his subject wants to hear, Deville made his 'diagnosis'. D'Urville, by simple virtue of the shape of his head, was supposedly very kind to children, animals and the unfortunate; generous, even-tempered and untormented by 'the baser passions'; steadfast when 'moved to act from a sense of justice or duty'; endowed 'with a very strong sense of honour'; inclined to acquire 'natural history collections or interesting objects'; likely to 'expend a lot of time or money, or take personal risks to attain lofty goals'; un-attracted by religious fanaticism; imbued with 'languages, grammar, the classics, history, the sciences'; very capable of 'the most profound physiological and metaphysical researches'; a lover of travel with an excellent memory for places and an ability to estimate 'dimensions, distances and parallel lines'; likely to be 'proficient in the arts if he applied himself'; a 'very powerful dialectician', ultimately in possession of an extraordinary 'organisation [cranial structure?] such as one rarely encounters'![61]

By 1837, d'Urville had already read the phrenological works of Franz Joseph Gall, Johann Spurzheim and Joseph Vimont. Vimont, born in Caen, was perhaps known personally to him. He also acquired a copy of Théodore Poupin's *Caractères phrénologiques*. When the Parisian phrenologist Pierre-Marie-Alexandre Dumoutier approached him and asked to join his forthcoming expedition, d'Urville agreed. Yet despite his dalliance with phrenology, he also owned a critical rejection of this pseudo-science: Laurent Cerise's *Exposé et examen critique du système phrénologique*.

D'Urville left London on 6 May, pleased with his enquiries and efforts. Despite the 'civilities' of his fellow explorers in England and their 'obliging offers', he tells us that 'it was easy to distinguish the regret that they felt to see someone other than an Englishman pursue a career that they looked upon as an exclusive preserve of their nation'.[62] Although d'Urville admitted to a past 'childish prejudice' of a 'hereditary antipathy'[63] of the British, his attitude had long changed. In his poem 'Au peuple anglais', he saw the Revolution of July 1830 as negating the injustices of the past and establishing a foundation for equality and enduring peace between Britain and France. Thus, he wrote:

> Et bien! oublions tout deuil, trahison, défaite,
> Confondons notre histoire, et que la paix soit faite;
> Juillet sur nous et vous n'aurez pu luire en vain
> Et l'air d'un peuple libre épure tout levain:
> Rougissons des vieux temps de nos tristes querelles,
> L'océan tout entier a ruisselé sur elles.

[Well! let grief, treason and defeat be allayed,
Let us confound our history, and peace be made;
July upon us and you could not have shone in vain
And the air of a free people purifies any leaven:[64]
Let us blush over our sad bad blood,
Over it whole oceans are now in flood.][65]

D'Urville was back in Paris on 8 May, and on the 19th, he accompanied the minister to meet with the king to discuss final preparations for the voyage. He was warmly received, and the discussions with Louis-Philippe were aided by a map of the circumpolar region of the southern hemisphere, which d'Urville had brought with him.[66] He then left the capital and was back in Toulon on 3 June.

Despite strong royal support, not everyone viewed the expedition favourably. The physicist, astronomer and mathematician François Arago, who had entered politics after the Revolution of 1830 and represented the Pyrénées–Orientales in the Chamber of Deputies, had a reputation for scrutinising government expenditure. At the chamber's sitting of 5 June 1837, Arago turned his attention to the navy and d'Urville's forthcoming expedition. If d'Urville found a 'vein' of water through the ice to reach the south pole, what would it achieve? Just as he disparaged those who climbed mountains simply because they were there, Arago declared his 'repugnance for voyages of simple curiosity'. He believed d'Urville's vessels were not constructed for a descent towards the South Pole. He made contrasting reference to vessels purpose-built by the Americans for such exploration and emphasised the fact that the polar mission was a mere 'episode' in a much longer voyage. No doubt with Lapérouse and, more recently, Jules-Alphonse Poret de Blosseville in mind, Arago even asserted that he and his fellow deputies would be 'forced to vote next year for funds to go and search' for d'Urville. As for the equatorial legs of d'Urville's expedition, he believed that if one were to be asked where the *Astrolabe* should go to have the least prospect of discovery, it would be little different from d'Urville's prescribed itinerary. He dismissed the need to do more surveys in the Strait of Magellan, Torres Strait and Cook Strait following protracted British efforts. He also made it clear that he was disturbed by the hasty approval of the expedition and its projected departure before its scientific instruments were properly tried. In his opinion, the enormous number of Lottin's magnetic observations during d'Urville's previous voyage had been squandered for lack of sufficient instrument trials prior to departure.[67]

These were stinging criticisms by a deputy who was no mere scientific dilettante and whose brother Jacques Arago had accompanied Freycinet on the *Uranie*. François Arago had been elected to the Académie des sciences in 1809 at the extraordinary age of 23. In the same year, he succeeded Gaspard Monge as professor of descriptive geometry at the École polytechnique, where he had been a student six years before. After the death of the astronomer and surveyor Pierre Méchain[68] in 1804, Arago had attracted attention for his work with Jean-Baptiste Biot measuring the arc of the meridian. With Biot, he had also studied the refraction of light passing through the earth's atmosphere. Arago had then conducted geodetic studies on the coasts of France, England and Scotland, and he was a member of the Bureau des longitudes (and for 40 years the principal contributor to its *Annuaire*) and had long been in charge of the Paris observatory, where he lived with his wife and children. Furthermore, he had made important discoveries in electromagnetism, including the creation of the first primitive solenoids with André-Marie Ampère. In 1825, the Royal Society of London awarded him the Copley Medal for his discovery that the rotation of non-magnetic metals engendered a magnetic effect on a magnetised needle, a phenomenon later explained by Faraday's theory of induction. In the field of optics, Arago pioneered the study of chromatic polarisation and rotary polarisation of light in certain crystals. This work led him to invent the polariscope, which passed light through a crystal polariser for analytical purposes, and then the polarimeter, which measured the incident of the ray on graduated plates.[69] The breadth of his experimental research and the foundations he laid for other seminal scientific discoveries are beyond the scope of d'Urville's biography, but suffice it to say that the fiery Catalan was a veritable Prometheus of science who spoke with authority and conviction.

The navy minister, Admiral Rosamel, rose in the chamber and replied to Arago. He acknowledged that Phillip Parker King had made a detailed survey of the southern coast of Tierra del Fuego and had also visited and surveyed the Strait of Magellan, but he asserted that the latter survey of the strait was 'very inexact'. Furthermore, he disputed whether British hydrography was the best in the world. As to the choice of vessels, Rosamel noted that the *Astrolabe* and the *Zélée* were 'in the hands of the engineers at Toulon', and that after repairs, they would be 'in the best possible state for this kind of navigation'. He also noted that the unfortunate Blosseville had disappeared while in command of a vessel in the Arctic very much like the American vessels extolled by Arago – and the vessel itself had made no difference to his fate. Aside from perfecting geographical knowledge, d'Urville's expedition would also search for favourable locations for whaling, which would soon be exhausted on the coast of Tierra del Fuego.[70] Not surprisingly, given the public forum, Rosamel mentioned neither renewed political interest in New Zealand and the Pacific nor broader intelligence-gathering considerations that might be of value to France in a future conflict.

On 14 June, an outraged d'Urville penned a response to Arago's criticisms that was published a week later in *Le Toulonnais* and also appeared in the *Journal des Débats*, *La Presse*, *Le Garde National de Marseille*, *La Gazette du Midi* and the *Annales maritimes et coloniales*. He would have been wiser to ignore Arago's comments, or at the very least to have replied succinctly with polite dignity, as the minister had. However, not known for restraint or tact, d'Urville wove a fierce personal attack into his public response. He blamed Arago for the rebuff he had received from the Académie des sciences in 1829 and accused him of ill-will, jealousy, absurd reasoning and ignorance. He asserted that Arago had dishonourably denigrated present French attempts in the Antarctic, yet in 1825 he had praised Weddell's discoveries in front of Humboldt and himself. After defending the suitability of the *Astrolabe* and the *Zélée*, he accused Arago of 'despotic tyranny' as a member of the academy and mocked him as the 'Sultan of the Observatory', who had failed to supply d'Urville's officers with instructions for geophysical observations despite repeated requests.[71]

Arago's long polemical response was published in *Le National* on 12 July 1837 and in the *Journal des Débats*. He reminded his readers of the numerous personal insults d'Urville had slung at him and then methodically outlined his own and the academy's contribution to the science of the first *Astrolabe* voyage. He poked fun at some of d'Urville's geophysical observations and stated that if he had declared that he was happy with some, it was because they were too simple to be subject to error. He recounted, with minute and humiliating personal detail, d'Urville's failed attempt to be elected to the Académie des sciences. He ridiculed the notion that he was jealous of d'Urville and said that he had 'examined and analysed all, absolutely all, that M. d'Urville had done regarding meteorology, geophysics, terrestrial magnetism' and found it 'insignificant'. He added: 'I am jealous. Jealous of what, great God? The mariners say that M. d'Urville is a botanist, the botanists assert that he is a mariner.' He made an oblique reference to the *Voyage pittoresque autour du monde* and called it 'very mediocre'. He reminded his readers of his own immense efforts undertaking geodesic triangulations on the Mediterranean coast of Spain and the Balearic Islands; that he had been a prisoner in Spain and Algeria; that at the age of 21, he had traversed the Mediterranean in an open longboat, in a Spanish prison ship, on a Greek vessel that had foundered on the North African coast and on an Algerian privateer. As to the approaches of d'Urville's officers to the observatory, he was adamant that there had been only one such approach and that it was at a time when he was bedridden with illness. To conclude, he quoted from Sir John Herschel's description of his instructions for Auguste-Nicolas Vaillant's *Bonite* expedition as 'scientific nourishment of the first order'.[72]

Still determined to have the last word, d'Urville penned yet another response to Arago on 17 July, but this time, he was more cautious and moderate in tone and sought to retain the moral high ground. In particular, he reflected on Arago's assertion that the *Astrolabe's* prescribed itinerary had the least prospect of discovery. He told his readers that the plan for the voyage was based on 15 years' study, meditation, personal observation and gathering on location. Of Arago's charge, he asked: 'Is it possible to imagine a personal attack more direct, more violent and more brutal?' Although he conceded to Arago's criticisms of the geophysical observations of the first *Astrolabe* voyage, he blamed him for providing poor instruments in the first place. Nevertheless he was adamant about the scrupulousness of the expedition's sea-water temperature studies at depth and pointed out that they accorded with those of Frederick Beechey. Finally, he declared: 'As for the work of hydrography, navigation, natural history, ethnography and philology, M. Arago has not engaged the testimony of the honourable men who accompanied me on my last voyage.'[73] There the bitter dispute ended – in the public arena at least – although d'Urville would continue to refer to Arago as a 'charlatan' in his journal.

For Camille Vergniol and two of d'Urville's subsequent modern biographers, Arago was described identically (and almost dismissively) as a member of the 'extreme left'.[74] This perhaps tells us more of their views than it does of Arago's. It is ironic that, in many respects, d'Urville and Arago were ideological soul-mates. Under other circumstances, they might even have been natural allies. Both were liberal constitutional republicans and both were critical of government spending priorities after the Revolution of 1830. Both believed in social reform, in the education and uplift of the lower classes and in the progressive role of the sciences. A decade later, in the wake of the Revolution of 1848 and the fall of the Orléanist monarchy, Arago became a member of the provisional government and signed decrees abolishing slavery in French colonies, ending corporal punishment and improving the nutrition of sailors. Although Arago, the scientist-politician, remained aloof from the socialist radicalism of Blanqui, Blanc and Ledru-Rollin,[75] d'Urville, who had died a decade before this radicalism was publicly expressed, owned eight instalments of the overtly socialist *Encyclopédie nouvelle ou dictionnaire philosophique, scientifique, littéraire et industriel* of Pierre Leroux and Jean Reynaud.[76] And at the time of his death, d'Urville was also in possession of undated correspondence from the editor of the centre-left newspaper *Le Temps*, whose presses were the first to be seized by police at the outbreak of the Revolution of 1830. Despite his deliberate attempt to lie low ideologically, 'to get rid of demagogue visitors, to refuse their printed papers and seldom read, without choice, some newspapers',[77] d'Urville's journals leave no doubt of his democratic political sympathies.

24

Astrolabe & Zélée

There is a history in all men's lives,
Figuring the nature of the times deceased;
The which observed, a man may prophesy,
With a near aim, of the main chance of things
As yet not come to life, which in their seeds
And weak beginnings lie intreasured.
Such things become the hatch and brood of time ...
William Shakespeare [Warwick]*

Fitting-out the *Zélée* began on 8 June 1837 and the *Astrolabe* five days later. At first, preparations proceeded very slowly, mainly because there were other priorities in the port: the departure of the prince de Joinville for Brazil with the *Hercule* and the *Favorite*. On the departure of these vessels in August, the workers in the Toulon arsenal were reallocated to the preparations for d'Urville's expedition.[1] He acknowledged receipt of British and Dutch letters of safe conduct on 3 August. Instruments, books and charts were delivered to him in Toulon via the maritime prefect around the same time.[2] The instruments included five reflective circles, three artificial horizons and a theodolite, all manufactured by Henri-Prudence Gambey, supplier to the Paris Observatory; specialised telescopes and other astronomical equipment; numerous hygrometers, barometers and thermometers for meteorological and sea-water temperature studies; a compass for measuring magnetic intensity; a galvanometer for measuring small electric currents; and even a Régnier dynamometer[3] like the one François Péron had used nearly 40 years before to test the physical strength of different races during the Baudin expedition.[4]

D'Urville's public dispute with Arago and his criticisms of Freycinet – the latter and d'Urville now held the same naval rank – probably did not help him in his dealings with the Académie des sciences. A 'Commission of Instruction' was nominated, and although Arago was not part of it, Freycinet was. The other four members were the botanist Charles-François Brisseau de Mirbel, the mineralogist Pierre-Louis-Antoine

* *Henry IV, part II* (ca.1596–99), act iii, scene i, lines 80–86

Cordier, the zoologist Henri de Blainville and the astronomer Félix Savary. At the academy's meeting of 7 August 1837, doubts were cast on the usefulness of d'Urville's expedition, and it was made clear that the academy had not been consulted with regard to its itinerary. The members declared that they did not have 'much to add to the instructions which have been adopted by the Academy for the voyage of the *Bonite*'.[5] Yet this expedition, which left France in February 1835 under the command of Auguste-Nicolas Vaillant, was not essentially scientific. The commission members listed their 'desiderata' in a mere 20 printed pages, mainly relating to the natural sciences; Freycinet contributed a perfunctory one and a half pages. Despite this lukewarm response, d'Urville received pleasing letters of goodwill from two of the academy's distinguished foreign members: Alexander von Humboldt and Adam von Krusenstern.[6]

The muster rolls for the two vessels also began to fill and included many impressive young men. As his executive officer aboard the *Astrolabe*, d'Urville was joined by Lieutenant Gaston de Roquemaurel. Born in Auriac-sur-Vendinelle (Haute-Garonne), he was the son of a cavalry officer in the service of Spain and a descendant of an ancient noble family originally from Auvergne. Thirty-three years old, Roquemaurel stood 172 centimetres tall, had brown hair, brown eyes and a snub nose, and he was an asthmatic. In 1825, he graduated from the École polytechnique, which still has three volumes of his beautifully illustrated lecture notes, including the only surviving historical record of François Arago's lectures there! On leaving the École polytechnique, he joined the navy and served in Admiral de Rigny's squadron in the Mediterranean. He had also participated in the Algerian campaign and more recently had taken part in the prince de Joinville's expedition to the Levant (1835–37).[7] The *Astrolabe*'s other lieutenant was the recently promoted 27-year-old François-Edmond-Eugène Barlatier-Demas. He was born in Saussay (Eure et Loire), but his naval family originally hailed from the upper Var. He had spent his childhood in Dunkirk and, in 1828, had graduated from the naval training vessel *Orion* in Brest. Barlatier-Demas had then sailed to Brazil before taking part in the Algerian campaign. In 1831, he had participated in the French intervention in Portugal – in support of the liberal Dom Pedro against his absolutist brother Dom Miguel – before once again being posted to the Mediterranean fleet.[8]

As his hydrographer, d'Urville recruited a talented 26-year-old named Clément-Adrien Vincendon-Dumoulin. Blond, blue-eyed and with a large nose, he stood 170 centimetres tall, was the son of a judge and hailed from Chatte, near Saint-Marcellin (Isère). He had graduated from the École polytechnique in 1833 and had then trained under the famous hydrographer Charles-François Beautemps-Beaupré.[9]

Three ensigns joined the *Astrolabe*. The eldest was Jacques-Marie-Eugène Marescot du Thilleul, who was of small stature but had a striking presence, with long curly black hair and large azure-blue eyes. Gentle, studious and agreeable, but also 'adventurous' and 'intrepid', he was liked by all who met him. Born in Boulogne, Marescot had studied at the prestigious Lycée Henri-IV in Paris before entering the École navale in Angoulême in 1826 and joining the training vessel *Orion* in 1827. At one stage, his father fell 300 francs in arrears with his tuition fees, and his graduation was delayed. We know that his family means remained limited because he had been obliged to support his brother from 1833. By the time Marescot joined d'Urville's expedition, he had served in Mediterranean waters and had participated in the Algerian campaign. Landing at Sidi Ferruch to guard the French retrenchment camp, he contracted an illness that appears to have weakened his constitution for the rest of his short life; he was also wounded in the chest by a musket ball but not seriously. In 1831, he too had taken part in the French intervention in Portugal. He had also sailed to Pondicherry, India, on the *Oise* with the new French governor, the marquis de Saint-Simon. When destined for Africa on the *Égérie* in 1835, he was forced to take six months' leave because of illness.[10] Given his precarious health, he was an unlikely candidate for a three-year voyage of exploration involving climatic extremes, but it would seem that his father, Jean-Augustin Marescot, who now lived in Caen, was a good friend of d'Urville.

Although Marescot was the eldest of the ensigns, Joseph-Antoine Duroch had seniority because he had graduated from the training vessel *Orion* at the age of 16 in 1828. Born in Bastia, Duroch was the son of an army pharmacist and a Corsican mother. Prior to entering the navy, he had studied for three years at the Collège de Toulon.[11] Adélie refers to him by his first name in a number of letters, which suggests that he might have been a family friend. The remaining and youngest ensign was Jean-Marie-Émile Gourdin, the son of a government official. He was born in Port Louis (Morbihan) and had studied at the Collège de Lorient before entering the École de la marine in Brest. After graduation, he had seen service in the Antilles and in Brazilian and Algerian waters. It seems likely that he gained his place in d'Urville's expedition because he was the nephew of Vice-Admiral Jurien, veteran of d'Entrecasteaux's expedition.[12]

The *Astrolabe*'s new purser was Jacques-Louis Ducorps, from Saint-Piat (Eure et Loire). The son of a humble *vigneron* who died young, he was raised by his widowed mother and, at the age of 17, having studied English, Spanish and Italian, Ducorps plucked up the courage to write to the navy minister to ask for a job. The minister offered him a position as an écrivain (scribe) in the port of Rochefort, and Ducorps seized the opportunity and took his mother too. D'Urville came to hold him in high regard, describing him as 'an educated young man, devoted and of excellent conduct', who 'always exhibited the best spirit'.[13]

The surgeon-major of the *Astrolabe* was Jacques-Bernard Hombron. Born in Paris, the son of a lawyer from Fribourg in Switzerland, he studied surgery in Lyon (1818–19) then attended the École de médecine navale, graduating in December 1821. After service as provost in the Hôpital de Pointe-à-Pitre in Guadeloupe, he returned to Paris and, in April 1826, submitted a thesis on yellow fever for the degree of Doctor of Medicine.[14] In the following decade, he married in Brest and sailed as a surgeon on a succession of French naval vessels – the *Meuse, Ibis, Alcibiade, Alerte, Orion* and *Naïade* – including two return voyages to Brazil and around Cape Horn to Chile and Peru, before joining the *Astrolabe*. Hombron was passionate about natural history, in particular geology and mineralogy, and frequently accompanied d'Urville during his botanical excursions. Like d'Urville, he also published a popular compendium of historic voyages: *Aventures les plus curieuses des voyageurs.*[15] Aboard the *Astrolabe*, Hombron was assisted by Louis Le Breton, a round-faced, flat-nosed young man with widely spaced eyes, originally from Douarnenez (Finistère). Le Breton's father, uncle and maternal grandfather were all doctors, and he graduated from the École de médecine navale in Brest in March 1836. He joined the *Astrolabe* in Toulon on 23 July 1837. Although he was designated as a junior medical officer, he is particularly remembered for his important artistic contribution to the record of d'Urville's expedition.[16]

There were four midshipmen aboard the *Astrolabe*. Charles-François Eugène Gervaize was born in Dinan (Côtes-du-Nord), the son of an advocate and a graduate of the École polytechnique, which meant that he immediately gained the rank of *élève de 1ère classe* on entering the École navale. He was 163 centimetres tall with brown hair, brown eyes, an oval face and a large nose.[17] Pierre-Antoine Delafond was yet another graduate of the École polytechnique. Blond and blue-eyed, he stood 170 centimetres tall and came from Villié-Morgon (Rhône). He had entered the École navale in 1835 and had seen service on the brig *Couëdic* in the Levant.[18] His fellow midshipman, Louis-Emmanuel Le Maistre Duparc, was the son of a rural landowner in the village of Bosc-Bénard-Crescy in upper Normandy. He had begun his career at sea on his fourteenth birthday – as a *mousse* aboard a merchant brig trading with Saint Petersburg. In November 1831, however, he entered the École navale and, after graduation, served for three and a half years on the frigate *Ariane*. He gained his place on the *Astrolabe* by virtue of his exemplary service record. Unfortunately, he appears to have suffered from tuberculosis.[19]

There were two civilians on the staff of the *Astrolabe*. One was the enigmatic phrenologist Pierre-Marie-Alexandre Dumoutier, a round-faced man with a snub-nose, thick upper lip and narrow beard who had pleaded with d'Urville to join the expedition. Keen to broaden the scientific scope of the expedition, d'Urville gained ministerial approval for Dumoutier's appointment, not only as a phrenologist but as an 'anatomical preparator';[20] he would also serve as an additional medical officer. Born in Paris, he apparently commenced medical studies in the capital but never completed his course. For a time, he was an anatomical assistant at the medical school. In 1827, he

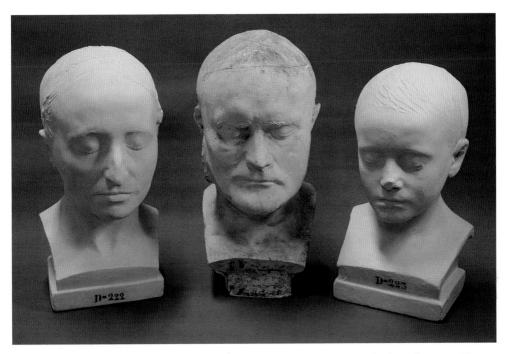

Phrenological busts, ca. 1836, by Pierre-Marie-Alexandre Dumoutier, of Jules-Sébastien-César Dumont d'Urville (centre) with his wife Adèle-Dorothée (left) and son Jules-Eugène-Hector (right). The busts of Adèle and young Jules are the only known images from life. The central bust of the explorer also played a crucial role in identifying d'Urville's remains after his death. Jean-Christophe Domenech, Musée de l'homme, Paris

was a regular member of the Société anatomique, but between 1836 and 1846, he was only a corresponding member. His interest in phrenology seems to have begun around 1820, probably when he attended lectures by Johann Spurzheim. In 1831, he helped to found the Société phrénologique in Paris, and in January 1836, he established a phrenological museum at his home, 37, rue de Seine, in the 6th arrondissement. He returned to this same address after his voyage with d'Urville, so it was perhaps his mother (who is known to have been alive and in her eighties in 1841) or his wife who cared for his collection during his absence, along with his daughter Valérie.[21] Dumoutier's museum contained plaster busts of hundreds of prominent savants (including d'Urville's nemesis Arago), cultural figures, statesmen, monarchs and generals. There were also death masks and skulls from different ethnicities, convicted criminals (thieves, murderers, rapists, etc.) and sufferers of specific medical conditions (deaf-mutes, insanity cases and even a nymphomaniac). D'Urville was perhaps introduced to Dumoutier by his colleague Paul Gaimard, who was also the subject of one of the busts (or at least his forehead was). Around 1836, when d'Urville was living in Paris with his family, and his gifted son Jules was about 10 years old, they all submitted to having casts of their heads taken. The busts of Adélie and young Jules – among the hundreds acquired in 1873 by the Muséum national d'histoire naturelle from Dumoutier's landlord, a Monsieur Barbier – appear to be the only contemporary images of d'Urville's wife and child.[22] As we shall see, in a codicil to his last will and testament, d'Urville even left his own skull to Dumoutier, to 'prepare it and conserve it as a subject of phrenological study'.[23]

The other civilian recruit for the *Astrolabe* was d'Urville's secretary, 21-year-old César-Louis-François Desgraz.[24] He was born in Smyrna (modern Izmir) in Turkey, the son of a Swiss merchant and the orphaned daughter of a merchant from Marseille.[25] It would seem that when Desgraz was two years old, his father had moved the family to Constantinople to work in or take charge of his firm's principal office in the Levant but also to develop trade in the Black Sea and the Crimea. In the wake of the instability and danger posed to foreigners as a result of the Greek War of Independence, Desgraz's father apparently sent César and his brother Édouard to France and then to Switzerland to be educated. The family was reunited in Paris after Desgraz's father returned from Turkey via Trieste and Vienna. Sometime after October 1832, when Desgraz was 16, his family moved to the Protestant quarter of Marseille.[26] There his father resumed trade with Smyrna and became the sole owner of the Marseille-registered vessel *Calisman*. How Desgraz came to join the expedition remains something of a mystery. D'Urville certainly knew him before the expedition and he is mentioned in his journal as a correspondent in Marseille. They shared an interest in linguistics and ethnology. According to Jacquinot, Desgraz spoke several languages,[27] including English. His erudite and exuberant father also shared d'Urville's interest in Confucius and was a published poet and essayist.[28] D'Urville could easily have met the Desgraz family during the *Chevrette*'s visit to the Ottoman capital, or in Paris or Marseille. Adélie also corresponded with Desgraz[29] during d'Urville's final expedition, so perhaps there was a connection on the Swiss side of her family.

While Desgraz' father was Protestant, his mother was Catholic, and he was baptised a Catholic in Smyrna. Nevertheless, he appears to have had a Protestant education and to have identified as a Protestant (at least when writing to his father). Although he has been accused of anti-clericalism,[30] this is too simple an assessment. He had Calvinist doctrinal differences with Catholic missionaries but wrote very positively of the manner in which they improved the lives of Polynesians.[31] Ironically, in 1850, Desgraz was made a papal knight when the Pope decorated him with the cross of the order of Saint Sylvester, apparently for his contribution to French protection of Catholic missionaries in the Pacific. Desgraz was also known to have frequented Christian socialist circles – perhaps another bond he had with d'Urville. He was popular with the other members of the crew, despite the initial apparent handicap of closeness to d'Urville and the fear that he might be the captain's ears on board.

Aboard the *Zélée*, Jacquinot's executive officer was Lieutenant Joseph-Fidèle-Eugène Dubouzet. Born in Paris to a noble family – his mother referred to herself as comtesse in 1816 and he inherited the title of marquis in 1862 – Dubouzet was a graduate of the naval college in Angoulême, a veteran of the *Thétis* on Hyacinthe de Bougainville's expedition and had already exercised independent command aboard the transport *Lionne*[32] on the Algerian coast. That May, not yet 32 years of age, he was made a *chevalier de la Légion d'honneur*. D'Urville held him in high regard as an 'officer of perfect merit, of the best conduct, of the most honourable character and of very remarkable learning'.[33] Dubouzet himself was excited to be part of a voyage destined for 'the exploration of icy seas where the dangers will heighten the glories to be acquired'. He added, in a 'time of peace' it was the only opportunity 'to reap some laurels'.[34]

The other lieutenant of the *Zélée* was the recently promoted Charles-Jules-Adolphe Thanaron. He was from Toulon and, like many of the officers, was a graduate of the École navale d'Angoulême. His father, a decorated former captain in the Garde impériale maritime, had been forced into retirement by Louis XVIII on his return from Belgium in 1816, presumably because of his Bonapartist affiliations.

As on the *Astrolabe*, there were three ensigns aboard the *Zélée*. The most senior was Louis-François-Marie Tardy de Montravel. He was born in Vincennes while his father, an artillery officer, was serving in Napoleon's Garde imperiale. He joined the navy in 1828 after studying at the Collège royal de Nancy. In the decade prior to joining the *Zélée*, he had served in Brazilian, Caribbean, Belgian, African and Mediterranean waters.[35] The second-eldest ensign was Antoine-Auguste-Thérèse Pavin de La Farge, highly regarded for his 'aptitude for work and his good conduct'. He had written directly to the minister asking for the 'favour' of joining d'Urville's expedition and had at least one influential friend who also wrote on his behalf with the same request. Known as 'Tony', he was born in Viviers (Ardèche), the son of a former officer. Pavin de La Farge came from a close family, to whom he wrote regularly. Around his neck, he wore a small gold cross given to him by a devout sister. After studying at the Collège de La Flèche, he was admitted to the École navale de Brest and was one of the top students in his class. Like many of his fellow officers, he had already taken part in operations on the Algerian coast, the expedition to Portugal and various transport missions to the Levant and Africa.[36] The remaining ensign was Aimé-Auguste-Élie Coupvent-Desbois. Born in Dunkirk, he had chestnut hair, blue eyes, an oval face with a small nose and mouth, and was 160 centimetres tall. A graduate of the École polytechnique, he would have a distinguished naval career.[37]

Following pages: *Map 6. The circumnavigation and Antarctic descents of the* Astrolabe *and the* Zélée, *7 September 1837 to 6 November 1840*

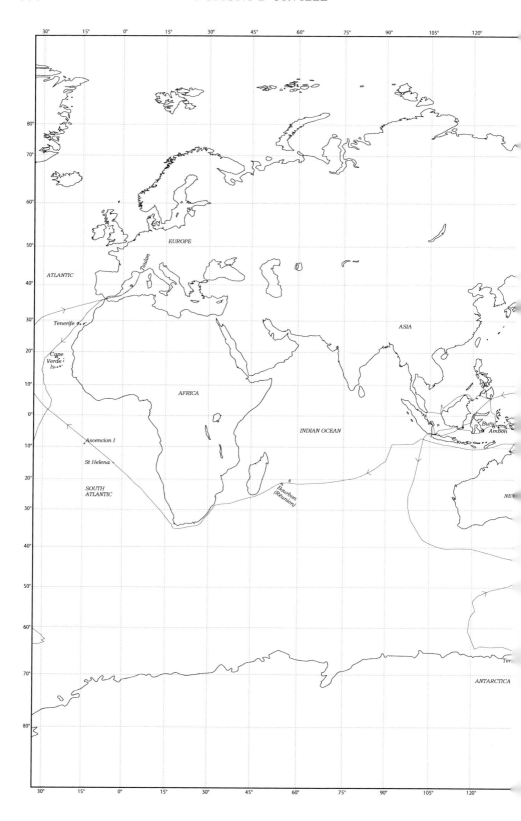

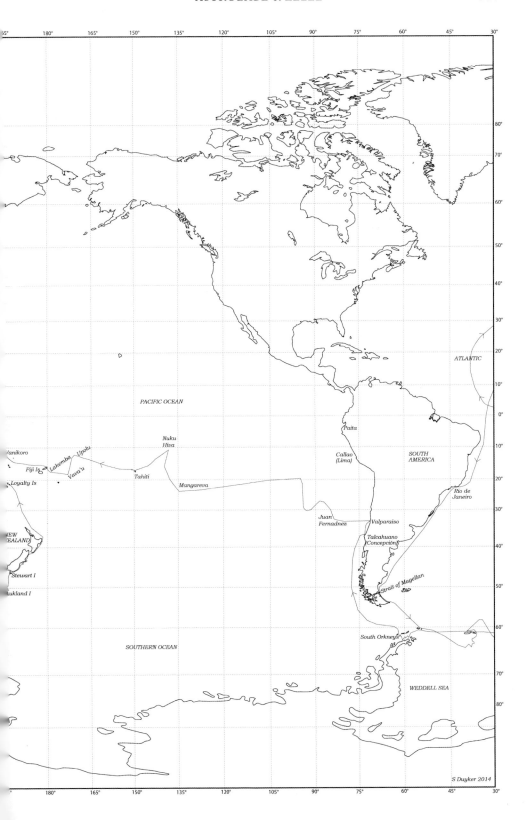

Terres Australes et Antarctiques Françaises stamps honouring: (left) Dumont d'Urville (1990), engraved by Jacques Gauthier; (centre) Clément-Adrien Vincendon-Dumoulin (1994), engraved by Jacky Larrivière; (right) Charles-Hector Jacquinot (1996), engraved by Marie-Noëlle Goffin. Author's collection

The purser of the *Zélée* was Félix-Casimir-Marie Huon de Kermadec, who came from a famous naval family that included the second-in-command of d'Entrecasteaux's expedition of 1791–93. The son of a sub-inspector in the naval administration, he had joined the navy in 1831.[38] The surgeon of the *Zélée* was Élie-Jean-François Le Guillou, who was born in Quimperlé, Brittany. The son of a doctor, he graduated from the École de médecine navale in 1824. In 1835, he had served with Paul Gaimard on the *Recherche* in search of Blosseville in Arctic waters. It was Gaimard who recommended Surgeon Le Guillou to Jacquinot for the *Zélée* because of his additional skills as a naturalist and his ability to sketch. He was undoubtedly a capable scientist, but he was also deeply egocentric and uninterested in any other opinion but his own. His former commander aboard the *Recherche*, François-Thomas Tréhouart, did not have a high opinion of him and wrote that Le Guillou would 'fulfill his duties in a more satisfactory manner, if in addition to his capacities he was less uncouth and behaved more graciously'. D'Urville certainly read Tréhouart's report but exactly when is unclear. Perhaps he and Jacquinot chose to give the surgeon the benefit of the doubt because of Gaimard's high opinion of him as a naturalist.[39]

During the voyage, Le Guillou was assisted by Jacquinot's half-brother Honoré. Nineteen years younger than the captain of the *Zélée*, he was known as 'Jacquinot jeune'. Clearly, his older half-brother took him under his wing, perhaps at the behest of their wealthy banker father. Born illegitimate in Moulins-Engilbert (Nièvre), Honoré Jacquinot was officially recognised by his father only two years before the expedition. A graduate of the École de médecine navale in 1836, he appears not to have gone to sea prior to the expedition, or indeed after it. Gracious and good-humoured, with a passion for herpetology and ornithology, he was well regarded by d'Urville, who made representations for his promotion on his return.[40]

There were four midshipmen aboard the *Zélée*. The eldest was Jean-Edmond Gaillard, born in Marennes (Charente-inférieure), the younger son of a merchant and landowner of recent wealth. He had studied first at the lycée in Rochefort and then the École navale, graduating in 1831. Among the five vessels he had served aboard, prior to the expedition, was the *Astrolabe* in the Mediterranean.[41] His colleague Germain-Hector Périgot was from Devant-les-Ponts (Moselle), the son of a retired army officer. He graduated from the École navale in 1832 without glowing academic references but with an acknowledgment of his aptitude for ship-handling.[42]

The remaining midshipman – although yet another would embark at Tahiti – was Joseph-Emmanuel-Prosper Boyer. He was born in Avignon (Vaucluse), the son of a merchant, and had joined the navy's training vessel, the *Orion*, in 1831. He resigned in June 1834, ostensibly because of ill health but in reality to sit for the École polytechnique examination. When he did not pass, he rejoined, only to attempt to resign again in February 1836 for family reasons.[43] He was certainly very family-minded, for he married his own niece in 1849!

The *Zélée*'s staff also included a civilian, the artist Auguste-Ernest Goupil, the son of a pharmacist from Châteaudun. Born prematurely the day before Napoleon's first abdication and as foreign troops were about to occupy his native Loire Valley,[44] Goupil had had a frail constitution from childhood. Although he commenced university studies in Paris, his passion for art led him, instead, to enter the studio of a relative, the landscape painter Louis-Étienne Watelet. He then studied under Jules-Louis-Philippe Coignet before painting in Auvergne, on the Somme estuary, in Algeria and along the French Mediterranean coast for a time in the company of the celebrated Camille Corot. By October 1836, Goupil had returned to Paris to exhibit his work. There, in 1837, he met d'Urville and showed him his portfolio, and soon after, he gained the minister's approval for his appointment as the expedition's official artist. With his 'gentle and jovial' temperament and his 'frank and open countenance', Goupil gained the affection of all his fellow voyagers.[45]

Filling the ordinary ranks was more problematic. At the end of July, the 800-tonne corvette *Dordogne* arrived in Toulon from Brest. She carried 80 reserve sailors, who were put at d'Urville's disposal. He, Jacquinot, Roquemaurel and Dubouzet began to review these men and their dossiers but found most to be very mediocre candidates for the expedition, despite being categorised as 'elite'. Only 20 were selected. D'Urville then requested permission from Vice-Admiral Jurien de la Gravière to make an appeal for volunteers from among the other vessels in Toulon harbour. Jurien was sympathetic and permission was granted. These volunteers still had to meet d'Urville's high standards, but with the minister's agreement, they were all promised promotions.[46] A royal ordinance also promised bonuses of 150 francs for every officer in charge who reached 75°S, 100 francs for other officers and sailors, and 50 francs for cabin boys and domestics. Respectively, for the same ranks, an additional 30, 20 and 10 francs were promised for each degree of latitude south thereafter.[47] The ranks of the *Astrolabe* and *Zélée* soon filled. D'Urville himself appears not to have inspired a great deal of confidence at this time. Walking 'slowly and heavily' after a recent attack of gout, he recorded overhearing some of the men, surprised to learn that he was their commander, exclaim: 'Oh! that fellow won't take us very far'. Steeled with determination, d'Urville tells us that 'from that moment on, I promised them that, if God let me live, that *fellow* would show them something of the art of navigation like they had never seen'.[48]

Most of the crew were from Toulon and the Var or Brittany, but others were from the Gironde, Charente-Maritime, Loire-Atlantique and the Vendée. There were also individuals from Alsace-Lorraine, the Alps, Italy and even Germany. The latter was the chief helmsman Charles (Carl) Kosmann, from Burbach, Westphalia, the 29-year-old son of a lieutenant-colonel of cavalry in the Grande Armée. (His father had served with distinction in Austria, Prussia, Spain and Portugal, and was wounded at both Jena and Heilsberg.) Although Kosmann began his naval career as a humble apprentice sailor in 1826, his intelligence, learning and devotion to duty gained him rapid promotion. He had served in the Algerian campaign, had been badly wounded in the shoulder during the capture of Bougie in 1833 and had joined d'Urville's expedition after a long convalescence. On his return to France, he was commissioned as an officer and later had a distinguished naval career, commanding five different warships before retiring with the rank of *capitaine de vaisseau*.[49] There were other men of surprising erudition and experience among the lower ranks. Aboard the *Astrolabe*, as a sailor third class, was Joseph Le Jeune, a tall, athletic former seminarian, pharmacist and whaler from Amiens. His friend Charles Rochefort, from Bordeaux, who served with the same rank initially on the *Zélée* and then on the *Astrolabe*, was a man of refined (even effeminate) manners and speech, who had a marvellous operatic singing voice and 'fertile' memory, according to Le Guillou.[50]

The sailors were accommodated on the 'tween deck, forward of the officers' cabins. As in the previous *Astrolabe* and *Coquille* voyages, the seven officers' cabins were accessed off the great cabin at the stern. Four of these were double cabins. Those allocated to the surgeon and pharmacist opened onto the area designated for the preparation of natural history specimens and for conducting experiments. The library and armoury were aft of the captain's cabin and illuminated by the stern windows.

Water on the vessels was stored in metal tanks of 900 and 1000 litres. We know that the *Zélée* was provisioned with 27,435 litres of wine, laid down in barrels of 250, 500 and 750 litres, intended to last 432 days; 1600 litres of brandy, intended to last 92 days; 590 kilograms of coffee, intended to last almost 14 months; 700 kilograms of sugar for 426 days; 74 kilograms of butter for 60 days; 3400 kilograms of salted lard for 230 alternate days; 550 kilograms of cheese to last 55 alternate days; 1395 kilograms of vegetables for 283 alternate days; over 4.5 tonnes of flour to last 92 days; and over 14 tonnes of sea biscuits to last 288 days. Furthermore, 642 kilograms of tinned beef, 400 kilograms of sauerkraut and 450 kilograms of rice were stowed. Some of the beef was preserved in 30-kilogram drums using the 'Noël and Taboureau' process, which involved the injection of carbon dioxide. Three of the drums exploded during the voyage, rupturing their soldered seams. Although the beef looked fine, it smelt of putrefaction and, not surprisingly, was unpopular with the crew, who preferred salted beef.[51] To nourish the expected dysentery cases, the infirmary was supplied with a reserve of 100 kilograms of gelatine and 3700 kilograms of tinned meat and vegetables. The relative perishability, availability en route, cost and bulk of particular victuals influenced the quantities loaded, but so too did the demands of French cuisine. Each vessel had its own baker, and aside from the already mentioned wine, cheese, butter and flour, 400 litres of olive oil, to last 813 alternate days, and 50 kilograms of mustard were laid down, as were 400 litres of vinegar. The latter was used as dressing for salad and for pickling, but it was also added to the drinking water (as was quick lime, presumably depending on the pH) to prevent putrefaction. Similarly, 726 kilograms of salt was stowed on the *Zélée* for seasoning but also for preserving fresh supplies en route. Only modest quantities of salted beef (300 kilograms for 18 alternate days) and cod (80 kilograms for eight alternate days) were loaded; they would soon have to be replenished. Forty-one cubic metres of firewood, to last almost 11 months, were also taken aboard.[52]

The *Zélée*, her belly full, left the arsenal and entered the harbour of Toulon on 14 August; a week later, the *Astrolabe* followed, similarly provisioned.[53] On 7 September, the expedition was ready to leave. Of his intense emotions on that day, d'Urville wrote:

> At precisely midday, I bade farewell to my wife and my children. This moment was quite painful for me. Twice I had already undergone this cruel test; but then I was a young person, robust, full of hope and promise, and under illusions. But in 1837, I was old, prone to the attacks of a cruel disease, completely disenchanted and without any illusions. I thus left all that was dear to me in the world, I voluntarily renounced the only happiness which I could taste, to launch myself again in a painful, ungrateful career which might not offer me any real compensation. Thus, when I gave a final kiss to my Adèle, all these notions assaulted me, I could not hold back my tears, and I cursed my sad destiny. But it was too late; I had filled the chalice; it was necessary to empty it. I cast a last glance at the walls of my humble retreat, then went quickly away and returned aboard.[54]

25

To the Antarctic Peninsula

… I turn'd, and fixed my mind
On the other pole attentive, where I saw
Four stars …
Dante Alighieri [on the South Pole and the Southern Cross]*

The *Zélée* was able to leave the outer harbour of Toulon with ease on 7 September 1837, but the *Astrolabe* had to be towed from the inner harbour by the steamboat *Crocodile*. This offered a marked contrast to d'Urville's experience in April 1826, when it had taken the lone *Astrolabe* three days to depart because of adverse winds. According to Joseph Seureau, quartermaster of the *Zélée*, both vessels were farewelled by craft bearing the wives and parents of many crew members. The mood was sombre and tearful because word had spread of 'Monsieur Harago's' [*sic*] attacks in the press, and it was said that the expedition would 'not return'.[1] D'Urville does not mention the depressing effect of Arago's attacks on the morale of the families of his men, nor the sad flotilla that escorted them from the harbour. For his part, Seureau confidently declared in the preface of his journal that 'Monsieur d'Urville, a man of intellect, knowing as much as him [Arago] in astronomy, wanted to show to him that he would not lead them to butchery, and would return them to France.'[2]

The following night, the expedition caught sight of the island of Minorca, but approaching Gibraltar, they were becalmed for some days and took the opportunity to conduct their first sea-water temperature studies at depth. On the evening of 19 September, the two corvettes left the Mediterranean. This, too, contrasted with the *Astrolabe*'s experience in 1826, when d'Urville had spent an excruciating month trying to enter the Atlantic.

D'Urville's first port of call was meant to be Cape Verde, but instead he chose to visit Santa Cruz in the Canary Islands, to purchase wine and to enable his hydrographer Vincendon-Dumoulin to climb the Peak of Tenerife to conduct base reference observations and rate his instruments – something he had been criticised for not

---

* *Purgatorio* (*ca.*1300), canto i, lines 22–24, Cary trans.

doing in 1826. After anchoring on 30 September and undergoing a medical inspection, the officers were allowed to land. D'Urville soon renewed the acquaintance of the French consul, Alexandre Brétillard, and called on the Spanish governor, Brigadier-General Juan Manuel de Pereyra y Soto-Sánchez, marqués de la Concordia. D'Urville recorded that he was glad of the governor's reserve and lack of acknowledgement of their special scientific status. He was not in the mood for galas, balls and boring questions at 'pompous gatherings'. He tells us that he wanted rest before leaving his 'floating prison' again![3] This was a tired, depressed d'Urville, not the mariner of old. He was, nevertheless, very pleased to meet the visiting British hydrographer Captain Alexander Vidal, who, armed with 12 chronometers, was seeking to calculate the meridian arc length between Cape Verde and the west coast of Africa aboard HMS *Aetna*.[4]

D'Urville permitted a quarter of his crew at a time to go ashore. Unfortunately, there were soon problems, as his sailors got drunk on the strong local wine and picked fights with the inhabitants. Two of his men were arrested and imprisoned by the Spanish for the duration of their visit. Desgraz, who had not visited the Canary Islands before, was shocked by the poverty, filth and prostitution he saw but enjoyed exploring the 'fresh and elegant interior' of the Franciscan church in Santa Cruz.[5] While the other officers began their assigned scientific or victualling tasks, the phrenologist Dumoutier set off on an ultimately successful search for skulls of the exterminated indigenous inhabitants, the Guanche.[6]

Although d'Urville once again enjoyed private hospitality and wine in Laguna, he did not return to the Jardín de Aclimatación outside the charming highland town of La Orotava. In 1826, he had established a lifelong friendship with its then director, Sabin Berthelot. Surgeon Le Guillou, however, visited the gardens, having earlier met Berthelot's successor, 'Miguel' Daguerre, another Frenchman.[7] D'Urville appears to have confined his excursions to horseback, perhaps because of his recurrent gout, but he had no mishaps – unlike Coupvent-Desbois, who was thrown from his horse and broke a barometer while descending Mount Teide in the company of Vincendon-Dumoulin, Le Guillou, Lafarge and Dubouzet. With scientific observations and revictualling completed, the expedition left the Canary Islands on 8 October.

Three weeks later, on the evening of 28 October, the *Astrolabe* and *Zélée* crossed the equator. The customary 'baptisms' for the first-timers were followed by plentiful libations. By this time, d'Urville had become very concerned about the health of one of his midshipmen, Louis-Emmanuel Le Maistre Duparc, aboard the *Astrolabe*. Surgeon Hombron had counselled the young man to leave the expedition while it was still in the Canary Islands, but he had been determined to press on. Now d'Urville was advised that there was 'no longer any hope' for him,[8] so he decided to alter course and

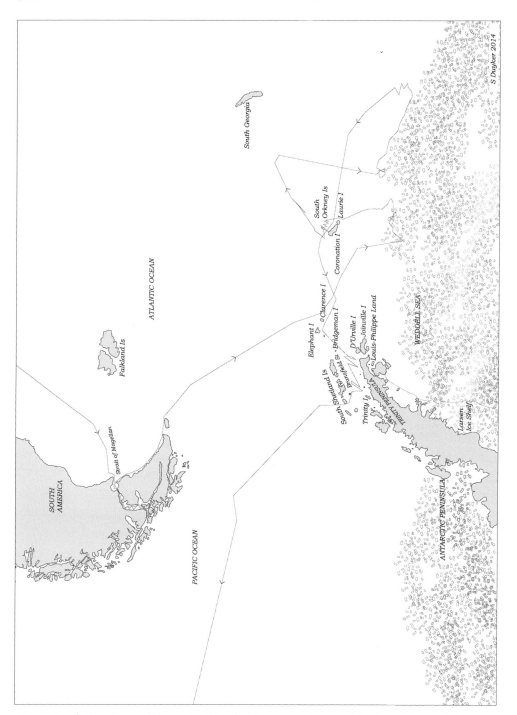

Map 7. South America and the route of the first Antarctic descent of the Astrolabe and the
Zélée, January–April 1838

put him ashore at Rio de Janeiro. Although he hoped that Duparc could be transferred to Rear Admiral Louis Leblanc's squadron, this did not prove possible for the moment, so Duparc was left in the care of the French consul. Surprisingly, despite Hombron's pessimistic prognosis, he would outlive d'Urville by four and a half years.[9]

While Duparc was taken ashore in a boat under the command of Lieutenant Barlatier-Demas, the *Astrolabe* and the *Zélée* stood some five kilometres off the coast. D'Urville followed their progress with his telescope until the pouring rain made visibility impossible. He was joined briefly by Jacquinot, who informed him that all his men were fit, save for the *Zélée*'s cook, who was suffering from homesickness and anxiety over the approaching ice. When the expedition set sail again, there was 'great disappointment' among many of the officers (and presumably the crew) that they could not have a 'longer stay in a town which promised them so much enjoyment and distractions'.[10] D'Urville, however, was determined not to compound their delayed schedule, already problematic after their departure a week late from Toulon.

On the evening of 24 November, a dense fog settled on the sea and necessitated the regular firing of cannons for the corvettes to avoid separating. Although d'Urville's instructions were to sail via the South Shetland Islands to the Antarctic Peninsula and then to pass through the Strait of Magellan, on 10 December, he informed Jacquinot that he had decided to reverse this itinerary and survey the strait first. He apparently believed that this would maximise the window of opportunity for exploration afforded by the southern hemisphere summer. Two days later, the expedition reached Cape Virgenes and the entry to the 560-kilometre-long strait. Discovered in 1520 by Fernão de Magalhães (Magellan), the Strait of Magellan separates southern Patagonia from Tierra del Fuego and other offshore islands. At its narrowest, it is just three kilometres wide, and the currents are strong and fast. D'Urville was amused to hear his sailors say of his passage through these waters: 'That devil is mad! He had us shaving the rocks, reefs and land as if he had never sailed otherwise in his life ... And we thought he had no spine!'[11]

On 16 December, the *Astrolabe* and *Zélée* anchored at Puerto Hambre – or rather, what had long been known as Port Famine – on San Juan Bay. The original Port Famine – as we shall see, the bay immediately to the north – received its bleak name in 1587, when the British navigator Thomas Cavendish found the remains of Pedro Sarmiento de Gamboa's Spanish settlement destroyed by cold, starvation and lack of external support. It had been established just three years before, in a failed attempt to prevent British privateers entering the Pacific.[12] When Charles Darwin visited in May 1834 aboard HMS *Beagle*, he wrote: 'I never saw a more cheerless prospect.'[13] Yet Seureau tells us that at the mouth of the Sedger River, which emptied into the strait, 'a single cast [of the seine] was sufficient to feed the crew' with fish.[14] D'Urville also wrote that the 'rocks of the coast are literally covered in mussels, limpets, fissurellas, whelks, etc., which will offer a delicious supplement to the mess-tins of the crew'.[15] On the beach, he also noted tufts of 'celery' (*Apium* sp.) and a kind of dandelion that he thought would make excellent salad greens, and not long after, he found geese that were particularly good eating. Furthermore, he found a favourable location for the expedition's observatory, protected from the winds by a small hill. Ashore, members of the crew encountered a small barrel suspended from a tree and, close by, a pot inscribed with the words 'Post Office'. The barrel, the brainchild of an American skipper named Cunningham in April 1833, contained letters 'posted' by the crews of visiting vessels in the hope that they would be collected by homeward-bound vessels. It also contained advice for other captains, together with notes, observations and newspapers. D'Urville decided to refurbish it with a proper box and make use of the simple but ingenious clearing station in the hope that, as he put it, 'our families will be agreeably surprised to receive our news from this wild and lonely land at the moment when we launch towards the polar ice'.[16]

D'Urville crossed the Sedger River in a whaleboat and found himself in a 'large and beautiful forest' of Antarctic beech (*Nothofagus antarctica*), winter's bark (*Drimys winteri*) and *Berberis*.[17] Although he was disappointed not to find any mammals, reptiles or terrestrial snails, he filled his specimen box with mosses and lichens, collected a few insects and noted a number of birds before recrossing the river with Dr Hombron. A number of new species were collected by the expedition's naturalists on the strait. The animals included the Magellanic plover (*Pluvianellus sociabilis*), a rare wader with grey and white plumage, a black beak, bright pink eyes and a dove-like coo, now included in a distinct ornithological family of its own, the Pluvianellidae;[18] a new king crab, *Lithodes granulata* (*Paralomis granulata*);[19] two new species of carabid beetle, *Acupalpus erythroderes* and *Antarctica complanata* (*Antarctonomus complanatus*);[20] and a new species of longhorn beetle, *Microplophorus magellanicus*.[21] A number of new mollusc species were collected (the expedition undertook dredging for five consecutive days), but delays in publishing the expedition's malacological results rendered their published names mere synonyms.[22]

In the plant kingdom, the holotype specimen of an entirely new genus of marine alga, *Heterosiphonia berkeleyi*, was collected on the strait and later described and published by Camille Montagne.[23] So too, a new species of leafy liverwort belonging to the Acrobolbaceae was personally collected by d'Urville and later named *Scapania urvilliana* (*Tylimanthus urvilleanus*) in his honour.[24] *Uncinia macrolepis*, a new species belonging to the Cyperaceae, was also collected; it was later described by Joseph Decaisne, who compiled the expedition's volume on vascular plants.[25] Hombron collected a new species of *Valeriana* on the strait: *V. magellanica*.[26] Even specimens of species already described by other botanists were of value. D'Urville was well aware of the great paucity of botanical specimens from this part of the world in French collections, with the exception of those collected by Philibert Commerson during Bougainville's landfalls in December 1767–January 1768.[27]

While the hydrographer Vincendon-Dumoulin and Lieutenant Roquemaurel were responsible for the broad survey of the coast and precise determination of the latitude and longitude of the observatory as a reference point, Ensign Duroch was charged with surveying Port Famine, while Lieutenant Thanaron and Ensign Pavin de la Farge were ordered to survey neighbouring Voces Bay. One of the helmsmen, Jean-Marie Coste, from Paramé in Brittany, was ordered to observe tidal movements. The sailors, when their duties were completed, were allowed to go ashore to explore the forest, go fishing and stuff themselves with shellfish. D'Urville described them as 'joyful and content'. So, it seems, was he, although he was annoyed that some of the sailors were responsible for starting a major forest fire, which enveloped the coast in smoke. Nevertheless it enabled him to understand how human intervention, or simply lightning, could occasion vast fires that ultimately cleared 'singular plains'.[28] It was yet another example of d'Urville's appreciation of anthropogenic ecological change.

On 18 December, d'Urville boarded the yawl with Dumoutier and rounded Punta Santa Ana to enter 'Rocky Bay' to the north. Although the weather was fine at the outset, they were lashed by extremely cold rain when they landed. Dumoutier was in search of the indigenous Patagonians, no doubt in the hope of measuring their heads or rifling their graves for skulls. On the coast bounded by lush grassland, they did find native habitations made of branches covered in dry grass, but they were unoccupied. D'Urville wrote that these shelters reminded him very much of the habitations 'of the miserable Australians of King George Sound'.[29] Dumoutier left empty-handed.

D'Urville had his own quest: to search for the ruins of the Spanish settlement of 'Philippeville' (Ciudad del Rey Don Felipe), which the American navigator Benjamin Morrell claimed to have visited in May 1823 (D'Urville incorrectly stated June 1827). Morrell had written that the fort built by the Spanish less than a century after Columbus 'appeared to be but little decayed considering the length of time it had been abandoned' and that only the town bore 'much stronger marks of the withering touch of time'.[30] D'Urville owned the 1832 New York edition of Morrell's book and circulated the author's remarkable account of the Spanish ruins to his officers. From a purely defensive perspective, d'Urville and his men thought that they had determined the most likely position of the Spanish settlement, but the search for vestiges only yielded the recent graves of several mariners dating from 1828 and 1829.

It was not until May 1955 that the remnants were discovered north of Punta Santa Ana by the Spanish-born Chilean historian Jesús Veiga Alonso, who realised that

Pedro Sarmiento de Gamboa's description of the location of the settlement did not accord with the long-assumed location of Port Famine (San Juan Bay). D'Urville had unwittingly searched the wrong bay. By 1958, it was clear that the chapel was the only structure in the original Spanish settlement that had stone foundations. Its rectangular plan was excavated in the early 1970s. Some European pottery fragments, iron nails and lead shot were also found, but the other civilian and military structures were no longer evident.[31] D'Urville was probably correct in his assumption that the Spanish colonists had used 'only wood and earth', which had long disappeared. Modern archaeology certainly did not vindicate Morrell and would appear to have upheld d'Urville's judgement that the American had 'toyed utterly with the good faith of his readers'.[32]

D'Urville spent Christmas Day collecting mollusca and botanising (including the gathering of useful salad herbs) – an excursion that he considered salutary, agreeable and useful. When the expedition weighed anchor at 8.00 am on 28 December, d'Urville was very pleased with the hydrography, geophysics and natural-history work undertaken during their visit.[33] Before leaving, he had sent his chief helmsman, Charles Kosmann, to post the expedition's mail at the 'post office', refurbished on d'Urville's orders.[34]

The expedition continued sailing south, traversing the mouth of the Boquerón Passage and passing through the mountain-lined waters between the Brunswick Peninsula and Dawson Island to round Cape Froward – the southernmost tip of the Brunswick Peninsula and thus continental South America – and then entered nearby Port Gallant on Fortescue Bay. Here, once again, d'Urville had great pleasure in botanising ashore – until the cold weather drove him back aboard the *Astrolabe*. The freezing conditions also appear to have decided him on a change of plan for the expedition, or rather, a reversion to its original orders. The first month of the southern hemisphere summer was almost over. On 30 December, d'Urville informed Jacquinot that the corvettes would no longer sail to the western exit of the strait; instead, they would sail back to the Atlantic and head for the Antarctic. After ancillary surveys of Cordès Bay and Port San Miguel, the two corvettes returned to Cape Froward and anchored for two days in Saint Nicholas Bay, which was teeming with sardines. There, d'Urville marked the New Year of 1838 with a feast of sausage, salted pork, chicken, roast goose, vintage white wine and finally a bottle of champagne from Aÿ (Marne). He also distributed silver expedition medals to all the officers and bronze medals to the midshipmen and the men of all other ranks he was pleased with.

The corvettes sailed north back through the waters between the Brunswick Peninsula and Dawson Island. On 3 January 1838, they were once more off Punta Santa Ana, so d'Urville yet again dispatched Charles Kosmann to leave an additional report to the minister at the 'Post Office'. The system worked. In March, the letters were collected by Captain Abraham B. Lawton, master of the American whaling ship *McDonnough*, and on his return to New London, Connecticut, in June 1838, Lawton forwarded them (with an explanatory declaration sworn before a notary public)[35] to the French consul in New York. They reached the minister in Paris in July.

The following day, the *Astrolabe* and the *Zélée* skirted Elizabeth Island (Isla Isabel), which offered significant protection from the Antarctic winds, before anchoring in Pecket Harbour (Bahia Pecket) on the northeastern side of the upper neck of the Brunswick Peninsula. Here, the French finally encountered some of the indigenous inhabitants. D'Urville thought their features reminiscent of Mongols, though he later saw Māori likenesses in some. All were barefoot but wearing guanaco skins or cast-off European uniforms. D'Urville wrote that they had a 'generally soft, indolent attitude … one would more likely take them for women of a seraglio of the East than savages so close to the state of nature'.[36] The French were also surprised to be greeted by two European castaways, who were living among the native Patagonians after being deposited by an American sealing vessel that had either abandoned them or had foundered before being able to return. One was a German speaker, and with the aid of Kosmann, d'Urville questioned him and discovered that his name was 'John' Niederhauser and that he was originally a watchmaker from Berne, Switzerland. His companion was a young Londoner named George Birdine. Both were embarked as passengers, Niederhauser aboard the *Astrolabe* and Birdine aboard the *Zélée*.

D'Urville profited from the ethnographic information that the Swiss castaway, in particular, was able to share with him. He ordered his Swiss-educated secretary, Desgraz, and another German-speaking crew member, Charles Baur, from Strasbourg, to interrogate Niederhauser systematically in German and compile Patagonian equivalents for his existing multilingual vocabularies. Niederhauser also provided other general information, dismissing as fables reports that the Patagonians were giants. He also asserted that the Patagonian women were 'singularly lascivious' – a response perhaps tailored to tantalise men long deprived of female company. D'Urville wrote that he did not know whether Dumoutier, Ducorps or Desgraz, who had all sought permission to spend the night ashore, had 'tried to assure themselves of this fact'.[37] Although the phrenologist Dumoutier once more failed to 'palpate any a skull',[38] while ashore, the purser, Ducorps, encountered a valuable ethnographic informant in the form of a gaucho from Montevideo, who was married to two local women and had eight children. For his part, d'Urville thought that the local women – some of whom he noted had skin as fair as the women of his beloved Provence – were only 'passably' attractive for their sex. His comments about the appearance of an elderly woman he encountered the following day were even less gracious although not devoid of compassion. Aside from a survey of the bay (and Gente-Grande Bay on the opposite Tierra del Fuegan shore of the strait), the expedition naturalists collected a new species of *Senecio* (*S. laseguei*)[39] and a new species of tree iguana, *Proctotretus magellanicus* (*Liolaemus magellanicus*).[40] The vast expanse of the Patagonian pampas reminded d'Urville of the Crimean steppes he had seen during his service aboard the *Chevrette*. Satisfied with their combined efforts and with his men healthy and in good spirits, d'Urville left the Strait of Magellan on 8 January.

The corvettes then sailed to Staten Island – separated from the southeastern tip of Tierra del Feugo by Le Maire Strait – before plunging east-southeast. Increasingly, they were swallowed up by fog. The temperature also fell rapidly as they entered the belt of water we now know as the Antarctic Convergence. On 15 January, the first floating ice was sighted, and the icebergs appeared larger and larger as the day progressed. Aboard the *Astrolabe*, Lieutenant Barlatier-Demas recorded ice that peaked 39 metres above the surface of the sea and made him puzzle over the forces and the lapse of time required to create such a frozen mass.[41] In the rain, sleet and fog, heightened vigilance became crucial – not simply to guard against icebergs, but for the two corvettes just to maintain visual contact. D'Urville hoped to catch sight of Clarence Island, part of the South Shetland group, but by 18 January, the current and the wind had already driven him beyond 61°S. That day, d'Urville also recorded an iceberg that was at least 50 metres above the level of the sea.

On 20 January, at 62° 3′S, the expedition reached the same latitude where the British sealing captain George Powell had encountered pack ice. As they were about to intersect with Weddell's route of 1823, they encountered an iceberg at least two kilometres wide and extending 66 metres above the sea. Plentiful numbers of petrels, penguins and finback whales were also observed. So far south in the southern summer, there was no longer any true night, just a crepuscular half-light that persisted between 11.00 pm and 1.00 am. By 21 January, a dozen icebergs were regularly in view. D'Urville remarked that at the level they battled the waves, the ice was 'the most beautiful blue of ultramarine'; the rest was 'snow white with large fissures'. Yet the beauty of the marvellous spectacle was ever tinged with dread. The following day, d'Urville wrote: 'nowhere else can man feel more strongly the conviction of his own impotence … It is a new world unfolding before our eyes, but a world that is inert, lugubrious and silent, where everything menaces the extinction of the faculties. If anyone had the misfortune to be abandoned there, no resources, no consolation, no spark of hope, would ease his last moments.' He added that it brought to mind the inscription on the gates of Dante's Inferno (Canto III): *Lasciate ogni speranza, voi ch' entrate*/All hope abandon, ye who enter.[42]

The expedition soon encountered the edges of the ice shelf, so d'Urville decided to follow its frozen length eastwards in the hope of then taking Weddell's route further south. The sea itself was very calm, and there was profound silence, not even broken by the few wheeling petrels in the sky. However, by 24 January, at 64° 23′S, it became obvious that where Weddell had supposedly found open sea in 1823, it was now frozen. Clearly, if Weddell had sailed south from here (and d'Urville was not entirely convinced), it must have been during a significantly warmer season. Nevertheless, d'Urville had now confirmed the non-existence of Benjamin Morrell's 'New South Greenland'.

The corvettes then sailed north, with the ice continuing to offer remarkable displays. At sunrise on 25 January, it seemed to d'Urville that he was in view of 'an immense city of white marble, with its palaces, domes, spires, arcades and bridges fallen into ruin'.[43] On 26 January, the summits of the South Orkney Islands were seen projecting from the mist some 50 kilometres ahead. D'Urville had hoped to chart these islands more accurately and to replenish his meat supplies by hunting for seals and penguins ashore. Unfortunately, an attempted landing was thwarted by violent contrary winds, sleet and fog in the Lewthwaite Strait. On deck for long periods, shivering uncontrollably and in constant pain, d'Urville was obviously gripped in hypothermia by the wind chill and, not surprisingly, reduced to near 'total exhaustion'.[44] He wisely decided to stand off Cape Faraday for the night, but his renewed attempt to land the following day was equally successful, and he had to content himself with a running survey of the islands. However, even this remained no simple matter in the heavy seas and severe weather conditions. For d'Urville, the wind blew 'with unequal violence', but the obligations of command in such dangerous waters forced him to remain on deck. Once more, he manifested the symptoms of exposure: 'a frightful headache, accompanied by nausea and uncontrollable shivering'.[45]

On 31 January, the swell diminished, but d'Urville spent much of the day prostrate in his cabin. He was informed that three other crewmen were similarly affected by their ordeal and he was convinced that there would be more if the bad weather continued. By 3 February, the expedition's route once more intersected with Weddell's route. D'Urville decided on yet another southern descent. While there was renewed optimism among the entire crew, no doubt mindful of the bonuses they had been promised, the men worried that their commander might give up prematurely. For his part, d'Urville declared: 'When I give up, none of them, I believe, will have any desire to push on any further.'[46]

The following day, they once again encountered the ice shelf at 62° 20′S and 39° 28′E (Paris meridian), but shortly after midday, through the fog and falling snow, there seemed to be an opening or at least penetrable ice ahead. D'Urville decided to gamble on the strength of the corvettes' reinforced hulls and crash through. It would also be the first trial of the ice-saw fixed to the beakheads of the bows. The *Astrolabe* led

'Coup de vent près des Îles Powell le 27 janvier 1838, parages Antarctiques', lithograph by E. de Laplante, after a sketch by Louis Le Breton, Voyage au pôle sud et dans l'Océanie, Atlas pittoresque, Paris, 1846, vol. i, plate no. 16. The expedition first sighted the summits of the South Orkney Islands, which include Powell Island, on 26 January 1838. D'Urville had hoped to chart these islands more accurately and to replenish his meat supplies by hunting for seals and penguins ashore. Unfortunately, an attempted landing was thwarted by violent contrary winds, sleet and fog in the Lewthwaite Strait. National Library of Australia, PIC S11149

the way. Unfortunately, the first impacts quickly loosened the nails that held her ice-saw in place, and it soon detached and sank without trace. The *Zélée* followed in the *Astrolabe*'s wake. Her ice-saw was also quickly loosened as she battered the ice, but it was secured with a rope and heaved on deck just before the last nail gave way. Despite the continuous snow, which reduced visibility to a mere 600 metres, just before 3.00 pm, it became evident that the two corvettes had entered a basin of about three kilometres in diameter. This was presumably a pocket of sea between icebergs calved from the shelf and the floes and pack-ice, swirling and re-congealing with the force of the wind and currents, and the temperature changes on the periphery. Seals lay on the low-lying ice watching them. It was obvious that there would be no progress beyond this frozen ice-strewn cauldron, but to exit from the channel they had just cut, the corvettes would firstly have to come about and avoid entering the lee of the walls of ice; otherwise they would have no wind for manoeuvre. It was decided to moor the vessels to seemingly stable floes and conduct magnetic inclination observations before departure. The

Astrolabe was even visited by a group of officers from the *Zélée* bearing a celebratory bowl of punch. After weighing up the potential hazards, a weary d'Urville allowed himself to fall into a deep sleep. Unfortunately, he had underestimated the stability of their mooring and, indeed, the whole basin, and at 11.00 pm, he was awakened by a strange new sound, as if the corvette was 'touching against rocks'.[47] The prolonged noise and shuddering was in fact the sound of floes and pack ice colliding and scraping along the *Astrolabe*'s sides with the force of the wind. Powerless to do anything in the icy morass, d'Urville decided to return to his cabin but asked the officer of the watch to call him if the wind menaced them with an iceberg.

D'Urville woke at 2.00 am on 5 February and at first he could not find the *Zélée* in the fog of the basin. When he finally located her, she was 800 metres off and, like the *Astrolabe*, surrounded by ice and completely blanketed with snow. At 4.30 am, he signalled Jacquinot to set sail. Both corvettes began to batter their way through the ice, with the *Astrolabe* in the lead. Like captive birds hoping for freedom and flinging themselves against the bars of a cage, it did not take long for them to come to an abrupt halt. If the cage would not yield to the corvettes under sail, then they would have to be hauled forward with the capstan. Accordingly, men were lowered onto the ice to attach ropes to stable anchoring points and to use picks, crowbars and mattocks to pry free the bows and flanks of each vessel. Despite the zeal of the sailors for the exhausting work, their progress was suddenly thwarted by a change in the wind direction. Fearful that his ships would be trapped and crushed, d'Urville saw no option but to retreat and try to smash his way through the west-southwestern perimeter. This also failed. During one of their deliberate collisions with the ice, he was even pitched head first over the poop deck, but fortunately, he was spared injury by a quick-thinking Barlatier-Demas, who managed to grab his commander's sleeve. Increasingly anxious about their dangerous predicament, d'Urville visited the *Zélée* to confer with Jacquinot. He returned buoyed by Jacquinot's steadfast confidence. Together they agreed to renew their attempt to breech the northern flank of the basin. Should they become separated in the process, they would rendezvous at 'Soledad Bay' (Berkeley Sound) in the Falkland Islands and then proceed to Valparaiso or return to France, depending on the damage inflicted by the ice and the extent of necessary repairs.

With a favourable wind, the two corvettes made rapid progress some five to six kilometres to the north, sailing parallel, but at exactly 10.00 am, the wind no longer sufficed to propel them through the ice. Once more the crews were put to work winching the corvettes forward with their capstans and ropes, and with picks and crowbars to break the ice at the bows. Progress was painfully slow. At one point, no impression could be made on a floe that was 'harder and more encased than its neighbours'.[48] This obliged a long and laborious diversion. Ten hours of labour had given them an additional one and a half kilometres. Despite the danger and frustration – or perhaps because of it – when off duty, the officers and men played like schoolboys on the ice and hunted seals to feast on their dark oily flesh. (D'Urville would eat only seal livers, which he declared tasted like pork; unwittingly, in the process he was ingesting potentially toxic quantities of Vitamin A.[49])

More than 24 hours had now elapsed since they had first made their way into the ice basin. At 8.00 pm, the *Astrolabe* had to be secured with ropes when strong winds threatened her with a piled-up mass of floating ice in what d'Urville called the form of a 'dolmen'.[50] As they waited for the danger to pass, he managed to sleep for an hour and a half. When he awoke, the floating mass was a mere 30–40 metres away, but soon after, he was amazed to find the *Astrolabe* in an area of clear water. He seized the opportunity to sail another two or three kilometres in the direction of the open sea – despite the reservations of Roquemaurel and Marescot, who were worried about exposing the corvette to further risks in the diminishing light. At midnight, he went to sleep again and was roused at 3.00 am (already daylight in the Antarctic summer), only to learn that the *Astrolabe* was surrounded by consolidated ice. The *Zélée* was less than two kilometres away to her lee. Despite three hours' labour attacking the ice around the *Astrolabe* with hand tools and attempting to haul with the capstan, she would not budge, and the sails could offer no assistance because the wind was contrary. Enormous pressure was now bearing on her hull, which had risen 20–30 centimetres above what had been the waterline. The snow that covered the rigging had also turned to ice.

On 8 February, as the swell began to rise, the immense sheet of floating ice that surrounded the corvettes started to oscillate discernibly. At one stage, it was as if the French were witnessing an earthquake when a valley of ice, covered in snow, subsided before their eyes. D'Urville ordered the reinforcing of the rudder to protect it from the shock of the moving ice. Spirits were still high, and the crews were still healthy, although more and more cases of ophthalmia were reported because of the 'perpetual whiteness and monotony of the snow and ice'.[51] Throughout that day, all they could do was deal with individual threats. A floe that menaced the *Astrolabe*'s chain-wale was demolished. It seems that this heavy labour was harnessed for additional purpose: d'Urville appears to have been referring to his water tanks when he wrote that 'five double kilolitres were filled with ice' as a consequence. Yet still, the 'corvette did not move a centimetre'.[52]

The following day, there was renewed hope when the wind changed to the southeast. The *Zélée* remained less than two kilometres astern of the *Astrolabe*, but d'Urville was determined that they should break out together. For more than two hours, the *Zélée* made little appreciable progress, but at 10.00 am, the wind suddenly

'L'Astrolabe *arrêtée par un glaçon avant sa sortie de la banquise, 9 février 1838',* lithograph
by Auguste-Etienne-Francois Mayer, after a sketch by Louis Le Breton, Voyage au pôle sud et
dans l'Océanie, *Atlas pittoresque, Paris, 1846, plate no. 24. During its first Antarctic descent, the
expedition repeatedly had to batter its way through the ice. If the ice did not yield to the corvettes
under sail, then they had to be hauled forward with the capstan. Accordingly, men were lowered
onto the ice to attach ropes to stable anchoring points and to use picks, crowbars and mattocks
to pry free the bows and flanks of each vessel. It was exhausting work in sub-zero conditions.*
National Library of Australia, PIC S11157

grew stronger and she quickly made up the distance to her sister ship. The *Astrolabe*
now cast off her moorings and managed to plough through several hundred metres
of the ice sheet before coming to an abrupt halt in front of 'a more voluminous' floe.
Labour at the capstan, with rope and grappling hook anchored on the ice, enabled
her to round the obstacle, and by the time she reached the outer ring of the pack ice,
she had covered about five kilometres. After another three hours and 45 minutes of
similar concerted labour, the *Astrolabe* had cut through the ice sheet, and d'Urville
was relieved to discover that ahead of them was only unconsolidated frazil ice.[53] He
ordered all his men back on board immediately but to his horror, Antoine-Henri Aude,
the chief caulker, was left behind as the corvette pulled away. Aude ran in pursuit of the
Astrolabe, jumping from one piece of ice to another and, amazingly, caught up and was
dragged aboard. It would seem that he was drenched in the process, for he developed a
very serious case of pleurisy and took a year to recover. In the meantime, the *Zélée* had

broken free. Five minutes later, the *Astrolabe* was also delivered from the jaws of the ice. There were spontaneous expressions of joy from the sailors, and d'Urville made a promise to himself 'to be more prudent in the future and to have much more respect for the ice floes'.[54]

D'Urville's immediate priority on escaping the ice was to confer with Jacquinot and determine what damage the *Zélée* had sustained. He was relieved to learn that, aside from the loss of her ice-saw, a 'good part' of her copper sheathing and some spars, the *Zélée* was intact and had not taken in 'a drop of water more than before'. They could resume their itinerary according to their instructions. The sky remained dark and brooding, but the iceblink from the vast frozen apron of the Antarctic illuminated the horizon. Heavy seas and a gale from the south-southeast made for a piercing wind chill. The corvettes remained festooned with icicles, and the encumbered ropes could not pass through the pulley-blocks. The slightest manoeuvre became extremely arduous for the crews. Both vessels pressed on, although the *Zélée* lagged behind, presumably because of drag engendered by the ragged copper sheathing on her hull.

On 10 February, d'Urville profited from a sufficiently clear sky to conduct astronomical observations and determine their precise position. For another five days, they followed the edge of the ice pack east with the intention of sailing to the South Sandwich Islands. However, on 15 February, when the winds thwarted this prospect, d'Urville decided to sail west back to the South Orkneys and then to the South Shetland Islands. The bleak weather and frequent fog made this passage dangerous. On the way, they passed a massive ice floe 11 kilometres long, in company with smaller floes of two and a half and three kilometres in length. The next day, the corvettes passed within five or six kilometres of the north coast of mountainous Laurie Island in the South Orkneys, which they had first sighted three weeks before. They also approached the northern coast of Saddle Island, a little more than three kilometres long and so named by Weddell for its twin peaks and rocky waist, reminiscent of a pommel, seat and cantle. A party from the *Astrolabe*, under the command of Ensign Marescot and with Vincendon-Dumoulin, Gourdin and Le Breton on board, was ordered to land on the island's south coast. Marescot was frustrated by the strong currents so instead landed on Weddell Island immediately to the south, followed by Dubouzet and Le Guillou in another boat from the *Zélée*. Despite a covering of snow and ice on a collapsed cliff, clues to the island's sedimentary and metamorphic past were revealed by specimens of 'whitish-grey limestone and phyllitic schists'.[55] The landing parties also added to the expedition's store of fresh provisions by killing a large number of sea birds.

After passing Cape Bowles on the southern tip of Clarence Island and then Cape Lookout on the southern coast of Elephant Island, d'Urville wanted to sail between Gibb Island and Aspland Island (also part of the South Shetland group), but the westerly wind and the increasing swell dictated a more prudent south-southeasterly course. On the morning of 26 February, the corvettes reached Bridgeman Island, essentially the eroded tip of a volcano that rises 240 metres above sea level. Ensign Duroch was ordered to attempt a landing on its steep, burnt-brick-coloured flanks, in company with Hombron and Ducorps. A boat crew from the *Zélée* was also dispatched. The attempt failed because of the strong westerly swell and because even the leeward side of the island offered no landing place.

D'Urville counted 72 icebergs and floes as they approached 63°S and proceeded into what is now known as the Bransfield Strait. On 27 February, the expedition headed due south. Between 6.00 and 8.00 pm, the sky cleared and a high mountain was sighted on the southern horizon. D'Urville was convinced that this was one of the mountains the Irish-born navigator Edward Bransfield had reported sighting in early 1820, despite a discrepancy of more than 10′ in latitude and 20′ in longitude, so he named the mountain in Bransfield's honour. The cape below the mountain he named Cape Dubouzet in honour of Jacquinot's second-in-command.[56] Extending to the southwest, he could see a coast, which he named 'Terre Louis-Philippe' in honour of the monarch who had sponsored his expedition. To the east, he could also see land, which he named 'Terre Joinville' in honour of the king's son, the prince de Joinville. In honour of the navy minister, he named an island between the two land masses 'Île Rosamel'. In 1902, the Swedish polar explorer Otto Nordenskjöld realised that part of what d'Urville had named 'Terre Joinville' was, in fact, an island divided by a strait. That island was named in honour of d'Urville, whom Nordenskjöld declared 'must be esteemed the real discoverer of the whole of this coast'.[57] D'Urville followed the ice-bound northern coast of Terre Louis-Philippe in a southwesterly direction, approaching the Antarctic mainland on two occasions and naming one mountain on the elevated coast after Jacquinot and another after himself; in addition, he named capes after Roquemaurel[58] and Goupil.

During a period of calm on 1 March, a boat party made a failed attempt to use a grappling hook to mount the ice and then go ashore to conduct magnetic intensity studies; the ice was simply too hard for the hook to bite and hold. Aside from sea-water temperature studies at depth, some natural science was undertaken in these waters with the collection of the type specimen of a new species of brown marine alga, named in honour of Honoré Jacquinot. Camille Montagne initially placed this seaweed in the genus *Scytothalia*, but in 1907 the Swedish botanist Carl Skottsberg, who took part in Nordenskjöld's expedition, placed *S. jacquinotii* in the genus *Cystosphaera* (Phaeophyceae).[59]

Late on the morning of 2 March, not long after sighting a small offshore island, which d'Urville named after the *Astrolabe*, the wind blew them to the southeast at a speed of three knots. Vast glaciers appeared to dominate the coast when they could see it, but in the gathering fog they were frequently forced to navigate blind. On 3 March, d'Urville thought that he had entered the mouth of a 'channel or a deep recess', which he named the 'Canal d'Orléans' in honour of King Louis-Philippe's family. This seemed to him to separate Louis-Philippe Land from the Trinity Peninsula (and what we now know as Trinity Island), first sighted by Edward Bransfield. D'Urville thought it might connect to Hugues Bay. It would be six decades before the Belgian explorer Adrien de Gerlache de Gomery would disprove the existence of such a channel.[60] Louis-Philippe Land was, in fact, the tip of the Antarctic Peninsula. However, Otto Nordenskjöld retained d'Urville's name 'Orléans Channel' on his chart for the waters between the offshore Trinity, Pendleton (Tower) and Astrolabe islands to the north and the Antarctic coast of the Louis-Philippe Peninsula to the south. Today it is sometimes called the 'Orléans Strait', but it remains a mere sub-strait of the Bransfield Strait.

On 5 March, d'Urville named the Dumoulin Islets in honour of Vincendon-Dumoulin, but as the weather conditions began to deteriorate – bringing falling temperatures, rain and almost continuous fog – he was forced to reconsider his continued survey of the perilous waters of the Antarctic coast. The *Astrolabe* and the *Zélée* began their retreat across the Bransfield Strait early on the morning of 6 March. Although d'Urville hoped to sight Middle Island (part of the South Shetlands group), the fog en route made this impossible. Rain and snow also beat down on the corvettes, and the wind began to rage from the south-southwest. After rounding ice-bound Deception Island and then Snow Island, the expedition entered the Drake Strait and finally the Pacific Ocean. By then there was another menace to contend with: scurvy had made an ominous appearance among the men. D'Urville ordered the distribution of fruit punch, but by 20 March, aboard the *Zélée* alone, there were 31 cases of the disease, 20 of them bedridden. D'Urville ordered a course for the Chilean port of Talcahuano via the tempestuous seas south of Cape Horn. Their first Antarctic foray was at an end.

26

Return to Chile

… whole oceans away, from that young girl-wife I wedded …
leaving but one dent in my marriage pillow – wife? wife? –
rather a widow with her husband alive!

Herman Melville [Ahab]*

The two corvettes reached Talcahuano on 8 April 1838. The return to the verdant coast of Chile was very welcome after weeks amid ice, snow and fog. By now, both d'Urville and Jacquinot had signs of scurvy, and one sailor aboard the *Zélée*, Aristide-Robert Le Preux, had succumbed to the disease. Another, Casimir Rouxel, would die less than a fortnight after their arrival, but the exact cause of his death is uncertain. D'Urville dispatched his medical officers and pursers to meet with the French vice-consul, Auguste Bardel, and to reprovision. Fresh fruit, meat and vegetables were soon distributed among the crews, and the worst scurvy cases were taken ashore. The expedition's passengers, Niederhauser and Birdine, finally returned to civilisation.

Since d'Urville's previous visit, the port of Talcahuano had been destroyed by a tsunami in the wake of an earthquake that also flattened nearby Concepción in 1835.[1] He was surprised to learn that General Ramón Freire was now an exile in Australia, a reminder of the political instability he had witnessed in Chile during his visit of 1823. (In fact, Freire soon left Sydney; d'Urville would meet him in Tahiti that September, and Dubouzet would even carry a letter to him from his wife.[2]) Freire had been on the losing side during the Civil War of 1829 and had failed in an armed expedition against Chile, launched from Peru, in 1836. This expedition, unpaid Peruvian debts, and a trade and tariff dispute in the wake of the Bolivian invasion of, and 'confederation' with, strife-torn Peru precipitated a Chilean declaration of war. At the Battle of Yungay in January 1839, the Chileans would smash the military power of the 'Supreme Protector' of the confederation, Andrés de Santa Cruz y Calahumana. No territory was annexed, but Chile's independence and commercial supremacy were thereby secured.[3]

France, like Britain, had recognised Andrés de Santa Cruz's Peruvian–Bolivian

* *Moby Dick* (1851), ch. 132

Confederation but, unlike Britain, had become directly embroiled in conflict with Chile's ally, Argentina, over trade and diplomatic issues. A week before d'Urville's arrival in Talcahuano, France's Rear Admiral Louis Leblanc had even begun an ill-considered blockade of the Río de la Plata and Buenos Aires. Fortunately for d'Urville, French naval intervention did not extend to Chile. While the British did not become active belligerents, they continued to maintain vessels in Chilean waters to protect their commercial interests. Vice-Admiral Charles Ross, the Royal Navy's commander-in-chief, Pacific Station, was in Talcahuano when d'Urville arrived. A short rotund man, he was aboard his flagship HMS *President*, a 52-gun frigate that had been stationed in South American waters since 1835. D'Urville and Jacquinot were invited aboard, but Ross apparently did not speak 'a word of French', and the pleasantries were left to Ross's second wife (who had lived in France) and to Captain James Scott, commander of the admiral's flagship. D'Urville and his officers would no doubt have been surprised to learn that Ross had commanded HMS *Northumberland* when she took Napoleon to exile on Saint Helena. While Ross seems to have remained circumspect about his part in Napoleon's far-flung banishment, d'Urville allowed the British officers to see all his 'charts, drawings and observations'.[4] The British were effusive in their praise and compliments, but d'Urville detected a certain irony in their comments, which led him to believe that they would have been less fulsome in their praise had his expedition surpassed the southern limits of Weddell's voyage. For his part, d'Urville could not resist a certain irony of his own when he commented in his journal on the domestic arrangements aboard HMS *President*: aside from Mrs Ross, the admiral had his sister-in-law, a child and several personal servants on board. D'Urville made reference to 'certain noises' emanating from his 'neighbours', normally 'more grave and more reserved' than the French. With confirmed condescension, he concluded that 'the presence of women on a vessel is excusable only in a case of absolute necessity'.[5]

Returning to the *Astrolabe*, d'Urville found Vice-Consul Bardel waiting for him. Aside from fresh provisions, one of the pressing matters d'Urville wanted to discuss was replacement copper sheathing for his ice-damaged corvettes. Bardel informed him that there was no copper to be had in Talcahuano or Valparaiso but suggested approaching the British. Consequently, d'Urville asked the consul to ask the commander of HMS *President* for 150 sheets and to provide an official undertaking to replace them as soon as fresh supplies became available. Captain Scott, who was about to sail for Valparaiso, agreed, but subject to the final approval of his admiral – now ashore with his family. Although Admiral Ross subsequently approved the arrangement, he was only prepared to release 70 sheets. This gave d'Urville sufficient copper for repairs – supervised by Roquemaurel, who careened the corvettes in Talcahuano – but left him no reserves.

Numerous French whalers were also anchored in the harbour during the expedition's sojourn. Two, the *Héva* and the *Georges* (500 tonnes) were from Le Havre. D'Urville was surprised by the youth and the American origins of the commander of the *Georges*, Captain Martin Caspar, who had taken up French citizenship in 1838.[6] He was also impressed by the intelligence and bearing of the skipper of the *Héva*, Captain Édouard Le Lièvre, destined at 35 years of age to become the first person to be buried in the French cemetery in Akaroa, New Zealand.[7] Although d'Urville did not meet Captain Pierre Largeteau, commander of the *Ville de Bordeaux* (826 tonnes), the finest whaler in the harbour, he was surprised to learn that the commander of such a magnificent French vessel had previously lost several ships yet still had 'enough confidence of the owners'.[8] Among three other French whalers was the *Rubens*, commanded by Captain Louis Rogerie. From the latter, Dumoutier would acquire the biggest skull in his collection: that of a young humpback whale. Yet another French whaler, the *Havre*, arrived on 23 April and anchored very close to the *Astrolabe* and *Zélée*. This was intentional, as her skipper, Captain Jean-Louis Privat, believed that his crew was on the verge of mutiny. D'Urville promised his assistance in re-establishing order, and within two days, Privat made a formal charge against his second-in-command. D'Urville had the insubordinate officer arrested and held in chains aboard the *Astrolabe* until the captain of the *Havre* requested his release – presumably after receiving an undertaking of good conduct.

The day before, d'Urville had court-martialled and punished two of his own sailors charged with insolence aboard the *Astrolabe*. One was sentenced to five days in irons on the deck; the other, a Breton sailor named Louis-Marie Brasquerh, received 12 lashes at the capstan. D'Urville, who had developed a repugnance for the use of the lash, wanted to punish both men with irons but bowed to his officers, who were determined to reassert what he called 'the big word *discipline*'.[9] To underline how counterproductive he thought violent punishment was, he noted that Brasquerh deserted soon after. Ultimately, there were seven desertions from the *Astrolabe* and two from the *Zélée* in Chile. Another two French whalers, the *Salamandre* (Captain James Thomas) and the *Aglaé* (Captain J. Labrée), arrived on 1 May, and a third, the *Courrier des Indes* (Captain Jacques Renouf) arrived on 12 May. The presence of so many French whaling vessels and possible financial inducements might explain the number of desertions d'Urville faced.

While in Talcahuano, d'Urville met the British vice-consul Robert Cunningham, whom he considered intelligent, able and well travelled. The conversation soon turned to the botanist Allan Cunningham (it is not known if they were related), whom d'Urville had befriended in New South Wales in 1824.[10] From the consul, d'Urville learned of the death of Allan's brother Richard, colonial botanist and director of the Sydney Botanic Gardens.[11] Consul Cunningham also shared reminiscences of James

Weddell and Peter Dillon. He discussed recent developments in the Pacific and informed d'Urville that Britain would soon annex New Zealand's North Island. (In his historical account, d'Urville declared that this 'did not surprise' him, adding that he was 'very surprised that they had not done so earlier'.[12]) On 25 April, d'Urville and Cunningham climbed nearby La Sentinelle together and enjoyed expansive views of Concepción and Penco (both devastated by the earthquake three years before), the Biobío River, Talcahuano harbour and the vast Pacific Ocean he was about to traverse yet again.

Although d'Urville would return to the heights of La Sentinelle to botanise[13] during the busy weeks ahead, he had no interest in visiting the ruins of Concepción – by then razed for the sixth time in its 300-year history (because of its unfortunate proximity to the convergent boundaries of the Nazca and South American tectonic plates). On 13 May, however, he took the *Astrolabe*'s yawl, in company with his Piedmontese servant Joseph (Giuseppe?) Camagne and Le Breton, to visit the settlement of Penco. After the earthquake, all that remained of its old Spanish fort were a few cannons poking from the rubble. While Camagne sought out provisions from the remaining locals and Le Breton sketched the ruins, d'Urville went hunting on the forested shore. He was not simply after game or natural history specimens, he was also looking for the site of the lignite deposit that had been used to supply the *Coquille* with stove fuel during his visit of 1823. D'Urville remembered that it was on a small eminence seven or eight minutes' walk above the village. With the aid of a local proprietor and miller, a Monsieur Mège – originally from Marseille but resident in Chile for nearly 20 years – he found it and located another deposit that had been used by the British explorer Frederick Beechey during the visit of HMS *Blossom* in 1826; the latter site appears to have been subject to subterranean fires and was abandoned. D'Urville's comments about these deposits are interesting because they reveal his appreciation of new technology and strategic commodities. He attempted to impress upon Mège that coal was valuable because 'steam navigation' was bound to 'arrive very soon' on the coasts of Chile and Peru.[14]

During their sojourn in Talcahuano, Dumoutier also undertook a number of excursions, mainly in pursuit of phrenology. However, the local Araucanían (Mapuche) Indians steadfastly avoided him and would not let him measure or feel their heads. In mid-May, he did manage to excavate seven or eight skulls from an indigenous burial ground in the Valle de la Mocha (on the Biobío River), but this was because the Christianised locals believed the cranial sutures marked the skulls as 'infidel'! When he raided Talcahuano cemetery on the same night and took 'another eight or ten skulls', d'Urville felt obliged to admonish him, politely it would seem, with 'some observations'.[15]

While in Talcahuano, d'Urville also met the American consul, Captain Paul

Delano.[16] He had lost his home in the earthquake and had built another on a hill overlooking the port. Originally from Fairhaven, Massachusetts, he too had lived in Chile for almost two decades and had played an important part in the development of the Chilean navy. D'Urville was particularly interested to learn that Delano had known Benjamin Morrell since 1823. Delano apparently also distrusted Morrell's 'veracity' and had nothing to say regarding Morrell's 'alleged meeting with the children of one of the surgeons of La Pérouse' – claims made on 20 June 1837 in a letter to the Société de géographie de Paris. D'Urville would later make additional enquiries about this matter with George Hobson, the American consul in Valparaiso, but gained no new information.[17]

With the corvettes careened, repaired and partially reprovisioned, and navigational astronomy and other scientific observations completed at Fort Galvez, the expedition made its farewells and set sail for Valparaiso on the morning of 23 May. This was to purchase additional supplies, to collect and forward mail, to rendezvous with the French corvette *Ariane* and to address the shortfall in crew numbers. D'Urville had already experienced his first difficulties with Le Guillou, who, unlike Hombron, 'continued to say that illness still existed among his men'. D'Urville believed that Le Guillou was only acting under a 'pretext of humanity',[18] but if men were to leave the expedition for medical reasons, arrangements had to be made for them. Replacements also had to be found, as they also had to be found for those who had deserted in Talcahuano.

The *Astrolabe* and *Zélée* made a rapid passage north and by midnight of the following day were outside Valparaiso harbour. Unfamiliar with the port, d'Urville decided not to enter in the dark; unfortunately, when the winds dropped the next morning, he was further delayed. The corvettes were greeted by a boat dispatched by the *Ariane* bearing a midshipman who delivered the expedition's mail. At first, d'Urville thought the bundle of letters contained nothing personal for him, but towards the bottom of the pile, there was an envelope addressed to him by Adélie in a barely legible hand. His heart was now beating wildly. Something about the envelope made him open it with dread. In it was a letter, dated 10 November 1837, that informed d'Urville of the death of his youngest son Émile (on 8 October 1837) in a renewed cholera epidemic in Toulon.[19] Adélie's letter, a flood of pain and despair, is today preserved among d'Urville's papers in the Archives nationales in Paris. The ink is visibly blotched with tears and it cannot fail to touch the heart of anyone who reads it:

> D'Urville, my friend, why are you not beside me, alone, isolated, without support, without help against my despair, forcing myself to live for the one who remains for us, for you, for whom I would give my life. Overwhelmed by my sorrows, when

all my memories assail me hearing the piercing cries of my children without seeing them again, what tragic fate, what punishment, why haven't I listened to you …
Oh, my Émile, so good, so affectionate, who had healed my wounds, why have you
been torn from me, why has heaven sent me children that I adore only to take them
back so cruelly. I am therefore accursed! You will receive two letters, without alarm.
That I was happy according to the first one. I had saved my son, he was returned to
life and I to happiness; when he was so well, I was to pay the doctor. In the middle
of the street the cholera struck. His face contorted, he was seized by diarrhoea, by
vomiting, everything went to the head, a much stronger cerebral fever. He gave out
heart-rending cries! In the convulsions the tongue was retracted. His eyes stared va-
cantly, he tore and bruised his head. The ignorant doctor did not heed me. After 12
days alternating between despair and hope, invoking the great God who punished
me, conserving to the last a mistaken hope … That cruel prophecy of your mother;
in your last days you will have no children. I understand. My head hurts so much,
it burns and I am always cold. The days are long, they were so short. I await Jules,
he thinks of his lessons, nothing but his lessons, no more love of children, no more
caresses. D'Urville my friend, return quickly. What will become of the one who remains. All day long alone and at night. I do not know where to write to erect a tomb.
I do not have him close to me. He was so beautiful. He did not [remain?] more than
20 hours. They took him from me. His hands so beautiful. When you receive this
letter you will have finished the work in the ice. You could return, could you not? It
is the only desire that I can have. Glory, honour, riches, I curse you, you have cost
me too much. I am still to blame for this voyage, it is still me who caused the death
of my son. Why was I born, wretch that I am? What a beautiful head my Émile had,
what suffering inside it. Come home, I beg you by the prayers that I send you, by
those of our angels. I no longer pray, God has cursed me.[20]

There was an additional letter from his son Jules, dated 20 November 1837, which
also pleaded for his return and reiterated the fragility of Adélie's health. Her hands now
shook so much, he told his father, that she could no longer write herself. Young Jules
informed his father that his mother had sought permission to reunite the remains of
all her deceased children in one tomb. He also told him of the friends who had been
the most support to his grief-stricken mother and of those who had written to her. The
reader senses his intelligence but also the early maturity so frequently engendered in
children who are forced to assume great responsibilities. (Not yet 12, he told his father
that Le Brun had written 'like an old bachelor and an egotist'![21]) The letters shocked
d'Urville profoundly and filled him with grief and regret. He struggled and failed to
compose himself as the expedition entered Valparaiso harbour with the aid of boats
sent by the *Ariane* and HMS *President*, both berthed nearby. Vincendon-Dumoulin
and other members of the crew 'could see the tears streaming down his face afflicted
with pain'.[22]

Despite his distress and anxieties for his wife and son, d'Urville would not cut short his voyage, and Adélie – despite her grief, isolation and fear – was forced to wait for her husband. In an era in which psychiatry and psychology were in their infancy, the only record we have of the treatment she received (for what must have been post-traumatic stress and severe depression) is Surgeon Jean-René Quoy coming to bleed her with leeches! In spite of this unpromising therapy, Adélie's letters to her husband eventually became calmer and more controlled, though not devoid of reference to her suffering. Surprisingly, they were written in near-faultless English, and it seems she took up the language in order to occupy herself more constructively as she waited for d'Urville's return.

Even before he had anchored in Valparaiso harbour, d'Urville had received a personal visit from Captain Malo-Bernard Duhaut-Cilly of the *Ariane* and a dinner invitation from Captain Scott and Admiral Ross aboard HMS *President*. He gave his apologies, explaining his bereavement and distress, and retired to his cabin to write a long letter to Adélie (which has not survived). The next morning, d'Urville and Jacquinot called on Duhaut-Cilly, who received them courteously. Born in Saint-Malo, he was the brother of Auguste-Bernard Duhaut-Cilly (whose two-volume account of circumnavigation d'Urville owned),[23] and had had a distinguished career at sea under the famous privateer Robert Surcouf aboard the *Revenant*, under Duperré on the *Bellone* at the Battle of Grand-Port (in which he was badly wounded), and aboard an earlier frigate named *Ariane* during a bloody engagement with HMS *Northumberland* off the Breton coast in 1812.[24] When d'Urville requested men to help meet the shortfall in his crew, it is not surprising that it brought a visible frown to Duhaut-Cilly's face. Officially, he was homeward bound, but he still had to round the tip of South America and traverse the South and North Atlantic, and was reluctant to part with men. (In fact, the *Ariane* was soon ordered to join Admiral Leblanc's blockade of the Río de la Plata.) D'Urville held the same rank as the battle-seasoned Duhaut-Cilly but had been promoted earlier. The latter replied that if the request for replacement crew members was an order based on d'Urville's technical seniority, he would comply. Ultimately, three of the five French sailors who joined the expedition in Chile were from the *Ariane*.

D'Urville soon met with the acting French consul-general in Valparaiso, Charles-Ferdinand de Cazotte, who took d'Urville and Jacquinot to call on 'Governor' Victorino Garrido. Rather than the 'Governor', Garrido was the elected deputy for Valparaiso and intendant of the army.[25] D'Urville was perhaps the willing tool of Cazotte, who was unhappy at the lack of diplomatic courtesies extended to France at the time. A few weeks before, the Chileans had ignored the feast day of King Louis-Philippe's patron saint, Phillip, on 1 May. As d'Urville put it, there had been 'no demonstration of politeness towards the French flag'.[26] Also, Garrido had supposedly slighted the commander of the French naval station, Henri de Villeneuve, by taking eight months to call on him. Garrido's lack of warmth towards France was perhaps not surprising, given French intervention on the Río de la Plata and diplomatic support for Chile's enemy the Peruvian–Bolivian Confederation.

Garrido had had a prominent role in the early stages of the conflict with the confederation. In August 1836, four months before war was officially declared, he had sailed to the Peruvian port of Callao, ostensibly on a good-will visit but actually to launch a surprise night attack, which captured three confederate ships. He had then been acting under the orders of the Chilean minister of war, the conservative Diego Portales. D'Urville was aware that Portales was now dead, murdered the previous October, and that Garrido – now the intendant in command of the campaign against Peru – had become one of the most powerful men in Chile. Despite this, d'Urville was surprised that he lived in a 'not very sumptuous' quarter of Valparaiso. On meeting Garrido, he found him to be 'a small man of about fifty years [in fact, he was almost 60], dry, sallow, with a bilious temperament. His manner, like his appearance, was embarrassing, without dignity, and nothing in him announced the habitual exercise of high office.'[27] Although the meeting had unpromising beginnings, d'Urville was clearly pleased that Garrido received him and Jacquinot amiably and was soon visibly impressed by the scientific status of their expedition. D'Urville was also charmed by Garrido's attractive and intelligent young wife and regretted that he did not have more Spanish to converse with her.

Before he left Valparaiso, d'Urville sought to learn more about the activities of French Catholic missionaries in the Pacific. Not only were they a potential source of assistance to his expedition (as interlocutors for supplies from island communities and for linguistic and ethnographic information), he had responsibilities towards them as French citizens. Such intelligence gathering was characteristic of d'Urville and his preparations for an expedition or any leg of an expedition. He had already quizzed Captain Duhaut-Cilly about French missionaries. On 26 May, Consul de Cazotte took him to meet Father Charles-Auguste 'Chrysostôme' Liausu, a native of La Gardelle (Lot) and a member of the Congrégation des Sacrés-Cœurs de Jésus et de Marie, more commonly known as the 'Picpus Fathers' after their clandestine house, established in the rue de Picpus, Paris, during the Revolution. As early as 1825, Pope Leo XII had entrusted Catholic evangelism in the Sandwich (Hawaiian) Islands to this same religious order and appointed Father Alexis Bachelot, from Saint-Cyr-la-Rosière (Orne), as prefect-apostolic.[28] In 1833, Pope Gregory XVI had further divided 'Oceania' into several vicariates. The Picpus fathers were given jurisdiction over southern and eastern Oceania. Liausu – whom d'Urville met at Valparaiso's Franciscan friary – had been appointed vicar-apostolic for southern Oceania and had sailed to Valparaiso from

Bordeaux in December 1833. The following year, Father Étienne 'Jérôme' Rouchouze, from Chazeau (Loire), had been appointed vicar-apostolic of eastern Oceania, with the title of 'Bishop of Nilopolis', and had sailed from Le Havre on the *Delphine* to establish himself with a group of Catholic missionaries on Mangareva in the Gambier Islands.[29] Pope Gregory gave jurisdiction over western Oceania to the 'Société de Marie', better known as the Marists, an order founded in Lyon in 1816. Consequently, Jean-Baptiste Pompallier was consecrated 'Bishop of Maronea'. He had left Le Havre in December 1836 and sailed to Valparaiso, and then Tahiti and Sydney, before establishing himself in New Zealand in January 1838. Pompallier would become the first Catholic bishop of Auckland, but at the time, Liausu had no real idea where he was. He told d'Urville that he thought Pompallier was in the Caroline Islands. Liausu's own ministry was short-lived; he would die in September the following year of typhoid contracted from Chilean troops returning from the war with Peru.

D'Urville was also informed that his compatriot Abel-Aubert Dupetit-Thouars had taken two Picpus missionary priests to the Marquesas aboard the frigate *Vénus*: Father Laurent 'Louis de Gonzague' Borgella, from Sainte-Marie de Campan (Hautes-Pyrénées), and Father Joseph 'Dosithée' Desvault from Longaulnay (Ille-et-Vilaine). D'Urville was also informed that two Catholic missionaries had been expelled from Tahiti as a result of 'Methodist intrigue'. In 1837, this was also the fate of Father Alexis Bachelot in the Hawaiian Islands; he died soon after and was buried on the small islet of Na, off the coast of Pohnpei in Micronesia.[30] This sectarian rivalry would soon have profound repercussions, and protection of French Catholic missionaries would be the pretext used by Dupetit-Thouars for French annexation of Tahiti and other islands in Polynesia.

On the day d'Urville met Father Liausu, he was informed by Jacquinot of a bizarre rumour circulating in Valparaiso and, in particular, aboard the French vessels in the harbour. This rumour suggested that d'Urville's expedition was a failure, and that the *Astrolabe* and *Zélée* had not even entered the Strait of Magellan and had instead taken refuge at Concepción. One of the officers aboard the *Astrolabe* had even received a letter from an officer aboard Dupetit-Thouars' *Vénus* that suggested that the only option left open to d'Urville was to 'blow his brains out'. D'Urville declared that it was yet another proof of the 'base jealousy and lack of patriotism so common among the officers of our nation'.[31] He promptly resolved to counter the rumours with a public relations exercise and extended a dinner invitation aboard the *Astrolabe* to Charles-Ferdinand de Cazotte, Captain Duhaut-Cilly and two prominent local French merchants, Messrs. Hubert and Lamotte-Duportail. He then regaled them with sketches from the portfolios of his artists Goupil and Le Breton, and the charts drafted by Vincendon-Dumoulin and his other officers. They could not help but be impressed and soon realised that d'Urville had been the victim of calumny. Soon after, d'Urville showed the same sketches and charts to Victorino Garrido, who made a surprise visit to the *Astrolabe* dressed in a colonel's uniform and accompanied by his Italian-born aide-de-camp. D'Urville further flattered him by arranging a salute from the guns of the *Ariane*.

As a result of his successful ship-board reception for these dignitaries, d'Urville was invited to have a personal tour of Valparaiso with Auguste Lamotte-Duportail, who was originally from Saint-Servan in Brittany. He was particularly impressed by the elegant homes of the English residents overlooking the city, and his attention was also drawn to an artillery exercise in preparation for a planned offensive against the Peruvians by 5000 Chilean troops. D'Urville believed the war was very unpopular (and it certainly had been), but he failed to realise how the murder of Diego Portales had ultimately rallied public opinion in favour of the military campaign.

Despite the political gulf between them – Lamotte-Duportail was the conservative son of a royalist émigré and discernibly unsympathetic to the Revolution of 1830 – the two got on well enough for d'Urville to be invited to dinner. During their promenade, d'Urville had been surprised to learn that his guide was the son of Jacques-Malo La Motte du Portail, a veteran of d'Entrecasteaux's voyage in search of Lapérouse.[32] He was further surprised to learn that Lamotte-Duportail possessed his father's four-volume manuscript account of the historic voyage.[33] During dinner, d'Urville pleaded with his host to be able to see the manuscript and was soon entranced. He found the narrative to be in the form of letters written in a 'simple … pure and agreeable' style, but the account also filled him with melancholy when he reflected on the dangers, illnesses and privations he and d'Entrecasteaux had faced on their respective expeditions. In particular, d'Entrecasteaux's death, without being able to complete his personal account of his voyage, made d'Urville dread the prospect of others, with 'malevolent passions', misrepresenting his own intentions and actions should he die in the course of his expedition.[34]

On the eve of his departure from Valparaiso, d'Urville was visited by Father Liausu and two other clergymen. Liausu had taken up d'Urville's offer to carry letters to Bishop Étienne Rouchouze and Bishop Jean-Baptiste Pompallier in the Pacific. He also asked d'Urville to take them 283 and 1417 grams of gold respectively, and a quantity of chests and parcels, which he brought the following morning. The day of their departure, Liausu also wrote a letter pleading with d'Urville to use all his influence to dissuade his sailors from 'seducing the women of Manga-Reva' and destroying the 'pious efforts of the missionaries'. D'Urville sent a polite reply that he would have 'regard to his recommendation', and that he would seriously invite all his men to submit to his orders and to 'respect religion and good manners'.[35] On 29 May 1838, the *Astrolabe* was towed from Valparaiso harbour by the *Ariane*'s longboat. D'Urville had already authorised Jacquinot to depart as soon as the *Zélée* was ready and had nominated the Gambier Islands as their rendezvous point in case of separation. Both corvettes were soon under full sail.

27

The missionary isles

Consider this,
That in the course of justice none of us
Should see salvation.

William Shakespeare [Portia]*

D'Urville's first landfall, as he began his traverse of the Pacific, was Más a Tierra Island, in the Juan Fernández Archipelago, formed by volcanic eruptions some four million years ago. The archipelago was discovered and named by the Spanish navigator Juan Fernández in 1574, but d'Urville was very much aware that it was most famous for the four-year sojourn of the castaway Alexander Selkirk, who inspired Daniel Defoe's novel *Robinson Crusoe* (1719). On 3 June 1838, the *Astrolabe* and *Zélée* were not able to anchor because of contrary winds and calms, but Barlatier-Demas was given command of a boat and rowed ashore to conduct navigational astronomy and fix the island's longitude. He was accompanied by Vincendon-Dumoulin, who undertook geophysical (magnetic inclination) observations, and Hombron and Gourdin, who collected natural history specimens. To assist them, Jacquinot dispatched his half-brother Honoré and Tardy de Montravel in a boat from the *Zélée*.

The landing party encountered the vestiges of a small fort, fruit trees, several rusting cannons and a recently abandoned Chilean 'Botany Bay' – the same ragged penal settlement described by Richard Henry Dana in his memoir *Two Years Before the Mast*.[1] At first, the island seemed unoccupied, but when Honoré Jacquinot and Goupil examined some nearby caves (perhaps the same caves Dana recalled being used to confine convicts 'nearly half-way up the mountain' in November 1834[2]), they were surprised to encounter an elderly hermit with long white hair living with five or six large dogs. A bed, hunting equipment and goat and seal skins were seen inside the clean and tidy interior. In an age when many dreamt of distant islands either untouched by the corrupting hand of man, as encountered by Defoe's Robinson Crusoe, or as the setting for idyllic innocence and simplicity, as portrayed by Bernardin de Saint-

---

* *The Merchant of Venice* (*ca.*1596–98), act iv, scene i, lines 193–95

Pierre in his celebrated novel *Paul et Virginie* (1787), the underground refuge struck a romantic chord with Goupil, who sketched it. However, the hermit's dogs, goat and seal skins were all emblematic of profound ecological changes on the island. The local Juan Fernandez fur seals (*Arctocephalus philippii*) were driven nearly to extinction in the nineteenth century. The hermit was also a fisherman, and garlands of dried fish hung from the walls of his spacious cavern. At the entrance to the cave, the younger Jacquinot noticed two large recently caught groupers and sought to acquire one. The hermit made a gift of the fish, saying he could easily replace it, but Jacquinot insisted on reciprocating with the contents of his gunpowder flask – a precious commodity for a man so isolated.[3]

Both boats had returned to their mother-ships by 7.30 pm. The reports of the landing parties no doubt increased d'Urville's personal desire to visit an island with such interesting literary associations, but three days of contrary winds made it an unappealing prospect. While standing off Más a Tierra, he auctioned the personal effects of the sailors who had deserted the expedition. Ever mindful that the winning bids would ultimately be deducted from the modest wages owed to the sailors, d'Urville intervened when the prices became exorbitant, which was typical of his concern for his men and their families. He was happy that they were cheerful and content, yet he understood their capriciousness, their fateful resignation to perhaps not returning home and their tendency to live for the moment. Death could come suddenly. On 4 July, André Geolier, a small, gentle, even-tempered man from Le Palais (Morbihan), who was popular with the officers and his fellow sailors, lost his life. He had only recently recovered from scurvy when he was tragically knocked overboard by the flapping sheet of the foretop staysail while answering a call of nature perched on the portside guardrail of the bow. Caution would have dictated the use of the heads. With his trousers unbuttoned and his body very likely struck by the *Astrolabe*'s hull as she passed over him,[4] Geolier quickly disappeared. A boat was launched to search for him, but he was never seen again. D'Urville was left wondering how anyone could have embarked on such an expedition without being able to swim and why the naval authorities did not have a policy of instructing such men.

In late June, the expedition encountered the brig *Friends* (203 tonnes), with a crew of 37 English, American and Chilean sailors under the command of the English-born Captain Christopher James Rugg. She was bound for Tahiti[5] (and later Tonga, New South Wales and New Zealand)[6] via Mangareva. There was also a purported 'naturalist' on board, a man named Richardson, the captain's brother-in-law. Although Rugg claimed to be on a half-scientific, half-commercial voyage, Roquemaurel would later pass a severe judgement on his purported natural history and geographical work, and dismiss him and his crew as among the 'marauders' seeking to exploit 'all the industries' of the Pacific.[7] At this stage, d'Urville still intended to visit Easter Island, so he gave

Rugg mail for Tahiti and asked him to advise the French missionaries on Mangareva of his expedition's impending arrival. Because of adverse winds and days already lost, d'Urville was forced to abandon his plan to visit Easter Island (the eastern limits of the Polynesian world and famous for its megalithic sculptures), even though he was no more than 385 kilometres away from the island by 13 July. With frequent calms, the expedition continued to make slow progress toward Mangareva. D'Urville tried to occupy his men with target practice, using four new Potet breech-loading rifles that he had been assigned to trial, and by conducting sea-water temperature observations at depths of up to a 1000 fathoms (1828.8 metres).

Finally, at 6.30 am on 31 July, the *Astrolabe*'s lookout sighted Mount Duff (441 metres), the highest point on the central basaltic ridge of Mangareva. At 9.00 am on 1 August, a whale boat was seen approaching. It contained several Europeans and half a dozen islanders. Thanks to Captain Rugg, the expedition had been expected. The first person to greet d'Urville was comte Alonso de Florit de La Tour de Clamouze, known as 'Brother Urbain' on the island. He was an impoverished nobleman from Meyrueis (Lozère), the son of a former senior cleric who had contracted a civil marriage during the Revolution. Baptised at the age of 10 and educated by the Picpus fathers, he began his novitiate in October 1817 but did not to take his final vows or seek ordination.[8] Something of a free spirit,[9] he had joined the order's mission on Mangareva to teach literacy, numeracy and geography but also to offer important manual skills.[10] Lieutenant Dubouzet described him as 'the engineer, the architect and master carpenter of the islands'.[11] La Tour reminded d'Urville that they had already met in a Paris street some years before. Aside from the Mangarevan boat crew, La Tour was accompanied by two French sailors: one, named Alexis Marion, was from Normandy;[12] the other, Jacques (or Jacob) Guilloux, was a Breton from Audierne (Finistère); both were married to local women.[13] In the constant company of clergy, they appear to have lost the roughness that usually characterised the speech of sailors, and they seemed genuinely committed to the missionary enterprise on Mangareva. However, Guilloux was also engaged in lucrative pearling (the island's waters are rich in black-lipped pearl oysters) and had a 'singular mania', according to Ensign Pavin de La Farge, to become the monarch of one of the islands in the Pomotou Archipelago![14]

The *Astrolabe* and *Zélée* negotiated the passage through the coral and at 6.00 pm anchored in the lagoon between Mangareva and the southwest point of the smaller neighbouring island of Akamarou. After 64 days at sea, d'Urville was keen to enjoy some fresh food. The sailors aboard the two corvettes had already been fishing on the reef, so d'Urville sat down to dine from their catch. This was despite warnings from the Mangarevans that particular species were 'bad to eat'.[15] Almost certainly, the locals were warning of the risk of ciguatera poisoning. The symptoms of stomach pain, nausea and violent headache that d'Urville, Roquemaurel and Barlatier-Demas soon experienced would appear to confirm this. In some parts of the tropical Pacific (including northern Australian waters), the Caribbean and the Indian Ocean, humans can suffer from ciguatera if they eat fish that have fed on seaweed infested with toxic benthic dinoflagellates. Ciguatera poisoning can also occur after eating the flesh of larger carnivorous fish that have eaten smaller herbivorous fish already contaminated – thereby bio-accumulating the toxin.[16]

Soon after anchoring, d'Urville assigned Marescot to deliver the parcels addressed to the Catholic missionaries on the island. Vincendon-Dumoulin, Dumoutier and Le Breton went ashore with him to begin their work. Dumoutier had already been permitted to measure the heads of some of the Mangarevans who had come aboard the *Astrolabe* with La Tour. Soon after, another boat bearing the new local flag – adopted in 1837 and coloured white and blue, with stars representing each of the islands in the Gambier group[17] – delivered chickens and numerous breadfruit and coconuts as a gift from the island's monarch, King Te Maputeoa, who, when he was baptised in August 1836, had taken the name 'Gregorio I' in honour of Pope Gregory XVI.

Meanwhile, Roquemaurel and Barlatier-Demas began to search the coast for a suitable location for astronomical observations, and they, or Vincendon-Dumoulin, decided on using the summit of Mount Duff.[18] Although d'Urville continued to use Wilson's name for the mountain in his account, after questioning La Tour, he promptly reinstated local Polynesian names instead of those bestowed by European navigators.

On 5 August, d'Urville visited Bishop Rouchouze at the modest four-room, coral-block residence he shared with La Tour in the village of Rikitéa at the foot of Mount Duff. His initial purpose was to give Rouchouze the gold that he had carried from Valparaiso. The bishop's personal appearance seems to have matched his modest home. When Rouchouze visited the *Astrolabe*, d'Urville's secretary, Desgraz, described him as 'short in stature and ugly in appearance', and added that 'his bishop's robe, dirty and shabby, contributes nothing to the majesty of his person, but engenders feelings of pity by recalling the impoverished state of the man wearing it'.[19]

D'Urville was keen to see more of the island, so the bishop provided him with a Polynesian and a French guide. He soon 'rediscovered with joy' a coastal 'equatorial' flora of coconut palms, banana trees, *Pandanus*, breadfruit (*Artocarpus*), Tahitian chestnut (*Inocarpus*), candlenut (*Aleurites*), mulberry (*Broussonetia*), *Barringtonia*, *Thespesia* and *Hibiscus*. This was a cultural landscape containing many species introduced to Mangareva by the Polynesian settlers who began colonising the island in the ninth and tenth centuries. Yet d'Urville seems to have had a sense of deforestation when he observed that, as he climbed away from the coast, the mountainous centre of the island was '*no longer covered* other than with tall grasses'.[20]

Thanks to archaeological excavations and geochemical analysis of stone tools by Professor Marshall Weisler, we know that the Gambier Islands were once part of a wider trading network with the Polynesian islands of Pitcairn and Henderson. The local black-lipped pearl oyster shells (which made up to 10 fish-hooks each) were traded on Pitcairn for fine-grained basalt (unavailable in Mangareva and used to make adzes), and for obsidian on Henderson. In addition, fine-grained Pitcairn basalt was also transported by Mangarevans to Henderson for tool-making, while Mangareva's coarser vesicular basalt was exported for oven stones. The end of this trade around 1450 – apparently as a result of social collapse on Mangareva induced by unsustainable population growth and deforestation – had profound implications for Pitcairn and Henderson, resulting in the complete extinction of their populations by about 1600.[21] Even the echoes of Mangareva's comparatively recent past were traumatic. Roquemaurel recorded oral history that suggested that, as a result of 'cruel wars', the population that had been 'estimated in the past at 5[000] or 6000 souls, had been reduced to 2000 or 2800'. Both Desgraz and Roquemaurel recorded missionary references to past cannibalism, but the latter added that 'infanticide was very common' and that 'ultimately famine came several times to help war in the destruction of the children'.[22]

D'Urville returned to the bishop's residence to dine on roast duck and to discuss Polynesian linguistic questions. He had already grasped that the Mangarevan language 'belonged to the great Polynesian language', but ventured to assert that it was 'closer to the dialect of New Zealand than all the others'.[23] Despite remarkable affinities with Māori, it is closer to the languages of Tahiti, the Marquesas and Hawaii. Perhaps for this reason, Bishop Rouchouze gave d'Urville a Hawaiian grammar, which pleased him greatly. The bishop also proudly showed him a new chapel that had been constructed of coral blocks, with narrow windows and a thatched palm-leaf roof. D'Urville, however, found it hot and stuffy and expressed his decided preference for timber architecture in the tropics. Despite a number of misgivings, he was generally positive about the endeavours of the Catholic missionaries on Mangareva and sought to assist them as best he could with all the iron tools he could spare.[24] He and his men attended Mass, arriving in military formation, and did their best to lend prestige to the missionaries as their compatriots. D'Urville also used the guns of the corvettes to salute Bishop Rouchouze and bestowed gifts on the island's monarch in the name of King Louis-Philippe. Many of d'Urville's men were genuinely devout; but one did not have to be a believer to appreciate the beauty of the Latin rite given Polynesian choral form on Mangareva. Pavin de La Farge, for example, wrote poignantly:

Suddenly and as if by enchantment, there rose at the same astonishing time from the natives, a solemn, serious and expressive song, a form of canticle in the language of the country, which made me shiver with emotion, and stopped, so to speak, the beat of my heart. I have never felt such emotions. There was this magical impression that the ceremonies of the Middle Ages must have produced, when a whole people sang the canticles. The picturesqueness of the place and the people, the sea on one side, even the large drops of rain which fell from time to time, all had a character, all impressed ...[25]

Aside from his acolyte La Tour, and the resident former sailors Marion and Guilloux, Bishop Rouchouze was aided in his missionary efforts by Father Antoine 'Cyprien' Liausu from Vaylats (Lot), who had done some medical studies under Joseph Récamier in Paris and had established an infirmary on the island; and the turbulent theocrat Father Honoré-Louis-Jacques Laval, originally from Saint-Léger-des-Aubées near Chartres (Eure et Loire) but recently expelled from Tahiti as a result of the machinations of the Protestant missionary and British consul George Pritchard. D'Urville's patriotic fibres began to tingle as Laval recounted his experiences of ill-treatment in Tahiti. He would devote an entire chapter to documenting the affair and his officers were also affronted by the manner in which the British Methodists reportedly caricatured France.[26]

Like d'Urville, most of his officers were impressed by what the missionaries had achieved in so short a time and in such isolation: ending violent customs and superstitions, commencing formal education, improving agriculture, introducing European weaving techniques, easing arduous labour with simple machines and building impressive edifices of stone.[27] Some, like Desgraz, were amused by the manner in which the islanders adopted and mangled liturgical songs, which they sang at odd times and in odd circumstances in Latin, ironically, 'the language of a people who had disappeared from the globe so long ago'.[28] Others, like Coupvent-Desbois, questioned whether the Mangarevans were truly happier with their new wants. With eyes as blue as d'Urville's, he looked on and lamented the loss of charm suffered by women now wrapped head to toe in large camisoles for the sake of 'decency' and men 'enveloped in rags'. He wondered whether the 'free and proud' Mangarevans who had battled William Beechey might have been happier than those now 'disgracefully clad' in threadbare trousers and dirty ragged shirts. With admirable sensitivity, he asked: 'Was not Christian law large enough to accommodate the differences of climate and location, and to allow each people their distinctive character?'[29] While d'Urville did not specifically decry the burning of the effigies of the local gods that once stood on the ancient marae of Managareva, he seems to have been pleased to find surviving carved examples in the interior of the island[30] and to confirm a consistent theogony

'*Messe célébrée par Monseigneur l'évêque de Nilopolis à Manga-Reva*', *lithograph by Adolphe-Jean-Baptiste Bayot, from a sketch by Ernest Goupil,* Voyage au pôle sud et dans l'Océanie, *Atlas pittoresque, Paris, 1846, vol. i, plate 44. D'Urville and his men attended Mass on the Pacific island of Mangareva, arriving in military formation to lend prestige to their compatriots, Bishop Rouchouze and his fellow French Catholic missionaries.* National Library of Australia, PIC S11179

with New Zealand and Tonga. There is also a definite tone of pity in his comments about the arduous labours of the islanders who were cutting large coral blocks for the island's planned Catholic cathedral. He felt their efforts could have been better directed and, in contrast, gave his approval to their road-building work. He also wrote with compassion and sensitivity of his meeting with a dignified elderly man who was determined to die adhering to the faith of his ancestors.

A week before departing from the island, d'Urville returned to botanise on the slippery precipitous slopes of Mount Duff with the *Astrolabe*'s Strasbourg-born storeman, Charles Baur, and Motoua, the uncle of King Gregorio Te Maputeoa. Normally d'Urville towered above everyone he met, but at 190 centimetres, Motoua – the island's wizened former high priest, now zealous Christian neophyte – was a giant of a man six centimetres taller than d'Urville. The excursion yielded no plant species that d'Urville had not already collected in Tahiti or Tonga; similarly, the entomology of the island proved very limited, and the personal selection he was permitted to make from La Tour's collection of local seashells also yielded no new species. The most spectacular event of the day, which gave the Mangarevans great amusement, was the near-sighted Charles Baur stumbling and then sliding down much of the flank of Mount Duff on his posterior. One new plant species was collected on Mangareva by Hombron and published by Camille Montagne: *Phragmicoma aulacophora* (*Acrolejeunea aulacophora*).[31] A liverwort that grows among mangroves, it was probably found on the coast. Surveying the shore, Hombron and Honoré Jacquinot also discovered two new crab species: *Etisus punctatus* (Xanthidae)[32] and *Thalamita coeruleipes* (Portunidae).[33]

As a final gesture of goodwill, on 13 August, the day after attending Mass with his men, d'Urville put the carpenters of both the *Astrolabe* and *Zélée* to work on a number of unfinished building projects on the island. Two days later, the expedition set sail for the Marquesas.

The corvettes reached Nuku Hiva on 25 August and anchored the following day in Taio Hai Bay, alongside a three-masted American whaler, the *Roscoff*. Female islanders, wearing nothing more than loincloths, soon swarmed around the vessels seeking to trade sexual favours. Some were little more than children. To avoid chaos, d'Urville ordered the raising of the boarding nets but promised to allow the women on board that evening. The pent-up frustrations of months at sea and the sojourn in prudish Mangareva exploded in orgiastic copulation when the evening gun was fired at 6.00 pm and the nets were dropped. D'Urville, constrained by the proprieties expected of him and personal fidelity to Adélie, withdrew monastically to his cabin, giving strict orders that he was not to be disturbed by any of the women. Despite his racist dismissal of the physical charms of the Marquesan women and proffering the notion that his age and infirmities made sexual restraint easier for him than for his ardent young officers and men, the carnal mayhem on deck cannot have banished all sensual reveries or made sleep easy. And mindful of the finger-pointing of pious wowsers once he returned home, he excused the liberties he had permitted by suggesting that it was better that his men were safe on board than lured ashore and subject to danger. Despite turning a blind eye to the women prostituting themselves on his vessels, he gave orders that none were to be transported in any of the expedition's boats; they would have to swim. He had already forbidden any trade in gunpowder for sexual favours, worried that precious munitions would be debased as a currency for fresh provisions and have other negative social consequences. Unfortunately, the trinkets that had served d'Urville so well in the past on other islands were now unwanted, and Ducorps had to trade 9 kilograms of gunpowder for just five pigs, although one of these beasts weighed almost 90 kilograms.

Ashore, d'Urville found no sign of the French missionaries that Dupetit-Thouars had supposedly left on the island, but he did find eight foreigners, mostly deserters of dubious character. One, an American named Hutchinson, became d'Urville's guide ashore; two others – an American named Rodgers and an Englishman named Alfred –

would apparently join the expedition as temporary crewmen as far as the Netherlands East Indies. They are not listed on the muster-rolls, but an Englishman named Frederick Cuwths (if that was his real name) is recorded as having been recruited at Nuku Hiva.[34]

The *Astrolabe* and *Zélée* spent a week in Nuku Hiva, during which Vincendon-Dumoulin conducted survey work and also sowed the seeds of the book (of more than 360 pages plus charts) that he and Desgraz would co-author: *Îles Marquesas ou Nouka-Hiva* (Arthus Bertrand, Paris, 1843). Marescot was assigned to draft a chart of the bay. Meanwhile, Dumoutier made still more comically inept attempts to measure the heads of the locals. Goupil had more success sketching a local chief named Nia-Nidou, and Le Guillou drafted portraits of one of the local women and of a chief named Maté-Oumo, both heavily tattooed, that were later re-worked and lithographed for publication in the first volume of his *Voyage autour du monde*. Le Guillou also visited the interior of the island with an American named Hamilton. Not long after he set off, a disturbing rumour reached Midshipman Gervaize, from another two Americans, that Le Guillou had been killed by the islanders. This was promptly reported to d'Urville, who immediately considered punitive action. Jacquinot, however, counselled d'Urville to use his planned official inspection of both corvettes, heralded with a four-gun salute, as a means of making an impression of French power. He also conducted small arms and gunnery drill that left the island's monarch, Queen Patini,[35] quivering. In fact, it frightened off all the local women, who did not visit the corvettes that night. Fortunately, the reports about Le Guillou proved groundless, and he was soon seen in the distance, returning in good health and spirits. His visit had awakened strong Rousseauist sentiments, and he declared to his European readers: '... man here is naked, completely naked, he does not want your clothes; the houses here are incomplete, he does not want your very closed habitations; the commerce he had, gave some enjoyments of life, he does not want your commerce'.[36]

On 3 September, d'Urville ordered the expedition to weigh anchor and set a southwesterly course for Tahiti. From the captain of the *Roscoff*, he had received further disturbing news of events in the Society Islands, in particular that the American consul, Jacques-Antoine Moerenhout, had been stripped of his office for giving sanctuary to the Picpus fathers Honoré Laval and François Caret, and that he and his wife had then been severely beaten by thugs supposedly incited by the Methodists. Although his men were excited at the prospect of visiting an island made famous by Wallis, Bougainville and Cook, d'Urville had less romantic notions, thanks to his visit of May 1823.

En route, d'Urville searched for an island named 'Tiberonnes' (perhaps derived from *tiburón*, Spanish for shark), which his American guide on Nuku Hiva, Hutchinson, had reported to him. Despite a very clear horizon, it could not be located within 40 kilometres of the nominated position, so d'Urville concluded that it was probably an imaginary isle. On 9 September, the expedition sighted Point Venus on the north coast of Tahiti, where James Cook observed the transit of Venus in 1769, and then the entry to Matavai Bay to the southeast, where Cook anchored. Some five kilometres off the point, they were approached by a canoe bearing a Polynesian man (a chief named Pewewe), dressed in European clothes, expecting to pilot the corvettes to an anchorage in the bay. However, he was dismissed because d'Urville wanted to impress upon him that he knew the harbour and because he did not want to submit to the 'rights of pilotage established by the missionaries'.[37] Shortly after anchoring, yet another canoe approached the *Astrolabe*. It bore a former shipbuilder turned missionary named John Rodgerson, who genuinely sought to extend a warm welcome. He was no doubt taken aback when d'Urville, pacing the deck, immediately began a tirade about George Pritchard and the treatment of the French missionaries Laval and Caret. D'Urville declared that he had come expressly to 'gather definite information on this event' and that his conduct 'would depend' on what he learned. Rodgerson replied defensively that it was 'unfair to hold a whole society responsible for the faults of one man' and added that he thought that the 'war was finished' and that 'peace was made between the French and Tahiti'.[38] Now it was d'Urville's turn to be surprised. He was unaware that the *Vénus* had anchored a few days earlier at Papeʻete to the northwest and that Captain Dupetit-Thouars had extracted 2000 piastres in reparations. Furthermore, he had appointed Jacques-Antoine Moerenhout French consul and had even given him a 21-gun salute. All French citizens would now ostensibly be received in Tahiti as the subjects of a friendly nation.

A conciliatory d'Urville now assured Rodgerson of the 'goodwill and interest' he had for the British missions and which he had 'publicly manifested in his writings'.[39] Rodgerson and his wife, Ellen, were recent arrivals in Tahiti after spending three fruitless years attempting to spread the Christian gospel in the Marquesas. When Rodgerson politely offered assistance to the French expedition, d'Urville seized the opportunity to have Desgraz 'procure from him information on the idioms of Nouka-Hiva and Taïti'.[40] He also invited Rodgerson to join him in his cabin for refreshments. The two clearly became friends. D'Urville would later meet Rodgerson's family, delight in his young children, share his remaining European seed stock with him and give him one of the expedition's commemorative medallions.

At 6.30 pm, d'Urville and Jacquinot went ashore to visit Charles Wilson, the 68-year-old doyen of the missionaries, whom they had both met during their first visit to Tahiti in 1823. Not surprisingly, the recent actions of George Pritchard and Dupetit-Thouar's response soon became a topic of conversation, but d'Urville thought it advisable to change the subject and reaffirm his respect and friendly intentions. Although it was clear that the arrival of another two French naval vessels had caused serious anxiety in

Tahiti, the missionaries appear to have been relieved to learn that a restrained d'Urville had more than three years' seniority over Dupetit-Thouars.

Earlier in the day, d'Urville had received a letter from Dupetit-Thouars, extolling the harbour of Pape'ete and suggesting that he relocate the *Astrolabe* and *Zélée* from their anchorages at Matavai Bay. D'Urville declined on the grounds that he intended to prepare a detailed plan of Matavai Bay. Their paths, nevertheless, crossed the following day (10 September), and d'Urville asked to visit the *Vénus*. Dupetit-Thouars invited him to dinner, and they were joined by the newly appointed Moerenhout. Although Flemish-born, he had served in the Napoleonic army and had studied in Paris. Prior to arriving in Tahiti as a merchant, he had also served as secretary to the French consul in Valparaiso. He was still recovering from the beating he had received, and his wife remained gravely ill from the attack. Not surprisingly, the British missionaries dissociated themselves from this violence; the culprits were alleged to be Spanish and French. D'Urville was warned to expect a formal complaint against Dupetit-Thouars from George Pritchard (appointed British consul the previous year).

D'Urville declined to make a formal inspection of the *Vénus*, an impressive 52-gun frigate, already a veteran of the Battle of Navarino and the conquest of Algeria. However, he did accept an invitation to meet her officers. Given the malicious rumours that had been spread in Valparaiso about his expedition and the letter sent by one of these very officers suggesting that he had little choice but to 'blow his brains out', it was presumably a good public-relations opportunity. Dupetit-Thouars apparently still doubted d'Urville had reached the Antarctic ice shelf until he was shown the expedition's charts, sketches and reports aboard the *Astrolabe* on the morning of 12 September. Conversely, d'Urville was flattered to learn, from Dupetit-Thouars and Moerenhout, that his *Voyage pittoresque autour du monde* had been well received in Rio de Janeiro, Concepción, Valparaiso and Tahiti.

After leaving the *Vénus*, d'Urville visited Moerenhout's modest home and was also introduced, it would seem, to Samuel Pinder Henry, who was seeking to acquire business as the expedition's chandler and provisioner during its sojourn. The son of the pioneering missionary William Henry, he had grown up in Tahiti, spoke the language, and offered to act as d'Urville's interpreter when he called on Queen Pomare. Before d'Urville took up this offer, he decided to pay a visit to the exiled former Chilean president, Ramón Freire. In Talcahuano, d'Urville had been informed that Freire was in Australia. He had indeed arrived in Sydney in June 1837 but had soon recrossed the Pacific hoping to return home. In Tahiti, however, he thought better of his actions and was now residing in a simple cottage that Moerenhout had put at his disposal. D'Urville and Jacquinot were delighted that Freire recognised them immediately, but they were also touched by the old man's painful fate and the fact that he did not know how long he would remain exiled from his country. The visit was very cordial, and d'Urville was also grateful to Freire for the loan of a number of French newspapers, albeit very old ones, to catch up on news at home. For his part, Freire was very grateful to learn that the expedition was carrying a letter to him from his wife.[41]

D'Urville and Jacquinot then called on Queen Aimata Pomare IV, along with Moerenhout, Henry and Dupetit-Thouars. D'Urville asserted that he remembered her as a teenager during his visit of 1823, but in fact she was only 10 years old at the time. The queen was the sister of the previous Tahitian ruler – the boy monarch Pomare III – and had acceded to the throne in 1827. The missionaries had already imported guns for her father, Pomare II, from New South Wales in exchange for Tahitian hogs. In helping to centralise the power of the dynasty established by her grandfather – the ruthless despot Tu (later Pomare I) at Matavai Bay – over some 20 local chiefdoms, the missionaries gained a powerful leverage for converting Tahiti, Mo'orea, Tetiaroa and Mehetia to Christianity.[42] The British missionaries, in particular George Pritchard, still had enormous influence over the Tahitian sovereign, and d'Urville suspected that the queen had been coached by him to refuse any invitations to call on any of the three visiting French vessels and to give maternal obligations to her infant child as an excuse. Both French commanders had made their acceptance of gifts from the queen (pigs, chickens and fruit) contingent on her agreeing to make official visits. D'Urville's objective was to ensure that French citizens and Catholic missionaries would be respected in the future, and he had conveyed this message; he saw no point in prolonging the standoff over diplomatic courtesies or 'tormenting the poor woman any longer' and decided to go immediately to the power behind the throne: George Pritchard.

In contrast to Queen Pomare's humble residence,[43] Pritchard, the thin, dark-haired son of a Birmingham brass founder, lived in a large house 'which immediately announced', according to d'Urville, 'the true sovereign of these islands'. A Union Jack flew from an enormous adjacent pole. D'Urville haughtily declared Pritchard to be a proud man with a 'cold dignity and reserve, so natural to the English, whom fortune has found in the lowest classes and raised to a certain rank'.[44] According to d'Urville, even before entering Pritchard's house, he came straight to the point:

> Mr. Pritchard, I come to visit you as a representative of a great nation, a long-time rival and enemy of another great nation, but today her friend and her ally. I would have been happy to have extended to you this courtesy, with only the title of English missionary, to whom I have always been a friend on my previous voyages; I would have been flattered to learn that you had always reconciled the duties that impose the title of Christian with that of humanity, [but] it has been otherwise and I am angry. I at least want to believe that from now on, in your capacity as an English

citizen, you will better understand the duties imposed on you, and that you will protect, even with the risk of your life, all French citizens that might still be exposed to similar affronts.[45]

Pritchard, perhaps surprised by such an eloquent and forthright salvo, made no initial reply, so d'Urville broke the awkward silence by asking him if he had spoken correctly in English and even offered to ask Moerenhout to repeat his words. Helen Rosenman, alluding to remarks by René Lesson and Élie Le Guillou, has commented that d'Urville 'spoke English with a funny whistling sound through his teeth and was hard to understand',[46] but Pritchard *had* understood and willingly affirmed his moral responsibilities. With the tension eased, d'Urville was welcomed into the missionary-consul's beautifully appointed home. The two men continued a civilised dialogue, and Pritchard informed d'Urville of Wesleyan evangelical efforts in Samoa and Fiji. This conversation only hinted at Pritchard's sectarianism. Little did he realise that, in fostering intolerance of other Christian denominations, particularly Catholics, Pritchard would ultimately undermine Tahitian independence and that he himself would soon be expelled from the island, despite repeated appeals to the British government, and lose property to the value of £4000.[47]

After taking cordial leave of Pritchard (whom he later unsuccessfully invited to dinner) and making a tour of Papeʻete, d'Urville returned to the *Vénus*, where Dupetit-Thouars insisted that he dine before going back to the *Astrolabe* with a local pilot. It was perhaps this coastal traverse that occasioned the collection of the only new botanical type specimen of d'Urville's visit to Tahiti: a marine alga that Camille Montagne named *Conferva patentiramea*,[48] which was later included in the genus *Cladophora* by the German botanist Friedrich Traugott Kützing. Despite his previous reservations about revisiting Tahiti, stating that bathing in the Matavai River engendered his only 'agreeable memories'[49] of the island, d'Urville seems to have enjoyed returning to numerous locations where he had botanised years before. It would be hard not to be entranced by Tahiti's azure-blue coastal waters, lush mountain slopes, fern-filled valleys and cascading streams. Yet there can be little doubt that the island's physical beauty was not enough for d'Urville's officers. The sad state of its people jarred with their romantic reveries. Lieutenant Roquemaurel perhaps best summarised their emotions when he wrote:

> Taïti is no longer what it was in the time of Wallis, Bougainville and Cook. To see these shores still green, watered by a multitude of limpid freshwater streams, to see these deep ravines crowned with trees to the summits, one would believe that one had rediscovered the Queen of Oceania. But a glance cast over this dirty and ragged population, which has exchanged its gentleness, its naïveté, its primitive virtues, for thievery, drunkenness and prostitution, such a glance suffices to disabuse the voyager.[50]

Honoré Jacquinot wrote scathingly of the missionaries, whose fines imposed on women for prostitution had evidently proved quite lucrative. While he acknowledged that 'among the Methodists, like among the Catholics, there are men of deep conviction and of blind devotion, capable of any sacrifice to a few souls for their religion', he also saw men 'hiding behind sacred masks', whose only interest was 'material speculation'.[51] The Protestant Desgraz also criticised the British missionaries in a letter to his father: 'Since 1797, English missionaries have taught the Tahitians. They are Protestant; unfortunately the Reformation is not as complete as was hoped. Christian charity is still backward, money has become the objective, the lust of the natives. Greed has replaced the generous sentiments of ancient times.'[52]

Prior to his departure, d'Urville agreed to the transfer of a young Breton midshipman from the *Vénus* to the *Zélée*. His name was vicomte Paul-Louis-François-René de Flotte, born in Landerneau (Finistère), the son of a naval artillery officer. Flotte had graduated from the École navale five years earlier with a glowing report, and had served in North African waters and the Antilles before joining the *Vénus*. Dupetit-Thouars had also praised his abilities and his character. Like d'Urville, Flotte came from the nobility, yet he was probably even more to the left politically than his new commander.[53]

After giving Moerenhout a brace of pistols, which the consul had requested for personal protection, and entrusting him with his official report to the navy minister, d'Urville set sail from Tahiti on 16 September, bound for the Navigator (Samoan) Islands. En route, his trust in Cook's location of 'Maupelia' (Maupihaa) atoll in the Leeward Islands nearly had disastrous consequences. The atoll proved to be 40 kilometres further to the west than Cook had stated, and the expedition unwittingly strayed into dangerous coral-laced waters. After passing Rose Island (named by Freycinet in honour of his wife in 1819), the Manu'a group and Tutuila (where a dozen members of Lapérouse's expedition were massacred in 1787), the expedition reached the western Samoan island of Upolu on 25 September. Two Englishmen piloted the corvettes into the port of Apia on the north coast of the island – below Mount Vaea (475 metres), where the novelist Robert Louis Stevenson now lies buried. One of the English pilots, a man named Frazier, had lived on the island for six years and would serve d'Urville ashore as a guide. In the harbour, the *Astrolabe* and *Zélée* were soon visited by a local chief named Pea Pongui, who bore a piece of paper demanding 'dollars' for port dues (in particular for taking fresh water), countersigned by Captain Charles Drinkwater-Bethune, commander of HMS *Conway*, a 28-gun sloop that had apparently anchored in the port only a few days before in search of escaped British convicts.[54] D'Urville was surprised that a British naval officer could have 'put his signature to such a swindle', which he considered a missionary revenue-raising exercise, and replied, via Frazier, that although he was prepared to pay for firewood, he believed that water 'belonged to all who had need of it'.[55]

D'Urville soon met one of the resident missionaries, the Reverend William Mills, a thin man with a sickly appearance, who, with some embarrassment, declared that the port dues were for commercial rather than naval vessels. D'Urville described him as a carpenter by trade who had constructed a 'little palace' for himself. (Although Mills also instructed the locals in carpentry, their indigenous construction techniques so impressed d'Urville that he described a communal *fale* that he visited as a 'masterpiece of savage industry'.[56]) Mills spoke no French but in any case appears to have been reticent, if not inarticulate. D'Urville addressed most of his questions to the missionary's intelligent young wife, who readily volunteered information on the local language, native customs and the names of islands. Jacquinot wrote that she 'appeared to be perfectly familiar with all that concerned the country'.[57] Later, d'Urville sent his English-speaking secretary, Desgraz, to quiz the Reverend Mills (and presumably Mrs Mills) on Samoan linguistic matters. Despite these ostensibly cordial relations, Jacquinot would later report to d'Urville his suspicions that Mills 'had by no means prejudiced the natives in our favour'. D'Urville, however, declared that it was undoubtedly possible 'that the wretched prejudices of the sect' and 'nationality' of the English missionaries could have 'reduced Mr. Mills to such baseness', but given the lack of 'obvious evidence', he preferred 'to doubt it'.[58] Ultimately, d'Urville was grateful to Mills for his gift of a number of books printed in Samoan[59] and for a manuscript vocabulary.

D'Urville quizzed Frazier, as he had Mills, about Samoan ethnography and language. He was also tantalised by a story (probably apocryphal) that Frazier told of three Frenchmen who were reputedly survivors of the massacre of Lapérouse's landing party. One was said to have married a Samoan and had numerous children. According to Frazier, one of these children (who spoke no French) was supposedly still alive, yet they had never met. There were indeed at least two survivors of the massacre in 1787, but they swam back to the *Astrolabe* rather than to the shore. One was the Franciscan naturalist Père Receveur, wounded above the eye, who died (probably of his wound) at Botany Bay in February 1788;[60] the other was the surgeon Simon Lavaux, who suffered a depressed fracture of the skull and had to be trepanned. Ironically, it was Lavaux whom Benjamin Morrell later alleged had survived the shipwreck of Lapérouse's ships at Vanikoro and fathered children on an island he had visited. One wonders whether Lavaux's name was simply plucked by Morrell from Milet-Mureau's published version of Lapérouse's journal because he was mentioned in the text and because he was a proven survivor of the massacre at Tutuila. More tangible vestiges of that terrible day, however, were several pieces of glass that William Mills had been given by a Samoan who had participated in the massacre. Mills in turn gave them to d'Urville when he dined aboard the *Astrolabe* on 28 September.

Just as seemingly amicable relations deteriorated into violence for Lapérouse in 1787, the next day, d'Urville contemplated violence of his own. One of his midshipmen, the blonde and blue-eyed Delafond, returned to the *Astrolabe* having been stripped of all his clothes and possessions, with the exception of his trousers, after attempting to skirt marshland near the hamlet of Savalalo (now a suburb of Apia). (He was perhaps in search of female 'company'; the women in missionary-dominated Apia proved resolutely chaste, and the French were directed to an outlying village.) D'Urville initially laughed at Delafond's misfortune but then decided that a deterrent was required to prevent such affronts in the future. There was no talk of turning the other cheek; even Reverend Mills, we are told, saw the need for action! Although d'Urville favoured the essentially immoral notion of collective punishment, he was opposed to rash punitive action as advocated by the furious Delafond. Thus he drafted an ultimatum, which he asked Frazier to deliver to the chief of Savalalo. This demanded that the culprits be handed over for punishment and that 25 pigs be given in compensation. Only then would the matter be forgotten. Should these demands not be met, d'Urville declared that he would set the village on fire and shoot any who resisted. Some negotiation took place, with the aid of Pea Pongui, the chief who had earlier demanded port dues from the French. The villagers pleaded poverty to Pea Pongui and declared their inability to provide any more than 10 pigs. Furthermore, they declared that the principal culprit had already been driven from the village and had fled into the mountains. D'Urville remained determined to present a show of force, even if the amount of compensation had now been more than halved. He dispatched Barlatier-Demas and Thanaron with a detachment of armed sailors in tight formation, with bayonets fixed and with a drummer at their head, accompanied by Pea Pongui. As in Tonga in 1827, D'Urville was prepared to bombard the village from his ships if his men required support, but fortunately, this did not prove necessary. Ten pigs and all of Delafond's stolen clothes were soon handed over, and the chief repeatedly hugged Barlatier-Demas with such a tight embrace that he turned the psychological tables and effectively defused any possibility of his being taken hostage by the French.

Yet there were also infractions on the part of d'Urville's men. Three or four men from the *Zélée* – d'Urville described them as 'marauders' but without much detail – became involved in a quarrel with locals, ostensibly over provisions. In response to their presumed or attempted thefts, d'Urville asked Jacquinot to restrict the men to the immediate environs of the bay. How understanding would he have been if the Samoans had inflicted collective punishment on the French, threatening to burn their ships if arbitrary compensation were not paid and killing all who resisted?

By now, Pavin de La Farge had completed a plan of Apia harbour. Dumoutier succeeded in making casts of the heads of a number of local chiefs, but when he enlisted the help of one of the European deserters on the island to raid burial sites for skulls, his plans went awry; he was shadowed and frustrated by suspicious locals and had to give up his goal. D'Urville also found time for an inland excursion. The beauty of the forest of Upolu made a deep impression on him. 'Never,' he wrote, 'have I seen more beautiful trees, either in New Zealand, or in New Guinea.'[61] It was easy to walk between the trunks because of their immense height, and because the dense canopy shut out the sun and prevented the development of a thick understorey. Although d'Urville considered this virgin scientific territory for the naturalists, they would publish few descriptions of Samoan plant and animal species and none new to science. As for the Samoans, d'Urville found them a handsome vigorous people, whose homes were elegant and clean and whose canoes were well built. He left Upolu on 2 October, well satisfied with the expedition's brief visit and particularly its linguistic research, and having recruited another sailor: a Chilean named 'Joseph' (José?) Poso.

After passing through the strait that separates Upolu from the island of Savai'i, d'Urville set a southeasterly course for the Tongan island of Vava'u. The *Astrolabe* and *Zélée* anchored in Port of Refuge on 5 October. Soon after mooring, d'Urville was visited by a young man who wanted to join the ranks of the expedition. His name was Mafi Kelepi, and he was the exiled son of Faka-Fanua, a chief from Tongatapu who had fallen foul of both the British missionaries and their ally Taufa'ahau. D'Urville was reluctant to employ a disgruntled young man of such high rank as a sailor but eventually agreed. Soon after came a pilot named Mackenzie, bearing a copy of port regulations just like those the missionaries had tried to enforce in Apia. To d'Urville's surprise, it was also signed by Captain Charles Drinkwater-Bethune. D'Urville told Mackenzie to keep his regulations for others but that he would recompense him if he would serve as his interpreter, to which Mackenzie promptly agreed.

D'Urville soon learned that Mackenzie had moved to Vava'u a few years before with the Reverend John Thomas, the blacksmith-missionary whom d'Urville had met on Tongatapu in 1827. He also learned that Charles Simonet, who had deserted from the *Astrolabe* during his previous visit, was on Vava'u. When the Reverend Thomas visited the *Astrolabe*, he was accompanied by William Brooks, a young man who ran a printing press on the island. The contrast between the two missionaries was striking: Brooks was as trim and as fit as Thomas was now fat and slow. When d'Urville eventually called on Brooks and his wife, Mary Anne, and young family, he noted that while the islanders 'seemed to fear Mr Thomas', in the young printer they recognised goodwill, gentleness and a 'spirit of humanity'.[62]

From the Reverend Thomas, d'Urville learned that the chief Taufa'ahau had converted to Christianity and that a civil war had ensued. Tahofa, d'Urville's erstwhile adversary, and several other chiefs whom he had known in 1827 were now dead. The sacred site of Ma'ufanga, bastion of the old Polynesian faith and burial place of Tonga's high chiefs, which d'Urville had bombarded a decade earlier, had also been destroyed. Thomas seems not to have made any mention of his own direct involvement in the brutal civil war of 1837. He remained a key advisor to the pragmatic and ruthless convert Taufaʻahau, now calling himself King George Tupou, who had invaded Tongatapu in support of his 'Christian' allies. John Garrett, historian of Christianity in the Pacific, has written that before the conflict, 'New Testament counsels of peace-making and gentleness prevailed', but then Methodist sermons bore quotes from the Old Testament 'books of Joshua, I Samuel, Chronicles and … Psalms of victory and physical vengeance'.[63] Thomas had not sat on the fence with such Old Testament references: the war became a religious crusade, marred by massacres and atrocities as the newly converted Christian chiefs stormed the fortified strongholds of their non-Christian opponents. Visiting Tongatapu and Vavaʻu shortly after, Peter Dillon learned of the 'torture, death and destruction', and the floggings and brandings (of non-Christians) that characterised the rule of the 'monster' Taufaʻahau – a 'complete despot', supported and counselled by John Thomas. Outraged at behaviour that he believed was completely anathema to Christianity, Dillon wrote a long personal letter of condemnation, which he sent to the Reverend Thomas on 20 November 1837 and which later appeared in print.[64]

Nor did Thomas reveal to d'Urville his role in having Taufaʻahau prevent Bishop Pompallier from establishing a Catholic mission on Vavaʻu after the Marist missionary arrived on Moerenhout's schooner *Raiatea* in October 1837.[65] Indeed, when Thomas and his wife, Sarah, entertained d'Urville at their home, they made only passing reference to Pompallier's 10-month sojourn and reported that he had been opposed by 'many chiefs'. D'Urville was told that, although he was protected by one local chief, he had 'made no progress' before departing.[66] In fact, Pompallier had initially been warmly received by Taufaʻahau, but the latter's attitude had suddenly changed, and the French bishop had then been 'encouraged' to move to distant Wallis Island (Uvea). Pompallier had also been ably assisted by the deserter Charles Simonet, whom Thomas now implored d'Urville to arrest. D'Urville agreed, but he was not prepared to hunt him down personally.

Thomas was only too happy to ask Taufaʻahau for assistance. On 9 October, Simonet, bound with a garrotte, was delivered to the *Astrolabe*. Now thin and pale, he tried to exculpate himself in d'Urville's eyes but without success. Furthermore, he told d'Urville that the 'Methodist missionaries had very badly received our Catholic priests', and that because Bishop Pompallier had 'accorded him his confidence', he had 'become an object of hatred for the English pastors'. While d'Urville was prepared to believe that there was 'much truth in these declarations', he remained convinced that Simonet's past actions as a deserter had to be punished. He ordered him kept in chains until further notice.[67] However, he was already planning to tap into Simonet's valuable Tongan linguistic knowledge and he would keep him in fetters for only five days.

By now, d'Urville's officers had completed their local surveys and astronomical observations. No new plants were collected, but among the many insects gathered on Vava'u were the type specimens of a previously unknown beetle, *Lagria dimidiata* (Tenebrionidae), and two new species of weevil, *Sphaerorhinus villosus* and *Otiorhynchus rotundipennis* (Curculionidae), later described by Emile Blanchard.[68] Reverend Thomas made a gift of some shells, but they did not impress d'Urville.

The day before the expedition's departure, d'Urville gave a shipboard dinner for Taufa'ahau, his consort Salote and the missionaries. He also entertained them by showing them Sainson's illustrations from the *Astrolabe*'s previous voyage, including his illustrations of Tongatapu. As a final gesture of goodwill, d'Urville offered to take the missionaries to Lefuga in the Ha'apai Islands south of Vava'u for a meeting with their Methodist brethren. They gladly accepted and were embarked with their families on 9 October. D'Urville even gave up his cabin to accommodate them for the voyage and slept under the poop deck. It was a short but rough passage. When the corvettes anchored off Kounla on the northern coast of Lefuga on 11 October, they were apparently the first French vessels ever to visit the island. Consequently, d'Urville ordered his midshipmen Delafond and Boyer to sound and draft a plan of their anchorage. D'Urville found the village ashore clean and tidy and demarcated with elegant palisades. He and his men were politely received by the missionaries and by the local people, whose chief owed allegiance to Taufa'ahau.

D'Urville considered the Tongans to be even more impressive and handsome than the Samoans, although he noted their tendency to obesity (a problem that would worsen with western dietary influences). For their part, the Tongans on both Vava'u and Lefuga were keenly aware of the bombardment of Ma'ufanga in 1827 and seem to have respected d'Urville and Jacquinot as warriors not to be trifled with. However, on Lefuga (and very likely earlier on Vava'u), the islanders argued about who was in command. Not surprisingly, they were confused by d'Urville's straw hat, shabby jacket and badly tarnished epaulettes, which contrasted sharply with Jacquinot's peaked cap, smart frock coat and gleaming insignia!

On 12 October, the expedition set sail for Viti Levu in the Fiji Islands. En route, two days later, the *Astrolabe* and the *Zélée* stood off the island of Lakemba, and d'Urville dispatched Duroch, Desgraz and the Chilean sailor Poso in the whaleboat to deliver mail to the Scottish Methodist missionary David Cargill, who resided there with his wife, Margaret (*née* Smith), and their five children. (In his short life, Cargill, with the aid of his wife, printed some of the first Fijian books and also published a memoir and a pamphlet that sought to refute the accusations made against the Methodists by Peter Dillon.) The landing party returned from Lakemba with Latchika, a chief with Herculean physique, who was the only local prepared to pilot the whaleboat back to the *Astrolabe*. The same day, d'Urville released Simonet from his shackles and restored him to full rations.

28

Vengeance & pilgrimage

Honour is like an island, rugged and without shores;
One cannot return when one has left it.

Nicolas Boileau-Despréaux*

D'Urville's immediate objective was now the small island of Viwa,[1] close to Bau off the southeastern coast of the Fijian island of Viti Levu. After negotiating the hazardous fringing coral, the corvettes anchored about three kilometres off this island on 16 October 1838. It was here, in 1834, that the French brig *Aimable Joséphine* was captured and her skipper, Captain Adolphe Bureau, and most of her crew massacred, supposedly on the orders of a chief d'Urville calls 'Nakalassé' but whose real name was Namosimalau. The Fijians had then roasted and eaten Bureau and his slain crewmen. After unsatisfactory attempts to sail the brig, they had stripped and abandoned her. In Tahiti, Dupetit-Thouars had provided d'Urville with a copy of a signed deposition by a young Peruvian survivor named José-Manuel Muños. It soon became clear to d'Urville that Bureau – who had initially come in search of trepang and tortoiseshell – had become involved in internecine wars and, according to d'Urville, 'with his arms and his ship he had aided the vengeance of these islanders and had not even recoiled from cannibalism, authorising one of the horrible meals aboard his ship'.[2] David Cargill later suggested that the covetous chiefs of Bao had, in fact, conceived the plan to kill Bureau and to seize his ship, and that it was they who put pressure on Namosimalau and his nephew (already on intimate terms with the French captain) to execute the massacre.[3] Surprisingly, d'Urville now sent Ensign Gourdin and Midshipman Gervaize (with Latchika as an interpreter) to Bao's newly reinstated *vunivalu* or paramount chief, Tanoa Visawaqa, to inform him of the expedition's intention to avenge the death of Bureau. Tanao responded with demonstrations of friendship and support for the French, predicated by explanations that he had already been driven into exile once by his powerful vassal Namosimalau (in 1832). In fact, he had only been reinstated as *vunivalu* in 1837 by his son, the future monarch of the first united Fijian kingdom,

---

* 'Satire X' (1667), lines 167–68.

Seru Epenisa Cakobau. While Tanao was powerless to hand over Namosimalau, he was clearly happy to see him destroyed or seriously weakened, and he purportedly sought to affirm a mutual contempt for Namosimalau by offering Gervaize a still-unfinished morsel of one of his rival's men, killed and roasted a few days before. Gervaize politely declined to sample the local cuisine!

At 3.00 am on 17 October, d'Urville sent 80 of his men in his five largest boats, under the command of Lieutenant Dubouzet, to wreak vengeance on the small island of Viwa. By 5.15 am, the French had occupied the island's fortified principal settlement, and within an hour, they had reduced its defences, some 60 houses and several large buildings, including its impressive chiefly residence and citadel, to ashes. Despite earlier reports of bravado and resolve, the island's inhabitants, including Namosimalau, had fled before the superior French force and had not attempted to defend their homes. In any case, they appear to have had ample warning of the assault: Namosimalau was married to Tanoa's niece. Although Dubouzet's account suggests that the punitive party only fired their blunderbusses into the plantations of breadfruit, banana and taro – because they were 'intermixed' with brush 'in which it would have been imprudent to engage'[4] – David Cargill later wrote that the French not only 'burned the town and property of the natives', they also 'laid waste their plantations' and that only 'an old temple, in a retired part of the island, escaped the ravages of their vengeance'.[5] Assuming the veracity of Cargill's report and given the severe damage that shrapnel or grapeshot in a blunderbuss can do to maturing fruit and the soft trunks of banana trees, it is hard to avoid the conclusion that, even if d'Urville's men did not kill or wound any of the islanders with their rifles, in laying waste to Viwa's plantations, they probably condemned many to starve in the succeeding months. Perhaps it was not just hunger for the Lord that induced Namosimalau to become a Christian soon after these events!

After speaking personally with Tanao through Charles Simonet and reiterating his reasons for destroying Viwa, d'Urville bestowed gifts of white cloth, yellow handkerchiefs, knives and expedition medals, then replenished his water supplies and fresh provisions at Bau. Meanwhile, the naturalists made a number of interesting discoveries, including the type specimen of the Pacific tree boa *Enygrus bibroni* (*Candoia bibroni*),[6] the endemic frog *Hylodes vitianus* (*Platymantis vitianus*),[7] and the tiger beetle *Cicindela vitiensis* (*Oceanella vitiensis*).[8]

The *Astrolabe* and *Zélée* set sail again on 19 October. Despite being piloted through the reef by an Englishman whom d'Urville once again named 'Williams' (his real name was Martins), the departure from Bau was tricky, and both corvettes scraped coral while making for the open sea. The following day, they reached Levuka on the east coast of the rugged volcanic island of Ovalau and were promptly greeted by a trader and former sailor named David Whippy. He was a dark-haired man with close-set eyes, a flattened nose and a weathered, somewhat unsymmetrical face that suggested a tough past. He was also well on his way to fathering at least 12 children by at least six different partners. D'Urville thought he was English, but he was in fact an American, born in Nantucket and later appointed United States consul. When Whippy next visited the *Astrolabe*, d'Urville was amused to discover that he carried a reference, signed by Peter Dillon – the self-styled 'Consul of France in the Viti Islands' – extolling his virtues as an interpreter, guide and pilot. For d'Urville, his best recommendation was the fact that he had lived for '13 years among savages' and lacked 'neither energy nor intelligence'. The American explorer Charles Wilkes would later hold Whippy in high regard and gain much valuable ethnographic and historical information from him on Fiji and the rise of the Bau chieftaincy.[9] It seems likely, therefore, that he was also an important informant for d'Urville and, in particular, Desgraz, who was given the task of compiling a vocabulary of the language of the Viti Islands.

David Whippy was not the only European living in Levuka. According to d'Urville, there were about nine others – beachcombers, deserters and drifters, it would seem – enjoying the charms of about 40 local women in the coastal settlement, with no missionaries to spoil their libertinage. The port had also been visited recently by Captain Drinkwater-Bethune and the *Conway*. This time, however, d'Urville was not presented with any of Drinkwater-Bethune's signed port regulations or fees.

The expedition remained almost a week at Levuka. While there, Coupvent-Desbois and Flotte drafted a plan of the port, and the naturalists collected a new subspecies of the many-coloured fruit dove *Ptilinopus perousii mariae*[10] and five entomological type specimens. The latter included a new weevil – perhaps collected by d'Urville himself, since it would be named *Elytrurus durvillei* in his honour – and the lobed leaf-insect *Phyllium lobiventre* (*Chitoniscus lobiventris*), a master of camouflage.[11] On 26 October, after taking on more fresh water but finding few pigs and chickens, d'Urville set sail for Bua Bay (sometimes referred to as Sandalwood Bay) on the coast of southwestern Vanua Levu, guided by a skilful English pilot named Thomas Grandy.[12]

Vanua Levu had become known as a source of sandalwood after the wreck of the American schooner *Argo* in 1800, but d'Urville noted that this valuable timber had now become very rare. The corvettes reached the magnificent harbour of Bua on the morning of 27 October. It appealed immediately to d'Urville, and he wrote: 'It is perhaps one of the most beautiful places in the world to found beautiful and flourishing colonies.' In clarification, he added: 'By colonies I mean places to gather and generously nourish the excess of Europe's population, or even speculative commercial settlements.'[13] Ultimately, it was Levuka rather than Bua that would be the cradle of colonial ambitions in Fiji, but British rather than French. D'Urville did not linger long to savour the beauty of Bua. On 29 October, after Barlatier-Demas and Vincendon-Dumoulin had fixed the longitude of 'Lacumba' (Lekumbi) Point on the southeastern arm of the bay, the expedition set sail again.

The Fijians impressed d'Urville as 'well-built and well-proportioned' and did 'not have, as in the Tongan Islands, and especially in the Society Islands, the propensity to obesity'. Their faces were not 'disagreeable', and 'their physiognomy'[14] indicated that they were intelligent – the latter suggesting phrenological preconceptions (or rather misconceptions) perhaps advanced by Dumoutier. Despite the fate of Bureau, d'Urville believed that 'if one was more versed in the language of these people one could recover all the testimonies; one could perhaps also explain what were the motives which engaged these people, for whom vengeance is a duty, to capture European ships and to massacre inoffensive crews'. He also felt that one could not ignore the fact that Europeans were able to live among them 'alone and without defence'.[15] Of their material culture, d'Urville wrote: 'It is above all by their industry that the Viti people take an important place among the savage nations of Oceania.' Their houses were often 'very beautiful and above all remarkable for the finish of their detail', and their canoes were 'much superior' to all those made in Oceania. While he considered Fijian weapons primitive, he thought the pottery of the archipelago 'remarkable' for its elegance, dimensions and ornamentation – the latter frequently featuring bizarre forms including 'monsters created by their imagination'.[16] Sadly, many of the fine examples noted were in the homes burned on Viwa.

D'Urville's instructions, mirrored in his initial expedition proposal, were to sail to Vanikoro and Santa Cruz in the Solomon Islands for follow-up survey work. The northwesterly passage from Vanua Levu was initially very uncomfortable for their Tongan recruit Mafi Kelepi, who suffered badly from seasickness during a heavy swell from the south. And even when he could eat, Mafi missed the fresh food of his native islands. Everyone aboard would suffer from the increasing heat and humidity, made worse by the failing wind. The listlessness aboard the corvettes was worsened by the lack of wildlife, 'neither birds, nor fish, nor cetaceans'. Then, on 4 November, the lush green form of Bougainville's 'Aurore Island' (Maewo, Vanuatu) was sighted through the saturating tropical mist, followed by the summit of the mountain Bougainville named 'Pic de l'Étoile' on Mera Lava in the southern Banks Islands. On the same day, shortly after sighting William Bligh's 'Sugar Loaf Island' (Mota) in the mist, a sailor on the *Zélée* fell overboard; given the poor visibility, he was very lucky to be rescued.

By 5 November, the corvettes had cleared the Banks Islands, and the following day, the island of Vanikoro was sighted. Standing off Paiu, d'Urville's thoughts naturally turned to Lapérouse and his crewmen who had lost their lives on this very shore 50 years before. In his account, d'Urville gave no precise reasons for his return to Vanikoro;

aside from additional surveys, we know that he had already made an effort to gather oral history relating to possible survivors of the Lapérouse expedition, including their purported descendants. A personal desire to visit Paiu must surely have been a major reason for his return to Vanikoro. In 1828, his responsibilities as expedition leader and then malarial fever had kept him from visiting the wreck site in person, despite his determination that each of his officers should make the pilgrimage and bear witness to the vestiges. On this voyage, d'Urville would be one of the first to land at Paiu.

On his way to the shore, d'Urville tried to scan the seabed for further remnants of Lapérouse's vessels, but the choppy waters made visibility poor, and nothing new was seen. Ashore, he noticed an area cleared of trees, which he thought might have been the campsite of those who reached land in 1788. Unfortunately, the site was covered with rotten vegetation and creepers almost a metre in height, which he was not prepared to clear to search for artefacts. Nor could he find any visible cairn that might mark where perhaps a bottle containing documents might have been buried five decades before. Only a very tall coconut tree appeared to bear the marks of a European axe. In one deserted habitation, Marescot found a piece of polished wood that d'Urville believed might have come from a French wreck, yet there was no sign of any European metalwork. Strangely, the abundant oysters on the shore seemed to him to have a strong taste of copper. Was it d'Urville's imagination, or did they perhaps hint at the many bronze cannons and copper artefacts that still remained undiscovered off shore?

Although fleeting contact was made with one local man, the other inhabitants kept a timid distance. D'Urville made no mention of the wooden cenotaph that he had ordered built at Paiu in 1828 to commemorate Lapérouse and his men. If it was now gone – perhaps destroyed by an intervening cyclone – it is possible the locals were expecting the vengeance d'Urville had promised during his previous visit. But d'Urville had his own fears: he had ordered Vincendon-Dumoulin and Dumoutier to rendezvous with him on the shore at Paiu, and when they failed to arrive by 3.00 pm, he became anxious. Nevertheless, he departed with the *Zélée*'s boat and ordered Gourdin to wait for them with the *Astrolabe*'s boat. His memories of the terrible fever he endured in 1828 also made him very reluctant to linger on the shore. Within two hours, he learned what had happened to Vincendon-Dumoulin and Dumoutier. They had entered the dense littoral forest and got lost, then followed a stream that they assumed would take them back to the shore; in fact, it flowed inland from a marsh. It was only when the rain stopped and the sky cleared long enough for them to see the position of the sun that they were able to find their way back to Gourdin and the boat. There was great joy at their safe return to the *Astrolabe*. With everyone back on board their respective vessels by 5.00 pm, the expedition continued its route along the reef that borders Vanikoro's western coast. There was no sign of human settlements, only continuous forest and very few coconut trees.

While the tropical winds were feeble, the currents were strong. The corvettes drifted to within 30–40 kilometres of Utupua Island on 7 November but could not get any closer. On the same day, 'Nitendi' (Nendö) Island was sighted and later the active volcanic island of Tinakula, its smoking plume visible just as it had been for the Spanish explorer Álvaro de Mendaña de Neira in 1595. Leaving the Santa Cruz group behind, the expedition sailed along the northern coast of San Cristobal, then the southwestern coast of Malaita (which occasioned the naming of Cape Zélée and Cape Astrolabe on the respective southern and northern ends of the island) and reached San Jorge Island off the southern tip of Santa Isabel Island. Here the corvettes anchored in newly christened Astrolabe Cove on 18 November. Fresh water and firewood were taken on board, and the bay was sounded. D'Urville showed the locals his ship's cat, which caused surprise and some fear. The sight of a black pig on deck caused them to flee in horror – a source of great amusement to the sailors but a sign to d'Urville that the island was unlikely to be a source of fresh pork for his crew.

On 20 November, Dumoutier thought he had found a local man prepared to submit to a plaster moulding of his head. The phrenologist began with the back of his subject's head, but when he began to plaster his face, the man took fright and began to smash the casting plaster free by banging his encrusted head against the ship's timbers – no doubt to the further amusement of the crew. Desgraz had better co-operation gathering words for a local vocabulary. Because d'Urville did not trust the islanders, he sought to restrict his men to the vicinity of the immediate anchorage, but Ducorps, Boyer, Gervaize, Delafond and Desgraz, accompanied by the Tongan Mafi Kelepi, made a successful excursion to the neighbouring island of Santa Isabel. Meanwhile, d'Urville found time to botanise ashore. Although no new plant species were found on San Jorge, a number of significant zoological discoveries were made. The birds collected for the first time included the midget flower-pecker (*Dicaeum aeneum*) and a honeyeater, the red-capped *Myzomela lafargei*, eventually named in honour of Ensign Pavin de La Farge.[17] The entomological collection was enriched by five new beetle species and a new species of earwig *Forficula grandiventris* (*Tagalina grandiventris*).[18] Early on the morning of 27 November, the corvettes weighed anchor and left San Jorge Island, but not before the *Astrolabe* had briefly scraped her keel and slowed dramatically on the coral fringe of her eponymous cove.

D'Urville stated that it was his intention to then sail through the waters between 'Guadalcanar [here he used the original Spanish spelling], Marsch and Isabelle Islands'. This suggests that he probably intended to survey the still-uncharted northern coasts of the Russell Islands and Guadalcanal, and then perhaps fulfil his orders to pass through Torres Strait to reach Ambon. In 1828, the number of fever cases aboard the *Astrolabe* had made him reconsider the same plan. This time, the westerly monsoonal winds were against him and made him decide to follow the northeastern coasts of Choiseul (Lauru) and Bougainville. By this stage, he had probably already decided to reprovision in Guam if he could. Buka was sighted on 7 December, and the following day, the mountains of New Ireland were seen in the distance. On 12 December, as they headed roughly north-northeast for the Caroline Islands, the *Astrolabe* and *Zélée* made their second crossing of the equator.

Ten days later, the expedition reached the Chuuk (formerly Truk) Islands group,[19] entering through the southern pass in the reef that encircles the cluster of volcanic islands (some rising 300–400 metres above the sea) on the atoll's enormous lagoon of over 60 kilometres in diameter. The expedition anchored off 'Tsis' (Siis), one of these islands. It will be remembered that d'Urville had passed Chuuk with Duperrey in 1824, but the atoll had been known to Europeans since it was sighted by the Spanish navigator Alonso de Arellano in January 1565.

D'Urville landed on Siis early on the afternoon of 22 December. The apparent friendliness of the islanders and the presence of many coconut, breadfruit and banana trees, as well as taro, augured well for acquiring fresh provisions. Importantly, plentiful fresh water was also located. The hospitable reception Marescot and Desgraz received on the neighbouring island of 'Periadik' (Parem) encouraged d'Urville to send Duroch and Vincendon-Dumoulin – accompanied by Thanaron, Delafond and Desgraz – to survey the island of 'Rouk' (Fefan). They left early on the morning of 26 December in the *Astrolabe*'s boat, armed with a blunderbuss and other small arms, and made for the southeastern coast of Fefan, opposite the northern tip of Uman Island. Soon after, a flotilla of canoes approached them from a bay on this same northern tip of Uman. The occupants seemed friendly and appeared to want them to visit their village, but given their orders, they could not do this. The survey party continued sailing around the eastern coast of Fefan, and as they approached the channel between Fefan and Tonowas Island (Dublon), a large number of very different canoes approached them from eastern Tonowas. They then noticed that their escorts from Uman had abandoned them. In the narrowest part of the channel, the survey boat was obstructed by the canoes, and Duroch and his companions were pelted with a derisive hail of native citrus.

Vincendon-Dumoulin was convinced that events were about to take a nastier turn, with their boat bottled up in the reef and their pursuers believing that they were grounded. Sure enough, a chief in one of the canoes stood up and flung a spear at them, and his companions readied their weapons for an attack. Meanwhile, another 50 islanders appeared to be making their way on foot along the reef to encircle the

French. Duroch acted decisively, setting his sails so that the wind carried the boat clear of the rocks, his men aiming their guns but still holding fire. Their attackers seemed to have no knowledge of European weapons, but they sensed Duroch's leadership role in the stern of the boat and flung a spear at him. It glanced off his shoulder and then hit Vincendon-Dumoulin's hat without causing any injury. Other spears struck the boat and were embedded in its timbers. Then a group of 21 canoes from Fefan, carrying between five and 10 warriors each, began to pursue them. One large canoe also carried two naked men, who taunted the French with what Vincendon-Dumoulin called 'a very indecent dance', and the canoe carrying the chief now bore down on them astern. The chief let down his hair, removed his poncho-like cape and seemingly entreated the French to come closer, yet at the same time readied his warriors with their spears. Meanwhile, the large canoe bearing the taunting dancers gained on them abeam. Their predicament seemed critical but within seconds, the balance of power would shift. The blunderbuss was fired into what appears to have been the hull of the chief's canoe. Heavily laden with warriors, the craft failed catastrophically and broke apart; its occupants were soon floundering in the water among its splintered debris. Duroch and Vincendon-Dumoulin then aimed their hunting rifles at the convenient target of the dancers in the other boat and felled them. The psychological effect was immediate: the would-be attackers now scrambled for the shore with their casualties, some apparently dead.

The French were still not completely out of danger: another attempt was made to attack their boat as it tried to pass through yet another set of narrows in the reef between Fefan and Tonowas. This time, Duroch fired grapeshot at their pursuers, and it took an even more terrible toll as its metal fragments tore through the canoes and their occupants. Until that moment, there were also many spectators watching the contest from the trees, and they too now fled at the sound of the terrible discharges. As the surveying party passed Tonowas, all the women could be seen fleeing to the mountains. After sighting the island of 'Moen' (Weno) and two or three isolated reefs, Duroch and Vincendon-Dumoulin decided that it was probably wiser to return to the corvettes rather than continue their survey work. D'Urville could see how visibly shaken they were when they arrived unexpectedly at noon.

After these unfortunate events, the only islanders who came to trade with the corvettes were from Parem and Totiw, to the northeast of their anchorage. The following day, d'Urville was disturbed to learn that on hitherto peaceful Siis, Honoré Jacquinot had had stones thrown at him by angry islanders. He was collecting bird specimens at the time – probably including the previously unknown Oceanic flycatcher (*Myiagra oceanica*), discovered during their sojourn.[20] Despite being shadowed and having a spear pointed at him, the younger Jacquinot, armed with a double-barrelled shotgun, kept his nerve and retreated safely to the shore, where he encountered Hombron, Gervaize and two sailors from the *Astrolabe*, all armed. Dubouzet and Goupil were bathing nearby but dressed quickly when Jacquinot recounted what had happened to him. Earlier, Goupil had had branches thrown at him as he tried to sketch. Soon after, Hombron and Gervaize, originally dismissive of any threat, encountered the menacing warriors and anxiously made a quick departure in the *Zélée*'s boat with Dubouzet, Goupil and Jacquinot.

Despite these warning signs, after lunch, Hombron landed again with Vincendon-Dumoulin, Ducorps and Delafond from the *Astrolabe*, each armed with a double-barrelled shotgun. They visited a familiar village without incident but with fear and tension in the air. While there, a canoe arrived, like one that Vincendon-Dumoulin had seen the day before, and it bore men similarly covered in red war-paint and costumed in what appeared to be battle-dress. When these men entered the village, they were astonished to find the French in one of the houses. One can only guess that they had arrived to seek support from the islanders of Siis for reprisals. Embarrassed to find the object of his anger in the midst of his allies, one of these men, with that universal expression that we all understand for puzzlement, struck his own head with the palm of his hand. When another warrior entered the same house and recognised Vincendon-Dumoulin, still dressed in the uniform he had worn the day before, the hydrographer was addressed in a strange psalm-like manner with a very low voice. The worried French, who could not understand what was being said to them, made their exit from the village. Despite discernible attempts by the islanders to separate them and to disarm them by encouraging them to discharge their firearms at birds, they returned safely to the shore together. There, they encountered Roquemaurel and Barlatier-Demas, who had arrived to rate the *Astrolabe*'s chronometers, along with Ducorps, who had come to trade for coconuts. They learned that stones had rained down on the purser, and that Barlatier-Demas had shot one of the assailants in the shoulder and, for the moment, put the attackers to flight. Continuing their observations and using their instruments under such conditions proved very stressful. They withdrew to the *Astrolabe* at 7.00 pm on 28 December. The expedition then left Chuuk lagoon via the same southern passage it had entered.

29

Guam & the Moluccas

… we sailed from place to place and from isle to isle; and whenever we
anchored we met a crowd of merchants and notables …

Anon.

On New Year's Day 1839, the corvettes anchored in Umatac Bay, Guam. D'Urville was soon visited by the curate of nearby Merizo and the local deputy-*alcade* (magistrate), a man named Domingo. From them, he learned that the Spanish governor, Lieutenant-Colonel José Medinilla y Pineda, who had been so kind to him and his men in 1828, had died five years earlier in Manila. D'Urville also learned that Medinilla was not remembered with affection by the locals, mainly because he had grown rich on a trade monopoly that dictated the debased prices at which the inhabitants could sell their produce and the inflated prices they had to pay for imported necessities. The current governor, appointed just 14 months before but without such trading privileges, was another soldier, Lieutenant-Colonel José Casillas y Salazar. D'Urville's friend José Flores, the *alcade* of Umatac, had been replaced by the gushingly polite Antonio Herrera, who soon offered d'Urville accommodation at his residence. There was an immediately familiar face in the Scotsman, John Anderson, who was still port captain and was still fathering children.[1] Anderson offered his services to d'Urville as a pilot and also offered to take him to the capital, Agaña, in his whaleboat. The latter offer appears to have been taken up by d'Urville's officers instead. D'Urville wrote immediately to Casillas y Salazar to inform him of his arrival and to request his assistance on a number of matters. He also ordered Ducorps to begin buying fresh provisions and distributing them to the crew. Later, d'Urville would ask Anderson to obtain rice, sugar, rum and tar for the expedition.

Umatac remained an isolated backwater; there was still no road across the steep mountains that separated it from Agaña to the north. (It would remain unconnected until the First World War, when the Americans built a road via the coastal settlements of Merizo and Inarajan.) In 1828, d'Urville and his men had been effectively quarantined

---

* *The Second Voyage of Sinbad Hight the Seaman* (*ca.* ninth century), Burton trans., vol. vi

'*Couvent abandonné à Umata*', *unknown engraver, for Dumont d'Urville's* Voyage pittoresque
autour du monde, *L. Tenré, Paris, vol. ii, 1835, plate lxi. The abandoned convent at Umatac, on
the island of Guam, is where the Spanish permitted the* Astrolabe's *sick cases to be housed in May
1828. When d'Urville returned, in January 1839, it was no longer habitable.* Author's collection

in Umatac because of the fever and dysentery they had carried from Vanikoro, the lack
of road access making that quarantine easy to enforce.

Revisiting Umatac, d'Urville was surprised at the lack of New Year celebrations that
would have been so common in Europe. Rather than a state of hope and excitement,
Umatac was in visible decline, like the Spanish colonial empire itself. There were
even fewer houses than there had been a decade before, and the local electorate had
shrunk to just 12 people. The former convent, which served the ailing crew of the
Astrolabe as a hospital in 1828, was no longer habitable, with half the floorboards of the
upstairs rooms destroyed by rot. Decrepit Fort San Ángel, which was meant to defend
the harbour, had neither the two bronze guns it had ranged in 1828 nor a garrison.[2]
The outside of the governor's misleadingly named 'palace' had been repainted, but
its shabby interior remained unchanged. In a letter, the governor offered to let the
French commander reside there during his visit, but d'Urville declined it in favour
of Vincendon-Dumoulin, who used it as a base for his navigational astronomical
observations, as Jacquinot had done in 1828.

On the morning of 3 January, d'Urville was visited by Padre Bernardo, curate of Agaña, and the Franciscan friar Fra Manuel, curate of Agat. They were accompanied by the commissaire, Don Felice Calvos, and a prominent local Hispano-Chamorran, Luis de Torres, who normally resided in the capital and claimed descent from the illustrious navigator Luis Vaez de Torres, discoverer of Torres Strait. In 1828, d'Urville had met Torres's now 69-year-old father and remembered him with affection. In Agaña, Torres's wife would also warmly receive a number of d'Urville's officers, including Duroch and Desgraz. Although d'Urville discussed his experiences in the Caroline Islands with his visitors, his principal concern remained how to re-provision his expedition. Later that day, he accompanied Jacquinot on a visit to Merizo, five kilometres to the south. Banana, coconut and breadfruit trees were plentiful, as were taro plantations, but pigs and chickens were very scarce. They did, however, encounter one young Chamorro who was prepared to sell them a cow, and when d'Urville returned to the *Astrolabe*, he found that 24 pigs had also been purchased.

Initially, Casillas y Salazar had sent his apologies, saying he could not greet the commander of the French expedition in person. However, on 7 January, d'Urville met him when he made a brief visit to Umatac, en route to Inajaran, and invited him to dinner when he returned to Umatac. A small thin man with a pale sickly complexion, he was greeted with a nine-gun salute, and after dinner he was presented with a pair of pistols as a souvenir of the expedition's visit. Apart from this, d'Urville had little to say about him. Robert Rogers, a historian of Guam, has described him as an alcoholic.[3]

The crews of the *Astrolabe* and *Zélée* appear to have enjoyed their 10-day visit to Guam and the hospitality of its impoverished inhabitants. Even the local clergy lacked the reserve that was so typical of their French counterparts, and d'Urville was very amused at the bizarre sight of the curates of Agaña and Agat striding and swirling on the dance-floor of the governor's palace in their flowing white soutanes – unembarrassed substitute partners for his men with a shortage of local women – to the accompaniment of a mediocre violinist and several guitarists. Although d'Urville could smile at these priests, he was nevertheless critical of them. When he visited the church of San Dimas in Merizo, he found it in a state of 'dilapidation that was painful to see'.[4] He noted that when Freycinet had visited Guam, the College of Agaña was flourishing; now he was informed that Padre Bernardo, who held the title of prefect apostolic and was officially director of the college, had no students but instead raised fighting cocks! He also augmented his stipend through private commerce. As Dubouzet saw it, the four priests on the island fulfilled their sacramental duties with the greatest pomp, but it was paid for by their impoverished parishioners to the last penny. In his opinion, 'the greatest service one could do for the natives would be to make them lose these ruinous habits, and, to do this, one would have to change … all the members of the Guam clergy'.[5]

On the morning of 10 January, farewells were made to the ever-gracious Luis de Torres, Don Calvos and the dancing clerics. The scientific staff ashore packed up their astronomical instruments and reboarded the corvettes, along with the naturalists. Visited by European explorers since 1521 and colonised by Spain for over 170 years, Guam was hardly virgin territory for naturalists. Nevertheless, during their sojourn, a previously unknown tenebrionid beetle, *Epilasium incisum* (*Gonocephalum incisum*), was collected on the island.[6] After mustering his sailors, Jacquinot soon discovered that two had deserted from the *Zélée*: Yves-Sylvain Le Bris, from Quimper, and Simon-Jean Touchard, from Lyon. He sent a message to the governor asking for them to be arrested, but no time could be spared to search for them or wait for their apprehension. In any case, they were not well-regarded crewman, and d'Urville suggested they would not be missed. No sailors had deserted from the *Astrolabe*. By midday, the expedition had already lost sight of Guam and was heading southwest.

On 13 January, the summits of the Yap island group were sighted, and d'Urville was soon able to scan the shore with his telescope. In 1828, he had not landed on Yap, only conversed with some of the friendly locals who had come out to greet the *Astrolabe*. He regretted that this occasion was much the same. Two days later, the expedition reached the Palau Islands. Three boats approached the expedition, bearing some 20 men eager to trade. While they were aboard the *Astrolabe*, d'Urville learned from one of the men, Nohor, that he and another man, Gueberar, were actually Bandanese who had spent 11 months in this island group after being shipwrecked. They had been sailors aboard a barque with seven crewmen, and their captain and most of their shipmates had been massacred; they had been spared but reduced to slavery. Nohor pleaded with d'Urville in Malay to be allowed to remain on board with his shipmate, and d'Urville promptly agreed. Aside from a clear moral imperative, he was glad of the linguistic opportunity the two new recruits offered. The Palauans, however, were angry when their slaves refused to obey the order to return to shore, and d'Urville resolved the standoff by ordering several of his biggest sailors to eject the islanders from the *Astrolabe* without their human chattel. The two naked Bandanese were then given a pair of trousers each.

On 16 January, the expedition changed course to the west-southwest to take advantage of the trade winds. After passing through the Sarangani Strait on 23 January, the corvettes were becalmed close to the verdant coast of Mindanao. D'Urville seized the opportunity to send Thanaron, Marescot and Vincendon-Dumoulin ashore to conduct geophysical and navigational observations, along with the naturalists to collect specimens. Despite feeble winds, the currents were so strong that they posed a serious threat to the safety of the corvettes off the Sangihe group. On 27 January, d'Urville was convinced that he was about to see the *Zélée* smashed against the walls of rock on the southeastern cape of Sangihe Island; the *Astrolabe* seemed only to have a temporary reprieve after her anchor held in 10 fathoms (18.2 metres) of water. Instead of disaster, the wind suddenly came up from the northeast and both crews rallied with extraordinary speed to sail clear of the rocks.

The expedition anchored at Ternate in the Netherlands East Indies on 29 January. There, the Dutch resident, A.J. van Olphen, did all he could to assist d'Urville and supply him with fresh provisions (including 120 litres of arrack). An extraordinary 400 birds of paradise from New Guinea were also purchased by the crew during their stay, not as scientific specimens but as souvenirs – sustaining a troubling predatory trade. D'Urville, immobilised with another bad attack of gout, could not indulge in his favourite pastimes of walking and botanising. His scientific staff, however, climbed Mount Gamalama during their sojourn; this 1715-metre conical stratovolcano, which dominates the entire island, erupted the following year with devastating consequences. D'Urville and his officers were entertained not only by van Olphen but also with 'princely magnificence' by the turbaned Dutch-pensionary sultan of Ternate, Taj ul-Mulki Amiruddin Iskandar Kaulaini Shah, on the eve of the expedition's departure. In pain, irritable and never very interested in the performing arts, d'Urville was clearly ill-disposed to enjoy the colourful traditional dances, let alone the songs and shimmering percussive gamelan music of the northern Moluccas. While in the isolated military outpost of Ternate, he reflected on the Dutch trading monopoly in the East Indies and its vulnerability to the rising tide of British imperial power on the Malay Peninsula: 'It is from there, that … she surveys this vast Asian archipelago where only the Dutch flag still flies. The Moluccas, if they were given up, would soon be invaded by the masters of India and Australia.'[7]

The *Astrolabe* and *Zélée* left Ternate on 1 February and, four days later, anchored below Fort Victoria in the harbour of Ambon. D'Urville was promptly visited by the port captain and by the senior magistrate enquiring about his business in Ambon. He no doubt presented his expedition's passports, for he was soon warmly welcomed. This was his third visit to the southern Moluccas, and he was clearly pleased to be back. His friend Andries Ellinghuijsen, who had become governor and served in the post for some seven years, had died in 1837. So too had J.R. Paape, who had been the governor's secretary and had then served as acting resident; d'Urville, however, did see Paape's widow. Although the acting governor and military commander of the Moluccas, François de Stuers, was then absent, d'Urville and Jacquinot were courteously received by his intelligent and attractive wife, Adriana (*née* Kock), who spoke fluent French.[8] Armed with a list of provisions required by both corvettes, d'Urville went to see the resident, Adrian Hendrik Rijkschroeff, and requested assistance. Unfortunately, only a small part of his needs were met, but every night d'Urville and his officers received invitations to dinner parties, which delayed their departure from the island.

Still afflicted with gout, d'Urville could not venture far beyond the walls of Ambon, but he seems to have had some amusement in being carried through thick forest on a palanquin to a volcanic cave (which he names as 'Seang-Kang'),[9] 60–90 metres long, with several narrow and tortuous connections between its chambers. He was accompanied by Jacquinot and eight of his officers. A new skink, *Euprepes concolor* (*Emoia concolor*)[10] and two new beetles[11] were also collected by the expedition in Ambon, presumably in this same forest.

Although d'Urville's orders gave him the freedom to dispatch the *Zélée* home from Ambon with his natural history specimens and any sick cases if he wished, his men were healthy and he did not want the *Astrolabe* to sail into the ice again without a consort, so the two corvettes would remain together. Both vessels required work on their masts, but this would have to wait until they had access to a proper shipyard. Having stowed the limited provisions to be had in Ambon, the corvettes weighed anchor on the morning of 18 February. Still in search of substantial supplies, particularly fresh meat (and presumably intending to drop off the two Bandanese, Nohor and Gueberar, he had rescued earlier in the Palau group), d'Urville set sail for the Banda Islands, some 200 kilometres to the southeast, arriving two days later. The group comprises 10 small volcanic islands that thrust some 5000 metres from the seabed. On Banda Neira, d'Urville finally met François de Stuers, the acting governor of the Moluccas, a man of refined manners, who, like his wife Adriana, spoke fluent French. He and Stuers soon established a warm rapport.

It is not clear what additional supplies d'Urville obtained from the Dutch or at what price. In his letter to the minister, written four months later, he stated that his reason for visiting the island was simply 'to have an idea of its famous nutmeg plantations'.[12] The Banda Islands annually produced 227,000 kilograms of nutmeg and 68,000 kilograms of mace (the reddish aril of the nutmeg seed) from their monocultural plantations. There were general stores there, since the garrisons at Fort Belgica and Fort Nassau and the plantation labourers (including convicts) all had to be fed by the colonial administration. We know that Stuers gave d'Urville a number of natural history specimens, including a live dugong. There was little hope of keeping the hapless creature alive outside its aquatic environment, and its body was soon preserved by Hombron in a barrel of arrack. Stuer also gave d'Urville 'a small black kangaroo'[13] (probably a black tree-kangaroo (*Dendrolagus ursinus*) from the Vogelkop region of New Guinea) and took him to visit one of the island's nutmeg plantations. He and his officers were also invited to a ball on 23 February; however, d'Urville left his young subordinates to enjoy the evening and retired early to the *Astrolabe*. His gout was probably still an impediment to such socialisation, let alone the kind of long exploratory trek on land that he once relished. He did not, for example, join Vincendon-Dumoulin, Hombron and Gourdin when they set off to climb the nearby 282-metre active stratovolcano of Gunungapi early on the same day.

The expedition left Banda on the morning of 25 February and set a course for the coast of New Guinea, which was sighted three days later. In early March, the coast of Adi Island and part of the wild and beautiful coast of West Papua's vast Triton Bay (Teluk Kamrau) were charted before the corvettes broke off their survey and made for Cape Vals (Tanjung Vals). The waters of the Arafura Sea between New Guinea and New Holland were laden with vegetable matter discharged from rivers swollen by the rains of the westerly Indo-Australian monsoon – the very monsoonal system d'Urville still hoped might carry him through Torres Strait. But by 11 March, after a fortnight of battling a series of violent squalls and contrary winds, which exhausted his crews,[14] he realised that he was at a crucial juncture. The winds had now swung to the east, and there was no prospect of passing through Torres Strait from the west before resupplying in Port Jackson (Sydney). Furthermore, summer in the southern hemisphere was nearly at an end. Even if he sailed directly to Hobart via the Western Australian coast and then attempted an immediate second Antarctic descent, he would be doing so in autumn or early winter. The sea ice would be more extensive, and the weather would be increasingly unfavourable. With the approaching southern winter solstice in June, the hours of sunlight would also be their most limited, and d'Urville realised that he had no choice but to occupy himself with other hydrographic tasks until the approach of the following summer. He sent a boat to the *Zélée* to inform Jacquinot of his decision to sail west-southwest to Raffles Bay, northern New Holland. This would appear to have been to enable the precise determination of a northerly point on the Australian mainland (for the moment as an alternative to Cape York). It also offered some hope of replenishing water supplies. Although we have no evidence of specific orders regarding Raffles Bay, the manner in which d'Urville framed his subsequent report to the minister suggests general (or secret) instructions to gather information of strategic significance regarding anchorages where vessels might find resources.

30

Northern New Holland

… it would be a most humiliating mortification,
to witness the tri-coloured flag … waving over Dampier's Land.*

At dawn on 27 March 1839, the lookouts sighted land clearly extending from the southeast to the southwest on the horizon. This was the flat, forested and deeply indented Cobourg Peninsula, which juts into the Arafura Sea from western Arnhem Land. As the French corvettes approached one of its inlets, Raffles Bay, several Aborigines could be seen on its western shore. About 20 Makassan *praus* of some 20–25 tonnes displacement[1] could also be seen fishing for trepang[2] in the bay. Their crews immediately hauled up Dutch colours as the *Astrolabe* and *Zélée* entered.

The following day, d'Urville dispatched Vincendon-Dumoulin to establish an observatory on a small island near their anchorage. Barlatier-Demas and Tardy de Montravel were ordered to join him there to rate the expedition's chronometers. Gourdin was ordered to draft a map of Raffles Bay, and Coupvent-Desbois was tasked with exploring Bowen Strait between Croker Island and the mainland. Another boat crew was ordered to search for fresh water. Although a 'rather large river' was found (possibly Sleemans Creek), it was only navigable at high tide, and the water remained brackish more than one and a half kilometres inland. Meanwhile, d'Urville and Jacquinot took a whaleboat to search for the ruins of Fort Wellington, a British outpost that had existed on the eastern shore of the bay between 1827 and 1829. Little remained of the settlement, abandoned because its isolated military garrison and convict workforce were unable to establish viable agriculture, create a commercial entrepôt or attract free colonists. D'Urville found a very thick wall, which he thought might have been the vestige of a powder magazine. He also found what he thought were the remnants of a forge and of a well, which yielded only salty water. In his opinion, the indigenous inhabitants had hastened the destruction of the buildings after the British had left. The cemetery, in particular, showed signs of graves plundered for nails (but presumably not robbed of skulls in the manner of Dumoutier!) D'Urville could find no

* Royal Geographical Society deputation to the British Secretary of State, 10 December 1836

trace of the crops or trees that the British had reportedly planted.

He had few kind words for the indigenous inhabitants of Raffles Bay, whom he described as 'men presenting a hideous appearance' and 'unfortunate savages who appeared even deprived of the qualities of the heart which constitute the bonds of society', adding that 'one notices among them no sign indicating gratitude'.[3] However, he did not question their very humanity, as Le Guillou did when he wrote of the Aborigines of Raffles Bay as 'nature at its poorest and most imperfect … the milieu between the monkey and the man'. Although referring to their mouths as 'monstrous furnaces', Le Guillou's prejudices were challenged when, suddenly, he heard them utter 'rather well articulated sounds'![4] For his part, Pavin de La Farge was surprised when, after aiming his gun at what he thought was a kangaroo in a rustling bush, two Aborigines fled shouting at the top of their voices: 'Wattaloo [Waterloo]! Welleton [Wellington]!'[5] Perhaps the most sensitive observer among the ranks of the expedition was d'Urville's secretary, Desgraz. He appears to have asked linguistic questions of about 10 Aborigines and concluded the likely existence of two dialects at Raffles Bay. 'All these men,' he wrote, 'conducted themselves perfectly on board; gentle, calm, nonchalant, they appeared not to have desires to satisfy other than hunger and rest.'[6]

Returning to the *Astrolabe*, d'Urville realised that a small cutter the size of a longboat and flying a British flag had anchored nearby. She was under the command of Lieutenant Peter Benson Stewart RN, who promptly called on the French. Just a few years before, Stewart had served as the mate of HMS *Beagle* and had circled the globe with Robert Fitzroy and Charles Darwin. In 1838, he had arrived at nearby Port Essington with Captain Sir James Bremer aboard HMS *Alligator* to establish a new British settlement. Stewart informed the French that their presence had been reported by the visiting Makassan trepangers. It seems that they also reported the hoisting of the French tricolour from a mast on Observatory Island, which d'Urville suggested might have seemed like confirmation of rumours that the French 'had the intention to found an establishment on this part of the north of New Holland'.[7] D'Urville would have been very surprised to learn that he had helped to precipitate the voyage of HMS *Alligator* and the establishment of the nascent settlement at Port Essington.

In December 1836, Commander John Washington and Captain Francis Beaufort – with whom d'Urville later dined at the Raleigh Club during his visit to London – were part of a deputation to the British secretary of state that urged an enhanced British presence on the northwestern coast of Australia. In the report that they signed, along with Sir John Barrow, second undersecretary to the admiralty, they stated:

> … two splendid expeditions of survey and discovery are about to proceed, next year, to the South Seas and the Pacific, one French, and the other American; both

of which, it can hardly be doubted, will refit and replenish at Sydney. England has hitherto taken the lead in expeditions of this kind and it would be a most humiliating mortification, to witness the tri-coloured flag, or that of the stripes and stars waving over Dampier's Land.[8]

While the deputation might initially have alluded to the French expeditions of Abel-Aubert Dupetit-Thouars or Cyrille Laplace, and most certainly the American expedition of Charles Wilkes, by the time the House of Commons published their report, d'Urville's expedition had also been approved. This was not the end of the matter. The British government was repeatedly lobbied to establish a new settlement on the northern Australian coast by John Barrow (who argued that this could be financed from within the naval budget)[9] and by a young English merchant skipper and author named George Windsor Earl, who was convinced that the potential of the region had been recognised by the French. In the appendix of his book *The Eastern Seas* (1837), Earl alluded to d'Urville's previous visits to Australia:

> Prompt measures enabled us to anticipate their intentions to settle at King George's Sound and at Swan River, neither of which places would have been taken possession of at the time, had not the French been fitting out vessels for the same purpose. We should be unable to shut them out in the same manner from the North coast, which possesses so many secure harbours, that, were they forestalled in one, they might fix themselves in another.[10]

In concluding his appendix (perhaps just before his book went to press in 1837), Earl made yet another apparent reference to d'Urville and what he believed were renewed French ambitions in Australia:

> An expedition for discovery is also fitting out in France, and the overflow of malefactors in that country, together with other circumstances, render it extremely probable that the chief object of the expedition consists in the selection of a spot for the purpose of forming a penal settlement, and that the N. and N.W. coasts of Australia will be examined with this view. It is to be hoped that the project will be thwarted, sufficient sin and misery having already been created by Britain vomiting forth her outcasts to people a country well deserving of a better system of colonisation.[11]

Ironically, d'Urville soon met the man who penned these words. George Earl accompanied Bremer to Port Essington on HMS *Alligator* as an official translator and draughtsman. D'Urville recorded that Earl was with Lieutenant Stewart and a young midshipman named 'Flinders' (almost certainly not his name)[12] on the cutter that came to investigate the arrival of the French at Raffles Bay.

D'Urville was certainly aware that his was the first French expedition to visit this part of Australia. When he later wrote to the navy minister, he made it clear that the British officers who called on him

> … came under the pretext of offering me the services of their commander; but I think, very quickly, to determine our intentions. After having thanked them and especially making clear that we did not have the intention to take possession of Raffles Bay, which they seemed to fear, I promised to make a visit on their governor, if the winds permitted me.[13]

Lieutenant Stewart, George Earl and the young midshipman left Raffles Bay for Port Essington on the morning of 30 March. The French remained at Raffles Bay, completing their surveys, observations and natural history collecting until the morning of 6 April. According to d'Urville, they were 'pursued incessantly and devoured by the mosquitoes, the flies and the ants'.[14] In his journal, he wrote, '… never was there a landfall that was more dejected than that of Raffles Bay. The heat there is intolerable; the excursions ashore – very fatiguing.' And he added that almost every crew member suffered from 'violent colic' and that he was 'not exempt'.[15] Despite the difficulties of labouring in the oppressive heat and humidity of the tropics, the expedition had a number of firm achievements. In addition to its geophysical and navigational observations, including Gourdin's chart of the bay,[16] the naturalists discovered a new terrestrial gastropod named in d'Urville's honour, *Helix urvillei* (*Xanthomelon durvillii*); two marine gastropods, *Nerita alveolus* and *Cerithium kieneri* (*Cerithium (Cerithidea) anticipata*);[17] two crab species, *Pinnotheres latipes* (related to the New Zealand pea crab) and the mole crab *Remipes marmoratus*;[18] and several new beetles, including *Nitidula latens* (*Aethina [Idaethina] latens*), *Onthophagus parvus*[19] and *Anoplostethus roseus*.[20]

Just after the expedition had dismantled its observatory and was about to depart, the British cutter reappeared, this time carrying two midshipmen and a hydrographer, ostensibly under orders to do survey work on the coast. Although they did evidently carry out some soundings and asserted that they entered Raffles Bay to visit the French, one suspects that they were under orders to shadow the *Astrolabe* and *Zélée*. The corvettes reached the open sea by 8.00 am. Despite the assurances of the British surveying party that there were no obstructions between Raffles Bay and Port Essington, the *Zélée* foundered on a pointed rock in three and a half metres of water soon after. Jacquinot unsuccessfully attempted to kedge her off but after sending a diver overboard to investigate, decided to wait for the next high tide to do the job. The *Zélée* floated free at 4.00 pm, just as a combined early dinner for the officers and men had begun.[21] With night approaching, d'Urville decided to anchor and enter Port Essington the following day. Ashore, Bremer became anxious that the French might not call at all, so he sent a boat carrying his European dispatches and a request that d'Urville take them to Hobart if the expedition did not stop at any other British establishment. Once again, warm offers of hospitality were extended, which were no doubt genuine; the newly founded outpost of Victoria had few visitors or distractions.

On 7 April, the corvettes anchored in Port Essington, and d'Urville sent an officer to call on Captain Bremer to tell him that he would visit the following day. Several of his other officers took advantage of a boat sent by the British to conduct them to the settlement. D'Urville, however, chose to land with Jacquinot on Record Point, a long narrow tongue of land opposite the British settlement. Aside from gathering natural history specimens on the shell-covered beach and in the open sclerophyll forest beyond, he had an opportunity for a private discussion and a review of his plans with his second-in-command. To avoid the midday heat, d'Urville visited Captain Bremer and the settlement of Victoria early the following morning. Bremer, a dark bald-headed veteran of the Battle of Trafalgar, who later commanded British naval forces during the First Opium War with China,[22] immediately made a favourable impression on d'Urville, who wrote that he was an 'officer of amenity, of gentleness of character and of a noble simplicity of manners'.[23] Had they discussed their very early careers, they would have been surprised to learn that they had both gone to sea on ships with the same name: in Bremer's case, the 98-gun guard-ship *Sandwich*, stationed at the Nore in 1794, and in d'Urville's case, the little 16-gun cutter *Sandwich*, captured by the French in 1799.

In d'Urville's opinion, Bremer was animated by 'very ardent zeal' and was convinced of the 'success of the nascent colony'.[24] D'Urville, however, later reported to his minister that he was 'far from sharing the high hopes' that Bremer had for Port Essington. Yet, he acknowledged

> … that an establishment in this location … will be a great benefit for ships intending to make the passage through Torres Strait. At least after this thorny navigation, they can count on a place of resources and refreshments, and in the event of disaster … assured assistance. Moreover, to judge by work already carried out, it seems to me that in six months the sailors and the soldiers of the corvette *Alligator* assigned to the service of this colony have used their time profitably.[25]

In his official account, d'Urville recognised that the settlement at Port Essington had already succeeded as a British strategic manoeuvre to retain sovereignty over the whole continent: '… it is principally to mark this taking of possession and to assure themselves of this vast territory that they have put so much effort into raising a settlement on these not very fertile shores'.[26]

As at Raffles Bay, there was no peace from the flies and the mosquitoes, and plunging

'*Port Essington*', *lithograph by Léon-Jean-Baptiste Sabatier after a sketch by Louis Le Breton,* Voyage au pôle sud et dans l'Océanie, *Atlas pittoresque, Paris, 1846, plate no. 120. D'Urville visited Port Essington, on the Cobourg Peninsula of western Arnhem Land, in April 1839. Ironically, his expedition appears to have helped precipitate the establishment of the recent British settlement. Many of the buildings in Louis Le Breton's sketch were destroyed by a cyclone nine months later.* National Library of Australia, PIC S11256

into the sea in an attempt to escape this airborne misery only offered an opportunity for small crabs to attach painfully to the body instead. D'Urville was impressed by the bounty of fish to be had in these same waters, recording that his men caught 68 kilograms of excellent-quality fish in just half an hour. Ashore, d'Urville noted how the 'ants' (*Isoptera* termites) built nests three to four metres in height and, despite mentioning how they rendered tree-trunks unusable for ship-building, he did not comment on their likely role in devouring the buildings he had previously blamed the Aborigines for destroying at Raffles Bay. The same termites had probably already begun to devour the prefabricated timber buildings that d'Urville noted, in admiration, had been transported from Port Jackson and erected at Port Essington. Seven such buildings housed the commandant (d'Urville continued to refer to him as 'governor'), the garrison of 37 marines (commanded by Captain John Macarthur and Lieutenant Phineas Priest) and a handful of civilian staff, and included a hospital, kitchen and storehouse; within a decade, termites would make the latter storehouse uninhabitable. In addition, a prefabricated church was shipped to Port Essington as a gift from William Broughton, the Church of England's Bishop of Australia. The wives of four soldiers lived with their husbands in separate cottages that they had constructed themselves. Sailors from HMS *Alligator*, HMS *Britomart* and the wrecked supply vessel *Orontes* assisted the marines in their labours.[27] Guns salvaged from the *Orontes* were also relocated to a provisional wooden fort erected on a small promontory overlooking the sea. Bremer's residence was 30 metres away on an elevated plateau, which enabled him to surveil the entire settlement and communicate readily with the *Alligator* and the *Britomart*. D'Urville was impressed by its design and comfort: 'salon, bedroom, workroom, toilet, bathroom, office, nothing was lacking'.[28] Yet the impression gained from Le Breton's sketch[29] of Bremer's domain is of a cluster of a dozen rudimentary buildings: small, airless, without verandahs and little suited to tropical heat and humidity, or the force of recurrent cyclones.[30]

D'Urville was drawn to a number of officers at Port Essington who had a passion for natural history. One was Lieutenant Phineas Priest of the Royal Marines, who was supervising the construction of cottages for his men. Priest showed d'Urville his extensive collection of local natural history specimens and made a gift of a number of prize examples to the French expedition. D'Urville also met the botanist John Armstrong, appointed to create a garden of useful plants at the settlement. This he had done with great difficulty because insects ravaged his seedlings and the settlement had no streams for irrigation, only five wells sunk 10 metres in depth. Immediately prior to his Port Essington appointment, Armstrong had been an assistant gardener to the orientalist and traveller Sir George Staunton.[31] Whether this fact ever came up in conversation with Armstrong's French visitors is unknown, but it would have interested d'Urville, who owned a copy of Staunton's *An Authentic Account of an Embassy from the King of Great Britain to the Emperor of China* (1797). Another local collector with a rich array of ethnographic items was Midshipman Edward Gordon Bremer, Captain Bremer's eldest son. A talented mimic, he entertained the French with a nose-flute and 'burlesque' (presumably mocking) impersonations of indigenous dance and music, but also adroit demonstrations of the woomera and spear.

The local Aboriginal people seem to have kept their distance during the visit of the *Astrolabe* and the *Zélée* to Port Essington. D'Urville thought that the reason was a death after the Aborigines and Makassans (who had a seasonal camp for smoking and drying trepang not far from the British settlement) had 'come to blows', a few days before he arrived.[32] However, the journal account of British Surgeon James Wallace suggests that on 2 March there was no death, only a 'quarrel … between the natives and the Malays which nearly ended in bloodshed'. Perhaps a more potent reason for why the Aborigines were shy of Port Essington is that on the same day, 'a native was whipped having been detected in an attempt to steal a knife from Government House'.[33] Of d'Urville's expedition, Wallace wrote warmly: 'The results of the voyage will be creditable to France & beneficial to the world. We have been happy together for two days & we only regret that a longer period of enjoyment has not been permitted.'[34] D'Urville visited the hospital, presumably then under Wallace's charge, and noted that there were only three patients with injuries and one 'nostalgic',[35] the latter case presumably suffering from debilitating depression, which hinted at difficulties that ultimately beset more than one member of the isolated British garrison.[36]

D'Urville saw little prospect of agriculture succeeding at Port Essington. Aside from the lack of water and poor fertility of the soil, there was a scarcity of suitable labour. He believed that it would take 'centuries' to bring the indigenous inhabitants 'to a more civilised state', and in the course of colonisation, they might share the tragic fate of the indigenous inhabitants of Van Diemen's Land. In any case, he could not see them tilling the land for the British – slavery was at an end – nor could he see the Malay people to the north abandoning their fertile fields to toil in the unproductive lands of northern Australia. Even the use of convicts, such as those that had been used to establish Sydney, would be predicated on what the soil could offer. D'Urville asked pointedly whether it would be 'sufficient compensation for the effort of its cultivation and the costs it would impose on its possessors?'[37] He probably already knew the answer. Unlike the settlement at Raffles Bay, convicts were employed at Port Essington for only four months in late 1844 and early 1845. Four years later, the settlement was abandoned.[38]

On the morning of 8 March, d'Urville had breakfast aboard the *Astrolabe* with Captain Bremer and his principal officers. (Bremer's first lieutenant was his son-in-law Augustus Leopold Kuper, who later rose to the rank of admiral.) He then made his farewells and offered a toast to the success of the colony and to the health of its 'governor'. D'Urville also ordered a seven-gun salute in Bremer's honour. The British reciprocated with their best wishes for the success of d'Urville's expedition and – once Bremer had returned to HMS *Alligator* – a salute of their own. By this time, the French corvettes had already set sail and were almost out of earshot of the settlement; d'Urville, however, was gracious enough to write that he and his men could still discern the smoke from the *Alligator*'s guns.

31

The augmentation of the Indies

… more lines than is in the new map,
with the augmentation of the Indies.
William Shakespeare [Maria]

If the expedition could not enter the Pacific through Torres Strait south of New Guinea, one alternative was to sail to the north and eventually to the east of the island. There were still potentially useful surveys to undertake en route – including determining the precise locations of the extremities of important landmasses. When such points had been fixed before, they offered an opportunity for reference, comparison and determination of error. In doing so, they would contribute to an ever-growing body of data that gave precision to the cartography of the globe. There were still opportunities to collect new species of plants and animals, and to conduct geophysical and oceanographic experiments. Nevertheless, the corvettes remained at the mercy of the prevailing easterly winds and the need to replenish food and water.

On leaving Port Essington, d'Urville set a north-northeasterly course for Dobo, a harbour on Wamar Island in the Aru group of the eastern Moluccas, not far from the island of Wokam (Tanahbesar). The corvettes arrived on 17 April 1839. The Dutch had established a settlement on western Wokam in 1793 but it was abandoned during the years of war that enveloped the Netherlands soon after. By now, scurvy had made an appearance among the crew: Hombron reported two men with symptoms that had appeared since leaving northern New Holland. To cure them and prevent further cases, d'Urville knew that fresh provisions were needed urgently. With the aid of a local Protestant minister and schoolmaster, he purchased some chickens and several baskets of sweet potatoes from a village but at 'an exorbitant price'.[1]

After four days of scientific work, the expedition set sail for Dubus Harbour, Triton (Kamrau) Bay, on the Papuan coast, and dropped anchor on 24 April. Here, too, there

---

* *Twelfth Night* (*ca.*1601–62), act iii, scene ii, lines 84–85

had been a Dutch settlement, established in 1829 (but abandoned in 1835) and named in honour of Leonard du Bus de Gisignies, then governor-general of the Netherlands East Indies. The Dutch fort had been named in honour of d'Urville's friend Pieter Merkus, governor of Ambon. D'Urville explored the abandoned settlement – rain-drenched and hemmed in by mountains – and delighted in the natural splendour of the dense forest that surrounded the area cleared by the Dutch. The local Papuans – long visited by Ceramese, who not only came in search of trepang, shells and birds of paradise but also carried off slaves – were at first wary of the French but proved hospitable when their fears were allayed. D'Urville even engaged some to gather natural history specimens for him. It was here that the expedition collected a number of new bird species, including a new riflebird, *Ptilotis similis*; the double-eyed fig parrot (*Cyclopsitta diophthalma*), also found in Australia; and the Stephan's dove (*Chalcophaps stephani*).[2] A large number of coconuts were also gathered on offshore islands, in addition to other fruits and even peppers – the latter presumably planted by the Dutch. By the time the expedition set sail on 30 April, d'Urville was pleased to learn that his two scurvy cases no longer had symptoms. However, departing proved no simple matter. Although towed out of Dubus Harbour by their longboats, the *Astrolabe* and the *Zélée* were forced by feeble winds and pouring rain to tack all day long to clear Triton Bay.

Having rounded Cape Van Den Bosch (Tanjung Katumin), the expedition sailed to Waru Bay on the northeastern coast of the island of Ceram, inhabited by Ceramese and their Papuan slaves. Here they purchased a number of goats and hunted wild pigs, which were not eaten by the Muslim Ceramese. Rounding the island of Buru, the corvettes then sailed to Makassar (Ujung Pandang), southeastern Sulawesi, dropping anchor on 21 May. At Fort Rotterdam, the French were very kindly received by the Dutch resident Reinier Filliettaz Bousquet, whose father d'Urville had met during one of his earlier visits to the Netherlands East Indies. For d'Urville, the visit was an opportunity to see where the Makassan trepangers hailed from. While Vincendon-Dumoulin had expressed admiration for 'brave'[3] individuals on the north coast of New Holland, in Makassar, d'Urville dismissed them as 'ignorant and lazy, seemingly only adept at fishing, navigation [and], above all else, that which facilitates piracy'.[4] What did impress him, however, was the gender equality of the Makassans, which he believed made them 'very superior to other Malays'.[5] Makassar also enabled d'Urville to renew his connection with the Chinese, whose language, literature and culture fascinated him and whose work ethic he admired. 'The Chinaman,' he wrote, 'whom one finds everywhere active and hardworking, carries on every trade, every kind of industry.' He added, 'no people of the world are more persevering, more indefatigable, more industrious'.[6]

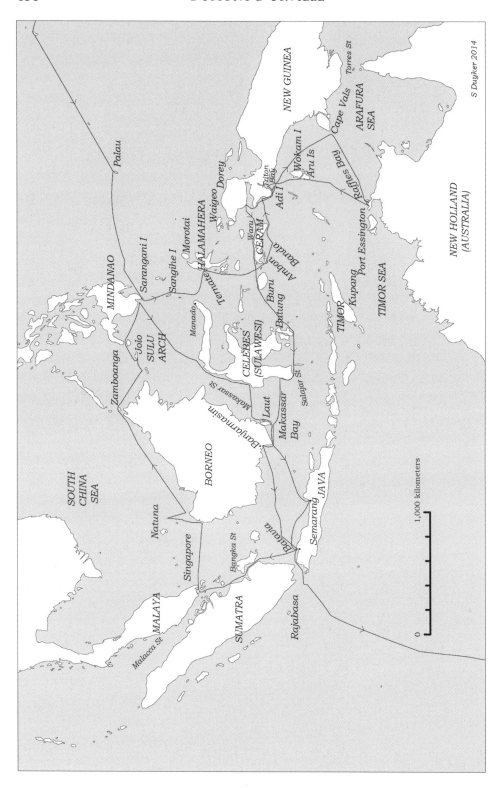

S Duyker 2014

The *Astrolabe* and the *Zélée* left Makassar on 28 May. After a very brief visit to Banjarmasin, southern Borneo – where a new subspecies of the yellow-vented bulbul[7] and two new beetle species were collected,[8] but little progress could be made penetrating the coastal mangrove swamp – the expedition continued on to Java. On 6 June, the corvettes anchored in the port of Batavia (Jakarta) among 47 merchant ships and two Dutch naval vessels (one a steamer). D'Urville immediately dispatched Marescot ashore to present his compliments to the governor-general of the Netherlands East Indies, Dominque de Eerens, but soon learned that the governor-general was not in Batavia but at his summer residence in Buitenzorg (Bogor).

D'Urville was disappointed not to receive any official correspondence from France on his arrival in Batavia and was particularly upset at the complete lack of acknowledgement of the efforts of his young officers and men. Nevertheless, he dispatched another official report to the minister.[9] In Batavia he purchased salted provisions, flour and biscuits from the firm of Tissot, Lagnier & Co, merchants originally from Marseille but established in Batavia for several decades and owners of a fleet of seven vessels.[10] In the office of Augustin Lagnier,[11] d'Urville encountered the French naturalist Pierre-Médard Diard, whom he had met on an earlier visit to Batavia. A former student of Georges Cuvier, Diard had left France for India in 1816 and had then collected zoological and botanical specimens in Bengal, Malacca, Sumatra, Singapore, Vietnam, Java and Borneo for the Muséum national d'histoire naturelle, Paris.[12] Subsequently, a dozen animal species were named in his honour by French zoologists. In early 1828, Diard entered Dutch service as a member of the Natuurkundige Commissie voor Nederlands-Indië (Natural History Commission for the Netherlands Indies).[13] D'Urville seems to have resented not only this foreign service but also Diard's 'mask' of amiability and his semblance of interest in the work of the naturalists of the expedition. Desgraz, usually one of the most charitable spirits of the expedition, was scathing of Diard, whom he held responsible for their cool reception in the Dutch colonial capital. Although Desgraz does not refer to Diard by name, the references to an individual previously employed by the 'Jardin des Plantes de Paris' leave little doubt who he meant. For Desgraz, Diard was not much more than a mendacious spy for the Dutch, and he considered it 'painful to see a Frenchman devoting himself to such reprehensible actions'.[14] Yet for all his duplicity, Diard took d'Urville to visit the museum of natural history and archaeology that he had established in Batavia in 1829. He also wrote a letter of introduction for Surgeon Le Guillou to visit the museum's young director, Dr Eltio Alegondas Forsten,[15] and he facilitated an invitation for d'Urville and Jacquinot to visit the governor-general in Buitenzorg.

Opposite: *Map 8. South-East Asia, New Guinea and Northern New Holland (Australia) and the route of the* Astrolabe *and the* Zélée, *January–October 1839*

Arriving at the governor-general's grand summer palace, built in Palladian style 60 kilometres south of Batavia, d'Urville found the vice-regal etiquette excessive and irritating. Fortunately, it became more relaxed by the time he and Jacquinot actually dined with their hosts. D'Urville even admitted to enjoying conversation with the governor-general (a former infantry divisional commander, who died less than a year later) and his family. The highlight of his overnight visit to Buitenzorg was seeing, for the first time, the world-famous botanical gardens that still surround the (now-presidential) palace.

On returning to Batavia, d'Urville and Jacquinot attended a meeting of the Bataviaasch Genootschap van Kunsten en Wetenschappen (Batavian Society of Arts and Sciences), chaired by d'Urville's old friend Pieter Merkus, who had retired to Batavia after service in Ambon. Although the meeting was in Dutch, Merkus extended a warm and flattering welcome in French to d'Urville, who had been a member since his visit of 1828. Pierre Diard took the opportunity to nominate Hector Jacquinot for honorary membership, which perhaps explains the latter's more charitable sentiments towards the expatriate French naturalist.[16]

After almost a fortnight in Batavia, the expedition weighed anchor on 19 June and sailed along the northern coast of Sumatra and then across the Strait of Malacca to the island of Singapore, arriving on 27 June. The island then had a population of 23,000, of whom only 270 were Europeans. Le Guillou described the large homes of the Europeans as 'small palaces with peristyles and terraces, clean, elegant, stylish, surrounded by plantations and delicious gardens', and he added that 'in the midst of all this, life slides along with a somnolence that would make the sore *lazzarone* [ruffian] of Naples envious'.[17] D'Urville dispatched Ensign Duroch to present his compliments to the British governor of the Straits Settlements, Samuel George Bonham, and the commander of the visiting French expedition was promptly invited to dinner. He was warmly received, but during the meal the conversation turned to the looming threat of war between Britain and China. D'Urville, the passionate Sinophile, clearly sympathised with the Chinese emperor Daoguang's attempts to stop the insidious opium trade but realised only later that Britain was using the heavy-handed actions of the mandarins as an excuse for broader ambitions. Bonham toed his government's free-trade line; the loyal servant of an ever-expanding empire, he was destined to become the third British governor of Hong Kong, an island ceded to Britain after the First Opium War, which began just five months after d'Urville left Singapore.[18]

D'Urville received neither personal nor official mail in the Straits Settlements but had word of Adélie and young Jules, thanks to Clara Jacquinot's letters to her husband. He had deliveries of his own to make: before leaving France, d'Urville had been given copies of the *Annales maritimes et coloniales* for distribution to various chambers of commerce during his voyage. In Singapore, this led him to the door of Joseph Balestier, a prominent local merchant and sugar planter but also the island's first American consul. Balestier was of French Huguenot descent, as was his wife Maria (whom d'Urville also met), the daughter of the famous American Revolutionary patriot Paul Revere. D'Urville declined their repeated invitations to stay at their home, just as he had declined a similar invitation from Governor Bonham. Nevertheless, he took the opportunity to exchange a number of rare seashells with Balestier and question him about the reliability of Benjamin Morrell's testimony on survivors and descendants of the Lapérouse expedition. D'Urville freely admitted his obsession with this question, but he was clearly not prepared to leave any stone unturned given public concern and reactions to Morrell's story at the time of his departure from France. Like Paul Delano (the American consul in Talcahuano), Balestier painted an unflattering portrait of Morrell and assured d'Urville that his story was an 'amusing tale'.[19]

On 29 June, d'Urville was aboard the *Astrolabe*, writing to his family, when he was visited by a French clergyman, Bishop Jean-Paul Courvezy, accompanied by two other Catholic priests, including one who was Chinese. Courvezy, originally from Narbonne and a former professor of dogma at the Catholic seminary in Chartres, was a member of the Société des missions étrangères de Paris. In April 1832, the pope appointed him *coadjuteur* (auxiliary bishop) of the 'apostolic vicariate of Siam'. As early as 1835, he recognised the growing importance of Singapore as a commercial hub that would facilitate communication with the 'diverse provinces of his immense vicariate' and moved there in 1838.[20] To d'Urville, however, he framed his relocation in the context of the 'ceaseless persecutions with which the missions were threatened in Japan' and what he thought was 'their interest'.[21] Courvezy also praised Cyrille Laplace's intervention in Vietnam to save the life of a condemned missionary. No doubt he expected a reaffirmation of the long-held French doctrine of the 'Protectorate of Missions'.[22] He invited all the expedition's officers to dinner, but d'Urville excused himself on the grounds of a pre-existing invitation to dine with (the Protestant!) Joseph Balestier. This seems to have displeased the bishop, who d'Urville soon learned had a reputation not only for intolerance but also for a dispute with the local Portuguese clergy.[23] Nevertheless, d'Urville, flattered him with a nine-gun salute on his departure from the *Astrolabe*.

On 2 July, the expedition left Singapore and set sail for the western coast of Borneo. Six days later, the corvettes anchored in the mouth of the Sambas River. D'Urville originally intended to call on the assistant resident Reinier Bloem and deliver packages for local missionaries, but initial investigations by Barlatier-Demas, Ducorps and Honoré Jacquinot in the *Astrolabe*'s longboat revealed that it would take at least three days to reach the Dutch settlement because of the river's strong contrary current.

D'Urville abandoned the idea but was grateful to entrust the packages to the skipper of a vessel belonging to the sultan of Sambas. Flying a Dutch flag, armed with one carronade and large enough to carry 15–18 men, it approached the French corvettes during an anti-smuggling cruise on the estuary. D'Urville's other consolations were his boat party's natural history observations and Honoré Jacquinot's capture of a pregnant female proboscis monkey (*Nasalis larvatus*). The younger Jacquinot thought it was a species particularly requested by the museum and the academy,[24] but they actually had gibbons and orangutans on their wish-list.[25] With her hairless face, long nose and other features that seemed almost human, she clearly fascinated d'Urville and the crew, but alas, wounded during her capture, she died two days after giving birth to a stillborn offspring. Although she did not belong to a hitherto unknown species, her body was preserved and was the second mammal specimen described in the third volume of the expedition's zoological results.[26]

After approaching the Natuna group, the expedition traversed the South China Sea and the northern coast of Borneo. During this leg of the voyage, Jean-Baptiste Pied, a sailor from Bayonne, died of dysentery aboard the *Zélée*. Less than a week later, on 21 July, the corvettes reached the island of Jolo in the Sulu Archipelago. In Singapore, d'Urville had been informed that the sultan of Sulu, Mohammed Jamalul Kiram I, was keen to further trade with France. However, the expedition soon discovered that the sultan's hereditary authority was 'only nominal'; he had little to trade and the island was essentially a nest of lawless pirates.[27] Midshipman Gervaize visited the centre of the island but was the only crew member to do so, under the protection of one local chief.[28] Dumoutier's attempt to buy skulls elicited a prompt offer from one man to sever the head of one of his enemies! Naturally, the offer was declined.[29] D'Urville considered the surrounding mountains too dangerous for his naturalists and even the town unsafe for his officers and men, so he decided not to linger any longer than was necessary. Despite this, the expedition made a significant ornithological discovery prior to departure: the collection of the type specimen of the Mindanao bleeding-heart dove, *Pampusanna criniger* (*Gallicolumba criniger*), so named for the scarlet spot on its breast.[30] After obtaining some fresh provisions and giving the sultan a seven-gun salute, the expedition set sail again on 25 July. The French departed with a man named Kakou, who gained a passage to freedom aboard the *Zélée*. Originally from the island of Buton, off Sulawesi, and about 40 years of age, judging by his portrait,[31] he had been kidnapped and taken by pirates to Jolo as a slave. Lieutenant Dubouzet, who spoke some Malay, took pity on him, and he remained with the expedition as far as Semarang. Le Guillou – who disobeyed orders and spent the night ashore at Jolo – was nearly left behind.

Three days later, on 28 July, the corvettes reached Zamboanga, on the western tip

'Kakou, esclave fugitif (Archipel Soulou)', lithograph by
Paul Petit, from a sketch by Charles Delhomme for Élie
Le Guillou's Voyage autour du monde de l'Astrolabe et de
la Zélée, Berquet et Petion, Paris, 1842, plate 27. Kakou,
a Boutonese slave, escaped Jolo pirates aboard the Zélée.
Author's collection

of Mindanao, and were guided to their anchorage by a boat dispatched by the Spanish governor, Lieutenant-Colonel Manuel Sanz. At dawn the following day, the corvettes saluted the Spanish fort with 21 guns; the Spaniards replied with a 21-gun salute of their own. But since this was also the anniversary of the commencement of the Revolution of 1830, d'Urville added another 21-gun salute to the deafening cycle. As he wryly put it: 'Thanks to our visit, the inhabitants of this peaceful city now know that, nine years ago, France had a revolution.'[32]

The French were warmly received by Governor Sanz, a veteran infantry commander. (A decade earlier, he had played a pivotal role in the final suppression of the long-running Dagohoy rebellion on the island of Bohol.) Like d'Urville, Sanz detested etiquette and excessive formality, and convinced the visiting French officers to change from their heavy naval uniforms into light, white, cotton clothes, more suitable for the tropics, which he supplied. He also offered the services of 'his house, his table, his horses and his carriage'.[33] D'Urville's account indicates that this hospitality was willingly accepted, perhaps before they realised that the governor requisitioned the only four horses in the town besides his own. Guided by Lieutenant Manuel de la Cruz, the Spanish naval officer who had piloted them to their anchorage, d'Urville, Dubouzet and Vincendon-Dumoulin rode out of Zamboanga on horseback, and Jacquinot followed in the governor's carriage. In the surrounding countryside, they crossed the Tumaga River and called on a very elderly military veteran, Don Mauricio de Léon, who 77 years before had taken part in the unsuccessful defence of Manila against the British. Significantly, it was after this same battle in 1762 that the Scottish hydrographer Alexander Dalrymple gained access to the contents of the secret Spanish naval archives and details of the voyage of Luis Vaez de Torres, who in 1606 passed through the strait now named in his honour. Although James Cook had confirmed the existence of Torres Strait in 1770, it was a passage that still eluded d'Urville.

On their return to Zamboanga, d'Urville and his senior officers dined with Governor Sanz. The table was set for eight but, according to d'Urville, there was enough food for 40. That evening, the local colonial naval and militia officers – commanding a garrison of some 300 men at Fort San Felipe and other posts – were presented to d'Urville. He was surprised that all, except the sergeant-major, were of mixed race, and that many were very elderly. Their large number also surprised him, although d'Urville realised that the Spanish could afford so many officers because they were paid much less than their Dutch and British counterparts. D'Urville was aware of the antipathy of local Christians towards the surrounding Muslim Moros, and he must have been aware, as Roquemaurel certainly was, that the local garrison comprised native Tagalog-speaking Filipino and mixed-race soldiers.[34] A social demarcation between the Spanish and their local and mixed-race subjects (including the attractive mistresses of many of the soldiers) was readily obvious: at a ball the French attended, the locals ate in a separate room from the Spanish and their guests. Desgraz noted:

> The familiarity in our manners astonishes these poor *Indios*; accustomed to the cold manners of the whites, they find us charming. This is very natural: we treat them as we would someone at home of any condition, while the pure-blooded Spaniards regard them as being of an inferior status; and though, in general, they act with benevolence towards them, nevertheless they make them feel this alleged superiority heavily.[35]

Aside from the governor, d'Urville appears to have been particularly grateful to Lieutenant Manuel de la Cruz for his assistance during their sojourn. He was working on an official geography of Mindanao and had also been involved in numerous anti-piracy operations in the region. He gave d'Urville vocabularies to aid his linguistic studies, and he gave Vincendon-Dumoulin a copy of his draft chart of southern Mindanao. Sadly, de la Cruz died some six months after d'Urville's visit to Zamboanga.[36]

The expedition had a death of its own in Zamboanga. On 5 August, Pierre Avril, a hardworking and respected sailor on the *Astrolabe*, died of tetanus after stepping on a nail while the corvette was mooring. Originally from Bordeaux, Avril had previously served in the merchant marine – for more than four years on a vessel based in Rio de Janeiro and for two years on a vessel based in Calcutta – before returning to France and joining d'Urville's expedition.[37] He was laid to rest in Zamboanga by the local curate and a burial party of more than 30 of his friends from both corvettes. It would be months before his 22-year-old wife and two young children would learn of his sad fate.

The next day, the expedition left Zamboanga. Jacquinot considered his sojourn there 'one of the most agreeable' of his 'adventurous life'.[38] Having determined the location of the western tip of Mindanao, d'Urville planned to fix the position of the island's southernmost point then re-enter the Pacific. In his report to the minister, dispatched from Zamboanga, he indicated his intention to traverse the Caroline Islands and cross the equator at a longitude of 160°E (of the Paris meridian) before sailing to 'Wangaroa'[39] in New Zealand, then replenishing in Sydney.[40] This suggests his intention to pass once more through the Solomon Islands and probably survey the still-uncharted northern coasts of the Russell Islands and Guadalcanal, which he had not been able to do in 1838. Although he was able to sight Sarangani Island off southern Mindanao, contrary winds soon resigned him to an alternative passage, through Makassar Strait, Sunda Strait and around western and southern New Holland to re-victual in Hobart (instead of Sydney) for his second Antarctic descent.

Shortly after crossing the equator on 29 August, the expedition encountered strong contrary winds and pouring rain. D'Urville decided to anchor near Pemarung, a low-lying island off the east coast of Borneo, and await more favourable weather. The tidal waters were very shallow, and the corvettes were briefly embayed at low tide but without much anxiety. D'Urville dispatched two boats, one under the command of Tardy de Montravel, the other under the command of Gourdin, to take Vincendon-Dumoulin (with his geophysical instruments) and the naturalists ashore. They were accompanied by Ducorps, who went hunting monkeys and who at one stage found himself perilously mired up to his waist. He killed two female proboscis monkeys and felled another with a musket ball to the arm. The latter, taken alive, was officially

'*Chasse aux Nasicas, Détroit de Makassar*', *lithograph by Rigo frères, for Élie Le Guillou's* Voyage autour du monde de l'Astrolabe et de la Zélée, *Berquet et Petion, Paris, 1842, plate 20. In late August 1839, d'Urville decided to anchor near Pemarung, a low-lying island off the east coast of Borneo, and await more favourable weather. During their visit the* Astrolabe's *purser, Jacques-Louis Ducorps, went hunting monkeys and at one stage found himself perilously mired up to his waist.* Author's collection

handed over to Hombron but quickly adopted by the crew; she was sketched by Le Breton. Alas, the monkey's wounded arm became gangrenous, and Hombron, refusing the combined requests of the crew to amputate, instead strangled the poor creature to end her suffering. D'Urville's account indicates that he was determined to preserve yet another intact museum specimen in alcohol. Five days later, on 8 September, this would be the fate of another adopted crew member, the Tongan Mafi Kelepi, who died gasping for breath, a victim of pulmonary tuberculosis. Despite his service as a valued member of the *Astrolabe*'s crew and despite d'Urville's acknowledgement of his humanity, 'very gentle character' and 'rare intelligence', he was accorded neither the dignity of a funeral like that of his close friend Pierre Avril, nor even a simple burial at sea. Instead, d'Urville glibly recorded: 'His body was conserved in a barrel of arrack and he was made part of the collection deposited by us at the Muséum d'histoire naturelle'![41] When Henri Ducrotay de Blainville came to report this to the Académie des sciences, he remarked that the expedition was 'not always limited to collecting fragments of skeletons of men, but that, it is the first … to bring us, entirely preserved in alcohol, the body …'[42] Before the expedition's departure, Blainville had urged the naturalists 'to occupy themselves constantly, in a special manner, with all that can be used to improve the natural history of man'. His very next instruction was 'to take all the suitable precautions of conservation, as for the animals which need to be in wine spirit'.[43] Hombron seems to have been little troubled by the notion of combining these two separate instructions and preserving the Tongan like an animal specimen. In the first zoological volume of the expedition's official reports, Hombron contributed a rambling 350-page essay entitled 'De l'homme dans ses rapports avec la création' ('Of man in his relations with creation'), a stridently racist and polygenist work published four years after d'Urville's death. Given its length and verbose meanderings, which had little to do with the expedition, one wonders whether it would have been included had d'Urville been alive. In Part V, Hombron declared that 'all leads us to believe that superior man did not appear on earth other than after inferior man'.[44] On the continent of Australia, Hombron informed his readers, 'there exist several species of man'.[45] Perhaps in search of proof of such diversity on the globe, he and Honoré Jacquinot would eventually remove Mafi's flesh and mount his bones as an exhibitable skeleton. His bones (and his separately catalogued hair in the Dumoutier collection) are still held by the Muséum national d'histoire naturelle in Paris.[46]

Before leaving Makassar Strait, the expedition visited the island of Laut and soon after effectively completed a circumnavigation of Borneo. As the corvettes traversed the Java Sea, d'Urville was confined to his cabin with severe colic. Hombron's journal indicates that he had also been suffering from recurrent gout, and it seems little wonder that he should have felt progressively worse as a result of his surgeon's ministering. Initially, d'Urville rejected Hombron's proposal to treat him with leeches and opium but agreed to daily drafts of 'wine of colchicum',[47] a preparation made from the bulbs of the autumn crocus (*Colchicum autumnale*), steeped in alcohol and then mixed with wine. As previously mentioned, it has been known since ancient times to be useful in the treatment of gout but contains an alkaloid, colchicine, that was very likely the cause of the severe intestinal pain the unfortunate d'Urville then suffered.[48] Some idea of the intensity of the side effects can be gleaned from the fact that Hombron then treated d'Urville with doses of sulphate of morphine.

On 24 September, the *Astrolabe* and *Zélée* anchored in the northern Javanese port of Semarang. Ensign Duroch was immediately sent ashore to present d'Urville's compliments to the Dutch resident, Guillaume-Louis Baud, who received him graciously. On hearing that the expedition's commander was ill, Baud invited him to stay at his country residence at Bajong. D'Urville declined but was happy to visit his home and the surrounding countryside in his company. He soon learned that the resident was well connected: he was a nephew of Jean-Chrétien Baud, the immediate predecessor of Dominque de Eerens as governor-general of the Netherlands East Indies. Like his uncle, Baud would eventually serve as the Netherlands' minister for colonies.[49]

Meanwhile, the purser Ducorps called on Joseph Tissot, the Semarang-based partner of Augustin Lagnier, to arrange for the re-provisioning of the expedition. Unfortunately, Tissot was not able to supply the corvettes with wine, which he asserted could only be found in Batavia, so d'Urville asked him to write to Lagnier to arrange for the required quantity to be readied (in addition to supplies of cheese) for immediate embarkation on their arrival in Batavia harbour, which he promptly did. Everything else that the expedition required was obtained from him in Semarang.

Tissot, then one of the richest men in Semarang, also offered d'Urville accommodation in his home, a mansion originally built for an Armenian who, having been bankrupted, was forced to sell it to Tissot for less than a tenth of its original cost. Ironically, within six years, Tissot and his partners would themselves be forced into liquidation. Once again, d'Urville declined an offer of accommodation but happily accepted an invitation to dine with Tissot and his family and his offer to facilitate his other visits ashore. These included a call on Pieter Boll, whom he had first met in Ambon and who had promised him specimens of two *Nautilus* – comprising the entire cephalopod animal, not simply the spiral shell. On the advice of Hombron, d'Urville arranged for the repatriation of the ailing Delafond, who was sent home on a merchant vessel, the Bordeaux-registered *Bombay*, recently arrived from the west coast of America. One wonders whether Delafond's greatest blessing was to be freed from Hombron's pharmacopœia; he survived the voyage (as we shall see, he was able to greet the expedition on its return to France) and lived another 50 years! Later he helped develop innovations for steam power in the navy and worked for a civilian steamship company for four years. On rejoining the navy, he took charge of the construction of the floating battery, the *Implacable*, and commanded the French naval station at the mouth of the Danube.[50]

Before d'Urville left Semarang, Tissot organised a party in the expedition's honour. Virtually everyone spoke French, and d'Urville felt that they had been 'transported into a French salon'.[51] Among those invited were a French sugar planter and former soldier named Louis Vitalis and a Captain Thébaud, a merchant skipper (probably from Nantes)[52] recently arrived from Batavia. Thébaud amused d'Urville and his officers by recounting gossip of their supposedly shabby dress during their recent visit to Batavia, ostensibly 'to insult the population', and that the officers 'more often wore only a solitary epaulette'.[53]

Tissot's party was graced with French wine and by a 'Malay' orchestra, which played European waltzes and contra-dances. As much as d'Urville enjoyed the evening, he was clearly unimpressed by those guests who whispered 'malign insinuations' in his ear regarding the presence of those of mixed race.[54] (Le Guillou's account indicates that those targeted included Tissot's wife[55] and daughters.[56]) D'Urville wrote: 'The stupid prejudice which, in the colonies tends to establish such deep differences between the mulatto and Europeans, exists here in all its force, and moreover a very large demarcation reigns between the noble families, the civil servants, the merchants and the Malay *metis*.'[57]

On the evening of 30 September, after further astronomical observations, the expedition set sail from Semarang with a northerly wind. Four days later, the corvettes anchored off Leyden Island (Pulau Nyamuk-besar) within view of Batavia. Ducorps was sent ashore to pay for and arrange delivery of the wine and cheese ordered from Lagnier. While the expedition waited for him, d'Urville visited Leyden Island with Vincendon-Dumoulin. They found it so infested with mosquitoes that their only escape was to dive in the sea.

Early the next day, 5 October, several praus loaded with the expedition's supplies arrived, but it was not until 11.00 am that Ducorps managed to return to the *Astrolabe*. It was not just the lack of wind that delayed him; he had neglected to negotiate a price for his own re-embarkation and, stranded ashore, was seemingly at the mercy of extortionate monetary demands. He resolved his dilemma by paying a heavy 30 francs to reach the closest French merchant vessel in the harbour, then her obliging second-in-command took him the rest of the way.

From Leyden Island, the corvettes sailed to Lampung Bay on the Sumatran side of Sunda Strait. On 8 October, they anchored off Rajabasa, nestled beneath the verdant volcanic peak of the same name. D'Urville went ashore with the naturalists and scientific staff charged with navigational astronomy and geophysical observations. The locals were friendly and welcoming, and he enjoyed the idyllic surroundings. The local water seemed pure and easily accessible, but no sooner were they underway again than dysentery, which had already afflicted some in Semarang, became widespread among the crew. D'Urville did not suspect contaminated water. Like the prevailing epidemiological explanations for cholera, he blamed 'deleterious miasmas' and 'malevolent humidity'. His only consolation was that the expedition was now directly bound for Hobart and 'the favourable temperature of more elevated latitudes'.[58]

32

Hobart

Faithful, below, he did his duty
And now he's gone aloft,
And now he's gone aloft.
Charles Dibdin*

Just prior to leaving the Sunda Strait, the expedition sailed into a thunderstorm and witnessed a spectacular waterspout, which twirled from sea to sky for a full 15 minutes. Torrential rain and a southerly swell heralded the entry of the corvettes into the Indian Ocean on 12 October 1839. Initially, d'Urville was not alarmed by the appearance of dysentery among the crew. The cases did not seem severe, but their number soon grew, and on 13 October, there were a dozen cases aboard the *Zélée* and eight on the *Astrolabe*. By the end of the month, there was only a marginal increase in the number of sick aboard the *Zélée*, but they included Pavin de La Farge and Goupil. Aboard the *Astrolabe*, the number of sick doubled and included Marescot du Thilleul (who had a weak constitution and was also suffering from fever since visiting Batavia) and Hombron.[1]

Then men began to die. On 1 November, Jean-Marie-Louis Le Blanc, a well-regarded sailor from Pordic in Brittany, died aboard the *Astrolabe*. Two days later, Louis Pflaum, from Strasbourg in Alsace, who served the staff officers, died aboard the *Zélée*. On 5 November, Jean-Baptiste Roux, a veteran gunner from Toulon, who was looking forward to a well-deserved retirement, died aboard the *Astrolabe*. The following day, Gilles-Lazare Bajat, a sailor from Bandol (Var), died aboard the *Zélée*, and Jean-Léopold Massé, a cook from Paris, died aboard the *Astrolabe*. Massé tried to treat himself with a strong infusion of pepper, cinnamon and other spices in spirits but only succeeded in giving himself 'appalling intestinal pains' and apparently an even earlier end.

D'Urville was probably also ill at this time and evidently thinking of his own death because, on 1 November, he drafted and signed a codicil to the already detailed will

* 'Tom Bowling' (*ca*.1790), verse i, lines 7–9

'*Vue de Hobart Town en Tasmanie*', engraving by Jean-Denis Nargeot from a sketch by Louis-Auguste de Sainson, for Dumont d'Urville's Voyage pittoresque autour du monde, *L. Tenré, Paris, vol. ii, 1835, plate xli.* Author's collection

he had made 11 days earlier, essentially leaving all his property to his son and all his money to his wife. He recorded his esteem and affection for his officers and thanked them for their goodwill. He left 350 litres of wine and 25 litres of arrack to be distributed in double rations to the sailors four days a week at the hour of his 'last breath'. Most surprisingly, d'Urville left his head to Dumoutier to be prepared and conserved as a 'subject of phrenological studies'! With the exception of his heart, which was to be preserved and given to his beloved wife on the expedition's return to Toulon, the rest of his body was to be consigned to the sea where it had 'tossed for so long'.[2]

The deaths in the first week of November and the worsening condition of Pavin de La Farge and Goupil emboldened Le Guillou to make representations to d'Urville – ostensibly at the behest of Dubouzet, Tardy de Montravel and Coupvent-Desbois – urging the commander to sail directly to Mauritius or the Swan River settlement on the Western Australian coast for the sake of his men. Le Guillou had come across to the *Astrolabe* in the boat that brought the report of Bajat's death. D'Urville was incredulous at such disregard for the usual chain of command. Although he doubted

Le Guillou's honesty, he wondered whether illness aboard the *Zélée* had thrown her officers into despondency. Determined to investigate, he made a personal visit to the *Zélée*. Jacquinot knew nothing of the supposed representations of his subordinate officers, and when d'Urville inspected the corvette, he could not kindle any pleas from these same officers when he raised the question of breaking off the voyage for the sake of the crew's health. Jacquinot's own investigations yielded no indication that his officers had entreated Le Guillou to act as he had, and these same officers wrote to d'Urville in the second week of November to disavow, absolutely, what Le Guillou had asserted in their name. Yet there can be little doubt of Le Guillou's genuine concern for the rising number of afflicted crewmen. He wrote:

> I was heartbroken; analysing the sufferings, the anguish of twenty dysentery cases piled up in a narrow, dark and damp orlop deck, infecting one another with miasmas … we did not have sufficient quarters for all our patients, and elsewhere space was lacking; our dysentery cases were lying side by side on mattresses on the deck, or in uncomfortable hammocks, robbed of sleep by serious anxieties … the concentration of air, the moans of their neighbours and the rails of death.[3]

Unfortunately, for all his concern for the sick, Le Guillou's treatment of the dysentery cases was only likely to make them worse. As Thierry Pendu put it in his thesis on the use of pharmaceuticals during d'Urville's final voyage:

> …one can say, with our current knowledge, that he made therapeutic errors including … the enema, sulphate of soda (purgative) and sometimes laxatives. However, at that time, the treatment of purging, whatever the patient, was a constant treatment. The frequent use of bloodletting, of leeches, corroborates this sentiment.[4]

D'Urville must have seen the sickbay during his inspection but made no mention of it. Instead, he declared that the *Zélée* had more fit men than the *Astrolabe* and resolved to press on, adding that unfavourable winds precluded Mauritius or Swan River. Timing was now crucial. Clearly, d'Urville was determined not to allow the window of opportunity to close yet again on a second Antarctic descent. However, the deaths continued. A day apart from each other, Jean-René Helies, a sailor from Antibes, and Thomas-Pascal Salusse, a master caulker from Toulon, died aboard the *Zélée*. On 14 November, they were followed by Auguste Billoud[5], a sailor from Lyon who joined the expedition in Valparaiso from the French corvette *Ariane*, and on 19 November, Jean-Baptiste Goguet, a first-class sailor from Le Havre.

For d'Urville, the most painful blow so far was the death of Marescot du Thilleul on 23 November, probably more personal given d'Urville's apparent friendship with his father and his family connections in Caen. Marescot was an exemplary officer who had gained the affection of all the ranks of the expedition, and his fellow officers cried as if they had lost a brother. His small ravaged body began to putrefy almost as soon as his eyes had closed. In order not to diminish the spirits of the many remaining sick cases below deck, he was consigned to the sea at midnight with 'the most profound silence' and without 'any military honours'.[6] Three days later, the Zélée's storeman, Joseph-Fortuné Reboul, died. Born in Genova during the French occupation, he too had suffered the additional misfortune of fever since the expedition's first visit to Batavia. On 27 November, 27-year-old Pavin de La Farge, whose condition had been precarious for weeks, finally succumbed aboard the Zélée. Hardworking, intelligent and sensitive, he had developed an interest in entomology and made collections of ethnographic artifacts during the voyage. He was also a gifted artist and surveyor. On 1 December, Raymond de Norgaret died aboard the Astrolabe. Born into a distinguished noble family in Tonneins in the valley of the Garonne, his ambition had been to skipper a merchant vessel, and to that end he had joined the expedition as a humble sailor and gunner. A week later, d'Urville's youngest ensign, Gourdin, died at the age of 26. He was one of the stalwarts of the expedition, taking part in many landings and scientific observations and also collecting natural history specimens. It was he who heightened British anxieties by raising the tricolour on Observatory Island during his survey of Raffles Bay. He is honoured, to this day, by a subspecies of the yellow-vented bulbul, *Pycnonotus goiavier gourdini*, a bird collected by the expedition at Banjarmasin, southern Borneo.[7]

On 11 December, just as the lookouts sighted the Tasmanian coast, Pierre Loupy was buried at sea. He was originally from Bordeaux and joined the Zélée in Talcahuano after deserting from the French whaler *John Cockerill*.[8] The next day, the expedition entered the Derwent estuary and at 1.00 pm, anchored off Hobart's Battery Point. Port Captain William Moriarty soon boarded the Astrolabe and offered his services. D'Urville requested his assistance establishing a temporary hospital ashore for his dysentery cases. He also allowed all his men without specific duties to go ashore. Two hours later, the corvettes were 'almost deserted'.[9] Since Governor Sir John Franklin (already a renowned polar explorer who disappeared during a later Arctic voyage) was away from Hobart, d'Urville and Jacquinot instead called on the colony's senior military officer, Lieutenant-Colonel William Elliot, who received them graciously.

D'Urville found Hobart very much changed since his previous visit. The population had almost tripled; the town was sensibly laid out on a grid, and the streets were lined with small but beautiful houses. Le Guillou even declared that 'without doubt' Hobart would 'soon rival Port Jackson',[10] but the surgeon had never visited New South Wales. That evening, d'Urville and Jacquinot went for a stroll in order to discuss future arrangements. D'Urville now envisioned leaving Jacquinot in Hobart for about two months while the Zélée's sick cases recovered and repairs were undertaken. After the

Astrolabe had completed a solo Antarctic descent, the two vessels would rendezvous in the Auckland Islands or New Zealand. Jacquinot was profoundly disappointed by such a suggestion and pleaded with d'Urville not to divide the expedition. Although the two corvettes did eventually set sail together, for the moment, d'Urville kept open the option of separation.

D'Urville decided to transfer Coupvent-Desbois and Boyer from the *Zélée* to the *Astrolabe*, with Boyer effectively promoted to acting ensign. If the *Zélée* was left behind in Hobart, Jacquinot agreed to transfer Tardy de Montravel to the *Astrolabe* for the duration of their separation, mainly because d'Urville held fears for the health of his youngest lieutenant, Barlatier-Demas. It also represented an indirect reprimand to Dubouzet, whose commitment to the expedition had been compromised by Le Guillou. Ultimately, Dubouzet would work tirelessly in Hobart to restore the seaworthiness of the *Zélée*.

Meanwhile, Ducorps had found a building for a temporary hospital (apparently close to the Catholic chapel) and spent most of the day preparing beds and transporting the sick. At first all the medical officers served in the hospital, but then d'Urville forbade Le Guillou from having anything to do with its running. Given Le Guillou's later comments about men being sent back for duty too early,[11] it would seem that he refused to certify men as fit for service when they had not entirely recovered. D'Urville visited the sick each day. Another regular visitor, sometimes several times a day, was Father John Therry, the Cork-born Catholic vicar-general in Van Diemen's Land, whose usual flock mainly comprised Irish convicts and their emancipated brethren. In 1820, Therry had been one of the first Catholic priests in New South Wales. Dispatched to Hobart in April 1838 to replace the unstable Father Philip Connolly, his ministry was characterised by isolation, heavy responsibilities and significant construction debts. D'Urville was touched that Therry included the names of those who died during the expedition and those who were still ailing among the 'prayers of the faithful' at Sunday Mass.

Three men from the *Astrolabe* were hospitalised. One of them, Félix Balthasar Simon, the first mate, originally from Saint-Tropez (Var), did not survive. He was the oldest member of both crews and, like Roux, had been looking forward to imminent retirement. D'Urville, who intended to nominate Simon for a decoration, considered him a 'victim of his [own] zeal and devotion'.[12] From the *Zélée*, 15 men were hospitalised; of these, six would die: apprentice sailor Jean-Baptiste Beaudoin, master carpenter Joseph Couteleng, the courageous young cabin boy Pierre Moreau, artist Ernest Goupil, second mate Honoré Argelier and, finally, sailor Alexandre Deniel. The expedition's dead were subsequently buried in the Catholic cemetery in Barrack Street, Hobart, apparently after requiem masses in Father Therry's chapel (St Joseph's Church was still unfinished).

During his first Antarctic descent, d'Urville had gained first-hand knowledge of the extreme climatic forces that could test his corvettes. In Hobart, therefore, after thoroughly cleaning the vessels as a sanitary measure, all the rigging was carefully checked, sails were mended, and the *Astrolabe*'s rudder was taken ashore for inspection and repair. It was exhausting work for a weakened crew, but d'Urville was determined to set sail before New Year's Day 1840. He himself had a renewed attack of gout, and Jacquinot had to deputise for him when he was invited to a reception by Lieutenant-Colonel Elliot and the Hobart garrison. D'Urville's spirits were buoyed when Governor Franklin wrote to say that he hoped to return to Hobart soon and, with his message, forwarded a packet of letters, including a number from d'Urville's family.

D'Urville and Jacquinot finally met Sir John and Lady Franklin on the evening of 19 December. They were well received, and d'Urville found Jane, Lady Franklin (*née* Griffin) particularly 'intelligent and engaging, with simple and agreeable manners' and 'conversation as instructive as interesting'.[13] Le Guillou later observed that both she and her daughter 'spoke French perfectly'.[14] Although d'Urville was clearly touched by the numerous social invitations he and his men received, Christmas proved mournful and sad because of the number of deaths among the crew. Invitations and visitors were also potential distractions from the preparations at hand, but among those whom d'Urville was especially pleased to meet in Hobart were Sir John Pedder, who was chief justice during his previous visit, and Captain John Biscoe, who had completed the third circumnavigation of Antarctica eight years before. From Biscoe, d'Urville learned that his American rival, Charles Wilkes, had been stopped by ice at latitude 63°S. Biscoe also assured him that several mariners believed 'that land existed south of Macquarie Island'.[15] While this assertion was without any apparent empirical basis, it reaffirmed d'Urville's hope of significant discoveries.

For the expedition to continue, replacements had to be found for the sick and dead crew members. Two new men were embarked on the *Astrolabe* in Hobart: Adolphe Poidecœur, from Le Havre, and William Cobans, who claimed to have been born at sea on an English vessel. Four French sailors were recruited for the *Zélée*. Constant Goudoin, from Caen, and Anthelme Dumoulard, from Lyon, were both deserters from the French whaler *Élisabeth*, commanded by the Basque skipper Pierre Darmandaritz. François Hoché from Ambon (Morbihan), and Pierre Voisin, a carpenter from Saint-Lô (Manche), were respectively deserters from the French whalers *Avenir* and *Rubens*.[16] Six other British nationals were also recruited: Malcolm Macpherson, from St John's, Newfoundland, had deserted from Cyrille Laplace's French naval frigate *Artémise* in Hobart ten months earlier;[17] John Roberts, Joseph Priseley and William Willon all claimed to be Londoners; John Jones said he was from Milford (Surrey); and William Watson declared he was from Aberdeen, Scotland. We know neither whether they gave their real names nor how long most had been in Van Diemen's Land. Although Hobart was a port of call for seamen from all over the world, Van Diemen's Land was still a penal colony, and it is worth considering that nine men named 'William Watson', 28 men named 'John Roberts' and 135 men named 'John Jones' were transported to the island as convicts prior to d'Urville's visit.[18] Le Guillou was unrestrained when he declared: 'a crowd of foreigners, from freed or escaped convicts to whaling deserters came to fill the void; new crews pressed themselves on the deck of the corvette in place of those that dysentery had devoured'.[19] It is indeed possible that there were some former or escaped British convicts among d'Urville's new recruits. As we have seen in the Pacific, he was not averse to recruiting men with questionable pasts. Given the time constraints and the limited pool of available men in Hobart, he could not afford to be too fussy. D'Urville himself indicated that reinforcements were found with 'much difficulty',[20] and Le Guillou recorded that 'employment contractors' were engaged, and that the quays and the taverns were scoured for recruits.[21] The expedition also used convict labour ashore.[22]

Although the brooding presence of Mount Wellington constantly beckoned d'Urville to re-climb and botanise the summit, he was determined not to be distracted from his preparations. On New Year's Eve, he and his officers attended a ball thrown by Lady Franklin, which provided a convenient opportunity to make their farewells. The next morning, the expedition set sail. The corvettes were battling contrary winds and struggling to leave the harbour when Port Captain William Moriarty caught up with them and delivered the sad news of Ernest Goupil's death. D'Urville was reluctant to delay his departure to attend the funeral of the popular young artist. Aside from anxieties about the limited amount of ice-free time to the south, he was particularly worried that some of his crew might desert if he lingered. However, given the contrary winds, he decided to anchor and allow Gervaize and (now Acting-Surgeon) Dumoutier to help Hombron lay Goupil to rest.

Pouring rain made Goupil's funeral a bleak affair, but Lieutenant-Colonel Elliot, on horseback, led a disciplined troop of redcoats from the garrison to form a guard of honour (apparently with the regimental band playing all the way to the cemetery) on the rough and sodden road. Then, after a dignified silence, four French officers removed the flag from Goupil's coffin and his remains were lowered into the grave to the sound of several volleys of rifle fire. Rarely, if ever, has a foreign artist been accorded such military honours in Australia. Yet, according to Joseph Seureau – one of the sick cases from the *Zélée* who was strong enough to attend – this was 'opposed by the priest who was not to be found'.[23] John Therry has been described as 'irenical rather than sectarian by conviction',[24] but it is hard to see an affirmation of common Christian bonds in this Irish priest's sullen absence from the interment that afternoon.

However, Hombron recorded that Therry's 'nephew' (in fact, they were not related), the Benedictine James Cotham, officiated at the funeral in his stead. Captain Emile-Adam Longuet and Captain Thomas Rossiter, respectively skippers of the French whalers *Nancy* and *Mississippi*, were also present.[25]

We know that Goupil and Couteleng were both given their own tombstones,[26] and the officers of the expedition subscribed to a joint monument in Hobart for all who had died during the expedition. By September 1866, according to comte Ludovic de Beauvoir, all the wooden crosses on the French graves had rotted away, and the stone monument was in such a poor state that it was replaced by King Louis-Philippe's grandson, Pierre d'Orléans, duc de Penthièvre, during his visit to Hobart aboard the *Omar Pacha*.[27] Unfortunately, d'Urville's men were not to rest in peace among the shrubs and weeds that had overgrown their graves by the beginning of the twentieth century.[28] In 1915, the Christian Brothers – seeking to expand Saint Virgil's College, opened three years earlier on land adjoining the Barrack Street Cemetery – were granted permission by the Parliament of Tasmania to relocate the remains to Cornelian Bay Cemetery.[29] There, another monument, with a large marble plaque, was erected in honour of the French dead. To this day, it lists the surnames, ranks and death-dates (although not always accurately) of all the expedition members who succumbed at sea or ashore – including the unfortunate Tongan, Mafi Kelepi.

33

Terre Adélie

The ice did split with a thunder-fit;
The helmsman steered us through!
Samuel Taylor Coleridge*

The *Astrolabe* and *Zélée* set sail from Hobart at 2.00 am on 2 January 1840. By the following morning, they had lost sight of the Tasmanian coast. D'Urville was well aware that the 'part of the polar circle which extended directly to the south of Tasmania had not been explored by any navigator'.[1] Although James Cook had traversed this region, he had not penetrated beyond a latitude of 60°S. D'Urville thought that it might even be possible to reach the south magnetic pole by sea and that this held the prospect of resolving 'the great problem of the laws of terrestrial magnetism'.[2] While he wished to maintain a course due south, the wind and current took the corvettes further to the east than he had hoped, and soon there was also a heavy swell. More worrying, after only four days at sea, was the news from Dumoutier that there were nine sick cases aboard the *Astrolabe*.

One wonders whether the men were unwittingly drinking from still-contaminated water tanks – despite all the sanitary efforts scrubbing down the vessels prior to leaving Hobart – or whether they were certified fit before they had truly recovered. Le Guillou certainly believed the latter, accusing Jacquinot of 'haranguing' his convalescents and declaring that they 'left hospital too early'.[3] From Gaillard, d'Urville learned that there were seven dysentery cases aboard the *Zélée*. Gaillard had braved the swell and come across to the *Astrolabe* to request an unused (indeed defective) compass for magnetic inclination studies. It would appear that many of the sick cases were men who had relapsed. D'Urville gave his men the lightest possible duties to spare them unnecessary exertion and, by 11 January, as the expedition crossed the 50th parallel, the number of dysentery cases had subsided. Four days later, as the crew began to sight the first floating ice, d'Urville learned that a sailor named Jean-Baptiste Poussou had died aboard the *Zélée*. Dubouzet considered him one of the expedition's best sailors. Originally from Antibes, he had joined the *Zélée* from the French vessel *Rose* at Valparaiso.

* 'The Rime of the Ancient Mariner' (1789), part i, lines 69–70

'Passage du cercle polaire, le 19 janvier, 1840, parages Antarctiques', lithograph by Adolphe-Jean-Baptiste Bayot, from a sketch by Louis Le Breton, Voyage au pôle sud et dans l'Océanie, Atlas pittoresque, Paris, 1846, vol. ii, plate no. 167. *Mimicking the tradition of baptising those who crossed the equator for the first time, the sailors of the* Astrolabe *celebrated the crossing of the Antarctic circle. D'Urville set the tone by being the first to submit to the sovereignty of 'Père Antarctique'. Nevertheless, because of the falling temperature, he forbade throwing water on deck or dunking any crewmen.* Author's collection

On 16 January, the lookouts sighted an iceberg 400 metres long and rising over 20 metres above the surface of the sea. According to d'Urville, most of his men gave it only a passing glance, which he attributed to the fact that on the *Astrolabe*, there were only about a dozen men who had not participated in the expedition's first Antarctic descent. Presumably a new recruit such as Malcolm Macpherson, from Newfoundland (a province which itself extends to 51° 38′N), would also have seen icebergs before, as would a good number of the men who had previously served on French whalers.

The expedition crossed the 64th parallel on the evening of 18 January. Given the moderate temperatures, optimism prevailed at the prospect of sailing further south than the corvettes had managed in early 1838. Soon after, however, they found themselves amid five enormous tabular icebergs, probably only recently calved from the ice sheet. During the night, heavy snow began to fall, and by 8.00 am the following day, d'Urville counted 16 islands of ice floating around them; by evening these would number nearly 60, with several over a kilometre in length. The presence of petrels, penguins and seals also suggested the proximity of a coast. At about 3.30 pm, Gervaize thought he saw land, grey and stationary, to the east. His colleagues on watch were doubtful, but Vincendon-Dumoulin climbed up one of the masts to see for himself and concurred that it did, indeed, have the appearance of land.

As the expedition prepared to cross the Antarctic Circle, the crew aboard the *Astrolabe* organised ritual celebrations that mimicked the crossing of the equator. D'Urville believed that such 'gross farces' had a 'good effect on board a ship where the distractions were so few for the sailors'. Although he was not against such 'burlesque scenes', he was determined to prevent matters getting out of hand. To set the tone, he declared that he would be the first to submit to the sovereignty of 'Père Antarctique', but because of the falling temperature, he forbade throwing water on deck or dunking any crewmen. Instead, rice and beans were showered from the mastheads, and a 'communion' of wine would replace 'the ceremony of the customary baptism of the line'.[4]

In such elevated latitudes in the southern summer, there was no more than half an hour of darkness each evening, and in the crepuscular light at midnight, it was even possible to read on deck. All this time, land remained a tantalising prospect on the distant horizon, but there was no wind to propel the corvettes closer. Aboard the *Zélée*, there were many who still doubted that land had even been sighted, but by midday on 20 January, their doubts had disappeared. Like those aboard the *Astrolabe*, they finally saw land extend from east to west – grey, snow-mantled and apparently sloping gradually to sea level. Then, at 3.00 am on 21 January, a weak south-southeasterly wind came up, and the corvettes began to advance at a speed of about one knot. As the wind strengthened, they made more rapid progress. D'Urville described what happened next:

> ... as we got nearer, the ice islands became more numerous and more menacing. Soon they even formed an enormous mass, divided by narrow sinuous channels. Nevertheless, I didn't hesitate to steer my corvettes towards them. At 8 am we were so enclosed by these floating masses of ice that I dreaded seeing our corvettes crash into them at any moment. This navigation was certainly not without danger, for the sea produced powerful eddies around all these bodies, which would not fail to drag a ship to her doom if she found herself cut off from the wind by one of the high ice cliffs. It was especially while passing their bases that we could judge the height reached by these icebergs. Their sheer walls were far higher than our masts; they overhung our ships, the size of which seemed ridiculously small in comparison with the enormous masses. The spectacle they presented was both grand and overawing. One could have believed oneself in the narrow streets of a city of giants. At the foot of these immense monuments, we saw vast caverns hollowed out by the sea, and into which the waves swept with great noise. The sun darted its oblique

rays onto immense walls of ice. The effects of light and shade were truly magical and startling. From the summits of these ice mountains many streams fed by the melting snows leapt down to the sea. It often happened that we saw two icebergs ahead of us so close together that we lost sight of the land we were making for. All we could see then were two menacing vertical walls up beside us. The commands of the officers were repeated by several echoes from these gigantic masses, which bounced the sounds of their voices from one to the other; when our eyes turned towards the *Zélée* which followed us a short distance behind, she appeared so tiny, her rigging so frail, that we were unable to suppress a feeling of terror. For nearly an hour we saw only vertical walls of ice around us. Then we came into a vast basin formed by the land on one side, and on the other by the chain of floating islands that we had just passed through. At noon we were no more than three or four miles from our new discovery.[5]

But land – with visible earth rather than a mantle of ice – remained unsubstantiated until Ensign Duroch spotted distant rocks with the aid of a telescope. D'Urville's whaleboat had already been put at the disposal of Vincendon-Dumoulin and Coupvent-Desbois, anxious to begin magnetic observations. Duroch was given command of the officer's yawl and ordered 'to gather palpable fragments' of the expedition's discovery.[6] What Duroch saw were exposed offshore islets, which were also seen from the *Zélée*, and Dubouzet asked permission of Jacquinot to command another yawl and landing party, accompanied by Le Guillou and Gaillard. There was probably some degree of rivalry between the two boats. It took about two and a half hours to cover the eleven kilometres from the corvettes to the most western and the most elevated of the exposed islands. The *Astrolabe*'s yawl had a head start and arrived just before the *Zélée*'s boat at 9.00 pm. Christened 'Rocher du Débarquement'[7] by Vincendon-Dumoulin,[8] the islet is among the northern Dumoulin Islands, about 500–600 metres from the frozen Antarctic coast. Duroch and some of his men managed to cling to the side of the rock. Armed with picks and hammers, they displaced the penguins and attempted to gather geological specimens. However, the hard, smooth flanks yielded only small fragments, and it was not until they reached the islet's crown that they found larger pieces of rock already loosened by periglacial conditions. Dubouzet first referred to the rock as granitic and then recognised gneiss identical to that among the gizzard stones of a penguin shot the day before. He was on the right track: the Dumoulin Islands are formed of mixed gneissic and granitic migmatite.

Dubouzet and his party had more flamboyant intentions than merely collecting rock specimens. In conscious mimicry of British practice, they raised the national flag on the top of the island and took formal possession in the name of France. Dubouzet wrote: 'Our enthusiasm and our joy were such as … we had added a province to French territory through this entirely peaceful conquest.' He even brought a bottle of

'Prise de possession de la Terre Adélie le 21 janvier 1840, parages Antarctiques', lithograph by Léon-Jean-Baptiste Sabatier, from a sketch by Louis Le Breton, Voyage au pôle sud et dans l'Océanie, *Atlas pittoresque, Paris, 1846, vol. ii, plate 171.* National Library of Australia, PIC S11308

Bordeaux to conclude the ceremony with hoorahs and libations, remarking that the wine also had 'advantages against the rigours of the temperature'.[9]

No molluscs were seen on the shore, and only a single piece of dried seaweed was found washed up on the rock. From their vantage point, they could see 'several entirely exposed summits' on the mainland coast, but Dubouzet realised that the base of these summits, covered in snow and ice – presumably part of the Astrolabe Glacier, later named by André-Frank Liotard – rendered an approach 'very difficult'. Nevertheless, their offshore geological efforts occasioned d'Urville's naming of Pointe-Géologie on the Antarctic mainland. More than a century later, the coastal islands would be grouped together under the name Archipel de Pointe-Géologie. France's Dumont d'Urville Antarctic base, which replaced the Port-Martin base (62 kilometres to the east) in 1956, is located on Petrel Island in this same group.

The two landing parties only remained on Rocher du Débarquement for half an hour. Because of the difficulty accessing the island (Gaillard actually fell into the water during the landing), the yawls remained partly manned and waiting offshore. Fortunately, the return journey to the corvettes took an hour less than the outward journey, presumably because of more favourable winds or currents, but the boats arrived completely frosted with ice in the sub-zero conditions. Le Guillou found the traverse 'perilous'. Although his account of the risk 'of death with all its horrors'[10] in the open yawl was perhaps deliberately exaggerated to pique the emotions of his readers, to be fair, he had with him the sodden Gaillard, whose hypothermia eventually developed into a fatal respiratory infection. Vincendon-Dumoulin and Coupvent-Desbois returned to the *Astrolabe* two hours earlier. Aside from geophysical and hydrographic observations, they had studied the movement of icebergs from the coast, presumably those recently separated from the tongue of the Astrolabe Glacier and propelled by katabatic drainage winds from the continent.

This new uninhabited coast would not be named after a monarch or minister; nor would it be named after d'Urville himself. Instead, it would be named after his beloved wife with the affectionate diminutive d'Urville used for her: 'Terre Adélie'. Although the now-famous Adélie penguins collected in this region would be named *Dasyramphus adelia* (*Pygoscelis adeliae*) by Hombron and Jacquinot, the specific epithet referred to the place rather than Madame d'Urville.[11] The land that was first sighted from the *Astrolabe* was named Cape Découverte. Cape Jules, further to the east, was almost certainly named after d'Urville's son.

Despite the feeble winds, d'Urville continued his survey in a westerly direction. At first, the nights were so short and the weather so clear that the expedition barely lost sight of the Antarctic coast, but this was still navigation amid immense floating ice fragments. Ravin Bay was named after the deep ravine-like fissures in the ice-bound shore, and nearby Cape Pépin was named after Adélie's family. The enormous blocks of ice on shore provoked d'Urville's geomorphological imagination and reminded him of the shape of rocks 'one often sees on recently created volcanic terrains'.[12] While the ice refracted light with many subtle and captivating tints, gazing at the darker hues, d'Urville recognised an intrinsic aspect of the glacial process, both with regard to the movement of ice sheets on the land and in the genesis of icebergs: 'It is probable,' he wrote, 'that all these islands of ice are formed near the coasts and that when they detach, they carry off with them debris which attests to their origin.'[13] It should be remembered that glacial geomorphology was then in its infancy. In that year, the Swiss geologist Louis Agassis published his *Études sur les glaciers*, which proposed that the earth had been subject to an Ice Age in which glaciers had played a major role in shaping the landscape.[14]

At 4.00 am on 23 January, the corvettes found the sea ahead of them blocked by a wall of ice extending roughly north–south. With the wind coming from the east, they had to beat windward in the hope of exiting the cul-de-sac near the coast. The next day, as the weather worsened, the expedition zig-zagged north, but the barrier still stretched to the northwest as far as the eye could see, and d'Urville realised he would not be able to tack his way out. Then thick snow began to fall, and the coast to the south was no longer visible. The snow not only obscured the corvettes from each other

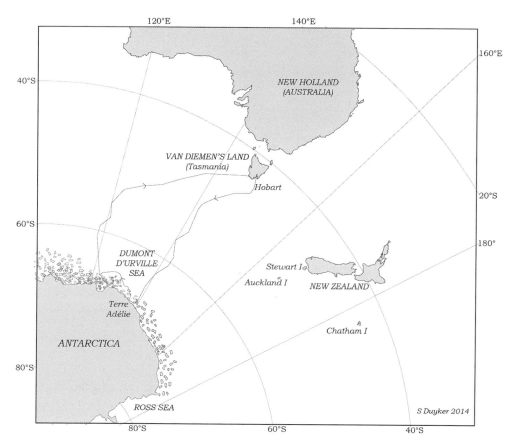

Map 9. Van Diemen's Land (Tasmania), and the route of the second Antarctic descent of the Astrolabe *and the* Zélée, *January 1840*

but also the icebergs, which were moving in the now gale-force winds. The risk of a collision was obvious. In order to maintain a means of propulsion, d'Urville retained a substantial spread of canvas, but as the squall worsened, he began to fear that his sails might be shredded or, worse, that his masts might snap. He ordered several sails clewed as a precaution. The wind-chill and heaving forces faced by men furling sails in such a pitching sea, amid rigging completely covered in snow and ice, can only be imagined. Even those on deck had to contend with waves of brine, barely above freezing temperature, constantly sweeping over the gunwales. At one stage, the *Astrolabe* listed so heavily to leeward that her gunports were almost completely submerged on one side. D'Urville was full of admiration for his men, who worked one-hour shifts to the point of exhaustion before being relieved by their crewmates. The compass, so close to the south magnetic pole, now became unreliable, and d'Urville recorded that, at one stage in the storm, the needle began to spin.

The tempest eased a little on 25 January, but for much of the day, d'Urville remained deeply anxious over the fate of the *Zélée*, which had become separated from the *Astrolabe*. Guns were fired in the hope of a return signal, but it was not until shortly after 6.00 pm that the corvettes were reunited – and when they were, it was obvious that the *Zélée* had suffered damage to her sails during the storm. When the sea calmed further and a southwesterly breeze came up, d'Urville hoped that the expedition, checked in the west by the ice, might instead be able to explore the coast to the east. Much of 26 January was spent hauling towards land but, by the middle of the day, they found themselves amid some 150 icebergs. (D'Urville thought they were probably the same icebergs he had passed through almost a week earlier on his first approach to the coast.) When the wind shifted to the south and then the southeast, the corvettes were forced to change direction yet again. Fortunately, they passed through the chain of icebergs before they were hit by an easterly gale and were once again pounded with heavy snow. Determined not to be pushed against the ice sheet, d'Urville ordered a northerly course. What seemed to be a solid ice-field ahead proved to be floes of ice that the corvettes were able to sweep aside, and by evening, they were completely clear of menace.

The following day, 28 January, the wind swung to the west. With stubborn tenacity, d'Urville once again plunged south in the hope of reaching the coast, despite boiling seas and heavy snow. When the winds swung east yet again, he ordered a southwesterly course, consoling himself that he would thereby cross the closely aligned magnetic meridians and aid Vincendon-Dumoulin's search for the magnetic pole. By now, the weather was much improved but still somewhat foggy. Through the mist, the lookout sighted a huge expanse of ice, which appeared to stretch from the southeast to the northwest. D'Urville promptly gave the order to haul to the wind and tack to starboard. No sooner had this been done than a brig, the *Porpoise* (227 tonnes) under Commander Cadwalader Ringgold, suddenly emerged from the fog, running before the wind under full sail. She quickly hoisted the flag of the United States. D'Urville correctly assumed that the brig belonged to Charles Wilkes's United States Exploring Expedition Squadron. The sighting brought all the *Astrolabe*'s crew on deck. Sharply contrasting accounts of what happened next would be published in the respective expedition records. Essentially, Ringgold, who wrote that he desired 'to pass within hail under the flag ship's stern', insinuated that d'Urville deliberately avoided him by putting on more sail.[15] D'Urville, supported by Vincendon-Dumoulin (but not by Le Guillou, who, in any case, was on the *Zélée*),[16] asserted that having just tacked to starboard, he had temporarily clewed his mainsail. When he saw the brig, he hoisted his own national colours, gave her time to catch up and then, expecting the American to communicate on the *Astrolabe*'s portside, ordered the mainsail reset in order to keep up with her as long as possible. D'Urville believed that this manoeuvre was misinterpreted by the commander of the American brig, which then (both agree) rapidly bore off to the south.[17]

It is hard to believe that d'Urville deliberately evaded Ringgold to avoid communicating his discoveries. In his historical account, he stated his firm opposition to secrecy in such hydrographic matters and also criticised Wilkes, who was aboard the *Vincennes*, for his tight-lipped behaviour in both Sydney and Hobart. Yet, in the *Sydney Morning Herald* of 13 March 1840, and two days earlier to the US secretary of the navy, Wilkes claimed to have sighted the Antarctic coast on the morning of 19 January. In Sydney, the latitude was given as 64° 20′S and the longitude 154° 18′E. On the same day, the *Sydney Morning Herald* also carried a report from the *Hobart Town Courier* that d'Urville claimed to have sighted the Antarctic coast at 66°S 130°E on the same day. Neither Wilkes's journal nor the logbooks of the *Vincennes* and the *Peacock* carried any record of such a sighting that day. Wilkes later gave evidence that he had recalled a sighting of land by a crew member, which he had then dismissed and not recorded.

Wilkes, a harsh, even fanatical disciplinarian, later brought a rash of charges against a number of his officers (ironically including a surgeon named Guillou!); they, in turn, brought charges against him. Among other indictments, Wilkes was accused of 'conduct unbecoming an officer' by fabricating his sighting of land in Antarctica. Although acquitted of the latter charge, thanks to the testimony of two officers from the *Peacock*, who attested that they had seen elevated land from the masthead on 16 January 1840, Wilkes was nevertheless convicted of 'illegal punishment', having exceeded the number of lashes commanding officers were allowed to inflict without a court martial.[18] Wilkes's reputation was undoubtedly tarnished by this and by James Clark Ross's assertion that he had sailed through waters Wilkes claimed to be land. Vincendon-Dumoulin – when he edited volume viii of the historical account of the voyage after d'Urville's death – couldn't resist making reference to the proceedings and casting doubt on his discoveries in an additional chapter (lxi) of reflections on recent polar exploration.

Despite this controversy, d'Urville would have found much in common with Charles Wilkes, who had visited many of the same landfalls he had visited in the Pacific and shared similar hydrographic ambitions in the Antarctic. Born in New York, he was a nephew of the famous English radical John Wilkes. He was raised (during part of his childhood) by his mother's sister, Elizabeth Ann Seton, later the first canonised Catholic saint in the United States. Both explorers were determined, driven and sometimes vain, but d'Urville appears to have been the more astute and accomplished leader of men. The geologist James Dwight Dana, who sailed with Wilkes, described him as 'overbearing and conceited' but added that he exhibited a 'wonderful degree of energy and was bold even to rashness in exploration.'[19]

On 30 January, the snow stopped falling during the night. Despite a swell, the wind was from the east, and by 6.00 am, the lookouts had sighted the coastal ice sheet. Four hours later, the expedition was once again five or six kilometres from the frozen edge of the continent, with uniform cliffs of ice plunging 30–50 metres to the sea. There were a few isolated icebergs in the vicinity, but the corvettes did not encounter another dense agglomeration of floating ice islands until the following day. D'Urville called this part of the Antarctic 'Côte Clarie', using Jacquinot's affectionate diminutive for his wife, Clara. We now know that Charles Wilkes did indeed pre-empt d'Urville to the west of Terre Adélie. It was later explored by Douglas Mawson, who would rechristen this part of the Antarctic coast (claimed by Australia) 'Wilkes Land', in honour and vindication of the American.[20] To this day, Australia does not recognise the toponym 'Clarie Coast'.[21]

On 31 January, d'Urville began to search for an accessible, stable iceberg or floe on which to land Vincendon-Dumoulin and Coupvent-Desbois so they could conduct magnetic declination studies. The next day, 1 February, conditions seemed promising. The swell was very weak, almost calm, but the manifest movement of each potential ice platform thwarted the observations. D'Urville then tried to conduct them fore and aft on the deck of the *Astrolabe*, but the readings (no doubt influenced by the pitching of the vessel and the plentiful presence of iron aboard) proved so bizarre and unreliable that d'Urville was forced to abandon the idea altogether. He also decided that, although it was possible to sail further west and chart the extent of the ice, it would be unfair to his men and a 'cruelty to abuse their courage'. He made no mention of the probability that Wilkes had pre-empted him on the Antarctic coast to the west. Rather, he expressed his concern for the health of the crews, in particular that of the *Zélée*, and admitted that he himself was very tired of the 'rough trade' he had just undertaken and doubted very much that he would be 'able to stand it much longer'.[22] He therefore decided to break off his Antarctic survey and sail north to Hobart in order to replenish his vessels and allow his men to recover before the next leg of their voyage.

34

Return to Hobart

*There is a city in [Van] Diemen's Land, where three newspapers are
published; the roads are macadamised; there are inns where one can dine
magnificently if one agrees to pay a guinea; there are learned and literary
societies; no slaves, and we do not know the name of it.*

Victor Jacquemont [on Hobart]*

The return to Hobart was not without challenges. The fog soon returned, and it
was necessary for both vessels to sound their bells and fire cannon at frequent
intervals to avoid separation. For some days, icebergs also remained a threat, but there
were still more wonders to behold. On the evening of 7 February 1840, all the men were
called on deck to witness a spectacular luminous display of the aurora australis – the
southern hemisphere's equivalent of the aurora borealis, caused by charged particles in
the upper atmosphere. Ten days later, the expedition entered Storm Bay and dropped
anchor in Hobart harbour.

The *Astrolabe* and *Zélée* remained in Van Diemen's Land for a week after their
return from Antarctica. On arrival, d'Urville was promptly informed by Hombron
of the deaths that had occurred during the expedition's absence, and he ordered him
to embark the remaining sick cases as quickly as possible. Most were convalescents,
whom he did not want frequenting local taverns 'so fatal to the pockets and health'[1]
of his sailors. However, he was forced to leave two men from the *Zélée* in the colonial
hospital: the second mate Honoré Argelier[2] and the sailor Alexandre Deniel. Normally,
d'Urville would not have been authorised to do this – Hobart had no French consul
who could arrange repatriations should the men recover – but in the opinion of
Hombron and the local British medical officers, there was no hope for the two men.
Argelier died in Hobart Hospital on 12 March, and Deniel died the following day.[3]
A sum of several pounds was left over from the amount raised by the expedition's
officers for the original monument at the Barrack Street Catholic Cemetery. According
to Hombron, it was donated to the Catholic poor of Hobart[4] – presumably with some
contingency for the burial of Argelier and Deniel.

* 29 January 1829 [after speaking to d'Urville], Correspondence, 1836, vol. i, p. 67

'Groupe de convicts dans un défrichement' [group of convicts in a clearing], engraving from a sketch by Louis-Auguste de Sainson, for Dumont d'Urville's Voyage pittoresque autour du monde, *L. Tenré, Paris, vol. ii, 1835, plate xlii. D'Urville greatly admired Governor Lachlan Macquarie's policies aimed at uplifting emancipated convicts.* Author's collection

There was only one deserter from the expedition in Hobart: Charles Bidal, who worked as a servant to the midshipmen on the *Zélée*. Originally from the Vendée, he had been recruited in Valparaiso but chose not to return to France. Concern was also growing for the health of 25-year-old Gaillard, who had suffered hypothermia during the landing on Rocher du Débarquement and now had a pulmonary infection. Jacquinot had to find replacements for Bidal and those who had died or were unfit for duty aboard the *Zélée*. He managed to recruit an experienced sailor named Joseph Digs from Harwich, England, and four deserters from four different French whalers.[5] Another two, Jean-Marie Legard and Jean-Louis Mouyou, both from Brittany, appear to have transferred legally from the French whaler *Asia*. On one particular day, Barlatier-Demas counted 13 French whalers at anchor in Hobart and wrote that the 'crews were in open mutiny'.[6] Although he was a naval officer who knew the importance of discipline and authority at sea, he openly sympathised with these sailors because of the manner in which they were exploited by their whaling captains. Typically, there were 60–80 men aboard such vessels, including the officers. Frequently improvident, the sailors were given meagre advances when recruited and promised a bare minimum percentage of the catch (1/220th to 1/230th). Generally ill-equipped on departure for voyages of up to two years, they inevitably had to buy replacement clothes or additional protective garments for harsh subantarctic conditions. The whaling captains sold these at 'twenty times their value' and at an enormous interest rate if the men had no money, initiating a cycle of indebtedness and, effectively, bonded labour. Barlatier-Demas wrote: 'If the fishing is bad, even mediocre, the poor devil, who for two years has been doing one of the hardest of jobs, far from having earned something, returns to France with debts contracted to the owner; debts he cannot repay except by signing on again.'[7] Under such conditions, desertions were inevitable, and it is little wonder that Jacquinot's offer of a passage back to France aboard the *Zélée* was attractive. Another three British men also stowed away on the *Zélée*,[8] probably including escaped convicts; one wonders whether this was with the complicity of members of the crew.

There can be no doubt of d'Urville's personal sympathy for the island's convicts and his uneasiness over the assignment system, the means by which free settlers (or rather 'the speculator, the capitalist',[9] as d'Urville called them, with economic if not socialist precision) had the use of convict labour without charge, except for the cost of food, clothes and, if necessary, medicine. D'Urville also recoiled from the severe and degrading physical punishments inflicted on the convicts, some of whom he knew were political prisoners rather than common criminals. Though he would have been well aware of the Irish nationalists transported to Australia over the previous half-century,[10] he made specific mention of the French-Canadian *patriotes* (transported after the insurrection of 1837) who had arrived in Hobart on 8 February 1840 on the transport *Buffalo*,[11] believing that they had embarked on the desperate course of rebellion only out of 'honourable sentiments'.[12] Had the opportunity presented itself, it is hard to believe that d'Urville would not have acted like those who helped the *patriote* Louis Bourdon escape New South Wales for the United States aboard a French whaler in September 1842.[13] Nevertheless, in Hobart he might still have urged patience rather than escape. According to Beverley Boissery, historian of the *patriotes* transported to Australia, some of d'Urville's officers visited the *Buffalo*, raising the spirits of the prisoners by giving them hope of a quick return and comparing their banishment to a turn in fortune's wheel.[14]

Aside from replenishing supplies of food and water while the corvettes were anchored in the Derwent estuary, d'Urville ordered the masts struck, the rigging reviewed and both vessels repainted. In addition, he sent a detailed report of his Antarctic explorations, together with charts, to the minister. This and the expedition's other correspondence were entrusted to the captain of an English vessel, the *Calcutta*, which set sail for Europe on the evening of 18 February. D'Urville also called on Governor Sir John and Lady Franklin and gave them a personal account of his recent discoveries. Word had already spread rapidly in Hobart of the coast that the French had found, and many locals thought that there was a sealing bonanza to be had immediately to the south, a misapprehension D'Urville was keen to correct. On his last day in Hobart, he visited the Museum of Natural History, which had been established by Lady Franklin under the direction of Ronald Campbell Gunn, Franklin's private secretary, whom d'Urville already knew by reputation as a respected botanist and collector.[15] D'Urville also learned that he had been elected a member of the Tasmanian Natural History Society, founded by Franklin, and appears to have been genuinely touched by this honour. This same society would later become the parent organisation of the Royal Society of Tasmania, the first royal society outside the British Isles.

D'Urville respected Sir John Franklin, not only as a man of science and culture but as a humane and enlightened advocate of reform who had attempted to draw the British government's attention to the abuses of the convict system. D'Urville shared many of these concerns. Although he recognised the enormous benefits Britain had enjoyed from the transportation of convicts to the antipodes, he also understood the other strategic factors that had enabled the Australian colonies to succeed, in particular, Britain's control of the 'Cape of Good Hope, Mauritius and India'.[16] Despite the secret orders he had borne in the past to search for locations for potential French convict colonies, d'Urville knew that if France had undertaken so onerous a task, 'she would have found it very difficult to get similar results [as the British had achieved in Australia], with her feeble colonial resources'. He believed that France had already lost the opportunity to colonise New Zealand, but even if she had not, he doubted whether France could have created an 'enduring and flourishing settlement' that would have linked together 'distant countries by continual [trade] exchanges'.[17] D'Urville believed that the French were more inclined to speculate at home, unlike the British, who sought individual opportunities overseas. Thus he wrote:

> … the French nation, unlike the English, does not display the very special abilities needed for colonising. Every day, in fact, one sees free men arriving in Australian ports, in possession of considerable capital, with large families to support, coming to establish themselves in these distant countries, seeking to enlarge their fortunes, and often not entertaining the thought of returning to the mother country after a voluntary exile. In France, emigration only draws into the colonies men who possess nothing. If a man possesses a small fortune, he soon seeks to augment it in speculation, without ever leaving the country of his birth. One must not ignore the fact that Australia has not simply been conquered by the convicts that England

sends there each year; the British Government, through its penal laws, has indeed furnished the manpower to people this new world, but it is the free colonists who have brought capital and made the labour of the condemned bear fruit.[18]

In his historical account, d'Urville quoted copiously from a book by Franklin's former private secretary, the Scottish reform advocate Alexander McConochie, *Thoughts on Convict Management and Other Subjects Connected with the Australian Penal Colonies* (1838). McConochie was probably already known to d'Urville as foundation secretary of the Geographical Society of London. His book was one of only two Australian-published works in d'Urville's library at the time of his death.

After several visits to Australia, d'Urville knew that local opinion was deeply divided on the future of convict transportation and the assignment system. So entrenched were the differences between free settlers and the emancipists that d'Urville believed Australia was destined to have 'its revolutions, perhaps bloody', the result of which would be 'freedom from the mother country', unless the majority emancipists were 'not totally repressed'.[19] He was wrong, perhaps because he tended to see events through the mental prism of the American Revolution or Paris in July 1830 rather than through that of British democratic experience. Convict transportation ended in 1839 in Queensland; in 1840 in New South Wales; in 1853 in Van Diemen's Land; and in 1868 in Western Australia. Although parliamentary self-government was also progressively established, tensions persisted. For example, Van Diemen's Land, renamed Tasmania in 1856, did not introduce universal male suffrage until 1898. The closest thing to a democratic rebellion in Australia that d'Urville might have recognised as proto-revolutionary was the Ballarat Eureka Stockade in 1854. Although it was precipitated by the issue of taxation on the Victorian goldfields and had nothing to do with convict transportation or emancipation, d'Urville would very likely have agreed with Karl Marx, who declared that the Eureka rebellion was engendered by 'in essence, motives similar to those which led to the Declaration of Independence of the United States'.[20]

Despite d'Urville's lengthy musings on British colonialism and the convict system, the principal descriptive chapter on Van Diemen's Land in the expedition's historical account was drawn from the journal of Barlatier-Demas. He had not participated in the expedition's second Antarctic descent because of illness, but after three weeks in bed, he was well enough to see something of the environs – indeed much more than any other member of the expedition.[21]

Because the medical officers had to tend the sick (and Honoré Jacquinot was actually one of the sick cases himself), their time as naturalists in Hobart was more limited than usual. Nevertheless, in Hobart, a new liverwort, *Plagiochila pusilla*, was added to the expedition's botanical collection.[22] Hombron also collected a new species of *Richea* (belonging to the Ericaceae), which was named *R. desgrasii* in honour of d'Urville's secretary, César Desgraz.[23]

Less satisfying were the expedition's zoological achievements in Van Diemen's Land. Although Hombron and Jacquinot collected a specimen of Tasmania's endemic spotted skink, which was named *Lygosoma hieroglyphicum* and was illustrated (plate, 5, fig. 1) in the expedition's 'Atlas d'historie naturelle, Zoologie', André and Auguste Duméril did not publish a matching description until 1851.[24] In the meantime, in 1845, John Edward Gray published his description from one of John Gould's specimens and thereby secured taxonomic priority for the name *Mocoa ocellata* (*Niveoscincus ocellatus*).[25] There were also problems with a supposedly new species of crab found at Hobart and named *Cyclograpsus tasmanicus*. No matching specimen was deposited with the Muséum national d'histoire naturelle, and the published description by Honoré Jacquinot and Hyppolyte Lucas[26] was based entirely on the illustration published in the expedition's atlas; if it is a synonym of another known species of *Cyclograpsus*, it is not known which.[27] It would appear that all the beetles collected by the expedition in the vicinity of Hobart had already been described by other entomologists – in many cases by Jean-Baptiste Alphonse Dechauffour de Boisduval in the entomological volume of the *Astrolabe*'s first voyage.

At 3.00 am on 25 February, despite a feeble breeze, the *Astrolabe* and *Zélée* left Hobart with the aid of the outgoing tide on the Derwent. D'Urville then set a southeasterly course across the Tasman Sea for the Auckland Islands 425 kilometres south of New Zealand's South Island.

35

Rivals in New Zealand

A rival in the case, is there? –
and you think he has supplanted you unfairly?
Richard Sheridan [Sir Lucius]*

On 11 March 1840, the *Astrolabe* and *Zélée* approached the expansive embrace of 'Sarah's Bosom' (now Port Ross) between Enderby Island, Green Island and the deeply indented north coast of Auckland Island, from which the whole group takes its name. As the corvettes entered this natural channel, another vessel could be seen leaving and could also be heard signalling with one of its guns. D'Urville later learned, from an inscription that he and his men found ashore, that she was the brig *Porpoise*, under the command of Cadwalader Ringgold, whom he had encountered off the Antarctic coast on 28 January. D'Urville thought that the brig had signalled under the mistaken impression that the *Astrolabe* and *Zélée* were also part of Wilkes's United States Exploring Expedition Squadron. Be that as it may, yet again there was no direct communication with the *Porpoise*, which was bound for the Bay of Islands.

The principal reason for the visit to the Auckland Islands was to enable Vincendon-Dumoulin to conduct further geomagnetic observations aimed at estimating the location of the south magnetic pole and to undertake longitudinal determinations. Discovered in 1806 by Captain Abraham Bristow of the whaler *Ocean* (owned by Samuel Enderby & Sons, London) and revisited by him the following year in the whaler *Sarah* (hence the naming of 'Sarah's Bosom'),[1] the Auckland Islands had subsequently been visited by other whalers and sealers. It was in a hut bearing an inscription that stated that it was built by whalers from the *Nancy* that Vincendon-Dumoulin set up his observatory. D'Urville might have been informed in advance of the hut's existence by Charles Barrois, a sailor aboard the *Zélée*, who had sailed on the *Nancy* before deserting in Hobart.[2]

It rained every day while the expedition was in the Auckland Islands, but there were some moments of good weather to conduct navigational astronomy. Despite

* *The Rivals* (1775), act iii, scene iv, lines 73–74

impromptu repairs, the *Nancy*'s hut leaked badly and barely sheltered Vincendon-Dumoulin and his companions from the wind. They were also isolated from the rest of the expedition. During a storm on 13 March, the wind was so fierce that it was impossible for a boat to reach them, but a supply of biscuits was flung ashore to sustain them. Continually wet, chilled by the wind, harassed by swarms of biting flies during the day and gnawing rats at night, it is little wonder that the hydrographer fell ill during his sojourn. Near the hut was another grim reminder of the island's dispiriting powers: a small wooden cross and the recent grave of the owner and *chef de pêche* of the whaler *Avenir*, Jacques François, from the Nantes whaling company of Jacques François frères. He had invented a harpoon launched from a pivoted gun,[3] which might have prefigured the heavier harpoon guns that would one day dominate whaling, but aiming the device from a whaleboat proved impractical other than in quiet bays. Fearing ridicule after taking a much smaller number of whales than he expected, François committed suicide in March 1839 with two pistols attached to a piece of wood.[4] D'Urville possibly learned of this tragic story in the Hobart press,[5] but he had a first-hand informant in François Hoché, who joined the *Zélée* in Hobart after deserting the *Avenir*.[6]

Ensign Tardy de Montravel and Acting Ensign Boyer were tasked with drafting a plan of the bay. They were accompanied by César Desgraz, and a longboat crew was also dispatched to replenish the expedition's water supplies. Another was ordered to go fishing, but unfortunately, the flesh of almost every fish that was caught in the bay was infested with thin parasitical worms (almost certainly *Pseudoterranova decipiens*)[7] that rendered the catches so unappealing that most of the sailors resigned themselves to eating salted provisions during their stay. The remaining crewmen, without specific duties, were allowed to go ashore, but their exploratory excursions must have been wet and bitterly cold. D'Urville also went ashore at the head of the bay with Jacquinot and Dubouzet. Though the coastal vegetation was sodden and sparse, inland they found some open 'forests' of lichen-covered *Metrosideros umbellata* (southern rata). Vincendon-Dumoulin also saw these trees in sheltered valleys but described them as 'thin, frail, twisted',[8] and Roquemaurel found their timber useless for construction. Even as firewood, it gave off a nauseating smell of 'rotten fish'![9] The wind-stunted stands were certainly nothing like the 'verdant groves' and the 'forests of lofty trees, flourishing with … extraordinary vigour'[10] that Benjamin Morrell claimed to have seen in the Aucklands in January 1830. Instead, they offered further proof of the American's fabrications. Although seabirds were present on the coast, there were very few birds inland, and those that were seen had no fear of humans. A number of specimens were easily taken, most species d'Urville already knew were common in New Zealand, but one was entirely new: the Auckland Island merganser (sea duck), *Mergus australis*.[11]

In the next 62 years, fewer than 24 additional specimens were collected.[12] It was one of only two species of merganser in the southern hemisphere and, sadly, is now extinct.[13]

Also anchored in the bay was a Portuguese vessel, the *Especulação de Lisboa*, commanded by an Englishman, James Robinson, who had availed himself of a Portuguese government subsidy to establish a whaling industry.[14] He was engaged in both sealing and whaling, and he permitted Coupvent-Desbois and Dumoutier to join his men in their daily forays in the whaleboat. Dumoutier's cranial obsessions were once more assuaged when Robinson severed and gifted him the intact head of a large seal that had been killed a few days earlier with a lance. Robinson also enabled Coupvent-Desbois to bring back a live seal to the *Astrolabe*. Though spared the carnage that had befallen its kin ashore, it remained tethered on deck until one day it broke free and caused mayhem, 'upturning everything it could find in front of it'.[15] Sadly, it would not regain its freedom. To restore order – and perhaps because of the difficulties of transporting an aquatic animal back to France – it was killed and handed over to the naturalists. This seems to have been rather pointless. It was not mentioned in the expedition's zoological volumes, probably because it was a southern fur seal (*Arctocephalus forsteri*), already described by René Primevère Lesson from a specimen collected during the *Coquille* expedition 16 years before.

With welcome relief, Vincendon-Dumoulin and his stoic observatory assistants were finally embarked aboard the *Astrolabe* on the night of 19 March. D'Urville's last act before setting sail on the morning of 20 March was to nail an inscribed plank below the one left by the brig *Porpoise*. It bore details of his own visit and recent explorations, including a bold claim regarding the 'determination of the south magnetic pole'.[16] Perhaps a more enduring memorial was the naming of Mount D'Urville (630 metres), the highest summit in the Auckland Islands.

Although briefly colonised by Polynesians around the thirteenth century, the Auckland Islands were uninhabited at the time of d'Urville's visit, but in the spring of 1842, they would be re-colonised by Ngāti Mutunga, from New Zealand's North Island. Their chief, Matioro, chartered a Sydney brig, the *Hannah*, to take 40 of his people and 20 enslaved Moriori from the Chatham Islands to form the southernmost Polynesian settlement in the world. Seven years later, Charles Enderby would establish the British whaling settlement of Hardwicke – with prefabricated houses – but it was doomed to failure within less than three years because of the island's isolation, harsh climate and the catastrophic collapse in whale stocks through over-exploitation. The British settlers departed in 1852, and the remaining Chatham Islanders were repatriated in 1856.[17]

D'Urville now set a northerly course. Soon after clearing the Aucklands, the corvettes encountered very heavy seas. While several sailors were attempting to secure

'Port Otago', charcoal and watercolour, 1840, by Louis Le Breton. Hocken Collections, University of Otago

the *Astrolabe*'s starboard anchor, a wave suddenly swept one of them over the gunwale. He was François-Daniel Grouhand, from Montoir on the Loire estuary. Miraculously, he grabbed hold of the anchor stock and got back on board with the aid of the chain. Had Grouhand fallen into the water, d'Urville doubted whether it would have been possible to launch a boat to rescue him in such turbulent seas.

The Snares were sighted on 22 March, and the following day, the mountainous peaks of Stewart Island were seen. Although contrary winds prevented the corvettes approaching for several days, on 26 March, they were able to sail close enough for Vincendon-Dumoulin to draft a basic description of Stewart Island.[18] On its southeastern coast, they encountered a boat containing a number of Englishmen. One offered his services as a pilot, but d'Urville did not intend to anchor. Instead, the expedition traversed the mouth of Foveaux Strait and began to sail along the east coast of the South Island of New Zealand – or rather 'Tavaï-Pounamou', as d'Urville continued to call it with ethnographic precision and sensitivity. On 30 March, the *Astrolabe* and *Zélée* entered Otago Harbour. There, along with two American and one English vessel already at anchor, they found the French whaler *Havre* under the command of Captain Jean-Louis Privat, whom they had previously met at Talcahuano in April 1838. In the meantime, Privat had returned to France and dispensed with his mutinous second-in-command. So far, his new expedition had not been marred by disagreements, but he had only just begun whaling. Privat also informed d'Urville that French whalers had now abandoned the Chilean coast in favour of New Holland and New Zealand.

D'Urville asked Duroch to draft a plan of their anchorage, and Vincendon-Dumoulin once again undertook observations to fix their longitude. Aboard the *Zélée*, d'Urville met Taiaroa, a chief of the Ngāi Tahu, who arrived with his son. A well-built man of medium height, he had visited Sydney and was later a convert to Christianity, taking the name 'Te Matenga' in honour of Samuel Marsden.[19] D'Urville found him insatiably demanding. Above all, he wanted European cloth. In the interests of those French vessels that might visit in his wake, d'Urville decided to grant Taiaroa's wish when he visited the *Astrolabe* with his retinue on 2 April. However, d'Urville was clearly annoyed at the chief's suggestions of 'a price, increased yet again, for a protection of which he was incapable and of which he gave no manifest proof'.[20] Taiaroa overstayed his welcome and, fed up with such ungracious insinuations and greed, d'Urville turned his back on him and apparently withdrew to his cabin.

D'Urville was also disgusted by the manner in which the Māori openly prostituted their women among visiting sailors. Some women were employed by Europeans to grow potatoes, turnips and lettuce, but even then their menfolk appropriated their wages in the form of alcohol. D'Urville noted that the local Ngāi Tahu squandered hard-won wages earned as sailors on whaling vessels on 'very high priced … execrable brandy'.[21] Other signs of acculturation were evident. Traditional cloaks of native flax (*Phormium*), which d'Urville so admired and had collected on at least one of his earlier visits, had been largely replaced by European woollen clothes. Even tattoos seemed to d'Urville to no longer bear complicated traditional motifs of rank. Diseases also afflicted the local population. D'Urville made specific mention of two women, including Tartaro (one of Taiaroa's wives), who appeared to have tuberculosis, but this was not necessarily introduced by Europeans.[22] D'Urville had his own ongoing battle with illness, and yet another painful attack of gout forced him to limit the extent of his visits ashore.

About a month before the *Astrolabe* and *Zélée* arrived at Otago Harbour, an American had been killed in a dispute with a drunken local Māori man. Fearful of arrest, the murderer had killed his wife (whose favours were perhaps at the heart of the dispute) and then committed suicide. These tragic deaths had heightened anxieties among Europeans living and trading on the coast. A man named Brown, who was in fear of his life, pleaded with d'Urville to be taken to the Bay of Islands with his Māori wife. Initially, d'Urville refused him but then changed his mind because Brown had lived 22 years in New Zealand and was potentially useful as an interpreter. Other Europeans made similar requests of d'Urville, but he refused them all, with the exception of an 'Englishman' who had rendered his officers a number of services. The heightened tensions in Otago did not deter two of the three British stowaways aboard the *Zélée* – Thomas Webb and John Jones – from leaving the expedition. This was perhaps not surprising, as Dubouzet pointed out: 'The European community established at Otago … is composed in great part of ship-deserters and escaped convicts from Sydney, for whom all ideas of evasion are today turned towards New Zealand'.[23] The *Astrolabe* had no desertions in Otago, but d'Urville allowed one of his sailors, Blaise Isnard, who had joined in Valparaiso, to transfer voluntarily to the whaler *Havre* after a request from Captain Privat.

After resupplying, mainly with an 'ample provision of excellent potatoes',[24] the corvettes left Otago on 3 April. Their next landfall was Akaroa on Banks Peninsula, and they arrived outside the entrance to the splendid harbour, a flooded volcanic crater, on 8 April. Because of the limited charts at his disposal, d'Urville initially hesitated entering without sounding but then accepted pilotage advice from one of the sailors he had recruited in Hobart (either Adolphe Poidecœur or William Cobans) and who had visited the harbour a number of times on whaling vessels. Unfortunately, while he hesitated, the wind dropped, and the *Astrolabe* was soon at the mercy of a strong tidal current dragging her towards the reefs below the cliffs. Mercifully, her yawl and a whaleboat sent by the visiting French whaler *Gange* were able to tow her to safety, with the aid of a timely breeze. The *Zélée*'s longboat also came to help, but d'Urville sent it back to advise Jacquinot to await a favourable wind and to rendezvous with him the following day. Aside from the *Gange*, which was about to return to France, there were three other French whalers anchored in the harbour: the *Adèle*, the *Pauline* and the *Héva*. The latter, from Le Havre, was the same whaler under the command of Captain Édouard Le Lièvre that the expedition had encountered in Talcahuano. D'Urville lent Le Lièvre his longboat to help him transport an anchor he had purchased from Captain Pierre-François Robin of the *Gange*. He also took advantage of the *Gange*'s departure on 10 April to send the expedition's mail and dispatches to France. Unfortunately, no official report to the minister survives from Akaroa. In the main body of his account, d'Urville did publish significant musings on the prospects for French colonisation at Akaroa, but they bear the mark of editorial additions in the wake of other events, which deserve review.

On 2 August 1838, Jean-François Langlois, captain of the French whaler *Cachalot*, with minimal knowledge of the Māori language, negotiated what he believed to be the purchase of most of Banks Peninsula from a dozen Ngāi Tahu chiefs, who had equally minimal knowledge of French. The deposit was a pitifully small amount of European clothing and a pistol – ostensibly valued at 150 francs in total. Provision was made for

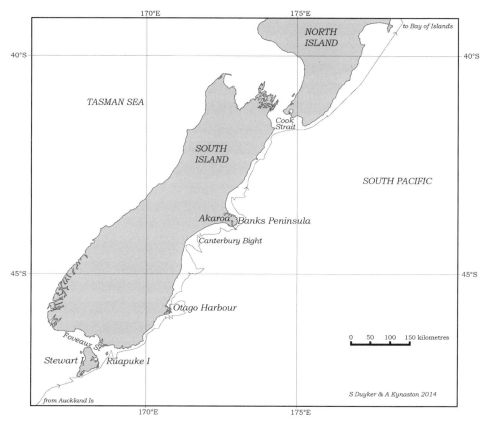

Map 10. The track of the Astrolabe *and the* Zélée, *March–April 1840, Stewart Island and the South Island of New Zealand*

the payment of the balance in the form of muskets, powder, swords, clothes and other trade goods (valued at 5850 francs) when Langlois took possession. Though provision was made for Iwikau, who was at Peraki and whose people lived on the peninsula, he did not sign the deed. As the historian Thomas Lindsay Buick put it, the payment was 'made with more or less irresponsible individuals, loose as to its terms and light as to its payments.'[25]

While d'Urville might have learned of Langlois' purported acquisition during his visit to New Zealand, perhaps from Captain Privat at Otago Harbour, he is unlikely to have known of Langlois' role in the formation of the Compagnie Nanto-Bordelaise to establish a colony at Akaroa. Nor could he have known of the agreement this company signed with the French government, on 11 December 1839, to use the 550-tonne *Comte de Paris* (the former naval transport *Mahé*) to carry its colonists to the South Island. She sailed from Rochefort with 63 emigrants on 8 March 1840. Accompanied by the 800-tonne naval corvette *Aube,* under the command of Charles-François Lavaud, the *Comte de Paris* reached the Bay of Islands on 11 July. There the colonists learned, as d'Urville soon would, that pursuant to the signing of the Treaty of Waitangi with the principal Māori chiefs on 6 February 1840, Britain had proclaimed sovereignty over all of New Zealand, and that Captain William Hobson RN had been appointed the first British lieutenant-governor on 21 May. The Compagnie Nanto-Bordelaise colonists did not reach Akaroa until 18 August, but on arrival, they discovered that Captain Owen Stanley RN and two British magistrates had been despatched on HMS *Britomart* – the same British sloop that had accompanied HMS *Alligator* to Port Essington – to enforce British law. Faced with what was effectively a fait accompli, the settlers had to resign themselves to living under British rule.[26]

There had been far bloodier conquests of the region in the previous decade. The most notorious was when the unscrupulous Captain John Stewart agreed to secrete a war party of 100 Ngāti Toa from Kapiti Island, led by Te Rauparaha, aboard his brig *Elizabeth* to wreak vengeance on the Ngāi Tahu at Akaroa. The Ngāi Tahu chief Tama-i-hara-nui was lured aboard the *Elizabeth* by Stewart on the pretext of trading muskets for flax, and was captured along with his wife and young daughter. His people ashore were also surprised and slaughtered. Tama-i-hara-nui strangled his daughter to spare her slavery, but he and his wife, Te Whe, were tortured to death when the *Elizabeth* returned to Kapiti. Two years later, in 1832, Te Rauparaha returned to capture Onawe pa, which occupied a peninsula in the centre of Akaroa harbour, and enslave its inhabitants.[27] Little wonder the neighbouring Ngāi Tahu chiefs were prepared to sell land to the French that Tama-i-hara-nui's brother Iwikau might claim but only partly controlled. They were not the only ones to seize an opportunity from these tragic events. Pierre Dumoutier would scour the battlefield for the skulls of the fallen Ngāi Tahu to take back to France to illustrate the expedition's anthropological atlas,[28] along with three plaster casts of living Māori from Otago and another from the Bay of Islands.[29]

D'Urville was quite negative about the choice of Akaroa as the prospective seat of French colonial ambitions in the region. With an eye for broader strategic considerations, he wrote:

> Akaroa would have been a very bad choice for a first settlement: it is not enough, in effect, for a nascent colony to possess a vast and safe harbour, to shelter vessels, to have a chance of success; the colonists must be assured, not only of being able to live off the land, but also of producing food from the land which nurtures trade. A nascent colony must also establish easy communication with the interior of the country, in a manner which extends measurably as emigration brings new colonists. From all these perspectives, the port of Akaroa appeared to me disadvantageous to the foundation of a settlement; indeed, in my opinion, it would be a foolish enterprise to go and create, at the other extremity of the globe, French agricultural colonies in

New Zealand, opposite England's Australian settlements, today undoubtedly successful. One cannot repeat sufficiently, if France ever wanted to enter into a system of distant colonisation, it would be exposed to certain failure by commencing the transportation of colonists as far away as New Zealand, without possessing intermediate [staging] points. Furthermore, in time of war with England, one would not think of defending such isolated possessions against British forces. In less than eight days, forces stationed in Australian ports would swoop on these colonies, which could only hope for help from the far too distant shores of the mother country … Since our passage to Akaroa, everyone knows, that England has taken possession of New Zealand as a whole. Some French colonists have been transported to the port of Akaroa; what will be their fate? … perhaps it is already too late today, to adopt any settlement project on lands henceforth under the British flag.[30]

Fortunately, Britain and France (if one excludes the collaborationist Vichy régime during World War II) would not go to war again, but the scenario d'Urville outlined was certainly one that afflicted German colonial possessions in the Pacific during World War I. Recognising the significance of the whaling industry to France, d'Urville recommended the establishment of a military post at Akaroa. This would ensure a safe haven for French whalers, facilitate reprovisioning and help control the behaviour of 'frequently undisciplined crews'.[31] Effectively, this happened by default; France could do little more. In 1843, Lieutenant Auguste Bérard (who had sailed with d'Urville as an ensign aboard the *Coquille*)[32] arrived with the 800-tonne corvette *Rhin*[33] to relieve the *Aube*. The French naval station was maintained at Akaroa until 1847.

Before leaving Akaroa, d'Urville provided Captain Charles Billard of the *Pauline* with some sheets of copper to repair his rudder. He also allowed one of his sailors, Pierre Voisin, to transfer to the same whaler. However, another sailor, Constant Goudoin, who had joined the *Zélée* in Hobart and had participated in the exploration of Terre Adélie, absconded without permission.

The *Astrolabe* and *Zélée* departed from Akaroa on 17 April. Five days later, they reached Poverty Bay on the North Island of New Zealand and anchored 'a great distance from land'.[34] Gervaize was given command of the largest yawl and ordered to draft a sketch plan of the bay. Unlike James Cook (who named the bay for the poverty of the supplies he obtained there in October 1769), d'Urville was delighted when Gervaize returned with about 50 pigs purchased from the locals; they were subsequently divided among the two corvettes. Duroch was then given command of the yawl and ordered to take Ducorps ashore to buy further provisions. They were accompanied by Barlatier-Demas, who undertook astronomical observations, possibly because Vincendon-Dumoulin was still ill after his ordeal on the Auckland Islands. With a southeasterly wind and in pouring rain, the expedition left Poverty Bay on 24 April.

Two days later, the *Astrolabe* and the *Zélée* anchored at Kororareka (now Russell) in the deeply indented basin of the Bay of Islands and learned that Britain had 'definitively taken possession' of New Zealand.[35] Little wonder that rumours soon began to spread that the French corvettes had arrived to contest this act of possession and establish a rival colony. In the harbour, a dozen whalers and HMS *Buffalo* were at anchor, the latter having discharged her remaining French-Canadian prisoners in Sydney and having transported a detachment of the 80th Regiment of Foot to Okiato to support Lieutenant-Governor Hobson. Another British naval vessel, HMS *Herald*, was seen departing. D'Urville felt as if he had been 'transported to a European port', despite the fact that the non-Māori population was only around 800 people at Kororareka and the nearby Okiato Peninsula. Yet only water supplies were easily replenished in this 'European port'; fresh food was virtually impossible to find. The local European population was unable to subsist 'without the aid of supplies sent from Sydney'.[36] D'Urville's first call was the modest three-room residence of Bishop Pompallier at the southern end of Kororareka beach. D'Urville was still carrying 'forty quadruples in gold'[37] (what the British called Spanish doubloons), entrusted to him by Father Chrysostôme Liausu in Valparaiso for Bishop Pompallier. The matter had obviously weighed on d'Urville's mind, because he had noted the sum in the codicil to his will lest he die before discharging the obligation. Although Pompallier was absent, d'Urville called on his subordinate, the French Marist missionary Father Maxime Petit, who had arrived in New Zealand in June the previous year, and gave him the gold.[38]

From Father Petit, d'Urville learned that Charles Wilkes, commander of the United States Exploring Expedition Squadron, had left the Bay of Islands just a few days before. Like Wilkes, d'Urville had no instructions from his government with regard to the British declaration of possession of New Zealand and, also like Wilkes, d'Urville resolved not to recognise the contestable authority of the British, which he believed would have dire consequences for French and American whaling companies, particularly through the imposition of onerous port dues. While he was at Pompallier's residence, he met Pierre-Michel Bonnefin, a former officer of the Napoleonic French navy,[39] and eventually he also met Bonnefin's younger sister Perinne, who was married to a French-born Mauritian merchant named Fortune Isidore Delarbre.[40] D'Urville described Bonnefin as having 'sought his fortune more or less everywhere' and having 'been brought, by a bizarre destiny, to live, at least for the moment, under the flag he hated most in the world'.[41] He added that his compatriot Bonnefin was in a state of 'great excitement and gave proof of much animosity against the English government'.[42]

D'Urville considered Bonnefin a man of integrity, but he recorded his prejudices to qualify his very anti-British account of the signing of the Treaty of Waitangi. Not only did Bonnefin cast doubt on the extent to which the Māori chiefs understood what they were signing, but he asserted that the majority had, in fact, refused to sign. Bonnefin and the other 'five or six'[43] French residents at Kororareka protested the declaration of possession and, as a result, were exposed to the 'vexations of the agents of Mr Hobson'.[44] They learned that there were also Māori who protested. Tardy de Montravel recorded the remonstration of one dissenting chief, who, with Socratic eloquence,

> … posed a trenchant question of Mr Hobson during the conference, a question so simple that it appeared to embarrass His Excellency very much. 'Do you believe,' said he, 'that if I, who am a great chief, went to England to propose my protection to Parliament and to ask for the place of the Queen, that my offers and my request would be accepted?' 'Certainly not,' Mr Hobson replied, biting his lips in annoyance. 'Well then! Why have you come here? Who asked for your protection? Believe me, return home, we are happy with our circumstances and we don't want anything to do with you.'[45]

Lieutenant Roquemaurel declared his belief that the most effective way to protect the Māori was to 'tear up the act of spoliation'.[46] To be fair, many of those who resented the creation of the new British administration particularly resented the order halting Māori land sales that had proved so lucrative to European speculators. D'Urville commented that the lack of fresh produce for sale at the Bay of Islands was a reflection of the fact that few of these speculators were seriously interested in cultivating the land.

On 1 May, d'Urville and his men once again celebrated the feast day of King Louis-Philippe's patron saint, Phillip. Thrice during the day, the corvettes shattered the silence of the bay with 21-gun salutes, but even before dawn, HMS *Buffalo*, the only remaining British naval vessel in the harbour, had been ordered to anchor next to the corvettes in what d'Urville thought was a deliberate attempt to neutralise the French presence. Although poorly armed – some of d'Urville's officers had seen the extent of her ordnance when they visited her in Hobart – the lumbering transport weighed 598 tonnes and was thus 218 tonnes heavier than either the *Astrolabe* or the *Zélée*. She fired no return salutes as was customary on such occasions, and d'Urville was quick to note her lack of courtesy. However, he himself had given no formal salute to Lieutenant-Governor Hobson on arrival. Is it any wonder that relations were cool?

Pierre Bonnefin also complained to d'Urville of the beginnings of sectarian rivalry between British Protestant and French Catholic missionaries on the bay, adding that his compatriots had fewer rights because of the 'ill-will of the [British] authorities'.[47] Although Bishop Pompallier resolved to be neutral on the question of British possession, insisting only on guarantees of religious freedom, he would eventually diffuse accusations of disloyalty by becoming a naturalised British subject in 1851.[48] In his correspondence, Pompallier tended to use the word 'heretic' rather than 'Protestant' to refer to British missionaries, but he himself was so often referred to as 'Anatikaraiti'

(Māori = Antichrist) by derogatory Protestants that many Māori innocently thought that this was his real name and accordingly addressed him as such! To his credit, Pompallier recognised that the insult had thereby lost its potency.[49] D'Urville also noted that the Protestant missionaries seemed to 'stir up hatred among the natives against the French name and they constantly represent our missionaries as envoys of Satan.'[50] One of their methods was to capitalise on local memories of the violent reprisals taken by the French in the wake of Marion Dufresne's murder at the Bay of Islands in 1772. Despite Protestant accusations that the French Catholic clergymen were intent on stripping the islanders of their possessions, d'Urville commented that the 'incontestable disinterestedness'[51] of the priests deflected the slanders. It was certainly true that the celibate Catholic missionary priests did not seek to purchase land. They did not have wives or children to support and, in addition to their vows of celibacy, they had also taken vows of poverty.

Despite sectarian tensions, d'Urville sought to reaffirm friendships with the Protestant missionaries at the Bay of Islands. On 1 May he called at the home of Reverend Henry Williams, whom he had met during his two previous visits to New Zealand. Most recently, Williams had acted as Hobson's interpreter prior to the signing of the Treaty of Waitangi. However, Williams was away, and d'Urville found his wife Marianne (née Coldham) 'cold but polite.'[52] The following day, he visited the missionary printing press[53] and was given the New Testament[54] and other Protestant devotional texts in Māori.[55] When he returned to the Astrolabe, he learned that three missionaries from Paihia had called during his absence, but by then it was too late to return the compliment.

On 1 May, d'Urville also acquired two kiwi from a local Māori. He was well aware that this strange flightless bird was endemic to New Zealand and that the specimens would be highly prized in France. The kiwi was illustrated in the expedition's zoological atlas (plates 24 and 25) and referred to in the expedition's third zoological volume under the specific name Apteryx australis, which George Shaw had published in 1813.[56] When Honoré Jacquinot and Jacques Pucheran began to draft their ornithological descriptions, published in 1853, they were informed[57] of a publication two years earlier by the British zoologist Abraham Dee Bartlett, which described another kiwi species, Apteryx mantelli.[58] To their credit, they acknowledged a 'point of doubt in the determination' of the bird collected on d'Urville's expedition.[59] Recent DNA analysis has confirmed the distinction between the southern brown kiwi, Apteryx australis, described by George Shaw (and confined to the South Island), and the northern brown kiwi, Apteryx mantelli, described by Abraham Dee Bartlett.[60] What d'Urville collected at the Bay of Islands would have been the latter species, which is restricted to the North Island.[61]

Despite his lack of official instructions on the subject of British possession, d'Urville resolved to make his visit to the Bay of Islands as useful as possible to his beleaguered countrymen. His principal action was to refuse to give any recognition to Captain Hobson as governor. When Hobson's secretary[62] called on the *Astrolabe*, d'Urville made his position clear: he would be happy to visit Captain Hobson but only as 'an officer of the British Royal Navy and the natural protector of British subjects resident at the Bay'. Hobson's secretary, according to d'Urville, assured him that his captain understood 'perfectly' the position his French visitor found himself in. Diplomatic niceties were preserved by Hobson's supposed 'indisposition' and his inability to offer his services in person. However, the diplomatic dance continued, with Hobson's secretary declaring that his superior would be 'flattered to receive the visit of the French commander'.[63] Yet when d'Urville and Jacquinot called at Hobson's residence, they were informed that he was absent.

As in Mangareva, d'Urville agreed to lend prestige to the Catholic mission by attending Mass on Sunday 2 May. Almost all of d'Urville's officers attended in full uniform, and the crews of both corvettes responded in sufficient numbers to make up two detachments under arms. With local Māori Catholics, the congregation swelled to 150 worshippers. This was too many for Kororareka's small Catholic church to hold, so a tent, decorated with all the expedition's signal flags, was erected in advance to cover an outside altar. Most of the Māori faithful were dressed in European rags, but d'Urville was particularly pleased to see a few richly tattooed warriors of noble bearing, mostly elderly, clad in traditional 'cloaks of flax trimmed with dogskin'.[64] Less dignified on that same day was the misconduct of two senior sailors from the *Astrolabe* towards a Māori women in, of all places, the bishop's residence. Despite Father Petit's pleas for leniency, the men were arrested and immediately punished on board.

Yet d'Urville did heed Father Petit's request that Charles Simonet be allowed to leave the expedition at the Bay of Islands. He recognised that Simonet, despite his desertion during the *Astrolabe*'s first voyage, had been torn from his wife (Louise Finao, whom he married according to Catholic rites in 1837) and children when he was arrested on Vava'u, and that France was no longer Simonet's home. Furthermore, d'Urville admitted that he had 'personally pardoned him long ago', that Simonet had rendered 'services to the expedition' and that he would be 'very useful to the mission'.[65] In this, he was probably reminded of the assistance that Simonet had given Bishop Pompallier during his ten months on Vava'u – under constant pressure from the Protestant missionary John Thomas, who was determined to drive him from the island. Consequently, Simonet was allowed to disembark and was paid all the wages that were due to him. D'Urville's compassion and forgiveness towards Simonet contrasts strikingly with the command style of captains such as William Bligh and Charles Wilkes. In 1841, Simonet settled on Wallis Island (Uvea); in 1848, serving the Marists as a pilot, he moved to Tahiti,[66] where three of his daughters married. He appears to have left Tahiti for Tonga with his son around 1862. There was still a Simonet living in Nukualofa in 1925.[67]

On his last day in the Bay of Islands, despite persistent gout and now colic – the latter perhaps a side effect of taking *Colchicum* as medication – d'Urville used his whaleboat to go ashore and explore Waitangi. He also visited the estate of James Busby, who had been appointed the official British resident in New Zealand in 1832 and had much to do with the drafting of the Treaty of Waitangi, signed on his front lawn. Busby was absent, but d'Urville was warmly received by John Flatt,[68] a former catechist of the Church Missionary Society who had arrived in New Zealand in 1834 on the schooner *Blackbird*.[69] Flatt had been allowed to reside in the 'back premises', but during Busby's absence in Sydney, he had 'taken the liberty' of occupying the main residence at Waitangi.[70] It seems Flatt also gained access to the cellar, and it was thanks to him that d'Urville was able to savour a light sparkling white wine made from Busby's grapes.[71] D'Urville found this New Zealand wine delicious and predicted that it would soon be exported to 'English possessions in India'.[72] He also took advantage of his meeting with Flatt to discuss the pronunciation of Māori words and to learn of his travels in the interior.[73]

D'Urville's final obligation before leaving New Zealand was to meet with the mercurial baron Charles de Thierry. He found him respectably dressed and waiting at Pompallier's home in the company of Dubouzet and Vincendon-Dumoulin. D'Urville had long followed Thierry's career and his ridiculous personal claims to sovereignty in New Zealand (and even Nuku Hiva), but he recognised that Thierry had documents of land title that were no less credible than those of many British residents in New Zealand. He also recognised that, although born in England of émigré parents, Thierry was fluent in French and identified himself as a French subject, and d'Urville, therefore, had obligations towards him. Moreover, he understood that Thierry's dogged persistence was a thorn in the side of the British. While he did not want to raise the baron's hopes, d'Urville promised to make representations on his behalf in France and drafted a sympathetic personal letter in which he drew attention to his own published references to Thierry's purchases of land.[74]

After final farewells aboard the *Astrolabe*, and giving replacement astronomical instruments to a mysterious Belgian naturalist named Lacour (who had apparently lost his instruments in a shipwreck en route from Port Essington to Sydney),[75] the expedition set sail from the Bay of Islands on 4 May. To d'Urville's surprise, they were followed from their anchorage by HMS *Buffalo*. At first, he thought that this was coincidental and that the *Buffalo* had a 'special mission' on the coast, but he soon realised that the British transport was shadowing the expedition to ensure that it was not about to anchor elsewhere in the bay. When it became clear that the *Astrolabe* and *Zélée* were headed for the open sea, the *Buffalo* returned to her anchorage – much to the amusement of d'Urville and his officers. Less than three months later, she was totally wrecked at Mercury Bay on the east coast of Coromandel Peninsula.[76] Tardy de Montravel wrote derisively of Lieutenant-Governor Hobson and the orders he had given the *Bufffalo*:

> How could he think that he could intimidate us with such a howker carrying only six miserable guns? Besides, weren't we at peace? and even if France had been at war with England, hadn't we passports which guaranteed us shelter and immunity from all the hazards of war? Really, if the New Zealand authorities do not give proof of greater sagacity in their administration, than they did in these circumstances, one must pity the colonists consigned to their care.[77]

In the next five years, the British flagstaff at Kororareka would be chopped down four times by indignant Māori. Despite a guard detachment from the 96th Regiment of Foot and the stationing of the 18-gun sloop HMS *Hazard*, a Māori attack in March 1845 forced the evacuation of the civilian population. A stockade full of gunpowder was blown up, and Māori began to loot the settlement. When HMS *Hazard* responded by shelling the looters, a fire began that consumed most of the town by the following evening. The Anglican and Catholic churches escaped destruction, but most of the European inhabitants took refuge in the new capital of Auckland. The hostilities that ensued until January 1846 came to be known as the 'Flagstaff War'. Kororareka, however, rose from the ashes as the new settlement of Russell.[78]

36

Homeward Bound via Torres Strait

We spake of storm and shipwreck,
The sailor and how he thrives,
And how betwixt heaven and ocean,
And joy and sorrow he strives.

Heinrich Heine*

The *Astrolabe* and the *Zélée* were now, effectively if not officially, on their way home. D'Urville remained determined to fulfil remaining orders en route, in particular to sail through Torres Strait. More than a year before, the end of the monsoon and the reversal of the winds had thwarted his passage from west to east, and now he hoped that the seasonal easterly winds would usher him through the strait from the opposite direction. The expedition's initial course, however, was via the Loyalty Islands, which the *Astrolabe* had sailed past 13 years earlier. On 12 May 1840, Britannia Island (Mare) was sighted, and during its coastal reconnaissance, Cape Boyer was named after Midshipman Boyer and Cape Desgraz after d'Urville's secretary. Then, tiny Hamelin Island (Leliogat) came into view; the following day, the expedition sighted Chabrol (Lifou) and Halgan (Ouvéa) islands; and on 15 May, Beaupré Island (Heo) was sighted. Then, for a week, the corvettes sailed without sight of any land. The weather was extremely hot, and every day it rained and thundered. Throughout this same week, d'Urville suffered constant intestinal pain, very likely caused by his gout medication. Rossel[1] Island (Yela), in the eastern Louisiades, was sighted on 22 May, and the following evening, the *Astrolabe* and *Zélée* rounded Cape Deliverance and tiny Adele Island (Loa Boloba) from a distance of some 30 kilometres. The northern Coral Sea was then traversed by skirting Sudest Island (Tagula), the Calvados Chain, the Montemont Islands and Ouessant Island. On 27 May, Orangerie Bay on the New Guinea coast, the western limit of Bougainville's discoveries, was reached. Here, a number of locals in canoes approached the corvettes and traded a few coconuts, a stone axe and some shells.[2]

* 'Die Heimkehr', verse vii, lines 9–12 [Lazarus trans.]

The expedition then sailed west along the New Guinea coast but near Hood Point, made for Australian waters and the entry to William Bligh's 1789 passage[3] through Torres Strait. On 31 May, after passing Anchor Cay, the French corvettes anchored safely for the night three kilometres off Darnley Island (Erub). D'Urville ordered Duroch to take the yawl ashore with the naturalists Gervaize and Coupvent-Desbois. (The latter was sent instead of Vincendon-Dumoulin, who once again was too ill to conduct geophysical observations.) Although the locals were keen to acquire iron and axes, they were reluctant to part with any fresh food, even coconuts. The following day, 1 June, the corvettes entered the North East Channel of Torres Strait near Dalrymple Island, and then sailed between Arden Island and the Warrior Reef with the intention of anchoring behind William Bligh's Warrior Island (Tudu). D'Urville's chart suggested that the reef was unbroken and completely exposed, and that he could sail along its edge to reach his prospective anchorage. Unfortunately, what he thought was a pass proved to be a cul-de-sac, and the *Astrolabe* came to a jolting halt on the edge of a wall of coral and quickly listed to one side. The *Zélée*, which had entered the same false passage, went aground windward of the *Astrolabe*. Jacquinot promptly signalled what had happened and sent an officer to report to d'Urville. Both corvettes were trapped by the wind and were being buffeted against the coral.

D'Urville and Jacquinot immediately acted to save their vessels from wreckage. The sails were furled, and the topgallants were stripped and dismantled. Soundings were taken around the corvettes, and 500-kilogram anchors were taken out and dropped in an attempt to prevent the vessels from being battered on the reef. By the time this task was completed, the tide had dropped, and it was clear that there was little hope of re-floating the corvettes before the next high tide. Meanwhile, the Tudu Islanders had flocked onto the reef to witness the strange spectacle on their doorstep. Despite darkness falling, the *Astrolabe*'s boat took out and dropped a second anchor in the deepest nearby water. The rudder was eased[4] to stop it snapping off and being swept away, but there was nothing that could be done to save the *Astrolabe*'s false keel; at 7.00 pm, part of it was seen floating beside the corvette. It was deeply troubling to d'Urville to think that so much of the timber spine of his vessel was now resting directly on the reef without any additional protection.

At 9.00 pm, a third anchor was taken out and dropped to offer another vector of security. Nevertheless, during the pitch darkness and pouring rain of the night that followed, violent squalls and gale-force winds continually lifted the *Astrolabe* up and dropped her against the reef, threatening to break her up. So violent was this battering that d'Urville began to think it would be preferable to be completely grounded. With the vessel listing heavily to portside off the edge of the reef, he attempted to use his spare masts as crutches to right the hull. The attempt failed and left the entire starboard flank

'*Échouage des corvettes l'*Astrolabe *et la Zélée dans le Détroit de Torrès*', *lithograph by Paul Petit, from a sketch by [Francesco?] Belloni after Louis Le Breton, for Élie Le Guillou's* Voyage autour du monde de l'Astrolabe *et de la Zélée, Berquet et Petion, Paris, 1842, plate 17.* Author's collection

of the *Astrolabe*'s hull exposed, posing the added risk of a complete capsize. The next high tide offered little comfort; it seemed to be lower than the previous one. D'Urville now contemplated unloading the most precious contents of the *Astrolabe* and ferrying them to Tudu Island for protection. Some of the locals had already walked across the reef to reach the *Astrolabe*, and d'Urville discovered that they spoke a few words of English. He gave them gifts and was determined to maintain good relations with them, particularly because it seemed likely that he would have to establish a camp on their island.

Another unsuccessful attempt was made to right the *Astrolabe*'s hull with a crutch. Then an attempt was made to reduce the overbalancing weight on her port side by striking the topmasts, but this failed because the altered centre of gravity had jammed the fids.[5] D'Urville held off unloading her, mainly because further sounding of the reef by boats he dispatched had revealed a practical leeward passage. Up until then, he had thought that they would have to retrace their movements if they ever succeeded in refloating the corvettes, but the southeasterly gale-force winds and currents meant there was no question of backtracking. By 6.00 pm on 2 June, darkness had enveloped the *Astrolabe*, and her hull heeled over to an angle of 32°, according to her onboard wheel pendulum. Still fearful of her capsizing, her carpenters readied their axes to chop

'Réservoirs d'eau de l'Île Toud, Détroit de Torrès', lithograph by P. Blanchard from a sketch by Louis Le Breton, Voyage au pôle sud et dans l'Océanie, *Atlas pittoresque, Paris, 1846, vol. ii, plate no. 188. Giant clam shells were used by the Tudu islanders of Torres Strait to collect rain water runoff from pandanus leaves.* National Library of Australia, PIC S11325

the masts clear. Water had reached the deck, and it was only a matter of time before her hull would begin to fill. The men, many still ill, had laboured unceasingly for 48 hours in the gale, and they now waited in silence, in the pouring rain, for d'Urville to give the order to abandon ship. The expedition's papers were readied for the boats; baggage covered the angled deck, now impossible to walk on. Louis Le Breton's painting of the corvettes floundering in the strait (now in the collection of the Peabody Essex Museum, Salem, Massachusetts), with the *Astrolabe* completely heeled over in the foreground, offers powerful testimony of the grave circumstances.[6]

Still, d'Urville held off giving the fateful order. Although the tide had been outgoing, it had not reached the lowest ebb of the previous day before it began to rise again. By some happy miracle, the *Astrolabe*'s hull had shifted onto a ramp of coral that supported her more favourably and made a capsize less likely. Despite another anxious hour, the new coral bed also offered hope of pivoting the hull and, with the aid of the rising tide, gradually leveraging and righting it. By 10.00 pm, there was general relief among all the officers and crew as the list progressively lessened. Camped on deck, they awaited the order to heave at the capstan and haul the *Astrolabe* clear of the reef. Unfortunately, when the order came, the anchors dragged. There was insufficient time to lay out new anchors before the tide fell again, but the *Astrolabe*'s crew could sense that deliverance was at hand. There was also consolation in seeing the *Zélée* successfully re-floated. As the men waited for the next high tide, they struck the topmasts to steady the *Astrolabe* further and propped her hull as an added precaution, but the high tide on the afternoon of 3 June was disappointingly low.

In the early hours of 4 June, the men began to work the capstan and were joined by 30 sailors from the *Zélée*. A northwesterly current also aided their labours, and the first signs of movement gave added impetus to their efforts. There were soon shouts of joy and triumph when the *Astrolabe* was finally refloated. Although it would become evident, on their return to France, how seriously the coral had damaged the corvettes, mercifully they took in very little water. If d'Urville offered religious thanks for his deliverance, it might have been in the form of a giant clam shell from Tudu Island.

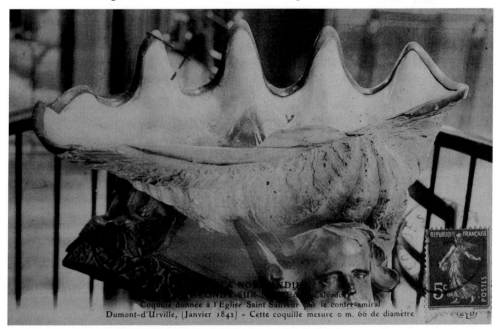

'Coquille donnée à l'Eglise Saint Sauveur par le contre-amiral Dumont-d'Urville (janvier 1842)'.
Postcard, ca. 1930s, of giant clam shell from Torres Strait donated by d'Urville, four months before his death, to the church where he was baptised. Courtesy Jean-Jacques Thomas, Condé-sur-Noireau

Just before his death, he would donate such a shell (66 centimetres in diameter) from Tudu Island to be used as a *bénitier*, or holy-water font, in the church where he was baptised: Saint-Sauveur in Condé-sur-Noireau.[7] These same giant clam shells were used by Tudu Islanders to collect rain water runoff from pandanus palm leaves – a clever survival technique that was sketched by Le Breton.[8]

D'Urville allowed his men a mere two hours' rest before putting them back to work weighing the anchors, repairing the rigging and restoring order to the chaos inside the *Astrolabe*'s hull after days on her side and being jolted against the reef. It was also necessary to spend a number of days surveying the tight leeward channel through the reef, but even with her boats marking and leading the way, the *Astrolabe* scraped the coral two or three times before clearing the reef[9] and dropping anchor in 10 fathoms (18.2 metres) of water at 3.00 pm on 8 June. The next day, the *Zélée* followed. While waiting for his consort, d'Urville had an opportunity to draft a few paragraphs of ethnographic notes on the tall and well-built Tudu Islanders. He noted that their island was low and sandy, with little shade and not a trickle of water (hence the need to capture rain water in clam shells). The inhabitants lived mainly off seafood, but d'Urville was unsure if this included marine mammals such as dugongs. He recognised the ritual treatment of dugong bones to mark what he thought were graves, however these were ritualised middens rather than tombs.[10] Unlike the Aborigines of the Australian mainland, the Tudu Islanders were armed with bows and arrows, which, like their hollowed log canoes, d'Urville thought must have come from New Guinea. Their spears were tipped with iron, and some had axes, which suggested contact with Europeans. Yet their huts were deserted, and their women and children were seemingly hidden, out of fear of Europeans.

On 10 June, with a favourable easterly breeze, the expedition sailed past Gueborar Island (Gabba) and then sighted Banks (Mua), Mulgrave (Badu) and Jervis (Mabuiag) islands to the south. Despite the strong current and the *Astrolabe*'s dragging one of her anchors, they anchored overnight. In the morning, they found that the *Astrolabe* had broken a fluke on the anchor that had dragged. Fires indicated these islands were heavily populated, and a canoe from Jervis Island – bearing men similar in appearance to those of Tudu Island – made a wary approach, but it did not come alongside the corvettes. With their boats cautiously surveying the way ahead, on 12 June, the *Astrolabe* and *Zélée* left the dangerous reef-strewn waters of Torres Strait and entered the Arafura Sea.

The coast of Timor was sighted on 19 June, but contrary winds kept the expedition from anchoring in busy Kupang harbour, beneath Fort Concordia, until the morning of 21 June. A 21-gun salute was fired by the *Astrolabe*, and the gesture was promptly reciprocated by the battery of the Dutch fort. D'Urville was courteously received by the

Dutch resident, Diederik van den Dungen Gronovius, who facilitated the replenishment of the expedition's stores of fresh food, firewood and water, even supplying Timorese men and boats to transport the water barrels to the corvettes. D'Urville, mindful of Timor's reputation for disease and still under the sway of miasmic theories of the causes of cholera and dysentery, wanted to avoid sending his own men to the watering point. Regardless of his mistaken notions, he was justified in his grave concerns for the health of Gaillard and Vincendon-Dumoulin.

Fort Concordia, built in 1653 overlooking the estuary of the Koinino River, did not impress d'Urville. Harking back to his travels in the Ottoman Empire, he described it as a fortress 'à la turque', incapable of any resistance.[11] It had no moat or exterior entrenchments, and its walls were a mere three or four metres high. What impressed d'Urville most was Kupang's Chinese temple. It seems likely that he also went in search of more Chinese books in the neighbouring Chinese quarter. Resident Gronovius probably did not share d'Urville's passion for things Chinese: originally from Leiden, he had previously been the Dutch resident in Borneo, and he informed Desgraz that he had drowned one Chinese man in a sack thrown into a river as a reprisal for Chinese rebels allegedly feeding Dutch prisoners-of-war to their pigs!

D'Urville also met a Dutchman named Jacob Tielman, who, with his half-French, half-Javanese wife, had graciously received Louis and Rose de Freycinet during their visit to Timor in October 1818.[12] The only other person d'Urville mentioned meeting in Kupang was a Captain J.M. Moyle, who was in command of one of Joseph Tissot and Augustin Lagnier's vessels, the schooner *Diana*.[13] He had recently visited Port Essington and told d'Urville of the great devastation caused by the cyclone of November 1839, and that Captain Bremer's residence had been blown 6 metres from its original footings by the wind.[14] He also informed d'Urville of the complete destruction of Ternate in the Moluccas by an earthquake and the eruption of Mount Gamalama in the same month. (D'Urville's scientific staff had climbed this very volcano at the end of January 1839.) D'Urville would have met more members of the local European community had he attended a reception given by the Dutch resident; although most of his staff attended, he was once again indisposed by chronic pain.

At 8.00 am on 26 June, d'Urville assembled all his officers, including the midshipmen. He informed them that the expedition had now fulfilled its mandate and that all that remained to be done was to return to France. An hour later, both corvettes were under sail. Three weeks later, on 17 July, the island of Rodrigues was sighted, and two days later, the peaks of the island of Mauritius. Soon after, torrents of lava could be seen spewing from the active shield volcano of Piton de la Fournaise on the east coast of Bourbon (now La Réunion). The next day, the meagre harbour of Saint-Denis was sighted, but unfavourable winds prevented the expedition from entering until 7.00 am on 21 July. The island had been claimed by France as early as 1638, when it was uninhabited, but was first colonised in 1665; unlike Mauritius, it had been returned to France by Britain after the Treaty of Paris in 1814. In the exposed harbour, d'Urville counted 14 French vessels, of which two – the transport *Lionne* and the brig *Lancier* – were naval vessels. On arrival, he sent one of his officers to present his compliments to the governor, Rear Admiral Anne-Chrétien-Louis de Hell. D'Urville soon learned that he was in a state of deep bereavement after losing 'one of his parents'[15] (presumably his mother, since his father, a member of the Constituent Assembly, was guillotined in April 1794).[16] Family news also occupied d'Urville's men: they spent all day reading letters and catching up on the latest events in France. We know that Adélie had sent a letter in English to Bourbon for d'Urville via the frigate *Junon* in late February that year.[17] Tardy de Montravel, Duroch, Boyer, Flotte and the ailing Gaillard all received official word of promotions. D'Urville was genuinely disappointed for the others he had nominated but commented that their spirits were high given the success of the expedition. Although the grieving governor was not disposed to entertain all the officers that evening, his aide-de-camp informed d'Urville that he had been extended a private invitation.

D'Urville's principal concern was to arrange for the care of his ailing men. Vincendon-Dumoulin's condition had improved, but Gaillard (apparently his pneumonia now looked more like tuberculosis) was incapable of continuing the return voyage; he would die on Bourbon five months later. Two other crewmen – Victor Duilliet and Auguste-Constant Malesieux – would be left at the naval hospital. Because of this separation, on 26 July, d'Urville assembled all his men and distributed medals to 20 sailors (including non-commissioned masters), distinguished for 'their courage, their zeal and their irreproachable conduct'.[18] On the same day, he also succeeded in presenting his officers to the governor.

After replenishing 40,000 litres of water, loading provisions for four months and replacing a 900-kilogram anchor, the corvettes were ready to set sail again. D'Urville also agreed to transport a number of military personnel who had finished their tours of duty on Bourbon, insisting they all be fit. Having been away from France so long, he feared arriving in a French port and then being subject to an additional lengthy period of quarantine. He also insisted that the passengers not include any officers as he simply had no spare cabins to accommodate them. They were embarked on the morning of 30 July, along with an unnamed ensign to replace Gaillard on the *Zélée*. That evening, the corvettes departed with a favourable wind.

Despite continuing favourable winds, the seas were heavy and tiring for the crews as they traversed the rest of the Indian Ocean. Two weeks later, the expedition rounded the Cape of Good Hope and entered the Atlantic in unusually tranquil conditions. The

'*Tombeau de Napoléon*', *unknown engraver, from Dumont d'Urville's* Voyage pittoresque autour du monde, *L. Tenré, Paris, vol. ii, 1835. D'Urville first visited the island of Saint Helena in January 1825, three and a half years after Bonaparte's death in exile. He visited the island twice more, in 1829 and 1840. Although he was not a Bonapartist, after the July Revolution of 1830, d'Urville offered to command an expedition to repatriate the former emperor's remains. The task was ultimately undertaken by the prince de Joinville in 1840.* Author's collection

next port of call, on 7 September, was the island of Saint Helena, to replenish the water they had consumed. D'Urville had already visited the island twice before, but many of his men were anxious to visit Napoleon's tomb. The fallen emperor would not rest there much longer.

Exactly two months before, King Louis-Philippe's son, the prince de Joinville, had left Toulon in the *Belle Poule* with orders to exhume Napoleon's remains and return them to France. This was the so-called '*retour des cendres*'. (Literally, the word *cendres* means ashes, but in French it is used very generally for mortal remains.) It was no doubt hoped that some of the emperor's past glory might rub off on the July Monarchy and that the funerary pomp and circumstance of the return might somehow lift its flagging fortunes. This proved a misguided hope. Even in death, Napoleon would cost the French taxpayer dearly: one million francs were earmarked for the exhumation, transport and eventual reinterment of his remains beneath the dome of Les Invalides in Paris. The prince de Joinville sailed with a large retinue, including luminaries from the Empire or their sons. He took 93 days to reach Saint Helena, partying all the way. Napoleon's empire might have crumbled, but his body, disinterred by Joinville and his entourage in October that year, was found to be remarkably well preserved. His face, although noticeably stubbled, appeared serene. His green and red colonel of chasseurs' uniform was still intact, as was the medal of the *Légion d'honneur* on his chest. Only the seams of his boots had split, allowing his toes to poke through. His long white fingernails were also clearly visible.[19]

It will be remembered that d'Urville had offered to undertake just such a mission to Saint Helena immediately after the Revolution of 1830. Very likely, he reflected on how simple and inexpensive it would have been for him to fulfil such a task now. He was already carrying Mafi Kelepi's body in a barrel of arrack, not to mention the skulls Dumoutier had gathered during their far-flung landfalls! And a hearse had already been constructed locally to convey Napoleon's coffin from his willow-shaded grave to the waterfront at Jamestown. The islanders expected Joinville's imminent arrival but would have to wait another five weeks for him to come.

Regardless of his republican and left-wing democratic beliefs, d'Urville made reference to Napoleon's sojourn on Saint Helena as that of 'the most extraordinary man of modern times'. He added a religious glow by describing all his officers 'hastening to make the pious pilgrimage' to the banished emperor's grave and recorded that his sailors, despite the weather, were also 'heading piously for the valley of Longwood'.[20] Yet, it does not appear that d'Urville made another 'pious pilgrimage' of his own. Despite his chronic pain, he instead went in search of the magnetic observatory set up that January by a capable young artillery lieutenant named John Henry Lefroy as part of a global study of terrestrial magnetism under the direction of Edward Sabine. Lefroy had been dropped on the island with his instruments by the Antarctic expedition of James Clark Ross in January 1840 and had established his observatory in a building that originally accommodated the exiled Napoleon but was never occupied by him.[21] Although only 23 years of age, Lefroy's 'merit' and 'very broad knowledge'[22] left a very favourable impression on d'Urville.

At 2.00 pm on 9 September, with his water replenished and all his pilgrims aboard, d'Urville gave the order to set sail. The rest of the voyage was relatively uneventful. The Azores were sighted on 20 October, and 11 days later, the Spanish coast came into view. On 1 November, the corvettes passed through the Strait of Gibraltar. After a rapid traverse of the western Mediterranean, they rounded Cape Sicié on the afternoon of 6 November 1840. Soon after, the *Astrolabe* and *Zélée* anchored in Toulon harbour. Despite pouring rain, all the men were on deck. They had been away from France exactly three years and two months.

37

Toulon & Paris:
The final years

*Fortune sometimes lies in wait to surprise the last hour of our lives,
to show the power she has, in a moment, to overthrow
what she was so many years in building …*

Michel de Montaigne*

At 6.00 am on 7 November 1840, presumably after a medical inspection, d'Urville and his men obtained permission to land at the port of Toulon.[1] Among those who came to greet the expedition was Pierre-Antoine Delafond, the midshipman who had been invalided home over a year earlier from Java. D'Urville was delighted to see that Delafond had recovered his health and that he had promptly reported for duty aboard the *Astrolabe* to free those officers anxious to see their families. Word would have spread quickly of the arrival of the expedition in the home town of so many of its members. Although La Juliade was some distance outside the then-walled port of Toulon, Adélie had frequently been visited by the wives of many members of the expedition, regardless of rank. She had acted as a conduit of news for these women (some of whom were illiterate) and passed on messages to their husbands via d'Urville. It seems likely that someone would have taken the trouble to inform her of the expedition's arrival and that Adélie and d'Urville were in each other's arms that day. The following day was a Sunday, so they also had the remains of the weekend together before Jules, now a maturing adolescent, returned to class.

Despite the minister's orders to report immediately to Paris, d'Urville remained in Toulon for another 'two months'.[2] He rendered accounts (including a stock-take of trade goods used during the expedition)[3] and was relentless in his demands for the recognition of his men; very likely, he also did further editing of his journal prior to official publication. Had he been in Paris, as Jacquinot soon was, he might have witnessed the arrival of Napoleon's remains and the funerary procession for the reburial

---

* *Essais* (1580), 'Qu'il ne faut juger de nostre heur, qu'après la mort', livre i, ch. xviii [Cotton trans.]

'Toulon', steel engraving by Émile Rouargue (ca. 1795–1865) and Adolphe Rouargue (1810–187?), published by Fourne, Fournier, Perrotin, ca. 1845. Courtesy Georgette Deslettres

at Les Invalides on 15 December 1840; Jacquinot complained that these events made it impossible for him to gain an audience with the minister.[4] Although family pressure probably contributed to d'Urville's extended sojourn in Toulon, there can be no doubt of his poor state of health at the time. We have the testimony of his old friend Aimable Matterer, who was shocked to find him 'no more than a spectre, a worn body, that dragged itself about painfully with the aid of a humble walking stick'. Yet d'Urville's 'calm and austere features were still very expressive, and his eagle-eyes shone' when he recounted episodes from his 'great voyage'.[5] Matterer visited him almost daily and, during a severe attack of gout, d'Urville declared: 'I feel that I don't have much time left in this world, but what consoles me is that I die in the gentle satisfaction of never having done ill to anyone, and that my name will perhaps not be forgotten in the annals of our maritime history.' He still hoped that his reports to the minister would lead to the acknowledgement of his men. If he himself was not promoted, he intended to retire. He told Matterer: 'I will finish my days here, under this beautiful sun; I will give instructions to be buried in this modest garden, next to my three children, who have rested in peace here for several years.'[6] However, d'Urville did receive recognition. Officially he was promoted to the rank of *contre-amiral* (rear admiral) on 31 December 1840,[7] but he appears to have received notification earlier because Tardy de Montravel wrote to congratulate him on 11 December.[8] Matterer was there when the brevet arrived, and d'Urville 'placed it on his heart and his eyes filled with tears'.[9]

From Adélie's passionate letters to d'Urville during his voyage, we can have no doubt that she had longed desperately for her husband's return. 'God grant,' she wrote (in English), in February 1840, '[that] you be entirely delivered and that I might press you on my heart – this fortunate moment will be softness for me and will [re]pay me of all my sufferings … I hope that you will never leave me at your return.'[10] Despite this, d'Urville set off alone for Paris. According to Isidore Le Brun, he arrived in February 1841, but d'Urville's dated correspondence indicates that he was in the capital by 27 January. Le Brun, perhaps on the basis of d'Urville's own admission, recorded that he was still so feeble that he had to be 'carried' (or perhaps lifted up) to the coach taking him on the first leg of his journey from Toulon to Lyon.[11]

Why did Adélie not accompany him to Paris? There were several reasons. She wanted Jules to finish his academic year at the Collège de Toulon, where he had excelled in his studies, and she clearly did not want to leave before the 'distribution [of prizes]' in August. She was also anxious over Jules' health. In the letter that she wrote to d'Urville for collection at the island of Bourbon, she declared (once again in English): 'This child is weak and sickly and he needs of the heat.'[12] Toulon's Mediterranean winters are undoubtedly milder than those in Paris. And she repeatedly asserted that her own health was precarious and prevented her from travelling. On 3 April, she wrote to d'Urville that she could not leave Toulon before the 'beginning of September', but that she was fearful of the journey because of a 'desire to urinate frequently without the power [to do so]' and because her current condition was 'a complete lowering of the womb'. This suggests that she was suffering from a uterine prolapse or perhaps a cystocele, both complications of childbirth. Given her condition, she readily conceded that consulting a doctor in Paris might benefit her.[13] She would almost certainly have been treated with a pessary of metal, or waxed cork or wood, with a cord for removal.[14] Adélie also wrote of being 'horribly' tired. She still suffered from the serious depressive illness that afflicted her after the deaths of her children. As René Lesson commented in 1846:

> Madame d'Urville, whom I knew personally, was a witty woman, who wrote with the finesse that is the prerogative of her sex, but the loss of [three] of her children soon wounded her naturally impressionable and enthusiastic spirit; soon blighted the purity of her character and brought forth some of the mental instability that made her life one long convalescence, seeded with sickly relapses.[15]

'Anxiety' is the word Adélie herself used to describe what most assailed her. Two years before, she had written to d'Urville (in English): 'You will find me much changed at your return, the anxiety more than the age have attended [my] features and it remains to me but a heart which knows to love you.'[16] Anxiety disorders are frequently a concomitant of depression, and very likely this also made Adélie overly protective of her remaining son.[17] If she was prescribed laudanum as a soporific to help her deal with her anxious temperament, insomnia or even the physical shaking that her son described during the worst stages of her emotional collapse in November 1837, she might now have been habituated to opiates, which could perhaps explain her chronic fatigue. She was also bled immediately after Émile's death, and how frequently (and uselessly) her subsequent depression was treated this way is unknown, although we do know that it was still happening at the time of her death. Depending on frequency, such bleedings could easily have caused anaemia and constant tiredness. For the moment Adélie remained in Toulon with Jules.

On arriving alone in Paris, Rear Admiral d'Urville lodged in the Hôtel de France, rue Saint-Thomas du Louvre, one of several ancient streets that once ran down to the Seine between the Louvre and the Jardin des Tuileries, now obliterated by the place du Carrousel.[18] His first obligation was to submit an official report to the minister with his plan for publishing the expedition's historical account and scientific results.[19] Even before d'Urville arrived in Paris, two commissions established by the Académie des sciences had reported on the expedition. D'Urville's past vocal critic, François Arago, was a member of both commissions, but he was neither the *rapporteur*[20] nor a dissenting voice. For hydrography (assessing 72 maps and 42 harbour and port plans), the *rapporteur* for the nine commission members was Charles-François Beautemps-Beaupré. On behalf of the commission, he asked the academy to solicit the government to publish the immense hydrographic results of d'Urville's expedition, described presciently as 'a scientific monument which will be consulted fruitfully, for many years, by the navigators of all nations'.[21] All the members of the hydrographic commission – Arago, Beautemps-Beaupré, Blainville, Augustin Serres, Léonce Élie de Beaumont, Brongniart, Geoffroy Saint-Hilaire, Victor Audouin and Henri Milne-Edwards – also served on the zoological commission, however its *rapporteur* was Blainville, aided by Milne-Edwards, who drafted a separate five-page note on crustaceans and insects. Although the number of new species collected on d'Urville's expedition was not as large as those brought back on some earlier French voyages, many were gathered in very isolated areas, and these efforts were judged to be of 'powerful interest for questions of zoological geography'.[22] Surprisingly, it was the work of the phrenologist Pierre Dumoutier that particularly impressed the commissioners. They declared: '… one of the most important, most interesting results of this expedition, the one that we now primarily have to call to the Academy's attention, is the rich and large collection of skulls and especially plaster busts, moulded from nature, of all races of man in various stages of civilisation'.[23] The zoologists of the expedition were judged to have 'perfectly fulfilled the mission that they had been charged with' and it was recommended to publish the 'results of their work in the most prompt manner and the most convenient for the interest of science and the glory of our country'.[24] Yet, it was not until 1 May 1841 that the scientific collections were actually released by customs in Toulon.[25] The following month, they were deposited in the largest greenhouse at the Jardin des plantes in Paris. It was there that they were inspected by the navy minister, Admiral Duperré, on 28 June 1841. He was received by the professors and administrators of the museum and a number of the naturalists from the expedition, who then guided him through the various parts of the collection. The minister was not a scientist, so in such a 'show and tell', it was hard for the dried and pressed botanical specimens to compete with the many colourful birds (the Adélie penguin drew particular attention) and Dumoutier's striking series of moulded plaster heads. Once again, these heads received a glowing report and were described in the *Annales maritimes et coloniales* as the 'beginning of a new genre of collection which will be more useful to give a solid basis to the study of the natural history of the human species'. According to the anonymous author of the article, the botanical specimens, brought together by locality, 'proved' that the medical officers had 'gathered examples of the vegetation of all the points that they had visited'. The 'able brush' of the artist Louis Le Breton and his collection of sketches were also praised.[26]

The minister needed little convincing. At the beginning of April, he had already assigned the Jacquinot brothers, Tardy de Montravel, Vincendon-Dumoulin and Hombron to work on the official publication of the expedition's findings under d'Urville's orders. Despite the praise Élie Le Guillou received from the zoological commission of the Académie des sciences, he was deliberately excluded from the editorial team. Instead, a young naval surgeon named Jules-Joseph-François Grange, who had already earned two of the five university degrees he would attain before the end of the decade, was chosen to edit the expedition's geological results, based on 5000 mineral and rock specimens.[27] Because Ernest Goupil had died in Hobart, Admiral Duperré seconded Louis Le Breton to the editorial team since he had assumed responsibilities as the expedition's artist. Three months before, d'Urville had been pleased to learn that, of his editorial staff, Vincendon-Dumoulin, Hombron, Honoré Jacquinot and Le Breton had all been decorated with the *Légion d'honneur*. In addition, Ducorps, Thanaron, Barlatier-Demas and Dumoutier were decorated, as were three non-commissioned officers: the master helmsman, Pierre-Joseph Augias, and the master of manoeuvres, Jean-Gaspard Gras, on the *Zélée*; and the master gunner, Indative-Paul Plagne, on the *Astrolabe*.[28] D'Urville would lobby for still more promotions and decorations for his men.[29]

The earliest surviving letter d'Urville received from Adélie while he was alone in Paris is dated 22 February 1841. Perhaps because of this, it has been asserted that she 'did not write to him for weeks'.[30] Although it is possible that Adélie suffered another serious depressive episode in the wake of d'Urville's departure from Toulon and stopped writing, there are no surviving letters from their son, Jules, during this period either. It is more likely that part of her correspondence has not been preserved, as appears to be the case with most of d'Urville's letters to his wife. In November 1839, Adélie beseeched d'Urville not to let anyone read her letters, and she pleaded with him not to tell anyone of their contents. Those that survive from this period (22 February to 3 June 1841) profess enduring love but also give evidence of her resistance to moving to Paris for the duration of the editorial and publishing project.

D'Urville had no choice but to get on with his life and fulfil his duties. On 4 March, he purchased a new three-buttoned uniform tunic, a pair of trousers, a hat of fine felt, a scarf with a gold clasp and a new sword from a Monsieur Claes, tailor to His Majesty the King of the Belgians – on the rue de Rivoli, near the Bourse. The account, when it arrived the following day, was a hefty 1091 francs (more than half his annual salary when he was an ensign). On that day, d'Urville was guest of honour at a banquet at the 'Caveau' (Société littéraire parisienne), where the Bonapartist writer Albert Montémont – after whom d'Urville named the Montemont Islands off New Guinea – recited a long ode glorifying the explorer's achievements.[31] D'Urville was rarely one for dressing up, but with his promotion to rear admiral came other obligations. According to Le Brun, he attended a dinner at the Tuileries, and the king 'addressed a few words … to encourage him to take care of his health'.[32] There is a hint of awkwardness about this encounter. Perhaps Louis-Philippe remembered d'Urville's unflattering comments about 'the direction' of the Orléanist government published in 1834.[33] Louis-Philippe might not have wanted to linger in conversation with the rear admiral, but his daughter-in-law, the duchesse d'Orléans, Princess Hélène, certainly did. Soon after, d'Urville was informed that he would be received by her husband, the duc d'Orléans, Crown Prince Ferdinand-Philippe, on 21 March. The duke then invited him to attend the baptism of his first-born son, the comte de Paris, Prince Philippe d'Orléans, at Notre-Dame cathedral on Sunday 2 May.[34] If he did attend this important event – and it would have been politically astute to do so since the infant was the second in line to the throne – d'Urville did not mention it in his journal.[35] Nor did he mention meeting Father Jean Barran of the Société des missions étrangères de Paris and discussing the Latin words 'ne nos inducas in tentationem', the penultimate petition in the Pater Noster and, it would seem, the theological debate over whether God leads us into temptation![36] Yet d'Urville did record going, as he frequently did, to the famous chess café La Régence, on the corner of the rue Saint-Honoré and the place du Palais-Royal[37] (where, two years later, Karl Marx is believed to have met Friedrich Engels for the first time), before dining with his friend Le Brun. The day before the baptism, d'Urville was also invited to dinner by Louis-Isidore Duperrey and his wife, but, once again, if he accepted, he did not record the evening in his journal,[38] so we do not know if the two were finally reconciled. D'Urville now outranked his old commander, who was never promoted to admiral and who had retired from the navy in January 1837. However, in November 1842, Duperrey achieved an honour that completely eluded d'Urville: election to the Académie des sciences and, furthermore, election to its presidency eight years later.[39] D'Urville had to content himself with the gold medal of the Société de géographie de Paris.

Beside Le Brun, d'Urville's old friends (including Phillip Barker Webb and Sabin Berthelot) were back in touch, and with celebrity came other admirers and approaches. One correspondent, evidently unaware of his painful gout, invited him to a Left Bank address on the rue de Vaugirard (the longest street in Paris) and signed simply 'on dansera' ['we will dance']! On 4 April, another proffered medical advice for his illness, recommending filtered water, milk, soup, baths and (impossibly!) brisk walks. Others, such as Father Jean Barran – with his letter strewn with Latin, Greek and Hebrew references – acknowledged d'Urville the polymath and scholar. On 6 June, Ambroise-Firmin Didot sent him a copy of the third instalment of Champollion's Egyptian grammar and touted for the contract to publish the expedition's historical account and scientific results. Minor artists also sought employment illustrating the volumes, but aside from engraving and lithography, this task had already been accomplished by Goupil and Le Breton.

Five individuals sought to publish the results of the expedition: Ambroise-Firmin Didot, Arthus Bertrand, Casimir Gide, Pierre-Paul Didier and [Jean-Jacques?] Lefevre,[40] so the minister ordered the establishment of a commission of five naval officers, headed by d'Urville, to conduct individual interviews, evaluate quotations and make the selection. This commission appears to have met in early June, and in the end, the publishing contract went to Casimir Gide. Although the conditions and price accepted were identical to that of Arthus Bertrand, the selection commission appears to have been swayed by Gide's assurances of collaboration with baron Isidore Taylor, already famous for editing almost half of the monumental multi-volume, illustrated folio catalogue of French heritage, *Voyages pittoresques et romantiques dans l'ancienne France* (1820–78). Under the terms of the final contract, the navy undertook to purchase 300 copies of the finished publication, and Gide agreed to complete publication by January 1848.[41] In fact, the botanical, zoological, geological and anthropological volumes would not be completed until 1854.

With a publisher chosen, on 15 June, d'Urville notified the minister that he was leaving Paris for 'two or three months'.[42] Although his extended family in Normandy hoped he might visit them, they would be disappointed; his understandable priority was to see his wife and son in Toulon. He headed south three days later – travelling via Fontainebleau, Nevers, Moulins, Lyon, Avignon and Aix-en-Provence – and was

Detail from a photograph by H. Blancard, ca. 1887, looking from the Jardin du Luxembourg down the rue de Fleurus, Paris. In 1841–42, d'Urville and his family resided on the first and second floors of 26 rue Madame – the cream-coloured building (centre right) – on the intersection with the rue de Fleurus. The building was demolished in the 1970s. Bibliothèque historique de la Ville de Paris, 4° 21, 15 H.

reunited with Adélie and Jules at La Juliade on 22 June.[43] They would not be separated again, but d'Urville's letters and private journal contain many references to the shifting compass of Adélie's emotions and her chronic depressive illness. Upon arrival in Toulon, he informed Le Brun that he found his 'good Adélie in a better state';[44] on 19 July, less than a month later, he wrote: 'Adélie is more tranquil.' Four days later, he noted, 'Adélie still suffers', and on 27 July, he wrote, 'Adélie has been sad again.'[45] Jules, her sole surviving child, now 15 years old, remained the anchor of both her happiness and her anxieties. At the end of the academic year of 1841 at the Collège de Toulon, he won the 'Prix d'honneur', topped his class in French and Latin dissertation, gained first prize in physics, chemistry and natural history, and received the 'first honourable mention' in mathematics. His future education was clearly a priority for his parents, who hoped he would qualify for the École polytechnique.[46] On arrival in Paris, probably on 21 September,[47] Jules was enrolled at the prestigious Collège royal (now Lycée) Louis-le-Grand, founded in 1563, on the rue Saint-Jacques. Two years before, Baudelaire had been a student there, but he was only one of many celebrated individuals to have attended this school, including Molière, Voltaire, Diderot and Victor Hugo.

While surgeons Hombron and Jacquinot moved into lodgings close to the Muséum national d'histoire naturelle, respectively in the rue du Pont Louis-Philippe and the rue Saint-Jacques, the d'Urville family moved into an apartment in a three-storey building at 26, rue Madame, close to the Jardin du Luxembourg. This was after initial lodgings at 3, rue du Battoir Saint-Andre.[48] Admiral Willaumez had his *pied-à-terre* in the same fashionable street. Although the building no longer stands, and the street has been renumbered,[49] we know from a notarial inventory and a cadastral plan that it was on the corner of the rue de Fleurus.[50] The d'Urvilles' landlord was an engraver named Joseph Molé,[51] who lived in the same building with his adopted son, Paul-Henri-Joseph Molé-Gentilhomme, the author of many melodramatic novels and plays.[52] As early as March 1841, d'Urville had suggested to Adélie that the family live on the rue Madame. Adélie ultimately agreed, although she was initially unenthusiastic because she thought it too far from the rue de Seine,[53] where Dumoutier resided with his wife and daughters; in fact, the two streets were in the same *arrondissement*. Although we know that Adélie's doctor in Paris was Jean-Baptiste Boisduval, it is possible she, or perhaps d'Urville, also sought the opinion of Dumoutier. As we shall see, he appears to have been privy to intimate details of Adélie's condition.

It is uncertain exactly when the family settled into the apartment, but it was presumably by 24 October 1841, when d'Urville rented furniture from a merchant named Denis Durel in the rue de Condé.[54] The d'Urvilles occupied the first floor, which had a small private staircase that gave access to at least part of the top floor, where a kitchen overlooked a courtyard, and a linen room was illuminated by a hinged skylight. D'Urville and Adélie slept separately. D'Urville's bedroom had a bunk bed and step, a desk with a lockable cashbox and two sofas upholstered in red. The only decorative items in the room were two bladed weapons: one from the Mariana Islands, the other, 'Malay', probably a kris from the Netherlands East Indies. Adélie's bedroom had two casement windows, which overlooked the rue de Fleurus, but also an east-facing window with a view of one of the gates of the Jardin du Luxembourg.[55] It is not known if the two bedrooms connected. Although separate sleeping arrangements might have been a reflection of a changed marital relationship, perhaps caused by Adélie's gynaecological problems, there is no evidence of any serious emotional rupture. The domestic configuration at 26, rue Madame continued what d'Urville's years at sea had already necessitated: both he and Adélie were used to sleeping alone. It is also possible that d'Urville's work habits – signalled by a desk in his bedroom – might have occasioned separate rooms to spare Adélie disturbance rather than deliberately to curtail physical intimacy.

Adélie's wardrobe in Paris was overwhelmingly dominated by black dresses. On 8 October 1841, she would have marked the fourth anniversary of Émile's death, so the other colours in her wardrobe, particularly whites and blues, might have represented a formal transition to partial mourning. In her room, she also kept a white satin baptismal robe. Her children lay buried in Toulon, but in Paris she could still hold the robe in which they were once held, full of life and hope, over the baptismal font. We have few documents to plumb the depths of her continuing anguish during these months, but it is remarkable that, by early May 1842, she had accumulated 21 pairs of gloves in her Paris bedroom! Were they purchased compulsively, on a near-weekly basis, in response to obsessive ruminations and anxieties over cleanliness? We will probably never know.

The d'Urvilles appear to have eaten all their meals, including breakfast, in the dining room. A cupboard near one of the casement windows held an olive-wood bread box, a bread warmer, a coffee grinder and coffee maker. There was also a crystal cabinet that held some four dozen bottles of Bordeaux, Champagne, liqueur and other wine, together with glasses and carafes. The living room contained another crystal cabinet and a gilded copper pendulum clock made by Adélie's father. Most of the furniture was of mahogany, with sofas and chairs upholstered variously in black, green, blue or red, and the curtains, depending on the room, were either blue or white. Compared to La Juliade, the apartment contained relatively few books: just over a hundred volumes, including Jules' school texts. Since he had no siblings, Jules also had the privilege of his own bedroom, which doubled as a study. It was accessed by a corridor from the living room and overlooked the rue Madame.[56]

While Jules settled in as a student in the *rhétorique* class – the final year of secondary education – at the Collège royal Louis-le-Grand and once again began to excel,[57] d'Urville returned to work on the official account of his recent voyage. Casimir Gide's printer, Ange Pihan de la Forest, in the rue des Noyers, soon had the first of the 10 historical volumes of his *Voyage au pôle sud et dans l'Océanie* typeset and in press.[58] On 11 December 1841, the *Bibliographie de France* announced its publication and the plan for the other nine projected historical and 13 scientific volumes and seven atlases.[59] The first octavo volume, with its dark-turquoise paper cover and a fold-out map of the Strait of Magellan, sold for 3 francs. In early 1842, the second historical volume, in identical format, appeared with a fold-out map of the expedition's surveys of the South Shetlands, South Orkneys and the tip of the Antarctic Peninsula. D'Urville, however, did not live to see the publication of the third volume, which appeared later the same year. Nor would he ever see his native Normandy again, although he intended to visit Caen, Condé-sur-Noireau and Vire for 'eight or ten days' in June 1842. On 1 May, he entrusted Le Brun with a letter for his nephew abbé Dumont de la Londe and copies of the first two historical volumes.[60]

Despite avoiding the fashionable intellectual salons of the capital in favour of the company of his family, d'Urville still sought out what was new in Paris. Steam rail

Bronze bas relief panel (1846) by Dominique Molknecht, representing the railway catastrophe in which Dumont d'Urville, his wife and only son were killed on 8 May 1842; it decorates the pedestal that supports the explorer's statue in Condé-sur-Noireau. Author's collection

transport was one of these novelties. On Sunday 8 May 1842, a week after the feast of Louis-Philippe's patron saint, the d'Urville family travelled to Versailles to enjoy the festival of the 'Grandes Eaux' – the release of some 10,000 cubic metres of water through the fountains of the royal gardens – in honour of the monarch. Initially, Adélie had not intended to travel to Versailles that Sunday. Presumably unwell, she had asked her physician, Jean-Baptiste Boisduval, to bleed her that day, but he instead arranged to come on the Monday (coincidentally what would have been her forty-fourth birthday).[61] The early spring weather was splendid, and perhaps d'Urville – who had his own predisposition to depression – understood instinctively that a family outing would do her more good. He, himself, had been tormented by almost unceasing headaches since his return to Paris, and he hoped the better weather would ease his pains.[62]

After a day in the festive throng, among a populace once excluded from such royal preserves, at 5.30 pm the d'Urvilles boarded the second covered carriage of the train for Paris on the Rive Gauche line. Among their fellow passengers in the first six carriages were an English family, a Prussian from Cleves, a money-changer from Nantes, two landholders from Lyon, a banker from Turin with his wife and sister-in-law, three Americans, two young Greeks, the sons of several local notables,[63] the concierge of the

Théâtre des folies-dramatiques, students of medicine, law and chemistry, merchants from Paris, Rouen and the Netherlands East Indies,[64] and two brothers from Lorient (Morbihan).[65] The train had 12 covered carriages, each seating 48 passengers, followed by three *diligences*, also seating 48 passengers, and two uncovered carriages seating 30 passengers. This configuration was pulled by two steam locomotives in tandem: the four-wheeled, 10-horsepower 'Matthew Murray' and the more powerful six-wheeled 'Éclair', both of British manufacture. Together with their tenders, the train was some 127 metres long. After leaving the railway station at Sèvres and picking up speed, a violent wobble in the wheels of the lead locomotive was reported by a number of witnesses.[66] The consequence was soon catastrophic.

At 7.00 pm, in a cutting near Bellevue, northwest of Meudon, the 'Matthew Murray' broke an axle and collapsed onto the rails, and the second locomotive, weighing 17 tonnes (but with the added momentum of perhaps 10 times this weight in tow), ploughed into it, resulting in a derailment to the left of the track within seconds. The locomotives were overturned, and one after another, the first six carriages crashed into each other and piled up on the lower flank of the cutting. Moments later, glowing coke from the fire boxes of the locomotives ignited a conflagration among the splintered timber carriages, fanned by a strong wind in the cutting. Blistering steam escaping from the boilers added to the horror of those trapped in the now-flaming pyre. In less than a quarter of an hour, six carriages and most of the screaming terror-stricken passengers inside were consumed by fire. There was little that the shocked and dazed survivors[67] in the dozen carriages still on the rails could do to aid those in the burning carriages ahead of them. Tragically, the doors were locked and the keys were in the custody of three conductors, of whom only one emerged from the tangled wreckage.[68] The chief engineer, an Englishman named George, tried to open the doors but was asphyxiated before he could do so.

We know that d'Urville, Adélie and Jules survived the initial crash but, like so many others, remained trapped. D'Urville was recognised by a passenger who had escaped from the fourth carriage – possibly a Dutch merchant from Batavia who earlier had seen the admiral carrying a letter bearing d'Urville's name. He (d'Urville) was heard to cry out 'Save my wife; save my son!', but fire appears to have driven the would-be rescuers back. D'Urville covered his eyes with his hands as 'a vortex of flame and smoke' robbed him of visibility.[69] One can only begin to imagine the terror of the family as searing flames began to consume their clothes, hair and skin, and also supplanted oxygen with toxic gases. Intense heat, agonising pain, circulatory shock and cardiac arrest soon united them in death. The physiologist François Magendie, who would perform post-mortem examinations on their remains at the Collège de France, noted that their internal organs had erupted from their bodies and had also been consumed by the flames.[70] Even the metal jewellery of the trapped passengers melted in the inferno.

It was initially believed that around 250 people died that evening, but the exact toll was uncertain because the casualties were taken to different hospitals and temporary mortuaries. More than a century later, the number was revised down to around 200 dead, including those who died in hospital. At the time, it was the worst railway accident that had occurred in Europe, claiming some ten-times the number killed in railway accidents in England in the previous two years. The remains of d'Urville and his family were among just over 30 charred and disfigured corpses initially deposited near the mill (which still stands) in the cemetery of Montparnasse. Only two of the corpses still had limbs, and another two still had their heads.[71] These two charred skulls attracted the attention of Dumoutier, who was convinced that he could identify d'Urville's remains based on the plaster phrenological busts he had cast in the previous decade. The admiral was a tall heavily built man with a large and distinctive head, and Dumoutier's identification 'did not permit the least doubt'.[72] Magendie would later comment on the 'prodigious hardness' of d'Urville's skull.[73] Dumoutier also identified Adélie's body, based on 'some particular circumstances of a recent malady'. Since all that remained of her body were two superior incisors and a charred, limbless, headless torso, it is possible that what Dumoutier identified (but discretely avoided revealing to the press) was a pessary used to treat her gynaecological problem. If it was made of metal and still lodged internally, it might indeed have survived the flames, unlike superficial metal jewellery. Other scientific evidence, perhaps the known proximity of other remains, enabled the identification of the body of d'Urville's gifted and promising son, Jules. Ultimately, the family physician, Dr Boisduval, surgeons Hombron and Jacquinot, hydrographer Vincendon-Dumoulin, botanist Charles Gaudichaud-Beaupré and the ethnographer Grégoire Domeny de Rienzi, who all knew d'Urville and his family, concurred with Dumoutier and formally identified the remains.[74]

On learning of the tragic events, Admiral Duperré ordered seals placed on the doors of the d'Urville family homes in Toulon and Paris prior to the sorting of 'papers, charts, plans, memoirs and all other documents of interest to science' that belonged to the navy.[75] After Magendie's post-mortems at the Collège de France, the remains were placed in coffins and taken back to 26, rue Madame. It was from there that the funeral cortege left for the church of Saint-Sulpice at 11.00 am on 12 May 1842, via the rues Vaugirard, de Tournon and Petit Bourbon (now the rue Saint-Sulpice). Two companies of grenadiers, together with the sappers, drummers and band of the navy's 12th Regiment of Infantry of the Line, accompanied the three hearses. The band also played funeral airs during the Requiem Mass. The municipal guard was called out to control the crowds of curious onlookers. D'Urville's hearse was surrounded by sailors. Among those in attendance were the navy minister, Admiral Duperré, and 15 other admirals (including Halgan, Jurien and Bougainville); virtually the entire naval officer and hydrographic corps, and the senior naval administrative staff present in Paris at the time; three peers of the realm; at least eight (and probably more) deputies from the National Assembly; deputations from the Institut de France, the Bureau des longitudes and various learned societies; and the mayor and deputy mayor of the 11th arrondissement. Jules' fellow students from the Collège royal Louis-le-Grand followed his hearse, which was draped in white and silver. Although no members of the royal family attended – Crown Prince Ferdinand-Philippe had escorted the duchesse d'Orleans to Plombières (Vosges) and two months later would himself be killed in a coaching accident en route to Saint-Omer – the court was represented by a naval ordnance officer. D'Urville's family in Calvados and Adélie's family in Var, Haute-Savoie and over the border in Switzerland were all too far away to attend and were represented by Hombron and Vincendon-Dumoulin. In Adélie's case, however, some distant cousins and perhaps her friend Antoinette Dombrowski accompanied her hearse. The pall-bearers included the botanist Adrien de Jussieu from the Académie des sciences, the hydrographer Charles-François Beautemps-Beaupré and the historian Abel-François Villemain. The latter was presumably present in his capacity as minister for public instruction, responsible for Jules' education, rather than as a particular friend of the d'Urville family. Unfortunately, those who were truly closest to d'Urville – Hector Jacquinot and Isidore Le Brun – had both left Paris just before the railway accident and were not present. The eulogy was delivered by Domeny de Rienzi.[76]

D'Urville and his family were buried at Montparnasse Cemetery in a perpetual concession granted by the city of Paris. This was despite d'Urville's stated wish (and almost certainly Adélie's) to be buried with their children in Toulon. The tomb, designed by the architect Simon Constant-Dufeux, was erected with private and government funds in 1845. It is a rounded, tapered, stupa-like column of limestone, without a capital. The sides are inscribed with bas-relief images from the most important events of d'Urville's life, with the explorer portrayed wearing a toga![77]

A chapel was also constructed near the site of the catastrophe in memory of all the victims; it has since been demolished and replaced with a commemorative plaque beside the railway line. In his birthplace, Condé-sur-Noireau, d'Urville was soon honoured with a statue. A posthumous portrait by the painter Jérôme Cartelier was also commissioned by the French government for the Palais de Versailles in 1846. Although d'Urville was alive during the early years of French photography and had a keen interest in new technology, no daguerreotype image of him is known to exist. Had he visited Calvados, in June 1842, as he had planned, his good friend the botanist

Louis-Alphonse de Brébisson (who pioneered photography in Normandy from 1839) might very easily have taken his portrait for posterity, but it was not to be.

In the wake of d'Urville's death, elegies and biographical memoirs were soon published by a number of individuals who knew the explorer personally. They all shed light on various aspects of his life, but one of the most cogent summations came from Vincendon-Dumoulin, the hydrographer who had lived and worked closely with d'Urville aboard the *Astrolabe* and at the Dépôt des cartes et plans in Paris. He described him as

> … sensitive and honest to excess, energetic, persevering, bold, enterprising, courageous at every test, just with his inferiors, but severe and rigid in the execution of his duties; [a] skilful sailor, embracing almost all areas of knowledge at a glance, perhaps not deeply, but certainly wonderfully clever! Seemingly cold at first, but gentle and affectionate in intimacy; republican but of little danger … because of his democratic ideas. That was Dumont d'Urville! After having united on his head the crowns of the naturalist [and] that of the geographer, he still aspired to other glories; he wanted to see his name mentioned among philologists and philosophers! He wanted the same names relived happily in his son, and no doubt dreamt of an even brighter future than his own for the child when death came to destroy everything![78]

To a modern biographer, the qualities Vincendon-Dumoulin enunciated – d'Urville's force of intellect, skilful resolute leadership, courage, gentleness and generosity – are as compellingly evident as his tendency to self-pity, melancholy depression and arrogance. They are an intrinsic part of what drove him to greatness.

Epilogue

Seeking the bubble reputation
Even in the cannon's mouth.
William Shakespeare [Jaques]*

Had he lived longer, d'Urville would certainly have retired to Toulon, but he was too restless an individual to have simply tended the garden of his beloved La Juliade. One can only guess at the linguistic, ethnographic, ecological and other scientific subjects that he might have explored in writing – ensconced, like Montaigne, in his library. It is hard to imagine that he would have been deaf to the grand conversation of progressive democratic politics in France, particularly during the Revolution of 1848. He would surely have been as capable of fulfilling the office of navy minister as François Arago was in the first few months of the Second Republic, and he would certainly have been as eager a reformer. If death had any mercy for d'Urville, it spared him the thwarted democratic promise of Louis-Napoléon Bonaparte's presidency, the coup d'état of December 1851, and the establishment of the autocratic, war-mongering and ultimately disastrous Second Empire.

D'Urville's name is honoured by an island, a mountain, a peninsula and a valley in New Zealand; a channel in Fiji; a pass in Vanikoro; streets, avenues, squares, places or quais in at least 24 French cities and towns, one in Tahiti, one in Australia, five in New Zealand and formerly two in North Africa (Algiers and Casablanca); an island, a sea and a base in Antarctica; schools in Toulon, Caen and Condé-sur-Noireau; a genus of kelp; a genus of sea slug; and the specific epithets of at least seven plants and three animals (a crab, a mollusc and a beetle).[1] Even the great Australian Antarctic explorer Sir Douglas Mawson christened his favourite Greenland dog in honour of his famous French predecessor![2]

Charles-Hector Jacquinot supervised the editing of the expedition's historical volumes after the death of his close friend and colleague. He was promoted to *contre-amiral* in February 1852 and distinguished himself in command of a naval squadron in the Black Sea during the Crimean War. He commanded the Levant station in 1855 and

---

* *As You Like It* (*ca.* 1599), act ii, scene vii, lines 152–53

Dumont d'Urville's grave in Montparnasse Cemetery,
Paris. He was buried with his wife and son, who died
with him in the same railway catastrophe. Designed
by the architect Simon Constant-Dufeux, it was
erected with private and government funds in 1845.
Author's collection

was promoted to *vice-amiral* the following year. In June 1857, he was appointed maritime prefect of Toulon. Jacquinot retired from the navy in 1861 and died in Toulon in 1879.[3]

Jacquinot's half-brother Honoré did not go to sea again because of the editorial responsibilities for the expedition's zoological and botanical volumes in Paris. He would otherwise have been sent to Pondicherry to administer the naval hospital there. Because he forgot to decline this posting formally, his colleagues in India were left wondering why he never arrived. Ill-health subsequently obliged him to decline a similar post in Senegal. Under new academic rules, he was granted the degree of Doctor of Medicine in 1847 by virtue of 15 years' practice rather than the submission of a thesis. In 1852, aged 37, he retired from the navy because of 'incurable infirmity'. Nevertheless, he lived another 25 years and died in 1887.[4]

Jacques-Bernard Hombron co-edited the expedition's botanical and zoological volumes with Honoré Jacquinot, heavily intruding his racial theories into the latter volumes. Aside from articles on zoological and ethnographic subjects, in 1843, he published an article on the Methodists in the Pacific. His personal dossier is missing from the naval archives at the Château de Vincennes, but since he is known to have died in 1852,[5] he probably never again served at sea as a surgeon.

Louis Le Breton worked on the publication of the expedition's results in Paris until April 1844. He then served aboard the corvette *Berceau*, stationed at Bourbon and Madagascar, before returning to France aboard the *Oise* in January 1846. Suffering from an inflammation of the urethra and the prostate, he resigned from the navy on 1 January 1848, two weeks before his thirtieth birthday, and gave up medicine.[6] Le Breton then settled in Paris, working at the Bibliothèque nationale and as an academic artist. He died in the capital in 1866, the victim of a cholera epidemic.

Clément-Adrien Vincendon-Dumoulin was also intimately involved in the task of editing the historical account of the expedition after d'Urville's death, assisted by the Jacquinot brothers and Hombron. He and his colleagues were all sued for including d'Urville's unfavourable comments about Élie Le Guillou, however the disgruntled surgeon lost his case. The Civil Tribunal found that there was an absence of malice: as editors they were simply reporting their late commander's opinion and, in any case, the account was published with the approbation of the navy minister. In 1847, Vincendon-Dumoulin went on a study mission to the Netherlands, gathering information on the islands of the Pacific. In 1852–3, he undertook hydrographic work on the Spanish coast aboard the corvette *Newton* and, in July 1854, on the coast of Morocco and the Strait of Gibraltar. He became ill during this latter mission and was only 48 years old when he died in Chevrières, in his native Isère, in May 1858.[7]

Gaston de Roquemaurel reached the rank of *capitaine de vaisseau* in July 1848. He retired from the navy in August 1862 and died in 1878.[8] Cape Roquemaurel, on the Trinity Peninsula in Antarctica, is named in his honour. Jacques-Louis Ducorps retired from the navy in February 1868 with the rank of assistant *commissaire* 1st class. By this time, he was married with five children; he died in 1892.[9] Charles-François-Eugène Gervaize was decorated *chevalier de la Légion d'honneur* in 1846.[10] In the same year, he was promoted to *lieutenant de vaisseau* and served in the Mediterranean for the rest of his career. In 1857, the King of Sardinia decorated him with the Order of Saints Maurice and Lazarus for rescuing the crew of the brig *Solon*, destroyed by fire in Marseille harbour. He retired in 1859, became a port officer in the merchant navy and died in 1895.[11]

César Desgraz was decorated *chevalier de la Légion d'honneur* in 1846.[12] He would play an important part in the publishing of the expedition's results, particularly after its leader's death. Jacquinot personally requested his secondment because he 'read perfectly the handwriting of Monsieur Dumont d'Urville which is so illegible'.[13] In 1855, he married in Wimbledon, England, according to Anglican rites. The novelist Charles Kingsley, author of *The Water Babies*, and Francis Carnac Brown, advocate of reform in India, were his two witnesses. It seems he also knew Thomas Hughes, the author of *Tom Brown's School Days*, and was related by marriage to another Christian socialist, John Ludlow (who co-owned a house with Thomas Hughes). Although Desgraz was a civilian prior to the expedition, he remained in the navy for more than two decades after it, retiring because of ill-health in 1862. He died in 1865.[14] Surprisingly, one of his sons, Sir Charles Des Graz, was the British envoy extraordinary and minister plenipotentiary to Serbia throughout World War I. Because of his British heirs, some of Desgraz's papers from the expedition are preserved in England. His personal journal from his time aboard the *Astrolabe* is held by the Royal Geographical Society, London, and 21 of his letters are held by Cambridge University Library.[15]

Joseph-Fidèle-Eugène Dubouzet, whom d'Urville described as an 'officer of perfect merit', returned to New Zealand in 1841 in command of the *Allier*. D'Urville had a letter written by him from Akaroa, on 18 November 1841, in his home at the time of his death. In 1844, Dubouzet married Catherine Chichagov, daughter of Russian Admiral Pavel Vasilevich Chichagov (aka Tschitchagoff). He was appointed governor of French establishments in Oceania in 1854 (which was probably less emotionally problematic than fighting his wife's countrymen in the Crimea), inherited the title of marquis in 1862 and rose to the rank of *contre-amiral*. Dubouzet died in 1867.[16]

Louis-François-Marie Tardy de Montravel also served as a French colonial administrator in the Pacific (founding Nouméa in New Caledonia) and reached the rank of *contre-amiral*. By that time, he was much bemedalled, receiving decorations from the French, Portuguese, Netherlands and Mexican governments. He died in 1864.[17] Aimé-Auguste-Élie Coupvent-Desbois rose to the rank of *vice-amiral* and was decorated *grand officer de la Légion d'honneur*.[18] Germain-Hector Perigot, who left the expedition in Valparaiso (because of ophthalmia that began in Antarctic waters), would be one of the longest-surviving veterans of d'Urville's expedition. He eventually rose to the rank of *vice-amiral* and, for four years, commanded the French naval division in the Pacific. He died in 1900.[19]

Vicomte Paul-Louis-François-René de Flotte (who joined the *Zélée* in Tahiti) was promoted to the rank of *lieutenant de vaisseau* in 1846. Two years later, he took part in the revolution against Louis-Philippe. Imprisoned on Belle-Île for insurrection, he escaped, was recaptured and was imprisoned again in Lorient. Ironically, he was shipped there on the *Darrien* and was surprised to find that Élie Le Guillou was her surgeon. Flotte narrowly avoided transportation to a penal colony by resigning from the navy.[20] In 1850, he was elected a left-wing republican deputy for the department of the Seine, and the following year, he published a passionate 466-page social-democratic manifesto, *La Souveraineté du peuple, essais sur l'esprit de la Révolution*. In the wake of Louis-Napoléon Bonaparte's coup d'état, he was forced to flee to Belgium. Returning to France under an assumed name, he worked as an engineer on the Paris-Strasbourg railway. In 1860, he joined Garibaldi's legion with the rank of colonel and was killed in the attack on Reggio – his death chronicled by Friedrich Engels in the *New York Daily Tribune*.[21]

Charles-Jules-Adolphe Thanaron would languish as a *lieutenant de vaisseau* for 13 years and even then was only promoted to the intermediate rank of *capitaine de frégate* in 1850. He still held this rank when he retired from the navy in 1855, despite his recognisable intelligence and learning. The reasons for his stalled career are uncertain, but perhaps they lie in his ferocious, even caustic, sense of humour and his slovenly tendencies. Whatever his failings, he was decorated *chevalier de la Légion d'honneur* in 1841. Thanaron Point, on the Trinity Peninsula in Antarctica, is named in his honour. He died in 1886.[22]

Victor-Charles Lottin, d'Urville's steadfast companion on the *Coquille*, on the first *Astrolabe* voyage and on two special missions (taking Louis-Philippe, duc d'Orléans to Palermo in 1814 and the exile of Charles X in 1830) was promoted to *capitaine de frégate* on 3 May 1848. He was elected a corresponding member of the Académie des sciences in 1852. Lottin retired on 25 May 1855 and died in Versailles on 8 February 1858. [23]

The sturdy corvette *Astrolabe* continued to serve as a naval transport for another decade. In May 1852, after being stationed in the Río de la Plata, between Argentina and Uruguay, she was condemned and then broken up in Toulon.[24] In 1877, the impasse Béranger in Paris (15th arrondissement) was renamed 'impasse de l'Astrolabe' in her honour and in honour of Lapérouse's unfortunate vessel of the same name.[25] The *Zélée* survived longer, serving as a transport during the Crimean War and for a decade after. In 1863, however, she was stripped of her masts and converted into a pontoon in the port of Lorient. Between 1876 and 1885, she was used as a floating powder magazine before being broken up in Lorient in 1887.[26]

APPENDIX

D'Urville's library

The deaths of d'Urville, his wife and his son on the same day occasioned the drafting of inventories of the contents of both the d'Urville family home, 'La Juliade', in the parish of Saint-Roch outside Toulon, and their Paris apartment at 26, rue Madame. Both these inventories were located in the course of research for this biography. Surprisingly, no previous biographer had cited them. The inventory for the Paris apartment, compiled by François-Alexandre Demanche, Étude C, is held in the Archives nationales and was readily accessible.[1] The Toulon inventory,[2] although a public document, was in the hands of private notaries[3] who were successors to the notarial practice of Maître Elzéar Vallavielle.[4] The latter, who had known the d'Urvilles personally while they were alive, drafted the list of contents on 30 July 1842.[5]

Both inventories list books in the possession of d'Urville and his family. Valuations for these books in the Toulon inventory are by numbered lots with the same general binding. Only occasionally are formats given and even less frequently the colours of bindings. Furthermore, the historian is frequently left guessing which volumes of incomplete sets were present. It would seem that the titles of the lots in Toulon were read out loud by one person and recorded by another. This is evident from the fact that the dates for years of voyages of exploration, etc., were in words rather than Hindu-Arabic numerals.

Both inventories offer a precious snapshot of the explorer's life at the time of his death and provide valuable insights into his and his family's interests. Because many books were not individually itemised – only grouped together as a general lot and valued – it is not possible to state the actual size of the library. Nor is it possible to distinguish the personal collection of Madame Dumont d'Urville from that of her husband. However, the various textbooks and juvenile literature almost certainly belonged to their son Jules. Despite being in abbreviated form, over 200 of the most significant and valuable titles (many multi-volume works) were listed in the inventories.

Some months after the inventories were compiled, towards the end of 1842, another list of d'Urville's books appeared. This was an auction catalogue: *Notice des livres français, anglais, arabes, persans, sanscrits, chinois, etc., etc., composant la bibliothèque de feu M. Le contre-amiral Dumont-d'Urville, dont la vente aura lieu les jeudi 5, vendredi 6 et samedi*

7 janvier 1843 à six heures du soir, rue des Bons-Enfants, no. 30, salle du premier, par le ministère de M[aîtr]e Guérin, commissaire-priseur, rue Chabanais, No. 7, H. Labitte, Paris, 1842. Copies of this rare catalogue are held by the Bibliothèque nationale de France in Paris and the Newberry Library in Chicago. It is a list of 287 books divided into five sections: i. *Théologie*; ii. *Jurisprudence, Sciences et Arts*; iii. *Belles-Lettres*; iv. *Histoire*; v. *Livres Chinois*. This, however, was not the order of the auction. Theological works, for example, were sold only on the second day, while historical works and Chinese books were sold each day, and *belles lettres* were sold only on the first two days of the auction.

A great many titles in the auction catalogue do not appear in the original notarial inventories; conversely, a great many of the titles in the notarial inventories do not appear in Maître Guérin's auction catalogue. Aside from the fact that the notaries did not list everything, many books must have been taken by d'Urville's heirs or were otherwise disposed of. The printed catalogue is the ultimate reference for many of the mysteriously abbreviated titles and unspecified editions listed in the inventories, but only if they were selected for auction.

The object of this appendix (first published in an expanded form as an article in *Explorations*, No. 50, 2011) is to offer an analysis of the manuscript inventories, with reference to the printed catalogue and to d'Urville's correspondence and journals. It also draws attention to important omissions and inconsistencies. With the aid of the catalogues of the Bibliothèque nationale de France and a number of other major national libraries, together with the *Bibliographie de la France* and several other specialised reference works, it has been possible to decipher and identify most of the books listed.

The d'Urville library contained many of the classics of French literature, with works by Chateaubriand, Casimir Delavigne, La Harpe, Malherbe, Montaigne, Montesquieu, Racine, Regnard, Rousseau and Madame de Sévigné, together with the work of lesser writers, such as Louis-François Jauffret and Amable Tastu. With the exception of works by Montesquieu, Chateaubriand and Jauffret, these authors were not represented in Guérin's auction catalogue.

D'Urville had a strong interest in languages and comparative linguistics. In 1834, he published a two-volume philological work as part of the official account of the *Astrolabe* voyage. In a letter to Isidore Le Brun, dated 6 January 1837, he wrote: 'I have returned to my philological studies and I am working on a comparative paraglottic vocabulary.'[6] The manuscript inventories list many dictionaries and grammars dealing with Ancient Egyptian (including ground-breaking works by Jean-François Champollion), Arabic, Chinese, Coptic, Dutch, French, Greek, Japanese, Latin, Malay, Persian, Sanskrit and Turkish. Guérin's auction catalogue lists further dictionaries, vocabularies and grammars of Anamese, Armenian, Bengali, Chaldean (one published in 1569, the oldest book in d'Urville's library), Eastern Polynesian, English, Ethiopian,

Georgian, Hebrew, Hindustani, Italian, Tahitian, Tartar, Tibetan, Manchu and several West African languages. D'Urville also had a very rich collection of Egyptology, and he owned six volumes of the works of Sir William Jones, one of the first scholars to propose a relationship between the languages of India and Europe, together with the companion volume to Jones' Persian grammar, *The Flowers of Persian literature* (1805).

Among the several Chinese dictionaries in d'Urville's possession was a solitary volume of Chrétien-Louis-Joseph de Guignes' three-volume *Dictionnaire chinois, français et latin*, published on Napoleon's orders in 1813. This work was based on the scholarship of the seventeenth-century Italian missionary Father Basile de Glemona, who translated some 9000 characters into Latin, which were, in turn, translated into French by de Guignes.[7] D'Urville also owned over 60 volumes in Chinese and numerous books in English and Latin, together with the Qur'an in Arabic (with a Latin introduction), the Bible in Hebrew and the *De idolatria* of Maimonides in Latin translation. The latter, with a full Hebrew text, was almost certainly a seventeenth-century Amsterdam edition, but this cannot be confirmed because it did not appear in Guérin's auction catalogue.

D'Urville was also a very capable botanist, and his library contained numerous regional French floras (by Giovanni-Battista Balbi, Jean-Baptiste de Lamarck, Jean Loiseleur Deslongchamps, Louis-François-Henri Lefébure and others) and important botanical works by Benjamin Delessert, Sabin Berthelot, Augustin de Candolle, Carlo Allioni, Alire Raffeneau-Delile, Achille Richard, almost certainly Joseph Pitton de Tournefort, and very likely John Sibthorpe's and James Edward Smith's *Prodromus* to the *Flora Græca*. Despite this, only 11 botanical works are listed in the auction catalogue. Although d'Urville began his botanical career as a Linnaean (he even joined the Société Linnéenne de Paris), the notarial inventories make no mention of the works of the Swede Carl Linnaeus, founder of modern binomial classification. However, the auction catalogue (no. 21) does list a 1774 Göttingen edition of the *Systema vegetabilium*. It is also surprising that the notarial inventories do not list any volumes of Phillip Barker Webb's and Sabin Berthelot's *L'Histoire naturelle des Îles Canaries*, since Webb also lived in the rue Madame (no. 45) at the time of d'Urville's death, and he and Berthelot were good friends of the explorer.[8] The anomaly, however, is addressed in Guérin's catalogue: see no. 25 and no. 28. In spite of d'Urville's numerous visits to Australia, he owned neither Jacques-Julien Houtou de Labillardière's pioneering *Novæ Hollandiæ plantarum specimen* (1804–06) nor Robert Brown's *Prodromus floræ Novæ Hollandiæ et Insulæ Van Diemen* (1810) – the latter arranged according to the 'natural' rather than the Linnaean 'sexual' system.[9] However, d'Urville did own Labillardière's *Relation du voyage à la recherche de La Pérouse*, which contains important descriptions of several new Australian plant genera. He also owned Charles Gaudichaud-Beaupré's botanical volume from Louis de Freycinet's expedition of 1817–20 and the botanical volumes he himself helped produce during the *Coquille* expedition of 1822–25 and the *Astrolabe* expedition of 1826–29. All had significant Australian botanical content.

D'Urville's scientific and technical interests extended to astronomy, chemistry, entomology, *materia medica*, geology, geography, glass-blowing, hydrography, forestry, naval architecture, trigonometry and even 'tachygraphie' (shorthand). Furthermore, he had an interest in the nascent science of psychology, owning Jean-Louis-Marie Alibert's two-volume *Physiologie des passions* (1825).[10] Furthermore, d'Urville had an interest in the Scottish analytical philosophers of the mind, owning an 1836 edition of Thomas Brown's *Lectures on the Philosophy of the Human Mind*. Surprisingly, while Brown's work found its way into Guérin's auction catalogue, few of the other scientific works on the above-mentioned subjects were included.

The notarial inventories also confirm d'Urville's interest in phrenology. It was not an uncommon interest; he shared it with many of the luminaries of his age. D'Urville's phrenological works, however, were not numerous and none would be listed in Guérin's catalogue. He had either Joseph Vimont's *Traité de phrénologie* (1832) or a French translation of the work of the Scottish phrenologist George Combe, published under the same title, together with Théodore Poupin's *Caractères phrénologiques* (1837). In focusing on phrenology as a pseudo-science, we tend to forget that some of its practitioners made pioneering discoveries in the behavioural sciences, and that others were progressive reformers of penal and medical institutions. One such reformer (and phrenologist) was Alexander McConochie, whose book *Thoughts on Convict Management and Other Subjects Connected with the Australian Penal Colonies* (1838) was one of two Australian-published works in d'Urville's library. It is also important to note that d'Urville owned a critical rejection of phrenology: Laurent Cerise's *Exposé et examen critique du système phrénologique*. Significantly, when one compares the Toulon and the Paris inventories, it is clear that d'Urville left all his phrenological works in Toulon and took none with him to the capital.

Although doubt has been cast on the extent to which d'Urville was a 'political animal',[11] he clearly supported the Revolution of 1830 and accepted responsibility for taking Charles X into exile. In his library (although it did not find its way into Guérin's auction catalogue) was a copy of Louis Rozet's *Chronique de juillet 1830*, which contains a lengthy account of d'Urville's role in these momentous events. While John Dunmore hinted that d'Urville had Bonapartist sympathies or at least ambitions to bring the late emperor's remains back from the island of Saint Helena, d'Urville himself referred to his spirit as 'naturally republican'. He also admitted that, at the beginning of the Revolution of 1830, his 'possibly immoderate ardour inspired him with very advanced opinions'.[12] The Paris inventory would appear to confirm this: d'Urville owned eight *livraisons* (instalments) of three volumes (1839–40) of the overtly socialist work of the writers Pierre Leroux and Jean Reynaud: *Encyclopédie nouvelle ou dictionnaire philosophique, scientifique, littéraire et industriel.* However, this work did not make the pages of Guérin's catalogue. D'Urville also owned a number of other encyclopaedias, including apparently thematic volumes reprinted from the famous *Encyclopédie méthodique* and instalments of François Malapeyre's *Mémorial encyclopédique et progressif des connaissances humaine,* which covered the sciences, literature, fine arts, industrial technology, history, geography and voyages of exploration.

D'Urville's library offers particularly valuable insights into his theoretical readings on the differences between the peoples of the world. Significantly, neither the notarial inventories nor the auction catalogue lists the third, or indeed any, edition of Johan Friedrich Blumenbach's *De generis humani varietate nativa* (1795), or Frédéric Chardel's French translation of 1804 (*De l'unité du genre humain et de ses variétés*), which divided humanity into five races on the basis of craniological measurements and skin colour: Caucasian, Mongolian, American, Ethiopian (Negroid) and Malay. Despite d'Urville's dalliance with phrenology and his voyaging with those (such as the surgeons Prosper Garnot, Jean-René-Constant Quoy, Paul Gaimard and later Pierre Dumoutier and Jacques-Bernard Hombron) who placed great emphasis on facial angles and craniological measurement in racial differentiation, his primary interest in the study of human difference remained linguistic. Of the relevant works in the notarial inventories, we know that he owned a four-volume French translation of the British philologist John Leydon's *Discoveries and Settlements of Europeans in Northern and Western Africa,* published by Arthus Bertrand in 1821. He appears to have owned a volume of Antoine Court de Gébelin's *Le Monde primitif* (1773–82), which, aside from an enormous amount of esoteric scholarship on the interpretation of symbols, contained a comparative grammar and proposed a theory of the universal origins of languages. Significantly, d'Urville owned abbé Jérôme Richard-Sabin's *Voyages chez les peuples sauvages* (1800–01), which sought to define the cultural commonalities of primitive societies. Edited by François Babié de Bercenay, Sabin's three-volume work did not seek to biologise human difference, nor did it seek to idealise 'savage' society as Rousseau had. It considered religion, violence, morality, social structure, customs and the knowledge of primitive peoples from historical literature, be it in the early European past or as revealed by the recent explorations of the Pacific. It is also possible that the 'Histoire de la Louisiane' d'Urville owned was one of Antoine-Simon Le Page Du Pratz's sympathetic volumes on the manners, customs and religion of the Amerindians published in 1758. But perhaps most importantly, he possessed a copy of Adriano Balbi's *Introduction à l'Atlas ethnographique du globe* (1833). This significant work classified the peoples of the globe primarily according to their languages, rather than the supposed anatomical differences of 'races' isolated by physical anthropologists. Balbi resided in Paris between

1821 and 1832, and it is very possible that d'Urville knew him personally. It was Balbi who proposed the term '*ethnographie*' for his rigorous, essentially linguistic, discipline. Once again, none of these works was included in Guérin's auction catalogue. However, Balbi's *Abrégé de géographie* (1834) is listed (no. 113) and so is Court de Gébelin's *Dictionnaire étymologique de la langue française*, Paris, 1778 (no. 83). Guérin also lists (no. 195) one of the last books d'Urville purchased: Gustave Séligmann d'Eichthal's *Histoire et origine des Foulahs ou Fellans: Études sur l'histoire primitive des races océaniennes et américaines* (1841). D'Eichthal was another socialist author represented in d'Urville's library.

Not surprisingly, d'Urville owned many accounts of travel and exploration by authors such as Beechey, Bougainville (father and son), Dampier, Desfontaines, Dillon, Demidoff, Douville, Duhaut-Cilly, Dupaty, Duperrey, Du Petit-Thouars, Freycinet, Gaimard, Krusenstern, Labillardière, almost certainly Lapérouse (edited by Milet-Mureau), Laplace, Lesson, Péron, Phipps, Raffet, Thunberg and Vaillant. He also owned Dominique Vivant Denon's *Voyage dans la basse et la haute Egypte* and Charles Sigisbert Sonnini's work with the same title. Furthermore, he had copies of the *Journal of the Royal Geographical Society* and the *Bulletin de la Société de géographie*, and owned voyage compilations by Henri Lemaire, Alcide d'Orbigny, Alexis Rochon and Albert Montémont, together with accounts of whaling and missionary voyages. Guérin's auction catalogue provides evidence of even greater bibliographic riches in the area of travel literature: d'Urville owned (no. 140) George Staunton's *An Account of an Embassy from the King of Great Britain to the Emperor of China; taken chiefly from the papers of the Earl Macartney* (1797); (no. 142) William Price's *Journal of the British Embassy to Persia* (1832); (no. 141) Francis Hamilton's *An Account of the Fishes found in the River Ganges* (1832); (no. 146) Frederic Louis Norden's *Voyage d'Egypte et de Nubie* (1795); (no. 148) Riffaud's *Tableau de l'Egypte, de la Nubie et des lieux circonvoisins* (1830); (no. 147) a French translation of Henry Salt's *Voyage to Abyssinia* (1812); (no. 132) Edmund Fanning's *Voyages Round the World* (1833); (no. 157) Charles Stewart's *A Visit to the South Seas* (1832); (no. 154) William Ellis's *Narrative of a Tour through Owhyhee* (1828); and (no. 158) Benjamin Morrell's *A Narrative of Four Voyages to the South Sea* (1832).

Aside from Alexander McConochie's *Thoughts on Convict Management*, d'Urville owned a number of books relating specifically to Australia. These included Phillip Parker King's *Narrative of a Survey of The Intertropical and Western Coasts of Australia* (1826), William Henry Breton's *Excursions in New South Wales* (1833) and very likely John Oxley's account of his survey expedition to *Port Curtis, Moreton Bay, and Port Bowen* (1825). In his Paris apartment, d'Urville also had a book by the Australian-by-adoption, John Dunmore Lang: *View of the Origin and Migrations of the Polynesian Nation* (1834). Once again, these aforementioned works are curiously absent from Guérin's catalogue, but other new titles augment the list, including (no. 151) James Dixon's *Narrative of a*

Voyage to New South Wales and Van Diemen's Land (1822); (no. 155) Henry Widowson's *Present State of Van Diemen's Land* (1829); and (no. 160) Phillip Parker King's *A Voyage to Torres Strait, in Search of the Survivors of the Ship* Charles Eaton (1837).

D'Urville came from a deeply religious family and professed his orthodox Catholicism well into his thirties; however, by 1842, the inventories would suggest that he owned few Christian religious works beside the New Testament (in his Latin Bible) and a volume of the selected works of Bishop Jean-Baptiste Massillon, who was born in Hyères, close to Toulon. There is no sign of the Jesuit Isaac-Joseph Berruyer's *Histoire du peuple de Dieu*, a multi-volume work published between 1728 and 1757, which, according to Isidore Le Brun, d'Urville read and re-read from the age of seven. Le Brun, the explorer's life-long friend and a fellow Norman, also witnessed the drafting of the Paris inventory. Furthermore, his own strongly anti-clerical, two-volume work *La bonne ville, ou le maire et le jésuite* (1826) was one of the books listed in the inventory of d'Urville's library, but not in the auction catalogue. The latter catalogue, however, offers some notable surprises not listed in the inventories, including the Christian gospels in Aramaic, Arabic, Chinese, Japanese, Malay, Mongolian, Sinhala and Turkish, together with the Psalms and the Song of Songs in Ethiopian, and Bossuet's *Oraisons funèbres*.

As previously mentioned, d'Urville owned a number of Jewish religious texts together with the Qur'an, but it is possible that his interest in these works was more linguistic than theological. We know from Le Brun's biographical account that, as a young man, d'Urville engaged the services of a rabbi to learn Hebrew. Linguistic interests aside, he was clearly interested in other religions and philosophical traditions. According to Guérin's catalogue (no. 164), he owned an early Amsterdam edition of Lagrue's French translation of Alexander Ross's *Pansebeia, or View of all the Religions in the World* (1652). He also owned a 1760 edition of Thomas Hyde's classic work on the religion of Ancient Persia: *Historia religionis veterum Persarum* (no. 186). Although the notaries did not have the language skills to transcribe the many Chinese titles in d'Urville's library, the commissaire-priseur Guérin obviously did find someone (perhaps a missionary) who had the skills to work on the catalogue. Mentioned among d'Urville's papers and in the auction catalogue, but not in the notarial inventories, is a printed copy of Zǐsī's 子思 (also known as Kǒng Jí 孔伋) *Zhōng yōng* or 'Doctrine of the Mean' 中庸 (published by Levasseur in Paris), one of the principal works in the Confucian canon. D'Urville also had the first published translation of the Confucian 'Book of Documents' (書經 *Shū-jīng*): Joseph de Guignes' *Le Chou-King* (1770), based on a manuscript translation by the French Jesuit Father Antoine Gaubil sent from Beijing but with reference to another manuscript of the original in the Royal Library in Paris. D'Urville had a number of other Confucian works, including Lacharme's and Mohl's Latin edition of Confucius published in Stuttgart in 1830 and Aignan-Stanislas Julien's partial Latin translation of Mèng Zǐ's (孟子) *The Four Books* (Sì Shū四書), published in Paris in 1824. Furthermore, he owned the *Mnavadharmastra* in Sanskrit (with notes by Loiseleur Deslongchamps), Abel Rémusat's *Nouveaux mélanges asiatiques* and several other books dealing with Chinese society and culture, such as the final volume of Joseph-Marie Amiot's (et al.) 16-volume *Mémoires concernant l'histoire, les sciences, les arts, les mœurs, les usages, &c. des Chinois* (1776–1814).

The book inventories include the titles of works of ancient history by authors such as Plutarch and Herodotus, together with many other classical studies. D'Urville, for example, owned Ennio Visconti's magnificent *Iconographie ancienne* (1808–26), the first part of which (three volumes), was given to him by Louis XVIII as a reward for his part in the acquisition of the Vénus de Milo.[13] This work, perhaps because of its distinguished provenance, was notably absent from the auction catalogue and was probably kept by members of the explorer's family. D'Urville owned Nicolas Furgault's *Dictionnaire des antiquités grecques et romaines* (1824), and numerous gazetteers and collections of classical texts. Guérin's auction catalogue (no. 167) indicates that d'Urville owned an edition of Pausanias in Greek and Latin, published in Hanover in 1613. Shortly before his death, d'Urville purchased (no. 86) a four-volume set of Sophocles and Aristophanes (1841). Furthermore, the Guérin catalogue reveals a rich collection of books on Egyptian, Persian, Chinese, Indian and Arab history and literature. Finally, all the sources indicate that d'Urville's library was well-endowed with multi-volume biographical reference works and works of French history.

Of the groups of unlisted titles in the inventories, the Guérin catalogue provides considerable information – particularly with regard to multi-volume Chinese books (nos 241–287). D'Urville's published works and his private papers provide further information on his voracious reading habits. In his private journal, for example, he mentions numerous books in the days immediately before the outbreak of the Revolution of 1830. On 23 July he notes '*The New Zealanders*, London, 1830, in-12–424 pages', undoubtedly the ethnohistorical work of the Scottish author George Lillie Craik, published by Charles Knight that year. The next day he mentions 'Spindler translated by Cohen entitled *L'élixir du diable*'. In fact, this was Jean Cohen's translation of a work by Ernst Theodor Amadeus Hoffman (rather than Karl Spindler), published by Mame et Delaunay-Vallée, Paris, 1829, 4 vols, in duodecimo format. On 26 July, d'Urville wrote: 'I read the novel by [Alexander] Bronikowski, translated by Loève-Veimars, entitled *Claire-Hébert* [1828]'. In the months after the revolution, there are similar references to the pulp fiction of the period. On 22 September 1830, for example, d'Urville records reading a 'bad novel entitled *Marie Stuart* by Horace Raisson, 1828'. On 2 October 1830, he records yet another 'bad novel', this time '*Ludsac, ou le Monastère de Saint-Basile* by Mme de Flesselles, 1824', but he has kinder words for '*Les chaperons blancs* par Cohen'. The latter was, in fact, a liberal translation by Jean Cohen of Anna Elza Bray's *The White Hoods* (1828). On 5 October, d'Urville notes 'a novel of Victor Ducange, *Isaurine et Jean Pohl*, *[ou les Révolutions du château de Gîl-au-Diable]*, en quatre volumes, 1830'.[14] While research among d'Urville's journals will no doubt yield many more titles of the same genre, we cannot be certain whether they were borrowed, bought, gifted or sold. They are listed neither in the inventory at the time of the explorer's death nor in Guérin's printed auction catalogue. Nevertheless, they tell us something of d'Urville's taste in historical fiction and gothic romance, and they give us some hint of the literary influences on his own novel, *Les Zélandais: Histoire australienne* (1825), translated and published by Carol Legge in 1992.

Unlike many of the explorer's manuscripts (the fate of which I have reviewed in my introduction), the fate of d'Urville's books is unclear. We do not know who the buyers were in January 1843. We know that the d'Urville estate was divided between the explorer's heirs in Normandy and Madame d'Urville's heirs in Toulon. It is not known whether any of the unauctioned printed books remained in Provence or went to Normandy. Although Dumont d'Urville's personal herbarium is preserved in the Herbier du Laboratoire de botanique, Faculté des sciences, Université de Caen,[15] the online catalogues of the university and of the Bibliothèque de Caen would not suggest that any of d'Urville's inventoried books are today preserved in public collections there. A possible buyer of the botanical works, perhaps even before the auction catalogue was compiled (which might explain the omission of so many botanical titles), was the wealthy Englishman Phillip Barker Webb, who had prior knowledge of d'Urville's collection. Webb's library was in turn bequeathed (with his herbarium of 300,000 specimens) to the Museo di storia naturale of Grand Duke Leopold II of Tuscany. It is significant that duplicates of d'Urville's plant specimens are today held in the herbarium of this same museum in Florence. Webb certainly had some of d'Urville's specimens from New Zealand and Greece, but these might have been given to him by d'Urville before his death. Webb also obtained some of d'Urville's specimens from the Society Islands when he purchased Labillardière's library and herbarium in 1834. Similarly, he acquired some of d'Urville's French, Crimean and Australian specimens when he purchased the complete herbarium of Joseph-François Soleirol.[16] Only a detailed study of the provenance of Webb's books, now in Florence, might determine whether at least part of d'Urville's library ended up in Italy. Be that as it may, the surviving inventories and the published auction catalogue provide enduring evidence of d'Urville's extraordinary range of interests and his ownership of an exceptional private library, containing printed titles dating back to the sixteenth century and important Asian and colonial imprints (including books published in Calcutta, Colombo, Constantinople, Hobart, Nanking, Peking, Serampore, Singapore, Sydney, Macao and New York).[17]

Acknowledgements

This biography was written without any direct funding, other than a six-month residency in Paris in the first half of 2007. This sojourn unquestionably laid the foundations for the book. I daily blessed the name of Dr Mark Hertzberg, who provided funds to pay for the rental of a studio in the Cité internationale des arts, for 70 years after the death of his wife, the writer Nancy Keesing, in 1993. This remarkable gift to Australian writers, the Keesing Studio, is administered by the Literature Board of the Australia Council, the Commonwealth Government's arts funding and advisory body. In conjunction with my residency, the board provided my airfares and a six-month stipend. I will always be deeply grateful for this assistance.

My greatest debt, nevertheless, is to my wife, Susan, for her patience and support during seven years of work. Some writers have peaks and troughs in their income; I had an ice sheet riddled with crevasses. Despite this, Susan was my steadfast companion during three research trips to France and on visits to a number of d'Urville's landfalls. On several occasions, her forensic abilities searching cadastral plans and examining photographs and models of historic streetscapes led to important discoveries. Furthermore, she prepared the 10 maps herein (with assistance from Allan Kynaston, Dunedin, for the two New Zealand maps). I am also grateful to our sons, Samuel and Pierre, particularly for their help while we were overseas: caring for our animals, paying bills and sometimes searching my library and files to answer questions from a distance of 17,000 kilometres.

My mother, Maryse Duyker, assisted me greatly in deciphering d'Urville's extremely difficult handwriting in numerous documents and, in particular, large sections of his *Coquille* journal. She only handed the task back to me when cranial nerve palsy afflicted her with double vision for an anxious six months! I still worry that d'Urville was the cause.

My late mother-in-law, Betty Wade, was usually the first to read my draft chapters and was an important source of encouragement, support and constructive critical comment. I am also deeply grateful to her for the gift of the very laptop computer on which this biography was written and ultimately for the generous bequest that subsidised its publication. It saddens me deeply that she did not live to see it in print. A decade ago, I dedicated my biography of Labillardière to her and to my mother Maryse.

In turn, they heartily approved of my decision to dedicate *Dumont d'Urville* to our mutual friend Ivan Barko, emeritus professor of French at the University of Sydney, for the wisdom and advice he has extended over many years in relation to this book and three of my previous biographies.

I wish to acknowledge the work of the late Helen Rosenman who, in 1987, published a two-volume abridged translation of the historical accounts of d'Urville's voyages. Although her children, Linda and Stephen, graciously gave me permission to quote from her work, the massive breadth of d'Urville's publications obliged me as a biographer to go to all the original volumes and do my own selective translations. Nevertheless, I frequently felt that I was following in Helen's footsteps, and her work was an important source of inspiration and guidance for me. Similarly, despite choosing to do my own translations from d'Urville's manuscript novel *Les Zélandais*, I wish to acknowledge the impressive scholarship of Dr Carol Legge, whose pioneering translation, published by Victoria University Press in 1992, is frequently referenced in my text.

I am particularly grateful to Pascal Allizard, mayor of Condé-sur-Noireau, for facilitating my use of Dumont d'Urville's previously unknown personal journals in the possession of his municipality. In the explorer's birthplace, I also thank Isabelle Vazard, Hélène Moisan, Julie Riberot and Marie-Pierre Lefèvre, of the Médiathèque Condé-sur-Noireau. Amid 55,000 books in boxes and with concrete dust in the air, they assisted me when they were officially closed for renovations and when they would have had every right to turn me away. I also thank three other generous townsfolk: Jean-Jacques Thomas, for access to his rich collection of historic local postcards, which opened up a window on Condé-sur-Noireau prior to the devastation of 1944; Alain Seguin, who (with the mayor's approval), helped me copy documents long after his usual work hours ended at the Hôtel de Ville; and the encyclopaedic archivist Philippe Cyprien, who answered numerous questions about the families and history of old Condé-sur-Noireau.

In d'Urville's adopted home, the wonderful port city of Toulon on the Mediterranean, I thank Madame Georgette Deslettres, who very generously accommodated my wife and me in her home during my research. That she should take two Australians whom she hardly knew under her roof at the advanced age of 88 is all the more extraordinary. I am also grateful to her daughter Josette Debard for her help during our stay, and to Madame Deslettre's neighbours Rear Admiral and Madame Le Dantec for access to their library of works on the history of Toulon. I thank François Deydon, Service du cadastre de Toulon; Henri Bouvet and Françoise Auriault, Société des amis du vieux Toulon et de sa région; Magali Bérenger, Archives municipales; M. Vincent Mollet, Corine Babeix, Service historique de la défense, Toulon; Jacqueline Cardona and the ever-helpful Véronique Gillain, Bibliothèque municipale, Toulon.

In Paris, I thank Hélène Richard, formerly head of the Département des cartes et plans, Bibliothèque nationale, now of the Inspection générale des bibliothèques, Ministère de la culture (and co-editor of Joseph Seureau's journal aboard the *Zélée*), who answered numerous questions, gently nudged others and with her family extended warm hospitality over dinner; Bruno Galland and Edith Pirio, Archives nationales de France; Dr Suzanne Débarbat, Observatoire de Paris, for assistance with d'Urville's critic François Arago and for several welcoming soirées at her apartment in the rue Hallé; Olivier Azzola, Chargé des archives, Bibliothèque de l'École polytechnique, for help with the dossiers of many of d'Urville's officers; Jacques Damade (descendant of the comte de Marcellus), Éditions La Bibliothèque; Florence Greffe, Archives et patrimoine historique, Institut de France, Académie des sciences; Élisabeth Peyré, Anne Cavero, Pascale Heurtel, Nadia Zouaq, Bibliothèque centrale du Muséum national d'histoire naturelle, Paris; Ratiba Mazighi, École doctorale VI, Université de Paris IV-Sorbonne; Sonia Bosc, Jean-Christophe Domenech, Philippe Mennecier and Aurélie Roux, Musée de l'homme; Bernadette Molitor, Bibliothèque interuniversitaire de médecine and Bibliothèque de l'histoire de médecine; Christine Minjollet, Musée de la Légion d'honneur; Marie-Hélène Thiault, Musée d'archéologie nationale, Château de Saint-Germain-en-Laye; Monique Boukhedid, Christine Françonnet, Antoine Monaque and Laurent Pinon, Bibliothèque nationale; Frédérick Lions, Bibliothèque historique de la Ville de Paris; Henri Prévost-Brouillet, Bibliothèque de la Société de l'histoire du Protestantisme français; and Isabel Ollivier, for permission to quote from her article on Pierre-Adolphe Lesson.

In other parts of France, I thank my cousin Dr Françoise Rousseau and her husband, Claude Rousseau, Issy-les-Moulineaux, for their warm hospitality, for taking me to the site of d'Urville's death near Meudon and for Françoise's help with Hebrew words in d'Urville's scholarly correspondence; Dr Maurice Recq, Landerneau, for very many useful editorial comments; my cousin Patrice Lionnet, Marseille, for help researching the family background of Esprit-Justin-Gustave Girard-Dudemaine; Jeannine Le Pontois-Menot, Mézidon-Canon, Calvados, for assistance with the genealogy of the d'Urville family; and Thierry Pendu, La Bruffière (Vendée), for permission to quote from his thesis 'La Pharmacopée de Dumont d'Urville lors de son voyage en Terre Adélie'. I also thank the following individuals and institutions: Romain Zechser, Service patrimoine, Abbeville; Patrick Brunet-Moret, Musée Trochu, Belle-Ile; Louis Le Roch Norgere and Jean-François Holvas, Archives départementales du Calvados, Caen; Nadège Orange, Service accueil de l'Hôtel de Ville, Caen; Bernard Huchet, Erik Calvet, Marie-Noëlle Vivier and Valérie Cauchon, Bibliothèque de Caen; Audrey Joly, Service des archives municipales, Caen, and Serge Lemonnier, maire adjoint, Mairie de Caen; Yves Renault, Secrétaire, Société nationale académique de Cherbourg; Pascale Brus, Archives municipales et documentation, Châteaudun; Florence Poirier,

Service des archives et du patrimoine, Cluses; Kelig-Yann Cotto and Mikael Riou, Douarnenez (Finistère); Elisabeth Masson, Médiathèque du Pays de Flers; Chantal de Gaye, Muséum d'histoire naturelle, La Rochelle; Brigitte Jaunatre, Mairie, Le Chesnay (Yvelines); Olivier Gorse, Archives départementales des Bouches-du-Rhône, Marseille; Patricia Guyard and Evelyne Guillaume, Archives départementales du Jura, Monmorot; Père André Mark, archivist, Congrégation des Sacrés-Cœurs de Jésus et de Marie, Montgeron; Pran Cojs Oudjani, Bibliothèque Université de Nantes; Kathrin Hentschel and Nathalie Martin, Service des archives et du patrimoine, Communauté d'agglomération Pau-Pyrénées, Pau; Yvonne Bouvier-Graux and Olivier Desgranges, Médiathèque de Rochefort; Isabelle Laurin, Chargée de la documentation, Département des collections, Manufacture de Sèvres; Cécile Boulaire, Université François-Rabelais, Tours; and Thi Siu Bernard, Laurent Boulogne, Monique Frêlon, Abudulla Hamada, Martine Hos, Patrice Krieff, Max Pineau and especially Gilles Roussel, Service historique de la défense, Château de Vincennes.

In Athens, I thank Sandra Pepelasis, Assistant Librarian, British School at Athens, and Antonios Katsiadas, Areos Hotel. On the island of Milos, I thank: Virginia Grigoriou, Adamas, who was a very generous guide and interlocutor and who introduced me to the work of a number of important Greek historians; Filio Kypreou and Maria Nikolao, Archaeological Museum of Milos, Plaka; and Antonia Kamakari Venizelou, Plaka, for access to the library of her late father, Professor George Kamakaris. On the island of Spetses, I thank Philip Demertzis-Bouboulis, Bouboulina Museum.

In Belgium, I thank Claire Pascaud, Librarian, Académie royale des sciences, des lettres et des beaux-arts de Belgique, Bruxelles. In Britain, I thank my cousin Pauline McGregor Currien, Cheltenham, for assistance researching aspects of d'Urville's visit to England in 1837 and the wife and in-laws of his secretary, César Desgraz. In Denmark, I thank Jarle Aadna, Mette Colding Dahl, Anne Dyhr and Lis Michelsen, Kongelige Bibliotek, Copenhagen. In Germany, I thank Steffi Wolf, Deutsche Nationalbibliothek, Leipzig; and Gerhard Moisel, Siegen, Westphalia. In Switzerland, I thank Yorio and Allison Tanimura, Crans-près-Céligny; Jacques Barrelet, Anouk Dunaut Gonzenbach, Danielle Proz, Martine Piguet, Archives d'État de Genève, for helping me research Adélie Dumont d'Urville's Swiss relatives; and Gilbert Coutaz and Pierre-Yves Favez, Archives cantonales vaudoises, Chavannes-près-Renens, for assistance researching the family background of César Desgraz. In the Netherlands, I thank: René M. Haubourdin, Nationaal Archief, Den Haag; and my cousin Martin Duijker, Heerhugowaard, for assistance with a number of sources relating to the former Netherlands East Indies. In the Canary Islands, I thank Elsa González Tabares, Biblioteca Municipal Santa Cruz de Tenerife. In Russia, I thank Dr Natalia Dushkina, Moscow Architectural Institute. At the Vatican, I thank Dr Adalbert Roth, Department of Printed Books, Vatican Library.

In the Americas, I thank: Erika Werner, Biblioteca Instituto de Botánica Darwinion, Buenos Aires, Argentina; Alexandra Hickey, Nicole Watier, Library and Archives Canada, Ottawa, Canada; Dr Elizabeth Hawthorne, former Dean, School of Education, University of Guam; Linda B. MacIver, Reference Librarian, Boston Public Library, Boston, Massachusetts; and Gregory Curtis, University of Texas, Austin, for kind permission to quote from his book *Disarmed: The Story of the Venus de Milo*, even though I have a different interpretation of the events.

On my mother's native island of Mauritius, I thank Dr Raymond d'Unienville, Professor Marc Serge Rivière and Philippe la Hausse de Lalouvière. In Kosrae, Federated States of Micronesia, I thank Berlin Sigrah, Historic Preservation Officer, Tofol.

In Australia, I thank Jeremy Spencer, formerly of the National Museum of Australia, Canberra, who loaned me his voluminous personal notes and files relating to d'Urville in New Zealand, introduced me to the pioneering work of S. Percy Smith, alerted me to several important ancillary documents and maps in public collections and aided me with many cogent comments on my typescript. I also thank Jeremy's wife, Diane Spencer, who gave me access to her collection of books on New Zealand ornithology. For scholarly support and assistance with a numerous questions, I thank Professor Gail Crossley, Trish D'Arcy, Dr Elaine Lindsay, Geraldine Marsh and Dr Laurie Woods, Australian Catholic University, Sydney; Donna Worland, Librarian, Department of Employment, Economic Development & Innovation, Brisbane; Lynn Meyers, State Library of Queensland, Brisbane; Leoné Lemmer and Fran Smith, Australian Museum Research Library, Sydney; Amelia Hartney, Australian War Memorial Research Centre, Canberra; Catriona Anderson, Scotia Ashley, Kylie Brooks, Sue Chan, Heather Clark, Damian Cole, Claire Cruickshank, Rachael Eedowes, Michael Herlihy, Bushra Khanum, Denise Kovacs, Alice Leung, Lucy Nuttall, Di Pin Ouyang, Rachel Pryor, Barbara Rozmus, Ralph Sanderson, Andrew Sergeant, Matthew Stuckings, Erin Williams, Dr Brendan Whyte, Renee Wilson and Martin Woods, National Library of Australia, Canberra; Tony Marshall, State Library of Tasmania, Hobart; Sister Carmel Hall, Archives, Catholic Archdiocese of Hobart; Louise Gilfedder, Department of Primary Industries, Water and Environment, Hobart; and Irene Schaffer, Hobart; Maxine Briggs (Koorie Liason Librarian), Sandra Burt, Des Cowley (Rare Printed Collections Manager), David Flegg, Jan McDonald, Mew Leng Mouy, Mark Showalter, Zoe Velonis, State Library of Victoria, Melbourne; Dr Anita Dewi, Monash University Library, Melbourne; Anne Harris, Lady Denman Maritime Museum, Huskisson (Jervis Bay); Rebecca Hawcroft and Jane Vernon, Godden Mackay Logan Pty. Ltd., Heritage Consultants, Sydney; Matthew Richardson, Halstead Press, Sydney; Dr Bronwyn Hanna, Heritage Branch, Office of Environment and Heritage, Parramatta;

Dr Alex Byrne (State Librarian), Helen Beneczec, David Berry, Ronald Briggs, Ben Clark, Joe Coelho, Mark Hildebrand, Wendy Holz, Susan Mercer, Richard Neville (Mitchell Librarian), Julie Sweeten, Maggie White, State Library of New South Wales, Sydney; Lindsay Allen, State Records Office, Sydney; Liz Rouse, Librarian, Royal Australian College of Physicians, Sydney; Max Bancroft, Lyn Barakat, Jacinta Crane, Diane Ollerenshaw, Kristin Ovidi, Wendy Lewis and Janet Samerski, Sutherland Shire Library Service; and Rachel Spangaro and Hirofumi Yada, Japan Foundation Library, Sydney. At the University of Sydney, I thank Professor Jeffrey Riegel, Jacqui Brocker, Shauna Crick, Rosemary Go, Wayne Isbister, Phil Jones, Michael McCabe, Drasko Mitrikeski and Qing Shi, School of Languages and Cultures; Craig Beavis, Richard Black, Cong Tam Dao, Lucy Davy, Rod Dyson, Bruce Isaacs, Dean Jones, Jim Nicholls, the ever-helpful Aleksandra Nikolic, Megan O'Brien, Luke Shepherd, Elly Sutandar and Cassie Zielonko, Fisher Library; and Erin Whitney, Badham Library. I also thank Dr Richard Johnson, Dr Ian Younger and Sue Hinton, Sydney, for help with the medical problems of the d'Urville family; Emeritus Professor Wallace Kirsop, Monash University, Melbourne, for help identifying a number of nineteenth-century French publishers; my sister-in-law Linda Chen, Brighton Grammar School, Melbourne, for help with Chinese sources; Robert Kennedy, Sydney, for his philatelic expertise; Christina Kanellaki Low and Kenneth Sheedy, Sydney, for assistance with Greek sources; Karen Lindsay, Canberra, for providing information on the history of the Bonnefin family; Gaynor Lovett, Northern Territory Library, Darwin, for aiding me with sources relating to Port Esssington and Raffles Bay; and John Low, Joëlle Legoux and Justice Robert Buchanan for help in the Blue Mountains. For kind permission to quote from her late husband W. G. (Greg) McMinn's biography of Allan Cunningham, I thank Martha McMinn. I also thank Emeritus Professor John Mulvaney for permission to quote from *The Prehistory of Australia*, David de Giustino for permission to quote from *Conquest of Mind*, David Garrett and his family for permission to quote from the late John Garrett's *To Live Among the Stars* and Neal Forster for permission to quote from his late father Colin Forster's *France and Botany Bay*.

In New Zealand, I thank Kaye Mathews, Akaroa Library; Lynda Wallace and Patsy Turner, Akaroa Museum; Associate Professor Peter Tremewan, Canterbury University, Christchurch, for sharing his enormous knowledge of French settlers and whalers in New Zealand; Dr Roger Collins, Dunedin, for help with the artists of Dumont d'Urville's expeditions and giving me many other useful comments on my typescript; Joan Druett, Wellington, for answering numerous New Zealand questions and generously gifting me books on Louis-Isidore Duperrey and Charles Wilkes; Sharon Dell, Debbie Gale and Richard Munro, Hocken Collections, University of Otago, Dunedin; Peter Attwell, Mary Cobeldick, Catherine Bisley, Fiona Gray, Séan McMahon, Marian Minson, Nigel

Murphy and David Retter, Alexander Turnbull Library, Wellington; Tania Te Whenua, Te Papa Museum, Wellington; Ken Scadden, Marist Archives, Wellington; Dinah Holman and Janis Fairburn for permission to quote from their father A.R.D. Fairburn's poem 'The Voyage'; Dr Mervyn McLean for permission to quote from his book *Māori Music*, and Duncan Ross for permission to quote from his mother Ruth Miriam Ross's article on Baron de Thierry. I am especially grateful to my editor, Jane Connor, for her sensitivity, understanding and patience – particularly with my linguistic and taxonomic obsessions, and my sometimes labyrinthine references and notes. Jane immediately inspired trust and it would have been hard to find someone better suited to the task, given her long editorial experience, award-winning accomplishments in natural history publishing and earlier studies in anthropology and French. The surprising bonus was her work as designer of the handsome final product. D'Urville is not the only polymath represented here! I also thank Imogen Coxhead and Fiona Moffat for their work on the final proofs, and Diane Lowther for her index and for including my hard-won biodates for individuals mentioned in the text. Finally, I thank retired publisher Wendy Harrex for her faith in this book, and publisher Rachel Scott, Otago University Press, for her collaboration across the Tasman and her considerable efforts bringing it to fruition.

Notes

INTRODUCTION

1. Lefaivre, *Condé occupé, Condé détruit, Condé reconstruit 1940–1963*, pp. 22–23.
2. Ibid., p. 121.
3. Judging from a photograph taken by local historian and teacher Jean-Pierre Lafontaine in 1944 and exhibited during celebrations for the bicentenary of d'Urville's birth; see Lafontaine, J.-P., 'Mémoire de ma ville: Condé-sur-Noireau et Dumont d'Urville: Exposition présenté à l'Hôtel de Ville de Condé-sur-Noireau du 19 mai au 24 juillet 1990', Fonds musée, 4535314174, Médiathèque Condé-sur-Noireau.
4. Including a monumental mason named André Gauquelin, his son Jean Gauquelin and other brave accomplices; see Guedon, 'Jules Dumont d'Urville ou l'histoire de sa statue'; see also Anon., 'Une figure condéene s'est éteinte: Jean Gauquelin n'est plus'.
5. Louis-Auguste-Camille Vergniol was born in Libourne (Gironde) on 20 October 1862, the son of a civil engineer. He resided on the boulevard Montparnasse, Paris, for many years and taught at the Lycée Michelet.
6. Guillon, *Dumont d'Urville*, p. 343. Guillon can be forgiven for thinking no records survived in Condé-sur-Noireau. Although a naval officer, he commanded a tank unit during the Normandy campaign in 1944 and witnessed the destruction first hand; see Johnson, 'Obituary: Admiral Jacques Guillon'.
7. Louis-Charles-Henry Dumont de la Londe died on 20 December 1903 at his home in the hamlet of Fouc, commune of Saint-Germain-du-Crioult, canton of Condé-sur-Noireau. It is possible his surviving unmarried sister, Marie-Barbe-Isabelle Dumont de la Londe, played a part in the donation. Their father was Dr Anselme-Prosper Dumont de la Londe, the son of d'Urville's eldest sister, Adélaïde-Jeanne-Victoire Dumont d'Urville. Aside from manuscripts, the donation included d'Urville's Légion d'honneur decoration, epaulettes, general officer's [rear admiral's] cap, sword, dirk and commemorative voyage medals; see Anon., 'Musée municipal de Condé: Souvenir de M. Dumont de la Londe'. A postcard of the interior of the museum (*ca.* 1910) suggests that the collection also included ethnographic items collected by d'Urville during his voyages.
8. On 10 May 2007, these manuscripts were housed in an underground bank vault in Condé-sur-Noireau. I remain very grateful to Mayor Pascal Allizard (who had the only key!) for his assistance accessing them. We left the bank like a medieval reliquary procession prior to examining and copying the documents at the Hôtel de Ville.
9. Dumont d'Urville papiers, 1838–41, Archives nationales, Marine 5JJ 158 Bis.
10. For Malcor, agent principal de commissaire de la marine, Toulon, see Archives nationales, Fond Léonore, LH/1703/50.
11. Presumably Louis-Thomas-Barthélemy Salvy, who described himself as Captain Salvy's nephew on the title page of the biographical memoir he published: Salvy, *Clément Salvy, capitaine de vaisseau*.
12. See Malcor's 'avertissement' setting out the provenance of the documents in papiers du Contre-Amiral Jules-Sébastien-César Dumont d'Urville, SHDDM, Vincennes, Fonds Privés, 7 GG^2 carton 1 [previously GG^2 30].
13. Acte de marriage, Toulon, 24 novembre 1817, 7E146_74, Archives départementales du Var, Toulon; for Louis-Clément-Emmanuel-Marie Salvy, who was born in Nice, see Archives nationales, Fond Léonore, LH/2451/70; see also Salvy, op. cit.
14. Acte de décés, Toulon, 10 décembre 1861, 7E146_253, Archives départementales du Var, Draguignan.

15. Bibliothèque municipale de Toulon, Mss 65, 131–33.
16. Vergniol, *Dumont d'Urville*, p. 22.
17. This was Paul-Joseph Colein[-Dubusq], a former director of the Compagnie des chemins de fer de l'Ouest. He was the son of Frédéric Colein, 'professeur de philosophie', and Louise-Noemie Manson and was residing in the rue de Vire, Condé-sur-Noireau, when he died on 5 September 1938. The fate of his 'archive' is unknown. His daughter Jeanne-Marie-Louise-Françoise Colein married a pharmacist named Paul Bobay and eventually moved to Acquigny (Eure). She died in Le Chesnay (Yvelines) on 24 March 1985; see Registres d'état civil, NMD, Condé-sur-Noireau, Paris (17e arrondissement) and Le Chesnay (Yvelines).
18. Vergniol, op. cit., p. 22.
19. Ibid., p. 12.
20. Colein-Dubusq's maternal grandmother was Honorine Davoult. She had a sister, Ernestine-Bénédictine Davoult, who married d'Urville's nephew Anselme-Prosper Dumont de La Londe on 1 February 1830. Colein-Dubusq was thus the first cousin of Louis-Charles-Henry Dumont de La Londe, who inherited d'Urville's previously mentioned personal effects and manuscripts donated to the municipality of Condé-sur-Noireau in 1904; see Registres d'état civil, NMD, Service documentation et archives, Médiathèque municipale, Condé-sur-Noireau.
21. The model could just as easily have been of the *Chevrette*, on which d'Urville sailed in the Mediterranean and the Black Sea earlier in his career; it was built to an identical plan. My model was made by José Ramar, who purchased my mother's family home in rue Remono, Curepipe Road, as a workshop in 1973 and used the plan by Javault, Joubert and Lagarlière, *L'Astrolabe* (ex: *La Coquille*), corvette de 380 tonneaux … modèle N° 17 MG 14 exposé au Musée de la marine (1962).
22. See Bagnall, 'Smith, Stephenson Percy (1840–1922)'.
23. It was not until the fifth edition (1909) of *Murihiku* that Robert McNab was able to make reference to S. Percy Smith's translations. D'Urville was not included in McNab's *Historical Records of New Zealand*.
24. See his articles in *Transactions and Proceedings of the Royal Society of New Zealand*, vol. 40, 1907, pp. 412–33; vol. 41, 1908, pp. 130–39; vol. 42, 1909, pp. 412–33.
25. See Duyker, 'Olive Wright (1886–1975), teacher and translator'.
26. In *New Zealand 1826–1827*, published privately in 1950, Olive Wright declared that her translation was 'an attempt to make readily available part of the record of the early exploration of New Zealand' (p. x). Five years later, after the 'kindly reception' of her first book, she published another volume, *The Voyage of the Astrolabe – 1840*, based on d'Urville's account of his final visit to New Zealand. While she recognised the importance of d'Urville's work for historians, she wanted 'to present Dumont d'Urville to the reading public of New Zealand, that some at least may come to appreciate his personality and read his narrative, even if only in translation, "for delight" ' (p. x).
27. For a biographical summary, see Rosenman, 'Helen Rosenman (1921–2009)'.
28. Aside from Isabel Ollivier's important contributions to the 'Early Eyewitness Accounts of Maori Life' series, published between 1985 and 1987, she donated a large collection of manuscript notes, transcriptions and translations of French explorers' journals to the Alexander Turnbull Library; see also her survey of French manuscript sources relating to New Zealand (1769–1840) in the *Turnbull Library Record*, vol. 16, no. 1, May 1983, pp. 5–19 and vol. 16, no. 2, October 1983, pp. 95–110.
29. Ollivier, 'Pierre-Adolphe Lesson, surgeon-naturalist: A misfit in a successful system'.
30. For a biographical summary, see Glynnis M. Cropp's introduction in Cropp, Watts, Collins and Howe, *Pacific Journeys*, pp. 9–14.
31. See Vincendon-Dumoulin and Desgraz, *Îles Marquises ou Nouka-Hiva*, and Vincendon-Dumoulin & Desgraz, *Îles Taïti*.
32. I discuss Bory de Saint-Vincent's essay 'Homme' and his polygenist ideas in chapter 14.
33. Garnot, who accompanied d'Urville on the *Coquille*, published separate entries on man and negroes in Guérin-Méneville's (ed.) *Dictionnaire pittoresque d'histoire naturelle*. The latter entry on negroes was published as a separate extract *ca.* 1837. In it, Garnot professed racist polygenist views. He considered negroes a separate species (in which he included not only Africans but the

Australian Aborigines and the peoples of New Guinea, New Caledonia, New Britain, New Ireland and Madagascar) and characterised them as having essentially negative traits of jealousy, arrogance, deceit, vindictiveness and thievery! Although he considered the slave trade 'infamous', he believed the institution of slavery benign and the condition of slaves better than agricultural labourers in many parts of France; see Garnot, *Quelques considérations sur les Nègres en général, du Nègre de la Nouvelle-Hollande en particulier.*

34. For Hombron's polygenism, see 'De l'homme dans ses rapports avec la création', in Dumont d'Urville [& Jacquinot], *Voyage au pôle sud*, 'Zoologie', vol. i.

35. Dumont d'Urville [& Jacquinot], op. cit., 'Histoire du voyage', vol. viii, p. 47.

36. Dumont d'Urville, *Voyage de la corvette l'Astrolabe*, sixième division, 'Philologie', vol. i, pp. 11–13.

37. Dumont d'Urville, op. cit., première division, 'Histoire du voyage', vol. i, p. 147.

38. Ibid.

39. See his comments on two South Australian Aborigines at King George Sound in Western Australia who were much darker than the locals; Dumont d'Urville, *Voyage de la corvette l'Astrolabe*, première division, 'Histoire du voyage', vol. i, p. 106.

40. D'Urville frequently accorded more intellectual respect to the women than the men he met during his landfalls.

41. Christie, *The Antarctic Problem*, p. 131.

42. Rimsky-Korsakov, Летопись моей музыкальной жизни [Chronicles of my Musical Life], p. 5.

43. *Autour de la lune* (1869), *Vingt mille lieues sous les mers* (1870), *Un capitaine de quinze ans* (1878), *Les grand navigateurs du XVIIIème siècle* (1879), *Robur-le-Conquérant* (1886), *Mistress Branican* (1891), *L'Île à hélice* (1895), *Le sphinx de glaces* (1895), *Les frères Kip* (1898) and *Bourse de voyage* (1903).

44. Christie, op. cit., p. 133.

45. Chevalier, 'Au souvenir de l'amiral J. Dumont d'Urville', p. 28.

46. Darwin, *The Voyage of the* Beagle, footnote p. 16, p. 446.

47. However, Charles Lyell made reference to some of d'Urville's observations in West Papua in his *The Geological Evidences of the Antiquity of Man*, p. 38.

48. See de Beer, 'Darwin's notebooks on transmutation of species', p. 83 and de Beer, Rowlands & Skramovsky (eds), 'Darwin's notebooks on transmutation of species', p. 142.

49. For a transcription of the notebook, see Burkhardt & Smith (eds), *The Correspondence of Charles Darwin*, vol. 4, 1847–1850, appendix iv.

50. Dumont d'Urville, 'Notice sur les îles volcaniques de Santorin'.

51. In November 2008, I informed Dr Rob Allan of the Atmospheric Circulation Reconstructions over the Earth (ACRE) project of the breadth of d'Urville's records. This international initiative (with Australian, United States, British, German and Swiss partners) undertakes and facilitates the recovery and linking of historical instrumental surface terrestrial and marine global weather observations to enable weather reconstruction, reanalysis and modeling over the past 250 years.

52. Further clarification of certain terms can be found in the glossary.

53. Mulvaney, *The Prehistory of Australia*, p. 20.

54. Map 32, vol. xli, of the Atlas Blaeu-Van der Hem of Prince Eugene of Savoy, in the Österreichische Nationalbibliothek, Vienna. The Amsterdam lawyer Laurens van der Hem (1621–1678) augmented the original 600 maps published in Joan Blaeu's *Atlas Maior* (11 vols, 1662) with 1800 additional maps, landscapes, coastal profiles and town views from all over the world. The resulting 46 folio volumes even included four volumes of confidential manuscript maps used by Dutch East India Company (VOC) officers. In 1730, this extraordinary collection of seventeenth-century maps was sold by Van der Hem's heirs to Prince Eugene of Savoy. On the Prince's death in 1736, it was inherited by his niece Princess Maria Anna Victoria, who sold it to the imperial library in Vienna, now the Österreichische Nationalbibliothek.

55. For additional background, see Duyker (ed.), *The Discovery of Tasmania*, and Sharp, *The Voyages of Abel Janzoon Tasman*.

56. Taxon (plural taxa), a general term for any taxonomic rank from subspecies to division.

57. I have not sighted the first edition, but in the edition of 1893, the 'Notes biographiques du capitaine Jules-César-Sébastien Dumont d'Urville' appear on pp. 183–226. Although there is a factual skeleton to Soudry du Kerven's text, it is riddled with errors and ridiculous assertions, such as d'Urville's having had three elder brothers who died serving as volunteers in the revolutionary army. In fact he had only one *younger* brother, who died in Paris in 1812. In the same imaginary text, all of d'Urville's sisters are said to have predeceased him in adolescence, when we know that his elder sister, Adélaïde-Jeanne-Victoire, married her first cousin Louis-François-Charles Dumont de La Londe and had five children. Similarly, although we know that d'Urville's wife was an only child, Soudry du Kerven gives her an elder brother serving on the *Suffren*. D'Urville's uncle's name is given as abbé Bertrand de Croisilles when we know his real name was Jean-Jacques-François de Croisilles. Although it is pointless to list all the errors, it should be mentioned that there is no overlap with the two known transcriptions of d'Urville's own autobiographical account.

58. SHDDM, Vincennes, Fonds Privés, 7 GG^2 carton 1.

59. Bibliothèque nationale de France, NAF 9439, ff. 152–64.

60. The *Coquille* journal in the possession of the Mairie de Condé-sur-Noireau spans the period 24 October 1823 to 5 June 1824. D'Urville reworked parts as footnotes for his manuscript novel *Les Zélandais ou histoire australienne*. He also published sections as notes in the account of his later *Astrolabe* voyage. Other parts (missing in manuscript) survive as extracts in his *Voyage pittoresque autour du monde*.

61. Vergniol, op. cit., pp. 20–21.

1. CHILDHOOD

1. Registres paroissiaux, Saint-Sauveur, 5 MI 33 R 5 B. M. S., Service documentation et archives, Médiathèque municipale, Condé-sur-Noireau; see also extrait de naissance, 24 mai 1790, dossier personnel, Dumont d'Urville, SHDDM, Vincennes, CC^7 Alpha 772, pièce 1.

2. Emedy, *L'amiral Dumont d'Urville*, p. 16.

3. Le Brun, *Biographie du contre-amiral Dumont d'Urville*, p. 5.

4. Laissez-passer, Citoyen Gabriel-Charles-François Dumont, 21 messidor an 2, Archives départementales du Calvados, Caen, 4L 216.

5. Emedy, op. cit., p. 15.

6. Le Brun, op. cit., p. 5.

7. Henri Emedy states this was in June 1709 for 10,000 livres, but Le Brun stated this was in 1689 for 12,000 livres.

8. Emedy, op. cit., p. 9.

9. I am grateful to M. Jean-Jacques Thomas for giving me access to his collection of pre-war postcards of Condé-sur-Noireau, including one of the house in which d'Urville was born.

10. The son of d'Urville's sister Adélaïde-Jeanne-Victoire, who married her first cousin Louis-François-Charles Dumont de La Londe.

11. Emedy, op. cit., p. 14.

12. Ibid.

13. I am very grateful to Madame Jeannine Le Pontois-Menot, Mézidon-Canon, Calvados, for assistance with d'Urville's maternal ancestry.

14. Between 1674 and 1806, the population of Condé-sur-Noireau grew from 3000 to 3925 people; see Barette, *Histoire de la ville de Condé-sur-Noireau*, p. 101, and Lafontaine, *Mémoire de mon canton*, p. 2.

15. Barette, op. cit., p. 70.

16. Huet, *L'histoire de Condé-sur-Noireau*, p. 142.

17. Tulard, Fayard & Fierro in *Histoire et dictionnaire de la Révolution française 1789–1799*, p. 317.

18. Matterer, 'Notes nécrologiques et historiques sur M. le contre-amiral Dumont d'Urville', p. 751.

19. Cautru, *L'histoire de Condé-sur-Noireau*, p. 155.

20. Ibid., pp. 157–58.

21. Emedy, op.cit., p. 32.

22. Cautru, op. cit., p. 161.

23. Ibid., p. 162.

24. Archives départementales du Calvados, Caen, 4L 216, administration de la période révolutionnaire 1789–an VIII: Comité de surveillance: Condé-sur-Noireau an II.

25. See Bodinier, *Les gardes du corps de Louis XVI*, p. 223.

26. Archives départementales du Calvados, Caen, 4L 216, administration de la période révolutionnaire 1789–an VIII: Comité de surveillance: Condé-sur-Noireau an II.

27. In particular, the Prince de Condé.

28. The 'mountain' faction took its name from the fact that its members sat on the highest benches of the left side of the chamber. Its members were revolutionary radicals who espoused a highly centralised government for France.

29. See Watson, *Carnot*, pp. 73–74.

30. See Greer, *The Incidence of the Terror during the French Revolution*, pp. 26, 37, 97 & 106.

31. Tulard, Fayard & Fierro, op. cit., p. 363.

32. Matterer, op. cit., p. 751.

33. See Joubert, Fr. [Just-Jean-Étienne Roy], *Dumont d'Urville*.

34. A copy of the illustrated 1889 edition was acquired by the Mitchell Library, Sydney, in 2012.

35. Vergniol, *Dumont d'Urville*, pp. 29–30.

36. Archives départementales du Calvados, Caen, 4L 216, administration de la période révolutionnaire 1789–an VIII: Comité de surveillance: Condé-sur-Noireau an II.

37. Archives départementales du Calvados, Caen, 4L 216, Comité de surveillance de Noireau, District de Vire, Départment du Calvados: État des personnes mises en arrestation par le comité, procès-verbaux en conséquences, motifs de leurs arrestations … 1 pluviôse an 2 [20 January 1794], signé par Martin, Devoult, Allard, Farein, Colein-Dubusq et autres.

38. Archives départementales du Calvados, Caen, 4L 216, réponse du comité de Noireau auquel fut remis la pétition de la citoyenne Durville.

39. Archives départementales du Calvados, Caen, 4L 216, [Gabriel-Charles] Dumont d'Urville au comité de surveillance de la commune de Noireau, 21 pluviôse an 2 [9 February 1794].

40. Archives départementales du Calvados, Caen, 4L 216, réponse du comité de Noireau auquel fut remis la pétition de la citoyenne Durville.

41. Robert, Bourloton & Cougny, *Dictionnaire des parlementaires français*, vol. i, p. 441.

42. Archives départementales du Calvados, Caen, 4L 216, administration de la période révolutionnaire 1789–an VIII: Comité de surveillance: Condé-sur-Noireau an II, certificat de Robert Benard, commissaire de police de la commune de Caen, au Bureau de surveillance, le 24 germinal an 2 [13 April 1794].

43. Archives départementales du Calvados, Caen, 4L 216, ordres de transférer de cette commune et du domicile de la citoyenne Durville à la maison d'arrestation des Bénédictines de la commune de Caen.

44. Archives départementales du Calvados, Caen, 4L 216, décret portant sur la déportation de La Durville.

45. Huet, op. cit., pp. 159–62.

46. Isidore Le Brun (sometimes written Lebrun) was born in Caen, the son of a manufacturer. In 1808 he became a teacher, and in 1816 he was appointed professor of literature at the Université de Caen. Although he initially favoured the Restoration, he was an anti-clerical liberal and a strong advocate of the education of women. He resigned his teaching position to pursue a career in political journalism with *Le Constitutionnel*, which was suppressed five times. He also founded an Anglo-French journal *Le Recueil*, published in New York in 1825. For further details of his publications and a study of his novel *La bonne ville*, see Thuillier, 'L'administration sous La Restauration'.

47. Robillard de Beaurepaire & Carbonnier, *Caen illustré*, pp. 393–94.

48. In 2007, the former Collège du bois at 17, rue Saint-Sauveur, Caen, housed a hairdressing salon.

49. Navel, *Monographie de Feuguerolles-sur-Orne*, pp. 353–59.

50. However, there was dissent regarding this document and the freedom it conferred. One local Jacobin named L'Aisné argued that all those with suffrage were entitled to participate in 'all deliberations and were authorised to continue to determine these arrests', but that they could not all sign passports and their differing opinions could not all be entered into the registers. He did not countersign the old man's passport and nor did Colein-Dubusq; see Archives départementales du Calvados, Caen, 4L 216, L'Aisné au comité de surveillance: [Condé-sur-]Noireau, 28 thermidor an II, délibérations du comité au sujet du passeport pour Gabriel Charles Dumont d'Urville.
51. Navel, op. cit., p. 386.
52. Extrait de l'acte de décès, Gabriel Charles Dumont d'Urville, 21 vendémiaire an V [12 October 1796], dossier personnel, Dumont d'Urville, SHDDM, Vincennes, CC^7 Alpha 772, pièce 14; see also Navel, op. cit., pp. 386–87.
53. Dumont d'Urville, in Collection Margry, 'Mers Australes', Bibliothèque nationale, NAF 9439, f. 152.
54. Le Brun, op. cit., p. 5.
55. Woods, 'Isaac Joseph Berruyer'.
56. Le Brun, op. cit., p. 11; Berthelot, 'Éloge du contre-amiral Dumont d'Urville', p. 363.
57. Le Brun, op. cit., p. 6; Berthelot (op. cit., pp. 362–63) also quotes this passage from Dumont d'Urville's now-missing manuscript memoirs.
58. Matterer, op. cit., p. 752.
59. Lesson, R.P., *Notice historique sur l'amiral Dumont d'Urville*, pp. 15–17.
60. Quoted by Le Brun, op. cit., p. 6, from Dumont d'Urville's now-missing manuscript memoirs.
61. Quoted by Le Brun, ibid., pp. 6–7.
62. Le Brun, op. cit., p. 6.

2. THE LYCÉE & THE SEA

1. One of my own forebears, Jacques-Marie Prenat (1777–1818), began a distinguished career in the French Navy at the age of five and a half during the closing months of the American War of Independence.
2. In October 1803, the *Sandwich* was recaptured by the British and restored to her private owner; see Roche, *Dictionnaire des bâtiments de la flotte de guerre française*, vol. i, p. 403; see also Colledge, *Ships of the Royal Navy*, vol. ii, p. 320.
3. État de services, 23 juillet, 1808, dossier personnel, Dumont d'Urville, SHDDM, Vincennes, CC^7 Alpha 772, pièce 3; this same document restates later service on the *Aquilon* but does not mention service on *Les Deux Amis*. The two periods of service, however, are not mutually exclusive. As a comparable example, it is interesting to note that Horatio Nelson was rated on the books of the *Raisonable* as a midshipman, aged 12, on New Year's Day 1771 yet with the real prospect of returning to school when term resumed.
4. Le Roy, *Louis de Frotté*, pp. 187–96.
5. Goyau, 'The French Concordat of 1801'.
6. Emedy, *L'amiral Dumont d'Urville*, p. 32.
7. Charles Brault was made a baron by Napoleon; under the Bourbons, he became archbishop of Albi in 1823 and a peer of France in 1827; see Michaud, *Biographie universelle*, vol. 59 (supplement), p. 198.
8. Le Brun, *Biographie du contre-amiral Dumont d'Urville*, p. 6.
9. Ibid., pp. 7–8.
10. État de services, 3 novembre, 1808, dossier personnel, Dumont d'Urville, SHDDM, Vincennes, CC^7 Alpha 772, pièce 3; this same document restates later service on the *Aquilon* but does not mention the earlier period of service on the *Sandwich*.
11. Le Brun, op. cit., p. 7.
12. Cited by Le Brun, ibid., p. 10.
13. The word *lycée* is derived from the Latin *lyceum*, in turn derived from the Greek *lykeion*, the name of one of the gymnasia of classical Athens.

14. Le Brun, op. cit., p. 8.
15. Ibid.
16. Cahier de physique appartenant à Dumont d'Urville de Condé-sur-Noireau: Elève au Lycée de Caen, commencé le 22 pluviôse an 13, Bibliothèque de Caen, ms in 4° 334.
17. Musset, *Le Lycée Malherbe*, p. 31.
18. Ibid., p. 30.
19. A surviving miniature of Jules' life-long friend Louis-Charles Lefébure de Cerisy, when a student at the Lycée de Caen between 1804 and 1807, shows him wearing this uniform; see SHDDM, Toulon, 23S 753.
20. Musset, op. cit., p. 31, and Beck & Le Poire, *Le Lycée Malherbe*, p. 24.
21. Musset, op. cit., p. 30.
22. Musset, op. cit., appendix iii, pp. 85–87.
23. Le Brun, op. cit., p. 8.
24. Chevalier, 'Au souvenir de l'amiral J. Dumont d'Urville', p. 11.
25. Le Brun, op. cit., p. 16.
26. Grey-eyed with chestnut-blond hair and only 168 centimetres in height – d'Urville dwarfed him by 16 centimetres – Cerisy later achieved fame as 'Cerisy Bey' rebuilding the Egyptian fleet after it was destroyed during the Battle of Navarino; see Lackany, *Cerisy Bey*; Caieu, 'M. Lefébure de Cerisy (Louis Charles)'; and Goldschmidt, *Biographical Dictionary of Modern Egypt*, p. 41.
27. Le Brun, op. cit., pp. 8–10.
28. See Rose, *A New General Biographical Dictionary*, vol. v, pp. 386–88.
29. Le Gallo, *Histoire de Brest*, pp. 196–97.
30. Le Brun, op. cit., p. 10.
31. Matterer, 'Notes nécrologiques et historiques sur M. le contre-amiral Dumont d'Urville', p. 752; see also Roche, *Dictionnaire des bâtiments de la flotte de guerre française*, vol. i, p. 326.
32. See Duflot & Duyker, 'Jacques-Rémy Maingon (1765–1809)'.
33. Le Brun, op. cit., p. 11.
34. See Levot, *Histoire de la ville et du port de Brest*, vol. ii, pp. 293–98.
35. Quoted in Le Brun, op. cit., p. 11, from d'Urville's now-missing memoirs.
36. Rosenman, *An Account in Two Volumes of Two Voyages to the South Seas*, vol. ii, p. 360.
37. Dossier personnel, Dumont d'Urville, SHDDM, Vincennes, CC[7] Alpha 772.
38. Roche, op. cit., vol. i, p. 21.
39. Matterer, op. cit., p. 752.
40. Rousseau, Bernard-Louis, Archives nationales, LH/2400/37.
41. Dumont d'Urville, in Collection Margry, 'Mers Australes', Bibliothèque nationale, NAF 9439, f. 153.
42. Le Brun, op. cit., p. 12.
43. Dumont d'Urville, in Collection Margry, 'Mers Australes', loc. cit., f. 153; also quoted in [Vincendon-Dumoulin] 'Notice biographique' in Dumont d'Urville [& Jacquinot], *Voyage au pôle sud*, 'Histoire du voyage', vol. x, p. 80.
44. See Feuardent, 'La perte de la frégate "L'Amazone"'. Rousseau's service dossier in his Légion d'honneur file (Archives nationales, Fond Léonore, LH/2400/37) glosses over these events; a seaman since 1775, he then commanded the French garrison in Danzig and was taken prisoner there in 1813 in the wake of Napoleon's ill-fated Russian campaign.
45. See abbé de Croisilles (et l'évêque de Bayeux) au ministre de la marine, avril 1810 and 29 août 1811, and Dubois-Dubais au ministre de la marine, 18 août 1811, in dossier personnel, Dumont d'Urville, SHDDM, Vincennes, CC[7] Alpha 772, pièces 6 & 7.
46. Agulhon, *Histoire de Toulon*, p. 203.
47. Dumont d'Urville, *Voyage pittoresque autour du monde*, vol. i, p. 1.
48. Ibid., p. 2.
49. Ibid., pp. 1–2.
50. The caryatids were sculpted in 1657 by Pierre Puget and can still be seen.
51. Dumont d'Urville, *Voyage pittoresque autour du monde*, vol. i, p. 2.

52. Ibid.

53. After graduation from the École polytechnique in 1809; see 'Cerisy, Louis Charles Lefébure de', in Goldschmidt, *Biographical Dictionary of Modern Egypt*, p. 41.

54. Dumont d'Urville, *Voyage pittoresque autour du monde*, vol. i, p. 2.

55. Dumont d'Urville, ms journal de la *Coquille*, Mairie de Condé-sur-Noireau, ms 11, p. 61.

56. Dubois-Dubais married Louise-Françoise Le Prévost de Miette on 30 August 1781.

57. See Bodinier, *Les gardes du corps de Louis XVI*, pp. 223 & 250; see also Robert, Bourloton & Cougny, *Dictionnaire des parlementaires français*, vol. ii, pp. 425–27.

58. See dossier personnel, Dumont d'Urville, SHDDM, Vincennes, CC^7 Alpha 772, pièce 11; d'Urville appears to have been granted leave between 28 August and 17 November 1812.

59. D'Urville paid for the repair of his grave and a cemetery concession in 1841; on the receipt for the latter, his death date is given as 24 January 1812; see Archives nationales, Paris, Marine 5JJ 158 Bis.

60. Senez, Louis-André, Archives nationales, Fond Léonore, LH/2501/30.

61. Dumont d'Urville, 'Au peuple anglais', *ca*.1830, Malcor transcription, SHDDM, Vincennes, Fonds Privés, 7 GG^2, carton 1, papiers du contre-amiral Dumont d'Urville.

62. Abbé de Croisilles au ministre de la marine, 18 October 1813, dossier personnel, Dumont d'Urville, SHDDM, Vincennes, CC^7 Alpha 772, pièce 12.

63. Louis-Philippe had already made the voyage from Sicily in a British frigate without his family to present himself to Louis XVIII. Because of his father's ('citoyen Philippe Égalité's) active participation in the Revolution and vote for Louis XVI's death, Louis-Philippe was unsure of the reception he would receive, but he was warmly received and re-appointed lieutenant-general; see Poore, *The Rise and Fall of Louis-Philippe*, pp. 115–17.

64. Guérin, *Notice des livres … composant la bibliothèque de feu M. Le contre-amiral Dumont-d'Urville*, p. 20, item 177.

65. For Hausleutner's German translation, see [Vella], *Geschichte der Araber in Sicilien und Siciliens unter der Herrschaft der Araber*.

3. ADÉLIE

1. Dumont d'Urville, *Voyage pittoresque autour du monde*, vol. i, p. 2.

2. Adèle-Dorothée Pépin was born on 20 floréal an VI (9 May 1798).

3. According to local historian Dr Tony Marmottans, Adélie's father arrived in Toulon 'without doubt soon after the siege of [17]93'; see Marmottans, *Art et commerce toulonnais (1830–1870)*, p. 85.

4. Adélie's paternal aunt Jeanne-Françoise 'Fanny' Pépin, whom she described as her godmother, was born in Chêne-Thônex in the year French troops invaded this part of Savoie. In the European negotiations that followed the fall of Napoleon, Chêne-Thônex was ceded to the Swiss Confederation and eventually became an outer suburb of Geneva. In a surviving letter to Isidore Le Brun, now held in the Dixson Library, Sydney, Adélie wrote that her aunt was married to a doctor in Geneva, named Favre. In fact, Jean-Claude Favre was a veterinarian, originally from Annecy. She wrote to Le Brun of other Swiss relatives, including the daughter of her great-uncle (Pépin de Cornière, the man who had raised her father), married to a well-to-do Genevois named Magnin, and yet another cousin, whom she did not name, 'married to a rich proprietor living on the shores of Lake Léman'; see Adèle Dumont d'Urville to Isidore Le Brun, 4 février 1841, Dixson Library, Sydney, MSQ355; see also Naissances, Chêne-Thônex, Archives d'état de Genève, E.C.3. p. 514; Recensement K3, p. 119.

5. At the end of his life, d'Urville and his wife owned at least one pendulum clock and two watches made by Pépin in addition to two English watches (one by Morris Tobias of London) and others by Roff, Dujardin, Berthoud and two by Landry. D'Urville also had others by anonymous makers and two incomplete watch movements; Archives nationales, ET/C/1200 Minutier central des notaires de Paris, '13 Juin 1842, Inventaire après décès de Mr. Dumont d'Urville' & '21 Juin 1842, Décharge donnée à M. Demanche'.

6. Adélie's parents divorced on 30 March 1812, according to the record of her mother's re-marriage on 24 November 1817; see 7E146_74, Archives départementales du Var, Toulon.

7. Consentement de Madame Dumont d'Urville, Vassy, 26 janvier 1815, in dossier personnel, Dumont d'Urville, SHDDM, Vincennes, CC^7 Alpha 772, pièce 14 (2).

8. Préfet maritime de Toulon au ministre de la marine, 17 février 1816, in Dumont d'Urville, dossier personnel, loc. cit., pièce 14.

9. Contrat de mariage de Dumont d'Urville et Adèle-Dorothée Pépin passé devant Maître Fournier, notaire à Toulon, le 28 avril 1815, Office notarial Pieroni-Mignon, Toulon.

10. Mariage de Dumont d'Urville et Adèle-Dorothée Pépin, 1 mai 1815, Archives municipales de Toulon, 3E1, Registres des mariages, 1815, folio 108; the witnesses were Théodore de Loffre, *enseigne de vaisseau*; Stanislas-Antoine-Alexis Banon, *pharmacien de la marine*; Jean Reynaud, *capitaine d'artillerie de la marine*; Jean-Jacques Mabille, *juge au tribunal civil*; Dame Josephine-Hélène Las de Guérin.

11. Vergniol, *Dumont d'Urville*, p. 53.

12. [Frédéric-Luc-Antoine Malcor], ms étude sur Dumont d'Urville (1884), SHDDM, Vincennes, Fonds Privés, 7 GG^2 carton 1.

13. Le Brun, *Biographie du contre-amiral Dumont d'Urville*, p. 64.

14. Lesson, 'Portrait de l'état-major de l'*Astrolabe*', p. 167.

15. Dumont d'Urville, ms journal de la *Coquille*, Mairie de Condé-sur-Noireau, ms 11, p. 62.

16. 'Abbé de Croisilles au ministre de la marine, 27 avril 1816' in Dumont d'Urville, dossier personnel, loc. cit., pièce 15.

17. Louis-François-Charles Dumont de la Londe (*ca.* 1761–1834).

18. See Acte de décès, Vassy, 20 février 1872, Louis-Napoléon Dumont de La Londe, Archives départementales de Calvados, 1868–1872, Vassy, NMD (no. 10). His parents' names are given as Louis-François-Charles Dumont de La Londe and Adélaïde Jeanne Victoire Dumont. Although the witnesses declared that he was 61 years old and that he was born and died in Vassy, there is no record of his birth in the local registers for 1810–13.

19. Dumont d'Urville, 'Au peuple anglais', *ca.* 1830, Malcor transcription, SHDDM, Vincennes, Fonds Privés, 7 GG^2, carton 1, papiers du contre-amiral Jules-Sébastien-César Dumont d'Urville (1790–1842).

20. Vergniol, op. cit., p. 56.

21. Dumont d'Urville, ms journal de la *Coquille*, loc. cit.

22. Ibid.

23. Registre des naissances de 1816, Archives municipales, Toulon, L121 E35.

24. Nettement, *Mémoires historiques de S.A.R. Madame, duchesse de Berry*, vol. i, pp. 138–46.

25. Cited by Vergniol, op. cit., p. 56.

26. For a fine study of this period, see Bertier de Sauvigny, *The Bourbon Restoration*.

27. Roche, *Dictionnaire des bâtiments de la flotte de guerre française*, vol. i, p. 36.

28. Dumont d'Urville, in Collection Margry, 'Mers Australes', Bibliothèque nationale, NAF 9439, f. 154.

29. 'Cerisy, Louis-Charles Lefébure de', in Goldschmidt, *Biographical Dictionary of Modern Egypt*, p. 41.

30. Le Brun, op. cit., p. 14.

31. Matterer, 'Notes nécrologiques et historiques sur M. le contre-amiral Dumont d'Urville'.

32. Dumont d'Urville, ms journal de la *Coquille*, loc. cit., p. 62.

33. Roche, op. cit., vol. i, p. 36.

34. Dumont d'Urville, ms journal de la *Coquille*, loc. cit, p. 62.

35. See, for example, Bassett, *Realms and Islands*.

36. Dumont d'Urville, in Collection Margry, 'Mers Australes', Bibliothèque nationale, NAF 9439, f. 154.

37. Lesson, *Notice historique sur l'amiral Dumont d'Urville*, p. 20.

38. See Duyker, *François Péron*.

39. Roche, op. cit, vol. i, p. 113–14.

40. Lesson, op. cit., p. 21.

41. Taillemite, *Dictionnaire des marins français*, p. 135.

4. APHRODITE AND THE ISLES

1. Higgins & Higgins, *A Geological Companion to Greece and the Aegean*, pp. 182–86.
2. See Shelford, Hodson, Cosgrove, Warren & Renfrew, 'The sources and characterisation of Melian obsidian', pp. 183–91.
3. See Stos-Gale and Gale, 'The sources of Mycenaean silver and lead'.
4. See Croon, 'Hot springs and healing gods', p. 231.
5. Dumont d'Urville, 'Notice sur les îles volcaniques de Santorin', pp. 598–99.
6. Higgins & Higgins, op. cit., pp. 187–95.
7. See Freidrich, *Fire in the Sea*.
8. Le Brun, *Biographie du contre-amiral Dumont d'Urville*, p. 15.
9. Dumont d'Urville à Théodose-Cyriaque Prost, Toulon, 23 février 1820, in Marie, 'Lettres de Dumont d'Urville (1819–1825)', p. 78.
10. This same view appears in Louis Dupré's portrait of Fauvel on his terrace in the same year that d'Urville met him. One of the Parthenon *metopes* can be seen lying beside him. The original painting is now in the David and Alfred Smart Museum of Art, University of Chicago.
11. Dyson, *In Pursuit of Ancient Pasts*, p. 67; see also Clairmont, *Fauvel*.
12. Dumont d'Urville à Théodose-Cyriaque Prost, Toulon, 23 février & 13 octobre 1820, in Marie, op. cit., pp. 78, 80–81.
13. Le Brun, op. cit., pp. 15–16.
14. Dumont d'Urville à Théodose-Cyriaque Prost, Toulon, 16 janvier 1820, in Marie, op. cit., pp. 75–76.
15. D'Urville retained the support of the bishop of Bayeux; see 'Lettre de l'évêque de Bayeux demandant de l'avancement et un service plus actif pour Dumont d'Urville', 17 mai 1819', dossier personnel, Dumont d'Urville, SHDDM, Vincennes, CC[7] Alpha 772, pièce 18.
16. Gauttier au ministre de la marine, rade de Milo, 17 avril 1820, Campagnes, 1820, vol. 2, Station du Levant, gabarre la *Chevrette*, Gauttier-Duparc, capitaine de vaisseau, SHDDM, Vincennes, BB[4] 411, folios 269 recto et verso.
17. Marcellus, *Souvenirs de l'Orient*, p. 236.
18. For Louis Brest, whose family had lived on the neighbouring island of Kimolos for two centuries before moving to Milos, see [Dalampira], Δαλαμπίρα, *Ο Κόνσολας*; see also Reinach, 'Louis Brest et la Vénus de Milo d'après des documents inédits'. In the first part of this article, published in *La Chronique des Arts*, 20 février 1897, and later included in the collection, *Amalthée* (vol. 1, p. 291), Reinach incorrectly states that Brest died around 1870; in fact, he died on 14 October 1862 and is buried inside the Catholic church of Our Lady of the Rosary, Plaka. His first wife, Aekaterini (*née* Bosari), is buried outside the church.
19. Kastro offers a commanding view of the island and contains the remains of a Frankish fort. In the nineteenth century, this panoramic view offered warning of pirates, while the thick exterior walls of the village offered refuge. It was devastated by an earthquake in 1918 and much of its stone reused for construction in Plaka. The original church that stood on the summit was dynamited by the Germans during World War II.
20. Dumont d'Urville, 'Notice sur les galeries souterraines de l'île de Melos', p. 146.
21. Matterer, 'Notes nécrologiques et historiques sur M. le contre-amiral Dumont d'Urville', p. 755.
22. Dumont d'Urville thought that the statue was discovered three weeks before the *Chevrette*'s arrival. However, a letter written by Captain Dauriac, commander of the *Bonite*, to Monsieur David, the French consul in Smyrna, on 11 April 1820 refers to the marble Venus discovered three days before; thus the statue was probably discovered on 8 April 1820; see Goeler von Ravensburg, *Die Venus von Milo*, appendix ii, p. 188; whose source is marquis Melchior de Vogüé's 'Lettre sur la découverte de la Vénus de Milo, séance du 29 mai 1874'; see also Alaux, *La Vénus de Milo et Olivier Voutier*, pp. 12 & 175.
23. In a letter dated 3 June 1862, Louis Brest wrote that the farmer's name was Theodore Kendrotas; see Brest, 'Rapport de Louis Brest', p. 84.

24. [Vaos] , ʾΒάος, "Η Αφροδίτη της Μήλου", [Aphrodite of Milos]ʾ, p. 376. In 1873, Antonios, whose nickname was ʾBottonisʾ, was interviewed by Jules Ferry, then the French ambassador to Greece. Solomon Reinach cast doubt on the identity of Antonios (see Reinach, ʾLouis Brest et la Vénus de Milo dʾaprès des documents inéditsʾ, [Part 1] p. 73. Ferryʾs account is reproduced in Aicard, *La Vénus de Milo*, p. 188. Less credible is the assertion of Takis Théodoropoulos that Kendrotas was working with a Kytheran apprentice named Andreas Kalokairinos, who later settled in Heraklion on Crete and became a wealthy merchant. His son Minos (a passionate amateur archaeologist) discovered Knossos in 1878, a site later excavated by Sir Arthur Evans; see Théodoropoulos, *Lʾinvention de la Vénus de Milo*, pp. 34–35. This story seems as apocryphal as Théodoropoulosʾs assertion that Olivier Voutier was having an affair with Louis Brestʾs wife, Aekaterini!

25. [Vaos], op. cit., pp. 391–92.

26. Parian = from the nearby island of Paros.

27. Voutier, ʾDécouverte et acquisition de la Vénus de Miloʾ.

28. [Vaos] op. cit., pp. 364–65.

29. See Reinach, op. cit., p. 382.

30. See, for example, Boardman, *Greek Art*, p. 193, and Steibing, *Uncovering the Past*, p. 283. Even Alaux, op. cit., writes of ʾYorgosʾ [Kendrotas] as a ʾ*chaumier*ʾ (lime-maker).

31. Sublime Porte (from French *porte* = gate, door), the open (rather than the private) court of the Ottoman sultan. It takes its name from the gate to the Topkapi Palace where the grand vizir would facilitate the sultanʾs official greeting of foreign ambassadors in Constantinople.

32. Voutier, op. cit., p. 102.

33. See Clark, *The Nude*, pp. 80–84.

34. Olivier Voutier to Marcellus, Hyères, 3 mars 1860, in Alaux, op. cit., appendix, p. 177.

35. Ibid.

36. Salomon Reinach refers to a letter from David, the French consul in Smyrna, dated 25 April 1820, to the marquis de Rivière, ambassador in Constantinople, which suggests that Captain Robert of the *Estafette* was with the rest of the French squadron at Smyrna at the time, since he also reported details of the statue; see Reinach, *Amalthée*, vol. i, note p. 276. This letter was published by Goeler von Ravensburg, op. cit., appendix ii, p. 190.

37. See Captain Dauriac to Consul David, Smyrna, 11 April 1820, in Alaux, op. cit., appendix, pp. 175–76.

38. Matterer, op. cit., p. 756; his other reminiscences of the statue, particularly with regard to its arms, published in Aicard, op. cit., have been shown to be unreliable.

39. Dumont dʾUrville, ʾSeconde relation de la campagne hydrographique de la gabare du roi la *Chevrette*ʾ, p. 153.

40. Ibid.

41. Ibid.

42. Ibid.

43. Inventaire des effets mobiliers dressé par Maître Vallavieille, notaire à Toulon, le 30 juillet 1842 … dépendant des successions réunies de feu M. Dumont DʾUrville … , Office notarial Boyer, Toulon.

44. There, dʾUrville recorded that he collected *Daphne pontica*, *Lilium chalcedonicum* and *Borago orientalis* in the woods; see Dumont dʾUrville, ʾSeconde relation de la campagne hydrographique de la gabare du roi la *Chevrette*ʾ, p. 154.

45. A pencil portrait of Marcellus, by Jean-Auguste-Dominique Ingres, is preserved in the Louvreʾs cabinet des dessins, RF 31136, recto, fonds des dessins et miniatures, petit format.

46. Anon., ʾMarcellus, Marie-Louis-Jean-André-Charles Demartin du Tirac, comte deʾ; see also Dumaine, *Quelques oubliés de lʾautre siècle*, pp. 1–64.

47. Marcellus, op. cit., pp. 237–39.

48. Dumont dʾUrville, ʾSeconde relation de la campagne hydrographique de la gabare du roi la *Chevrette*ʾ, p. 152.

49. Chazet, *Mémoires posthumes, lettres et pièces authentiques*, p. 166.

50. Agulhon, *Histoire de Toulon*, p. 209.

51. See Anon., 'Rivière, Charles-François de Riffareau, marquis'; see also Chazet, op. cit.

52. The following year, Olivier Voutier resigned his naval commission and joined the Greek insurgents, serving under Alexander Ypsilantis in the Greek War of Independence. He eventually rose to the rank of colonel in the Greek army. He is buried in Hyères near Toulon.

53. See Brest, op. cit., p. 85; but Marcellus says his name was Œconome.

54. Mourouzi belonged to the old Byzantine Phanariot nobility (the posts of dragoman to the fleet and grand dragoman to the Porte were reserved for these Christian aristocrats). His father, Alexandros, had previously been *hospodar* (prince) of the Ottoman vassal states of Moldavia and Wallachia; see Papachristou, 'The Three Faces of the Phanariots', p. 7.

55. Chazet, op. cit., p. 167.

56. Nicolaki Mourouzi was an early casualty of the Greek Revolution. He was murdered by the Ottomans on 6 May 1821 for his role in fomenting rebellion on Hydra, Spetses and Psara; see Marinescu, *Étude généalogique sur la famille Mourouzi*, pp. 85–87; see also Marcellus, op. cit., p. 254, and Marcellus, *Les Grecs anciens et modernes*, pp. 288–89.

57. According to Brest, op. cit., p. 85, it was the vessel of a 'raya' (a non-Muslim Ottoman subject) from Galaxidi (a Greek port on the Crisaean Gulf). But, according to Marcellus, it was a Greek brig with an Albanian skipper. In 1874, Voutier asserted it was a Ragusan (Sicilian) brig; see Voutier, op. cit., p. 98. None of these eyewitnesses name the vessel.

58. Early in 1820 (it was still winter), Marcellus had attended a select reading of Aeschylus's *Persians* with Mourouzi and other Greek nationalist intellectuals at Büyükdere. Forty years later, Marcellus published an account of the remarkable evening and reflected on the fate of the small gathering in the Revolution which followed soon after; see 'Les Perses d'Eschyle à Constantinople Scène orientale' in Marcellus's *Les Grecs anciens et modernes*, pp. 225–89.

59. See Brest, op. cit., p. 85; Marcellus, *Souvenirs de l'Orient*, p. 250, and Chazet, op. cit., p. 168; for further details of Mourouzi's controversial behaviour towards his fellow Greeks, see Kriezis, *Histoire de l'Île d'Hydra*, pp. 67–68.

60. For a discussion of this question, see Alaux, op. cit., chapter v.

61. [Simopoulou] Σιμοπουλου, Ξενοι Ταξιδιωτες Στην Ελλαδ, [Foreign Travellers in Greece], vol. 4, pp. 547–49.

62. [Vaos], op. cit., p. 408.

63. The immediate area where Kendrotas found the statue was later subject to so much additional excavation by those in search of the missing arms or other treasures that the cavity no longer exists.

64. For a map of the route of the *Estafette*, see Alaux, op. cit., pp. 82–83.

65. In February 1820, as he left the opera on the rue de Rivoli, the duc de Berry was mortally stabbed by a 37-year-old saddler named Louis-Pierre Louvel (1783–1820). A fanatical Bonapartist, Louvel hoped to extinguish the direct Bourbon line of Louis XIV. In this he failed: the duchesse was already two months' pregnant and, on 29 September 1820, gave birth to a son.

5. THE BOSPHORUS & BEYOND

1. Gauttier au ministre de la marine, rade de la Caffa (Crimée), 17 mai 1820, Campagnes, 1820, vol. 2, Station du Levant, gabarre la *Chevrette*, Gauttier-Duparc, capitaine de vaisseau, SHDDM, Vincennes, BB^4 411, f. 271 recto.

2. Dumont d'Urville, 'Seconde relation de la campagne hydrographique de la gabare du roi la *Chevrette*', p. 154.

3. Le Brun, *Biographie du contre-amiral Dumont d'Urville*, p. 18, footnote 1 (on the basis of his reading of d'Urville's now-missing private journal).

4. See Dumont d'Urville à Théodose-Cyriaque Prost, Toulon, 13 octobre 1820, in Marie, 'Lettres de Dumont d'Urville (1819–1825)', p. 81.

5. Dumont d'Urville, 'Seconde relation de la campagne hydrographique de la gabare du roi la *Chevrette*', p. 155.

6. Gauttier au ministre de la marine, rade d'Odessa, 17 juillet 1820, Campagnes, 1820, vol. 2, Station du Levant, gabarre la *Chevrette*, Gauttier-Duparc, capitaine de vaisseau, loc. cit., f. 273 recto.

7. Dumont d'Urville, 'Seconde relation de la campagne hydrographique de la gabare du roi la *Chevrette*', p. 156.

8. Dumont d'Urville à Théodose-Cyriaque Prost, Toulon, 13 octobre 1820, in Marie, op. cit., p. 81.

9. Ibid., p. 158; see also Gauttier au ministre de la marine, rade d'Odessa, 17 juillet 1820, Campagnes, 1820, vol. 2, Station du Levant, gabarre la *Chevrette*, Gauttier-Duparc, capitaine de vaisseau, loc. cit., f. 273 recto.

10. D'Urville spells his name as Mogilianski and records his rank as colonel, but according to Russian military archives, he was still a major the following year. I am very grateful to Dr Natalia Dushkina, Moscow Architectural Institute, for her assistance in identifying him.

11. It is possible that d'Urville confused the Russian-installed Prince of Abkhazia, Sefer Ali-Bey Shervashidze, also known as 'Giorgi' Shervashidze (after his conversion to Orthodox Christianity), with his deposed elder brother Hassan (also known as Aslan) Bey Shervashidze, then in exile; see Manvelichvili, *Histoire de la Géorgie*, pp. 391–93, and Gvosdev, *Imperial Policies and Perspectives Towards Georgia, 1760–1819*, p. 124.

12. Dumont d'Urville, 'Seconde relation de la campagne hydrographique de la gabare du roi la *Chevrette*', p. 160.

13. Pierre Dupré became vice-consul in Trébizonde in 1803 then consul in 1811; he died in his post on 6 September 1820; see the biographical note in Cordier, *Voyage de Pierre Dupré de Constantinople à Trébizonde: 1803*.

14. Gauttier au ministre de la marine, rade d'Odessa, 17 juillet 1820, Campagnes, 1820, vol. 2, Station du Levant, gabarre la *Chevrette*, Gauttier-Duparc, capitaine de vaisseau, loc. cit., f. 273 verso.

15. The duc de Richelieu's statue, erected six years after his death by the grateful Odessans, still graces the top of the famous Potemkin Steps.

16. Gauttier au ministre de la marine, rade de Constantinople, 9 août 1820, Campagnes, 1820, vol. 2, Station du Levant, gabarre la *Chevrette*, Gauttier-Duparc, capitaine de vaisseau, loc. cit., f. 275 recto.

17. Dumont d'Urville, 'Seconde relation de la campagne hydrographique de la gabare du roi la *Chevrette*', pp. 172–73.

18. The surviving fragment of d'Urville's personal navigational journal for this part of the voyage provides a detailed account of these movements; see Dumont d'Urville, [ms Journal on the *Chevrette*] 'Evénements historiques et remarques, dimanche 23 juillet 1820–dimanche 20 août 1820', Mairie de Condé-sur-Noireau, ms 10.

19. Dumont d'Urville, 'Seconde relation de la campagne hydrographique de la gabare du roi la *Chevrette*', p. 173.

20. Bouboulina was also associated with the Stroganoff family and had spent time in exile in the Crimea; for a biography see [Demertzis-Bouboulis] Δεμερτζής-Μπούμπουλης, *Λασκαρίνα Μπουμπουλίνα* [*Laskarina Bouboulina*].

21. According to Florin Marinescu, Nicolaki Mourouzi visited Spetses in March 1821 to help rouse the islanders into rebellion; see Marinescu, *Étude généalogique sur la famille Mourouzi*, p. 87.

22. D'Urville would correctly remark that this former crusader fortress, rebuilt by the Venetians in 1711, was 'almost impregnable'; the Turkish defenders surrendered because of starvation rather than because the walls were breached.

23. Dumont d'Urville, 'Seconde relation de la campagne hydrographique de la gabare du roi la *Chevrette*', p. 173.

24. Ibid., p. 178.

25. [Vaos] Βάος, 'Η Αφροδίτη της Μήλου' [Aphrodite of Milos], p. 383.

26. Dumont d'Urville, 'Notice sur les galeries souterraines de l'île de Melos', pp. 157–58.

27. According to some accounts, the catacombs of Milos were discovered in 1844 by Ludwig Ross, a Danish-German archaeologist of Scottish descent; see [Belivanakis] Μπελιβανάκης, *Οι κατακόμβες της Μήλου* [*The catacombs of Milos*], p. 91. Ross was followed by the French archaeologist Charles-Marie Bayet in 1877 (see his 'La nécropole chrétienne de Milo') and by Georgios Lambakis in 1907. While d'Urville thought the catacombs might have had a role as a place of refuge during pirate attacks (and this may indeed have been the case), in 1927, the distinguished Greek Byzantinist

Georgios Soteriou speculated that their use might have ended as a result of just such an attack or perhaps because of an earthquake; see Σωτηρίου [Soteriou], Ἡ χριστιανικὴ κατακόμβη τῆς νήσου Μήλου' [The Christian catacombs of Milos island]; for a more recent survey, see Laskaris, *Monuments funéraires paléochrétiens (et byzantins) de Grèce*, pp. 429–59.

28. None of this embarrassing episode was recorded in d'Urville's published account. In 1842, Le Brun had access to d'Urville's (now-missing) private journal and included a brief reference to the incident in a footnote in his obituary; see Le Brun, op. cit., p. 19.

29. Gauttier au ministre de la marine, 9 octobre 1820, Campagnes, 1820, vol. 2, Station du Levant, gabarre la *Chevrette*, Gauttier-Duparc, capitaine de vaisseau, loc. cit., f. 277 recto.

30. Dumont d'Urville à Théodose-Cyriaque Prost, Toulon, 13 octobre 1820, in Marie, op. cit., p. 80.

31. Aicard, *La Vénus de Milo*, appendix iv, pp. 169–71.

6. PARIS & PLANS

1. During the *ancien régime*, the corvée system of compulsory labour had kept roads in relatively good repair, but this harsh unpaid imposition on the peasantry had been abolished during the Revolution. Under Napoleon, strategic frontier roads in the north and east had been maintained and, in the case of the Alps, even extended. However, well before the tide of empire turned, more than a third of the road system was already in serious disrepair: narrow-shouldered, pot-holed and mired. With Napoleon's defeats from 1812 onwards came a fiscal crisis and an even greater deterioration in the road network. Furthermore, many bridges were destroyed as the army retreated within France's borders. The bridge across the Rhône at Tournon, for example, was not rebuilt until 1823, and more than 45 per cent of roads were still officially 'un-maintained' in 1824; see Bertier de Sauvigny, *The Bourbon Restoration*, pp. 201–12.

2. Dumont d'Urville à Théodose-Cyriaque Prost, Toulon, 28 novembre 1828 [*sic* = 1820], in Marie, 'Lettres de Dumont d'Urville (1819–1825)', p. 82.

3. Adélie d'Urville, Toulon [*sic*] (corrected 'Paris' in blue pencil), 1? janvier 1821, à Louis-Charles Lefébure de Cerisy, Toulon, Papiers de Louis-Charles Lefébure de Cerisy: SHDDM, Toulon, 23S 710.

4. See Hillairet, *Dictionnaire historique des rues de Paris*, vol. ii, pp. 373–76. Around the corner from d'Urville's hotel was the narrow cour du commerce, which runs between the rue Saint-André-des-Arts and the rue de l'Ancienne Comédie. One of its buildings (now the Catalan Cultural Centre) embraces an original tower from the walls of Paris; another is where Marat produced his revolutionary newspaper *Ami du Peuple*, and yet another is the rear of the famous Café Procope, the oldest restaurant in Paris (founded in 1686).

5. Adèle d'Urville, Toulon [*sic*] (corrected 'Paris' in blue pencil), 1? janvier 1821, à Louis-Charles Lefébure de Cerisy, Toulon, loc. cit.

6. Ibid.

7. Still earlier, Antoine Dubois had served the republic as a military surgeon in Egypt, and even earlier he was the last professor of surgery appointed by Louis XVI; see Dupont, *Dictionnaire historique des médecins dans et hors de la médecine*, p. 203.

8. Le Brun, *Biographie du contre-amiral Dumont d'Urville*, p. 19.

9. Dumont d'Urville, Paris, 2 février 1821, à Louis-Charles Lefébure de Cerisy, Toulon, Papiers de Louis-Charles Lefébure de Cerisy, SHDDM, Toulon, 23S 693.

10. Le Brun, op. cit., p. 19.

11. The society had originally been founded on 28 December 1787 but disappeared in 1790 (according to Louis-Augustin Bosc d'Antic) because word spread that young naturalists who aspired to election to the Académie des sciences would harm their prospects by remaining members; see Gillispie, *Science and Polity in France and the End of the Old Regime*, pp. 192–93; see also Hahn, *The Anatomy of a Scientific Institution*, p. 112. On 28 December 1821, the *Société linnéenne de Paris* held a meeting to commemorate the centenary of the death of Pitton de Tournefort, which d'Urville attended; see Lacépède & Thébaut de Berneaud, 'Société linnéenne de Paris: Procès-verbal de la séance publique du 28 décembre 1821, jour anniversaire de la mort de Tournefort', p. 6.

12. Duris, *Linné et la France (1780–1850)*, p. 169.
13. One of the leading French Linnaeans of the previous generation, Jacques-Julien Houtou de Labillardière was conspicuously absent from the ranks of the resurrected Société linnéenne, despite the fact that his most important botanical works, including his pioneering general flora of Australia, the *Novæ Hollandiæ plantarum specimen* (1804–06, 2 vols), was organised on strict Linnaean principles. However, Labillardière's final major botanical work, his flora of New Caledonia, the *Sertum austro-caledonicum* (1824–25), would be characterised by an abandonment of the Linnaean system of classification in favour of the natural system first established by Antoine-Laurent de Jussieu in his *Genera plantarum* (1789); see Duyker, *Citizen Labillardière*.
14. Those present included the astronomers Arago, Cassini, Delambre and Lalande; the botanists Bosc, Desfontaines, Jussieu, Labillardière and Richard; the zoologists Cuvier, Duméril, Geoffroy Saint-Hillaire, Lamarck (also a famous botanist) and Latreille; the chemists Brongniart, Gay-Lussac and Vauquelin; the physicists Ampère, Biot and Fourier; the physiologist Pinel; and the hydrographers Rossel and Dupetit-Thouars.
15. Dumont d'Urville, Paris, 2 fevrier & 3 mars 1821, à Louis-Charles Lefébure de Cerisy, Toulon, loc. cit., 23S 693–4.
16. Nussac, *Les débuts d'un savant naturaliste*, pp. 25–43.
17. Dumont d'Urville, Paris, 17 juin 1821, à Louis-Charles Lefébure de Cerisy, Toulon, loc. cit., 23S 700.
18. Dumont d'Urville, Paris, 3 mars 1821, à Louis-Charles Lefébure de Cerisy, Toulon, loc. cit., 23S 694.
19. Dumont d'Urville, 'Seconde relation de la campagne hydrographique de la gabare du roi la Chevrette', p. 179, on which it is stated: 'Ce mémoire a été lu à l'Académie royale des sciences, le 22 [*sic*] janvier 1821.'
20. Aicard, *La Vénus de Milo*, appendix iv, pp. 169–71.
21. The Café Procope had been the meeting place of Voltaire, Rousseau, Diderot and Franklin prior to the Revolution, and during the Revolution it was frequented by Robespierre, Danton, Jefferson and many other famous figures.
22. Curtis, *Disarmed*, p. 20.
23. For a comparison of the parts of the manuscript and the published text dealing with the Venus, see Aicard, op. cit., appendix v, pp. 173–81.
24. There is no doubt that Matterer was deeply moved by d'Urville's words, regardless of the fact that they were not published. He annotated d'Urville's manuscript with the words 'The last lines of this interesting journal flatter my heart and honour me'; see Aicard, op. cit., appendix vi, p. 185.
25. Curtis, op. cit., p. 73.
26. Dumont d'Urville, Paris, 3 mars 1821, à Louis-Charles Lefébure de Cerisy, Toulon, loc. cit., 23S 694.
27. Dumont d'Urville à Théodose-Cyriaque Prost, Toulon, 8 avril 1821, in Marie, op. cit., p. 84.
28. Dumont d'Urville, Paris, 25 août 1821, à Louis-Charles Lefébure de Cerisy, Toulon, loc. cit., 23S 701.
29. Dumont d'Urville, Paris, 31 août 1821, au président de l'Académie des sciences, Belles lettres de Caen, Bibliothèque de Caen, ms in-fol. 178 / 1 (f. 208).
30. Dumont d'Urville, Paris, 2 février 1821, à Louis-Charles Lefébure de Cerisy, Toulon, loc. cit., 23S 693.
31. Le Brun, op. cit., p. 19.
32. Dumont d'Urville, Paris, 25 août 1821, à Louis-Charles Lefébure de Cerisy, Toulon, loc. cit., 23S 701.
33. Inventaire des effets mobiliers dressé par Maître Vallavieille, notaire à Toulon, le 30 juillet 1842 … dépendant des successions réunies de feu M. Dumont D'Urville, de son épouse et de son fils décédés ensemble le 8 mai 1842 domicilé à Paris, Office notarial Boyer, Toulon.
34. Visconti, E.Q., *Iconographie ancienne, ou recueil des portraits authentiques des empereurs, rois et hommes illustres de l'antiquité par le chevalier E.Q. Visconti puis le chevalier A. Mongez; planches dessinées et gravées sous la direction de Claude Laguiche*, 7 vols, P. Didot l'aîné, Paris, 1808–26.
35. Dumont d'Urville à Théodose-Cyriaque Prost, Toulon, 6 mai 1821, in Marie, op. cit., p. 84.
36. Dumont d'Urville, Paris, 13 mai 1821, à Louis-Charles Lefébure de Cerisy, Toulon, loc. cit., 23S 698.
37. Nomination de Dumont d'Urville dans l'ordre royal de la Légion d'honneur, 8 juin 1821, in dossier personnel, Dumont d'Urville, SHDDM, Vincennes, CC[7] Alpha 772, pièce 19.

38. Quoted by Le Brun, op. cit., pp. 17–18; this same text was quoted by Vergniol and referred to as an extract from a letter from d'Urville to Le Brun. Subsequent biographers slavishly followed suit. Le Brun, however, did not refer to it as a quotation from a letter; rather he wrote that it was from d'Urville's 'Confessions', which suggests that Le Brun took it from the now-missing manuscript of d'Urville's autobiographical memoir (ca.1830).

39. Dumont d'Urville, Paris, 6 septembre 1821, à Louis-Charles Lefébure de Cerisy, Toulon, loc. cit., 23S 702; Prosper-Abbeville Tillette de Clermont and d'Urville would both build substantial private herbaria and botanical libraries; for his earlier military career, see Boucher de Perthes, 'M. Tillette de Clermont-Tonnerre'.

40. Le Brun, op. cit., p. 20.

41. Vergniol, *Dumont d'Urville*, p. 77.

42. Adèle d'Urville, 18 octobre 1821, à Louis-Charles Lefébure de Cerisy, Toulon, Papiers de Louis-Charles Lefébure de Cerisy, loc. cit., 23S 712.

43. Ibid.

44. Ibid.

45. Ibid.

46. Dumont d'Urville, ms journal de la *Coquille*, Mairie de Condé-sur-Noireau, ms 11, p. 63.

47. Duperrey was born in Paris to a Parisian family, so he probably spent his leave there before starting work at the Dépôt. Although Duperrey's seniority in rank was of only a few months' standing, he was nearly four and a half years older than d'Urville, had seen combat, had significant survey experience in the Mediterranean and had participated in a major voyage of circumnavigation and exploration, albeit one that had ended in shipwreck; dossier personnel, Duperrey, Louis Isidore, SHDDM, Vincennes, CC[7] Alpha 777.

48. Dumont d'Urville, ms journal de la *Coquille*, loc. cit., ms 11, p. 63.

49. Dumont d'Urville, Paris, 25 août 1821, à Louis-Charles Lefébure de Cerisy, Toulon, loc. cit., 23S 701.

50. Dumont d'Urville, ms journal de la *Coquille*, loc. cit., p. 64.

51. Ibid.

52. Duperrey, *Voyage autour du monde*, 'Partie Historique', pp. 4–5.

53. See Bertier de Sauvigny, op. cit., pp. 168–81.

54. 'Marine–Colonies', *Le moniteur universel*, jeudi, 9 mai 1822, p. 698.

55. Duchêne, A., *La politique coloniale de la France*.

56. The minister was also a cousin of d'Urville's botanist friend Prosper-Abbeville Tillette de Clermont-Tonnerre.

57. Dumont d'Urville, ms journal de la *Coquille*, loc. cit, p. 66.

58. Mémoire pour M. Duperrey commandant la corvette la *Coquille*, SHDDM, Vincennes, BB[4] 1000, f. 38.

59. Ibid., ff. 57–58.

60. Roche, *Dictionnaire des bâtiments de la flotte de guerre française*, vol. i, p. 128; Boudriot, 'L'Astrolabe', p. 45.

61. See also Javault, Joubert, & Lagarlière, *L'Astrolabe (ex: la Coquille) corvette de 380 tonneaux du lieutenant de Vaisseau Duperrey.*

62. Jacquinot, Charles-Hector, SHDDM, Vincennes, CC[7] 2 moderne, carton 3, dossier 11.

63. Dossier personnel, Lottin, Victor-Charles, SHDDM, Vincennes, CC[7] Alpha 1610; see also Duyker, 'Lottin, Victor-Charles (1795–1858)'.

64. Dossier personnel, Bérard, Auguste, SHDDM, Vincennes, CC[7] Alpha 164.

65. Dossier personnel, Deblois de la Calande, Théodore-Julien, SHDDM, Vincennes, CC[7] Alpha 622.

66. Taillemite, *Dictionnaire des marins français*, p. 37.

67. Dossier personnel, Lejeune, François-Louis dit Jules, SHDDM, Vincennes, CC[7] Alpha 1503.

68. See 'Le Jeune', in Sarrut & Saint-Edme, *Biographie des hommes du jour*, vol. iv, part 2, p. 286.

69. In Dorinda Outram's *The Letters of Georges Cuvier*, there is no clue to this man's identity, yet Cuvier mentioned numerous protégés in his correspondence, before and after the planning for the *Coquille* voyage. Interestingly, Cuvier did eventually correspond with both René-Primevère Lesson

and Prosper Garnot. The latter eventually sent him a copy of the zoological results of the *Coquille* expedition.

70. Dumont d'Urville, ms journal de la *Coquille*, loc. cit., p. 68.
71. For this expedition, see Duyker & Duyker (ed. & trans), *Bruny d'Entrecasteaux: Voyage to Australia and the Pacific 1791—1793*.
72. Dossier personnel, Lesson, René Primevère SHDDM, Vincennes, CC^7 Alpha 1565.
73. Dossier personnel, Garnot, Prosper SHDDM, Vincennes, CC^7 Alpha 967.
74. Dossier personnel, Lesage, Charles-Félix-Victor SHDDM, Vincennes, CC^7 Alpha 1557.
75. Dumont d'Urville, ms journal de la *Coquille*, loc. cit., p. 68.
76. Ibid.

7. LA COQUILLE

1. Dumont d'Urville, ms journal de la *Coquille*, Mairie de Condé-sur-Noireau, ms 11, p. 69. Soon after Cerisy would travel to England to study naval architecture; he would later achieve fame for his part in rebuilding the Egyptian navy in the wake of its destruction at the Battle of Navarino; see 'Cerisy, Louis-Charles Lefébure de', in Goldschmidt, *Biographical Dictionary of Modern Egypt*, p. 41.
2. Duperrey, *Voyage autour du monde*, 'Partie Historique', pp. 9–10.
3. See 'Procès-verbal touchant la question qui a été faite à bord de la corvette de Sa M[ajesté]. la Coquille des viandes préparées & des tablettes à bouillon d'Appert', 30 mars 1823, Voyage de la *Coquille*, Duperrey (1822–1825), SHDDM, Vincennes, BB^4 1000.
4. Duperrey, op. cit., 'Partie Historique', pp. 10–12.
5. These included a Gambey compass, two inclination compasses (for studying magnetic variation and intensity), Borda repeating circles, Berthoud and Bréguet marine chronometers, an astronomical and two prismatic telescopes, four marine barometers, two hygrometers, nine thermometers, a 20-metre measuring chain, copies of the *Connaissance des temps* (the official French astronomical annual), solar and lunar tables, Arrowsmith's map of the Pacific, James Horsburgh's *Directions for Sailing to and from the East Indies, China, New Holland, Cape of Good Hope, Brazil and Interjacent Ports*; see 'État des Instrumen[t]s, livres et cartes détaché, remis à M. Duperrey, commandant la Coquille …', Voyage de la *Coquille*, Duperrey (1822–1825), SHDDM, Vincennes, BB^4 1000; see also Duperrey, op. cit., 'Partie Historique', p. 8.
6. Dumont d'Urville, ms journal de la *Coquille*, loc. cit., mercredi, 31 décembre 1823, pp. 68–69.
7. Rolland, in Rivière & Einam (eds), *Any Port in a Storm*, p. 43.
8. Ibid; the French army did ultimately invade Spain and ushered in a period of violent and cruel reaction.
9. Dumont d'Urville, *Voyage pittoresque autour du monde*, vol. i, p. 25.
10. Lesson, *Voyage autour du monde*, vol. i, p. 9.
11. Dumont d'Urville, *Voyage pittoresque autour du monde*, vol. i, p. 34.
12. Bory de St-Vincent, in Duperrey, op. cit., 'Botanique: Cryptogamie', p. 122.
13. Dumont d'Urville, *Voyage pittoresque autour du monde*, vol. i, p. 25.
14. Péron, *Voyage de découvertes aux Terres Australes*, vol. i, p. 41.
15. Dumont d'Urville, *Voyage pittoresque autour du monde*, vol. i, p. 26.
16. Ibid.
17. Duperrey, op. cit., 'Partie Historique', p. 24.
18. See Bertier de Sauvigny, *The Bourbon Restoration*, p. 197.
19. Quoted by Bertier de Sauvigny, ibid., p. 269.
20. Duperrey, op. cit., 'Partie Historique', p. 27.
21. Lesson, op. cit., vol. i, p. 17.
22. He contrasted this lush flora with that of the Falklands; see Dumont d'Urville, 'Flore des Malouines', p. 573.
23. For an account of the difficult circumstances under which this species of *Tillandsia* was first collected in late 1768, see Duyker, *Nature's Argonaut*, pp. 115–21.
24. Brongniart in Duperrey, op. cit., 'Botanique: Phanérogamie', pp. 186–87.

25. Ibid., pp. 196–97

26. At Santa Catarina, aside from numerous ferns and lycopodes, d'Urville collected the type specimens of *Pleurostachys urvillii* (named in his honour by Brongniart) and *Abildgaardia polycephala*, as well as a syntype of *Becquerelia cymosa*, all three belonging to the Cyperaceae.

27. Guérin-Méneville, in Duperrey, op. cit., 'Zoologie', vol. ii, part ii, 1ère division: 'Crustacés, Arachnides et Insectes', p. 51.

28. Dumont d'Urville, 'Flore des Malouines', p. 581.

29. Dumont d'Urville, *Voyage pittoresque autour du monde*, vol. ii, p. 545.

30. Rolland, in Rivière & Einam (eds), op. cit., p. 49.

31. Dumont d'Urville, *Voyage pittoresque autour du monde*, vol. ii, p. 545.

32. Dumont d'Urville, ms journal de la *Coquille*, loc. cit., 1 décembre 1823, p. 70.

33. Lesson, *Notice historique sur l'amiral Dumont d'Urville*, pp. 55–56.

34. Dumont d'Urville, 'Flore des Malouines', pp. 573–74.

35. See Godley, 'Botany of the southern zone', p. 155; see also Wright, 'Flora of the Falkland Islands'.

36. Lesson, op. cit., vol. i, p. 17.

37. Dumont d'Urville, *Voyage pittoresque autour du monde*, vol. ii, p. 545.

38. Darwin, *The Voyage of the* Beagle, p. 188.

39. On the way, d'Urville collected the type specimen of the fern *Aspidium mohrioides*, later described by Bory de Saint-Vincent; see Dumont d'Urville, 'Flore des Malouines', p. 583.

40. Dumont d'Urville, *Voyage pittoresque autour du monde*, vol. ii, p. 545.

41. Dumont d'Urville, 'Flore des Malouines', p. 579.

42. D'Urville does not provide a bibliography in his article, but from the names of several of the species he lists, it is clear that he consulted Lamarck's *Encyclopédie méthodique: Botanique* and Forster's 'Fasciculus plantarum magellanicarum . . .'.

43. Ibid., p. 577.

44. Ibid.

45. For this voyage, see Duyker (ed.), *Mirror of the Australian Navigation by Jacob Le Maire*.

46. Ibid., p. 541.

47. Duperrey, op. cit., 'Partie Historique', p. 127.

48. Dumont d'Urville, ms journal de la *Coquille*, loc. cit., 1 décembre 1823, p. 69.

49. Ibid., p. 70.

50. Ibid., p. 71.

8. THE PACIFIC

1. Lesson, *Voyage autour du monde*, vol. i, p. 91.

2. Ibid., p. 93.

3. Ibid.

4. Ibid., pp. 98–99.

5. Duperrey, *Voyage autour du monde*, 'Partie Historique', p. 165.

6. Lesson, op. cit., vol. i, p. 113.

7. Duperrey, op. cit., pp. 166–68.

8. Brongniart, in Duperrey, op. cit., 'Botanique: Phanérogamie', pp. 14–15.

9. Bory de Saint-Vincent, in Duperrey, op. cit., 'Botanique: Cryptogamie', p. 273.

10. The other five species were *Gigartina contorta*, *Gelidium filicinum*, *Sphaerococcus chauvinii* (*Chondracanthus chauvinii*), *Halymenia variegata* (*Callophyllis variegata*), and *Ulva nematoidea*; see Bory de Saint-Vincent, in Duperrey, op. cit., 'Botanique: Cryptogamie', pp. 153, 162–63, 166–67, 179–80, 190; for *Polyides durvillei* (*Ahnfeltiopsis durvillei*), see Bory de Saint-Vincent, op. cit., p. 138; and *Dawsonia durvillaei* (*Hymenena durvillaei*), see Bory de Saint-Vincent, op. cit., pp. 183–84.

11. Guérin-Méneville, in Duperrey, op. cit., 'Zoologie', vol. ii, part ii, 1ère division, 'Crustacés, Arachnides et Insectes', p. 50.

12. Duperrey, op. cit., p. 131; Duperrey does not mention the name of the ship, but Lesson, op. cit.,

vol. i, p. 105, does. For more about Choyce, who had earlier been a prisoner of war in France, see Cameron, *The Log of a Jack Tar*.

13. Dumont d'Urville, 'Note sur les collections et les observations recueillies par M. J. D'Urville', p. 67.

14. Lesson, op. cit., vol. i, pp. 154–55.

15. Brongniart, in Duperrey, op. cit., 'Botanique: Phanérogamie', pp. 17–18, 20–21, 48–49, 51, 138–39.

16. Where the magnetic field is parallel to the earth's surface and where a balanced magnetic needle stabilises horizontally without a dip; it should not be confused with the more familiar equator equidistant from the poles.

17. Lesson, op. cit., vol. i, p. 206.

18. André-Paul Gabert had earlier served as Freycinet's secretary during the voyage of the *Uranie*; see SHDDM, Vincennes, CC7 Alpha 937.

19. Dumont d'Urville, ms journal de la *Coquille*, Mairie de Condé-sur-Noireau, ms 11, 31 décembre 1823, p. 79; see also Duyker, 'Gabert, André-Paul (1797–1855)'.

20. Stone, 'Age of the Chira Group, Northwestern Peru'.

21. Gabert, in Lesson, op. cit., vol. i, pp. 172–84.

22. Dumont d'Urville, ms journal de la *Coquille*, loc. cit., 31 décembre 1823, p. 79.

23. Gabert, in Lesson, op. cit., vol. i, p. 198.

24. Ibid., p. 184.

25. See Procès-verbal touchant la question qui a été faite à bord de la corvette de Sa M[ajésté]. la *Coquille* des viandes préparées & des tablettes à bouillon d'Appert, 30 mars 1823, Voyage de la *Coquille*, Duperrey, SHDDM, Vincennes, BB^4 1000.

26. Rolland, in Rivière & Einam (eds), *Any Port in a Storm*, pp. 60–63; Lesson, op. cit., vol. i, pp. 225–28.

27. Dumont d'Urville, *Voyage pittoresque autour du monde*, vol. i, p. 528.

28. Lesson, op. cit., vol. i, p. 310.

29. Lesson misspelt the names of both these captains: 'Debs' instead of 'Dibbs' and 'Charton' instead of 'Charlton'. The *Endeavour* had previously been owned by the Port Jackson merchant Henry Kable, but at the time of the *Coquille*'s visit, she was owned by the chiefs (Lesson says 'King') of Raiatea. In July 1823, she was chartered by the missionary John Williams to explore the southern Cook Islands, and Dibbs 'discovered' Mitiaro and Mauke during this expedition. For Charlton, later a controversial British consul in Hawaii, see MacAllan, 'Richard Charlton: A reassessment'.

30. Wilson, W., et al. *A Missionary Voyage to the Southern Pacific Ocean: Performed in the years 1796, 1797, 1798 in the Ship* Duff, *Commanded by Captain James Wilson …*, Printed by S. Gosnell for T. Chapman, London, 1799.

31. Dumont d'Urville, *Voyage pittoresque autour du monde*, vol. i, p. 528.

32. Lesson, op. cit., vol. i, pp. 264.

33. Bouge, 'Première législation tahitienne: Le Code Pomare de 1819'.

34. Chateaubriand, *Travels in America and Italy*, p. 53.

35. Rolland, op. cit., p. 71.

36. For more on this custom, see Finney, 'Notes on bond-friendship in Tahiti'.

37. Lesson, op. cit., vol. i, pp. 269–70.

38. Ibid., pp. 288–89.

39. Dumont d'Urville, *Voyage pittoresque autour du monde*, vol. i, p. 527.

40. Lesson, op. cit., vol. i, pp. 275–79.

41. Dumont d'Urville, *Voyage pittoresque autour du monde*, vol. i, pp. 530–31.

42. Ibid., p. 531.

43. Guérin-Méneville, in Duperrey, op. cit., 'Zoologie', vol. ii, part ii, 1ère division, 'Crustacés, Arachnides et Insectes', p. 9.

44. For the published description, see Brongniart, op. cit., pp. 132–34.

45. Lesson, op. cit., vol. i, p. 322.

46. Lesson also gave Charles Wilson's wife medical treatment; see Lesson, op. cit., vol. i, p. 264.

47. According to Lesson, participation in the religious services of the missionaries was from 'pure conviction' (*Voyage autour du monde*, vol. i, p. 444), a comment that was perhaps the foundation

for John Dunmore's assertion that Duperrey was a Protestant (*From Venus to Antarctica*, p. 38). However, the reformed church in France has no record of him or his family belonging to any of their congregations. Furthermore, he was a Chevalier de Saint-Louis, an order that required an oath (a copy of which was preserved in his service dossier) that he was Catholic and that he would live and die in the Catholic faith; see dossier personnel, Duperrey, Louis-Isidore, SHDDM, Vincennes, CC[7] Alpha 777.

48. Lesson, op. cit., vol. i, p. 288.
49. Ibid., p. 302. Lesson, when concluding his account of this incident, declared that d'Urville was 'characterised by brusqueness (to use a polite term) too long standing for this not to be inherent in his makeup'.
50. Dumont d'Urville, ms journal de la *Coquille*, loc. cit., 31 décembre 1823, pp. 76–77.
51. Ibid., p. 77.
52. Although John Orsmond's chapel was constructed in 1822, Henry Nott had preached on the island in 1807, and the two principal chiefs of Bora Bora, Mai and Tefaaroa, had converted to Protestant Christianity in 1813.
53. Lesson, op. cit., vol. i, p. 458.
54. Duperrey, op. cit., 'Hydrographique, Atlas', p. 12.
55. Duperrey, 'Sur les opérations géographiques faites dans … la *Coquille*', p. 196.
56. Brongniart, in Duperrey, op. cit., 'Botanique: Phanérogamie', pp. 93–94, 179–80, 199–200.
57. Lesson, op. cit., vol. i, p. 456.
58. See Wallis (ed.), *Carteret's Voyage Round the World 1766–1769*, vol. i, p. 179, footnote 3.
59. Bougainville, *Voyage autour du monde*, pp. 210–13.
60. Rolland, op. cit., pp. 86–89.
61. Lesson, op. cit., vol. ii, pp. 23–24.
62. Bory de Saint-Vincent, in Duperrey, op. cit., 'Botanique: Cryptogamie', pp. 123–24 & 180–81.
63. Duperrey, 'Sur les opérations géographiques faites dans … la *Coquille*', pp. 196–98.
64. D'Urville calls him 'Williams' in the extract from his journal published in his *Voyage pittoresque autour du monde* (vol. ii, pp. 200–01) but refers to the 'aid of the intelligent and indefatigable Williams [*sic*] Taylor' at Offak Bay in his manuscript journal; see Dumont d'Urville, ms journal de la *Coquille*, loc. cit., 31 décembre 1823, p. 78. D'Urville refers to him as 'an intelligent American' who had 'been living in these islands for several years and appeared to speak their language fluently', in note 26, canto iii, of 'Les Zélandais ou histoire australienne', SHDDM, Vincennes, Fonds Privés, 7 GG2, carton 1.
65. Dumont d'Urville, *Voyage pittoresque autour du monde*, vol. ii, pp. 200–01.
66. Lesson, op. cit., vol. ii, p. 82–83.
67. Dumont d'Urville, *Voyage pittoresque autour du monde*, vol. ii, p. 201.
68. Loureiro, *Flora cochinchinensis*, vol. 1, pp. 606–07.
69. By George Claridge Druce; see 'Nomenclatural notes; chiefly African and Australian', p. 637.
70. Rolland, op. cit., p. 87.
71. Dumont d'Urville, *Voyage pittoresque autour du monde*, vol. ii, p. 202.
72. Ibid.
73. The original description was published under the name *Oxyanthera micrantha* by Brongniart, in Duperrey, op. cit., 'Botanique: Phanérogamie', pp. 198–99. The taxonomy was revised by the Dutch botanist Johannes Jacobus Smith (1867–1947) in 1905.
74. The original description was published under the name *Polypodium brongniartii* by Bory de Saint-Vincent, in Duperrey, op. cit., 'Botanique: Cryptogamie', pp. 263–64. The revision was by Richard Eric Holttum in the *Kew Bulletin*, vol. 29, 1974, p. 350.
75. Duperrey, 'Sur les opérations géographiques …de la corvette de S. M. la *Coquille*', p. 202.
76. Lesson, op. cit., vol. ii, p. 158.
77. Dumont d'Urville, *Voyage de la corvette l'*Astrolabe, 'Histoire du voyage', vol. iv, p. 624.
78. *Eriachne gracilis, Ischaemum digitatum* and *Pogonatherum contortum*; see Brongniart, in Duperrey,

op. cit., 'Botanique: Phanérogamie', pp. 25, 70–72, 90–91.

79. Duperrey, 'Sur les opérations géographiques …de la corvette de S. M. la *Coquille*', p. 202.

80. Rolland, op. cit., p. 108–09.

81. Ibid.

82. Ibid.

83. Dumont d'Urville, ms journal de la *Coquille*, loc. cit., 25 octobre 1823, p. 2.

84. Ibid., 24 Octobre 1823, p. 1.

85. See Brongniart, in Duperrey, op. cit., Botanique: Phanérogamie', pp. 50–51.

86. [Xiè] 谢宗, et al., 汉拉英对照中药材正名词典[Chinese, Latin, English/Chinese herbal medicines dictionary], p. 925; for example, the National Library of Australia holds a rare copy of the materia medica of Wāng Áng 汪昂 (born 1615), 增訂本草備要 [Herbal preparations up to date], published in Kyoto in 1728, which contains a woodblock illustration of this species.

87. Stuart & Smith, *Chinese Materia Medica: Vegetable kingdom*, p. 247.

88. Dumont d'Urville, ms journal de la *Coquille*, loc. cit., 24 Octobre 1823, p. 1.

89. Published as *Platanthera rumphii* in Brongniart, in Duperrey, op. cit., Botanique: Phanérogamie', pp. 194–95.

90. For Georg Eberhard Rumphius (Rumpf), see Boxer, *The Dutch Seaborne Empire 1600–1800*, pp. 202–03, and Heniger, 'Dutch Contributions to the Study of Exotic Natural History in the Seventeenth and Eighteenth Centuries'.

91. Rumphius, *Herbarium amboinense* , vol. vi, p. 118 & tabula 54.

92. 'cette promesse dignement accompli', Lesson, op. cit., vol. ii, p. 181.

93. Blosseville, journal, 4–28 octobre 1823, cited by Dunmore, *French Explorers in the Pacific*, vol. ii, p. 137.

94. Only 'John Smith' and 'William Taylor' remained until the following year, according to the Rôle d'equipage, La *Coquille*, SHDDM, Toulon, 2E6 138.

95. Dumont d'Urville, ms journal de la *Coquille*, loc. cit., 28 octobre 1823, p. 7.

96. Roll d'equipage, La *Coquille*, loc. cit.

97. Dumont d'Urville, ms journal de la *Coquille*, loc. cit., 28 octobre 1823, p. 7.

98. Ibid., p. 72.

99. Ibid.

100. Lesson, op. cit., vol. ii, p. 226.

101. Dumont d'Urville, ms journal de la *Coquille*, loc. cit., 1 décembre 1823, p. 25.

102. Mémoire pour M. Duperrey commandant la corvette La *Coquille*, SHDDM, Vincennes, BB[4] 1000, ff. 57–58.

103. Duperrey au ministre de la marine et des colonies, Port Jackson, SHDDM, Vincennes, BB[4] 1000, 15 février 1824.

104. Marchant, *France Australe*, p. 241.

105. Ibid.

106. Dumont d'Urville, ms journal de la *Coquille*, loc. cit., 1 décembre 1823, p. 39.

107. Ibid., 31 décembre 1823, p. 73.

108. Ibid., p. 75.

109. The evidence, however, does not support Lesage's suffering a 'nervous breakdown' as asserted by John Dunmore; see *French Explorers in the Pacific*, vol. ii, p. 139.

110. Dumont d'Urville, ms journal de la *Coquille*, loc. cit., 31 décembre 1823, p. 75.

111. Ibid.

112. Ibid., p. 76.

113. Dossier personnel, Lesage, Charles-Félix-Victor, SHDDM, Vincennes, CC[7] Alpha 1557.

114. Personal communication, Madame Yvonne Bouvier-Graux, conservatrice de la Médiathèque de Rochefort, 29 May 2009; Lesage's death is not recorded in his service dossier; however, René Lesson refers to it in Rochefort but does not give a date in his *Voyage autour du monde*, vol. ii, p. 270.

115. Dumont d'Urville, ms journal de la *Coquille*, loc. cit., 5 janvier 1824, p. 88.

9. NEW SOUTH WALES

1. Barnard, 'Piper, John (1773–1851)'.
2. Dumont d'Urville, ms journal de la *Coquille*, Mairie de Condé-sur-Noireau, ms 11, samedi, 17 janvier 1824, p. 96.
3. Rolland, in Rivière & Einam (eds), *Any Port in a Storm*, pp. 120–21.
4. Dumont d'Urville, ms journal de la *Coquille*, loc. cit., 22 janvier 1824, p. 104.
5. 'As for Sydney, even Europeans cannot help but admire the imposing spectacle and the magnificent view which the sight of the nascent city already presents. One day it will probably play an important role among the most famous ports and perhaps within a century Australasia will be peopled by a race similar to the Americans of the United States'; see Dumont d'Urville, footnote 42, canto ii, 'Les Zélandais ou histoire australienne', SHDDM, Vincennes, Fonds Privés, 7 GG² [Legge translation, *The New Zealanders: A Story of Austral lands*, p. 296–97].
6. Dumont d'Urville, ms journal de la *Coquille*, loc. cit., 19 janvier 1824, p. 92.
7. See, for example, Yarwood, *Samuel Marsden*.
8. Dumont d'Urville, ms journal de la *Coquille*, loc. cit., 19 janvier 1824, pp. 93–94.
9. See the many notes referring to Marsden in the three cantos of Dumont d'Urville's manuscript 'Les Zélandais ou histoire australienne', SHDDM, Vincennes, Fonds Privés, 7 GG², carton 1.
10. Brisbane, *Reminiscences of General Sir Thomas Makdougall Brisbane*, chapters vi & vii.
11. Ibid., p. 67.
12. See note 53 for canto ii of Dumont d'Urville's manuscript 'Les Zélandais ou histoire australienne', loc. cit. [Legge, trans., op. cit., p. 300]. D'Urville soon became aware that Rümker, despite his initial 'important services', had completely renounced the 'cult of Urania' for the 'cult of Ceres' and was now devoting himself to agriculture. Rümker was also assisted by the Scottish-born James Dunlop. All that now remains of Brisbane's observatory are the stone supports for his transit telescope. A commemorative marker was erected by astronomer John Tebbut in 1880. For an account of Governor Brisbane's astronomical work, including a plan and elevations of his observatory, see Bhathal & White, *Under the Southern Cross*, pp. 17–21.
13. See 'Angleterre', *Le moniteur universel*, no. 154, published lundi, 5 [*sic* = 3] Juin 1822, p. 792.
14. Mémoire pour M. Duperrey commandant la corvette La *Coquille*, SHDDM, Vincennes, BB⁴ 1000, f. 37.
15. Duperrey, 'Sur les opérations géographiques … de la corvette de S. M. la *Coquille*', pp. 204–06.
16. Mémoire pour M. Duperrey commandant la corvette La *Coquille*', loc. cit., f. 37.
17. Duperrey, op. cit., p. 204.
18. Dumont d'Urville, ms journal de la *Coquille*, loc. cit., 20 mars 1824, p. 195.
19. Ibid., 19 janvier 1824, pp. 93–94.
20. Dumont d'Urville, *Voyage pittoresque autour du monde*, vol. ii, p. 324.
21. Ibid.
22. See note 50 for canto ii of Dumont d'Urville's manuscript 'Les Zélandais ou histoire australienne', loc. cit.
23. See Duyker, *Nature's Argonaut*, ch. 14.
24. See Duyker, *Père Receveur*.
25. Lesson, *Voyage autour du monde*, vol. ii, pp. 266–67.
26. Dumont d'Urville, ms journal de la *Coquille*, loc. cit., 22–25 janvier 1824, pp. 101, 104, 107–10.
27. Ibid., 28 janvier 1824, p. 115. The *Sydney Gazette* contains an advertisement on 29 January 1824 of the intended departure of the *Castle Forbes* for the Isle of France (Mauritius) and then London on or about the 10th or 15th of the following month (February).
28. Ibid., 29 janvier, p. 122.
29. See note 45 for canto ii of Dumont d'Urville's manuscript 'Les Zélandais ou histoire australienne', loc. cit.
30. Dumont d'Urville, *Voyage pittoresque autour du monde*, vol. ii, p. 290.
31. Dumont d'Urville, ms journal de la *Coquille*, loc. cit., 29 janvier 1824, p. 223.
32. See Duyker, *François Péron*, pp. 143–44.

33. [René-Primevère] Lesson, Voyage de *Coquille*, journal, 29 janvier 1824, Hélouis transcript, Mitchell Library, State Library of New South Wales, B1298 [Havard & Havard, trans. 'Some early French visitors to the Blue Mountains and Bathurst', p. 262].

34. Dumont d'Urville, ms journal de la *Coquille*, loc. cit., 18 février 1824, p. 151.

35. For a detailed account, see McMinn, *Allan Cunningham*, chapters 1–3.

36. McMinn, op. cit., chapter 4.

37. Dumont d'Urville, ms journal de la *Coquille*, loc. cit., 29 janvier 1824, p. 122; 23 février 1824, pp. 156–59.

38. Lesson, Voyage de *Coquille*, journal, 29 janvier 1824 [Havard & Havard trans., p. 264].

39. Dumont d'Urville, ms journal de La *Coquille*, loc. cit., 29 janvier 1824, p. 123.

40. Lee, *Early Explorers in Australia: From the Log-books and Journals, including the Diary of Allan Cunningham* ... , p. 516.

41. Perry, 'Cunningham, Allan (1791–1839)'.

42. McMinn, *Allan Cunningham*, p. 61.

43. Ibid., p. 116; McMinn, however, incorrectly states that d'Urville's visit spanned the years 1823–24.

44. Dumont d'Urville, ms journal de la *Coquille*, loc. cit., 16 février 1824, p. 149; 18 février 1824, p. 151; 23 février 1824, p. 155.

45. Brongniart, in Duperrey, op. cit., 'Botanique: Phanérogamie', pp. 183–84.

46. Boisduval, 'Faune entomologique de l'Océan Pacifique', in Dumont d'Urville, *Voyage de la corvette l'Astrolabe*, quatrième division, 'Entomologie', première partie: Lépidoptères, p. 31.

47. *Panagaeus australis* (*Craspedophorus australis*) was first published by Pierre Dejean; he attributed his specimen to the collection of d'Urville's friend Pierre Latreille; see Dejean, *Species général des Coléoptères de la collection de M. le comte Dejean*, vol. v, pp. 601–02. Significantly, Boisduval was the curator of Dejean's collection. For Boisduval's reference to Cunningham, see Boisduval, op. cit., deuxième partie, Coléoptères, pp. 29–30.

48. Boisduval, op. cit., deuxième partie, Coléoptères, pp. 32–33 & 34–35.

49. Dumont d'Urville, ms journal de la *Coquille* journal, loc. cit., 29 janvier 1824, p. 123.

50. Lesson, Voyage de *Coquille*, journal, 29 janvier 1824 [Havard & Havard trans., p. 262].

51. Dean was transported in 1799; see Anon., 'Obituary of William Dean', *Sydney Morning Herald*, 11 November 1847.

52. Lesson, Voyage de *Coquille*, journal, 30 janvier 1824 [Havard & Havard trans., p. 265].

53. Dumont d'Urville, ms journal de la *Coquille*, loc. cit., 30 janvier 1824, p. 124.

54. Lesson, 'Observations générales d'histoire naturelle', p. 244.

55. Dumont d'Urville, ms journal de la *Coquille*, loc. cit., 30 janvier 1824, p. 125.

56. Eldershaw, 'Murdoch, Peter (1795–1871)'.

57. Dumont d'Urville, ms journal de la *Coquille*, loc. cit., 30 janvier 1824, p. 125.

58. Ibid., 31 janvier 1824, p. 126.

59. Ibid.

60. Dumont d'Urville, *Voyage pittoresque autour du monde*, vol. ii, p. 288.

61. Dumont d'Urville, ms *Coquille* journal, loc. cit., 31 janvier 1824, p. 126.

62. Dumont d'Urville, *Voyage pittoresque autour du monde*, vol. ii, p. 324.

63. Lesson, *Voyage autour du monde*, vol. ii, pp. 256–57.

64. Blosseville, 'Projet d'une colonie pénale sur la côte S. O. de la Nouvelle-Hollande', Bibliothèque nationale de France, NAF 6785.

65. Forster, C. *France and Botany Bay*, p. 72.

66. Dumont d'Urville, *Voyage de la corvette l'Astrolabe*, 'Histoire du voyage', vol. i, chap. ix, 1830, pp. 211–76; his subsequent chapters on the present state of New South Wales and on the indigenous inhabitants are also noteworthy.

67. Barker, *A History of Bathurst*, vol. i, p. 22.

68. Lesson, Voyage de *Coquille*, journal, 30 janvier 1824 [Havard & Havard trans., p. 269].

69. Ibid., 31 janvier 1824 [Havard & Havard trans., p. 270].

70. Dumont d'Urville, ms journal de la *Coquille*, loc. cit., 31 janvier 1824, p. 127.

71. Ibid., p. 272.
72. 'Campbell's Cataract' was the name given to the falls by Lachlan Macquarie in honour of his secretary.
73. Lesson, Voyage de *Coquille*, journal, 1 février 1824 [Havard & Havard trans., p. 273].
74. Water collects in many small depressions on the weathered sandstone plateau, and one can still see numerous Aboriginal sharpening grooves where stone tools were fashioned with the aid of water on Kings Tableland.
75. Cunningham found this same species in a 'peaty bog on the Cox's River' during John Oxley's expedition.
76. Dumont d'Urville, ms journal de la *Coquille*, loc. cit., 1 février 1824, p. 129.
77. Lesson, Voyage de *Coquille*, journal, 1 février 1824 [Havard & Havard trans., p. 273].
78. Dumont d'Urville, ms journal de la *Coquille*, loc. cit., 1 février 1824, p. 129.
79. See Duyker & Low, 'A Church on Pulpit Hill: Unlocking a Blue Mountains mystery'.
80. Whether d'Urville recorded the inscription in situ or at the end of his day's travel is unknown. It is possible he unconsciously recorded the common French spelling 'Edgard' and perhaps wrote 'Juny' because he could not discern (or remember) clearly whether Church died in June or July and therefore fudged the two months.
81. Dumont d'Urville, ms journal de la *Coquille*, loc. cit., 1 février 1824, p. 130.
82. See Duyker & Low, op. cit.
83. Lesson, Voyage de *Coquille*, journal, 1 février 1824 [Havard & Havard trans., p. 274].
84. He did later record meeting the eldest Macarthur son and recording his testimony of Aboriginal cannibalism in the mountains; see note 60 for canto ii of Dumont d'Urville's manuscript 'Les Zélandais ou histoire australienne', SHDDM, Vincennes, Fonds Privés, 7 GG², carton 1.
85. Lesson, ms journal de la *Coquille*, loc. cit., 1 février 1824 [Havard & Havard trans., p. 274].
86. Lesson, *Notice historique sur l'amiral Dumont d'Urville*, pp. 57–58.
87. For a summary of Sieber's life, see Gunn & Codd, *Botanical Exploration of Southern Africa*, pp. 322–33; see also Duyker, 'Sieber, Franz Wilhelm (1789–1844)'.
88. The dollar (from German *thaler* and Dutch *daler*) was a large silver coin dating from the sixteenth century. It also became the English name for the Spanish *peso* or pieces of eight (*reales*) circulating in the Americas, hence the Spanish dollar. The latter was one of the ubiquitous forms of international currency circulating in the early Australian colonies during d'Urville's visits. In 1813, in an attempt to regularize the sterling value in New South Wales, a circular piece was removed from the centre of the Spanish dollar. This small 'dump' was stamped with a crown on one side and the value of 'fifteen pence' on the other. The remaining 'holey' dollar was stamped with the state name on one side and the value 'fifteen shillings' on the other.
89. Dumont d'Urville, ms journal de la *Coquille*, loc. cit., 2 février 1824, p. 131.
90. Garnot, 'Observations sur l'échidné épineux'.
91. Dumont d'Urville, ms journal de la *Coquille*, loc. cit., 2 février 1824, pp. 131–32.
92. Lesson's mention of a 'natural granite bridge' in his journal was probably a reference to the same granite stepping stones crossed by members of Freycinet's expedition in 1819 and portrayed in Friedrich Schroeder's engraving (after Alphonse Pellion's sketch), published in the 'Atlas historique' of Freycinet's *Voyage autour du monde* (1822), plate 98; see also Havard & Dowd, *Historic Glenroy, Cox's River, Hartley NSW*.
93. Darwin, *The Voyage of the* Beagle, p. 425.
94. Lamarck, *Philosophie zoologique*, pp. 26–27.
95. Cuvier, *Le règne animal*, vol. 1, pp. 226–27.
96. For a useful survey, see Moyal, *Platypus*.
97. Lesson spelt his name as 'Shennon' and d'Urville spelt it as 'Schennon', but a 'William Webb Shannon', residing at Raineville, near Bathurst, was, 'at the direction of the Commandant, on the 19th of June [1824], present at the medical enquiry upon the bodies of several Aboriginal women who had been killed by settlers and interred within half a mile of his residence'; see the *Sydney Gazette*, 12 August 1824. Shannon may have been the William Shannon who arrived in New South Wales as a soldier in the 1st/3rd Foot (The East Kent, The Buff's) Regiment, among one of four detachments between 1821 and 1824. This regiment did indeed see action against the French and

famously took part in the Battle of Albuera in May 1811, losing 643 out of 755 men; see Anon., *Historical record of the Third Regiment of Foot, or, The Buffs*, p. 230.

98. Dumont d'Urville, ms journal de la *Coquille*, loc. cit., 3 février 1824, p. 135.

99. Ibid., 4 février 1824, p. 136.

100. Lesson, 'Observations générales d'histoire naturelle', p. 252.

101. Dumont d'Urville, ms journal de la *Coquille*, loc. cit., 5 février 1824, p. 135 & ibid., 12 février 1824, p. 145.

102. Lesson, in Duperrey, op. cit., 'Zoologie', vol. ii, part i, 'Reptiles, Poissons, Mollusques', pp. 194–95; see also Cuvier & Valenciennes, *Histoire naturelle des poissons*, vol. v, 1830, p. 377, plate cxxxi.

103. Dumont d'Urville, ms journal de la *Coquille*, loc. cit., 6 février 1824, p. 139.

104. Ibid., 12 février 1824, p. 145.

105. See Dumont d'Urville's manuscript 'Les Zélandais ou histoire australienne', loc. cit., canto ii, note 41 [Legge trans., op. cit., p. 296].

106. Brongniart, in Duperrey, op. cit., 'Botanique: Phanérogamie', pp. 223–25 and Brongniart, 'Note sur quelques Euphorbiacées de la Nouvelle-Hollande', pp. 386–87.

107. Brongniart, in Duperrey, op. cit., 'Botanique: Phanérogamie', pp. 219–23; see also Brongniart, 'Note sur quelques Euphorbiacées de la Nouvelle-Hollande', pp. 385–86. The species collected by d'Urville, *Poranthera corymbosa*, has drawn considerable attention from chemists because it is the source of the alkaloid porantheridine, remarkable for its (9b-azaphenalene) ring-like molecular structure; see Bick, 'Alkaloids from Australian Flora', pp. 102–03.

108. In the latter case, Brongniart incorrectly attributed the specimen to Anselm Riedlé, who died in Timor well before the expedition reached Van Diemen's Land.

109. Dumont d'Urville, ms journal de la *Coquille*, loc. cit., 27 février 1824, pp. 164–65; 2 mars 1824, p. 178.

110. See, for example, ibid., 18 février 1824, p. 151; 24 février 1824, p. 160; 9 mars 1824, p. 186.

111. Ibid., 19 février 1824, p. 152.

112. Ibid., 28 février 1824, p. 165.

113. Duyker, 'Prosper Garnot (1794–1838), An Early French Naturalist in New South Wales'.

114. Uniacke arrived in Van Diemen's Land aboard the *Competitor* in August 1823 then made his way to Sydney. Soon after, he became supercargo (but also collector of mineral and bird specimens and ethnographic notes) on John Oxley's *Mermaid* expedition to Port Curtis and Moreton Bay in November 1823. This was to undertake survey work for a penal settlement, a subject of great interest to d'Urville. Uniacke's account: 'Narrative of Mr Oxley's expedition to survey Port Curtis and Moreton Bay with a view to form convict establishments there in pursuance of the recommendation of the commissions of enquiry' was published in Barron Field's *Geographical Memoirs on New South Wales*, pp. 27–67. Significantly, the manuscript of Uniacke's account was loaned to the officers of the *Coquille*, transcribed by Auguste Bérard and translated by Jules de Blosseville. It was published in the *Journal des voyages*, vol. xxvii, Paris, 1825; see Lesson, *Voyage autour du monde*, vol. ii, p. 241; see also Rivière, 'An unknown 1824 French version of Oxley's exploration of the Brisbane River' & 'Découverte de la Rivière Brisbane /Discovery of the Brisbane River'. It has been argued that Justice Barron Field, whom d'Urville also met, appropriated at least one of Uniacke's other manuscripts without attribution after the latter's death in 1825; see Steele, 'Pamphlet, Uniacke and Field'.

115. Dumont d'Urville, ms journal de la *Coquille*, loc. cit., 28 février 1824, p. 165; McCarthy, 'Bungaree (?–1830)'.

116. See d'Urville's published account extracted from his journal (28–29 février 1824, pp. 165–70) in his *Voyage de la corvette l'Astrolabe*. 'Histoire du voyage', vol. i, 1830, p. 442.

117. Lesson, *Voyage autour du monde*, vol. ii, p. 283.

118. Dumont d'Urville, ms journal de la *Coquille*, loc. cit., 28–29 février 1824, pp. 165–70.

119. Dumont d'Urville, *Voyage de la corvette l'Astrolabe*, 'Histoire du voyage', vol. i, 1830, p. 443.

120. Ibid., p. 444.

121. See Harman, 'Aboriginal Convicts: Race, law, and transportation in colonial New South Wales', p. 18.

122. For Duall's life, see Harman, pp. 1–59.

123. See Kohen and Lampert, 'Hunters and fishers in the Sydney region', p. 351.

124. Dumont d'Urville, *Voyage de la corvette l'*Astrolabe, 'Histoire du voyage', vol. i, 1830, p. 446.

125. Ibid., p. 450.

126. Ibid., p. 453.

127. Ibid.

128. Ibid., p. 454.

129. Dumont d'Urville, ms journal de la *Coquille*, loc. cit., 28–29 février 1824, pp. 165–70; Dumont d'Urville, *Voyage pittoresque autour du monde*, vol. ii, pp. 292–300.

130. Dumont d'Urville, ms journal de la *Coquille*, loc. cit., 19 mars 1824, p. 194.

131. See Steele, 'Pamphlet, Uniacke and Field', op. cit., and Rivière, *Discovery of the Brisbane River, 1823, Oxley, Uniacke and Pamphlet*.

10. NEW ZEALAND

1. See George Clarke's childhood memoir: *Notes on Early Life in New Zealand*.

2. Dumont d'Urville, ms journal de la *Coquille*, Mairie de Condé-sur-Noireau, ms 11, 9 mars 1824, p. 186 & 16 mars, 1824, p. 192.

3. See Cloher, *Hongi Hika Warrior Chief*.

4. Dumont d'Urville, 'Les Zélandais ou histoire australienne', footnote 51, canto iii, SHDDM, Vincennes, Fonds Privés, 7 GG², carton 1 [Legge (trans.), *The New Zealanders*, p. 350].

5. Dumont d'Urville, 'Les Zélandais ou histoire australienne', footnote 40, canto ii, loc. cit. [Legge (trans.), op. cit., p. 296].

6. Ibid., footnote 38, canto ii, [Legge (trans.), op. cit., p. 295].

7. Ibid., footnote 37, canto ii, [Legge (trans.), op. cit., p. 295].

8. Marion Dufresne was killed after unwitting breaches of etiquette and religious observance (in particular tapu), and imposing stress on the local subsistence economy at a time of shifting tribal boundaries; see Duyker, *An Officer of the Blue*, pp. 137–63.

9. Duperrey, 'Sur les opérations géographiques … de la corvette de S. M. la *Coquille*', p. 207.

10. See Wilson, 'Tooi, Teeterree and Titore'; see also Wilson, 'The Letters of Tooi and Teeterree'.

11. Dumont d'Urville, ms journal de la *Coquille* [summary], Muséum national d'histoire naturelle, Paris, ms 1602, 3 avril 1824, p. 192.

12. Dumont d'Urville, 'Les Zélandais ou histoire australienne', footnote 72, canto i, loc. cit. [Legge (trans.), op. cit., p. 259].

13. Ibid., footnote 46, canto i, [Legge (trans.), op. cit., p. 246].

14. Ibid., footnote 40, canto ii, [Legge (trans.), op. cit., p. 296].

15. Ibid., footnote 41, canto ii, [Legge (trans.), op. cit., p. 296].

16. Dumont d'Urville, ms journal de la *Coquille*, MNHN, Paris, ms 1602, 4 avril 1824, p. 193.

17. Duperrey, op. cit., p. 209.

18. Dumont d'Urville, in his *Voyage de la corvette l'*Astrolabe, 'Histoire du voyage', vol. iii, 1831, p. 690; see also Dumont d'Urville, 'Les Zélandais ou histoire australienne', footnote 72, canto i, loc. cit., [Legge (trans.), op. cit., p. 259].

19. While 'Tuhi' is now the accepted Ngā Puhi spelling of this chief's name, d'Urville renders him 'Touï' in his manuscript and 'Touai' in printed form. For more on this question of spelling, see Wilson, 'Tooi, Teeterree and Titore'.

20. Dumont d'Urville, 'Les Zélandais ou histoire australienne', footnote 19, canto i, loc. cit., [Legge (trans.), op. cit., p. 234]. The Musée Quai Branly, Paris, has conserved just such a Māori cloak (flax with brown/black geometric border), collected by Dumont d'Urville in New Zealand: SG 84 432.

21. Duperrey, op. cit., p. 207; for accessible transcriptions and translations of the officers' accounts of their visit and survey work, see Ollivier, *Extracts from New Zealand Journals*, pp. 83–219; see also Sharp, *Duperrey's Visit to New Zealand*.

22. Dumont d'Urville, ms journal de la *Coquille*, Mairie de Condé-sur-Noireau, ms 11, 1 avril 1824, p. 208.

23. The CMS was founded in London on 12 April 1799 (as the Society for Missions to Africa and the East) by evangelical members of the Church of England, including anti-slavery campaigner William Wilberforce. It published the *Missionary Register*, which was a major source of ethnographic and other information for d'Urville. The first CMS missionary in New Zealand was the Reverend Samuel Marsden in 1814.
24. Dumont d'Urville, ms journal de la *Coquille*, Mairie de Condé-sur-Noireau, ms 11, 5 avril 1824, p. 221; Dumont d'Urville [MNHN Paris ms], 5 avril 1824, p. 193.
25. Blosseville mentions these pallisades around the homes, courtyards and gardens of the missionaries William Hall and John King at Rangihoua during his visit; see Blosseville, 'Notes', in Ollivier, op. cit., pp. 178–79.
26. Dumont d'Urville, 'Les Zélandais ou histoire australienne', footnote 56, canto i, loc. cit., [Legge (trans.), op. cit., pp. 250–52].
27. Ibid., footnote 56, canto i [Legge (trans.), op. cit., p. 250].
28. Davidson, 'Kendall, Thomas (1778–1832)'.
29. Dumont d'Urville, 'Les Zélandais ou histoire australienne', footnote 27, canto i, loc. cit., [Legge (trans.), op. cit., p. 237].
30. Ibid., footnote 35, canto i, [Legge (trans.), op. cit., p. 239].
31. Ibid., footnotes 39–40, canto i, [Legge (trans.), op. cit., p. 241]. Nevertheless, phylogenetic research has established that emus and kiwis are related; see Cooper, Lalueza-Fox, Anderson, Rambaut, Austin, & Ward, 'Complete mitochondrial genome sequences of two extinct moas clarify ratite evolution'.
32. Wilson, 'Tooi, Teeterree and Titore', p. 267.
33. Dumont d'Urville, in his *Voyage de la corvette l'Astrolabe*, 'Histoire du voyage', vol. iii, pp. 687–88.
34. Dumont d'Urville, 'Les Zélandais ou histoire australienne', footnote 56, canto i, loc. cit., [Legge (trans.), op. cit., pp. 249–50].
35. McLean, *Maori Music*, p. 71.
36. The author made oblique reference to d'Urville, stating that Tuhi's 'conduct was admired by Captain Duperrey and another Gentleman on board, who invited him to dine with them'; see Anon., 'Some Account of Tooi, The Late New-Zealand Chief', p. 304.
37. [Caw, J.L.,] 'Williams, Henry (1792–1876)'.
38. His grandson was the Australian 'bush' poet and author Henry Kendall (1839–1882), who appears to have inherited his melancholy alcoholic traits; see Binney, *The Legacy of Guilt: A life of Thomas Kendall*.
39. The *Cossack* was under the command of a Captain Dix and left Sydney on 18 March 1823. She was totally wrecked at Hokianga, but all the crew were saved; see *The Sydney Gazette and New South Wales Advertiser*, Thursday, 20 March 1823, p. 2 & Thursday, 4 December 1823, p. 2.
40. Dumont d'Urville, 'Les Zélandais ou histoire australienne', canto ii, loc. cit., [Legge (trans.), op. cit., p. 132].
41. Lesson, *Notice historique sur l'amiral Dumont d'Urville*, p. 17.

11. COMPLETING THE CIRCLE

1. The Wesleyan Protestants would come in 1842 and the Marist Catholics in 1847; their alliances with rival chieftains ultimately precipitated violent conflict and provided the pretext for British annexation. Today the island is part of the Republic of Fiji.
2. Although d'Urville alludes to only six deserters from the *Rochester*, Duperrey says there were eight; see Duperrey, 'Sur les opérations géographiques … de la corvette de S. M. la *Coquille*', p. 210.
3. Lesson, *Voyage autour du monde*, vol. ii, p. 419.
4. Dumont d'Urville, *Voyage pittoresque autour du monde*, vol. ii, pp. 435–40.
5. Duperrey, op. cit., pp. 209–12.
6. Dumont d'Urville, op. cit., vol. ii, pp. 435–36.
7. Duperrey, op. cit., p. 212.

8. Kiribati is a local rendering of 'Gilbert'. The Gilbert Islands were named after Thomas Gilbert, captain of the 'First Fleet' transport *Charlotte*. In company with the *Scarborough*, the *Charlotte* sailed from New South Wales to China in 1788 and made numerous discoveries en route. The Marshall Islands were named in honour of John Marshall, captain of the *Scarborough*.

9. Dumont d'Urville, op. cit., vol. ii, p. 442.

10. Formerly Sydenham Island.

11. Duperrey, op. cit., p. 213.

12. He introduces his quotation as follows: 'Voici ce que dit M. d'Urville dans son journal inédit de la *Coquille*, au sujet des habitans de cette île'; see Dumont d'Urville, op. cit., vol. ii, p. 441.

13. For Marshall's chart, see [Phillip], *The Voyage of Governor Phillip to Botany Bay*, chapter xxi.

14. Dumont d'Urville, op. cit., vol. ii, pp. 442–43; Duperrey, op. cit., p. 215.

15. Dumont d'Urville, op. cit, vol. ii, p. 443.

16. Duperrey, op. cit., p. 215.

17. Dumont d'Urville, op. cit, vol. ii, p. 443.

18. Duperrey, op. cit., pp. 217–18.

19. Sharp, *The Discovery of the Pacific Islands*, p. 202.

20. Duperrey, op. cit., p. 219; see also [Paterson],'Situation of Islands Seen in the Pacific Ocean', p. 154.

21. Duperrey, op. cit., p. 220.

22. Ibid., p. 221; see also the *Mercantile Advertiser* (New York), 15 November 1805, page 3, in which his name is spelt 'Crocker'.

23. Dumont d'Urville, op. cit, vol. ii, p. 457.

24. Lesson, op. cit., vol. ii, p. 480.

25. Dumont d'Urville, op. cit, vol. ii, p. 457.

26. According to René Lesson, they had difficulty finding 'twenty plants in flower', and the botany of the island 'did not differ at all from that of the South Sea islands', except that there were some 'plants of the Molluccas'; see Lesson, op cit., vol. ii, p. 465.

27. Bory de Saint-Vincent, in Duperrey, op. cit., 'Botanique: Cryptogamie', pp. 273–74.

28. Dumont d'Urville, op. cit., vol. ii, p. 458.

29. Duperrey would rename it Chabrol Harbour.

30. Lesson thought the population a little smaller – perhaps 500–600 inhabitants; see Lesson, op. cit., vol. ii, p. 493.

31. Dumont d'Urville, op. cit., vol. ii, p. 459.

32. Ibid.

33. Ibid., p. 460.

34. Morgan, *Prehistoric Architecture in Micronesia*, pp. 86–115.

35. Dumont d'Urville, op. cit., vol. ii, p. 462.

36. Guérin-Méneville, in Duperrey, op. cit., 'Zoologie', vol. ii, part ii, 1ère division, 'Crustacés, Arachnides et Insectes', pp. 37–38.

37. Spamer and Bogan, 'Type Specimens of Crustacea Surviving in the Guérin-Méneville Collection', p. 43.

38. Duperrey, op. cit., p. 228.

39. Lesson, op. cit., vol. ii, p. 524.

40. According to Andrew Sharp, the first European to sight this island, like Mokil and Pingelap, might have been Alvaro de Saavedra Ceron; see Sharp, op. cit., pp. 16–23.

41. Duperrey, op. cit., pp. 236–37.

42. Dumont d'Urville, op. cit., vol. ii, p. 477.

43. Ibid., vol. ii, pp. 182–83.

44. Duperrey, op. cit., pp. 243–45.

45. Dumont d'Urville, op. cit., vol. ii, p. 249.

46. Duperrey, op. cit., p. 245.

47. Dumont d'Urville, op. cit., vol. ii, p. 249.

48. Ibid., vol. i, p. 54.
49. Ibid.
50. Darwin, *The Voyage of the* Beagle, ch. xxi, p. 465.
51. Dumont d'Urville, op. cit., vol. i, p. 54.
52. Duperrey, op. cit., p. 246.
53. Barnwell, 'Cole, Sir Galbraith Lowry (1772–1842)'.
54. Duperrey, op. cit., pp. 246–50.
55. D'Urville mentions meeting Telfair in 1824 in his *Voyage de la corvette l'*Astrolabe: 'Histoire du voyage', vol. v, p. 503. D'Urville also noted in his journal that the botanist Allan Cunningham gave Prosper Garnot a letter of recommendation to 'his friend M. Telfair' before leaving New South Wales. At the time, d'Urville mistakenly thought Telfair was governor of Mauritius! It seems likely he had a similar letter of introduction; see Dumont d'Urville, ms journal de la *Coquille*, Mairie de Condé-sur-Noireau, 29 février 1824, p. 175.
56. These 270 plants included 36 ferns; see Dumont d'Urville, 'De la distribution des fougères sur la surface du globe terrestre', p. 63.
57. Rouillard & Guého, *Le Jardin des Pamplemousses 1729–1979*, p. 61.
58. D'Urville mentions meeting Lislet Geoffroy in 1824 in his *Voyage de la corvette l'*Astrolabe, 'Histoire du voyage', vol. v, p. 509.
59. Béchet, 'Geoffroy, Jean Baptiste Lislet (1755–1836)'.
60. Dumont d'Urville, *Voyage pittoresque autour du monde*, vol. i, p. 64.
61. Ibid., vol. ii, p. 546.
62. Duperrey, op. cit., p. 250.
63. Dumont d'Urville, *Voyage pittoresque autour du monde*, vol. ii, p. 546.
64. Duperrey, op. cit., p. 251.
65. Dumont d'Urville, *Voyage de la corvette l'*Astrolabe, 'Histoire du voyage', vol. v, p. 562.
66. Bumstead, 'Walker, Alexander, explorer and author …'.
67. See Abell [*née* Balcombe], *Recollections of the Emperor Napoleon*.
68. A reference to the hermits of the early Christian period in Egypt; see Dumont d'Urville, *Voyage pittoresque autour du monde*, vol. ii, p. 548.
69. On 28 October 1818, Napoleon's doctor on Saint Helena, Barry Edward O'Meara, dispatched a letter to the Admiralty 'insinuating that Napoleon's life was not safe in Lowe's hands', see [Knollys], 'O'Meara, Barry Edward (1786–1836)'.
70. See Weider & Forshufvud, *Assassination at St. Helena*.
71. Jones & Ledingham, 'Arsenic in Napoleon's Wallpaper'; it should also be remembered that Napoleon attempted suicide with poison in April 1814.
72. Dumont d'Urville, *Voyage pittoresque autour du monde*, vol. ii, p. 548.
73. Ibid.
74. Lesson, op. cit., vol. ii, pp. 536–37.
75. See Humbert, *Napoléon aux Invalides*.
76. Dumont d'Urville, *Voyage pittoresque autour du monde*, vol. ii, p. 548.
77. Ibid.
78. Ibid., p. 549.
79. Heidler, *Encyclopedia of the War of 1812*, pp. 388–89.
80. Dumont d'Urville, *Voyage pittoresque autour du monde*, vol. ii, pp. 550 & 552. D'Urville, nevertheless, set his account of Ascension Island during the command of Nicolls' successor, Captain William Bates.
81. Ibid., vol. ii, p. 550.
82. See Ashmole & Ashmole, *St Helena and Ascension Island*, pp. 214–15.
83. Dumont d'Urville, *Voyage pittoresque autour du monde*, vol. ii, p. 551.
84. Duperrey, op. cit., p. 256.

12. COMMAND

1. In March 1823, d'Urville's mother, who had also had no letters from him, wrote to the navy minister requesting news of her son; see lettre de Madame Dumont d'Urville [née de Croisilles], 23 mars 1823, demandant des nouvelles de son fils, dossier personnel, Dumont d'Urville, SHDDM, Vincennes, CC[7] Alpha 772, pièce 21.

2. Dumont d'Urville, mémoire, quoted by Frédéric Malcor in 'Dumont-d'Urville, Contre-amiral, d'après ses manuscrits', f. 10, Papiers du contre-amiral Jules-Sébastien-César Dumont d'Urville, Fonds Privés, SHDDM, Vincennes, 7 GG[2] carton 2.

3. The aerial télégraphe was invented by Claude Chappe during the Revolution; see Bertier de Sauvigny, The Bourbon Restoration, p. 211.

4. Dumont d'Urville, mémoire, quoted by Frédéric Malcor in 'Dumont-d'Urville, Contre-amiral, d'après ses manuscrits', loc. cit., f. 1.

5. Ibid.

6. Lettre de Dumont d'Urville [18, rue des Petits Augustins] au ministre, demandant de l'avancement à la suite du voyage de la Coquille, 6 mai 1825, Dumont d'Urville, dossier personnel, SHDDM, Vincennes, CC[7] Alpha 772, pièce 22.

7. In 1916, the building became the headquarters for Czech nationalists and it remains a Czech centre; see Hillairet, Dictionnaire historique des rues de Paris, vol. 1, p. 211.

8. Nomination de Dumont d'Urville dans l'ordre de Saint-Louis, 12 juillet 1825, Dumont d'Urville, dossier personnel, SHDDM, Vincennes, CC[7] Alpha 772, pièce 23.

9. See the introduction to Dumont d'Urville, The New Zealanders: A story of Austral lands, translated by Carol Legge, pp. 19–20.

10. See Cretella, 'The complete collation and dating of the section Zoologie of the Coquille voyage'.

11. Dumont d'Urville, ms journal de la Coquille, Mairie de Condé-sur-Noireau, ms 11, 31 décembre 1823, p. 82.

12. Dumont d'Urville, ms journal de la Coquille, loc. cit., 1 décembre 1823, p. 71.

13. Dumont d'Urville, 'Note sur les collections et les observations recueillies par M.J. D'Urville', and Dumont d'Urville, 'De la distribution des fougères sur la surface du globe terrestre'.

14. Cuvier, 'Zoologie', in Humboldt, Cuvier, Desfontaines, Cordier, Latreille, Rossel & Arago, 'Rapport fait à l'Académie royale des sciences', p. xl.

15. 'Suite de rapport de M. Arago', in Humboldt, Cuvier, Desfontaines, Cordier, Latreille, Rossel & Arago, op. cit., p. xlii.

16. According to d'Urville, Duperrey 'each day made me listen to indecent mocking of natural history and that which it occupied itself with', Dumont d'Urville, ms journal de la Coquille, loc. cit., 31 décembre 1823, p. 69.

17. Quoted by William E. Lyons, in Matters of the Mind, p. 222.

18. 'Suite de rapport de M. Arago', in Humboldt, Cuvier, Desfontaines, Cordier, Latreille, Rossel & Arago, op. cit., p. xlii.

19. Dumont d'Urville, Projet d'une campagne d'exploration sur les côtes de la Nouvelle-Guinée, de la Nouvelle-Bretagne et de la Louisiade, 23 mai 1825, SHDDM, Vincennes, BB[4] 1002.

20. Dumont d'Urville, Voyage de la corvette l'Astrolabe, 'Histoire du voyage', vol. i, pp. 1–2.

21. Ibid., p. 2.

22. Although the comte de Chabrol did not have a naval background – he had originally studied for the priesthood and was imprisoned during the Terror after refusing to swear allegiance to the civil constitution – he was a pragmatic political moderate with ample experience as an administrator, serving Napoleon (who made him a count of the Empire) in Italy and the northwestern Balkans, and then the Bourbons as under-secretary of state for the interior and registrar-general of domains, before accepting the navy portfolio; see Robert, Bourloton & Cougny, Dictionnaire des parlementaires français, vol. ii, p. 17.

23. Ministre de la marine et colonies, Paris, rapport au roi, Paris, le 4 décembre 1825, SHDDM, Vincennes, BB[4] 1002.

24. Ross, 'Thierry, Charles-Philip-Hippolytus, Baron de (1793?–1864)'.

25. Baron de Thierry, 'Projet de colonisation de la Nouvelle-Zélande', Paris, 21 avril 1825, SHDDM, Vincennes, BB^4 1002.

26. Ruth Ross believed baron de Thierry was in Paris in October 1825. This may be correct, but his proposal is dated Paris, 21 April 1825; see Ross, op. cit.

27. See Ginouvier, *Le Botany-Bey* [*sic*] *français*.

28. Ministre de la marine et colonies, Paris, rapport au roi, Paris, le 4 décembre 1825, SHDDM, Vincennes, BB^4 1002.

29. Direction des mouvements, note au ministre de la marine et des colonies, Paris, le 12 septembre 1825, SHDDM, Vincennes, BB^4 1002.

30. Anon., 'M. l'amiral anglais Manby, récemment arrivé à Paris …', *Le moniteur universel*, Paris, jeudi, 8 septembre 1825, p. 1270; see also Anon., 'De Englische Admiraal Manby …', *Algemeene Konst en Letterbode voor het jaar 1825*, no. 37, vrijdag den 16den september 1825, Haarlem, deel ii, pp. 177–78.

31. Ministre de la marine et colonies à M. le Chev[alier]. de Rosily, vice-amiral, directeur général du Dépôt [des cartes et plans] de la marine, Paris, 15 décembre 1825, SHDDM, Vincennes, BB^4 1002.

32. Manby to Dumont d'Urville, Chantilly, 26 December 1825, in Dumont d'Urville, *Voyage de la corvette l'*Astrolabe, 'Histoire du voyage', vol. i, p. 6.

33. [Chabrol, Christophe comte de], Lettre du ministre de la marine à M. Dumont d'Urville … pour lui servir d'instruction relativement au voyage de découvertes qu'il va entreprendre, Paris, le 8 avril 1826', p. liii.

34. Ministre de la marine et colonies, Paris, à M. le commandant et M. l'intendant de la marine, Toulon, 15 décembre 1825, SHDDM, Vincennes, BB^4 1002.

35. Ministre de la marine et colonies à M. le Chev[alier]. de Rosily, vice–amiral, directeur général du Dépôt [des cartes et plans] de la marine, Paris, 15 décembre 1825, loc. cit.

36. Ministre de la marine et colonies à [Ange-Hyacinthe-Maxence] baron de Damas [de Cormaillon], ministre des affaires étrangères, Paris, 15 décembre 1825, SHDDM, Vincennes, BB^4 1002.

37. Ministre de la marine et colonies au baron Aimé de Puymaurin, directeur de la monnaie royale, Paris, 15 décembre 1825, SHDDM, Vincennes, BB^4 1002.

38. See Etat des livres à faire venir de l'Angleterre and Ministre de la marine et colonies à M. le Baron Séguier, consul général de France à Londres, 5 janvier 1826, SHDDM, Vincennes, BB^4 1002.

39. Ministre de la marine et colonies à M. le directeur de la forge royale à Guérigny, Paris, 9 février 1826, SHDDM, Vincennes, BB^4 1002.

40. Dumont d'Urville, *Voyage de la corvette l'*Astrolabe, 'Histoire du voyage', vol. i, p. 9.

41. I have not found the letter of 26 December 1825, but it is referred to in the following letter: Ministre de la marine et des colonies à baron Cuvier et baron Jean-Joseph Fourier, secrétaires perpétuels de l'Académies des sciences, Paris, 2 mars 1826, SHDDM, Vincennes, BB^4 1002.

42. Ministre de la marine et des colonies à M. D'Arcet, membre de l'Académie des sciences, 12 janvier 1826, SHDDM, Vincennes, BB^4 1002.

43. Dawson, *A Biography of François Magendie*, p. 33.

44. Ibid., pp. 32–35.

45. Ministre de la marine et des colonies, Paris, à M. le commandant et M. l'intendant de la marine, Toulon, 15 décembre 1825, SHDDM, Vincennes, BB^4 1002.

46. Ministre de la marine et des colonies, Paris, à M. Dumont d'Urville, capitaine de frégate, le 26 décembre 1825, SHDDM, Vincennes, BB^4 1002.

13. ASTROLABE

1. Dumont d'Urville, ms journal de la *Coquille*, Mairie de Condé-sur-Noireau, ms 11, mercredi, 31 décembre 1823, p. 75. Pierre-Adolphe Lesson, however, considered Lottin an 'egotist and a mocker'; see Lesson, 'Portrait de l'état-major de l'*Astrolabe*', p. 177.

2. Dossier personnel, Béringuier, Alexandre, SHDDM, Vincennes, CC^7 Alpha 167.

3. Anne Bataille, who made a detailed study of Lesson and his journal, concluded that he was perhaps 'too partial' in his treatment of d'Urville (see Bataille, 'Un document inédit', p. 163), while Isabel Ollivier saw him as a 'misfit in a system that worked well for others' (see Ollivier, 'Pierre-Adolphe Lesson, Surgeon-Naturalist', p. 55).

4. See Duyker, 'Lesson, Pierre Adolphe (1805–1888)'.

5. Lesson, op. cit., p. 178.

6. Dossier personnel, Gressien, Victor-Amédée, SHDDM, Vincennes, CC^7 Alpha 1080.

7. Dossier personnel, Guilbert, Pierre-Edouard, SHDDM, Vincennes, CC^7 Alpha 1117; Lesson, op. cit., pp. 180–81.

8. Dossier personnel, Quoy, Jean-René-Constant, SHDDM, Vincennes, CC^7 Alpha 2074; see also Duyker, 'Quoy, René Constant (1790–1869)'.

9. Lesson, op. cit., p. 184.

10. Ibid., p. 189.

11. Gaimard would later be decorated by the French, Swedish and Danish governments; see dossier personnel, Gaimard, Joseph-Paul, SHDDM, Vincennes, CC^7 Alpha 944; see also Taillemite, *Dictionnaire des marins français*, pp. 31–32.

12. Dossier personnel, Sainson, Louis-Auguste de, SHDDM, Vincennes, CC^7 Alpha 2233; see also Collins, 'Louis-Auguste de Sainson'; and (with particular regard to Mauritius) Duyker, 'Sainson, Louis-Auguste de (1800–1887)'.

13. Dossier Faraguet, Archives départementales du Jura, M53.

14. Dossier personnel, Faraguet, Henry-Antoine, SHDDM, Vincennes, CC^7 Alpha 847; see also Duyker, 'Faraguet, Henry Antoine (1802–*post* 1859)'.

15. Pâris was also elected a member of the Académie des sciences in 1863 and later served as its vice-president and president. He is still remembered for the classic *Dictionnaire de la marine à voile et à vapeur*, co-authored with his father-in-law, Pierre-Marie-Joseph Bonnefoux; see dossier personnel, Pâris, François-Edmond, SHDDM, Vincennes, CC^7 Alpha 1908; see also Duyker, 'Pâris, François-Edmond (1806–1893)'.

16. [Louis XVIII], Ordonannce du roi portant nomination d'élèves au Collège royal de la marine à Angoulème, Paris, le 26 avril 1823.

17. His maternal great-great grandfather, Antoine de la Pôterie de la Garrigue, was an alderman of Carcassonne; for details of Dudemaine's father, see Woelmont de Brumagne, *Notices généalogiques*, vol. 3. p. 764.

18. Lauvergne was decorated *chevalier de la Légion d'honneur* at the age of 35 in 1841. He married in 1854 and retired from the navy in 1863 with the rank of *sous-commissaire*; see dossier personnel, Lauvergne, Barthélémy, SHDDM, Vincennes, CC^7 Alpha 1401.

19. For the muster roll of the expedition, see Dumont d'Urville, *Voyage de la corvette l'*Astrolabe, 'Histoire du voyage', vol. i, pp. xxxiv–xlvii.

20. Ministre de la marine et des colonies à M. Dumont d'Urville, capitaine de frégate, commandant la corvette du roi l'*Astrolabe*, à Toulon, instruction relatives au voyage de découvertes qu'il doit entreprendre, Paris, le 8 avril 1826, SHDDM, Vincennes, BB^4 1002.

21. Ibid.

22. Deacon, *Scientists and the Sea 1650–1900*, p. 232.

23. Lesson, op. cit., p. 167.

24. If the ship had been moving, the thermometrograph would not have settled vertically beneath the ship but would have been dragged towards the surface, preventing temperature readings at any significant depth.

25. When one converts from Celsius back to the older Reaumur scale.

26. See Duyker, *François Péron*, p. 61, and Deacon, op. cit., p. 204.

27. Dumont d'Urville, op. cit., 'Histoire du voyage', vol. i, 1830, pp. 16–17.

28. Rosenman (ed. & trans.), *An Account in Two Volumes of Two Voyages to the South Seas*, vol. i, p. 18.

29. D'Urville had acquired King's two-volume *Narrative of a Survey of the Intertropical and Western*

Coasts of Australia: Performed between the years 1818 and 1822, John Murray, London, 1826, for his personal library and had King's charts aboard the *Astrolabe*.

30. According to d'Urville, King wrote to him on 4 May 1832; see Dumont d'Urville, MS 65, Bibliothèque municipale de Toulon, 2 juin 1832.

31. Hernandez Suárez, 'Breves biographifias actualizadas de personajes Canarios'.

32. The author visited this botanical garden in Tenerife in December 2002; it now contains numerous Australian species and a herbarium of some 30,000 specimens.

33. Pierre-Adolphe Lesson was annoyed that these specimens were destined for d'Urville's private herbarium; see Ollivier, 'Pierre-Adolphe Lesson, Surgeon-Naturalist', pp. 59–60.

34. Found in altitudes of up to 2800 metres; see Bramwell & Bramwell, *Wildflowers of the Canary Islands*, p. 163.

35. D'Urville employed the older synonym *Spartium supranubium*.

36. Viera y Clavijo, J. de, *Noticias de la historia general de las islas de Canaria: Contienen la descripción geográfica de todas, una idea del origen, caracter, usos y costumbres de sus antiguos habitantes, de los descubrimientos … que … hicieron los Europeos, de su gobierno … del establecimiento y succesión de su primera nobleza, de sus varones ilustres … de sus fábricas*, impr. de B. Román, Madrid, 1772–83, 4 vols.

37. Dumont d'Urville, *Voyage de la corvette l'*Astrolabe, 'Histoire du voyage', vol. i, pp. 49–50.

38. See Owen, *Narrative of voyages to explore the shores of Africa, Arabia and Madagascar*.

39. Dumont d'Urville, *Voyage de la corvette l'*Astrolabe, 'Histoire du voyage', vol. i, p. 62.

40. Ibid., p. 66.

41. Dumont d'Urville, *Voyage de la corvette l'*Astrolabe, 'Observations nautiques, météorologiques, hydrographiques et de physique', 1833, pp. 20–28.

42. Dumont d'Urville, *Voyage de la corvette l'*Astrolabe, 'Histoire du voyage', vol. i, p. 82.

43. Ibid., p. 84.

14. NEW HOLLAND

1. Dumont d'Urville, *Voyage de la corvette l'*Astrolabe, 'Histoire du voyage', vol. i, 1830, p. 81.

2. Marchant, *France Australe*, p. 247.

3. Ministre de la marine et des colonies à M. Dumont d'Urville, capitaine de frégate, commandant la corvette du roi l'*Astrolabe*, à Toulon, instruction relatives au voyage de découvertes qu'il doit entreprendre, Paris, le 8 avril 1826, SHDDM, Vincennes, BB⁴ 1002.

4. Mémoire pour M. Duperrey commandant la corvette La *Coquille*, ff. 57–58, SHDDM, Vincennes, BB⁴ 1000.

5. Blosseville, 'Projet d'une colonie pénale sur la côte S. O. de la Nouvelle-Hollande', Bibliothèque nationale de France, NAF 6785.

6. Dumont d'Urville, op. cit., 'Histoire du voyage', vol. i, 1830, p. 88.

7. This was a 'buka' cloak, traditionally made from kangaroo skin.

8. Dumont d'Urville, op. cit., 'Histoire du voyage', vol. i, 1830, p. 90.

9. D'Urville spells his name 'Maukorraï' in his *Voyage pittoresque autour du monde*, vol. ii, p. 280.

10. Sainson's portrait of Mokaré (with his name) appears in the form of a lithograph by Antoine Maurin (1793–1860) on the bottom right-hand corner of plate 8 of Dumont d'Urville, *Voyage de la corvette l'*Astrolabe, 'Atlas historique', 1833.

11. For a substantial account of his life, see Ferguson, 'Mokaré's domain'.

12. Dumont d'Urville, op. cit., 'Histoire du voyage', vol. i, 1830, p. 92.

13. Ibid., pp. 92–94.

14. Ibid., p. 100.

15. Ibid., p. 93.

16. Ibid.

17. The original of Guilbert's journal aboard the *Astrolabe* was in the possession of a member of his family, M. Ludovick Pruche, in December 2000. With his permission, a microfilm copy was made for the Service des archives de la Nouvelle-Calédonie in Nouméa. I am grateful to the director, M. Ismet

Kurtovitch, for his kindness in alerting me to this previously unknown document.

18. Dumont d'Urville, op. cit., 'Histoire du voyage', vol. i, 1830, pp. 98–99.

19. Ibid., p. 103.

20. Ibid., p. 105.

21. Ibid., pp. 105–06.

22. Dumont d'Urville, op. cit., 'Philologie', vol. ii, pp. 1–10.

23. Bory de Saint-Vincent, 'Homme', p. 331.

24. Ibid., p. 323.

25. Ibid., p. 308.

26. Bory de Saint-Vincent believed that, for a voyager like d'Urville, 'knowledge of a species or a race of men' was as valuable as that of 'a Medusa, a kangaroo or a *Metrosideros*'; ibid., p. 303.

27. Dumont d'Urville, op. cit., 'Histoire du voyage', vol. i, 1830, p. 106.

28. Sloan, 'The Idea of Racial Degeneration in Buffon's *Histoire naturelle*'.

29. In the first part of Blumenbach's *De generis humani varietate native*, there is a detailed discussion of 'degeneration'. According to Blumenbach, 'it is white in colour, which we may fairly assume to have been the primitive colour of mankind, since … it is very easy for that to degenerate into brown, but very much more difficult for dark to become white'; see Bendyshe (ed.), *The Anthropological Treatises of Johann Friedrich Blumenbach* … , p. 269.

30. 'Mémoire d'instruction', in Dumont d'Urville, op. cit., 'Histoire du voyage', vol. i, pp. lxii–iii; d'Urville's instructions also alluded to seemingly anomalous racial preconceptions of physical appearance, intelligence and cultural sophistication. It was troubling, he was told – with perhaps a hint of phrenology – that the people of Fiji were 'less beautiful', 'less tall', not very well proportioned and had 'less regular' features, yet their faces and attitudes 'were somewhat more characterful' and their material culture 'indicated a people more industrious' than those of the Friendly Islands who from time to time captured them.

31. Dumont d'Urville, 'Les Zélandais ou histoire australienne', canto ii, SHDDM, Vincennes, Fonds Privés, 7 GG², carton i, [Dumont d'Urville (trans. Legge), *The New Zealanders*, p. 131].

32. Robert Brown spent 24 days at King George Sound and collected nearly 500 species, of which about 300 were entirely new. They would form a significant part of his *Prodromus floræ Novæ Hollandiæ et insulæ Van Diemen, exhibens characteres plantarum quas annis 1802–1805* (Typis Richardi Taylor et socii, Londini, 1810); see Estensen, *The Life of Matthew Flinders*, p. 181.

33. D'Urville included a significant ethnobotanical detail in his historical account, that the Aborigines at King George Sound carried glowing *Banksia* cobs wherever they went in order to light their fires with ease; see Dumont d'Urville, *Voyage de la corvette l'*Astrolabe, 'Histoire du voyage', vol. i, 1830, p. 95.

34. One of the '*Xanthorrhoea*' species d'Urville noted was in fact a member of an entirely new genus and not even a member of the same family, despite its appearance. D'Urville would add a footnote that Brown had recently named it *Kingia australis* (Dasypogonaceae) in the botanical appendix to volume ii of Phillip Parker King's *Narrative of a Survey of the Intertropical and Western Coasts of Australia,* a copy of which he owned.

35. Lesson & Richard, in Dumont d'Urville, op. cit., 'Botanique', pp. 89–91.

36. Quoy & Gaimard, in Dumont d'Urville, op. cit., 'Zoologie', vol. i, pp. 175, 197–98, 237–38.

37. For background on these magnetic studies, see Cawood, 'Terrestrial magnetism and the development of international collaboration in the early nineteenth century'.

38. Dumont d'Urville, op. cit., 'Histoire du voyage', vol. i, 1830, p. 122.

39. During Hamelin's visit to Western Port, Pierre Faure spent eight days surveying, and Léon Brèvedent circumnavigated French Island.

40. Dumont d'Urville, op. cit., 'Histoire du voyage', vol. i, 1830, p. 126.

41. Quoy & Gaimard, in Dumont d'Urville, op. cit., 'Zoologie', vol. i, pp. 215–16.

42. *Notoxus pantomelas* (*Eleale pantomelas*), *Notoxus ephippium* (*Trogodendron ephippium*), *Anoplognathus suturalis, Macrothops rufipennis* (*Phyllotocus rufipennis*), *Cneorhinus stygmatipennis* and *Amycterus tomentosus.*

43. Quoy & Gaimard, in Dumont d'Urville, op. cit., 'Zoologie', vol. iii, pp. 618–19; *Polyclinum cylindrica* (*Clavelina cylindrica*).
44. Ibid., pp. 77–79, 89–90, 340–41.
45. Lamarck, 'Sur une nouvelle espèce de Trigonie'.
46. Quoy & Gaimard, in Dumont d'Urville, op. cit., 'Zoologie', vol. iii, pp. 474–77.
47. Dumont d'Urville, op. cit., 'Histoire du voyage', vol. i, p. 143.
48. Dumont d'Urville, op. cit., 'Philologie', vol. i, pp. 11–13.
49. Dumont d'Urville, op. cit., 'Histoire du voyage', vol. i, pp. 147–49.
50. Ibid., p. 149.
51. Ibid., p. 154.
52. Barnwell, 'Darling, Sir Ralph (1775–1858)'.
53. See Fletcher, *Ralph Darling*.
54. *The Australian*, no. 150, Wednesday, 6 December 1826, p. 3, col. 2.
55. Dumont d'Urville, op. cit., 'Histoire du voyage', vol. i, p. 160.
56. Ministre de la marine et des colonies à [Ange-Hyacinthe-Maxence] baron de Damas [de Cormaillon], ministre des affaires étrangères, Paris, 13 février 1826, SHDDM, Vincennes, BB^4 1002.
57. Lord Bathurst to Darling, 1 March 1826, *Historical Records of Australia*, series 1, vol. xii, pp. 192–93.
58. Ibid., pp. 194–95.
59. See Rivière (ed. & trans.), *The Governor's Noble Guest*.
60. Lord Bathurst to Darling, 11 March 1826, *Historical Records of Australia*, series 1, vol. xii, p. 218.
61. Darling to Lord Bathurst, 24 November 1826, *Historical Records of Australia*, series 1, vol. xii, p. 699.
62. The then Lieutenant Wright is listed among the wounded at Albuera; see Anon., *Historical Record of the Third Regiment of Foot, or, The Buffs*, p. 230.
63. Turner, *A History of the Colony of Victoria*, vol. i, p. 63.
64. Darling to Captain Wright, 4 November 1826, *Historical Records of Australia*, series 1, vol. xii, p. 701.
65. In his confidential instructions to Major Lockyer, Darling wrote: 'As the French Discovery Ships, which are understood to have been preparing for these Seas, may possibly have in view the Establishment of a Settlement on some part of the Coast of this Territory, which has not yet been colonized by us, I think it necessary to apprize you confidentially, of what may possibly be their object; and I am to desire, in the event of their touching at King George's Sound that you will be careful to regulate your language and Communications with the Officers, so as to avoid any expression of doubt of the whole of New Holland being considered within this Government, any division of it, which may be supposed to exist under the designation of New South Wales being merely ideal, and intended only with a view of distinguishing the more settled part of the Country. Should this explanation not prove satisfactory, it will be proper in that case to refer them to this Government for any further information they may require. But should it so happen that the French have already arrived, You will, notwithstanding, land the Troops agreeably to your Instructions, and signify that it is considered the whole of New Holland is subject to His Britannic Majesty's Government, and that orders have been given for the Establishment of King George's Sound as a settlement for the reception of Criminals accordingly'; see Governor Darling to Major Lockyer, Government House, 4 November 1826, *Historical Records of Australia*, series 1, vol. xii, p. 701; see also Sweetman, *The Military Establishment and Penal Settlement at King George Sound*.
66. Governor Darling to Under-Secretary Hay, 4 December 1826, *Historical Records of Australia*, series 1, vol. xii, p. 730.
67. Dumont d'Urville, op. cit., 'Histoire du voyage', vol. i, p. 154.
68. 'Through misplaced pride, this edifice was begun on too vast a plan and there are not enough funds,' wrote Dumont d'Urville, op. cit., 'Histoire du voyage', vol. i, pp. 162–63.
69. The lithograph 'Vue de George's Street à Sydney (Nouvelle Galles du Sud)' by Alexis-Nicolas Noël, *Voyage de la corvette* l'Astrolabe, 'Atlas historique', pl. 32, is attributed to a sketch by Louis-Auguste de Sainson, but despite replacement figures in the street by Victor-Jean Adam, it is obviously copied directly from Augustus Earle's earlier 'View from the Sydney Hotel', *Views in Australia*, Earle's Lithography, Sydney, *ca*. 1825, plate 2.

70. This was despite Jean-Baptiste de Boisduval's publication of a substantial two-part volume on the entomology of the voyage, containing descriptions of 86 Australian lepidoptera and nearly 400 Australian beetles. In fact, many were previously described species and even species collected by other French expeditions. He made reference to many Australian beetles in the collections of Pierre Dejean (1780–1845), the brothers Léonard Puech Dupont (1795–1828) and Henry Dupont (born 1798), Hippolyte Gory (1800–1852), Jean-Baptiste Buquet (1807–1889), and even Jacques-Julien Houtou de Labillardière. He also included several species of coleoptera collected by François Péron on Kangaroo Island in January 1803. A number had been collected at Port Jackson by Dumont d'Urville during the visit of the *Coquille*. They included the Australian beetles *Acupalpus piceus* (*Egodroma piceus*) and *Elater scapularis* (*Conoderus scapularis*); see Boisduval, in Dumont d'Urville, op. cit., 'Entomologie' (Latreille ed.), 'Faune entomologique', première partie, pp. 47 & 104.
71. Ibid., pp. 227–28, 231–39.
72. Quoy & Gaimard, in Dumont d'Urville, op. cit., 'Zoologie', vol. iv, pp. 118–20.
73. Cherbonnier, 'Sur une Holothurie de Quoy et Gaimard'.
74. Dumont d'Urville, op. cit., 'Histoire du voyage', vol. iv, p. 628.
75. Ibid., vol. i, p. 277.
76. Ibid., vol. iv, p. 511.
77. Lesson, 'Portrait de l'état-major de l'*Astrolabe*', p. 172.

15. RETURN TO NEW ZEALAND

1. Sharp, *The Voyages of Abel Janszoon Tasman*.
2. Dumont d'Urville, *Voyage de la corvette* l'Astrolabe, 'Histoire du voyage', vol. ii, p. 2.
3. See Duyker, *An Officer of the Blue*.
4. Doak, *The Burning of the* 'Boyd'.
5. In fact, on his return in 1773, James Cook named it Murderers Bay, a translation of Tasman's 'Moordenaar's Bay'.
6. Dumont d'Urville, op. cit., 'Histoire du voyage', vol. ii, pp. 20–21.
7. Ibid., p. 22. D'Urville does not itemise or describe these particular objects, but the ethnographic collection from the expedition was deposited with the Musée de marine du Louvre in 1828. Items from d'Urville's later voyage were added in 1841. In 1905 (but effectively between 1908 and 1911), they were divided between the Musée des antiquités nationales (later the Musée d'archéologie nationale) in the Château de Saint-Germain-en-Laye, the Musée de la marine du Trocadéro and the Muséum d'histoire naturelle de La Rochelle. The objects at Saint-Germain-en-Laye were later transferred to the Musée national des arts d'Afrique et d'Océanie, which in turn merged with the Musée Quai Branly in 2003; see Extrait de l'Inventaire du Musée des antiquités nationales: 'Collection Dumont d'Urville', Musée Quai Branly, cote D003691/45392; see also Jacquemin, *Objets des Mers du Sud*.
8. I have relied on the positions stated in Dumont d'Urville, op. cit., 'Observations nautiques, météorologiques, hydrographiques, et de physique', p. 42.
9. Dumont d'Urville, op. cit., 'Histoire du voyage', vol. ii, pp. 28–29.
10. Ibid., p. 26.
11. Ibid., p. 40.
12. Ibid., p. 41.
13. See Guilbert, 'Plan de l'anse de l'*Astrolabe* dans la Baie de Tasman, (Détroit de Cook) …' in Dumont d'Urville, op. cit., 'Atlas (Hydrographie)', plate 14.
14. Ibid.
15. According to James Drummond (1869–1940), citing 'O. Caldwell', the specific name *igata* was perhaps a corruption of the Māori name *inaka*, reportedly a reference to this bird having a nest shaped like an eel basket; see Drummond, 'Nature Notes'.
16. Quoy & Gaimard, in Dumont d'Urville, op. cit., 'Zoologie', vol. i, pp. 201, 255–26; *Bowdleria punctatus* was originally included in the genus *Synallaxis*.

17. Richard, 'Essai d'une flore de la Nouvelle-Zélande', in Dumont d'Urville, op. cit., 'Botanique [part i]', pp. 175–76, 221–22, 356–57.

18. Ibid., pp. 27–28, 31–32.

19. Ibid., p. 258.

20. Quoy & Gaimard, in Dumont d'Urville, op. cit., 'Zoologie', vol. ii, pp. 148–49, 214 & vol. iii, pp. 256–58.

21. Lesson, 'Portrait de l'état-major de l'*Astrolabe*', p. 167.

22. Percy Smith (see Smith, 'Captain Dumont d'Urville's Visit to Tasman Bay in 1827') did not identify this hill in 1907, but it seems to have been on the ridge (rising to 214 metres) between Lesson Creek, d'Urville's Pointe Percée (Yellow Point) and the Torrent River.

23. Dumont d'Urville, op. cit., 'Histoire du voyage', vol. ii, pp. 32–33.

24. Ibid., p. 66.

25. See 'L'*Astrolabe* dans la Passe des Français, Nouvelle Zélande', lithograph by Achille Saint-Aulaire, from a sketch by Louis-Auguste de Sainson, in Dumont d'Urville, op. cit., 'Atlas historique', plate no. 40.

26. Dumont d'Urville, op. cit., 'Histoire du voyage', vol. ii, p. 54.

27. Richard, 'Essai d'une flore de la Nouvelle-Zélande', in Dumont d'Urville, op. cit., 'Botanique [part i]', pp. 251–52.

28. Both were sketched by Sainson, and a lithograph by Antoine Maurin appeared as plate 34 in the expedition atlas.

29. Dumont d'Urville, op. cit., 'Histoire du voyage', vol. ii, p. 80.

30. Young Nick's Head was named by James Cook in honour of the surgeon's boy, Nicholas Young, who first sighted the New Zealand coast from the *Endeavour* on 6 October 1769.

31. Dumont d'Urville, op. cit., 'Histoire du voyage', vol. ii, p. 109.

32. Guilbert, journal [copy], 15 février 1827, Service des archives de la Nouvelle-Calédonie, Nouméa.

33. Still known as the Astrolabe Reef, it was the location of the wreck of the MV *Rena* on 5 October 2011. The resultant oil spill is regarded as 'New Zealand's worst maritime environmental disaster'; see *New Zealand Herald*, 11 October 2011, p. 1.

34. Dumont d'Urville, op. cit., 'Histoire du voyage', vol. ii, p. 132.

35. Milne, 'Secret documents reveal French mutiny on NZ coast'.

36. Lesson, 'Voyage de découverte de l'*Astrolabe*', 16 février 1827, Médiathèque de Rochefort, Fonds Lesson, ms 8122.

37. Guilbert, journal [copy], 15 février 1827, loc. cit.

38. See Dumont d'Urville, journal de bord de la corvette *Astrolabe*, 16 février 1827, SHDDM Vincennes, Fonds Privés, 7 GG^2, carton ii.

39. Lesson, 'Portrait de l'état-major de l'*Astrolabe*', p. 169.

40. Ibid.

41. D'Urville spelt Hauraki as 'Shouraki'.

42. Smith, 'Wars of the northern against the southern tribes of New Zealand in the nineteenth century: Part VII', p. 85.

43. Smith, 'Captain Dumont d'Urville's visit to Whangarei, Waitemata, and the Thames in 1827', p. 412.

44. See Dumont d'Urville, op. cit., 'Observations nautiques, météorologiques, hydrographiques et de physique', p. 46.

45. Ibid.

46. S. Percy Smith identifies him; see 'Captain Dumont d'Urville's Visit to Whangarei, Waitemata, and the Thames in 1827', p. 422.

47. Dumont d'Urville, op. cit., 'Histoire du voyage', vol. ii, p. 181.

48. Ibid., pp. 171–72.

49. Ibid., pp. 176–77.

50. A mere 1200 metres wide (between Otahuhu Creek and Mangere Inlet), this was an ancient canoe portage route, reputedly dating from the ancestral Tainui canoe of the first Māori settlers; see Grey, *Polynesian Mythology*, p. 108. Hongi Hika used the Tamaki portage when he invaded Waikato,

according to the testimony of the respected Ngā Puhi centenarian Eruera Mahi Patuone (*ca.* 1764–1872); see 'Native Land Court', *Daily Southern Cross*, 24 October 1868, p. 4. As Francis Dart Fenton (1821–1898), chief judge of the Native Land Court, put it, 'the history of this isthmus … is almost an epitome of the history of New Zealand during many years, for this was the highway of the armies of the tribes in old days, and, whether going North or South, all war parties passed through or touched at Tamaki'; see Fenton, 'The Orakei Case', p. 4. As early as the 1850s, it was proposed as the location for a canal; see *Daily Southern Cross*, 6 August 1852, p. 4. I am very grateful to Jeremy Spencer, Canberra, for his assistance in researching the historic Tamaki portage route.

51. Dumont d'Urville, op. cit., 'Histoire du voyage', vol. ii, pp. 167, 173.
52. Beaglehole, *The Discovery of New Zealand*, p. 82.
53. Ibid., p. 179.
54. See Lottin, 'Carte générale de la partie de la Nouvelle-Zélande, reconnue par le Cap'ne de frégate Dumont D'Urville', in Dumont d'Urville, op. cit., 'Atlas hydrographique', plate 9.
55. Presumably the same sand bank Cook's *Endeavour* grounded on off Motukiekie Island in December 1769.
56. Yarwood, *Samuel Marsden*, p. 256.
57. D'Urville also visited Kendall's home at Matauwhi Bay and found it destroyed; only the missionary cemetery was intact.
58. Dumont d'Urville, op. cit., 'Histoire du voyage', vol. ii, p. 228.
59. Ibid., p. 222.
60. D'Urville recorded how William Williams flattered himself that he could negotiate his way through what the missionary considered the 'ridiculous' obstacle of a tapu sweet potato field; he did not succeed; see Dumont d'Urville, op. cit., 'Histoire du voyage', vol. ii, p. 216.
61. Ibid., p. 233.
62. The version of Sainson's sketch engraved by Jean-Denis Nargeot for Dumont d'Urville's *Voyage pittoresque autour du monde* (opposite page 358) does not include the field gun on the foreshore.
63. Dumont d'Urville, op. cit., 'Histoire du voyage', vol. ii, p. 209.
64. For further background, see Orchiston, 'Preserved Human Heads of the New Zealand Māoris'.
65. Dumont d'Urville, op. cit., 'Histoire du voyage', vol. ii, pp. 209, 236.
66. Groube, 'Excavations on Paeroa Village Bay of Islands' and Groube, 'Rescue excavations in the Bay of Islands'; see also Dansey, 'Digging for the stories from long ago'.
67. Richard's *Epilobium cinereum* (see Richard, 'Essai d'une flore de la Nouvelle-Zélande', in Dumont d'Urville, op. cit., 'Botanique', pp. 330–31) is now *Epilobium billlardierianum* subsp. *cinereum*.
68. Richard's *Podocarpus zamiaefolius*, ibid., pp. 360–61, a synonym for *Agathis australis*.
69. Richard's *Metrosideros tomentosa*, ibid., pp. 336–67, a synonym for the familiar *Metrosideros excelsa* or pohutukawa.
70. Quoy & Gaimard, in Dumont d'Urville, op. cit., 'Zoologie', vol. iii, pp. 293–94, 611–12.
71. Ibid., vol. iv, pp. 290–91.
72. Dumont d'Urville, op. cit., 'Histoire du voyage', vol. ii, chapter xvii ('Essai sur la Nouvelle-Zélande'), pp. 289–630.
73. Dumont d'Urville, op. cit., 'Histoire du voyage', vol. ii, pp. 114–16. The Royal Society of New Zealand was established in 1867 and soon functioned as a national academy of science. In 2011, the Council for the Humanities (which had established the New Zealand Academy of the Humanities in 2007) became a committee of the Royal Society of New Zealand, and its fellows joined the ranks of the Academy of the Royal Society of New Zealand. Among its 372 fellows are indeed those who argue over the 'narratives of the earliest navigators'!

16. ILL WINDS IN TONGA

1. Named by William Crompton Sever, master of the *Lady Penrhyn*, one of the six transports that carried convicts to New South Wales in 1788; Sever's voyage is described in chapter xx and tables vii and viii of [Phillip], *The Voyage of Governor Phillip*.

2. Unfortunately, many of those who came aboard the *Astrolabe* were not chiefs and were 'openly mocked' by their compatriots.

3. For more on John Read, see Campbell, *'Gone native' in Polynesia*, pp. 60–61.

4. Dumont d'Urville, *Voyage de la corvette l'*Astrolabe, 'Histoire du voyage', vol. iv, p. 23.

5. According to Peter Dillon, who visited Tongatapu three months after d'Urville, Singleton might have been American; see Dillon, *Narrative and Successful Result of a Voyage in the South Seas*, vol. i, p. 266.

6. Another survivor from the privateer *Port-au-Prince* was 15-year-old William Mariner, whose recollections are a precious source of information about early Tonga; see Martin, *An Account of the Natives of the Tonga Islands* (William Singleton is mentioned on p. 77).

7. Dumont d'Urville, op. cit., 'Histoire du voyage', vol. iv, p. 24.

8. Ibid., p. 27.

9. Ibid., p. 33.

10. Ibid., p. 41.

11. For John Thomas, see Latukefu, 'The case of the Wesleyan Mission in Tonga'.

12. Dumont d'Urville, op. cit., 'Histoire du voyage', vol. iv, p. 46.

13. Ibid., pp. 49–51.

14. Ibid., p. 52.

15. Ibid.

16. Ibid., p. 59.

17. Dumont d'Urville, op. cit., 'Histoire du voyage', vol. iv, pp. 100–01.

18. Tamahā (from *tama* child and *ha* sacred) was a title applied to the eldest daughter of the Tu'i Tonga *fefine* (the eldest sister of the Tu'i Tonga monarch). There is dispute over the succession of the women who held the title and whether they were formally invested or acquired the designation automatically on the death of the previous title holder. However, there is no doubt that Amelia Fakahiku'o'uiha was the last tamahā and that the title lapsed on her death in 1852; see Burley, 'Sacred child and sacred place: On the intersection of myth, narrative, genealogy and landscape for the study of dynastic Tongan history'.

19. Dumont d'Urville, op. cit., 'Histoire du voyage', vol. iv, p. 138.

20. Martin, op. cit., vol. i, pp. 92–93.

21. Dumont d'Urville, op. cit., 'Histoire du voyage', vol. iv, p. 153.

22. Ibid., p. 149.

23. Ibid., p. 161.

24. According to Peter Dillon, op. cit., vol. i, p. 269.

25. 'Tonga-Tabou, Vadodai vient demander la fin des hostilités', lithograph by Victor-Jean Adam, from a sketch by Louis-Auguste de Sainson, in Dumont d'Urville, op. cit., 'Atlas historique', plate no. 88.

17. ANY OTHER CAPTAIN WOULD PROBABLY HAVE HESITATED

1. It has been suggested that William Oliver, master's mate of the *Pandora*, might have sighted the islands of Totoya and Matuku in 1791 when he was in command of the captured schooner *Resolution*, built by the *Bounty* mutineers on Pitcairn; see Sharp, *The Discovery of the Pacific Islands*, p. 216.

2. For his account of surveys in the Fijian archipelago, see Dumont d'Urville, *Voyage de la corvette l'*Astrolabe, 'Histoire du voyage', vol. iv, chapter xxv, pp. 398–458.

3. See Duyker, 'Coutance and the Voyage of the *Adèle*'.

4. Dumont d'Urville, op. cit., 'Histoire du voyage', vol. iv, p. 485.

5. Ibid., p. 473.

6. See Wallis (ed.), *Carteret's Voyage Round the World 1766–1769*, vol. i, pp. 180–81.

7. Dumont d'Urville, op. cit., 'Histoire du voyage', vol. iv, p. 501.

8. Ibid., p. 499.

9. Quoy & Gaimard, in Dumont d'Urville, op. cit., 'Zoologie', vol. i, pp. 166–67.

10. Hohnen, *Geology of New Ireland, Papua New Guinea*, p. 14.
11. Richard, 'Sertum astrolabianum: Description des espèces nouvelles ou peu connues, recueillies par M. Lesson Jeune, chirurgien de la marine royale, pendant la circumnavigation de la corvette l'*Astrolabe*', in Dumont d'Urville, op. cit., 'Botanique, (part ii, 1834)', pp. xii, xiv & 6–7.
12. Lesson, 'Portrait de l'état-major de l'*Astrolabe*', p. 172.
13. In August 1770, Joseph Banks recorded that one or two members of the *Endeavour* crew 'were violently affected by them both upwards and downwards'; see Beaglehole, (ed.). *The Endeavour Journal of Joseph Banks 1768–1771*, vol. ii, p. 128.
14. Labillardière, *Relation*, vol. i, p. 236 (Stockdale trans., p. 163).
15. Freycinet recorded that cycad nuts were 'soaked to remove their poisonous quality' to produce 'a kind of flour or sago which the inhabitants now use a lot'. Earlier in his narrative he asserted that it was only after the arrival of the Spanish that the inhabitants of Guam 'learned the art of extracting this nutrient, and stripping the deleterious juice which previously had prohibited the use [of cycads]'; see Freycinet, *Voyage autour du monde*, vol. ii, pp. 259 & 262.
16. Dumont d'Urville, op. cit., 'Histoire du voyage', vol. iv, p. 503.
17. Chang, et. al., 'Acute Cycas seed poisoning in Taiwan'.
18. See Sacks, *The Island of the Colourblind and Cycad Island*, pp. 109–201.
19. For a further review of cycad toxicity, see Hill & Osborne, *Cycads of Australia*, pp. 10–11.
20. Lesson, op. cit., p. 167.
21. Ibid., pp. 167–71.
22. John Dunmore has suggested that d'Urville might have suffered from paranoia and manic depression; see *From Venus to Antarctica*, p. 235. Such a bi-polar disability is perhaps too strong a judgement, given d'Urville's impressive achievements in an age prior to mood-stabilising, anti-psychotic medication. Nevertheless, periods of depression are certainly evident throughout his career.
23. Dumont d'Urville, op. cit., 'Histoire du voyage', vol. iv, p. 508.
24. Ibid., p. 511.
25. Lesson, op. cit., p. 171.
26. Dumont d'Urville, op. cit., 'Histoire du voyage', vol. iv, p. 577.
27. Ibid., p. 515.
28. Ibid., p. 528.
29. Dampier, *A Voyage to New Holland*, p. 224.
30. D'Urville did not give a reference, but he appears to have alluded to Brosses's translated extracts from the accounts of William Dampier and Woodes Rogers; see Brosses, *Histoire des navigations aux Terres Australes*, vol. ii, pp. 168 & 385.
31. Quoy & Gaimard, in Dumont d'Urville, op. cit., 'Zoologie', vol. i, pp. 172–73.
32. Ibid., pp. 208–09.
33. Ibid., pp. 207–08.
34. Ibid., p. 227.
35. Ibid., pp. 245–46.
36. Richard, 'Sertum Astrolabianum', in Dumont d'Urville, op. cit. 'Botanique', p. xix.
37. Dumont d'Urville, op. cit., 'Histoire du voyage', vol. iv, p. 582.
38. Ibid.
39. Ibid., p. 591.
40. Lesson, op. cit., p. 167.
41. Baal, Galis & Koentjaraningrat, *West Irian*, p. 110.
42. D'Urville misspelt his name as Elgeneuze. In 1828, he spelt his name Elgenhuizen. Andries Ellinghuijsen was indeed in West Java in 1824. He was collector of duties and then president of the court of chancery in Semarang, before being posted to Ambon. In 1829, he became governor of the Moluccan Islands.
43. Dumont d'Urville, op. cit., 'Histoire du voyage', vol. iv, p. 627.

44. Ibid., p. 629.
45. Lesson, op. cit., pp. 167–68.
46. Dumont d'Urville, op. cit., 'Histoire du voyage', vol. iv, p. 635.
47. Ibid., pp. 628–29.
48. Ibid., p. 636.
49. Ibid., p. 639.
50. Ibid., p. 637.
51. Ibid., p. 632.
52. Ibid., p. 652.

18. VAN DIEMEN'S LAND

1. Dumont d'Urville, *Voyage de la corvette* l'Astrolabe, 'Histoire du voyage', vol. iv, p. 659.
2. Ibid., p. 657.
3. For further information, see Henn, 'The Tryal Rocks'.
4. Dumont d'Urville, op. cit., 'Histoire du voyage', vol. iv, p. 672.
5. Dumont d'Urville to the minister, 9 April 1829, in dossier personnel, Béringuier, Alexandre, SHDDM, Vincennes, CC7 Alpha 167.
6. Dumont d'Urville, op. cit., 'Histoire du voyage', vol. v, p. 10.
7. For a fine biography, see Davidson, *Peter Dillon of Vanikoro*.
8. Quoted by Dillon in his letter to Charles Lushington, chief secretary to the government of Bengal, 19 September 1826, in Dillon, *Narrative and Successful Result of a Voyage in the South Seas*, vol. i, pp. 39–40.
9. French archaeologists did indeed find evidence of a French camp at Paiu in 1999; see Galipaud, et al., *Naufragés à Vanikoro*. Initially, Dillon thought that Paiu and 'Wannow' (Fono) were offshore islands of Vanikoro rather than coastal locations.
10. Dillon, op. cit., p. 44.
11. Tytler served in the 34th Native Bengal Infantry at Midnapur. He was the father of Robert Christopher Tytler, famous for his pioneering photographs of India.
12. Dillon, op. cit., vol. i, p. 249.
13. Ibid., vol. ii, p. 359.
14. Ibid., vol. ii, p. 364.
15. Dumont d'Urville, op. cit., 'Histoire du voyage', vol. v, p. 16.
16. Ibid., p. 17.
17. Ibid., p. 22.
18. Ibid., p. 23.
19. Ibid.
20. Dillon, 'Postscript: La Peyrouse'.
21. Lettre de Madame Dumont d'Urville [chez Madame veuve Lamouroux, rue des quais no. 54, Caen] 25 décembre 1827 au ministre de la marine, demandant des nouvelles de son fils, dossier personnel, Dumont d'Urville, SHDDM, Vincennes, CC^7 Alpha 772, pièce 24.
22. D'Urville named the sailors as 'Grasse' (probably Joseph Gras, born 1806) and 'Jean' (probably Jean Jacques, born 1806).
23. Dumont d'Urville, op. cit., 'Histoire du voyage', vol. v, p. 32.
24. Richard, 'Sertum Astrolabianum: Description des espèces nouvelles ou peu connues, recueillies par M. Lesson Jeune, chirurgien de la marine royale, pendant la circumnavigation de la corvette l'*Astrolabe*', in Dumont d'Urville, op. cit. 'Botanique', pp. 92–95, 119–21, 125–26.
25. Dumont d'Urville, op. cit., 'Histoire du voyage', vol. v, p. 30.
26. Quoy & Gaimard, op. cit., 'Zoologie', vol. i, pp. 177–78.
27. *Nomen oblitum* (Latin forgotten name, plural *nomina oblita*): name that has remained unused for many years and is effectively a senior synonym. In this particular case, generic revision was

inevitable; Gould correctly recognised that this beautiful robin belonged to the genus *Petroica*, established in 1829 by the English ornithologist William Swainson (1789–1855).

28. Boisduval, in Dumont d'Urville, op. cit., 'Faune entomologique', Coléoptères, pp. 588–89.
29. Quoy & Gaimard, in Dumont d'Urville, op. cit., 'Zoologie', vol. iv, pp. 145–46.
30. Ibid., vol. iv, pp. 150–51.
31. Ibid., vol. iv, pp. 91–92.
32. Ibid., vol. ii, pp. 327–29. Significantly, in the early 1980s, this species yielded two exciting new polypropionate antibiotics (diemenensin A and B), the first of which has been shown to inhibit the growth of *Staphylococcus aurea* bacteria; see Hochlowski & Faulkner, 'Antibiotics from the marine pulmonate *Siphonaria diemenensis*'.
33. Dumont d'Urville, op. cit., 'Histoire du voyage', vol. v, p. 89.
34. Ibid., p. 96.
35. See Evans, '19 June 1822, Creating "An Object of Real Terror"'.
36. Dumont d'Urville, op. cit., 'Histoire du voyage', vol. v, p. 48.

19. VANIKORO

1. Sharp, *The Discovery of the Pacific Islands*, pp. 152–53.
2. The earliest population count, 1278 people, was conducted by the anthropologist Raymond Firth in 1928–29. Jared Diamond discusses Tikopia's sustainable agricultural practices and traditional population-control methods, including abortion and infanticide. The later practices only began to end with missionary contact from 1900 onwards; see Diamond, *Collapse*, pp. 286–93.
3. Dumont d'Urville, *Voyage de la corvette l'Astrolabe*, 'Histoire du voyage', vol. v, p. 117.
4. Peter Dillon also failed to persuade Achowlia to accompany him to Vanikoro, and in his account he tells us that he was 'an old man' who felt he would 'beg or starve' if he returned to India, having 'lost his caste'; furthermore, he was married to a Tikopian woman 'whom he loved tenderly', and he considered Tikopia a land of plenty; see Dillon, *Narrative and Successful Result of a Voyage in the South Seas*, vol. ii, pp. 116–17; see also Duyker, 'Achowlia, aka Joe (*ca.* 1790–*ca.* 1840)'.
5. Helen Rosenman excluded the end of d'Urville's possibly gratuitous but nonetheless racist comment in her translation of this text; see Rosenman (ed. & trans.), *An Account in Two Volumes of Two Voyages to the South Seas*, vol. i, p. 201.
6. D'Urville would call the American William Taylor (who joined the *Coquille* at Bora Bora) 'Williams' in his *Voyage pittoresque autour du monde* (vol. ii, pp. 200–01), and he had already named one of the English sailors who joined the *Astrolabe* at King George Sound in October 1826 (and guided the expedition into Western Port) 'Hambilton'. Given the unusual spelling of Hambilton, this is an unlikely coincidence. Guilbert spelt his name 'Ambelton', but this may simply have been a phonetic rendering. The fact that these men were either deserters or escaped convicts, and that France might have had international legal obligations to apprehend them, might explain the pseudonyms d'Urville employed. Peter Dillon (op. cit., vol. ii, pp. 118–19) suggested that one of these Englishmen might have been named Cleft or Cleff and that he had served as second mate on a vessel named *Mary* prior to a conviction for forgery in London and then transportation to New South Wales. However, the Old Bailey's records offer no confirmation of any such London conviction for anyone by these names, as asserted by Dillon.
7. Dillon, op. cit., vol. ii, p. 118.
8. Dumont d'Urville, op. cit., 'Histoire du voyage', vol. v, pp. 124–25.
9. In identifying modern place names, I have been greatly assisted by Dr Alexandre François' 'Carte toponomique de Vanikoro' Centre National de la Recherche Scientifique, Paris, 2005.
10. Dumont d'Urville, op. cit., 'Histoire du voyage', vol. v, p. 144.
11. Ibid., pp. 145–46.
12. Ibid., p. 155.
13. Lesson, 'Portrait de l'état-major de l'*Astrolabe*', p. 188–89.
14. Dumont d'Urville, op. cit., 'Histoire du voyage', vol. v, p. 162.

15. Ibid., p. 166.

16. Ibid., pp. 166–67.

17. Ibid., pp. 181–82.

18. D'Urville specifically uses the word '*pierrier*', which generally refers to a swivel gun but can also be a kind of mortar.

19. Lesson, op. cit., p. 188.

20. Dumont d'Urville, op. cit., 'Histoire du voyage', vol. v, p. 186.

21. Ibid., p. 191.

22. Gaimard, in Dumont d'Urville, op. cit., 'Philologie', vol. ii, Vocabulaires des idiomes des habitans de Vanikoro, pp. 165–74.

23. Richard, 'Sertum Astrolabianum', in Dumont d'Urville, op. cit. 'Botanique', pp. xxxviii & xli.

24. Quoy & Gaimard, in Dumont d'Urville, op. cit., 'Zoologie', vol. i, pp. 188–89.

25. Ibid., p. 206.

26. Ibid., p. 183.

27. Ibid., pp. 77–80.

28. Simmons, 'Order Chiroptera', p. 340.

29. See Desmarest, *Mammologie, ou, description des espèces de mammifères*, supplement, vol. ii, p. 547.

30. Quoy & Gaimard, in Dumont d'Urville, op. cit., 'Zoologie', vol. ii, pp. 163–65.

31. Ibid., pp. 337–38.

32. Ibid., vol. iii, pp. 195–96.

33. These included: *Mitra vanikorensis* (*Imbricaria vanikorensis*), *Cerithium inflatum* (*Clypeomorus inflata*) and *Stomatella maculata* (*Granata maculata*); see Quoy & Gaimard, in Dumont d'Urville, op. cit., 'Zoologie', vol. ii, pp. 649–50; vol. iii, pp. 130 & 305–07.

34. Dumont d'Urville, op. cit., 'Zoologie', vol. iv, pp. 137, 141–42, 147–48, 182–83 & 260–63.

35. See, for example, Chang-Yih Duh et al., 'New cytotoxic constituents from the Formosan soft corals *Clavularia viridis* and *Clavularia violacea*'.

36. Boisduval, in Dumont d'Urville, op. cit., 'Faune Entomologique', Coléoptères, pp. 400–01.

37. See Aberlenc, 'Les insectes de Vanikoro'.

38. Bellamy, 'Type species designations in the family Buprestidae (Coleoptera)', p. 10.

39. Boisduval, in Dumont d'Urville, op. cit., 'Faune Entomologique', Coléoptères, pp. 79–80.

40. Boisduval, in Dumont d'Urville, op. cit., 'Faune Entomologique', Lepidoptères, pp. 138–39.

41. For an account of both monuments, see Rivière, 'In Honour of a Fellow Explorer'.

42. Dumont d'Urville, op. cit., 'Histoire du voyage', vol. v, p. 188.

43. Ibid., p. 189.

44. See, for example, Thorpe, 'A probable relic of La Perouse'.

45. Galipaud et al., *Naufragés à Vanikoro*.

46. See Association Salomon, *Le mystère Lapérouse*.

47. 'Inauguration du monument élevé par l'*Astrolabe* à Lapérouse à Vanikoro, de Sainson pinx.; Vanderburch lith.; fig. par V. Adam', in Dumont d'Urville, op. cit., 'Atlas historique', plate 187.

48. Dumont d'Urville, op. cit., 'Histoire du voyage', vol. v, pp. 202–03.

49. Ibid., pp. 203–04.

50. Ibid., pp. 208–09.

20. THE VOYAGE HOME

1. Dossier personnel, Collinet, Pierre-Jean-François, SHDDM, Vincennes, CC[7] Alpha 519.

2. Bataille, 'Un document inédit', p. 63.

3. D'Urville would later learn that despite his title, Flores held only the military rank of sergeant; a further surprise was that his niece was married to a former French sailor from Le Havre named Baptiste.

4. According to Rose de Freycinet, Medinilla was already in his fifties in 1819, 'of average build and quite handsome', with 'lively and intelligent eyes, a pleasant face with a distinguished air and

considerable nobility in his deportment. Among his many attributes, the attention he gives to his grooming makes him good company; his hair is always well powdered and perfumed; his clothes are very becoming and his shoes polished'; see Rivière, *A Woman of Courage: The journal of Rose de Freycinet on her voyage around the world*, pp. 89–90. A conservative royalist, Medinilla had spent 23 years as an infantry officer in South America (of which 14 years were in Lima, Peru) before being posted to the Philippines in 1809. He was first appointed governor of Guam in 1812 but was removed from office in 1822. After a four-year liberal interregnum (largely under Captain José Ganga Herrero), he was reinstated by the Spanish Bourbons in August 1826 and would remain in office until 1831. He died in Manila *ca.* 1834. The plant genus *Medinilla* (Melastomataceae) was named in his honour by Freycinet's botanist Charles Gaudichaud-Beaupré; see Freycinet, *Voyage autour du monde*, vol. ii, p. 224 and Henige, *Colonial Governors*, p. 298.

5. Dumont d'Urville, *Voyage de la corvette l'*Astrolabe, 'Histoire du voyage', vol. v, p. 261.

6. 'Couvent d'Umata servant d'hopital aux marins de l'*Astrolabe*, Guam', lithograph by Achille Saint-Aulaire, figures by Victor-Jean Adam, from a sketch by Louis-Auguste de Sainson, in Dumont d'Urville, op. cit., 'Atlas historique', plate 199.

7. Dumont d'Urville, op. cit., 'Histoire du voyage', vol. v, pp. 257–58.

8. Richard, 'Sertum Astrolabianum', in Dumont d'Urville, op. cit. 'Botanique', pp. xliii & xlviii.

9. Gaimard, 'Vocabulaires de la langue des habitans de Gouaham', in Dumont d'Urville, op. cit., 'Philologie', vol. ii, pp. 190–92.

10. Surgeon Quoy also requested to treat the governor in Agaña.

11. Quoy & Gaimard, in Dumont d'Urville, op. cit., 'Zoologie', vol. iii, pp. 191–92. It should be noted that Governor Medinilla also gave the expedition a case of local shells, so we cannot be certain whether Quoy and Gaimard personally collected *Nerita guamenis*.

12. Although Freycinet does not mention this Scotsman by name in his historical account, Jacques Arago (1790–1855) recorded that he was enrolled during a landfall before Timor (possibly Mauritius). He described him as 'agile, strong, robust, patient [and] adroit'; see Arago, *Souvenirs d'un aveugle*, pp. 85–86; see also pp. 126–27. Surgeon John Wilson of the visiting whaling ship *Gipsy* wrote that 'he is the Government Pilot, Interpreter, Port-Adjutant, &c., &c., he speaks Spanish, & Chemora fluently & is a tolerable French scholar: he is a tall very stout man; full of conversation & anecdote, but rather too fond of the bottle: it is reported he was Lieutenant in the English navy, was guilty of a breach of Trust, & fled here'; see Forster (ed.), *The Cruise of the 'Gipsy'*, p. 90.

13. Dumont d'Urville, op. cit., 'Histoire du voyage', vol. v, p. 267.

14. Ibid., p. 280.

15. Wa'ab would perhaps have been more accurate, but it was certainly closer to the mark than Yap, the name by which the island and indeed the state of the Federated States of Micronesia are still officially known.

16. Dumont d'Urville, op. cit., 'Histoire du voyage', vol. v, p. 392.

17. Ibid., p. 393.

18. In his private library, d'Urville owned a 1793 French translation of George Keate's (1729–1797) account of these islands based on the journals of Henry Wilson and his officers, who were shipwrecked there in August 1783 aboard the *Antelope*. He was also aware of the survey work of Lieutenant John McCluer (1759–1795) and the crew of the *Panther* in the Palau Islands in June 1791 and January to March 1793.

19. The remnants of d'Entrecasteaux's expedition also sought assistance at Cajeli in October 1793.

20. Boisduval, in Dumont d'Urville, op. cit., 'Faune Entomologique', Coléoptères, pp. 3, 70–71, 82–83, 95–96, 132–33, 187–88, 224, 252, 269, 271–72, 285 & 573–74.

21. Despite its unpleasant side effects as an emetic and purgative (which can also affect the muscles of the heart), ipecac, derived from the root of the ipecacuanha plant, is a proven anti-protozoal. A safer synthesised version, dehydroemetine, is still used and administered in the form of intramuscular injections to treat amoebic dysentery.

22. Bataille, op. cit., pp. 138–39; his name was recorded as 'Langaker', but this was perhaps Nicolaus Lange (1807–1855), later city apothecary at the dispensary of the hospital in Batavia; see Bloys van

Treslong Prins, *Genealogische en heraldische gedenkwaardigheden betreffende Europeanen op Java*, vol. iii, p. 167.

23. Boisduval, in Dumont d'Urville, op. cit., 'Faune Entomologique', Coléoptères, pp. 99–100, 162–63, 224–26, 256–57, 395–96, 443–44, 470–71, 495–96, 503–04, 518–19 & 591–92.

24. Dumont d'Urville, op. cit., 'Histoire du voyage', vol. v, pp. 421–22.

25. See Quoy & Gaimard, in Dumont d'Urville, op. cit., 'Zoologie', vol. i, pp. 143–48.

26. Barbier was a former naval officer who had served as an *enseigne de vaisseau* aboard the 32-gun frigate *Sémillante* in Admiral Linnois' squadron in the Indian Ocean, but, according to d'Urville, he was dismissed for his political opinions (presumably republican or Bonapartist) in 1815; see Dumont d'Urville, op. cit., 'Histoire du voyage', vol. v, p. 432.

27. Quoy & Gaimard, in Dumont d'Urville, op. cit., 'Zoologie', vol. i, pp. 136–39.

28. Ibid., pp. 125–32.

29. Gaimard refers to d'Urville's fresh-water temperature studies at Lake Tondano, see 'Extrait du Journal de M. Gaimard', in Dumont d'Urville, op. cit., 'Histoire du voyage', vol. v, p. 672. Although Lake Poso in Sulawesi is one of the deepest lakes in the world (450 metres), Lake Tondano is only 20 metres deep. D'Urville was no doubt disappointed not to be able to plunge his 'thermometrograph' deeper than a few fathoms. At the village of Passoun, the waters of the lake (33.3°) proved to be 9° warmer than the air temperature at the surface (24.5°).

30. Gaimard, in Dumont d'Urville, op. cit., 'Philologie', vol. ii, Vocabulaire de la langue des harfours de Manado, pp. 193–94.

31. 'Mr Merkus, Gouverneur des Moluques, offrant des babi-rousses a l'expédition de l'*Astrolabe*, Célèbes', lithographed by Victor-Jean Adam from a sketch by Louis-Auguste de Sainson, in Dumont d'Urville, op. cit., 'Atlas historique', plate no. 216.

32. Dumont d'Urville, op. cit., 'Histoire du voyage', vol. v, pp. 486.

33. Ibid., pp. 486–87.

34. Ibid., p. 488.

35. Known to the English as Anjerie, the port town was completely destroyed by a tsunami in the wake of the eruption of Karakatoa (facing it in the Sunda Strait) in 1883.

36. 'Extrait du Journal de M. Gaimard', in Dumont d'Urville, op. cit., 'Histoire du voyage', vol. v, p. 673.

37. Dumont d'Urville, op. cit., 'Histoire du voyage', vol. v, p. 509.

38. For an excellent survey of Telfair's life, see Rivière, *'No Man is an Island'*, chapter iv.

39. Dumont d'Urville, op. cit., 'Histoire du voyage', vol. v, p. 506.

40. Barclay, 'A picture of the negro slavery existing in the Mauritius'; Charles Telfair is specifically mentioned on p. 376: 'the case of the estate of Bel Ombre, belonging to Mr. Telfair, the private Secretary of Sir Robert Farquhar … one of the best regulated in the island.' There is also a separate section on 'Cases of cruelty at Bel Ombre', pp. 380–81.

41. Telfair, *Some Account of the State of Slavery at Mauritius*.

42. With British prohibition of the importation of new slaves and the voice of abolition growing louder and louder, the days of slavery in Mauritius were numbered. D'Urville even mentions meeting a Breton captain named Guilbaud, who was engaged in the profitable trade in French mules, which fetched high prices as replacements for slaves in many areas of heavy labour.

43. See Toussaint, 'Epinay, Antoine Zacharie Adrien d' (1794–1839)'; see also Toussaint (ed.), *Les Missions d'Adrien d'Epinay (1830–1834)*.

44. Dumont d'Urville, op. cit., 'Histoire du voyage', vol. v, p. 515.

45. Elénore Lapérouse (*née* Broudou) is buried in the Hocquart de Turtot family tomb in Père Lachaise Cemetery, Paris.

46. The *Sydney Gazette* article in question appears to have been published on Saturday, 24 September 1827, p. 2. The article stated that he 'commenced cannonading the island, in which several natives were brutally and unnecessarily murdered. It is true that Captain D'Urville lost one of his men whilst engaged in pursuing the natives, destroying their villages, and insulting their sacred places of interment, but common humanity should have prompted another spirit [than] that which was manifested by the French commander. He should have kept a better guard over his men, and then

the sacrifice of life – which is deliberate murde[r] in the sight of an avenging Creator – would have been spared. After all, Captain D'Urville was obliged to depart without men, threatening to proceed to Valparaiso, return with two frigates, and in blowing up the island exterminate the race of Tongese!'

47. In return, d'Urville gave Bennett a bronze medallion commemorating the *Astrolabe* expedition.
48. Dumont d'Urville, op. cit., 'Histoire du voyage', vol. v, p. 528.
49. Under the agreement, Farquhar undertook to have the French-Malagasy dictionary printed in England and to share any resulting profits with Froberville. However, the book was never published, mainly because of pressure from members of the London Missionary Society, who had competing English-Malagasy publishing ambitions. Farquhar died in 1830, and 20 years later, his son Walter donated Froberville's manuscripts to the British Library. They are preserved there to this day, along with two others apparently entrusted by Froberville to Matthew Flinders in 1810; see Pier M. Larson's masterly study *Ocean of Letters*, ch. 4, pp. 147–95.
50. Dumont d'Urville, op. cit., 'Histoire du voyage', vol. v, p. 528.
51. See Chapelier [Antoine Flageollot], 'Grammaire de la langue madécasse (Madagascar)'
52. Larson, op. cit., p. 175; d'Urville also cited Étienne de Flacourt's *Dictionnaire de la langue de Madagascar*, published in 1658, and Père Claude-Bernard Challan's *Vocabulaire malgache* (1773), the first book ever published in Mauritius. Whether he also sought access to manuscripts on the language of Madagascar in the library of Charles Telfair is unclear.
53. See Relandus, 'De linguis insularum quarundam orientalium'.
54. Hurles, et al., 'The dual origin of the Malagasy in island Southeast Asia and East Africa'.
55. See chapters by Adelaar, Blench and Dewar in Reade (ed.), *The Indian Ocean in Antiquity*; see also Dahl, *Migration from Kalimantan to Madagascar*.
56. Quoy & Gaimard, in Dumont d'Urville, op. cit., 'Zoologie', vol. ii, pp. 311–12.
57. Ibid., vol. iv, pp. 151–52 & 166.
58. Ibid., vol. iii, pp. 397–98.
59. Ibid., pp. 712–13.
60. Dumont d'Urville, op. cit., 'Histoire du voyage', vol. v, p. 518.
61. Ibid., p. 524.
62. Ibid., p. 535.
63. Dossier personnel, Faraguet, Henry Antoine, SHDDM, Vincennes, CC[7] Alpha 847.
64. McIntyre, *Comets in Old Cape Records*.
65. Faraguet appears to have returned to France around the time of the Revolution of 1848 and settled in Villers Rotin (Côte d'Or) in the same canton as his father's native Auxonne. In the wake of Louis-Napoléon's coup d'état, he was arrested, imprisoned until February 1853 and then temporarily exiled to Belgium because he was a leading freemason and seen as a possible source of organised dissent (see dossier Antoine Henry Faraguet, Archives départementales du Jura, M53 & Archives nationales BB/22/154/1). Between 1858 and 1860, he was in Paris and the partner of François-Joseph Leiber (died 1869), publishing numerous astronomical, mathematical and other scientific texts. Thereafter he disappears from the historical record; see also Duyker, 'Faraguet, Henry Antoine (1802–*post* 1859)'.
66. Jacquemont to his father, 28 December 1828, in Jacquemont, *Correspondance,* vol. i, pp. 53–54.
67. Dumont d'Urville, op. cit., 'Histoire du voyage', vol. v, p. 556.
68. Quoy & Gaimard, in Dumont d'Urville, op. cit., 'Zoologie', vol. iv, pp. 120–21.
69. Dumont d'Urville, op. cit., 'Histoire du voyage', vol. v, p. 553.
70. If a gynaecological allusion, it cannot be divorced from the intersecting categories of race and gender in the nineteenth century, particularly when one reflects on the tragic fate of Saartje Baartman (*ca.*1790–1815), the so-called 'Hottentot Venus', exhibited like a circus freak in Britain and France in the years immediately before d'Urville's marriage. Her genitalia and brain were displayed at the Musée de l'Homme in Paris until as recently as 1985 but were returned to South Africa in 2002; see my discussion of this subject in Duyker, *François Péron*, pp. 207–08 & 215.
71. Dumont d'Urville, op. cit., 'Histoire du voyage', vol. v, pp. 554–55.
72. See Solomon, *Saul Solomon*.

73. Dumont d'Urville, op. cit., 'Histoire du voyage', vol. v, p. 564.

74. Kauffmann, *The Black Room at Longwood*, pp. 10 & 14.

75. Dumont d'Urville, op. cit., 'Histoire du voyage', vol. v, pp. 561–62.

76. Quoy & Gaimard, in Dumont d'Urville, op. cit., 'Zoologie', vol. iii, pp. 706–07.

77. Dumont d'Urville, 'De la distribution des fougères sur la surface du globe terrestre', pp. 64–65.

78. In 1988, 150 years after his death from influenza, William Bates appeared on a set of five Ascension Island stamps. D'Urville appeared on a French stamp in the same year.

79. Although France and other European powers had long been vexed by the pirates that had used safe havens on the Algerian coast, the blockade of Algiers was precipitated by a long-standing commercial dispute over Bonaparte's refusal to pay for a grain shipment to the Republic made by the Algerian-Jewish merchants David ben Joseph Cohen Bakri (1770–1811) and Naphtali Busnach (died 1805) in 1797. Bonaparte had considered their price excessive, but in 1820, the restored Bourbons decided to pay them half of the 14 million francs they demanded. Hussein, the Dey of Algiers (1765–1838), also claimed 250,000 francs as repayment for a loan made to the same merchants and demanded direct payment from the French government. These demands were ignored by both Louis XVIII and Charles X because France had no obligation to pay the creditors of Bakri and Busnach (who by now had relocated to Livorno). The Dey then blamed the French consul Pierre Deval (1757–1829) for this and not only castigated him but struck him thrice with his fly-swish. Outraged, the French government demanded reparations and sent warships to evacuate its citizens and commence a blockade; see Bertier de Sauvigny, *The Bourbon Restoration*, pp. 434–35.

80. Extrait d'une lettre, Toulon, 26 mars 1829, adressée au ministre [Hyde de Neuville] par Dumont d'Urville, annoçant le retour de l'*Astrolabe*, dossier personnel, Dumont d'Urville, SHDDM, Vincennes, CC^7 Alpha 772, pièce 26.

21. FRANCE & REVOLUTION

1. See, for example, d'Urville's comment: 'M. Freycinet wanted to travel as a great lord and with all the comforts of life, indeed all; but this is not, in my opinion, the point of these voyages', Dumont d'Urville, *Voyage de la corvette l'*Astrolabe, 'Histoire du voyage', vol. v, p. 604.

2. See Rivière (ed. & trans.), *A Woman of Courage*.

3. Extrait d'une lettre, Toulon, 26 mars 1829, adressée au ministre [Hyde de Neuville] par Dumont d'Urville, annonçant le retour de l'*Astrolabe*, dossier personnel, Dumont d'Urville, SHDDM, CC^7 Alpha 772, pièce 26.

4. Ibid.

5. Hyde de Neuville to Turpinier, marginal note on d'Urville's letter to the minister of 26 March 1829, loc. cit.

6. Lettre du baron Tupinier à Dumont d'Urville, 23 mars 1829, accusant réception des rapports rédigés pendant le 1er voyage de l'*Astrolabe* (copy), dossier personnel, Dumont d'Urville, SHDDM, Vincennes, CC^7 Alpha 772, pièce 25.

7. Dossier personnel, Jacquinot, Honoré, SHDDM, Vincennes, CC^7 Alpha 1222.

8. Dossier personnel, Lottin, Victor-Charles, SHDDM, Vincennes, CC^7 Alpha 1610.

9. Dossier personnel, Gressien, Victor-Amédée, SHDDM, Vincennes, CC^7 Alpha 1080.

10. Sainson would soon take up an administrative position in the navy before resigning; see dossier personnel, Sainson, Louis-Auguste de, SHDDM, Vincennes, CC^7 Alpha 2233; see also Collins, 'Louis-Auguste de Sainson'.

11. On behalf of Bertrand, d'Urville wrote a separate letter to the minister from Mauritius requesting his advancement; see dossier personnel, Bertrand, François-Esprit, SHDDM, Vincennes, CC^7 Alpha 191.

12. Dumont d'Urville, op. cit., 'Histoire du voyage', vol. v, p. 588.

13. Dossier personnel, Lesson, Pierre-Adolphe, SHDDM, Vincennes, CC^7 Alpha 1563.

14. Ollivier, 'Pierre-Adolphe Lesson, Surgeon-Naturalist', pp. 55.

15. This system of semaphore messaging was invented by Claude Chappe (1763–1805) during the

Revolution. In 1821, the Paris–Lyon line of signal stations was extended to Toulon, with significant benefits for the navy, since Brest and Paris had already been connected before 1814. The telegraph, which relied on lines of sight, could not operate at night or in foggy inclement weather, yet in April 1829, news received in Toulon at 4.00 am from Rome, announcing the election of Pope Pius VIII, was transmitted by the cumbersome counterweighted arms of the telegraph to Paris within eight hours; see Bertier de Sauvigny, *The Bourbon Restoration*, p. 211.

16. Dumont d'Urville, op. cit., 'Histoire du voyage', vol. v, p. 582.
17. Hillairet, *Dictionnaire historique des rues de Paris*, vol. ii, pp. 515–16.
18. See Dumont d'Urville, Journal, MS 65, Bibliothèque municipale de Toulon, 3 & 28 juillet 1830.
19. Ibid., 9 septembre 1830.
20. While he was in Hobart in December 1827, d'Urville had written to the secretary of the Académie des sciences reporting on his sea-water temperature studies at depths of up to 820 fathoms. His letter was not received in Paris until mid-September the following year. 'Dossier de la séance de l'Académie des sciences du 15 septembre 1828; lettre de Dumont d'Urville du 27 xbre 1827 de Hobart-town, reçu par le secrétaire le 15 septembre 1828', Archives de l'Académie des sciences. Dumont d'Urville, 'Rapport à l'Académie royale des sciences de l'institut sur la marche et les opérations du voyage de découvertes de la corvette l'*Astrolabe* en 1826, 1827, 1828 et 1829, lu dans la séance du 12 mai 1829'. Ironically, the final article in the same issue of the *Annales* was a report on a new British colony on the west coast of Australia, a colony that effectively negated the secret political significance of d'Urville's survey work on the same coast; see Anon, 'Nouvelle colonie anglaise sur la côte occidentale de la Nouvelle-Hollande'.
21. Rossel, *Rapport sur la navigation de* l'Astrolabe. This report would be followed, on 16 November, by Georges Cuvier's report on the zoological collections and, on 20 November, by René Desfontaines' report on the botanical work of the voyage. All these reports were republished at the beginning of the first volume of d'Urville's historical account of the *Astrolabe* voyage; see Dumont d'Urville, op. cit., 'Histoire du voyage', vol. i, pp. lxxv–cxvi.
22. État des services, 31 décembre 1829, dossier personnel, Dumont d'Urville, SHDDM, Vincennes, CC[7] Alpha 772, pièce 29.
23. The candidates were Admiral Albin-Reine Roussin, Captain Anne-Chrétien-Louis de Hell, Captain Louis-Isidore Duperrey, Captain Jules Sébastien César Dumont d'Urville, Pierre Daussy, Colonel Charles-Rigobert Bonne and Colonel Jean-Baptiste Corabœuf.
24. Institut de France, *Index biographique de l'Académie des sciences*, p. 445.
25. Arago, 'Réponse de M. Arago, député, à une lettre de M. le capitaine de vaisseau Dumont d'Urville, et examen critique du premier voyage de circumnavigation de l'*Astrolabe*', p. 94.
26. Dumont d'Urville, op. cit., 'Histoire du voyage', vol. v, p. 591.
27. Rozet, *Chronique de juillet 1830*, vol. ii, p. 144.
28. Bertier de Sauvigny, *The Bourbon Restoration*, pp. 434–39.
29. For the ordinances and all their articles, see Turnbull, *The French Revolution of 1830*, pp. 32–39; for further background, see Bertier de Sauvigny, op. cit., chapter 23; also Rémond, *La droite en France*, chs 1 & 2.
30. Dumont d'Urville, Journal, MS 65, Bibliothèque municipale de Toulon, lundi 26 juillet 1830.
31. Fortescue, *France and 1848*, pp. 15–16.
32. Dumont d'Urville, Journal, loc. cit., mardi, 27 juillet 1830.
33. Ibid., mercredi, 28 juillet 1830.
34. Ibid., mardi, 27 juillet 1830.
35. Ibid.
36. Marmont, *Mémoires*, vol. viii, p. 254. Marmont would show d'Urville his manuscripts for these very memoirs during their traverse of the Channel in the following month.
37. Dumont d'Urville, Journal, loc. cit., mercredi, 28 juillet 1830.
38. Less than a month later, Marmont would confide to d'Urville his opinion that Polignac was 'a fool'; Dumont d'Urville, Journal, loc. cit., mercredi, 18 août 1830.
39. There were deeper connotations. Because Marmont had entered into negotiations with the allies in

1814 and surrendered Paris to them, Bonapartists coined the term *ragusade* as a synonym for treason.

40. Dumont d'Urville, Journal, loc. cit., jeudi, 29 juillet 1830.

41. Rozet, op. cit., vol. ii, p. 104.

42. [Vincendon-Dumoulin, C.D.], 'Notice biographique: Jules-Sébastien-César Dumont d'Urville', p. 117.

43. See Vergniol, 'La chute de Charles X: I. Les "Trois Glorieuses"' and II. 'Une mission de confiance'.

44. Dumont d'Urville, Journal, loc. cit., jeudi, 29 juillet 1830.

45. Ibid.

46. Dumont d'Urville, Cherbourg, au ministre de la marine, Paris, 27 août [1830], '[dossier] Embarquement de Charles X à Cherbourg 1830', SHDDM, Vincennes, BB^4 530 Bis, f. 232 recto.

47. [Vincendon-Dumoulin, C.D.], op. cit., pp. 117–18.

48. Dumont d'Urville, in Collection Margry, 'Mers Australes', Bibliothèque nationale, NAF 9439, ff. 153 & 161.

49. Bertier de Sauvigny, op. cit., p. 452.

50. Dumont d'Urville, Journal, vendredi, 30 juillet 1830.

51. See Duyker, 'Bailly, Joseph-Charles (1777–1844)'.

52. 'Ange René Armand de Mackau', in Robert, Bourloton & Cougny, *Dictionnaire des parlementaires français*, vol. iv., pp. 212–13.

53. Dumont d'Urville, Journal, loc. cit., samedi, 31 Juillet 1830. In English and French, the words 'Jesuit' and 'Jesuitical' are used to describe political prevarication and cunningly dissembled policy. D'Urville appears to have used the word Jesuit a number of times to describe the royalist 'ultras', but he was probably also making a direct reference to the role of the church as one of the pillars of Bourbon France. In the lead up to the Revolution, one deep source of resentment and heated debate – because many saw it as a violation of the principle of freedom of thought and religion – was the draconian anti-sacrilege law (January 1825), which specified capital punishment for those who profaned consecrated hosts and sacred vessels.

54. Dumont d'Urville, Journal, loc. cit., samedi, 31 juillet 1830.

55. Ibid., dimanche, 1 août 1830.

56. Bertier de Sauvigny, op. cit., p. 454.

57. Dumont d'Urville, Journal, loc. cit., lundi, 2 août 1830.

58. [Tupinier, J.-M.] Directeur des ports à Dumont d'Urville, capitaine de vaisseau, Paris, 2 août 1830, 'Embarquement de Charles X à Cherbourg 1830', loc. cit., f. 41 recto & verso.

59. Dumont d'Urville, Journal, loc. cit., lundi, 2 août 1830.

60. Ibid., mardi, 3 août 1830.

61. Ibid., mercredi, 4 août 1830; I am at odds with Camille Vergniol, who transcribed 'Harfleur' as 'Honfleur'; see Vergniol, *Dumont d'Urville*, p. 134. Although d'Urville's handwriting is frequently open to guesswork (especially when it comes to two very similar toponyms), it stands to reason that travelling via Caudebec from Rouen, he was already on the northern bank of the Seine. He would not have re-crossed the Seine and gone to Honfleur (rather than Harfleur), which required a diagonal crossing of the estuary at its widest point, to reach Le Havre 'shortly after'.

62. See Denois, Etienne François, Archives nationales, LH/733/47.

63. The *Great Britain* s[hip], c[opper] s[heaved], [Captain] F. French, 725 tons, N[ew] York, [owned by the] Capt. & Co., *Lloyd's Register of Shipping for the year 1830*, Society for the Registry of Shipping, London, entry no. 471.

64. The *Charles Carroll* does not appear in Lloyd's Register in 1830, but the *Carroll* s[hip], c[opper] s[heaved], [Captain] J. Clark, 411 tons, N[ew] York, [owned by the] Capt. & Co., A[merican property], does appear in *Lloyd's Register of Shipping for the year 1833*, Society for the Registry of Shipping, London, entry no. 479. According to Lloyd's, the individual captains were part-owners of the vessels, but Marshal Marmont was told that the vessels belonged to Joseph Bonaparte (1768–1844); see Marmont, *Mémoires*, vol. viii, p. 328. The comte de Montbel believed that they belonged to Jérôme Bonaparte's (1784–1860) former father-in-law, William Patterson; see Montbel, *1787–1831: Souvenirs du comte de Montbel*, p. 339. Jérôme Bonaparte and his American first wife,

Elizabeth Patterson (1785–1879), William Patterson's daughter, were married by John Carroll (1735–1815), Archbishop of Baltimore, a cousin of Charles Carroll (1737–1832), the only Catholic and the last surviving signatory of the American Declaration of Independence, after whom the *Charles Carroll* was named. The brother of Elizabeth Patterson was also married to Charles Carroll's granddaughter.

65. Dumont d'Urville, Journal, mercredi, 4 août 1830, loc. cit. In a letter written to the director of ports on the same day, d'Urville used almost the same words as he had in his journal: the vessels 'far surpassed the opinion I had formed'; see Dumont d'Urville, Cherbourg, au [Tupinier, J.-M.] directeur des ports, Paris 4 août 1830, 'Embarquement de Charles X à Cherbourg 1830', loc. cit., f. 170 recto & verso.

66. Ministre de la marine [Marie-Henri-Daniel Gauthier, comte de Rigny] à M. [Charles-Toussaint] Pouyer, préfet maritime à Cherbourg, Paris, 3 août 1830, 'Embarquement de Charles X à Cherbourg 1830', loc. cit., ff. 4–5.

67. See, for example, Dumont d'Urville, Cherbourg, au [Tupinier, J.-M.] directeur des ports, Paris, 7 août 1830, 'Embarquement de Charles X à Cherbourg 1830', loc. cit., f. 217 recto & verso, where Naples is explicitly mentioned.

68. Tupinier, J.-M., Rapport au ministre, 6 août 1830, 'Embarquement de Charles X à Cherbourg 1830', loc. cit., f. 250 recto & verso.

69. Ministre de la marine à M. Pouyer, préfet maritime à Cherbourg, Paris, 6 août 1830, 'Embarquement de Charles X à Cherbourg 1830', loc. cit., f. 6.

70. Dumont d'Urville, Journal, loc. cit., samedi, 7 août 1830.

71. Dumont d'Urville, Cherbourg, au [Tupinier, J.-M.] directeur des ports, Paris, 7 août 1830, 'Embarquement de Charles X à Cherbourg 1830', loc. cit., f. 217 verso.

72. [Tupinier, J.-M.] Directeur des ports, Paris, à Dumont d'Urville, capitaine de vaisseau, Cherbourg, 10 août 1830, 'Embarquement de Charles X à Cherbourg 1830', loc. cit., f. 44 recto.

73. Marmont, op. cit., vol. viii, livre xxiv, passim.

74. Dumont d'Urville, Cowes, au ministre de la marine, Paris, 16 août 1830, 'Embarquement de Charles X à Cherbourg 1830', loc. cit., f. 227 recto & verso, f. 228.

75. 'Note des personnes embarquée sur le *Great Britain* et le *Charles Carroll*, le 16 août 1830' and 'Liste des personnes qui ont été transportées par les deux pacquebots … *Great Britain* et *Charles Carroll*', 'Embarquement de Charles X à Cherbourg 1830', loc. cit., f. 130 & ff. 132–35.

76. Dumont d'Urville, Journal, loc. cit., lundi, 16 août 1830.

77. Ministre de la marine [Horace Sébastiani] au préfet maritime, Cherbourg, 14 août 1830, 'Embarquement de Charles X à Cherbourg 1830', loc cit., f. 13 recto & verso.

78. [Tupinier, J.-M.] Directeur des ports, Paris, à Dumont d'Urville, capitaine de vaisseau, Cherbourg, 10 août 1830, 'Embarquement de Charles X à Cherbourg 1830, loc. cit., ff. 42 recto & verso, 43 recto.

79. Dumont d'Urville, Cherbourg, au [Tupinier, J.-M.] directeur des ports, Paris, 7 août 1830, 'Embarquement de Charles X à Cherbourg 1830, loc. cit., f. 217 recto. D'Urville uses the word 'espingoles', which I have translated as swivel guns rather than blunderbusses.

80. Roche, *Dictionnaire des bâtiments de la flotte de guerre française*, vol. i, pp. 179, 385 & 410; Rozet, op. cit., vol. ii, pp. 106–07.

81. Rozet, op. cit., vol. ii, p. 108.

82. Dumont d'Urville, Journal, loc. cit., lundi, 16 août 1830.

83. Dumont d'Urville, 'Adieux de Charles X au Capitaine Dumont d'Urville'.

84. Rozet, op. cit., vol. ii, pp. 118–19.

85. Rozet, op. cit., vol. ii, p. 124.

86. Dumont d'Urville, Journal, loc. cit., mardi, 17 août 1830.

87. Rozet, op. cit., vol., ii, p. 125.

88. See, for example, Dumont d'Urville, Journal, loc. cit., jeudi, 19 août; vendredi, 20 août; dimanche, 22 août 1830.

89. Ibid., dimanche, 22 août 1830.

90. Ibid., jeudi, 19 août 1830.

91. Ibid., vendredi, 20 août 1830.

92. Ibid., samedi, 21 août 1830.

93. In a letter to Dr Alexandre de La Motte, the mayor of Condé-sur-Noireau, on 9 August 1843, published in *La Quotidienne*, 12 février 1844; the text appears in Du Saussois, *Henri de France*, pp. 23–24.

94. *La France*, 15 février 1844, cited by Vergniol in the 'Annexes et pièces justificatives', of his *Dumont d'Urville*, p. 285.

95. See Rozet, op. cit., vol. ii, pp. 109–11.

96. It is possible d'Urville was making a humorous pun on her status as royal governess facing *le gouvernail* (French = the rudder); Gontaut-Biron, *Mémoires de madame la duchesse de Gontaut*, p. 366.

97. Montbel, *1787–1831: Souvenirs du comte de Montbel*, p. 339.

98. Haussez, *Mémoires du baron d'Haussez*, vol. ii, pp. 347–48.

99. Saint-Albin, *Histoire d'Henri V*, p. 85.

100. Dumont d'Urville, op. cit., 'Histoire du voyage', vol. v, pp. 593–94.

22. PARIS & THE PEN

1. See Dumont d'Urville, Cowes, au ministre de la marine [Horace Sébastiani], 23 août 1830, 'Embarquement de Charles X à Cherbourg 1830', SHDDM, Vincennes, BB^4 530 Bis, f. 230 recto.

2. See Norvins, *Translation des cendres de Napoléon*; see also Humbert (ed.), *Napoléon aux Invalides*.

3. Dumont d'Urville, Cherbourg, au ministre de la marine [Horace Sébastiani], 27 août [1830], 'Embarquement de Charles X à Cherbourg 1830', loc. cit., ff. 231 recto & verso, 232 recto.

4. Jean-Augustin Marescot was the father of the ill-fated Jacques Marescot du Thilleul, who grew up in Caen and served as an officer on d'Urville's final voyage aboard the *Astrolabe*; one letter from d'Urville to Lair survives from the previous year; see Bibliothèque de Caen, ms in-fol. 178 / 1 (f. 124) Dumont d'Urville, Paris, 20 mai 1829, à Monsieur Lair, conseiller de préfecture, Caen.

5. Dumont d'Urville, Journal, MS 65, Bibliothèque municipale de Toulon, mardi, 31 août 1830.

6. Ibid., mercredi, 1 septembre 1830.

7. Ibid., jeudi, 2 septembre 1830.

8. See Poore, *The Rise and Fall of Louis-Philippe*.

9. Dumont d'Urville, Journal, loc. cit., jeudi, 2 septembre & vendredi, 3 septembre 1830.

10. Billault de Gérainville, *Histoire de Louis-Philippe*, vol. ii, pp. 489–90.

11. Dumont d'Urville, Journal, loc. cit., jeudi, 2 septembre & vendredi, 3 septembre 1830.

12. Dumont d'Urville, Journal, loc. cit., dimanche, 5 septembre 1830.

13. Presumably one of the fixed-route, horse-drawn omnibuses carrying up to 16 passengers, established by Stanislas Baudry (1777–1830).

14. Dumont d'Urville, Journal, loc. cit., dimanche, 5 septembre 1830.

15. Dumont d'Urville [& Jacquinot], *Voyage au pole sud*, 'Histoire du voyage', vol i, p. lxii. It is clear that for this introduction, d'Urville drew upon his autobiographical memoir; for transcribed extracts, see Dumont d'Urville, in Collection Margry, 'Mers Australes', Bibliothèque nationale, NAF 9439, f. 161 verso.

16. Dumont d'Urville, *Voyage de la corvette* l'Astrolabe, 'Histoire du voyage', vol. v, pp. 594–95. Although this volume bears the imprint date of 1833, d'Urville's conclusion and reflections are dated 25 November 1834.

17. Le Brun, *Biographie du contre-amiral Dumont d'Urville*, p. 31.

18. Dumont d'Urville [& Jacquinot], op. cit., 'Histoire du voyage', vols i, pp. lxii–lxiii.

19. Dumont d'Urville, lettre de remerciements pour son élection au poste de secrétaire de la Société de géographie, 2 avril 1830, Manuscrits de la Société de géographie, carton Du-Ey, °374, Bibliothèque nationale de France, Paris, Département des cartes et plans.

20. Dumont d'Urville, 'Sur les îles du Grand Océan'.

21. See Lapie, *Atlas complet du précis de la géographie universelle de M. Malte-Brun*.

22. See Brue, *Carte de l'Océanie ou cinquième partie du monde*.

23. Brosses, *Histoire des navigations aux Terres Australes*, vol. i, p. 80.

24. Dumont d'Urville, 'Sur les îles du Grand Océan', pp. 11–12.

25. Ibid., p. 12.

26. Ibid., pp. 13–14.

27. Ibid., p. 16.

28. Ibid.

29. Ibid., p. 19.

30. Ibid., p. 17.

31. Ibid., p. 19.

32. FIFA: Fédération Internationale de Football Association.

33. Dumont d'Urville, lettre de remerciements pour son élection au poste de vice-président, Société de géographie, 6 avril 1832, Manuscrits de la Société de géographie, carton Du-Ey, °374, loc. cit.

34. The son of d'Urville's sister Adélaïde-Jeanne-Victoire, who married her first cousin Louis-François-Charles Dumont de La Londe (*ca.*1761–1834).

35. Dumont d'Urville, Journal, loc. cit., dimanche, 6 mai 1832.

36. Adèle Dumont d'Urville to Dumont d'Urville, Toulon, 10 novembre 1837, Archives nationales, Marine, 5JJ 158 bis.

37. Anon., 'France', *Gazette médicale de Paris*, vol. 3, no. 80, 4 septembre 1832, p. 555.

38. Boulay de La Meurthe, *Histoire du choléra-morbus dans le quartier du Luxembourg*, p. 33.

39. Dumont d'Urville [& Jacquinot], op. cit., 'Histoire du voyage', vol. i, p. lxii–iii.

40. Dumont d'Urville to Isidore Le Brun, 29 juin 1833, Dixson Library, Sydney, MSQ355.

41. Le Brun, op. cit., p. 32.

42. Dumont d'Urville, Journal, loc. cit., dimanche, 16 mars 1834.

43. Dumont d'Urville, Journal, loc. cit., samedi, 6 juillet 1833.

44. Dumont d'Urville, 'Rapport sur le voyage du Capitaine Beechey', p. 203.

45. Roche, *Dictionnaire des bâtiments de la flotte de guerre française*, vol. i, p. 287.

46. Solé, *Le grand voyage de l'obélisque*.

47. Dumont d'Urville, *Voyage de la corvette* l'Astrolabe 'Histoire du voyage', vol. v, p. 607.

48. Lacouture, *Champollion*, pp. 444, 479 & 483.

49. D'Urville revealed this in his *Voyage au pôle sud*, 'Histoire du voyage', vol. iv, p. 66.

50. Le Brun, op. cit., p. 33.

51. Adèle Dumont d'Urville to Isidore Le Brun, 18 février 1839, Dixson Library, Sydney, MSQ355.

52. Possibly Chef de Bataillon Alexandre Dombrowski [Aleksander Dąbrowski] (1787–1836), born in Kamienieck, Poland, who joined the Napoleonic army in October 1807 (1st regiment of the Vistula), was wounded several times, decorated *chevalier de la Légion d'honneur* in 1811 and, according to his naturalisation certificate of 31 January 1816, was married to a French woman; Archives nationales, Fond Léonore, LH/786/9; 'M. Dombrowski was a very brave man,' wrote Adélie to Isidore Le Brun in August 1838, Dixson Library, Sydney, MSQ355.

53. See, for example, Dumont d'Urville, Journal, loc cit., 7 avril 1833 & 1 juin 1835.

54. [Boulger], 'Webb, Philip Barker (1793–1854)'; see also Steinberg, 'The collectors and collections in the Herbarium Webb'.

55. Webb helped both d'Urville and his son Jules with questions relating to English translations; see Dumont d'Urville, Journal, loc. cit., vendredi, 28 mars 1834; see also Webb's letter to d'Urville of 29 December 1840, Archives nationales, Paris, Marine 5JJ 158Bis.

56. Le Brun, op. cit., pp. 35–36. According to Le Brun, d'Urville had known the royal librarian for some 20 years. However, he was surprised and affronted when he sought to borrow a number of works relating to ethnography and linguistics and was told by this librarian to make a written submission and to await a written reply. D'Urville was particularly offended because he believed that the same librarian had liberally indulged the loan requests of the families of ministerial secretaries. Proud, angry and stubborn, he left without making any reply and resolved to buy the books he required, despite their forbidding cost of more than 800 francs.

57. Dumont d'Urville [& Jacquinot], op. cit., 'Histoire du voyage', vol i, p. lxi.

23. LA JULIADE

1. Although d'Urville stated that he left Paris in June 1835 (see Dumont d'Urville [& Jacquinot], *Voyage au pôle sud*, 'Histoire du voyage', vol. i, p. lxi), d'Urville's private journal does not substantiate this assertion.
2. Pollitzer, 'Cholera Studies', p. 435.
3. Minutier central des notaires de Paris, 13 Juin 1842, Inventaire après décès de M[onsieu]r. Dumont d'Urville, and 21 Juin 1842, décharge donnée à M. Demanche, Archives nationales, Paris, ET/C/1200; d'Urville mentions the transaction for the property on the place de l'Intendance in Toulon in his journal.
4. See Matrice des propriétés bâties et non bâties de l'Ouest de la banlieue, partie rurale, f. 464, Archives municipales de Toulon, 1G9-2; also Plan du cadastre napoléonien, 1827, Section D de St Antoine, 2eme Feuille levée par M. Fouque, cadet géomètre de 1ère classe, 6Fi60, loc. cit.
5. Lesson, *Notice historique sur l'amiral Dumont d'Urville*, p. 96.
6. The name 'La Juliade' also appears to include the suffix 'ade' (with strong provençal roots in the word *ada*), used, in both English and French, to create new words of action, process and product (blockade, crusade, etc.), but also architectural terms such as 'arcade' and 'colonnade'.
7. Toulon Mémoire, *Le nom des rues*, vol. iv, p. 8.
8. Lochouarn (ed.), *Histoire d'un coin de Toulon*, p. 92; see also Fédoroff & Roché, *Au fil du Béal*.
9. Minutier central des notaires de Paris, 13 Juin 1842, Inventaire après décès de M[onsieu]r. Dumont d'Urville, and 21 Juin 1842, décharge donnée à M. Demanche, loc. cit.
10. See Hempel, *The Strange Case of the Broad Street Pump*.
11. Ibid., p. 273.
12. Acte de décès, Sophie Adèle Julie Dumont d'Urville, 31 juillet 1835, Toulon, no. 2550, 7E146_144, Archives départementales du Var, Draguignan.
13. Sophie's name is listed among the victims in Lavergne, *Choléra-Morbus en Provence*, p. 458.
14. Dossier personnel, Bertrand, François-Ésprit, SHDDM, Vincennes, CC[7] Alpha 191.
15. Dominique, *Le Choléra à Toulon*, p. 30.
16. Adèle Dumont d'Urville to Isidore Le Brun, 25 juin 1841, Dixson Library, Sydney, MSQ355.
17. Lochouarn (ed.), op. cit., p. 92.
18. The description of the 'dépendance' comes from Minutier central des notaires de Paris, 13 Juin 1842, Inventaire après décès de Mr. Dumont d'Urville, & 21 Juin 1842, décharge donnée à M. Demanche, loc. cit.
19. Although the property outline of 'La Juliade' is readily discernable on the scale model of Toulon completed in 1800 and still surviving in the remarkable Musée des plans-reliefs (housed in the roof space of Les Invalides in Paris), no model of the actual house appears on it. The d'Urvilles' home might have post-dated the model, but it is also possible that the rectangular representation of the house simply fell off when the ensemble was moved. 'La Juliade' would have been located where the mounting boards are joined. For some background, see Petit, 'Toulon au Musée des plans-reliefs des Invalides'. This and other models in the museum were constructed to instruct army offices in the defence of France's strategic ports and forts. They were based on meticulous sketches by artists.
20. Le Brun, *Biographie du contre-amiral Dumont d'Urville*, p. 36.
21. Ibid., pp. 36–37.
22. Dumont d'Urville, testament, 20 octobre 1839; codicille 1er novembre 1839, SHDDM, Toulon, ms 11.
23. Inventaire des effets mobiliers dressé par Maître Vallavieille, notaire à Toulon, le 30 juillet 1842 … dépendant des successions réunies de feu M. Dumont d'Urville, de son épouse et de son fils décédés ensemble le 8 mai 1842 domicilé à Paris', Office Notarial Boyer, Toulon.
24. Jules Dumont d'Urville (*fils*) to Dumont d'Urville, 2 novembre 1839, Archives nationales, Paris, Marine 5JJ 158 Bis.
25. Inventaire des effets mobiliers dressé par Maître Vallavieille, notaire à Toulon, le 30 juillet 1842 … dépendant des successions réunies de feu M. Dumont D'Urville …, loc. cit.

26. See Duyker, 'An Explorer's Books', and Duyker, 'Dumont d'Urville's Library'.

27. Recent forensic examination of the frozen remains of crewmen from the Franklin expedition suggests that lead poisoning was a significant factor in Franklin's disappearance. Owen Beatie and John Geiger (*Frozen in Time: The fate of the Franklin expedition*) suggested that lead solder in canned foods was responsible. However, in 2008, William Battersby pointed out that similar canned food had been used by many other Royal Navy vessels and on earlier polar expeditions. Instead, he drew attention to the lead plumbing on Franklin's vessels, which integrated their auxiliary steam power (refurbished locomotive engines) with steam-based heating (for arctic conditions) and condensed drinking water; see Battersby, 'Identification of the probable source of the lead poisoning observed in members of the Franklin expedition'. Lead solder in canned food could still have been a source of kidney damage for d'Urville.

28. Lesson, op. cit., p. 56.

29. Ibid., note 1.

30. Hombron (note 1), in Dumont d'Urville [& Jacquinot], op. cit., 'Histoire du voyage', vol. viii, p. 269.

31. Hartung, 'History of the use of colchicum and related medicaments in gout'.

32. Acte de naissance, Émile-Jules-Léon Dumont d'Urville, 30 juillet 1836, Toulon, no. 922, 7E146_145, Archives départementales du Var, Draguignan.

33. Dumont d'Urville [& Jacquinot], op. cit., 'Histoire du voyage', vol. i, p. lxiii.

34. Duperré and the British commander Nesbit Willoughby (1777–1849) were both wounded in the Battle of Grand Port (Mauritius) and both were treated in the same room of the Château de Robillard (Mahébourg) when it was over. The author's great-great-great grandfather, Pierre-Henry Lionnet (1773–1829) a native of the Vendée, also took part as a medical officer on the *Victor*. The battle is the only naval victory commemorated on the Arc de Triomphe in Paris; see Huet de Froberville, *Île de France: Le Combat de Grand-Port*.

35. Dumont d'Urville [& Jacquinot], op. cit., 'Histoire du voyage', vol. i, p. lxii.

36. Ibid., note 1, p. lxx.

37. Taillemite, *Dictionnaire des marins français*, pp. 102 & 296.

38. Dumont d'Urville[& Jacquinot], op. cit., 'Histoire du voyage', vol. i, p. lxv.

39. Acte de décè, Joseph-Marie Pépin, 15 janvier 1837, Toulon, no. 82, 7E146_152R, Archives départementales du Var, Draguignan.

40. Dumont d'Urville, Toulon, au ministre de la marine et des colonies, Paris, 2 février 1837, and Notes relatives à l'expédition … proposées par le Capt. de vais. Jules d'Urville, SHDDM, Vincennes, BB[4] 1009.

41. Dumont d'Urville [& Jacquinot], op. cit., 'Histoire du voyage', vol. i, p. lxiv.

42. Ibid., p. lxviii.

43. Dumont d'Urville, 'Mission projéttée de l'*Astrolabe*, notes pour le ministre', Toulon, 25 février 1837, SHDDM, Vincennes, BB[4] 1009.

44. See Roche, *Dictionnaire des bâtiments de la flotte de guerre française*, vol. i, pp. 127 & 477; see also Couturaud, 'Le troisième voyage de circumnavigation de J.S.C. Dumont d'Urville 1837–1840', pp. 34–37.

45. Dossier personnel, Lottin, Victor-Charles, SHDDM, Vincennes, CC[7] Alpha 1610; Archives nationale, LH2789/134.

46. Dossier personnel, Guilbert, Pierre-Édouard, SHDDM, Vincennes, CC[7] Alpha 1117; Archives nationales, LH1231/67.

47. Dossier personnel, Gressien, Victor-Amédée, SHDDM, Vincennes, CC[7] Alpha 1080; Archives nationales, LH1199/22.

48. Dumont d'Urville [& Jacquinot], op. cit., 'Histoire du voyage', vol. i, p. lxx.

49. Collinet was decorated *chevalier de la Légion d'honneur* on 30 May 1837 (a fact not mentioned in his service dossier because he retired in 1833); see dossier personnel, Collinet, Pierre-Jean-François, SHDDM, Vincennes, CC[7] Alpha 519; Archives nationales, Fond Léonore, LH570/62.

50. See Duyker, 'Lottin, Victor-Charles (1795–1858)'.

51. Dossier personnel, Dumont d'Urville, SHDDM, Vincennes, CC^7 Alpha 772, pièce 32, mars–septembre 1837, dépèche et ordres concernant l'expédition de la *Zélée*.

52. Dossier personnel, Dumont d'Urville, SHDDM, Vincennes, CC^7 Alpha 772, pièce 37, 8 mai 1842, état des services.

53. Dumont d'Urville [& Jacquinot], op. cit., 'Histoire du voyage', vol. i, p. lxxi; see also dossier personnel, Dumont d'Urville, SHDDM, Vincennes, CC^7 Alpha 772, pièce 32, mars–septembre 1837, dépèche et ordres concernant l'expédition de la *Zélée*; pièce 33, 13 avril 1837, fixations du traitement de M. Dumont d'Urville pendant son séjour à Paris; pièce 34, 11 mai 1837, décompte de M. Dumont d'Urville pendant son séjour à Londres, SHDDM, Vincennes, BB^4 1009.

54. Dumont d'Urville [& Jacquinot], op. cit., 'Histoire du voyage', vol. i, p. lxxi.

55. Décompte de M. Dumont d'Urville pendant son séjour à Londres, 11 mai 1837, in dossier personnel, Dumont d'Urville, SHDDM, Vincennes, CC^7 Alpha 772, pièce 34.

56. See Friendly, *Beaufort of the Admiralty*.

57. Marshall-Cornwall, *History of the Geographical Club*, p. 14. In 1854, the Raleigh Club was reconstituted as the Geographical Club.

58. See Savours, 'John Biscoe, Master Mariner'; see also [Biscoe] 'Recent discoveries in the Antarctic Ocean communicated by Messrs Enderby'.

59. Dumont d'Urville [& Jacquinot], op. cit., 'Histoire du voyage', vol. i, p. lxxii.

60. Giustino, *Conquest of Mind*, p. 94.

61. For M. Berrier-Fontaine's translation of Deville's phrenological report, dated London, 4 May 1837, see Malcor, 'Dumont d'Urville d'après ses manuscrits', p. 29, SHDDM, Vincennes, Fonds Privés, 7 GG^2, carton i, Papiers du contre-amiral Jules-Sébastien-César Dumont d'Urville; for an English retranslation of the same report, see Rosenman, *An Account in Two Volumes of Two Voyages to the South Seas*, vol. ii, appendix ii, pp. 564–65.

62. Dumont d'Urville [& Jacquinot], op. cit., 'Histoire du voyage', vol. i, p. lxxii.

63. Dumont d'Urville, 'Au peuple anglais', *ca.* 1830, Malcor transcription, SHDDM, Vincennes, Fonds Privés, 7 GG^2, carton i, papiers du contre-amiral Jules-Sébastien-César Dumont d'Urville.

64. D'Urville appears to use the word 'leaven' in the sense of reactionary prejudices, perhaps an allusion to Saint Paul's plea to 'purge out therefore the old leaven, that ye may be a new lump', 1 Corinthians 5:7.

65. Dumont d'Urville, 'Au peuple anglais', loc. cit.

66. Dumont d'Urville [& Jacquinot], op. cit., 'Histoire du voyage', vol. i, p. lxxiii–lxxiv.

67. Arago, 'Service scientifique [Chambre des députés, séance du lundi 5 juin 1837]'.

68. For Méchain's remarkable life, see Alder, *The Measure of All Things*.

69. Hahn, 'Arago, Dominique François Jean'.

70. [Rosamel, C. du Campe de,] Ministre de la marine, 'Service scientifique [Chambre des députés, séance du lundi 5 juin 1837]'.

71. Dumont d'Urville, 'Note sur l'expédition de l'*Astrolabe* et de la *Zélée* en réponse aux critiques de M. Arago'.

72. Arago, 'Réponse de M. Arago, député, à une lettre de M. le capitaine de vaisseau Dumont d'Urville ...'

73. Dumont d'Urville, '2e et dernière note de M. Dumont d'Urville sur l'expédition de l'*Astrolabe* et de la *Zélée* ...'

74. See Vergniol, *Dumont d'Urville*, p. 216; Guillon, *Dumont d'Urville*, p. 179 and Jacob, *Dumont d'Urville*, p. 219.

75. Hahn, op. cit.

76. Minutier central des notaires de Paris, 13 Juin 1842, Inventaire après décès de Mr. Dumont d'Urville, and 21 Juin 1842, décharge donnée à M. Demanche, loc. cit.

77. Le Brun, *Biographie du contre-amiral Dumont d'Urville*, p. 31.

24. ASTROLABE & ZÉLÉE

1. Dumont d'Urville, Toulon, au ministre de la marine et des colonies, Paris, 3 août 1837, SHDDM, Vincennes, BB⁴ 1009.

2. Dépêches des 27 juillet et 1er, 4 & 5 août 1837, caisses d'instruments, livres et autres objets d'envoi du depôt des cartes et plans reçus par Mr d'Urville pour l'expédition de l'*Astrolabe* et de la *Zélée*, and bordereau des cartes, livres et atlas destinés à Mr Dumont d'Urville, Capitaine de vaisseau, commandant l'*Astrolabe* à Toulon, SHDDM, Vincennes, BB⁴ 1009.

3. Ibid.

4. The Régnier dynamomètre was designed by the engineer Édmé Régnier (1751–1825) as a portable device – weighing around a kilogram – to measure the strength of men of different ages and states of health. Its central, almost elliptical steel spring could be clasped and compressed to record the strength of the hands, or a 'T'-shaped handle and a foot piece could be fitted to test the strength of the back and arm muscles through traction. The results were read from an arrow on a graduated semi-circular brass disc, with each degree on the scale equivalent to 500 grams pressure. The author found one in working order in the collection of the Musée d'histoire de la médecine in Paris in the course of research for his biography of the naturalist François Péron in January 2003.

5. Mirbel, Cordier, Blainville, Freycinet & Savary, 'Rapport de la commission chargée sur l'invitation de M. le Ministre de la Marine …'

6. Dumont d'Urville [& Jacquinot], *Voyage au pôle sud*, 'Histoire du voyage', vol. i, pp. lxxiv–lxxvi.

7. Fiche matricule, Rocquemaurel [*sic*], Gaston de, École polytechnique, Paris; Archives nationales, Fond Léonore, LH/2363/46; Pradel de Lamase, 'Avec Dumont d'Urville: Souvenirs du commandant de Roquemaurel'.

8. Dossier personnel, Barlatier-Demas, François-Edmond-Eugène, SHDDM, Vincennes, CC⁷ Alpha 102; Archives nationales, Fond Léonore, LH/116/53.

9. Vincendon-Dumoulin, Clément-Adrien, Fiche matricule, École polytechnique, Paris; dossier personnel, Vincendon-Dumoulin, Clément-Adrien, SHDDM, Vincennes, CC⁷ Alpha 2475; Archives nationales, Fond Léonore, LH/2724/22.

10. Dossier personnel, Marescot du Thilleul, Jacques-Marie-Eugène, SHDDM, Vincennes, CC⁷ Alpha 1675; see also 'Eugène Marescot du Thilleul' in Dumont d'Urville [& Jacquinot], op. cit., 'Histoire du voyage', vol. viii, pp. 363–72.

11. Dossier personnel, Duroch, Joseph-Antoine, SHDDM, Vincennes, CC⁷ Alpha 802; Archives nationales, Fond Léonore, LH/874/22.

12. Dossier personnel, Gourdin, Jean-Marie-Émile, SHDDM, Vincennes, CC⁷ Alpha 1056; see also 'Émile Goudin' in Dumont d'Urville [& Jacquinot], op. cit., 'Histoire du voyage', vol. viii, pp. 374–80.

13. Dumont d'Urville au ministre de la marine, Hobart Town, 19 février 1840, in dossier personnel, Ducorps, Jacques-Louis, SHDDM, Vincennes, CC⁷ Alpha 753.

14. Hombron, *Réflexions sur la fièvre jaune*.

15. Rigaudeau, 'Un document: les journaux de bord du "chirurgien navigant" Jacques Bernard Hombron (1798–1852)', p. 13; Ehrhardt, 'Les médecins des explorations de Dumont d'Urville (1826–1840)'; see also Couturaud, 'Le troisième voyage de circumnavigation de J.S.C. Dumont d'Urville 1837–1840', pp. 158–61.

16. Dossier personnel, Le Breton, Louis Raymond Marie, SHDDM, Vincennes, CC⁷ Alpha 1432; see also Collins, *Louis Le Breton*.

17. Gervaize, Charles-François Eugène, Fiche matricule, École polytechnique, Paris; dossier personnel, SHDDM, Vincennes, CC⁷ Alpha 1006; Archives nationales, Fond Léonore, LH/1126/13.

18. Fiche matricule, Delafond, Pierre-Antoine, École polytechnique, Paris; dossier personnel, Delafond, Pierre-Antoine, SHDDM, Vincennes, CC⁷ Alpha 858; Archives nationales, Fond Léonore, LH/695/68.

19. Dossier personnel, Le Maistre Duparc, Louis-Emmanuel, SHDDM, Vincennes, CC⁷ Alpha 1511; Archives nationales, Fond Léonore, LH/695/44.

20. Dumont d'Urville [& Jacquinot], op. cit., 'Histoire du voyage', vol. i, p. lxxvii.

21. Dumoutier also had a daughter Angélina, but she appears to have died in infancy because he cast her death mask, which survives to this day.

22. See Ackerknecht, 'P.M.A. Dumoutier et la collection phrénologique du Musée de l'homme'.

23. Dumont d'Urville, testament, 20 octobre 1839; codicille 1er novembre 1839, SHDDM, Toulon, ms 11.

24. Dossier personnel, Desgraz, César Louis François, SHDDM, Vincennes, CC^7 Alpha 686; Archives nationales, Fond Léonore, LH/1194/40.

25. César Desgraz's father, François-Louis Desgraz [later Desgraz-Bory] (1787–1853), was born illegitimate in Lausanne, the son of a Coblenz-born father (Pierre Lienhardt) and a Swiss mother. When he was three years old, his mother married a Belgian Catholic named François-Joseph-Ghillain Bertrand on 10 September 1790, but his stepfather died less than three months later. He then returned with his mother to her native village of Saint-Saphorin, Vaud. Although César Desgraz's father's book *Paroles d'un négociant* contains a great deal of fiction to conceal his illegitimate origins, it suggests that in early 1810, he travelled to Paris and found work with a firm trading in cloth. In the midst of the war shortages, he convinced his employers to let him go overland to Turkey to find supplies of cotton. His return journey, laden with merchandise, took nearly four years. In May 1814, as the Bourbons were restored, he appears to have sailed from Marseille to Smyrna to avail himself of the commercial contacts he had made in the Levant. There, in 1815, he married Anne-Madeleine Bory. César, who became d'Urville's private secretary, was their eldest son; the youngest was Édouard, who followed his father trading with Smyrna. I am grateful to M. Pierre-Yves Favez of the Archives cantonales vaudoises (Chavannes-près-Renens, Switzerland) and Olivier Gorse of the Archives départementales des Bouches-du-Rhône (Marseille) for their assistance in uncovering the truth of Desgraz' father's Swiss origins and discerning fact from fiction in his *Paroles d'un négociant* (pp. 7–21) and his *Mélanges–Économie sociale*, p. 209.

26. To 23, rue 3e Calade (today rue Dieudé), sometime between October 1832 and 25 October 1833; see Chardon, *Nouveau guide marseillais … pour l'année 1834*, p. 164.

27. Hector Jacquinot, Paris, 19 août 1842, à amiral Duperré, ministre de la marine, SHDDM, Vincennes, BB^4 1009.

28. See [Desgraz-Bory], *Paroles d'un négociant*; the essay on Confucius is 'Le juste-milieu des Chinois', pp. 148–56.

29. See, for example, Adèle Dumont d'Urville to her husband [in English], 5 November 1837, Archives nationales, Paris, Marine 5JJ 158 Bis.

30. See, for example, Dunmore, *From Venus to Antarctica*, p. 175.

31. In a letter to his father from Tahiti, dated 14 September 1838, Desgraz wrote: '… despite the difference of opinion with regard to their beliefs or superstitions, the efforts of these priests do good to these people. They destroyed cannibalism, made their subsistence more certain, introduced cotton cultivation and spinning, and finally iron implements, the construction of more airy houses, more solid canoes.' Desgraz also believed that the pomp of Catholic religious ceremonies was more attractive to Polynesians than 'acting only by persuasion like ours'; Cambridge University Library, MS. Add. 7540/44.

32. It will be remembered that the *Lionne* was the vessel that transported the Vénus de Milo to the marquis de Rivière in Constantinople.

33. Dossier personnel, Dubouzet, Joseph-Fidèle-Eugène, SHDDM, Vincennes, CC^7 Alpha 742.

34. Journal, Dubouzet, SHDDM, Vincennes, ms 379, cited by Couturaud, op. cit., p. 134.

35. Dossier personnel, Tardy de Montravel, Louis-François-Marie, SHDDM, Vincennes, CC^7 Alpha 2334; Archives nationales, Fond Léonore, LH/2568/99; see also Taillemite, *Dictionnaire des marins français,* pp. 317–18.

36. Dossier personnel, Pavin de La Farge, Antoine-Auguste-Thérèse, SHDDM, Vincennes, CC^7 Alpha 1922; see also 'Tony de Pavin de La Farge' in Dumont d'Urville [& Jacquinot], op. cit., 'Histoire du voyage', vol. viii, pp. 372–74.

37. Fiche matricule, Coupvent-Desbois, Aimé-Auguste-Élie, École polytechnique, Paris; dossier personnel, Coupvent-Desbois, Aimé-Auguste-Élie, SHDDM, Vincennes, CC^7 Alpha 561; Archives nationales, Fond Léonore, LH/609/15.

38. Dossier personnel, Huon de Kermadec, Félix-Casimir-Marie, SHDDM, Vincennes, CC[7] Alpha 1025; Archives nationales, Fond Léonore, LH/1327/12.

39. Dossier personnel, Le Guillou, Élie-Jean-François, SHDDM, Vincennes, CC[7] Alpha 1498.

40. Dossier personnel, Jacquinot, Honoré, SHDDM, Vincennes, CC[7] Alpha 1222; Archives nationales, Fond Léonore, LH/1346/36.

41. Dossier personnel, Gaillard, Jean-Edmond, SHDDM, Vincennes, CC[7] Alpha 994; see also Couturaud, op. cit., pp. 147–51.

42. Périgot, Germain-Hector, Archives nationales, Fond Léonore, LH/2100/15; see also Couturaud, op. cit., pp. 196–99.

43. Dossier personnel, Boyer, Joseph-Emmanuel-Prosper, SHDDM, Vincennes, CC[7] Alpha 320; Archives nationales, Fond Léonore, LH/347/47.

44. Acte de naissance, Auguste-Ernest Goupil, 10 avril 1814, Archives municipales, Châteaudun.

45. 'Ernest Goupil' in Dumont d'Urville [& Jacquinot], op. cit., 'Histoire du voyage', vol. viii, pp. 381–91.

46. Dumont d'Urville [& Jacquinot], op. cit., 'Histoire du voyage', vol. i, pp. lxxix–lxxx; see also Dumont d'Urville, mémoires intimes, Malcor transcription *ca.* 1884, ff. 46–47, Papiers du contre-amiral Jules-Sébastien-César Dumont d'Urville (1790–1842), SHDDM, Vincennes, Fonds Privés, 7 GG[2], carton 1.

47. Louis-Philippe, Roi des Français, 'Ordonnance du roi qui accorde aux équipages des gabares l'*Astrolabe* et la *Zélée*'.

48. Dumont d'Urville [& Jacquinot], op. cit., 'Histoire du voyage', vol. i, p. 89.

49. For Kosmann's origins, see Evangelische Kirchengemeinde, Burbach (Siegen, Westphalia), Abschrift aus dem Taufbuch 1796–1810, S. 38 Nr. 26 and S. 206 Nr. 79; also dossier personnel, Kosmann, Charles-Henry-Georges, SHDDM, Vincennes, CC[7] Alpha 1295; see also Couturaud, op. cit., pp. 264–68; for his father's military service, see Archives nationales, Fond Léonore, LH/1407/29.

50. Le Guillou, *Voyage autour du monde*, vol. i, p. 48.

51. See notes on the tins of preserved meat by Duroch and Jacquinot in Dumont d'Urville [& Jacquinot], op. cit., 'Histoire du voyage', vol. i, p. 209.

52. Journal, du Bouzet, SHDDM, Vincennes, ms 379, cited by Couturaud, op. cit., pp. 307 & 319.

53. Dumont d'Urville, Toulon, au ministre de la marine et des colonies, Paris, 21 août 1837, SHDDM, Vincennes, BB[4] 1009.

54. Dumont d'Urville [& Jacquinot], op. cit., 'Histoire du voyage', vol. i, pp. lxxxi–lxxxii.

25. TO THE ANTARCTIC PENINSULA

1. Seureau, in Méhaud & Richard (eds.), *Dumont d'Urville en Antarctique*, p. 32.

2. Ibid., p. 31.

3. Dumont d'Urville [& Jacquinot], *Voyage au pôle sud*, 'Histoire du voyage', vol. i, p. 17.

4. Dawson, *Memoirs of Hydrography,* part i, pp. 94–95.

5. Journal (extract), Desgraz, in Dumont d'Urville [& Jacquinot], op. cit., 'Histoire du voyage', vol. i, pp. 202–06.

6. See Dumoutier, 'Anthropologie', pp. 249–51, in Dumont d'Urville [& Jacquinot], op. cit.

7. Le Guillou, *Voyage autour du monde*, vol. i, pp. 11–12 & 17–19.

8. Dumont d'Urville [& Jacquinot], op. cit., 'Histoire du voyage', vol. i, p. 39.

9. Dossier personnel, Le Maistre Duparc, Louis-Emmanuel, SHDDM, Vincennes, CC[7] Alpha 1511; Archives nationales, Fond Léonore, LH/695/44.

10. Dumont d'Urville [& Jacquinot], op. cit., 'Histoire du voyage', vol. i, p. 46.

11. Ibid., p. 90.

12. Support for the nascent Spanish settlement was not forthcoming because, on his return voyage, Pedro Sarmiento de Gamboa's (*ca.*1530–1592) ship was captured by an English privateer belonging to Sir Walter Raleigh. He arrived in Plymouth in September 1586 and was presented to Queen Elizabeth I of England, who freed him and gave him funds to return to Spain (in the hope that he might help to avert war and the coming armada). Unfortunately, in Bayonne, he fell into the hands

of French Huguenots and was imprisoned for three years. He did not reach Spain until September 1590; see Duro, 'Pedro Sarmiento de Gamboa, El Navigante', pp. 285–87.

13. Darwin, *The Voyage of the* Beagle, p. 222.
14. Méhaud & Richard (eds), op. cit., p. 37.
15. Dumont d'Urville [& Jacquinot], op. cit., 'Histoire du voyage', vol. i, p. 93.
16. Ibid., p. 96.
17. Ibid., pp. 97–98.
18. It was named *Pluvianellus sociabilis* by Hombron and Jacquinot, and appeared in the expedition's zoological atlas of 1845 (plate no. 30, figure 1). Although Jacques Pucheran's (1817–1894) description of the expedition's ornithological results did not appear until 1853, Hombron's and Jacquinot's names were included in George Robert Gray's (1808–1872) *The Genera of Birds*, vol. 3, p. 549.
19. Jacquinot & Guichenot, in Dumont d'Urville [& Jacquinot], op. cit., 'Zoologie' [Hombron & Jacquinot (eds)], vol. iii, Reptiles et Poissons, pp. 94–96.
20. Blanchard, in Dumont d'Urville [& Jacquinot], op. cit., 'Zoologie' [Hombron & Jacquinot (eds)], vol. iv, Description des insectes, pp. 18 & 37–38; see also Emberson, 'Tentative dates of publication of the zoology plates of Dumont d'Urville's *Voyage au Pôl[e] Sud*'.
21. In the expedition's 'Zoologie Atlas', there were 19 hand-painted, engraved plates of coleoptera, each with 13–20 figures of individual beetles. The livraisons (instalments) for these plates were issued between 1842 and 1847; see Emberson, 'Tentative Dates of Publication of the Zoology Plates of Dumont d'Urville's *Voyage au Pôl[e] Sud*, with particular reference to the Coleoptera'. The new species of longhorn beetle, *Microplophorus magellanicus*, collected on the Strait of Magellan, was illustrated as figure 1 of plate 16. This was issued in 1846 and denoted with the Latin abbreviation 'Nob.' (for *nobilitare* to make known), but Blanchard's accompanying description was not published until 1853. In the meantime, in 1851, the French-born Chilean zoologist Claude 'Claudio' Gay (1800–1873) published a description of *Microplophorus magellanicus*, retaining the name coined by Blanchard and referencing Hombron and Honoré Jacquinot as the expedition's zoological editors, but incorrectly giving figure 1, plate 29, instead of figure 1, plate 16, as the type illustration; see Gay, *Historia fisica y politica de Chile*, 'Zoologia', vol. v, p. 456; see also Blanchard, op. cit., pp. 260–61.
22. For example, Hombron and Jacquinot's *Natica magellanica*, a gastropod belonging to the Naticidae, appeared as figures 28–29 of plate 16 in the expedition's zoological atlas in 1848 and with a description in the fourth zoological volume in 1854; by then it had already been described, in 1845, by the Prussian-born Chilean zoologist Rudolf Amandus Philippi (1808–1904) under the name *Natica patagonica* (*Euspira patagonia*); see Philippi, [R.]A. 'Diagnosen einiger neuen Conchylien', pp. 50–71. For a study of the dates of the 40 plates in the 'Atlas d'Histoire Naturelle, Zoologie' (Dumont d'Urville [& Jacquinot], op. cit.), which were distributed in 28 'livraisons' (installments) between 1842 and 1854, see Clark & Crosnier, 'The zoology of the *Voyage au pôle sud …*' They propose that date-stamps on the atlas in the British Library should be adopted as dates of publication.
23. Montagne, *Prodromus generum specierumque phycearum novarum …* , p. 5.
24. Montagne, in Dumont d'Urville, [& Jacquinot], op. cit., 'Botanique' [Hombron & Jacquinot (eds)], vol. i, Plantes cellulaire, pp. 222–24; see also Hässel de Menéndez & Solari, 'Sinopsis de las especies Andinopatagónicas del género *Tylimanthus* (Hepaticae)', p. 580.
25. Decaine, in Dumont d'Urville, [& Jacquinot], op. cit., 'Botanique' [Hombron & Jacquinot (eds)], Description des plantes vasculaires, vol. ii, p. 13–14.
26. Ibid., p. 54.
27. Dumont d'Urville [& Jacquinot], op. cit., 'Histoire du voyage', vol. i, p. 116.
28. Ibid., p. 101.
29. Ibid., p. 102.
30. Morrell, *A Narrative of Four Voyages to the South Sea*, p. 89.
31. Ortiz-Troncoso, 'A 16th-century Hispanic harbour in the Strait of Magellan, South America'.
32. Dumont d'Urville [& Jacquinot], op. cit., 'Histoire du voyage', vol. i, p. 106.
33. Ibid., p. 115.

34. Dumont d'Urville, Port Famine [Détroit de Magellan], au ministre de la marine et des colonies, Paris, 27 décembre 1837, in which he sent a report on the geophysics and natural science executed up to that date; Vincendon-Dumoulin, 'Les observations qui ont été faites au Port Famine pendant la visite des corvettes françaises l'*Astrolabe* et *Zélée*', 27 décembre 1837, SHDDM, Vincennes, BB⁴ 1009.

35. Declaration by Abraham B. Lawton, 19 June 1838, before Thos. S. Pirkins, Notary Public, New London, Connecticut; SHDDM, Vincennes, BB⁴ 1009.

36. Dumont d'Urville [& Jacquinot], op. cit., 'Histoire du voyage', vol. i, pp. 146–47.

37. Ibid., p. 157.

38. Ibid., p. 158.

39. Decaine, op. cit., pp. 48–49; *Senecio laseguei* was illustrated earlier in a plate: tab. 13, fig. D.

40. Jacquinot & Guichenot, in Dumont d'Urville [& Jacquinot], op. cit., 'Zoologie' [Hombron & Jacquinot (eds)], vol. iii, Reptiles et poissons, pp. 6–7.

41. Barlatier-Demas, note 13, in Dumont d'Urville [& Jacquinot], op. cit., 'Histoire du voyage', vol. ii, p. 206.

42. Dumont d'Urville [& Jacquinot], op. cit., 'Histoire du voyage', vol. ii, p. 49.

43. Ibid., p. 61.

44. Ibid., p. 69.

45. Ibid., pp. 76–77.

46. Ibid., p. 80.

47. Ibid., p. 88.

48. Ibid., p. 101.

49. Cleland & Southcott, 'Illness following the eating of seal liver in Australian waters'; see also Shearman, 'Vitamin A and Sir Douglas Mawson'.

50. Dolmen: a megalithic portal tomb consisting of several standing stones supporting a horizontal stone cap. The earliest in Western Europe date from about 5000 BC. As a child in Calvados, d'Urville might have been familiar with the Dolmen de la Loge aux Sarrazins at Saint-Germain de Tallevende (south of Vire), or the ruined Pierres Branlantes in Biéville-Beauville (north of Caen).

51. Dumont d'Urville [& Jacquinot], op. cit., 'Histoire du voyage', vol. ii, p. 109.

52. Ibid.

53. Frazil ice (Canadian, from French *fraisil* = cinders): unstructured slushy ice formed in turbulent open waters; see May (ed.), *The Greenpeace Book of Antarctica*, p. 41; also the *Oxford English Dictionary* (vol. vi, p. 156),which equates frazil ice with 'anchor ice' in streams.

54. Dumont d'Urville [& Jacquinot], op. cit., 'Histoire du voyage', vol. ii, p. 115.

55. Grange, in Dumont d'Urville [& Jacquinot], op. cit., 'Géologie, minéralogie, géographie physique', part i, p. 32.

56. For a photograph of this cape, see Nordenskjöld, *Antarctica*, p. 41.

57. Nordenskjöld, ibid., pp. 46 & 414.

58. For a photograph of this cape, see Nordenskjöld, ibid., p. 37.

59. Skottsberg, 'Zur Kenntnis der subantarktischen und antarktischen Meeresalgen I, Phaeophyceen', p. 146, fig. 177; ibid., pl. 35.

60. Yelverton, *Quest for a Phantom Strait*, p. xii.

26. RETURN TO CHILE

1. Charles Darwin experienced this earthquake personally at Valdivia on 20 February 1835, then entered tsunami-devastated Talcahuano aboard the *Beagle* on 4 March, and bore personal witness to the scene of complete destruction of the port and nearby Concepción. 'Both towns,' he wrote, 'presented the most awful yet interesting spectacle I ever beheld'; see Darwin, *The Voyage of the Beagle* (ch. xiii), pp. 288–99.

2. Jacquinot, note 12, in Dumont d'Urville [& Jacquinot], *Voyage au pôle sud*, 'Histoire du voyage', vol. iv, pp. 305–06.

3. Villalobos, *A Short History of Chile*, pp. 112–15.

4. Dumont d'Urville [& Jacquinot], op. cit., 'Histoire du voyage', vol. iii, p. 7.

5. Ibid., p. 6.

6. D'Urville spells his name Gaspard. He married in Hobart in 1844 and later became the landlord of the Sir John Franklin Hotel in Sunbury, Victoria; see *The Argus* (Melbourne), Thursday 19 May 1859, p. 6. I am grateful to Peter Tremewan, Canterbury, New Zealand, for other biographical details.

7. Buick, *The French at Akaroa*, p. 216.

8. Dumont d'Urville [& Jacquinot], op. cit., 'Histoire du voyage', vol. iii, p. 31.

9. Ibid., p. 46.

10. Surprisingly, while d'Urville was in Talcahuano, Allan Cunningham was aboard the French naval corvette l'*Héroïne*, bound for New Zealand, under the command of Jean-Baptiste Cécille (1787–1873), who had orders to protect French whalers and missionaries in the Pacific; see McMinn, *Allan Cunningham*, p. 112.

11. Richard Cunningham was killed by Aborigines after he became separated from Thomas Mitchell's (1792–1855) expedition in search of the source of the Darling River; see Hoare, 'Botany and society in Eastern Australia', p. 202.

12. Dumont d'Urville [& Jacquinot], op. cit., 'Histoire du voyage', vol. iii, p. 39.

13. Neither d'Urville nor the other naturalists of the expedition appear to have collected any new plant species during their visit. Some zoological specimens were thought to be new and were published, but they later proved to be synonyms for previously described species.

14. Dumont d'Urville [& Jacquinot], op. cit., 'Histoire du voyage', vol. iii, p. 75.

15. Ibid., p. 77.

16. Delano, *The Genealogy, History, and Alliances of the American House of Delano, 1621 to 1899*, pp. 469–72.

17. Dumont d'Urville [& Jacquinot], op. cit., 'Histoire du voyage', vol. iii, pp. 32 & 106. Morrell had asserted that Simon Lavaux, surgeon on the Lapérouse expedition, had died as late as 1834 on an island in the Pacific, leaving two children. Morrell did not name the island in his letter, but two years after d'Urville's death, Thomas Jefferson Jacobs, in his fanciful work *Scenes, Incidents, and Adventures in the Pacific Ocean*, p. 83, named the island as 'Riger' in the so-called 'Morrell Group', vaguely located northeast of Papua. The tale has fuelled speculation ever since.

18. Dumont d'Urville [& Jacquinot], op. cit., 'Histoire du voyage', vol. iii, p. 64.

19. Acte de décès, Toulon, no. 2089, Émile-Jules-Léon Dumont d'Urville, 8 octobre 1837, Archives départementales du Var, Draguignan, 7E146_152R2.

20. Adélie to Dumont d'Urville, 10 novembre 1837, Archives nationales, Paris, Marine 5JJ 158 Bis.

21. Jules Dumont d'Urville *fils* to Dumont d'Urville, 20 novembre 1837, Archives nationales, Paris, Marine 5JJ 158 Bis.

22. [Vincendon-Dumoulin, C.-D.], 'Notice biographique: Jules-Sébastien-César Dumont d'Urville', in Dumont d'Urville [& Jacquinot], op. cit., 'Histoire du voyage', vol. x, p. 133.

23. Duhaut-Cilly, A.B., *Voyage autour du monde, principalement à la Californie et aux Îles Sandwich, pendant les années 1826, 1827, 1828, et 1829*, 2 vols, Arthus Bertrand, Paris, 1834–35.

24. Levot, 'Biographie des frères Bernard Duhaut-Cilly'.

25. Victorino Garrido was born in Castilla la Vieja, Spain, in 1779. He arrived in Chile in 1818 as a royal commissioner but soon deserted to the forces of the Chilean independence leader Bernardo O'Higgins. He was elected a senator in 1855 and died in July 1864; see Castillo infante & Fuentes y Liá Cortés, *Diccionario Histórico y Biográfico de Chile*, p. 197.

26. Dumont d'Urville [& Jacquinot], op. cit., 'Histoire du voyage', vol. iii, p. 89.

27. Ibid., pp. 89–90.

28. Yzendoorn, 'Alexis John Augustine Bachelot'.

29. Anon., 'Missions de l'Océanie'.

30. Yzendoorn, op. cit.

31. Dumont d'Urville [& Jacquinot], op. cit., 'Histoire du voyage', vol. iii, p. 92.

32. See Duyker, 'La Motte du Portail, Jacques-Malo de (1761–1812)'.

33. I have made extensive use of a transcription of La Motte du Portail's account in my biography of the naturalist Jacques-Julien Houtou de Labillardière. La Motte du Portail constructed his narrative in the form of 36 letters to a supposed fiancée named 'Zélie'. This may have been a means of avoiding handing over his journal at the end of the voyage, for he did not marry anyone by the name of 'Zélie', rather he married Julienne Guillemaut-Despeche in Saint-Malo on 5 January 1804. The letters reveal a shrewd observer with a comic (albeit politically conservative) journalistic eye, who was well read in poetry and other literature.
34. Dumont d'Urville [& Jacquinot], op. cit., 'Histoire du voyage', vol. iii, pp. 101–03.
35. Ibid., p. 108.

27. THE MISSIONARY ISLES

1. Richard Henry Dana described the settlement (which he visited less than four years before d'Urville) as 'a variety of huts or cottages, nearly a hundred in number, the best of them built of mud or unburnt clay, and whitewashed, but the greater part Robinson Crusoe like – only of posts and branches of trees. The governor's house, as it is called, was the most conspicuous, being large, with grated windows, plastered walls, and roof of red tiles; yet, like all the rest, only of one story [sic]. Near it was a small chapel, distinguished by a cross; and a long, low, brown-looking building, surrounded by something like a palisade, from which an old and dingy-looking Chilian [sic] flag was flying'; see Dana, *Two Years Before the Mast*, chapter vii.
2. Ibid.
3. Honoré Jacquinot, note 53, in Dumont d'Urville [& Jacquinot], *Voyage au pôle sud*, 'Histoire du voyage', vol. iii, p. 337.
4. Desgraz, note 57, in Dumont d'Urville [& Jacquinot], op. cit., 'Histoire du voyage', vol. iii, p. 342.
5. British consular records described the *Friends* as 'a ship of war seeking seals and whales'; Rugg had sailed from Valparaiso and had three sojourns in Tahiti: 28 September–26 October 1838, 2–22 May 1839 and 15 November–28 December 1839; see Richards, *Tahiti and the Society Islands Index to Ships 1800–1852*, pp. 40 & 152.
6. After visiting Tonga, Rugg reached Sydney on 9 February 1840 (see *Australasian Chronicle*, Tuesday 11 February 1840, p. 2) and then apparently sailed for New Zealand (*The Sydney Monitor and Commercial Advertiser*, Friday 6 March 1840, p. 1).
7. Roquemaurel, note 85, in Dumont d'Urville [& Jacquinot], op. cit., 'Histoire du voyage', vol. iii, p. 386.
8. In the eyes of the church, La Tour was illegitimate, which was a barrier to ordination.
9. Ironically, Marie-Joseph Coudrin, the founder of the order, believed Brother Urbain (La Tour) would be 'a bad note' in the congregation and was happy to be rid of him; see his letter to père Joachim Delétang, 8 août 1822, in Mark, A., & Hœdemaekers, P. (eds), *P. Marie-Joseph Coudrin: Correspondance*, Maison générale, Congrégation des Sacrés-Cœurs de Jésus et de Marie, Rome, vol. 5, p. 142.
10. Ibid.; see also Garrett, J., *To Live Among the Stars*, p. 93. D'Urville refers to him as Urbain de Fleury de la Tour or M. de la Tour.
11. Dubouzet, note 95, in Dumont d'Urville [& Jacquinot], op. cit., 'Histoire du voyage', vol. iii, p. 396.
12. Marion had previously served under Captain Adolphe Bureau (died 1834) on the ill-fated *Aimable Joséphine*.
13. Laval, *Mémoires pour servir à l'histoire de Mangareva: Ère chrétienne, 1834–1871*, p. 151, note 1. & p. 152, note 2; see also O'Reilly, *Tahitiens: Supplément*, pp. 30–31 [also numbered 570–71]. Alexis Marion's wife's Christian name (in the most literal sense) was Geneviève. Jacques (or Jacob) Guilloux married a Mangarevan woman named Keretia-Célestine Toamagiti in 1834.
14. La Farge, note 77, in Dumont d'Urville [& Jacquinot], op. cit., 'Histoire du voyage', vol. iii, pp. 372–73. Despite these dreams, Guilloux had at least five children in Mangareva and it would remain his home until his death. In 1862, he built and skippered the whaler *Notre-Dame-de-la-Paix*; see O'Reilly, op. cit., p. 31 [also numbered 571].

15. Dumont d'Urville [& Jacquinot], op. cit., 'Histoire du voyage', vol. iii, p. 138.

16. Julien Crozet (1728–1782) made reference to ciguatera during his visit to Guam in late 1772, writing that some fish were 'very unwholesome, for they nourish themselves on the little polyps, which form the coral'; however, his account was not published until 1783; see Crozet, *Nouveau voyage à la mer du sud*, p. 197. The first published description was by William Anderson (1750–1778), surgeon's mate aboard James Cook's *Resolution*, in 1776; see Anderson, 'An account of some poisonous fish in the South Seas'. More than two centuries later, in 1979, the principal toxic culprit in the Pacific, *Gambierdiscus toxicus*, was identified and named after the Gambier Islands (where ciguatera remains endemic) by two Japanese marine scientists, Adachi Rokur (born 1931) and Fukuyo Yasuo (born 1948).

17. The flag is described, though not the symbolism of the stars, in Desgraz, note 67, in Dumont d'Urville [& Jacquinot], op. cit., 'Histoire du voyage', vol. iii, p. 354.

18. Named by the British missionary James Wilson in honour of his ship the *Duff*, after he sighted the Gambier Islands in 1797.

19. Desgraz, note 84, in Dumont d'Urville [& Jacquinot], op. cit., 'Histoire du voyage', vol. iii, p. 384.

20. Dumont d'Urville [& Jacquinot], op. cit., 'Histoire du voyage', vol. iii, pp. 144–45.

21. Weisler, 'The settlement of marginal Polynesia'; this case is also summarised in Diamond, *Collapse*, pp. 120–33.

22. Roquemaurel, note 97, in Dumont d'Urville [& Jacquinot], op. cit., 'Histoire du voyage', vol. iii, p. 398.

23. Dumont d'Urville [& Jacquinot], op. cit., 'Histoire du voyage', vol. iii, p. 147.

24. Ibid., pp. 161 & 168. The tools were delivered by Barlartier-Demas on 9 August.

25. La Farge, note 104, in Dumont d'Urville [& Jacquinot], op. cit., 'Histoire du voyage', vol. iii, pp. 411–12.

26. For example, Marescot du Thilleul wrote that the British missionaries 'faked a French history, worthy of their imagination, and in their low and coarse jibes, they said that the French nation was hardly larger than that of Mangareva and that one day England had been obliged to give a thrashing to a certain Napoleon, king of this region'; see Marescot, note 103, in Dumont d'Urville [& Jacquinot], op. cit., 'Histoire du voyage', vol. iii, pp. 410–11.

27. See, for example, Desgraz, note 84, in Dumont d'Urville [& Jacquinot], op. cit., 'Histoire du voyage', vol. iii, pp. 384–86; Hombron, note 121, in Dumont d'Urville [& Jacquinot], op. cit., 'Histoire du voyage', vol. iii, pp. 437–41.

28. Desgraz, note 82, in Dumont d'Urville [& Jacquinot], op. cit., 'Histoire du voyage', vol. iii, p. 381; writing to his father from Tahiti, Desgraz took up this theme again. Of the Tahitian converts to Catholicism, he wrote: 'They sing Latin songs that they do not understand. It has undoubtedly been difficult to explain what the Pope [and] Rome are … but they seem delighted with religious ceremonies and repeat each instant the words learned from missionaries such as *Catolico, Apostolico, Romano* … This new religion is more brilliant than the old, and they love it'; César Desgraz to his father, Tahiti, 14 septembre 1838, Cambridge University Library, MS. Add. 7540/44.

29. Coupvent, note 122, in Dumont d'Urville [& Jacquinot], op. cit., 'Histoire du voyage', vol. iii, p. 441.

30. D'Urville collected one of these statues, which was deposited with the Musée de marine du Louvre in 1841. In the early twentieth century, it was transferred to the Muséum d'histoire naturelle de La Rochelle (H2442); see Jacquemin, *Objets des Mers du Sud*.

31. Montagne, in Dumont d'Urville [& Jacquinot], op. cit., 'Botanique' [Hombron & Jacquinot (eds.)], vol. i, Plantes cellulaires, pp. 219–21.

32. Hombron & Jacquinot (eds), in Dumont d'Urville [& Jacquinot], op. cit., 'Zoologie', vol. iii, pp. 51–53.

33. Ibid., pp. 53–54.

34. 'Équipage de l'Astrolabe', in Dumont d'Urville [& Jacquinot], op. cit., 'Histoire du voyage', vol. i, p. xlii.

35. Ironically, Queen Patini had a rival for the title of monarch of Nuku Hiva. The officers of d'Urville's expedition were amused to learn that baron Charles de Thierry had visited the island briefly in July 1835, in his ridiculous capacity as 'chief sovereign of New Zealand and king of Nouka-Hiva', and had

drafted a letter of recommendation in English, for one of the chiefs, bearing these purported titles. The letter is quoted by Jacquinot, note 1, in Dumont d'Urville [& Jacquinot], op. cit., 'Histoire du voyage', vol. iv, p. 269. Jacquinot could not resist a mocking comment on the same page: 'Lucky king! lucky subjects! His majesty, the baron Thierry had made, in the course of his reign, a brief apparition at Nouka-Hiva, without doubt to receive some tributes of pigs and other refreshments.'

36. Le Guillou, *Voyage autour du monde*, vol. i, p. 117.
37. Dumont d'Urville [& Jacquinot], op. cit., 'Histoire du voyage', vol. iv, p. 56.
38. Ibid., pp. 59–60.
39. Ibid., p. 61.
40. Ibid.
41. Jacquinot, note 12, in Dumont d'Urville [& Jacquinot], op. cit., 'Histoire du voyage', vol. iv, pp. 305–06.
42. Barclay, *A History of the Pacific*, p. 67.
43. In fact, Queen Pomare had fled her usual residence on the harbour of Pape'ete after Dupetit-Thouars' arrival.
44. Dumont d'Urville [& Jacquinot], op. cit., 'Histoire du voyage', vol. iv, p. 71.
45. Ibid., pp. 71–72.
46. Rosenman, (ed. & trans.), *An Account in Two Volumes of Two Voyages to the South Seas*, vol. ii, p. 360.
47. Timmins, 'Pritchard, George (1796–1883)'.
48. Montagne, *Prodromus generum specierumque phycearum novarum*, p. 15.
49. Dumont d'Urville [& Jacquinot], op. cit., 'Histoire du voyage', vol. iv, p. 85.
50. Roquemaurel, note 14, in Dumont d'Urville [& Jacquinot], op. cit., 'Histoire du voyage', vol. iv, p. 312.
51. Jacquinot jeune, note 15, in Dumont d'Urville [& Jacquinot], op. cit., 'Histoire du voyage', vol. iv, p. 317.
52. César Desgraz to his father, Tahiti, 14 septembre 1838, loc. cit.
53. Dossier personnel, Deflotte, Paul-Louis-René, SHDDM, Vincennes, CC[7] Alpha 629; Taillemite, *Dictionnaire des marins français*, p. 121; additional information from Mikael Riou, Douarnenez (Finistère).
54. Bach, *The Australian Station*, p. 35.
55. Dumont d'Urville [& Jacquinot], op. cit., 'Histoire du voyage', vol. iv, pp. 99–100.
56. Ibid., p. 101.
57. Jacquinot, note 19, in Dumont d'Urville [& Jacquinot], op. cit., 'Histoire du voyage', vol. iv, p. 332.
58. Dumont d'Urville [& Jacquinot], op. cit., 'Histoire du voyage', vol. iv, p. 109.
59. The range of Samoan books d'Urville received was limited and they are not recorded in either the notarial inventories or the sale catalogue of his private library. In 1834, Charles Barff (1792–1866) of the London Missionary Society printed the first book in Samoan, a 12-page primer prepared by John Williams, at the Leeward Press at Huahine (Society Islands). The Methodists produced a four-page Samoan primer of their own at Tongatapu in March 1835, shortly before their press was moved to Vava'u; see Lingenfelter, *Presses of the Pacific Islands, 1817–1867*, p. 69. According to Barff, as quoted by Richard Moyle in his editorial notes for *The Samoan Journals of John Williams, 1830 and 1832*, the publications distributed in 1834 comprised 'the first elementary books printed in the Samoan dialect – a small reading and spelling book – a small catechism and a small hymn book. These little works had been drawn up by Mr Williams before he left for England and we printed them at Huahine' (footnote 62 on p. 119).
60. See Duyker, *Père Receveur*.
61. Dumont d'Urville [& Jacquinot], op. cit., 'Histoire du voyage', vol. iv, p. 102.
62. Ibid., p. 140.
63. Garrett, op. cit., p. 76.
64. One of Dillon's principal informants was Joseph Meyrick, former surgeon of the whaler *Thetis*. Dillon's letter to Reverend Thomas eventually appeared in French translation in Dupetit-Thouars' *Voyage autour du monde*, vol. ii, pp. 414–19; see Davidson, *Peter Dillon of Vanikoro*, pp. 270–74.
65. Ibid., pp. 270–71.

66. Dumont d'Urville [& Jacquinot], op. cit., 'Histoire du voyage', vol. iv, p. 139–40.
67. Ibid., p. 148.
68. Blanchard, in Dumont d'Urville [& Jacquinot], op. cit., 'Zoologie' [in Hombron & Jacquinot (eds.)], vol. iv, Description des insectes, pp. 186–87, 237 & 239.

28. VENGEANCE & PILGRIMAGE

1. D'Urville used an idiosyncratic spelling 'Piva'. Viwa should not be confused with the island of the same name in the Yasawa group.
2. Dumont d'Urville [& Jacquinot], *Voyage au pôle sud*, 'Histoire du voyage', vol. iv, p. 190.
3. Cargill, *Memoirs of Mrs. Margaret Cargill*, p. 114.
4. Du Bouzet, report quoted in Dumont d'Urville [& Jacquinot], op. cit., 'Histoire du voyage', vol. iv, p. 200.
5. Ibid., p. 115.
6. Duméril & Bibron, *Erpétologie générale*, vol. 6, pp. 483–84.
7. Duméril, 'Mémoire sur les Batraciens anoures de la famille des Hylaeformes ou Rainettes', p. 177.
8. Blanchard, in Dumont d'Urville [& Jacquinot], op. cit., 'Zoologie' [Hombron & Jacquinot (eds.)], vol. iv, Description des insectes, pp. 7–8.
9. Brown, *Men from Under the Sky*, pp. 100–02.
10. Jacquinot & Pucheran, in Dumont d'Urville [& Jacquinot], op. cit., 'Zoologie' [Hombron & Jacquinot (eds)], vol. iii, Mammifères et oiseaux, pp. 115–17; see also Voisin et al., 'Liste des types d'oiseaux des collections du Muséum national d'histoire naturelle de Paris', p. 116.
11. The other insects were the weevils *Isomerinthus lineolatus* and *I. rufipes*; and a previously undescribed mantid, *Mantis fuscescens* (*Hierodula fuscescens*); see Blanchard, in Dumont d'Urville [& Jacquinot], op. cit., 'Zoologie' [Hombron & Jacquinot (eds)], vol. iv, Description des insectes, pp. 221–22, 226–27, 354 & 359–60.
12. These were hazardous waters. Despite his experience, Thomas Grandy drowned during a cyclone that wrecked the *Venus* (a vessel he part-owned) off Ovalau in April 1848; see Henderson (ed.), *The Journal of Thomas Williams, Missionary in Fiji, 1840–1853*, vol. ii, pp. 431–34.
13. Dumont d'Urville [& Jacquinot], op. cit., 'Histoire du voyage', vol. iv, p. 236.
14. Ibid., p. 247.
15. Ibid., p. 250.
16. Ibid., pp. 258–61.
17. Jacquinot & Pucheran, in Dumont d'Urville [& Jacquinot], op. cit., 'Zoologie' [Hombron & Jacquinot (eds)], vol. iii, Mammifères et oiseaux, pp. 97–99; *Myzomela lafargei* might have been collected earlier on Vanikoro.
18. The tiger beetle *Cicindela sanguineomaculata*; a shining leaf chafer, *Parastasia rufolimbata*; a scarab, *Lomaptera rugata*; and two longhorn beetles, *Clytus aureicollis* (*Demonax aureicollis*) and *Heteroclytomorpha quadrinotata*; see Blanchard, in Dumont d'Urville [& Jacquinot], op. cit., 'Zoologie' [Hombron & Jacquinot (eds)], vol. iv, Description des insectes, pp. 5–6, 269–70, 277–78 & 349–50; see also Blanchard, *Catalogue des Cétonides de la collection du Muséum d'histoire naturelle de Paris*, p. 18.
19. D'Urville refers to them as the Hogoleu Islands.
20. Jacquinot & Pucheran, in Dumont d'Urville [& Jacquinot], op. cit., 'Zoologie' [Hombron & Jacquinot (eds)], vol. iii, Mammifères et oiseaux, p. 77.

29. GUAM & THE MOLUCCAS

1. According to Surgeon John Wilson of the whaling ship *Gipsy*, by 12 September 1840, Anderson and his wife (Josefa de Castro), had a family of six boys and five girls; see Forster (ed.), *The Cruise of the 'Gipsy'*, p. 111. Anderson ultimately fathered 12 children; see Souder, 'Heritage', unpublished MS 1978, Micronesian Area Research Center, University of Guam; see also Rogers, *Destiny's Landfall: A history of Guam*, p. 96.

2. Dubouzet noted that 150 soldiers from Manila were stationed on Guam but that Spanish defence seemed posited on the island's 'uselessness' to any other power; see Dubouzet, quoted in Dumont d'Urville [& Jacquinot], *Voyage au pôle sud*, 'Histoire du voyage', vol. v, p. 202.

3. Rogers, *Destiny's Landfall*, p. 98.

4. Dumont d'Urville [& Jacquinot], op. cit., 'Histoire du voyage', vol. v, p. 175.

5. Dubouzet, quoted in Dumont d'Urville [& Jacquinot], op. cit., 'Histoire du voyage', vol. v, p. 198.

6. Blanchard, in Dumont d'Urville [& Jacquinot], op. cit., 'Zoologie' [Hombron & Jacquinot, (eds.)], vol. iv, Description des insectes, p. 157.

7. Dumont d'Urville [& Jacquinot], op. cit., 'Histoire du voyage', vol. v, pp. 246–47.

8. D'Urville does not mention that the acting governor's wife was the daughter of General Hendrik Mercus de Kock (1779–1845), the former governor-general of the Netherlands East Indies (1826–1830) and, from 1836, the foreign minister of the Netherlands, who had an intimate role in providing the very passports that he had just presented in Ambon; see Molhuysen & Blok (eds), *Nieuw Nederlands Biografisch Woordenboek*, vol. 2, pp. 692–95.

9. Dumont d'Urville [& Jacquinot], op. cit., 'Histoire du voyage', vol. v, p. 267.

10. Jacquinot & Guichenot, in Dumont d'Urville [& Jacquinot], op. cit., 'Zoologie' [Hombron & Jacquinot (eds)], vol. iii, Reptiles et poissons, pp. 12–14.

11. *Lomaptera virens* and *Prioneta albosignata* (*Pterolophia albosignata*), see Blanchard, in Dumont d'Urville [& Jacquinot], op. cit., 'Zoologie' [Hombron & Jacquinot, (eds.)], vol. iv, Description des insectes, pp. 134–35 & 293.

12. Dumont d'Urville, Rade de Batavia, *Astrolabe*, au ministre de la marine et des colonies, Paris, 18 Juin 1839, SHDDM, Vincennes, BB^4 1009.

13. Dumont d'Urville [& Jacquinot], op. cit., 'Histoire du voyage', vol. vi, p. 6.

14. Dumont d'Urville, Rade de Batavia, *Astrolabe*, au ministre de la marine et des colonies, Paris, 18 Juin 1839, loc. cit.

30. NORTHERN NEW HOLLAND

1. Méhaud & Richard (eds), *Dumont d'Urville en Antarctique*, p. 89.

2. Trepang are holothurians, also known as sea slugs or bêches-de-mer. The Makassan voyages probably began sometime after the Dutch restricted other trading enterprises from Sulawesi in 1667. No mention of the trade appears in Dutch sources prior to 1754, despite the probability that Makassan skippers had access to Dutch maps long before. Many Makassan boats were owned by Dutch merchants, and their voyages continued until the first decade of the twentieth century. Smoked and dried trepangs were sold to an eager Chinese market. They are still used in soups and cooked with vegetables in China. They also have a reputation as aphrodisiacs – probably because of their phallic shape; for an excellent survey, see Macknight, *The Voyage to Marege*.

3. Dumont d'Urville [& Jacquinot], *Voyage au pôle sud*, 'Histoire du voyage', vol. vi, p. 37.

4. Le Guillou, *Voyage autour du monde*, vol. i, p. 865.

5. Barlatier-Demas, note 10, in Dumont d'Urville [& Jacquinot], op. cit., 'Histoire du voyage', vol. vi, p. 264.

6. Desgraz, note 14, in Dumont d'Urville [& Jacquinot], op. cit., 'Histoire du voyage', vol. vi, p. 275.

7. Dumont d'Urville [& Jacquinot], op. cit., 'Histoire du voyage', vol. vi, p. 41.

8. Barrow, Beaufort, Marcheson & Washington, 'Report of the Deputation from the Council of the Royal Geographical Society…', pp. 10–11 [vol. xl, pp. 350–51].

9. Statham, *The Origins of Australia's Capital Cities*, pp. 285–86.

10. Earl, *The Eastern Seas*, appendix, note, p. 441.

11. Ibid., p. 461.

12. D'Urville described 'Flinders' as a *jeune élève* (young student, trainee or midshipman). It is possible that his name was misread when volume vi of the official account was typeset. On the muster roll of HMS *Alligator*, there was no Midshipman Flinders; see James C. Wallace, Journal aboard HMS *Alligator*, 1838–39, National Library of Australia, MS 179. Nor does a Flinders appear in other

contemporary naval records or on the list of marines aboard HMS *Alligator*; see Spillet, *Forsaken Settlement*, p. 178. The midshipmen listed were Bremer and Baker; there were also two first-class volunteers: Meynell and Balfour. Midshipman Edward Bremer, Captain Bremer's son, was mentioned separately by d'Urville. The journal of Francis Meynell (who was later described as a 'midshipman'), preserved in the Northern Territory Library, Darwin (MS61), indicates that he was in Port Essington with Captain Bremer at the time and *not* in Raffles Bay with Lieutenant Stewart and George Earl. The balance of probability is that 'Flinders' was in fact Midshipman Horace Mann Baker (*ca.*1815–1848), the second son of Admiral Sir Thomas Baker (1771?–1845). He was promoted to mate of HMS *Alligator* in 1840, took part in the First Opium War, was promoted lieutenant in 1841 and served on HMS *Pique*; see O'Byrne, *A Naval Biographical Dictionary*, p. 38. Baker is buried in the Hospital Burial Ground, Haslar, Hampshire.

13. Dumont d'Urville, Rade de Batavia, *Astrolabe*, au ministre de la marine et des colonies, Paris, 18 Juin 1839, SHDDM, Vincennes, BB^4 1009.

14. Ibid.

15. Dumont d'Urville [& Jacquinot], op. cit., 'Histoire du voyage', vol. vi, pp. 43–44.

16. Unfortunately, Gourdin's nautical remarks were found to be missing after his death later that year; see Vincendon-Dumoulin, in Dumont d'Urville [& Jacquinot], op. cit., 'Hydrographie', vol. ii, p. 148.

17. Rousseau, in Dumont d'Urville [& Jacquinot], op. cit., 'Zoologie' [in Hombron & Jacquinot (eds)], vol. v, Description des mollusques, coquilles et zoophytes, pp. 1, 66 & 96; the name *Cerithium kieneri* had already been used by the Belgian zoologist François-Joseph Cantraine in 1835; in 1929, Tom Iredale (1880–1972) applied the new name *Cerithium (Cerithidea) anticipata* to this species, which is found on mangrove trees; see Iredale, 'Queensland molluscan notes, no. 1', p. 278.

18. Jacquinot & Lucas, in Dumont d'Urville [& Jacquinot], op. cit., 'Zoologie' [Hombron & Jacquinot (eds)], vol. iii, Zoologie crustacés, pp. 57–58 & 97–98.

19. Blanchard, in Dumont d'Urville [& Jacquinot], op. cit., 'Zoologie' [Hombron & Jacquinot (eds)], vol. iv, Description des insectes, pp. 36 & 101.

20. Blanchard, *Museum d'histoire naturelle, catalogue de la collection entomologique*, vol. ii, p. 224.

21. Méhaud & Richard (eds), op. cit., p. 89.

22. [Laughton], J.K.L. 'Bremer, Sir James John Gordon (1786–1850)'.

23. Dumont d'Urville, Rade de Batavia, *Astrolabe*, au ministre de la marine et des colonies, Paris, 18 Juin 1839, loc. cit.

24. Ibid.

25. Ibid.

26. Dumont d'Urville [& Jacquinot], op. cit., 'Histoire du voyage', vol. vi, p. 42.

27. Allen, 'The archaeology of nineteenth-century British imperialism'.

28. Dumont d'Urville [& Jacquinot], op. cit., 'Histoire du voyage', vol. vi, p. 65.

29. Le Breton's sketch of Port Essington was later lithographed by Léon-Jean-Baptiste Sabatier and published as plate 120 in Dumont d'Urville [& Jacquinot], op. cit., 'Atlas pittoresque', vol. ii.

30. Nine months later, one such cyclone struck with devastating force, killing a dozen men at Port Essington. Government House was swept up off its stone piers and flung some 3 metres away. The unfinished church was flattened, and the NCOs' cottages were either smashed to pieces, unroofed or rendered uninhabitable; see Spillet, op. cit., pp. 56–63. D'Urville learnt of these events when he visited Timor on his return voyage to France.

31. Armstrong later became a plant collector in Timor, where he died; see Desmond, *Dictionary of British and Irish Botanists and Horticulturists*, p. 18.

32. Dumont d'Urville [& Jacquinot], op. cit., 'Histoire du voyage', vol. vi, p. 66.

33. James C. Wallace, Journal aboard HMS *Alligator*, 1838–39, loc. cit.

34. Ibid.

35. Dumont d'Urville [& Jacquinot], op. cit., 'Histoire du voyage', vol. vi, p. 67.

36. It was already clear to d'Urville that Bremer's subordinates did not share their commander's faith in the fledgling colony; see Dumont d'Urville, Rade de Batavia, *Astrolabe*, au ministre de la marine et des colonies, Paris, 18 Juin 1839, loc. cit.

37. Dumont d'Urville [& Jacquinot], op. cit., 'Histoire du voyage', vol. vi, p. 79.
38. Spillet, *Forsaken Settlement*, pp. 156–68.

31. THE AUGMENTATION OF THE INDIES

1. Dumont d'Urville [& Jacquinot], *Voyage au pôle sud*, 'Histoire du voyage', vol. vi, p. 89.
2. Jacquinot & Pucheran, in Dumont d'Urville [& Jacquinot], op. cit., 'Zoologie' [Hombron & Jacquinot (eds)], vol. iii, Mammifères et oiseaux, pp. 89, 107–08 & 119–21.
3. Vincendon-Dumoulin, in Dumont d'Urville [& Jacquinot], op. cit., 'Histoire du voyage', vol. vi, p. 55.
4. Dumont d'Urville [& Jacquinot], op. cit., 'Histoire du voyage', vol. vi, pp. 187–88.
5. Ibid., p. 196.
6. Ibid., p. 188.
7. *Pycnonotus goiavier gourdini*; see Gray, G.R., *The Genera of Birds*, vol. 1 [instalment of October 1847], p. 237 'P[ycnonotus]. Yourdini [*sic*] "(Homb. & Jacq.)"'; this bird was named in honour of Ensign Gourdin; see Jacquinot & Pucheran, in Dumont d'Urville [& Jacquinot], op. cit., 'Zoologie' [Hombron & Jacquinot (eds)], vol. iii, Mammifères et oiseaux, pp. 79–80; see also Delacour, 'A revision of the genera and species of the family Pycnonotidae (bulbuls)'.
8. *Onthophagus armatus* and *Opatrum aequatoriale* (*Gonocephalum aequatoriale*); see Blanchard, in Dumont d'Urville [& Jacquinot], op. cit., 'Zoologie' [Hombron & Jacquinot (eds)], vol. iv, Description des insectes, pp. 98–99 & 152–53.
9. Dumont d'Urville, Rade de Batavia, *Astrolabe*, au ministre de la marine et des colonies, Paris, 18 Juin 1839, SHDDM, Vincennes, BB^4 1009.
10. Registers van het Europese personeel op Java en Madoera … 1 januari 1819, Nationaal Archief, Den Haag, 3106–3125; see also Broeze, 'The Merchant Fleet of Java (1820–1850)', pp. 263–64.
11. Augustin Bonaventure Désiré Lagnier, son of Joachim Lagnier, born Marseille, 27 August 1793 [registre 4], table décennale, naissances, 1792–1802, Archives départementales des Bouches-du-Rhône, Marseille.
12. See Peyssonnaux, 'Vie, voyages et travaux de Pierre Médard Diard'.
13. See Husson & Holthuis, 'The dates of publication of "Verhandelingen over de natuurlijke Geschiedenis der Nederlandsche overzeesche Bezittingen" edited by C.J. Temminck', p. 17.
14. Desgraz (note 6), in Dumont d'Urville [& Jacquinot], op. cit., 'Histoire du voyage', vol. vii, pp. 270–71.
15. Le Guillou, *Voyage autour du monde*, vol. ii, p. 25.
16. Hector Jacquinot, note 1, in Dumont d'Urville [& Jacquinot], op. cit., 'Histoire du voyage', vol. vii, p. 244.
17. Le Guillou, op. cit., p. 53.
18. [Douglas, R.K.], 'Bonham, Sir Samuel George (1803–1863)'.
19. Dumont d'Urville [& Jacquinot], op. cit., 'Histoire du voyage', vol. vii, p. 84.
20. See Costet, *Archives des missions étrangères*, pp. 208–13.
21. Dumont d'Urville [& Jacquinot], op. cit., 'Histoire du voyage', vol. vii, p. 85.
22. See Brucker, 'Protectorate of Missions'.
23. Ibid., pp. 89–90; officially, Singapore was under the jurisdiction of the Diocese of Malacca, which was in turn a suffragan of the Portuguese Archdiocese of Goa in India.
24. Dumont d'Urville [& Jacquinot], op. cit., 'Histoire du voyage', vol. vii, p. 106.
25. Blainville, H. Ducrotay de, 'Instructions relatives au voyage de circumnavigation de l'*Astrolabe* et de la *Zélée*', extrait des *Comptes-rendus des séances de l'Académie des sciences*, séance du 7 août 1837, in Dumont d'Urville [& Jacquinot], op. cit., 'Zoologie' [Hombron & Jacquinot (eds)], vol. i, p. 11.
26. Jacquinot & Pucheran, in Dumont d'Urville [& Jacquinot], op. cit., 'Zoologie' [Hombron & Jacquinot (eds)], vol. iii, Mammifères et oiseaux, pp. 17–22.
27. Le Guillou (op. cit., p. 48) wrote sarcastically: 'M. d'Urville thought that a treaty of commerce with this redoubt of brigands might become useful to France.'

28. For Gervaize's colourful account of his adventures, see Dumont d'Urville [& Jacquinot], op. cit., 'Histoire du voyage', vol. vii, pp. 178–83.

29. Blainville, 'Rapports sur les résultats scientifiques du voyage de circumnavigation de l'*Astrolabe* et de la *Zelée*: Partie zoologique'.

30. Jacquinot & Pucheran, in Dumont d'Urville [& Jacquinot], op. cit., 'Zoologie' [Hombron & Jacquinot (eds)], vol. iii, Mammifères et oiseaux, pp. 118–19.

31. Le Guillou, op. cit., facing p. 61.

32. Dumont d'Urville [& Jacquinot], op. cit., 'Histoire du voyage', vol. vii, p. 210.

33. Ibid., p. 212.

34. Roquemaurel, note 23, in Dumont d'Urville [& Jacquinot], op. cit., 'Histoire du voyage', vol. vii, p. 326.

35. Desgraz, note 27, in Dumont d'Urville [& Jacquinot], op. cit., 'Histoire du voyage', vol. vii, p. 345.

36. See Vincendon-Dumoulin's footnote in Dumont d'Urville [& Jacquinot], op. cit., 'Histoire du voyage', vol. vii, pp. 228–29.

37. Dossier personnel, Avril, Pierre, SHDDM, Vincennes, CC[7] Alpha 77.

38. Hector Jacquinot, note 21, in Dumont d'Urville [& Jacquinot], op. cit., 'Histoire du voyage', vol. vii, p. 319.

39. 'Wangaroa' (or 'Wangaloa') was an alternative name for Akaroa on the east coast of the South Island of New Zealand. Given d'Urville's orders, it seems a more likely destination than Whangaroa on the east coast of the North Island. I am grateful to Dr Roger Collins, Dunedin, for his assistance with this question.

40. Dumont d'Urville, Samboangan (Zamboanga), Île Mindanao, *Astrolabe*, 4 août 1839, au ministre de la marine et des colonies, Paris, in Dumont d'Urville [& Jacquinot], op. cit., 'Histoire du voyage', vol. x, Pièces justificatives, p. 174.

41. Dumont d'Urville [& Jacquinot], op. cit., 'Histoire du voyage', vol. viii, p. 14.

42. Blainville, 'Rapports sur les résultats scientifiques du voyage de circumnavigation de l'*Astrolabe* et de la *Zelée*: Partie zoologique'.

43. Blainville, 'Instructions relatives au voyage de circumnavigation de l'*Astrolabe* et de la *Zélée* : Partie zoologique', extrait des *Comptes-rendus des séances de l'Académie des sciences*, séance du 7 août 1837, in Dumont d'Urville [& Jacquinot], op. cit., 'Zoologie' [Hombron & Jacquinot (eds)], vol. i, p. 6.

44. Hombron, in Dumont d'Urville [& Jacquinot], op. cit., 'Zoologie' [Hombron & Jacquinot (eds)], vol. i, De l'homme dans ses rapports avec la création, p. 98.

45. Ibid., p. 312.

46. MNHN-HA-1789 & MNHN-HA-8518.

47. Hombron, note 1, in Dumont d'Urville [& Jacquinot], 'Histoire du voyage', op. cit., vol. viii, p. 269.

48. Hartung, 'History of the use of colchicum and related medicaments in gout'.

49. Zuidema, 'Baud, Guillame Louis'.

50. Fiche matricule, Delafond, Pierre-Antoine, École polytechnique, Paris; dossier personnel, Delafond, Pierre-Antoine, SHDDM, Vincennes, CC[7] Alpha 858; Archives nationales, Fond Léonore, LH/695/68.

51. Dumont d'Urville [& Jacquinot], op. cit., 'Histoire du voyage', vol. viii, p. 45.

52. Possibly the same Captain Thébaud who commanded the whaler *Cap Horn*, owned by Veuve Thomas Dobrée & Cie, Nantes, in the early 1830s.

53. Dumont d'Urville [& Jacquinot], op. cit., 'Histoire du voyage', vol. viii, p. 47.

54. Ibid.

55. Madame Tissot (*née* de Jong); see Bloys van Treslong Prins, *Genealogische en heraldische gedenkwaardigheden betreffende Europeanen op Java*, vol. iii, p. 93.

56. Le Guillou, op. cit., pp. 158–59.

57. Dumont d'Urville [& Jacquinot], op. cit., 'Histoire du voyage', vol. viii, p. 47.

58. Ibid., pp. 66–67.

32. HOBART

1. Dumont d'Urville [& Jacquinot], *Voyage au pôle sud*, 'Histoire du voyage', vol. viii, pp. 74–75.
2. Dumont d'Urville, testament, 20 octobre 1839; codicille 1er novembre 1839; ms 11, SHDDM, Toulon.
3. Le Guillou, *Voyage autour du monde*, vol. ii, pp. 169–70.
4. Pendu, 'La pharmacopée de Dumont d'Urville lors de son voyage en Terre Adélie', p. 210.
5. According to Le Guillou's medical journal, Billoud also suffered from syphilis.
6. Dumont d'Urville [& Jacquinot], op. cit., 'Histoire du voyage', vol. viii, p. 89.
7. For the taxonomy of this species, see my note 7 in chapter 31.
8. Muster Roll *Zélée* 1837–40, Archives nationales, JJ/5/158/bis.
9. Dumont d'Urville [& Jacquinot], op. cit., 'Histoire du voyage', vol. viii, p. 96.
10. Le Guillou, op. cit., vol. ii, p. 184.
11. Ibid., p. 188.
12. Dumont d'Urville [& Jacquinot], op. cit., 'Histoire du voyage', vol. viii, p. 108.
13. Ibid., p. 106.
14. Le Guillou, op. cit., vol. ii, p. 184; Jane, Lady Franklin was of French Huguenot descent on both her mother's and her father's side; she had also visited France and Switzerland.
15. Dumont d'Urville [& Jacquinot], op. cit., 'Histoire du voyage', vol. viii, p. 111.
16. Muster Roll *Zélée* 1837–40, Archives nationales JJ/5/158/bis. The *Rubens*, wrecked in January 1844 off Tubuai Island, was one of the whaling vessels the expedition encountered in Talcahuano; it will be remembered that her captain, Louis Rogerie, gave Dumoutier a young humpback whale skull.
17. Muster Roll *Zélée* 1837–40, loc. cit.; according to the muster roll of the *Artémise*, MacPherson joined Laplace's expedition in Libourne (Gironde); see Laplace, *Campagne de circumnavigation de la frégate l'*Artémise, *pendant les années 1837, 1838, 1839 et 1840*, vol. 1, p. xxxi.
18. Index to Tasmanian convicts (1804–1893), Archives Office of Tasmania.
19. Le Guillou, op. cit., vol. ii, p. 186.
20. Dumont d'Urville [& Jacquinot], op. cit., 'Histoire du voyage', vol. viii, p. 123.
21. Le Guillou, op. cit., vol. ii, p. 186.
22. Five convicts were put at the disposal of Vincendon-Dumoulin and Ensign Coupvent-Desbois to carry their scientific instruments to the top of Mt Wellington to conduct geophysical and other observations; see Vincendon-Dumoulin, quoted in Dumont d'Urville [& Jacquinot], op. cit., 'Histoire du voyage', vol. viii, p. 111.
23. Seureau, in Méhaud & Richard, (eds), op. cit., p. 117.
24. Eddy, 'Therry, John Joseph (1790–1864)', p. 510.
25. Hombron, note 4, in Dumont d'Urville [& Jacquinot], op. cit., 'Histoire du voyage', vol. ix, pp. 259–61. Hombron spells Rossiter's name 'Roster' and mistakenly refers to him as the captain of the *Nancy*.
26. Joseph Seureau recorded the inscriptions on both Goupil's and Couteleng's graves; see Méhaud & Richard (eds), *Dumont d'Urville en Antarctique*, p. 117.
27. See Beauvoir, *Australie*, pp. 233–34.
28. See Anon., 'Stories in Stone: Scotch settlers and French circumnavigators'.
29. See Anon., 'Notice', and Anon., 'Removal of Bodies'.

33. TERRE ADÉLIE

1. Dumont d'Urville [& Jacquinot], *Voyage au pôle sud*, 'Histoire du voyage', vol. viii, p. 127.
2. Ibid.
3. Le Guillou, *Voyage autour du monde*, vol. ii, pp. 187–88.
4. Dumont d'Urville [& Jacquinot], op. cit., 'Histoire du voyage', vol. viii, pp. 137–38.
5. Ibid., pp. 142–43.
6. Ibid., p. 147.
7. The location of Rocher du Débarquement is 66° 36′S 140° 4′E.

8. Service hydrographique et océanographique de la marine, *De l'Île Hélène au rocher du Débarquement: Archipel de Pointe Géologie: Océan Antarctique–Terre Adélie* [1:20,000 map].

9. Dubouzet, in Dumont d'Urville [& Jacquinot], op. cit., 'Histoire du voyage', vol. viii, p. 151.

10. Le Guillou, op. cit., p. 192.

11. Hombron & Jacquinot, 'Description de plusieurs oiseaux nouveaux ou peu connus', p. 320.

12. Dumont d'Urville [& Jacquinot], op. cit., 'Histoire du voyage', vol. viii, pp. 155–56.

13. Ibid., p. 157.

14. In the eighteenth century, Horace-Bénédict de Saussure (1740–1799) had recognised the link between glaciers and moraines but still thought that glaciers moved on a bed of water. In 1802, the Scot John Playfair (1748–1819), disciple of the 'uniformitarian' James Hutton (1726–1797), argued that the mass and weight of glacial ice had a vast power to shape landscape and move rocks. However, it was the German-born Swiss geologist Jean de Charpentier (1786–1855) who, in 1834, first argued that glaciation had once been much more extensive and that glaciers had moved and deposited vast boulders, so called 'erratic' rocks. His ideas were taken up by Louis Agassiz (1807–1873); for a useful overview, see Wilson, *The Spiritual History of Ice*, pp. 86–94.

15. Ringgold, in Wilkes, *Narrative of the United States Exploring Expedition*, vol. ii, pp. 344 & 371.

16. Le Guillou, op. cit., p. 198.

17. At the time, Ringgold was separated from the other vessels of Wilkes's squadron. Initially, he thought that the *Astrolabe* and the *Zélée* were the *Vincennes* and the *Peacock*. Then he thought they were vessels of the British expedition under James Clark Ross: HMS *Erebus* and HMS *Terror*. They were only identified as French after they hauled up the tricolour.

18. Leonhart, 'Charles Wilkes: A biography', p. 196; see also Jones & Jones, *Oceanography in the Days of Sail*, pp. 194–200.

19. Quoted by Viola in 'The Story of the U.S. Exploring Expedition', p. 23.

20. See Price, *The Winning of Australian Antarctica*, appendix A: 'Mawson's part in the Wilkes controversy', pp. 174–81; see also appendix B (gazetteer), p. 192.

21. A February 2002 National Geographic Society map of Antarctica bears the toponyms Adélie Coast and Clarie Coast but no Adélie Land; instead, Wilkes Land, in bold capitals, straddles 100–140° E. longitude!

22. Dumont d'Urville [& Jacquinot], op. cit., 'Histoire du voyage', vol. viii, p. 180.

34. RETURN TO HOBART

1. Dumont d'Urville [& Jacquinot], *Voyage au pôle sud*, 'Histoire du voyage', vol. ix, p. 2.

2. Honoré-Antoine-Étienne Argelier, *2e maître de manœuvres de 1ère classe*, was born on 4 April 1791 at La Ciotat, Bouche du Rhône, the son of Charles-Étienne Argelier and Marguerite Girard. He joined the navy as a novice on 9 July 1806 on the *Mohawk* then served for nearly five years on the *Proserpine* and, successively, on the *Ulm*, *Montebello* and *Ville de Marseille*. After the final abdication of Napoleon, he left the navy for almost eight years (probably then in merchant service) before rejoining and serving successively on the *Fanne*, *Cayenne*, *Sylène* and *Cornélie*. Between 9 September 1833 and 7 June 1837, he served in the port (presumably Toulon) before joining the *Zélée* on 7 June 1837. Hospitalised in Hobart on 13 December 1839 with dysentery, he died on 12 March 1840. He was married to Marie-Virginie-Athanasie Martinenq at La Seyne on 1 August 1817; see dossier personnel, Argelier, Honoré Antoine Étienne, SHDDM, Vincennes, CC[7] Alpha 44/0.

3. Epitaphs, St Mary's Old Cemetery, archives, Archdiocese of Hobart; alas, the death dates on the Cornelian Bay Cemetery monument predate the expedition's departure from Hobart and are incorrect.

4. Hombron, note 4, in Dumont d'Urville [& Jacquinot], op. cit., 'Histoire du voyage', vol. ix, p. 259.

5. Pierre Texsier, from Marans (Charente-Maritime), deserted from the *Félicon*; Pierre Sivade, from Antibes (Var) deserted from the *Mississippi*; Charles Desmaretz (born 1818), from Dunkerque (Nord), deserted from the *Courrier des Indes*; and Charles Barrois (born 1818) deserted from the *Nancy*; see Muster Roll *Zélée* 1837–40, Archives nationales JJ/5/158/bis.

6. Barlatier-Demas, in Dumont d'Urville [& Jacquinot], op. cit., 'Histoire du voyage', vol. ix, p. 67.
7. Ibid.
8. The stowaways gave the following names: Thomas Wabb [Webb?] (born 1818), from Bristol; George Bassell (born 1804), from Kingston [upon Hull]; and yet another man who called himself John Jones (born 1819), from Liverpool; see Muster Roll *Zélée* 1837–40, loc. cit.
9. Dumont d'Urville [& Jacquinot], op. cit., 'Histoire du voyage', vol. ix, p. 12.
10. In his chapter 'Histoire de la colonie de la Nouvelle-Galles du Sud', in the first volume of the historical account of the first *Astrolabe* voyage, d'Urville mentions unrest among prisoners who arrived from Ireland in 1798, but he does not mention the Castle Hill uprising in 1804; Dumont d'Urville, *Voyage de la corvette l'Astrolabe*, 'Histoire du voyage', vol. i, chap. ix, p. 237; his subsequent chapters on New South Wales and on the indigenous inhabitants are also noteworthy.
11. See Boissery, *A Deep Sense of Wrong*, p. 186.
12. Dumont d'Urville [& Jacquinot], op. cit., 'Histoire du voyage', vol. ix, p. 32.
13. Bourdon's account of his escape was later published (see *La Patrie*, 21 October 1933). He did not mention the name of the French whaler, probably to protect the captain's identity. However, the departure from Sydney of the French whaler *Roland*, under the command of Captain Olivier Le Cozannet, would appear to be more than coincidental; see *Sydney Morning Herald*, 12 September 1842, p. 2.
14. Boissery, op. cit., p. 187.
15. See Desmond, *Dictionary of British and Irish Botanists and Horticulturalists*, p. 275.
16. Dumont d'Urville [& Jacquinot], op. cit., 'Histoire du voyage', vol. ix, p. 10.
17. Ibid., p. 11.
18. Ibid., pp. 11–12.
19. Dumont d'Urville [& Jacquinot], op. cit., 'Histoire du voyage', vol. ix, pp. 32–33.
20. Marx, 'Stellenkauf-Aus Australien'.
21. Barlatier-Demas was invited to stay with Lieutenant William Henry Breton (1799–1887), district magistrate at Richmond. There he witnessed a court session in which Breton sentenced one convict after another to be flogged (from 15 to 50 lashes) or to serve days on bread and water in solitary confinement. Although Barlatier-Demas also alluded to Alexander McConochie's reform campaign, under the apparent influence of Lieutenant Breton and his neighbours (the francophone Villeneuve-Smith family, originally from Santo-Domingo), he expressed sympathy for the assignment system, even declaring that the convicts in Van Diemen's Land were 'better off than most day labourers in France' (Barlatier-Demas, in Dumont d'Urville [& Jacquinot], op. cit., 'Histoire du voyage', vol. ix, p. 59). But by the time he had visited Port Arthur, his tune had begun to change. In particular, Barlatier-Demas was appalled by the treatment of child convicts and political prisoners.
22. Montagne, 'Quatrième centurie de plantes cellulaires exotiques nouvelles, pp. 246–47; see also Montagne, in Dumont d'Urville [& Jacquinot], op. cit., 'Botanique' [Hombron & Jacquinot (eds)], vol. i, Plantes cellulaires, pp. 270–71.
23. Decaisne, in Dumont d'Urville [& Jacquinot], op. cit., 'Botanique' [Hombron & Jacquinot (eds.)], vol. ii, Plantes vasculaires, p. 85.
24. Duméril & Duméril, *Muséum d'histoire naturelle de Paris*, p. 166.
25. Gray, *Catalogue of the Specimens of Lizards in the Collection of the British Museum*, p. 82.
26. Jacquinot & Lucas, in Dumont d'Urville [& Jacquinot], op. cit., 'Zoologie' [Hombron & Jacquinot (eds), vol. iii, [part iii] 'Zoologie crustacés', pp. 76–77. However, it should be noted that the Dutch carcinologist Lipke Holthuis (1921–2008) offered convincing proof that Hippolyte Lucas drafted the original text alone and that Honoré Jacquinot had little to do with the final version; see Holthuis, 'A few notes on the authors and dates of the names of crustacea'.
27. Campbell & Griffin, 'The Australian Sesarminae (Crustacea: Brachyura)', p. 141.

35. RIVALS IN NEW ZEALAND

1. Jones, 'Captain Abraham Bristow and the Auckland Islands'; McLaren, *The Auckland Islands*, p. 20.
2. Muster Roll *Zélée* 1837–40, Archives nationales, JJ/5/158/bis.
3. A reference to Jacques François' invention appears in the following work: *Dessin du canon harpon à pivot, du fusil harpon, du harpon ouvrant, de la lance à tuer, et de leurs accessoires pour la pêche de la baleine, représentant leur installation sur les pirogues. De l'invention de MM. Jacques François frères, armateurs à Nantes*, Impr. lith. de Charpentier, Nantes. Although it does not appear in the Catalogue Collectif de France, it is listed (no. 485) in the *Bibliographie de la France* [chez Charles Pillet ainé, Paris], année xxiv, no. 25, samedi, 20 juin, 1835, p. 431.
4. Dubouzet, note 6, in Dumont d'Urville [& Jacquinot], *Voyage au pôle sud*, 'Histoire du voyage', vol. ix, p. 267; McLaren, op. cit., p. 31.
5. *Colonial Times*, Hobart, Tuesday 18 July 1839; I am very grateful to Associate Professor Peter Tremewan, University of Canterbury, for generous assistance unravelling Jacques François' past.
6. Very likely Jacques François' emotional problems were compounded by financial difficulties and litigation by British insurers over entitlements to a French government bounty for his company's whaler *Henri*, totally wrecked, with its entire cargo of whale oil, off the Chilean coast in December 1835; see 'Devaux and another v. Steele', in Bingham, *New Cases in the Court of Common Pleas and Exchequer Chamber*, vol. vi, pp. 358–72.
7. See Johnston & Mawson, 'Endoparasites of the subantarctic islands of New Zealand'.
8. Vincendon-Dumoulin, in Dumont d'Urville [& Jacquinot], op. cit., 'Hydrographie', vol. ii, p. 184.
9. Roquemaurel, note 7, in Dumont d'Urville [& Jacquinot], op. cit., 'Histoire du voyage', vol. ix, p. 270.
10. Morrell, *A Narrative of Four Voyages*, pp. 360–61.
11. See Hombron & Jacquinot, 'Description de plusieurs oiseaux nouveaux', p. 320.
12. Oliver, *New Zealand Birds*, p. 229.
13. Last collected in 1902, this marine duck was probably driven to extinction as a result of predation by introduced mammals; see Williams & Weller, 'Unsuccessful search for the Auckland Islands merganser (*Mergus australis*)'.
14. Dubouzet, note 6, in Dumont d'Urville [& Jacquinot], op. cit., 'Histoire du voyage', vol. ix, p. 267; see also Headland, *Chronological List of Antarctic Expeditions and Related Historical Events*, p. 151; and McLaren, op. cit., p. 31.
15. Dumont d'Urville [& Jacquinot], op. cit., 'Histoire du voyage', vol. ix, p. 113.
16. Ibid., p. 116.
17. Peat, *Coasting*, pp. 91–95; McLaren, op. cit., pp. 37–38 & 73.
18. Vincendon-Dumoulin, in Dumont d'Urville [& Jacquinot], op. cit., 'Hydrographie', vol. ii, pp. 186–88.
19. Taiaroa belonged to the Ngai Te Ruahikihiki and Ngāti Moki hapu; see Oliver, 'Taiaroa, Te Matenga'.
20. Dumont d'Urville [& Jacquinot], op. cit., 'Histoire du voyage', vol. ix, p. 133.
21. Ibid., p. 128.
22. See Suzuki, 'Tuberculosis in Polynesia'.
23. Du Bouzet, in Dumont d'Urville [& Jacquinot], op. cit., 'Histoire du voyage', vol. ix, p. 134.
24. Dumont d'Urville, *Voyage de la corvette l'Astrolabe*, 'Histoire du voyage', vol. ix, p. 131.
25. Buick, *The French at Akaroa*, p. 8.
26. For a detailed study of the colony, see Tremewan, *French Akaroa*.
27. Oliver, 'Te Rauparaha (?–1849)'.
28. Dumoutier, in Dumont d'Urville [& Jacquinot], op. cit., 'Anthropologie', p. 147; see also 'Atlas Anthropologie', plate 32.
29. For an important anthology on Dumoutier's casts, see Baker & Rankin, (eds), *Fiona Pardington*.
30. Dumont d'Urville [& Jacquinot], op. cit., 'Histoire du voyage', vol. ix, pp. 155–57.
31. Ibid., p. 157.
32. Although d'Urville considered Bérard a man of 'relatively mediocre abilities', he enjoyed his company ashore, recognised that he had 'real talents in hydrography' and predicted that one day

he would be 'charged with some important reconnaissance'; see Dumont d'Urville, ms journal de la *Coquille*, Mairie de Condé-sur-Noireau, ms 11, pp. 74–75.

33. Among the officers of the *Rhin* was Charles Meryon (1821–1868), who made an important artistic record of the settlement at Akaroa; see Collins, *Charles Meryon*.

34. Dumont d'Urville [& Jacquinot], op. cit., 'Histoire du voyage', vol. ix, p. 160.

35. Ibid., p. 162.

36. Ibid., p. 165.

37. The exact quantity of gold coins for Bishop Pompallier is specified by d'Urville in his will; see Dumont d'Urville testament, 20 octobre 1839; codicille 1er novembre 1839; ms 11, SHDDM, Toulon.

38. Keys, *The Life and Times of Bishop Pompallier*, p. 141.

39. Pierre Michel Bonnefin was born in Saint-Malo on 27 August 1787. He married in Saint-Helier, Jersey, on 7 April 1815 and had a daughter Louise 'Lise' Marie Bonnefin, who married Didier Numa Joubert at the Bay of Islands on 23 November 1839 (see BMS/État Civil, Saint-Malo, Archives départementales, Ille-et-Vilaine; *Sydney Monitor and Commercial Advertiser*, Monday 30 December 1839, p. 2). They were later founders of the Sydney suburb of Hunters Hill, where there is still a Bonnefin Street.

40. D'Urville thought Delarbre was Mauritian. Although he married Perrine Bonnefin in Port Louis, Mauritius, in September 1828, Delarbre was in fact born in Le Havre. In April 1842, after she was widowed, Perrine left New Zealand for France on the French whaler *Élisabeth*.

41. Dumont d'Urville [& Jacquinot], op. cit., 'Histoire du voyage', vol. ix, pp. 168–69; curiously, César Desgraz uses almost identical words in his manuscript account; see 'Journal, impressions et remarques pendant la voyage des corvettes l'*Astrolabe* et la *Zélée*', vol. iii, f. 226, Royal Geographical Society, London, SSC/58/1-3.

42. Dumont d'Urville [& Jacquinot], op. cit., 'Histoire du voyage', vol. ix, pp. 168–69.

43. Ibid., p. 174; aside from Bonnefin and his sister Perinne and brother-in-law Fortune Delarbre, there was a Frenchman named Victor Desentis, whom Desgraz described as a 'speculator from Toulouse', and a 'M. Kafler', whom Desgraz described as 'the richest of the French cultivators'. He added that Kafler's wife was a 'creole from the île de France [Mauritius]'; see Desgraz, 'Journal, impressions et remarques …', vol. iii, f. 224 & 236, loc. cit. According to surgeon Élie Le Guillou, Desentis was a 'Bordelais' who arrived six months earlier with 500 francs in his pocket and had amassed a fortune valued at 35,000–40,000 francs; see Le Guillou, *Voyage autour du monde*, vol. ii, pp. 248–49. Peter Tremewan has identified 'Kafler' as Eugène-Édouard Cafler (*ca*.1798–1893) and his wife as Uranie Dioré (died 1866).

44. Dumont d'Urville [& Jacquinot], op. cit., 'Histoire du voyage', vol. ix, p. 174.

45. Tardy de Montravel, note 24, in Dumont d'Urville [& Jacquinot], op. cit., 'Histoire du voyage', vol. ix, p. 322.

46. Roquemaurel, note 22, in Dumont d'Urville [& Jacquinot], op. cit., 'Histoire du voyage', vol. ix, p. 314.

47. Dumont d'Urville [& Jacquinot], op. cit., 'Histoire du voyage', vol. ix, p. 174.

48. Although Pompallier died in the Paris suburb of Puteux in 1871, his remains were exhumed in 2001 and reinterred in Saint Mary's Motuti (Hokianga) the following year.

49. Wright, *The Voyage of the Astrolabe – 1840*, p. 133.

50. Dumont d'Urville [& Jacquinot], op. cit., 'Histoire du voyage', vol. ix, p. 188

51. Ibid.

52. Ibid., p. 183.

53. Presumably the press established by William Colenso; see Bagnall & Petersen, *William Colenso*.

54. Presumably William Williams' Māori translation of the New Testament, printed by Colenso: *Ko te Kawenata Hou o to Tatou Ariki te Kai Wakaora a Ihu Karaiti: He mea wakaMāori i te reo kariki*, Paihia, 1837. It was not listed in d'Urville's library at the time of his death.

55. In 1839 and 1840, Colenso printed the *Book of Common Prayer* in Māori: *Ko te Pukapuka o nga Inoinga, me te Minitatanga o nga Hakarameta, ko era Tikanga Hoki o te Hahi, ki te Ritenga o te*

Hahi o Ingarani. In January 1840, he also began printing 10,000 copies of the catechism, *Ko nga Katikihama Ewa: Ka oti nei te wakaMāori ki te reo o Nu Tireni*. In the same year, Colenso printed William Gilbert Puckey's (1805–1878) Māori translation of the Book of Daniel (which he also revised).

56. Shaw, *The Naturalist's Miscellany*, vol. 24, no page numbers, plates 1057 (showing the kiwi) & 1058 (showing the bill, wing, leg and feathers), by Richard Polydore Nodder, who succeeded his artist father Frederick. The kiwi in question was collected from 'the south coast' by Captain Andrew Barclay of the *Providence*.

57. They were informed of Bartlett's publication by ornithologists Jules Verreaux (1807–1873) and Philip Sclater (1829–1913).

58. Bartlett, 'On the Genus *Apteryx*', p. 275.

59. Jacquinot & Pucheran, in Dumont d'Urville [& Jacquinot], op. cit., 'Zoologie' [Hombron & Jacquinot (eds)], vol. iii, Mammifères et oiseaux, p. 127.

60. See Burbidge, Colbourne, Robertson & Baker, 'Molecular and other biological evidence supports the recognition of at least three species of brown kiwi'.

61. However, while the expedition was at Akaroa, surgeon Bacherau of the whaler *Adèle*, commanded by Captain James Walsh (1797–1879), had undertaken to provide one or more kiwi to César Desgraz (see Desgraz, 'Journal, impressions et remarques …', vol. iii, f. 210, loc. cit.). There is no indication that he fulfilled his undertaking, but if he did, the specimens would almost certainly have been of the southern brown kiwi, *Apteryx australis*. Ultimately, Jacquinot and Pucheran did not provide a habitat statement.

62. D'Urville does not name the secretary in his journal, but presumably this was James Stuart Freeman (died 1855), after whom Freemans Bay, Auckland, is named. He was later acting colonial secretary; see Platts, *The Lively Capital*, pp. 55–59.

63. Dumont d'Urville [& Jacquinot], op. cit., 'Histoire du voyage', vol. ix, p. 179.

64. Ibid., p. 185.

65. Ibid., p. 181.

66. Girard, *Lettres des missionnaires maristes en Océanie, 1836–1854*, pp. 103, 377 & 723.

67. O'Reilly & Teissier, *Tahitiens*, pp. 426–27.

68. In d'Urville's published historical account, his name is incorrectly given as 'Mr Flint'. D'Urville often guessed the spelling or gave phonetic approximations of the names of those he met, but this error was probably made by those who transcribed or typeset this part of his manuscript for publication after his death.

69. 'Old Colonists Roll', *New Zealand Herald*, 10 October 1892; according to the New Zealand Biographies Index, Alexander Turnbull Library, Wellington, Flatt had a wife, Caroline (*née* Haslip) (*ca*.1813–1887) and two children.

70. Busby, Sydney, 18 July 1840, to Mair, quoted in Ramsden, *Busby of Waitangi*, p. 262, footnote 23.

71. Originally from Edinburgh, Busby had learned his viticultural skills in Bordeaux and had already pioneered vine growing in the Hunter Valley of New South Wales. The vineyard at Waitangi appears to have been planted in late 1836 by Edward Callender, from stock that James Busby gave earlier to the Botanical Gardens in Sydney; see McLean, *The Garden of New Zealand*, p. 76.

72. Dumont d'Urville [& Jacquinot], op. cit., 'Histoire du voyage', vol. ix, p. 194.

73. In d'Urville's published account, 'Mr Flint' (John Flatt) is said to have visited a place named 'Roto-Rocia' where there was a live volcano. This cannot be identified with certainty, but very likely the live volcano was a reference to the geothermal activity at Lake Rotorua. The fact remains that d'Urville wasn't alive to edit or proofread his historical account before it went to press.

74. The text of the letter (addressed to 'M. le baron') appears in Dumont d'Urville [& Jacquinot], op. cit., 'Histoire du voyage', vol. ix, pp. 199–202.

75. The naturalist–astronomer Lacour's story is intriguing. His date of arrival in the Bay of Islands is unknown. Most Belgians are Catholic, and his name suggests he was francophone, so presumably he associated with Bishop Pompallier. He probably also had letters of introduction and spoke with sufficient erudition to satisfy d'Urville of his bona fides. There were apparently two Messieurs

Lacour who were sent to Australia by the Société des missions belges scientifiques et commerciales de l'Océanie in 1837. This was a private company associated with the Établissement géographique de Bruxelles, which was founded in 1830 by the celebrated Belgian cartographer Philippe Vandermaelen (1795–1869) on a 20,000-square-metre site on the left bank of the Charleroi Canal near the Porte de Flandre. It combined cartographic enterprise, a lithographic press, a splendid library (which by 1836 held the published accounts of d'Urville's two previous voyages), a 'mappothèque', an ethnographic and natural history museum, a botanical garden (including glasshouses), a free school – which taught 14–18 year olds mathematics, drawing, science and lithography – and a centre for exchanging documents and specimens. Presumably, Lacour's natural history specimens were destined for this 'établissement', and his astronomical observations were to provide Vandermaelen with further cartographic precision. The latter was already the author of the famous lithographed *Atlas Universel de Géographie* (1825–27, 6 vols.), which included a volume on Oceania with numerous maps of New Holland and New Zealand. By 1846, Vandermaelen also had collections of insects from New Holland and was cultivating specimens of *Eucalyptus*, *Melaleuca*, *Banksia* and *Hakea* from Australia and *Metrosideros* from New Zealand in his glasshouses; see Drapiez, *Notice sur l'Établissement géographique de Bruxelles*, pp. 59, 65, 70 & 79; see also Silvestre, 'Notes sur l'*Atlas Universel* de Philippe Vandermaelen (1825–1827)'.

76. Bateson, *Australian Shipwrecks*, p. 147.
77. Tardy de Montravel, note 24, in Dumont d'Urville [& Jacquinot], op. cit., 'Histoire du voyage', vol. ix, p. 323.
78. Lee, 'I have Named it the Bay of Islands …', pp. 253–71.

36 HOMEWARD BOUND VIA TORRES STRAIT

1. Named in honour of the Rear Admiral Élisabeth-Paul-Édouard Rossel, d'Urville's friend and patron. He took part in Bruny d'Entrecasteaux's expedition in search of Lapérouse, was a member of the Académie des sciences and, in 1827, became director-general of the Dépôt des cartes et plans in Paris.
2. Dumont d'Urville [& Jacquinot], *Voyage au pôle sud*, 'Histoire du voyage', vol. ix, pp. 205–13.
3. During Bligh's 6700-kilometre open-boat voyage to Timor after the *Bounty* mutiny.
4. Presumably by raising the pintles (vertical metal pins) of the rudder out of the gudgeons affixed to the sternpost.
5. In this instance, the fids are square bars of wood or metal, with a wider shoulder at one end, used to secure and support a topmast stepped on a lower mast. They are slotted into a mortice in the heel of the topmast, aligned with a mortice in the head of the lower mast. Fids are also used to secure bowsprits. They should not be confused with the pointed conical hardwood fids used to open the strands of large ropes prior to splicing.
6. Louis Le Breton, '*Astrolabe* et *Zélée*, Détroit de Torrès', M10920, Peabody Essex Museum, Salem, Massachusetts.
7. See Dumont d'Urville à son neveu [abbé Louis-François-Paul Dumont de La Londe], rue aux Lisses, Caen, 1 mai 1842, text quoted in full by Vergniol, *Dumont d'Urville*, pp. 257–58, but without reference to an archival repository.
8. See Le Breton, 'Réservoirs d'eau de l'île Toud, Détroit de Torrès'; lithographed by P.Ph. Blanchard in 1846, it appeared as plate 188 in volume ii of the 'Atlas pittoresque' of Dumont d'Urville [& Jacquinot], *Voyage au pôle sud*.
9. This does not appear to have been the Basilisk Pass discovered in 1872 by John Morseby (1830–1922) and named in honour of his ship.
10. See McNiven & Wright, 'Ritualised marine midden formation in western Zenadh Kes (Torres Strait)'.
11. Dumont d'Urville [& Jacquinot], op. cit., 'Histoire du voyage', vol. x, p. 4.
12. See Rivière, *A Woman of Courage*, pp. 54–55 & 57.
13. See Spillett, *Forsaken Settlement*, p. 65; in 1840, Tissot, Lagnier & Co. had a fleet of seven vessels

weighing a total of 968 *lasts* (1210 tonnes) engaged in inter-island and European trade. These vessels, however, varied considerably in size. In 1835 they ranged from 202 to a mere 35 *lasts* (275–43 tonnes); see Broeze, 'The merchant fleet of Java (1820–1850): A preliminary survey', pp. 263–64.

14. Other eyewitness accounts would suggest Bremmer's residence was propelled from its footings about half the distance Captain Moyle asserted; see Spillet, *Forsaken Settlement*, p. 57.
15. Dumont d'Urville [& Jacquinot], op. cit., 'Histoire du voyage', vol. x, p. 19.
16. Taillemite, *Dictionnaire des marins français*, p. 159.
17. Adèle Dumont d'Urville, Juliade, 20 février 1840, à Dumont d'Urville, Archives nationales, Paris, Marine 5JJ 158 Bis.
18. Dumont d'Urville [& Jacquinot], op. cit., 'Histoire du voyage', vol. x, p. 24.
19. See Humbert, *Napoléon aux Invalides*.
20. Dumont d'Urville [& Jacquinot], op. cit., 'Histoire du voyage', vol. x, pp. 26–27.
21. Ross, *A Voyage of Discovery and Research in the Southern and Antarctic Regions*, vol. i, p. 27.
22. Dumont d'Urville [& Jacquinot], op. cit., 'Histoire du voyage', vol. x, p. 28.

37. TOULON & PARIS: THE FINAL YEARS

1. Dumont d'Urville [& Jacquinot], *Voyage au pôle sud*, 'Histoire du voyage', vol. x, p. 29.
2. Ibid.
3. Expédition de l'*Astrolabe* et de la *Zélée*: extrait du rapport de Dumont d'Urville et récompenses, novembre 1840; dossier personnel, Dumont d'Urville, SHDDM, Vincennes, CC^7 Alpha 772, pièce 35.
4. Hector Jacquinot to Dumont d'Urville, 17 décembre 1840, Archives nationales, Paris, Marine 5JJ 158 Bis.
5. Matterer, 'Notes nécrologiques et historiques sur M. le contre-amiral Dumont d'Urville', pp. 772–73.
6. D'Urville, quoted by Matterer, op. cit., p. 773.
7. Dossier personnel, Dumont d'Urville, SHDDM, Vincennes, CC^7 Alpha 772, pièce 37 (État des services).
8. Tardy de Montravel to Dumont d'Urville, 11 décembre 1840, Marine 5JJ 158 Bis, loc. cit.
9. Matterer, op. cit., p. 773.
10. Adèle Dumont d'Urville, Juliade, 20 February 1840, [in English] to Dumont d'Urville, Marine 5JJ 158 Bis, loc. cit.
11. Le Brun, *Biographie du contre-amiral Dumont d'Urville*, p. 52.
12. Adèle Dumont d'Urville, Juliade, 20 February 1840, [in English] to Dumont d'Urville, Marine 5JJ 158 Bis, loc. cit.
13. Adèle Dumont d'Urville, 3 avril 1841, to Dumont d'Urville, in which she uses the word 'precarious' to describe her health; see Marine 5JJ 158 Bis, loc. cit. On 21 April 1841, when she wrote a letter of condolence to d'Urville's cousin Adolphe, she also apologised for her inability to leave Toulon because of her health, and her inability to express her sentiments in person; Marine 5JJ 158 Bis, loc. cit.
14. See Downing, 'Uterine Prolapse'.
15. Lesson, *Notice historique sur l'amiral Dumont d'Urville*, pp. 26–27.
16. Adèle Dumont d'Urville, avril 1839, to Dumont d'Urville, Marine 5JJ 158 Bis, loc. cit.
17. Adélie also had fears regarding the career her husband had in mind for her son Jules. She wrote quirkily in English: 'Well mean you destine without any doubt this boy to the marine – No Sir, it is enough to have my husband a seaman; I have lost all my children and I keep near me the only one that heaven has left me – it is not possible ma'am, the son of Mr D'Urville must be a seafaring man – will never be with my consent'; see Adèle Dumont d'Urville, 4 November 1837 [*sic*], to Dumont d'Urville, Marine 5JJ 158 Bis, loc. cit.
18. Hillairet, *Dictionnaire historique des rues de Paris*, vol. i, pp. 277–78.
19. Dumont d'Urville, 'Rapport sur les opérations exécutées par les corvettes l'*Astrolabe* & la *Zélée*, dans leur second campagne aux régions polaire antarctiques, janvier, février 1840', Paris, 27 janvier 1841, SHDDM, Vincennes, BB^4 1009.

20. French, reporter (from Latin *reportare* = to bring back), a person who is appointed by an organisation to provide an account of the proceedings of a meeting, conference or commission of enquiry.

21. Beautemps-Beaupré, 'Rapport sur les travaux hydrographiques', p. 772.

22. Blainville, 'Rapports sur les résultats scientifiques', p. 711.

23. Ibid., p. 713.

24. Ibid., pp. 715–16.

25. Clark & Crosnier, 'The zoology of the *Voyage au pôle sud et dans l'Océanie*, p. 419.

26. Anon., 'Visite de M. l'amiral Duperré, ministre de la marine, au muséum'.

27. Grange, Jules Joseph François, Archives nationales, Fond Léonore, LH/1189/86.

28. Plagne had joined the navy at the age of 14, in 1808, and had sailed with d'Urville on the *Chevrette* in 1820–21; for his long record of service, see Archives nationales, Fond Léonore, LH/2175/29.

29. Dumont d'Urville, Paris, au ministre de la marine et des colonies, Paris, 9 avril 1841 [regarding decorations for his men], BB^4 1009, loc. cit.

30. Dunmore, *From Venus to Antarctica*, p. 224.

31. See Montémont, *À M. l'Amiral Dumont d'Urville*.

32. Le Brun, op. cit., p. 53.

33. Dumont d'Urville, *Voyage de la corvette l'Astrolabe*, 'Histoire du voyage', vol. v, pp. 594–95. Although this volume bears the imprint date of 1833, d'Urville's conclusion and reflections are dated 25 November 1834.

34. The invitation (see Archives nationales, Paris, Marine 5JJ 158 Bis) was dated 29 April 1841; alas, neither the prince, nor his son would inherit the throne, thanks to the Revolution of 1848. However, the comte de Paris grew up a committed democrat and even served as a captain in the Army of the Potomac during the American Civil War.

35. Dumont d'Urville, ms journal de la *Coquille*, 6 avril 1841–16 septembre 1841, ms 12, Mairie de Condé-sur-Noireau.

36. Barran wrote a long letter to d'Urville dated (at the very end) 11 May, without stating the year, but presumably 1841. This was a Tuesday, and in the letter he mentioned their meeting and conversation on 'Sunday' and, later, 'last Sunday'. Depending on when the letter was begun and then finished, this might have been a reference to Sunday 2 May rather than Sunday 9 May. Barran drew d'Urville's attention to the words of the Lord's Prayer in the Greek text of Saint Matthew's gospel (6:13) and that the word πμον (translated into Latin as *tentatio*) has the meaning of 'test, proof, effort'. He also drew d'Urville's attention to the Hebrew equivalents in the book of Job to suggest that it is a plea to be spared such trials, and made further reference to Hebrew words such as *masah* and *nisah* which mean 'to test'. (The latter was the word used in the Genesis 22:1 '… and God tested Abraham'. I am grateful to my cousin Dr Françoise Rousseau, Issy-les-Moulineaux, and Dr Laurie Woods, School of Theology, Australian Catholic University, for their assistance with this difficult correspondence.

37. Lepage, *Les cafés artistiques et littéraires de Paris*, pp. 125–32.

38. Dumont d'Urville, ms journal de la *Coquille*, 6 avril 1841–16 septembre 1841, loc. cit.

39. Taillemite, *Dictionnaire des marins français*, pp. 102–03 and Institut de France, *Index biographique de l'Académie des sciences*, p. 231.

40. See Lettres reçues 1841, SHDDM, Vincennes, BB^4 1009; see also Mellot, Queval & Monaque, *Répertoire d'imprimeurs-libraires (vers 1500–vers 1810)*, p. 359.

41. Clark & Crosnier, op. cit., pp. 420–21.

42. Dumont d'Urville, Paris, au ministre de la marine et des colonies, Paris, 15 juin 1841, BB^4 1009, loc. cit. Despite his absence from Paris, d'Urville remained in contact with Casimir Gide by mail; see his letter of 8 July 1841, MS Acc07/37, National Library of Australia, Canberra.

43. Dumont d'Urville, ms journal de la *Coquille*, 6 avril 1841–16 septembre 1841, ms 12, Mairie de Condé-sur-Noireau, pp. 72–75.

44. In a note at the end of a letter Adélie wrote to Le Brun on 25 June 1841, informing him of her joy at d'Urville's safe arrival but also of the 'fatigue of travel'; Dumont d'Urville, Correspondance

autographe, Dixson Library, State Library of New South Wales, DLMS Q355 (microfilm CY 293).

45. Dumont d'Urville, ms journal de la *Coquille*, 6 avril 1841–16 septembre 1841, ff. 90–91 loc. cit.

46. Marmottans, 'Un enfant surdoué'.

47. The next day d'Urville wrote from his Paris address (3, rue du Battoir Saint-André) to invite Le Brun to dine with his family on the evening of 26 September; Dumont d'Urville to Isidore Le Brun, 22 septembre [1841], Dumont d'Urville, Correspondance autographe, Dixson Library, State Library of New South Wales, DLMS Q355 (microfilm CY 293). The final entry in d'Urville's last surviving journal is dated 17 septembre 1841, when he was apparently still in Toulon; the family must have travelled to Paris over the next four or five days.

48. Dumont d'Urville to Isidore Le Brun, 22 septembre [1841], loc. cit.

49. Saunier, 'Le numérotage de la rue Madame'.

50. Juin 1842, inventaire après décès de M[onsieu]r. Dumont d'Urville, and 21 Juin 1842, décharge donnée à M. Demanche, Archives nationales, Minutier central des notaires de Paris, ET/C/1200; the building appears in a photograph taken by Henri Blanchard in 1887, Paris Album Blancard, 1887–1889 (rue Madame), Bibliothèque historique de la Ville de Paris, 4° 21, 15 H; see also: 'Plan géométrique du Quartier du Luxembourg (11me arrondissement)' in Vasserot & Bellanger, *Atlas général des quarante-huit quartiers de la Ville de Paris*.

51. Sommiers des biens immeubles [ancien no. 26, rue Madame = nouveau no. 60], Archives de Paris, Sommier foncier DQ^{18} Art. 349, p. 72 verso, 75 recto. Joseph Molé also owned the adjoining property at no. 24 (now 58, rue Madame, the Église Réformée de Pentemont-Luxembourg).

52. Molé-Gentilhomme's works include *Manon la dragonne* (1837), *Rêve d'une mariée* (1838) and *Romans du cœur: La marquise d'Alpujar* (1842). After d'Urville's death, he published another 20 novels and plays with similar melodramatic titles.

53. Rue de Seine is, in fact, in the same arrondissement as rue Madame.

54. Juin 1842, inventaire après décès de M[onseiu]r. Dumont d'Urville, and 21 Juin 1842, décharge donnée à M. Demanche, loc. cit.

55. Ibid.

56. Ibid.

57. Pinard, *Relation exacte de l'affreuse catastrophe du 8 mai !!!*, p. 87.

58. The manuscript of this first volume is today preserved in the collection of the Bibliothèque municipale de Toulon, MS 65, pièce iv.

59. *Bibliographie de la France, ou Journal général de l'imprimerie et de la librairie*, Pillet Aîné, xxxe année, 1841, p. 610.

60. Dumont d'Urville à son neveu [abbé Louis-François-Paul Dumont de La Londe], rue aux Lisses, Caen, 1 mai 1842, text quoted in full by Vergniol, *Dumont d'Urville*, pp. 257–58, but without reference to an archival repository.

61. Pinard, op. cit., pp. 86–87.

62. Dumont d'Urville à son neveu [abbé Louis-François-Paul Dumont de La Londe], 1 mai 1842, loc. cit.

63. Luxel, 'Le tragique destin de l'amiral Dumont d'Urville'.

64. Pinard, op. cit., pp. 26, 40, 80 & 87.

65. Philippe-Mathieu Le Pontois (1793–1842), a former naval ensign turned merchant, and his half-brother Charles-Philippe Le Pontois (1817–1842), a lawyer in Paris. Their father, Pierre Le Pontois (1770–1837), was from Agon (Manche), as was my own ancestor (their cousin), Barbe Leonore Le Pontois (died Agon, 24 December 1784) and Jacques Le Pontois (born Agon, 14 September 1742), maternal ancestor of the novelist Marcel Pagnol (1895–1974). D'Urville was also distantly related to the Le Pontois family; I am grateful to Jeannine Le Pontois-Menot, Mézidon-Canon, Calvados, for alerting me to these connections.

66. Maintenance was haphazard. The axles of the *Matthew Murray* had not been changed since the end of September 1839. Although replacement wheels and axles had been ordered from England, they had languished in the customs office for lack of funds to pay the duty owing; see Vergniol, 'La fin tragique de Dumont-d'Urville', p. 100.

67. The survivors included the mathematician Joseph-Louis-François Bertrand (1822–1900), who had injuries to his face, and his fellow Polytechnicien (and future brother-in-law), the engineer Pierre-Marcel Aclocque (1820–1887), whose leg was fractured. Prior to the accident, Bertrand had visited Aclocque's family in Versailles; he would marry Aclocque's sister, Louise-Céline Aclocque (1825–1907) in December 1844; see Struik, 'Bertrand, Joseph Louis François'; see also fiches matricules, Bertrand, Joseph Louis François (X 1838), and Aclocque, Pierre Marcel (X 1839), École polytechnique, archives. Half a century later, there was an absurd apocryphal addendum to this story. Several newspapers told their readers that Bertrand was d'Urville's secretary (in fact, he was then a teacher at the Collège Saint-Louis) and, having effectively confused Adélie with Louise Aclocque, asserted that d'Urville had thrust her from the burning carriage via a 'narrow aperture into young Bertrand's arms, crying: "Save her! Save her! my friend, and marry her!"' The secretary was then declared to have 'fulfilled his dying master's injunctions, and two years later led the widow to the altar'; see *Sydney Morning Herald*, 2 February 1895, p. 5; *Bruce Herald*, 26 March 1895, p. 2; *Otago Witness*, 2 May 1895, p. 49. I am grateful to Jeremy Spencer for alerting me to this story, even though I then had to disappoint him with the truth.

68. Pinard, op. cit., p. 8.

69. Ibid., p. 86.

70. Magendie, 'Collège de France – M. Magendie', pp. 261–62.

71. Ibid.

72. Pinard, op. cit., p. 87.

73. Magendie, op. cit., p. 261–62.

74. Pinard, op. cit., p. 88.

75. Ministre de la marine au M. Clément Salvy, capitaine de vaisseau, commandant le v[aisse]au le *Diadième*, a Toulon, 4 juillet 1842, SHDDM, Vincennes, BB^4 615, ff. 275–76; see also SHDDM, Vincennes, CC^7 Alpha 772, dossier personnel, Dumont d'Urville, pièce 38, 1842, succession et inhumation.

76. [Duperret, F.] 'Obsèques de M. Dumont d'Urville'.

77. Today the monument is much weathered, and Adélie's family name Pépin has been incorrectly rendered Périn, probably during restoration work.

78. [Vincendon-Dumoulin, C.A.], 'Notice biographique: Jules-Sébastien-César Dumont d'Urville', pp. 134–35.

EPILOGUE

1. I have updated and enlarged John Dunmore's list of d'Urville commemorations; see *Venus to Antarctica*, p. 236.

2. Ayres, *Mawson*, p. 117.

3. Dossier personnel, Jacquinot, Charles-Hector, SHDDM, Vincennes, CC^7 2 Moderne, carton 3, dossier 11; Archives nationales, Fond Léonore, LH/1346/12; Taillemite, *Dictionnaire des marins français*, pp. 167–68; and Blandin, 'Souvenirs sur l'amiral Jacquinot'.

4. Dossier personnel, Jacquinot, Honoré, SHDDM, Vincennes, CC^7 Alpha 1222; Archives nationales, Fond Léonore, LH/1346/36.

5. See Couturaud, 'Le troisième voyage de circumnavigation de J.S.C. Dumont d'Urville 1837–1840', pp. 158–61.

6. Dossier personnel, Le Breton, Louis Raymond Marie, SHDDM, Vincennes, CC^7 Alpha 1432; see also Collins, *Louis Le Breton*.

7. Dossier personnel, Vincendon-Dumoulin, Clément-Adrien, SHDDM, Vincennes, CC^7 Alpha 2475; Archives nationales, Fond Léonore, LH/2724/22.

8. Archives nationales, Fond Léonore, LH/2363/46; see also Couturaud, op. cit., p. 124.

9. Dossier personnel, Ducorps, Jacques-Louis, SHDDM, Vincennes, CC^7 Alpha 753; Archives nationales, Fond Léonore, LH/826/41.

10. Gervaize, Charles-François Eugène, Archives nationales, Fond Léonore, LH/1126/13.

11. Fiche matricule, Gervaize, Charles-François Eugène, École polytechnique, Paris; dossier personnel, Gervaize, Charles-François Eugène, SHDDM, Vincennes, CC[7] Alpha 1006; Archives nationales, Fond Léonore, LH/1126/13.

12. Desgraz, César Louis François, Archives nationales, Fond Léonore, LH/1194/40.

13. Hector Jacquinot, Paris, 19 août 1842, à amiral Duperré, ministre de la marine, SHDDM, Vincennes, BB[4] 1009.

14. Dossier personnel, Desgraz, César Louis François, SHDDM, Vincennes, CC[7] Alpha 686; Archives nationales, Fond Léonore, LH/1194/40.

15. Papers of John Ludlow and of the Ludlow, Liot and Des Graz families, MS.Add.7348 & MS.Add.7450, Cambridge University Library.

16. Dossier personnel, Dubouzet, Joseph-Fidèle-Eugène, SHDDM, Vincennes, CC[7] Alpha 742; Archives nationales, Fond Léonore, LH/344/75; see also Anon., 'Nécrologie: Le contre-amiral m[arqu]is du Bouzet'.

17. Dossier personnel, Tardy de Montravel, Louis-François-Marie, SHDDM, Vincennes, CC[7] Alpha 2334; Archives nationales, Fond Léonore, LH/2568/99; see also Taillemite, *Dictionnaire des marins français*, pp. 317–18.

18. Fiche matricule, Coupvent-Desbois, Aimé Auguste Élie, École polytechnique, Paris; dossier personnel, Coupvent-Desbois, Aimé Auguste Élie, SHDDM, Vincennes, CC[7] Alpha 561; Archives nationales, Fond Léonore, LH/609/15.

19. Archives nationales, Fond Léonore, LH/2100/15; see also Couturaud, op. cit., pp. 196–99.

20. Dossier personnel, Deflotte, Paul-Louis-René, SHDDM, Vincennes, CC[7] Alpha 629; Taillemite, *Dictionnaire des marins français*, p. 121; additional information from Mikael Riou, Douarnenez (Finistère).

21. Engels, F., 'Garibaldi's Progress', *New York Daily Tribune*, No. 6056, 21 September 1860, p. 1.

22. Dossier personnel, Thanaron, Charles-Jules-Adolphe, SHDDM, Vincennes, CC[7] Alpha 2349; Archives nationales, Fond Léonore, LH/2583/24; see also Couturaud, op. cit., pp. 204–05.

23. See Duyker, 'Lottin, Victor-Charles (1795–1858)'.

24. Roche, *Dictionnaire des bâtiments de la flotte de guerre française*, vol. i, pp. 54 & 128.

25. See Hillairet, *Dictionnaire historique des rues de Paris*, vol. i, p. 115.

26. Roche, op. cit., vol. i, p. 477.

APPENDIX

D'Urville's Library

1. '13 Juin 1842, Inventaire après Décès de M[onsieu]r. Dumont d'Urville' & '21 Juin 1842, Décharge donnée à M. Demanche', Archives nationales, Minutier central des Notaires de Paris, ET/C/1200.

2. 'Inventaire des effets mobiliers dressé par Maître Vallavieille, notaire à Toulon, le 30 juillet 1842 … dépendant des successions réunies de feu M. Dumont D'Urville, de son épouse et de son fils décédés ensemble le 8 mai 1842 domicilié à Paris.'

3. Maîtres Eric, Michel & Stéphane Boyer, 60 rue Jean Jaurès, Toulon.

4. Toulon notarial études were not numbered like their Parisian counterparts.

5. Vallavieille is mentioned in d'Urville's journal (see, for example, his entry for 20 février 1836, MS 65, Bibliothèque municipale de Toulon) and his wife's correspondence (Archives nationales, Marine 5JJ 158 BIS).

6. Dumont d'Urville, correspondance, autographe, Dixson Library MSQ355.

7. Most of the Chinese characters printed were engraved on wood in the first half of the eighteenth century, under the direction of Étienne Fourmont (1683–1745), and are still held by the Imprimerie nationale; see Leung, *Étienne Fourmont*, p. 245.

8. See Phillip Barker Webb's letter to d'Urville, 31 March 1841, Archives nationales, Marine 5JJ 158 BIS.

9. Robert Brown's *Prodromus* was published in 1810, while Britain and France were still at war. Nevertheless, in that year Napoleon permitted the importation of books from enemy states, legalising what was already a flourishing trade in contraband through neutral ports. Labillardière's

personal copy of Brown's work was sent by the author himself; see Duyker, *Citizen Labillardière*, pp. 234 & 239.

10. For a discussion of Alibert's theories and substantial extracts from his introduction, translated into English, see Goshen, 'The psychology of Jean Louis Alibert'.

11. Dunmore, *Venus to Antarctica*, p. 123.

12. Dumont d'Urville, in Collection Margry, 'Mers Australes', Bibliothèque nationale, NAF 9439, ff. 153 & 161.

13. See d'Urville's letter of 25 August 1821 to his friend Louis Charles Lefébure de Cerisy, SHDDM, Toulon, 23S 701.

14. See Dumont d'Urville, Journal, 1830, MS 65, Bibliothèque municipale de Toulon.

15. Stafleu & Cowan, *Taxonomic literature*, vol. 1, pp. 696–98. D'Urville's 'official' collections, upon which the botanical publications of his voyages are based, are held at the Laboratoire de Phanerogamie and Laboratoire de Cryptogamie of the Museum national d'histoire naturelle, Paris.

16. Steinberg, 'The Collectors and Collections in the Herbarium Webb'.

17. This appendix is an abridged version of my article, 'An Explorer's Books: The library of Dumont d'Urville', *Explorations*, no. 49, part ii, December 2010, pp. 66–81. For the list of known book titles, see Duyker, 'Dumont d'Urville's Library: The Notarial Inventories'; it follows in the same issue of *Explorations*, pp. 82–121.

Glossary of terms, titles & institutions

ABBÉ (father). A title given to abbots, priests without the charge of parishes and members of the secular clergy.

ACADÉMIE [ROYALE] DES SCIENCES (Royal Academy of Sciences). Founded in 1666 by Jean-Baptiste Colbert during the reign of Louis XIV to promote scientific endeavours in France. Although suppressed by the National Convention in 1793, it was effectively reconstituted as a principal part of the Institut national (q.v.) in 1795. In 1816, the name Académie des sciences was resurrected, but to this day it remains part of the Institut.

ANCIEN RÉGIME (old regime). The social and political structure in France prior to the Revolution, based on absolute monarchy. It consisted of three orders: the clergy, the nobility and the third estate or commons (peasantry and bourgeoisie).

BRUMAIRE (from French *brume* = fog). The second month of the French republican calendar; the equivalent of the northern hemisphere autumn period 22 October–20 November. It is particularly remembered for the coup d'état of 18 brumaire (9 November 1799) and the establishment of the Consulate (q.v.).

CABLE. A heavy rope, 32–65 centimetres in circumference, comprising three strands and used for anchoring, berthing or towing a vessel. Such ropes were at least 100 fathoms (182.8 metres) in length, but as a formal unit of measure, a 'cable-length' is 1/10 of a nautical mile or 185.2 metres.

CAPITAINE DE VAISSEAU (ship's captain). The most important rank among the French navy's *officiers particuliers*. The immediate superiors of the *capitaines des vaisseaux*, after 1791, were the *contre-amiraux* (q.v.) or rear admirals.

CHEVALIER (knight). A title by which the upper level of the French nobility separated itself from the rest of the nobility, who were merely *écuyers* (esquires). The title was used by high officers of the royal household, the chancellor and holders of *fiefs de dignité* but was appropriated by lesser nobles toward the end of the *ancien régime* (q.v.). Members of the order of Saint-Louis, created by Louis XIV in 1693 as a reward for outstanding military conduct, were also entitled to call themselves *chevalier*. Orders of chivalry were abolished by the Constituent Assembly in 1791, but the title *chevalier* was reinstated by Napoleon for those who were members of the *Légion d'honneur* (q.v.) which he created in 1802 as First Consul. Louis XVIII retained the *Légion d'honneur* after the Restoration (q.v.). He also reinstated the Order of Saint-Louis, which was restricted to Catholics and was finally abolished by King Louis-Philippe after the July Revolution of 1830.

CHOUAN (tawny owl). A family nickname and later *nom de guerre* of Jean Cottereau, a leader of the counter-revolutionary insurgents in Mayenne. It was later applied generally to royalist insurgents (other than the Vendéens, 1793–96) in the west of France, particularly in Brittany, Maine and Normandy.

COMTE (count). A title of landed nobility ranking next after a *marquis* and corresponding to the British earl.

CONSULATE. The name of the French government that existed after the military-backed coup d'état of 18 brumaire (9 November 1799) until the commencement of the Empire (q.v.) on 18 May 1804. General Napoleon Bonaparte firstly outmanoeuvred his fellow conspirator and fellow provisional consul, abbé Emmanuel-Joseph Sieyès – who intended to head the new government himself – and Pierre-Roger Ducos, who had been a member of the Council of the Ancients under the Directory (q.v.). The provisional consulate was replaced by a triumvirate comprising Bonaparte, Jean-Jacques-Régis de Cambacérès and Charles-François Lebrun. They took their title *consul* from the highest elected office of the Roman Republic. Ducos became conservateur (and later vice-president) of the senate. With his military authority, Bonaparte soon consolidated personal dictatorial power as 'first consul', confirmed by a referendum on 14 pluviôse (q.v.) an VIII (7 February 1800), and then as 'first consul for life', confirmed by a referendum on 14 thermidor (q.v.) an X (2 August 1802). The Consulate was a repressive police state with no free press and few remaining republican virtues – a state at war and subordinate to the needs of the military. On 18 May 1804, the senate proclaimed Bonaparte emperor.

CONTRE-AMIRAL (rear admiral). A naval rank equivalent to an army *lieutenant-général*, superior to a *capitaine de vaisseau* (q.v.), but junior to a *vice-amiral* (q.v.). D'Urville was promoted to this rank on 31 December 1841.

CORVETTE (sloop). A flush-decked, lightly armed, highly manoeuvrable vessel with three masts. The term initially applied to a variety of smaller French naval vessels, including those that served as light frigates. They were divided between *corvettes à gaillards*, *corvettes sans gaillards* and *corvettes avisos*, respectively corvettes with and without decks (particularly gun decks) and dispatch *corvettes*. By 1829, heavy-transport vessels, such as *flûtes* of 800 tonnes, were designated *corvettes de charge* by the French navy. Although *gabares* (vessels of burden), between 300 and 550 tonnes, were not designated as corvettes, the 380-tonne *Astrolabe* (ex-*Coquille*), originally built as a *grande gabare-écurie* (horse and livestock transport) and armed with only 14 guns, was listed as a *corvette*, as was the *Zélée*.

CRYPTOGAM. A plant (such as a fern, moss or alga) that reproduces with spores rather than visible flowers and seeds.

DIRECTORY. The constitution of 22 August 1795 vested executive authority in five directors: Paul de Barras, Jean-François Reubell, Étienne-François Letourneur, Louis-Marie de La Réveillière-Lépeaux and Emmanuel Joseph Sieyès. The latter promptly retired and was replaced by Lazare Carnot. They were assisted by the Council of Five Hundred and the Council of Ancients (made up of 250 members). The Directory was overthrown by the coup d'état of 9 November 1799, which initiated the dictatorship of the Consulate (q.v.).

DRAGOMAN (translator). The title of those who provided diplomatic and linguistic services to the Ottoman sultan. It was dominated by Greek Christian *phanariotes*, descendants of the Byzantine nobility, for whom grand dragoman positions were reserved.

DUC (duke). A hereditary title of nobility ranking after a prince; the holder of a duchy. Aside from the 17 mediaeval French dukedoms, there were 120 dukedoms (held by more than one person, for 30 years or more) during the *ancien régime* (q.v.). During the empire, Napoleon created 24 dukedoms to reward his marshals and senior ministers. Still more were created after the Restoration (q.v.).

ÉCOLE POLYTECHNIQUE. An élite French government school founded in 1794 to provide a comprehensive scientific education based on mathematics, physics and chemistry. It aimed to prepare students for entry into specialised schools of engineering (military and civilian) and artillery, but also the École navale. Admission was highly selective, and the École polytechnique attracted some of France's most brilliant students. Although d'Urville failed the entrance exam in September 1807, he would later serve with, and then command, a number of its accomplished graduates, known as *polytechniciens* and designated with the letter 'X' and class year after their names. At first, students boarded with host families, but in 1804, under the Empire (q.v.), Napoleon militarised the school and moved its now uniformed students into barracks. During the Restoration (q.v.), the école was demilitarised, but students remained boarders, wore a civilian uniform, were subject to strict discipline (the whole school was dismissed by Louis XVIII in 1817!), and the military continued to attract a large proportion of its graduates.

EMPIRE. The French government that existed after the senate's proclamation of 'First Consul for Life' Napoleon Bonaparte as Emperor Napoleon I on 18 May 1804, until his first abdication on 11 April 1814, and then during the so-called 'Hundred Days' (q.v.) between 20 March and 22 June 1815. It is sometimes referred to as the First Empire to distinguish it from the Second Empire of Napoleon III (Louis-Napoléon Bonaparte), which existed between 2 December 1852 and 4 September 1870.

ENSEIGNE DE VAISSEAU (ship's ensign). French naval rank junior to *lieutenant de vaisseau* (q.v.) but generally with more responsibility than a sub-lieutenant in the British Royal Navy.

ESTATES-GENERAL (French = États généraux). An ancient assembly of the three estates (clergy, nobility and third estate or commons), first summoned by the king of France in 1301; prior to the Revolution, they had not met since 1614. Summoned by Louis XVI to resolve France's financial crisis, it met at Versailles on 5 May 1789. From the ranks of the third estate and a number of reformist members of the clergy and nobility emerged the self-declared National Assembly on 17 June.

FLORÉAL (from Latin *floris* = a flower). The eighth month of the French republican calendar; the equivalent of the spring period 20 April to 19 May.

FRANC. French monetary unit. On 7 December 1793, the National Convention decreed that the principal monetary unit of the ancien régime (q.v.), the *livre* (q.v.), was to be decimalised and henceforth known as the *franc*. The following year, the convention decreed that the new one-franc coin would weigh 5 grams. The old coins coexisted with the new until Napoleon, who issued coins bearing his own image, ordered their removal from circulation. After the Restoration (q.v.), the franc was retained as a monetary unit, but new coins bearing the image of Louis XVIII and subsequently Charles X were minted. After more than two centuries, the French franc was replaced by the single European currency unit, the euro, on 1 January 2002.

FRIMAIRE (from Latin *frigus* = cold). The third month of the French republican calendar; the equivalent of the northern hemisphere autumn period 21 November to 20 December.

FRUCTIDOR (from Latin *fructus* = fruit). The final month of the French republican calendar; the equivalent of the northern hemisphere summer period 18 August to 16 September.

GERMINAL (from Latin *germino* = to sprout). The seventh month of the French republican calendar; the equivalent of the northern hemisphere spring period of 21 March to 19 April.

HOLOTYPE. A single specimen (except in the case of a hapantotype representing different stages in the life cycle of a species) designated the type specimen (q.v.) by the original botanical or zoological author when the description of a species was first published.

HUNDRED DAYS (French = *Cent-Jours*). The period between the First and Second Bourbon Restorations (q.v.). On 8 July 1815, comte Gilbert-Joseph Gaspard de Chabrol-Volvic, prefect of the department of the Seine, greeted Louis XVIII on his return to Paris after Napoleon's final defeat at Waterloo with the words: 'A hundred days have passed since the fatal moment when Your Majesty left his capital.' In fact, Louis had fled Paris 110 days before.

INSTITUT (Institute). In 1666, during the reign of Louis XIV, Jean-Baptiste Colbert founded the Académie [royale] des sciences (q.v.) to promote scientific endeavours in France. Although suppressed by the National Convention (q.v.) in 1793, it was effectively reconstituted as a principal part of the new Institut national in 1795 (and Institut impérial after Napoleon crowned himself emperor). In 1816, the name 'Académie des sciences' was resurrected, but to this day it remains part of the Institut de France. The Institut originally had three 'classes': physical sciences and mathematics; literature and fine arts; and moral and political sciences. In January 1803, Bonaparte reorganised the Institut into four classes: physical sciences and mathematics; French language and literature; history and ancient literature; and fine arts. In the process, he rid himself of his ideological critics by abolishing the class of moral and political sciences.

INTENDANT. During the *ancien régime* (q.v.), the senior administrator of a province, roughly equivalent to a governor. In the navy, an *intendant de la marine et des colonies* held a royal commission equivalent to a *lieutenant-général* and was responsible for the fiscal supervision of a naval base or *arsenal* – in ports such as Toulon, Marseille, Rochefort, Brest and Le Havre or in colonies such as Martinique, Saint-Domingue and the Île-de-France. In 1799, the intendants were replaced by the prefects (q.v.). The rank of *intendant* was briefly resurrected during the Restoration (q.v.).

JACOBINS. The most radical of revolutionary associations, which took its name from its meeting place in the former Dominican convent in the rue Saint-Jacques. Its members included the 'Mountain' faction of Maximilien Robespierre, Jean-Paul Marat and Louis Florelle de Saint-Just. The Jacobins ruled France during the Terror (q.v.) and were overthrown on 9 thermidor (27 July 1794). Their principal leaders were guillotined.

JARDIN DES PLANTES. Originally the Jardin du Roi, the royal botanical garden, it was established in 1635 on a six-hectare site by Louis XIII. Initially it functioned as a physic garden for medicinal and useful plants. Together with the *ménagerie*, where exotic animals were kept, it gradually became a centre for the study of all branches of the natural sciences. Renamed the Jardin des plantes in 1792, the following year it became home to the new Muséum national d'histoire naturelle. It was also an institution with influential professorial chairs.

LÉGION D'HONNEUR (Legion of honour). A French order of civil and military merit created on 19 May 1802 by the Consulate (q.v.). It initially had three grades: *grand officier*, *commandeur* and *légionnaire*. With the establishment of the Empire (q.v.), *légionnaires* also became *chevaliers* (q.v.) *de l'Empire*. The ribbon of the order was red (like that of the order of Saint-Louis abolished during the Revolution); the medal was a five-armed star of white enamel (each double-pointed and edged with gold) and overlaying a laurel wreath. Its gold centre was charged with the effigy of Napoleon. An imperial crown joined the ribbon with the medal. The back of the medal bore the imperial eagle. At the time of the Battle of Waterloo, there were some 48,000 members, of whom only 1400 were civilians. During the Restoration (q.v.), the *Légion d'honneur* was retained by a pragmatic Louis XVIII who required recipients to swear an oath of allegiance. He also replaced the central effigy of Napoleon with that of Henri IV (the first Bourbon monarch) and the imperial crown with one bearing the *fleurs de lys*. The imperial eagle on the back of the medal was also replaced with three *fleurs de lys*, the heraldic emblem of the Bourbon dynasty. It was this version of the decoration that Dumont d'Urville wore after he was made a *chevalier de la Légion d'honneur* on 8 June 1821. After the Revolution of July 1830, Louis-Philippe removed the *fleurs de lys* from the crown and the reverse of the medal, replacing the latter with crossed tricoloured French flags. He also introduced the military grade of *officier* in 1837. During the Second Empire, Napoleon's image was once again restored to the centre of the medal. The modern decoration, however, bears the image of Marianne, symbol of the republic, and the ribbon is attached to a wreath instead of a crown.

LIEUTENANT DE VAISSEAU (ship's lieutenant). French naval rank junior to a *capitaine de vaisseau* (q.v.).

LIVRE (from Latin *libra* = pound). The common monetary unit of France prior to the introduction of the franc. It was equivalent to the value of a *livre* or pound of silver and was divided into 20 *sols* (or *sou*) and each *sol* into 12 *deniers*. The famous gold coin the *Louis d'or* was valued at 24 livres. Prior to the Revolution, a modest meal or a seat at the *Comédie française* could be purchased for 1 livre. A bowl of *café au lait* at a street stall cost about 2 sols. A Paris labourer earned between 300 and 500 livres a year. A professorial stipend was about 1900 livres a year. It was replaced by the decimal *franc* (q.v.) on 7 December 1793.

MARQUIS. A title of landed nobility ranking immediately below a *duc* (duke) and above a *comte* (count). It originally referred to the ruler of a *marche* or frontier territory.

MESSIDOR (from Latin *messis* = harvest). The tenth month of the French republican calendar; the equivalent of the northern hemisphere summer period of 19 June to 18 July.

MUSÉUM NATIONAL D'HISTOIRE NATURELLE. See Jardin des plantes.

NATIONAL ASSEMBLY (French = *Assemblée nationale*). On 17 June 1789, the representatives of the Third Estate in the Estates-General (q.v.) were joined by reform-minded representatives of the nobility and clergy, and declared themselves to be the National Assembly. After refusing Louis XVI's orders to disband and sit as separate estates, on 9 July, the representatives proclaimed themselves to be a National Constituent Assembly (*Assemblée nationale constituante*). On 22 December 1789, the voting procedures drafted by the assembly gave suffrage to adult males over 25 years of age with tax and residential qualifications. The National Assembly was succeeded by the National Legislative Assembly (*Assemblée nationale législative*) on 1 October 1791, which in turn was succeeded by the National Convention on 21 September 1792. The National Convention, which proclaimed the republic on 22 September, was succeeded by the Directory (q.v.) in 1795. It was overthrown by Napoleon Bonaparte in the coup d'état of 18 brumaire (9 November 1799), which initiated the Consulate (q.v.) and laid the foundations of the Empire (q.v.).

THE NATIONAL CONVENTION. See National Assembly.

NATIONAL GUARD (French = *Garde nationale*). Citizen militia established in Paris on 13 July 1789 to ensure law and order. The first commander was the marquis de Lafayette, hero of the American War of Independence. Although abolished in 1827, it was resurrected during the Revolution of 1830. D'Urville joined it on the evening of 29 July 1830.

NATIONAL LEGISLATIVE ASSEMBLY. See National Assembly.

NIVÔSE (from Latin *nivosus* = snowy). The fourth month of the French republican calendar; the equivalent of the northern hemisphere winter period of 21 December to 19 January.

PHANEROGAM. A plant that produces seeds (from visible fertilised flowers).

PIROGUE. A small, flat-bottomed, shallow-draught boat, of varying descriptions but often dug out of a single tree trunk and propelled by a paddle, sail or punt pole.

PLUVIÔSE (from Latin *pluvia* = rain). The fifth month of the French republican calendar; the equivalent of the northern hemisphere winter period 20 January to 18 February.

PRAIRIAL (from French *prairie* = meadow). The ninth month of the French republican calendar; the equivalent of the northern hemisphere spring period 20 May to 18 June.

PREFECT (French = *préfet*). By means of the Law of 28 pluviôse an VIII (17 February 1800), the First Consul Bonaparte installed prefects as representatives of his highly centralised authoritarian state in each of France's regional *départements*. The previous year the title had already been applied to the *Intendants* (q.v).

PROCUREUR (attorney, advocate, lawyer). They acted as legal representatives in seigneurial courts and provincial *parlements* (courts), and were generally equivalent to English 'solicitors'. A *procureur du roi* acted as a public prosecutor in a royal court of law.

RESTORATION (from French *Restauration* = reinstatement, reestablishment). The name given to the French Government under the Bourbon monarchs Louis XVIII and Charles X. Effectively there were two Restorations divided by the so-called 'Hundred Days' (q.v.). The First Restoration, between 5 April 1814 and 20 March 1815, began after Napoleon's first abdication and ended three weeks after his escape from Elba. The Second Restoration, between 28 June 1815 and 29 July 1830, began after Napoleon's final defeat at Waterloo and ended with the Revolution of July 1830.

SIEUR (gentleman). Honorific title denoting a male landholder or member of the gentry, hence *monsieur* (my sir, mister).

SYNTYPE. A plant or animal specimen belonging to a type series from which a holotype (q.v.) has not been selected or designated. The syntypes constitute the name-bearing type collectively.

TERROR (French = *La Terreur*). The intensely fearful period of denunciations, mass-arrests and executions that began with the fall of the Girondins on 2 June 1793 and ended with the fall of Robespierre and the Jacobins (q.v.) on 9 thermidor an II (27 July 1794). Initially, those accused of being enemies of the Revolution were tried, and almost invariably condemned, by the *Tribunal révolutionnaire*, but in the final six weeks of the Terror (after a law passed on 10 June 1794), those arrested were executed without trial.

THERMIDOR (from Greek *thermos* = hot) The eleventh month of the French republican calendar; the equivalent of the northern hemisphere summer period 19 July to 17 August. It is particularly remembered for the fall of Robespierre on 9 thermidor an II (27 July 1794) and the end of the Terror (q.v.) – hence the term 'post-thermidor'.

TYPE SPECIMEN. The museum or herbarium specimen selected by a taxonomist to serve as a basis for naming and describing a new species. Where the original specimen has disappeared, an illustration can have 'type' status.

VAUBAN FORTIFICATIONS. Defences designed by Sébastien Le Prestre de Vauban, Louis XIV's famed military engineer who constructed fortifications on France's borders, coasts and off-shore islands. In 2008, 12 of these surviving fortified complexes were inscribed on UNESCO's list of World Heritage Sites.

VENDÉMIAIRE (from Latin *vindemia* = grape harvest, vintage). The first month of the French republican calendar; the equivalent of the northern hemisphere autumn period 22 September to 21 October. It is particularly remembered for Bonaparte's dispersal of royalist insurgents in Paris on 13 vendémiaire (4 October 1795).

VENTÔSE (from Latin *ventosus* = windy). The sixth month of the French republican calendar; the equivalent of northern hemisphere winter period 19 February to 20 March.

VICE-AMIRAL (vice-admiral) A naval rank superior to *contre-amiral* (q.v.) (rear admiral) and an army *lieutenant-général*, but junior to *amiral* and *maréchal de France*. After the naval reforms of 1791, the officer corps comprised nine *vice-amiraux*.

Archival, bibliographic & periodical sources

ABBREVIATIONS

BMS: Actes de baptêmes, mariages et sépultures
MNHN: Muséum national d'histoire naturelle, Paris
NAF: Nouvelle acquisition française
NMD: Actes de naissances, mariages et décès
SHDDM: Service historique de la défense, Département de la marine

ARCHIVAL SOURCES

FRANCE

Archives de l'Académie des sciences, Paris
Dossier de séance de l'Académie des sciences du 15 septembre 1828.

Archives de Paris
DQ^{18} Art. 349, Sommier foncier.
Registres paroissiaux et d'état civil, NMD.

1. Archives départementales des Bouches-du-Rhône, Marseille
Registres paroissiaux et d'état civil, table décennale, naissances, 1792–1802.

Archives départementales du Calvados, Caen
4L 216, Administration de la période révolutionaire 1789–an VIII: Comité de Surveillance: Condé-sur-Noireau an II.
Registres paroissiaux et d'état civil, NMD, Vassy, 1762–1872; Caen, 1793–1832.

Archives départementales du Jura, Monmorot
M53, dossier Antoine-Henry Faraguet.

Archives départementales du Var, Draguignan
7E146_74–253 Registres paroissiaux et d'état civil, 1817–61

Archives municipals, Toulon

3E1 [formerly E66], folio 108, Acte de mariage: Dumont d'Urville et Adèle-Dorothée Pépin, 1 mai 1815.

1G9-2, Matrice des propriétés bâties et non bâties de l'Ouest de la banlieue, partie rurale, folio 464.

6Fi60, Plan du cadastre napoléonien, 1827, Section D de St Antoine, 2ème Feuille levée par M. Fouque, cadet géomètre de 1ère classe.

L121 E35, Registre des naissances de 1816.

Archives nationales de France, Paris

Marine 5JJ 154–5, Observations du Lieutenant de vaisseau Tardy de Montravel.

Marine 5JJ 158 Bis, Dumont d'Urville papiers, 1838–1841.

Marine JJ5 80A–87B, Voyage de Duperrey sur la *Coquille*, 1822–1825.

Marine JJ5 99–102c, Voyage de Dumont d'Urville sur l'*Astrolabe*, 1825–1829.

Marine JJ5 127, Voyage de Dumont d'Urville sur l'*Astrolabe* et la *Zélée*, 1836–1841.

Marine JJ5 128, Journaux des officiers de l'*Astrolabe*.

Marine JJ5 129, Journaux des officiers de la *Zélée*.

Marine JJ5 130, Journaux de timonerie de l'*Astrolabe*.

ET/C/1200, Minutier central des notaires de Paris, '13 Juin 1842, Inventaire après décès de Mr. Dumont d'Urville'; '21 Juin 1842, Décharge donnée à M. Demanche'.

Fond Léonore: LH/74/77– LH2789/134.

Bibliothèque de Caen

Ms in 4° 334, Cahier de physique appartenant à Dumont d'Urville de Condé-sur-Noireau: Élève au Lycée de Caen, commencé le 22 Pluviôse an 13.

Ms in-fol. 178 / 1 (f. 124), Dumont d'Urville, Paris, 20 mai 1829, à Pierre-Aimé Lair, Conseiller de Préfecture, Caen.

Ms in-fol. 178 / 1 (f. 208), Dumont d'Urville, Paris, 31 août 1821, au Président de l'Académie des sciences et belles lettres de Caen.

Bibliothèque historique de la Ville de Paris

Paris Album 4° 21, 15 H. Blancard, 1887–1889 (Rue Madame).

Bibliothèque municipale de Toulon

Ms 65, Manuscrits de Dumont d'Urville:

Pièce i, Relation présentée à l'Académie des sciences de la campagne hydrographique faite par la gabare 'La *Chevrette*' dans le Levant et la Mer Noire 1819–1820, p. 45 [R 1347 [1]].

Pièce ii, Manuscrit d'une partie du voyage de l'*Astrolabe* 1826–1829, ff. 1358 [R 942 [b]].

Pièce iii, Journaux particuliers, 1830–1837, 7 carnets de ff. 93, in °4 [R 1347 [2]].

Pièce iv, Manuscrit du premier volume de la publication de la campagne de 'l'*Astrolabe*' et de la 'Zélée' 1837–41, ff. 258 [R 942 [a]].

Ms 131, Manuscrits de l'amiral Dumont d'Urville.

Ms 132, Expédition *Astrolabe* et *Zélée* (7 septembre 1837–6 novembre 1840).

Ms 133, Manuscrits de l'amiral Dumont d'Urville.

Bibliothèque nationale de France, Paris
Département des cartes et plans
Manuscrits de la Société de géographie, Carton Du-Ey, °374, Dumont d'Urville,
    lettre de remerciements pour son élection au poste de secrétaire de la Société de géographie, 2
    avril 1830 and de vice-président, 6 avril 1832.

Département des manuscrits
NAF 6785, Blosseville, 'Projet d'une colonie pénale sur la côte S. O. de la Nouvelle-Hollande', 31
    décembre 1828; Blosseville, 'Projet d'une colonie pénale à la Nouvelle-Zélande, 1 juillet 1829'.
NAF 9439, Collection Pierre Margry, 'Mers Australes'; ff. 151–255 [comprising biographical notes
    on Dumont d'Urville and extracts from his 'mémoire auto-biographique' (ff. 152–64), formerly
    in the collection of the Bibliothèque municipale de Toulon, now lost].

École polytechnique, Paris
Archives
Fiches matricules: X 1822–39.

Mairie de Condé-sur-Noireau
Ms 10, Dumont d'Urville, 'Événements historiques et remarques, dimanche 23 juillet 1820–
    dimanche 20 août 1820'.
Ms 11, Dumont d'Urville, Ms journal de la *Coquille* '24 octobre 1823–5 juin 1824'.
Ms 12, Dumont d'Urville, Ms journal, 6 avril 1841–16 septembre 1841.

Médiatheque de Rochefort
Fonds Lesson, Ms 8122, Pierre-Adolphe Lesson, 'Voyage de découverte de l'*Astrolabe*'.

Médiathèque municipale, Condé-sur-Noireau
Service documentation et archives
5 MI 33 R 5 BMS., Registres paroissiaux Saint-Martin & Saint-Sauveur
État civil, NMD, Condé-sur-Noireau, 1800–2001.
Fonds musée, 4535314174, Lafontaine, J.-P., 'Mémoire de ma Ville: Condé-sur-Noireau et Dumont
    d'Urville: Exposition présenté à l'Hôtel de Ville de Condé-sur-Noireau du 19 mai au 24 juillet
    1990'.

Muséum national d'histoire naturelle (MNHN), Paris
Bibliothèque centrale
Ms 62, Lesson, R.P. Voyage de l'*Astrolabe*–botanique [1826–29].
Ms 165, Dumoutier, 'Notes sur les races humaines: rapport sur la collection d'anthropologie
    recueillie pendant l'expédition de l'*Astrolabe* et de la *Zélée*'.
Ms 354 ,'Voyage autour du monde sur la corvette la *Coquille*'.
Ms 1602, Dumont d'Urville, 'Journal d'un voyage autour du monde entrepris sur la corvette de sa
    Majesté' [not to be confused with the personal journal in the possession of the Mairie de Condé-
    sur-Noireau].

Musée de l'homme, Paris
Collections d'Anthropologie biologique
MNHN-HA-29266, buste de Jules Sébastien César Dumont d'Urville.
MNHN-HA-D-222, buste d'Adèle Dumont d'Urville.
MNHN-HA-D-223, buste de Jules Dumont d'Urville, enfant.
MNHN-HA-1789, 'squelette monté de Mafy, naturel de Tonga-Tapou, voyage de l'*Astrolabe* et de la
  Zélée; préparé par Hombron et Jacquinot'.
MNHN-HA-8518, 'cheveux de Maphi, Kanake de Tonga Tabou, archipel Tonga'.

Office notarial Boyer, Toulon
Inventaire des effets mobiliers dressé par Maître Vallavieille, notaire à Toulon, le 30 juillet 1842
  … dépendant des successions réunies de feu M. Dumont d'Urville, de son épouse et de son fils
  décédés ensemble le 8 mai 1842 domicilé à Paris.

Office notarial Pieroni-Mignon, Toulon
Contrat de mariage de Dumont d'Urville et Adèle Dorothée Pépin passé devant
  Maître Fournier, notaire à Toulon, le 28 avril 1815.

Service des archives de la Nouvelle-Calédonie, Nouméa
Pierre-Edouard Guilbert, journal, 1826–28 [copy from the library of Ludovick Pruche].

Service historique de la défense, Département de la marine (SHDDM), Château de Vincennes
CC^7 2 Moderne, carton 3, dossier 11; dossier personnel, Jacquinot, Charles-Hector.
CC^7 Alpha 44/0–2475, dossiers personnels (including CC^7 Alpha 772, Dumont d'Urville, Jules-
  Sébastien-César).
BB^4 411, Campagnes, 1820, vol. 2, Station du Levant, gabarre la *Chevrette*, Gauttier-Duparc,
  capitaine de vaisseau, 8 février–28 novembre 1820;
'Relation de la Campagne hydrographique de la gabare du roi la *Chevrette* dans le Levant et la
  Mer Noire par M. d'Urville chargé par le commandant de l'expédition de la partie de l'histoire
  naturelle année 1820.'
BB^4 507, Lettres du ministre de la marine, Voyage de l'*Astrolabe*.
BB^4 530 Bis, embarquement de Charles X à Cherbourg 1830.
BB^4 615, folios 275–76, ministre de la marine au M. Clément Salvy, Capitaine de Vaisseau,
  Commandant le v[aisse]au. Le *Diadième*, à Toulon, 4 juillet 1842.
BB^4 1000, Voyage de la *Coquille*, Duperrey (1822–25).
BB^4 1002, Voyage de l'*Astrolabe*, Dumont d'Urville (1826–29).
BB^4 1009, Voyage de l'*Astrolabe* et la *Zélée*, Dumont d'Urville (1837–40).
Fonds Privés, 7 GG^2 cartons 1 & 2 [previously GG2 30 & GG2 31], Papiers du Contre-Amiral
  Jules-Sébastien-César Dumont d'Urville.

Service historique de la défense, Département de la marine (SHDDM), Toulon
Ms 11, Dumont d'Urville, testament, 20 octobre 1839; codicille 1er novembre 1839; portrait, avril
  1826.

Papiers de Louis Charles Lefébure de Cerisy:

23S 693–709, Lettres de Jules Dumont d'Urville (1821–22).

23S 710–712, Lettres d'Adèle Dumont d'Urville (1821).

23S 753, [portrait] Louis Charles Lefébure de Cerisy, Élève au Lycée de Caen, de 1804 à 1807.

2E6 1386, Rôle d'Équipage, *La Coquille*.

NETHERLANDS

Nationaal Archief, Den Haag

3106–3125, Registers van het Europese personeel op Java en Madoera, alsmede van hun mannelijke afstammelingen boven de zestien jaren. Opgemaakt 1 januari 1819. Ingezonden bij brief van de gouverneur-generaal dd. 3 januari 1831 nr. 3 1831, 30 delen.

UNITED KINGDOM

Cambridge University Library, Cambridge

MS.Add.7348 & MS.Add.7450, 'Papers of John Ludlow and of the Ludlow, Liot and Des Graz families'.

MS. Add. 7540/44, César Des Graz, letters 1838–40.

Royal Geographical Society, London

SSC/58/1-3, César Des Graz, 'Journal, impressions et remarques pendant la voyage des corvettes l'*Astrolabe* et la *Zélée*', 7 septembre 1837–22 juin 1840 [3 vols].

SSC/58/5, 'Tableau comparatif des idiomes des différentes peuplades visitées par l'expédition'.

AUSTRALIA

National Library of Australia, Canberra

MS Acc07/37, Dumont d'Urville to his publisher Gide, 8 July 1841.

MS 693, Dumont d'Urville, to Monsieur de Paravey, 12 June 1832.

MS 179, James C. Wallace, Journal aboard HMS *Alligator*, 1838–39.

MS 9061, (Duyker Papers) Gaston Sarré, *Recueil de renseignements généalogiques sur les familles de l'île Maurice*, photocopied typescript, Port Louis, *c*.1945.

Archives Office of Tasmania, Hobart

Index to Tasmanian Convicts (1804–93).

Archives, Catholic Archdiocese of Hobart

Epitaphs, St Mary's Old Cemetery.

State Library of New South Wales, Sydney

Dixson Library

DLMS Q355 (microfilm CY 293), Dumont d'Urville 'Correspondance autographe' with Isidore Le Brun, (25) letters, 6 janvier 1830–6 septembre 1841; Adèle Dorothea Dumont d'Urville, (44) letters to Isidore Le Brun, 12 février 1830 to janvier 1842; Dumont d'Urville and Adèle Dorothée

Dumont d'Urville to Isidore Le Brun (3) dinner invitations; Jules Dumont d'Urville to Monsieur Le Brun, (6) letters, octobre 1838–1 mars 1840.

DL Add 207, Dumont d'Urville, Copy of letter, aboard *Astrolabe*, Bay of Islands, dated 4 mai 1840, to the Baron de Thierry.

Mitchell Library
B1298, [René-Primevère] Lesson, Voyage de *Coquille*, journal, 1823–24, Hélouis transcript.

Northern Territory Library, Darwin
Ms 61, Log of HMS *Alligator* kept by Francis Meynell, 22 May 1838 to 9 September 1840.

GUAM

University of Guam, Mangilao
Richard Flores Taitano Micronesian Area Research Center
Paul B. Souder, 'Heritage: A Genealogy of the Souder-Torres and Affiliated Families throughout the Nineteenth and Twentieth Centuries', unpublished MS 1978.

NEWSPAPERS

The Auckland Star (Auckland), 1965
The Australasian Chronicle (Sydney), 1840
The Australian (Sydney), 1826
The Argus (Melbourne), 1859
Bruce Herald (Milton), 1895
Daily Southern Cross (Auckland), 1852–1868
The Dominion (Wellington), 1966, 2001
L'Echo de la Suisse-Normande et du Bocage (Condé-sur-Noireau), 1983
The Independent (London), 1997
La Patrie (Montréal), 1933
Le moniteur universel (Paris), 1822–1830
L'Orne Combattante (Flers), 1997–2001
Mercantile Advertiser (New York), 1805
Mercury (Hobart), 1910–15
Journal de Condé (Condé-sur-Noireau), 1904
Journal des Débats (Paris), 1837
Le National (Paris), 1830–37
New Zealand Herald, 1915
Sydney Gazette and New South Wales Advertiser (Sydney), 1823–27
Sydney Morning Herald (Sydney), 1839–42, 1847, 1895
Le Toulonnais (Toulon), 1837
Otago Witness (Dunedin), 1895

THESES

Bataille, A., 'Un document inédit: Le journal médical de Adolphe Pierre Lesson, chirurgien de Dumont d'Urville sur l'*Astrolabe* (1826–1829)', thèse médicale [no. 2025], Université de Nantes, 1978.

Couturaud, C., 'Le troisième voyage de circumnavigation de J.S.C. Dumont d'Urville 1837–1840', thèse doctorale, Université de Provence, Aix-en-Provence, 1986.

Harman, K.E., 'Aboriginal Convicts: Race, law, and transportation in colonial New South Wales', Ph.D. thesis, University of Tasmania, 2008.

Papachristou, P.A., 'The Three Faces of the Phanariots: An inquiry into the role and motivations of the Greek nobility under Ottoman rule, 1683–1821', M.A. thesis, Simon Fraser University, 1988.

Parquet, F., 'Le chirurgien navigant [*sic*] du Pacifique Pierre Adolphe Lesson (1805–1888)', thèse médicale [no. 107M/1988], Université de Nantes, 1988.

Pendu, T., 'La pharmacopée de Dumont d'Urville lors de son voyage en Terre Adélie', thèse D. Pharm. [no. 036P/1993], Université de Nantes, 1993.

Rigaudeau, J., 'Un document: Les journaux de bord du "chirurgien navigant" Jacques Bernard Hombron (1798–1852)', thèse médicale [no. 1956], Université de Nantes, 1978.

Suzuki, K.K., 'Tuberculosis in Polynesia: A discussion of its occurrence before initial European contact', MA (anthropology) thesis, University of Hawai'i, 2008.

BOOKS & MONOGRAPHS

Abell, L.E.B., *Recollections of the Emperor Napoleon during the First Three Years of his Captivity on the Island of St Helena*, John Murray, London, 1844.

Agulhon, M. (ed.), *Histoire de Toulon*, privately published, Toulouse, 1980.

Aicard, J., *La Vénus de Milo: Recherches sur l'histoire de la découverte*, Sandoz et Fischbacher, Paris, 1874.

Alaux, J.-P., *La Vénus de Milo et Olivier Voutier, frontispice gravé par Decaris, sept bois gravés par Gustave Alaux*, Jean-Paul Alaux, Paris, 1939.

Alder, K. *The Measure of All Things: The seven-year odyssey and hidden error that transformed the world*, The Free Press, New York, 2002.

Anon., *Historical Record of the Third Regiment of Foot, or, The Buffs: Formerly designated the Holland Regiment: Containing an account of its origins in the reign of Queen Elizabeth and of its subsequent services to 1838*, Longman, Orme, London, 1839.

Arago, J., *Souvenirs d'un aveugle: Voyage autour du monde*, H. Lebrun, Paris, 1868.

Ashmole, P., & Ashmole, M., *St Helena and Ascension Island: A natural history*, Anthony Nelson, Owestry, 2000.

Association Salomon, *Le Mystère Lapérouse, ou le rêve inachevé d'un roi*, Editions de Conti, Paris, 2008.

Ayres, P., *Mawson: A life*, Miegunyah/Melbourne University Press, Carlton, 1999.

Baal, J. van, Galis, K.W., & Koentjaraningrat, R.M., *West Irian: A bibliography*, Foris Publications, Dordrecht, 1984.

Bach, J., *The Australian Station: A history of the Royal Navy in the south west Pacific 1821–1913*, New South Wales University Press, Kensington, 1986.

Bagnall, A.G., & Petersen, G.C., *William Colenso, Printer, Missionary, Botanist, Explorer, Politician: His life and journeys*, A.H. & A.W. Reed, Wellington, 1948.

Baker, K., & Rankin, E., (eds), *Fiona Pardington: The pressure of sunlight falling*, Otago University Press, Dunedin, 2011.

Barclay, G., *A History of the Pacific*, Sidgwick & Jackson, London, 1978.

Barette, Abbé, *Histoire de la ville de Condé-sur-Noireau ... Suivie d'une notice sur Dumont-d'Urville*, Auger, Condé-sur-Noireau, 1844.

Barker, T., *A History of Bathurst*, 2 vols, Crawford House, Bathurst, 1992–98.

Bassett, M., *Realms and Islands: The world voyage of Rose de Freycinet in the corvette* Uranie, *1817–1820: From her journal and letters and the reports of Louis de Saulces de Freycinet, capitaine de corvette*, Oxford University Press, London, 1962.

Bateson, C., *Australian Shipwrecks Including Vessels Wrecked en Route to or from Australia, and some Strandings*, volume 1: 1622–1850, A.H. & A.W. Reed, Frenchs Forest, 1982.

—— *The Convict Ships, 1787–1868,* Library of Australian History, Sydney, 1983.

Beaglehole, J.C. (ed.), *The Discovery of New Zealand*, second edition, Oxford University Press, Wellington, 1961.

—— *The* Endeavour *Journal of Joseph Banks 1768–1771*, 2 vols, Public Library of New South Wales/Angus and Robertson, Sydney, 1962.

Beatie, O., & Geiger, J., *Frozen in Time: The fate of the Franklin expedition*, Bloomsbury, London, 1987.

Beauvoir, L. de, *Australie: Voyage autour du monde*, Henri Plon, Paris, 1869.

Beck, B., & Le Poire, J.-G., (eds), *Le Lycée Malherbe: Deux siècles d'histoire*, Association du bicentenaire du Lycée Malherbe, Caen, 2004.

[Belivanakis, G.] Μπελιβανάκης , Γ., *Οι κατακόμβες της Μήλου*, Αθήνα [Athens], 1994.

Bendyshe, T. (ed.), *The Anthropological Treatises of Johann Friedrich Blumenbach ...*, Published for the Anthropological Society by Longman, Green, Roberts & Green, London, 1865.

Bertier de Sauvigny, G., *The Bourbon Restoration*, translated from the French by Lynn M. Case, University of Pennsylvania Press, Philadelphia, 1966.

Bhathal, R. & White, G., *Under the Southern Cross: A brief history of astronomy in Australia*, Kangaroo Press, Kenthurst (NSW), 1991.

Billault de Gérainville, A.-E., *Histoire de Louis-Philippe*, 3 vols, chez tous les libraires, Paris, 1870–75.

Bingham, P., *New Cases in the Court of Common Pleas and Exchequer Chamber*, 6 vols, Saunders and Benning, London, 1835–41.

Binney, J., *The Legacy of Guilt: A life of Thomas Kendall*, Published for the University of Auckland by Oxford University Press, Auckland, 1968.

Blais, H., *Voyages au Grand Océan: Géographie du Pacifique et colonisation 1815–1845*, CTHS, Paris, 2005.

Blanchard, [C.]-E., *Catalogue des Cétonides de la collection du Muséum d'histoire naturelle de Paris*, Paris, 1842.

—— *Museum d'histoire naturelle, catalogue de la collection entomologique, classe des insectes,* vol. ii : *Ordre des Coléoptères,* Gide et Baudry, Paris, 1851.

Blosseville, E. Poret de, *Histoire des colonies pénales et des établissements de l'Angleterre en Australie,* Adrien le Clère et Cie, Paris, 1831.

Bloys van Treslong Prins, P.C., *Genealogische en heraldische gedenkwaardigheden betreffende Europeanen op Java,* 3 vols, Drukkerij Albrecht, Batavia, 1934–39.

Boardman, J., *Greek Art,* Thames and Hudson, London, 1973.

Bodinier, G., *Les gardes du corps de Louis XVI: Étude institutionnelle, sociale et politique, dictionnaire biographique,* Service historique de l'armée de terre, Vincennes, 2005.

Boissery, B., *A Deep Sense of Wrong: The treason, trials, and transportation to New South Wales of lower Canadian rebels after the 1838 rebellion,* Dundurn Press, Toronto, 1995.

Bonnefoux, P.-M.-J. de, & Pâris, E., *Dictionnaire de la marine à voile* (1856), facsimile edition, Fontaine au Roi, Paris, 1987.

Bougainville, L.-A. de., *Voyage autour du monde: Par la frégate la* Boudeuse *et la flûte l'*Etoile, Editions la Découverte, Paris, 1989.

Boulay de La Meurthe, H., *Histoire du choléra-morbus dans le quartier du Luxembourg,* Chez Paul Renouard, Paris, 1832.

Boxer, C., *The Dutch Seaborne Empire 1600–1800,* Penguin, Harmondsworth, 1973.

Brisbane, T., *Reminiscences of General Sir Thomas Makdougall Brisbane,* Thomas Constable, Edinburgh, 1860.

Brosses, C. de, *Histoire des navigations aux Terres Australes,* 2 vols, Durand, Paris, 1756–57.

Brown, S. *Men from Under the Sky: The arrival of Westerners in Fiji,* Charles E. Tuttle Company, Rutland, Vermont, 1973.

Brue, A.-H., *Carte de l'Océanie ou cinquième partie du monde … publiée pour la première fois en 1822 par J. Goujon; revue et augmentée par l'éditeur d'après de nouveaux matériaux,* Chez J. Goujon et J. Andriveau, Paris, 1829.

Buick, T.L., *The French at Akaroa: An adventure in colonization,* New Zealand Book Depot, Wellington, 1928.

Burkhardt, F., & Smith, S. (eds), *The Correspondence of Charles Darwin,* [30 vols projected], Cambridge University Press, Cambridge, 1985–.

Cameron, V.L. (ed.), *The Log of a Jack Tar; or, the life of James Choyce, master mariner … with O'Brien's captivity in France,* T. Fisher Unwin, London, 1891.

Campbell, I.C., *'Gone native' in Polynesia: Captivity narratives and experiences from the South Pacific,* Greenwood Press, Westport, Conn., 1998.

Cargill, D., *Memoirs of Mrs. Margaret Cargill, Wife of the Rev. David Cargill, A.M., Wesleyan Missionary: Including Notices of the Progress of Christianity in Tonga and Feejee by her Husband,* John Mason, London, 1841.

Castillo infante, F., & Fuentes y Liá Cortés, J., *Diccionario Histórico y Biográfico de Chile,* Editorial Zig-Zag, Santiago, 1996.

Cautru, C., *L'Histoire de Condé-sur-Noireau,* Imprimerie-Librairie Ch. Corlet, Condé-sur-Noireau, 1965.

Cerise, L.A., *Exposé et examen critique du système phrénologique, considéré dans ses principes, dans sa méthode, dans sa théorie et dans ses conséquences*, Trinquart, Paris, 1836.

Chardon, J., *Nouveau guide marseillais ou véritable indicateur marseillais, l'almanach historique et commercial de Marseille et du département des Bouches-du-Rhône pour l'année 1834*, Chaudon, Marseille, 1834.

Chateaubriand, F.-A., *Travels in America and Italy*, London, H. Colburn, 1828.

[Chazet, R. de,] *Mémoires posthumes, lettres et pièces authentiques touchant la vie et la mort de Charles-François, duc de Rivière*, L'advocat, Paris, 1829.

Chevalier, A., *La vie et l'œuvre de René Desfontaines, fondateur de l'herbier du Muséum: La carrière d'un savant sous la Révolution*, Editions du Muséum, Paris, 1939.

Choiseul-Gouffier, M.-G.-A.-F., comte de, *Voyage pittoresque de la Grèce*, 3 vols, Chez J.J. Blaise, Paris, 1782–1822.

Christie, E.H., *The Antarctic Problem: An historical and political study*, George Allen & Unwin, London, 1951.

Clairmont, C.W., *Fauvel: The first archaeologist in Athens and his philhellenic correspondents*, Akanthus, Zurich, 2007.

Clark, K., *The Nude: A study of ideal art*, Penguin, Harmondsworth, 1960.

Cloher, D.U., *Hongi Hika, Warrior Chief*, Viking, Auckland, 2003.

Colledge, J.J., *Ships of the Royal Navy: An historical index*, 2 vols, David & Charles, Newton Abbot, 1970.

Collins, R., *New Zealand Seen by the French (1769–1846) / La Nouvelle-Zélande vue par les Français,* National Library of New Zealand in association with UTA French Airlines, Wellington, 1991.

Collins, R., *Charles Meryon: A life*, Garton & Co., Devizes, 1999.

—— *Louis Le Breton: À la découverte du Pacifique et de l'Antarctique*, Coop Breizh, Spézet, 2012.

Cordier, H., *Voyage de Pierre Dupré de Constantinople à Trébizonde: 1803*, Imprimerie nationale, Paris, 1919.

Costet, R., *Archives des missions étrangères: Études et documents 17: Siam-Laos, histoire de la mission*, 'Églises d'Asie', Paris, 2003.

Cropp, G.M., Watts, N.R., Collins, R.D.J. and Howe, K.R., *Pacific Journeys: Essays in honour of John Dunmore*, Victoria University Press, Wellington, 2005.

Crozet, J. (edited by Rochon, A.), *Nouveau voyage à la mer du sud*, Barrois, Paris, 1783.

Curtis, G., *Disarmed: The story of the Venus de Milo*, Alfred A. Knopf, New York, 2003.

Cuvier, G., *Le règne animal distribué d'après son organisation: Pour servir de base à l'histoire naturelle des animaux et d'introduction à l'anatomie comparée*, 4 vols, Déterville libraire, Paris, 1817.

—— *Éloge historique de M. Richard*, no imprint details, [Paris, *ca.* 1821].

Cuvier, G., & Valenciennes, A., *Histoire naturelle des poissons*, 22 vols, F.G. Levrault, Paris, 1828–49.

Dahl, O.C., *Migration from Kalimantan to Madagascar*, Norwegian University Press, Oslo, 1991.

[Dalampira, C.E.] Δαλαμπίρα, Χ.Ε., *Ο Κόνσολας* , Αθήνα [Athens], 1999.

Dallaway, J., *Constantinople Ancient and Modern: With excursions to the shores and islands of the archipelago*, T. Cadell junr. & W. Davies, London, 1797.

Dampier, W., *A Voyage to New Holland: The English voyage of discovery to the South Seas in 1699*, edited with an introduction by James Spencer, Alan Sutton, Gloucester, 1981.

Dana, R.H., *Two Years Before the Mast and Twenty-four Years After*, first published 1840, [Harvard Classics] P.F. Collier & Son, New York, [1909].

Darwin, C., *The Voyage of the* Beagle, first published 1839, J.M. Dent, London, 1936.

Davidson, J.W. (edited by O.H.K. Spate), *Peter Dillon of Vanikoro, Chevalier of the South Seas*, Oxford University Press, Melbourne, 1975.

Dawson, L.S., *Memoirs of Hydrography: Including brief biographies of the principal officers who have served in H.M. Naval Surveying Service between the years 1750 and 1885*, Henry W. Keay, Eastbourne, 1885.

Dawson, P.A., *A Biography of François Magendie*, A.J. Huntington, Brooklyn–New York, 1908.

Dayrat, B., *Les botanistes et la flore de France: Trois siècles de découvertes*, Muséum national d'histoire naturelle, Paris, 2003.

Deacon, M., *Scientists and the Sea 1650–1900: A study of marine science*, Academic Press, London, 1971.

Dejean, P.-F.-M.-A., *Species général des Coléoptères de la collection de M. le comte Dejean*, 5 vols, Méquignon-Marvis, Paris, 1825–31.

Delano, J.A., *The Genealogy, History, and Alliances of the American House of Delano, 1621 to 1899*, New York, no imprint details, 1899.

[Demertzis-Bouboulis, P.,] Δεμερτζής-Μπούμπουλης, Φ., *Λασκαρίνα Μπουμπουλίνα*, Μουσείο Μπουμπουλίνα, Σπέτσες [Spetses], 2001.

Denon, D.V., *Voyage dans la basse et la haute Égypte pendant les campagnes du général Bonaparte*, 2 vols, P. Didot l'aîné, Paris, 1802.

Désert, G., *La Révolution française en Normandie, 1789–1800*, Editions Privat, Toulouse, 1989.

[Desgraz-Bory, F.-L.], *Paroles d'un négociant*, Cherbuliez, Paris/l'auteur, Marseille, 1834.

[Desgraz-Bory, F.-L.], *Mélanges–Économie sociale*, Hivert, Paris, 1836.

Desmond, R., *Dictionary of British and Irish Botanists and Horticulturalists including Plant Collectors and Botanical Artists*, Taylor & Francis, London, 1977.

Diamond, J., *Collapse: How societies choose to fail or succeed*, Viking, New York, 2005.

Dibie, P., *La passion du regard: Essai sur les sciences froides*, Metailié, Paris, 1998.

Dillon, P., *Narrative and Successful Result of a Voyage in the South Seas Performed by Order of the Government of British India, to Ascertain the Actual Fate of La Pérouse's Expedition. By the Chevalier Capt. P. Dillon*, 2 vols, Hurst, Chance, London, 1829.

Doak, W., *The Burning of the* Boyd: *A saga of culture clash*, Hodder and Stoughton, Auckland, 1984.

Dominique, A., *Le Choléra à Toulon: Étude historique, statistique et comparative des epidémies de 1835, 1849, 1854, 1865 et 1884*, A. Isnard, Toulon, 1885.

Doré, F., Larsonneur, C., Juignet, P., Pareyn, C., & Rioult, M., *Normandie* (*Guides géologiques régionaux*), Masson, Paris, 1977.

Douglas, B., & Ballard, C., *Foreign Bodies: Oceania and the science of race 1750–1840*, ANU E Press, Canberra, 2008.

Drapiez, P.-A.-J., *Notice sur l'Établissement géographique de Bruxelles*, Bruxelles, 1836 & 1846.

Duchêne, A., *La politique coloniale de la France: Le ministère des colonies depuis Richelieu*, Payot, Paris, 1928.

Dumaine, A., *Quelques oubliés de l'autre siècle*, Vélin d'Or, Paris, 1928.

Duméril, A.-M.-C., & Bibron, G., *Erpétologie générale ou histoire naturelle complète des reptiles*, 9 vols, Librairie Encyclopédique de Roret, Paris, 1834–54.

Duméril, A., & Duméril, A., *Muséum d'histoire naturelle de Paris: Catalogue méthodique de la collection des reptiles*, Gide et Baudry, Paris, 1851.

d'Urville, J.-S.-C. Dumont, *Voyage de la corvette* l'Astrolabe *exécuté par ordre du roi pendant les années 1826–1827–1828–1829 sous le commandement de M. J. Dumont d'Urville*:

première division, 'Histoire du voyage', 5 vols & Atlas historique, rédigée par J. Dumont d'Urville, J. Tastu, Paris, 1830–33;

deuxième division, 'Botanique', par A. Lesson & A. Richard, J. Tastu, Paris, 1832–34;

troisième division, 'Zoologie', 4 vols, rédigée par Quoy & Gaimard, J. Tastu, Paris, 1830–33;

quatrième division, 'Faune entomologique', rédigée par Latreille: première partie, Lepidoptères, par Boisduval, J. Tastu, Paris, 1832; deuxième partie, Coléoptères, par Boisduval, J. Tastu, Paris, 1835;

cinquième division, 'Hydrographie' Atlas & 'Observations nautiques, météorologiques, hydrographiques, et de physique', par J. Dumont d'Urville, Ministère de la Marine, Paris, 1833;

sixième division, 'Philologie', 2 vols, par J. Dumont d'Urville, Ministère de la Marine, Paris, 1833–34.

—— *Voyage pittoresque autour du monde: Résumé général des voyages de découvertes*, 2 vols, L. Tenré, Paris, 1834–35.

—— *The New Zealanders: A story of Austral lands*, translated by Carol Legge, Victoria University Press, 1992.

d'Urville, J.-S.-C. Dumont, [& Jacquinot, C.-H.] *Voyage au pôle sud et dans l'Océanie sur les corvettes* l'Astrolabe *et la Zélée, exécuté par ordre du roi pendant les années 1837–1838–1839–1840 sous le commandement de M. J. Dumont d'Urville*:

'Histoire du voyage', vols i–x, par J.S.C. Dumont d'Urville, Gide, Paris, 1841–46;

'Atlas pittoresque', vol. i [plates 1–96]–vol. ii [plates 97–192], Paris, Gide, 1846;

'Botanique', rédigée par Hombron, H., & Jacquinot, C.-H., vol. i., Plantes cellulaire, par C. Montagne, Gide, Paris, 1845;

'Botanique', rédigée par Hombron, H., & Jacquinot, C.-H., vol. ii., Plantes vasculaire, par J. Decaisne, Gide, Paris, 1853;

'Zoologie', rédigée par Hombron, H., & Jacquinot, C.-H., vol. i, De l'homme dans ses rapports avec la création, par Hombron, H., Gide, Paris, 1846;

'Zoologie', rédigée par Hombron, H., & Jacquinot, C.-H., vol. ii, Considérations générales sur l'anthropologie suivies d'observations sur les races humaines de l'Amérique méridionale et de l'Océanie, par H. Jacquinot, Gide, Paris, 1846;

'Zoologie', rédigée par Hombron, H., & Jacquinot, C.-H., vol. iii, Mammifères et oiseaux par Jacquinot, H., & Pucheran, J., Gide, Paris, 1853;

'Zoologie', rédigée par Hombron, H., & Jacquinot, C.-H., vol. iv, Description des insectes, par E. Blanchard, Gide, Paris, 1853;

'Zoologie', rédigée par Hombron, H., & Jacquinot, C.-H., vol. v, Description des mollusques, coquilles et zoophytes, par L. Rousseau, Gide, Paris, 1854;

'Atlas d'histoire naturelle, zoologie', [40 plates in 28 installments], Gide et J. Baudry, Paris, 1842–54;

'Atlas hydrographique', Dépôt-général de la marine, Paris, 1847;

'Atlas anthropologie', Gide et J. Baudry, Paris, 1842–47;

'Atlas géologie' [maps 1–4, plates 1–3 (Volcan, Île Bridgeman, Île Deception, Matauriki), Paleantologie, plates 4–9], Gide et J. Baudry, Paris, 1847;

'Atlas botanique' [Phanérogamie: Monocotyledones, plates 1–8; Dicotyledones, plates 1–31; Cryptogamie, plates 1–20; Cryptogames vasculaires, plates 1–5], Gide et J. Baudry, Paris, 1852;

'Physique', par MM. [C.-A.] Vincendon-Dumoulin et [A.-A.-E.] Coupvent-Desbois, Gide, Paris, 1842;

'Hydrographie', par [C.-A.] Vincendon-Dumoulin, vols i–ii, Gide, Paris, 1843–51;

'Géologie, minéralogie, géographie physique', [parts i & ii], par M.J.-[J.-F.] Grange, Gide, Paris 1848–54;

'Anthropologie', par [P.-M.-A.] Dumoutier, Gide, Paris, 1854.

Dunmore, J., *French Explorers in the Pacific*, 2 vols, Clarendon Press, Oxford, 1965–69.

———— *From Venus to Antarctica: The Life of Dumont d'Urville*, Exisle Publishing, Auckland, 2007.

Du Pasquier, J.-T., *Les baleiniers français au XIXe siècle: 1814–1868*, Editions Terre et Mer–4 Seigneurs, Grenoble, 1982.

Duperrey, L.-I. (ed.), *Voyage autour du monde: Exécuté par ordre du roi sur la corvette de sa majesté, La* Coquille, *pendant les années 1822, 1823, 1824 et 1825, sous le minstère de S.E.M. Le marquis de Clermont-Tonnerre, et publiée sous les auspices de son excellence M. le comte de Chabrol, ministre de la marine et des colonies*, Arthus Bertrand, Paris, 1826–1830:

'Partie Historique' [incomplete], par L.-I. Duperrey, 1825;

'Histoire du voyage, atlas', 1826;

'Zoologie, atlas', part i: Mammifères, oiseaux; part ii: Reptiles, poissons, mollusques, par Lesson; part iii: Crustacés, insectes, zoophytes, 1826[–31], [157 plates in 27 installments];

'Botanique, atlas', 2 vols, 1826;

'Hydrographie, atlas', 1826;

'Hydrographie', par L.-I. Duperrey, 1829;

'Hydrographie et physique', par L.-I. Duperrey, 1829;

'Botanique', rédigée par M.M. d'Urville, Bory de Saint-Vincent & Ad. Brongniart: Cryptogamie, par J.-B. Bory de Saint-Vincent, 1828; Phanérogamie, 2 vols [vol. ii, incomplete], par Ad. Brongniart, 1829;

'Zoologie', rédigée par R.-P. Lesson & P. Garnot: vol. i, part i, 1826[–29], [in 9 installments]; vol. i, part ii [in 7 installments]; vol. ii, part i: Reptiles, poissons, mollusques par R.-P. Lesson, 1830[–31], [in 3 installments]; vol. ii, part ii, première division: Crustacés, arachnides et insects, par F.-C. Guérin-Méneville, 1830[–38]; deuxième division: Zoophytes, par R.-P. Lesson, 1830[–38], [in 1 installment].

Dupont, M., *Dictionnaire historique des médecins dans et hors de la médecine*, Larousse, Paris, 1999.

Du Saussois, A., *Henri de France, le C[om]te de Paris et le peuple français*, l'auteur, Paris, 1884.

Duyker, E. (ed.), *The Discovery of Tasmania: Journal extracts from the expeditions of Abel Janszoon Tasman and Marc-Joseph Marion Dufresne, 1642 & 1772*, St David's Park Publishing/Tasmanian Government Printing Office, Hobart, 1992.

Duyker, E., *An Officer of the Blue: Marc-Joseph Marion Dufresne, South Sea explorer, 1724–1772*, Miegunyah/Melbourne University Press, Carlton, 1994.

—— *Nature's Argonaut: Daniel Solander 1733–1782, Naturalist and voyager with Cook and Banks*, Miegunyah/Melbourne University Press, Carlton, 1998.

—— (ed.), *Mirror of the Australian Navigation by Jacob Le Maire: A facsimile of the 'Spieghel der Australische Navigatie …' Being an account of the voyage of Jacob Le Maire and Willem Schouten 1615–1616 published in Amsterdam in 1622*, Hordern House for the Australian National Maritime Museum, Sydney, 1999.

—— *Citizen Labillardière: A naturalist's life in revolution and exploration (1755–1834)*, Miegunyah/Melbourne University Publishing, Carlton, 2003.

—— *François Péron: An impetuous life: Naturalist and voyager*, Miegunyah/Melbourne University Publishing, Carlton, 2006.

—— *Père Receveur: Franciscan, scientist and voyager with Lapérouse*, Dharawal Publications, Sydney, 2011.

Duyker, E., & Duyker, M. (eds & trans.), *Bruny d'Entrecasteaux: Voyage to Australia and the Pacific 1791–1793*, Miegunyah/Melbourne University Press, Carlton, 2001.

Dyson, S.L., *In Pursuit of Ancient Pasts: A history of classical archaeology in the nineteenth and twentieth centuries*, Yale University Press, New Haven, 2006.

Earl, G.W., *The Eastern Seas, or, Voyages and Adventures in the Indian Archipelago, in 1832–33–34, Comprising a Tour of the Island of Java – Visits to Borneo, the Malay Peninsula, Siam &c.; also An Account of the Present State of Singapore with Observations on the Commercial Resources of the Archipelago*, W.H. Allen and Co., London, 1837.

Emedy, H., *L'amiral Dumont d'Urville: Origines ancestrales et familiales*, Imprimerie-Librairie Ch. Corlet, Condé-sur-Noireau, 1963.

Estensen, M., *The Life of Matthew Flinders*, Allen and Unwin, Sydney, 2002.

Field, B., *Geographical Memoirs on New South Wales*, John Murray, London, 1825.

Fédoroff, I., & Roché, Y., *Au fil du Béal: De la source de la foux au Moulin de Tourris*, Autre temps, Marseille, 1999.

Ferguson, J., *Bibliography of Australia* (facsimile edition), 7 vols, National Library of Australia, Canberra, 1975–1986.

Fletcher, B.A., *Ralph Darling: A governor maligned*, Oxford University Press, Melbourne, 1984.

Forster, C., *France and Botany Bay: The lure of a penal colony*, Melbourne University Press, Carlton, 1996.

Forster, H. (ed.), *The Cruise of the 'Gipsy': The journal of John Wilson, surgeon on a whaling voyage to the Pacific Ocean, 1839–1843*, Ye Galleon Press, Fairfield, Wash., 1991.

Fortescue, W., *France and 1848: The end of monarchy*, Routledge, Milton Park, 2005.

Freycinet, L.-C. de Saulces de, *Voyage autour du monde: Entrepris par ordre du roi … exécuté sur les corvettes de S.M. l'Uranie et la Physicienne, pendant les années 1817, 1818, 1819 et 1820 … *, 8 vols, Chez Pillet Aîné, Paris, 1824–44.

Friedrich, W., *Fire in the Sea: The Santorini volcano: Natural history and the legend of Atlantis*, translated by Alexander R. McBirney, Cambridge University Press, Cambridge, 2000.

Friendly, A., *Beaufort of the Admiralty: The life of Sir Francis Beaufort 1774–1857*, Random House, New York, 1977.

Galipaud, J.-C., de Biran, A., Beaumont, E., Boré, J.-M., Le Breüs, A., & Aberlenc, H.-P., *Naufragés à Vanikoro, les rescapés de l'expédition Lapérouse à Païou*, IRD, Nouméa, 2006.

Garnot, P., *Quelques considérations sur les Nègres en général, du Nègre de la Nouvelle-Hollande en particulier* [extrait de *Dictionnaire pittoresque d'Histoire naturelle*], Imprimerie de Cosson, Paris, *ca.* 1837.

Garrett, J., *To Live Among the Stars: Christian origins in Oceania*, WCC [World Council of Churches] Publications, Geneva, 1982.

Gay, C., *Historia física y política de Chile segun documentos adquiridos en esta republica durante doce años de residencia en ella y publicada bajo los auspicios del supremo gobierno*, 28 vols, En casa del autor, Paris, 1844–71.

Gillispie, C.C., *Science and Polity in France and the End of the Old Regime*, Princeton University Press, Princeton, 1980.

Ginouvier, J.-F.-T., *Le Botany-Bey [sic] français, ou colonisation des condamnés aux peines afflictives et infamantes et des forçats libérés*, Paris, Béchet, 1826.

Girard, C. (ed.), *Lettres des missionnaires maristes en Océanie, 1836–1854: Anthologie de la correspondance reçue par Jean-Claude Colin, fondateur de la Société de Marie pendant son généralat*, Karthala, Paris, *ca.* 2008.

Giustino, D. de, *Conquest of Mind: Phrenology and Victorian social thought*, Croom Helm, London, 1975.

Goeler von Ravensburg, F., *Die Venus von Milo: Eine kunstgeschichtliche monographie*, C. Winter, Heidelberg, 1879.

Goldschmidt, A., *Biographical Dictionary of Modern Egypt*, Lynne Rienner, Boulder (Colorado), 2000.

Gontaut-Biron, M.-J.-L. de Montaut de Navaille, *Mémoires de madame la duchesse de Gontaut: Gouvernante des enfants de France pendant la restauration, 1773–1836*, sixème edition, Plon Nourrit, Paris, 1909.

Gray, G.R., *The Genera of Birds: Comprising their generic characters, a notice of the habits of each genus and an extensive list of species referred to their several genera*, 3 vols, Longman, Brown, Green and Longmans, London, 1844–49.

Grey, G., *Polynesian Mythology and Ancient Traditional History of the New Zealanders: As furnished by their priests and chiefs*, G. Routledge & Sons, London, 1854.

Gray, J.E., *Catalogue of the Specimens of Lizards in the Collection of the British Museum*, The Trustees of the British Museum, London, 1845.

Greer, D., *The Incidence of the Terror during the French Revolution: A statistical interpretation*, Harvard University Press, Cambridge, 1935.

Guérin, Maître, *Notice des livres français, anglais, arabes, persans, sanscrits, chinois, etc., etc., composant la bibliothèque de feu M. Le contre-amiral Dumont-d'Urville, dont la vente aura lieu les jeudi 5, vendredi 6 et samedi 7 janvier 1843 à six heures du soir, rue des Bons-Enfants, no. 30,* salle du premier, par le ministère de M[aîtr]e Guérin, commissaire-priseur, rue Chabanais, no. 7, H. Labitte, Paris, 1842.

Guillon, J., *Dumont d'Urville: 1790–1842*, Editions France-Empire, Paris, 1986.

Gunn, M., & Codd, L.E.W., *Botanical Exploration of Southern Africa: An illustrated history of early botanical literature on the Cape flora: Biographical accounts of the leading plant collectors and their activities in Southern Africa from the days of the East India Company until modern times*, Published for the Botanical Research Institute by A.A. Balkema, Cape Town, 1981.

Gvosdev, N.K., *Imperial Policies and Perspectives Towards Georgia, 1760–1819*, St. Martin's Press, New York, 2000.

Hahn, R., *The Anatomy of a Scientific Institution: The Paris Academy of Sciences, 1666–1803*, University of California Press, Berkeley, 1971.

Haussez, C., Le Mercher de Longpré, baron d', *Mémoires du baron d'Haussez, dernier ministre de la marine sous la Restauration*, 2 vols, Calmann Lévy, Paris, 1897.

Havard, W.L. & Dowd, B.T., *Historic Glenroy, Cox's River, Hartley NSW*, Blaxland Shire Council, ca.1937.

Headland, R., *Chronological List of Antarctic Expeditions and Related Historical Events*, Cambridge University Press, Cambridge, 1989.

Heidler, D.S., *Encyclopedia of the War of 1812*, Naval Institute Press, Annapolis, 2004.

Hempel, S., *The Strange Case of the Broad Street Pump: John Snow and the mystery of cholera*, California University Press, Berkeley, 2007.

Henderson, C.C. (ed.), *The Journal of Thomas Williams Missionary in Fiji, 1840–1853*, 2 vols, Angus & Robertson, Sydney, 1931.

Henige, D.P., *Colonial Governors from the Fifteenth Century to the Present*, University of Wisconsin Press, 1970.

Higgins, M.D. & Higgins, R., *A Geological Companion to Greece and the Aegean*, Cornell University Press, Ithaca (New York), 1996.

Hill, K., & Osborne, R., *Cycads of Australia*, Kangaroo Press, Sydney, 2001.

Hillairet, J., *Dictionnaire historique des rues de Paris*, 2 vols. Les Editions de Minuit, Paris, sixth edition, 1963.

Hippeau, C., *Dictionnaire topographique comprenant les noms de lieux anciens et modernes*, Imprimerie nationale, Paris, 1883.

Hohnen, P.D., *Geology of New Ireland, Papua New Guinea*, Australian Government Publishing Service, Canberra, 1978.

Hombron, J.-B., *Réflexions sur la fièvre jaune, thèse présentée et soutenue à la faculté de médecine de Paris, le 14 avril 1826*, Imprimerie de Didot le jeune, Paris, 1826.

—— *Aventures les plus curieuses des voyageurs: Coup d'œil autour du monde, d'après les relations anciennes et modernes et des documents recueillis sur les lieux*, 2 vols, Belin-Leprieur et Morizot, Paris, 1847.

Honigman, J., *The Development of Anthropological Ideas*, Dorsey Press, Homewood, 1976.

Huet, L., *L'histoire de Condé-sur-Noireau: Ses seigneurs, son industrie*, F. Le Blanc-Hardel, Caen, 1883.

Huet de Froberville, L., *Île de France: Le Combat de Grand-Port et la fin de l'occupation française*, Standard, Île Maurice, 1910.

Humbert, J.-M. (ed.), *Napoléon aux Invalides: 1840, le retour des cendres*, Éditions de l'Albaron, Thonon-les-Bains, *ca.* 1990.

Hunt, S., Terry, M., & Hunt, N., *Lure of the Southern Seas: The voyages of Dumont d'Urville 1826–1840*, Historic Houses Trust of New South Wales, Sydney, 2002.

Institut de France, *Index biographique de l'Académie des sciences*, Gauthier Villars, Paris, 1979.

Jacobs, T.J., *Scenes, Incidents, and Adventures in the Pacific Ocean, or, The Islands of the Australasian Seas, During the Cruise of the Clipper* Margaret Oakley *under Capt. Benjamin Morrell*, Harper & Brothers, New York, 1844.

Jacquemin, S., *Objets des Mers du Sud: Histoire des collections océaniennes dans les musées et établissements parisiens, XVIIIème–XXème siècles*, École du Louvre, Paris, 1991.

Jacquemont, V., *Correspondance de V. Jacquemont, avec sa famille et plusieurs de ses amis pendant son voyage dans l'Inde*, 2 vols, Garnier frères, Paris, 1861.

Javault, R., Joubert, P. & Lagarlière, R. de, *L'Astrolabe (ex: la Coquille), corvette de 380 tonneaux du Lieutenant de vaisseau Duperrey et du capitaine de vaisseau Dumont d'Urville, 1811–1851, monographie comprenant 1 notice descriptive, 1 plan à l'échelle de 1/100e , 2 phototypies, modèle No. 17 MG 14 exposé au Musée de la marine*, Association des amis des musées de la marine, Paris, 1962.

Jones, I., & Jones, J., *Oceanography in the Days of Sail*, Hale & Iremonger, Sydney, 1992.

Joubert, Fr. [Just-Jean-Étienne Roy], *Dumont-d'Urville*, A. Mame et Fils, Tours, 1871.

Jussieu, A.L. de, *Genera plantarum secundum ordines naturales disposita, juxta methodum in Horto Regio Parisiensi exaratum, anno M.DCC.LXXIV*, Viduam Herissant et Theophilum Barrois, Paris, 1789.

Kauffmann, J.-P., *The Black Room at Longwood: Napoleon's exile at Saint Helena*, Four Walls Eight Windows, New York, 1999.

Kendall, T., *A Korao no New Zealand; or, the New Zealander's First Book; Being an Attempt to compose some Lessons for the Instruction of the Natives*, Printed by G. Howe, Sydney, 1815.

Keys, L., *The Life and Times of Bishop Pompallier*, The Pegasus Press, Christchurch, 1957.

Kriezis, G.-D., *Histoire de l'Île d'Hydra*, H. Chassefière fils, Marseille, 1888.

Labillardière, J.-J. Houtou de, *Relation du voyage à la recherche de La Pérouse fait par ordre de l'assemblée constituante, pendant les années 1791, 1792, et pendant la 1ère. et la 2e. année de la République Françoise*, 2 vols & atlas, H.J. Jansen, Paris, an VIII [1800].

Labillardière, J.-J. Houtou de, *NovæHollandiæ plantarum specimen*, 2 vols, Dominae Huzard, Paris, 1804–06.

—— *Sertum austro-caledonicum*, Dominae Huzard, Paris, 1824–25.

Lackany, R., *Cerisy Bey, fondateur de l'arsenal d'Alexandrie et constructeur de la flotte égyptienne*, Alexandrie, 1989.

Lacouture, J., *Champollion: Une vie de lumières*, France Loisirs, Paris, 1988.

Lafontaine, J.-P., *Mémoire de mon canton*, Médiathèque municipale de Condé-sur-Noireau, 1992.

Lamarck, J.-B.-P.-A. de Monet de, *Encyclopédie méthodique: Botanique*, 8 vols, Pancoucke, Paris, 1783–1808.

—— *Philosophie zoologique ou exposition des considérations relatives à l'histoire naturelle des animaux*, Dentu, Paris, 1809.

Lapie, M., *Atlas complet du précis de la géographie universelle de M. Malte-Brun*, Chez Francois Buisson, Paris, 1812.

Laplace, C.P.T., *Campagne de circumnavigation de la frégate l'Artémise, pendant les années 1837, 1838, 1839 et 1840, sous le commandement de M. Laplace*, 6 vols, Arthus Bertrand, Paris, 1841–54.

Larson, P.M., *Ocean of Letters: Language and creolization in an Indian Ocean diaspora*, Cambridge University Press, Cambridge, 2009.

Laskaris, N.G., *Monuments funéraires paléochrétiens (et byzantins) de Grèce*, Basilopoulos, Athènes, 2000.

Laval, H., *Mémoires pour servir à l'histoire de Mangareva: Ére chrétienne, 1834–1871*, Musée de l'homme, Paris, 1968.

Lavergne, M., *Choléra-Morbus en Provence*, Aug. Hurel, Toulon, 1836.

Le Brun, I., *Biographie du contre-amiral Dumont d'Urville* [extrait de l'*Annuaire Normand*], Imprimérie de H. Le Roy, Caen, 1843.

Le Gallo, Y. (ed.), *Histoire de Brest,* privately published, Toulouse, 1976.

Le Guillou, E., *Voyage autour du monde de l'Astrolabe et de la Zélée sous les ordres du contre-admiral Dumont-D'Urville, pendant les années 1837, 38, 39 et 40 par Élie Le Guillou … mis en ordre par J. Arago*, Berquet et Petion, Paris, 1842.

Le Roy, C., *Louis de Frotté: Dernier général des Chouans*, Editions H & D, Milon-La Chapelle, 2006.

Lee, I., *Early Explorers in Australia: From the Log-books and Journals, Including the Diary of Allan Cunningham, Botanist, from March 1, 1817, to November 19, 1818*, Methuen, London, 1925.

Lee, J. '*I have Named it the Bay of Islands …*', Hodder and Stoughton, Auckland, 1983.

Lee, S., & Kendall, T., *A Grammar and Vocabulary of the Language of New Zealand*, The Church Missionary Society, London, 1820.

Lefaivre, F., *Condé occupé, Condé détruit, Condé reconstruit 1940–1963*, Éditions Charles-Corlet, Condé-sur-Noireau, 2004.

Lepage, A., *Les cafés artistiques et littéraires de Paris*, Martin-Boursin, Paris, 1882.

Lesson, R.P., *Voyage autour du monde entrepris par ordre du gouvernement sur la corvette la Coquille*, 2 vols, P. Pourrat frères, Paris, 1838.

—— *Notice historique sur l'amiral Dumont d'Urville: Mémoire envoyé au concours ouvert par l'Académie de Caen en 1844*, Imprimerie de Henry Loustau, Rochefort, 1846.

Leung, C., *Etienne Fourmont, 1683–1745: Oriental and Chinese languages in eighteenth-century France*, Leuven University Press, Leuven, 2002.

Levot, P., *Histoire de la ville et port du Brest*, 3 vols, privately published, Brest, 1864–66.

Lingenfelter, R.E., *Presses of the Pacific Islands, 1817–1867: A history of the first half century of printing in the Pacific Islands,* Plantin Press, Los Angeles, 1967.

Lochouarn, D. (ed.), *Histoire d'un coin de Toulon: Le Quartier Armand Barbès*, Imprimerie du Sud-Est, Toulon, 2003.

Loureiro, J. de, *Flora cochinchinensis: Sistens plantas in regno Cochinchina nascentes. Quibus accedunt aliæ observatæ in Sinensi imperio, Africa Orientali, Indiæque locis variis. Omnes dispositæ secundum systema sexuale Linnæanum Labore*, 2 vols, typis, et expensis academicis [Acadamia real das Sciencias], Ulyssipone [Lisbon], 1790.

Lucas-Dubreton, J., *Le comte d'Artois, Charles X: Le prince, l'émigré, le roi*, Hachette, Paris, 1927.

Lyell, C., *The Geological Evidences of the Antiquity of Man*, John Murray, London, 1863.

Lyons, W.E., *Matters of the Mind*, Routledge, New York, 2001.

McIntyre, D., *Comets in Old Cape Records*, Cape Times Limited, Cape Town, 1949.

Macknight, C.C., *The Voyage to Marege: Macassan trepangers in Northern Australia*, Melbourne University Press, Carlton, 1976.

McLaren, F.B., *The Auckland Islands: Their eventful history*, A.H. & A.W. Reed, Wellington, 1948.

McLean, Martin, *The Garden of New Zealand: A history of the Waitangi Treaty House and grounds from pre-European times to the present*, Department of Conservation, Wellington, 1990.

McLean, Mervyn, *Maori Music*, Auckland University Press, Auckland, 1996.

McMinn, W.G., *Allan Cunningham: Botanist and explorer*, Melbourne University Press, Carlton, 1970.

McNab, R. (ed.), *Historical Records of New Zealand*, 2 vols, Government Printer, Wellington, 1908–14.

McNab, R., *Murihiku: A history of the South Island of New Zealand and the islands adjacent and lying to the South, from 1642 to 1835*, Whitcomb & Tombs, Wellington, 1909.

Manvelichvili, A., *Histoire de la Géorgie*, Nouvelles Éditions de la Toison d'or, Paris, [*ca.* 1951].

Marcellus, [M.-L.-J.-A.-C. Demartin du Tirac] comte de, *Souvenirs de l'Orient*, 2 vols, Debécourt, Paris, 1839.

—— *Les Grecs anciens et modernes*, Michel Levy frères, Paris, 1861.

Maréchal, D. & Bouvet, S., *Dumont d'Urville: 'Les tours du monde d'un Normand'*, Les cahiers des Archives départementales du Calvados, no. 21, Caen, 2002.

Marinescu, F., *Étude généalogique sur la famille Mourouzi*, Centre de recherches neo-helléniques de la fondation nationale de la recherche scientifique [Collection: Tetradia ergasias, no. 12], Athens, 1987.

Mark, A., & Hœdemaekers, P. (eds), *P. Marie-Joseph Coudrin: Correspondance*, 8 vols, Maison Générale, Congrégation des Sacrés-Cœurs de Jésus et de Marie, Rome, 1994–2000.

Marmont, A.-F.-L. Viesse de, *Mémoires du Maréchal Marmont, duc de Raguse, de 1792 à 1841*, 9 vols, Perrotin, Paris, 1857.

Marmottans, A. *Art et commerce toulonnais (1830–1870): 123 factures à en-tête classées et commentées*, Éditions Valettoises, La Valtette-du-Var, 2004.

Marshall-Cornwall, J., *History of the Geographical Club*, The Geographical Club, London, 1976.

Martin, J., *An Account of the Natives of the Tonga Islands in the South Pacific Ocean Compiled and Arranged from the Extensive Communications of Mr William Mariner, Several Years Resident in Those Islands*, 2 vols, John Murray, London, 1818.

May, J. (ed.), *The Greenpeace Book of Antarctica: A new view of the seventh continent*, Child & Associates, Frenchs Forest (NSW), 1988.

Méhaud, C., & Richard, H. (eds), *Dumont d'Urville en Antarctique: Journal de bord de Joseph Seureau, quartier-maître de la Zélée (1837–1840)*, Publisud, Paris, 1995.

Mellot, J.-D., Queval, E., & Monaque, A., *Répertoire d'imprimeurs-libraires (vers 1500–vers 1810)*, Bibliothèque nationale de France, Paris, 2004.

Michaud, L.-G. (ed.), *Biographie universelle ancienne et moderne, ou Histoire par ordre alphabétique de la vie publique et privée de tous les hommes qui se sont fait remarquer par leurs écrits, leurs actions, leurs talents, leurs vertus ou leurs crimes,* ouvrage entièrement neuf, rédigé par une société de gens de lettres et de savants, 85 vols, Michaud frères, Paris, 1811–62.

Molhuysen, P.C., & Blok, P.J. (eds), *Nieuw Nederlands Biografisch Woordenboek*, 10 vols, A.W. Sijthoff, Leiden, 1911–37.

Montagne, C., *Prodromus generum specierumque phycearum novarum, in itinere ad polum antarcticum Regis Ludovici Philippi jussu ab illustri Dumont d'Urville peracto collectarum, notis diagnosticis tantum huc evulgatarum, descriptionibus verò fusioribus nec no iconibus analyticis jam jamque illustrandarum*, Gide editorem, Paris, 1842.

Montbel, G.I. de, *1787–1831: Souvenirs du comte de Montbel, ministre de Charles X*, publiés par son petit-fils Guy de Montbel, Plon Nourrit, Paris, second edition, 1913.

Montémont, A., *À M. L'Amiral Dumont d'Urville: Sur sa nouvelle expédition dans le grand océan: Ode, lue au Caveau, le 5 mars 1841 en présence de M. L'Amiral, invité au banquet*, [Paris, ca. 1841].

Morgan, W.N., *Prehistoric Architecture in Micronesia*, University of Texas Press, Austin, 1989.

Morrell, B., *A Narrative of Four Voyages to the South Sea*, J. & J. Harper, New York, 1832.

Moyal, A., *Platypus*, Allen & Unwin, Crows Nest, 2001.

Moyle, R. (ed.), *The Samoan Journals of John Williams, 1830 and 1832*, Australian National University Press, Canberra, 1984.

Mulvaney, D.J., *The Prehistory of Australia*, Thames and Hudson, London, 1969.

Musset, L., *Le Lycée Malherbe: Notice historique publiée à l'occasion du cent-cinquantenaire*, Imprimerie Caron et Cie, Caen, 1954.

Nadin, M., *Histoire de Condé-sur-Noireau: Jardins ouverts – Jardins secrets: Des origines à l'an 2000*, vol. i, Éditions Ch. Corlet, Condé-sur-Noireau, 1998.

Navel, H., *Monographie de Feuguerolles-sur-Orne (Calvados), des origines à la Révolution*, Caen, Jouan et Bigot, 1931.

Nettement, A., *Mémoires historiques de S.A.R. Madame, duchesse de Berry, depuis sa naissance jusqu'à ce jour*, 3 vols, Allardin, Paris, 1837.

Nordenskjöld, O., *Antarctica or Two Years Amongst the Ice of the South Pole*, Hurst & Blackett, London, 1905.

Norvins, J. Marquet de Montbreton de, *Translation des cendres de Napoléon*, Furne, Paris, 1840.

Nussac, L. de, *Les débuts d'un savant naturaliste, le prince de l'entomologie, Pierre-André Latreille à Brive de 1762 à 1798*, G. Steinheil, Paris, 1906.

O'Byrne, W.E., *A Naval Biographical Dictionary*, John Murray, London, 1849.

Oliver, W.R.B., *New Zealand Birds*, Fine Arts (N.Z.) Ltd., Wellington, 1930.

Olivier, G.A., *Voyage dans l'Empire Othoman, l'Égypte et la Perse, fait par ordre du gouvernement pendant les six premières années de la République*, 3 vols, H. Agasse, Paris, 1801–07.

Ollivier, I., (transcription & translation), *Extracts from New Zealand Journals Written on Ships Under the Command of d'Entrecasteaux and Duperrey: 1793 and 1824* [Early Eyewitness

Accounts of Maori Life: 3 and 4], Alexander Turnbull Library Endowment Trust with Indosuez New Zealand Limited, Wellington, 1986.

O'Reilly, P., *Tahitiens: Supplément: Répertoire bio-bibliographique de la Polynésie Française*, Musée de L'homme, Paris, 1966.

O'Reilly, P., & Teissier, R., *Tahitiens: Répertoire bio-bibliographique de la Polynésie française,* Musée de l'homme, Paris, 1962.

Outram, D., *The Letters of Georges Cuvier: A summary calendar of manuscript and printed materials preserved in Europe, the United States of America, and Australasia*, British Society for the History of Science, Chalfont St. Giles, 1980.

Owen, W.F.W., *Narrative of voyages to explore the shores of Africa, Arabia and Madagascar performed in H.M. ships* Leven *and* Barracouta *under the direction of W.F.W. Owen by command of the Lords Commissioners of the Admiralty*, 2 vols, Richard Bentley, London, 1833.

Patry, R., *Une ville de Province: Caen pendant la Révolution de 1789*, Éditions Charles Corlet, Condé-sur-Noireau, 1983.

Peat, N., *Coasting: The sea lion and the lark*, Longacre, Dunedin, 2001.

Péron, F., *Voyage de découvertes aux Terres australes, exécuté par ordre de sa Majesté, l'Empereur et Roi, sur les corvettes le* Géographe*, le* Naturaliste *et la goëlette le* Casuarina*, pendant les années 1800, 1801, 1802, 1803 et 1804*, 3 vols and atlas, L'Imprimerie Impériale, Paris, 1807–17.

[Phillip, A.,] *The Voyage of Governor Phillip to Botany Bay*, John Stockdale, London, 1789.

Pinard, C., *Relation exacte de l'affreuse catastrophe du 8 mai !!!, chemin de fer de Versailles (rive gauche) suivie de détails circonstanciés sur l'incendie de Hambourg*, Berquet-Pétion, Pinard, 1842.

Platts, U., *The Lively Capital: Auckland 1840–1865*, Avon, Christchurch, 1971.

Poore, B.P., *The Rise and Fall of Louis-Philippe, Ex-King of the French*, W.D. Tricknor & Co., Boston, 1848.

Poupin, T., *Caractères phrénologiques et physiognomoniques des contemporains les plus célèbres selon les systèmes de Gall, Spurzheim, Lavater, etc. avec des remarques biblio-graphiques, historiques, physiologiques et littéraires,* Germer Baillière, Paris, 1837.

Prévost, M., Roman d'Amat, J.-C., Tribout de Morembert, H. (eds), *Dictionnnaire de biographie française*, 19 vols, Librairie Letouzay, Paris, 1933–97.

Price, A.G., *The Winning of Australian Antarctica: Mawson's B.A.N.Z.A.R.E. voyages 1929–31 based on the Mawson papers*, Angus & Robertson, Sydney, 1962.

Ramsden, E., *Busby of Waitangi: H.M.'s resident at New Zealand, 1833–40*, A.H. and A.W. Reed, Wellington, 1942.

Reade, J. (ed.), *The Indian Ocean in Antiquity*, Kegan Paul, London, 1996.

Reinach, S., *Amalthée: Mélanges d'archéologie et d'histoire*, 2 vols, Librairie Ernst Leroux, Paris, 1930–31.

Richards, R., *Tahiti and the Society Islands Index to Ships 1800–1852*, Pacific Manuscripts Bureau, Research School of Pacific & Asian Studies, Australian National University, Canberra, 2008.

[Rimsky-Korsakov, N.A], Римский-Корсаков, Н.А., *Летопись моей музыкальной жизни*, С-Петербург [St Petersburg], 1909.

Rivière, M.S. (ed. & trans.), *A Woman of Courage: The journal of Rose de Freycinet on her voyage around the world*, National Library of Australia, Canberra, 1996.

———— *Discovery of the Brisbane River, 1823, Oxley, Uniacke and Pamphlet: 175 years in retrospect*, Royal Historical Society of Queensland, Brisbane, 1998.

———— (ed. & trans.), *The Governor's Noble Guest: Hyacinthe de Bougainville's account of Port Jackson, 1825*, Miegunyah/Melbourne University Press, Carlton, 1999.

———— 'No Man is an Island': *The Irish presence in Isle de France/Mauritius*, Éditions de l'Océan Indien, Rose Hill, 2008.

Rivière, M.S. & Einam, T.H. (eds), *Any Port in a Storm: From Provence to Australia: Rolland's journal of the voyage of* La Coquille *(1822–1825)*, James Cook University of North Queensland, Townsville, 1993.

Robert, A., Bourloton, E. & Cougny, G., *Dictionnaire des parlementaires français: Depuis le 1er mai 1789 jusqu'au 1er mai 1889*, 5 vols, Bourloton, Paris, 1889–91.

Robillard de Beaurepaire, E. & Carbonnier, P., *Caen illustré: Son histoire, ses monuments*, F. Leblanc-Hardel, Caen, 1896 [facsimile edition], Bruxelles, 1977.

Roche, J.-M., *Dictionnaire des bâtiments de la flotte de guerre française de Colbert à nos jours*, 2 vols, privately published, Toulon, 2005.

Rogers, R.F., *Destiny's Landfall: A history of Guam*, University of Hawaii Press, Honolulu, 1995.

Rose, H.J., *A New General Biographical Dictionary*, 12 vols, T. Fellowes, London, 1857.

Rosenman, H. (ed. & trans.), *An Account in Two Volumes of Two Voyages to the South Seas by Captain (later Rear-Admiral) Jules S.C. Dumont D'Urville of the French Navy to Australia, New Zealand, Oceania 1826–1829 in the Corvette* Astrolabe *and to the Straits of Magellan, Chile, Oceania, South East Asia, Australia, Antarctica, New Zealand and Torres Strait 1837–1840 in the Corvettes* Astrolabe *and* Zélée, 2 vols, Melbourne University Press, Carlton, 1987.

Ross, J.C., *A Voyage of Discovery and Research in the Southern and Antarctic Regions in the Years 1839–43*, 2 vols, John Murray, London, 1847.

Rossel, E.P.E. de, *Rapport sur la navigation de* l'Astrolabe *commandé par M. Dumont d'Urville, capitaine de vaisseau lu à l'Académie royale des sciences, dans la séance du 17 août 1829*, J. Tastu, Paris, 1829.

Rouillard, G., & Guého, J., *Le Jardin des Pamplemousses 1729–1979: Histoire et botanique*, General Printing and Stationery, Les Pailles, 1983.

Rozet, L., *Chronique de juillet 1830*, T. Barrois et B. Duprat, Paris, 1832.

Rumphius, G.G., *Herbarium Amboinense: Plurimas complectens arbores, fructices, herbas, plantas terrestres, & aquaticas, quae in Amboina, et adjacentibus reperiuntur insulis …*, 6 vols, Meinardum Uytwerf, Amstelaedami [Amsterdam], 1741–55.

Sacks, O., *The Island of the Colourblind and Cycad Island*, Picador, London, 1996.

Saint-Albin, A. de, *Histoire d'Henri V*, Palmé, Paris, 1871.

Salvy, L.-T., *Clément Salvy, capitaine de vaisseau*, Imprimérie d'Eugène Aurel, Toulon, 1864.

Sarrut, G. & Saint-Edme, B., *Biographie des hommes du jour*, 7 vols, H. Krabbe, Paris, 1835–43.

Service hydrographique et océanographique de la marine, *De l'Île Hélène au rocher du Débarquement: Archipel de Pointe Géologie: Océan Antarctique–Terre Adélie* [1:20,000 map], SHOM, Brest, 2002.

[Simopoulou, K.] Σιμοπουλου, K., *Ξενοι Ταξιδιωτες Στην Ελλαδα*, 4 vols, Εκδόσεις ΣΤΑΧΥ [Editions STAHI], Αθήνα [Athens], 1970–75.

Sharp, A., *The Discovery of the Pacific Islands*, Clarendon Press, Oxford, 1960.

—— *The Voyages of Abel Janszoon Tasman*, Oxford University Press, London, 1968.

—— *Duperrey's Visit to New Zealand*, Alexander Turnbull Library, Wellington, 1971.

Shaw, G., *The Naturalist's Miscellany: Or, coloured figures of natural objects; Drawn and described immediately from nature*, 24 vols, Nodder & Company, London, 1789–1813.

Solé, R., *Le grand voyage de l'obélisque*, Éditions du Seuil, Paris, 2004.

Solomon, W.E., *Saul Solomon: 'The member for Cape Town'*, Oxford University Press, Cape Town, 1948.

Soudry du Kerven, A., *Dumont d'Urville pages intimes*, Téqui, Paris, MDCCCLXLIII [*sic*, 1893].

Spillet, P.G., *Forsaken Settlement: An illustrated history of Victoria, Port Essington, North Australia 1838–1849*, Landsdowne, Melbourne, 1972.

Stafleu, F.A., & Cowan, R.S., *Taxonomic Literature: A selective guide to botanical publications and collections with dates, commentaries and types*, 7 vols, Bohn, Scheltema & Holkema, Utrecht/Antwerp, 1976–88.

Statham, P., *The Origins of Australia's Capital Cities*, Cambridge University Press, Melbourne, 1990.

Staum, M.S., *Labeling People: French scholars on society, race and empire 1815–1848*, McGill-Queen's University Press, Montreal & Kingston, 2003.

Staunton, G., *An Authentic Account of an Embassy from the King of Great Britain to the Emperor of China: Including cursory observations made, and, information obtained in travelling through that ancient empire, and a small part of Chinese Tartary*, G. Nicol, London, 1797.

Steibing, W.H., *Uncovering the Past: A history of archaeology*, Oxford University Press, Oxford, 1994.

Stuart, G.A., & Smith, F.P., *Chinese Materia Medica: Vegetable kingdom*, American Presbyterian Mission Press, Shanghai, 1911.

Sweetman, J., *The Military Establishment and Penal Settlement at King George Sound (Frederickstown), 25th December 1826–19th March 1831*, Hesperian Press, Carlisle, W.A., 1989.

Taillemite, E., *Dictionnaire des marins français*, Éditions Maritimes et d'Outre-Mer, Paris, 1982.

Telfair, C., *Some Account of the State of Slavery at Mauritius: Since the British Occupation in 1810; in refutation of anonymous charges promulgated against government and that colony*, James Ridgway, London, 1830.

Théodoropoulos, T., *L'invention de la Vénus de Milo*, traduit du grec par Michel Grodent, Sabine Wespieser, Paris, 2008.

Toulon Mémoire, *Le nom des rues*, vol. iv: Le Pont du Las, Service culture et patrimoine, Toulon, 2000.

Toussaint, A. (ed.), *Les Missions d'Adrien d'Epinay (1830–1834)*, Société de l'histoire de l'Île Maurice/General Printing & Stationery Cy., Port Louis, 1946.

Tremewan, P., *French Akaroa: An attempt to colonise southern New Zealand*, Canterbury University Press, Christchurch, 2010.

Tulard, J., Fayard, J-F., & Fierro, A., *Histoire et dictionnaire de la Révolution française 1789—1799*, Robert Laffont, Paris, 1987.

Turnbull, D., *The French Revolution of 1830; The events which produced it, and the scenes by which it was accompanied*, Henry Colburn and Richard Bentley, London, 1830.

Turner, H. G., *A History of the Colony of Victoria: From its Discovery to its Absorption into the Commonwealth of Australia*, 2 vols, Longmans, Green and Co., 1904.

[Vella, G.], *Geschichte der Araber in Sicilien und Siciliens unter der Herrschaft der Araber*, 4 vols, Aus dem Italiänischen, Mit Anmerkungen und Zusäzen von Philipp Wilhelm Gottlieb Hausleutner, Nicolovius, Königsberg, 1791–92.

Vasserot, P., & Bellanger, J.-H., *Atlas général des quarante-huit quartiers de la Ville de Paris*, Ph. Vasserot et J.-H. Bellanger, Paris, [1827–1836].

Vergniol, C., *Dumont d'Urville*, La Renaissance du livre, Paris, 1931.

Villalobos, S., *A Short History of Chile*, Editorial Universitaria, Santiago, 1996.

Vincendon-Dumoulin, C.-D., & Desgraz, C., *Îles Marquises ou Nouka-Hiva: Histoire, géographie, mœurs et considérations générales, d'après les relations des navigateurs et les documents recueillis sur les lieux*, A. Bertrand, Paris, 1843.

——— *Îles Taïti: Equisse historique et géographique, précédée de considérations générales sur la colonisation française dans l'Océanie*, A. Bertrand, Paris, 1844.

Wallis, H. (ed.), *Carteret's Voyage Round the World 1766–1769*, 2 vols, Hakluyt Society, Cambridge, 1965.

[Wāng, Á.] 汪昂, 增訂本草備要, 林喜兵衛, 享保戊申, 京都 [Hayashi Kihei, Kyoho Boshin, Kyoto (1728)].

Watson, S.J., *Carnot*, The Bodley Head, London, 1954.

Weider, B., & Forshufvud, S., *Assassination at St. Helena: The poisoning of Napoleon Bonaparte*, Mitchell Press, Vancouver, 1978.

Wilkes, C., *Narrative of the United States Exploring Expedition During the Years 1838, 1839, 1840, 1841, 1842*, 5 vols, George P. Putnam, New York, 1851.

Williams, J., *A Narrative of Missionary Enterprises in the South Seas With Remarks Upon the Natural History of the Islands, Origin, Languages and Usages of the Inhabitants*, J. Snow, London, 1837.

Wilson, E., *The Spiritual History of Ice: Romanticism, science and the imagination*, Palgrave Macmillan, New York, 2003.

Woelmont de Brumagne, H. de, *Notices généalogiques*, 9 vols, Champion, Paris, 1923–35.

Wright, O. (ed. & trans.), *New Zealand 1826–1827, from the French of Dumont d'Urville: An English translation of the voyage of the* Astrolabe *in New Zealand waters with an introductory essay by Olive Wright*, printed by the Wingfield Press for Olive Wright, Wellington, 1950.

——— *The Voyage of the* Astrolabe*–1840: An English rendering of the journals of Dumont d'Urville and his officers of their visit to New Zealand in 1840, together with some account of Bishop Pompallier and Charles Baron de Thierry*, A.H. & A.W. Reed, Wellington, 1955.

[Xiè, Z.] 谢宗, et al., 汉拉英对照中药材正名词典, 北京科学技术出版社, 北京 [Beijing science and technology press, Beijing], 2004.

Yarwood, S., *Samuel Marsden: The great survivor*, Melbourne University Press, Carlton, 1977.

Yelverton, D.E., *Quest for a Phantom Strait: The saga of the pioneer Antarctic Peninsula expeditions, 1897–1905*, Polar Publishing Limited, Guildford, Surrey, 2004.

ARTICLES

Aberlenc, H.-P., 'Les insectes de Vanikoro', *Journal de bord: Journal des membres de l'Association Lapérouse*, vol. 27, no. 2, 2006, p. 2.

Ackerknecht, E.H., 'P.M.A. Dumoutier et la collection phrénologique du Musée de l'Homme', *Bulletins et mémoires de la Société d'anthropologie de Paris*, Xe série, vol. 7, 1956, pp. 289–308.

Adachi, R., & Fukuyo, Y., 'The thecal structure of a marine toxic dinoflagellate *Gambierdiscus toxicus* gen. et sp. nov. collected in a ciguatera-endemic area', *Nippon Suisan Gakkaishi* [= Bulletin of the Japanese Society of Scientific Fisheries], vol. 45, 1979, pp. 67–71

Allen, J., 'The archaeology of nineteenth-century British imperialism: An Australian case study', *World Archaeology*, vol. 5, no. 1, Colonization (June 1973), pp. 44–60.

Anderson, D.M., & Lobel, P.S., 'The Continuing Enigma of Ciguatera', *The Biological Bulletin*, vol. 172, no. 1, February 1987, pp. 89–107.

Anderson, W., 'An account of some poisonous fish in the South Seas', *Philosophical Transactions of the Royal Society of London*, vol. lxvi, 1776, pp. 544–74.

Anon., 'M. l'amiral anglais Manby, récemment arrivé à Paris …', *Le moniteur universel*, Paris, jeudi, 8 septembre 1825, p. 1270.

——— 'De Englische Admiraal Manby …', *Algemeene Konst en Letterbode voor het jaar 1825*, no. 37, vrijdag 16 september 1825, Haarlem, deel ii, pp. 177–78.

——— 'Some Account of Tooi, The Late New-Zealand Chief', *Missionary Register*, June 1826, pp. 302–04.

——— 'Nouvelle colonie anglaise sur la côte occidentale de la Nouvelle-Hollande', *Annales maritimes et coloniales*, vol. i, 1829, pp. 678–80.

——— 'France', *Gazette médicale de Paris*, vol. 3, no. 80, 4 septembre 1832, p. 555.

——— 'Missions de l'Océanie', *Annales de la propagation de la foi*, vol. 8, 1835, pp. 5–15.

——— 'Plan et itinéraire approuvés par le roi d'une prochaine expédition au pôle antarctique et autour du monde sous les ordres de M. Dumont-d'Urville, capitaine de vaisseau', *Annales maritimes et coloniales*, 22e année, 2e série, vol. 1, 1837, pp. 575–80.

——— 'Visite de M. l'amiral Duperré, ministre de la marine, au muséum, à l'occasion des objets d'histoire naturelle rapportés par l'expédition autour du monde, commandée par M. le capitaine Dumont d'Urville', *Annales maritimes et coloniales*, 26e année, 2e série, vol. ii, 1841, pp. 101–03.

——— 'Catastrophe du chemin de fer de Versailles (Rive Gauche)', *Revue générale de l'architecture et des travaux publics*, vol. iii, 1842, pp. 134–35.

——— 'Marcellus, Marie-Louis-Jean-André-Charles Demartin du Tirac, comte de', in Hoefer [J.C.F.] de (ed.) *Nouvelle biographie générale depuis les temps les plus reculés jusqu'à nos jours*, vol. 33, Firmin-Didot, Paris, 1860, pp. 461–63.

——— 'Rivière, Charles-François de Riffareau, marquis', in Hoefer [J.C.F.] de (ed.), *Nouvelle biographie générale depuis les temps les plus reculés jusqu'à nos jours*, vol. 42, Firmin-Didot, Paris, 1863, pp. 345–46.

——— 'Nécrologie: Le contre-amiral m[arqu]is du Bouzet', *Revue maritime et coloniale*, vol. 2, novembre 1867, pp. 695–700.

—— 'Musée municipal de Condé: Souvenir de M. Dumont de la Londe', *Journal de Condé*, dimanche 20 mars 1904, p. 2.

—— 'Stories in Stone: Scotch settlers and French circumnavigators', *The Mercury* (Hobart), 13 May 1910, p. 7.

—— 'Notice', *The Mercury* (Hobart), 20 July 1915, p. 1.

—— 'Removal of Bodies', *The Mercury* (Hobart), 20 September 1915, p. 1.

—— 'Dumont d'Urville, Jules Sébastien César', *Australian Encyclopaedia*, The Grolier Society of Australia, Sydney, 1958, pp. 309–10.

—— 'Une figure condéene s'est éteinte: Jean Gauquelin n'est plus', *L'Orne Combattante*, Edition 'Flers-Suisse-Normande', jeudi, 21 juin 2001, p. 16.

Arago, F., 'Chambre des Députés … Séance du 5 juin [1837]: Discours de M. Arago sur le chapitre des travaux scientifiques', *Journal des Débats*, 6 juin 1837, p. 3.

—— 'Service scientifique [Chambre des députés, séance du lundi 5 juin 1837]', *Annales maritimes et coloniales*, vol. 63, 1837, pp. 914–35.

—— 'Réponse de M. Arago, député, à une lettre de M. le capitaine de vaisseau Dumont d'Urville, et examen critique du premier voyage de circumnavigation de l'*Astrolabe*' [ex- *Le National*, 12 juillet 1837], *Annales maritimes et coloniales*, vol. 64, 1837, pp. 71–98.

Bagnall, A.G., 'Smith, Stephenson Percy (1840–1922)' in McLintock, A.H. (ed.), *Encyclopaedia of New Zealand*, R.E. Owen, Government Printer, Wellington, 1966, vol. iii, pp. 265–66.

Barclay, A., 'A picture of the negro slavery existing in the Mauritius', *Anti-Slavery Monthly Reporter*, no. 44, January 1829 [no. 20, vol ii], pp. 373–96.

Barnard, M., 'Piper, John (1773–1851)', *Australian Dictionary of Biography*, vol. 2, Melbourne University Press, Carlton, 1967, pp. 334–35.

Barnwell, P.J., 'Darling, Sir Ralph (1775–1858)', *Dictionnaire de biographie mauricienne*, no. 2, avril 1941, p. 41.

—— 'Cole, Sir Galbraith Lowry (1772–1842)', *Dictionnaire de biographie mauricienne*, no. 3, juin 1941, pp. 71–72.

Barrow, J., Beaufort, F., Marcheson, R., & Washington, J., 'Report of the Deputation from the Council of the Royal Geographical Society, to the Secretary of State for the Colonies, concerning Discoveries in New South Wales, 10 December 1836', in [House of Commons], *Accounts and Papers (2.) Estimates; Army; Navy; Ordnance etc.*, Session 31 January–17 July 1837, vol. xl, 1837 (III. Estimates &c. Miscellaneous Services for the Year 1837–38), House of Commons, London, 23 March 1837, pp. 10–11 [pp. 350–51].

Bartlett, A.D., 'On the genus *Apteryx*', *Proceedings of the Zoological Society of London*, part xviii, 1850, pp. 274–76.

Battersby, W., 'Identification of the probable source of the lead poisoning observed in members of the Franklin expedition', *Journal of the Hakluyt Society*, September 2008 [electronic form only], pp. 1–10.

Bayet, C.M., 'La nécropole chrétienne de Milo', *Bulletin de correspondance hellénique*, vol. 2, année 1878, pp. 347–59.

Beautemps-Beaupré, C.-F., 'Rapport sur les travaux hydrographiques exécutés dans l'expédition au pôle austral et dans l'Océanie commandée par Dumont d'Urville, *Comptes-rendus hebdomadaires des séances de l'Académie des sciences*, 1841, vol. 13, p. 764–76.

Béchet, R.-O., 'Geoffroy, Jean Baptiste Lislet (1755–1836)', *Dictionnaire de biographie mauricienne*, no. 6, octobre 1942, pp. 167–68.

Beer, G. de (ed.), 'Darwin's notebooks on transmutation of species: Part II. Second notebook [C] (February to July 1838)', *Bulletin of the British Museum (Natural History). Historical Series* 2, vol. 3, May 1960, pp. 75–118.

Beer, G. de, Rowlands, M.J., & Skramovsky, B.M. (eds), 'Darwin's notebooks on transmutation of species: Part VI. Pages excised by Darwin', *Bulletin of the British Museum (Natural History), Historical Series* 3, vol. 5, 21 March 1967, pp. 129–76.

Bellamy, C.L., 'Type species designations in the family Buprestidae (Coleoptera)', *Mitteilungen aus dem Museum für Naturkunde in Berlin, Deutsche Entomologische Zeitschrift*, vol. 45, no. 1, 1998, pp. 9–15.

Bergounioux, A., 'L'activité de l'enseigne de vaisseau Dumont d'Urville comme membre de la Société des Sciences, Belles Lettres et Arts du département du Var, aux environs de 1820, d'après des documents inédits, *Bulletin de l'Académie du Var*, 106ème année, 1938, pp. 160–70.

Berthelot, S., 'Éloge du contre-amiral Dumont d'Urville', *Bulletin de la Société de géographie*, mai 1843, pp. 361–89.

Bertier de Sauvigny, G. de, 'French Politics, 1814–47', in Crawley, W., *The New Cambridge Modern History*, vol. ix, War and Peace in an Age of Upheaval, 1793–1830, Cambridge University Press, Cambridge, 1965, pp. 337–66.

Besnier, M., 'La Vénus de Milo et Dumont d'Urville', *Revue des études anciennes*, vol. 10, 1908, pp. 205–48.

Bick, I.R.C., 'Alkaloids from Australian Flora', in Pelletier, W., *Alkaloids: Chemical and biological perspectives*, vol. 10, Pergamon, Oxford, 1996, pp. 1–154.

[Biscoe, J.,] 'Recent discoveries in the Antarctic Ocean communicated by Messrs Enderby', *Journal of the Royal Geographical Society*, vol. iii, 1833, pp. 103–12.

Blainville, H. Ducrotay de, 'Instructions relatives au voyage de circumnavigation de l'*Astrolabe* et de la *Zélée*: Partie zoologique' (Extrait des *Comptes-rendus des séances de l'Académie des sciences*, séance du 7 août 1837), in Hombron, J.-B., & Jacquinot, H., (eds), 'Zoologie', vol. i, pp. 5–12, in Dumont d'Urville, [& Jacquinot,] *Voyage au pôle sud …*

——— 'Rapports sur les résultats scientifiques du voyage de circumnavigation de l'*Astrolabe* et de la *Zélée*: Partie zoologique', *Comptes-rendus hebdomadaires des séances de l'Académie des sciences*, 1841, vol. 13, pp. 691–716.

Blandin, G., 'Souvenirs sur l'amiral Jacquinot', *Bulletin de la Société nivernaise*, tome xxxii, no. 34, 1959, p. 81.

Bonnome, S., 'Dumont-d'Urville à Toulon', *Bulletin de la Société des amis du Vieux Toulon*, no. 60, janvier–mars 1939, pp. 27–30.

Bory de Saint-Vincent, J.-B.-G.-M., 'Homme', in Audoin, J.V. et al., *Dictionnaire classique d'histoire naturelle*, vol. 8, septembre 1825, Rey et Gravier, Paris, pp. 269–346.

Boucher de Perthes, J., 'M. Tillette de Clermont-Tonnerre', *Mémoires de la Société impériale d'émulation d'Abbeville, 1857, 1858, 1859 et 1860*, typographie P. Briez, Abbeville, 1861, pp. 667–72.

Boudriot, J., 'L'*Astrolabe*', *Neptunia*, no. 123, 1976, pp. 45–53, 3e tr.

Bouge, L.J., 'Première législation tahitienne: Le Code Pomare de 1819', *Journal de la Société des océanistes*, vol. 8, no. 8, 1952, pp. 5–26.

[Boulger, G.S.], 'Webb, Philip Barker (1793–1854)', *Dictionary of National Biography*, Oxford University Press, London, vol. xx, 1973, pp. 1016–18.

Bramwell, D., & Bramwell, Z.I., *Wildflowers of the Canary Islands*, Stanley Thornes, London, 1974.

Brest, L., 'Rapport de Louis Brest', in Reinach, S., 'Louis Brest et la Vénus de Milo, d'après des documents inédits', *Chronique des Arts*, 27 février 1897, pp. 84–87.

Broeze, F.J.A., 'The merchant fleet of Java (1820–1850): A preliminary survey', *Archipel*, vol. 18, 1979, pp. 251–69.

Brongniart, A., 'Note sur quelques Euphorbiacées de la Nouvelle-Hollande', *Annales des sciences naturelles*, série 1, vol. 29, 1833, pp. 382–87.

Brown, P., 'Dumont d'Urville et les voyages d'exploration anthropologiques en Nouvelle-Zélande', *Le Colloque d'Akaroa 16–19 août 1990, Bureau d'Action linguistique et Fédération des Alliances françaises*, Heritage Press (for the Bureau d'Action linguistique de l'Ambassade de France à Wellington), Waikanae, 1991, pp. 18–29.

Brucker, J., 'Protectorate of Missions', *The Catholic Encyclopedia*, vol. 12, Robert Appleton Company, New York, 1911, pp. 488–92.

Bumstead, J.M., 'Walker, Alexander, explorer and author …', *Dictionary of Canadian Biography*, vol. vi, University of Toronto Press, Toronto, 1987, pp. 797–98.

Burbidge, M.L., Colbourne, R.M., Robertson, H.A., & Baker, A.J., 'Molecular and other biological evidence supports the recognition of at least three species of brown kiwi', *Conservation Genetics*, vol. 4, no. 2, 2003, pp. 167–77.

Caieu, A. de, 'M. Lefebvre de Cerisy (Louis Charles)', *Mémoires de la Société impériale d'émulation d'Abbeville*, 1861–66, deuxième partie [vol. xi], pp. 688–704, Abbeville, 1867.

Campbell, B.M., & Griffin, D.J.G., 'The Australian Sesarminae (Crustacea: Brachyura): Genera Helice, Helograpsus Nov., Cyclograpsus and Paragrapsus', *Memoirs of the Queensland Museum*, vol. 14, part 5, 1966, pp. 127–74, plates xx–xxiii.

[Caw, J.L.,] 'Williams, Henry (1792–1876)', in Smith, L., & Lee, S., *Dictionary of National Biography*, vol. xxi, Oxford University Press, London, 1973, pp. 405–07.

Cawood, J., 'Terrestrial magnetism and the development of international collaboration in the early nineteenth century', *Annals of Science*, vol. 34, 1977, pp. 551–87.

[Chabrol, C., comte de,] 'Lettre du ministre de la marine à M. Dumont d'Urville, capitaine de frégate, commandant la corvette du roi l'*Astrolabe*, à Toulon, pour lui servir d'instruction relativement au voyage de découvertes qu'il va entreprendre, Paris, le 8 avril 1826', in Dumont d'Urville, *Voyage de la corvette l'*Astrolabe, première division, 'Histoire du voyage', vol i, 1830, pp. il–lvi.

Chang, S.-S., Chan, Y.-L., Wu, M.-L., Deng, J.-F., Chiu, T.F., Chen, J.-C., Wang, F.-L. & Tseng, C.-P., 'Acute Cycas seed poisoning in Taiwan', *Clinical Toxicology*, vol. 42, no. 1, 2004, pp. 49–54.

Chang-Yih Duh et al., 'New cytotoxic constituents from the Formosan soft corals *Clavularia viridis* and *Clavularia violacea*', *Journal of Natural Products*, vol. 65, 2002, pp. 1535–39.

Chapelier, L.-A. [Antoine Flageollot], 'Grammaire de la langue madécasse (Madagascar), par feu M. Chapelier, naturaliste du gouvernement à Madagascar, publiée par R.P. Lesson', *Annales maritimes et coloniales*, 1827, 2ème partie, vol. 1, pp. 90–121.

Cherbonnier, G., 'Sur une Holothurie de Quoy et Gaimard, type d'un nouveau genre: Plesiocolochirus', *Bulletin du muséum national d'histoire naturelle*, Paris, 2ème série, vol. 18, no. 3, 1946, pp. 280–86.

Chevalier, A., 'L'amiral J. Dumont d'Urville et ses découvertes scientifiques spécialement en Océanie et dans les Terres australes', *Comptes-rendus hebdomadaires des séances de l'Académie des sciences*, 23 octobre 1950, pp. 805–08.

Chevalier, A., 'Au souvenir de l'amiral J. Dumont d'Urville: Prospecteur de la flore de l'Océanie et de l'hémisphère austral de 1822 à 1840', *Revue internationale de botanique appliquée & d'agriculture tropicale*, 31e année, janvier–février 1951, pp. i–ii, 1–37.

Clark, P.F., & Crosnier, A., 'The zoology of the *Voyage au pôle sud et dans l'Océanie sur les corvettes l'Astrolabe et la Zélée exécuté par ordre du roi pendant les années 1837-1838-1839-1840 sous le commandement de M. Dumont-d'Urville (1842-1854)*: titles, volumes, plates, text, contents, proposed dates and anecdotal history of the publication', *Archives Natural History*, vol. 27, no. 3, 2000, pp. 407–35.

Cleland, J.B., & Southcott, R.V., 'Illness following the eating of seal liver in Australian waters', *Medical Journal of Australia*, 12 April 1969, pp. 760–63.

Collins, R.D.J., 'Louis-Auguste de Sainson', *Bulletin of New Zealand Art History*, no. 18, 1997, pp. 5–27.

Constant-Dufeux, S.-C., & Roux de la Rochelle, J.-B.-G., 'Discours prononcés à l'inauguration du monument de Dumont d'Urville au cimetière du Montparnasse, le 1er novembre 1844', *Bulletin de la Société de géographie de Paris*, 3e série, ii, 1844, pp. 211–42.

Cooper, A., Lalueza-Fox, C., Anderson, S., Rambaut, A, Austin, J., & Ward, R., 'Complete mitochondrial genome sequences of two extinct moas clarify ratite evolution', *Nature*, vol. 409, no. 6821 (8 February 2001), pp. 704–07.

Cretella, M., 2010 'The complete collation and dating of the section *Zoologie* of the *Coquille* voyage', *Bollettino Malacologico*, vol. 46, no. 2, 2010, pp. 83–103.

Croon, J.H., 'Hot springs and healing gods', *Mnemosyne*, fourth series, vol. 20, fascicule 3, 1967, pp. 225–46.

Dansey, H., 'Digging for the stories from long ago', *The Auckland Star*, 20 February, 1965, p. 7.

Davidson, J.W., 'Kendall, Thomas (1778–1832)', *Australian Dictionary of Biography*, Melbourne University Press, Carlton, 1967, vol. 2, pp. 42–43.

Delacour, J., 'A revision of the genera and species of the family Pycnonotidae (bulbuls)', *Zoologica*, vol. 28, no. 1, 1943, pp. 17–28.

Dillon, P. 'Postscript: La Peyrouse', *The Sydney Gazette and New South Wales Advertiser*, Wednesday 5 December 1827, p. 2.

[Douglas, R.K.], 'Bonham, Sir Samuel George (1803–1863)', *Dictionary of National Biography*, vol. ii, Oxford University Press, London, 1973, p. 807.

Downing, K.T., 'Uterine Prolapse: From antiquity to today', *Obstetrics and Gynecology International*, vol. 2012 (2012), [article ID 649459], pp. 1–9.

Druce, G.C., 'Nomenclatural notes; chiefly African and Australian', *Report of the Botanical Society and Exchange Club of the British Isles*, vol. iv, 1916, second supplement (July 1917), pp. 602–55.

Drummond, J., 'Nature Notes', *New Zealand Herald*, 27 November 1915, p. 5.

Duflot, Y., & Duyker, E., 'Jacques-Rémy Maingon (1765–1809)', *Dictionnaire de biographie mauricienne*, no. 62, mai 2013, pp. 2474–76.

Duméril, A.-M.-C., 'Mémoire sur les Batraciens anoures de la famille des Hylaeformes ou Rainettes, comprenant la description d'un genre nouveau et de onze espèces nouvelles', *Annales des sciences naturelles*, série 3, vol. 19, 1853, pp. 135–179.

Dumont d'Urville, J.-S.-C., 'Seconde relation de la campagne hydrographique de la gabare du roi la *Chevrette* dans le Levant et la mer noire pendant l'année 1820 (histoire naturelle)', *Annales maritimes et coloniales*, 2ème partie, 1821, pp. 149–79.

—— 'Notice sur les îles volcaniques de Santorin et plus particulièrement sur la nouvelle Camini lue à la Société linnéenne le 28 décembre', *Mémoires de la Société linnéenne de Paris*, vol. i, deuxième partie, 1822, pp. 598–608.

—— 'Enumeratio plantarum quas in insulis archipelagi aut littoribus Ponti-Euxini annis 1819 et 1820', *Mémoires de la Société linnéenne de Paris*, vol. i, deuxième partie, 1822, pp. 255–387.

—— 'Notice sur les galeries souterraines de l'île de Melos', *Nouvelles annales des voyages*, 1825, pp. 145–59 & plates.

—— 'Note sur les collections et les observations recueillies par M.J. d'Urville, durant la campagne de la *Coquille* autour du monde, en 1822, 1823, 1824 et 1825', *Annales des sciences naturelles*, vol. v, May 1825, pp. 62–82.

—— 'De la distribution des fougères sur la surface du globe terrestre', *Annales des Sciences naturelles*, septembre 1825, pp. 51–73.

—— 'Flore des Malouines', *Mémoires de la Société linnéenne de Paris*, vol. 4, 1826, pp. 573–621.

—— 'Rapport à l'Académie royale des sciences de l'institut sur la marche et les opérations du voyage de découvertes de la corvette l'*Astrolabe* en 1826, 1827, 1828 et 1829, lu dans la séance du 12 mai 1829', *Annales maritimes et coloniales*, vol. i, 1829, pp. 633–76.

—— 'L'*Astrolabe* à Vanikoro', *Bulletin de la Société de géographie*, vol. 12, no. 75, juillet 1829, pp. 249–67.

—— 'Rapport sur le guide des marins pendant la navigation nocturne, etc., par M. Coulier', *Bulletin de la Société de géographie*, vol. 13, no. 81, janvier 1830, pp. 32–34.

—— 'Rapport sur le projet d'un voyage par M. de Buckingham', *Bulletin de la Société de géographie*, vol. 13, no. 90, octobre 1830, pp. 153–80.

—— 'Du tabou et des funérailles à la Nouvelle-Zélande (Voyage inédit de l'*Astrolabe*)', *Revue des deux mondes*, vol. iii, 1831, pp. 197–213.

—— 'Adieux de Charles X au Capitaine Dumont d'Urville', *Revue des deux mondes*, vol. iii, 1831, pp. 288–91.

—— 'Rapport sur le voyage du Capitaine Beechey', *Bulletin de la Société de géographie*, vol. xv, no. 97, mai 1831, pp. 201–53.

—— 'Sur les îles du Grand Océan', *Bulletin de la Société de géographie*, vol. 17, no. 105, janvier 1832, pp. 1–21.

—— 'Note sur les expériences de température sous-marine, exécutées par M. Bérard dans la Méditerranée, en 1831', *Bulletin de la Société de géographie*, vol. 17, no. 105, janvier 1832, pp. 82–86.

—— 'Analyses: *Voyage au Congo et dans l'Afrique équinoxiale* de M. Douville', *La France Littéraire*, vol. iia, 5e livraison, 1832, pp. 5–46.

—— 'Observation sur les découvertes du capitaine américain J. Morrell', *Bulletin de la Société de géographie*, vol. 19, no. 121, mai 1833, pp. 270–77.

—— 'Notice sur la température de la mer à diverses profondeurs (Extrait du voyage de l'*Astrolabe*)', *Bulletin de la Société de géographie*, no. 122, juin 1833, pp. 313–32.

—— 'Croisière du schooner le *Dolphin* dans les îles de l'Océan Pacifique, par le lieutenant H. Paulding', *Bulletin de la Société de géographie*, vol. 20, juillet 1833, p. 144–57.

—— 'Observation sur la note précédente [Extrait du *Moniteur* du 4 octobre 1833 relatif à un groupe d'îles découvertes par le capitaine Harwod, accompagné d'observations]', *Bulletin de la Société de géographie*, vol. 20, no. 123, juillet 1833, p. 245.

—— 'Rapport sur un manuscrit espagnol présenté à la Société de géographie par M.H. Ternaux', *Bulletin de la Société de géographie*, deuxième série, vol. 1, no. 123, mars 1834, pp. 145–64.

—— 'Cook, Jacques', *Encyclopédie des gens du monde*, vol. 6, deuxième partie, 1834, pp. 742–46.

—— 'Note sur le voyage de découvertes au pôle austral, et dans l'Océanie, de l'*Astrolabe* et de la *Zélée*', *Bulletin de la Société de géographie*, deuxième série, vol. vii, no. 38, mai 1837, pp. 281–86.

—— 'Note de M. le capitaine Dumont d'Urville en réponse au discours prononcé par M. Arago à la Chambre des Députés, dans la séance du 5 juin', *Annales maritimes et coloniales*, vol. 64, 1837, pp. 64–71 [same text as *Le Toulonnais* article below].

—— 'Note sur l'expédition de l'*Astrolabe* et de la *Zélée* en réponse aux critiques de M. Arago', *Le Toulonnais*, 5ème année, no. 387, mercredi, 21 juin 1837, pp. 3–4.

—— '2e et dernière note de M. Dumont d'Urville sur l'expédition de l'*Astrolabe* et de la *Zélée*, au sujet des critiques à M. Arago', *Annales maritimes et coloniales*, vol. 64, 1837, pp. 98–105.

—— 'Expédition de l'*Astrolabe* et de la *Zélée* pour un voyage d'exploration au pôle sud et dans l'Océanie (Lettre de M. le capitaine Dumont d'Urville, commandant de l'expédition, à M. le ministre de la marine)', *Bulletin de la Société de géographie*, deuxième série, vol. 10, no. 55, juillet 1838, pp. 118–23.

—— 'Exploration des Îles Arrou: Par les corvettes l'*Astrolabe* et la *Zélée*: Fragment inédit du journal de l'amiral Dumont-d'Urville', in Lacroix, F. (ed.), *Annuaire des voyages et de la géographie pour l'Année 1844*, Guillaumin, Paris, 1844, pp. 58–77.

[Duperret, F.,] 'Obsèques de M. Dumont d'Urville', *La Renommée: Biographie générale*, vol. ii, 2e année, 1842, pp. 527–29.

Duperrey, L.-I., 'Sur les expériences du pendule invariable, faites dans la campagne de la corvette de S.M. la *Coquille*, pendant les années 1822, 1823, 1824 et 1825', *Connaissance des temps … pour l'an 1830*, Bachelier, Paris, 1827, pp. 83–99.

—— 'Résumé des Observations de l'inclinaison et de la déclinaison de l'aiguille aimantée, faites dans la campagne de la corvette de S.M. la *Coquille*, pendant les années 1822, 1823, 1824 et 1825', *Connaissance des temps … pour l'an 1830*, Bachelier, Paris, 1827, pp. 100–14.

———— 'Sur les opérations géographiques faites dans la campagne de la corvette de S.M. la *Coquille*, pendant les années 1822, 1823, 1824 et 1825', *Connaissance des temps … pour l'an 1830*, Bachelier, Paris, 1827, pp. 172–271.

Duro, C. F., 'Pedro Sarmiento de Gamboa, El Navigante', *Boletín de la Real Academia de la Historia*, vol. xxviii, no. iv, abril 1896, pp. 273–87.

Duyker, E., 'Coutance and the voyage of the *Adèle*', *Explorations*, no. 4, March 1987, pp. 21–25.

———— 'La Motte du Portail, Jacques-Malo de (1761–1812)', *Dictionnaire de biographie mauricienne*, no. 54, octobre 2000, pp. 1752–53.

———— 'Bailly, Joseph-Charles (1777–1844)', *Dictionnaire de biographie mauricienne*, no. 58, décembre 2006, pp. 2027–29.

———— 'An Explorer's Books: The Library of Dumont d'Urville', *Explorations*, no. 49, part ii, December 2010, pp. 66–81.

———— 'Dumont d'Urville's Library: The Notarial Inventories', *Explorations*, no. 49, part ii, December 2010, pp. 82–121.

———— 'Achowlia, aka Joe (*ca.* 1790–*ca.* 1840)', *Dictionnaire de biographie mauricienne*, no. 61, avril 2012, pp. 2319–21.

———— 'Faraguet, Henry Antoine (1802–*post* 1859)', *Dictionnaire de biographie mauricienne*, no. 61, avril 2012, pp. 2345–47.

———— 'Gabert, André-Paul (1797–1855)', *Dictionnaire de biographie mauricienne*, no. 61, pp. 2348–49, avril 2012.

———— 'Lesson, Pierre Adolphe (1805–1888)', *Dictionnaire de biographie mauricienne*, no. 61, avril 2012, pp. 2357–59.

———— 'Lottin, Victor-Charles (1795–1858)', *Dictionnaire de biographie mauricienne*, no. 61, avril 2012, pp. 2364–67.

———— 'Pâris, François-Edmond (1806–1893)', *Dictionnaire de biographie mauricienne*, no. 61, avril 2012, pp. 2382–84.

———— 'Quoy, René Constant (1790–1869)', *Dictionnaire de biographie mauricienne*, no. 61, avril 2012, pp. 2384–86.

———— 'Sainson, Louis-Auguste de (1800–1887 [*sic*])', *Dictionnaire de biographie mauricienne*, no. 61, avril 2012, pp. 2392–94.

———— 'Sieber, Franz Wilhelm (1789–1844)', *Dictionnaire de biographie mauricienne*, no. 61, avril 2012, pp. 2394–96.

———— 'Olive Wright (1886–1975), Teacher and Translator', *Doryanthes*, vol. 6, no. 2, May 2013, pp. 16–18.

———— 'Prosper Garnot (1794–1838): An Early French naturalist in New South Wales', *Doryanthes*, vol. 7, no. 1, February 2014, pp. 22–26.

Duyker, E. & Low, J., 'A Church on Pulpit Hill: Unlocking a Blue Mountains mystery', *Doryanthes*, vol. 2, no. 3, August 2009, pp. 33–36.

Eddy, J., 'Therry, John Joseph (1790–1864)', *Australian Dictionary of Biography*, vol. 2, pp. 509–12.

Ehrhardt, J.-P., 'Les médecins des explorations de Dumont d'Urville (1826–1840)', *Médecine et armées*, vol. 9, no. 2, 1981, pp. 147–54.

Eldershaw, P.R., 'Murdoch, Peter (1795–1871)', *Australian Dictionary of Biography*, vol. 2, Melbourne University Press, Carlton, 1967, p. 269.

Emberson, R.M., 'Tentative dates of publication of the zoology plates of Dumont d'Urville's *Voyage au pôl[e] sud*, with particular reference to the Coleoptera', *Archives of Natural History*, vol. 19, no. 2, 1992, pp. 251–60.

Evans, R., '19 June 1822, Creating "An Object of Real Terror": The tabling of the first Bigge Report', in Crotty, M. & Roberts, D., (eds), *Turning Points in Australian History*, University of New South Wales Press, Sydney, 2009, pp. 48–61.

Fenton, F.D., 'The Orakei Case: Interlocutory judgement', *Daily Southern Cross*, 30 December 1868, p. 4.

Ferguson, W.C., 'Mokaré's domain', in Mulvaney, D.J. & White, J.P., *Australians to 1788*, Fairfax, Syme & Weldon Associates, Sydney, 1987, pp. 121–45.

Feuardent, R., 'La perte de la frégate "L'Amazone"', *Mémoires de la Société nationale académique de Cherbourg*, vol. 28,1975, pp. 67–74.

Finney, B.R., 'Notes on bond-friendship in Tahiti', *Journal of the Polynesian Society*, vol. 73, no. 4, 1964, pp. 431–35.

Flagellot, A., *see* Chapelier, L.-A.,

Forster, J.G.A., 'Fasciculus plantarum magellanicarum oblatus societati in ipso consessu sollennium Academiae Georgae augustae semisaecularium d. xvii Sept mdcclxxxvii', *Commentationes Societatis Regiae Scientiarum Gottingensis*, vol. 9, 1789, pp. 13–45.

Franceschini, P., 'La scoperta del bacillo del colera: Firenze, 29 agosto 1854', *Physis*, no. 3–4, 1976, pp. 349–65.

Garnot, P., 'Observations sur l'échidné épineux', *Annales des sciences naturelles*, série 1, vol. 6, 1825, pp. 504–08.

Garnot, P., 'Notes sur quelques peuples de la mer du Sud', *Journal des voyages*, vol. xxxiii, 1827, pp. 271–81.

—— 'Excursion dans les environs de Sydney', *Journal des voyages*, vol. xlii, 1829, p. 139.

—— 'Homo', in Guérin-Méneville, F.E. (ed.), *Dictionnaire pittoresque d'histoire naturelle*, vol. 4, Paris, Bureau de souscription,1836, pp. 6–16.

—— 'Nègre', in Guérin-Méneville, F.E. (ed.), *Dictionnaire pittoresque d'histoire naturelle*, vol. 5, Paris, Bureau de souscription,1837, pp. 628–32.

Godley, E.J., 'Botany of the southern zone: Exploration to 1843', *Tuatara*, vol. 13, issue 3, November 1965, pp. 140–81.

Goshen, C.E., 'The psychology of Jean Louis Alibert', *Journal of the History of the Behavioral Sciences*, vol. 2, 1966, pp. 357–70.

Goyau, G., 'The French Concordat of 1801', *The Catholic Encyclopedia*, vol. iv, Robert Appleton Company, New York, 1908, pp. 204–06.

Groube, L.M., 'Excavations on Paeroa Village Bay of Islands', *The New Zealand Historic Places Trust Newsletter*, no. 9, June 1965, pp. 5–7.

—— 'Rescue Excavations in the Bay of Islands', *New Zealand Archaeological Association Newsletter*, vol. 9, 1966, pp. 108–14.

Guedon, C., 'Jules Dumont d'Urville ou l'histoire de sa statue', *L'Orne combattante*, Edition 'Flers-Suisse-Normande', jeudi, 15 mai 1997, p. 1 [& Condé-sur-Noireau regional page].

Hahn, R., 'Arago, Dominique François Jean', in Coulston, C.C. (ed.), *Dictionary of Scientific Biography*, vol. i, Charles Scribner's Sons, New York, 1981, pp. 200–03.

Hartung, E.F., 'History of the use of colchicum and related medicaments in gout: With suggestions for further research', *Annals of the Rheumatic Diseases*, vol. 13, 1954, pp. 190–200.

Hässel de Menéndez, G.G., & Solari, S.S., 'Sinopsis de las especies Andinopatagónicas del género *Tylimanthus* (Hepaticae)', *Darwiniana*, vol. 17, 1972, p. 568–91.

Havard, O., & Havard, W.L., 'Some early French visitors to the Blue Mountains and Bathurst', *Royal Australian Historical Society Journal and Proceedings*, vol. xxiv, part iv, 1938, pp. 245–90 [part ii, Lesson's journal, pp. 260–90].

Heniger, J., 'Dutch Contributions to the Study of Exotic Natural History in the Seventeenth and Eighteenth Centuries' in Eisler, W., & Smith, B., *Terra Australis: The furthest shore*, Art Gallery of New South Wales/International Cultural Corporation of Australia, Sydney, 1988, pp. 59–66.

Henn, P.U., 'The Tryal Rocks', *Journal and Proceedings of the Western Australian Historical Society*, vol. 2, part 17, 1935, pp. 38–43.

Hernandez Suárez, M., 'Breves biographifias actualizadas de personajes Canarios', in Torres, A.M. (ed.), *Historia General de Las Islas Canarias*, vol. vi, Edirca, Las Palmas, 1981, pp. 76–77.

Hoare, M., 'Botany and society in Eastern Australia', in Carr, D.J., & Carr, S.G.M. (eds), *People and Plants in Australia*, Academic Press, Sydney, 1981, pp. 183–219.

Hochlowski, J.E. & Faulkner, D.J., 'Antibiotics from the marine pulmonate *Siphonaria diemenensis*', *Tetrahedron Letters*, vol. 24, issue 18, 1983, pp. 1917–20.

Holthuis, L.B., ' A few notes on the authors and dates of the names of crustacea collected by the *Voyage au pôle sud et dans l'Océanie sur les corvettes l'*Astrolabe *et la Zélée*', *Crustaceana*, vol. 75, nos. 3–4, 2002, pp. 413–22.

Hombron, J-B., 'Race jaune étudiée en Amérique et dans la Polynésie', *Annales maritimes et coloniales*, vol. 82, no. 2, 1842, pp. 1298–1322.

—— 'Des méthodistes dans l'Océanie', *Annales maritimes et coloniales*, 2e partie, tome 1, 1843, pp. 1055–58.

Hombron, J-B., & Jacquinot, H., 'Description de quelques mollusques provenant de la campagne de l'*Astrolabe* et de la *Zélée*', *Annales des sciences naturelles*, 2e série, vol. 16, 1841, pp. 62–64 & 190–92.

—— 'Description de plusieurs oiseaux nouveaux ou peu connus provenant de l'expédition autour du monde faite sur les corvettes l'*Astrolabe* et la *Zélée*', *Annales des sciences naturelles*, 2e série, vol. 16, 1841, pp. 312–20.

Humboldt, A. von, Cuvier, G.-F., Desfontaines, R.-L., Cordier, P.-L.-A., Latreille, P.-A., Rossel, E.-E., & Arago, D.-F.-J., 'Rapport fait à l'Académie royale des sciences, le lundi 22 août 1825, sur le voyage autour du monde de la corvette de S.M., La *Coquille* commandée par M. L.-I. Duperrey', in Duperrey, L.-I., *Voyage autour du monde: Exécuté par ordre du roi sur la corvette de sa Majesté, la* Coquille, *pendant les années 1822, 1823, 1824 et 1825 …*, Arthus Bertrand, Paris, Histoire, vol. i, 1825, pp. i–xlvxl.

Hurles, M.E. et al., 'The dual origin of the Malagasy in island Southeast Asia and East Africa: Evidence from maternal and paternal lineages', *American Journal of Human Genetics*, vol. 76, 2005, pp. 894–901.

Husson, A.M., & Holthuis, L.B., 'The dates of publication of "Verhandelingen over de natuurlijke Geschiedenis der Nederlandsche overzeesche Bezittingen" edited by C.J. Temminck', *Zoologische Mededelingen*, vol. xxxiv, no. 2, 1955, pp. 17–24.

Iredale, T., 'Queensland molluscan notes, no. 1', *Memoirs of the Queensland Museum*, vol. 9, no. 3, 1929, pp. 261–97.

Johnson, D., 'Obituary: Admiral Jacques Guillon', *The Independent*, 27 December 1997, p. 16.

Johnston, T.H., & Mawson, P.M., 'Endoparasites of the subantarctic islands of New Zealand', *Records of the South Australian Museum*, vol. 7, no. 3, 1943, pp. 237–43.

Jones, A.G.E., 'Captain Abraham Bristow and the Auckland Islands', *Notes and Queries*, October 1970, pp. 369–71.

Jones, D.E.H., & Ledingham, K.W.L., 'Arsenic in Napoleon's Wallpaper', *Nature*, vol. 299, 14 October 1982, p. 626–27.

Jore, L., 'Le drame du brick bordelais l'*Aimable Joséphine* aux Îles Fidji en 1834', *Revue historique de Bordeaux et du département de la Gironde*, vol. iv, nouvelle série, 1959, pp. 268–89.

[Knollys, W.W.,] 'O'Meara, Barry Edward (1786–1836)', *Dictionary of National Biography*, Oxford University Press, London, vol. xiv, 1973, p. 1065.

Kohen, J.L., & Lampert, R., 'Hunters and fishers in the Sydney region', in Mulvaney, D.J., & White, J.P., *Australians to 1788*, Fairfax, Syme & Weldon, Sydney, 1987, pp. 343–65.

Kunth, R. 'Richard, Louis Claude Marie', in Michaud, L.G. (ed.), *Biographie universelle*, Paris, vol. xxxvii, 1824, pp. 561–70.

Lacépède, B. de, & Thiébaut de Berneaud, A., 'Société linnéenne de Paris: Procès-verbal de la séance publique du 28 décembre 1821, jour anniversaire de la mort de Tournefort', *Mémoires de la Société linnéenne de Paris*, vol. i, 1822, pp. 1–6.

Lagrange, L., 'Dumont d'Urville et la Vénus de Milo', *Archives de l'Art français*, série ii, vol. ii, 1863, pp. 202–24.

Lamarck, J.-B. de, 'Sur une nouvelle espèce de Trigonie, et sur une nouvelle huître, découvertes dans le voyage du capitaine Baudin', *Annales du Muséum national d'histoire naturelle*, vol. 4, 1804, pp. 351–59 & pl. 67.

Latukefu, S., 'The case of the Wesleyan Mission in Tonga', *Journal de la Société des océanistes*, vol. 25, issue no. 25, 1969, pp. 95–112.

[Laughton J.K.L.], 'Bremer, Sir James John Gordon (1786–1850)', *Dictionary of National Biography*, Oxford University Press, London, vol. ii, 1973, pp. 1164–65.

Legge, C., 'Dumont d'Urville's Novel "Les Zélandais – Histoire Australienne"', *The Turnbull Library Record*, vol. xxii, no. 2, October 1984, pp. 77–83.

Le Guillou, É.-J.-F., 'Description des orthoptères nouveaux recueillis pendant son voyage autour du monde sur la *Zélée*', *Revue zoologique*, vol. 4, 1841, pp. 292–95.

——— 'Description de quatorze nérites nouvelles', *Revue zoologique*, vol. 4, 1841, pp. 343–47.

——— 'Description de quelques espèces nouvelles des genres Natice, Sigaret et Ampullaire', *Revue zoologique*, vol. 5, 1842, pp. 104–05.

—— 'Description de vingt-sept espèces d'Hélices nouvelles', *Revue zoologique*, vol. 5, 1842, pp. 130–41.

—— 'Description de sept diptères nouveaux recueillis pendant le voyage autour du monde de l'*Astrolabe* et de la *Zélée*', *Revue zoologique*, vol. 5, 1842, pp. 314–16.

—— 'Description de vingt insectes coléoptères recueillis pendant le voyage autour du monde de l'*Astrolabe* et de la *Zélée*', *Revue zoologique*, vol. 7, 1844, pp. 220–25.

Leonhart, J., 'Charles Wilkes: A Biography', in Viola, H.J. & Margolis, C. et al. (eds), *Magnificent Voyagers: The U.S. Exploring Expedition, 1838–1842*, Smithsonian Institution Press, Washington D.C., 1985, pp. 189–203.

Lesson, A.-P., 'Portrait de l'état-major de l'*Astrolabe*', in Bataille, A., 'Un document inédit: Le journal médical de Adolphe Pierre Lesson, chirurgien de Dumont d'Urville sur l'*Astrolabe* (1826–1829)', thèse méd. [no. 2025], annexe i, Université de Nantes, 1978, pp. 167–93.

Lesson, R.-P., 'Observations générales d'histoire naturelle, faites pendant un voyage dans les Montagnes-Bleues de la Nouvelle-Galles du Sud', *Annales des sciences naturelles*, Paris, série 1, vol. 6, [1825], pp. 241–66.

Levot, P., 'Biographie des frères Bernard Duhaut-Cilly', *Revue des provinces de l'ouest*, vol. i, part i, 1853, pp. 305–09.

[Louis XVIII,] 'Ordonance du roi portant nomination d'élèves au Collège royal de la marine à Angoulême, Paris, le 26 avril 1823', *Annales maritimes et coloniales*, 1823, partie 1, p. 365–66.

Louis-Philippe, Roi des Français, 'Ordonnance du roi qui accorde aux équipages des gabares l'*Astrolabe* et la *Zélée* dans leur voyage de découvertes au pôle antarctique, une prime proportionnée aux divers degrés de latitude qu'ils atteindront', *Annales maritimes et coloniales*, 22e année, 2e série, partie officielle, 1837, pp. 433–34.

Luxel, P., 'Le tragique destin de l'amiral Dumont d'Urville', *Revue maritime*, février 1953, pp. 227–39.

MacAllan, R., 'Richard Charlton: A reassessment', *Hawaiian Journal of History*, vol. 30, 1996, pp. 53–76.

McCarthy, F.D., 'Bungaree (?–1830)', *Australian Dictionary of Biography*, Melbourne University Press, Carlton, vol. 1, 1966, p. 177.

McNiven, I.J., & Wright, D., 'Ritualised marine midden formation in western Zenadh Kes (Torres Strait)', in Clark, G., Leach, F., and O'Connor, S., (eds), *Islands of Inquiry: Colonisation, seafaring and the archaeology of maritime landscapes*, Terra Australis 29, ANU Press, Canberra, 2008, pp. 133–48.

Magendie, F., 'Collège de France – M. Magendie: Accident arrivé sur le Chemin de Fer de Versailles (Rive Gauche)', *La Lancette française: Gazette des hôpitaux civils et militaires*, 13e année, no. 37, vol. 4, jeudi 12 mai 1842, pp. 261–62.

Maher, C., 'Quoy', *Archives de médecine navale*, vol. xii, 1869, pp. 401–22.

Marie, A. (ed.), 'Lettres de Dumont d'Urville (1819–1825)', *Revue rétrospective: Recueil de pièces intéressantes et de citations curieuses*, 10e semestre, janvier–juin 1889, pp. 74–90.

Marmottans, A., 'Un enfant surdoué', *Bulletin de la Société des amis du vieux Toulon*, no. 126, 2004, pp. 321–22.

Marx, K., 'Stellenkauf-Aus Australien' [ex-*Neue Oder-Zeitung* (Breslau), Nr. 111, 7 März 1855], in

Institut für Marxismus-Leninismus, *Karl Marx, Friedrich Engels Werke*, Dietz Verlag, Berlin/
DDR, 1961, band 11, pp. 104–07.

Matterer, A.-T., 'Notes nécrologiques et historiques sur M. le contre-amiral Dumont d'Urville',
Annales maritimes et coloniales, Octobre 1842, vol. 2, pp. 750–74.

Mercier, P., 'L'opinion publique après le déraillement de Meudon en 1842', *Paris et Île de France*, vol.
44, 1993, pp. 53–174.

Milne, J., 'Secret documents reveal French mutiny on NZ coast', *The Dominion*, Tuesday, 11
January 2001, p. 13.

Milne-Edwards, H., 'Note sur les animaux annelés recueillis par MM. les officiers de l'*Astrolabe* et
de la *Zélée*', *Comptes-rendus hebdomadaires des séances de l'Académie des sciences*, vol. 13, 1841,
pp. 716–20.

Mirbel, C.-F. de, Cordier, P.-L.-A., Blainville, H.-M. de, Freycinet, L.-C. de, & Savary, F., 'Rapport
de la commission chargée sur l'invitation de M. le ministre de la marine, de rédiger des
instructions pour les observations scientifiques à faire pendant le voyage des corvettes de l'état,
l'*Astrolabe* et de la *Zélée*', *Comptes-rendus hebdomadaires des séances de l'Académie des sciences*,
vol. 5, 1837, pp. 133–35.

Montagne, C., 'Quatrième centurie de plantes cellulaires exotiques nouvelles: Décades I–VI',
Annales des sciences naturelles; Botanique, série 2, vol. 19, 1843, pp. 238–66.

Oliver, S., 'Taiaroa, Te Matenga', in [Oliver, W.H., & Orange, C. (eds)] *The People of Many Peaks:
The Maori biographies from the Dictionary of New Zealand Biography*, vol. 1, 1769–1869, Bridget
Williams Books/Department of Internal Affairs, Wellington, 1991, pp. 121–24.

Oliver, S., 'Te Rauparaha (?–1849)' in [Oliver, W.H., & Orange, C., (eds)] *The People of Many Peaks:
The Maori biographies from the Dictionary of New Zealand Biography*, vol. 1, 1769–1869, Bridget
Williams Books/Department of Internal Affairs, Wellington, 1991, pp. 270–77.

Ollivier, I., 'Pierre-Adolphe Lesson, Surgeon-Naturalist: A misfit in a successful system', in R.
Macleod & P.E. Rehbock, *Nature in Its Greatest Extent: Western science in the Pacific*, University
of Hawaii Press, Honolulu, 1988, pp. 44–64.

Orchiston, D.W., 'Preserved Human Heads of the New Zealand Maoris', *Journal of the Polynesian
Society*, vol. 76, 1967, pp. 297–329.

Ortiz-Troncoso, O.R., 'A 16th century Hispanic harbour in the Strait of Magellan, South America',
International Journal of Nautical Archaeology, vol. 5, issue 2, May 1976, pp. 176–79.

[Paterson, Capt.,] 'Situation of Islands Seen in the Pacific Ocean, by the Brig *Elizabeth*, from Port
Jackson to China', in Purdy, J., *Of The Positions, Or Of The Latitudes And Longitudes, Of Places,
Composed To Accompany The 'Oriental Navigator', Or Sailing Directions For The East-Indies,
China, Australia, &c. With Notes, Explanatory And Descriptive,* Printed by Rider and Weed, for
James Whittle and Richard Holmes Laurie, London, 1816, pp. 153–54.

Perry, T. M., 'Cunningham, Allan (1791–1839)', *Australian Dictionary of Biography*, Melbourne
University Press, Carlton, vol. 1, 1966, pp. 265–67.

Petit, R., 'Toulon au Musée des plans-reliefs des Invalides', *Bulletin de la Société des amis du Vieux
Toulon*, no. 100, 1978, pp. 125–33.

Peyssonnaux, J.H., 'Vie, voyages et travaux de Pierre Médard Diard', *Bulletin des amis du vieux Hué*,
no. 1, 22e année, janvier–mars 1935, pp. 1–68 (annexes, pp. 69–120).

Philippi, [R.]A. 'Diagnosen einiger neuen Conchylien', *Archiv für Naturgeschichte*, Band 11, 1845, pp. 50–71.

Pisier, G., 'Dumont d'Urville et la découverte des Îles Loyauté', *Bulletin de la Société d'études historiques de la Nouvelle-Calédonie*, 1975, pp. 20–32.

Pollitzer, R., 'Cholera Studies: History of the disease', *Bulletin de l'Organisation mondiale de la Santé/Bulletin of the World Health Organization*, vol. 10, 1954, pp. 421–61.

Pradel de Lamase, M. de, 'Avec Dumont d'Urville: Souvenirs du Commandant de Roquemaurel', *Revue Maritime*, vol. 1, 1924, pp. 203–26.

Reinach, S., 'La Vénus de Milo', *Gazette des Beaux-Arts*, vol. 3, 3e période, 1890, pp. 376–94.

Reinach, S., 'Louis Brest et La Vénus de Milo d'après des documents inédits', *La Chronique des arts*, [part 1], 20 février 1897, pp. 72–74; [part 2], 27 février 1897, pp. 84–87.

Relandus, H. [Adriaan van Reeland], 'De linguis insularum quarundam orientalium', in *Dissertationum Miscellanearum*, pars tertia et ultima, Guilielmus Broedelet, Trajecti ad Rhenum [Utrecht], 1708, pp. 55–139.

Renneville, M., 'Un musée anthropologique oubliée: Le cabinet phrénologique de Dumoutier', *Bulletins et Mémoires de la Société d'Anthropologie de Paris*, nouvelle série, vol. 10, nos. 3–4, 1998, pp. 477–84.

Renneville, M., 'Un terrain phrénologique dans le Grand Océan autour du voyage de Dumoutier sur l'*Astrolabe* en 1837–1840', in Blanckaert, C. (ed.), *Le terrain des sciences humaines XVIIIe–XXe siècles*, L'Harmattan, Paris, 1996, pp. 89–138.

Rivière, M.S., 'An unknown 1824 French version of Oxley's exploration of the Brisbane River', *Royal Historical Society of Queensland Journal*, vol. 16, no. 4, November 1996, pp. 143–58.

——(trans.), 'Découverte de la Rivière Brisbane: Extrait du journal de Mr Uniak/Discovery of the Brisbane River: Extract of the journal of John Fitzgerald Uniacke', *Royal Historical Society of Queensland Journal*, vol. 16, no. 4, November 1996, pp. 159–88.

—— 'In honour of a fellow explorer: Flinders' and Bougainville's monuments to La Pérouse in Mauritius and at Botany Bay', *Humanities Research*, vol. 10, no. 2, 2003, pp. 9–20.

Rochette, M., 'Dumont d'Urville's phrenologist: Dumoutier and the Aesthetics of Races [Translated from French by Isabel Ollivier]', *Journal of Pacific History*, vol. 38, no. 2, September 2003, pp. 251–68.

[Rosamel, C. du Campe de,] Ministre de la Marine, 'Service scientifique [Chambre des députés, séance du lundi 5 juin 1837]', *Annales maritimes et coloniales*, vol. 63, 1837, pp. 935–40.

Rosenman, L., Rosenman, S., & Rosenman, S., 'Helen Rosenman (1921–2009), *Explorations*, no. 53, December 2012, pp. 50–52.

Ross, R.M., 'Thierry, Charles-Philip-Hippolytus, Baron de (1793?–1864)', McLintock, A.H. (ed.), *An Encyclopaedia of New Zealand*, vol. iii, R.E. Owen, Government Printer, Wellington, 1966, pp. 394–95.

Sainson, L.-A. de, 'Souvenirs des Îles des Amis', *Revue des deux mondes*, 1831, vol. iii, pp. 1–14.

Saunier, C., 'Le numérotage de la rue Madame', *Bulletin de la Société historique du VI° arrondissement de Paris*, vol. xxix, 1928, pp. 75–86.

Savours, A. 'John Biscoe, Master Mariner: 1794–1843', *Polar Record*, vol. 21, no. 134, 1983, pp. 485–91.

Shelford, P., Hodson, P., Cosgrove, M.E., Warren, S.E., & Renfrew, C., 'The sources and characterisation of Melian obsidian', in Renfrew, C. & Wagstaff, M. *An Island Polity: The archaeology of exploitation in Melos*, pp. 182–92, Cambridge University Press, Cambridge, 1982.

Shearman, D.J.C., 'Vitamin A and Sir Douglas Mawson', *British Medical Journal*, 4 February 1978, pp. 283–85.

Silvestre, M., 'Notes sur *l'Atlas Universel* de Philippe Vandermaelen (1825–1827)', *Ngogne: Carnets de sciences humaines*, no. 7, 2012, pp. 7–13.

Simmons, N.B., 'Order Chiroptera', in Wilson, D.E., & Reeder, D.M., *Mammal Species of the World: A taxonomic and geographic reference*, Johns Hopkins University Press, Baltimore, 2005, vol. i, pp. 312–529.

Skottsberg, C., 'Zur Kenntnis der subantarktischen und antarktischen Meeresalgen I, Phaeophyceen', in Svenska Sydpolar-Expeditionen, *Wissenschaftliche Ergebnisse der Schwedischen Südpolar-Expedition 1901–1903 unter Leitung von Dr. Otto Nordenskjöld*, Stockholm, vol. 4, fasc. 6, 1907, pp. 1–172.

Sloan, P., 'The idea of racial degeneration in Buffon's *Histoire naturelle*', in Pagliaro, H. (ed.), *Studies in Eighteenth-Century Culture*, vol. 3, 'Racism in the eighteenth century', pp. 293–321.

Smith, S.P., 'Wars of the northern against the southern tribes of New Zealand in the nineteenth century: Part VII', *Journal of the Polynesian Society*, vol. 10, no. 2, June 1901, pp. 78–88.

—— 'Captain Dumont d'Urville's visit to Tasman Bay in 1827', *Transactions and Proceedings of the Royal Society of New Zealand*, vol. 40, 1907, pp. 412–33.

—— 'Captain Dumont d'Urville's visit to Tolaga Bay in 1827', *Transactions and Proceedings of the Royal Society of New Zealand*, vol. 41, 1908, pp. 130–39.

—— 'Captain Dumont d'Urville's visit to Whangarei, Waitemata, and the Thames in 1827', *Transactions and Proceedings of the Royal Society of New Zealand*, vol. 42, 1909, pp. 412–33.

[Soteriou, G.] Σωτηρίου Γ., 'Ἡ χριστιανικὴ κατακόμβη τῆς νήσου Μήλου', *Πρακτικά Ακαδημίας Αθηνών*, vol. 3, part 1, 1928, pp. 33–46.

Spamer, E.E., & Bogan, A.E., 'Type specimens of crustacea surviving in the Guérin-Méneville Collection', *Proceedings of The Academy of Natural Sciences of Philadelphia*, vol. 145, 1994, pp. 35–46.

Steele, J.G., 'Pamphlet, Uniacke and Field', *Queensland Heritage*, vol. 2, no. 3, 1970, pp. 3–14.

Steinberg, C.H., 'The collectors and collections in the Herbarium Webb', *Webbia*, vol. 32, no. 1, 1977, pp. 1–49.

Stone, B. 'Age of the Chira Group, Northwestern Peru', *Journal of Palaeontology*, vol. 23, no. 2, March 1949, pp. 156–60.

Stos-Gale, Z.A., & Gale, N.H., 'The sources of Mycenaean silver and lead', *Journal of Field Archaeology*, vol. 9, no. 4 (winter), 1982, pp. 467–85.

Struik, D.J., 'Bertrand, Joseph Louis François', *Dictionary of Scientific Biography*, vol. 1, pp. 87–89.

Thorpe, W.W., 'A probable relic of La Perouse', *The Australian Museum Magazine*, January–March 1926, pp. 303–04.

Thuillier, G., 'L'administration sous la Restauration: "La Bonne Ville" (1826) d'Isidore Lebrun', *La Revue administrative*, 36e année, no. 213, mai–juin 1983, pp. 232–40.

Timmins, S., 'Pritchard, George (1796–1883)', *Dictionary of National Biography*, vol. xvi, Oxford University Press, London, 1973, pp. 406–07.

Toussaint, A., 'Epinay, Antoine Zacharie Adrien d' (1794–1839)', *Dictionnaire de biographie mauricienne*, no. 14, juillet 1944, pp. 426–27.

[Vaos, Z.A.] Βάος, Z. A., Ἡ Ἀφροδίτη τῆς Μήλου', *Ἐπετηρίς τῆς Ἑταιρείας Κυκλαδικῶν Μελε*, vol. 3, 1963, pp. 359–409.

Vergniol, C., 'La chute de Charles X: I. Les "Trois Glorieuses"', *La Revue de France*, vol. 10, 15 juin 1930, pp. 674–79.

——— 'La chute de Charles X: II. Une mission de confiance', *La Revue de France*, vol. 10, 1 juillet 1930, pp. 102–34.

——— 'La fin tragique de Dumont-d'Urville', *Lecture pour tous*, juillet 1930, pp. 99–106.

[Vincendon-Dumoulin, C.-D.], 'Notice biographique: Jules-Sébastien-César Dumont d'Urville', in Dumont d'Urville, J.-S.-C. [& Jacquinot, C.-H.], *Voyage au pôle sud …*, 'Histoire du voyage', vol. x, pp. 55–150.

Vincendon-Dumoulin, C.-D., 'Exposé des observations concernant la physique du globe faites à bord des corvettes l'*Astrolabe* et la *Zélée*, du 1er juin 1838 au 15 décembre 1839', *Bulletin de la Société de géographie*, 2e série, vol. 13, 1840, pp. 313–17.

Viola, H.J., 'The story of the U.S. Exploring Expedition', in Viola, H.J. & Margolis, C. et al. (eds), *Magnificent Voyagers: The U.S. Exploring Expedition, 1838–1842*, Smithsonian Institution Press, Washington D. C., 1985, pp. 9–23.

Vogüé, M. de, 'Lettre sur la découverte de la Vénus de Milo, séance du 29 mai 1874', *Comptes rendus de l'Académie des inscriptions*, vol. 18, no. 2, année 1874, pp. 152–60.

Voisin, C., Voisin, J.-F., Jouanin, C., & Bour, R., 'Liste des types d'oiseaux des collections du Muséum national d'histoire naturelle de Paris. 13: Gangas et pigeons (Pteroclididae et Columbidae), première partie', *Zoosystema*, vol. 26, no. 1, 2004, pp. 107–28.

Voutier, O., 'Découverte et acquis8ition de la Vénus de Milo', in Lorris, A. de (ed.), *Enlèvement de Vénus: Dumont d'Urville, Marcellus et Voutier*, pp. 95–111, Éditions la Bibliothèque, Paris, 1994.

Weisler, M.I., 'The settlement of marginal Polynesia: New evidence from Henderson Island', *Journal of Field Archaeology*, vol. 21, 1994, pp. 83–102.

Williams, G.R., & Weller, M.W., Unsuccessful search for the Auckland Islands merganser (*Mergus australis*)', *Notornis*, vol. 21, no. 3, 1974, pp. 246–49.

Wilson, O., 'The Letters of Tooi and Teeterree: 1818–19', *The Turnbull Library Record*, October 1969, pp. 62–67.

——— 'Tooi, Teeterree and Titore', *Journal of the Polynesian Society*, vol. lxxii, September 1963, pp. 267–69.

Woods, J.M., 'Isaac Joseph Berruyer', *The Catholic Encyclopedia*, Robert Appleton Company, New York, 1907, vol. ii, pp. 516–17.

Wright, C.H., 'Flora of the Falkland Islands', *Journal of the Linnean Society of London*, Botany, vol. 39, no. 273, July 1911, pp. 313–39.

Yzendoorn, R. 'Alexis John Augustine Bachelot', *The Catholic Encyclopedia*, vol. xvi, Encyclopedia Press, New York, 1914, p. 6.

Zuidema, E., 'Baud, Guillame Louis', in Molhuysen, P.C. & Blok, P.J., *Nieuw Nederlandsch biografisch woordenboek*, vol. 1, 1911, pp. 244–45.

Index

Page numbers in **bold** refer to illustrations.

4 février.